DATE DUE

DEMCO 38-296

THE

DICTIONARY

OF

NATIONAL BIOGRAPHY

1986–1990

THE

DICTIONARY

OF

NATIONAL BIOGRAPHY

1986–1990

EDITED BY

C. S. NICHOLLS

Consultant Editor: Sir Keith Thomas

With an Index covering the years 1901–1990
in one alphabetical series

OXFORD UNIVERSITY PRESS

1996

The dictionary of national biography, 1986-1990

Walton Street, Oxford OX2 6DP
New York
Bangkok Bombay
Dar es Salaam Delhi
ng Istanbul Karachi
Kuala Lumpur Madras Madrid Melbourne
Mexico City Nairobi Paris Singapore
Taipei Tokyo Toronto
and associated companies in
Berlin Ibadan

Oxford is a trade mark of Oxford University Press

Published in the United States
by Oxford University Press Inc., New York

© Oxford University Press 1996

First Published 1996

British Library Cataloguing in Publication Data
Data available

Library of Congress Cataloging in Publication Data
Dictionary of national biography, 1986–1990:
with an index covering the years 1901–1990
in one alphabetical series/edited by C. S. Nicholls;
consultant editor, Sir Keith Thomas.
Includes index.
1. Great Britain—Biography—Dictionaries.
I. Nicholls, C. S. (Christine Stephanie).
II. Thomas, Keith, 1933–   .
DA28.D525 1996 920.041—dc20 95–47330
ISBN 0–19–865212–7

1 3 5 7 9 10 8 6 4 2

Typeset by Interactive Sciences, Gloucester
Printed in Great Britain
on acid-free paper by
Bookcraft (Bath) Ltd
Midsomer Norton, Avon

PREFATORY NOTE

THE 450 people noticed in this, the final volume of the *Dictionary of National Biography*, died between 1 January 1986 and 31 December 1990. Those who died after 1 January 1991 will be included in the *New Dictionary of National Biography*, which will appear in the early years of next century and will be a thorough revision and updating of the *DNB*, the first volume of which was published in 1885. Suggestions for entrants to the *New DNB* can be sent to the Oxford University Press.

As usual, the entrants to this volume are drawn from every walk of life and they range in age from 101 (Sir Thomas Sopwith) to 42 (Jacqueline du Pré). There are several centenarians, but, for the first time, there are also a few cut down in their prime by AIDS. In the selection of entrants we took note of the advice of experts in various fields of endeavour, who gave their time freely and generously to us. We are most grateful to them, as we are also to those who wrote the articles. The latter had to follow strict guidelines and obtain facts frequently not readily available, a task they undertook cheerfully.

I am particularly grateful to Sir Keith Thomas, for his assistance as Consultant Editor, to the Bodleian Library, without whose facilities this book would be the poorer, and to Jane Bainbridge and Lorna Lyons, whose efficiency in computing and administrative matters enabled the compilation of this book to progress smoothly.

As I leave the *DNB* after having been associated with the last five volumes over a period of almost twenty years, I am fully conscious of the debt I owe to the thousands of people who have assisted the book in their various ways and to the general public, many of whom wrote to express their appreciation of the new volumes. To all these people I say farewell and thank you.

C. S. Nicholls

LIST OF CONTRIBUTORS

AHM, Povl:
Arup, Sir Ove Nyquist
ALLEN, Douglas. See Croham
ALLEN, Sir Geoffrey:
Davies, Duncan Sheppey
ALLEN, John Anthony:
Yonge, Sir (Charles) Maurice
AMIS, Sir Kingsley William:
Braine, John Gerard
AMORY, (Ian) Mark (Heathcoat):
Boxer, (Charles) Mark (Edward) ('Marc')
ANDERSON, William Francis Desnaux:
Collins, Cecil James Henry
APPLEYARD, (Walter) Philip:
Ross, (John) Carl
ARCHER OF SANDWELL, Peter Kingsley
Archer, Baron:
*Silkin, Samuel Charles, Baron Silkin of
Dulwich*
ARDWICK. See Beavan
ASKONAS, Brigitte Alice:
Humphrey, John Herbert
AVERILL, June Rose:
Madden, Cecil Charles
AVERY JONES, John Francis:
Wheatcroft, George Shorrock Ashcombe

BACKHOUSE, Janet Moira:
Pächt, Otto Ernst
BAKER, Anne Pimlott:
*De Manio, Jack; Fraser, Sir Hugh; Glass,
Ruth Adele; Halliwell, (Robert James)
Leslie; Hurst, Margery; Johnson, Sir Henry
Cecil; Mercer, Joseph; Moore, Doris
Elizabeth Langley; Revie, Donald; Russell,
Dora Winifred; Russell, (Muriel) Audrey;
Solomon; Tinling, Cuthbert Collingwood
('Ted')*
BAND, George Christopher:
Odell, Noel Ewart
BARBER, Giles Gaudard:
Shackleton, Robert
BARDSLEY, Gillian Anne:
Issigonis, Sir Alexander Arnold Constantine
BEAVAN, John Cowburn, Baron Ardwick:
*Hamilton, Sir (Charles) Denis; King, Cecil
Harmsworth*
BELLENGER, (Dominic) Aidan:
Butler, Basil Edward ('Christopher')
BENNER, Patrick:
Marre, Sir Alan Samuel
BENNETT, Alan:
Harty, (Fredric) Russell
BESSBOROUGH, Frederick Edward Neuflize
Ponsonby, Earl of:
Clements, Sir John Selby

BEW, Paul Anthony Elliott:
*O'Neill, Terence Marne, Baron O'Neill of
the Maine*
BIRK, Ellis Samuel:
Sosnow, Eric Charles
BLAKE, Robert Norman William Blake,
Baron:
*Gibbs, Sir Humphrey Vicary; Macmillan,
(Maurice) Harold, first Earl of Stockton*
BLUNDEN, Sir George:
Salomon, Sir Walter Hans
BOARDMAN, Sir John:
Ashmole, Bernard
BONE, Quentin:
Smith, Sir (James) Eric
BONNER, (William) Nigel:
Matthews, (Leonard) Harrison
BOWNESS, Sir Alan:
Moore, Henry Spencer
BRADING, Alison Frances:
Bülbring, Edith
BRAND, David William Robert Brand, Lord:
*Shaw, Charles James Dalrymple, Baron
Kilbrandon*
BRIGGS, Asa Briggs, Baron:
*Fulton, John Scott, Baron; Hill, Charles,
Baron Hill of Luton*
BROCK, Michael George:
Peterson, Alexander Duncan Campbell
BROWN, Jeremy John Galbraith:
Keswick, Sir William Johnston
BROWN, (Lionel) Neville:
Phillips, Owen Hood
BRUCE LOCKHART, John Macgregor:
*Dunderdale, Wilfred Albert; Easton, Sir
James Alfred; Young, George Kennedy*
BRUDENELL, (John) Michael:
Clayton, Sir Stanley George
BUDDEN, Kenneth George:
Ratcliffe, John Ashworth
BULLARD, Sir Julian Leonard:
*Berthoud, Sir Eric Alfred; Johnston, Sir
Charles Hepburn*
BURCHFIELD, Robert William:
Laski, Esther Pearl ('Marghanita')
BURROWS, Eva:
Bramwell-Booth, Catherine
BUTLER, David Edgeworth:
Chester, Sir (Daniel) Norman
BUTLER-SLOSS, Dame (Ann) Elizabeth
(Oldfield), Lord Justice Butler-Sloss:
Lane, Dame Elizabeth Kathleen
BYRON, Reginald Francis:
Blacking, John Anthony Randoll

CADOGAN, Sir John Ivan George:
Hey, Donald Holroyde
CAIN, John Clifford:
Scupham, John
CAIRNCROSS, Sir Alexander Kirkland:
Burn, Duncan Lyall; Hall, Robert Lowe,
Baron Roberthall; Jewkes, John; Sayers,
Richard Sidney
CALDECOTE, Robert Andrew Inskip, Viscount:
Atkins, Sir William Sydney Albert
CALIGARI, Peter Douglas Savaria:
Mather, Sir Kenneth
CAMPBELL, Peter Nelson:
Dickens, Frank
CARBON, John Joseph:
Fricker, Peter Racine
CECIL, Robert
Bentinck, Victor Frederick William
Cavendish-, ninth Duke of Portland
CHADD, David Francis Lanfear:
Harrison, Francis Llewelyn ('Frank')
CHADWICK, (William) Owen:
Ramsey, (Arthur) Michael, Baron Ramsey
of Canterbury; Rupp, (Ernest) Gordon
CHALLENS, (Wallace) John:
Cook, Sir William Richard Joseph
CHAMBERS, David John:
Hassall, Joan
CHAPMAN, (Francis) Ian:
Maclean, Alistair Stuart
CHARTERIS OF AMISFIELD, Martin Michael
Charles Charteris, Baron:
Cooper, Lady Diana Olivia Winifred Maud,
first Viscountess Norwich
CHIBNALL, Marjorie McCallum:
Cheney, Christopher Robert
CHISHOLM, Michael Donald Inglis:
Steers, James Alfred
CLAPP, Susannah:
Chatwin, (Charles) Bruce
CLARKE, Sir Cyril Astley:
Ford, Edmund Brisco
CLARKE, Roger Howard:
Pochin, Sir Edward Eric
CLENSHAW, Charles:
Wilkinson, James Hardy
CLIVE, Nigel David:
Philby, Harold Adrian Russell ('Kim')
COLLIER, Leslie Harold:
Miles, Sir (Arnold) Ashley
COMYN, Sir James:
Pearce, Edward Holroyd, Baron
COOK, Sir Alan Hugh:
Jeffreys, Sir Harold
COOPER, Joseph Elliott Needham:
Moore, Gerald
CORK, Richard Graham:
Fuller, Peter Michael
CORTAZZI, Sir (Henry Arthur) Hugh:
Pilcher, Sir John Arthur

COUPE, George:
Robinson, Sir David
COX, Ernest Gordon:
Robertson, John Monteath
CROHAM, Douglas Albert Vivian Allen,
Baron:
Part, Sir Antony Alexander
CRUICKSHANK, Alan Hamilton:
Sheehan, Harold Leeming
CULLEN, Alexander Lamb:
Barlow, Harold Everard Monteagle

DACIE, Sir John Vivian:
Macfarlane, (Robert) Gwyn
DAINTON, Frederick Sydney Dainton, Baron:
Morris, Charles Richard, Baron Morris of
Grasmere
DALTON, (Henry) James (Martin):
Thalben-Ball, Sir George Thomas
DALYELL, Tam:
Stewart, (Robert) Michael (Maitland),
Baron Stewart of Fulham
DARRACOTT, Joseph Corbould:
Topolski, Feliks
DAVIDSON, Malcolm Alexander:
Moores, Cecil
DAVIES, James Atterbury:
Williams, (George) Emlyn
DAVIES, (Thomas) Gerald (Reames):
Jones, (William) Clifford
DAVIS, Veronica Mary:
Edwards, James Keith O'Neill ('Jimmy')
DAY, Peter:
Anderson, (John) Stuart
DEEDES, William Francis Deedes, Baron:
Cotton, (Thomas) Henry
DENISON, (John) Michael (Terence
Wellesley):
Byam Shaw, Glencairn Alexander ('Glen')
DENMAN, Sir (George) Roy:
O'Neill, Sir Con Douglas Walter
DENSELOW, Robin Nicholas:
MacColl, Ewan
DOLL, Sir (William) Richard (Shaboe):
Cochrane, Archibald Leman
DRURY, Sir (Victor William) Michael:
Hunt, John Henderson, Baron Hunt of
Fawley
DUGGAN, John Francis:
Church, Charles James Gregory
DUNNETT, James Inglis:
Goldfinger, Ernö
DUTHIE, Robert Buchan:
Platt, Sir Harry

EAMES, Robert Henry Alexander:
Armstrong, John Ward
EDWARDS, David Lawrence:
Bliss, Kathleen Mary Amelia

EGREMONT, (John) Max (Henry Scawen)
Wyndham, Baron:
Zulueta, Sir Philip Francis de
ELLIS, Roger Wykeham:
Abell, Sir George Edmond Brackenbury
EMSLIE, George Carlyle Emslie, Baron:
Fraser (Walter) Ian (Reid), Baron Fraser of Tullybelton
ENTWISTLE, Kenneth Mercer:
Bowden, (Bertram) Vivian, Baron
ERDMAN, Edward Louis:
Samuel, Harold, Baron Samuel of Wych Cross

FARRAR-HOCKLEY, Sir Anthony Heritage:
Lea, Sir George Harris; Stockwell, Sir Hugh Charles
FAWKES, Richard Brian:
Trinder, Thomas Edward ('Tommy')
FERMOR, Patrick Michael Leigh:
Durrell, Lawrence George
FIRTH, Rosemary:
Leach, Sir Edmund Ronald
FLECK, Adam:
Cuthbertson, Sir David Paton
FLOWERS, Brian Hilton Flowers, Baron:
Merrison, Sir Alexander Walter
FLOWERS, Mary Frances Flowers, Lady:
Fuchs, (Emil Julius) Klaus
FOOT, Michael Mackintosh:
Lee, Janet ('Jennie'), Baroness Lee of Asheridge
FOOT, Michael Richard Daniell
Wynne, Greville Maynard
FORD, Sir Edward William Spencer:
Lane-Fox, Felicity, Baroness
FORSTER, Margaret:
Du Maurier, Dame Daphne
FORTUNE, Nigel Cameron:
Arnold, Denis Midgley
Fox, Sir Paul Leonard:
Greene, Sir Hugh Carleton; Wheldon, Sir Huw Pyrs
FREEMAN, Sir Ralph:
Wex, Bernard Patrick

GAMMOND, Peter:
Loss, Joshua Alexander ('Joe')
GENNARD, John:
Keys, William Herbert
GENTLEMAN, David William:
Bawden, Edward
GERE, John Arthur Giles:
Pouncey, Philip Michael Rivers
GILLES, Herbert Michael:
Maegraith, Brian Gilmore
GLAUERT, Audrey Marion:
Fell, Dame Honor Bridget
GOLDBERG, Sir Abraham:
Wayne, Sir Edward Johnson

GOMBRICH, Richard Francis:
Burrow, Thomas
GOODE, Royston Miles:
Schmitthoff, Clive Macmillan
GOODHART, Sir William Howard:
Sargant, Thomas; Sieghart, (Henry Laurence) Paul (Alexander)
GOODING, Melvyn Graham:
Scott, William George; Trevelyan, Julian Otto
GOODISON, Sir Nicholas Proctor:
Wilkinson, Sir (Robert Francis) Martin
GOODMAN, Geoffrey George:
Cousins, Frank
GOUDIE, Andrew Shaw:
Shotton, Frederick William
GRAY, Donald Clifford:
Jasper, Ronald Claud Dudley
GRAY (Denison), Dulcie Winifred Catherine:
Bennett, (Nora Noel) Jill
GRAY, Sir John Archibald Browne:
Matthews, Sir Bryan Harold Cabot
GREENHILL, Basil Jack:
Cayzer, (Michael) Anthony (Rathborne); Runciman, (Walter) Leslie, second Viscount Runciman of Doxford
GREGORY, Richard Langton:
Zangwill, Oliver Louis
GRIFFIN, Jasper:
Meiggs, Russell
GRIGG, John Edward Poynder:
Boothby, Robert John Graham, Baron; Cazalet-Keir, Thelma; Sylvester, Albert James

HACKER, Peter Michael Stephan:
Hayter, Stanley William
HACKETT, Sir John Winthrop:
Urquhart, Robert Elliott
HALSEY, Albert Henry:
Wootton, Barbara Frances, Baroness Wootton of Abinger
HARCOURT, Geoffrey Colin:
Kahn, Richard Ferdinand, Baron
HARRIS, Frank:
Illingworth, Ronald Stanley
HARRISON, Martin Lewis:
Parkinson, Norman
HART-DAVIS, (Peter) Duff:
Chipperfield, James Seaton Methuen
HEAP, Robert Brian:
Parkes, Sir Alan Sterling
HEATH, Sir Edward Richard George:
Trend, Burke Frederick St John, Baron
HILL, William George:
Robertson, Alan
HILLIER, Bevis:
Lancaster, Sir Osbert
HINDE, Robert Aubrey:
Tinbergen, Nikolaas

HOFFENBERG, Sir Raymond:
  Bull, Sir Graham MacGregor
HOOSON, (Hugh) Emlyn Hooson, Baron:
  Jones, (Frederick) Elwyn, Baron Elwyn-Jones
HOPE-HAWKINS, Richard John:
  Terry-Thomas
HOPKIRK, Peter:
  Teague-Jones, Reginald (Ronald Sinclair)
HOWARD, Anthony Michell:
  Fairlie, Henry Jones; Paget, Reginald Thomas Guy Des Voeux, Baron Paget of Northampton; Watt, (John) David (Henry)
HOWARD, Philip Nicholas Charles:
  Dahl, Roald
HOWELL, David:
  Brockway, (Archibald) Fenner, Baron; King, Horace Maybray, Baron Maybray-King
HOWKINS, Alun John:
  Evans, George Ewart
HUGHES, David John:
  Lehmann, (Rudolph) John (Frederick)
HUGHES, William Hughes, Baron:
  Ross, William, Baron Ross of Marnock
HUNT, Sir David Wathen Stather:
  Harding, Allan Francis ('John'), first Baron Harding of Petherton; Stephenson, Sir William Samuel
HUNT, Giles Butler:
  Fleming, (William) Launcelot (Scott)
HUTTON, Patrick:
  Howarth, Thomas Edward Brodie

IGGO, Ainsley:
  Robertson, Sir Alexander
INGLIS, Kenneth Stanley:
  Hancock, Sir (William) Keith
INGRAMS, Richard Reid:
  Muggeridge, (Thomas) Malcolm
ISAACS, Jeremy Israel:
  Moore, (Charles) Garrett (Ponsonby), eleventh Earl of Drogheda

JACKSON, Archibald Stewart:
  Bennett, Donald Clifford Tyndall
JAHODA, Marie:
  Himmelweit, Hildegard Therese
JAMES, Eric Arthur:
  Lacey, Janet
JAMES, Ioan MacKenzie:
  Adams, (John) Frank
JAY, Sir Antony Rupert:
  Cawston, (Edwin) Richard
JEGER, Lena May Jeger, Baroness:
  Foot, Hugh Mackintosh, Baron Caradon
JELLICOE, George Patrick John Rushworth Jellicoe, second Earl:
  Cave, Sir Richard Guy
JENKIN, Ian Evers Tregarthen:
  Coldstream, Sir William Menzies

JENSEN, John Peisley:
  Emett, (Frederick) Rowland
JOLOWICZ, John Anthony:
  Hamson, Charles John Joseph ('Jack')
JUDD, Frank Ashcroft Judd, Baron:
  Kirkley, Sir (Howard) Leslie

KEEGAN, John Desmond Patrick:
  Hull, Sir Richard Amyatt
KEEN, Maurice Hugh:
  Oakeshott, Sir Walter Fraser
KELLY, John Stephen:
  Ellmann, Richard David
KENNET, Wayland Hilton Young, Baron:
  Grigson, (Heather Mabel) Jane
KESSEL, (William Arthur) Neil:
  Pond, Sir Desmond Arthur
KIRBY, Stephanie Anne:
  Dreyer, Rosalie
KLINE, Paul:
  Vernon, Philip Ewart
KNOX, (Ernest) George:
  McKeown, Thomas

LAMB, Richard Anthony:
  Sandys, (Edwin) Duncan, Baron Duncan-Sandys
LANCASTER, Terence Roger:
  Jacobson, Sydney, Baron
LANGLEY, Bernard William:
  Rose, Francis Leslie
LARMINIE, (Ferdinand) Geoffrey:
  Kent, Sir Percy Edward ('Peter')
LAYTON, Robert Edward:
  Abraham, Gerald Ernest Heal; Rubbra, (Charles) Edmund (Duncan)
LEA, Kathleen Marguerite:
  Gardner, Dame Helen Louise
LE BAILLY, Sir Louis Edward Stewart Holland:
  Mason, Sir Frank Trowbridge
LEES-MILNE, James:
  Sitwell, Sir Sacheverell
LESLIE, Sir Peter Evelyn:
  Seebohm, Frederic, Baron
LEWISON, Jeremy Rodney Pines:
  Ede, Harold Stanley ('Jim')
LLEWELLYN SMITH, Christopher Hubert:
  Bell, John Stewart
LLOYD, Brian Beynon:
  Sinclair, Hugh Macdonald
LOCK, Stephen Penford:
  Fox, Sir Theodore Fortescue
LOW, Rachael:
  Carreras, Sir James Enrique; Grant, Cary; Greenwood, Joan Mary Waller; Lockwood, Margaret Mary; Manvell, (Arnold) Roger; Quayle, Sir (John) Anthony
LUCAS, Percy Belgrave:
  Balfour, Harold Harington, first Baron Balfour of Inchrye

LUNT, James Doiran:
 Glubb, Sir John Bagot
LYALL, Sutherland:
 Banham, (Peter) Reyner
LYNDEN-BELL, Donald:
 Woolley, Sir Richard van der Riet

McAVOY, Douglas Newton:
 Gould, Sir Ronald
MACCARTHY, Fiona:
 Reilly, Paul, Baron
McCARTHY, Kevin:
 Downie, Allan Watt
McCARTHY, William Edward John
 McCarthy, Baron:
 Fisher, Alan Wainwright
McCREA, Sir William Hunter:
 Woolley, Sir Richard van der Riet
McEWEN, John Sebastian:
 Willing, Victor James Arthur
McKITTERICK, David John:
 Cockerell, Sydney Morris
MACLAGAN, Michael:
 Laithwaite, Sir (John) Gilbert
MACLEAN OF DUNCONNEL, Sir Fitzroy Hew,
 Bart.:
 Stirling, Sir (Archibald) David
McLEAN, (John David) Ruari (McDowall
 Hardie):
 Wolpe, Berthold Ludwig
McMULLAN, Dennis:
 Cosslett, (Vernon) Ellis
McNALLY, Thomas:
 Stonehouse, John Thomson
MACNAUGHTON, Sir Malcolm Campbell:
 Baird, Sir Dugald
MALPAS, James Spencer:
 McElwain, Timothy John
MANKTELOW, Michael Richard John:
 Moorman, John Richard Humpidge
MANSFIELD, Eric Harold:
 Wittrick, William Henry
MARSH, Arthur Ivor:
 Boyd, Sir John McFarlane
MARSH, Norman Stayner:
 Gardiner, Gerald Austin, Baron
MARSHALL, Sir Colin Marsh:
 Granville, Sir Keith
MASEFIELD, Sir Peter Gordon:
 *Lockspeiser, Sir Ben; Sopwith, Sir Thomas
 Octave Murdoch*
MASON, Philip:
 Moon, Sir (Edward) Penderel
MATTHEWS, Robert Charles Oliver:
 Hicks, Sir John Richard
MATTHEW-WALKER, Robert:
 Ogdon, John Andrew Howard
MELLOR, (David) Hugh:
 Braithwaite, Richard Bevan
MENNELL, Stephen John:
 Elias, Norbert

MENUHIN, Yehudi Menuhin, Baron:
 Du Pré, Jacqueline Mary
MIALL, (Rowland) Leonard:
 *Goldie, Grace Murrell Wyndham; Vaughan-
 Thomas, (Lewis John) Wynford*
MIDWINTER, Eric Clare:
 *Edrich, William John ('Bill'); Ramsey,
 (Mary) Dorothea (Whiting); Wall, Max*
MILLAR, Fergus Graham Burtholme:
 Syme, Sir Ronald
MILLS, Ivor Henry:
 Mitchell, Joseph Stanley
MINOGUE, Kenneth Robert:
 Oakeshott, Michael Joseph
MITCHELL, Donald Charles Peter:
 Pears, Sir Peter Neville Luard
MITCHISON, (Nicholas) Avrion:
 Medawar, Sir Peter Brian
MONTGOMERY, Doreen:
 Strong, Patience
MOORE, David Moresby:
 Tutin, Thomas Gaskell
MORETON, Sir John Oscar:
 Wates, Sir Ronald Wallace
MORGAN, Kenneth Owen:
 Shinwell, Emanuel, Baron
MORLEY, Sheridan Robert:
 Lillie, Beatrice Gladys, Lady Peel
MORRIS, Alfred:
 Peart, (Thomas) Frederick, Baron
MORRIS, Malcolm Simon:
 Andrews, Eamonn
MOSER, Sir Claus Adolf:
 Kentner, Louis Philip
MUIR, Frank:
 Marshall, (Charles) Arthur (Bertram)
MUIR WOOD, Sir Alan Marshall:
 Harding, Sir Harold John Boyer
MURLEY, Sir Reginald Sydney:
 *Riches, Sir Eric William; Sellors, Sir
 Thomas Holmes*
MURRAY, Oswyn:
 Momigliano, Arnaldo Dante

NEVILLE, Jill:
 Gibbons, Stella Dorothea; Smart, Elizabeth
NEWSAM, Sir Peter Anthony:
 Clegg, Sir Alexander Bradshaw
NICHOLLS, Christine Stephanie:
 *Bergel, Franz; Elliot, Sir John; Fisher, Alan
 Wainwright; Markham, Beryl; Stonehouse,
 John Thomson; Terry-Thomas;
 Winterbotham, Frederick William*
NICHOLS, Roger David Edward:
 Berkeley, Sir Lennox Randal Francis
NICOLL, Douglas Robertson:
 Jones, Sir Eric Malcolm
NISBET, Robin George Murdoch:
 Mynors, Sir Roger Aubrey Baskerville

SHERFIELD, Roger Mellor Makins, Baron:
*Caccia, Harold Anthony, Baron; Millar,
Frederick Robert Hoyer, first Baron Inchyra*

SHERRIN, Edward George ('Ned'):
*Baddeley, Hermione Youlanda Ruby
Clinton; Gingold, Hermione Ferdinanda*

SHIPLEY, Stanley Albert:
*Farr, Thomas George ('Tommy'); Petersen,
John Charles ('Jack')*

SHONE, Richard Noël:
Moynihan, (Herbert George) Rodrigo

SIMON, Brian:
Pedley, Robin

SINCLAIR-STEVENSON, Christopher Terence:
Hamilton, Hamish

SLACK, Paul Alexander:
*Hunt, Norman Crowther, Baron Crowther-
Hunt*

SLATER, Stephen:
Van Damm, Sheila

SMITH, David Burton:
Williams, Raymond Henry

SMITH, Sir David Cecil:
Harley, John Laker ('Jack')

SNOW, Michael Neville Seward:
Graham, (William) Sydney

SOUTHBY-TAILYOUR, (Simon) Ewen:
Hasler, Herbert George ('Blondie')

STALLWORTHY, Jon Howie:
Reed, Henry

STEARN, William Thomas:
Holttum, (Richard) Eric

STEWARTBY, Bernard Harold Ian Halley
Stewart, Baron:
Blunt, Christopher Evelyn

STIRRAT, Gordon Macmillan:
Turnbull, Sir Alexander Cuthbert

STORR, (Charles) Anthony:
Bowlby, (Edward) John (Mostyn)

STREET, Sarah Caroline Jane:
*Clarke, Thomas Ernest Bennett; Neagle,
Dame Anna; Powell, Michael Latham;
Pressburger, Emeric*

STROUD, Barry:
Grice, (Herbert) Paul

SWALLOW, Norman:
Mitchell, Denis Holden

SYKES, Geoffrey Robert:
Croft, (John) Michael

SYKES, Sir (Malcolm) Keith:
Macintosh, Sir Robert Reynolds

TAYLOR, Arnold Joseph:
Myres, (John) Nowell (Linton)

TAYLOR, Elizabeth Julia ('Lib'):
Howard, Trevor Wallace

TAYLOR, Peter Arthur Storey:
Cobbold, Cameron Fromanteel, first Baron

TEMPLEMAN, Sydney William Templeman,
Baron:
*Russell, Charles Ritchie, Baron Russell of
Killowen*

TESLER, Brian:
Thomas, Howard

THIRLWALL, Anthony Philip:
Kaldor, Nicholas, Baron

THOMPSON, Arthur Frederick:
*Acland, Sir Richard Thomas Dyke; Taylor,
Alan John Percivale*

THOROGOOD, Bernard George:
Slack, Kenneth

THWAITE, Anthony Simon:
Nicholson, Norman Cornthwaite

TODD, Alexander Robertus Todd, Baron:
Bergel, Franz

TOMKINS, Oliver Stratford:
Milford, (Theodore) Richard

TOMKINS, Stephen Portal:
Hutchinson, Sir Joseph Burtt

TOOK, Barry:
*Murdoch, Richard Bernard; Williams,
Kenneth Charles*

TOOLEY, Sir John:
Goodall, Sir Reginald; Turner, Dame Eva

TRAPP, Joseph Burney:
De Beer, Esmond Samuel

TRELFORD, Donald Gilchrist:
Hutton, Sir Leonard

TREWIN, Wendy Elizabeth:
Albery, Sir Donald Rolleston

TRICKETT, (Mabel) Rachel:
*Cecil, Lord (Edward Christian) David
(Gascoyne-)*

TYRRELL, David Arthur John:
Andrewes, Sir Christopher Howard

ULLENDORFF, Edward:
Coke, Gerald Edward

VAIZEY, Marina Vaizey, Lady:
Spear, (Augustus John) Ruskin

VARAH, (Edward) Chad:
Morris, (John) Marcus (Harston)

VERNON, (William) Michael:
Forbes, Sir Archibald Finlayson

WALBANK, Frank William:
Finley, Sir Moses I.

WALKDEN, Paul
Scott, Sir Peter Markham

WALKER, David Maxwell:
Smith, Sir Thomas Broun

WALKER, Richard John Boileau:
Piper, Sir David Towry

WALLACE, Ian Bryce:
*Hall, Henry Robert; Semprini, (Fernando
Riccardo) Alberto*

WALTERS, (Stuart) Max:
Gilmour, John Scott Lennox

WARDLE, (John) Irving:
Dexter, John; Olivier, Laurence Kerr, Baron
WARNOCK, Sir Geoffrey James:
Grice, Paul; Warner, Reginald Ernest ('Rex')
WARRACK, John Hamilton:
Goossens, Léon Jean; Matthews, Denis James; Sorabji, Kaikhosru Shapurji
WAUGH, Auberon Alexander:
Sykes, Christopher Hugh
WEBB, Kaye:
Streatfeild, (Mary) Noel
WELLS, Alan Arthur:
Weck, Richard
WELLS, John Campbell:
Cleverdon, (Thomas) Douglas (James)
WENHAM, Brian George:
Trethowan, Sir (James) Ian (Raley)
WILLIAMS, Sir Robert Evan Owen:
Wilson, Sir Graham Selby
WILLIAMS, Val:
McBean, Angus Rowland
WILLMOTT, Phyllis Mary:
Aves, Dame Geraldine Maitland
WILLOCKS, James:
Donald, Ian
WILSON, John Francis:
Ferranti, Basil Reginald Vincent Ziani de
WINCHESTER, David Henry:
Basnett, David, Baron

WINDSOR, Alan Ernest:
Buhler, Robert; Middleditch, Edward Charles
WINTON, John:
Davis, Sir William Wellclose; Hopkins, Sir Frank Henry Edward
WINTOUR, Charles Vere:
Hopkinson, Sir (Henry) Thomas
WOLFF, Otto Herbert:
Dudgeon, (John) Alastair
WOLLHEIM, Richard Arthur:
Ayer, Sir Alfred Jules
WOODCOCK, John Charles:
Allen, Sir George Oswald Browning ('Gubby')
WORLOCK, Derek John Harford:
Dwyer, George Patrick
WRIGHT, (Arthur Robert) Donald:
Hamilton, Walter
WYATT OF WEEFORD, Woodrow Lyle Wyatt, Baron:
Hastings, Francis John Clarence Westenra Plantagenet, fifteenth Earl of Huntingdon

YOUNG, Alec David:
Owen, (Paul) Robert

ZIEGLER, Philip Sandeman:
Colville, Sir John Rupert; Windsor, (Bessie) Wallis, Duchess of

NOTE TO THE READER

An asterisk (*) in front of a name indicates that there is a separate entry for this person in the *DNB*.

DICTIONARY

OF

NATIONAL BIOGRAPHY

(TWENTIETH CENTURY)

PERSONS WHO DIED 1986–1990

ABELL, SIR George Edmond Brackenbury (1904–1989), private secretary to the viceroy of India, was born 22 June 1904 in Sanderstead, Surrey, the eldest in the family of two sons and two daughters of George Foster Abell, director of Lloyds Bank, and his wife, Jessie Elizabeth Brackenbury. His brother, (Sir) Anthony Abell, became governor of Sarawak. He was a scholar and senior prefect of Marlborough College, and scholar of Corpus Christi College, Oxford, where he obtained a first class in classical honour moderations (1925) and a second in *literae humaniores* (1927). A triple blue, in rugby, cricket, and hockey, he captained the Oxford rugby XV in 1926, and played cricket for Worcestershire.

He joined the Indian Civil Service as a district officer in the Punjab in 1928, becoming deputy registrar of co-operative societies and a settlement officer. He enjoyed the work, and coped effectively with crises, quelling a riot in Dera Ghazi Khan gaol by walking into the middle of it, while the warders were taking refuge on the roof. In 1941 the governor of the Punjab appointed him as his private secretary, and in 1943 he was promoted deputy secretary to the viceroy, the second Marquess of *Linlithgow. In 1945 he took over as private secretary to the viceroy, by then Viscount (later first Earl) *Wavell, and he continued to hold this post under Louis *Mountbatten (later first Earl Mountbatten of Burma) until the end of the Raj, thereafter serving as Mountbatten's secretary when he became governor-general of India.

His role in government during the critical years leading up to the partition and transfer of power in India was of central importance. Although the Hindus regarded his Punjab background with suspicion, Wavell, whom he liked and admired, used him to coax M. K. *Gandhi, describing him as 'diplomatic and persuasive'. He wrote the first draft of the hand-over scheme to be presented to the new Labour government, and was on the small committee used by Wavell to work out the details of his 'breakdown plan'.

He tended to moderate Wavell's tougher telegrams, but respected his soldierly directness. However, he came to feel that the British position in India was untenable, that partition was inevitable, and that the British should extricate themselves quickly. Although less comfortable with Mountbatten's personality, he therefore worked happily to implement his policy. He drafted the partition plan for the viceroy with General Hastings (later Baron) *Ismay, and helped to keep him from some of the mistakes inevitably made in the rush to meet the deadline. 'The Lord needs George or Ismay to steady him,' commented a diarist close to the scene.

On his return to England in 1948 he joined the Bank of England as an adviser, serving as a director from 1952 until 1964. He was responsible for all matters connected with staff, and for the buildings. He developed the new graduate entry, organizing a career structure which made proper use of graduates' talents. He also ended the old division between men and women, and integrated them into one staff. He had directorial responsibility for three major new Bank buildings, including the New Change office block at the top of Cheapside.

He was first Civil Service commissioner from 1964 until 1967, chairman of the Rhodes trustees from 1969 until 1974 (having been a trustee from 1949), chairman of the governors of Marlborough College from 1974 until 1977, and president of the council of Reading University between 1970 and 1974. This was at a time of rapidly increasing numbers and general student restlessness. That Reading did not suffer the disruption of many other universities had much to do with the confidence which Abell engendered in dons and students. They respected his mind and his sense of humour defused many a difficult situation.

He enjoyed the outdoor life, shot well, and tied his own flies. He remained the all-rounder throughout his life, and brought his common sense and his clear mind to a wide range of problems. He retained the discretion of the civil servant, and his response to biographers and journalists who wanted to get behind the scenes of the closing years of the Raj was that he continued to regard his role as that of a private secretary.

He was appointed OBE (1943), CIE (1946), and KCIE (1947). He received an honorary LL D from Aberdeen University in 1947, and became an honorary fellow of Corpus Christi College in 1971. He married in 1928 Susan, daughter of Frank Norman-Butler, inspector of schools, and they were close companions throughout the rest of his life. They had two sons and a daughter. Abell died at their home in Ramsbury, Wiltshire, 11 January 1989.

[Philip Ziegler, *Mountbatten, the Official Biography*, 1985; Penderel Moon (ed.), *Wavell: the Viceroy's Journal*, 1973; private information from relatives and from Sir George Blunden, Sir Harry Pitt, and Judge Christopher Beaumont; personal knowledge.] ROGER ELLIS

ABRAHAM, Gerald Ernest Heal (1904–1988), musical scholar and leading authority on Russian music, was born 9 March 1904 in Newport, Isle of Wight, the only child of Ernest Abraham, manufacturer, and his wife, Dorothy Mary Heal, a jeweller's daughter. In spite of his strong musical interests, he planned a naval career, attending a naval crammer in Portsmouth. Ill health forced him to abandon this, though he retained a lifelong interest in naval history, and after studying for a year in Cologne he published his first book on music, a study of Alexander Borodin (1927), an autodidact like himself. Apart from some early piano lessons, he was self-taught but, during the following years, he contributed widely to musical periodicals and also published monographs on Nietzsche (1933), Tolstoy (1935), and Dostoevsky (1936), as well as an introduction to contemporary music, *This Modern Stuff* (1933), renamed *This Modern Music* in later reprints. He taught himself Russian and published two collections of his primarily analytical essays, *Studies in Russian Music* (1935) and *On Russian Music* (1939). In collaboration with M. D. Calvocoressi, he wrote *Masters of Russian Music* (1936). In 1935 he joined the BBC as assistant editor of the *Radio Times* and subsequently served as deputy editor of the *Listener* (1939–42), remaining its music editor until 1962.

During World War II, when interest in Russian music was at fever point, he published *Eight Soviet Composers* (1943) and made a valuable behind-the-scenes contribution to broadcasting as director of gramophone programmes (1942–7), helping to lay the foundations of the Third Programme in 1946. He returned to the BBC in 1962, as assistant controller of music, after having spent the intervening years (1947–62) as the first professor of music at Liverpool University.

He spent a further year as chief music critic of the *Daily Telegraph* (1967–8), before becoming the Ernest Bloch professor of music at the University of California at Berkeley (1968–9). His lectures there were subsequently published under the title, *The Tradition of Western Music* (1974).

Although the public tended to associate him with Slavonic and Romantic music, his scholarship was of quite unusual breadth and depth. He edited symposia on Tchaikovsky (1945), Schubert (1946), Sibelius (1947), Grieg (1948), Schumann (1952), and Handel (1954). He set in motion The History of Music in Sound (gramophone records and handbooks) and the *New Oxford History of Music*. The latter occupied him for the best part of three decades; he edited three of its ten volumes personally—the third, *Ars Nova and the Renaissance, 1300–1450*, in collaboration with Dom Anselm Hughes (1960), the fourth, *The Age of Humanism, 1540–1630* (1968), and the eighth, *The Age of Beethoven, 1790–1830* (1982). He also brought out his magisterial, synoptic overview of western music, *The Concise Oxford History of Music* (1979). He was closely involved in *The New Grove Dictionary of Music and Musicians* (1980). His selfless work as an editor is nowhere better exemplified than in his completion of Calvocoressi's Master Musicians study of Mussorgsky (1946) and his work on seeing Calvocoressi's larger study through the press in 1955 (published in 1956).

Abraham was of medium height, with a genial and warm personality. His writings are exceptional in the field of musicology for not only their scholarship, which was always worn lightly, but also their freshness, originality, and readability. He had the rare ability to stimulate the interest and engage the sympathies of the less informed as well as the specialist reader, and commanded a ready wit with the gift for a felicitous and memorable phrase. Although Abraham wrote widely on Russian music and literature, he was also the author of a penetrating study of *Chopin's Musical Style* (1939), which was a model of lucidity, economy, and good style. Always a Wagnerian, Abraham long planned a book on Wagner's musical language. In the 1940s he even made a conjectural reconstruction of a quartet movement that was published by the OUP. He also made a conjectural completion of Schubert's 'Unfinished' Symphony in 1971.

He held honorary doctorates from Durham, Liverpool, Southampton, and Berkeley in California, was a fellow of the British Academy (1972), and president of the Royal Musical Association (1969–74). He was appointed CBE in 1974. From 1973 to 1980 he was chairman of the British Academy's Early English Church Music committee. Some of his finest and most absorbing writing is to be found in *Slavonic and*

Romantic Music: Essays and Studies (1968). Whether as a lecturer or broadcaster, Abraham's erudition was always tempered by a keen sense of humour. The publication of *Slavonic and Western Music: Essays for Gerald Abraham*, edited by Malcolm Hamrick Brown and Roland John Wiley (1985), paid him fitting and timely tribute.

In 1936 he married (Isobel) Patsy, daughter of Stanley John Robinson, pharmacist; they had one daughter. Abraham had an abiding love of the English countryside and the music of Sir Edward *Elgar, and from the early 1960s lived in a converted school in Ebernoe near Petworth, until his death at the King Edward VII Hospital, Midhurst, 18 March 1988.

[Malcolm H. Brown and Ronald J. Wiley, *Slavonic and Western Music: Essays for Gerald Abraham*, 1985; Sir Jack Westrup (ed.), 'A Birthday Greeting to Gerald Abraham', *Music and Letters*, vol. lv, 1974; personal knowledge.] ROBERT LAYTON

ACLAND, SIR Richard Thomas Dyke, fifteenth baronet (1906–1990), politician and publicist of 'good causes', was born 26 November 1906 at Broadclyst, Devon, his ancestral home, the eldest in the family of three sons and a daughter of Sir Francis Dyke Acland, fourteenth baronet, landowner, member of Parliament, and PC, minister in the governments of H. H. *Asquith (later the first Earl of Oxford and Asquith), and his wife, Eleanor Margaret, the outspoken anti-war daughter of Charles James Cropper, of Ellergreen, Westmorland, landowner and grandee. He was educated at Rugby and Balliol College, Oxford, where he received a second class in philosophy, politics, and economics in 1927. His career epitomized a family tradition of reformist public service, both nationally and in the west country.

Acland stood unsuccessfully as a Liberal for Torquay in 1929 and Barnstaple in 1931, capturing the latter seat in 1935. Radical by temperament, he became involved in the efforts of the Left Book Club to create a progressive alliance, and by the beginning of World War II had moved from conventional, secular Liberalism towards a Christian Socialist concern for the transformation of the privileged world in which he grew up. His Penguin best seller of 1940, *Unser Kampf*, eloquently summed up the aspirations of many who saw the war as an opportunity to escape from the disillusionments of the 1920s and 1930s and establish a more egalitarian, less class-ridden society. This message was repeated in *The Forward March* (1941) and *What It Will Be Like* (1942), and then elaborated, after the proposals of Sir William (later Baron) *Beveridge, in *How It Can Be Done* (1943).

Having served briefly as a lieutenant in the Royal Devon Yeomanry, initially as a ranker, Acland returned to politics and brought together Forward March, a loose alliance of the discontented but hopeful, and the dissident intellectuals of the 1941 Committee under J. B. *Priestley, to found the Common Wealth party in July 1942. Sheltered by the electoral truce between the major parties, Common Wealth was active in wartime by-elections, and by 1945 had four MPs. Its appeal was essentially to the more modest, professional middle classes, notably in London and on Merseyside; though its membership was never more than 15,000, the party was organized with panache by R. W. G. Mackay and the evangelistic Acland proved himself a master of electioneering tactics. For funding they could also rely upon sympathetic businessmen such as Alan Good and Denis Kendall.

In the general election of 1945 Common Wealth lost all its MPs and the deposits of every candidate, as politics reverted to the familiar two-party pattern. Nevertheless, Acland's creation had helped to prepare the way for Labour's victory, and in this he was the crucial element. Rarely effective in the House of Commons, he was an inspired and tireless propagandist, who packed wartime meetings across the country; tall, gangling, and intense, with hawklike features, always putting his case in a rasping voice in simple, moralistic terms but with a socialist slant, he was seen by many as the true prophet of a better future. As an earnest of his personal commitment to common ownership, he made over the family's vast Killerton estates in Devon to the National Trust in 1943 and always lived frugally if generously. But Labour's first attainment of full power meant that his moment of historical importance had passed.

Acland returned to the House of Commons in 1947 as MP for Gravesend under the sponsorship of Herbert *Morrison (later Baron Morrison of Lambeth) and remained committed to Labour for the rest of his life. Increasingly a maverick, divorced from mainstream politics, he resigned his seat in 1955 in protest against the development of the H-bomb and never returned to Parliament. More and more his interests had become one-dimensional. A devout Anglican since 1940, Acland served as a church estates commissioner in 1950–1 and maintained his friendship with left-wing bishops thereafter; but his attention came to centre upon education, a traditional concern of both his father and grandfather (Sir A. H. D. *Acland). Abandoning Westminster, he was senior lecturer at St Luke's College of Education, Exeter, from 1959 to 1974.

In retirement Acland wrote freely on educational matters, the problems of securing world peace, and, in his last years, the difficulties facing the third world. Now that he was a figure of the past, having outlived his period of influence during World War II, he had few readers. He continued to cherish his beloved Devon countryside and protect its traditions, including, somewhat surprisingly, stag hunting.

Acland succeeded his father in the baronetcy in 1939, having married in 1936 Anne Stella, ARIBA, architect daughter of Robert Greenwood Alford, of Cheyne Walk, London. They had four sons, the youngest of whom died when five days old, in 1945. Acland died at Broadclyst 24 November 1990 and was succeeded in the baronetcy by his eldest son, John Dyke Acland (born 1939).

[Acland's own publications; Paul Addison, *The Road to 1945*, 1975; Angus Calder, *The People's War*, 1969.]

A. F. THOMPSON

ADAMS, (John) Frank (1930–1989), mathematician, was born 5 November 1930 in Woolwich, the elder son (there were no daughters) of William Frank Adams, civil engineer, and his wife Jean Mary Baines, biologist, both of London. He was educated at Bedford School and then spent 1948–9 doing his national service in the Royal Engineers. He went to Trinity College, Cambridge, where he was a wrangler in part ii (1951) and gained special credit in part iii (1952) of the mathematical tripos. He continued at Cambridge as a research student, first under A. S. *Besicovitch and then, more significantly, under Shaun Wylie. His Ph.D. thesis (1955) was on algebraic topology, which remained his main research interest for the rest of his life. Adams spent the year 1954 at Oxford, as a junior lecturer, where he came under the influence of J. H. C. *Whitehead, then the leading topologist in the country.

Returning to Cambridge in 1956 as a research fellow at Trinity College, Adams developed the spectral sequence which bears his name, linking the cohomology of a topological space to its stable homotopy groups. In 1957–8 he was a Commonwealth fellow at the University of Chicago, where he proved a famous conjecture about the existence of H-structures on spheres, using the same ideas. On his return from America Adams became fellow, lecturer, and director of studies at Trinity Hall, Cambridge. There, in 1961, he confirmed his already high international reputation by solving another famous problem, concerning vector fields on spheres. For this he invented some operations in K-theory, which later bore his name, and these proved to be of fundamental importance.

In 1962 Adams left Cambridge for Manchester University, where in 1964 he became Fielden professor in succession to M. H. A. Newman, and was elected a fellow of the Royal Society at the early age of thirty-four. At Manchester he took much further the powerful methods he had originated at Cambridge in a celebrated series of papers 'On the groups J(X)', which opened up a new era in homotopy theory. In the first of these he made a bold conjecture about the relation between the classification of vector bundles by stable isomorphism and their classification by stable homotopy equivalence of the associated sphere-bundles. Reformulated in various ways this Adams conjecture (later a theorem) became one of the key results in homotopy theory.

By 1970 Adams was the undisputed leader in his field and his reputation was such that he was seen as the obvious person to succeed Sir William *Hodge as Lowndean professor of astronomy and geometry at Cambridge. He was delighted to return to Trinity, his old college, although he never became very active in its affairs. Among Adams's various research interests in this later phase of his career three subjects predominated: finite H-spaces, equivariant homotopy theory, and the homotopy properties of classifying spaces of topological groups. Although he published important papers on these and other subjects throughout this period he also began to publish more expository work, notably his lecture notes on *Stable Homotopy and Generalised Homology* (1974) and his monograph on *Infinite Loop Spaces* (1978), based on the Hermann Weyl lectures he gave at Princeton. The latter, especially, gives a good idea of his magisterial expository style and particular brand of humour.

Adams was an awe-inspiring teacher who expected a great deal of his research students and whose criticism of work which did not impress him could be withering. For those who were stimulated rather than intimidated by this treatment, he was generous with his help. The competitive instinct in Adams was highly developed, for example in his attitude to research. Priority of discovery mattered a great deal to him and he was known to argue such questions not just as to the day but as to the time of day. In a subject where 'show and tell' is customary he was extraordinarily secretive about research in progress.

Although Adams enjoyed excellent physical health he suffered a serious episode of depressive illness in 1965 and there were further episodes of depression later. To what extent his professional work was adversely affected by the nature of the treatments he received to help control the condition is not clear, but certainly his contributions to research in later years were not as innovative as those of his youth. Moreover, he never played the prominent role in the academic and scientific world to which his professional standing would have entitled him. Even so, his influence was great; those who turned to him for an opinion were seldom left in any doubt as to his views.

His great contributions to mathematics were recognized by the awards of the Junior Berwick

(1963) and Senior Whitehead (1974) prizes of the London Mathematical Society and the Sylvester medal (1982) of the Royal Society. He received a Cambridge Sc.D. in 1982. He was elected a foreign associate of the National Academy of Sciences of Washington (1985) and an honorary member of the Royal Danish Academy of Sciences (1988), and he received an honorary Sc.D. (1986) from the University of Heidelberg. His *Collected Works* were published in 1992.

In 1953 Adams married Grace Rhoda, daughter of Charles Benjamin Carty, time and motion engineer. Soon after the marriage she became a minister in the Congregational Church. They had a son and three daughters (one adopted). Family life was extremely important to Adams, although he preferred to keep it separate from his professional life. The family used to do many things together, especially fell-walking in the Lake District. Adams acted as treasurer of the local branch of the Labour party and might be described as an intellectual Fabian in outlook. Adams, who was driving, died immediately following a car accident at night, on the A1 near Brampton, 7 January 1989.

[I. M. James in *Biographical Memoirs of Fellows of the Royal Society*, vol. xxxvi, 1990.]   I. M. JAMES

ALBERY, SIR Donald Rolleston (1914–1988), theatrical manager, was born 19 June 1914 at 33 Cumberland Terrace, London, the elder son and second of four children of (Sir) Bronson James *Albery, theatrical manager, and his wife Una Gwynn, daughter of Thomas William Rolleston, Irish scholar and poet. Educated at Alpine College, Switzerland, he joined the family firm of Wyndham & Albery, the owners and managers of three London theatres: the Criterion in Piccadilly Circus, and Wyndham's and the New (after 1972 the Albery), both built by his grandmother, the actress Mary *Moore, and Sir Charles *Wyndham, her partner and second husband. His first position of importance, as general manager of the Sadler's Wells Ballet (1941–5), was complicated by wartime emergencies. On one occasion he arrived in Bath to find that the trucks containing scenery and costumes were immobilized in a siding close to unexploded bombs.

On first nights at his theatres Donald Albery, a tall lean figure, would be seen walking about the auditorium with a slight limp. He was prematurely bald, with a long narrow face, and in later years his resemblance to his father became more marked. He inherited the family business sense, though his taste in plays was modern whereas Sir Bronson was known for his classical productions. In 1953 he formed his own company, Donmar, and his choice of dramatists included Graham Greene, Tennessee Williams, Edward Albee, Jean Anouilh, and (Dame) Iris Murdoch (adapted by J. B. *Priestley). Greene's

The Living Room, with Dorothy Tutin, was his favourite production, and *I am a Camera*, John van Druten's adaptation from Christopher *Isherwood, gave him 'enormous pleasure'.

Although he ran his theatres with an eye to commercial success he could spring surprises, and on occasions was prepared to take risks. He had youthful memories of going to Paris with his parents to see the Compagnie des Quinze, which Bronson admired and brought to London knowing that their appeal would be limited. On hearing about Samuel Beckett's *Waiting for Godot*, Albery went to Paris and decided to put it on in London. He hoped to cast the play with star names for the tramps, but after two years of failing to persuade any of them—including Sir Laurence (later Baron) *Olivier and Sir Ralph *Richardson—the play went on at the Arts Theatre Club directed by the young (Sir) Peter Hall and without stars (1955). Greatly daring, he transferred it to the Criterion in the heart of the West End, where it survived for nearly 300 performances though the audiences were frankly puzzled. Many left at the interval; the performances were disturbed by shouts of 'Take it off!', 'Rubbish!', and 'It's a disgrace!' The run was dogged by illness in the cast and inadequate understudies. In these unhappy circumstances the high teas provided by the management between the Saturday performances were greatly appreciated.

During the late 1950s and 1960s the idiosyncratic productions of Joan Littlewood at the Theatre Royal, Stratford East, appealed to Albery. Under his management they came to the West End and some went to New York—another example of his adventurous spirit. These included *A Taste of Honey* and Brendan Behan's *The Hostage* (both 1959) and *Fings Ain't What They Used T'Be* (1960). Out of gratitude to Joan Littlewood he presented a crystal chandelier to the Theatre Royal. This connection brought him his greatest success, the musical *Oliver!* (1960) by Lionel Bart (who also wrote the score of *Fings Ain't*). *Oliver!* had been turned down by three managements and opened so disastrously at Wimbledon that doubts were expressed at the wisdom of bringing it into the West End, where advance bookings (at the New) amounted to just £145. A new musical director had to be found at the last moment, but the first night changed these gloomy expectations, and the Sean Kenny revolving set on which everything in Dickens's novel happened was rapturously received. *Oliver!* ran for 2,618 performances and has since been revived.

In 1960, against strong competition from Bernard (later Baron) Delfont, Albery added the Piccadilly to the Wyndham–Albery empire. Thus 3,360 seats were offered to the public at every performance in these four theatres. At one point, when it looked as if the Criterion, the oldest of them, would be endangered by a Piccadilly Circus development scheme, Albery leaped eagerly into the fray and fought hard—enjoying the battle—and finally won. After *Oliver!* he produced several other musicals: in 1966, a failure, *Jorrocks*, which lost £70,000; and in 1968 a success, *Man of La Mancha*, which called for extensive structural alterations to the Piccadilly stage, and so, by special permission of the lord chamberlain, the safety curtain was never lowered during the run. Albery was the first manager to investigate the tourist trade in relation to the theatre. This pioneering survey proved beyond doubt that without overseas visitors the theatres would suffer irreparably (though this situation had been suspected for years).

When Sir Bronson Albery died in 1971 Donald Albery took control. In 1977 he became the third member of his family to receive a knighthood; in the following year he sold the theatres and retired to Monte Carlo. Ian Albery, his son by his first wife, carried on for a time. During the Albery regime their theatres were regarded as being among the best run in London, and the two back-to-back theatres, Wyndham's in Charing Cross Road and the Albery in St Martin's Lane, housed some of the most interesting productions of the period. From 1958 to 1978 Albery was also a director of Anglia Television.

Albery was married three times. In 1935 he married Rubina ('Ruby'), daughter of Archibald Curie Macgilchrist, medical officer in India; she died in 1956 as a result of injuries incurred in a World War II air raid. They had one son. In 1946, the year of his divorce from Ruby, he married (Cicely Margaret) Heather, daughter of Brigadier-General Reginald Harvey Henderson Boys. They had two sons and one daughter. The marriage was dissolved in 1974 and in 1978 he married Nobuko, daughter of Keiji Uenishi, businessman, and former wife of Professor Ivan Morris. Albery died in Monte Carlo 14 September 1988.

[Wendy Trewin, *All on Stage, Charles Wyndham and the Alberys*, 1980; Peter Bull, *I Know the Face, But...*, 1959; family papers; personal knowledge.]

WENDY TREWIN

ALLEN, SIR George Oswald Browning ('Gubby') (1902–1989), cricketer and cricket administrator, was born 31 July 1902 in Sydney, Australia, the younger son and second of the three children of (Sir) Walter Macarthur Allen and his wife, Marguerite Julie ('Pearl'), daughter of Edward Lamb, of Sydney, minister of lands in Queensland. His sister married Sir William *Dickson, marshal of the Royal Air Force. His brother died on active service in 1940. Although by birth a third-generation Australian—his father's brother had played cricket for Australia against England at Sydney in 1887—Allen was taken to England at the age of six, so that he should be educated there. In the event, his parents chose to settle in England, his father becoming commandant-in-chief of the Metropolitan Special Constabulary, in which post he was appointed KBE in 1926.

It was not long before 'Gubby' Allen, as he came to be known, was resolutely English. After showing early promise as a cricketer at Summer Fields School, Oxford, he had three years in the Eton XI (1919–21) before winning a blue at Cambridge in 1922 and 1923. After two years at Trinity College, Cambridge, he left without a degree and became a stockbroker in the City. By 1923 he was making the occasional appearance for Middlesex, and gaining a reputation as a genuinely fast bowler and no mean batsman. Of no more than medium build, Allen achieved his pace through timing, thrust, and a fine follow-through. He made the most of an elastic strength, while managing, at the same time, to play the game with style. Between the late 1920s and the mid-1930s there was no English fast bowler, apart from Harold Larwood, capable of more dangerous spells.

Allen was essentially an amateur. Even when, in 1929, he took all ten Lancashire wickets for 40 runs for Middlesex at Lord's, he had done some stockbroking in the City first and arrived on the ground too late to open the bowling. He never played first-class cricket regularly enough in England to score 1,000 runs or take 100 wickets in a season. Not surprisingly, perhaps, it was in Australia, when he went back there as a member of the MCC sides of 1932–3 and 1936–7 and had plenty of bowling, that he was at his most consistent.

On the first of these tours Allen's refusal to resort to 'leg theory' distanced him from his captain Douglas *Jardine. Despite that, he took twenty-one wickets in the five test matches. Four years later he took another seventeen test wickets at the same time as enduring, as England's captain, the mortification of seeing Australia recover from the loss of the first two test matches so effectively that they won the last three and, with them, the Ashes. There developed on the tour of 1936–7 a friendship between Allen and his opposite number, (Sir) Donald Bradman, which was to last for over fifty years and have a major influence within the corridors of cricketing power: this, although it was Bradman with his prodigious scoring who did more than anyone to turn the tables on England.

In the seventeen years which passed between the last of Allen's twenty-five test matches, at Melbourne in 1937, and his last first-class match, against Cambridge University at Fenner's in 1954, he played very little first-class cricket, even for Middlesex. This was partly because of World War II, during which he served, to the rank of lieutenant-colonel, in military intelligence (MI15) at the War Office, partly because of the time he gave to the City, and partly through choice. He did, however, accept an invitation to take a somewhat experimental MCC side to the West Indies in 1947–8, a decision which he considered afterwards to have been a mistake. He was forty-four by then, older than any England captain since W. G. *Grace in 1899, and he tore the first of many hamstrings on the outward voyage.

Elected to the MCC committee for the first time in 1935, at what was then an unusually young age, Allen became in time the *éminence grise*. As a cricket administrator of dominance and durability he ranks with the seventh Baron *Hawke of Towton (1860–1938), the fourth Baron *Harris (1851–1932), and Sir Pelham *Warner (1873–1963). For half a century there was scarcely an issue connected with the game in which he was not closely involved. He was chairman of the England selectors from 1955 to 1961, president of the MCC in 1963–4, treasurer of the MCC from 1964 to 1976, a member of the Cricket Council from its formation in 1968 until 1982, a prime mover in founding the national coaching scheme, and co-author, with H. S. *Altham, of the *MCC Cricket Coaching Book* (1952), the standard work of its kind.

Allen's other main sporting interest was golf, a game to which he applied himself diligently and which he played well enough to have, at his best, a handicap of four. His own account of a good round, stroke by stroke, was always something of a ceremony. As a source of cricketing reference he had no equal, and in the summers after his retirement from the City (he was a member of the Stock Exchange from 1933 to 1972) there was never much doubt where to find him: he would be in his customary place in the window of the committee room at Lord's.

He was appointed CBE in 1962 and knighted in 1986. He was awarded the TD (1945) and US Legion of Merit (1946) for his war services. Allen died 29 November 1989 at his home overlooking the Lord's pavilion in St John's Wood, London. He never allowed himself to be talked into marriage, though he always enjoyed feminine company.

[E. W. Swanton, *Gubby Allen, Man of Cricket*, 1985.]

JOHN WOODCOCK

ANDERSON, (John) Stuart (1908–1990), chemist, was born 9 January 1908 in Islington, the only son and younger child of John Anderson, master cabinet-maker, and his wife, Emma Sarah Pitt. His parents, both widowed, married about 1901–2. From his father's previous marriage there were two stepsisters about twenty

years older. Family circumstances declined catastrophically in 1916, when his father died. Just before that, his mother went to work in a munitions factory. His sister left school early and the family suffered ten years of acute poverty. These years, during which he was solitary, made Anderson permanently shy, and awkward in relationships. He was educated at Highbury County School, Acton Technical College, and Imperial College, where he topped the first-class honours list in 1928 and received the prize in advanced chemistry. After his Ph.D. in 1931, he spent two semesters in Heidelberg, returning to Imperial College (the Royal College of Science) in 1932 as a demonstrator.

From discussions with his colleague Harry Emeleus about how inorganic chemistry should be taught, came their landmark textbook *Modern Aspects of Inorganic Chemistry* (1938). Nevertheless, believing that his future at the RCS was blocked, in 1937 Anderson obtained a senior lectureship at the University of Melbourne, where his leaning towards the chemistry of the solid state increased, and he became especially interested in the constitution of non-stoichiometric compounds.

In 1946 the Atomic Energy Research Establishment was being set up at Harwell and 'J. S.', as his colleagues always knew him, was invited to join the chemistry division as a deputy chief scientific officer. Among other work he was responsible for analysis on fallout from atomic tests. Before the first British nuclear test on Montebello Island in 1952 Anderson went to Melbourne to arrange for analysis of the air particles that would result. He had been offered senior positions in Britain, but deep apprehension about the danger of a nuclear war led him to accept a chair at Melbourne University (1954–9). Although Ph.D. degrees were now possible in Australian universities, research funds and students were lacking and his stay in Melbourne was something of a disappointment. He left after only five years. He had become FRS in 1953.

In 1951 he had been urged to accept the directorship of the National Chemical Laboratory in England, and in 1959 he received another invitation, which eventually he accepted. Nevertheless, he was frustrated by the difference between his assessment of the purpose and possibilities of the NCL and those of the bureaucracy. Within a year of his arrival he was approached about a new chair of inorganic chemistry at Oxford, but he felt committed to the NCL. However, two years later the invitation was renewed and he accepted, arriving at Oxford in October 1963. This was the time of the first systematic application of electron microscopy to solid-state chemistry, and hence to understanding non-stoichiometry at the atomic level. He retired from the Oxford chair in 1975.

Aiming to continue work with another active solid-state research group free of administrative chores, he joined the University College of Wales, Aberystwyth. He renovated a cottage in the country a few miles inland from Aberystwyth, and while the work was in progress he lived alone through an unusually cold and miserable winter in a caravan on the property. Finally, in 1979, the year he received an honorary D.Sc. from Bath University, the Andersons returned once again to Australia, where three of their four children (and their grandchildren) lived. They settled in Canberra. Anderson's continued pleasure in working 'at the bench', even as a senior academic, amazed everyone. When the new 'high-temperature' superconducting oxides were discovered in 1987 his enthusiasm (at the age of seventy-nine) ensured that over a short period he was co-author of eight publications in the field.

Anderson was of medium height and spare frame with a face which, in later years, took on a weathered texture from life outdoors. He was an unusually private man: he seldom relaxed, even with close colleagues. But this was a mask, for he loved an argument, especially on scientific matters, about which he was passionate. A very 'British' chemist, he delighted in 'string and sealing-wax' methods, and practical work in general, especially glass-blowing. His ability to concentrate deeply, excluding all surrounding activities and people, was also remarkable. When a question was put to him, the answer was invariably a thoughtful silence preceding a well-phrased reply. His main contributions to science lay in exploiting the electron microscope to study reaction mechanisms in the solid state, and in the influential 'Emeleus and Anderson' textbook.

In 1935 he married Joan Habershon, daughter of Hugh Habershon Taylor, of Enfield, Middlesex. They had three daughters and a son. Anderson's drive decreased only when, in 1989, he contracted throat cancer. For the last two years of his life his wife was confined to a nursing home, but his children and young colleagues guarded his welfare. His phenomenal memory, puckish humour, and sharpness of intellect persisted to the last days; he died 25 December 1990 in Woden Valley Hospital, Canberra.

[B. G. Hyde and P. Day in *Biographical Memoirs of Fellows of the Royal Society*, vol. xxxviii, 1992; personal knowledge.]   P. DAY

ANDREWES, SIR Christopher Howard (1896–1988), virologist, was born 7 June 1896 in London, the elder child and only son of (Sir) Frederick William *Andrewes, pathologist, and his wife Mary Phyllis, daughter of John Hamer, publisher. He was educated as a day-boy at Highgate School, but he was frequently ill and spent many weeks in bed at home, where he watched and recorded the wildlife in the garden below. He was an unusually able and enthusiastic schoolboy naturalist and produced remarkable diaries recording the plants, insects, and birds of his neighbourhood. He entered St Bartholomew's Hospital as a medical student in 1915. In 1916 he obtained an open scholarship, and other prizes followed later. After war service in the Royal Navy in the winter of 1918–19 he returned to London and qualified MB, BS in 1921, with a gold medal. He became MD and MRCP in 1922 and FRCP in 1935.

He worked at St Bartholomew's until 1923, and then spent two years in the laboratories and wards of the Rockefeller Institute, New York. He returned to St Bartholomew's in 1925 and in 1927 joined the staff of the Medical Research Council. Apart from brief wartime secondments he worked for the Council at the National Institute for Medical Research, first at Hampstead and then at Mill Hill. He rose to be head of the division of bacteriology in 1940 and deputy director in 1952. He retired in 1961.

He was not interested in detailed administration, but in 1946 he promoted the idea of a research station to work on common colds in human volunteers. He persuaded the authorities to set up the Common Cold Research Unit at Salisbury, Wiltshire, and he was in charge there until he retired. He also wrote in 1947 the original memorandum proposing to the World Health Organization that it set up a World Influenza Centre (WIC), to study viruses from around the world collected by a network of national laboratories. The original WIC was established in his department and the network continued long afterwards, being the model for WHO reference laboratories and networks on other subjects.

At first Andrewes was interested in cancer viruses, but then he worked with a biophysicist, W. J. Elford, on the fundamental properties of virus particles, their size, density, and interactions with antibodies. In the 1930s he lectured on the possibility of virus vaccines being developed. His joint paper with K. G. V. Smith and P. Laidlaw in 1933, describing the transmission of a human influenza virus to ferrets, was a landmark and his research was involved with the study of influenza viruses for decades thereafter. The Common Cold Research Unit did pioneering work on the transmission of colds and in 1953 reported that a common cold virus had been grown in human cells cultured in a test-tube.

Out of Andrewes's interest in natural history in general grew his interest in the natural history of viruses and in virus classification and taxonomy. He was a leader in getting virus taxonomy established on a sound basis and internationally agreed and recognized. The environment of free but focused enquiry and individual initiative at the Institute suited him admirably. He was a lively person, good at debate and repartee; a big man, he loved to walk, to a park or to a good place for collecting flies, and his red face and wind-blown white hair showed it. He could be a tough scientific opponent, but he treated the laboratory as an extension of his family and visited most members daily, stimulating and helping them in their experimental work and, at times, in their careers.

He was a member of many scientific committees on subjects ranging from respiratory disease and influenza vaccines to poliomyelitis, myxomatosis, foot-and-mouth disease, and cancer. He wrote many scientific papers and a number of books, including the classic *Viruses of Vertebrates* (1964). He received honorary degrees from Aberdeen (1963) and Lund (1968) and many medals and prizes from institutions in Britain and abroad. He was elected FRS (1939) and a foreign member of the US National Academy of Science (1964), and he received the Robert Koch gold medal from West Germany in 1979. He was knighted in 1961.

In 1927 he married Kathleen Helen (died 1984), a trained physicist and daughter of Robert Bell Lamb, wool merchant. They had a simple home life and raised three sons. The eldest, John, and one of two twins, David, became highly regarded general practitioners, while the other twin, Michael, engaged in research in electronics. Andrewes died 31 December 1988 in Michael's house at Redlynch, near Salisbury. Until the end he was able to identify by its botanical or common name any plant which was brought in from the garden.

[D. A. J. Tyrrell in *Biographical Memoirs of Fellows of the Royal Society*, vol. xxxvii, 1991; private information; personal knowledge.]   D. A. J. TYRRELL

ANDREWS, Eamonn (1922–1987), radio and television broadcaster, was born 19 December 1922 at 11 Synge Street, Dublin, Ireland, the second of five children and elder son of William Andrews, carpenter, and his wife, Margaret Farrell. He was educated at a Dublin convent and the Synge Street Christian Brothers School, where he became an altar boy. In spite of being tall for his age (he was later over six feet and fourteen stones) he was bullied at school and to overcome this he started taking boxing lessons. He was so successful that he became the all-Ireland juvenile middleweight boxing champion.

His first job was as a clerk with the Hibernian Insurance Company, from which he was dismissed when he was discovered doing a boxing commentary for Radio Éireann. After many applications he was finally given more broadcasting work for Irish radio. In 1948 he compèred the stage show *Double or Nothing* from the Theatre Royal, Dublin. The show was seen by

the English bandleader, Joe *Loss, who liked Andrews's voice and personality and invited him to take the programme on tour with the band in England.

In 1949, when Stewart MacPherson gave up his job as compère on a BBC radio programme, *Ignorance Is Bliss*, Andrews wrote to the BBC stating his experience with Irish radio and asked to be considered for the job, which he got. The programme was a great success and Andrews's distinctive voice became known to his English audience. He was then asked to present the live weekly BBC radio programme, *Sports Report*. Although he was badly paid for this, Andrews undertook the programme in order to consolidate his position with the BBC, and he went on to present many successful worldwide boxing commentaries.

In 1951 a chairman was needed for a new BBC television panel game called *What's My Line?* and two people were considered for the job—Andrews and Gilbert *Harding. As it happened, Harding joined the game's panel and Andrews became its chairman. The programme was such a national success that Andrews gained first-class status in television, being voted the top television personality of the year for four years running from 1956. He also appeared on a children's programme, *Crackerjack*.

The BBC bought a new American television programme, *This Is Your Life*, in 1955, even though there was some doubt about its intrusive nature, which was not in the BBC style. Andrews presented the programme, which became an instant success and lasted until 1964, when for internal BBC reasons it was dropped. Greatly concerned, he accepted the chance to change channels to the new independent television station, ABC TV. In 1964 he presented a late-night live talk programme, featuring five guests at the same time. Thus *The Eamonn Andrews Show*, live from London, became the first television programme to broadcast at eleven o'clock at night and get into the top twenty television ratings.

One of Andrews's biggest challenges was to bring back his favourite programme, *This Is Your Life*, on Thames Television in 1969. However, it became an even greater success, rising to the number one position in the national television ratings. It remained in the top ten programme lists and was watched by over fourteen million people weekly. Andrews continued to present it until he died. The current affairs programme, *Today*, was also presented by Andrews on three nights a week, which meant that at some part of the year he was on television for four nights every week. In spite of this schedule, he found time to write for *Punch* magazine and was a member of the exclusive Punch lunch club. He was also (from 1960) chairman of the Irish independent television service, Telefis. He became one of the highest paid entertainers on British television, and was reputed to be a millionaire when some of his business activities failed towards his later years.

In 1964 he became a papal knight of St Gregory (an honour given to him personally by the pope), and in 1970 he was appointed honorary CBE. Even at the height of his success he was always shy and reticent with strangers. Andrews, who never lost his Irish brogue, had an open face, with brown eyes, a broad smile, and a large chin. When he was at the Theatre Royal, Dublin, he met Grace (who was always known by the Gaelic version of her name, Grainne), daughter of Lorcan Bourke, a Dublin impresario. They married in 1951 and had two daughters and a son. Andrews died from heart failure in Cromwell Road Hospital, London, 5 November 1987. His memorial service at Westminster Cathedral attracted over three thousand people.

[Eamonn Andrews, *This Is My Life*, 1963; Gus Smith, *Eamonn Andrews: his Life*, 1989; personal knowledge.]
MALCOLM MORRIS

ANSTEY, Edgar Harold Macfarlane (1907–1987), documentary film-maker, was born in Watford 16 February 1907, the younger child and only son of Percy Edgar Macfarlane Anstey and his wife, Kate Clowes. His father was a chef, distinguished in his occupation. He was able to attend Watford Grammar School and Birkbeck College, London University, graduating in sciences. In June 1926 he was appointed junior scientific assistant at the Building Research Establishment, Department of Scientific and Industrial Research, where he served for five years, 'eagerly looking for something more creative to do', developing a keen interest in film, and joining the London Film Society, where he had an opportunity to see films of the Soviet and continental avant-garde directors. In 1931 he left the security of the Civil Service to join the nascent documentary film unit at the Empire Marketing Board under John *Grierson.

Anstey's creative career fell into two phases. Until 1949 he followed the mercurial path of John Grierson, making the types of documentaries which Grierson was currently championing, and moving posts in accordance with Grierson's wishes. *Housing Problems* (1935) and *Enough To Eat?* (1936), both made jointly with (Sir) Arthur *Elton, were landmarks in the development of the documentary, being the first (and effectively the only) Griersonian documentaries addressing social issues with party political implications. They employed the starkly pedagogical, unvisual style, deliberately devoid of aesthetically pleasing features, which Grierson argued for at the time. Following Grierson's interest in the kind of screen journalism developed by the American *March of Time* series, designed not so much to

report but to editorialize about contemporary issues, Anstey became *March of Time*'s London editor and then went to the USA as foreign editor (1936–8). *March of Time* issues touching on British concerns, such as appeasement, were banned in Britain, much to the regret of (Sir) Winston *Churchill.

Always a patriot and a family man first, Anstey returned to Britain as war was approaching, although he loved America and was set fair for a career there offering both greater scope and better financial prospects. He was turned down for military service, much to his anger, because he was more useful to the war effort as a filmmaker. Between 1940 and 1945 he directed, produced, or supervised the making of some seventy films, concentrating on instructional films, the most unglamorous but most useful type of film during the war.

After the war something went wrong with the documentary movement. There was a loss of purpose, creative development, and young talent—Grierson called it 'the dereliction'. Some of the leading figures—such as Harry Watt and Paul *Rotha—tried their hands, with varying success, at feature films and television; others, such as Stuart Legg and Basil *Wright, gradually gave up film-making altogether, and Grierson himself took charge of a feature-film studio (Group Three) and never returned to documentary production. Anstey turned to writing in 1947, publishing a book on *The Development of Film Techniques in Britain*, and worked as film critic for the *Spectator* (1946–9), but unlike the others he then returned to production, with drive and purpose undimmed. In 1949 he became films officer for the British Transport Commission and established there a new documentary film unit, British Transport Films, which he headed until his retirement in 1974.

Thus began the second phase of Anstey's creative career. His unit succeeded in attracting young talent, such as that of John Schlesinger, and adopted new technologies and creative ideas as they came along. In addition to making many instructional, informational, and public relations films of impeccable technical standards as well as cost efficiency, it produced a regular flow of documentaries, gaining some of the highest awards nationally and internationally, including those of the British Film Academy, the Venice Film Festival, and the Hollywood Oscar. Anstey showed that the solution to the 'dereliction' of the documentary was to give the audience aesthetic enjoyment as well as ideas, and that those 'arty' and 'commercial' techniques which make films attractive need not be incompatible, as Grierson had so disastrously argued, with the documentary purpose. *Journey into Spring* (1957), *Between the Tides* (1958), *Under Night Streets* (1958), *Terminus* (1961), and *Wild Wings*

(1965) are some of the most mature and flawless manifestations of the British documentary film genre. As Anstey later put it with characteristic simplicity: 'Without art there is no effective communication, anyway.'

Anstey was also an outstanding manager, of people as well as organizations, a much liked and effective committee man, lecturer, and public speaker. He served as chairman of the British Film Academy (1956 and 1967), president of the British and the International Scientific Film Associations (1961–3), governor of the British Film Institute (1965–75), and adjunct professor at Temple University, Philadelphia (from 1982). He was appointed OBE in 1969, but it pleased him particularly to have been made an honorary member of the Association of Cinematographic and Television Technicians and of the Retired Railway Officers.

In appearance he was the image of the tall, slim Englishman, with a small moustache and regular features, made for the classic Savile Row suit; in manner he was courteous, rather formal at first, but with great warmth and charm. His private life was entirely devoid of the eccentric preferences, tastes, and lifestyles common in the film world. In 1949 he married (Marjorie) Daphne, who worked with Grierson at the National Film Board of Canada, the daughter of Leslie Dalrymple Lilly, of the Canadian Bank of Commerce and the Lilly Adjustment Agency. They had a son and a daughter. Anstey died suddenly 26 September 1987, in the Royal Free Hospital, London. He had been suffering from leukaemia, which sapped his physical energies, but his intellectual zest and vigour remained unimpaired to the last.

[Elizabeth Sussex, *The Rise and Fall of the British Documentary*, 1975; G. Roy Levin, *Documentary Explorations*, 1971; private information; personal knowledge.]   NICHOLAS PRONAY

ARMSTRONG, John Ward (1915–1987), archbishop of Armagh and Anglican primate of all Ireland, was born in Belfast 30 September 1915, the eldest of four sons (there were no daughters) of John Armstrong, Belfast corporation official, and his wife, Elizabeth Ward. While attending Belfast Royal Academy he became a chorister of St Anne's Cathedral, Belfast, and developed an interest in church music, which was to be a lifelong passion. At an early age he became an accomplished pianist and organist and at one time gave serious consideration to a career as a musician. However, largely because of his family's strong church involvement (his father was organist of St Simon's parish church in Belfast), he decided to seek ordination in the Church of Ireland. He went to Trinity College, Dublin, where he won the Toplady, pastoral theology, Archbishop King's biblical Greek, and Downes

prizes. He obtained first-class honours in Hebrew (1936 and 1937) and a first class in divinity testimonium (1938). In 1945 he became BD and in 1957 MA.

He was ordained deacon for the diocese of Dublin and Glendalough in 1938 and became a priest on 24 December 1939. His first curacy was in the Dublin suburban parish of Grangegorman, from 1938 to 1944. He was appointed honorary clerical vicar of Christ Church Cathedral, Dublin, in 1940 and became dean's vicar on the staff of St Patrick's Cathedral, Dublin, in 1944. In 1950 he was elected prebendary of Tassagard on the chapter of St Patrick's. He was appointed rector of Christ Church, Leeson Park, Dublin, in 1951 and in 1958 took up the important position of dean of St Patrick's Cathedral. He encouraged good music in all his churches, arranging the restoration of St Patrick's organ, and used his fine speaking voice to good effect in his sermons. As dean and ordinary of the national cathedral he was to become a most influential and popular churchman in Dublin and throughout the Republic of Ireland. During that period he combined the duties of the deanery with that of Wallace lecturer in Trinity College, Dublin (1954–63), and lecturer in liturgy at the Divinity Hostel, which at that period was the centre for training Anglican ordinands in Ireland.

On 2 May 1968 he was elected bishop of Cashel, Emly, Waterford, and Lismore and was consecrated bishop in his own cathedral of St Patrick on 21 September 1968. Following the amalgamation of southern dioceses in 1977, he became bishop also of Ossory, Ferns, and Leighlin from 29 April 1977. On the retirement of George Otto Sims, Armstrong was elected archbishop of Armagh and primate of all Ireland, on 25 February 1980. He was enthroned in St Patrick's Cathedral, Armagh, on 7 May 1980 and led the Church of Ireland as primate until his retirement, due to ill health, on 1 February 1986. This was a period of intense violence and division in Northern Ireland and his leadership was often tested in an atmosphere of inseparable religious and political allegiances. He challenged recalcitrant elements on both sides of the conflict, condemning murder and attempting to effect reconciliation. In 1981 he was awarded an honorary DD by Trinity College, Dublin. He was a trustee of the National Library of Ireland (1964–74).

Although such people were almost unknown among Irish Protestants until the 1960s, he was a committed ecumenist throughout his ministry and in 1980 acted as co-chairman, with the Roman Catholic primate, Cardinal Tomás O'Fiaich, of the Ballymascanlan inter-church talks. He was a member of the British Council of Churches from 1966 to 1980 and in November 1979 became chairman of the Irish Council of

Churches, to which he gave courageous leadership during years when the churches of Northern Ireland faced immense challenge through growing sectarianism. Within the Anglican communion Armstrong was an elected member of the Anglican Consultative Council (1971–81) and attended meetings at Limuru, Kenya, in 1971, Dublin in 1973, Trinidad in 1976, and Canada in 1979. He was a good administrator and in his hands meetings were effective and businesslike. He was essentially an ecumenical pastor who felt grieved by the divisions of the Northern Ireland community and based his sincere love for Anglicanism on an abiding affection for all things liturgical.

Armstrong, whose hobbies were carpentry and bird-watching, was of average height and stature, with irrepressible good humour and an engaging smile. In later years he had a slight limp. In 1941 he married Doris Winifred, daughter of William James Harrison, chief clerk of the Dublin circuit court. They had two sons and two daughters, the younger of whom died in 1950 at the age of eighteen months. Typically, during the last six months of his retirement, Armstrong was in charge of the little parish at Skerries, twenty miles north of Dublin, during a vacancy in the rectory. He died at his home in Swords, county Dublin, 21 July 1987, and was buried in the grounds of his beloved St Patrick's Cathedral.

[Records at the Representative Church Body library, Dublin; private information; personal knowledge.]

R. H. A. EAMES

ARNOLD, Denis Midgley (1926–1986), musicologist, was born 15 December 1926 in Sheffield, the only son and younger child of Charles Arnold, company director, and his wife, Bertha Ball. He was educated at High Storrs Grammar School in Sheffield, and Sheffield University. He graduated BA in 1947 and B.Mus. in 1948, and received an MA in 1950 for a dissertation on Thomas *Weelkes, partly written during service in the Royal Air Force.

The orientation of his life's work as a musicologist was determined by the award in 1950 of an Italian government scholarship enabling him to go to Bologna to study Italian music of the years around 1600. In 1951 he was appointed lecturer (reader, 1960) in music in the department of adult education at the Queen's University, Belfast; he also worked for the music department. His experience in adult education confirmed another of Arnold's conspicuous qualities: his powers as an educator and communicator, addressing widely varying audiences in plain language and with engaging enthusiasm. This stance, moreover, informs all his writings, even the most specialized. It was during his Belfast years that he began publishing the stream of articles in learned journals that continued up to

his death. Through them he quickly made a name as a major scholar on the music, mainly secular vocal, of late Renaissance and early baroque Italy, and as one of Britain's leading musicologists, a reputation reinforced by his many editions of the music itself.

In 1964 Arnold moved as senior lecturer in music to the University of Hull at about the time he published his first book, the 'Master Musicians' volume on *Monteverdi* (1963). He was joint editor of, and a contributor to, the *Monteverdi Companion* (1968; new edition as *The New Monteverdi Companion*, 1985) and, perhaps surprisingly, the *Beethoven Companion* (1971). It was natural that he should welcome the chance to communicate with a potentially larger readership through a series of short studies of composers with whom he was particularly identified: *Marenzio* (1965), *Monteverdi Madrigals* (1967), *Giovanni Gabrieli* (1974), *Monteverdi Church Music* (1982), and *Gesualdo* (1984), as well as *Bach* (1984).

In 1969 Arnold became professor of music at the University of Nottingham and from 1975 to his death was Heather professor of music at the University of Oxford. He had always been a keen conductor, and he threw himself into performance at both universities with renewed zeal. He increasingly became a public figure on a wider scale too. For many years he toiled as editor of, and contributor to, *The New Oxford Companion to Music* (1983); he was president of the Royal Musical Association (1978–83) and British representative on the directorium of the International Musicological Society (IMS) from 1978 to his death; and he served as chairman of the Oxford Playhouse and the music panel of Southern Arts. Amid this activity he wrote his largest study, *Giovanni Gabrieli and the Music of the Venetian High Renaissance* (1979) and, with his wife, *The Oratorio in Venice* (1986), the fruit of an increasing interest in his later years in Italian, especially Venetian, music of the century and a half after the period on which he concentrated for much of his career.

Arnold was short of stature but in every other respect a 'big' man: ebullient, generous, and gregarious, as well as informal and unpretentious; an industrious scholar who produced eminently approachable books and practical editions that helped transform the general view of music and its contexts in Italy in the age of Gabrieli and Monteverdi. All were based on solid research: a public figure in his element as lecturer, conductor, or conference-goer, he was perhaps never happier than when working in libraries and archives, especially in his beloved Venice.

Arnold was appointed CBE in 1983. In 1980 the honorary degree of D.Mus. was conferred on him by two universities, Sheffield and Queen's, Belfast. He was an honorary fellow of the Royal

Academy of Music (1971) and Royal College of Music (1981). He became FBA and an honorary foreign member of the Accademia Nazionale dei Lincei, Rome (both 1976), and in 1977 was awarded the Premio Internazionale Galileo Galilei dei Rotary Italiani at Pisa University for services to the study of Italian music.

In 1951 Arnold married Elsie Millicent, a trained musicologist, daughter of John William Dawrant, schoolmaster, of Liverpool. They had two sons. Arnold died suddenly, of a heart attack, 28 April 1986 in Budapest while representing Britain at a meeting of the directorium of the IMS.

[Nigel Fortune in *Proceedings of the British Academy*, vol. lxxiii, 1987; private information; personal knowledge.]   NIGEL FORTUNE

ARUP, SIR Ove Nyquist (1895–1988), civil engineer, was born 16 April 1895 in Newcastle upon Tyne, the elder son and second of three children of (Jens Simon) Johannes Arup and his wife, Mathilde Bolette Nyquist. Johannes Arup was Danish veterinary consul in Newcastle upon Tyne at the time but was shortly afterwards transferred to Hamburg, Germany, as Danish consul there. Ove Arup's early schooling was in Hamburg, but he received his secondary education at Sorø Academy in Denmark and in 1913 went to the University of Copenhagen, where he studied mathematics and philosophy. He then moved to the Polyteknisk Laereanstalt (later the Technical University of Denmark, DTH) to study engineering. He graduated in 1922 with a first-class honours degree.

He joined, as an engineer in their Hamburg office, the Danish international firm of civil engineers, Christiani & Nielsen. In 1923 he transferred to their London office, for the firm was one of a number of Danish-led civil engineering contractors carrying out novel and major works in Britain, especially in reinforced concrete, which at that time was a little-used material.

In 1925 he became the firm's chief designer, a post he held until 1934. His main activity was the design of harbours and jetties, but it was during this period that he became actively interested in architecture, and particularly in what became known as the Modern movement. He did not, however, become professionally involved with architectural projects until 1933, when he was invited to collaborate in the design and construction in Highgate village of a block of apartments which became known as Highpoint. This gave Ove Arup the opportunity to apply to a major building the techniques of reinforced concrete, which he had used in many civil engineering projects. As a consequence in 1934 he accepted the post of chief designer and director with J. L.

Kier & Co., another London firm with Danish roots.

Ove Arup's interest in what he later called 'total architecture' developed and grew, and he became associated with most of the significant architects in Britain and in Europe. He became a leading figure in the MARS (Modern Architectural Research Society) group and he was active in the Architectural Association. He designed and built with the architectural group Tecton, one of whose partners was Berthold *Lubetkin, a number of projects, notably the penguin pool at London Zoo.

In 1938 he left Kier to form, together with his cousin Arne Arup, the firm of Arup & Arup, engineers and contractors. During World War II his inventive mind turned to the design of air-raid shelters, which he felt could be converted into underground car parks after the war, but he invariably experienced great frustration in promoting his novel ideas. He also designed and built parts for Mulberry harbour, which in 1944 helped make the Normandy landing possible.

For some years Arup felt torn between contracting and design, but in 1946 he set up practice as a consulting engineer; the firm became Ove Arup & Partners in the same year. Its subsequent expansion and diversification resulted in a practice which became one of the largest and most important in the world. In 1978 the firm was transformed from a partnership, in which Ove Arup was still a partner, into a company, Ove Arup Partnership, owned by a trust for the purpose of making it independent—financially and professionally—of outside influence. The projects which gave Arup personally the greatest pleasure were those in which essentially simple structural concepts were elegantly expressed. An outstanding example is the Kingsgate footbridge over the river Wear at Durham, which was completed in 1963. Other projects for which Arup and his partners will be remembered include the Sydney Opera House, the Maltings at Snape, Coventry Cathedral, and the Centre Pompidou in Paris.

Physically tall and lean, though somewhat stooped in old age, he remained active almost till his death. His face was warm, intelligent, and quizzical, his well-known inability to finish a sentence marking a constant search for exactness and truth, rather than vagueness. This, as well as the strong Danish accent he always retained despite decades of residence in Britain, made any encounter or conversation with him a memorable experience.

Ove Arup was always a visionary and an idealist who hated compromise. He worked for greater understanding between the professions, particularly between architects and engineers. This found its most visible embodiment with the formation in 1963 of Arup Associates, a practice of architects, engineers, and quantity surveyors. Arup was fortunate in attracting talented collaborators, but all those who worked with him were deeply influenced and inspired by him. He stood for both quality and excellence, professionally and personally. At the same time he enjoyed life in all its aspects.

He did not involve himself with professional institutions, though he belonged to and was honoured by many. He was eventually persuaded to become a vice-president of the Institution of Civil Engineers (1968–71). Appointed CBE in 1953 and knighted in 1971, he was made a chevalier of the Order of Dannebrog (Denmark) in 1965 and a commander (first class) in 1975. He received the RIBA gold medal for architecture (1966) and the Institution of Structural Engineers' gold medal (1973). Universities honoured him with doctorates: Durham (1967), East Anglia (1968), the Technical University of Denmark (DTH) (1974), Heriot-Watt (1976), and City University (1979). In 1976 he became one of the original fellows of the Fellowship of Engineering (from 1992 the Royal Academy of Engineering). He was a member of the Danish Academy for Technical Sciences (1956), and in 1986 he was elected to the Royal Academy.

In 1925 he married Ruth, daughter of Poul Sørensen, managing director of the Danish Water Authority and an eminent engineer. They had one son and two daughters. Arup died 5 February 1988 at his home in Highgate, London.

[Ove Arup Partnership archives; personal knowledge.]
POVL AHM

ASHMOLE, Bernard (1894–1988), classical archaeologist and art historian, was born 22 June 1894 in Ilford, Essex, the youngest in the family of two sons and three daughters of William Ashmole, auctioneer and estate agent, and his wife, Sarah Caroline Wharton Tiver. Both his parents had strong literary and religious interests. He was educated at Forest School (1903–11) and in 1913 went to Hertford College, Oxford, with a classics scholarship. In 1914, having taken pass moderations, he was commissioned in the 11th Royal Fusiliers, served in France, and was severely wounded on the Somme. He was awarded the MC in 1917. Back in Oxford, he obtained an ordinary pass degree and went on to study for the diploma in classical archaeology under the guidance of Percy *Gardner and (Sir) John *Beazley. He developed an interest in numismatics, but classical sculpture was to be his main interest for the rest of his academic career and he helped catalogue the collection in the Palazzo dei Conservatori in Rome and, later, that in Ince Blundell Hall (1929).

In 1923 he had taken his B.Litt. at Oxford and joined the staff of the coin room in the Ashmolean Museum there (he was a collateral descendant of the founder). He was persuaded in 1925 to take up the directorship of the British School at Rome, which he held until 1928. He was then appointed (1929) to the Yates chair of classical archaeology at University College London, adding to this the part-time keepership of the Greek and Roman department in the British Museum in 1939. Here he had to supervise the packing of its treasures on the outbreak of war in 1939.

He was commissioned as a pilot officer in the Royal Air Force Volunteer Reserve, serving in Britain, Greece, and the Middle and Far East, and returning as a wing commander. He was twice mentioned in dispatches. After the war ended in 1945, he supervised the reinstallation of his department in the British Museum, giving up his chair in 1948 to become a full-time keeper. In 1956 he was persuaded to succeed Beazley to the Lincoln chair of classical archaeology and art at Oxford, where, as a fellow of Lincoln College, he served until his retirement in 1961. This was followed by busy travelling and visiting appointments at Aberdeen, Yale, Cincinnati, and Malibu, where he advised J. Paul Getty on the purchase of antiquities, and also by fieldwork, at the mausoleum of Halicarnassus in Turkey.

Ashmole was not a prolific scholar, but all his writing was characterized by a precision of learning and perceptivity that made him an unrivalled and internationally recognized authority on classical sculpture. This was displayed by concise articles, not without some acidity when dealing with the inadequacy of others, and perhaps best enjoyed in his lectures, notably the Semple lectures (*The Classical Ideal in Greek Sculpture*, 1964), and the books *Olympia* (with N. Yalouris, 1967) and *Architect and Sculptor in Classical Greece* (1972). By looking beyond connoisseurship of Greek sculpture to the problems of its context and logistics of its creation he demonstrated the value of the study to many other fields of classical archaeology. His memorable lecturing style was quiet yet dominating, but as a teacher he was probably most influential through the example he set. He had a remarkable organizing skill, which showed in his scholarship no less than in his work on the British Museum collections before and after the war, in his installation of the cast collections in University College London, and in Oxford in the Ashmolean's new building in 1961.

His interest in art did not stop with antiquity but he was the friend of contemporary artists, even adviser to the fated *I, Claudius* film with Charles *Laughton, and in the late 1920s commissioned from the architect A. D. *Connell one of the first concrete-frame houses in Britain, High and Over, near Amersham. His practicality ranged from the design of garden fountains cast in concrete in upturned umbrellas to a rare skill with the camera which he employed to good effect on ancient sculpture. His collection of sculpture photographs was given to King's College London (the Ashmole archive), with copies in the cast gallery at the Ashmolean. He was in many respects not the last of an older generation of scholars but the first of the new, displaying in his work and life the finer standards of his predecessors and adding an almost non-academic breadth and originality.

He was made a fellow of the British Academy in 1938, was appointed CBE in 1957, and became honorary ARIBA in 1928. He was an honorary fellow of Hertford (1961) and Lincoln (1980) colleges, Oxford, and of University College London (1974). Aberdeen awarded him an honorary LL D (1968). He was an honorary member of the Archeological Institute of America (1940) and the Archaeological Society of Athens (1978), and was awarded the Kenyon medal of the British Academy in 1979.

Ashmole was a tall, slim man; his bearing was almost military but tempered by a sprightliness of step and unforced charm. In 1920 he married Dorothy Irene, daughter of Everard de Peyer, chartered accountant. She survived him by three years; a biographer remarked that 'anyone who knew the couple finds it hard to think of them apart'. They had two daughters and a son. In 1972 Ashmole and his wife moved to Peebles, to be near their son, and there he died 25 February 1988.

[Bernard Ashmole, *One Man in his Time*, 1993; Martin Robertson in *Proceedings of the British Academy*, vol. lxxv, 1989; personal knowledge.] JOHN BOARDMAN

ASHTON, SIR Frederick William Mallandaine (1904–1988), dancer, and founder and choreographer, with (Dame) Ninette de Valois, of the Royal Ballet, was born 17 September 1904 in Guayaquil, Ecuador, the youngest of four sons of George Ashton, a minor diplomat working for a cable company, and his wife, Georgiana Fulcher, who came from a Suffolk family. Later there was a much-loved younger sister, Edith. The family moved to Peru, where Ashton attended the Dominican School in Lima. In 1917 he was taken to see a performance by Anna *Pavlova—'she injected me with her poison'— and resolved to make dancing his life. In 1919 he was sent to England, to Dover College, which he hated, and to spend holidays in London with family friends. With them he saw Isadora Duncan and many dance companies, including that of Sergei Diaghilev in his disastrous production of *The Sleeping Princess* in 1921.

In 1922, aged eighteen, he began dance lessons with Léonide Massine and, later, with (Dame) Marie *Rambert. Lacking height, he was nevertheless slim and elegant with a long, large-featured face and melancholy eyes, which would be effective in his future stage career. His dancing talent was not great, and his 'passionate laziness' was noted by Rambert, but this perceptive woman already sensed choreographic talent in the young man. The suicide of Ashton's father in South America brought his impoverished mother to England to join her son. They shared a series of inadequate lodgings while Ashton attended Pavlova's London performances and the last seasons of Diaghilev's Ballets Russes. At one of these he met the Russian designer, Sophie Fedorovitch, who would become his lifelong friend and collaborator.

Rambert, with her group of pupils, gave Ashton an enviable springboard as a budding choreographer; her generous encouragement launched his future career. He composed solos, *pas de deux*, and short ballets for revues, musical shows, the Camargo Society, and the Ballet Club, which later became the Ballet Rambert. His first work of importance was *A Tragedy of Fashion* in 1926 for the revue, *Riverside Nights*. In the thirty years which followed, Ashton choreographed many of his best ballets: *Façade* for the Camargo Society (1931); *Les Rendezvous*, Vic-Wells Ballet for Ninette de Valois (1933); an American interlude to arrange dances for the Virgil Thomson/Gertrude Stein opera, *Four Saints in Three Acts* (1934); and *Le Baiser de la Fée* at Sadler's Wells in 1935, which inaugurated his long partnership with (Dame) Margot Fonteyn. Leaving Rambert for the larger stage of de Valois' company, his most successful works were *Apparitions* and *Nocturne* (1936), *Les Patineurs* and *A Wedding Bouquet* (1937), *Horoscope* (1938), and *Dante Sonata* and *The Wise Virgins* (1940–1).

Ashton served with RAF intelligence during World War II, but was given leave in 1943 to choreograph a new ballet, *The Quest*, with a score by (Sir) William *Walton. After the war, with the Sadler's Wells company resident at the reopened Royal Opera House, Covent Garden, Ashton choreographed the ballet considered by many his most perfect—César Franck's *Symphonic Variations* (1946). He ventured into opera production in 1947, at Covent Garden and Glyndebourne, and in 1948 choreographed two short works, *Scènes de Ballet* and *Don Juan*, and Sergei Prokofiev's *Cinderella*, the first three-act British ballet. In 1949 and 1950 ballets in Paris and New York were less successful. In 1951 Ashton also choreographed his first film, *The Tales of Hoffmann*, and this was followed in 1952 by *The Story of Three Loves*. At Covent Garden his highly successful ballet *Daphnis and Chloë* was performed in 1951, to be followed in 1952 by Léo Delibes' three-act *Sylvia*.

Ashton's entire life was lived in the ballet world. From 1953 until the late 1970s he continued to invent and produce work of varying shades and character. Among his notable achievements were *Homage to the Queen* (1953); *Romeo and Juliet* for the Royal Danish Ballet (1955); *Ondine* (1958); *La Fille Mal Gardée* (1960); *Marguerite and Armand* (1963); *The Dream* (1964); *Enigma Variations* (1968); and *A Month in the Country* (1976). He may have reached his largest public with the charming dances for the 1970 film, *Tales of Beatrix Potter*, in which he appeared as Mrs Tiggywinkle. He was both principal choreographer (1933–70) and director (1963–70) of the Royal Ballet.

Ashton was a lyrical choreographer, considered by many to be peerless in this field, though his approach to choreography was idiosyncratic. He seemed to plan little in advance, to arrive for first rehearsals without original ideas, and to use music suggested, occasionally even chosen, by friends. He would ask dancers to invent steps to musical phrases, sometimes selecting ones he liked and discarding others, sometimes discarding everything and commanding new inventions. In this unorthodox manner many of his best-known ballets were built; the original cast of dancers in each production took a considerable part in its creation, the resulting choreography reflecting their particular talents and style. Margot Fonteyn, for whom he made the majority of his ballets, brought into every Ashton role her love of floating, aerial movements while carried by her partner.

Ashton was homosexual and had several enduring relationships during his long life. Over the years he lived in charming, comfortable apartments and small houses in London and in a large country house at Eye in Suffolk, with ten acres, a lake, and a terraced room filled with his collection of Wemyss pottery, vividly displayed in well-lit glass cabinets. He was a supreme socialite, loving gossip and good living, which caused a certain florid portliness in his later years. His sense of humour was delightful and he was an amusing, often witty, companion. He adored everything connected with royalty and became a particular friend of his near contemporary, the queen mother. He was much honoured, receiving the CBE (1950), a knighthood (1962), CH (1970), and the OM (1977). He was given the freedom of the City of London (1981) and the Legion of Honour (1960). He had honorary degrees from Durham (1962), East Anglia (1967), London (1970), Hull (1971), and Oxford (1976). He died 18 August 1988 at his house in Eye.

[Z. Dominic and J. S. Gilbert, *Frederick Ashton, a Choreographer and his Ballets*, 1977; David Vaughan, *Frederick Ashton*, 1977; personal knowledge.]

MOIRA SHEARER

ATKINS, SIR **William Sydney Albert** (1902–1989), engineer, was born 6 February 1902 in Bow, east London, the second of three sons (there was also a daughter, who died at the age of eight) of Robert Edward Atkins and his wife, Martha Mary Ann Sully, who, when her husband died in 1908, set up a millinery business to support her family. He was educated at the Coopers' Company School, where he won a competition to become an articled pupil to (Sir) E. Graham Wood's firm of structural engineers. Wood paid the fees for Atkins to attend evening classes, enabling him to become a fully qualified draughtsman after three years. During the final two years of his apprenticeship he gained experience of practical work on construction sites and in workshops; at the same time he attended further evening classes at Manchester College of Technology and took an external London degree at intermediate B.Sc. level. At the age of nineteen he began a two-year degree course in engineering at University College London, from where he obtained second-class honours in 1923.

During the next five years he undertook a variety of jobs—with Dr Oscar Faber, Dorman Long, and the Foundation Company, which was building the Deptford power station. The chief engineer responsible for this major job died suddenly and, at the age of twenty-six, Atkins was appointed in his place. After completion of the power station, he moved to Smith Walker Ltd. as structural designer and rose rapidly to become chief engineer in 1928.

Soon after this, Atkins started his own business by buying out a Smith Walker subsidiary company, specializing in reinforced concrete, which he had helped to form. His new company, London Ferro-Concrete, prospered and attracted more and more work, as the recession of the early 1930s gave place to activity in preparation for the coming World War II. His policy of employing the best people he could get was a major factor in building up this successful design and building firm and in the growth of the international engineering consultancy, W. S. Atkins & Partners, which he set up in 1938. During the war 'London Ferro' made a major contribution to the war effort by constructing a wide variety of defence works, including part of the Mulberry harbour used in the Normandy landings.

At the end of the war Atkins arranged another management buy-out by the directors of London Ferro, and in 1950 he severed his connections with the firm to concentrate all his energy on W. S. Atkins & Partners. The next few years saw the start of the rapid growth of the firm, which formed the heart of the later international company, W. S. Atkins Ltd. In 1945 Atkins had been invited to discuss the appointment of his firm as consulting structural engineers for a major new steel works at Port Talbot (the Abbey works).

With characteristic honesty, he pointed out that he was virtually the whole staff of W. S. Atkins & Partners. Notwithstanding, Atkins got this huge job. The works, which became the Steel Company of Wales, were opened in 1951 by Hugh *Gaitskell, the chancellor of the Exchequer, who said: 'There has been no single project of this size in the British Isles since the great days of the railway age.'

The Abbey works project, with the special skills it required in project management over a wide field, provided the basis for the development of the later multi-disciplinary international business. Atkins was associated with most of the large steelworks developments in Britain and many overseas. Other projects included Berkeley and Drax power station, Selby coalfield, the Channel tunnel, and major parts of motorway construction. In 1986 Atkins decided to stand down as chairman of his company. He did not find this easy but, with characteristic generosity, he arranged to transfer a substantial part of the equity to the staff on advantageous terms.

Atkins, a well-built short man, achieved his success through strongly held opinions and innovative ideas, combined with determination and toughness to carry them through. He was never arrogant or pompous, and his toughness was not unkind. Occasionally he could seem hard when dealing with people, but only because of the high standards which he himself maintained and expected others to follow. The moment of hardness quickly passed, often to be followed by words of encouragement and a twinkle in his eye, preserved to the last. His innovation inevitably led to some mistakes, towards which he had a rare and very constructive attitude. He freely admitted errors, and often wrote a paper on them to prevent their repetition, whether in his own organization or elsewhere. He thrived on competition, but never descended to vilifying his rivals, often giving them unstinting praise. His work absorbed much of his energy and there was little time left for recreation and hobbies, although he was a keen gardener and founded in 1965 the Round Pond Nurseries on his estate near Chobham, Surrey.

For his work Atkins was appointed CBE in 1966 and knighted in 1976. His company twice won the Queen's award for industry. He was a fellow of the Fellowship of Engineering (later the Royal Academy of Engineering), and was awarded the Sir William Larke medal and Telford premium prize by the Institution of Civil Engineering, of which he was also a fellow. In 1982 he became an honorary freeman of Epsom and Ewell.

In 1928 he married Elsie Jessie, daughter of Alfred Edward Barrow, police officer, of Hockley, Essex. They had two daughters. Atkins died in Woking, after a short illness, 15 August 1989.

[Sir William Atkins, *Partners* (autobiography, privately published), 1988; private information; personal knowledge.]   CALDECOTE

AVES, DAME Geraldine Maitland (1898–1986), public servant and social reformer, was born 22 August 1898 at Jay's Hatch, a gamekeeper's cottage in a wood near the village of Bovenden, Hertfordshire, because her mother wanted her first child to be born in the depths of the country. She was the elder daughter (there were no sons) of Ernest Harry Aves, social investigator (and collaborator of Charles *Booth), who later, as an expert on minimum wage rates and working conditions, became first chairman of the trades boards set up in 1909. His wife, Eva Mary, the youngest of the six children of Frederick Maitland, of the East India Company, was politically active, a suffragist and one of the first women members elected to the London School Board. Geraldine and her sister attended Frognal, a small private school in Hampstead. In March 1917 their father unexpectedly died. It was a blow that Geraldine Aves described even in old age as 'the worst of my life'.

She went to Newnham College, Cambridge (1917–20), and obtained a third class in both parts of the economics tripos (1919 and 1920). While at Cambridge she became president of the Women's University Settlement Society and this helped her to decide that 'doing something with and for people was how I should spend my days'. She was appointed in early 1924 as a 'temporary assistant organizer' in the care committee service of the London county council's education department. By 1938, under the threat of World War II, she was engaged at County Hall in the complex plans for the evacuation of London schoolchildren. In 1941 she was seconded to the Ministry of Health as chief welfare officer responsible for the general co-ordination of evacuation and wartime welfare services, including the recruitment of social workers. Drawn into the plans for postwar reconstruction, in June 1945 she served as the United Nations Relief and Rehabilitation Administration's chief child-care consultant in Europe, returning to the Ministry in 1946 to become the established head of a permanent welfare division, where, apart from undertaking various short-term assignments to the United Nations, she remained until retiring in 1963. She played a key part in developing the postwar reforms in welfare services, the subsequent development of personal social services, and social work training.

Her retirement from the Ministry of Health was the beginning of a second career in the voluntary sector. She was fully occupied in promoting, enabling, and chairing (at which she excelled) numerous projects and organizations that were eager for her support. She served on the National Institute of Social Work Training (board of governors, 1961–71), the Council for Training in Social Work (member, 1962–72), the London Diocesan Synod and Bishop's Council (member, 1971–9), the London Diocesan Board for Social Responsibility (vice-chairman, 1979–84), the North London Hospice (founder-president, 1986), the Harington scheme (a horticultural training scheme for young people with learning difficulties, of which she became chairman in 1980 and later vice-president in 1984), and many other organizations.

Amongst the achievements in which she took most pride in this second career was that of chairing the independent committee of inquiry into the place of and scope for voluntary workers in the social services, which was set up in 1966. Following vigorous campaigning under her leadership, the committee's report, *The Voluntary Worker in the Social Services* (1969), led to the creation of The Volunteer Centre, a national organization which aimed to promote and encourage volunteering at all levels and in all spheres of society. She became a founder member of its board of governors and, from 1974, vice-president. It was this work that led to her appointment as DBE in 1977—an honour she had long coveted and, rightly, felt she deserved. She had been appointed OBE in 1946 for her contribution to wartime social services, and CBE in 1963. All through her working life she maintained close links with Newnham College. In 1956 she was elected associate, in 1962 associate fellow, and in 1981 honorary fellow.

Geraldine Aves was one of that band of educated single women who, following World War I, looked for personal fulfilment in a professional career. She found it in a lifetime devoted to the common good. A handsome woman, of regal appearance, she charmed many and overawed—on occasion bullied—some others, although her authoritarian manner softened in later years. From the age of thirty-four, when she was baptized, her Christian faith meant a great deal to her. She never married, but enjoyed a rich private life of travels and companionship with close friends and relatives. It was while visiting, in Swanage, Dorset, a former colleague, Sibyl Clement Brown (who in 1927 became Britain's first qualified psychiatric social worker) that she was taken ill, entered a nursing home, and died 23 June 1986.

[Dame Geraldine Aves, *1924 to 1983: Commentary by a Social Servant*, 1983; Phyllis Willmott, *A Singular Woman: the Life of Geraldine Aves 1898–1986*, 1992; personal knowledge.]   PHYLLIS WILLMOTT

AYER, SIR Alfred Jules (1910–1989), philosopher, was born 29 October 1910 at Neville Court,

Abbey Road, north-west London, the only child of Jules Louis Cyprien Ayer, financier, later in the timber trade, who came from a Swiss Calvinist family, and his Jewish wife, Reine Citroën, who came from the Citroën car family and ultimately from Holland. He had no religious upbringing, and his childhood years, which he described as lonely, were spent in London. At the age of seven he was sent to Ascham, at Eastbourne, and from there went on, first to Eton as a scholar, and then, with an open scholarship in classics, to Christ Church, Oxford. Choosing not to read classical honour moderations, he obtained in 1932 a first in *literae humaniores*, which, so out of sympathy was he with the prevailing tone of Oxford philosophy, he owed entirely to his marks in ancient history.

On the advice of his tutor, Gilbert *Ryle, who had already introduced him to the ideas of Bertrand (third Earl) *Russell and Ludwig *Wittgenstein—and to the latter personally—Ayer spent the winter of 1932–3 in Vienna, attending Moritz Schlick's lectures and the meetings of the Vienna Circle, and then returned to a lectureship at Christ Church, to which he had been elected while still an undergraduate, and which he held until 1939.

In 1936 Ayer published his most famous book, *Language, Truth and Logic*, written at the age at which (as he liked to recall) David *Hume had written his *Treatise of Human Nature* (1739). It was his version of Viennese logical positivism, though he also saw it as a recasting of the traditional theses of British empiricism into linguistic terms. The book is full of passionate iconoclasm, expressed in a fine cadenced prose. Its central thesis is the verification principle, which divided all statements into the verifiable or the unverifiable. Verifiable statements were either reducible to observation statements (everyday beliefs, science) or transformable by means of definitions into tautologies (logic, mathematics), and only they were meaningful. Unverifiable statements (metaphysics, ethics, religion) were literally nonsense. Difficulties found in formulating the principle were treated as comparatively insubstantial, though, when the book was reissued in 1946, the new thirty-six-page introduction, itself a model of philosophical frankness, gave them much greater weight.

Ayer's ideas scandalized established philosophy, not least through their self-assurance, and they infiltrated pre-war Oxford mainly through a discussion group of younger dons that met in (Sir) Isaiah Berlin's rooms in All Souls College. The young J. L. *Austin was an early convert, but only briefly, and was then, for over twenty-five years, Ayer's relentless critic. The more open-minded of the older philosophers, such as William Kneale and H. H. Price, regarded Ayer's impact on Oxford philosophy as salutary.

Ayer's next book, *The Foundations of Empirical Knowledge*, philosophically his most refined work, supplemented the earlier attempt to set the limits of human knowledge with an account, based on sense-data, of how we attain this knowledge. The book appeared in 1940, by which time Ayer was in the army. He was commissioned in the Welsh Guards, but mostly served in the Special Operations Executive. He ended the war as a captain, attached to the British embassy in Paris.

In 1945 Ayer went to Wadham College, Oxford, as philosophy tutor, a post to which he had been appointed in 1944, but in 1946 he obtained the Grote chair of the philosophy of mind and logic at University College London. Here Ayer's charismatic powers as a teacher, enhanced by his swiftness in discussion, and his broad and growing fame as the author of *Language, Truth and Logic*, came into their own, and he converted a run-down department into the rival of Oxford and Cambridge. This was the happiest period of his career. In 1956 he published *The Problem of Knowledge*, in which, abandoning reductionism, he justified our everyday beliefs by their power to explain our sense-experience. This line of argument was developed in such later works as *The Origins of Pragmatism* (1968) and *Russell and Moore* (1971), in which the history of philosophy was deftly blended with philosophical argument, and *The Central Questions of Philosophy* (1973), which aimed at updating Russell's *The Problems of Philosophy* (1912).

In 1959 Ayer had accepted the Wykeham chair of logic at Oxford, which was held at New College, partly to continue his polemic with Austin, who died the following year. Ayer always held that philosophy, to be worth while, must aim at generality: Austin saw no reason to believe this. Though perhaps no longer at the epicentre of debate, Ayer fought with immense skill and undiminished speed and agility against such developments as ordinary-language philosophy, Wittgensteinianism, and the new essentialism. He liked philosophy to be high-spirited as well as serious. He remained a great and generous teacher, and a prolific writer, with twenty-six publications before his death and one after. He shone at international conferences. He retired in 1978 and was a fellow of Wolfson College, Oxford, from 1978 to 1983.

Like his friend and hero, Bertrand Russell, Ayer did not treat philosophy as a cloistered enterprise. In the postwar years he reached a wide audience through the BBC *Brains Trust*, and later was active against anti-homosexual legislation.

'Freddie', as he was known, was highly gregarious, elegant, and an animated conversationalist. He was short, with large, dark brown eyes, and a sudden smile which irradiated his fine, slightly simian features. He spoke very fast, and to the accompaniment of quick, fluent gestures. His friends included writers, painters, politicians, and journalists. He hated religion, and followed competitive sport, particularly football, avidly. He loved the company of women, and was much loved in turn. Vanity was in his nature, but he combined this with great charm and total loyalty to his friends.

Ayer was made FBA in 1952, and a foreign honorary member of the American Academy of Arts and Sciences in 1963: he was knighted in 1970, and became a chevalier of the Legion of Honour in 1977. He received honorary degrees from Brussels (1962), East Anglia (1972), London (1978), Trent in Canada (1980), Bard in the USA (1983), and Durham (1986). He became an honorary fellow of New College (1980).

Ayer was married four times: first, in 1932 to (Grace Isabel) Renée, daughter of Colonel Thomas Orde-Lees, explorer, of the Royal Marines; there was one son and one daughter. The marriage was dissolved in 1941 and in 1960 he married Alberta Constance ('Dee'), former wife of Alfred Wells, American diplomat, and daughter of John Chapman, business executive, from the local newspaper-owning family in Providence, Rhode Island: they had one son. The marriage was dissolved in 1983 and in the same year he married Vanessa Mary Addison, former wife of Nigel Lawson MP (later Baron Lawson of Blaby), and daughter of Felix Salmon, businessman. She died in 1985 and in 1989 he remarried Alberta Ayer, who survived him. Ayer also had a daughter with Sheilah Graham, the Hollywood columnist (see Wendy W. Fairey, *One of the Family*, 1993). When Ayer died in University College Hospital, London, 27 June 1989, the event received much publicity in the press, serious and popular, and it was seen as bringing to an end a long line of outspoken arbiters of liberal or secular opinion.

[A. J. Ayer, *Part of My Life*, 1977, and *More of My Life*, 1984; A. Phillips Griffiths (ed.), *A. J. Ayer, Memorial Essays*, 1992; information from friends; personal knowledge.]   RICHARD WOLLHEIM

B

BADDELEY, Hermione Youlanda Ruby Clinton (1906–1986), actress, was born 13 November 1906 in Broseley, Shropshire, the youngest of four daughters (there were no sons) of William Herman Clinton-Baddeley, composer, and his wife, Louise Bourdin. A descendant both of Sir Henry *Clinton, a British general in the American War of Independence, and Robert Baddeley, the actor and pastry-cook who bequeathed the annual fruit cake to the cast playing at Drury Lane, she combined aspects of both these ancestors in her long and eventful career. Her immediate senior sister, Angela Baddeley, was also a successful actress. Their theatrical education was at the Margaret Morris School of Dancing in Chelsea, where the pupils considered themselves vastly superior to the more competitive Italia Conti children.

Hermione's first great success was under Basil *Dean's management, playing a badly behaved waif from the slums with a famous plate-smashing scene in Charles McEvoy's *The Likes of Her* at the St Martin's theatre (1923). The next year Dean cast her as a murderous Arab urchin in *The Forest*, by John *Galsworthy. Having established a career as a dramatic actress she switched to comedy in *The Punch Bowl* (1924), a revue at the Duke of York's, where she danced with Sonny Hale and credited her formidable comic technique to lessons learned from the comedian Alfred Lester. She joined *The Co-optimists*, at the Palace theatre, in the same year. In *On with the Dance* (1925), (Sir) Noël *Coward's revue for (Sir) Charles *Cochran, she created (with Alice Delysia) Coward's topically satirical 'poor little rich girl'. This was the first of four productions for Cochran and then, among a number of undistinguished comedies, farces, and musicals, she also played Sara in *Tobias and the Angel* by James *Bridie (Westminster, 1932). She had a long run in *The Greeks Had a Word for It*, which transferred from Robert Newton's Shilling theatre in Fulham to the Duke of York's in 1934.

With *Floodlight* by Beverley *Nichols (Saville, 1937) she began a long period as a queen of revue, having also plunged into an increasing social whirl with her husband, David Tennant, for whom she often performed in cabaret at his club, the Gargoyle. Herbert Farjeon's wit in *Nine Sharp* (subsequently *The Little Revue*, 1940) provided the perfect launching-pad for her inspired clowning, bravura characterization, and skill at quick costume and make-up changes. Her most popular characters included an old girl at Torquay, a Windmill girl in 'Voilà les Non-Stop Nudes', and her prototype funny ballerina, Madame Allover. When she was ill, five understudies barely kept the curtain up.

In her autobiography she suggests that she recruited Hermione *Gingold to *Rise Above It* at the Comedy (1941). It was a legendary, explosive partnership, with Gingold's daunting control of laughter and Baddeley's penchant for wild improvisation. They were reunited less successfully in *Sky High* at the Phoenix the next year. Their final joint venture, Noël Coward's *Fallen Angels* at the Ambassador's in 1949, inspired the fury of the author at the liberties they took. He was mollified when the show became a fashionable success. Meanwhile, as a dramatic actress Hermione Baddeley's two outstanding successes were as Ida in Graham Greene's *Brighton Rock* (Garrick, 1943), which she repeated in the Boulting Brothers' film (1947), and in *Grand National Night* (Apollo, 1946), by Dorothy and Campbell Christie. Her American début in *A Taste of Honey* (1961) led to an invitation from Tennessee Williams to create the role of Flora Goforth in *The Milk Train Doesn't Stop Here Anymore* at the Spoleto festival (1962) and on Broadway a year later. A newspaper strike killed the play but Williams greatly admired her performance.

In England she played in many films from 1926 (*A Daughter in Revolt*)—most notably in *Kipps* (1941), *It Always Rains on Sunday* (1947), *Quartet* (1948), *Passport to Pimlico* (1949), and *The Pickwick Papers* (1952). She was nominated for an Oscar in 1959 for *Room at the Top* (1958) and had a Hollywood success as the housekeeper, Ellen, in *Mary Poppins* (1964). For the last twenty years she lived mainly in Los Angeles and became a familiar face on television in situation comedies, especially *Bewitched* and *Maude*.

Always known as 'Totie', and originally a petite and delicate gamine, Hermione Baddeley grew into a still small, but fuller figured beauty and this lent authority to her later blowsier characterizations. In 1928 she married David Pax Tennant, son of Edward Priaulx Tennant, first Baron Glenconner, MP for Salisbury. They had a son and a daughter. The marriage was dissolved in 1937 and in 1941 she married Captain J. H. ('Dozey') Willis, MC, of the 12th Lancers, the son of Major-General Edward Henry Willis, of the Royal Artillery. This marriage was later dissolved. She enjoyed a stormy romance with the actor Laurence Harvey, but they did not marry. She died in Los Angeles, at the Cedars Sinai Hospital, 19 August 1986.

[Hermione Baddeley, *The Unsinkable Hermione Baddeley* (autobiography), 1984; *The Times*, 22 and 27 August 1986; *Contemporary Theatre, Film and Television*, vol. iv, 1987; Phyllis Hartnoll (ed.), *The Oxford Companion to the Theatre*, 1983; Ephraim Katz, *The International Film Encyclopaedia*, 1980; David Quinlan, *The Illustrated Directory of Film Character Actors*, 1985; personal knowledge.]   NED SHERRIN

BAIRD, SIR Dugald (1899–1986), professor of midwifery, was born 16 November 1899 in Beith, Ayrshire, the eldest in the family of three sons and one daughter of David Baird, head of the science department at Greenock Academy, and his wife May, daughter of John Allan, farmer, of Alloway. He was educated at Greenock Academy and then studied science and medicine at Glasgow University, graduating MB, Ch.B. in 1922. He proceeded MD with honours and was awarded the Bellahouston gold medal in 1934. He was elected a fellow of the Royal College of Obstetricians and Gynaecologists in 1935. After he qualified he worked in Glasgow Royal Maternity and Women's Hospital and Glasgow Royal Infirmary.

His experiences as a medical student and junior doctor in Glasgow, where he attended home births, had a fundamental effect on his career. He was appalled at the conditions in which women had their confinements and the lack of concern about them among his senior colleagues. During his term as senior lecturer in the University of Glasgow (1931–7) he introduced sterilization for the many women who had had several children that he attended and also, in some cases, performed abortions for social reasons. He was shocked by the high maternal and infant mortality rates in the Glasgow Royal Maternity Hospital, where two mothers died each week from complications of childbirth. Baird became aware of the wide discrepancy in the health and reproductive efficiency of women in different socio-economic groups and quickly realized the importance of social factors in obstetrics.

When he moved to Aberdeen in 1937, as regius professor of midwifery, he saw opportunities for research in this field. Since the population was relatively stable and not too large, proper arrangements could be made for obstetric care and the keeping of statistics. Baird set up a records system based on good data and accurate measurements and introduced epidemiology into obstetric practice. Initially in Aberdeen he had conducted a thriving private practice in addition to his hospital work, but when the National Health Service was introduced in 1948 he gave up private practice to concentrate on his academic work and research.

Realizing that a multi-disciplinary approach was most likely to succeed in improving obstetric care and reproductive performance, Baird persuaded the Medical Research Council to support this type of research. In 1955 the Obstetric Medicine Research Unit was established, with himself as the honorary director. It consisted of dietitians, sociologists, physiologists, endocrinologists, statisticians, and obstetricians, who worked together to elucidate the factors affecting reproduction in women. Baird was thus the instigator of social obstetrics. Much of what he pioneered later became commonly accepted practice.

He was also instrumental in altering the pattern of reproduction in Britain. He lectured on the fifth freedom—freedom from the tyranny of excessive fertility. He introduced the first free family planning clinic in Britain in Aberdeen, and offered abortion to Aberdeen women. This was very important in influencing the reform of the abortion law in 1967. Baird also encouraged women who had completed their family to be sterilized.

Baird was concerned with long-term effects in obstetrics. Because of the excellent record system in the Aberdeen Maternity Hospital he was able to study generations of women and the influence on daughters of their mothers' pregnancies. He saw deaths from cervical cancer as avoidable and instituted the first screening programme, the results of which showed that mortality could be reduced by this method.

Baird, who retired from his chair in 1965, sat on many local, national, and international committees and was a consultant to the World Health Authority. He was knighted in 1959 and received honorary degrees from Glasgow (1959), Manchester (1962), Aberdeen and Wales (both 1966), and Newcastle and Stirling (both 1974). He became honorary FRCOG in 1986.

Baird was a big man with a strong physical presence. He had a quizzical face and the smile on his lips illustrated his marked sense of humour. In his earlier years he was a fine rugby football player and had a trial for the Scottish international team. In later life he played a good game of golf. In 1928 he married May Deans (died 1983), daughter of Matthew Brown Tennent, grocer, of Newton, Lanarkshire. She was also a doctor and was involved in local and national politics. She was appointed CBE (1962) and both she and her husband were made freemen of Aberdeen (1966). There were two sons and two daughters of the marriage. Baird died in Edinburgh 7 November 1986.

[Personal knowledge.]   MALCOLM MACNAUGHTON

BALFOUR, Harold Harington, first BARON BALFOUR OF INCHRYE (1897–1988), airman, businessman, and politician, was born 1 November 1897 in Farnham, Surrey, the younger son and second of three children of Colonel Nigel Harington Balfour, OBE, a serving officer, of Belton, Camberley, Surrey, and his wife Grace Annette Marie, youngest daughter of Henry Robarts Madocks and granddaughter of Field-Marshal Baron *Napier of Magdala. His elder brother was killed in January 1941 when his ship, HMS *Southampton*, was sunk in the Mediterranean. Balfour was educated at Chilverton Elms, Dover, and the Royal Naval College, Osborne.

Soon after the outbreak of World War I in 1914, he volunteered for service with the 60th Rifles, but his urge to fly encouraged him to transfer to the Royal Flying Corps when a chance was offered the next year. There then began a distinguished, yet hazardous spell as a fighter pilot on the western front, which culminated in his promotion, in 1917, to command a flight in the famous No. 43 (Fighter) Squadron, in which he had served earlier under the command of Major William Sholto *Douglas (later Marshal of the Royal Air Force Baron Douglas of Kirtleside). Once wounded in action and, by temperament, by no means fitted for war, he was awarded the MC and bar for gallantry. He remained with the newly formed Royal Air Force until 1923.

Faced with a continuing need to earn a living, he became, initially, a news reporter on the *Daily Mail* before joining Whitehall Securities in the Pearson Group in 1925, when the organization was then entering the field of commercial aviation. Politics also beckoned and, after standing unsuccessfully as the Conservative candidate for the Stratford division of West Ham in 1924, Balfour was elected to the House of Commons in 1929 as the member for the Isle of Thanet, which he represented until 1945, when he was created Baron Balfour of Inchrye, of Shefford, in the county of Berkshire.

In 1938, as the Royal Air Force was rearming for war, he accepted Neville *Chamberlain's invitation to join the government as parliamentary under-secretary of state for air, first, under Sir H. Kingsley *Wood, and later in (Sir) Winston *Churchill's national government, under Sir Archibald *Sinclair (later first Viscount Thurso). It was an inspired appointment in which he served with signal ability until 1944, often flying himself about in a Spitfire and forming a first-hand judgement of Fighter Command's 'big wing' controversy in the Battle of Britain. Balfour adorned the office which he was to hold for six-and-a-half years, always championing the cause of the Service he loved. His achievements at the Air Ministry were many. Outstanding among them was the establishment, in the spring of 1940, of the great Empire Air Training Scheme of which he was a prime instigator and which, in the next five years, was responsible for training more than 130,000 aircrew in countries of the Commonwealth and empire. Its contribution to victory was undoubted. Moreover, his relationship with the Royal Air Force's senior officers, from the chief of the air staff, Sir Charles *Portal (later Viscount Portal of Hungerford), and the air staff, to the heads of operational commands, was both effective and forthright, not least because they respected his knowledge of aviation and his own Service record in World War I.

Eventually Churchill, having earlier failed to persuade him to accept, first, the office of financial secretary to the Treasury and, later, a civil department of state (Balfour refused each to remain loyal to the Royal Air Force), appointed him resident minister in West Africa until the dissolution of the national coalition in 1945.

Senior privy councillor (sworn on 5 August 1941), Balfour remained active in politics for much of his life, speaking frequently for Tory friends in the country and often intervening in House of Lords debates. This he combined with his business interests, which included a directorship of British European Airways from 1955 to 1966 and chairmanship of BEA Helicopters Ltd. in 1964–6. He also held the presidency of the Chambers of Commerce of the British Empire from 1946 to 1949 and of the Commonwealth and Empire Industries Association from 1956 to 1960. His autobiography, *Wings Over Westminster* (1973), one of his three published works, was well received, reflecting his early training as a Fleet Street journalist and his feeling for words. He wrote touching little stanzas and verses on the back of old envelopes.

An upstanding and attractive man, who was intensely loyal, Balfour was a persuasive speaker on a public platform, his sensitivity and humour enabling him quickly to catch the mood of an audience. His all-round judgement was acute. Although he lived happily in London at End House, St Mary Abbot's Place, Kensington, with his family often around him, his love of fishing and shooting took him regularly to Scotland. There, in his contented twilight years, he once confided in a member of his family: 'You know, I would sooner be stone deaf on a grouse moor than able to hear a pin drop in a bath chair.'

Balfour married, first, in 1921 Diana Blanche (died 1982), daughter of Sir Robert Grenville Harvey, second baronet; they had one son. The marriage was dissolved in 1946 and he married, secondly, in 1947 Mary Ainslie, daughter of Albert Peter Anthony Profumo, barrister; they had one daughter. Balfour died 21 September 1988 in King Edward VII Hospital, London. He was succeeded in the barony by his son Ian (born 1924).

[Harold Balfour, *Wings Over Westminster* (autobiography), 1973; family information; personal knowledge.]
P. B. LUCAS

BALL, SIR George Thomas Thalben- (1896–1987), organist. [See THALBEN-BALL, SIR GEORGE THOMAS.]

BANHAM, (Peter) Reyner (1922–1988), architectural critic and historian, was born 2 March 1922 in Norwich, the elder son (there were no daughters) of Percy Banham, gas engineer, and his wife, Violet Frances Maud Reyner. Reyner Banham (Peter only to his close friends) had a typical Norfolk upbringing in the Nonconformist and Labour tradition, in which education was highly valued. His father's family had been Primitive Methodists and an influential maternal uncle was Edwin George Gooch, a Labour MP. His parents were not well off and he had a scholarship at the local public school, King Edward VI School in Norwich, which wanted him to go to Cambridge to read French. But Banham, whose interest in technology had been formed early, won a national scholarship to train as an engineer with the Bristol Aeroplane Company, with which he spent much of the war (1939–45). Back in Norwich he became involved with the Maddermarket theatre, lecturing on art and writing arts reviews in the local Norwich paper.

In the late 1940s, now married, he enrolled at the Courtauld Institute in London. Having graduated BA in 1952 and commenced a Ph.D., he joined the staff of the *Architectural Review*, where his doctoral supervisor, (Sir) Nikolaus *Pevsner, was an editor. Already Banham and his wife had instigated weekly open houses to study contemporary art and design and he soon became a prominent member of the Independent Group of the Institute of Contemporary Art, whose fellow members were the leading figures of the postwar revolt against Modernism in art and architecture. Its major outcomes were the New Brutalism in architecture and Pop Art—of which Banham was the leading proselytizer and chronicler.

His incisive writing in the influential *Architectural Review* established him as a major commentator on contemporary architecture and design. His reputation was confirmed by the publication of his doctoral thesis, *Theory and Design in the First Machine Age* (1960). This dazzling, densely argued, and meticulously researched work became the seminal reassessment of the history of the Modern movement in architecture.

In 1964 Banham became a senior lecturer at the Bartlett School of Architecture, University College London. He became a reader in 1967 and in 1969 was given a personal chair in the history of architecture at the Bartlett. Meanwhile he had published *The New Brutalism* (1966), a history of the movement which he had espoused from the late 1950s onwards and which he felt had run its natural course. After *The Architecture of the Well-tempered Environment* (1969), about architecture as determined by its mechanical services, he published three books, the most successful of which, especially among the locals, was *Los Angeles: the Architecture of Four Ecologies* (1971).

In 1976, tired of the post-1968 gloom which had settled on British architectural academic life, he took up the post of chairman of the department of design studies at the University of New York at Buffalo. This turned out to be a disappointment and in 1980 he moved to a chair in art history at the University of California, Santa Cruz, where his wife became director of the Eloise Pickard Smith Gallery. A powerful figure in her own right, she was an essential part of Banham's life and career. Happy living in a house overlooking the sea at Santa Cruz, cycling up to the university, where he taught art history as well as architectural history, and travelling widely, Banham published the lyrical *Scenes in America Deserta* (1982) about the great American deserts in whose thrall he had been since the early 1960s. He became honorary FRIBA in 1983 and was awarded an honorary D.Litt. by East Anglia University in 1986.

Tall, well built, a prodigious conversationalist, and, from the early 1960s onwards, patriarchally bearded, he had a penchant for string ties, silver belt buckles, unexpected headgear, and the small-wheeled Moulton bicycle.

Banham was the towering architecture and design critic and polemicist of the postwar era. His great gift was in looking at major issues from vantage points which nobody else had thought of occupying. Last in the line of that school of German art history which placed primary valuation on meticulousness in dealing with source material, Banham's point of departure from this tradition was only in the subjects to which he applied it. His position was that the design of a new refrigerator, automobile, or the latest film could and should be analysed with the same rigour and methodology as a painting by Piero della Francesca.

In 1987 he was appointed to the Sheldon H. Solow chair at the Institute of Fine Arts, New York University. Before he could take up this prestigious post it was found he had cancer. After returning to London for his final months he wrote the text of a book about his old friend and Archigram member, Ron Herron.

On 16 August 1946 he married Mary, daughter of John Mullett, park-keeper in south London. They had a son and a daughter. Banham died 18 March 1988 in University College Hospital, London, with this and the inaugural lecture, which he knew he could never deliver in person, just completed.

[Personal knowledge.]   SUTHERLAND LYALL

BARLOW, Harold Everard Monteagle (1899–1989), professor of electrical engineering, was born 15 November 1899 at 45 Balfour Road, Islington, London, the second child in the family of four sons and two daughters of Leonard Barlow, professional electrical engineer, and his wife, Katharine Monteagle, of Glasgow. After Wallington Grammar School, at the age of fifteen he entered the City and Guilds College at Finsbury, and in June 1917 obtained the college certificate in electrical engineering. He then wanted to follow his elder brother Leonard into the Royal Flying Corps, but was persuaded to make better use of his training in experimental work with the Signal School at Portsmouth, as a sub-lieutenant in the Royal Naval Volunteer Reserve (1917–19).

After the war he studied electrical engineering at University College London, graduating with first-class honours in 1920. Research under Professor Sir Ambrose Fleming, FRS, led to a Ph.D. three years later. He then joined his father's electrical engineering consulting firm, but was not altogether happy with the work. So when Fleming offered him an assistant lectureship, he gladly returned to UCL in 1925. He soon became an excellent all-round academic, producing a substantial research output, seeming equally at home in power and communications. His research included a fundamental experimental study of Ohm's law at high current densities. He also invented a valve ammeter and a protective system for fluorescent tubes.

With war again threatening, the Air Ministry was selecting suitable academics to be told the secrets of radar. Barlow, by now a reader, was a natural choice, and when war broke out in 1939 he was deeply involved. He eventually became superintendent of the radio department at the Royal Aircraft Establishment (1943–5), with about 800 staff. During this time he realized that microwave techniques, essential to radar, could also be important in civil applications.

On his return to UCL after the war as professor of electrical engineering (1945–50) and Pender professor (1950–67), he built up a strong research school in microwaves, and an undergraduate course with a firm foundation of electromagnetic theory. His principal research interest now was in the use of millimetre-wave waveguides for telecommunications, and he was influential in persuading the Post Office to initiate a major programme of research and development in this area, to which UCL made considerable contributions. Barlow was a strong advocate of the use of *guided* waves wherever possible, so releasing frequency bands for mobile services, for which free-wave communication was imperative. He was also very active in surface-wave research, and in the application of electromagnetic forces and the Hall effect to the measurement of microwave power.

He was a regular and always welcome participant in scientific conferences, especially those of the International Union of Radio Science, from which in 1969 he received the Dellinger gold medal. His other honours included: FRS (1961), honorary doctorates of Heriot-Watt (1971) and Sheffield (1973), foreign membership of the Polish Academy of Sciences (1966), foreign associateship of the US National Academy of Engineering (1979), the Microwave Career award of the (American) Institute of Electrical and Electronics Engineers (1985), and a Royal medal of the Royal Society (1988).

Barlow retired from the UCL Pender chair in 1967, but remained in the department as an honorary research fellow. Optical fibres were then emerging as an alternative to waveguides for telecommunications. It was characteristic of Barlow that, once convinced of the superiority of optical fibres, he switched his own research in that direction. He had a delightful personality, with a characteristic and infectious laugh, frequently heard in the laboratory. He was interested in everything that was going on in the department, and retained this interest to the end of his life. In his last few years illness prevented him from getting up to his beloved University College, but it did not stop him working on optical fibres.

Barlow was of average height and build, with clear blue eyes, a healthy complexion, and a ready smile. He had a forward-looking attitude, an enthusiasm for research, and a zest for life. In 1931 he married Janet Hastings, daughter of the Revd Hastings Eastwood, minister at Christ Church (Presbyterian), Wallington, Surrey, and the marriage was a very happy one. They had three sons and a daughter. Barlow's own modest comment on his career was: 'Finally, I regard such success as I have been able to achieve as largely dependent upon my good fortune in having a happy home and a healthy life.' He died at his home in Epsom 20 April 1989, after a long and painful period of suffering, first with arthritis, and later also cancer.

[Alex L. Cullen in *Biographical Memoirs of Fellows of the Royal Society*, vol. xxxvi, 1990; personal knowledge.]   ALEX CULLEN

BASNETT, David, BARON BASNETT (1924–1989), general secretary of the General and Municipal Workers' Union (GMWU), was born 9 February 1924 in Liverpool, the son of Andrew Basnett, regional secretary of the GMWU, and his wife, (Mary) Charlotte Kerr. His mother died when he was six. After attending a local elementary school he won a scholarship to Quarry Bank High School in Liverpool. His first job after leaving school was as a bank clerk. During World War II he served as a pilot in the Royal Air Force, in Sunderland flying boats involved in reconnaissance missions over the Atlantic.

Basnett joined the GMWU as a Liverpool regional official in 1948 and was appointed as the union's first national education officer in 1955. Five years later he was promoted to the post of national industrial officer, with responsibility for negotiations in the chemicals and glass industries. He gained a reputation as one of the most intelligent and progressive of the new generation of union officials, not least through his active participation in the innovative phase of productivity bargaining at ICI and elsewhere in the chemicals industry. He was a tall, thin, and quietly spoken man, whose demeanour was more like that of an academic or civil servant than of a manual workers' trade-union official.

Basnett achieved wider public recognition during the dramatic seven-week strike at the Pilkington Glass Company in St Helens in 1970. The dispute exposed chronic weaknesses in union. organization and in union–management relations. The closed-shop agreement covering nearly 8,000 workers had produced complacency on the part of local union officials and management, the virtual collapse of union membership participation, and the absence of effective joint procedures. Within a few days the strike became a national *cause célèbre*, and Basnett was subjected to intense public scrutiny as he struggled to defeat a putative 'breakaway union', to negotiate an end to the bitter dispute, and thereafter to reconstruct the credibility of the GMWU in St Helens.

The courage and expertise shown by Basnett at Pilkington undoubtedly contributed to his success in the election for the post of GMWU general secretary in 1973. The dispute confirmed also that the union required substantial reorganization and improved services in order to encourage growth and effective membership participation. Basnett was not wholly successful in his attempts to reform the GMWU. In the thirteen years before he retired in 1986, he was able to conclude mergers with several unions, most notably with the Boilermakers to form the General, Municipal, Boilermakers, and Allied Trades Unions (GMBATU) in 1982. The tradition and practices of regional autonomy, however, impeded the implementation of other reforms that might have allowed the union to benefit more from the growth of overall union membership in the 1970s and strengthen it for the more difficult challenges of the 1980s.

Basnett was appointed to the general council of the Trades Union Congress (TUC) in 1966 and became one of its most prominent members during the following twenty years. He served as chairman of the finance and general purposes committee and the economic committee. He represented the TUC on the National Economic Development Council from 1973 to 1986, as a founder member of the National Enterprise Board (1975–9), and as a member of several committees of inquiry and three royal commissions—most notably the 1974–7 royal commission on the press, for which he co-authored a minority report.

Basnett's contribution to the trade-union movement can be divided into two distinct periods, separated by the year when he was chairman of the TUC in 1977–8. Throughout the 1970s he worked closely with Jack Jones of the TGWU in the 'inner cabinet' of the TUC, negotiating with the Heath, Wilson, and Callaghan governments on a wide range of economic, industrial, and social policies. In his 1978 presidential address to Congress, Basnett outlined his strong commitment to the view that union leaders had a right and a duty to participate with government in developing policies designed to improve economic performance and reduce social inequality. A few days later, James Callaghan (later Baron Callaghan of Cardiff) astonished the TUC by his decision to delay the expected general election. Over the following six months, the widespread industrial disruption of the 'winter of discontent' buried what was left of the 'social contract' with the Labour government, contributed to its electoral defeat in the spring of 1979, and ended the first, most successful, phase of Basnett's career.

The Conservative governments of the 1980s were determined to weaken the power of trade unions, and to exclude their leaders from any involvement in policy-making. The focus of Basnett's activity therefore shifted to the relationship between unions and the Labour party; he helped to create a new organization in 1979, Trade Unionists for a Labour Victory (TULV), promoted conferences between union and Labour party leaders, and pressed for reforms in the party's structure and organization. The failure of many of these initiatives and the weakness of trade unions throughout the 1980s may have contributed to Basnett's decision to retire early in 1986. More important, one of his two sons, Ian, a doctor, had suffered serious neck and spinal injuries on a rugby field in 1984. Basnett chose to strengthen further the close family life that he shared with his wife, Kathleen Joan Molyneaux, whom he had married in 1956, Ian, and his other son, Paul. Kathleen was the daughter of John

Joseph Molyneaux, general practitioner. Basnett was made a life peer in 1987 and derived considerable satisfaction from his contributions to the House of Lords. He died of cancer, at home in Leatherhead, 25 January 1989.

[TUC annual reports 1978 and 1989; *Independent*, 27 January 1989; personal knowledge.]

DAVID WINCHESTER

BAWDEN, Edward (1903–1989), draughtsman, painter, and designer, was born 10 March 1903 in Braintree, Essex, the only child of Edward Bawden, a Braintree ironmonger of Cornish stock, and his wife, Eleanor Game, the daughter of a Suffolk gamekeeper. He went to Braintree High School, to the Friends' School in Saffron Walden, and to the Cambridge Art School, and then—on a Royal Exhibition scholarship—to the Royal College of Art. Here he studied writing and illumination, but took his diploma in book illustration. His design tutor was the painter Paul *Nash; other RCA contemporaries were Barnett *Freedman, Henry *Moore, and Douglas Percy Bliss, his future biographer. But his closest student friendship, and the most fruitful artistically, was with someone who was in many ways his opposite, Eric *Ravilious.

Paul Nash helped Bawden to get his earliest commissions—posters for London Transport and designs for the Curwen Press. In 1928 Bawden and Ravilious worked together on a large mural in Morley College, London, the first of many mural designs; while Bawden's line drawings of English place-names for petrol advertisements—'Stow-on-the-Wold but Shell on the Road'—made him familiar to a wider audience.

In 1932 Bawden married his RCA contemporary Charlotte Epton, the daughter of Robert Epton, solicitor, of Lincoln. They had a son and a daughter, both of whom became artists. In the same year, the Bawdens and Eric and Eileen ('Tirzah') Ravilious moved to Brick House in Great Bardfield, Essex, which they had previously visited at weekends. Here Bawden began painting the local Essex landscapes; and in 1933 he held his first one-man show at the Zwemmer Gallery.

In 1940 Bawden was appointed an official war artist. He went to France, where he drew the evacuation from Dunkirk; he was among the last to leave; and then to the Middle East and Africa: Egypt, the Sudan, Ethiopia, Eritrea, and Libya. He made many fine water-colours both of the fighting and of the historic background, landscape and architectural, against which it took place. Returning by sea from Africa in 1942, he was torpedoed; after five days in an open boat, he was rescued by a Vichy French warship and interned for two months in Casablanca. But he returned to the war, to Arabia, Egypt, Iraq,

Persia, and Italy. Much of his war work is in the Imperial War Museum.

After the war Bawden lived in Bardfield and taught part-time at the RCA under (Sir) Robin *Darwin; he was an excellent teacher. Although in the postwar climate his work now seemed less fashionable than it had before the war, he was always busy. His dexterity was not impaired by an operation he had in 1946 to remove the poisoned top joint of his index finger. He worked industriously on book illustrations—for *Life in an English Village* (King Penguin Books, 1949), *The Arabs* (Puffin Picture Books, 1947) by Richard B. Serjeant, and for Faber & Faber, the Kynock Press, the Nonesuch Press, and the Limited Editions Club of New York—and lino-cutting, of which seemingly humble yet intractable craft he was a master. 'Liverpool Street Station' and 'Brighton Pier' are outstandingly original among many fine prints. He also made several mural designs—that for the Lion and Unicorn Press pavilion in the Festival of Britain was perhaps the most notable, and there is a striking example in Blackwells bookshop in Oxford. But it was his landscape water-colours, technically adventurous and highly individual, that he always considered his central activity.

Photographs, self-portraits, and the early Ravilious portrait at the RCA show him as tall, spare, and serious; his expression sharp-eyed, ironic, and humorous. In character, he was paradoxical: not strong as a child, but a tenacious survivor as an adult; shy and diffident but unstoppable; insecure and highly self-critical, yet self-reliant; imaginative yet very organized; possessing curious blind spots, like his inability to drive or enjoy music, yet extraordinarily versatile and capable of learning anything he set his hand to—from engraving on copper to designing a cast-iron garden seat. He was not an easy man to get on with and his ruthless determination to work bore heavily on his family. Shyness sometimes made him seem dry, mocking, and contrary, and he hated sentimentality.

Bawden's style was individual, clear, and economical; people, landscapes, and buildings were simply and unambiguously delineated. He drew animate and inanimate subjects with equal ease, simplifying complicated subject-matter and making epigrammatic or decorative images out of seemingly unlikely material, and he was as skilful with a fine pen as with the thick, solid technique of linocutting. Although he abhorred influences, Bawden has been likened to Edward *Lear, whose work he admired and who in some respects—shyness, solitariness, and precision—he resembled. He was a skilful and resourceful designer, a brilliant creator of pattern when this skill was out of fashion, and a draughtsman of wit and individuality. His life's work reveals him also as a serious artist whose vision of the world around him was personal and comprehensive. His clarity may have been for him a mixed blessing; for by removing ambivalence and leaving the observer with little to puzzle over, it made Bawden seem simpler and less profound than other artists whose work is harder to fathom. That, and the fact that he did many different things, meant that Bawden's work was accorded respect and admiration, rather than the renown it merited.

He became CBE in 1946, ARA in 1947, RDI in 1949, and RA in 1956, and received honorary doctorates from the RCA and Essex University. From 1951 to 1958 he was a trustee of the Tate Gallery. His work was given a retrospective exhibition at the Victoria and Albert Museum in 1989. When his wife died in 1970 he moved to Saffron Walden, where he worked steadily and fruitfully to the end of his days. On 21 November 1989, after a morning spent working on a linocut, he had a stroke and died later that day at home in Saffron Walden.

[J. M. Richards, *Edward Bawden*, Penguin Modern Painters, 1946; Douglas Percy Bliss, *Edward Bawden*, 1980; Robert Harling, *Edward Bawden*, 1950; Justin Howes, *Edward Bawden, a Retrospective Survey*, 1988; work in Cecil Higgins Museum, Bath; personal knowledge.]　　　　　　　　　DAVID GENTLEMAN

BAXTER, (Mary) Kathleen (1901–1988), advocate of women's rights, was born 30 May 1901 to a Roman Catholic family in Bradford, Yorkshire, the eighth child in the family of three daughters and five sons (one of whom died in infancy) of Richard Aloysius Young, woollen-manufacturer, and his wife, (Mary) Ann Barker. Her father died during her infancy. She was educated at St Joseph's College, Bradford, and won an open scholarship to the Society of Oxford Home Students (later St Anne's College), Oxford, where she obtained a third class in modern history in 1922 and a second in philosophy, politics, and economics in 1923.

She entered the Department of Inland Revenue and was inspector of taxes in Bradford and Leeds until her marriage in Westminster Cathedral on 12 September 1931 to Herbert James ('H. J.') Baxter, barrister, who later became a county court judge. He was the son of James Baxter, whose career was in the army and Civil Service. There were two daughters of the marriage, and a son, who became a Roman Catholic priest. When she married she was obliged by the Income Tax Act to resign from the DIR. She became a tax consultant to a London firm of chartered accountants. During World War II she worked in the Ministry of Supply at the wool control in Ilkley.

After the war the family moved from London to a house in Bessel's Green, Kent, which remained their home for forty years. Kathleen

Baxter used her intellectual and analytical abilities to further causes she believed in. In her career she had experienced discrimination against women. She worked for equal rights, better education, and better job opportunities for women, to enable them to take their place in decision-making and become an effective voice for the improvement of society.

In 1951 she joined the National Council of Women, founded in 1895, a non-party-political organization affiliated to the International Council of Women. She held high office on many of the Council's specialist committees. In the 1950s she led a campaign, with their education committee, which achieved improvement in the university grants system. She also founded the Council's science and technology committee, which pressed for better education in science and mathematics for girls, and inaugurated a status-of-women committee, which submitted important points for incorporation into the 1975 Sex Equality Act. She was elected vice-president (1961–4), and subsequently, as president (1964–6), she was involved with national and international issues. In 1966, as vice-chairman of the European Centre of the International Council of Women, she led the British women's delegation to the international conference in Tehran, at which Britain's resolution on slavery was passed unanimously. She served on the UK Human Rights Year national executive in 1968. As a governor of the British Institute of Human Rights she was asked by the United Nations' secretary-general to write a background paper on the advancement of women's rights for the 1968 international conference on human rights, and she gave evidence to the UN session on human rights in Geneva. At the time of Britain's application for membership of the European Economic Community, she successfully pressed the government to consult the major women's organizations and was largely responsible for the establishment of the Women's Consultative Council (renamed in 1969 the Women's National Commission): its first co-chairmen were herself and a government minister.

In late middle age she studied law, from both interest in her husband's profession and knowledge that it would further her own work; she was called to the bar (Inner Temple) in 1971, but ceased taking cases when her husband became gravely ill in 1974. After his death in the same year, she was appointed honorary legal adviser to the National Council of Women, while still continuing to serve on the executive of the Women's National Commission. In her dual capacity she chaired working parties commenting on documents from the Law Commission and the criminal law revision committee relating to women, children, and the family.

In 1978 she was awarded the papal cross 'pro ecclesia et pontifice' for outstanding service to the church. She was president of the National Board of Catholic Women (1974–7), a founder-member of the Catholic bishops' conference legislation committee, and a member of their bio-ethical advisory committee on artificial insemination, *in vitro* fertilization, and genetic engineering, helping to foster a broad social concern in these Catholic circles. In Kent she served on the hospital, maternity wing, and old people's home committees, and as a governor of four schools. She was devoted to her family and four grandsons, and greatly enjoyed music and tennis.

Kathleen Baxter combined high intelligence with an affectionate nature. She was a good-looking woman with an appearance of natural dignity and authority; silver hair framed a broad forehead, beneath which strikingly blue eyes claimed attention, and a smile of warmth and charm promised interest and encouragement. She died 25 October 1988 in hospital in Bromley, Kent.

[National Council of Women archives at NCW head-quarters, London; private information; personal knowledge.]   DIANA GRANTHAM REID

BEER, Esmond Samuel de (1895–1990), historian and benefactor. [See DE BEER, ESMOND SAMUEL.]

BELL, John Stewart (1928–1990), theoretical physicist, was born into a Protestant working-class family in Belfast 28 July 1928, the eldest of three sons and second of four children of John Bell. The latter worked as a horse dealer, but his health was poor and after army service he had no real job, and his wife, (Elizabeth Mary) Ann Brownlee, did some casual sewing work. After leaving the Belfast Technical High School at sixteen, he worked for a year as a laboratory assistant in the physics department of the Queen's University, Belfast (1944–5); his supervisors gave him physics books to read and he was able to skip a year after he entered the university in 1946. He graduated with first-class honours in experimental physics in 1948 and in mathematical physics in 1949.

Bell worked for the Atomic Energy Research Establishment at Malvern and Harwell from 1949 to 1953 on the theory of particle accelerators; he applied Hamiltonian dynamics to develop various analytical approaches, and discovered the 'Courant–Snyder' invariant. He spent 1953 on leave working for a Ph.D. in Birmingham under P. T. Matthews and (Sir) Rudolf Peierls. Returning to Harwell, he completed his thesis in 1956 and began to work on many body problems and quantum field theory, with particular reference to atomic nuclei. His thesis contains a proof of the profound and fundamental parity–charge conjugation–time reversal (PCT) theorem, although his discovery of this theorem was anticipated by G. Lüders.

In 1960 Bell moved to the theoretical studies division at CERN, the European particle physics laboratory near Geneva, where he stayed until his death, apart from one year's leave in 1963–4 at the Stanford Linear Accelerator Center in California. He published a large number of important papers on particle physics, his contributions including articles on CP (charge conjugation–parity) violation, the discovery that, despite having a mean free path of millions of miles in matter, neutrinos are 'shadowed' in nuclei, the observation that the algebra of electroweak charges is strongly suggestive of a gauge theory, and an illuminating explanation of the upper limit on the polarization of particles in storage rings as a manifestation of interaction with the black body radiation experienced by accelerated observers. The best known of his 'conventional' contributions was his discovery (with R. Jackiw) of the 'Alder–Bell–Jackiw' anomaly, which leads not only to constraints on models of elementary particles, but also to surprising and deep connections between physics and geometry.

Bell was best known for work on what he described as 'his hobby—the problem of quantum mechanics'. His first contribution was to demolish John von Neumann's celebrated theorem that purported to show that 'quantum mechanics would have to be objectively false in order that another description of the elementary process than the statistical one be possible'. He then showed (Bell's Theorem) that certain predictions of quantum mechanics cannot be reproduced by any 'local' theory in which the results of a measurement, or experiment as he preferred to call it, on one system are unaffected by operations on a distant system with which it interacted in the past. The subsequent verifications of these predictions were of fundamental importance.

His masterly expositions of the 'rotten' state of the foundations of quantum mechanics (collected in *Speakable and Unspeakable in Quantum Mechanics*, 1987), in which he stressed that without a definition of a 'measurement' the predictions are in principle ambiguous, did much to shake the 'complacent' views of other physicists. He made the most important contribution to 'quantum philosophy' since the birth of quantum mechanics, although—by exposing its essential non-locality—he only deepened the fundamental mysteries of the subject. He also had a profound knowledge of the foundations of other pillars of theoretical physics, especially classical electromagnetism.

Bell's work was recognized by his election as a fellow of the Royal Society in 1972 and as a foreign honorary member of the American Academy of Arts and Sciences in 1987; the award of the Reality Foundation prize in 1982; the Dirac medal of the British Institute of Physics, an honorary D.Sc. from Queen's University, Belfast, and an honorary Sc.D. from Trinity College, Dublin (all 1988); and the Dannie Heineman prize of the American Physical Society and the Hughes medal of the Royal Society in 1989.

John Bell had red hair and a beard and spoke with a lilting Ulster accent. He generally dressed informally and was a vegetarian. He and his wife were a rather private couple, but excellent company for those who got to know them. He was a brilliant writer and teacher, both in formal lectures and in private discussions, delighting in teasing out the truth by means of Socratic dialogue and paradox. He was amused by the widespread publicity that his theorem attracted, although perhaps also mildly resentful that it tended to obscure his other contributions. He enjoyed the encounters it generated with people such as the Dalai Lama, which he described in an amused and sceptical manner (Bernstein—see bibliography).

He married Mary, daughter of Alexander Munro Ross, a shipyard commercial manager in Glasgow, in 1954. They met when both were working for AERE on accelerator theory, publishing a joint report in 1952, and Mary joined CERN as an accelerator physicist when they moved there. They published several joint papers on electron cooling in storage rings and quantum beam- and brems-strahlung in the 1980s. Mary Bell's comments on the drafts of her husband's papers on quantum mechanics helped improve their clarity; he wrote that in them 'I see her everywhere'. The Bells had no children. John Bell died suddenly and unexpectedly of a cerebral haemorrhage in Geneva, 1 October 1990.

[*Europhysics News*, vol. xxii, no. 4, 1991; *Physics Today*, August 1991, p. 82; Jeremy Bernstein, *Quantum Profiles*, 1991; private information; personal knowledge.]

C. H. LLEWELLYN SMITH

BENNETT, Donald Clifford Tyndall (1910–1986), air vice-marshal and member of Parliament, was born 14 September 1910 in Toowoomba, Queensland, Australia, the fourth and youngest son and youngest of five children of George Thomas Bennett, cattle estate owner, of Brisbane, and his wife, Celia Juliana Lucas. His sister died in early childhood. He was educated at Brisbane Grammar School and enlisted in the Royal Australian Air Force.

In 1931 he was posted to England on a short-service commission in the Royal Air Force. He resigned in 1935 to join Imperial Airways, having successfully passed the examinations for a civil navigator's licence, first class, and both wireless

operator's and ground engineer's licences. In 1938 he gained the world's long-distance record for seaplanes in a flight from Dundee in Scotland to Alexandra Bay in South West Africa.

In 1940, as flight superintendent of the Atlantic Ferry service, he flew the first of thousands of American-built aircraft to the British Isles, a feat never before attempted in winter. Despite his technical brilliance and outstanding capacity for work, his relationship with his civilian masters was difficult and he returned to the RAF in 1941. He was posted to Leeming, Yorkshire, to command No. 77 Squadron operating Whitley bombers and in April 1942 to No. 10 Squadron, also at Leeming. During an attack on the *Tirpitz* in a Norwegian fiord his Halifax was shot down. After bailing out he escaped on foot to Sweden to be repatriated and to receive immediate appointment to the DSO.

When the Air Ministry ordered Bomber Command to create an élite target-finding force he was the obvious choice to command it. Promotion followed swiftly and as air officer commanding No. 8 Group his Pathfinder Force successfully mastered the identification and marking of chosen targets. In 1943 he was accorded the rank of air vice-marshal. Although regarded by many as the architect of the efficiency of Bomber Command his relationship with other long-serving bomber group commanders was not without friction. Few had any recent operational experience and most were reluctant to release their best crews to No. 8 Group.

In 1945, having resigned his commission, he was appointed chief executive of British South American Airways, a new airline founded by shipping interests. His policy of operating only British aircraft involved dependence upon a converted bomber, the Lancastrian, until the Avro Tudor was ready for service. The deficiencies of the airport facilities, together with the inexperience of the youthful crews, took their toll in accidents. In 1948, following the unexplained disappearance of a Tudor *en route* to Bermuda, the minister for civil aviation, the first Baron *Nathan, grounded the remainder, pending an investigation. Convinced that the Tudor was perfectly airworthy, Bennett angrily denounced the minister to the national press. In the ensuing furore he refused to resign and was dismissed.

Almost at once the Russian blockade of road, rail, and river routes to West Berlin provided him with an opportunity to prove the Tudor's merits. He founded Airflight, based at Langley, near Slough, equipping two Tudors as oil-tankers and personally flying 250 sorties to Berlin. In May 1949 he registered a new company, Fairflight, based at Blackbushe, Hampshire. Charter flights to the Middle and Far East were carried out before the company was sold in 1951.

At the invitation of Sir Archibald *Sinclair, leader of the Liberal party, he had accepted the vacant seat of Middlesbrough West in 1945. In the general election later that year he lost it to the Labour candidate. In 1948 he unsuccessfully contended North Croydon and, in 1950, Norwich North. Thereafter the Liberal party's enthusiasm for the European Economic Community and its posture on defence alienated Bennett, whose upbringing was founded on pride in the empire and the merits of imperial preference. He left the Liberal party in 1962 and five years later polled about 500 votes as a National party candidate at a by-election in Nuneaton. Although not a member of the National Front, he supported some of its policies, such as the voluntary repatriation of immigrants, when he organized, in 1969, the Association of Political Independents, and, later, the Independent Democratic Movement. He joined the National Council of Anti-Common Market Organizations, being its chairman from 1973 to 1976. From 1946 to 1949 he was chairman of the executive committee of the United Nations Association of Great Britain and Northern Ireland. His most notable publication, *The Complete Air Navigator* (1931), ran through many editions until 1967. He also wrote *The Air Mariner* (1938) and *Pathfinder* (1958), among other books.

He was appointed CBE (1943) and CB (1944). The Russian government awarded him the Order of Alexander Nevsky in 1944. For services to aviation, he was awarded the Johnston memorial trophy in 1937 and 1938, and the Oswald Watt medal in 1938 and 1946. In 1935 he married Elsa, daughter of Charles Gubler, jeweller, of Zurich. They had a son and a daughter. Bennett died 15 September 1986 at Wexham Hospital, Buckinghamshire.

[D. C. T. Bennett, *Pathfinder* (war memoirs), 1958; personal knowledge.]   ARCHIE STEWART JACKSON

BENNETT, (Nora Noel) Jill (1929?–1990), actress, was born possibly 24 December 1929 in Penang, Malaya, the only child of (James) Randle Bennett, owner of rubber plantations, and his wife, Nora Adeline Beckett. Her death certificate claims that she was born in 1931, but she was reticent about her date of birth. In *Who's Who* she said she was born in 1929. When war broke out in 1939 her mother took her to England. Her father was taken prisoner by the Japanese, and neither Jill nor her mother saw him again for five years. In England she attended several boarding schools, including Priors Field, Godalming, where, she claimed, she was good at games, French, riding, and the history of art. She was expelled at the age of fourteen. She showed an early talent for ballet too, but at fifteen decided to be an actress, and was accepted by the Royal Academy of Dramatic Art (1944–6). She made

her stage début in 1947 in *Now Barabbas* (Bolton's theatre, and, later, Vaudeville theatre).

In 1949 she was given one speaking part and walk-ons with the Shakespeare Memorial Theatre Company at Stratford-upon-Avon, where she met (Sir) Godfrey *Tearle, a fine actor, who was over forty years her senior. Until he died in 1953, they had what she called 'a passionate friendship'. In her book, *Godfrey: a Special Time Remembered* (written with Suzanne Goodwin in 1983), she makes it clear that he was the great love of her life. She was later married twice, both times to playwrights. In 1962 she married Willis Hall, the son of Walter Hall. This marriage was dissolved in 1965 and in 1968 she married John James Osborne, the son of Thomas Godfrey Osborne, copywriter in an advertising agency. They were divorced in 1977. There were no children of either marriage, although she had two miscarriages when married to John Osborne. Osborne's hostile picture of her in *Almost a Gentleman* (1991) is unrecognizable to those who knew her well.

She had a long and successful career in theatre, films, television, and radio. Her first parts in London were Anni in *Captain Carvallo*, directed by Sir Laurence (later Baron) *Olivier (St James's, 1950) and Iras in both *Antony and Cleopatra* and *Caesar and Cleopatra* in the Sir Laurence Olivier season, also at the St James's (1951). From 1955 she was much in demand, mostly in the West End, notably as Helen Eliot in *The Night of the Ball* (New theatre, 1955), Masha in *The Seagull* (Saville, 1956), and Isabelle in *Dinner with the Family* (New, 1957). In December 1962 she began her important association with the Royal Court theatre, as Hilary in *The Sponge Room*, and Elizabeth Mintey in *Squat Betty*. In 1965 she made the first of her three appearances there in a play by her future husband John Osborne, as Countess Sophia Delyanoff in *A Patriot for Me*. She was also in the film versions of Osborne's *Inadmissible Evidence* and *The Charge of the Light Brigade* (both 1968). Osborne wrote *Time Present*—based on her relationship with Godfrey Tearle—for her in 1968, and in it, as Pamela, she won the *Evening Standard* and Variety Club awards for best actress. Her final Osborne play (also at the Royal Court, and subsequently at the Cambridge theatre) was *West of Suez* (1971).

She was a memorable Hedda Gabler in 1972, and Fay, in Joe Orton's *Loot* in 1975 (both back at the Royal Court) and was highly successful in a revival of Sir Terence *Rattigan's *Separate Tables*, in which she played the contrasting emotional cripples Mrs Shankland and Miss Railton Bell (Apollo, 1977). This was followed by leading parts in successive Chichester seasons in 1978 and 1979, which included Miss Tina in *The Aspern Papers*. Other personal successes included

Gertrude in *Hamlet*—in the opinion of the director, Anthony Page, the best Gertrude he ever saw (Royal Court, 1980)—and the wife in August Strindberg's *Dance of Death* (Manchester Royal Exchange, 1981).

Her films included *Lust for Life* (1956), Joseph Losey's *The Criminal* (1960), *The Nanny* (with Bette Davis, 1965), *Britannia Hospital* (1982), and Bernardo Bertolucci's *Sheltering Sky* (1990). Her many television credits included *The Heiress, The Three Sisters, Design for Living, Rembrandt* (all 1970), Alan Bennett's *The Old Crowd* (1979), and John Mortimer's *Paradise Postponed* (1986).

No conventional beauty, she considered herself ugly. She was in fact extremely attractive, elegant, petite, blonde, and blue-eyed, with a distinctively turned-up nose, flared nostrils, strong teeth, and a small, amusingly jutting chin. She had quick intelligence and wit, and her laughter was companionable and infectious, but needed to be won. She often indulged in extravagant behaviour, which could be embarrassing. She wrongly believed that she was a failure in her relationships with men. Her friendships were many and long lasting. For instance, Anthony Page was a friend and colleague for over thirty years, and Lindsay Anderson, the film director, for longer still—as was her loving and much-loved secretary, Linda Drew.

She adored acting, but, being sensitive and nervous, preferred the cloistered security of rehearsal, the passionate search for character and motive, and the trusting relationship with her directors to the exposure of performance. When, however, she felt utterly secure in her part, in the play, and in her colleagues, she could be superb.

She committed suicide at home at 23 Gloucester Walk, London, by taking an overdose of sleeping pills 5 October 1990, having tried unsuccessfully to do so a month previously. Her relationship with a Swiss businessman, Thomas Schoch, had foundered and her ever-present sense of failure had finally overcome her.

[Jill Bennett and Suzanne Goodwin, *Godfrey: a Special Time Remembered*, 1983; John Osborne, *Almost a Gentleman*, 1991; information from Linda Drew and Anthony Page; personal knowledge.] DULCIE GRAY

BENTINCK, Victor Frederick William Cavendish-, ninth DUKE OF PORTLAND (1897–1990), diplomat and international businessman, was born 18 June 1897 at 16 Mansfield Street, London W1, the younger son and third of four children of Frederick Cavendish-Bentinck, barrister, who managed the ducal family's Marylebone estate, and his wife, Ruth Mary, who was the illegitimate daughter of Earl St Maur, a son of the Duke of Somerset, and was reputed to have gypsy blood. 'Bill' Bentinck was educated at Wellington College, but left at seventeen without

making a mark and was appointed in August 1916 honorary attaché at the British legation at Christiania (later Oslo). In 1918 he enlisted and trained with the Household Brigade, but saw no active service. He entered the Diplomatic Service in 1919, missing the chance of university education, and was posted as third secretary to the legation at Warsaw. It was as ambassador at Warsaw twenty-seven years later that he ended a diplomatic career in which he achieved special distinction as chairman of the wartime Joint Intelligence Committee (1939–45). In 1922 he began work in the Foreign Office and took charge of administrative arrangements for the Lausanne conference before moving to the embassy in Paris as second secretary. There in 1924 he contracted a marriage that soon cast a shadow over a very promising career. His wife, Clothilde, was the daughter of James Bruce Quigley, a Kentucky lawyer; her lifestyle was extravagant and she had a talent for quarrelling with other diplomatic wives. Bentinck was a conciliator by nature, though well able to fight his corner. His tall, stooping figure and rather myopic look belied the resolution he displayed in a crisis.

Back in the Foreign Office in 1925, he served in the League of Nations department and had a useful role at the Locarno conference. He was promoted first secretary and sent back to Paris in 1928; but, as his domestic problems worsened, assignments grew shorter and further from the 'inner circle': Athens in 1932 was followed by Santiago in 1933. In 1937, however, he was recalled to the FO as assistant in the Egyptian department and there acquired experience of handling military matters. In the summer of 1939 his wife left without warning for the USA, taking the two children, a boy and a girl. Her departure coincided with the high point of his diplomatic career, when the FO, which had been reluctant to pool intelligence with the armed services, appointed him chairman of the JIC and he found himself, as a civilian and relatively junior, reporting to the chiefs of staff. His perceptiveness and tact enabled him to overcome service rivalries and weld the JIC into a highly effective instrument. He was appointed CMG in 1942 and promoted counsellor to head the newly created services liaison department of the FO.

Despite wartime success, his diplomatic career was doomed. He had formed a close friendship with a Canadian, Kathleen Elsie, widow of Arthur Richie Tillotson and daughter of Arthur Barry of Montreal, but his absent wife refused to divorce him. He explained his difficulties to the FO, which persuaded him in July 1945 to take the key post of ambassador to Poland, which had fallen under Soviet control. The communist-dominated government did its utmost to sabotage his mission and in February 1947 the FO withdrew him and applied to Brazil for his *agrément* as ambassador. In March his suit for divorce came before the court and was exploited by his wife to discredit him. The resultant publicity obliged the FO to withdraw the request for *agrément*. He then resigned, thus forfeiting his pension under Treasury regulations. The Court of Appeal finally granted his divorce and in July 1948 he married Kathleen.

He had lost no time in finding remunerative work as vice-chairman of the Committee of Industrial Interests in Germany, becoming chairman in 1949. In addition to advancing the interests of major British companies, such as Unilever, he formed close connections with leading German companies, such as Bayer AG. He promoted the German and Belgian nuclear industries and was awarded a high German decoration (*Bundesverdienstkreuz*). On the death of his elder brother in 1979, he became the ninth Duke of Portland, Marquess of Titchfield, Viscount Woodstock, and Baron Cirencester; but he inherited neither land nor capital, since the entail had been broken eight years previously by the seventh duke. His son, William, had died of heart failure in 1966, leaving no children. When he himself died at his home, 21 Carlyle Square, London, 30 July 1990, the dukedom created in 1716 was extinguished.

[Patrick Howarth, *Intelligence Chief Extraordinary: the Life of the Ninth Duke of Portland*, 1986; private information; personal knowledge.]   ROBERT CECIL

BERGEL, Franz (1900–1987), biochemist, was born 13 February 1900 in the Alsergrund quarter of Vienna, the younger child and second son of Moritz Martin Bergel, a Hungarian immigrant and wine merchant, and his wife, Barbara Betty Spitz, daughter of a carpet manufacturer. He was educated at a Realgymnasium in Vienna and was called up into a cavalry regiment at the beginning of 1918. At the end of the war he returned to school, from which he went to the universities of Würzburg and Freiburg to study chemistry. He obtained his Ph.D. in 1924 and published some first-class work on amino-acid oxidation.

In 1928, having begun a whirlwind affair with Niddy Impekoven, a popular solo dancer and wife of a Freiburg University professor, he eloped with her following her divorce. They married in 1930. From then until he went to Edinburgh in 1933 he was mainly occupied as a kind of manager-impresario for his wife in dance tours all over Europe, and in 1932–3 he acted in this capacity in an extended tour of Ceylon and Indonesia. There was one daughter of this marriage, which ended in divorce in 1933, after which the child lived with her mother in Switzerland.

On Bergel's return to Freiburg in 1933 the National Socialists were already in power. He was totally opposed to National Socialism and immediately decided to leave Germany, although at that time he was under no necessity to do so, since although he was of Jewish descent he was an Austrian citizen and not, therefore, subject to persecution. Bergel went from Freiburg to Edinburgh, where, thanks to financial support from Hoffmann La Roche & Co. of Basle, he joined the laboratory of George *Barger, professor of medical chemistry in the university. He did not at first find this very congenial, but in the summer of 1934 he was joined by A. R. (later Baron) Todd, who had been brought to Edinburgh from Oxford to carry out research on the structure (and eventual synthesis) of vitamin B1, of which a very small quantity was in Barger's possession. Todd and Bergel struck up an immediate and lasting friendship and worked together on vitamin B1, for which, in 1936, they developed an effective synthesis which permitted the commercial development of the vitamin by Hoffmann La Roche.

When, in 1936, Todd moved to the Lister Institute of Preventive Medicine in London, Bergel moved with him (still supported by Hoffmann La Roche) and the two continued their joint work on vitamin E and the active principle of *Cannabis* resin. Bergel was naturalized in about 1938. Todd moved to Manchester in 1938 as professor of chemistry and Bergel to Welwyn Garden City as director of the new research laboratories of Roche Products Ltd. There he worked on synthetic analgesics, cannabinoids, antibacterials, and vitamins. With the enforced wartime separation of Roche Products from the mother firm in Basle, Bergel had to devote much time to the process control and development of vitamins and to the study of the various new vitamins that had been discovered.

He remained at Welwyn Garden City until 1952, when he succeeded G. A. R. Kon as professor of chemistry in the Chester Beatty Research Institute at the Royal Cancer Hospital, London, a post which he filled with great distinction until his retirement in 1966. He concentrated on cancer chemotherapy, enlarging Kon's programme of work on derivatives of 'nitrogen mustard' as possible chemotherapeutic agents. He also initiated and developed a substantial programme of research on the biochemical properties of tumours. He sought to exploit the emphasis of tumours on anabolic rather than catabolic pathways, and also to use enzyme therapy to deprive particular tumours of essential nutrients. In 1961 he published a comprehensive monograph, *Chemistry of Enzymes in Cancer*, in which he reviewed all that was known about the role of enzymes in cancer and the potential of some of them as therapeutic agents.

Bergel's outstanding contributions to cancer research are the more remarkable since he underwent a major operation for rectal cancer in 1957 which involved a colostomy; despite this handicap he continued his work and lived an active life. He was deputy director of the Chester Beatty Institute, serving on all its major committees and acting as dean from 1963 to 1966. He was an honorary lecturer at University College London (1946–72), served on the council of both the Chemical Society and the Society of the Chemical Industry, and was chairman of the Co-ordinating Committee for Symposia on Drug Action. He was elected FRS in 1959.

Bergel was a kind, compassionate, and gentle man. Widely read, with an active interest in European languages, he was an engaging conversationalist and a talented amateur artist. Tall, dark, and handsome, he was very much a 'ladies' man', similar to the typical Austrian aristocrats of Franz Lehar's operettas. In 1939 he married for the second time. His wife was Phyllis Edith, divorced wife of John Shuell (otherwise Shaw), daughter of John Thomas, of independent means. There were no children. He retired to Bel Royal in Jersey, where he died 1 January 1987.

[Lord Todd in *Biographical Memoirs of Fellows of the Royal Society*, vol. xxxiv, 1988.]   A. R. TODD
C. S. NICHOLLS

BERKELEY, SIR **Lennox Randal Francis** (1903–1989), composer, was born 12 May 1903 at Melford Cottage, Boar's Hill, near Oxford, the younger child and only son of Captain Hastings George FitzHardinge Berkeley, of the Royal Navy (the eldest son of George Lennox Rawdon Berkeley, seventh Earl of Berkeley), and his wife Aline Carla, daughter of Sir James Charles Harris, KCVO, former British consul in Monaco. His father did not succeed as eighth Earl of Berkeley because Captain Berkeley's parents were unmarried until prior to the birth of their third son, who succeeded to the earldom. After early schooling in Oxford, he was educated at Gresham's School in Holt, St George's School in Harpenden, and Merton College, Oxford, where he coxed the college rowing VIII and took a fourth class in French (1926). He became an honorary fellow of Merton in 1974.

He had shown no outstanding musical abilities at school (though a contemporary remembers him playing the piano with much flourishing of hands), but while at Oxford he had several of his compositions performed and eventually made up his mind to be a composer. In this he was supported by the young British conductor Anthony Bernard, who was to conduct first performances of a number of Berkeley's early works.

On advice from Maurice Ravel, he went to Paris in the autumn of 1926 to study with Nadia Boulanger, and stayed with her for six years. For the first of these she allowed him to do nothing but counterpoint exercises, a discipline which often reduced him to tears at the time, but for which he was to remain grateful all his life. He had works performed in Paris and London and his 'Polka for Two Pianos' (1934) was a notable success, inaugurating his ties with the publishers J. & W. Chester. But the BBC broadcast of his oratorio *Jonah* (1935) in 1936 and the Leeds festival performance of it the following year led many critics to look at him askance as a purveyor of modernism. From 1932 to 1934 he lived on the Riviera with his invalid mother.

In 1936 he met Benjamin (later Baron) *Britten and the two became close friends, sharing a house in Snape just before World War II. Although rather daunted by what he felt to be Britten's superior talent, Berkeley was able to find a distinctive voice in the 'Serenade for Strings' (1939), the First Symphony (1940), and the 'Divertimento' (1943). From 1942 to 1945 he worked for the BBC, first in Bedford and then in London, as an orchestral programme planner. The authorities noted with dismay that when Berkeley was labouring on a commission his BBC work suffered, and he was happy to accept an appointment as professor of composition at the Royal Academy of Music in 1946. He remained in the post until 1968 and numbered many of the country's best composers among his pupils, including David Bedford, Peter Dickinson, William Mathias, (J.) Nicholas Maw, and John Tavener.

Until he succumbed to Alzheimer's disease in the early 1980s, he produced a succession of works which made him many friends and admirers in the musical community, even if he never became famous outside it. He wrote for performers such as the pianist Colin Horsley, the oboist Janet Craxton, and the guitarist Julian Bream, and produced a considerable body of fine chamber music. He was particularly at home with the voice, and his vocal and choral works, such as the *Four Poems of St Teresa of Avila* (1947), the *Stabat Mater* (1947), and *The Hill of the Graces* (1975), show a love and understanding of words at least equal to Britten's. His four operas—*A Dinner Engagement* (1954), *Nelson* (1954), *Ruth* (1956), and *Castaway* (1967)—display at times an individual view of what constitutes opera, and one which critics and impresarios have not always shared; certainly he was not always fortunate with his librettists. But *Nelson* suffered from less than adequate London performances and deserves to be revived. From the late 1960s Berkeley, like many composers, experimented with serial techniques and, though they never took over his music, he admitted that thanks to them his musical language had expanded. The Third Symphony (1969) is perhaps his most impressive exercise in this new vein. The 1970s found Berkeley still true to his principles of writing with performance in mind and never *in vacuo*. At the time his last illness struck he was working on a fifth opera, 'Faldon Park'.

In 1959 he said, 'I know quite well I'm a minor composer, and I don't mind that.' It is true that he was not an Arnold Schoenberg or an Igor Stravinsky. His music made no revolutionary claims, partly because revolutionaries have to be destroyers and Berkeley was too respectful of tradition to set about it with a hatchet. If his studies with Boulanger taught him to be at ease with counterpoint, they also inculcated a love of 'la grande ligne', which Boulanger had inherited from Gabriel Fauré. Berkeley's music, like Fauré's, eschews surprises and, for the most part, grand gestures (though, again, *Nelson* showed what he could achieve in this more public, extrovert manner). His colleague Edmund *Rubbra referred to his work as offering 'so much insanity and honesty of purpose'. These attributes have in general been misprized in the twentieth century and Berkeley's refusal to jettison them meant that his reputation likewise matured without sudden surprises. He was notable for attending to the needs of the amateur: it is unusual, for example, to come across a flautist who has not at some time played his *Sonatina*. But his larger works, though always expertly written, demand patience and close attention to be fully appreciated. Even if his music always remains basically tonal, it can sometimes be fierce and gritty, very often as a result of his essentially linear thinking. Perhaps too much has been made of his music's Frenchness, and too often critics have used this as an excuse to deny his work profundity, but at the very least he managed to avoid the vapid pastoral meanderings of some of his English predecessors. The history of twentieth-century music may not have been greatly changed by his passing across it, but without him it would have been immeasurably the poorer. He was a man dedicated, as his pupil Peter Dickinson has said, to 'passing on the love of music as a spiritual imperative in a foreign, material age'.

He was appointed CBE in 1957 and knighted in 1974. Among many other honours were the papal knighthood of St Gregory (1973), honorary membership of the American Academy and Institute of Arts and Letters (1980), honorary doctorates of music from City University (1983) and Oxford (1970), and an honorary fellowship of the Royal Northern College of Music (1976). He also served as president of the Performing Right Society (1975–83), the Composers' Guild of Great Britain (from 1975), and the Cheltenham festival (1977–83).

Berkeley was, above all, graceful: he had been a good tennis player in his youth and remained all his life a tireless walker. As with his music, there was no hint of otiose flesh, rather of a strength which he was careful to hide beneath beautiful manners. As well as being a kind and approachable man, he was always quick to see the funny side of things. During his time with Boulanger, he and Igor Markevitch were members of a mildly disruptive 'back row', while in later life an eye would twinkle in response to persons on committees who treated 'criteria' as a singular noun or interposed with, 'Mr Chairman, I have a trepidation about that one.' Although determined to do what he saw as his civic duty, he never courted public notice unless forced by the strength of his own opinions. He had become a Roman Catholic in 1928 (when he took the name Francis), and, in the wake of the second Vatican council, wrote in the press urging the retention of the tridentine mass, since he believed the authorities were ignoring a legitimate desire expressed by a large body of Roman Catholic laymen. In private he wrote of those 'for whom the overthrow of the old tradition appears to be an end in itself', an end which, in religion as in music, he was unable to approve.

In 1946 he married Elizabeth Freda, daughter of Isaac Bernstein, a retired shopkeeper. They had three sons, of whom the eldest, Michael, became a composer. Berkeley died in St Charles's Hospital, Ladbroke Grove, London, 26 December 1989.

[Peter Dickinson, *The Music of Lennox Berkeley*, 1988; BBC archives; private information; personal knowledge.]   ROGER NICHOLS

BERNEY, Margery (1913–1989), recruitment agency founder. [See HURST, MARGERY.]

BERTHOUD, SIR Eric Alfred (1900–1989), oil executive, public servant, and diplomat, was born 10 December 1900 in Kensington, London, the second son and third child in a family of four sons and two daughters of Alfred Edward Berthoud, of the private merchant bank Coulon, Berthoud & Co., and his wife, Hélène Christ, who came from a Swiss-Alsatian banking family. As a boy at Gresham's School, Holt, Berthoud was greatly helped by his headmaster, G. W. S. Howson, who in 1914 found ways to keep him at the school when his father's bank collapsed and his relations proposed moving him to Switzerland. In 1918 Berthoud went up to Magdalen College, Oxford, where he played hockey for the university, did well at other sports, and took his degree in chemistry in 1922, paying his way with vacation tutoring and further help from Howson. His father, an alcoholic, died in 1920.

After four years with the Anglo-Austrian bank in Vienna and Milan (1922–6), Berthoud joined the Anglo-Persian Oil Co. (later BP), serving in Paris (1926–9), Berlin (1929–35), and again in Paris (1935–8). On leaving Germany he sent a detailed memorandum to the director of military intelligence in London on Hitler's military build-up. When war began he joined the petroleum division of the Ministry of Fuel and Power, and by November 1939 he was installed at the British legation in Bucharest. His colleagues included the eccentric (Sir) Edmund *Hall-Patch, who was later helpful to his career. Berthoud's instructions were to impede the supply of Romanian oil to Germany by non-violent means such as diplomatic pressure, pre-emptive buying, manipulating prices, and cornering railcars, barges, and tankers on the Danube. These and other British activities in Romania worried the Germans for a time, but both German vulnerability and British ability to exploit it were exaggerated in London; Berthoud himself was in agreement with the policy, but realistic as to its effectiveness, compared with other factors outside British control. In January 1941, by which time Romania had effectively thrown in its lot with Germany, Britain broke off relations and the legation in Bucharest was closed.

Berthoud spent the next four years in a variety of countries and tasks, all related to the objective of securing oil for the Allies and denying it to the Axis powers. One sensitive mission was to the Soviet Union, to which he travelled three times by adventurous routes in 1941–2. He soon became convinced of the need to support the Soviet Union by all possible means—this at a time when many in London were disinclined to spend scarce resources on what they saw as a hopeless cause.

The year 1945 found Berthoud in charge of the economic division of the British element of the Control Commission for Austria. Next he worked on east European peace treaties, on problems affecting the Anglo-Persian Oil Company, and finally on the Marshall plan, where his superiors valued his hard work and negotiating skill. After a long spell as assistant under-secretary in the Foreign Office (1948–52) he could have moved up to the deputy under-secretary's seat, but preferred to go as ambassador to Denmark (1952–6), where he made many friends. As ambassador in Warsaw (1956–60) he sympathized with the strivings of the ordinary Polish people, while unconditionally condemning the regime. He was appointed CMG in 1945 and KCMG in 1954, and retired in May 1960. From 1969 he was deputy lieutenant of Essex. In retirement BP made him a non-executive director on certain of its regional boards. Among other things he was deeply involved in the United World Colleges, the new University of Essex, and the Anglo-Polish round table conferences.

With his athletic build, countryman's face, and ready smile, Berthoud was a more complex character than he looked. Only one-quarter British by blood, he was as proud of his continental connections as of his own compensating 'Britishness'. As an ambassador he exacted a degree of deference (and punctuality) which some found

excessive. He could be thick-skinned and overbearing, but there was a vein of sensitivity in him too, nourished by a Protestant faith which strengthened as he grew older. In 1927 he married Ruth Tilston, daughter of Sir Charles Bright, electrical engineer and fellow of the Royal Society of Edinburgh, and granddaughter of Sir Charles Tilston *Bright, electrical engineer. A son who died in infancy was followed by two more sons and two daughters. They lived in a series of houses in Essex and finally in Suffolk, where Berthoud enjoyed cricket and country sports to the full. He died in Tunbridge Wells, Kent, 29 April 1989, his wife having predeceased him by a year.

[Sir Eric Berthoud, *An Unexpected Life* (privately printed), 1980; W. N. Medlicott, *The Economic Blockade*, 2 vols., 1952; *Documents on German Foreign Policy*, series D, vol. viii, pp. 502 ff.; private information; personal knowledge.]   JULIAN BULLARD

BISHOP, Richard Evelyn Donohue (1925–1989), mechanical engineer and naval architect, was born 1 January 1925 in Lewisham, London, the elder son (there were no daughters) of Norman Richard Bishop, chief accountant and director of Tar Residuals Ltd., and his wife, Dorothy Mary Wood, teacher of French. His father, through self-education, obtained the London external degrees of Bachelor of Commerce and Ph.D. (1944) and in 1949 was ordained a priest in the Church of England. 'Dick' Bishop's early years were spent in Catford, London, in a family whose main interests were music and the church. He attended Roan School for Boys, Greenwich, leaving in 1943 with a burning desire to join the Royal Navy, but no great ambition to go to university.

He volunteered as an ordinary seaman in the Royal Naval Volunteer Reserve, and impressed the authorities by the results of examinations taken while he was training. Subsequently a series of psychology tests indicated that he would make an engineer in the Fleet Air Arm. In mid-1944 he emerged from training with a first-class certificate of competency, as an air engineering officer, and was posted to a squadron.

Having become an engineer by accident and acquired a great interest in technology, after leaving the navy in 1946 he entered University College London, graduating with a first-class honours B.Sc. (Eng.) and a diploma with distinction in 1949. Before leaving in 1949 for Stanford University, California, as a Commonwealth Fund fellow to work under the supervision of J. N. Goodier, he married Jean ('Liz'), elder daughter of Hector Cross Buchanan Paterson, bank clerk; they had a daughter and a son. Bishop obtained his Ph.D. in 1951 with a thesis entitled 'The Analysis of Elastic Wave Propagation'.

Returning to England, he was employed as a senior scientific officer by the Ministry of Supply (1951-2) and then moved to the University of Cambridge on his appointment as an engineering demonstrator in 1952. He became a fellow of Pembroke College (1954) and a university lecturer (1955). His lifelong fascination for engineering and vibration, rather than his earlier commitment to applied mechanics and wave motions, were fostered in the Cambridge engineering laboratory. Returning to his old department in UCL as departmental head (1957-77), Kennedy professor of mechanical engineering (1957-81), and research professor (1977-81), he laid the foundations of modern rotor dynamics theory, devised the first successful method of balancing flexible shafts, and made significant advances in knowledge about the instability of high-speed rolling stock; aircraft resonance testing; torsional oscillating of rotating machinery caused by gear eccentricity; structural self-excitation by shedding of entrained vortices; measurement of forces transmitted by the human knee; and various aspects of ships' structural behaviour in waves based on hydroelasticity theory. In technical matters he was a man of vision, having the ability to simplify a complex dynamics problem to a discussion of fundamental principles. An excellent communicator, he wrote seven books and well over 200 papers.

In 1981, surprisingly, he moved from research into administration, as vice-chancellor and principal of Brunel University. Through his stress on academic excellence and scholarship, he successfully reorganized the apparatus and changed the culture of Brunel, laying the foundation of a flourishing university.

Bishop's fine clear mind brought him significant achievements and honours in the scientific world. He was a fellow of the Royal Society (1980) and appointed a vice-president and member of its council (1986-8). He was a fellow of the Royal Academy of Engineering (1977) and was appointed CBE in 1979. He received the Thomas Hawksley (I.Mech.E., 1965), Krizik (Czechoslovak Academy of Science, 1969), Rayleigh (British Acoustical Society, 1972), and the William Froude (RINA, 1988) gold medals; the Skoda silver (1967) and Anniversary (1980) medals; the Archibald Head (UCL, 1948) and Royal Institution of Naval Architects (1980) bronze medals; and the George Stephenson (1959) and Clayton (1972) prizes of the I.Mech.E.

Bishop was a severe critic and yet the staunchest of supporters. He thrived on technical discussion and debate—not argument—though at times this fine distinction depended on the sensitivity of the listener/combatant. By his probing he stimulated others, but he caused resentment in many, especially when he questioned the professionalism of engineers and engineering

practices. He was an independent, innovative research engineer, who spoke his mind on technical matters. An earnest man crowned by distinguishing white hair since his late twenties, he loved sailing and was always active. He died in Portsmouth 12 September 1989, from the effects of a hepatic abscess and septicaemia.

[W. Geraint Price in *Biographical Memoirs of Fellows of the Royal Society*, vol. xl, 1994; personal knowledge.]
W. GERAINT PRICE

BLACK, Dora Winifred (1894-1986), feminist writer and campaigner. [See RUSSELL, DORA WINIFRED.]

BLACKING, John Anthony Randoll (1928-1990), social anthropologist and ethnomusicologist, was born 22 October 1928 in Guildford, Surrey, the elder child and only son of William Henry Randoll Blacking, ecclesiastical architect, and his wife, (Josephine) Margaret (Newcombe) Waymouth. The family moved to 21 The Close, Salisbury, in 1930. Blacking attended Salisbury Cathedral School (1934-42) where, as a chorister and pianist, he showed early musical promise. Attendance at Sherborne School (1942-7) was followed by a commission in the Coldstream Guards and active service in Malaya (1947-9). The plight of the aboriginal peoples caught up in the conflict moved him deeply, and on his release from national service he went to King's College, Cambridge, to read archaeology and anthropology. While there, he was active in artistic life as a pianist and actor, and as a performer and promoter of contemporary music. He obtained second classes (division I in part i and division II in part ii) in his tripos (1952 and 1953).

He began to use his musical and anthropological talents in a variety of ways. For a time he considered becoming a professional pianist, he worked as a social worker in the East End, and he spent a summer studying ethnomusicology in Paris. In October 1953 he was invited by the Colonial Office to return to Malaya as assistant adviser on aborigines, which he did, only then to learn that his role was to provide the intelligence that would enable the forced removal of the forest peoples, all of whom were apparently suspected of being (or harbouring) terrorists. He refused, resigning after only six days.

He took a post as a musicologist at the International Library of African Music at Roodeport, South Africa, in 1954. In this capacity he carried out field studies in Zululand and Mozambique, and among the Venda and Gwembe Tonga peoples. In 1955 he married Brenda Eleonora, daughter of Herman Wilhelm Friedrich Gebers, farmer. They had a son and four daughters, two of whom died in childhood (1956 and 1963). In 1959 Blacking took up a lectureship in social anthropology and African government at the University of Witwatersrand, becoming professor and head of the department in 1965. Witwatersrand awarded him a Ph.D. in 1965 and a D.Litt. in 1972. His principal publications during this period included (as editor) *Black Background: the Childhood of a South African Girl* (1964) and (as author) *Venda Children's Songs: a Study in Ethnomusicological Analysis* (1967). A man of forceful personality and an enthusiastic evangelist in promoting understandings between people, and between people and the institutions they create, Blacking set up courses in African music and Asian studies, and took an increasingly outspoken role in anti-apartheid politics, which eventually led him to clash with the authorities. He was prosecuted under the notorious Immorality Act, which forbade sexual relations between people of different colours.

He left South Africa in 1969 with his second wife-to-be, Zureena Rukshana Desai, medical doctor, with whom he was later to have four daughters. After his divorce in 1975, they were married in 1978. She was the daughter of Suliman Mohamed Desai, company director. Offered a choice of chairs in Britain and the United States, he chose, after a short spell as professor of anthropology at Western Michigan University, to take up in 1970 the first appointment to the chair of social anthropology at the Queen's University of Belfast. This was at the very height of 'the troubles' in Northern Ireland, in which he saw many parallels with Malaya and South Africa. It was with a sense of mission that he guided the department from modest beginnings in 1970 to become one of the largest in the British Isles and an internationally recognized centre of ethnomusicology. His most influential book, *How Musical is Man?* (1974), stressed the importance of identifying the structural relationships between patterns of musical organization and those of social life. It argued that the human potential for musical creativity had been stifled in the West by an élitist conception of musical ability, whereas in pre-industrial societies everyone was an active musician. The book was soon in paperback and was translated into several languages. It brought students of ethnomusicology from all over the world to Belfast.

Blacking was a handsome man, tall and fair with clear blue eyes and the lean, broad-shouldered frame of a rugby player. He frequently wore his Regiment of Guards tie, which gave him a rather formal and military air that contrasted with the rebellious and iconoclastic things he often said. His impact upon an audience was both physical and intellectual. A gifted lecturer, always at his best playing to an audience, Blacking could, and did, teach anything in the syllabus with authority and flair. He served in various capacities on the committees of the International Folk Music Council, the Royal Anthropological Institute, the Social Science Research Council, the Council for National Academic Awards, and the British Council, gave dozens of guest lectures and addresses, and yet still found the time to do voluntary work for the homeless, handicapped, and unemployed as a council member in local charitable organizations. He regularly gave solo piano recitals at the university's lunchtime concerts. A man of great verve, wide interests, and an abiding belief in the creative genius of all humanity, he was constantly active. He believed that human beings were inherently musical and that music was an important means of communication across cultural boundaries.

In 1984 he was elected to the Royal Irish Academy. He was awarded the Rivers memorial medal of the Royal Anthropological Institute (1986), and the Koizumi Fumio prize in Tokyo (1989). His last works included a six-part series, *Dancing*, for Independent Television, and a book on the ethnomusicological work of the Australian composer Percy Grainger, *A Commonsense View of All Music* (1987). Blacking died of cancer in Belfast 24 January 1990.

[Obituaries in Queen's University *Newsletter*, March 1990; *Annals of the Association of Social Anthropologists of the Commonwealth*, 1990; *Guardian*, 30 January 1990; *Journal of Comparative Family Studies*, vol. xxii, no. 3, autumn 1991; Blacking's notes and letters in the department of social anthropology, Queen's University, Belfast; personal knowledge.]   REGINALD BYRON

BLISS, Kathleen Mary Amelia (1908–1989), Christian thinker and ecumenist, was born 5 July 1908 in Fulham, London, the elder child and only daughter of Thomas Henry Moore, local government officer, and his wife, Ethel Steward. She was educated at Fulham County High School before winning a scholarship to Girton College, Cambridge, where she obtained a second class (division II) in part i of the history tripos (1929) and a first class in part i of the theology tripos (1931). She was also active in the Student Christian Movement, widening her Congregational inheritance. After temporary posts teaching religious education, in 1932 she married Rupert Geoffrey Bliss, marine engineer. He was the son of Arthur Harold Antonio Bliss, traveller and big-game hunter. Sixteen years later her husband inherited the Portuguese barony of de Barreto and in 1950 he was ordained in the Church of England, but from 1932 to 1939 the young couple were missionaries with the London Missionary Society (mainly Congregational) in south India. Later Rupert Bliss became a teacher, administrator, and marriage consultant.

Kathleen Bliss's missionary experience developed her interests in education, in the problems of society at large, and in the possibilities of drawing Christians together in response to them. After a year's leave back in England she became assistant to J. H. *Oldham, the editor of the influential *Christian News Letter*. Her own contributions were recognized by her appointment as assistant editor (1942) and editor (1945), until the journal had to close in 1949, when the time had passed for its sophisticated discussion of Christian values amid wartime hatreds and post-war reconstruction. For four years from 1945 she also served on the staff of the British Council of Churches, organizing 'Religion and Life' weeks and local councils of churches. Having moved into the Church of England, she was in 1948 a delegate to the first assembly of the World Council of Churches. In the WCC she made such a mark that she was entrusted with drafting (she originated the unforgotten phrase 'we intend to stay together'), was appointed the part-time secretary of a commission on women in the churches, and was elected to serve energetically on the central and executive committees in 1954. In 1949 Aberdeen gave her an honorary DD.

For five years from 1950 she was a producer with the BBC. The discussions which she organized for the Third Programme, between Christians of various shades and non-believers, broke the Corporation's previous caution in presenting alternatives to Christianity. In 1958 she began her major work. In a time of optimism and new activity she was the first general secretary of the new board of education of the Church of England, charged with the co-ordination of work from primary schools through teacher training colleges to university chaplaincies, and from Sunday schools to the educational activities of the Mothers' Union. She resigned in 1966, exhausted and somewhat disillusioned.

A less complicated job awaited her after a rest, and her time as senior lecturer in religious studies in the University of Sussex (1967–72) brought fulfilment to her academic gifts as well as yet another pioneering opportunity: to develop theological (not only Christian) interests in a university excitingly new and not ecclesiastical. She continued to be an active participant in, and commentator on, religious and ecological movements in her retirement to the countryside near Shaftesbury, Dorset, and then to London. The admiration of many for her abilities and energies meant that invitations to preach, speak, or advise continued throughout her life. She was, for example, a member of the Public Schools Commission (1967–70) and was select preacher at Cambridge in 1967.

Her domestic background was unusual, but for her essential (she was thoroughly feminine) and fortunate. Her husband, a priest with independent means and part-time pastoral duties, was responsible for much of the upbringing of their three daughters, who like her were red-heads with clear-cut features and opinions (Deborah was to become a distinguished sur-

geon). A highly strung, incisively critical, often overworking intellectual, she could show the strain of her life when her wider commitments allowed her time at home, but from 1946 to 1974 she was supported by a Cambridge friend, Margaret Bryan, who lived in the family and was glad to absorb any outbursts. Family life was also helped by shared interests in music, reading, current affairs, and dressmaking.

She articulated and organized a phase in the ecumenical movement (for Christian renewal and reunion), when a definitely lay approach, which underplayed denominational customs, was not detached from academic standards or the routine of the churches. Being a perfectionist, she wrote fewer and shorter books than was to be expected and never completed her biography of her mentor J. H. Oldham, but she was for many years a director of the SCM Press. Her own publications put on record her most passionate interests: *The Service and Status of Women in the Churches* (arising out of the World Council of Churches, 1952), *We the People* (about the Christian laity, 1963), and *The Future of Religion* (about the response to secularization, 1969). She died of cancer 13 September 1989 in the King Edward VII Hospital, Midhurst.

[Susannah Herzel, *A Voice for Women: the Women's Department of the World Council of Churches*, 1981; private information; personal knowledge.]

DAVID L. EDWARDS

BLUMENFELD, John Elliot (1898–1988), railway manager and chief of London Transport. [See ELLIOT, SIR JOHN.]

BLUNT, Christopher Evelyn (1904–1987), merchant banker and numismatist, was born 16 July 1904 at the Vicarage, Ham Common, Surrey, the second of the three remarkable sons (there were no daughters) of the Revd (Arthur) Stanley (Vaughan) Blunt and his wife Hilda Violet, daughter of John Henry Master, of Montrose House, Petersham. He was educated at Marlborough but, unlike his brothers, Wilfrid, writer and artist, and Anthony *Blunt, art historian and Soviet agent, who were destined for academic careers, he did not go to university. After a year in Germany and Spain and two as a trainee accountant, in 1924 he joined the small banking house of Higginson & Co., which later became part of Hill Samuel. There he ultimately became head of corporate finance. Tall, fair, and patrician, he was a distinguished figure in the City for many years.

In 1930 Blunt married Elisabeth Rachel, daughter of Gardner Sebastian Bazley, barrister, of Hatherop Castle, Gloucestershire. They had one son and two daughters. The family moved from London to Hungerford in 1944, and in 1952 to Ramsbury Hill, near Marlborough. For most of the war Blunt had worked for Supreme

Headquarters, Allied Expeditionary Force (SHAEF), being mentioned in dispatches for his liaison work in the evacuation from Bordeaux in 1940, and later engaged in preparations for the Normandy invasion. He was demobilized as colonel, with the OBE and the US Legion of Merit (both 1945).

While at Marlborough Blunt had met John Shirley Fox, a leading student of medieval English coins, a subject to which Blunt himself was to devote the greater part of his leisure for the rest of his life. In 1935 Blunt became director of the British Numismatic Society and from 1946 to 1950 he was its president. The Society, which had acrimoniously spun off in 1903 from the Royal Numismatic Society, in order to give more attention to British coins, had lost momentum. Under Blunt's leadership its finances were strengthened, its membership increased, and its academic standing established.

From 1956 to 1961 Blunt served as president of the Royal Numismatic Society, finally laying to rest the lingering tensions between the two societies. In 1965 he was elected a fellow of the British Academy, an exceptional distinction for an amateur scholar without formal education after school, and one that recognized his leading role in establishing the Sylloge of Coins of the British Isles, a project for publishing fully illustrated catalogues of English coins in major collections in Britain and abroad. A committee was set up in 1953 with Sir Frank *Stenton as chairman, the first volume appeared in 1958, and when Blunt died the fortieth was in course of preparation.

Blunt's early numismatic work was devoted to the later middle ages, but after the war his interests turned towards the Anglo-Saxon series, largely neglected in the previous generation. Although increased responsibility in the City and his editorial duties with the *British Numismatic Journal* and the Sylloge left relatively little time for his own research, in conjunction with R. H. ('Michael') Dolley, appointed to the British Museum coin room in 1951, Blunt soon brought about a fundamental reappraisal of the early English coinage. After retirement from Hill Samuel in 1964, he remained a director of Eucalyptus Pulp Mills Ltd. and as chairman guided it through the difficulties of the political revolution in Portugal. But he was now able to devote most of his time to numismatics, moving on from the Heptarchic period between *Offa and *Alfred, on which he had previously concentrated, to the tenth century, during which previously fragmented English coinage gradually became unified. This work culminated in three seminal publications, a magisterial monograph on *Athelstan (1974) and, in collaboration, *British Museum: Anglo-Saxon Coins*, vol. v, *Athelstan to the Reform of Edgar* (with Marion M. Archi-

bald, 1986), and *Coinage in Tenth-Century England* (with B. H. I. H. Stewart and C. S. S. Lyon, 1989).

Blunt's contribution to English numismatics was exceptional. In addition to his own scholarly achievement, his judgement and diligence as editor had a pervasive influence on the standards of English numismatic literature for half a century. Through hospitality at Ramsbury and extensive correspondence Blunt was able to provide a focus and continuity for a subject in which professional scholars have always been in a minority. Although distressed by revelations about his brother Anthony in 1979 and by the loss of Elisabeth in 1980, he continued to work productively until a few weeks before his death at home at Ramsbury Hill, 20 November 1987. With the needs of future students in mind, one of his last acts was to provide for his magnificent coin collection (incorporating that of Shirley-Fox, which he inherited in 1939) to be offered to the Fitzwilliam Museum, Cambridge, in lieu of estate duty.

[D. F. Allen, *British Numismatic Journal*, vol. xlii, 1974, pp. 1–9; H. E. Pagan, *Numismatic Circular*, 1988, pp. 3–4; Ian Stewart in *Proceedings of the British Academy*, vol. lxxvi, 1990.]   STEWARTBY

BOOTH, Catherine Bramwell- (1883–1987), Salvation Army commissioner. [See BRAMWELL-BOOTH, CATHERINE.]

BOOTHBY, Robert John Graham, BARON BOOTHBY (1900–1986), politician, was born 12 February 1900 at 5 Ainslie Place, Edinburgh, the only child of (Sir) Robert Tuite Boothby, manager of the Scottish Provident Institution and a director of the Royal Bank of Scotland, and his wife Mabel Augusta, daughter of Henry Hill Lancaster, Edinburgh advocate. Robert, known throughout his life as Bob, was educated at Eton and Magdalen College, Oxford, where he enjoyed himself and made many friends, but secured only a pass degree in modern history (1921). Between Eton and Oxford he trained as a Guards officer, but was too young to take an active part in World War I.

In 1923 he contested Orkney and Shetland on behalf of the Conservative party, whose new leader, Stanley *Baldwin (later first Earl Baldwin of Bewdley), was a friend of his father. Though he did not win there, his campaign provided ample evidence of his political assets, which included dark and dramatic looks, a lively and independent mind, an easy way with people, and the ability to make compelling speeches enhanced by humour, wit, and a voice well described as 'of golden gravel'. He was soon selected as the Conservative candidate for another seat, East Aberdeenshire, which he won in 1924 and held for nearly thirty-four years, until he left of his own accord. He gave his constituents, mainly fishermen and farmers, superb service as their MP, and they showed their gratitude by backing him loyally through the many vicissitudes of his career.

In Parliament he at once made his mark with a successful maiden speech and was soon regarded as a rising star. But some of his views were unorthodox, notably on economics—he was an early Keynesian—and his sympathies, personal and political, were by no means confined to his own party. He was quick to denounce the decision by the chancellor of the Exchequer, (Sir) Winston *Churchill, to return Britain to the gold standard at the pre-war parity. Nevertheless, Churchill chose him as his parliamentary private secretary in 1926, and he held the post until the government fell at the next election, in 1929. Over the years his relations with Churchill, though intermittently close, were scarred by differences of opinion, for instance on India and the abdication of *Edward VIII, and above all by Boothby's natural incapacity to be a disciple or courtier.

From his position on the left of the party he contributed to the publication *Industry and the State, a Conservative View* (R. Boothby et al., 1927), to which another contributor was Harold *Macmillan (later the first Earl of Stockton), his closest associate in politics. In 1929 he began an affair with Macmillan's wife, Lady Dorothy, which lasted, on and off, until her death in 1966. The affair was soon well known in political circles and was used by Boothby's enemies to discredit him, though Macmillan himself remained ostensibly friendly. Lady Dorothy claimed that Boothby was the father of one of her daughters, Sarah, but there are grounds for doubting this; she may have been making the claim in the vain hope of provoking Macmillan into divorcing her. Boothby himself was doubtful, but nevertheless accepted responsibility and treated Sarah with much kindness and affection.

The liaison with Dorothy Macmillan added to the impression that Boothby was a raffish adventurer, while his attempts to make money in the City, necessitated by his extravagant and generous habits, earned him the reputation of a gambler, which was equally damaging to him politically. Yet he deserved to be taken seriously, not least because he was one of the very few MPs with a consistent anti-appeasement record in the 1930s. He took a stronger line than Churchill on Hitler's reoccupation of the Rhineland and on the Hoare–Laval pact, and he was among the thirty Conservatives, including Churchill, who refused to support the government over Munich. In May 1940 he was among the forty-one who voted against the government at the end of the Norway debate, with the result that Neville *Chamberlain resigned and Churchill came to power. In the coalition then formed he was appointed under-secretary at the Ministry of Food. Since the minister, the first Earl of *Woolton, was in the House of Lords, Boothby was spokesman for the department in the House of Commons.

He proved an excellent minister. The national milk scheme that he worked out was widely praised, and he reacted imaginatively to the problems created by the blitz. His regular broadcasts were practical and inspiring. He gained Woolton's warm confidence. Then suddenly, in October 1940, he was suspended from his duties while a select committee investigated his activities the previous year in connection with émigré Czech financial claims. When the committee reported that his conduct had been 'contrary to the usage and derogatory to the dignity of the House', he resigned. The verdict of (Sir) Robert Rhodes James, after careful analysis of the committee's report, is that it was 'heavily, and unfairly, loaded against Boothby'. Though he was not quite blameless in the matter, the penalty he paid was out of all proportion to his offence. After delivering a resignation speech (January 1941), which won him much support, he served for a time as a junior staff officer with RAF Bomber Command. Later in the war he worked with the Fighting French, and after it his services to France were recognized by his appointment as an officer of the Legion of Honour (1950).

In the late 1940s he worked enthusiastically in Churchill's movement for a United Europe, but when Churchill became prime minister again in 1951 there was no post for him. He had to be content with the award of the KBE in the coronation honours (1953). From 1949 to 1957 he was a British delegate to the consultative assembly of the Council of Europe, and from 1952 to 1956 vice-chairman of the committee on economic affairs. He opposed the Suez adventure in 1956, though he was a fervent Zionist. Macmillan's advent to the premiership brought him no office, perhaps understandably, but when a heart attack forced him to give up his seat, Macmillan recommended him, in 1958, for a life peerage. In the House of Lords he sat on the cross benches and was a frequent contributor to debates.

Meanwhile, in the 1950s, his appearances in current affairs programmes on television and radio had made him a household name, which did not endear him to colleagues lacking his eloquence and engaging personality. At the end of the decade he was elected rector of St Andrews University (1958–61), where he was immensely popular with the students. Music played a great part in his life; he was chairman of the Royal Philharmonic Orchestra (1961–3) and a founder member of the RPO Society.

In July 1964 the *Sunday Mirror* ran a story linking him with the gangster Ronald Kray. A photograph was published of the two men together at Boothby's flat, and the police were said to be investigating a homosexual relationship between them. Scotland Yard issued a denial, and Boothby wrote a powerful letter to *The Times*, in which he denied being a homosexual but admitted having met Kray three times at his flat to discuss a business proposal which he had turned down. He was quite unaware of the criminal activities for which Kray and his brother were later imprisoned. The *Mirror* management apologized unreservedly and made Boothby a voluntary payment of £40,000 as compensation. After his death, however, further evidence suggested that his *Times* letter had not been wholly candid. Boothby was, in fact, bisexual, and it seems possible that his connection with Kray involved some homosexual activity (then still criminal) with youths procured by Kray; but nothing worse. It is fair to assume that, if he had known what later came to light about Kray, he would have had nothing to do with him.

He published a volume of autobiography, *I Fight to Live*, in 1947, and another, *Boothby, Recollections of a Rebel*, in 1978. He also published *The New Economy* in 1943, and a collection of articles and speeches, *My Yesterday, Your Tomorrow*, in 1962. Boothby's ambition was insufficiently concentrated, and his temperament too reckless, for complete worldly success. Yet he was right on most of the major issues of his career, and showed outstanding promise during his brief innings as a minister. He was also, as Queen Elizabeth the queen mother said, '*such* a jolly man'.

He was twice married. In 1935 he married Diana, daughter of Lord Richard Cavendish, landowner and former politician. The marriage ended in amicable divorce in 1937. In 1967 he married Wanda, daughter of Giuseppe Sanna, a Sardinian import–export wholesaler. She gave him nearly twenty years of comfort and security at the end of his life. There were no children of either marriage. Boothby died in Westminster Hospital, London, 16 July 1986, and his ashes were scattered at sea off the coast of his old constituency.

[Robert Rhodes James, *Bob Boothby: a Portrait*, 1991; Robert Boothby, *I Fight to Live*, 1947, and *Boothby, Recollections of a Rebel*, 1978; private information; personal knowledge.]　　　　　　　　　JOHN GRIGG

BOWDEN, (Bertram) Vivian, BARON BOWDEN (1910–1989), scientist, educationist, and politician, was born 18 January 1910 in Chesterfield, Derbyshire, the elder child and only son of Bertram Caleb Bowden, primary school headmaster in Chesterfield, and his wife Sarah Elizabeth, daughter of John Thomas Moulton, of Throwley Hall, Staffordshire. He was educated at Chesterfield Grammar School and became a scholar at Emmanuel College, Cambridge, where he was awarded first-class honours in both parts of the natural sciences tripos (1930 and 1931). He was awarded a Ph.D. at Cambridge for a thesis on the structure of radioactive nuclei.

He then became an Imperial Chemical Industries fellow at the University of Amsterdam (1934–5), sixth-form master at Liverpool Collegiate School (1935–7), and chief physics master at Oundle School (1937–40), before moving to the Ministry of Defence Telecommunications Research Establishment, initially at Swanage and then in Malvern (1940–3). Here he investigated the use of radar to detect aircraft and precisely position them. This work began in Malvern and in May 1943 moved to Washington, where Bowden led a British team working with the Americans at the naval research laboratories. He showed his capacity to earn the trust of people at all levels in an organization and to cut through delaying bureaucracy to get things done. In 1973 he was given the Pioneer award by the American Institution of Electrical and Electronic Engineers. The citation, which recognized 'work done at least 20 years before but which remains important and in use', applauded Bowden's 'wartime radar identification system that has become an essential aid for modern air traffic control'.

After the war he had a brief period at the Atomic Energy Research Establishment at Harwell (July–December 1946) before becoming a partner with Sir Robert Watson-Watt & Partners (1947–50). He left the partnership when Sir Robert *Watson-Watt moved to Canada, and joined Ferranti (Digital Computers) Ltd. to attempt to sell digital computers at a profit. He thought it a most peculiar job until he met a man on the *Queen Mary* who sold lighthouses on commission. In the brief period of this appointment (1950–3) he successfully applied his great energy. He was particularly effective in explaining, with uncanny prescience, the dramatic effect that the digital computer was destined to have. Some of these thoughts he gathered together in his book *Faster than Thought* (1953).

In 1953 he became principal of the Manchester College of Science and Technology. At that time it taught a modest number of students on degree courses of the University of Manchester and a large number of part-time students, who studied for the National Certificate and other qualifications. Shortly after Bowden arrived, a period of rapid national expansion in higher education was launched, and he exploited this to the full. He attracted substantial resources, which transformed what he referred to as the surrounding dereliction and slums into an attractive campus with fine buildings. The university numbers expanded by a factor of about ten to the point where the city decided to transfer the non-university work to another college, much to Bowden's regret. The Manchester College then became an independent chartered body, the University of Manchester Institute of Science and Technology (UMIST), and was put on the University Grants Committee's list.

The development of UMIST was Bowden's great achivement. He had drive and energy, and a clear vision of what he wished to achieve. He did things by impulse, offering chairs to outstanding candidates at chance meetings in airport lounges and leaving his efficient and supportive registrar, Joe Burgess, to tidy up the legal processes afterwards. He made UMIST visible to the media by his public statements, in which he generated quotable aphorisms. He employed striking statistics to back his arguments. In these he often used the truth with some economy, but his conclusions were powerful. His national visibility led Harold Wilson (later Baron Wilson of Rievaulx) to make him a life peer (1963) and to appoint him minister for education and science (1964). Wilson hoped that Bowden would assist the development of the white-hot technological revolution, but it was not to be. Bowden has been described, accurately, as a man possessing candour without guile. This is not a quality that promises success in dealing with permanent civil servants, his relationship with whom Bowden described as 'like fighting a feather bed; you meet no resistance but you cannot get through it'. So he left the ministry in 1965, after having set up the Industrial Training Boards, which was a brave attempt to persuade industry to contribute to the cost of training the skills it needed. He returned to UMIST.

Here he continued to twinge consciences. He criticized the government for a fiscal policy that deterred industrial investment in new plant and processes. He counselled against the bifurcation of higher education. He despaired of the inadequate number of engineering and technology graduates entering British industry, and he was forever petitioning the city to act to reduce the 'decaying slums around the UMIST campus'. He retired in 1976.

He was a mixture of the ruthless and the humane. He had a portly figure which could be recognized at some distance by its rolling gait. As he said, 'I walk as if one leg is always shorter than the next one.' His door was always open. He was continually visible around the campus and took a keen interest in the problems and successes of all his staff, from the humble to the great. His concern with staff morale led him to pioneer the involvement of students in the decision-making bodies of UMIST. For this he was roundly criticized by the traditionalists, but later UMIST was to avoid the excesses of the student unrest of the 1960s. He was honorary FICE (1975) and

had honorary degrees from Rensellaer Polytechnic, USA (1974), Manchester (1976), and Kumasi, Ghana (1977).

He married in 1939 Marjorie Mary (died 1957), daughter of William G. H. Browne, chief government sanitary inspector in British Guiana. They had a son and two daughters. The marriage was dissolved in 1954. In 1955 he married Diana Stewart. They were divorced in 1961 and in 1967 he married Mary Maltby, who died in 1971. She was the daughter of Bernard W. Maltby, of Ilkeston, Derbyshire. In 1974 he married Phyllis, former wife of John Henry Lewis James, and daughter of Stanley Ernest Myson, postman. This marriage was dissolved in 1983. Bowden died 28 July 1989 in a nursing home in Bowdon, Cheshire.

[Citations presented at the 'Commemoration of the Life of Lord Bowden of Chesterfield' at UMIST, 13 October 1989; personal knowledge.]

K. M. ENTWISTLE

BOWLBY, (Edward) John (Mostyn) (1907–1990), psychiatrist, was born 26 February 1907 at 24 Manchester Square, London, the fourth child and second son in the family of three daughters and three sons of Major-General (Sir) Anthony Alfred *Bowlby, later first baronet, surgeon, and his wife Maria Bridget, daughter of the Revd Canon the Hon. Hugh Wynne Lloyd Mostyn, rector of Buckworth, Huntingdonshire. Bowlby was educated at the Royal Naval College, Dartmouth. He then read medicine at Trinity College, Cambridge, gaining first-class honours in part i of the natural sciences tripos (1927), and a second class in part ii of the moral sciences tripos (psychology, 1932). He went on to qualify in medicine (MB, B.Chir., 1933) at University College Hospital, London, proceeding to MD (Cambridge, 1939). Upon qualification, he began to specialize in psychiatry by becoming a clinical assistant at the Maudsley Hospital.

He was on the staff of the London Child Guidance Clinic from 1936 to 1940, and from 1940 to 1945 he served as a specialist psychiatrist in the Royal Army Medical Corps, attaining the rank of temporary lieutenant-colonel in 1944. From 1946 until his retirement in 1972 he was on the staff of the Tavistock Clinic, where he was director of the department for children and parents (1946–68). From 1962 to 1966 he was president of the International Association of Child Psychiatrists and Allied Professions. He was also consultant in mental health to the World Health Organization (1950–72), and a part-time member of the external scientific staff of the Medical Research Council (1963–72). Bowlby was elected a fellow of the Royal College of Physicians, London (1964), and a foundation fellow of the Royal College of Psychiatrists (1971). He held several visiting chairs abroad.

In 1946 he published a study of delinquent children: *Forty-Four Juvenile Thieves: their Characters and Home-Life*. The work which established his reputation began with an invitation from the World Health Organization in 1950 to advise on the mental health of homeless children. This led to the publication of *Maternal Care and Mental Health* (1951). *Attachment*, the first volume of Bowlby's massive trilogy *Attachment and Loss*, was published in 1969. Volume ii, *Separation: Anxiety and Anger*, followed in 1973. The trilogy was completed by the publication of *Loss: Sadness and Depression* (1980). Briefer, more popular expositions of Bowlby's views were *The Making and Breaking of Affectional Bonds* (1979) and *A Secure Base* (1988).

Bowlby was the originator of what later became known as 'attachment theory'. Having established that separation from the mother or mother-substitute in early childhood often had dire results, Bowlby set about investigating the way in which human beings establish ties of attachment with one another, and what consequences follow when these ties are severed. His conclusions were invariably backed up by objective research and extensive references. His interest led him to study ethology, and he became acquainted with, and indebted to, Konrad Lorenz, Nikolaas *Tinbergen, and Robert Hinde. Bowlby's studies of attachment in other species led him to conclude that the biological roots of attachment originated in the need to protect the young from predators. His interest in biological theory led to his last book, a biography of Charles *Darwin (1990).

Bowlby's studies of attachment had two main consequences. First, his theories prompted a large body of research, ranging from studies of attachment between infants and their mothers to the effects of bereavement and the severance of social ties in adult life. Second, his demonstration that even brief periods of separation of small children from their mothers can have serious emotional consequences led to important changes in hospital practice. It is because of Bowlby's research that it was later taken for granted that parents should be allowed free access to their sick children in hospital (and vice versa). Bowlby reinforced his case that such separations were traumatic by making a series of films with James Robertson, of which *A Two-Year-Old Goes to Hospital* (1952) is the best known. Bowlby saved hundreds of small children from unnecessary emotional distress.

Where most psychoanalysts assume that neurotic symptoms originate from the patient's inner world of fantasy, Bowlby remained firmly convinced that traumatic events in real life were more significant—not only actual separation and loss, but also parental threats of abandonment and other cruelties.

As a psychiatrist, Bowlby was a warm, caring human being who always remained entirely approachable. He was an excellent teacher and lecturer. His contributions to psychiatric knowledge and the care of children mark him as one of the three or four most important psychiatrists of the twentieth century. Underestimated by both biological scientists and psychoanalysts, his recognition was delayed. He was appointed CBE in 1972, and received honorary doctorates from Leicester (1971), Cambridge (1977), and Regensburg (1989). He was elected an honorary fellow of the Royal College of Psychiatrists (1980) and of the Royal Society of Medicine (1987). The British Paediatric Association gave him the Sir James Spence medal (1974) and he was elected a senior fellow of the British Academy in 1989.

Tall and courteous, with the manners of an old-fashioned English gentleman, Bowlby appeared reserved, but was never pompous. In 1938 he married Ursula, daughter of Dr Tom George *Longstaff, mountain explorer and president of the Alpine Club in 1947-9. They had two daughters and two sons. Bowlby died of a stroke while on holiday on the Isle of Skye, 2 September 1990.

[Bowlby papers in the Wellcome Institute, London; private information; personal knowledge.]

ANTHONY STORR

BOXER, (Charles) Mark (Edward) (1931–1988), caricaturist and cartoonist with the pseudonym 'Marc', and magazine editor, was born 19 May 1931 in Chorley Wood, Hertfordshire, the only son and younger child of Lieutenant-Colonel (Harold) Stephen Boxer, garage owner and car salesman, and his wife, Isobel Victoria Hughlings Jackson. He was educated at Boarsted, Berkhamsted School, and King's College, Cambridge.

He cut an immediate dash. To contemporaries his slender elegance, charm, and wit seemed immensely sophisticated, even intimidating. As a youth he appeared mature, as an adult boyish. In his first term he acted as Tybalt, all in white, for the Marlowe Society, and also drew for a comic magazine, *Granta*. He became editor the next year (1952), and took more interest in style than content; the content undid him. A poem contained the lines: 'You drunken gluttonous seedy God/ You son of a bitch, you snotty old sod.' This was deemed blasphemous and he was sent down for a week. Though he could have taken finals, he chose not to do so and left Cambridge in a hearse, followed by a crowd of perhaps a thousand protesters.

In London he worked briefly on the *Sunday Express*, a fashion export magazine called *Ambassador*, and *Lilliput*, and drew for the *Tatler*. In

1957 Jocelyn Stevens, a Cambridge friend, bought *Queen* and made him art director. Boxer hired the best photographers, displayed their work to maximum advantage, and was a large contributor to the magazine's conspicuous success. In 1962 he was the editor who launched the *Sunday Times Magazine*. Of the first issue Roy *Thomson (later first Baron Thomson of Fleet), who was paying for it, commented 'This is awful, absolutely awful', but though the losses continued for months, he held on and it became one of the major developments in British journalism of its time, much copied but rarely equalled. Boxer remained as editor until 1965 and stayed on as assistant editor until 1979. He was a director of the *Sunday Times* in 1964–6. In 1965 a listings magazine, *London Life*, of which he was editorial director, came and went, his only spectacular failure.

Over the same years 'Marc' had become famous as the outstanding pocket cartoonist of his time. His reputation was made at *The Times* (1969–83), where his work showed to best advantage, but he later worked for the *Guardian*. He had a detailed knowledge of the manners and customs of the establishment, the upper classes, and newly fashionable 'swinging London'. His own background and his left-wing views, conventional at the time, gave him the necessary distance. He did not deal directly with political issues, but reported what certain types would (revealingly) say about them. He also had an extraordinary eye for details of dress. He was Cartoonist of the Year in 1972. His caricatures, for profiles in the *New Statesman*, *Observer*, *London Review of Books*, and, after 1987, the *Sunday Telegraph*, were witty. Immediately pleasing because of his skill at catching a slightly distorted likeness, they were often sharp, even wounding. He said himself that the best compliment was when the subject asked if he could buy the original and then after a day or two reconsidered. He also developed, from one of Alan Bennett's ideas, the Stringalongs, who first appeared in a strip cartoon in the *Listener*. Based on friends, they were viewed without affection and with merciless accuracy.

Among his most effective illustrations for books were those which appeared in Clive James's *The Fate of Felicity Fark* (1975) and *Britannia Bright's Bewilderment* (1976) and in Alan Watkins's *Brief Lives* (1982), and on the jackets of the novels of Anthony Powell. In 1980 he became a director of the publisher Weidenfeld & Nicolson, but he returned to magazines to edit the *Tatler* in 1983–6. This time a dowdy magazine had already been livened up by Tina Brown, and his job, successfully carried out, was to maintain its vitality and widen its appeal. In 1986 he was made editorial director of Condé Nast in Europe, and in 1987 editor-in-chief of *Vogue*.

Thus he ended as he had begun; if he ever wished for a more serious role, there was no sign of it in his career. A stylish cricketer, he did everything that he did exceptionally well and left a precise and amusing portrait of the world he lived in.

In 1956 he married Lady Arabella Stuart, youngest daughter of Francis Douglas Stuart, eighteenth Earl of Moray; they had a daughter and a son. In 1982 they were divorced and in the same year Boxer married the television newscaster Anna Ford, daughter of John Ford, Church of England clergyman. They had two daughters. Boxer died 20 July 1988 of a brain tumour at his home in Brentford, London.

[*The Times We Live In: the Cartoons of Marc*, introduced by James Fenton, 1978; Mark Boxer, *The Trendy Ape*, 1968, and *Marc Time*, 1984; Mark Amory (ed.), *The Collected and Recollected Marc*, 1993; private information; personal knowledge.]   MARK AMORY

BOYD, SIR **John McFarlane** (1917–1989), trade-union official and Salvationist, was born 8 October 1917 in Motherwell, Lanarkshire, the only child of James Boyd, butcher, who died in the influenza epidemic of the following year, and his wife, Mary Marshall, who in 1920 married John Burns, collier, with whom she had two further sons. John was welcomed by his stepfather as his own son, but John Burns's earnings were irregular and after the 1926 general strike he had no work until the outbreak of World War II in 1939. Boyd was therefore brought up in considerable poverty and later recalled that until he was fourteen the only boots he possessed were supplied by the parish. He attended Hamilton Street Elementary School and Motherwell and Glencairn Secondary School, earning money for the family by delivering newspapers and milk. In 1932 he left school early to take up one of the few engineering apprenticeships at the Lanarkshire Steel Company and at the same time joined the apprentices' section of the Amalgamated Engineering Union. He thus added a second element to his future career, for he had at the age of ten joined the Salvation Army. In 1932 he signed the Salvationist articles of war, was sworn in as a senior soldier, and graduated to a BB♭ bass in the Motherwell Corps; his tuba, he noted, was 'easy to play but heavy'.

It was with a reputation as an open-air 'boy preacher' that in 1937 he took up the cause of junior workers at the Lanarkshire mill, on the claim of the AEU for the right to negotiate on their behalf. He found himself as one of the youthful leaders of a strike, which spread countrywide and achieved the union's objective on the apprenticeship question. After nine years as a craftsman and shop steward he was elected assistant divisional organizer in 1946, divisional organizer in 1949, and executive councillor for division 1 (Scotland) in 1953, the youngest member of the union ever to attain that office. He retained this post until 1975 when, following the untimely death of Jim Conway in an aeroplane crash, he was elected general secretary of the AEU until his retirement in 1982.

During almost three decades of working from AEU headquarters in London, Boyd held almost every post in the Labour movement available to him: president of the Confederation of Shipbuilding and Engineering Unions in 1964; member of the general council of the Trades Union Congress in 1967–75 and 1978–82; and chairman of the Labour party in 1967. He was also his union's chief negotiator in a number of industries including shipbuilding, atomic energy, electricity supply, paper-making, iron and steel, and aluminium. He was a member of the council of the Advisory, Conciliation and Arbitration Service (1978–82); a director of the British Steel Corporation (1981–6), of the United Kingdom Atomic Energy Authority (1980–5), of Industrial Training Services Ltd. from 1980, and of International Computers Ltd. (UK) from 1984; and a governor of the BBC (1982–7). He was appointed CBE in 1974, knighted in 1979, elected a fellow of the Royal Society of Arts in 1982, and in 1981, perhaps to his greatest satisfaction, received the Salvation Army's OF (Order of the Founder).

John Boyd was a tall, well-built, kindly man, craggy of face and rich in the intonations of the Clydesider. His devotion to the Salvation Army never faltered, nor his sincerity in combining this with his role as a trade unionist. To him they both were aspects of his mission of service. 'Yours, in the Joys of Service', the words with which he ended his address to members urging them to elect him as general secretary of the AEU in 1974, was to him no cant phrase. It was the expression of a form of Christian socialism pursued at a time when this had ceased to be fashionable, but recognizable as a creed which had inspired many of his forebears in the trade-union movement.

Much of his time within the AEU was spent weaning it away from communist and extreme left-wing influence. When he retired in 1982 the committed left had only two seats on the seven-man AEU executive. His hand was behind the introduction of the secret postal ballot for the election of AEU full-time officials, which was regarded with disfavour by many unions at the time, but later universally accepted. He was a doughty negotiator, persistent, fair, but sometimes tetchy, who sought to update his own organization. In this he did not wholly succeed before his retirement and he left much still to be done. His efforts to absorb the draughtsmen into the AUEW (as it was then called) proved, for both organizational and political reasons, to be an exercise in sentiment rather than reality. But he

did much to leave his union in better condition than he found it. Above all, Boyd laid great emphasis on decency and trust; 'ye can'na,' he commented in disgust with an employers' representative who had abused his confidence, 'negotiate with liars'.

In 1940 he married a fellow Salvationist, Elizabeth, daughter of James McIntyre, steelworker. They had two daughters. Boyd died 30 April 1989 at his home at 24 Pearl Court, Cornfield Terrace, Eastbourne, Sussex.

[Gordon Sharp, *Sir John Boyd*, Salvationist Publishing and Supplies Ltd., 1983; *Militant Moderate* (video, *c*.1980), Salvation Army Film and Video Unit; Gavin Laird, 'Sir John Boyd: a Tribute', *AEU Journal*, June 1989; J. B. Jefferys, *The Story of the Engineers*, 1946; personal knowledge.] ARTHUR MARSH

BRAINE, John Gerard (1922–1986), writer, was born 13 April 1922 in Bradford, the elder child and only son of Fred Braine, a sewage-works inspector, and his wife, Katherine Josephine Henry. By religion his father was a Methodist, his mother a Roman Catholic; he was brought up in the latter faith. He was educated at St Bede's (RC) Grammar School, Bradford, and attended the Leeds School of Librarianship—his mother had worked as a librarian. In 1938–40 he was in rapid succession a furniture-shop assistant, bookshop assistant, laboratory assistant, and progress chaser. Between 1940 and 1951 he was an assistant librarian at Bingley public library, becoming chief assistant in 1949. This part of his career was interrupted in 1942–3 by service in the Royal Navy, from which he was invalided out. In 1951 tuberculosis necessitated a long spell in hospital, from which he did not emerge till 1954. Over the next three years he worked as branch librarian successively at Northumberland and West Riding of Yorkshire county libraries. He had been writing various items, including a verse play, without much success for some time, and now, in 1957, published his first novel, *Room at the Top*.

Although earlier rejected by four publishers, this book immediately took its place as one of the significant novels of the postwar period. Its author's lack of a conventionally prolonged education may well have contributed to its freshness and vigour, and its story, of the material ascent and emotional coarsening of Joe Lampton, a northern working-class lad, owed something to a tradition of provincial writing that had become weakened. Before long its sales reached 100,000 in hardback and the film rights had been sold before publication. Within four months Braine was able to give up his career as a librarian and devote himself to writing. The film appeared in 1958.

His second novel, *The Vodi* (1959), an excursion into the supernatural influenced by his hospital experiences, has never done anything like so well either commercially or in esteem, but in his third, *Life at the Top* (1962, filmed 1965) he returned to Joe Lampton, now a capable but disaffected executive, and to commercial success. None of Braine's later novels, of which the last, *These Golden Days*, appeared in 1985, attracted the attention the Lampton books received. Joe enjoyed a kind of resurrection as the protagonist of two television series, *Man at the Top* (1970 and 1972), and several of Braine's other novels were effectively adapted for TV.

It is difficult not to see in his career after 1962 a decline in literary standards of performance as well as of popularity and standing with the public. Inexorably he came to be seen as a man, if not of one book, then of one character, the uncertainly attractive and far from inexhaustible Lampton. What at one stage had passed as a harsh northern critique of the affluent south seemed more and more to slide into tolerance at best. More than this, in the absence of the narrative thrust of the earlier novels, the general treatment and style was revealed as flatly pedestrian. Autobiography or wish-fulfilment took the place of invention, to the point of occasional embarrassment in late works like *One and Last Love* (1981).

Besides fiction, he published a critical study, *J. B. Priestley* (1978), and a handbook called *Writing a Novel* (1974), which, together with much sound practical advice to the tyro, includes a heartfelt warning, poignant in retrospect, of the dangers of success. He pursued a more ephemeral calling as a political polemicist in writing and in public appearances. At first a supporter of unilateral nuclear disarmament and other left-wing causes, he moved suddenly and spectacularly to the right, calling for the return of hanging and the ending of all foreign aid.

Though possessing strong views and vociferous dislikes, he showed no animosity towards anyone. He was indeed a man of great natural sweetness. Pale, chubby, bespectacled, a serious cigarette-smoker and drinker with a perpetual look of being out of condition, he had an expression of settled gloom that easily lightened into a genial smile. He showed an endearing pleasure in his prosperity and no resentment when his star began to fade.

In 1955 he married Helen Patricia, daughter of William Selby Wood, engineering fitter. They had a son and three daughters. The family moved from Bingley to Woking in 1966. Braine died of a gastric haemorrhage 28 October 1986, in a Hampstead hospital.

[Dale Salwak, *John Braine and John Wain, a Reference Guide*, 1980; *The Times*, 30 October 1986; *New Statesman*, 21 March 1975; information from family; personal knowledge.]   KINGSLEY AMIS

BRAITHWAITE, Richard Bevan (1900–1990), philosopher, was born 15 January 1900 in Banbury, Oxfordshire, the eldest in the family of three sons and one daughter of William Charles Braithwaite, of Banbury, barrister, banker, and historian of Quakerism, and his wife Janet, daughter of Charles C. Morland, of Croydon. He was educated at Sidcot School, Somerset (1911–14), Bootham School, York (1914–18), and as a scholar at King's College, Cambridge (1919–23), where he became a wrangler in part ii of the mathematical tripos (1922) and gained a first class in part ii of the moral sciences tripos (1923).

In 1924 he was elected to a fellowship at King's College, which he retained until his death. He was successively a university lecturer in moral sciences (later called philosophy) (1928–34), Sidgwick lecturer (1934–53), and Knightbridge professor of moral philosophy (1953–67). He did much to foster the philosophy of science in Cambridge, lecturing on it regularly for the philosophy tripos (his lectures on probability being particularly memorable). He also brought it into the natural sciences tripos, working with the historian (Sir) Herbert *Butterfield to found the department of history and philosophy of science.

His own work was in the Cambridge tradition of scientifically informed philosophy exemplified by Bertrand (third Earl) *Russell, J. Maynard *Keynes, Frank *Ramsey, and C. D. *Broad. His mathematical training showed most clearly in his philosophy of science, notably in his explication of the concept of probability invoked in modern science. This culminated in *Scientific Explanation* (1953), the published version of his Trinity College Tarner lectures of 1945–6, a classic work whose influence ranks him as a methodologist of science with Sir Karl Popper and Carl Hempel.

His philosophy ranged far wider than the philosophy of science. His 1955 inaugural lecture, *Theory of Games as a Tool for the Moral Philosopher*, showed the significance for moral and political philosophy of modern theories of games and decisions. His 1955 Eddington lecture, *An Empiricist's View of the Nature of Religious Belief*, showed his long-standing concern with religion. In this he was greatly influenced by his Quaker upbringing, as in the pacifism, later rejected, that made him serve in the Friends' Ambulance Unit in World War I. He eventually joined the Church of England, being baptized and confirmed in King's College chapel in 1948.

He took a keen interest in public affairs, and was active in college and university politics. He took especial satisfaction in helping to promote the grace admitting women to membership of Cambridge University and thus to its degrees. His principal recreation was reading novels.

It was the way he philosophized that most inspired his students, colleagues, and friends. In height and weight he may have resembled the average Englishman, but not in his intellectual exuberance. In discussion, even in old age, deaf, with spectacles and thinning hair, sometimes apparently asleep, his attention rarely flagged; and the intensity of his contributions—often prefaced with roars of 'Now look here, I'm sorry...'—was a continual refutation of the popular dichotomy of reason and passion. His curiosity was boundless, his grasp of issues quick and complete, his comments clear, forceful, and original. No one could be more passionate in the rational pursuit of truth, nor less concerned to impress, dominate, preach, or be taken for a guru. He was a great scourge of the obscure, the portentous, the complacent, and the slapdash—diseases to which philosophy is always prone and to which his incisive irreverence was the perfect antidote.

He received an honorary D.Litt. from Bristol University in 1963, and was visiting professor of philosophy at Johns Hopkins University in 1968, the University of Western Ontario in 1969, and the City University of New York in 1970. He was president of the Mind Association in 1946 and of the Aristotelian Society in 1946–7. In 1957 he became a fellow of the British Academy and in 1986 a foreign honorary member of the American Academy of Arts and Sciences. In 1948 he helped to found what later became the British Society for the Philosophy of Science, of which he was president from 1961 to 1963.

In 1925 he married Dorothea Cotter, daughter of Sir Theodore *Morison, principal of Armstrong College, Newcastle upon Tyne, which later became Newcastle University. She died in 1928, and in 1932 he married Margaret Mary (died 1986), daughter of Charles Frederick Gurney *Masterman, a noted Liberal MP and member of the 1914 cabinet. They had a son and a daughter. Braithwaite died of pneumonia 21 April 1990 at The Grange, a nursing home in Bottisham, near Cambridge.

[Mary Hesse in *Proceedings of the British Academy*, vol. lxxxii, 1992; *King's College Cambridge Annual Report*, October 1990; private information; personal knowledge.]   D. H. MELLOR

BRAMWELL-BOOTH, Catherine (1883–1987), Salvation Army commissioner, was born 20 July 1883 at Hadley Wood, Hertfordshire, the eldest in the family of two sons and five daughters of (William) Bramwell *Booth, Salvation Army general, and his wife, Florence Eleanor Soper. Bramwell was the eldest son of General William *Booth, the founder of the Salvation Army, and both he and his wife became Salvation Army leaders. Catherine spent all her childhood at Hadley Wood, which was 'so perfect that I

have never written about it, as no-one would believe me'. Her mother disapproved of outside influences acting on the tender minds of her children and taught them all herself for two hours every morning.

At the age of eighteen Catherine left her idyllic family life to become a full-time Salvation Army officer, an occupation she never left until her retirement. She added her father's forename to her surname. Following a period of study at the Salvation Army Training College, her first posting, in 1904, was as a captain in Bath. The pay was 7s.6d. a week and the duties, which started at 6 a.m., meant providing some counter-attraction to the pubs and gin houses every night of the week. She then held appointments in a number of important provincial centres, in charge of the Salvation Army's evangelical work, before commencing, in 1907, a period of ten years assisting with the training of women officers at the Army's International Training College. In 1913 she preached in Tsarist Russia and in 1917 made headlines when she led a rescue team into the area devastated by the Silvertown munitions factory explosion in West Ham, in which sixty people were killed. Later, she was involved with relief work in Europe after both world wars.

She vacated her post at the International Training College in 1917, to assume responsibility as international secretary for Salvation Army work in Europe, attached to the international headquarters in London. She was subsequently (1926–46) in charge of the movement's social work among women in Great Britain. In 1927 she was appointed a commissioner, concerned with all the Salvation Army's social welfare activities, meeting the needs of all types of people, from orphaned children to the elderly residents of Salvation Army eventide homes. From 1946 she was international secretary for Europe until she retired in 1948.

She was nominated three times for the generalship of the Salvation Army. On each occasion, in 1934, 1939, and 1946, the election resulted in one of the other candidates assuming the mantle of international leader. Possibly it was felt that the movement, at that stage, should not appear to be dependent on the Booth 'dynasty'. Certainly 'Commissioner Catherine', as she became affectionately known, was firmly in the Booth mould of charismatic leadership.

Throughout her life she remained true to the evangelical driving force of her parents and grandparents. Everyone confronted by her, from local tradesmen to distinguished national journalists, could expect a fearless cross-examination of their spiritual state and a presentation of the claims of her beloved Jesus Christ. She was a Salvation Army officer who never strayed from her roots and never lost her pioneering zeal. She had a keen analytical mind and a fund of knowledge which made her public addresses dynamic and inspiring, as well as informative.

She wrote several books, her best being a biography of her grandmother, *Catherine Booth, the Story of her Loves*. Published in 1970, this book brought her public recognition late in life, which resulted in her becoming something of a media personality, with a chirpy, engaging manner. During the last decade of her life she made frequent appearances as a stimulating guest on many radio and television programmes.

In 1971 she was appointed CBE. Six years later, at the age of ninety-three, she received the Guild of Professional Toastmasters best speaker award—to her own amusement because she was a lifelong teetotaller. In 1983 she was honoured with the Salvation Army's Order of the Founder. She died, unmarried, at the age of 104, 4 October 1987 at her home in Finchampstead, Berkshire, where she lived with two of her sisters.

[Mary Batchelor, *Catherine Bramwell-Booth*, 1987; Catherine Bramwell-Booth (with Ted Harrison), *Commissioner Catherine*, 1983; Salvation Army archives; personal knowledge.]   EVA BURROWS

BRENAN, (Edward Fitz)Gerald (1894–1987), writer and Hispanist, was born 7 April 1894 at Sliema, Malta, the elder son (there were no daughters) of Hugh Brenan, subaltern in the Royal Irish Rifles, and his wife Helen, daughter of Sir Ogilvie Graham, cotton and linen merchant. Gerald, as he was always called, spent the first seven years of his childhood either travelling with the regiment in South Africa and India, or living in the family home of the Grahams, Larchfield, near Belfast. However, in 1901 Hugh Brenan became almost stone deaf as a result of malaria, and had to leave the army. Gerald was a precocious, imaginative little boy, and devoted to his mother, who stimulated his love of books and his interest in history, travel, and especially botany. He won an exhibition to Radley, where he was extremely unhappy, and was awarded the Scott essay prize every year.

In obedience to his father's wishes, he passed into Sandhurst. Detesting this prospect, at seventeen he concocted and carried out a wildly romantic scheme to escape with an older friend, a donkey, and very little money, and walk to Asia. His friend got no further than Venice, but Gerald plodded on alone, braving wolves and snowstorms until he gave up in the Balkans, after having covered over 1,500 miles. His parents were relieved at the return of the prodigal, and —a year later—the outbreak of World War I temporarily settled his future. He was commissioned into the 5th Gloucesters and in due course was sent to France, serving first with the Cyclist Corps, and later in charge of observation posts, fighting at Ypres, Passchendaele, and the

Somme, and gaining the MC (1918) and the croix de guerre. It was in the army that he met Ralph Partridge and made the greatest friendship of his life, lasting as it did until Partridge's death in 1960, despite a violent breach over an affair with Partridge's first wife, Dora *Carrington.

Demobilized in 1919, Brenan was eager to get away from England, and acquire the education he felt Radley had failed to supply. With little equipment except his war gratuity and some 2,000 books in various languages, including the classics, he embarked for Spain, thinking his war gratuity would last longer there, and rented a little house in the village of Yegen on the beautiful slopes of the Sierra Nevada. Here he began life in his adopted country, devoting himself to reading, walking immense distances in the mountains, and writing quantities of long and brilliant letters. He considered himself a 'writer' from the first, though he never finished his projected life of Santa Teresa, and his first publication was a picaresque novel called *Jack Robinson* by 'George Beaton' (1933), which received élitist rather than wide acclaim.

During his visits to London he made many literary friends, and when in Spain he was visited by Lytton *Strachey, Virginia *Woolf, Bertrand *Russell, Roger *Fry, David *Garnett, and (Sir) V. S. Pritchett, with their consorts. At his best a brilliant and amusing talker, Brenan's character was full of contradictions: he had a great capacity for prolonged and concentrated study, as well as outstanding intelligence and originality in the interpretation of its results; he would often work far into the night, but he might collapse many times in a month with what he called 'flu'. *Jack Robinson* was followed by an unceasing output until the book of aphorisms in his eighties. *The Spanish Labyrinth* (1943), a penetrating study of the history of modern Spain, and *The Literature of the Spanish People* (1951) were much admired in academic circles, while Brenan's knowledge of Spain took a form designed to appeal to the general reader in *The Face of Spain* (1950) and *South from Granada* (1957). The latter was one of his most successful and often reprinted books. Two volumes of autobiography, *A Life of One's Own* and *Personal Record*, followed in 1962 and 1974; two more novels, and a life of St John of the Cross in 1973.

As a young man Brenan was tall, sparely built, and agile; he had straight fair hair and small, nearly black eyes set wide apart in a face that was expressive and charming rather than good-looking. He kept his agility until his seventies. In comparison with all his intellectual activity his emotional life ran an uneasy course. His love affair with Dora Carrington was far the most serious in his life, producing as it did an enormous two-way correspondence, some ecstasy, and considerable unhappiness on both sides.

Otherwise he was obsessed by sex, and inhibited by fears of impotence. A stream of prostitutes, hippies, and peasant girls occupied his agitated thoughts and feelings and directed his travels. In 1930, while in Dorset, he met the American poetess and novelist, (Elisabeth) Gamel Woolsey, who was then involved with the literary Powys family, especially Llewelyn. She was the daughter of William Walton Woolsey, plantation owner, of South Carolina. She and Gerald drifted into a relationship, and although their temperaments differed greatly—between his nervous excitability and her dreamy melancholy—they grew very close. In 1931 they went through a pseudo-marriage in Rome, ratified later in London. Gamel died of cancer in 1968. Brenan had one child, a daughter Miranda, whose mother was Juliana Pellegrino, an unmarried girl from Yegen village. She was born in 1931 and later legally adopted by her father and Gamel, who took her to England to be educated. She died of cancer in 1980.

After the end of Franco's regime most of Brenan's books were translated, and he became a hero in Spain, receiving the Pablo Iglesias award. He was also appointed CBE (1982). In 1970 Brenan moved inland to a smaller house built to his own design, and here he spent his last seventeen years, while his eyesight and health gradually declined. He was cared for by Lynda Price and her husband, Lars Pranger. In 1984 the burden of his rapidly declining state led to his consenting to be taken by Lars to a home in Pinner, near London, to the great indignation of his Spanish admirers. This resulted in the extraordinary and much publicized sequel when two members of the Junta de Andalucia flew to London, kidnapped Brenan, and took him back to Alhaurin, where they arranged for him to be nursed and cared for at his home. He died there 19 January 1987.

[Xan Fielding (ed.), *Best of Friends, the Brenan–Partridge Letters*, 1986; Jonathan Gathorne-Hardy, *The Interior Castle: a Life of Gerald Brenan*, 1992; personal knowledge.]   FRANCES PARTRIDGE

BROCKWAY, (Archibald) Fenner, BARON BROCKWAY (1888–1988), socialist campaigner and parliamentarian, was born 1 November 1888 in Calcutta, the only son and eldest of three children of the Revd William George Brockway, London Missionary Society missionary, and his wife, Frances Elizabeth, daughter of William Abbey. His mother died when he was fourteen. Educated at the School for the Sons of Missionaries at Blackheath (subsequently Eltham College), he became a journalist. He moved from Liberalism to the Independent Labour party and by 1912 was editor of the ILP newspaper, the *Labour Leader*. Still in his twenties, he worked closely with leading figures on the British left.

He played a heroic role in the ILP's opposition to the war of 1914–18, as a journalist, and then through the No-Conscription Fellowship as an opponent of military conscription. On four occasions he was sentenced to gaol—the last time in July 1917 to two years' hard labour. When released in April 1919, he had served a total of twenty-eight months, the last eight in solitary confinement. His war record increased his status in several sections of the Labour movement and in the election of 1929 he was returned as the Labour member for East Leyton. In 1919 he became editor of *India* and joint secretary of the British committee of the Indian National Congress. From 1926 to 1929 he was editor of the *New Leader*, the renamed organ of the ILP, of which he had become organizing secretary in 1922.

Brockway's continuing involvement in the ILP section of the wider Labour party made him an increasingly controversial figure. From 1926 the ILP moved to the left under the leadership of James *Maxton, and called for 'socialism in our time', a radicalization backed enthusiastically by Brockway. With the 1929 Labour government proving helpless in the face of rocketing unemployment, Brockway was prominent amongst a small group of ILP rebel members. This small section of left-wingers refused to accept the party's disciplinary guidelines, and were denied endorsement for the 1931 election. Like most Labour MPs, Brockway lost his seat. The dispute over discipline was symbolic of a much more fundamental division over policy. In July 1932, with Brockway in the chair, the ILP voted to disaffiliate from the Labour party.

There followed the most radical period of Brockway's career as he sought to articulate a socialism distinct from the pragmatism of Labour and the Stalinism of the Communist party. But the ILP's membership dwindled, and it was squeezed between its rivals. The Spanish civil war modified his pacifism and deepened his suspicion of the Communist party. In 1937 he visited Spain and observed the repression of the ILP's Spanish equivalent by the Communist party. During the war of 1939–45, he felt cross-pressured between his distaste for militarism and his thorough antipathy to fascism. In wartime by-elections he argued for socialism as a means of ending the war. After Labour's 1945 electoral success, he decided that the ILP offered no distinctive way forward and rejoined the Labour party. From 1942 to 1947 he was chairman of the British Centre for Colonial Freedom and in 1945 he helped establish the Congress of Peoples against Imperialism.

In February 1950 he returned to the Commons as the member for Eton and Slough. He remained firmly on the left, participating in the faction centred around Aneurin *Bevan, but his radicalism was always tempered by a concern not to reproduce what he had come to see as the disastrous split of 1932. His strong anti-militarism was expressed in his involvement with the Campaign for Nuclear Disarmament. His principal fame came from his championing of anti-colonial movements. His interest in Indian independence had been long-standing and from 1950 he began to visit Africa regularly. Some called him the member for Africa and he knew several of the first generation post-independence African leaders. From 1954 he was chairman of the Movement for Colonial Freedom. His anti-colonialism was reflected in a thorough opposition to racism in Britain. In nine successive sessions he introduced Bills into the Commons aimed at outlawing discrimination. Ironically, when the 1964 Labour government embarked on such legislation, Brockway had just lost his parliamentary seat. The margin was eleven votes and some commentators ascribed his defeat to the race issue. Despite misgivings, he accepted a life peerage (1964) and campaigned for his causes within the traditionalism of the upper house. His radicalism remained vibrant in his new environment. Brockway was a prolific writer, of books, pamphlets, and articles. These included four volumes of autobiography and major studies of two ILP contemporaries, Fred Jowett (*Socialism over Sixty Years*, 1946) and Alfred Salter (*Bermondsey Story*, 1949).

In 1914 he married Lilla, daughter of the Revd William Harvey-Smith. They had four daughters, two of whom predeceased him (1941 and 1974). As Brockway acknowledged later, the marriage was not a success and he had several, often short-lived, affairs in the interwar years. After a divorce in 1945, in 1946 he married Edith Violet, daughter of Archibald Herbert King, electrician; they had one son. Both his wives shared many of his political views.

Many found Brockway to be highly principled and warmly sympathetic. His style inherited something of his missionary background and his socialist politics owed much to a broader tradition of English radicalism. Not an intellectual, he was yet an independent thinker. Born in the age of *Gladstone, he died in the age of Thatcher 28 April 1988, at Watford General Hospital, Hertfordshire.

[*Guardian*, 29 April 1988; *The Times*, 30 April 1988; *Independent*, 2 May 1988; Fenner Brockway, *Inside the Left*, 1942, *Outside the Right*, 1963, *Towards Tomorrow*, 1977, and *98 Not Out*, 1986; personal knowledge.]

DAVID HOWELL

BUHLER, Robert (1916–1989), painter, was born 23 November 1916 at the French Hospital, Shaftesbury Avenue, London, the only son and elder child of Robert Buhler, a Swiss aircraft designer with Handley Page, who later became a journalist, and his wife, Lucy Kronig, who came from the village of Täsch in the Valais. He held Swiss-British nationality all his life. He attended Westbourne Park Grammar School in 1926–9, and was then further educated in Switzerland for a short time, before leaving school in his early teens to study commercial art at the *Kunstgewerbeschule* in Zurich and then at that in Basle.

In 1933 he returned to London, where he spent two terms at Bolt Court School of Photo-Engraving and Lithography. There he met (J.) Keith *Vaughan, who encouraged him to take up fine art. In 1934 he became a painting student at St Martin's School of Art, where he was taught by (R.) Vivian Pitchforth, (G. C.) Leon *Underwood, and Harry Morley. In 1935 he won a senior county scholarship to the Royal College of Art. He responded to the teaching of Barnett *Freedman and John *Nash, but only stayed there for six weeks.

Having inherited a little money, he relinquished his scholarship, and rented a studio in Camden Town. He made an income from teaching at Wimbledon School of Art and from illustrating for various newspapers. He was also commissioned by Jack Beddington of Shell to design a very successful poster depicting Hawker Hurricane fighter aircraft. He began to exhibit in 1936, and showed at the first British Artists' Congress (1937), organized by the Artists' International Association. His work attracted the attention of the collector and patron Sir Edward *Marsh, and his 'Portrait of Dickie Green' was illustrated in (Sir) Herbert *Read's review of the exhibition in the *Listener*.

His mother, by then separated from his father, ran a bookshop and café in Charlotte Street, which was frequented by staff and students of the nearby Euston Road School; from 1937 Robert Buhler became acquainted with them, but did not attend the school himself. He was, however, influenced by their approach to painting, using restrained colour and close tones for the composition of soberly executed portraits, still lifes, landscapes, and urban scenes. The Contemporary Art Society bought his portrait of (Sir) Stephen Spender, then a student at the Euston Road School, in 1938.

Buhler shared exhibitions with Vivian Pitchforth and also with (Sir) Lawrence Gowing in the early 1940s, whilst serving in the Auxiliary Fire Service during World War II. In 1945 he began teaching at the Central School of Arts and Crafts in London, and also at the Chelsea School of Art. He exhibited at the Royal Academy in 1945, at the New English Art Club (becoming a member in 1946), and at the Royal Society of British Artists. In 1947 he was elected ARA and the following year joined the London Group. He was invited in 1948 by (Sir) Robert ('Robin') *Darwin to teach at the Royal College of Art. He was an intelligent and sensitive teacher, who encouraged students of very varied talents. His first one-man show was at the Leicester Galleries in 1950, and in 1956 he was made an RA, one of the youngest until then to achieve that distinction.

In 1975 he became a trustee of the Royal Academy. In that year he resigned from the staff of the RCA, and travelled very widely in Europe and the United States over the next few years. In 1982 he won the Wollaston award for the most distinguished exhibit at the RA, 'Water-Meadow Dusk', and in 1984 he won the Hunting Group prize for 'Vineyards, Neufchâtel'. His work is in the permanent collections of national and provincial galleries all over the world. In addition to his many commissioned portraits, Buhler painted a number of portraits of his friends and fellow artists for his own satisfaction. In his later work he tended to seek an underlying geometry or pattern in nature. His oil paintings were matt in texture, brush strokes were almost suppressed, and detail was all but eliminated in favour of muted but luminous blocks of colour.

(H. G.) Rodrigo *Moynihan's group portrait, 'The Painting School Teaching Staff of the RCA' (1949–52), depicts Buhler, of average height, dark-haired, and handsome, with dark eyebrows and a markedly cleft chin, wearing a dark suit, standing at the centre of the composition with his hand on the back of a chair. A sophisticated man of cosmopolitan background, he was a sociable and witty person. In 1938 he married Eveline Mary, daughter of William Gadsby Rowell, joiner. They were divorced in 1951. They had one son, and Buhler was also the father of a daughter, the mother of whom he did not marry. In 1962 he married Prudence Mary Brochocka, whose previous marriage was dissolved, daughter of Hubert William Hastings Beaumont, solicitor. They had two sons, and were divorced in 1971. Buhler died at his home in Chelsea 20 June 1989.

[Colin Hayes, *Robert Buhler*, 1986; 'Robert Buhler, in Conversation with Mervyn Levy', September 1984, National Sound Archives, 29 Exhibition Road, London; private information; personal knowledge.]

ALAN WINDSOR

BÜLBRING, Edith (1903–1990), pharmacologist and smooth muscle physiologist, was born 27 December 1903 in Bonn, Germany, the youngest of four children and third daughter of Karl Daniel Bülbring, professor of English at Bonn University, and his wife Hortense Leonore Kann, a Dutch woman, daughter of a Jewish banker's family in The Hague. Edith's father died prematurely in 1917, and his eldest child, a son, was killed in action in 1918. Edith was educated at the Klostermann Lyzeum, Bonn. Her father's death and the hyper-inflation of the postwar years caused a financial strain, but her mother's brothers set up accounts for the three girls, giving each a modest income for life. After a period of private tuition she entered Bonn Gymnasium in 1922 to study chemistry, physics, and mathematics for the municipal examinations, which she passed at Easter 1923, entitling her to enter Bonn University, where she started preclinical studies for medicine.

Her decision to read medicine at university was a surprise and perhaps a disappointment to her mother, since she had early shown exceptional talent as a pianist, an accomplishment that gave her and her friends considerable pleasure in later life (she had two grand pianos in Oxford). Her clinical training was undertaken in Munich, Freiburg, and Bonn, and she qualified in May 1928. She then moved to Berlin, where she spent a year as house physician and two years as research assistant to Paul Trendelenburg, an eminent professor of pharmacology and an old family friend, who thought she was wasting her talents as a physician. Unfortunately, he died of tuberculosis before Edith had become sufficiently confident to decide on a research career, and she returned to medicine in 1931, as a paediatrician for a year in Jena (Germany). This seems to have been her first paid position. She then returned to Berlin, to the infectious disease unit of the Virchow Krankenhaus. This was during the rise of Adolf Hitler and National Socialism, and, when citizens were required by law to declare their ancestry, the fact that she was half Jewish caused her dismissal. She returned home to Bonn, in late 1933.

Intending to go to Holland to practise medicine, Edith Bülbring first joined a sister and a friend on a holiday in England. Whilst there, she visited her old chief at the Virchow Krankenhaus, Ulrich Friedemann, from Berlin, a refugee working in Sir Henry *Dale's laboratory in Hampstead. Dale assumed she also was looking for a job, and contacted J. H. Burn, who was setting up a biological standardization laboratory for the Pharmaceutical Society in Bloomsbury Square, London; he offered her a post. Thus began her scientific career. When Burn was appointed to the Oxford chair of pharmacology in 1937, she moved to Oxford, where she became successively a departmental demonstrator (1937), university demonstrator and lecturer (1946), *ad hominem* reader (1960), and finally, in 1967, *ad hominem* professor. She was elected to a professorial fellowship at Lady Margaret Hall in 1960. She had been naturalized in 1948.

Initially Edith Bülbring worked in collaboration with Burn on the autonomic nervous system, and the effects of catecholamines and acetylcholine and their interactions. She acted as Burn's research assistant for some fifteen years, but in her early forties began more independent research. She decided to concentrate on trying to unravel the physiology of smooth muscle, a tissue that had previously always irritated her by its unpredictability. It was here that she made the greatest impact, and she will be remembered as one of the world's most influential scientists in this field. Under her influence, the study of smooth muscles became first respectable, and then increasingly important. She published *Smooth Muscle* in 1970. The techniques developed in her laboratory led to increasing knowledge of the physiology of smooth muscle, and the activities of the many scientists who spent time working with her spread her interest and enthusiasm for these tissues throughout the world. Her influence and scientific skills were recognized in her election as a fellow of the Royal Society in 1958, by the conferment on her of honorary degrees from Groningen, Leuven, and Homburg (Saar), and by the award of the Schmiedeberg-Plakette of the Deutsche Pharmakologische Gesellschaft in 1974 and of the Wellcome gold medal in pharmacology in 1985.

Edith Bülbring's friends and close colleagues remember her with great affection for the warmth, keen interest, and whole-hearted generosity with which she treated them. She never married, but in Oxford lived first with her younger sister, Maud, in Cumnor, and then finally built a house at 15 Northmoor Road, where after Maud's death she lived with her elder sister Lucy. In appearance Edith was not distinguished, being of medium height and build. In early photographs she looked decidedly plain, and one would have guessed that she was quiet and unassuming, but her contemporaries do not remember her that way. Her vivacity and enthusiasm are what is remembered, not what she looked like. Later in life she became progressively more attractive and feminine in appearance. Her health was good and she continued active work well after her official retirement. Eventually atherosclerosis led to amputation of one leg below the knee when she was in her seventies. She did not allow this to handicap her, but she had progressive loss of circulation in her other leg, and could not tolerate the thought of a second amputation. Instead, she spent much of her last two years trying different treatments, culminating in her final operation, an attempt at a venous graft which she knew would be highly risky. The graft was probably a success, but there were multiple emboli which affected her heart and probably caused her minor strokes. She died three days later, 5 July 1990 in the John Radcliffe Hospital, Oxford.

[T. B. Bolton and A. F. Brading in *Biographical Memoirs of Fellows of the Royal Society*, vol. xxxviii, 1992; personal knowledge.]   A. F. BRADING

BULL, SIR Graham MacGregor (1918–1987), physician, was born 30 January 1918 in Nyaunghla, upper Burma, the eldest in the family of two sons and one daughter of Arthur Barclay Bull, medical practitioner to an oil company and later in practice in Simonstown, and his wife, Margaret Petrie MacGregor. He was educated at Diocesan College, Rondebosch, Cape Province, South Africa, and the University of Cape Town, where he obtained his MB, Ch.B. with distinction in 1939. He worked in the department of medicine at the University of Cape Town at Groote Schuur Hospital from 1940 to 1946, gaining an MD degree in 1947 on the subject of postural proteinuria. As a result of this work he was awarded a fellowship by the South African Council for Scientific and Industrial Research to continue his research at the Postgraduate Medical School in Hammersmith, London, the postwar Mecca of most Commonwealth medical academics.

Under the direction of (Sir) John McMichael, the Postgraduate Medical School provided an exciting environment in which bright young people were encouraged to think critically and pursue novel and intellectually challenging research. Bull thrived in this environment and in 1947 was appointed to a lectureship in the School. His research concerned the management of acute kidney failure, for which he devised a treatment that became internationally known as the 'Bull regime'. The basis of the regime was simplicity itself. Bull argued from the analogy of a blocked lavatory. One's natural reaction was to pull the chain, so that more water flowed into the basin, which then overflowed; it would be better to leave things as they were until the blockage was relieved. For patients who were unable to pass urine, Bull recommended replacement only of the fluid and electrolytes they lost. In this way they were not overloaded and were kept in balance until kidney function returned spontaneously. The Bull regime saved countless lives by preventing over-enthusiastic attempts to 'flush out' the kidneys, but was eventually superseded by dialysis techniques, through which a similar balance could be maintained.

The recognition of Bull's work soon led to his appointment in 1952 to a chair of medicine at Queen's University, Belfast, where he gained an immense reputation as an all-round clinician and teacher. A paper he published from Belfast examined marking systems applied to essay questions in medical examinations and he was able to demonstrate that individual variability led to highly discrepant and irreproducible outcomes. More than anyone else Bull was responsible for the switch from essays to multiple-choice questions, which later became the basis of most written examinations in medicine. He became FRCP (Lond.) in 1954.

Following the untimely death of the director designate, John Squire, Bull was asked in 1966 to become the director of the new Medical Research Council Clinical Research Centre at Northwick Park, Harrow. Squire's was a difficult place to fill, but Bull did so superbly, displaying the tact, wisdom, and concern for high standards that eased the centre into its role as a world-class clinical and investigative institution, despite many difficulties that stood in its path. His novel idea was to integrate a clinical research centre and a general district hospital, and, by the time he retired in 1978, he was in charge of an 800-bed hospital (Northwick Park Hospital) and a clinical research centre, designed as a single unit. His own research activity had, not unexpectedly, diminished over the years, but he remained abreast of the latest scientific advances and encouraged the excellent medical and scientific personnel at the centre to tackle big and exciting research problems—much in the same way as John McMichael had lent support to his young people some twenty to thirty years earlier.

Bull was a member of the Medical Research Council from 1962 to 1966, and for many years chairman of its tropical medicine research board. From 1970 to 1983 he was a member of the executive committee of the CIBA Foundation, serving as its chairman from 1977 to 1983. He was also vice-president of the Royal College of Physicians of London in 1978–9, and in 1988 the Sir Graham Bull memorial prize was founded there, to be awarded annually for meritorious research carried out by a scientist under the age of forty-five in the broad field of clinical research, in which Bull personally had excelled and guided so many young doctors. He had been knighted in 1976.

Bull was a kind and humane man, greatly respected and liked by patients, students, and colleagues. He was an excellent institutional head, always willing to listen sympathetically to people's ideas or problems and to offer sensible and helpful advice. He had many outside interests—travel, cooking, wine-making—and he and his wife were exceptional and popular hosts. A little above average height, he was of solid build and tended to put on weight latterly. His brown hair fell over his forehead; in later years it silvered and thinned and, with his rather aquiline nose, this gave him a distinguished, almost patrician appearance. His eyes were strikingly direct and penetrating. In 1947 he married Megan Patricia, daughter of Thomas Jones, doctor of medicine, of South Africa. She had been a fellow medical student of his at Cape Town and became governor of Holloway prison in 1973, having previously served as its medical officer. The Bulls had three sons and a daughter, whose occupations—doctor, accountant, biologist, and

musician—reflected the wide interests of their parents. Bull died suddenly 14 November 1987 after surgery, at the National Heart Hospital, London.

[*The Times*, 18 November 1987; *Independent*, 4 December 1987; *Lancet*, vol. ii, 5 December 1987; *MRC News*, March 1988; *Munk's Roll*, vol. viii, 1989; personal knowledge.]   RAYMOND HOFFENBERG

BURN, Duncan Lyall (1902–1988), economist, was born 10 August 1902 in Holloway, London, the younger child and younger son of Archibald William Burn, engineer, and his wife, Margaret Anne Mead, who, prior to her marriage, worked as a nanny. He was taught history at Holloway County School by (Sir) Arthur *Bryant and won a scholarship to Christ's College, Cambridge, where he took a first class (division II) in both parts of the history tripos (1923 and 1924). On graduation he won a Wrenbury scholarship, which enabled him to spend a year (1924) as a bachelor research scholar at Christ's. After two years at Liverpool as a university lecturer in economic history (1925–6) he returned to Cambridge in 1927 in the same capacity. There he remained until the outbreak of World War II in 1939, living out of Cambridge and with no college attachment. During that time he completed his authoritative study of the British steel industry, *The Economic History of Steelmaking 1867–1939* (1940). He was also a kindly and rigorous supervisor, some of whose students maintained a lifelong friendship with him.

A self-taught economist, he never ceased to be basically an academic, pursuing research in industrial economics throughout his life. He was not much interested in macroeconomics, dismissing demand management after the war as 'penny-in-the-slot-economics'.

Throughout the war he served with (Sir) Robert Shone in the iron and steel control of the Ministry of Supply, taking part in the later stages in government planning for the postwar steel industry. In 1946 he did not return to Cambridge but joined *The Times* as leader-writer and industrial correspondent, continuing in that capacity for the next sixteen years and displaying an impressive knowledge of industry in Britain and abroad. He won a high reputation in the main industrial countries and maintained close and frequent contact with Jean Monnet, the French economist and politician. He was a natural choice to edit a two-volume study of British industry (*The Structure of British Industry*, 1958), and contributed to it chapters on oil and steel, as well as an analytical survey. He continued to write on the steel industry, producing in 1961 a sequel to his earlier book, *The Steel Industry 1939–59*. When re-nationalization was under debate he argued (in *The Future of Steel*, 1965), that the proposal misconceived the problems of the industry and misjudged the likely effects. 'More scope,' he maintained, 'must be given to rebels in management' who backed far-sighted but unfashionable or unpopular projects.

In 1962 Burn left *The Times* and adopted a third career as an industrial consultant, acting for three years as director of the economic development office set up by four leading manufacturers of heavy electric generators. This increased his interest in nuclear energy, on which he wrote extensively over the next fifteen years, beginning with a lengthy study in 1965, after a visit to America, of 'The Significance of Oyster Creek', the first large boiling water reactor to be ordered. He also acted as consultant to firms in the aircraft and chemical industries, producing in 1971 a study of the chemical industry, *Chemicals under Free Trade*. He served on a number of official and academic committees such as the economic committee of the Department of Scientific and Industrial Research (1963–5) and had two further spells of academic life as visiting professor at the universities of Manchester (1967–9) and Bombay (1971). At his death he had been working for a number of years on a book on 'The Public Interest'.

In 1967 Burn developed his criticisms of British plans for a programme of gas-cooled reactors (AGRs) in *The Political Economy of Nuclear Energy*, maintaining that the AGR was well behind light water reactors in performance and likely to fall further behind. By the time he published *Nuclear Power and the Energy Crisis* in 1978 it was apparent that, instead of Britain leading the world in nuclear energy as ministers claimed even in the mid-1960s, no British nuclear reactors had ever been built abroad. Burn continued to interest himself in nuclear energy, acting from 1980 until his death as specialist adviser to the House of Commons select committee on energy.

The distinguishing feature of Burn's work was his deep interest in what made for successful industrial and technological development. He stressed the contribution made by competition in encouraging a variety of approaches and allowing scope for differences of opinion. His research was meticulous and quantitative, and aimed to single out the key elements in competitive success. He had many contacts in industry and, as he was a good listener with a retentive memory, he came to have a rare knowledge of expert industrial opinion as well as its divisions and weaknesses. In expressing his own views he was never daunted by the authority or eminence of those from whom he differed. He could be scathing in his criticisms, but his views were well documented and carefully argued.

Burn was short in stature, clean-shaven, with blue eyes and a slightly puckered face. He spoke slowly and quietly, but with assurance, and he enjoyed an argument. Normally serious-minded, he did not lack a sly humour and was given to an occasional quip and twinkle of the eye. On 30 December 1930 he married Jessie Mabel ('Mollie'), daughter of William Louis White, a chemist who worked in a retail pharmacy. It was an extremely happy marriage that lasted for nearly sixty years until his death from heart failure 9 January 1988 in the Royal Free Hospital, London. She was four years his senior. They had two daughters.

[Personal knowledge.]   ALEC CAIRNCROSS

BURROW, Thomas (1909–1986), professor of Sanskrit at the University of Oxford, was born 29 June 1909 in Leck, north Lancashire, the eldest in the family of five sons and one daughter of Joshua Burrow, farmer, and his wife, Frances Eleanor Carter. He was educated at Queen Elizabeth's School, Kirkby Lonsdale, and won a scholarship to Christ's College, Cambridge. He first read classics, specializing in comparative philology, and obtained first classes in both parts i and ii of the tripos (1929 and 1930). He then went on to study oriental languages, in which he also got firsts in both parts of the tripos (1931 and 1932). He began research for a year at the School of Oriental Studies, London University, and continued in Cambridge, where after two more years he was awarded the Ph.D. He became a research fellow of Christ's College (1935–7).

His first book, *The Language of the Kharoṣṭhī, Documents from Chinese Turkestan* (1937), was based on his doctoral thesis. The language in question, sometimes known as Niya Prakrit, was an official language in central Asia after the Kushan dynasty; the documents had been discovered and brought to Europe by Sir (M.) Aurel *Stein. Burrow published his translation of them in 1940.

Burrow was assistant keeper in the department of oriental printed books and manuscripts at the British Museum from 1937 to 1944. During this period he mainly devoted himself to studying Dravidian languages. In 1944 he was appointed Boden professor of Sanskrit at Oxford University and professorial fellow of Balliol College, positions which he held until his retirement in 1976. Until 1965 he was the university's sole teacher in classical Indology. Besides Sanskrit he had to teach Pali and Prakrit. His practice was to read a set Sanskrit text with a BA student (or students, on the rare occasions when there was more than one in a year) for three hours a week; those texts not covered in class the students read unaided in the vacations. He gave some extra classes in Pali or Prakrit and in Sanskrit composition, but he may never have set an essay.

Of Burrow's many publications on Sanskrit,

the best known are *The Sanskrit Language* (1955, revised edn. 1973) and *The Problem of Shwa in Sanskrit* (1979). His views on the development of the Sanskrit vowel system were at odds with those of most Indo-Europeanists, but otherwise his exposition of Sanskrit was orthodox in the mainstream of comparative philology. His early interest in Prakrit did not develop further.

Burrow was happiest as a Dravidologist and did his most important work in Dravidian linguistics. In 1949 he began to collaborate with Professor Murray B. Emeneau of Berkeley. Together they published *A Dravidian Etymological Dictionary* (1961) and *Dravidian Borrowings from Indo-Aryan* (1962). After retirement Burrow gave most of his energy to producing the second edition of the *Dictionary* (1984); it was, as he intended, his last book.

This work on comparative Dravidian linguistics was complemented by Burrow's research on hitherto unrecorded Dravidian languages which survive in small linguistic communities in central India. To record them, he undertook field trips with S. Bhattacharya of the Anthropological Survey of India; together they published *The Parji Language* (1953), *A Comparative Vocabulary of the Gondi Dialects* (1960), and *The Pengo Language* (1970). Further fruits of Burrow's research in this field are gathered in *Collected Papers in Dravidian Linguistics* (1968).

Burrow was widely respected as a singleminded scholar of great learning. A Sanskrit panegyric was presented to him by the Sanskrit College, Calcutta. He was elected a fellow of the British Academy in 1970. In 1974 he became a fellow of the School of Oriental and African Studies of London University and in 1979 a number of the *Bulletin of the School of Oriental and African Studies* (vol. xlii, no. 2) was devoted to articles in honour of his seventieth birthday.

In build Burrow was rather over middle size and his appearance, at least in later life, was somewhat lumbering, but he moved quietly. His habitual expression was mild, even vague. He had very short sight and blinked frequently. To his colleagues and students he was amiable but socially passive and taciturn. There were reports that of an evening he would visit his local pub in Kidlington, the village outside Oxford where he lived, and entertain companions with lively conversation; but in Oxford he was reticent about his private life to the point of secrecy. In 1941 he married Inez Mary, daughter of Herbert John Haley; but when she died at their home in 1976 it came as a surprise to his Oxford acquaintances, who believed him to be living alone. He never brought his wife into college, and explained after her death that her health was poor. It may be that she suffered from depression after their only child died in early infancy.

Burrow died of a heart attack in Oxford 8 June 1986.

[Private information; personal knowledge.]

RICHARD GOMBRICH

BUTLER, Basil Edward ('Christopher') (1902–1986), monk and theologian, was born in Reading 7 May 1902, the second of four sons and third of five children of William Edward Butler, wine merchant, and his wife, Bertha Alice Bowman, a schoolteacher originally from Suffolk. His intellectual gifts revealed themselves early and he proceeded from Reading School to St John's College, Oxford, on a scholarship. At Oxford he received the Craven scholarship and Gaisford Greek prose prize and was *proxime accessit* for the Hertford scholarship, as well as taking first classes in classical honour moderations (1922), *literae humaniores* (1924), and theology (1925).

In 1925 he began his life as a clerical don with a tutorship at Keble College, and the following year was ordained an Anglican deacon. His High Church upbringing came to maturity at university, but he was becoming increasingly convinced by Catholicism. He taught classics at Brighton College in 1927–8 and (after his reception into the Roman communion in 1928) at Downside School, Somerset, in 1928–9. Downside was to be his home until 1966. He entered the Benedictine community there in 1929, assuming the religious name Christopher, and was ordained priest in 1933. He was head master of Downside from January 1940 until his election as seventh abbot of Downside on 12 September 1946. He was re-elected in 1954 and 1962, remaining abbot until 1966, and he presided over the extensive building programme which followed the great fire at Downside in 1955. In August 1961 he was elected president of the English Benedictine congregation, a post he held until 1966.

It was in this capacity that he attended all four sessions of the second Vatican Council from 1962 to 1965, during which he emerged as perhaps the leading English-speaking participant. His fluency in Latin, and his wide theological learning, neither shared by many of the anglophones at the Council, gave him great authority. He was also assisted by his independence from local episcopal concerns. He was present as a major religious superior, not as a bishop. He was a member of the commission for doctrine and contributed to the chapter on the Virgin Mary, which was included (principally, it is said, at his instigation) in the decree on the church, *Lumen Gentium*, rather than appearing as a separate document. He also interested himself in the discussions on war and peace, with particular reference to nuclear deterrence. If Cardinal J. H. *Newman was 'the invisible father' of the second Vatican Council, then no one was better suited to be his spokesman than Christopher Butler. His Sarum lectures at Oxford in 1966 (published in 1967) presented his thoughts on *The Theology of Vatican II* and he was made an honorary fellow of St John's, the first Catholic priest to be so honoured by an Oxford college since Newman.

The Vatican Council made him a public figure and in 1966 he left Downside to go to Westminster as auxiliary bishop to Cardinal J. C. *Heenan. He was consecrated with the title of bishop of Nova Barbara in Westminster Cathedral on 21 December 1966. As auxiliary he became the first area bishop of Hertfordshire, last resident president of St Edmund's College, Ware, and vicar capitular of the archdiocese in the interregnum between Cardinals Heenan and Basil Hume. He became an elder statesman among the English hierarchy and an official Roman Catholic representative on many ecumenical bodies, including the Anglican/Roman Catholic International Commission. He was co-chairman of 'English ARC' from 1970 to 1981, and was twice honoured with the cross of St Augustine by the archbishop of Canterbury. In February 1980 he was appointed an assistant to the pontifical throne by Pope John Paul II.

The breadth of his activities and his popularity as a radio personality, especially on the *Any Questions?* programme in the 1960s, conceal from view the fact that his was chiefly an intellectual genius. In his books—which ranged in subject from scripture (he consistently supported the priority of St Matthew's gospel, as he demonstrated in *The Originality of St Matthew*, 1951) to spirituality via theology, ecumenism, and autobiography—and in the many hundreds of reviews and articles which he wrote, he revealed a wide sympathy. He owed most to the scriptures and the fathers but had a great attachment to the spiritual teaching of the French Jesuit master of contemplative prayer, Jean-Pierre de Caussade (1675–1751), and also, in later years, to the Canadian Jesuit, Bernard Lonergan (1904–1985). Like the abbot in the rule of St Benedict, he made full use of things '*nova et vetera*' and always retained much of that balance of the middle way, which distinguishes classical Anglicanism and to some extent English Catholicism. From 1972 he was a member of the editorial board of the *New English Bible*.

He was a man of deep spirituality, who put prayer at the centre of a timetable which always remained fixed and unvaried throughout his adult life. He loved, as a Benedictine, the stability of the regular life, and all he wrote and said reflected his deep life of prayer. As a junior monk he had been a disciple of Dom David *Knowles and had sought a deeper asceticism. He was of slightly more than average height and as a young man he had an ascetic appearance. Advancing

years made him more corpulent. His hair was always close-cropped, which gave great prominence to his head, very suitable given his intellectual gifts. He lived a simple life, although he enjoyed smoking a pipe, and was an expert chess player as well as a devotee of detective novels. He was a reserved man but became easier and more relaxed as a bishop. He remained a true Benedictine, one whose central vocation is seeking God. He died 20 September 1986, at St John and St Elizabeth's Hospital, St John's Wood, London.

[B. E. ('C.') Butler, *A Time to Speak* (autobiography), 1972; Anne T. Floyd, *B. C. Butler's Developing Understanding of Church: an Intellectual Biography*, 1981; Dom Daniel Rees (writing as 'Ceredig'), *Bishop Christopher Butler, Seventh Abbot of Downside and Bishop of Nova Barbara*, Downside, 1986; Valentine Rice, *Dom Christopher Butler, the Abbot of Downside*, Notre Dame, Indiana, 1965; *Tablet*, 27 September 1986; *The Times*, 22 September 1986; personal knowledge.]

AIDAN BELLENGER

BUTLER, Christopher (1902–1986), monk and theologian. [See BUTLER, BASIL EDWARD ('CHRISTOPHER').]

BYAM SHAW, Glencairn Alexander ('Glen') (1904–1986), actor and director of theatre and opera, was born 13 December 1904 in Addison Road, London, the fourth in the family of four sons and one daughter of John Byam Lister *Shaw, painter, illustrator, and founder of the Byam Shaw School of Art, and his wife, Evelyn Caroline Pyke-Nott, miniaturist. He went to Westminster School as a day-boy during World War I and his contemporaries included his elder brother, James, who became a distinguished art historian, and (Sir) John Gielgud, who was to be a lifelong friend and colleague.

While James won a scholarship to Christ Church, Oxford, and Gielgud to the Royal Academy of Dramatic Art, Glen next surfaced on 1 August 1923 as an apparently untrained professional actor in *At Mrs Beam's* at the Pavilion theatre, Torquay. In the era of the matinée idol Byam Shaw's dazzling and lifelong good looks, together with the reported encouragement of his cousin May Ward, a close friend of (Dame) Ellen *Terry, may have been enough to make him take the plunge into acting. His first London appearance in 1925 was as Yasha in *The Cherry Orchard* (John Gielgud was Trofimov) and in the next four years he had the good fortune to appear in three more Chekhov plays.

In 1929 he married the actress (Madeleine) Angela (Clinton) Baddeley, the elder sister of Hermione *Baddeley. Their father, William Herman Clinton-Baddeley, was an unsuccessful composer. The Byam Shaw marriage was a supremely happy one, both domestically and professionally, until Angela's death in 1976. They had a son and a daughter.

After a tour together to South Africa in 1931 Byam Shaw appeared memorably at the Lyceum in 1932 in Max Reinhardt's mime play *The Miracle*, which starred Lady Diana *Cooper as the Madonna. In 1933 the long and mutually rewarding association with John Gielgud began when Byam Shaw took over the Gielgud part in the long running *Richard of Bordeaux* by Gordon Daviot (i.e. Elizabeth *Mackintosh). In 1934 he was Darnley in Daviot's *Queen of Scots* and later Laertes in Gielgud's longest running *Hamlet*, each time directed by Gielgud. In 1935 he played Benvolio in the famous *Romeo and Juliet* with Laurence (later Baron) *Olivier, (Dame) Edith *Evans, and (Dame) Peggy Ashcroft. During the play's run there was the beginning of a sea change in Byam Shaw's career. He assisted Gielgud in directing *Richard II* for the Oxford University Dramatic Society—Vivien *Leigh was the Queen and Michael Denison played three small parts—and he was as stimulating, firm, and courteous to his undergraduate cast as he was always to be to professional companies. He had now found his true *métier*; he had never enjoyed acting. Until the war, however, he continued to act, mostly in supporting parts in prestigious Gielgud productions, but also, importantly for the future, with (Sir) Michael *Redgrave, George *Devine, and Peggy Ashcroft in Michel-St Denis's short season at the Phoenix. But he was now directing too, and in 1938 was engaged to direct Gielgud in Dodie Smith's *Dear Octopus*.

He had joined the Emergency Reserve of Officers before the war and with his brother James was commissioned into the Royal Scots in 1940. They both served in Burma from 1942 and were both wounded. Byam Shaw ended his service in 1945 as a major making training films in India. By 1946 he had joined St Denis and Devine in running the Old Vic Centre, which combined a school of acting, an experimental project, and the Young Vic Company. Byam Shaw also found time to direct *The Winslow Boy* by (Sir) Terence *Rattigan (with Angela in a key role)—the start of another rewarding association—and also three Shakespeare plays at the Vic. Despite much success in all fields the three partners fell foul of the Vic governors and of the

theatre's top-heavy and largely hostile administration and resigned in 1951.

Fortunately for Byam Shaw and the British theatre there followed his great work at Stratford, first as co-director with (Sir) Anthony *Quayle (1952–6) and then on his own, until handing over to his chosen successor (Sir) Peter Hall in 1959. Byam Shaw directed fourteen plays at Stratford, notably *Antony and Cleopatra* (Redgrave and Ashcroft), *Macbeth* (Olivier and Leigh), *As You Like It* (Ashcroft), *Othello* (Harry Andrews and Emlyn *Williams), and *King Lear* (Charles *Laughton and Albert Finney); and chose companies which were a magnet to directors of the calibre of Hall, Peter Brook, and Gielgud. He helped transform Stratford from a worthy tourist trap into the country's theatrical capital. Ironically the company became 'Royal' only after he left.

As a freelance director in the 1960s he was much in demand. Then suddenly, though self-confessedly tone deaf, he turned to opera; and, unencumbered by musical considerations, brought his special gift for clarifying texts to the service of outrageous operatic story-lines, inculcating in principals and chorus his passion for theatrical truth. From *The Rake's Progress* at Sadler's Wells (1962) to Wagner's *Ring* at the Coliseum (1973) he directed in all fifteen operas, sweeping the stage before first nights 'to calm his nerves'. The decoration of the Coliseum's safety curtain was taken from a painting by his father.

Byam Shaw was slim, neatly and untheatrically dressed, with shoes always highly polished; his white hair, ruddy complexion, and searching brown eyes were those of the archetypal senior officer. Even his quiet voice and beautiful manners cloaked a steely authority. He did not aspire to be a virtuoso director, manipulating the playwright's intentions to conform to a subjective vision. He was content to be an interpreter, but he brought to that characteristically modest role the highest level of research, intuition, and love of the theatre and its workers.

He was appointed CBE in 1954 and was given an honorary D.Litt. by Birmingham University in 1959. He died in a nursing home in Goring on Thames 29 April 1986, not far from his house at Wargrave.

[Michael Billington, *Peggy Ashcroft*, 1988; Michael Denison, *Double Act*, 1985; private information; personal knowledge.]   MICHAEL DENISON

C

CACCIA, Harold Anthony, BARON CACCIA (1905–1990), diplomat, was born 21 December 1905 in Pachmarhi, India, the only child of Anthony Mario Felix Caccia, of the Indian Forest Service, and his wife Fanny Theodora, daughter of Azim Salvador Birch, of Erewhon and Oruamatua, New Zealand. Caccia's great-grandfather had fled to England from Lombardy as a political refugee in 1826. Caccia went to Eton, where he was a popular all-rounder, and then to Trinity College, Oxford, where he gained a rugby blue and second-class honours in philosophy, politics, and economics (1927). In 1928 he won a Laming travelling fellowship from Queen's College, Oxford.

He entered the Foreign Office in 1929 and was appointed third secretary at Peking in 1932. He returned to London in 1935 as a second secretary and, from 1936, as assistant private secretary to the secretary of state until, in 1939, he was transferred to Athens. Driven from Athens in 1941, the Caccias with the embassy wives and children and some commandos, including Oliver Barstow, his wife's brother, had a perilous journey. Their ship was bombed *en route* to Crete and Barstow was killed. They reached Crete in another small craft and a destroyer took them to Cairo.

Caccia was appointed in 1943 to the staff of the resident minister in north Africa, Harold *Macmillan (later the first Earl of Stockton), at Algiers. He soon moved to Italy as vice-president of the Allied Control Commission and political adviser to General Harold *Alexander (later first Earl Alexander of Tunis). In 1944 he became the political adviser to the general officer commanding British land forces in Greece, and was in the embassy during the communist uprising in Athens in December 1944. Caccia was in his element in a military environment and got on well with the Allied commanders. In 1945 he became minister at the Athens embassy, before returning to the Foreign Office as chief clerk in 1949. In this post he was instrumental in putting into effect the administrative reforms which Anthony *Eden (later the first Earl of Avon) had announced in 1943.

In 1950 he went to Austria, then still under four-power administration, first as minister, then as British high commissioner, and finally as ambassador from 1951 to 1954. He was again in his element in Austria, *persona grata* to the Allied military commanders and popular with the Austrian authorities. For relaxation he pursued chamois in the mountains. In 1956 he became British ambassador in Washington. After the Suez débâcle, communications between the two governments were virtually suspended. In spite of his earlier relationship with the US president, Caccia received a frosty reception. However, after Harold Macmillan became prime minister normal relations were rapidly restored, and there were no further crises during his mission. A major success was the resumption of full co-operation on atomic energy in 1958, and the relationship was further enhanced by an official visit by the queen. Caccia soon got back on excellent terms with the administration and became a respected and popular figure in the United States.

In 1962 he became permanent under-secretary of state and in 1964 head of the Diplomatic Service until his retirement in 1965. He was appointed CMG (1945), KCMG (1950), GCMG (1959), and GCVO (1961). In 1965 he was created a life peer as Baron Caccia. He took the arms of his Florentine ancestors.

From 1965 to 1977 he was provost of Eton and also accepted many outside appointments in banking, finance, industry, and insurance. He was director of the National Westminster Bank, chairman of the Orion Bank, a director of the Foreign and Colonial Investment and European trusts, director of the Prudential, chairman of Standard Telephones and Cables and of ITT (UK) Ltd., and a member of the advisory council of Foseco Minsep PLC. He was chairman of the Gabbitas Thring Educational Trust, a member of the advisory committee on public records, and chairman of the Marylebone Cricket Club. In 1969 he became first chancellor and then lord prior of the Order of St John of Jerusalem. He was a regular attender at the House of Lords, where he sat on the cross benches, speaking mainly on foreign affairs. He was chairman of the Anglo-Austrian Society and became an honorary fellow of Trinity College, Oxford, in 1963, and of Queen's College in 1974.

In appearance he was short, stocky, and bald with a fair complexion. He was forthright in speech and energetic in action and he retained throughout his life a cheerful and light-hearted, almost boyish, manner, which concealed a serious and thoughtful disposition. He was a good administrator and universally popular in all that he undertook. He ended as he had begun, as a great all-rounder.

In 1932 he married Anne Catherine ('Nancy'), daughter of Sir George Lewis *Barstow, civil servant. They had two daughters and one son. Caccia was happy in his family life and he and his wife were a devoted couple. But his latter years were saddened by the untimely death of his son David in 1983. Caccia died of cancer at his home in Builth Wells, Powys, 31 October 1990.

[Private information; personal knowledge.]

SHERFIELD

CARADON, BARON (1907–1990), colonial administrator and diplomat. [See FOOT, HUGH MACKINTOSH.]

CARRERAS, SIR **James Enrique** (1909–1990), film executive, was born 30 January 1909 at 9 Chiswick Lane, Chiswick, as Jaime Enrique Carreras, the only child of Enrique Carreras, commission merchant, and his wife, Dolores Montousse. He was educated privately. In 1913 his father, who came from the Carreras tobacco family of Spain, became a film exhibitor and built the first of a small chain of cinemas in London, the Blue Halls. James joined the business as a youth and worked his way up from usher to assistant manager. In 1935 his father and William Hinds, known professionally as Will Hammer, founded Exclusive Films. James worked for this firm also. It distributed imported second features and a few films made by Hammer himself for a small company, Hammer Productions, which he had registered in 1934. This was moribund by 1937. During the war James rose from private to lieutenant-colonel in the Honourable Artillery Company. In his absence his own son Michael joined the company at sixteen and, like his father, began at the bottom. James rejoined the firm after the war.

Will Hammer now wished to return to production and revive the name of Hammer. He was associated with a few films made at Marylebone Studios in 1947. In 1948 he joined with Enrique and James Carreras to form a new company, Hammer Film Productions, as the production arm of Exclusive Films. Production proper began in 1948 at a mansion studio at Bray, near Windsor. The company was registered in February 1949 and James Carreras, who was to dominate the company, became chairman. They made routine second features, a number of them based on BBC radio serials, using the large house and nearby locations as inexpensive settings. Output was large, and films were quickly and cheaply made by a small permanent team. Much of the writing and direction was by James's son Michael and Will Hammer's son Anthony Hinds, and there was an informal and family atmosphere in the unit.

In 1955 they made a science fiction thriller, *The Quatermass Experiment*, in which the survivor of a space journey is gradually consumed by a mysterious fungus. This had been a popular BBC television serial, and its enormous success as a film encouraged Carreras to introduce a second seeping mass of something horrible in *X the Unknown* the next year. A third successful film, shown in 1957, was *Quatermass II*, which portrayed people taken over by menacing space organisms. The Gothic horror tale, a strain in English literature, was out of fashion at the time, but Carreras now took a well-considered gamble, and with *The Curse of Frankenstein* later that year found his niche. Christopher Lee and Peter Cushing first appeared as Hammer's favourite bogeymen in this lurid and profitable colour remake of the 1931 film, *Frankenstein*.

From now on an important part of Hammer Films' output featured vampires, werewolves, resurrected mummies, blood, and gore, and there were repeated appearances of Frankenstein and Dracula, producing delicious dread in the audience. Most other film-makers and the critics scorned these films, made in six to eight weeks and promoted with lurid posters and stunts. But they had a large and enthusiastic public in Britain and abroad, especially in America, where they had a huge cult following among teenagers. Ironically, it was Carreras who achieved the assured distribution in America which had so long eluded more serious British producers. His was the most consistently profitable film company in Britain, earning £1.5 million in foreign exchange one year. It received the Queen's Award for Industry in 1968. Carreras took no part in the creative side of film-making.

However, times changed. The studio was sold in 1968, and although production continued elsewhere the verve had gone. In 1972 Carreras sold his holding to Michael and resigned as chief executive, though he remained chairman. He moved to the EMI group of companies, where he acted as special adviser for some years. With the appearance in 1973 from America of *The Exorcist*, an exceptionally frightening film, the writing was on the wall for the escapist Hammer brand of horror. The last Hammer film was made in 1978 and the company was in the hands of the receivers by 1979. Carreras then had a remarkable idea: to sell the 'Hammer House of Horror' series to television in the early 1980s. This was then repackaged as video cassettes in the late 1980s for yet another set of youngsters going through the monsters stage.

In appearance and character Carreras, a good-looking, mild-mannered, soberly dressed businessman, who was a strong family man and devout Christian, was a surprising person to have brought about the phrase 'Hammer horror'. But the essential innocence of the genre, with its saving grace of absurdity, was very different from the sadistic and violent films produced by other companies in later years.

Carreras was a prominent member of the Variety Club, the show-business charity, being its chief barker in 1954–5. He was chairman of the board of Variety Clubs International for eleven years and president in 1961–3. In 1970 he was knighted for his extensive charity work over many years, especially in the cause of young people—he was president of the London Federation of Boys' Clubs for five years. He was appointed MBE in 1944, possibly for secret operations in Spain during the war. He became KCVO in 1980 and also received honours from Spain and Liberia.

In 1927, when he was very young, he married Vera St John (died 1986). Their one son Michael was born in 1927. Carreras died of a heart attack 9 June 1990 at home in Henley-on-Thames.

[*The Times*, 12 June 1990; *Daily Telegraph*, 20 June 1990; *Independent*, 18 June 1990; David Pirie, *A Heritage of Horror*, 1973.]   RACHAEL LOW

CAVE, SIR **Richard Guy** (1920–1986), industrialist, was born 16 March 1920 in Bickley, Kent, the youngest in the family of two sons and three daughters of William Thomas Cave, London solicitor, and his wife, Gwendoline Mary Nicholls. The already very tall Richard Cave ('Dick' to his many friends from an early age) was educated at Tonbridge School, where he was captain of the rowing IV and of swimming, and was in the rugby XV. In 1938 he went to Gonville and Caius College, Cambridge, to read mechanical engineering. His course was interrupted by the outbreak of war in 1939.

From 1940 Cave served with the 44th battalion of the Royal Tank Regiment in North Africa (taking part in the battle of El Alamein), Sicily, and mainland Italy. Landing in Normandy on D-Day plus three, he commanded A squadron of the 44th battalion with great distinction throughout the campaign in north-west Europe, being awarded the MC (1944). His tank was among the first to cross the Rhine. His brigade commander, Michael (later Baron) Carver, described him as 'a splendid squadron commander, brave, sensible, level-headed, always calm and resolute and unfailingly cheerful'.

After the war Cave decided not to return to Cambridge to complete his degree and instead joined Smiths Industries in 1946. The drive, intelligence, insight, and all-round competence of this big man—Cave stood a good six feet, five inches—were recognized from the outset. He was appointed export director of the motor accessory division in 1956 and managing director of that division in 1963, joining the main board at the same time. In 1967 he became managing director of the firm, in 1968 chief executive, and in 1973 chairman. Under his steady, firm, forceful, and also imaginative direction, Smiths Industries achieved remarkable progress and success, and diversified considerably.

In 1976 Cave left Smiths Industries to become chairman of Thorn Electrical Industries, taking over from its founder, Sir Jules Thorn. Cave's outstanding leadership qualities—humanity, humour, and warmth, combined when necessary with toughness and directness—were equal to the challenge. He quickly won the loyalty of the staff, recognizing at the same time that Thorn was perhaps unduly dependent on the home market and that too many of its businesses were in comparatively low-level technologies. His major achievement at Thorn was the merger with EMI in 1979, which, despite much criticism at the time from the newspaper press and the City, secured the twin objectives of establishing a truly international company and strengthening Thorn's technological base. Notwithstanding major lung surgery in 1980, Cave characteristically continued as an active chairman of Thorn until late in 1983.

Cave also played a positive and valuable role in many other companies. He served as non-executive chairman of Vickers from 1984, during a period in the company's history of significant divestments and some important acquisitions. He was also deputy chairman of British Rail (1983–5), and his directorships included those of Thomas Tilling (1969–76), Tate & Lyle (1976–86), Equity & Law (1972–9), and Thames Television (1981–4).

Throughout his business career Cave left a distinctive and personal mark on wider industrial policy. He had a long-standing belief in training, having created a training college for young entrants to Smiths Industries. He also had a deep interest, from the wider national viewpoint, in export promotion, as shown by his membership of the British Overseas Trade Board (1977–80), and in employment matters, as demonstrated by his chairmanship of the Confederation of British Industry's steering group on unemployment (1981–3). His active membership, from 1970 until his death, of the Industrial Society, of which he was chairman from 1979 to 1983, bore witness to his lasting concern for better industrial relations. He was knighted in 1976.

Cave was a many-sided man with several interests. He was a keen supporter of the arts, in particular of the Aldeburgh Festival close to his much-loved home in Suffolk, being chairman of the successful Aldeburgh appeal. He loved opera and ballet and, perhaps even more, sailing, and was commodore of the Aldeburgh Yacht Club (1975–6) and a member of the Royal Yacht Squadron.

In 1957 he married Dorothy Gillian, daughter of Henry Kenneth Fry, of Adelaide, a general physician who later specialized in psychiatry and neurology. They had two sons and two daughters. Cave, a devoted family man, died of cancer at his home in Aldeburgh 5 December 1986 after a long period of illness.

[Private information; personal knowledge.]

GEORGE JELLICOE

CAVENDISH-BENTINCK, Victor Frederick William, ninth DUKE OF PORTLAND (1897–1990), diplomat and international businessman. [See BENTINCK, VICTOR FREDERICK WILLIAM CAVENDISH-.]

CAWSTON, (Edwin) Richard (1923–1986), documentary film-maker, was born 31 May 1923 in Weybridge, Surrey, the elder child and elder son of Edwin Cawston, merchant, of Weybridge, and his wife Phyllis, daughter of Henry Charles Hawkins. He always wanted to make films; as a boy at Westminster School he and a friend made a documentary of the school's evacuation to Lancing. In 1941 he joined the Royal Signals and then spent two terms at Oriel College, Oxford, doing an army short course in radio, electricity, and magnetism. He became a captain in 1945, and a major in 1946, while serving in the Southern Command in India. When he was demobilized in 1947, he took a post as assistant film librarian with the newly reopened BBC television service in Alexandra Palace.

He did not stay a librarian for long. He soon became film editor and then the producer of the popular *Television Newsreel*. Between 1950 and 1954 he produced 700 editions and gained a depth of experience in the technicalities of film craftsmanship which few of his television contemporaries could equal. This early experience of volume production under pressure was the foundation of his success as one of Britain's (and later the world's) most respected television documentary producers over a period of thirty years. It is also a key to the kind of producer he became; he was a capable camera director, but he showed his greatest strengths in the cutting room and dubbing theatre after the film had been shot. The newsreel years gave him a grounding in the shaping and pacing of film and the adding of commentary, music, and effects, which were to be of great value in guiding the work of younger producers as well as in developing his own.

In 1954 *Television Newsreel* lost its battle to stay independent of the BBC news division and Cawston left to join the talks department of the television service, as a documentary producer.

The age of the old film documentary makers such as John *Grierson and (F.) Humphrey *Jennings was dead; Cawston was present at the birth of the new documentary on television. He produced a long series of major documentary films, many of which won national and international awards. He was especially interested in institutions and professions, with whom his frank and open approach and high professionalism created a trust which gained him an entrée that would have been refused to most producers. His films documented the worlds of lawyers, pilots, the National Health Service, the British educational system, and, perhaps most memorably, the BBC itself in *This Is the BBC* (1959). There was no 'typical Cawston' film because he did not impose his own views or slant on his subject-matter. His aim was to let the subject speak for itself, usually with the minimum of narration or (as in the BBC film) none at all. The common factor was meticulous craftsmanship.

In 1965, just after the start of BBC 2, he was made head of documentary programmes. It was here that for fourteen years he coached and developed a new generation of documentary makers. The sessions in which he looked at rough assemblies of their films were master-classes that refined the skills of many of today's leading documentary-makers. But he did not stop making his own films; *Royal Family*, in which he recorded a year (1968–9) in the private and public life of the queen, was at that time the most popular and widely seen documentary in television history and did much to restore the popularity the monarchy had lost in the mid-1960s. It led to his becoming the producer of the queen's Christmas day broadcast to the Commonwealth from 1970 to 1985, and to his appointment as CVO in 1972.

For most of his working life he was an active and influential member of BAFTA, the television and film-makers' professional body; he was chairman from 1976 to 1979, and a trustee from 1971 until his death. It was largely through his energy and enterprise that BAFTA secured its present home at 195 Piccadilly, and it was due to his advocacy that the queen made the initial major donation towards its funding out of the sales revenues of *Royal Family*.

Cawston left the BBC in 1979, having won almost all the major professional prizes, including the Italia prize (1962), three BAFTA awards, and the silver medal of the Royal Television Society (1961). He joined Video Arts Ltd. as special projects director, but continued producing programmes for the BBC as an independent executive producer, and acting as consultant to the government and tourist board of Hong Kong.

Cawston was tall, clean shaven, and well built; his dress was reassuringly conventional, more like that of a family solicitor than the usual image of a film-maker. In 1951 he married Elisabeth Anne ('Liz'), daughter of Richard Llewellyn Rhys, of St Fagans, canon of Llandaff. They had two sons. She died in 1977, and in 1978 he married Andrea, daughter of Michael Phillips, company director, of Cyprus. Cawston died of a heart attack in Cassis, France, 7 June 1986.

[BBC Written Archives Centre, Caversham Park, Reading; BBC Research Library, 80 Wood Lane, London W12; private information.]   ANTONY JAY

CAYZER, (Michael) Anthony (Rathborne) (1920–1990), shipowner and director of aviation companies, was born 28 May 1920 at Tylney Hall, Rotherwick, Hampshire, the second son in the family of two sons and two daughters of Major Herbert Robin Cayzer, later first Baron Rotherwick, shipowner and later chairman of the Clan Line, and his wife Freda Penelope, daughter of Colonel William Hans Rathborne, of county Cavan, Ireland. Anthony Cayzer grew up at Tylney and was educated at Eton, from where, with the intention of becoming a professional soldier—his father had a distinguished military record—he went to the Royal Military College, Sandhurst, and was commissioned into the Royal Scots Greys in 1939.

He would probably have had a successful and happy army career, but while serving in the Middle East, where he was mentioned in dispatches, he contracted poliomyelitis and was invalided out in 1944. He entered the Cayzer family's shipowning and financial empire and his business career was to span a period of great change in the shipping world. He was chairman of the Liverpool Steamship Owners' Association for ten years from 1956 to 1967. He was president of the Chamber of Shipping of the United Kingdom in 1967 and of the Shipping and Forwarding Agents from 1963 to 1965. He was also deputy chairman of the British and Commonwealth Shipping Company and a director of Cayzer, Irvine & Co. and of Overseas Containers (Holdings) Ltd.

Professional involvement with shipping matters on this scale was to be expected in a grandson of Sir Charles Cayzer, founder of the Clan Line, one of the most prestigious of the later British merchant shipping concerns. He was fascinated by the complexities of the freight conferences, the collective monopolies by which potentially destructive competition between shipping concerns was avoided. His knowledge of these organizations and their workings found expression when, as chairman of the trustees of the National Maritime Museum from 1977 to 1987 (he had been a trustee since 1968), he personally inspired and organized a gallery which made this important aspect of maritime history intelligible to the lay visitor in a thoroughly attractive way.

This involvement in the National Maritime Museum's development was typical of Cayzer's chairmanship. He was highly successful in this when as an academic institution it sought to interpret its themes to a mass public with accuracy and realism. Despite his interest and his background as an arbiter of power, he never sought to usurp the director's responsibility for initiating policy and managing its execution. He sought continuously for ways in which, with his immense circle of acquaintance and knowledge of the business world, he could further the aims of the museum. His association with it marked a considerable personal achievement.

Cayzer broke away from his family business tradition by becoming deeply involved with civil aviation. He was fascinated by the element of risk enterprise and competition involved in the industry at this stage in its development and by some of the more piratical business colleagues with whom he found himself working. A qualified pilot of multi-engined planes, he knew the handling characteristics of many of the aircraft his companies operated. He became deputy chairman of Air UK and of Aviation Services Ltd., chairman of Servisair (1954–87) and of Britavia, and a director of Bristow's Helicopter Group. In 1970 he was a moving force in the merger of British United with Caledonian Airways to form British Caledonian. He would have dearly liked to see the establishment of a national aviation museum to complement the National Maritime Museum.

A well-built, handsome man, Cayzer had all the social graces which went with his upbringing and considerable fortune. He held extensive shooting parties at his 1,500-acre estate in Hertfordshire. He was not an intellectual, though he frequently expressed great respect for academic achievement. He was open-minded, flexible in his approach to problems, and always ready to enter into new worlds. He greatly enjoyed Glyndebourne as he did his motor yacht *Patra*. In his attitude to women he was intensely conservative. To him they were essentially private and social creatures. He could not accept them as suitable for higher professional responsibilities or as reliable participants in confidential business affairs. His very brave struggle with the after-effects of polio, which impeded his mobility, was at times painful to watch and perhaps prevented him from reaching his full potential.

He married in 1952 the Hon. Patricia Helen Browne, elder daughter of Dominick Geoffrey Edward Browne, fourth Baron Oranmore and Browne; they had three daughters. She died in 1981 and in 1982 he married Baroness Sybille, daughter of Count de Selys Longchamps. He died of cancer in the Nuffield Hospital, Mayfair, London, 4 March 1990.

[C. Augustus Muir and M. Davies, *A Victorian Shipowner, a Portrait of Sir Charles Cayzer*, 1978; private information; personal knowledge.] BASIL GREENHILL

CAZALET-KEIR, Thelma (1899–1989), politician, was born 28 May 1899 at 4 Whitehall Gardens, London, the third of four children, the eldest of whom was killed in action in 1916, and only daughter of William Marshall Cazalet, a man of hereditary wealth and standing, whose family origins were Huguenot, and his wife Maud Lucia, daughter of Sir John Robert Heron-Maxwell, seventh baronet, of Springkell, Dumfriesshire, who was of modest means. The mother was the dominant parental influence, from whom Thelma derived her worldly sophistication and love of the arts; also her feminism and Christian Science, two creeds to which she held firmly throughout her life.

In London and at the Cazalets' country house, Fairlawne in Kent, she was introduced as a child to many leading figures in politics and literature, including Rudyard *Kipling, J. M. *Barrie, the *Pankhursts, and Sidney and Beatrice *Webb. After being taught at home by governesses, she attended lectures at the London School of Economics. The lure of politics was already strong, and in the years immediately following World War I she became an accepted member of the *Lloyd George family circle, through her close friendship with the prime minister's youngest child, *Megan.

She entered politics by way of local government, first in Kent and then as a member of the London county council for seven years (1924–31), after which she became an alderman. Despite her radical connections her party allegiance was Conservative, though her outlook was never narrowly partisan. In 1931 she unsuccessfully contested the parliamentary seat of East Islington at a by-election, but in the general election held later in the year she was returned as National Conservative MP for the same constituency with a majority of over 14,000.

In the House of Commons she joined her brother Victor, who was MP for Chippenham. (He was killed in 1943 in an air crash with the Polish General Sikorski.) Her best subject in Parliament was education, with which she had been particularly concerned on the LCC. She was a regular speaker on the education estimates, and from 1937 to 1940 was parliamentary private secretary to Kenneth Lindsay, when he was parliamentary secretary to the Board of Education. In March 1944, as a member of the Tory reform committee, she was put in charge of an amendment to the education bill introduced by R. A. *Butler (later Baron Butler of Saffron Walden), providing that there should be equal

pay for men and women teachers. When the amendment was carried by the margin of a single vote, (Sir) Winston *Churchill's wartime coalition suffered its only defeat.

Greatly angered, Churchill insisted that the clause be deleted, making the issue one of confidence in himself; and she then felt she had no option but to vote against her own amendment. An important point had been made, however, and Churchill announced the setting up of a royal commission to consider the question of equal pay for equal work (1944–6). From 1947 she was chairman of the equal pay campaign committee, and eventually saw the principle enshrined in legislation in 1970. Meanwhile Churchill had made personal amends by appointing her in May 1945 parliamentary secretary for education in his short-lived caretaker government. The 1945 general election, which swept that government away, also cost her her seat and brought her parliamentary career to an end.

For some time she remained active in public life outside Parliament. From 1946 to 1949 she was a member of the Arts Council, of whose precursor, the Council for the Encouragement of Music and the Arts (CEMA), she had been a founder member in 1940. She was also on the executive committee of the Contemporary Art Society, and from 1956 served a five-year term as a governor of the BBC. She was a keen supporter of the Fawcett Library, and in 1964 was president of the Fawcett Society. She was appointed CBE in 1952.

A friend of most of the prime ministers during her life, she was a special confidante of Edward Heath throughout his premiership, though their relations later cooled when she rebuked him for his attitude to Margaret (later Baroness) Thatcher. Rather surprisingly, she was never recommended for a life peerage.

After losing her parliamentary seat she started market gardening at her home in Kent, Raspit Hill, and for a time ran a flower shop in London. When she sold Raspit Hill, deliberately for much less than its true value, to an old friend, Malcolm *MacDonald, she moved to a flat in London. During her last years her sight failed, a particularly sad affliction for one who was, perhaps above all, a visual aesthete. Her collection of pictures included works by Sir Matthew *Smith, Sir Stanley *Spencer, Paul *Nash, Walter *Sickert, and Augustus *John. John knew her well, and his portrait of her in a bright yellow dress, with a piano—which she played more than adequately—behind her, is one of his finest. (It was painted in 1936, and is privately owned.)

In 1967 she published a short volume of memoirs, *From the Wings*, notable chiefly for its vivid description of Lloyd George, though also interesting about other characters in her life. She married, in August 1939, David Edwin, son of the Revd Thomas Keir. Her husband was lobby correspondent of the *News Chronicle*. He died in 1969, and there were no children. On her marriage she changed her surname to Cazalet-Keir. She died 13 January 1989 at her London flat, 90 Eaton Square.

[*The Times*, 16 January 1989; Thelma Cazalet-Keir, *From the Wings* (autobiography), 1967; private information; personal knowledge.]   JOHN GRIGG

CECIL, LORD **(Edward Christian) David (Gascoyne-)** (1902–1986), man of letters, was born 9 April 1902 at 24 Grafton Street, London W1, the fourth and last child and the second son of James Edward Hubert Gascoyne-*Cecil, fourth Marquess of Salisbury, politician, and his wife, Lady (Cicely) Alice Gore, second daughter of the fifth Earl of Arran, descended on her mother's side from the Melbourne family. A delicate child, he was much at home and benefited in this from the company of his brilliant aunts and uncles, notorious for their eccentricities, wit, and zeal. Between 1915 and 1919 he was at Eton, where the confidence fostered by this remarkable family carried him through an unfamiliar and in some ways uncongenial atmosphere. His experience of Oxford—he entered Christ Church in 1920—was different. He loved the life and the place. His exceptionally quick, associative mind served him well in his final examinations where he took a first class in modern history (1924). Though he failed to win an All Souls fellowship, he was elected to a fellowship at Wadham in 1924 to teach mainly history. At the same time, with characteristic independence, he was writing a life of the poet William *Cowper, *The Stricken Deer*, his first and one of his best books, which was published in 1929 and won the Hawthornden prize in 1930.

This success led to his decision to resign his fellowship in 1930 and take up the life of a writer in London. There he met and fell in love with Rachel, only daughter of (Sir) (C. O.) Desmond *MacCarthy, literary critic, one of the original members of the Bloomsbury group. Their marriage took place in 1932. Virginia *Woolf in a wry but affectionate entry in her *Diary* describes 'David and Rachel, arm-in-arm, sleep-walking down the aisle, preceded by a cross which ushered them into a car and so into a happy, long life, I make no doubt' (A. O. Bell (ed.), *The Diary of Virginia Woolf*, vol. iv, 1982, p. 128). She was not to know how accurate her ironic prediction would prove. A remarkable woman in her own right, Rachel MacCarthy was the perfect match for her husband. Of a simpler, more practical nature, she shared his vivacity and his unfailing curiosity about people, literature, and life. Like him, she was instinctively religious and a practising Christian. They were perfectly happy together, drawing their many friends into that happiness, for fifty years.

As he now moved into the country near Cranborne, David Cecil's new life, though congenial, showed him that he missed Oxford, especially the teaching. In 1939 he accepted a fellowship in English at New College and it was here as tutor and, from 1949, as Goldsmiths' professor that he exercised his widest influence and produced much of his best work. He had a genius for teaching, communicating enjoyment, and drawing out the best from others. A brilliant conversationalist, his wit consisted in verbal sharpness and accuracy, together with a peculiarly sympathetic humour that was always adapted to the company and the occasion. He was a celebrated lecturer, but his influence was most felt in tutorials, classes, or small, intimate groups. He and his wife, naturally hospitable, were eager to mix their friends and share them with young unknowns. Without condescension or pretension they spread over a wide circle of acquaintances and pupils the best-known cultural, political, and artistic influences of the mid-twentieth century.

In the 1960s David Cecil began to feel that his particular concern for English literature was under attack in an increasingly professional age. He never avoided, indeed enjoyed, debate, and was confident of his position, but he shared his family's clear-sightedness about the signs of the times. Developments in graduate studies, and the insistence on advanced degrees as a qualification for university teaching, made him feel his way was out of favour. In 1969 he reached retirement age and went happily to Cranborne, where he continued to write and entertain until his wife's death in 1982, and, though less happily, with remarkable resilience and little diminished powers of enjoyment until his own death.

David Cecil's writings, especially his biographies of William *Cowper (*The Stricken Deer*, 1929), Lord *Melbourne (1955), Jane *Austen (1978), and Charles *Lamb (1983), are a substantial contribution to the understanding of different kinds of personality and period. As such they had a value beyond the academic, and reached a wide readership. His literary criticism came to be badly underestimated. *Early Victorian Novelists* (1934) was ahead of its time in a subtle analysis and discussion of the structure of *Wuthering Heights*. *Hardy the Novelist* (1943) remains a classic exposition of the work of one of his favourite authors. His best essays, too often written off as *belles-lettres*, are as acute as they are sensitive. But most typical of his imagination is his response to extrovert, worldly figures like Melbourne, or balanced moral observers like Jane Austen, and, on the other hand, to introverted, despondent, but gentle and humorous spirits, like Cowper and Lamb. To their situation he was drawn by a sympathy typical of the depth and complexity of his own nature.

He considered himself, with good reason, the most fortunate of men. Born into one of the first families in the land, gifted with intellectual and imaginative sympathies of a high order, professionally successful, idyllically happy in his marriage and family life, he might well have grown complacent and a figure of envy. But complacency was not in his nature or his background: he was self-critical and self-aware. As for enemies, he had few if any. He was greatly loved because of the unusual sweetness of his temper and his genuine humility. Naturally high-spirited and with some vanity, he felt most strongly an inherited impulse of service and purpose. Himself a devout Christian, what he possessed he wanted to share, and he had been given precisely the gifts to enable this. His appearance was extraordinary and memorable: elegant and at the same time spontaneously gauche, continually in motion from the twirling thumbs to the enthusiastic forward lurch. His voice, too, was rapid, stuttering, and spasmodic, with Edwardian pronunciation. David Cecil was one of the most influential cultural figures of his age.

He was appointed CH in 1949 and C.Lit. in 1972. He had honorary doctorates from London, Leeds, Liverpool, St Andrews, and Glasgow universities. He died at Cranborne 1 January 1986.

[W. W. Robson (ed.), *Essays and Poems Presented to Lord David Cecil*, 1970; Hannah Cranborne (ed.), *David Cecil: a Portrait by his Friends*, privately printed, 1990; family information; personal knowledge.]

RACHEL TRICKETT

CHANCELLOR, SIR **Christopher John Howard** (1904–1989), news agency chief executive and company chairman, was born 29 March 1904 in Cobham, Surrey, the elder son and eldest of three children of (Sir) John Robert *Chancellor, soldier and later colonial administrator, and his wife Elsie, daughter of George Rodie Thompson, barrister, of Lynwood, Ascot. He was educated at Eton and Trinity College, Cambridge, where he obtained a second class (division I) in part i of the history tripos (1924) and a first class (division II) in part ii (1925). On graduation, friendship with the son of (Sir) Ernest Debenham led Chancellor into the Debenham & Freebody drapery chain. But his hopes of rising to manage the business collapsed when the family sold out in 1927. In 1929 his wife wrote to Sir G. Roderick *Jones, managing director of Reuters and a family friend, asking for a job for her husband. At interview, recollected Jones later, Chancellor revealed an 'executive outlook'—intelligence balanced by steadiness, energy and enthusiasm matched by prudence. These qualities, plus a necessary suave ruthless-

ness, were to serve Chancellor well throughout his business career. He was clean-cut and of medium build, with a distinctive, light voice. His piercing, enquiring eyes and expressive eyebrows gave him presence.

After starting in 1930 in the editorial department of Reuters, Chancellor progressed rapidly. He was appointed general manager for the Far East at Shanghai from the beginning of 1932. Although not himself a regular journalist, Chancellor understood the news business. He was particularly effective in negotiating contracts, and in smoothly representing Reuters within ruling circles. Mixing duty with pleasure, the Chancellors became prominent figures within Shanghai society.

In 1939 Chancellor returned to London to become a third general manager. On Jones's enforced resignation in 1941 he became joint general manager, and sole general manager in 1944. Reuters could not make much profit out of selling general news, and money was always short. But at the end of the war Chancellor gave priority to negotiating supportive contracts with the news agencies of liberated western Europe. He also turned to the Commonwealth for new partners to join the Press Association and the Newspaper Proprietors' Association in the ownership of Reuters. In recognition of his work, he was appointed CMG in 1948, and knighted in 1951 at the time of Reuters' centenary.

After 1951 Chancellor found himself increasingly frustrated by an unenterprising board. Fortunately, the daily conduct of news reporting was in the hands of the management; and here, at the time of the 1956 Suez crisis, Chancellor was able to make one last and crucial contribution. He had long been sympathetic towards colonial nationalism, and he was a personal friend of several Labour politicians, including Hugh *Gaitskell, who led the loud opposition to the Suez landings. Chancellor made sure that Reuters reported the Suez war from both sides and in language which favoured neither side. Personally, he was disgusted by the British military intervention. But, as head of Reuters, he was motivated by a wider awareness. Under his guidance and just in time, Reuters successfully set out to end its British imperial role and become a supra-national news agency.

In 1959 Chancellor chose to step down. One of his successors later likened him at Reuters to Horatius defending the bridge, successful in holding his chosen ground but restricted in what he could otherwise attempt. Chancellor's underlying achievement was to keep Reuters in competition with the much more affluent American agencies. He became deputy chairman and then chairman of Odhams Press (1959–61). He found himself plunged uncomfortably into one of the most controversial take-over battles of the 1960s, between Thomson Newspapers and the *Mirror* group. After the *Mirror*'s victory, Chancellor resigned. He disapproved of the new combined company gaining control of so many leading titles.

He next joined the Bowater Paper Corporation, becoming chairman in 1962. Chancellor pursued a necessary policy of drastic rationalization and decentralization. But when he retired in 1969 Bowaters was still vulnerable. Chancellor was chairman of Madame Tussaud's from 1961 to 1972, and of the Bath Preservation Trust from 1969 to 1976. With characteristic commitment to what he regarded as a moral duty of conservation, he successfully campaigned against proposals for the drastic modernization of the city.

In 1926 Chancellor married Sylvia Mary, daughter of Sir Richard Arthur Surtees Paget, second baronet, barrister and physicist. They had two sons and two daughters. Chancellor died 9 September 1989 in Wincanton, Somerset.

[Reuter archive, notably a 1976 interview by Stuart Underhill; conversations with contemporaries; *The Times*, *Daily Telegraph*, and *Independent*, 11 September 1989; D. J. Jeremy (ed.), *Dictionary of Business Biography*, vol. i, 1984; Sir Roderick Jones, *A Life in Reuters*, 1951; Donald Read, *The Power of News: the History of Reuters*, 1992.]   DONALD READ

CHATWIN, (Charles) Bruce (1940–1989), traveller and writer, was born 13 May 1940 in Sheffield, the elder child (his brother was born four years later) of Charles Leslie Chatwin, a Birmingham solicitor, and his wife, Margharita Turnell. He was educated at Marlborough College, where he was dreamily interested in classics and enthusiastic about acting; in his spare time he collected and restored odd pieces of furniture. In 1958 he joined Sotheby's auction house as a porter; he rose rapidly to become head of the department of antiquities and the newly founded and flourishing department of Impressionist painting. He was made a director of the firm in his twenties but left in 1966, variously citing failing eyesight and disillusion with the art business, to go to Edinburgh University.

While visiting the Sudan he had developed a fascination with nomads which was to last all his life: he identified with, and to some extent adopted, a travelling way of life, revered its disdain for possessions, and theorized in published and unpublished work about the importance of walking and the pernicious effects of settlement. At Edinburgh he studied archaeology with Professor Stuart Piggott; he left after two years, without taking his degree, and went to Mauritania, from which he returned with a sheaf of desert photographs and many more notes on nomads, which were subsequently extended by journeys to Iran and Afghanistan. In 1970 he helped to organize an exhibition of 'Animal Style Art' at the Asia House Gallery in New York. In the early 1970s he worked for the *Sunday Times Magazine*, first as an art consultant, and then as a journalist: his pieces included interviews with André Malraux, Indira *Gandhi, George Costakis, the Greek collector of Russian avant-garde art, and the dress designer Madeleine Vionnet, who had invented the bias cut which helped to abolish the corset. He is said to have left the paper with a characteristic flourish, sending a telegram which explained: 'Gone to Patagonia for six months.'

This trip resulted in his first published book, *In Patagonia* (1977), an imaginative investigation of that country which mixed crisp description with anthropology, biography, and history, relishing strange encounters and esoteric facts, and rendering these in a spare elliptical prose. *In Patagonia* was awarded the 1977 Hawthornden prize and the E. M. Forster award. Chatwin earned and retained a name as a redefiner of travel writing, though the books that followed were strikingly varied in subject-matter and style. *The Viceroy of Ouidah* (1980), luxuriant, highly wrought, and exotic, provided a fictionalized account of the life of a Brazilian slave-trader. The book was in part based on Chatwin's researches in Dahomey, where he had been arrested during a *coup d'état* on suspicion of being a mercenary; Werner Herzog filmed the story as *Cobra Verde* (1988). *On the Black Hill* (1982)—written, Chatwin claimed, in order to put paid to the label 'travel-writer', from which he recoiled—described in dense domestic detail the intertwined lives of a pair of Welsh twins who never moved from their farm in the border country; the book, which won the 1982 Whitbread award for the best first novel and the James Tait Black memorial prize, was made into a film directed by Andrew Grieve (1987). Five years later Chatwin produced *The Songlines* (1987), a capacious exploration of Aboriginal creation myths which incorporated some of his early speculations about nomads. *Utz* (1988), a coolly written study of an obsessional collector of Meissen porcelain, drew on his experience of the art world and his interest in the Soviet Eastern bloc; it was short-listed for the 1988 Booker prize and filmed by George Sluizer. His collection of articles, *What Am I Doing Here*, appeared in 1989, a few months after his death; a selection of his photographs and notebooks, edited by David King and Francis Wyndham, was published in 1993.

Chatwin was an animated talker, physically and mentally restless, prominently blue-eyed, and hugely enthusiastic. He was a vivid presence, in print and in person: he drew people to him during his lifetime and became the subject of myth-making after his death; he had both male and female lovers. In 1965 he married Elizabeth Margaret, the daughter of Gertrude Laughlin and Hubert Chanler, an American naval officer; there were no children. His wife, a shepherdess and a trekker, was one of his most stalwart travelling companions. They lived in Gloucestershire and later in the Chilterns; Chatwin, who liked to work away from home, also had a series of London rooms, which were uniformly small, bare, and white. In September 1986 he was diagnosed as having the AIDS virus; he died in Nice 18 January 1989, of a fungal infection.

[Nicholas Murray, *Bruce Chatwin*, 1993; Susannah Clapp, *A Portrait of Bruce Chatwin*, 1995; private information; personal knowledge.] SUSANNAH CLAPP

CHENEY, Christopher Robert (1906–1987), historian, was born 20 December 1906 in Banbury, Oxfordshire, the youngest of four sons (there were no daughters) of George Gardner Cheney, director of a family printing business established in the eighteenth century, and his wife, Christina Stapleton Bateman, schoolteacher. It was a close-knit family, with strong musical interests which he shared. He was educated at Banbury County School and Wadham College, Oxford, where he won the Gibbs scholarship in 1927 and took a first-class degree in modern history in 1928. He then began research in medieval English ecclesiastical history under (Sir) F. M. *Powicke. After spells of lecturing in Cairo, University College London (1931–3), and Manchester University (1933–7), in 1937 he succeeded V. H. *Galbraith as reader in diplomatic in Oxford and became a fellow of Magdalen College. He returned to Manchester as professor of medieval history in 1945, moving to Cambridge in 1955 on his election to the chair of medieval history, which he held until his retirement in 1972, and to a fellowship at Corpus Christi College. During World War II he worked in the War Office with MI5.

His greatest achievement was to lead the way in interpreting the records and history of the medieval English church and of the relations of the papacy with England, and in furthering the collaborative enterprises, both national and international, necessary to publish the original sources. His upbringing gave him a lasting interest in the practical process of making books, and he always took delight in good craftsmanship and typographical perfection.

Cheney's university lectures were the seeding ground for many of his published works. His Oxford courses on diplomatic led to his *Notaries Public in the Thirteenth and Fourteenth Centuries* (1972) and to his writings on English episcopal documents. These involved him in two major collaborative enterprises. A project to produce an edition of the corpus of medieval church councils, inspired by Powicke, was in danger of running into the quicksands of planning committees when he took control, brought out, and part edited one volume (1964) and assisted substantially in the completion of another. Later he directed and contributed to the British Academy series of *Episcopal Acta*. The field he made particularly his own was the age of Innocent III, especially the great pope's relations with England. Critical examination of Innocent's letters concerning England led to two definitive volumes of documents (1953 and, with Mary Cheney, 1967). These provided the groundwork for his Ford lectures, *From Becket to Langton* (1956), his monograph on Hubert *Walter (1967), and his fine book, *Pope Innocent III and England* (1976). All were remarkable for the lucidity, sanity, and breadth of imagination and knowledge they revealed.

A penetrating, but never unjust critic, he was an inspiring if exacting teacher, remembered for his inflexibly high standards, and for his kindness and humour, which, together with intelligence and imagination, were reflected in his face. His originality lay in going more deeply and critically, more precisely and less credulously, into the written materials preserved in archives and other collections. In the memorable words of his Cambridge inaugural lecture, he pointed out that 'Records, like the little children of long ago, only speak when they are spoken to, and they will not speak to strangers.' No one was better able than he to penetrate the minds of the men behind the medieval institutions that he described almost as if he had been there when they were being fashioned. He brought to historical study in England a mastery of the techniques of research in which English scholars hitherto had lagged behind continental writers. At the same time, his deeper penetration into the practical application of the jurisdiction of the medieval church in England provided a model for their future researches. Closely associated with Walther Holzmann, who worked in English archives on the ambitious *Papsturkunden* project sponsored by the Göttingen Academy, he carried his own researches on collections of papal decretals and the work of judges delegate in England to a point that has inspired French and German scholars to begin filling in gaps in the *Papsturkunden in Frankreich* series. As joint literary editor of the Royal Historical Society (1938–45), he guided many scholars' work to publication.

He was appointed CBE in 1984. In 1951 he was elected a fellow of the British Academy; other academic honours included honorary doctorates at Glasgow (D.Litt., 1970) and Manchester (D.Litt., 1978), and election as a corresponding fellow of the Mediaeval Academy of America and corresponding member of the Monumenta Germaniae Historica. Wadham College made him an honorary fellow in 1968.

Cheney was a small man with dark hair and an impish glance. In 1940 he married Mary Gwendolen (daughter of Gilbert Hall, of the Malayan Civil Service), a historian who collaborated with him in two of his books and supported him in his research all his life. There were two sons and one daughter of the marriage. Cheney died in Cambridge 19 June 1987.

[C. N. L. Brooke in *Proceedings of the British Academy*, vol. lxxiii, 1987; *Speculum*, vol. lxiii, 1988; personal knowledge.]   M. CHIBNALL

CHESTER, SIR **(Daniel) Norman** (1907–1986), warden of Nuffield College, Oxford, was born 27 October 1907 in Chorlton-cum-Hardy, Manchester, the elder son and eldest of three children of Daniel Chester, traveller in the cotton trade, of Chorlton-cum-Hardy, and his wife Edith, daughter of John and Elizabeth Robinson of Stretford, near Manchester. He was educated at St Clement's Church of England School, Chorlton-cum-Hardy.

Growing up in somewhat straitened circumstances, Chester left school at fourteen to work in the treasurer's department of Manchester city council. By the age of twenty-four he had won an external BA (1930) at Manchester University, where he also gained an MA (1933). This was followed by a research post and later a lectureship there. In 1935–6 he held a Rockefeller fellowship in the United States to study public utilities. On the outbreak of war in 1939 he was recruited to the economic section of the war cabinet secretariat, where he served from 1940 to 1945. He worked closely with Herbert *Morrison (later Baron Morrison of Lambeth) and Sir John *Anderson (later first Viscount Waverley), but the most memorable of his tasks was to act in 1941–2 as secretary to the committee on social insurance and allied services chaired by Sir William (later Baron) *Beveridge.

When the war ended in 1945 he went to Oxford as a fellow of the newly founded Nuffield College, where he was to remain for the rest of his life. In 1954 he was elected warden of Nuffield, a position he held until 1978. His experience of Whitehall and the contacts made there stood him in good stead. More than anyone else, Chester shaped the development of the college (founded in 1937), which was breaking new ground for Oxford in being the first graduate college for both men and women, and the first college to specialize, being devoted exclusively to the social sciences. Even before he was elected warden, he had become involved in every detail of college development—the finances and furnishing and, even more, the recruitment of fellows and students. The college was granted a royal charter in 1958. One of Chester's major achievements was, after early estrangements, to reconcile Viscount *Nuffield to the college that

bore his name. He took great pride in the fact that, when Nuffield died in 1963, he made the college his residuary legatee.

Chester was a man of enormous energy. His abiding commitment to local self-government led him to serve as an Oxford city councillor and later alderman from 1952 to 1974. He was a leading figure in the Royal Institute of Public Administration, serving as its chairman in 1953–4 and acting as editor of its journal from 1943 to 1966. After helping to found the Study of Parliament Group in 1960, he was its president from 1971 to his death. He chaired the 'Britain in Europe' campaign in Oxford during the 1975 referendum and was assiduous in building up Nuffield College's links with Europe, in particular with the Fondation Nationale des Sciences Politiques in Paris. He was one of the founders of the British Political Studies Association and then of the International Political Science Association, of which he was president in 1961–4. He played a central role in the establishment of the Oxford Centre for Management Studies (later Templeton College) and was its chairman from 1965 to 1975.

He had been a runner in his youth and remained dedicated to sport. His wartime friend, Harold Wilson (later Baron Wilson of Rievaulx), persuaded him to chair a government committee on association football in 1966–8 and he was a key figure in football for the rest of his life. He served as chairman of the Football Grounds Improvement Trust and finally as deputy chairman of the Football Trust, travelling assiduously to see games all over the country.

Chester was also a productive, meticulous, and wide-ranging scholar. He wrote with clarity and precision rather than with stylistic sparkle, his works making a notable and authoritative contribution to the study of Parliament and administration. His principal books included *Central and Local Government: Financial and Administrative Relations* (1951), (ed.) *Lessons of the British War Economy* (1951), *The Nationalisation of British Industry, 1945–51* (1975), *The English Administrative System 1780–1870* (1981), and *Economics, Politics and Social Studies in Oxford* (1986).

Chester remained very much a northerner, always keeping something of his Mancunian accent. His occasionally blunt rejection of the conventional Oxford style upset some people and earned him a reputation for abrasiveness. But behind the rough exterior there was a man who showed great kindness to colleagues and to students. He had great breadth of vision and an unfailing sense of duty. He left his mark on many sectors of national life—association football, local government, and the study of British government. But his main achievement was in giving shape to Nuffield College as a new model of collegiate life and of what he believed a graduate college dedicated to the social sciences should be. Under his guidance the college became a highly prestigious institution both in Oxford (its ex-students supplied a majority of tutorial fellows in the social sciences) and internationally.

He was appointed CBE in 1951 and knighted in 1974. He became a chevalier of the Legion of Honour in 1976 and received an honorary Litt.D. from Manchester University in 1968. On retirement in 1978 he became an honorary fellow of Nuffield. In 1936 he married Eva (died 1980), daughter of James H. Jeavons, master butcher. There were no children. Following an operation, he died in Oxford 20 September 1986 while still in full vigour and enjoying his hobbies of bridge playing, country walking, and ornithology. Nuffield College has drawings of him by David Hockney.

[D. E. Butler and A. H. Halsey (eds.), *Policy and Politics* (Festschrift), 1978; obituary by Nevil Johnson in *Public Administration*, vol. lxv, summer 1987; private information; personal knowledge.]   DAVID BUTLER

CHIBNALL, Albert Charles (1894–1988), biochemist and historian, was born 28 January 1894 in Hammersmith, London, the second of three sons and third of six children (two subsequent daughters died in infancy) of George William Chibnall, baker, and his wife Kate, daughter of Thomas Butler, restaurateur in London and minor landowner at Littlebury in Essex. At St Paul's School he developed an early interest in chemistry and geology. With an exhibition at Clare College, Cambridge, he embarked on the natural sciences tripos, intending to take the diploma in mining engineering. After completing part i of the tripos in 1914, in which he gained a second class, he joined the army (Army Service Corps) and saw service in Salonika, transferring to the Royal Flying Corps in 1917. His two brothers were killed in the war.

On demobilization Chibnall decided not to return to Cambridge and became a research student with S. B. Schryver, professor of plant biochemistry at Imperial College, London. Here he laid the foundations of a career in protein biochemistry which profoundly influenced the development of the subject. After two years in the laboratory of T. B. Osborne, at New Haven, Connecticut, in 1924 Chibnall returned to England, to University College as an assistant, doing further work on proteins and broadening his interests to plant waxes. He continued to publish on the latter subject even after retirement from active biochemistry. He succeeded Schryver as professor of biochemistry at Imperial College in 1929 and Sir F. G. *Hopkins in the chair of biochemistry in Cambridge in 1943. When he took up his Cambridge chair he became a fellow of Clare College.

In 1939 appeared his classic monograph, *Protein Metabolism in the Plant*, which was based on his research and the prestigious Silliman lectures he gave at Yale during the previous year. In later years at Imperial College and Cambridge, however, the structure and chemistry of proteins in general became his main interest. At this time the precise nature of protein structure was still unknown and theories abounded. The careful amino acid analyses carried out by his group before the advent of chromatography were the best of their kind and no structural theory could survive if it did not comply with their data. Chibnall and his group demonstrated directly that asparagine and glutamine were components of proteins. From the 1930s to the early 1950s he was the man to approach with a problem relating to protein chemistry. He was elected a fellow of the Royal Society in 1937. Collaboration with W. T. *Astbury and Kenneth *Bailey led to a patent for the conversion of groundnut protein into a fibre with the characteristics of wool. The process was promising enough to be put into commercial production by Imperial Chemical Industries, but it failed to compete successfully with the synthetic fibres. The importance of the scientific environment Chibnall built up at this critical time for the development of protein chemistry is reflected in the subsequent achievements of his young associates. He suggested that Frederick Sanger should investigate the amino groups of insulin, work which in the course of time led to the first determination of the sequence of a protein and the award of a Nobel prize. He also encouraged R. R. *Porter, a contemporary of Sanger, who was later to be similarly honoured for his work on the structure of immunoglobulin.

Chibnall played an important part in the development of biochemistry in the United Kingdom. From the mid-1930s he had strong links with the Agricultural Research Council and did much to strengthen biochemistry in its institutes. He served as a member of the council but turned down the secretaryship when it was offered to him. He was the longest serving secretary of the Biochemical Society, chairman of the society's committee, and president of the first international congress of biochemistry when it met in Cambridge in 1949. Ironically this was the year when, at the height of his academic distinction, he decided to give up the Cambridge chair and devote himself fully to research. There was altruism in this decision, for he felt that, with the tremendous advances and importance of animal and medical biochemistry, a person more versed in these aspects than himself should be in charge of the Cambridge department.

Historical research fascinated Chibnall for most of his life. His interest was first aroused when soon after demobilization he spent time at

Somerset House and the Public Record Office
seeking information about his sixteenth-century
ancestors, the Chibnalls of Sherington. He
taught himself the techniques of historical
research and from then onwards, when he could
spare time from his busy life as a scientist, he
meticulously collected material about medieval
Sherington. When in 1958 he finally gave up his
laboratory in Cambridge he was able to devote
himself full-time to historical research and enjoy
college life at Clare. In effect he started a second
career and produced a series of important books
on medieval Buckinghamshire. The most
remarkable of these, *Sherington, Fiefs and Fields
of a Buckinghamshire Village* (1965), was much
acclaimed by leading historians. In 1978 at the
age of eighty-four he was elected a fellow of the
Society of Antiquaries.

Chibnall was tall and well built, with an air of
distinction and quiet authority. His scholarship
crossed the normal boundaries. For an academic
he had a wide experience of life and was generous
and supportive to his junior associates. He followed their development with interest and drew
great pleasure from their successes.

In 1931 he married his cousin Cicely, daughter
of Herbert Barber Chibnall, businessman; they
had two daughters. Cicely died in childbirth in
1936. In 1947 he married Marjorie McCallum
Morgan, a history lecturer at the University of
Aberdeen and later a fellow of Girton College,
Cambridge. She was the daughter of John Christopher Morgan, farmer. They had a son and a
daughter. Chibnall died at his home in Cambridge 10 January 1988.

[E. Ashby, *Cambridge Review*, vol. cix, 1988; S. V.
Perry, *Biochemist*, vol. x, 1988; F. Sanger, *Annual
Review of Biochemistry*, vol. lvii, 1988; R. L. M. Synge
and E. F. Williams in *Biographical Memoirs of Fellows of
the Royal Society*, vol. xxxv, 1990; personal knowledge.]
                                          S. V. PERRY

CHIPPERFIELD, James Seaton Methuen
(1912–1990), circus proprietor and inventor of
the safari park, was born 17 July 1912 in a
mahogany wagon on land belonging to Paul,
third Baron *Methuen, near Corsham, Wiltshire,
the second son in the family of three sons and
two daughters of Richard Chipperfield, owner of
a small family circus, and his wife Maud, daughter of George Seaton, another circus man.
Because the show was constantly on the road,
'Jimmy' received almost no formal education,
rarely attending any school for more than a few
days; but he grew up richly imbued with the
traditions of the circus, in which his family had
performed for more than two centuries.

A short, stocky man with dark hair and strong
features, he inherited his father's ferocious appetite for hard physical work. Hours on the trapeze
equipped him with powerful arms and shoulders,
and from an early age he showed an exceptional
affinity with animals, not least with Rosie, the
elephant in which he and his elder brother Dick
invested all their capital of £400 during the
1920s. He also trained lions and tigers, wrestled
the bear, and played the clown.

At the age of sixteen he fell in love with
another Rosie, daughter of Captain Tom Purchase, circus proprietor and lion trainer, who had
been killed by a lion. In 1934, when Chipperfield
was twenty-two, the young couple eloped and
married, to circumvent his father's opposition,
and they remained happily married for nearly
sixty years. Their eldest son, also Jimmy, died of
tetanus at the age of six in 1941, but they had two
more sons and two daughters.

At the outbreak of war in 1939 Chipperfield
set his heart on becoming a fighter pilot in the
Royal Air Force. His handicaps would have
defeated most aspirants: he had no mathematics,
and only one kidney, the other having been
crushed during a bout with Bruni the bear.
Ignoring adverse medical reports, he put himself
into school, alongside children, and by sheer
determination mastered enough trigonometry to
win his wings and fly Mosquito fighter bombers
with No. 85 Squadron.

After the war he returned to the circus, and in
partnership with Dick built up the biggest travelling show in Britain. Then in 1955 he broke away
on his own, farming in Hampshire, training
animals for Walt Disney films, and founding a
zoo in Southampton. He began to travel in
Africa, and it was the sight of big game roaming
the plains of Kenya and Uganda that gave him
the most important idea of his life.

This was for a novel form of zoo, in which the
animals would run free in large paddocks, and
human beings would stay in cages—their cars—
to drive among them. It took him some time to
find an ideal site, but in 1964 he hit on Longleat,
the ancestral home of the Bath family. There,
in partnership with the sixth Marquess of Bath,
he built the world's first safari park. While
the fences were being installed, *The Times*
denounced the scheme as 'a dangerous folly', and
called for its suppression; this made excellent
publicity for the venture, which opened at Easter
1966 and proved a colossal success.

Other parks followed at Woburn, Knowsley,
Blair Drummond, and Bewdley. Their success
attracted the enmity of traditional zoo-keepers,
particularly Sir Solly (later Baron) Zuckerman,
then secretary of the London Zoological Society;
but Chipperfield claimed with obvious truth that,
apart from inventing a novel attraction, he had
established useful breeding groups of endangered
species. He became a rich man, bought expensive
cars, and enjoyed his association with landed
aristocrats such as the Marquess of Bath and the
Duke of Bedford.

In 1975 he and Rosie suffered a severe blow when their eldest surviving son, Richard, was killed in a car accident in Uganda. An outstanding animal man, with an attractive personality, he had been the natural heir to the business. With him gone, it was left to Mary, the elder daughter, to carry on the family's circus traditions.

During the 1960s Chipperfield settled comfortably, but without ostentation, into a substantial house on the outskirts of Southampton. In 1986 he moved to a farm at Middle Wallop, in Hampshire, where he remained surrounded by animals—there was usually a chimpanzee on the premises, and often a lion cub—and by the latest electronic gadgets. Although tough with anyone who crossed him, he was generous and loyal to friends, and retained a fierce pride in his family and their achievements. He published his autobiography, *My Wild Life*, in 1975, and died 20 April 1990 at his home, Croft Farm, near Middle Wallop.

[Jimmy Chipperfield, *My Wild Life*, 1975; private information; personal knowledge.]

DUFF HART-DAVIS

CHURCH, Charles James Gregory (1942–1989), house builder, was born 29 October 1942 in Windlesham, Surrey, the only son and younger child of Charles Church, farm labourer, of Windlesham, and his wife, Fuensanta Guisantes. He was educated at Strodes School, Egham, and studied civil engineering at the Regent Street Polytechnic in London. His interest in construction and house building became apparent very early and by the age of eleven he had become a competent electrician and was able to wire his parents' cottage for electric light. Five years later he single-handedly built a tennis court for a neighbour. During his college vacations he worked for the Turriff construction group as a junior engineer. His construction manager, Jack Hamer, was so impressed by the house builder in-the-making that he lent Church the deposit money for the purchase of his first site.

In 1964 he graduated and worked full-time for Turriff. A year later he moved to Laing as a junior engineer, as part of the team involved in the construction of the Wraysbury reservoir project. Laing moved him to Doncaster in 1966 to work on a new gas pipeline. Church felt that his determination and enterprise were going both unnoticed and unrewarded, and after only six months in his new job he decided to establish his own company. In partnership with Con Burke he established the civil engineering company, Burke & Church Ltd., in 1967, and quickly sold his first house at Prior Road, Camberley. The proceeds of the sale were ploughed back into the business and used to acquire more land, including a two-acre site in Wokingham, Surrey, on which sat a tumbledown cottage, in which he lived.

At this time he learned a valuable business lesson. He realized that trying to establish a land bank and develop houses was tying up his dwindling cash resources. The only way forward for a small house builder was to develop an option system on difficult sites, rather than buying them outright. Church was already adept at buying sites, but he knew he could not compete with cash-rich, large house builders for land which could be easily developed. Instead he turned to tracts of land which other builders would avoid. Sites without planning consent or those which would be difficult to develop because of drainage or construction problems began to attract him, not only because they were cheap but because he could secure an option to buy at a future date for very little money.

During the 1970s he not only honed these land buying skills, but also developed his own 'just-in-time' construction techniques more than a decade ahead of Japanese and American building companies. This entailed extremely efficient management of each construction site, to ensure that materials arrived only when they were needed and when they could be paid for. Simultaneously he recognized the need for a highly skilled, highly motivated, and loyal workforce. Although he demanded a lot from his workers, they were among the best paid in the industry. Church could also lead by example, as there was hardly a job on the site he could not do himself, and he imbued his workers with a sense of achievement and of fun.

While he was developing his reputation as a consummate house builder, who provided quality, up-market homes, mainly designed in Tudor or Georgian style, Church continued to be hamstrung by a lack of cash. He solved this problem in the mid-1970s by forming a partnership with Martin Grant, another Surrey-based house builder. Grant's cash injection allowed Church to start acquiring larger sites. This enabled the company to lay the solid foundations of growth, which ultimately resulted in a stock market flotation in 1988, when 750 houses a year were being built. The stock market had not fully recovered from its crash the previous autumn and house builders were out of favour with the City. Church became frustrated by investors' lack of confidence and a year later bought back all the shares. Once more Charles Church became a private company, whose posters, prominently displayed on London underground stations, gave it a high profile.

In the male-dominated world of building and construction he was unusual in that he employed a relatively high number of women in key positions. This was never a token gesture. He wanted to help people develop their intrinsic skills while at the same time encouraging them to widen their experience. He included his wife in this policy, for in the early days she was expected to do her share of the physical work and later was encouraged to become involved in all aspects of managing a house-building company. Ultimately she became a main board director in charge of architecture and was expected to take control of the business if anything happened to him.

Church was just over six feet tall, with long legs, broad shoulders, large eyes, and thick, brownish-red hair. He seemed to be a workaholic who believed his business was his life, but he found time to indulge his great passion for vintage aircraft. He bought a 1,000-acre farm and sporting estate in Hampshire, at which he based his company for refurbishing World War II aircraft and established his own vintage plane collection, which included various Spitfires, a Hurricane, a Mustang, an ME109, and a Lancaster bomber. He died at the controls of his beloved Mark V Spitfire, which developed engine failure and crashed near Hartley Wintney in Hampshire, 1 July 1989.

In 1967 he married a former air hostess, Susanna Bridgette, daughter of William Simms, dairy shop manager. They had two daughters and a son.

[Private information; personal knowledge.]

JOHN DUGGAN

CLAPHAM, (Arthur) Roy (1904–1990), botanist, was born in Norwich 24 May 1904, the eldest of three children and only son of George Clapham, schoolmaster, and his wife, Dora Margaret Harvey. His childhood was spent in Norwich, where he attended the City of Norwich School (1915–22), winning a scholarship to Downing College, Cambridge. At Cambridge he developed his interests in botany, retaining his love of the native flora but applying his knowledge of the physical sciences and mathematics to plant physiology. He obtained first classes in both parts of the natural sciences tripos (1924 and 1925) and then undertook research, supervised by Professor F. F. *Blackman, for his Cambridge Ph.D. (1929).

In 1928 he was appointed crop physiologist at Rothamsted Agricultural Experimental Station in Hertfordshire, where he worked closely and successfully with (Sir) R. A. *Fisher to establish reliable methods for using small samples to measure the yield of cereal crops. In 1930 Clapham was appointed to a teaching post in the botany department at Oxford University and in 1933 he and his wife set up their home in Wytham. His period at Oxford under (Sir) Arthur *Tansley was one of great activity. He lectured on a very wide variety of topics and published research in plant ecology, palaeoecology, cytotaxonomy, and physiology. His ability

as a teacher, both formally in lectures and informally in tutorials, was outstanding. His lectures concentrated on the essential steps in understanding a subject, and he had the rare gift of being able to express himself in clear, simple, often elegant language with perfect syntax.

In 1944 he moved to the chair of botany at the University of Sheffield, where he remained until his retirement in 1969. He fell in love with the Derbyshire countryside and soon became an expert on its vegetation.

He continued to develop both teaching and research in plant ecology and thus built upon the foundation already laid by his predecessor, W. H. *Pearsall. Several of his research students made important contributions, but his own time for research was devoted to the preparation, with T. G. *Tutin and E. F. *Warburg, of the *Flora of the British Isles*. This was published in 1952 and was followed by a revised second edition (1962) and by the *Excursion Flora* (1959). Initially his department was small, but Clapham's wide interests ensured that it offered a well-balanced treatment of modern botany, to which Clapham himself contributed a full share. During the following years the size and activities of the department were steadily expanded so that at his retirement it had acquired both a national and international reputation for its achievements.

Clapham enjoyed field classes and would seem oblivious of driving rain or wet undergrowth as he explained ecological processes. His colleagues never ceased to be surprised at the extent of his knowledge, not only of botany, nor indeed of physical sciences and mathematics, but of literature, languages, art, and history. He combined a retentive memory with a penetrating intellectual curiosity. He could be a fearsome critic, but he was always constructive.

His early scientific publications are notable for their precision and their clarity of presentation. Yet after moving to Sheffield he ceased publishing original research and increasingly became a source of ideas and a stimulus to others, both formally through his writing and informally through discussion. For example, he played a leading part in the scheme to map in detail the distribution of British flora, and in the United Kingdom's contribution to the International Biological Programme. He was an editor of the *New Phytologist* from 1930 to 1961.

At Sheffield an increasing proportion of Clapham's time was given to serving on committees of the university, of learned societies, and of national bodies, such as the Nature Conservancy, Field Studies Council, and the planning board of the Peak District National Park. He was a trustee of the British Museum (Natural History) from 1965 to 1975. In 1959 he was elected a fellow of the Royal Society. He also served the University of Sheffield as a pro-vice-chancellor (1954–8) and was acting vice-chancellor in 1965. He was appointed CBE in 1969 and in 1948 a fellow of the Linnean Society, of which he was president in 1967–70. He won the Linnean gold medal in 1972. In 1970 he received honorary doctorates from Sheffield (Litt.D.) and Aberdeen (LL D).

Following his retirement he moved to Arkholme in the Lune Valley near Lancaster. Clapham was of medium build and always wore glasses. His face was very attentive, with a quizzical look and a smile never far away. In 1933 he married Brenda North (died 1986), daughter of Alexander Goodwin Stoessiger, watch importer and wholesale jeweller, of London. They had two sons and two daughters. One of his sons died in infancy in 1934. Clapham died in Lancaster Royal Infirmary, 18 December 1990.

[Donald Pigott in *Journal of Ecology*, vol. lxxx, 1992, and *New Phytology*, vol. cxix, 1991; private information; personal knowledge.]   DONALD PIGOTT

CLARK, COLIN GRANT (1905–1989), economist, was born 2 November 1905 in London, the eldest in the family of three sons and one daughter of James Clark, a merchant of Scottish descent, who worked in South Africa, and his wife, Marion Jolly, who had travelled to London for the birth. He was educated at the Dragon School in Oxford, Winchester, and (from 1924) Brasenose College, Oxford. Though he read chemistry, obtaining a second-class degree in 1928, he developed a fascination for economics, partly influenced by G. D. H. *Cole and Lionel (later Baron) *Robbins.

He then took up a research post at the London School of Economics, moving in May 1929 to Liverpool University, to work on the Merseyside social survey. In February 1930 he was invited to join the Economic Advisory Council, which included J. Maynard (later Baron) *Keynes. Through that connection Clark became a Cambridge lecturer in statistics in the economics faculty (1931–7). His first book, *The National Income 1924–1931* (1932), was a landmark in national accounting. His reputation grew through the publication, with A. C. *Pigou, of *The Economic Position of Great Britain* (1936) and the appearance of his *National Income and Outlay* (1937). Keynes relied greatly on his estimates.

Clark also found time for Labour party politics, and unsuccessfully fought three parliamentary elections (North Dorset, 1929, Liverpool Wavertree, 1931, and South Norfolk, 1935). Although he assumed a non-party stance, he shifted after World War II across the political spectrum from Fabianism towards free market economics. While he retained sympathy towards the weak, he increasingly doubted the power of government to secure improvement without growth and monetary stability.

In 1937, with his outstanding *The Conditions of Economic Progress* (1940) in preparation, Clark obtained leave to visit Australian universities. Though expected back in Cambridge, he learned that the Labour premier of Queensland needed urgent assistance. Thus began a long spell, to 1952, as under-secretary of state for labour and industry and adviser to the Queensland government, which was combined with academic writing. Four books appeared quickly (*The National Income of Australia*, with J. G. Crawford, 1938; *A Critique of Russian Statistics*, 1939; *The Conditions of Economic Progress*, 1940; and *The Economics of 1960*, 1942), though much of his important work appeared in the official *Economic News*.

In October 1951 Clark's interest in world food supplies, stemming from Australian experience, brought him secondment to Rome to advise the Food and Agriculture Organization. It was then that he decided to apply for the vacant directorship of the Oxford University Institute for Research in Agricultural Economics and, to his surprise, was appointed (1953–69). *The Conditions of Economic Progress*, revised in 1951, was extended in 1957. He argued that progress involves shifts from primary into secondary and tertiary sectors, and he quantified the size of the movement and its resulting changes in income and productivity through intensive empirical study. Clark was a master of data assembly, possessing an uncanny ability to draw elegant and simple conclusions. There followed *The Economics of Subsistence Agriculture* (1964, with Margaret Haswell), *The Economics of Irrigation* (1967, revised with Ian Carruthers in 1981), and *Population Growth and Land Use* (1967).

In a broader context, Clark became controversial, relentlessly pursuing three themes. First, his conversion to Catholicism in 1942 provoked his interest in population growth, prompting him to attack Malthusian views. He became a key lay member of the pope's Commission on Population (1964–6), from which *Humanae Vitae* appeared. Though frequently regarded as extreme, Clark was able to demonstrate agriculture's remarkable capacity to increase food availability to support his contention that 'the earth can feed its people'. His other themes were equally prominent. By 1957 he found kindred free market advocates in London at the Institute of Economic Affairs. In *Growthmanship* (1961), one of several IEA pamphlets, he argued that progress would not be achieved by increased levels of nationally planned investment but by improving skills and fostering incentive. The latter, his third theme (*Taxmanship*, 1964), could only be damaged by attempts to secure welfare improvements by excessive redistribution of wealth.

In 1969 Clark retired to Australia, briefly joining Monash University before returning to Brisbane and an unofficial position at Queensland

University. There he continued avid writing, including his final book *Regional and Urban Location* (1982), in which, despite his normal stance, he expressed scepticism about market efficiency in guiding the geographical distribution of industry and population.

Clark held four honorary doctorates (the last fittingly from Queensland University, 1985) to add to his Oxford D.Litt. (1971), a Festschrift appeared in 1988 (Duncan Ironmonger *et al.*, *National Income and Economic Progress, Essays in Honour of Colin Clark*), and he became a corresponding fellow of the British Academy (1978) and, in 1987, a distinguished fellow of the Australian Economic Society. He was also a fellow of the Econometric Society.

Clark was regarded by some as a 'gadfly' or wayward genius; others thought he had been overlooked for a Nobel prize for his national income work or felt that his passion for data overwhelmed his capacity for deductive reasoning. With enormous zest for life he was never remote, singing to an accordion, reciting *Belloc, and engaging in rough rural living and walking, which admirably suited his physique. He was above average height, with a strong muscular body and short cropped hair, and often seemed to be untidily dressed. While his memory and powers of recall were undaunting, he was basically a sensitive man who was easy to approach and whose eyes would twinkle at the prospect of a friendly argument.

In 1935 he married Marjorie, daughter of Hugh Herbert Tattersall, sea captain in the merchant navy. They had eight sons and one daughter. Clark died in Brisbane, 4 September 1989.

[John Eatwell *et al.* (eds.), *The New Palgrave: a Dictionary of Economics*, 1987; *Economic Record*, vol. lxv, September 1989, and vol. lxvi, December 1990; David L. Sills (ed.), *Encyclopaedia of the Social Sciences*, vol. xviii, 1968; personal knowledge.]   G. H. PETERS

CLARKE, Thomas Ernest Bennett (1907–1989), author and screenwriter, was born 7 June 1907 in Watford, Hertfordshire, the younger son and third of four children of (Sir) Ernest Michael Clarke, a company director dealing in shipping and gold mines, and his wife Madeline, daughter of Ernest Bennett Gardiner, an Irish bank manager. Always known as 'Tibby', Clarke attended Charterhouse and spent a year at Clare College, Cambridge, studying law, before visiting Australia, where he edited the *Red Heart*, a girls' magazine. He then travelled to New Zealand, San Francisco, and Canada. On his return to England he secured employment as junior editorial assistant on the *Hardware Trade Journal*, moving on to work for the weekly magazine *Answers* and other papers.

Clarke's work in the late 1920s as publicity officer for the W. S. Crawford Advertising Agency brought him into contact with the film industry for the first time, publicizing sound equipment systems for Western Electric. Clarke was made redundant in 1930 and decided to visit Argentina, securing his passage by becoming a purser on a tramp steamer. On his return he resumed work for *Answers* and wrote *Go South–Go West* (1932), an account of his recent adventures abroad. Clarke secured another journalist/publicity job, editing the UK Temperance and General Provident Institution's monthly magazine. He then decided to go freelance, continued work on his novels, and reported for the *Daily Sketch*.

In World War II Clarke enlisted as a war reserve constable in the Metropolitan Police until asthma forced his discharge. He did not write screenplays until 1942, aged thirty-five, when Monja Danischewsky, director of publicity at Ealing Studios, asked Clarke to assist with unsatisfactory scripts before securing a contract as a screenwriter. His first screen credit was for 'doctoring' the script of *For Those in Peril* (1944), followed by *The Halfway House* (1944), a ghost story directed by Basil Dearden.

Clarke is best known for his Ealing comedies, and his first opportunity to work on comedy was to write a short sequence of the supernatural story film *Dead of Night* (1945). This was a prelude to his writing the first classic 'Ealing comedy', *Hue and Cry* (1946), an ingenious story about the revenge of youngsters who discover that criminals have been using their newspaper to pass information. One of his most famous comedies was *Passport to Pimlico* (1949), which celebrated its characters' discovery that an area of London belonged to Burgundy, thus freeing them from laws and petty restrictions, a theme that reflected its postwar audiences' desire to be rid of rationing. Clarke won an Oscar and an award at the Venice film festival for *The Lavender Hill Mob* (1951), about a Bank of England employee, played by (Sir) Alec Guinness, who steals bullion and turns it into souvenir models of the Eiffel tower. *The Titfield Thunderbolt* (1952), about a village community trying to save a branch railway from closure, similarly celebrated individuals who battled against authority. Although these films had no clear political message, their themes tapped into the mood of postwar austerity and reflected the concerns of many British people. Clarke also scripted *The Blue Lamp* (1949), a police drama from a play by Ted (later Baron) Willis, starring Jack *Warner and (Sir) Dirk Bogarde.

Clarke was associated with Ealing's most productive years, when it was a studio with a distinctive outlook and structure, which enabled its head, Sir Michael *Balcon, to initiate some of the British cinema's most famous films. In 1955

Ealing was sold to the BBC and Clarke went freelance, working in Hollywood and Britain. He scripted John Ford's *Gideon's Day* (1958) and adapted literary classics during this period. But his days of writing original screenplays were over and he was never again allowed the freedom or creative inspiration he enjoyed at Ealing. The last film with a 'Clarke' screen credit was *A Man Could Get Killed* (1966).

In 1952 he was appointed OBE. He published a witty and penetrating autobiography in 1974, *This Is Where I Came In*. He continued to write novels throughout his career as a screenwriter: *Jeremy's England* (1934), *Cartwright Was a Cad* (1936), *Two and Two Make Five* (1938), *What's Yours?* (1938), *Mr. Spirket Reforms* (1940), *The World Was Mine* (1964), *The Wide Open Door* (1966), *The Trial of the Serpent* (1968), *The Wrong Turning* (1971), *The Man Who Seduced a Bank* (1979), *Murder at Buckingham Palace* (1981), and *Grim Discovery* (1983).

Clarke was a courteous, sensitive man with a great sense of humour, who fulfilled his ambition to become a racehorse owner in the 1960s. He was genial and portly, with a youthful appearance; his distinctive brown hair had a silver streak. In 1932 he married Joyce Caroline Jenny (died 1983), daughter of Roy Rockwell Steele, engineer. They had a son, Michael, a film producer who died in a drowning accident in 1966, and a daughter, Ann. Clarke died 11 February 1989 in London.

[Charles Barr, *Ealing Studios*, 1977; T. E. B. Clarke, *This Is Where I Came In* (autobiography), 1974; British Film Institute microfiche jacket; private information.]

SARAH STREET

CLAYTON, SIR Stanley George (1911–1986), professor of obstetrics and gynaecology, was born 13 September 1911 in Hankow, China, the younger son (there were no daughters) of the Revd George Clayton, Methodist minister, and his wife, Florence Powell. At the age of eight he was sent to Kingswood School near Bath and from there in 1929 he went to King's College, London, with a Sambrooke scholarship to begin his medical studies. He went on to King's College Hospital and qualified MB, BS and MRCS, LRCP in 1934, gaining the Jelf medal in surgery and the Todd prize in medicine. He then took the primary FRCS (1936), gaining the Hallett prize. As a medical student he was noted not only for his academic brilliance but also as a first-class rugby player. After qualification and house appointments, he became a gynaecological registrar at King's in 1936 and obstetric registrar at Queen Charlotte's Hospital in 1938.

The war years saw him serving as a general surgeon and a gynaecologist in the Emergency Medical Services and latterly as a major in the Royal Army Medical Corps. On his return to civilian life he resumed work in his chosen speciality of obstetrics and gynaecology and he was soon appointed to the consultant staff of King's College Hospital (1947), Queen Charlotte's (1946), and the Chelsea Hospital for Women (1953). He obtained the London University degrees of MD (1941) and MS (1942). As a consultant he was noted for the excellence of his clinical judgement and the speed of his surgery, but above all for the clarity of his teaching, both at undergraduate and postgraduate levels. His pocket textbooks of obstetrics and gynaecology ran to many editions and were compulsory reading for most undergraduates—indeed they were often used by postgraduates as well. He became FRCOG in 1951.

The opportunity to develop the academic side of his professional life came when he was invited to take the chair of obstetrics and gynaecology at Queen Charlotte's Hospital and the Chelsea Hospital for Women in 1963. He returned to King's to take up the newly established chair of obstetrics and gynaecology in 1967 and set up the new academic department. He soon gathered round him a team of young and enthusiastic academics, who worked under his guidance to build the foundations of what was to become one of the outstanding departments in the country, with a growing international reputation. In later years, in spite of a heavy involvement in the work of the Royal College of Obstetricians and Gynaecologists (RCOG), he continued to devote much of his time to the department at King's and to the hospital and medical school. Clayton's association with the RCOG was long and distinguished. He served on many of its committees and was in turn vice-president (1971) and president (1972–5). During his presidency, his administrative skills and obvious integrity enabled him to guide the Australian gynaecologists through a minefield of legal and professional problems when they decided to separate from the parent college. The Australians made him an honorary fellow of their new college in 1985. Clayton also edited the *British Journal of Obstetrics and Gynaecology* from 1963 to 1975. He was knighted in 1974 and became honorary FRSM in 1985.

After his retirement from King's in 1976, Clayton took on that most onerous of tasks for a medical man, chairmanship of the consultants' merit awards committee. In this role he travelled widely around the country and did much to explain the workings of the committee to the often aggrieved consultant body.

Clayton was a well-built, balding, bespectacled, and shy man, with a somewhat austere outward appearance. He spoke his mind diffidently but was always to the point and impatient of the inessential. He had a delightful sense of humour, which quickly broke through his outer shell, and he was an entertaining and lively companion. A knowledgeable and keen gardener, he was also interested in embroidery, at which he became very skilled. He had a happy family life at home in Leatherhead with Kathleen Mary, daughter of Alfred Willshire. They were married in 1936 and had a son and a daughter. Kathleen died in 1983. Clayton continued to work as editor of *Ten Teachers' Obstetrics* (14th edn., 1985) and *Ten Teachers' Gynaecology* (14th edn., 1985) and took a close interest in developments in the speciality. He suffered a great deal from angina following a mild coronary thrombosis, but characteristically made light of the disability. Following an operation from which he was recovering satisfactorily, he suffered another coronary and died 12 September 1986 in King's, the hospital to which he had given devoted service for more than fifty years.

[*Munk's Roll*, vol. viii, 1989; *Daily Telegraph*, 17 September 1986; private information; personal knowledge.]   MICHAEL BRUDENELL

CLEGG, SIR Alexander Bradshaw (1909–1986), teacher, educator, and educational administrator, was born 13 June 1909 in Sawley, Derbyshire, the only son and youngest of five children of Samuel Clegg, headmaster of Long Eaton Grammar School, and his wife, Mary Bradshaw. 'Alec' Clegg attended his father's school before going on to the Quaker Bootham School, York, at the age of fifteen. He studied modern languages at Clare College, Cambridge, where he obtained a second class (division I) in all three of his examinations—part i (French) in 1929, part i (German) in 1930, and part ii (1931). He then qualified as a teacher at the London Day Training College.

Clegg served as an assistant master at St Clement Dane's Grammar School in London, where he taught languages and football. In 1936 he was appointed an administrative assistant to the Birmingham education committee. His notebooks of that period show a meticulous regard for the details of administrative procedures, which he was sometimes later at pains to conceal. In 1939 he became assistant education officer to Cheshire, before being appointed in 1942 as deputy education officer to Worcestershire. He became deputy education officer to the West Riding, one of the largest education authorities in the country, in January 1945. Within a few months the chief education officer moved to Lancashire and Clegg was appointed in his place. In later years he attributed this to the fact that the clerk to the West Riding, himself legally qualified, discovered that the preferred candidate also had a legal qualification. So began a remarkable career in creative educational administration.

Clegg concentrated on the essentials. Early on he established a number of specialist colleges for teachers: in 1949 Bretton Hall for teachers of the arts, and in 1952 Woolley Hall as the first in-service residential college. Others followed. Bringing teachers together, thinking with them, and learning from them, was a matter of personal commitment throughout Clegg's career. He had a gift for expressing complex ideas simply. He wrote *Ten Years of Change* (1953), which was the first of four major reports to the West Riding education committee. Unlike most such reports, it pointed sharply, with accompanying photographs, to the failures of the system as well as to its successes. As regards secondary schools, Clegg believed they should take responsibility for children of all abilities but insisted that there was no one way of achieving this. Local communities in the West Riding were encouraged to shape schools to their needs. So some comprehensive schools were large, some small; some had sixth forms, others did not. What worked was the test. Clegg had no interest in uniformity. He was one of the main architects of the comprehensive system of education.

In 1959 Clegg served on the central advisory council for education, chaired by Sir Geoffrey (later Baron) *Crowther, which dealt with the education of fifteen- to eighteen-year-olds, but his main interests lay with the changing primary school. After widespread discussion with teachers, he came to the view that a middle-school system would combine the best practices of the primary school with the needs of eleven- and twelve-year-olds. His reasoning convinced the secretary of state and enabling legislation was passed in 1964.

In 1964 the West Riding published his *The Excitement of Writing* to show what could be achieved by young children if the opportunity was given to them to express themselves freely. In 1963 he was invited to serve on the inquiry chaired by (Sir) John *Newsom, whose report, *Half Our Future* (1963), concluded that most children in secondary modern schools were undervalued, a view he shared. He was knighted in 1965, the year in which he became president of the Association of Chief Education Officers. In 1968 his most influential book, written with Barbara Megson, *Children in Distress*, was published. In 1970 he was invited by the Department of Education and Science to deliver the lecture in Central Hall, Westminster, to commemorate one hundred years of state education. In that lecture, published in *About Our Schools* (1980), he examined the failure over that period to achieve genuine educational opportunities for the disadvantaged and pointed to the disturbing social and economic consequences of this. After retiring from the West Riding in March 1974, he became chairman of the Centre for Information and Advice on Educational Disadvantage, a post he held between 1976 and 1979.

He was awarded honorary degrees by Leeds (1972), Loughborough (1972), and Bradford (1978), and was made a fellow of King's College, London (1972) and an honorary fellow of Bretton Hall (1981). The inspirational qualities which he brought to his achievements in the West Riding and elsewhere were remarkable. He was proud of his ability to pick and then trust colleagues of high quality. Informality mixed with firmness of purpose, good humour, and approachability were characteristics of his style. Absolute integrity and a commitment to put the interests of children above all else were at the heart of his achievement.

In 1940 he married Jessie Coverdale, daughter of Thomas Phillips, teacher; they had three sons. Clegg died in York, 20 January 1986.

[Clegg papers, Lawrence Batley Centre, Bretton Hall, Yorkshire; *Bramley Occasional Papers*, vol. iv, 1990; private information; personal knowledge.]

PETER NEWSAM

CLEMENTS, SIR **John Selby** (1910–1988), actor, manager, and producer, was born 25 April 1910 at 1 Carlton Terrace, Childs Hill, Hendon, Middlesex, the only child of Herbert William Clements, barrister, and his wife, Mary Elizabeth Stephens. He was educated at St Paul's School and spent one term at St John's College, Cambridge. He was forced to withdraw from the college, where he had begun to study history, because sudden financial loss meant his family could no longer afford the fees. His mother's great friend, Marie Löhr, gave him his first job at the age of twenty at the Lyric theatre, Hammersmith. In 1931 he joined the Shakespearian Company run by Sir (P. B.) Ben *Greet, and at twenty-five, in 1935, was sufficiently confident to found the Intimate Theatre, Palmers Green, as a weekly repertory company which he managed, directed, and acted in until 1940. In the first year he produced forty-two plays there, playing thirty-six leading parts.

In 1936 he married his first wife, Inga Maria Lillemor Ahlgren. They had no children and the marriage was dissolved ten years later. In 1946 he married the actress Kay Hammond, whose real name was Dorothy Katherine, daughter of Sir Guy Standing, KBE, of the Royal Naval Volunteer Reserve. Kay was formerly the wife of Sir Ronald George Leon, third baronet, and mother of Sir John Leon, fourth baronet, later better known as the actor John Standing. She and Clements had no children.

During the war Clements had produced many plays for ENSA and also organized a revue company to entertain the troops at out-of-the-way places. John Clements and Kay Hammond together became one of the best known theatrical couples of their day. In 1944 they acted at the Apollo in *Private Lives*, by (Sir) Noël *Coward,

an enchanting production with which Coward was delighted. In 1946 Clements appeared as the Earl of Warwick in *The Kingmaker* at the St James's theatre, which he himself managed. He presented and directed *Man and Superman* in 1951 at the New theatre, playing the role of John Tanner.

In addition to his many productions and performances, Clements was a successful broadcaster on the radio, taking part with Kay Hammond in the weekly discussion programme, *We Beg To Differ*. Their comic rivalry on the air delighted audiences. From 1955 Clements was adviser on drama for Associated Rediffusion, one of the first independent television companies, for which he was contracted to produce a number of television plays. In July 1955 he joined the board of directors of the Saville theatre, the management of which came under his personal control.

In 1960 Kay Hammond became paralysed after a stroke and was confined to a wheelchair for the remaining twenty years of her life. Clements joined the Old Vic Company in 1961, making his first appearance in New York in the title part of *Macbeth* in 1962. In 1966 he took on the challenge of directing the Chichester festival theatre when Sir Laurence (later Baron) *Olivier left to found the National Theatre. His boundless enthusiasm and love of the theatre overcame any initial reluctance on the part of the actors he approached for his first season at Chichester to join him 'in the wake of Larry'. He was able to recruit Celia *Johnson and Bill Fraser and splendid supporting casts, who were very loyal to him. His seasons were independent and enterprising and he was always encouraging, calm, and resourceful in times of crisis.

As a director he was businesslike, almost prosaic, and very logical, never selfish and always courteous. Six feet tall, with a handsome face and slightly 'jug' ears, he had kind eyes and excellent hands. He was one of the last actor-managers in the country. In Chichester he was not only the director of four plays each summer season, but also played, among other parts, Macbeth, Antony, and Prospero, as well as two of Jean Anouilh's heroes, the general in *The Fighting Cock* and Antoine in *Dear Antoine*. It was his appreciation of the literary tradition of drama that gave him the courage to present *The Fighting Cock*, which had been a great success in its original French version in Paris. *Heartbreak House*, in which he played Shotover, was one of his most memorable productions.

Clements also acted in a number of films, including *Things to Come* (1936), *South Riding* (1937), *The Four Feathers* (1939), *Oh What a Lovely War!* (1969), and *Gandhi* (1982). He was appointed CBE in 1956 and knighted in 1968. A member of the council of Equity in 1948–9 and vice-president in 1950–9, he was also a popular trustee of the Garrick Club.

He left Chichester in 1973 to spend more time with his wife, for they were a devoted couple. She died in 1980. Clements died 6 April 1988 at Pendean Convalescent Home near Midhurst, where he spent the last two years of his life.

[Personal knowledge.]   BESSBOROUGH

CLEVERDON, (Thomas) Douglas (James) (1903–1987), bookseller, publisher, and radio producer, was born 17 January 1903 in Bristol (he retained all his life a faint trace of a Bristol accent), the elder child and elder son of Thomas Silcox Cleverdon, master wheelwright, and his wife, Jane Louisa James. The only book in the house in those days was his mother's Welsh Bible. He was educated at Bristol Grammar School, where he learned his love of books from the headmaster, Ted Barton. While still an astonishingly good-looking schoolboy in a cap and blazer he went for a week to London, and walked into Francis Birrell's and David *Garnett's new bookshop. He was fêted by Clive *Bell and Roger *Fry, and introduced to the latest work in painting, engraving, and printing.

He published his first catalogue as an undergraduate at Jesus College, Oxford, immediately establishing his reputation as a lover of fine printing and exquisitely illustrated books. He became part of what he himself later called the 'typographical renaissance' made possible by Stanley *Morison's reintroduction of great typefaces of the past and (A.) Eric *Gill's sculptural lettering, and became a close friend and disciple of both. At Oxford he obtained a second class in classical honour moderations (1924) and a third in *literae humaniores* (1926).

In 1926 he opened his own bookshop in Charlotte Street, Bristol. Roger Fry painted the hanging sign, bought from an old pub, with Athena's owl perched on a pile of books, and Eric Gill painted the fascia over the shop window in sans-serif capitals. Cleverdon asked him for a copy of the alphabet, and it was from this that Morison commissioned the famous 'Gill Sans-serif'. At this time he also began publishing, with Gill's *Art and Love* (1927), printed in a limited edition, including thirty-five copies on full vellum, and S. T. *Coleridge's *The Rime of the Ancient Mariner* (1929), for which he commissioned ten copper engravings and an introduction from David *Jones. This venture was brought to an end by the economic depression, but Cleverdon continued to sell books until the end of the 1930s, when he was persuaded by Francis Dillon to begin working part-time for the BBC. In 1939 he worked for *Children's Hour* and in the same year became a west regional features producer. In 1940, as he himself put it, 'a bomb fell on the bookshop, and I was with the BBC for

thirty years'. In 1943 he became a features producer in London.

He was to bring to radio all his skills as a publisher: inspired commissioning of new work, patient encouragement and direction of writers, musicians, and actors, perfectionism in editing and production, and all the craftsmanship he had learned from Morison and Gill, and in his father's workshop.

It was shortly before the war that he met (Elinor) Nest, former head girl of the Clergy Daughters School in Bristol and daughter of James Abraham Lewis, canon, of Cardiff. They eventually married in 1944, though (Sir) John *Betjeman referred to her ever afterwards as 'Douglas's child bride'. They were to have two daughters, the elder of whom, born in 1948, died immediately, and three sons, the eldest of whom died at birth in 1952. Cleverdon, busy, bustling, chuckling, with sparkling blue eyes and a slightly irregular smile, would greet almost everyone as 'my dear' to save himself from having to remember names. He was a small man, and it was said that he 'towered over' his wife. But she was to be his strength and stay, making a home that gleamed with merriment like the bright china on the Welsh dresser, a house always full of friends.

Cleverdon's main achievement of the war years was the *The Brains Trust*, which he devised with Howard *Thomas, and which reached an audience of twelve million. He was sent briefly to Burma in 1945 as a BBC war correspondent, and on his return began by developing the already existing *Radio Portrait* series for the Third Programme. These included personal reminiscences of Joseph *Conrad, (G.) Norman *Douglas, and Henry *James. He dramatized David Jones's *In Parenthesis* (1948) and *The Anathemata* (1953), using the voices of Richard *Burton and Dylan *Thomas. He also launched Henry *Reed's satirical *Hilda Tablet* series in 1953, broadcast the poems of Sylvia *Plath, Ted Hughes, Thom Gunn, Wole Soyinka, John Betjeman, Siegfried *Sassoon, and Stevie *Smith, and produced the work of David Garnett, (Dame) Rose *Macaulay, Sir Compton *Mackenzie, and Jacob *Bronowski. He also travelled to Rapallo to record a series of broadcasts with Sir Max *Beerbohm.

Cleverdon produced programmes of folk-song with A. L. Lloyd and Alan Lomax, and commissioned new music from Humphrey *Searle, Alan *Rawsthorne, (Sir) Lennox *Berkeley, Alexander Tcherepnin, Peter Racine *Fricker, and Mátyás Seiber. He was the first to engage Michael *Flanders and Donald Swann for the radio. His most famous commission was *Under Milk Wood*, broadcast in 1954, which he succeeded in wringing out of Dylan Thomas shortly before his death in 1953.

Cleverdon retired from the BBC in 1969, and,

as well as organizing poetry festivals, returned to publishing, with his own Clover Hill Editions, called after the Anglo-Saxon meaning of his own name. His printer was his old friend Will Carter of the Rampant Lions Press, Cambridge. He preserved the same standards he had set himself as a young man, with beautifully produced work by (A.) Reynolds *Stone, Michael *Ayrton, and David Jones, and *The Story of Cupid and Psyche*, an unprinted Kelmscott Press book with wood blocks by William *Morris after Sir Edward *Burne-Jones.

Cleverdon died 1 October 1987 at his home at 27 Barnsbury Square, London N1.

[Douglas Cleverdon, *Fifty Years*, The Private Library, 1983; Nicolas Barker in *Book Collector*, vol. xxxii, no. 1, 1983; private information; personal knowledge.]

JOHN WELLS

COBBOLD, Cameron Fromanteel, first BARON COBBOLD (1904–1987), governor of the Bank of England, was born 14 September 1904 at 23 Eaton Terrace, London, the only child of Lieutenant-Colonel Clement John Fromanteel Cobbold, barrister, of Belstead Manor, Ipswich, and his wife Stella Willoughby Savile, daughter of Charles Cameron. He was educated at Eton and went to King's College, Cambridge, in 1923. However, academic life did not offer the challenge he was seeking and he left after the first year.

After brief experience in accountancy, he worked in France and Italy, where, as manager in Milan of an insurance company, his skill in unravelling the tangled affairs of a failed Italian bank came to the notice of Montagu (later Baron) *Norman, governor of the Bank of England. At Norman's invitation, he joined the Bank in 1933 and rapid advancement followed. He became adviser to the governor in 1935 and, in 1938, one of four executive directors appointed to the court with the object of easing the load upon the governor. After World War I and increasingly through the 1930s, problems of industrial reorganization and reconstruction had led the Bank into areas that hitherto had been regarded as outside the concerns of a central bank. Norman's solution was to create a specialist team of advisers working outside the formal structures of the Bank's staff. 'Kim' Cobbold occupied a special place in Norman's team.

His Bank apprenticeship was full and varied, both on the international and domestic fronts. Having joined shortly after the collapse of the gold standard, he immediately found himself closely involved in intricate international discussions, especially with the French, which led to the tripartite monetary agreement of 1936, designed to restore order in the troubled European foreign exchange markets. His domestic responsibilities were no less important and,

increasingly, his time was taken up with the preparation of emergency plans for wartime operations in the Bank and City. War finance itself, the transition from war to peace, problems of meeting the domestic financial needs of the country in the immediate postwar period and, of special importance, negotiations which led to the creation of the International Monetary Fund and World Bank were matters of state that commanded the attention and honed the skills of the Bank's young deputy governor, a post Cobbold attained in 1945.

As deputy governor he was closely involved in the negotiations with the government that preceded the nationalization of the Bank in 1946 and, with the example of Norman to encourage him, he took on the governorship in 1949 determined to maintain the Bank's integrity and independence of mind. Despite the pressures, crises, and uncertainties of his twelve years as governor, he succeeded in keeping the Bank out of politics. Pressures there were—a sterling crisis and devaluation within months of his becoming governor, the Bank Rate Tribunal of 1957, and the wide-ranging committee of inquiry into the operation of the monetary system chaired by Baron (later Viscount) *Radcliffe (1957–9)—but they were only episodes in what he saw as the proper role of the Bank, dedicated to serving the national interest and providing sound practical advice to government. He was essentially a pragmatist and an able administrator, a 'markets' man and not an academic, happy to hear the arguments and to make up his own mind. To some around him he appeared reserved, even unfriendly, and he never succeeded in overcoming a dislike of public speaking. Some part at least of this was probably due to an inherent shyness, which others wrongly attributed to a lack of personal warmth. He set himself high standards and, by example and encouragement, succeeded in getting the best out of others.

His public service did not end with his retirement as governor in 1961. He had for many years been a fellow of Eton (1951–67) and in 1962 he chaired the Malaysia commission of inquiry. A year later he was appointed lord chamberlain of the queen's household (1963–71) and brought to his new duties the same perceptive approach and professional expertise that had characterized his years at the Bank. Tall and powerfully built, with a commanding presence, he was able to find genuine and satisfying relaxation in country pursuits. Still active in mind and body, he spent his last years in retirement happily surrounded by family and friends at Lake House, Knebworth. Cobbold had an honorary LL D from McGill University (1961) and an honorary D.Sc.(Econ.) from London (1963). He was sworn of the Privy Council in 1959, was appointed GCVO in 1963 and KG in 1970, and was created first Baron Cobbold in 1960.

He met Lady (Margaret) Hermione (Millicent) Bulwer-Lytton in India in 1925 while staying with her father, Victor Alexander George Robert *Bulwer-Lytton, second Earl of Lytton, governor of Bengal. They married in 1930 and Lady Hermione inherited the family seat at Knebworth on the death of her father in 1947. They had two daughters, one of whom died in 1937 at the age of five, and two sons, the elder of whom, David Antony Fromanteel Lytton-Cobbold (born 1937), succeeded to the peerage. Cobbold died at Knebworth 1 November 1987.

[John S. Fforde, *The Bank of England and Public Policy 1941–58*, 1992; family records; personal knowledge.]
                                        PETER TAYLOR

COCHRANE, Archibald Leman (1909–1988), medical scientist and epidemiologist, was born in Galashiels 12 January 1909, the second child in the family of a daughter and three sons of Walter Francis Cochrane, of Kirklands, manufacturer of Scotch tweed, and his wife Mabel Purdom, daughter and granddaughter of lawyers from Hawick. His grandfather's family had become wealthy, but the death of his father on active service in April 1917 led to his mother's relative impoverishment. He gained entry scholarships to Uppingham and King's College, Cambridge, where he obtained first classes in both parts of the natural sciences tripos (1929 and 1931).

An inheritance gave him the means to continue study and in 1931 he began research in tissue culture at the Strangeways Laboratory, Cambridge, hoping to become a university lecturer. The results of his experiments, however, seemed trivial and the concomitant development of what he believed (erroneously) to be a psychological symptom led him to abandon the project and seek medical advice. British doctors were unsympathetic and he sought help at the Kaiser Wilhelm Institute in Berlin. He received sympathy there, but little else, and he turned to Theodor Reik, an early follower of Sigmund Freud, partly to obtain treatment and partly to learn enough about psychoanalysis to design ways of testing psychoanalytical hypotheses. The succeeding two and a half years did nothing for his complaint, but they provided an exceptional education, as he followed Dr Reik from Berlin to Vienna, and to The Hague, attending the clinical course in both the last cities.

Returning to Britain in 1934 with fluent German, a hatred of Fascism, and a sceptical attitude to all theories not validated by experiment, Cochrane enrolled as a medical student at University College Hospital, London. The outbreak of the Spanish civil war and the intervention of Fascist Germany and Italy led him to abandon his studies for membership of a field ambulance unit supporting the International Brigade, in which he was probably the only member with neither party political nor religious affiliation. After a year's service on the Aragon and Madrid fronts, he returned to University College Hospital, with valuable experience of wartime triage and the realities of left-wing politics.

Cochrane qualified MB, B.Chir. (Cambridge, 1938) in time to complete a house physician's job at the West London Hospital and obtain a research appointment at UCH before war again intervened. He joined the Royal Army Medical Corps in 1940 and was posted to a general hospital in Egypt. He was then sent to Crete, where he was soon taken prisoner. There followed the darkest period of his life when, as medical officer for a prisoner-of-war camp in Salonika, he was confronted by major epidemics, severe malnutrition, and extreme Nazi brutality. During this time he undertook what he later described as his 'first, worst, and most successful controlled trial' in search of a cure for famine oedema, finding it in small amounts of yeast obtained on the black market.

When he returned to Britain in 1945, a Rockefeller fellowship enabled him to take a course at the London School of Hygiene, where he became enthusiastic about the conduct of controlled trials by random allocation of treatments and obtained his DPH (1947). He then went for a year (1947) to the Phipps Clinic in Philadelphia, where he developed a lifelong interest in the scientific study of diagnostic and prognostic error. In 1948 he accepted an appointment with the Medical Research Council's pneumoconiosis research unit in Cardiff. There Cochrane designed and started an ambitious project to test the idea that tuberculosis played an important part in transforming the disease into its most disabling form.

In 1960 Cochrane was appointed David Davies professor of tuberculosis and diseases of the chest at the Welsh National School of Medicine and transformed his team into a new epidemiology unit, of which he became director in 1969, under the Medical Research Council. With this support, he continued his studies of the progress of pneumoconiosis and conducted population surveys to study the natural history and aetiology of anaemia, glaucoma, and other common diseases. He showed the importance of building in checks on the reproducibility of any diagnostic procedure and demonstrated that it was regularly possible to get over 90 per cent of the public to participate in health surveys. The social importance of his trials was lucidly expressed in his short book, *Effectiveness and Efficiency* (1971), which won him international acclaim. He became FRCP in 1965.

In 1972 Cochrane became the first president of the new faculty of community (subsequently public health) medicine of the Royal College of Physicians. He had never been attracted by administration or ceremony and was relieved to hand over after two years. In this period, however, he succeeded in welding into a harmonious whole two mutually suspicious groups: academics in social medicine and practising medical officers of health. He was appointed MBE in 1945 and CBE in 1968, and had honorary doctorates from York (1973) and Rochester, USA (1977).

'Archie', as Cochrane was generally known, combined concern for public welfare with that for the individual and discovered late in life, as a result of the trouble he took over an illness of his sister's, that they both suffered from hereditary porphyria, which may have been responsible for the sexual condition that so affected his early career. He created a garden included in the national garden scheme and collected with discrimination contemporary paintings and sculpture. A man of medium height and athletic build, he had reddish hair and a permanently quizzical expression. He never married, having resolved to have no more love affairs after an unfortunate experience in the USA in 1947. He died of cancer after a long illness, 18 June 1988, at his nephew's home in Holt, near Wimborne, Dorset. He is commemorated in Green College, Oxford, to which he left a substantial legacy, by a residence for students and a fellowship for the director of the Cochrane Centre, set up by the Department of Health to promote overviews of controlled trials.

[A. L. Cochrane with Max Blythe, *One Man's Medicine: an Autobiography*, 1989; personal knowledge.]

RICHARD DOLL

COCKAYNE, DAME **Elizabeth** (1894–1988), chief nursing officer, was born 29 October 1894 in Burton-on-Trent, the youngest in the family of two daughters and three sons of William Cockayne, brewer's traveller and licensed victualler, and his wife, Alice Bailey. One of her brothers was killed in World War I, the second died of tuberculosis, and the third died in 1943. Her father died when she was five. These distressing experiences sharpened Elizabeth Cockayne's deep commitment to Christianity and sense of duty to others. She went to Guild Street Girls' School in Burton-on-Trent. After contracting smallpox as a child, she contemplated a career in nursing. In 1912 she embarked upon a two-year training in fever nursing at the Borough Hospital, Plymouth. Although asked by the matron to stay on the staff after her training was completed, she decided to leave Plymouth in 1915.

She had four years' training at Sheffield Royal Infirmary, which gave her a dual qualification. She was rapidly promoted to the post of ward sister in 1919 and then night sister, a post in which she oversaw the administration of the 500-bed hospital. While she was on night duty she undertook a course in hygiene and sanitary science offered by the local education authority. Much against the wishes of her employers, she left Sheffield to undertake midwifery training at Birmingham Maternity Hospital (1920–1). She impressed her supervisors with her intelligence and judgement, and took charge of caring for premature babies. Her mother died at this time. She left Birmingham to become a peripatetic nurse-tutor, travelling between the Gloucester and Cheltenham General hospitals. As her headmistress had noted earlier, she had a natural flair for teaching. Throughout her life she maintained a keen commitment to her own education as well as that of others.

Although happy in Gloucester, she moved to London to be near her sister, a schoolmistress, who had fallen ill. She joined the West London Hospital as one of the first nurses to occupy a combined post as assistant matron and sister tutor. She excelled in her new position and by the age of twenty-nine was appointed to a matron's post first at the West London, then at the Saint Charles, and finally at the Royal Free Hospital. She was at the Royal Free from 1936 to 1948, having succeeded the formidable Rachael Cox-Davies as matron. She displayed calmness and courage after the outbreak of war, when the hospital was bombed and she was buried in the rubble. At the same time she was invited by the matron-in-chief of the London county council to act as an examiner to training schools and to review the policy on the length of the working week for nurses and domestics. She inspected work in training schools and factories, supervising the health of munitions workers during World War II. She had a continued interest in the effects of fatigue and strain on nurses' health and performance. She was honorary secretary of the Association of Hospital Matrons between 1937 and 1948, occupying one of the premier positions in nursing policy and politics. As a founding member of the sister tutor section of the Royal College of Nursing, she recognized the prejudice faced by tutors, who were regarded as superfluous and a luxury in training schools.

In 1945 Elizabeth Cockayne was appointed a member of the working party (chaired by Sir Robert Wood) on the recruitment and training of nurses, which reported in 1947. It aimed to improve the intellectual calibre of nurse training by reducing the repetitive and routine nature of practical nursing experience and stripping the nursing role of its domestic functions. It reported (HMSO, 1947) that this could only be achieved by radically reducing the jurisdiction of the matron-dominated General Nursing Council over nurse training and substituting it with regional nursing boards. These recommendations made Elizabeth Cockayne unpopular with her fellow matrons. In 1948 she was appointed the first chief nursing officer in the National Health Service, where she remained until her retirement in 1958.

She was of slender build, with striking features, a kindly face, and keen intelligent eyes. An enlightened, energetic, and progressive leader, she had charisma, charm, a generous nature, humanitarian values, and an understanding of the various groups whose differences often clashed in the sectarian politics of health care. A shrewd but subtle strategist, she determined that the nursing voice should be heard at the highest levels of policy-making. She was gifted with the rare capacity to influence without alienating, and to assume multiple roles without undermining her integrity. She was committed to nurses' welfare and high standards of patient care.

After her retirement she was a member of the South West Metropolitan Health Board (1959–65) and an adviser to the World Health Organization during the 1950s. In later life she cared for many old people near her home in Cobham, Surrey, some of whom were younger than herself. She lived alone in her cottage after the death of her sister in 1982. She received the Jubilee medal (1935), the Coronation medal (1953), and the Florence Nightingale medal of the International Red Cross committee in Geneva. She was appointed DBE in 1955. She died 4 July 1988 at her home in Cobham, Surrey. She was unmarried.

[Interview with Dame Elizabeth Cockayne, 27 March 1987, in membership file, Royal College of Nursing archives, 44 Heriot Row, Edinburgh; Dame Kathleen Raven's memorial speech in honour of Dame Elizabeth Cockayne, Royal Free Hospital, 31 October 1988.]

ANNE MARIE RAFFERTY

COCKERELL, Sydney Morris (1906–1987), bookbinder and conservator, was born 6 June 1906 at 96 Earls Court Road, London, the second of three children and elder son of Douglas Bennett *Cockerell, bookbinder, and his wife Florence Margaret Drew, daughter of Samuel Drew Arundel, box-maker, of London. His mother died in 1912 and his father married again two years later. His father's training and background influenced much of 'Sandy' Cockerell's own career. After St Christopher's School, Letchworth, in 1924 Cockerell joined his father as a partner in D. Cockerell & Son. Their workshop was in an extension to the family house at Letchworth and both there and, from 1963, in Grantchester, there was always an air of domesticity about Sydney Cockerell's surroundings. In partnership with his father, in 1935 he rebound the 'Codex Sinaiticus' after its purchase for the nation. In the same year they were joined by

Roger Powell, who remained as a partner until 1947, when he established his own workshop, remaining in close and amicable contact. Douglas Cockerell died in 1945.

Cockerell's long association with university, national, and other libraries, as he repaired manuscripts and early printed books, began in the 1920s. Cambridge University Library was among the first such customers, and the most longstanding. Some of that library's greatest treasures, including the 'Codex Bezae', the 'Book of Cerne', the 'Book of Deer', and Sir Isaac *Newton's papers all passed through his hands. For Trinity College, repairs included those for the twelfth-century 'Eadwine Psalter' and the autograph volume of John *Milton's poetry. The extensive task of repairing papers for the Wordsworth Trust, at Dove Cottage, was spread over many years, while for the Fitzwilliam Museum, Cambridge, Cockerell repaired *Handel's autographs and the Fitzwilliam virginal book, among others. In such work he was unsurpassed in his generation. He was also consulted widely from overseas, notably following the Florence floods in 1967.

As a binder of more recent books, the traditions shared with his father likewise led him to consider bookbinding as a process as much concerned with a book's structure and use as with its outward decoration. His many commissions included rolls of honour for both Houses of Parliament as well as for the armed services; he was regularly called on for lectern bibles in cathedrals. From 1948, collaboration with Joan Rix Tebbutt, of the Glasgow School of Art, led to a distinctive series of bindings in toned vellum, in which designer and binder co-operated in outstanding accord.

Adept with his hands, Cockerell was also of a highly practical turn of mind. Many of his tools he made himself, and the hydraulic ram (adapted from an aeroplane's wing flaps), with which he impressed gold leaf into his bindings, gave any visitor immediate notice of his ingenuity. Like his father, Cockerell insisted on the best materials appropriate to their purpose, paying especial attention to leathers (especially goatskins) and to papers with a neutral pH and of the right weight and fibre structure. In the 1920s his experiments on marbling paper for bindings soon led to its regular production by his workshop. This continued until his death, principally in the hands of William Chapman. The necessary combs to create the repeatable and distinctive (yet always subtly different) patterns were made in the workshop.

He was an influential teacher, succeeding his father at both the Central School of Arts and Crafts, London, and at the Royal College of Art. At University College London he lectured to students of librarianship in 1945–76, and thus sought to demonstrate how his practical skill and knowledge could be applied to the proper care of books and manuscripts. In his workshop he trained a series of assistants, most of whom subsequently either joined major libraries, or established their own practices. His book, *The Repairing of Books* (1958), was offered as a further means of closing the gap between the librarian or collector and the craftsman.

Cockerell's appearance was dominated by prominent and luxuriant eyebrows, which formed an inseparable part of his conversation, helping by turn to orchestrate his dry sense of humour or forcefully express criticism, as necessary. He was scathing about poor workmanship, and formidable when he perceived incompetence in those charged with the care of the nation's collections of books and manuscripts. He was appointed OBE in 1980 and was awarded an honorary Litt.D. by Cambridge in 1982.

In 1932 he married Elizabeth Lucy (died 1991), daughter of Harrison Cowlishaw, architect. She had been one of his father's students at the Central School, and she brought her own contribution to the workshop. They had a son and two daughters. Cockerell died in Addenbrooke's Hospital, Cambridge, 6 November 1987.

[*Book Collector*, summer 1974; *Cockerell Bindings, 1894–1980* (exhibition catalogue, Fitzwilliam Museum), 1981; *Independent*, 10 November 1987; personal knowledge.]   DAVID MCKITTERICK

COKE, Gerald Edward (1907–1990), industrialist, merchant banker, patron of music, art, and scholarship, collector, and creator of gardens, was born 25 October 1907 at Bruton Street, London, the only son and eldest of three children of (Sir) John Spencer Coke, major in the Scots Guards and royal equerry (seventh son of Thomas William *Coke, second Earl of Leicester, of Holkham Hall, Norfolk), and his wife Dorothy Olive, only child of Sir Harry *Lawson, second baronet, second baron, and first and only Viscount Burnham, newspaper proprietor and member of Parliament, of London. Coke was educated at Eton and New College, Oxford, where he obtained a third class in modern history (1929).

During the 1930s Coke worked at Barrow-in-Furness in a firm connected with haematite iron ore mining. He served throughout World War II in the Scots Guards and attained the rank of lieutenant-colonel. From 1945 to 1975 he was a director of the merchant bank S. G. Warburg & Co., and rose to be vice-chairman. He also served as a director of the Rio Tinto-Zinc Corporation (1947–75), and as chairman (1956–62). His success in these enterprises owed as much to his charm, patent sincerity, and integrity as it did to his commercial acumen. He was a JP from 1952

and deputy lieutenant of Hampshire from 1974. He was appointed CBE in 1967 and became an honorary FRAM in 1968.

The financial success of his work in commerce and banking allowed him to acquire his home, Jenkyn Place, Bentley, Hampshire, which he and his wife transformed into a residence of great beauty and refined taste, filled with libraries, precious porcelain, the great Handel collection, and many *objets d'art*. Both partners devoted long hours almost daily to the creation of the large and choice gardens surrounding their property, which were intermittently open, chiefly to connoisseurs and garden societies, and formed the subject of television programmes.

Coke's character obliged him to share the fruits of his wealth and accomplishments with many in the fields of music, scholarship, and similar concerns. His influence contributed much to the success of Glyndebourne, run by John *Christie and Sir George Christie, of whose arts trust he was chairman (1955–75). He also served as a director of the Royal Opera House, Covent Garden (1958–64), and of the Royal Academy of Music (1957–74). He was a governor of the BBC (1961–6). Particularly close to his heart was his long association, as treasurer and benefactor, with Bridewell Royal Hospital, and King Edward's School, Witley, where there is a portrait of him by Sir William *Coldstream. When Coke took over as treasurer, King Edward's School was a relatively small boys' school, which he made into a co-educational boarding school of some importance.

The *pièce de résistance* of his life as a scholar and collector was the Coke Handel collection, which embraced important musical manuscripts, libretti, and autographs. Coke also enabled Handel scholars, such as O. E. Deutsch and W. C. Smith, to persevere with and complete their studies. Towards the end of his life he was instrumental in arranging for the publication of a Handel iconography and for the eventual transfer of the Handel collection to the care of the Handel Institute. His 1983 book, *In Search of James Giles*, was the culmination of his other great enthusiasm, his porcelain collection.

If Coke was an amateur, then this term can only be understood in the sense that music, opera, porcelain, or the art of garden cultivation were not the source of his income but the objects of his expenditure. His knowledge and expertise in so many disparate fields were prodigious, but they were always imparted to others with that modesty and self-effacement which characterized him, and which perhaps led to his failure to receive higher official honours.

In appearance he was tall and slender, with an upright bearing. On 2 September 1939, the day before the outbreak of war, Coke married Patricia, daughter of Sir Alexander George Montagu

*Cadogan, diplomat. The marriage was one of exceptional happiness and harmony, and of shared interests in gardening, music, and collecting. They had a daughter and three sons, the third of whom died of meningitis suddenly in 1972, a day after his successful final degree examination at London University. Coke died at Jenkyn Place, Bentley, of heart failure, 9 January 1990. A concert in his memory was given at Glyndebourne on 5 August 1990, at which it was disclosed that Coke had persuaded his shipping heiress friend, the countess of Munster, to sell one of her ships and with the proceeds endow a trust for education in music. By 1994 well over 1,300 British musicians had benefited from the trust.

[Donald Burrows in the *Guardian*, 18 January 1990; Gerald Coke, *The Gerald Coke Handel Collection*, 1985; *The Countess of Munster Musical Trust*, annual reports; information from Henry Grunfeld at S. G. Warburg, Sir George Christie, and Leopold de Rothschild; personal knowledge.]   EDWARD ULLENDORFF

COLDSTREAM, SIR **William Menzies** (1908–1987), artist and arts administrator, was born 28 February 1908 at the Doctor's House, West Street, Belford, Northumberland, the youngest in the family of two sons and three daughters of George Probyn Coldstream, general medical practitioner, and his wife (Susan Jane) Lilian Mercer, elder daughter of Major Robert Mercer Tod (43rd Light Infantry), of Edinburgh.

He was two years old when the family moved to West Hampstead, London. Early interest in the natural sciences made him want to become a doctor but, at the age of twelve, with a suspected heart condition following rheumatic fever, he was removed from school and tutored at home. Although he went at sixteen to the University Tutorial Centre, Red Lion Square, to prepare for entry to medical school, by his eighteenth birthday he had failed matriculation, met W. H. *Auden, and started to draw and paint seriously. In April 1926, with his father's support, he enrolled at the Slade School of Fine Art.

While there he was awarded the Slade certificate for drawing (1926), a Slade scholarship, the figure and summer composition prizes (1927), the summer landscape prize, and the second Melville Nettleship prize for figure composition (1928). Meanwhile, he had become greatly impressed by the work of nineteenth-century French masters, especially Cézanne, Braque, and Matisse, and by artists like Walter *Sickert, Duncan *Grant, and Picasso; had attended outside lectures by Sickert on 'The Technique of Drawing and Painting'; and, to increase his manual graphic control, taken extra drawing instruction from a signwriter in Horseferry Road. By the time he left the Slade (1929) he was

working wholly from nature, with intense interest in the appearance of things.

In 1930 he got his first commission, met Victor Pasmore, and was elected to the London Artists' Association. Over the next two years he became increasingly concerned at the conflict between his real interest in visual facts and his appreciation that abstraction was gaining ground, in response to current aesthetic theories and the support for subjective painting then centred on Paris. In 1932 he became temporary art master at Wellington College and in 1933 briefly attempted 'objective abstraction', which Geoffrey Tibble and Rodrigo *Moynihan were then moving towards. When elected that year to the London Group, he already felt convinced that abstract art appealed only to an élitist minority and that broken communications between artist and public needed rebuilding.

Spurred by contemporary political and social problems and believing in film as a communicator, he got a job with the pioneering GPO Film Unit run by John *Grierson. In 1935 he directed *The King's Stamp* and edited *Coal Face*, with lyrics by Auden and music by Benjamin (later Baron) *Britten; but, after directing *Fairy of the Phone* (1936) and *Roadways* (1937), he decided to return to painting. The experience had convinced him that film was no answer to the current crisis in painting, that many of the approved preconceptions about art were for him unimportant, and that he had to start painting again—but now only in the way that interested him: directly from nature, as a pure transcription of what he saw.

To encourage an objective process in visual representation, in 1937 he joined with Claude *Rogers and Victor Pasmore in starting a School of Drawing and Painting at 12 Fitzroy Street (later 316 Euston Road). Although it closed on the outbreak of war (1939), it had much impact and created a 'new look' in English art.

In 1940 Coldstream enlisted in the Royal Artillery but was soon transferred to the Royal Engineers and commissioned as a camouflage officer (1940). He served in England until appointed an official war artist (1943). He then went first to Egypt, painting mostly portraits at No. 11 Indian transit camp, between the pyramids and Cairo. From 1944 he was in Italy, doing outstanding war landscapes in Capua, Pisa, Rimini, and Florence.

On demobilization (1945) he joined Victor Pasmore in teaching at Camberwell School of Art and Crafts, later (1948) becoming its inspiring head of painting. In June the following year he was appointed Slade professor at University College London, returning to the school he had always loved. During twenty-six dynamic years there he greatly strengthened its work, introduced postgraduate courses, and, for the first time, made film studies available at university level. Taking always a leading role in the life of University College, he was elected a fellow in 1953. During those years and after his retirement (1975), his paintings included a succession of outstanding nudes, a series of views of Westminster painted from the Department of the Environment in Marsham Street, and a number of commissioned portraits which rank among his most remarkable works. Among these are: 'Dr Bell, Bishop of Chichester' (1954, Tate Gallery), 'Sir Ifor Evans' (1958–60, University College London), 'Westminster Abbey I' (1973–4, Arts Council Collection, South Bank Centre, London), and 'Reclining Nude' (1974–6, Tate Gallery).

An exceptional chairman, he discharged a formidable range of public duties. He was chairman of the National Advisory Council on Art Education (1958–71) and largely responsible for the liberalizing transformation of art education in Britain; a trustee of the National Gallery (1948–55, 1956–63) and of the Tate Gallery (1949–55, 1956–63); a member of the Arts Council (1952–62), vice-chairman of the council (1962–70), and chairman of its art panel (1953–62); a director of the Royal Opera House (1957–62); chairman of the British Film Institute (1964–71); and vice-president of Morley College (1977–83). In 1977 he was elected to the Society of Dilettanti and became painter to the society. Appointed CBE in 1952, he was knighted in 1956 and received honorary degrees from the universities of Nottingham (1961), Birmingham (1962), and London (1984), and from the Council for National Academic Awards (1975).

First and foremost a painter, laden with self-doubt and ever diffident about his remarkable achievements, he was a good friend and immensely stimulating companion, whose outstanding work is a lasting tribute to his self-imposed discipline and the integrity of his painterly qualities. Small, wiry, grey-suited, and unobtrusive, he was highly intelligent and greatly respected, with an irrepressible wit which, in Rodrigo Moynihan's words, was 'an inspired sustained hilarity, directed towards the absurdities of art, the pretensions of artists, the shortcomings of friends'.

On 22 July 1931 he married Nancy, a student with him at the Slade and daughter of Hugh Culliford Sharp, doctor of medicine, of Truro. They had two daughters. The marriage was dissolved in 1942 and on 30 March 1961 he married Monica Mary, daughter of Alfred Eric Monrad Hoyer, journalist, of London. They had a son and two daughters. By 1982 his health had begun to decline, and by 1984 he could no longer paint. Although he attended the private view of his last solo exhibition (June 1984) at the Anthony D'Offay Gallery, he was by then unable to work. After a long illness, he died at the Homoeopathic Hospital in Camden, 18 February 1987.

[*The Times* and *Daily Telegraph*, 19 February 1987; *Independent*, 21 February 1987; *The Paintings of William Coldstream*, catalogue for Tate Gallery exhibition, 1990–1; *William Coldstream Memorial Meeting, 24 April 1987*, UCL booklet, 1988; private information; personal knowledge.]   IAN TREGARTHEN JENKIN

COLLAR, (Arthur) Roderick (1908–1986), mathematician and aeronautical engineer, was born 22 February 1908 in West Ealing, London, the second of three children and elder son of Arthur Collar, of Whitstable, Kent, who had a successful ironmonger's and builder's business, and his wife, Louie Gann, who also came from a Kent family. He was educated at the local board school in Whitstable, from where he gained a scholarship to Simon Langton School in Canterbury. Here he developed his mathematical and scientific ability, and became good at games and an accomplished piano-player and violinist. It was in a football match that, at the age of fifteen, he was struck a blow that led to the permanent loss of sight in his right eye. In 1926 he entered Emmanuel College, Cambridge, as an open scholar. He obtained a first in part i of the mathematical tripos in 1927 and a second in part ii of the natural sciences tripos in 1929.

Collar sought an appointment in 1929 in the National Physical Laboratory at Teddington, and soon found working there, in the aerodynamics department under E. F. *Relf, so congenial that he stayed from 1929 until the beginning of World War II in 1939. In 1930 the airship R101 crashed in France on its maiden voyage to India, and Collar's ability came to the fore when he made skilful step-by-step calculations on the airship's motion prior to the disaster. It was, however, for his work on the application of matrices to aeroplane flutter that Collar was best known at the NPL. Initiated by R. A. Frazer, this work had been fostered by the aeronautical research committee, which later brought Frazer, W. J. Duncan, and Collar together to produce in 1938 the first textbook on the subject—*Elementary Matrices*, which proved a best seller in Britain and the USA, and was later translated into Russian and Czech. This basic work on flutter was developed at the Royal Aeronautical Establishment (RAE) into a design tool in time to ensure that the new fighter aircraft being built prior to World War II—the Hurricane and Spitfire—were flutter free. With the onset of war, in 1941 Collar was transferred to the RAE, to help with this design work.

After the war several universities considered introducing aeronautical engineering into their engineering faculties. One of the first to do so

was Bristol University, which in 1945 invited
Collar to be the first holder of the Sir George
White chair in aeronautics. After he took up the
post in 1946 his new department prospered in
new accommodation. From 1954 to 1957 he was
dean of the faculty and in 1968, after the sudden
death of the vice-chancellor, he was persuaded to
hold this position for seventeen months, pending
the appointment of a successor. Collar's personality made all this seem natural; a sincere Christian and a born raconteur, with a slim athletic
build, who enjoyed cricket and music, he was an
attractive colleague.

Collar always took an active part in the Royal
Aeronautical Society (he was president in 1963–4
and became an honorary fellow in 1973), and
won a number of its principal prizes, including
the society's gold medal in 1966. He was
appointed CBE in 1964 and elected a fellow of
the Royal Society in 1965. His outstanding
aeronautical work led to his appointment as
chairman of the Aeronautical Research Council
(1964–8). He also served on the councils of the
Rolls-Royce Technical College, the Royal Military College of Science, Clifton College, the
Cranfield Institute of Technology, and the Royal
Society. He had honorary degrees from Bristol
(1969), Bath (1971), and Cranfield (1976).

In 1934 Collar married Winifred Margaret
Charlotte, of East Molesey, Surrey, daughter of
Ernest George Whittington Earl Moorman, a
clerk in the office of works at Hampton Court
Palace. They had two sons. After his retirement
in 1973 from Bristol University, Collar began to
suffer from rheumatoid arthritis in his hands and
feet. Following a fall in a friend's garden in 1983,
he developed leukaemia. This left him severely ill
for the last years of his life and led to his death at
his home in Bristol, 12 February 1986.

[R. E. D. Bishop in *Biographical Memoirs of Fellows of
the Royal Society*, vol. xxxiii, 1987; personal knowledge.]   A. G. PUGSLEY

COLLINS, Cecil James Henry (1908–1989),
artist, was born in Plymouth 23 March 1908, the
only child of Henry Collins, an engineer in a
Plymouth laundry, and his wife, Mary Bowie. He
won scholarships to the Plymouth School of Art
(1924–7) and the Royal College of Art (1927–31),
where he was a favourite pupil of (Sir) William
*Rothenstein. At the Royal College he met a
fellow student, Elisabeth Ward Ramsden, whom
he married in 1931. She was the daughter of
Clifford Ramsden, editor and proprietor of the
Halifax Courier and Guardian. There were no
children of the marriage.

The chief contemporary artistic influences on
him at this time were Picasso and Klee: other
strong influences were Byzantine art, the music

of Igor Stravinsky's classical period, and contemporary scientific illustrations, both of cell biology
and of astronomy. His early love of *Shelley and
*Shakespeare was now augmented by his studies
of *Coleridge and *Milton. When he and his
wife went to live in a lonely cottage in Buckinghamshire, these influences, together with
readings in the English mystics and the silence of
the place, inspired him to do his first visionary
paintings, which were successfully shown at
his first London exhibition, at the Bloomsbury
Gallery in 1935. (Sir) Herbert *Read, much
impressed, included his work in the London
International Surrealist Exhibition in 1936. Collins's association with the Surrealists was short-
lived, for he was accused of religious sympathies
and excluded from the movement.

He went to live near Dartington, where the
American artist Mark Tobey was teaching.
Tobey and Bernard *Leach aroused his interest
in eastern thought and art. There he painted
several great works, such as 'The Voice', 'The
Quest', and the double portrait, 'The Artist and
his Wife' (1939, Tate Gallery). The artistic and
intellectual stimuli at Dartington, together with
the threat of war, inspired Collins to paint his
most famous series of works, based on the image
of the Fool, which he began in late 1939. To him
the Fool signified 'purity of consciousness' and
he gave to his many depictions of the image all
the qualities that were most threatened by war:
charm, fun, compassion, and insight. Rejected
for war service at a time when the Dartington
community was depleted by the internment of
many of its teachers, who had taken refuge there
from Germany, Collins was asked to teach, and it
was then that he discovered his great gifts as a
teacher.

His exhibition at the Lefevre Gallery in 1944,
even though cut short by a flying bomb, was an
outstanding success. Collins and his wife had left
Dartington by this time and lived variously in
London, Yorkshire, Oxford, and Cambridge. In
this period Collins produced his 'paradisal drawings' and experimented with print-making. He
also published in 1947 his essay *The Vision of the
Fool*, a work that expresses his feelings about the
role of the artist (the Fool) in the modern world
of war and industrialization.

This time of success was to be followed by a
long period when some critics turned against him
and others neglected him. He took up teaching
again, at the Central School from 1951 onwards,
and leaned towards the traditional images of
Christianity. He found a new freedom in painting large works, based on the principle of what he
called the 'matrix': he would let the image come
to him out of a preliminary working with his
paints in a seemingly wild and chaotic manner.
Thus he independently discovered something of

what the American abstract expressionists had been doing for years. These new works were shown in a major retrospective of his work at the Whitechapel Gallery in 1959. The matrix period led him to explore in greater depth the three main images of his work: the Fool, the Lady or Anima, and the Angel. The matrix period was followed by a return to a calmer, more classical, style in which he continued to express the moods of the spiritual worlds these images conveyed to him. The Fool, the Lady, and the Angel all have access to the world of the Great Happiness, which is the true source of our creativity. In his portrayals of the Lady Collins gave new expression to the ancient tradition of Wisdom or Sapientia as a beautiful woman and in his angels he showed creatures who are constantly and mysteriously always present and ready to give us guidance.

When in 1975 the Central School tried to end his teaching contract, his students arose in rebellion on his behalf. His contract was extended for a year, but the battle had to be fought again with each new generation of students marching and demonstrating, and with correspondence in national newspapers supporting his cause. The conflict, which arose from objections to the originality of his teaching methods and the metaphysical ideas on which they were founded, often debilitated him and distracted him from painting. Nevertheless he received support from other quarters, notably from his association with the Anthony d'Offay Gallery from 1976 onwards, an Arts Council film of his work in 1978, and a Tate Gallery exhibition of his prints in 1981, the year in which his poems *In the Solitude of this Land* and a reprint of *The Vision of the Fool* were published. These were to be followed by two full-length television documentaries in 1984 and 1988.

In early manhood and into middle age Collins wore a beard. In later years the curvature of his spine, brought about by deprivations in his early life, became very pronounced, though it never affected his co-ordination. He had great physical calm, with long, fine, thin fingers with which he would seemingly shape his sentences in front of him as he spoke. He was very nervous of catching colds and would often be seen in the hottest weather wearing a tweed suit, a thick tweed greatcoat, and a hat. His eyes were expressive, witty, and sharply observant.

Collins was present at the opening of the retrospective exhibition of his work at the Tate Gallery in May 1989 and died shortly afterwards in the London Clinic, 4 June 1989. He was buried in Highgate cemetery. He had been appointed MBE in 1979 and elected RA in 1988. A man of deep metaphysical interests, and with a scholar's analytical mind, he was regarded by

some as Britain's greatest visionary artist since William *Blake.

[William Anderson, *Cecil Collins: the Quest for the Great Happiness*, 1988; *Cecil Collins, Paintings and Drawings, 1935–45*, 1946; Kathleen Raine, *Cecil Collins, Painter of Paradise*, 1979; Judith Collins, *Cecil Collins* (catalogue of Tate Gallery retrospective exhibition), 1989; private information; personal knowledge.]

WILLIAM ANDERSON

COLVILLE, SIR **John Rupert** (1915–1987), diplomat and private secretary, was born in London 28 January 1915, the youngest of three sons (there were no daughters) of the Hon. George Charles Colville, barrister, and his wife, Lady (Helen) Cynthia Crewe-Milnes, daughter of Robert Offley Ashburton *Crewe-Milnes, Marquess of Crewe, politician. He was educated at West Downs School and Harrow and continued on a senior scholarship to Trinity College, Cambridge, where he obtained a first class in part i of the history tripos and a second class (division I) in part ii (1936). In 1937 he joined the Diplomatic Service and after only two years was seconded to 10 Downing Street to act as assistant private secretary to Neville *Chamberlain. He liked and admired Chamberlain and would have favoured Viscount (later the Earl of) *Halifax to succeed him in May 1940—'I am afraid it *must* be Winston,' he wrote regretfully in his diary—but even then he conceded *Churchill's drive and determination and he was quickly converted into one of the most devoted of his supporters.

Exciting and congenial though he found the work in No. 10, after the outbreak of World War II Colville resolved to enter the armed forces, and in October 1941 he overcame the opposition of the Foreign Office and the handicap of bad eyesight and joined the Royal Air Force Volunteer Reserve. After training in South Africa he was commissioned as a pilot officer and joined No. 268 Squadron of the Second Tactical Air Force, flying Mustang fighters. In spite of periodic efforts by Churchill to recapture him, he remained with the air force until the end of 1943 and was allowed to rejoin his unit for the invasion of France, returning to Whitehall for good in August 1944.

Although in spirit a Conservative, who had contemplated standing as such in 1945, Colville greatly admired C. R. (later first Earl) *Attlee's honesty, efficiency, and common sense, and found no difficulty in serving under him when Labour came to power. However, his career was still diplomacy and in October 1945 he returned to the Foreign Office to work in the southern department. After the dramas of No. 10 the work lacked savour, and within two years he had moved away again to become private secretary to the twenty-year-old Princess Elizabeth (1947–9). It was a natural appointment for a former page of honour to King *George V, whose mother was a woman of the bedchamber to Queen *Mary. No one would have been surprised if he had remained in royal service, but after two years he returned to diplomacy and was posted to Lisbon (1947–51) as first secretary.

It was not for long; when Churchill became prime minister in October 1951, Colville was invited—commanded, almost—to rejoin him as principal private secretary. When Churchill suffered a severe stroke in June 1953 but refused to allow his powers to be delegated, Colville and the prime minister's son-in-law and parliamentary private secretary, Christopher (later Baron) *Soames, found themselves called on to make decisions on matters about which they would normally never have been consulted. For almost a month, with the encouragement and support of the secretary of the cabinet, Sir Norman *Brook (later Baron Normanbrook), they dealt with government departments which had no conception of the gravity of the prime minister's condition, acting in his name and articulating what they believed would have been his views. They handled their duties with tact and discretion, but the experience fortified Colville's resolve not to return yet again to diplomacy after Churchill's resignation in April 1955.

Instead, he embarked on two new careers. He joined Hill Samuel and became a director of the National & Grindlay, Ottoman, and Coutts's banks and chairman of Eucalyptus Pulp Mills. He also took to writing. His first book, a biography of the sixth Viscount *Gort, Man of Valour (1972), won excellent reviews and encouraged him to follow it with, among others, a study of Churchill's entourage, The Churchillians (1981), and an autobiographical volume, Footprints in Time (1976). His best known work, however, was his edition of the diaries which he had kept while at No. 10, The Fringes of Power (1985), a colourful, informative, and admirably honest account of the years he spent working for Churchill. He also served as treasurer of the National Association of Boys' Clubs and president of the New Victoria Hospital in Kingston. Colville was appointed CVO (1949) and CB (1955), and was knighted in 1974. He was an officer of the Legion of Honour and an honorary fellow of Churchill College, Cambridge (1971), in whose foundation he played a role.

By birth, upbringing, and career, Colville seemed a quintessential establishment figure, but any tendency to pomposity or undue conventionality was curbed by his keen eye for the ridiculous. His tact, charm, good judgement, and readiness always to tell the truth when necessary, made him an ideal private secretary. He was stocky and of medium height, very dark, with a roundish face and slightly Latin appearance— 'Who is that foreigner with an English wife?' people would sometimes ask when he was

abroad. His hair went grey when he was in his forties, which gave him a more distinguished air: this concerned him little; he took no particular trouble over his appearance and, without being scruffy, was rarely smart. He married in 1948 Lady Margaret Egerton, lady-in-waiting to Princess Elizabeth and daughter of John Francis Granville Scrope Egerton, fourth Earl of Ellesmere. They had two sons and a daughter. He was still leading and enjoying an active life when on 19 November 1987 he suffered a heart attack while at Winchester station and died almost immediately.

[John Colville, The Fringes of Power, 1985, and Footprints in Time, 1976; private information; personal knowledge.]   PHILIP ZIEGLER

COOK, SIR William Richard Joseph (1905–1987), scientific civil servant, was born 10 April 1905 in Trowbridge, Wiltshire, the elder son and eldest of three children of John Cook, railway inspector, and his wife, Eva Boobyer. A successful scholar at Trowbridge High School, he went on to Bristol University, graduating B.Sc. in 1925, with first-class honours in mathematics (specializing in applied maths). He took a diploma in education in 1926 and an M.Sc. in 1927. Success as a part-time lecturer almost persuaded him to become a teacher, but he settled for the Civil Service and joined the research department at Woolwich Arsenal in 1928, as librarian.

After working for a time on the external ballistics of guns, he joined the new rocket programme in 1935, becoming by 1940 deputy controller of projectile development, where he was responsible for many successful military applications of rockets. At the end of the war Cook became first director of a new rocket establishment at Westcott, but uncertainty and disagreement about the future of the work unsettled him so much that in 1947 he moved to become director of physical research at the Admiralty, where, although the field was new to him, he was instrumental in pioneering major advances in underwater warfare technology. He became deputy chief scientific adviser, Ministry of Defence, in 1950, as well as chief of the Royal Naval Scientific Service.

In 1954 the government decided to develop thermonuclear weapons and Cook, an ideal choice, was appointed to lead the programme, as deputy director at Aldermaston. The essence of his work was to test the bomb before a possible test ban treaty could be imposed. A crash programme, driven by Cook, culminated in a successful test series based on Christmas Island in 1957. He himself went to the island to play a vital role as directing scientist. Following this demonstration of British thermonuclear capability, he played a leading role in the successful negotiations to re-establish co-operation with the United States. Cook left Aldermaston early in 1958 to become member for engineering and development in the Atomic Energy Authority and took over the newly formed reactor group in 1961. Here he achieved a great deal, resolving problems in the advanced gas-cooled reactor, bringing the fast reactor to full power, and recommending the construction of a heavy-water steam-generating reactor.

Cook returned to the Ministry of Defence in 1964 where, as a deputy chief scientific adviser, he took responsibility for operational requirements and projects. His immediate problem was the disorganization that followed the cancellation of the fighter bomber TSR2. An Anglo-French project for a fighter aircraft quickly failed when the French withdrew, and was replaced by a joint British–German–Italian effort. After much difficult negotiation, in which Cook played a prominent part, the successful Tornado fighter was specified and produced. In 1968 he became chief adviser, projects and research, and set up a number of important international projects intended to reduce defence costs. He also initiated the studies which led eventually to the Chevaline system to improve the defence penetration of the Polaris missile.

He retired in 1970 but soon became involved in commercial directorships, which kept him very busy for another fifteen years. Nationally the most important of these was Rolls-Royce, which had gone bankrupt in 1971. He was appointed to chair a committee to decide very quickly whether the RB211 engine should be continued, and it is largely to his credit that the engine eventually became the backbone of Rolls-Royce's civil programme. He was appointed a director when the new government-owned company was set up later in 1971. In addition to his directorships, he continued to chair, very effectively, the nuclear safety committees for another ten years. He was appointed CB in 1951, and KCB in 1970, having been knighted in 1968. He held honorary degrees from Strathclyde (1967) and Bath (1975). He was elected a fellow of the Royal Society in 1962.

Cook, known as 'Bill' to his friends and colleagues, was slightly built and always neatly dressed. A man of great charm and ready wit, fond of his pipe and of a Scotch, he was known for his meticulous preparation for meetings, his ability to find and probe the weaknesses in a technical case, and his forceful but good humoured pressure on all to give of their best. In 1929 he married Grace, daughter of Frederick Arthur Purnell, treasurer for Burton-on-Trent council; they had one daughter. They were divorced in 1939 and in the same year he married Gladys, librarian at the Woolwich Arsenal department, the daughter of Sydney Edward

Allen, postman. They had one son and one daughter. When Gladys's health began to fail he looked after her devotedly. He died 16 September 1987 in Westminster Hospital, London, following a massive stroke.

[Lord Penney and V. H. B. Macklen in *Biographical Memoirs of Fellows of the Royal Society*, vol. xxxiv, 1988; *The Times*, 19 September 1987; *Daily Telegraph*, 22 September 1987; personal knowledge.]

JOHN CHALLENS

COOPER, LADY **Diana Olivia Winifred Maud**, first VISCOUNTESS NORWICH (1892–1986), beauty, actress, memorable hostess and guest, and autobiographer, was born 29 August 1892 in London into the Manners family where she was accepted as the third of three daughters and the fifth of five children. Her assumed father was Henry John Brinsley Manners, Marquess of Granby, later eighth Duke of Rutland, MP, and her mother was Marion Margaret Violet, daughter of Colonel Charles Hugh Lindsay. It was generally believed, and certainly by Diana, that her true father was Henry John Cockayne ('Harry') *Cust, politician, journalist, and brother of the fifth Baron Brownlow. She received no formal education, but was educated at home by governesses and the culture of her surroundings. She learned much, including great drifts of poetry, which she remembered to her dying day. In her voluminous correspondence and in the drafts for her books, her prose was vivid and imaginative and her idiosyncratic spelling added to its charm.

At ten years old, Diana contracted Urb's disease, a form of paralysis, and for five years was a semi-invalid. She never complained, but, because of her illness, was certainly over-indulged by the family. In 1910 she formally 'came out' and took her place at the centre of that so-called 'golden generation', soon so largely to perish in war. At this time her beauty was first acknowledged. She was hailed 'queen of beauty', but also acquired some notoriety. She and her immediate circle dubbed themselves the 'corrupt coterie' and lived their lives of privilege to the full and sometimes to excess. Diana was much criticized when, at a party on the Thames in 1914, Sir Dennis Anson swam for a dare and was drowned; this tragedy haunted her all her life. When war came in 1914, Diana Manners trained as a member of the Voluntary Aid Detachment at Guy's Hospital. She was hard-working and conscientious and acted as a nurse at Guy's and at the hospital established by her parents in their London house in Arlington Street.

Diana had many suitors and mourned the deaths of several of them in the fighting. (Alfred) Duff *Cooper, at first in the Foreign Office and then in the Grenadier Guards, was amongst her most ardent admirers. In 1916 she promised to marry him, but was prevented by lack of money and opposition from her ambitious mother. Even the DSO, to which Duff Cooper was appointed in 1918, failed to overcome this opposition. Eventually, however, agreement was given and they were married on 2 June 1919. It was a marriage which never staled. Diana had many who loved her and Duff was frequently unfaithful; but for each the relationship with the other remained the most important thing in both their lives.

To earn money, Diana acted in two unmemorable films before her marriage and gained the reputation of a hard-working actress as well as a transcendent beauty. Marriage and Duff Cooper's wish to enter politics increased the need for money and Diana was glad to accept Max Reinhardt's offer to play the madonna in a mime play, *The Miracle*. This was first staged in the USA from November 1923 to the following May, and again for the following three autumns and winters. It toured Europe in 1927, and London and the provinces in 1932; the last performance was in January 1933. *The Miracle* was a phenomenal success and Diana Cooper's triumphant part in it was remembered as long as she lived. The money earned allowed her husband to enter Parliament, as MP for Oldham, in 1924.

On 15 September 1929 she had a son, John Julius. He was her only child and she took a close and intelligent interest in his education. Once *The Miracle* was ended, she was primarily concerned with her husband's career rather than her own and she gave him powerful support, as chatelaine of Admiralty House (Duff Cooper became first lord of the Admiralty in May 1937). There she first had the opportunity to display her outstanding talent as a hostess in a splendid setting. In the 1930s the Coopers were friendly with King Edward VIII and Mrs Simpson and accompanied them on the cruise of the *Nahlin* in 1936. They were spoken of as belonging to Mrs Simpson's camp, but this was never the case.

Diana supported Duff throughout World War II, even accompanying him to Singapore and the Far East against convention and in the face of opposition. When in Britain, they lived in the Dorchester Hotel and at Bognor in a house given to Diana by her mother, where she found complete happiness running a smallholding farm. In January 1944 Duff Cooper became British representative to the French committee of liberation in Algiers and in November British ambassador in Paris. His wife was unfailingly at his side; her French was fluent but inaccurate, and she was by no means a conventional ambassadress, but she gave the embassy a glamour possessed by none other. With her remarkable ability to get on with people, she collected a group of artists and writers known as 'La Bande'; it was said with criticism that some of them had collaborated

with the Germans. Whilst at the embassy, Diana Cooper discovered and rented the house 'she loved best in the world', the Château St Firman at Chantilly. On leaving the embassy at the end of 1947, contrary to convention and to the aggravation of their successors, the Coopers returned to live at Chantilly.

In 1952 Duff Cooper was created first Viscount Norwich, but Diana would have none of it, announcing in *The Times* that she wished to retain her former name and title, so 'Lady Diana Cooper' she remained. In 1953 Duff Cooper was taken violently ill and, although he recovered, died 1 January 1954 on a cruise to Jamaica. He was buried at Belvoir castle, but Diana did not attend the funeral: she never attended the funerals of those she loved. Her life had been centred round Duff for thirty-five years and she was distraught without him.

She lived for a further thirty-two years. She disliked getting old, but found solace in writing a three-volume autobiography, which was a resounding success. She gained much comfort from John Julius, her grandchildren, and her many friends. She retained her love of travel and her interest in people: she still enjoyed each new experience, even, it seemed, two burglaries, when she displayed her courage and her enduring star quality. She will be remembered mostly for her outstanding beauty, but for most people this obscured that she was a shy, very clever, and sometimes extremely funny woman. She died 16 June 1986, at her London home in Warwick Avenue.

[Philip Ziegler, *Diana Cooper*, 1981; Diana Cooper, *The Rainbow Comes and Goes*, 1958, *The Light of Common Day*, 1959, and *Trumpets from the Steep*, 1960; personal knowledge.]   CHARTERIS OF AMISFIELD

COSSLETT, (Vernon) Ellis (1908–1990), physicist and electron microscopist, was born 16 June 1908 in Cirencester, Gloucestershire, the eighth child in the family of six boys and five girls of Edgar William Cosslett, carpenter, and his wife, Anne Williams. His father worked on the Earl of Eldon's Stowell Park estate, and they lived in an isolated house on the site of the Roman villa at Chedworth. Because of illness, Ellis was seven when he entered elementary school in Cirencester, eight miles from home. At twelve he won a junior county scholarship to Cirencester Grammar School, and in 1926 a county scholarship took him to Bristol University, where he obtained first-class honours in chemistry (1929).

In 1929 he was awarded an ICI research studentship to work for a Bristol Ph.D. in chemistry. He spent the second year at the Kaiser Wilhelm Institute for Physical Chemistry in Berlin, and took full advantage of the opportunity, having acquired some German while an undergraduate. However, he did not know that at that very time the electron miscroscope was being invented by M. Knoll and E. Ruska only a few miles away. Witnessing the rise of the Nazi party had a traumatic effect, making him a lifelong worker for left-wing causes, although he concealed these views from most of his colleagues. He obtained his Ph.D. in 1932 and a London M.Sc. in 1939.

He moved to London in 1935 to teach at Faraday House and research part-time on electron optics at Birkbeck College under P. M. S. (later Baron) *Blackett, and later J. D. *Bernal. In 1939 he was awarded a Keddey–Fletcher–Warr research fellowship but, in the autumn, Birkbeck was evacuated to Oxford and he spent the war years teaching physics to short-course officer cadets in the electrical laboratory of Oxford University. He maintained his interest in electron optics and became increasingly convinced of the possibilities of the electron microscope: although he had barely set eyes on one, he was a founder of the Electron Microscope Group of the Institute of Physics in 1946.

In the same year Cosslett was awarded an ICI fellowship at the Cavendish Laboratory, Cambridge, where there was an electron microscope, which had been received during the war under lend-lease arrangements with the USA. Cosslett's life's work was now beginning. Even before he was appointed lecturer in 1949, he started to attract bright young research students to his EM section, nearly all of whom made important contributions to electron microscopy then, and in their later careers. At its peak the section had forty members. Noteworthy projects which were brought to successful conclusions were: the X-ray projection microscope (1955), the X-ray scanning microprobe analyser (1959), a high voltage (750 kilovolts) electron microscope (1966), and, jointly with the Cambridge engineering department, a high resolution (<0.2 nm) electron microscope (1979). Commercial developments followed from all these projects. Writing occupied much of Cosslett's time and he published four books, including *Practical Electron Microscopy* (1951) and *Modern Microscopy* (1966), and many papers.

He was little involved with undergraduate teaching and was not elected to a college fellowship (at Corpus Christi) until 1963. In 1965 he became reader in electron physics and was also awarded the Sc.D. Cosslett's achievements, which were considerable, lay not in proposing new principles, or the design and engineering of new instruments, but in drawing together the many diverse strands of the rapidly developing subject that embraced the whole of biology and material sciences. He was adept in attracting good students, guiding them towards rewarding projects, obtaining grants to finance them, and

keeping them informed about work in progress in other laboratories all over the world. Early on, he very quickly built up an international reputation and was a founder member and first secretary (1955) of the International Federation of Societies for Electron Microscopy.

In 1972 he was elected a fellow of the Royal Society; he was awarded its Royal medal in 1979. He shared the Duddell medal of the Institute of Physics (1971), and received honorary degrees from Tübingen (D.Sc., 1963) and Gothenburg (MD, 1974). He was an honorary fellow (1965) of the Royal Microscopical Society and served as president (1961–3).

Cosslett was a mild-mannered and courteous man but there were fires within, which, on rare occasions and to the dismay of those present, would burst out spectacularly. Outside microscopy, interests that he shared with his second wife included mountain walking, listening to music, and gardening. In 1936 he married Rosemary, a teacher at Clifton Girls' College and daughter of James Stanley Wilson, graduate electrical engineer, of Barking, Essex. In 1940 the marriage was dissolved and in the same year he married Anna Joanna, daughter of Josef Wischin, a railway official in Vienna. She was a microscopist who had recently arrived in London as a refugee; they had a son and a daughter. She continued with her research and played an important part in the EM section until her death in 1969. After some years of increasing disability, Cosslett died at his home, 31 Comberton Road in the village of Barton near Cambridge, 21 November 1990.

[T. Mulvey in *Biographical Memoirs of the Royal Society*, vol. xl, 1994; V. E. Cosslett, 'The Development of Electron Microscopy and Related Techniques at the Cavendish Laboratory, Cambridge, 1946–1979', *Contemporary Physics*, vol. xxii, 1981, pp. 3–36 and 147–82; private information; personal knowledge.]

DENNIS McMULLAN

COTTON, (Thomas) Henry (1907–1987), golfer, was born 26 January 1907 in Holmes Chapel, Cheshire, the second son in the family of two sons and one daughter of George Cotton, industrialist, inventor, and Wesleyan lay preacher, and his second wife, Alice le Poidevin, a native of Guernsey. His early childhood was spent in Peckham. He and his brother Leslie went to Ivydale Road School, Peckham, and, after their evacuation from London in World War I, to Reigate Grammar School. Thereafter Cotton won a scholarship to Alleyn's School. The war over, George Cotton obtained junior membership for both boys at the Aquarius Golf Club, and both won the club championship before reaching their teens. From the time he left Alleyn's (after irritating the headmaster) to become a golf professional at sixteen, Cotton trod a path of his own. His aloofness lost him popularity with contemporaries, and his strong will brought him into conflict with golf's rulers, but he rarely deviated from his chosen course. His achievements were founded on intense application and self-reliance.

When he entered his profession, the status of golf professional was barely above that of a senior caddy. By personal example Cotton did more than anyone of his time to alter that. He sought the best: silk shirts from Jermyn Street, limousines rather than taxis, and the best restaurants. Though he was to win three British Open Championships and many famous victories, the impact he made on his own profession was his greatest attainment. He was not long content to be the junior of six assistants at Fulwell Golf Club on 12s. 6d. a week. Within a year he had moved to an assistant's post at Rye. There he made friends with Cyril *Tolley, a fine amateur golfer, who assisted his next move. At nineteen, Cotton went to Langley Park, the youngest head professional in the history of British golf.

At this point Cotton perceived that to reach the top in golf he must challenge American supremacy. With the blessing of his club, £300, and a first-class ticket on the *Aquitania*, he joined America's winter season of 1928–9. A year later he was invited to Argentina to teach and play exhibition matches with a fellow professional. There (Maria) Isabel Estanguet Moss booked him for fifty lessons. The daughter of Pedro Estanguet, a wealthy landowner, and his wife Epifania, and married to Enrique Moss, of Argentina's diplomatic service, 'Toots', as she became universally known, was five years Cotton's senior. They formed a close partnership, which transformed both their lives. Eventually, on the annulment in Latvia in June 1939 of her first marriage, they married at a Westminster register office in December 1939. They had no children, although there were two daughters from Isabel's first marriage. Passionately loyal to Cotton's interests, when occasion demanded she became his most trenchant critic.

Cotton won three Open victories (1934 at Royal St George's, 1937 at Carnoustie, and 1948 at Muirfield). After seven years at Langley Park, Cotton had taken a post at Waterloo, a fashionable club near Brussels. But after his first Open win, he was persuaded by the sixth Earl of *Rosebery to build up the reputation of Ashridge Golf Club. The outbreak of World War II interrupted a career at the peak of success. Cotton joined the Royal Air Force, and suffered a regime which aggravated his stomach ulcer. Medically discharged, with the rank of flight lieutenant, he raised £70,000 for the Red Cross and other war charities from 130 matches which he organized. He took appointments first at Coombe Hill and then Royal Mid-Surrey. From there he won his last Open in 1948. That was the apogee of a career in which he had dominated tournament golf for some twenty years. He was also captain of the British Ryder Cup team in 1939, 1947, and 1953. Though there were minor wins in 1953 and 1954, writing, teaching, and golf architecture became main outlets. He wrote several books on golf, as well as designing thirteen golf courses in Britain and ten more abroad.

In 1963 Cotton went to Portugal and on the Algarve coast created from a swamp the Penina Golf Course, which became his memorial. He became virtually squire of the place until the Portuguese revolution of April 1974, during which he was expelled. Profoundly depressed by enforced exile, Cotton was rallied by his wife and they moved for a spell to Sotogrande in Spain. After a two-year interlude they returned to Portugal. There, at Christmas 1982 Toots died, ending half a century's close partnership. In 1987 Cotton entered King Edward VII Hospital, and there received intimation of his knighthood. He had been appointed MBE in 1946. During his convalescence he died suddenly in King Edward VII Hospital, London, 22 December 1987, and was buried at Mexilhoeira Grande in Portugal. He was knighted posthumously in the New Year's honours of 1988.

Always an individualist, Cotton taught that golfing excellence demanded infinite pains. He believed in strong hands and could hit a succession of one-handed shots without regripping the club. A severe opponent, he was also an excellent host. Tireless in pursuit of his own goals, he freely shared with a generation of young golfers more insight into the game than any other figure of his time.

[Henry Cotton, *This Game of Golf*, 1948; Peter Dobereiner, *Maestro: the Life of Henry Cotton*, 1992; personal knowledge.]   W. F. DEEDES

COUSINS, Frank (1904–1986), trade-union leader, was born 8 September 1904 at 28 Minerva Street, Bulwell, Nottinghamshire, the eldest son in a family of ten (five sons and five daughters) of Charles Fox Cousins, miner, and his wife Hannah Smith, the daughter of a miner from Bulwell. He was educated at Beckett Road School in Wheatley, Doncaster, and King Edward Elementary School, Doncaster, which he left at the age of fourteen in 1918 shortly before the end of World War I. He immediately started work alongside his father, as a trainee at Brodsworth colliery in Doncaster, where he worked underground and joined the mineworkers' union (then the Yorkshire Miners' Association, which was part of the Miners' Federation of Great Britain, the forerunner of the National Union of Mineworkers).

After working in the colliery for more than

five years Cousins left to become a truck driver, first delivering coal locally and then, in 1931, as a long-distance road-haulage driver—by which time he had joined the Transport and General Workers' Union, led by Ernest *Bevin. He mostly ferried meat between Scotland and London until July 1938, when he became a full-time official of the TGWU, as an organizer in the Doncaster district. In one sense he was born into trade unionism as were so many of his generation—men of great natural ability but without extended education or social opportunities open to the more prosperous groups in society. Becoming a trade-union activist was a calling, quite the equal of similarly dedicated work for a political party. At this time Cousins first met Ernest Bevin, clashing with him over organizing road haulage workers into the union. It was a brotherly clash, but one which both men remembered, and especially Cousins, since he felt it may have been a turning-point in his own career, demonstrating as it did his characteristic style as a fearless, stubborn, awkward, and rebellious negotiator.

His physical stature helped to accentuate these characteristics: he was six feet four inches tall, powerfully built, and immensely strong. He spoke with a sharp rasping tone, especially when excited by events. His loyalty to his principles and political beliefs was absolute.

His development as a full-time official for the TGWU took him from Doncaster to Sheffield during World War II. In 1944 he was appointed to his first national trade-union post, as national officer for the road haulage section of the TGWU, based in London. In October 1948 Cousins was appointed national secretary for the group, a substantial achievement in view of his difficult relationship with the TGWU general secretary, Arthur *Deakin, with whom Cousins had frequently clashed, on industrial as well as political policy. Deakin, a rock of the established right-wing authority of the trade-union movement, sought to keep Cousins firmly under control and, where possible, deny him advancement in the union. But a series of remarkable circumstances thrust Cousins into the top ranks of the TGWU.

Deakin died in 1955 before he could secure his preferred successor. The job of general secretary of the TGWU, arguably the most important power-broking role in the British Labour movement, then went to Deakin's number two, Arthur Tiffin, and to everyone's surprise Cousins was appointed by the union's executive as Tiffin's deputy. Tiffin died unexpectedly within six months of taking over and on 2 January 1956 Cousins was appointed 'acting' general secretary. Later, on 11 May 1956, after a union ballot, he was confirmed as general secretary by 503,560 votes to 77,916—which was the largest ballot

return in the history of any British trade union. At that time the union ran membership ballots only for the general secretary's post.

The whole affair was an extraordinary sequence of events, which was to have far-reaching consequences for the entire Labour movement—especially for the Labour party, then under the leadership of Hugh *Gaitskell. The largest union in the country had a left-wing radical at the helm for the first time in its history. Cousins immediately made an impact on the industrial front, first in the motor industry, where he inherited a difficult and tense climate of industrial relations as automation was being introduced, and then in London buses, where he led a strike lasting nearly two months. At the same time he quickly sought to switch the TGWU's traditional political stance from staunchly pro-Gaitskell to the support of Aneurin *Bevan and the Bevanite left. In fact he went beyond this and personally associated himself and his family with the Campaign for Nuclear Disarmament. In 1960 Cousins led the campaign to 'Ban the Bomb' at the Labour party conference at which Gaitskell was defeated on defence policy. The defeat precipitated Gaitskell's famous 'fight, fight, and fight again' speech.

After Gaitskell's death in 1963 Cousins played a prominent part in helping to secure Harold Wilson (later Baron Wilson of Rievaulx) as leader of the Labour party. In October 1964, when Wilson won the general election, Cousins was invited into the Labour cabinet as the first minister of technology. At the same time he was sworn of the Privy Council. Yet the rebellious instinct refused to desert him even in the cabinet. He quickly found himself at odds with Wilson, as he opposed all moves by the Wilson government to establish a statutory incomes policy. When, in the end, he failed to persuade his cabinet colleagues, he resigned from the Wilson government in July 1966. Shortly afterwards he also resigned his parliamentary seat at Nuneaton—a seat that had been found for him in a by-election in 1964 and which he assumed in January 1965.

Cousins consistently resisted any form of state control over pay, carrying this opposition back with him to the TGWU where, after resigning from the government, he resumed as general secretary in 1966. Yet he never again quite recaptured the force of his earlier years. However, during the three years which remained before he retired from the TGWU in September 1969, he ensured the succession of his chosen 'crown prince', Jack Jones.

Cousins's final role was as the founding chairman of the Community Relations Commission, set up in 1968 by the Wilson government, and charged with improving race relations in Britain.

It was a cause close to Cousins's heart—so much so that he remained in the post for a short while even after the election of a Conservative government under (Sir) Edward Heath in 1970. Indeed, he was persuaded to do so by the home secretary, Reginald *Maudling. In November 1970 Cousins finally resigned his chairmanship of the CRC and went into retirement in the village of Wrington near Bristol, curiously enough only a few miles from where the founder of the TGWU, Ernest Bevin, was born. Cousins refused several invitations to return to public life and declined a seat in the House of Lords.

Cousins was the most forceful of all trade-union leaders to emerge in the postwar years; he had a remarkable and galvanizing effect on the rank and file of the entire Labour movement. He shifted the Labour party and the trade-union movement to the left and turned the Transport and General Workers' Union—the largest union in the country—from a pillar of the Labour right-wing establishment into a driving force for radical left-wing reform. Yet as a cabinet minister, the first minister of technology, he was a failure. Like so many 'imports' from industry, he could never come to terms with the climate of the House of Commons. Yet he did lay the foundations at the Ministry of Technology for a new approach to technological development.

In 1930 Cousins married Annie Elizabeth ('Nance'), daughter of Percy Judd, a railway clerk in Doncaster. They had two sons and two daughters. Cousins died 11 June 1986 in Chesterfield, Derbyshire.

[Geoffrey Goodman, *The Awkward Warrior*, 1979, and *Brother Frank*, 1969; Margaret Stewart, *Frank Cousins*, 1968; Jack Jones, *Union Man*, 1986; personal knowledge.]   GEOFFREY GOODMAN

CREDITOR, Dora (1901–1989), UK representative at the United Nations in the 1960s, and wife of Hugh Gaitskell, leader of the Labour party. [See GAITSKELL, ANNA DEBORAH ('DORA').]

CROFT, (John) Michael (1922–1986), founder and director of the National Youth Theatre, was born in Oswestry 8 March 1922, the child of Constance Croft, who was unmarried. As a young child he moved with his elder sister to live with his mother's sister in Manchester, where he was educated at Burnage Grammar School from 1933 to 1940. His adolescence was dominated by two passions, for literature (in particular, poetry, for which he had an almost photographic memory), and for team games, which he played with extreme gusto, but at which he achieved a limited effectiveness only in cricket, the rich lore of which always fascinated him.

He had little satisfaction or security from his home. He soon developed an uncompromising individualism and volunteered for aircrew duties

in the Royal Air Force in 1940. He became a sergeant-pilot and took part in daylight bombing raids over occupied France, but his manual dexterity proved unequal to the demands of flying, and he was offered the option of a discharge.

He had a variety of casual occupations, as an actor, professional 'fire-watcher' in ARP (Air Raid Precautions), credit salesman, and lumberjack, before he volunteered for the navy in 1943. After service in Mediterranean convoys, he finished the war as a radar operator on merchant ships.

In 1946 he went to Keble College, Oxford, to read English. He was a member of an exceptionally talented generation of ex-service students, and revelled in being able to indulge his love of literature, theatre, writing, and sport, while, at the same time, breaking university regulations by living in licensed premises. He took a special short-course degree and achieved a third class in English in 1948.

An unsettled period followed graduation. He did occasional journalism, poetry writing, broadcasting, and acting, and worked as a private tutor and a supply-teacher. From teaching, he gathered the material for his novel, *Spare the Rod* (1954), a minor *cause célèbre* amongst liberal educationists, which, after skirmishes with the Board of Censors, was filmed in 1961 with Max Bygraves as the sexually ambivalent schoolteacher. He also wrote *Red Carpet to China* (1958). Croft's final teaching post was at Alleyn's School, Dulwich (1950–5), where he staged a series of epic Shakespearian productions, involving the majority of the school's pupils, that aroused the interest of the London press and the professional theatre. His work was characterized by spectacle, vigour, commitment, and an unusual concern for verse-speaking: he wanted to envelop everybody in his huge enthusiasm and to make them share his fascination with the works of Shakespeare.

Spare the Rod gave him sufficient financial independence to resign from teaching, ostensibly to devote himself to writing, but it seems that he was persuaded by a group of ex-pupils, disconsolate at the loss of their Shakespeare play, to direct them in an out-of-term production of *Henry V* at Toynbee Hall in 1956. In effect, this was the first 'Youth Theatre' production and it determined the course of the rest of his life. The venture was self-supporting: ticket sales and donations were the only funding until, in 1958, King George's Jubilee Fund gave a grant which was continuous. Subsequently, the British Council and the Department of Education and Science provided support. There was a long and fairly acrimonious battle with the Arts Council before any funding was secured, only for it to be withdrawn after a few years. By 1970, Croft was able to claim, 'We have three companies touring in Europe, four in London, and one in the north-east of England—the whole being run by a full-time staff of four, with a handful of voluntary helpers.' Ahead lay the televising and broad-casting of youth theatre productions, the com-missioning of new works (significantly from Peter Terson and Barrie Keeffe in the 1970s), the visit to America, the acquiring of the Shaw theatre (1971), and, in 1977, official recognition of the National Youth Theatre of Great Brit-ain.

Croft gained an increasing reputation as an internationally respected director, and his com-panies added to the lustrous reputation of the English theatre, but the NYTGB struggled against inadequate funding. He saw his creation as the victim of national parsimony to the arts and he became more obviously an abrasive, militant publicist, enjoying a bare-knuckle approach to negotiation. He had a flair for discovering stars, such as Derek Jacobi, Helen Mirren, Ben Kingsley, and Diana Quick.

He was appointed OBE in 1971. After the straitened circumstances of his early days, his later success introduced him to an expansive lifestyle, which he delighted in sharing gen-erously with his vast number of friends and acquaintances. He was homosexual, but he had many friends of the opposite sex and, particularly in his early years, led a bisexual existence. He had few intimates, apparently finding it difficult to break down his core of loneliness. He was a man of gargantuan appetites in every way, espe-cially for food and drink, and his eventual failure to control these proclivities, allied to a dread of surgery, contributed to his comparatively early death. He died of a heart attack at his home in Kentish Town, 15 November 1986. A character-istic instruction in his will provided a party for a vetted list of some hundreds of his friends, 'at which the food shall be wholesome—and the drink shall not be allowed to run out'.

[Michael Croft's papers in private hands; personal knowledge.]   GEOFFREY SYKES

CROSS, (Arthur) Geoffrey (Neale), BARON CROSS OF CHELSEA (1904–1989), judge, was born in London 1 December 1904, the elder son and elder child of Arthur George Cross, quantity surveyor, of Hastings, and his wife, Mary Eliz-abeth Dalton. He was eight years older than his brother, (Sir) Rupert *Cross, a distinguished academic lawyer. He was a scholar of West-minster School, where his classical scholarship was firmly grounded. He then won a classical scholarship to Trinity College, Cambridge. First-class honours in both parts of the classical tripos (1923 and 1925) and the Craven scholar-ship (1925) followed. He was elected to a fellow-

ship of Trinity, which he held from 1927 to 1931. His book *Epirus*, published in 1932, became a classic.

But while he might have aspired to be a successor to Richard *Porson or Sir Richard *Jebb, he decided in favour of a career at the Chancery bar. He was called to the bar by the Middle Temple in 1930 and started to practise in Lincoln's Inn. His abilities were soon recog-nized. He built up a large junior practice, espe-cially in the somewhat esoteric field of estate duty, which amply justified him in taking silk in 1949. At that time the Chancery bar was excep-tionally strong. His contemporaries and rivals included Charles *Russell (later Baron Russell of Killowen), (Sir Edward) Milner *Holland, and (Sir) Andrew Clark, all formidable advocates. Cross's talents were less spectacular or rhetorical, but sometimes the more effective for that reason. Promotion to the Chancery bench was stagnant in the 1950s. There was no compulsory retire-ment age. Incumbents showed a marked reluc-tance to accept the limitations of increasing age and the inevitability of promotion was thus delayed. Ultimately however there were retire-ments and Milner Holland's refusal of the prof-fered appointment facilitated the promotion of Russell, Cross, and others. Thus the strong Chancery bar of the 1950s became the strong Chancery bench of the 1960s.

Cross's practice had been wide-ranging. He had been leading counsel for the Bank of Eng-land before the Bank rate leak enquiry in 1956. He was for many years closely involved on behalf of C. S. Gulbenkian and his family in the intricacies of the various agreements concerning the production and distribution of Middle East oil. Those who were involved with him at that time never ceased to admire his gifts for convert-ing the complex into the simple. His advice was widely sought because of his gifts of clarity of thought and expression. From 1960 (the year in which he was knighted) to 1969 he served as a judge of the Chancery Division, always charming and courteous to those appearing before him, quick to see the point and to reach his decisions. By chance, cases involving champagne, sherry, and toffee-apples came before him and not only brought him unaccustomed publicity, but revealed an enjoyment of life which had hitherto been known only to his family and friends.

He bought a house at Aldeburgh in Suffolk. This led him to sit as a deputy chairman of Suffolk quarter-sessions and to acquire for him the novel experience of the workings of the criminal law. He was fond of saying that the criticism of Chancery lawyers with their sup-posed love of technicality was misdirected. The criticism should be directed at criminal law-yers.

Promotion to the Court of Appeal came in 1969. After only two years, in 1971 he was promoted to the House of Lords as a lord of appeal in ordinary. But he decided to retire in 1975 upon the completion of his fifteen years' service. His relatively short time in the two appellate tribunals did not enable him to leave his mark as an appellate judge. He and his wife retired to Herefordshire, where they lived happily for the remainder of his life. He served for five years after his retirement as chairman of the appeal committee of the Takeover panel (1976–81) and occasionally chaired a select committee in the House of Lords. He had become a bencher of the Middle Temple in 1958 and an honorary fellow of Trinity College, Cambridge, in 1972. In his last years at the bar he was an admirable and sensitive chairman of the bar's charity, the Barristers' Benevolent Association. He was sworn of the Privy Council in 1969.

He had not only his intellectual gifts, but also warmth and charm. He was nearly six feet in height and somewhat short-sighted, but his thick lenses did not conceal his smile. He possessed a real humility and often wondered why so much had come his way when others had been less fortunate. He married in 1952 Joan, widow of Thomas Walton Davies and daughter of Lieutenant-Colonel Theodore Eardley Wilmot, who was killed in France in March 1918. There was a daughter of the marriage. Cross died in hospital in Hereford, 4 August 1989.

[*Independent*, 17 August 1989; private information; personal knowledge.]   ROSKILL

CROWTHER-HUNT, BARON (1920–1987), academic, constitutional expert, and broadcaster. [See HUNT, NORMAN CROWTHER.]

CUTHBERTSON, SIR David Paton (1900–1989), medical researcher and nutritionist, was born 9 May 1900 in Kilmarnock, Ayrshire, the only child of John Cuthbertson, MBE, FRSE, secretary of the West of Scotland Agricultural College, and his wife, Lilias Ann Bowman, formerly matron of Kilmarnock Infirmary. He was educated at Kilmarnock Academy. After army service (1918–19), first as a cadet, later as second lieutenant (temporary) in the Royal Scots Fusiliers, he entered Glasgow University, from which he graduated B.Sc. in 1921, with chemistry as the principal subject. He won the Dobie–Smith gold medal and was awarded a scholarship by the Scottish Board of Agriculture to undertake research in chemistry. He decided, however, that his interest in research required a medical degree and he graduated MB, Ch.B. from the University of Glasgow in 1926, having obtained the Hunter medal in physiology and the Strang–Steel scholarship for research, which enabled him to carry out the work during vacations for

his first scientific publication, in the *Biochemical Journal*, in 1925.

His first appointment (1926) was as lecturer in pathological biochemistry in the University of Glasgow and clinical biochemist to Glasgow Royal Infirmary. It was while holding this joint appointment that he carried out the initial studies on the changes in metabolism in surgical patients which led, later, to worldwide recognition. In the eight years he held this post, before being appointed to the Grieve lectureship in physiological chemistry in the University of Glasgow in 1934, he published twenty-seven papers, mainly on the effects of immobility, bed rest, infection, or injury, on metabolism in surgical patients. In 1934 he studied with Professor Karl Thomas in Leipzig University.

His nutritional investigations at this time included studies on the interactions of carbohydrate and fat with the metabolism of protein, some of which were carried out in collaboration with colleagues, of whom one, Hamish N. Munro, was to gain a considerable international reputation for his work in nutrition about thirty years later. In 1937 his MD was awarded with honours and he gained the Bellahouston medal of the University of Glasgow. Undoubtedly, however, it was the publication of his Arris and Gale lecture of the Royal College of Surgeons of England in the *Lancet* (1942, no. 1, pp. 433–7), entitled 'Post-shock Metabolic Response', which gained for him his greatest and enduring international recognition. Textbooks throughout the world came to refer to his general classification of the changes in metabolism which follow serious injury as the 'ebb' and 'flow' phases, the ebb phase corresponding to the period of clinical shock and the flow phase to the subsequent period of increased energy consumption, which gradually returns towards normal with healing and recovery.

During the later years of the 1939–45 world war business travel (to research or scientific committee meetings) became part of Cuthbertson's life and continued until his death. His secondment to the Medical Research Council in London in 1943 required frequent travel between Glasgow and London until 1945. In that year he became director of the Rowett Research Institute, Bucksburn, Aberdeen, a post which he held until retirement in 1965 with a knighthood, having been appointed CBE in 1957. Under his direction the Institute expanded with new buildings and facilities, such that in 1951 there were nine sections and in its jubilee year in 1963 the number of staff had increased fourfold. There were laboratories for studies with trace elements, radioactive isotopes, and a large animal calorimeter. The Rowett became internationally renowned in nutrition research.

On retirement Cuthbertson returned to full-time research on the changes in metabolism following injury, with support from the MRC and Glasgow Royal Infirmary. He continued to publish scientific papers and review articles, and travel widely to scientific meetings, being particularly welcome in the USA. Two of his notable attributes were his ability to obtain support for research and to encourage others. His eminence was recognized by honorary degrees from Rutgers (1958), Glasgow (1960), and Aberdeen (1972), and honorary fellowship or membership of royal colleges and societies.

Cuthbertson was six feet tall and had a pleasant personality and a gently positive approach. He found time for art, water-colours, and engraving, and many of his colleagues received personally engraved Christmas cards. Another activity was golf—he played in Scottish inter-university matches and for many years participated in the matches between the senates of the ancient Scottish universities. In 1928 he married a nursing sister in Glasgow Royal Infirmary, Jean Prentice (died 1987), daughter of the Revd Alexander Prentice Telfer, of Tarbet, Dunbartonshire. Cuthbertson died at home in Troon, 15 April 1989, having played golf in the morning. He is commemorated in the annual Cuthbertson lecture of the European Society for Parenteral and Enteral Nutrition and by a plaque in Glasgow Royal Infirmary.

[Personal records in the archives of the Royal Society of Edinburgh; personal knowledge.]   ADAM FLECK

CUTNER, Solomon (1902–1988), pianist. [See SOLOMON.]

D

DAHL, Roald (1916–1990), writer of children's fiction, was born 13 September 1916 in Llandaff near Cardiff, the youngest in a family of four daughters and two sons of Norwegian parents: Harald Dahl, who had given up farming near Oslo to make a fortune as a ship-broker in Wales, and his wife, Sofie Magdalene, daughter of Olaf Hesselberg, a meteorologist and classical scholar. His sister married the microbiologist (Sir) Ashley *Miles.

When Dahl was only three, a beloved older sister and, a few weeks later, his father both died. This was the first in a series of mortal disasters that dogged him, and, he said, gave his work a black savagery. His mother ran the family and gave Dahl a passion for reading. He was a rebel at Llandaff Cathedral School, St Peter's in Weston-super-Mare, and Repton. In his account of his childhood, he revealed the cruel flogging pleasurably inflicted by Repton's headmaster, G. F. *Fisher (later Baron Fisher of Lambeth, archbishop of Canterbury).

Resisting the attractions of a university education, at the age of eighteen he joined the Public Schools Exploring Society's expedition to Newfoundland, sponsored by Shell, and then joined Shell in 1934 and was sent to Dar-es-Salaam, Tanganyika. When war broke out in 1939, he drove to Nairobi, Kenya, to volunteer for the Royal Air Force. He served with No. 80 Fighter Squadron in the Western Desert (1940) and was severely wounded when his Hurricane crashed over Libya. He rejoined his squadron to serve in Greece and then Syria (1941). Invalided home to London, he was posted to Washington as assistant air attaché (1942–3), and worked in security (1943–5). He was appointed wing commander in 1943.

While he was in Washington in 1943, C. S. *Forester, creator of Captain Hornblower and author of many popular novels, asked Dahl to write an account of his most exciting RAF experience. Forester liked the contribution so much that he sent it to the *Saturday Evening Post*, which published it. Dahl's first book, originally written as a film script for Walt Disney, was *The Gremlins* (1943), which concerned a tribe of imaginary goblins who were blamed by the RAF for everything that went wrong with an aircraft.

Dahl claimed, mistakenly, to have invented the name.

His short stories, published in such noticeboards of the genre as the *New Yorker* and *Harper's Magazine*, tiptoed along the tightrope between the macabre and the comic in a manner reminiscent of Saki (H. H. *Munro) in that mode. In a typical Dahl plot, a woman murders her husband with a frozen leg of lamb and then feeds it to the investigating detectives, or a rich woman goes on a cruise, leaving her husband to perish in an elevator stuck between two floors in an empty house. When the stories were published as collections, *Someone Like You* (1954) and *Kiss Kiss* (1960), they made Dahl a celebrity, his fame being augmented by their translation to the television screen as *Tales of the Unexpected*, which ran for many years from 1965. They are bizarre examples of the fashionable genre of black comedy.

In 1953 Dahl married the film star Patricia Neal (on the rebound from her long affair with Gary Cooper). She was the daughter of William Burdett Neal, manager of the Southern Coal and Coke Company, of Packard, Kentucky. They had one son and four daughters, but one daughter died of measles in 1962, and their son was brain-damaged at the age of four months, when a cab hit his pram in New York. Dahl started writing children's books for his own children, characteristically because he thought the existing ones were 'bloody awful', and because he said he had run out of ideas for macabre short stories.

James and the Giant Peach (1967) was an instant new planet in the sky of children's books. Dahl also wrote, among others, *Charlie and the Chocolate Factory* (1967, filmed as *Willy Wonka and the Chocolate Factory*, 1971), *Fantastic Mr Fox* (1970), *Charlie and the Great Glass Elevator* (1973), *Danny, the Champion of the World* (1975), *The Enormous Crocodile* (1978), *The Twits* (1980), and *George's Marvellous Medicine* (1981). The books are rude, naughty, and violent, and children loved them, though some librarians and teachers did not. Children think that Dahl is on their side against the interfering and misunderstanding adult world.

While pregnant with their fifth child, Patricia Neal suffered a series of massive strokes, and was helped through her long recovery by Dahl, until she was well enough to resume acting. He then divorced her, in 1953, and in the same year married her best friend and his long-time mistress, Felicity Ann, former wife of Charles Reginald Hugh Crosland, businessman and farmer, and daughter of Alphonsus Liguori d'Abreu, thoracic surgeon, of Birmingham. They lived with the eight children of their previous marriages at Gipsy House, a white Georgian farmhouse in Great Missenden in Buckinghamshire. There Dahl wrote, always in pencil, in a hut in the garden.

Dahl wrote several scripts for films, among them the James Bond adventure, *You Only Live Twice* (1967), and *Chitty Chitty Bang Bang* (1968). He was six feet six inches tall, a chain-smoker, a lover of fine wine, a collector of contemporary painting, and a keen gambler on horses. His public statements were often intemperate, and some of his stories about himself were as tall as he was. But he had a magical touch for the macabre and the surrealist, and for a lord of misrule topsy-turvydom that made him the most popular children's writer of his age. He died 23 November 1990 in the John Radcliffe Hospital, Oxford.

[Barry Farrell, *Pat and Roald*, 1970; Roald Dahl, *Boy*, 1984, *Going Solo*, 1986, and *Ah Sweet Mystery of Life*, 1989 (autobiographies); Jeremy Treglown, *Roald Dahl: a Biography*, 1994; personal knowledge.]

PHILIP HOWARD

DAMM, Sheila Van (1922–1987), car rally driver and director of the Windmill theatre. [See VAN DAMM, SHEILA.]

DANIEL, Glyn Edmund (1914–1986), archaeologist and writer, was born 23 April 1914 at Lampeter Velfrey, Pembrokeshire, the only child of John Daniel, schoolmaster, and his wife, Mary Jane Edmunds. He was educated in his father's school at Llantwit Major (where they moved in 1919) and then at Barry County School, of which he had many happy memories, vividly recorded in his autobiography *Some Small Harvest* (1986). He gained a place for 1932 at St John's College, Cambridge, spending the preceding year at University College, Cardiff, studying geology and the organ. Turning to the archaeology and anthropology tripos at St John's, after getting a first in the qualifying examination for the geography tripos (1933), he graduated with first classes in both section A (1934) and section B (1935). He continued as a research student at St John's with a Strathcona studentship, receiving also an Allen scholarship in 1937.

The remarkable megalithic monuments of western Europe formed the subject of his research, both in Britain (his doctoral dissertation of 1938 being published in 1950 as *The Prehistoric Chamber Tombs of England and Wales*) and in France, where his first visit to Brittany in 1936 resulted eventually in *The Prehistoric Chamber Tombs of France* (1960), with an authoritative overview of the whole subject in *The Megalith Builders of Western Europe* (1958).

His doctoral dissertation won him a research fellowship at St John's in 1938, but his tenure was interrupted by the war. He served as an intelligence officer in the RAF (1940–5), becoming officer in charge of photo interpretation, India and south-east Asia (1942–5), rising to the rank of wing commander and being mentioned in dispatches. In India he met his future wife Ruth, daughter of the Revd Richard William Bailey Langhorne, headmaster of Exeter Cathedral Choristers' School. They were married in 1946, and their happy partnership formed thereafter a central part of his life. They had no children.

On his return from India he resumed his fellowship at St John's, another significant and enduring strand in his life, serving as steward from 1946 to 1955. He was made assistant lecturer in the department of archaeology in 1945, becoming lecturer, then reader, and then, in 1974, Disney professor and head of department until his retirement in 1981. He received a Cambridge Litt.D. in 1962.

Already with his first major publication, *The Three Ages* (1943), he showed an acute awareness of the relevance of the history of archaeology to current archaeological research. His *A Hundred Years of Archaeology* (1950), a pioneering study in the history of archaeology, perhaps his most important contribution, was followed by several others, including *The Idea of Prehistory* (1962).

As a teacher he excelled in kindling the enthusiasm of his pupils, many of whom became also his friends. He held that 'friendship is a conspiracy for pleasure', and while food and drink habitually formed part of that pleasure (a point well documented in *The Hungry Archaeologist in France*, 1963), people mattered more. His keen eye for character is deployed in his two detective novels (*The Cambridge Murders*, 1945, and *Welcome Death*, 1954), and his ebullient sense of humour comes over well in the small, privately published *The Pen of My Aunt* (1961). His love affair with France was consummated in 1964 by the purchase of a house in the Pas de Calais, which he and his wife visited frequently until the year of his death.

While his most influential academic work was in the history of archaeology, his greatest impact on the archaeology of postwar Britain was as a communicator, not least as chairman of the highly successful television panel game *Animal, Vegetable, Mineral?*, which made both Sir (R. E.) Mortimer *Wheeler and Glyn Daniel household names, and brought them the accolade of television personality of the year in 1954 and 1955 respectively. Daniel was a founding director of Anglia Television from 1959 to 1981. He was a brilliant and entertaining speaker and his public lectures and broadcasts made him widely known and recognized. As editor of the Ancient People and Places series for Thames & Hudson he commissioned over 100 volumes. He became editor of *Antiquity* in 1958, following the death of its founder-editor O. G. S. *Crawford the previous year. Yet he was not elected a fellow of the British Academy (where his role as a popularizer may have counted against him) until 1982.

He was a fellow of the Society of Antiquaries from 1942, and served as president of the Royal Anthropological Institute in 1977–9. A corresponding fellow of many learned societies overseas, he became a knight (first class) of the Dannebrog in 1961: Princess (later Queen) Margrethe of Denmark, like the prince of Wales, had been among his many distinguished pupils.

His scholarly contributions will be remembered, and yet the sheer humanity and zest that sparkle from his *Antiquity* editorials and from the pages of *Some Small Harvest* give as valid an insight into a remarkable teacher and scholar. A non-smoker, after a short illness he died of lung cancer at home in Cambridge, 13 December 1986.

[Glyn Daniel, *Some Small Harvest* (autobiography), 1986; Stuart Piggott in *Proceedings of the British Academy*, vol. lxxiv, 1988; J. D. Evans *et al.* (eds.), *Antiquity and Man: Essays in Honour of Glyn Daniel*, 1981; Glyn Daniel, *Writing for Antiquity*, ed. Ruth Daniel, 1992; personal knowledge.]   COLIN RENFREW

DAVIES, Duncan Sheppey (1921–1987), scientist, industrialist, and civil servant, was born in Liverpool 20 April 1921, the only child of Duncan Samuel Davies, stockbroker, and his wife, Elsie Dora, née May. He grew up in Liverpool and was educated at Liverpool College. He went to Oxford as a scholar at Trinity College, read chemistry, and graduated with first-class honours in 1943. His postgraduate research was supervised by (Sir) Cyril *Hinshelwood, a polymath and an internationally respected physical chemist. Unusually for that period he studied the kinetics of growth of bacterial cells, which was a field pioneered by Hinshelwood and a precursor to modern biotechnology. His D.Phil. was awarded in 1946. The years at Oxford formed him as a gifted scientist, a bounding spirit, and a warm and tolerant human being.

The principal part of his career was spent in Imperial Chemical Industries (ICI). In 1945 he joined the research department at the dyestuffs division in Blackley, Manchester, at a time when it teemed with chemical talent and spawned the fibres division and pharmaceutical division. He worked for ten years on the mechanism of organic reactions related to the manufacture and use of colours and fine chemicals. His exceptional talents began to be revealed when he took over a works experimental section in the colours department at Grangemouth works. Laboratory-derived techniques were applied with considerable ingenuity and success to full-scale operations. As research director of ICI general chemicals division at Runcorn (1959–62) he followed up this work and was involved in the initiation of major changes in the business portfolio and its associated research. The rebuilding of university relationships with the division proved to be a stepping-stone to his next post: director of the ICI petrochemical and polymer laboratory, 'charged with the creation of new innovative opportunities (products and processes) for ICI'. The hour and the man were well suited. He recruited about 400 scientists and managers from ICI, other companies, and universities all over the world. He introduced new ways of using the economics of the chemical industry to direct the choice of research programmes. He was one of the first people in the chemical industry to think automatically of it as a global business. Not surprisingly he introduced biotechnology into the laboratory.

Those around him, especially the young, were inspired to considerable achievement. Ideas of all sorts poured forth. He became a superb and challenging communicator, both in speech and writing. In this period he extended his influence to the universities and research councils. With Callum McCarthy he wrote *An Introduction to Technological Economics* (1967). He was one of the instigators of the much valued co-operative awards in science and engineering (CASE), in which a Ph.D. student was supervised by an industrial and an academic supervisor.

In 1967 he became deputy chairman of Mond division in Runcorn and in 1969 became general manager, research and development, at ICI headquarters. In this post he worked directly with the main board research and development director and was responsible for group research and development policy and connected matters, such as long-term future business and government contracts.

After a career spanning thirty-two years with ICI, Davies became chief scientist in the UK Department of Industry in 1977. He was the senior permanent civil servant responsible for policy in science, engineering, and technology. He gave renewed importance to the role of engineering in the UK and brought refreshing vigour to science in Whitehall. He championed biotechnology, as an exploitable technology. Davies himself became deeply attached to information technology, and when he retired from the department in 1982, he was an addict of personal computers.

He was a European and a member of the Club of Rome. As chairman he breathed new life into the British Ceramics Association. He was an ebullient president of the Society of Chemical Industry. Davies wrote, lectured, consulted, argued, and travelled. He was witty, erudite, loving, and lovable. His two great passions were Wagner and *Shakespeare. He was appointed CB in 1982, was an honorary fellow of UMIST, and received honorary degrees from the universities of Stirling (1975), Surrey (1980), and Bath (1981), and from the Technion in Haifa (1982), and he was a foreign associate of the US Academy of Engineering (1978).

Davies was a large bulky man, with a bluff cheerful face, warm welcoming personality, and an abundance of energy. In 1944 he married (Joan) Ann, daughter of Edward Noel Frimston, cotton broker, and Caroline Ethel Martin, a Liverpool artist. They had a son and three daughters. Davies died in Paris, 25 March 1987.

[Private information; personal knowledge.]

GEOFFREY ALLEN

DAVIS, SIR William Wellclose (1901–1987), admiral, was born in Simla 11 October 1901, the elder son and eldest of three children of Walter Stewart Davis, of the Indian Political Service, and his wife, Georgina Rose. Having been to Summer Fields School in Oxford, he joined the Royal Navy as a cadet in May 1915 and attended the naval colleges, Osborne and Dartmouth. He first went to sea as a midshipman in the battleship *Neptune* in 1917. He specialized in torpedoes in 1926 and quickly showed his ability as a staff officer. He was fleet torpedo officer to Admiral Sir Frederic *Dreyer on the China station and was promoted to commander in 1935. He then became fleet torpedo officer and staff officer, plans, to the commander-in-chief, Home Fleet, and was subsequently appointed executive officer of the battle cruiser *Hood* in January 1939. He served in her for the first eighteen months of World War II and was mentioned in dispatches.

Promoted to captain in December 1940, Davis went to the Admiralty as deputy director of plans. He was for a time seconded to the staff of Admiral of the Fleet Sir Roger (later first Baron) *Keyes, director of combined operations. Davis displayed his tact in his handling of Operation Workshop—the projected seizure of the Mediterranean island of Pantelleria, a plan proposed by Keyes and espoused by (Sir) Winston *Churchill, but fiercely resisted by the chiefs of staff and by Admiral Sir Andrew *Cunningham (later Viscount Cunningham of Hyndhope), the C-in-C, Mediterranean. Operation Workshop never took place, but Davis himself emerged with credit, Keyes calling him 'the admirable staff officer'.

In March 1943 Davis took command of the cruiser *Mauritius*, a ship in a very sensitive state of discipline, which was aggravated in January 1944 when she arrived in Plymouth Sound with her ship's company expecting to pay off. In spite of Davis's representations to the Admiralty, proper leave was not granted and the ship had to return almost at once to the Mediterranean. Her sailors believed, not unreasonably, that they were being punished for previous acts of indiscipline and there was further unrest, with outright refusals of duty. It was a discouraging start, but Davis, with his gift for making people work together, turned the commission into a triumph. *Mauritius* was the only major British warship to take part in the four invasions, of Sicily, Salerno, Anzio, and Normandy, bombarding enemy shore positions on more than 250 occasions. Later in 1944 *Mauritius* destroyed two enemy convoys in the Bay of Biscay. Davis himself was mentioned in dispatches three more times and appointed to the DSO with bar (1944).

After the war Davis was director of the underwater weapons division at the Admiralty, where he helped to form the new electrical branch, and then he became chief of staff to the C-in-C, Home Fleet (1948–9). Promoted to rear-admiral in 1950, he was naval secretary to three first lords of the Admiralty. From 1952 to 1954 he was flag officer, second in command, Mediterranean Fleet, when the first Earl *Mountbatten of Burma was C-in-C. It was made clear to Davis that he was to run the fleet while Mountbatten dealt with the numerous political and strategic problems in the Mediterranean.

A tall man, and extremely good-looking in his youth, Davis had great personal charm and a good brain. There was nothing bombastic or dramatic about him; he was no fire-eater. But when he went to the Admiralty in 1954, as vice-chief of the naval staff, he provided the competent, imperturbable staff work which ably supported the much more flamboyant Mountbatten, then first sea lord, during a seemingly interminable series of crises in the late 1950s, notably the 'Crabb affair', when Commander Crabb, a naval frogman, disappeared whilst allegedly inspecting the propellers of the Soviet cruiser which had brought Bulganin and Khrushchev to Portsmouth in 1956; the Suez operation, later that year, which Mountbatten himself deplored; and the navy's response to the swingeing cuts proposed by the 1957 white paper of Duncan *Sandys (later Baron Duncan-Sandys), a man whom Davis privately thought had little grasp of the strategic needs of the country.

His last appointment, as a full admiral, was from 1958 to 1960 as C-in-C, Home Fleet, and NATO C-in-C, eastern Atlantic. He was by then the only senior naval officer still serving who had served in World War I. He was also the first C-in-C to haul down his flag afloat and hoist it again ashore over the 'Führer Bunker', the NATO headquarters at Northwood in Middlesex. He was appointed CB in 1952, KCB in 1956, and GCB in 1959. After he retired in 1960 he devoted much time to county affairs in Gloucestershire. To the end of his life he took a close interest in naval history and naval affairs.

In 1934 he married Lady (Gertrude) Elizabeth, second daughter of Constantine Charles Henry Phipps, third Marquess of Normanby, canon of St George's chapel, Windsor. She died in 1985. They had two sons and two daughters. Davis died in hospital in Gloucester, 29 October 1987.

[*Daily Telegraph*, 2 November 1987; unpublished autobiography in the possession of the family; private information.]   JOHN WINTON

DE BEER, Esmond Samuel (1895–1990), historian and benefactor, was born 15 September 1895 in Dunedin, New Zealand, the second son and fourth and youngest child of Isidore Samuel de Beer, merchant, and his wife Emily, daughter of Bendix Hallenstein. His family on both sides was Jewish and had reached New Zealand from Germany, by way of Australia, during the 1860s, in his grandfather's generation. The continuing success of Hallensteins, the family clothing chain, gave de Beer ample means for a life of private research in England, where he lived from his school-days onwards. It was never necessary for him to hold a salaried post. From his early schooling in Dunedin, de Beer was sent in 1910 to Mill Hill School, from which he went up to New College, Oxford, in 1914 to read history. After army service, first in the ranks and then as a lieutenant in the 2/35th Sikh Regiment of the Indian Army (1916–19), he returned to Oxford, taking a special wartime BA in 1920 (MA 1925). He then studied at University College London and in 1923 received a London MA for a thesis on political parties during the ministry of Sir Thomas *Osborne, first Earl of Danby.

The later seventeenth century remained de Beer's lifelong intellectual centre. As he wrote of his mentor, Sir Charles *Firth, whose assistant he became, he was at home there and almost on terms of friendship with its men and women. He built up a large private library, most of which was dispersed by gift, chiefly to the University of Otago, in the 1980s, when he could himself no longer use it. An omnivorous reader, he retained so well what he read that, in his last bedridden years when his sight had failed, he could pass time by recalling it verbatim. Together with his sisters, Mary (1890–1981) and Dora (1891–1982), his companions in a succession of London houses, he made a small but well chosen art collection, which he gave to Dunedin Public Art Gallery in 1982. He and they had already given Iolo A. Williams's library of eighteenth-century

English literature to the university and made a succession of other substantial gifts to the Dunedin Public Art Gallery and the Otago Museum.

De Beer's scholarly reputation derived from his editions of the diary of John *Evelyn and the correspondence of John *Locke. They were carried through virtually single-handed, despite the impression given by the punctilio of his acknowledgements. Taken together, they provide a remarkable overview of the cultural and intellectual milieu of their time, being marked by an easy mastery of bibliographical, biographical, literary, and historical skills as well as of the circumstances of living in and out of seventeenth-century England. Their editor's curiosity and his conviction that the treatment of any topic should be complete, as far as its carefully weighed merits allowed, exactly balance his feeling for conciseness and his passion for eliminating the otiose. He began work on Evelyn in the late 1920s by revising an existing transcript. Early in the 1930s he was formally invited by the Clarendon Press to prepare their edition. As published in 1955 the six volumes are the first satisfactory rendering of the *Diary* and its author: a full and scrupulous text, sustained by an introduction and appendices and by some 12,000 footnotes, the whole made accessible by a large and exemplary index. Separately published by-products were magisterial essays on the origin and diffusion of the term 'Gothic', the development of the European guidebook, and the early history of London street lighting.

In 1956, after the task had been refused by another scholar, de Beer began the second great instalment of his life's work, his Clarendon Press edition of Locke's correspondence. He himself brought together much of the material. When its first two volumes appeared in 1976 he was already past eighty, but he followed them punctually with five more before his health began seriously to decline in 1982. The eighth, completing the record of some 3,650 items, came out in 1989.

De Beer's direct services to scholarship were supplemented by unstinting generosity to institutions, societies, and individuals, for preference through intermediaries, in his lifetime and by bequest. He gave generous and judicious support to the Bodleian, British, and London Libraries, where he was a regular reader; his subsidies ensured the publication of J. C. *Beaglehole's edition of the journals of Captain James *Cook and the Anglo-Australian edition of Cook's charts and views. He was both benefactor and practical helper of the Royal Historical Society, the Historical Association, the Bibliographical Society, and the London Topographical Society. Two London University institutes engaged his special loyalty: he was honorary librarian at the

Institute of Historical Research (1940–5), and he and his sisters established at the Warburg Institute a fund in memory of Fritz *Saxl. He was an honorary fellow of the Warburg (1978) and of New College, Oxford (1959), and a fellow of University College London (1967), the Society of Antiquaries (1942), the Royal Society of Literature (1958), and the Royal Historical Society (1927), besides being vice-president (1966) and president (1972–8) of the Hakluyt Society and vice-president of the Cromwell Association (1980). He held honorary doctorates from the universities of Durham (1956), Oxford (1957), and Otago (1963) and he was a trustee of the National Portrait Gallery (1959–67) and a member of the reviewing committee for the export of works of art (1965–70). In 1965 he was elected a fellow of the British Academy and in 1969 he was appointed CBE.

De Beer valued such recognitions. He prized more highly, however, the private, individual state that allowed him freedom personally and vicariously to advance learning. By disposition bookish, shy, and a little stiff, mildly pedantic, deliberate and precise in manner and speech, he was also courteous, friendly, and humorous. He had a knowledgeable love of comfort, food, wine, and travel, especially in Italy. His physical stamina matched his scholarly tenacity. A tireless walker and a climber, he took special pleasure in the far south of the South Island of New Zealand and the island of Raasay near Skye, where he spent summer holidays in company with his sisters and others. He had a wide acquaintance with literature, particularly drama, *Shakespeare and Ibsen being two of his heroes, and with music, principally opera. In adult life he neither practised the Jewish religion nor adopted another. De Beer's aspect was dapper and benevolent: he always wore spectacles and a small moustache. Of middle height, he was broad-shouldered but thinnish in build, with a large and powerful head. A confirmed and lifelong bachelor, he died 3 October 1990 in Stoke House, Stoke Hammond, north Buckinghamshire, a residential home for the aged.

[Charles Brasch, *Indirections: a Memoir 1909–1947*, 1980; *Addresses given at Memorial Gathering at the Warburg Institute, London, on 6 December, 1990*, 1990; Michael Strachan, *Esmond de Beer (1895–1990), Scholar and Benefactor: A Personal Memoir*, with a Bibliography by J. S. G. Simmons, 1995; personal knowledge.]
         J. B. TRAPP

DE FERRANTI, Basil Reginald Vincent Ziani (1930–1988), industrialist and politician. [See FERRANTI, BASIL REGINALD VINCENT ZIANI DE.]

DE MANIO, Jack (1914–1988), broadcaster, was born 26 January 1914 in Hampstead, London, the only child of Jean Baptiste de Manio, an Italian aviator, and his Polish wife, Florence Olga. Before he was born his father, the first person to fly across the English Channel in winter, was killed in a flying accident during a race to Lisbon. His mother, an eccentric and fashionable woman, never remarried but had many male admirers. She spoke eight languages, but her English was bad, and de Manio later attributed his poor progress in reading and writing to this. He claimed to have been born a Catholic and brought up for a time as a Jew. He left Aldenham School without any academic qualifications, and got a job as an invoice clerk in a brewery in Spitalfields, in the East End of London. For a time he then attempted to make a career in the hotel business, first on the kitchen staff at Grosvenor House and as assistant to the wine waiter at the Ritz, and later as a waiter at the Miramar Hotel, Cannes. Following his marriage in 1935 he lived in the United States for a short while, working on his wife's family's farm.

At the outbreak of World War II de Manio was called up into the Royal Sussex Regiment. In 1939–40 he fought with the 7th battalion, in the British Expeditionary Force, and from 1940 to 1944 he was with the 1st battalion, Middle East Forces. He was awarded the MC in 1940, and a bar was added to it in North Africa. In 1944 he joined the Forces Broadcasting Unit in Beirut.

On leaving the army in 1946 he was able to get a job with the BBC Overseas Service as an announcer, and he transferred to the Home Service in 1950. He managed to survive the furore over his slip of the tongue when he announced a talk by the governor of Nigeria, Sir John *Macpherson, on 'The Land of the Niger', as 'The Land of the Nigger', and in 1958 he was invited to join the new BBC programme *Today*.

Today was a daily breakfast-time magazine programme on the Home Service (renamed Radio 4 in 1967) 'bringing you news, views, and interviews'. Despite his inability to give the correct time, de Manio survived as presenter from 1958 until 1971. Although one listener demanded compensation after he had crashed his car in surprise after hearing the wrong time announced on his car radio, most listeners got used to his misreading the studio clock, and his mistakes made him seem more human, a real person. With his relaxed, informal style and his friendly manner, he became very popular, regarded by millions of listeners as a personal friend. To the listening public he *was* the *Today* programme, a national institution. In 1969 he was the first radio broadcaster to interview Prince Charles. In 1964, and again in 1971, he was voted radio personality of the year by the Variety Club of Great Britain. But in 1970 the new editor of morning current affairs programmes decided to add a co-presenter, and to make *Today* more of a current affairs programme. For a year de Manio was joint presenter with John Timpson. He never felt happy with the new format, feeling that two presenters tended to talk to each other, rather than directly to the listeners. On his retirement from *Today* in 1971 his BBC colleagues presented him with an old studio clock, with the inscription 'and parting Time toiled after him in vain' (Samuel *Johnson).

For the next seven years, until 1978, de Manio presented his own afternoon programme, *Jack de Manio Precisely*. His one venture into television, when he was asked to present *Wednesday Magazine*, a women's programme, was not a success. For a short time from 1979 onwards he was a contributor to *Woman's Hour*, but he did little broadcasting in the 1980s.

Jack de Manio's career and the development of the informal interview marked the end of the old style of impersonal and impartial radio broadcasting. On the air he behaved naturally, and Brian Johnston's advice, when asked how to become a good broadcaster, was 'be like Jack de Manio: be yourself'. The *Guardian* in 1971 referred to the 'cosy warmth' of de Manio's *Today* compared with that of his successors.

Jack de Manio was thickset, with large features and a wide mouth. As a radio broadcaster, it was his voice rather than his face which was well known. The slightly hoarse, gravelly tones became instantly recognizable, and despite his foreign antecedents, he was the epitome of the middle-class, middle-brow Englishman, a *Daily Telegraph* reader.

He was married twice. In 1935 he married Juliet Gravaeret Kaufman, an American. They had one son. His wife and son spent the war in the United States. They were divorced in 1946, and he was not reunited with his son, who remained in the United States, until the 1950s. In 1946 he married Loveday Elizabeth Matthews, a widow, daughter of Evelyn Robins Abbott, CIE, Indian civil servant, later chief commissioner, Delhi. They had no children. Jack de Manio died 28 October 1988 in hospital in London.

[*Independent*, 29 October 1988; Jack de Manio, *Life Begins Too Early, a Sort of Autobiography*, 1970; Jack de Manio, *To Auntie with Love*, 1967; John Timpson, *Today and Yesterday*, 1976; recordings in the National Sound Archive, 29 Exhibition Road, London SW7 2AS; private information.]   ANNE PIMLOTT BAKER

DENNIS, Nigel Forbes (1912–1989), writer, was born 16 January 1912 in Bletchingley, Surrey, the younger child and only son of Lieutenant-Colonel Michael Frederick Beauchamp Dennis and his wife Louise Marguerite Jermyn, youngest daughter of Theodore and Merelina Bosanquet, whose family were descendants of Huguenots from the Languedoc. His parents lived in north Devon. As a young man Colonel Dennis had tried his fortune in South Africa, fought in the Boer war, then settled in Southern Rhodesia, where Nigel's sister, Dorothy, was born. Returning to Britain on the outbreak of World War I, he enlisted in the King's Own Scottish Borderers and was killed in 1918. In 1920 his widow married his best friend, Fitzroy Griffin, and the whole family returned to Rhodesia. Nigel was sent first to Plumtree School, Southern Rhodesia, and then to St Andrew's, Grahamstown, South Africa, which he had to leave early on account of attacks of epilepsy, an affliction which had struck him at the age of about eleven and against which he bore up courageously for the rest of his life. He had one half-brother and one half-sister.

From South Africa he was dispatched to Kitzbühel in Austria, where an uncle, A. Ernan Forbes Dennis, husband of Phyllis Bottome, the novelist, and friend of Alfred Adler, the psychologist, was running a sort of crammer for would-be entrants to the Foreign Office (Peter *Fleming and Ian *Fleming were fellow pupils in Dennis's time) and also acting as British consul. From there he moved on, at his uncle's suggestion, to the Odenwaldschule in Bavaria, a progressive, co-educational establishment at the opposite pole, educationally speaking, to Plumtree and St Andrew's. Dennis, whose youthful literary ambitions had been expressed in stories contributed to the *Boy's Own Paper* (until a hot one from the Odenwaldschule caused the editor to disengage), was very soon writing a novel about this experience. Called *Chalk and Cheese*, it was published a few years later, in 1934, under the pseudonym of 'Richard Vaughan'. Dennis chose to disown it.

After a further unsettled period (more tutoring, this time in Wales; helping his family, by now repatriated, to run a small hotel in Chipping Campden called The Live and Let Live, where the young Graham Greenes were neighbours; and selling ladies' garments from door to door) Dennis got his lucky break. A legacy enabled him to travel steerage to New York and a dockers' strike prevented him from returning on the appointed date. He stayed eighteen years, working first as an assiduous freelance, writing stories and articles, helping to translate Adler, then landing salaried jobs. He became (improbably) secretary of the national board of the *Review of Motion Pictures* (1935), and was assistant editor and book reviewer of the *New Republic* (1937–8) and staff reviewer of *Time* magazine (from 1940). In 1949 he published his first acknowledged novel, *Boys and Girls Come Out to Play* (*A Sea Change* in the USA), which won the Anglo-

American novel award for that year (shared with Anthony West). It starts very personally, with a description of a young man having an epileptic fit.

Dennis returned to England in 1950 and five years later published *Cards of Identity*, the novel which made his name. Its theme—the ease with which modern man, uncertain of who he is, can be manipulated by charlatans—was advanced and piquant. At the request of George *Devine, of the English Stage Company, Dennis turned it into a play. It was produced at the Royal Court theatre in 1956. A second play, *The Making of Moo*, an anti-religious send-up which caused protests in the stalls, followed a year later and in 1958 both were published in book form as *Two Plays and Preface*—the preface being a Voltairean swipe at theologians like St Augustine and a paean of praise for satirists like Aristophanes. His last play, *August for the People*, was produced in 1961.

Dennis's books were few but distinguished: *Dramatic Essays* (1962), a collection worth pondering for its radical approach; a study of one of his heroes, *Jonathan Swift* (1964), which won the Royal Society of Literature award under the W. H. Heinemann bequest (1966); and a haunting last novel, *A House in Order* (1966), which showed the influence of Franz Kafka and the author's passion for gardening. In 1967 he moved to Malta and two final volumes—*Exotics* (1970), a book of Mediterranean poems, and a short, quirky, bellicose *An Essay on Malta* (1972), with illustrations by (Sir) Osbert *Lancaster—were inspired by this new scene.

From its launch in February 1961 until his retirement twenty years later Dennis was lead reviewer of the *Sunday Telegraph*. His admixture of wit, acuteness, and common sense made him an unfailing draw. Between 1963 and 1970 he was drama critic, contributor, and finally co-editor of *Encounter* magazine, but this association ended in acrimony. He wrote for, and read on, radio.

Dennis was tall, somewhat sardonic-looking, and with facial corrugations in his later years which rivalled, but could not quite match, those of his admired W. H. *Auden. A fine conversationalist when the mood took him, he could also be elusive and tortuous: not for nothing had he fielded in boyhood for B. J. T. Bosanquet, the famous cricketer who invented the googly. He was twice married: first, probably in 1934, 1935, or 1936, to Marie-Madeleine, daughter of Avit ('Jean') Massias, a peasant farmer from the Charente. They had two daughters. The marriage was dissolved and in 1959 he married Beatrice Ann Hewart Matthew, a most spirited support and scribe. She was the daughter of William Alexander Matthew, a director of his family's

shipping firm in Cardiff. Dennis died 19 July 1989 in Little Compton, near Moreton-in-Marsh, Gloucestershire, at the home of his elder daughter.

[Rachele Verrecchia, 'Westdown to Mosali: the Diaries of Louise Bosanquet', BA thesis for Manchester Metropolitan University, 1993; written recollections by Dorothy MacKendrick (sister) and E. J. Oliver; private information; personal knowledge.]　　　RIVERS SCOTT

DEXTER, John (1925–1990), stage director, was born 2 August 1925 in Derby, the only child of Harry Dexter, plumber, and his wife, Rosanne Smith. There were music, painting, and home theatricals in the family, but Dexter's only formal education was at the local elementary school (Reginald Street), which he left at the age of fourteen. He then took a factory job before joining the army as a national serviceman. Not having attended a university was a source of lifelong regret, particularly as his entry into the professional theatre coincided with the rise of the graduate director. For the same reason, he developed into a compulsive autodidact, a passionate scholar of stage history who never undertook a classical text without exhaustive research.

His career began in the Derby Playhouse, in a company that also included John Osborne. Osborne recommended Dexter to the English Stage Company's artistic director, George *Devine, who engaged him in 1957 as an associate director. Dexter had no previous directing experience, but he rapidly gained it at the Royal Court theatre, which he subsequently described as his university; there he forged relationships with working-class writers, notably Michael Hastings and Arnold Wesker. At the same time he formed his long alliance with the designer Jocelyn Herbert, crucially in the 1959 production of Wesker's *The Kitchen*, an elaborately choreographed show on a defiantly undecorated stage, where even the lighting rig was exposed to the audience. This marked the beginning of the text-centred, visually austere style which was to become his trademark.

At the Royal Court Dexter gained a double reputation: as an electrifying animator of spectacle and crowd movement, and as a 'playwright's director', who could spot not only the defects of a script but also the hidden potential, and coax the writer into achieving it. The success of his subsequent partnership with Peter Shaffer (*The Royal Hunt of the Sun*, 1964; *Black Comedy*, 1966; *Equus*, 1973) depended as much on pre-rehearsal textual analysis as on the physical staging.

In 1963 Dexter left the Royal Court to become assistant director to Sir Laurence (later Baron) *Olivier at the National Theatre when it was in its honeymoon phase. He began widening his range with productions of *Saint Joan* (1963), *Hobson's Choice* (1964), and the Olivier *Othello* (1964), shows that went lastingly into public memory. He also began another fertile partnership with the poet Tony Harrison, whose versions of Molière and Racine (*The Misanthrope*, 1973, and *Phaedra Britannica*, 1975) set a dazzling new standard for creative translation.

By the late 1960s Dexter was building a parallel career as a director of opera: a natural move given his flair as an animator and innate musicality (coupled with his temporary withdrawal from the National Theatre following disagreements with Olivier). His first venture, Berlioz' *Benvenuto Cellini* at Covent Garden (1966), was untypically ornate; but with Verdi's *I Vespiri Siciliani* at the Hamburg State Opera three years later he declared himself in a production of characteristically austere magnificence. Staged on Josef Svoboda's gigantic staircase between two vast watch-towers, this production carried his name round the world as a new force on the operatic scene; and although he maintained his connection with Hamburg until 1973 (Verdi's *Un Ballo in Maschera*), the main focus of his work during the 1970s was at New York's Metropolitan Opera House, where he was appointed director of productions in 1974. Dexter saw the Met. as a Babylonian anachronism, and he made it his mission to drag it into the twentieth century through simplified staging, technical reform, and enlargement of repertory. Against the odds, he won over the conservative public with a series of non-standard works, from Meyerbeer's *Le Prophète* and Poulenc's *Dialogues of the Carmelites* (both 1977) to *Parade* (1981), a French triptych which he assembled from Satie, Poulenc, and Ravel. By this time, however, his relationship had soured with the Met.'s administration and its musical director, James Levine; and during the early 1980s he returned to free-lance work.

He continued to direct major productions in London and New York, but never achieved his ambition of running a house and company of his own; and his final attempt to do so—with a classically based West End troupe—fell apart after its opening production of *The Cocktail Party* by T. S. *Eliot (Phoenix theatre, 1986).

Dexter was a stocky figure of medium height, with chubby features and a domed head that became increasingly prominent as he lost his hair. He had a biting tongue, which could wound actors and alienate patrons; he also suffered from declining health, due to diabetes and the aftermath of youthful polio, before his final heart attack. He was a homosexual and suffered a brief term of imprisonment for homosexuality in the 1950s. A collection of his writings, *The Honourable Beast: a Posthumous Autobiography*, was

published by his friend Riggs O'Hara in 1993. Dexter died 23 March 1990 in London, following a heart operation.

[John Dexter, *The Honourable Beast: a Posthumous Autobiography*, 1993; private information; personal knowledge.]   IRVING WARDLE

DE ZULUETA, SIR Philip Francis (1929–1989), civil servant and businessman. [See ZULUETA, SIR PHILIP FRANCIS de.]

DICKENS, Frank (1899–1986), biochemist, was born 15 December 1899 in Northampton, the youngest in the family of five sons and a daughter of (William) John Dickens, master currier and leather merchant, and his wife, Elizabeth Ann Pebody. His father, who built up a leather factory in Northampton, died when Frank was four years old. He had been an active member of the Baptist church at Walgrave, but his wife belonged to the Church of England. Frank's four brothers joined the family leather firm, Dickens Brothers Ltd., situated in Kettering Road, Northampton. He was educated at Northampton Grammar School from 1910 to 1918. From the age of sixteen he became seriously interested in science and was always grateful that his science masters were good teachers. In January 1918 he won an open scholarship to Magdalene College, Cambridge, but because of the war he could not take it up until January 1919. He enlisted in the army (Artists' Rifles, and then, as a second lieutenant, the Northamptonshire Regiment), but did not see active service. At Cambridge he took the shortened postwar course of eight terms and got a second class in both parts (1920 and 1921) of the natural sciences tripos (physics and chemistry). He then moved to Imperial College, London, to study for a Ph.D. in organic chemistry, which profoundly influenced his later work in biochemistry.

In October 1923 Dickens took his first appointment, at the Middlesex Hospital, to work with a newly qualified medical graduate, (Sir) E. Charles *Dodds. Two years beforehand, (Sir) Frederick *Banting and Charles H. Best in Canada had isolated insulin. Dickens set out to simplify the method of isolation and make the substance available for patients. He was thus precipitated into biochemistry, from 1924 to 1930 assisting Dodds in his work on the isolation of a female sex hormone. With Dodds he wrote *The Chemical and Physiological Properties of the Internal Secretions* (1925). He also developed a lasting interest in carbohydrate metabolism. In 1929 he spent a year with Otto Warburg in Berlin, which greatly influenced him. He translated into English Warburg's book, *The Metabolism of Tumours* (1930). On his return home he worked in the newly opened Courtauld Institute of Biochemistry at the Middlesex Hospital, searching for differences between the metabolism of tumour and normal tissue.

In 1933 Dickens moved to Newcastle upon Tyne to be the director of the cancer research laboratory at the Royal Victoria Infirmary. Apart from a year in London on war work (for the Royal Naval personnel committee of the Medical Research Council in 1943–4) he remained in Newcastle until 1946, when Dodds invited him back to the Courtauld Institute and he became the Philip Hill professor of experimental biochemistry. His research work on the mechanism whereby living tissues derive energy from the breakdown of carbohydrates culminated in the description of what is known as the 'pentose phosphate pathway', for which he is best known. He was a major contributor to the discovery of this important route of glucose metabolism, a significant marker of the rate of tumour growth. Dickens's happy relationship with Dodds was crucial: although Dickens had a more academic intellect, Dodds was the leader, being imaginative, ambitious, and a superb tactician in committee. Dickens admired Dodds even if he would not have wanted to be in his shoes. Dickens's last appointment was as director of the Tobacco Research Council's research laboratories at Harrogate, where he spent two years (1967–9) and was influential in advising the tobacco industry about a 'safer' cigarette.

In addition to his research, Dickens played a full part in the wider development of biochemistry and a decisive role in the organization of the first international congress of biochemistry in Cambridge in 1949. For eight years (1938–46) he was one of the editors of the *Biochemical Journal*. Throughout his career he was fortunate in the circumstances in which he worked, being supported first by the Medical Research Council and then by the Cancer Research Campaign. He was thus able to choose his research activities and never had to resort to self-promotion. He was an honorary member of the Biochemical Society (1967), of which he was chairman in 1950–1, and was elected FRS in 1946. In 1972 he received an honorary D.Sc. from Newcastle. He was also a fellow of the Institute of Biology (1968).

Dickens was a kind and gentle man, of medium height, spruce in appearance, with a healthy complexion and a welcoming air. He was an attentive host. He enjoyed good food and was very put out when as external examiner at the University of Leeds he was accommodated in a temperance hotel. In 1925 he married Molly, daughter of Arthur William Jelleyman, the owner of a rope-walk and tenting factory in Northampton, which among other items made special ropes for the local hangman. They had two daughters. Dickens died at his home in Ferring, near Worthing, 25 June 1986.

[R. H. S. Thompson and P. N. Campbell, *Biographical Memoirs of Fellows of the Royal Society*, vol. xxxiii, 1987; private information; personal knowledge.]

PETER N. CAMPBELL

DICKSON, SIR William Forster (1898–1987), marshal of the Royal Air Force, was born in Northwood, Middlesex, 24 September 1898, the only child of Campbell Cameron Forster Dickson, solicitor, and his wife, Agnes Nelson-Ward, a direct descendant of Lord *Nelson. He was educated at Haileybury and joined the Royal Naval Air Service in 1916.

After training as a pilot he served with the Grand Fleet aboard the aircraft-carrier *Furious*, where he pioneered deck landings and participated in the first carrier-based bombing raid, earning appointment to the DSO (1918). After the war he became a flying instructor in the newly independent Royal Air Force and flew as a test pilot, being awarded the AFC (1922). Then, after working in the Air Ministry (1923–6) as the expert on naval/air operations for Sir Hugh (later first Viscount) *Trenchard, he flew with No. 56 Squadron (1926–7), attended the Andover Staff College (1927–8), spent several years in India, commanded No. 25 Squadron (1935–6), and thoroughly enjoyed three years on the directing staff at Andover (1936–8), proving a fine instructor.

On the outbreak of war, having attended the Imperial Defence College (1939), he was called upon to use his exceptional staff skills in the joint planning staff, first as group captain (1940) and then air commodore (1941). He contributed greatly to the forward planning in the early years of the war, working directly for (Sir) Winston *Churchill and the chiefs of staff, joining in meetings with the Soviet ambassador to discuss military aid, and attending the Arcadia conference, where the future Anglo-American strategy was decided. After a year (1942–3) in Fighter Command (as air vice-marshal) he spent another year (1943–4) preparing No. 83 Group for the Normandy invasion, whereupon General B. L. *Montgomery (later first Viscount Montgomery of Alamein) insisted that the Group be handed over to (Sir) Harry Broadhurst, the commander whom he knew. Dickson, accepting the inevitable disappointment with good grace, departed for Italy to command the Desert Air Force, and for most of 1944 ably directed its intensive interdiction and close army support operations.

At the end of the year he returned to London as assistant chief of air staff (policy); in June 1946 he was promoted to air marshal and joined the Air Council as vice-chief of air staff, working under the first Baron *Tedder and devoting much of his attention to the RAF's postwar re-equipment programme; and in March 1948 he became commander-in-chief, Middle East. A year later he was criticized in Parliament after four reconnaissance Spitfires had been shot down by the Israelis, but the prime minister firmly defended him over what had been essentially a political air operation. Dickson returned to the Air Ministry in March 1950, as air member for supply and organization. Central to his work was the expansion programme necessitated by the Korean war, and he also negotiated an agreement with his American counterpart to cover the deployment of a large USAF contingent in the United Kingdom.

Dickson became chief of air staff on 1 January 1953. Churchill, again prime minister, remembered him well from wartime and fully supported him in his prime task: the planning and preparation for the RAF's nuclear deterrent. Recognizing the increasing importance of cold war operations Dickson also pressed forward the development of the air transport force, but was ever mindful of the growing economic pressures on the RAF budget. He became marshal of the Royal Air Force in 1954. Then on 1 January 1956 Sir Anthony *Eden (later the Earl of Avon), now prime minister, appointed him to the new position of separate chairman of the chiefs of staff. Dickson, convinced of the need for a stronger 'centre' in the Ministry of Defence, readily accepted the post, which he held throughout the Suez crisis and the subsequent defence review by Duncan *Sandys (later Baron Duncan-Sandys); unable to exercise much influence during this controversial debate he supported the proposal by Harold *Macmillan (later the first Earl of Stockton) in 1958 to convert his post to chief of defence staff. On 1 January 1959 he became the first incumbent, handing over to the first Earl *Mountbatten of Burma six months later. He had served at the top of the defence hierarchy for six and a half years, at a time of turmoil, defence cuts, and post-Suez reforms in the armed services. While short of stature, he always commanded attention, combining a razor-sharp brain with a great sense of fun. His sense of humour often defused awkward situations. His love of flying had enamoured him of the RAF, but he retained deep respect for the other services and was seen as an ideal choice for Britain's first chief of defence staff.

In retirement near Newbury his interests included the Royal Central Asian Society, the Ex-Services Mental Welfare Society, and the Forces Help Society and Lord Roberts Workshops, and he loved his golf. He was appointed OBE (1934), CB (1942), CBE (1945), KBE (1946), KCB (1952), and GCB (1953).

In 1932 he married Patricia Marguerite, sister of Sir George ('Gubby') *Allen, cricketer, and daughter of Sir Walter Macarthur Allen, com-

mandant-in-chief of the Metropolitan Special Constabulary. They had two daughters, one of whom died in childhood (1952). Dickson died 12 September 1987 at the RAF Hospital, Wroughton.

[Official records, Air Historical Branch, Ministry of Defence, London; private information; personal knowledge.]   HENRY A. PROBERT

DONALD, Ian (1910–1987), obstetrician and pioneer of the use of ultrasound in medicine, was born 27 December 1910 in Liskeard, Cornwall, the eldest in the family of two sons and two daughters of John Donald, medical practitioner, and his wife, Helen Barrow Wilson, concert pianist. His education was at Warriston School, Moffat, and Fettes College, Edinburgh, and then in South Africa at the Diocesan College, Rondebosch, and Capetown University (where he obtained a BA in French, Greek, English, and music). On his return to England he entered St Thomas's Hospital Medical School (MB, BS, 1937).

He served in the Royal Air Force medical branch from 1942 to 1946 and was mentioned in dispatches and appointed MBE (military, 1946) for acts of gallantry. He returned to St Thomas's Hospital and qualified MD and MRCOG in 1947 (FRCOG, 1955). In 1952 he became reader at Hammersmith Hospital, where he devised a respirator for the resuscitation of the new born. In 1954 he was appointed to the regius chair of midwifery in the University of Glasgow. The first edition of his eminently readable textbook, *Practical Obstetric Problems*, was published in 1955. It reflected his motto, 'the art of teaching is the art of sharing enthusiasm', his sparkling wit, and his deep knowledge of English literature and the Bible.

Familiar with radar and sonar from his RAF days, his mind turned to the idea that sonar could be used for medical diagnosis. With T. G. Brown of the electronics company Kelvin Hughes he produced the first successful diagnostic ultrasound machine, and with Dr John MacVicar the findings were reported in the *Lancet* of 7 June 1958 under the title 'Investigation of Abdominal Masses by Pulsed Ultrasound'. The idea of applying the principles of metal flaw detection to human diagnosis was received at first with scepticism and some hilarity, but Donald's vision of ultrasound as a new diagnostic science never faded and work with various colleagues followed, exploring the whole subject of foetal development. The impact of ultrasound on obstetric practice has been enormous and in later life Donald wrote: 'the innumerable difficulties, set-backs and disappointments have been more than compensated for by those who have turned the subject from a laughable eccentricity into a science of increasing exactitude.'

In 1964 the department moved from Glasgow Royal Maternity Hospital to a new hospital (the Queen Mother's Hospital), which he had campaigned for and helped to design. There he directed everything with verve and panache, like a great actor-manager of the old school. Striding its corridors he was an impressive figure, six feet two inches tall with red hair, blue eyes, and strong personal magnetism. He was impulsive, witty, and quick-tempered, but his sudden anger evaporated almost instantly. He had a great sense of fun and at the most solemn occasions could dissolve into helpless laughter. His hobbies were sailing, which he persisted in despite a cardiac condition, piano-playing (Chopin was his favourite composer), and landscape painting in watercolour. All these were pursued with characteristic enthusiasm.

He was appointed CBE in 1973 and received the Order of the Yugoslav Flag with gold star in 1982. He received honorary D.Sc. degrees from London (1981) and Glasgow (1983), the Eardley Holland gold medal (1970), Blair Bell gold medal (1970), Victor Bonney prize (1970–2), and MacKenzie Davidson medal (1975). Other distinctions included FCOG (SA) (1967), honorary FACOG (1976), honorary FRCOG (1982), and honorary FRCP Glasgow (1984).

In 1937 he married Alix Mathilde, daughter of Walter Wellesley Richards, a farmer in the Orange Free State, South Africa. Happily married for fifty years, he was the loving father of four daughters and was devoted to his women patients, as they were to him. From 1961 he was hampered by ill health, but continued active despite having three major heart operations. He showed enormous courage throughout and was greatly sustained by his profound Christian faith. His opposition to the Abortion Act of 1967 and its consequences stemmed from a deep respect for human life. He was opposed to experiments on embryos. His last research effort, pursued in retirement, was an attempt to achieve a perfect method of natural family planning using a device to warn the woman of the approach of ovulation. He died at his home in Paglesham, Essex, 19 June 1987.

[Private information; personal knowledge.]

JAMES WILLOCKS

DOWNIE, Allan Watt (1901–1988), professor of bacteriology, was born 5 September 1901 in Rosehearty, Aberdeenshire, the fifth child in the family of seven sons and one daughter of William Downie, deep sea fisherman, and his wife Margaret Watt, daughter of a fisherman from Fife. He was the younger of identical twins. Allan and his twin Ricky grew up close to Rosehearty harbour and became familiar with the sea. They were educated at Rosehearty School, where their unusual talent was spotted, and Fraserburgh Academy. In 1918 they entered Aberdeen University Medical School, from which in 1923 they graduated MB, Ch.B. with first-class honours and the distinction of collecting between them every subject prize in every year of the course.

From 1924 to 1926 Allan Downie was a lecturer in bacteriology at Aberdeen University. He obtained his MD in 1929 and D.Sc. in 1938. In 1927 he moved to the department of pathology in Manchester University, where he turned to the new science of virology. With a veterinary pathologist he for the first time demonstrated, in tissue culture, the cellular changes which characterized in its natural animal host, the disease mousepox, a model for human smallpox. This little-noted paper opened a new chapter in methods for studying viruses and virus diseases.

In 1935 Downie won the senior Freedom research fellowship at the London Hospital Medical School. First, however, he had to spend a nine-month academic year at the Rockefeller Institute in New York City, under O. T. Avery and alongside the future leaders of American microbiology. At the London Hospital Downie initiated work on pox viruses and defined for the first time the distinction between vaccinia and cowpox viruses. This later led him on to smallpox and to its ultimate eradication. The outbreak of World War II stalled his work on pox viruses when he was directed to head the emergency Public Health Service laboratory in Cambridge, one of the regional laboratories providing expertise in public health for disease control, water-supply monitoring, and possibly bacterial warfare. The east coast was a probable front line should invasion happen. Downie was in Cambridge till 1943, when he was appointed professor of bacteriology in Liverpool.

Returning troops and the resumption of foreign trade after the war brought numerous imports of smallpox into Britain. Downie's laboratory in Liverpool became the world centre for the study of smallpox: of how the virus entered its victims, spread inside them, and then passed to others; of precisely when the patient became infectious and for how long. These studies progressed for twenty-two years, and then the World Health Organization recognized that an effective smallpox eradication plan was possible. With Downie's guidance the intensified and successful programme was launched in 1966, the year of his retirement. Since 1978 there has been no smallpox case; there are no human carriers and no animal cases or carriers. The disease which in the 1960s was killing ten million people per year has ceased to exist. Many thousands of public health workers took part and the credit, as Downie would have wished, is spread worldwide.

None can doubt that in the laboratory in Liverpool, in the field in India, at WHO at Geneva, and in training courses in Denver Downie's contribution was paramount. It was the greatest medical triumph of the century.

Downie helped to train over 3,000 doctors and published 110 outstanding papers. A founder fellow of the Royal College of Pathologists, he had an honorary LL D from Aberdeen (1957). He became a fellow of the Royal Society in 1955 and FRCP in 1982.

Short and wiry, Downie had a great affection for sport. In Manchester he played left-half for Whalley Range Football Club in the Lancashire amateur league. Every summer found him in Rosehearty, with Ricky and his family, sailing in the heavy old family sailboat, with grandchildren or friends, happy to be on the water and under sail. Downie loved to fish and to identify sea birds, but it was at golf on the Royal Birkdale course that he excelled and was never satisfied, striving always to reduce his (most enviable) handicap. When he retired from his Liverpool chair in 1966, the *Southport Visitor* heralded the news with the headline 'Noted Local Golfer Retires'.

In 1935 he married Annie ('Nancy'), schoolteacher and daughter of William Alan McHardy, wood engineer. They had two daughters and a son. Downie died in Southport 26 January 1988. His twin brother had predeceased him in 1978. Both were smokers, both victims of lung cancer.

[*Independent*, 1 February 1988; *Journal of Medical Microbiology*, vol. lxxxviii, 1989, pp. 291–5; D. A. J. Tyrrell and K. McCarthy in *Biographical Memoirs of Fellows of the Royal Society*, vol. xxxv, 1990; Sir Cyril Clarke's tribute on Downie's retirement, University of Liverpool *Recorder*, 1966; personal knowledge.]

K. McCarthy

DREYER, Rosalie (1895–1987), nursing leader, was born 3 September 1895 in Berne, Switzerland, the eldest child in the family of four daughters and one son of Johann Dreyer, manager of a dairy co-operative, and his wife, Elisabeth Neuenschwander. The father's work necessitated travel in the Lausanne area, and this Lutheran family's two eldest daughters received their education from Roman Catholic nuns. The young 'Rosa' was encouraged to travel by a cosmopolitan aunt. She went to England in 1914 as an au pair girl to the Saltzburgers, a Swiss family settled there. She kept links with her young charges for many years.

In May 1918 she began to train as a nurse at Guy's Hospital, London. Despite a bout of glandular fever, she gained her state registration certificate in March 1922, excelling in practical nursing and sickroom cookery. After a year's private nursing she went back to Switzerland to work in the Rollier Clinic, a tuberculosis sanatorium in Leysin.

In 1924 she returned to the staff of Guy's. She gained her midwifery qualification in 1926 and rose through the nursing hierarchy to become assistant matron in 1931. In 1934 she secured the post of matron at the Bethnal Green Hospital, since the 1929 Local Government Act under the control of the London county council. The next fifteen years of her career were spent in the service of the LCC, as principal matron (1935–40), principal matron in charge (1940–8), and chief nursing officer (1948–50).

The move to the LCC was to a world vastly different from Guy's and the voluntary sector. The LCC nursing service had been built up from over 120 different institutions, employing approximately 8,000 female nursing staff. It offered a comprehensive training, uniformity of conditions of employment, and probably the most integrated service in existence prior to the inception of the National Health Service. In the course of her work Rosalie Dreyer frequently met Herbert *Morrison (later Baron Morrison of Lambeth), leader of the LCC from 1934 to 1940. She was well aware of her uniquely powerful position, seeing herself as a policy-maker and using her opportunities to promote nursing and to professionalize the former workhouse infirmary staff. Younger women at London matrons' meetings and her own ward sisters were in awe of her.

During World War II her organizational abilities were fully utilized. She had to deal with the immense challenges presented by the urgent need to evacuate and disperse hospitals into the surrounding countryside. Personnel and equipment had to be relocated and both had eventually to return together. Her memos give eloquent testimony to her managerial skills as patients, many of them chronically sick, staff, student nurses, their teachers, equipment, anatomical charts, and life-sized mannequins were moved about London and the Home Counties in what was logistically the most difficult task to face a nurse manager so far this century. With a car and a driver at her disposal, she visited bombed and evacuated hospitals, to assess the extent of damage and morale of her staff. Her opinion was esteemed by her LCC colleagues, for she had an acute grasp of the realities of the situation. In negotiations with the Ministry of Health on the production of a nursing recruitment film to be shown in cinemas, she stressed the need for the filming to be undertaken in a hospital where the uniform was up to date and visually appealing to potential new nurses.

Rosalie Dreyer had become a British citizen in 1934, shortly before her appointment to Bethnal Green Hospital. Her wartime experience was marred by the xenophobic agitation of Ethel

Bedford *Fenwick, who described her appointment as matron in chief as unpatriotic. Rosalie Dreyer received messages of support from the Royal College of Nursing and was publicly defended by the LCC leader, Charles (later first Baron) *Latham.

After the war she supervised the assimilation of the LCC nursing service into separate new National Health Service units, which had their own hospital management committees. She became chief nursing officer, in charge of domiciliary nursing services, but she disliked this work, which was in no way comparable with her previous post, and in 1950 she moved to the World Health Organization as nursing adviser, touring the war-torn countries of Europe and advising on nursing reconstruction, until her retirement in 1953. Despite her significant contribution to the health provision for Londoners, she received no civic or public honours.

Rosalie Dreyer was a life member of the Royal College of Nursing, president of one of its London branches (South East Metropolitan), and a member of the RCN committee on the assistant nurse, chaired by the first Baron *Horder. She believed in the formal recognition of the second-level nurse, and was chosen as first president of the National Association of State Enrolled Nurses.

Within the NHS she served on three hospital management committees (South West Middlesex in 1950–8, Stepney in 1952–64, and Lewisham in 1955–64) and was a governor and honorary secretary to the Friends of the Royal Ear, Nose and Throat Hospital on the Whitley council.

She was bird-like, tall and slim (until she worked for the WHO), with dark hair, which she complained was squashed by nurses' caps. While at Guy's she was an avid theatre-goer, with a wide circle of friends. She regarded her nurses as her family. Her retirement was an active one, sustained by her love of sewing, cooking, and travelling. She travelled to Australia in her sixties, partly by mail boat. She kept up her lifelong links with nursing friends, such as Dame Elizabeth *Cockayne. During her last illness she was nursed by one of her sisters and district nurses, some of whom knew her background. She died at her flat in Wimbledon 21 May 1987, from the effects of a cerebral tumour.

[Guy's Hospital records; London county council records; Royal College of Nursing membership archives; private information.]   STEPHANIE KIRBY

DROGHEDA, eleventh EARL OF (1910–1989), chairman of the *Financial Times* and the Royal Opera House, Covent Garden. [See MOORE, (CHARLES) GARRETT (PONSONBY).]

DUDGEON, (John) Alastair (1916–1989), microbiologist, was born 9 November 1916 in Stanhope Place, Bayswater, London, the youngest in the family of two sons and one daughter of Leonard Stanley *Dudgeon (later CMG and CBE), professor of pathology and dean of St Thomas's Hospital, and his wife Norah Edith, daughter of Sir Richard Orpen, solicitor and later president of the Irish Law Society. His childhood was spent in London, and his summer holidays in Aldeburgh, a place which was to mean much to him throughout his life. He was educated at Repton and Trinity College, Cambridge, where he obtained a second class in part i of the natural sciences tripos (1937). He then went to St Thomas's Hospital Medical School.

He had joined the Territorial Army in 1936 and at the outbreak of World War II in 1939 he interrupted his medical studies to serve as a combatant officer. His career in the North Africa campaign as a company commander in the 7th Rifle Brigade was distinguished. In 1942 he was awarded the MC, to which a bar was added in 1943. Having been wounded twice, he was evacuated back to Britain in 1943. His army service left a deep imprint on him. He cared for the soldiers under his command with the sense of responsibility which he was later to feel for patients, colleagues, research workers, and technicians, and his friendships made in the army were lasting.

He completed his medical studies at St Thomas's, qualifying MRCS, LRCP and MB, B.Ch. in 1944. He transferred to the Royal Army Medical Corps in 1944 and served in the Territorial Army until 1962, gaining the rank of colonel and the Territorial Decoration and three clasps (1947). He received a Cambridge MD in 1947. After qualification he specialized in microbiology, particularly virology. In 1945–6 he worked at the National Institute for Medical Research, under (Sir) Christopher *Andrewes. In 1948 he was appointed assistant pathologist (virus diseases) at the Hospital for Sick Children, Great Ormond Street—another institution to benefit from his lifelong loyalty. In 1953 he became senior lecturer in virology at St George's Hospital, keeping his links with Great Ormond Street as honorary consultant virologist. From 1958 to 1960 he was director of virus research at the Glaxo laboratories. He returned to Great Ormond Street in 1960, as consultant microbiologist and lecturer at the Institute of Child Health. He built up a splendid department and in 1972 became professor of microbiology and in 1974 dean of the institute. In 1963 he had become FRCPath. He was an excellent administrator, serving on many hospital and institute committees, usually as chairman.

His researches related to viral diseases of the foetus and newborn child. His most original contribution concerned the trials of a vaccine against the rubella virus. After a link between an attack of rubella during the early weeks of pregnancy and malformations in the offspring had been demonstrated, a live vaccine against the virus was produced in 1967 in the United States and was awaiting clinical trials. Dudgeon thought that the trials should be undertaken in closed religious communities, in order to avoid accidental transferral of rubella to pregnant women. With the enthusiastic co-operation of those communities he showed that the vaccine was not transmitted from person to person and was safe, and that the resulting immunity lasted for many years. These studies laid the foundation for the vaccine's routine use and resulted in the declining incidence of rubella malformations. For this contribution Dudgeon received the Harding award (1972) and the Bissett Hawkins medal of the Royal College of Physicians (1977), of which he had become a member in 1970 and a fellow in 1974.

His expertise in the field of immunization was recognized internationally and he became chairman of several government and World Health Organization committees. He was appointed an officer of the Order of St John of Jerusalem (1958), DL of Greater London (1973), and CBE (1977). After his retirement in 1981 he worked for medical charities and South-East Kent Health Authority. He became senior warden (1984–5) and master (1985–6) of the Society of Apothecaries.

Dudgeon valued tradition. He had a rocklike dependability and a strong sense of right. On first acquaintance he appeared austere, but underneath he had great warmth, a sense of humour, and a humility which prevented him from mentioning his achievements. He enjoyed gardening and collected antique porcelain, glass, silver, and apothecary jars. Always correctly dressed, he was of medium height, with a fine head of black hair, which remained unchanged into old age, and dark brown eyes.

In 1945 he married Patricia Joan, daughter of Gilbert Ashton, schoolmaster. They had two sons. She died in 1969. In 1974 he married Joyce Kathleen, widow of Stanley Tibbetts and daughter of James Counsell, farmer and businessman. Dudgeon died 9 October 1989 at home, Cherry Orchard Cottage, Bonnington, Kent.

[Private information; personal knowledge.]

OTTO WOLFF

DU MAURIER, DAME Daphne (1907–1989), novelist, was born 13 May 1907 at 24 Cumberland Terrace, Regent's Park, London, the second of three daughters (there were no sons) of Sir Gerald Hubert Edward Busson *du Maurier, actor-manager, and his wife Muriel, actress, daughter of Harry Beaumont, solicitor. She was educated mainly at home by governesses, of whom one, Maud Waddell, was highly influen-

tial, and afterwards spent three terms at a finishing school near Paris.

She began writing stories and poetry in her childhood and was encouraged by her father, with whom she had a very close relationship. He longed for her to emulate her grandfather, George *du Maurier, artist and author of three novels, including the best-selling *Trilby* (1894). But the circumstances of her upbringing, with its constant emphasis on pleasure and distraction, called for self-discipline of a kind she did not manage to exert until she was twenty-two, when she finally completed several short stories. The first published story was 'And now to God the Father', which appeared in the *Bystander* (May 1929), a magazine edited by her uncle. It was a cynical view of society as she saw it.

Her ambition then was to write a novel. She settled down to do so in the winter of 1929–30 at Bodinnick-by-Fowey in Cornwall, where her parents had bought Ferryside to be their country home. Here she wrote *The Loving Spirit*, the story of four generations of a Cornish family, which was published to considerable acclaim by Heinemann in February 1931. She immediately wrote second and third novels which confounded expectations by differing radically from her first, but it was her fourth book, *Gerald*, a frank biography of her father, written when he died in 1934, which made the greatest impact. It was published by (Sir) Victor *Gollancz, with whom she then began a long and fruitful partnership.

Gollancz recognized that her strengths lay in narrative drive and the evocation of atmosphere. He encouraged her to develop these and the result was *Jamaica Inn* (1936), an instant best seller. At this point in her career she was obliged, as an army wife, to go abroad, to Egypt, with her husband, Major (Sir) Frederick Arthur Montague ('Boy') *Browning, the son of Frederick Henry Browning. The latter ran various businesses and also worked for MI5, as well as having a distinguished army career. They had married in 1932 and in 1933 had a daughter, Tessa, who was later to marry the son of the first Viscount *Montgomery of Alamein (her second marriage).

This was a deeply unhappy period in Daphne du Maurier's life—she was an untypical army wife, being very anti-social, and she loathed Egypt and was profoundly homesick—but it produced *Rebecca* (1938). This was meant to be a psychological study of jealousy, and was based on her own feelings of jealousy towards a former fiancée of her husband's, Jan Ricardo, but was hailed as a romantic novel in the tradition of *Jane Eyre*. She was astonished by the success of *Rebecca*—hardback copies in Britain alone passed the million mark in 1992—and mystified by the readers' interpretation of the novel. In 1941 she produced *Frenchman's Creek* and in 1943 *Hungry Hill*.

In 1943, while her husband was away fighting in the war, she went to live in Cornwall with her three children, daughters Tessa and Flavia (1937), and son Christian (1940). She took on the lease of Menabilly, a house (owned by the Rashleigh family) with which she had become obsessed. The war years affected her marriage deeply and adversely. She felt estranged from her husband, in spite of her love for him, and wrote a play, *The Years Between* (performed in 1944), about how war affected marriages.

After the war her husband became comptroller of the household and treasurer to Princess Elizabeth, which meant that he lived in London while she stayed in Cornwall, with only weekends shared. This led to tensions which heavily influenced her work. Outwardly charming, witty, and light-hearted, she was struggling inwardly with feelings of rejection and uncertainty about her personal life. In two collections of short stories, *The Apple Tree* (1952) and *The Breaking Point* (1959), she expressed the extent of her confusion and frustration. These stories are of great biographical significance.

Her career flourished, though not precisely in the way she wished. *My Cousin Rachel* appeared in 1951. Her novels translated well into films and *Jamaica Inn* (1939), *Rebecca* (1940), *Frenchman's Creek* (1944), and *Hungry Hill* (1946) were notable successes. Her short story, *The Birds*, became famous in the hands of (Sir) Alfred *Hitchcock in 1963. *Rebecca* had made her a popular, worldwide, best-selling author, but she felt her later, more serious, work was not given its due. In *The Scapegoat* (1957) she was writing at a deeper level, but the novel was treated as a romantic thriller. She turned to biography, partly in an attempt to show she could do serious work, though it was also true that she had temporarily lost the creative urge to write fiction. *The Infernal World of Branwell Brontë* (1960) gave her tremendous satisfaction, and was well researched, but did little to alter her image.

In 1965 her husband died. Her grief, together with the distress caused by her fear that her imagination was deserting her, made her depressed. The news that she could not renew her lease on Menabilly again added to her misery but in 1969, the year in which she was appointed DBE, she moved to Kilmarth, the dower house of Menabilly, and wrote *The House on the Strand* (1969), which restored her confidence. Her last novel, *Rule Britannia* (1972), destroyed it again. She was unable to write any more fiction afterwards. In 1977 she wrote a slim volume of autobiography (*Growing Pains*), which she regretted producing. In 1981 she had a nervous breakdown and then a mild coronary. The last eight years of her life were spent mourning her lost talent, without which she felt her days were empty and meaningless.

Daphne du Maurier was in her youth an extremely beautiful woman, of medium height, fine-boned and slender, with thick blonde hair and arresting eyes of a startlingly bright, clear blue. She was a very complex person, well aware, through constant self-analysis, that she acted out her life to an extraordinary degree. Her novels were her fantasies and seemed more real to her than her actual life. She needed them, to give expression to what she called, through her fascination with Jungian theory, her 'no. 2' self. This was a darker, violent self, which she suppressed in a most determined manner. Part of this suppression was sexual: she believed she should have been born a boy and that she had to keep this masculine side of herself hidden, which she did, except while writing, for most of her life. The problem of her life she herself defined as 'a fear of reality'. Only when she was alone, and especially alone in Menabilly, was she able to still this fear.

Her work has been consistently underrated, in spite of critical acknowledgement that *Rebecca* and *The Scapegoat*, at least, are of literary worth. Her influence on the growth of 'women's writing' as a separate division, and on writing for the cinema (eight of her novels and stories were made into successful films), was significant in the 1930s and 1940s, but it is as a popular novelist that her position remains secure, especially among the young. She died at her home in Par, Cornwall, 19 April 1989.

[Margaret Forster, *Daphne du Maurier*, 1993; private information; family papers.]   MARGARET FORSTER

DUNCAN-SANDYS, BARON (1908–1987), politician. [See SANDYS, (EDWIN) DUNCAN.]

DUNDERDALE, Wilfred Albert (1899–1990), intelligence officer, was born in Russia 24 December 1899, the son of Richard Albert Dunderdale, a British shipowner, whose vessels traded between Constantinople and the Russian ports on the Black Sea, and his wife, Sophie. He was educated in Russia, at the gymnasium in Nikolayev, and was studying naval engineering at Petrograd University when the Russian revolution broke out in 1917. Much of the Russian navy remained in White Russian hands. Dunderdale was contacted by the Royal Navy, who found his great knowledge of the Russian language and the Russian navy invaluable.

At this time Constantinople, where Dunderdale had numerous friends, had been occupied by the Allies. On one occasion in 1919 a submarine was being handed over by the Allies to the White Russian navy. Dunderdale discovered that the crew were Bolsheviks who intended to murder the tsarist officers together with the liaison officer (himself) as soon as the vessel sailed. The crew were arrested and Dunderdale was appointed MBE (1920). In the same year he became a sub-lieutenant in the Royal Naval Volunteer Reserve. During this period he was also sent as the British observer and interpreter to accompany the imperial procurator on his investigation into the murder of the Russian imperial family at Ekaterinburg, which had been recaptured by the White Russian army. As a result he remained convinced of the falseness of the pretender Anastasia, who he said was merely the Polish girlfriend of one of the Bolshevik gaolers, who occasionally did some sewing for the tsarina.

The world of Constantinople, from the end of the war until Kemal Atatürk deposed Sultan Muhammad in 1922, was one of classical Byzantine intrigue on a grand scale. The only stabilizing factor was the heavy guns of the Royal Navy, which were trained on the centre of the city. Dunderdale was in his element and in 1921 he was recruited by MI6, with whom he remained until 1959. He had found his spiritual 'home'. He always maintained that his first job for MI6 was to pay off, with gold sovereigns, all the foreign members of the sultan's harem, and to repatriate them through the good offices of the Royal Navy.

In 1926 he was posted to Paris to represent MI6's interests, and to liaise with the French Deuxième Bureau. He stayed in Paris until 1940. The central weapon in his armoury was his own personality. He spoke several languages well, and was debonair and a wonderful host. There was about him an element of the pirate; he was a romantic with enormous vitality and a gift for friendship. If the truth of past dramatic events was occasionally expanded in telling the story, his friends readily forgave him. His flat in Paris became a meeting place for international visitors and political gossip. His relations with the Deuxième Bureau became close and he played a major role in one great intelligence coup. He had become a close personal friend of Colonel Gustave Bertrand, the Deuxième Bureau chief signals officer. They were both friendly with the Polish intelligence service in Paris. Shortly after the outbreak of World War II in 1939, they managed to smuggle out of Poland to Paris a model of the top secret German encoding machine known as 'Enigma'. Dunderdale brought it over to London himself, in romantic circumstances. It was the biggest single contribution to the vital intelligence results achieved by the British decoding centre at Bletchley Park, and was perhaps the greatest Allied intelligence coup of the war. Dunderdale was appointed CMG (1942).

In the summer of 1940 he had to return to London. He ran a small group of agents into French seaports, but his contribution gradually diminished. Part of the reason for this was that, as Charles de Gaulle became increasingly powerful in London and set up his own intelligence organization, Dunderdale's contacts with the old Deuxième Bureau became an object of suspicion: a number of its officers were indeed working with the Vichy government.

After the war Dunderdale refused to have an office in MI6's headquarters because the aura of Whitehall was intolerable to him; he was allowed to set up a small office nearby. There, with lovely oriental carpets, portraits of the queen and the tsar, a whiff of incense, and a fine model of a Russian destroyer of 1912, he provided a home from home for many foreign visitors from pre-war days. He made two further contributions. When de Gaulle resigned early in 1946 an intelligence amalgamation took place in Paris between those who worked for de Gaulle and the pre-war professionals. Dunderdale played a useful role in bridging the gap between the new generation of MI6 officers and his pre-war French colleagues. Secondly, in his final period with MI6 his company and his worldly knowledge was a constant pleasure and profit to his younger colleagues. He was an officer of the French Legion of Honour, a holder of the French croix de guerre (with palm), and an officer of the US Legion of Merit.

Always known as 'Biffy', Dunderdale was neat, dark, immaculately dressed, stubby in build, and always with a Balkan cigarette, in a long, black, ivory holder, in his hand. In 1928 he married June Woodbridge Ament-Morse, of Washington, USA. The marriage was dissolved in 1947 and in 1952 he married Dorothy Mabel Brayshaw Hyde, daughter of James Murray Crofts, D.Sc., CBE. The marriage was very happy and they lived in London until her death in 1978. After his wife died there was little left to keep Dunderdale in England and he went to live in New York, where he had some old friends. In 1980 he married Deborah, widow of Harry McJ. McLeod and daughter of Eugene B. Jackson, of Boston, Massachusetts. There were no children of any of the marriages. Dunderdale died 13 November 1990 in New York.

[Personal knowledge.]   JOHN BRUCE LOCKHART

DU PRÉ, Jacqueline Mary (1945–1987), cellist, was born 26 January 1945 in Oxford, the younger daughter and second of three children of Derek du Pré, financial writer and editor, who became secretary to the Institute of Cost and Works Accountants, and his wife, Iris Greep, who taught piano at the Royal Academy of Music. The family name had twelfth-century origins in Jersey. In 1948 the family went to settle in Purley, a suburb south of London. At four years of age, Jacqueline heard a cello for the first time and wanted to have such an instrument; she was given one for her fifth birthday. Her mother soon recognized that her daughter showed unusual talent; even when singing, neither her intonation nor her rhythms could be faulted. She arranged lessons and jotted down little tunes for her. With such support, coupled with Jacqueline's own outstanding talent and enthusiasm, the girl's early music lessons could not but succeed. After one year the six-year-old Jacqueline began studying at the London Cello School, directed by Herbert Walenn; when seven, she gave her first public performance at a children's concert.

The well-known teacher William Pleeth entered her life when she was ten; she was to stay with him for the next seven years. It was from him, she said later, that she learned to love the big concertos she was to play with unmatched brio, as well as the chamber music for which she always had a particular affection. She had a private tutor for general schooling. When she was eleven Jacqueline du Pré won London's first Suggia gift, an international cello prize, a remarkable result in a competition which set its age limit at twenty-one. From then on her tuition was financially secure, enabling her to study in Paris with Paul Tortelier, who predicted a great future for her. After being awarded all possible prizes at the Guildhall School of Music, London, including the gold medal 'for the outstanding instrumental student of the year', Jacqueline du Pré gave her first recital in March 1961, at the Wigmore Hall in a sonata programme, accompanied by Ernest Lush. This recital brought her to the attention of the public and of professional musicians, and from then on her career was assured.

In her first appearance in a chamber music recital for the National Trust Concert Society, she was joined by Yehudi (later Baron) Menuhin and his sister Hephzibah at Osterley Park. In March 1962 she played with the BBC Symphony Orchestra, at London's South Bank, Sir Edward *Elgar's Cello Concerto, which she was to repeat at two Promenade Concerts under Sir Malcolm *Sargent and which was to become the work with which her audiences would associate her for years to come. She then launched into a career that was to take her to the Continent and the USA. In 1966 there followed an intense time of study with Mstislav Rostropovich at the Conservatoire of Moscow, from where she wrote to Yehudi Menuhin: 'Over the past two years I have felt extremely lost with my work and generally fatigued by it. Now, under Rostropovich's tuition, I am finding a new freshness in it, and the old desire to go ahead with what I love so deeply is returning.' From this honest declaration it would appear that her meteoric rise to fame had taken its toll. The following year saw her return to London for concerts with the BBC Symphony

Orchestra. An extensive tour of the United States and Canada further established the fame which had followed her first visit in 1965. American critics wrote about 'waves of intensity and love', her 'awesome gifts', her 'dazzling technique'. Beyond her cultivated and deeply musical approach to her playing she almost compelled the music to yield its utmost intensity, passion, and emotional abandon and was at one with it.

A first casual meeting with the young Argentinian-born Israeli pianist Daniel Barenboim (only son of Enrique and Aida Barenboim, pianists) turned out to lead not only to a musical partnership which was to become legendary but to Jacqueline adopting his Jewish faith before their marriage on 15 June 1967 in Israel, a country then at war. The following day they were the soloists in a concert with the Israel Philharmonic in Tel Aviv. On the programme were Schumann's Cello Concerto, which Barenboim conducted, and a Mozart Piano Concerto which he played, the conductor being Zubin Mehta. From then on the young Barenboims were involved in three musical careers: his, hers, and theirs. Their knowledge of each other's interpretive ideas was almost uncanny; they thought as one and their performances radiated this complete understanding. Though visual opposites—Jacqueline tall, with long, flowing, blonde hair and lively light-blue eyes, Daniel slim and slightly shorter with dark curly hair and intense brown eyes—they were beautiful to behold as a pair; their exuberance and joy in music-making and their deep respect for composer and score, together with their love of performance, never failed to reach the audience. Their musical partnership, which began at great speed, was to last for just four years, but this short period was filled with recitals, concerts, and recordings, the latter embracing a large catalogue, mainly on the EMI label, with which Jacqueline du Pré had an exclusive agreement. She recorded virtually the entire cello concerto repertoire with the greatest orchestras and conductors of her time, as well as numerous sonatas and other cello pieces with eminent pianists, amongst them Gerald *Moore.

When in the autumn of 1973 odd symptoms, which had begun to disturb her playing two years earlier, were diagnosed as signs of the beginning of the crippling illness multiple sclerosis, which allows only brief periods of remission, all happiness and hope for the future were taken away and the musical world was stunned. Jacqueline du Pré took this fatal blow without complaint. With typical spirit she taught, gave master classes, cooked, and, whenever possible, played chamber music with her husband and friends. Her generosity of character and unselfish nature made her an ideal chamber music player. She became a familiar and beloved sight in her wheelchair at many London concerts, and she would ask people to come and play to her. Alexander Goehr wrote his *Romanze* for her (1968).

She was appointed OBE in 1976, was a fellow of the Guildhall School of Music (1975) and the Royal College of Music (1977), and was an honorary fellow of the Royal Academy of Music (1974) and of St Hilda's College, Oxford (1984). She won the gold medal of the Guildhall School of Music and the Queen's prize (both 1960), the City of London midsummer prize (1975), and the Incorporated Society of Musicians' musician of the year award (1980). She had honorary doctorates from Salford (1978), London (1979), the Open University (1979), Sheffield (1980), Leeds (1982), Durham (1983), and Oxford (1984). She had no children. In her final years she was saddened by her husband's relationship with Helena Bachkirev and the birth of their two children. At times she gave way to depression. She died 19 October 1987 in her flat at Chepstow Villas, and was buried at the Jewish cemetery in Golders Green.

[Carol Easton, *Jacqueline du Pré*, 1989; private information; personal knowledge.]   YEHUDI MENUHIN

DURRELL, Lawrence George (1912–1990), author and poet, was born 27 February 1912 at Jullundur in the Punjab, the eldest child in the family of three sons and a daughter of Lawrence Samuel Durrell, civil engineer, and his wife, Louise Florence Dixie, who was of Irish descent. Both families had worked in India for several generations. Gerald Durrell (died 1995), the zoologist and author, was a younger brother. Early days in the Himalayas left memories of 'a kind of nursery-rhyme happiness', the opposite of his reaction to England when he was sent there for his schooling. He felt stifled. He was educated at St Joseph's College, Darjeeling, and St Edmund's School, Canterbury. To his great disappointment he failed to be accepted for Cambridge. He threw himself into London bohemian life, tried motor racing, made friends with poets, and in 1935 married Nancy Myers, who left the Slade School of Art to help things out by acting, while he played jazz in a Soho nightclub, jumping out of the window during police raids. She was the daughter of Thomas Cyril Myers, dentist.

His family's migration to Corfu in 1934 was hilariously recounted by Gerald in *My Family and Other Animals* (1956). 'It was pure gold'; and the luminous but measured ecstasy of Lawrence's poems about the Ionian, the Aegean, and the Cyclades caught this exactly. His verse represented a wholly new approach to the Greek world. (The magic was recaptured later on in *Prospero's Cell*, 1945.) Nobody could have been better equipped for running wild among olive groves. Fast as a dolphin in the sea, short,

compact, and vigorous, Durrell would work and read all day, swim a couple of miles, then feast with island friends most of the night. He had an amusing and engaging face, a charming voice, skill at languages and painting and all stringed instruments, and an unhesitating fluency, which he attributed to his mother's Irish blood. He put new oxygen into the air; nothing seemed impossible; and his alert comic sense was balanced by a certain quiet authority.

For censorship reasons, because it was regarded as *risqué*, his first published volume, *The Black Book* (1938), was brought out in Paris by the Obelisk Press, and wider contacts and friendships soon began. On a return to London, T. S. *Eliot helped and advised, and then launched him at Faber & Faber; and a stay in Paris turned his correspondence with Henry Miller into lifelong friendship. Back in Greece his closest friends were the naturalist Theodore Stephanides, the poet Seferis (George Seferiades), and the polymath storyteller George Katsimbalis (Miller met him when visiting Durrell and immortalized him in *The Colossus of Maroussi*, 1942). He gravitated to the British Council, which sent him to Kalamata to teach English. When World War II broke out, he wanted to join the Royal Air Force, but the British embassy commandeered him for press officer in Athens.

After a last minute escape to Egypt in April 1941, with his wife and baby daughter, the only child of the marriage, he worked for the British embassy in Cairo and Alexandria, where the Greek poet Constantine P. Cavafy and E. M. *Forster were his spiritual guides. He helped to edit *Personal Landscape* (1945), an impressive Middle Eastern equivalent of *Horizon*, with Robin Fedden and Bernard Spencer; and when the Aegean was set free in 1944, he became press officer for the Dodecanese, based on Rhodes. After a divorce in 1947 he married in the same year Eve Cohen, a Shulamitish Alexandrian beauty; their only child, a daughter, was called Sappho. Eve was the daughter of Moise Cohen Arazi, jeweller and money-changer. The archipelago soon inspired *Reflections on a Marine Venus* (1953) and a new crop of poems; then the British Council sent him to Argentina (1947) for two unprofitable years, and in 1949 he was put in charge of the British embassy press office in Belgrade, where the siege atmosphere of embassy life later on prompted several comic novels about diplomacy.

In 1952, aged forty now, he settled down in Cyprus to write, but the EOKA unrest drove him to Nicosia, where he was press officer once again. It was a depressing time of conflicting loyalties, and his second marriage was breaking up; it only ended when he met Claude Forde, a Frenchwoman who shared his literary bent. She was the daughter of Jacques Marie Vincendon, banker. They married in 1957, the year of his divorce from Eve Cohen, moved to France, and finally put down roots near Nîmes, in the old Provençal town of Sommières. They had no children.

In a single year, 1957, he brought out *Bitter Lemons*, his account of the Cyprus troubles; *Esprit de Corps*, his first diplomatic novel; *White Eagles over Serbia*, an adventure story; and, momentously, *Justine*. This, followed hot-foot by *Balthasar* (1958), *Mountolive* (1958), and *Clea* (1960)—'The Alexandria Quartet'—made him world famous. There was no need for the reader to concur with the aphorisms or the philosophy, or to puzzle over the author's claim to an underlying Einsteinian framework; there was so much more besides: the interlock of real Alexandria with an imaginary city populated by fantastic but believable denizens, books within books, shifts of angle and focus and voice, shock twists of plot, tortuous erotic mazes, the brio and colour of the Levant, and, above all, atmospheric effects, which burst on that grey period like the ascent of a phoenix. It was an astonishing achievement.

It is tempting to try and pigeon-hole the stages of his progress; but whatever the influences at work—whether they were the Austrian psychoanalyst Georg Groddeck (about whom Durrell wrote a book in 1961) or Cavafy, an arcane school of philosophy, some dark historical byway, or hints from the Gnostics or the Manichees—the results cohered in something new, original, and hard to classify. If English critical opinion lagged behind his lasting fame in Europe, and especially in France, geography is partly to blame; also, perhaps, faults on both sides.

Claude's death (1967) was a hard knock and *Tunc* (1968) and *Nunquam* (1970), published together as *The Revolt of Aphrodite* (1974), reflected this mood. (His daughter Sappho's suicide in 1984 was another sombre time.) His 1973 marriage to Ghislaine (daughter of Bernard de Boysson, landowner) was dissolved in 1979, but the subsequent companionship of Françoise Kestsman lit up the rest of his life. This was largely devoted to *The Avignon Quintet* (1974–85), published in one volume in 1992, into which, with undiminished vigour, he wove the whole drama of the Knights Templar. Meanwhile his books won numerous prizes and the long list of his publications includes his correspondence with Henry Miller (1963 and 1988) and Richard *Aldington (1981); his assembled essays had appeared in *Spirit of Place* (1969) and his *Collected Poems, 1931–1974* in 1980. Exhibitions of his paintings had been well received and his verse dramas were acted and broadcast with success. Later, emphysema was an intermittent infliction but it left his diligence and his spirits triumphantly intact. He died in Sommières 7 Novem-

ber 1990, and *Caesar's Vast Ghost*, the last of several books inspired by Provence, came out a few days later. His house became the Centre d'Études et Recherches Lawrence Durrell.

[Ian S. MacNiven and Carol Peirce, in *Twentieth Century Literature* (journal), parts i and ii, Hofstra University, New York, 1987; *Independent*, 9 November 1990; private information; personal knowledge.]

PATRICK LEIGH FERMOR

DWYER, George Patrick (1908–1987), seventh Roman Catholic archbishop of Birmingham, was born in Manchester 25 September 1908, the eldest in the family of five sons and two daughters of John William Dwyer, a wholesale egg and potato merchant, and his wife, Jemima ('Ima') Chatham. He was educated at St Bede's College, Manchester (1919–26), and was then accepted as a candidate for the priesthood in the diocese of Salford and sent to study at the Venerable English College, Rome. He soon proved outstanding academically and was awarded doctorates in philosophy and theology at the Gregorian University, Rome, being ordained priest on 1 November 1932. On his return to England the following year he was sent to Christ's College, Cambridge, where he was Lady Margaret scholar and obtained second classes (division I) in both parts of the modern and medieval languages tripos (1935 and 1937). In 1937 he began a ten-year stint on the staff of St Bede's, Manchester, where he taught French.

Whilst in Rome Dwyer established a firm friendship with a fellow student three years his senior, John Carmel *Heenan, and their names were linked in partnership over nearly fifty years. Some saw Dwyer as frequently following in Heenan's footsteps, yet each achieved greatness in his own right. Possessing complementary talents, they were very different characters: Heenan, the brilliant communicator and preacher; Dwyer, the outstanding theologian and linguist, with a phenomenal memory, and an outspoken clarity of expression, which at times, especially in his younger days, reflected his inability to suffer fools gladly. Yet both had a wide circle of friends and were renowned for great personal kindness towards those less gifted than themselves.

In 1947 Heenan was invited to re-establish the Catholic Missionary Society, a group of diocesan clergy charged with preaching parish missions throughout England and Wales. Heenan promptly chose Dwyer as his principal assistant and together they organized a general mission nationwide in 1949. When Heenan was appointed bishop of Leeds in 1951, Dwyer was the automatic choice as superior of the Catholic Missionary Society. In this role he showed both leadership and initiative, and established the Catholic Enquiry Centre. He himself wrote the series of pamphlets used to answer postal enquiries about the Catholic faith. The success of this venture owed much to his clear style, human understanding, and sound theology.

In 1957 Heenan was appointed archbishop of Liverpool and Dwyer was named as his successor in Leeds. He was consecrated bishop on 24 September and set about the task of calming what had become known under Heenan as 'the cruel see'. His episcopal motto *Spe Gaudentes* described well his strong and joyful faith. By his energy, zeal, and learning he did much to prepare northern Catholics for their church's call for renewal. When the second Vatican Council was convened in 1962, Dwyer was elected to the commission for the rule of dioceses, where his polyglot prowess and pastoral common sense proved of great value.

At the end of the Council Dwyer was appointed to Birmingham, where he was installed as archbishop on 21 December 1965. Of average height, stocky build, and cheerful expression, he became in later years stout and florid in appearance, yet he was never the Rabelaisian character suggested by his relative Anthony Burgess in the latter's two-volume autobiography. He had a deep, straightforward, and traditional piety, with little sympathy for post-conciliar excesses. Yet, when the newly established Bishops' Conference of England and Wales entrusted to him oversight of the revision of the church's liturgy, he insisted, no matter what his personal feelings, on following each new decree of the church.

In the ten years which followed, Dwyer's influence throughout the country steadily increased. He took a firm line in dealing with Irish Republican Army troubles in Birmingham, yet increasingly won the admiration and affection of his priests, to whom he was known as 'Instant Wisdom'. Age added warm compassion and support to the strict disciplinarian. As Heenan suffered a series of heart attacks, Dwyer naturally supplied leadership to the Bishops' Conference, for which he wrote the widely acclaimed statement on moral questions.

When Heenan died in November 1975, it was inevitable that people should wonder whether once again Dwyer would follow him, this time to Westminster. But he recognized the danger and publicly informed the apostolic delegate that at sixty-seven he felt too old to be considered for the post. But he did not escape entirely. Whilst Archbishop Basil Hume became used to episcopal leadership, Dwyer was elected president of the Bishops' Conference for a three-year period, the only non-archbishop of Westminster ever to have filled that position. It was after this that his own health began to fail and in 1981, suffering from circulatory problems, he resigned his archdiocese, continuing as apostolic administrator until the appointment of his successor in March 1982. He had honorary degrees from Keele (1979) and Warwick (1980). He lived another five years in retirement at St Paul's Convent, Selly Park, Birmingham, showing exemplary patience as he lost the use of one faculty after another. He died 17 September 1987 at the Alexian Brothers' Nursing Home in Manchester.

[Private information; personal knowledge.]

DEREK WORLOCK

E

EASTON, Sir James Alfred (1908–1990), Royal Air Force officer and intelligence officer, was born in Winchester 11 February 1908, the youngest in the family of two sons and five daughters of William Coryndon Easton, chemist and botanist, and his wife, Alice Summers. He was educated at Peter Symonds School, Winchester. He passed into the Royal Air Force College at Cranwell in 1926, and was commissioned into the RAF in 1928. He held a series of flying appointments, including a spell in biplanes co-operating with the army on the North-West Frontier of India (1929-32) and duties in Egypt (1934-6). He was also increasingly regarded as an able young officer with a promising future. In 1937 he was posted to Canada as RAF armament liaison officer with the Canadian National Ministry of Defence (1937-9). There he met and married in 1939 Anna Mary, daughter of Lieutenant-Colonel John Andrew McKenna, of the Royal Canadian Engineers, from Ottawa. Not only was it a very happy marriage, but it had a strong influence on his subsequent career.

'Jack' Easton returned to England early in 1940, having been mentioned in dispatches that year, and was posted to the intelligence department at the Air Ministry. He gradually concentrated on the problem of technical innovations introduced by the *Luftwaffe*, particularly in the field of navigational aids and radar. In 1943 he became an air commodore, and was director of the intelligence (research) department at the Air Ministry. He represented the RAF's interests on (Sir) Winston *Churchill's Crossbow committee, whose function was to consider all means of countering the threat of the V1 flying bomb and the V2 rockets. He also became involved in the allocation of RAF aircraft for the clandestine dropping of agents into north-west Europe. All this brought him increasingly in touch with organizations and individuals outside the Air Ministry, including the Special Operations Executive and MI6, where he worked closely with the gifted young Professor R. V. Jones. His clear mind, considerable administrative ability, cool temperament, and gift for getting the best out of different groups with differing vested interests, made him an increasingly respected figure in the intelligence world.

Immediately after the war Easton was guided towards MI6, for which he had excellent qualifications. Sir Stewart *Menzies, the chief of the service at that time, was glad to accept him. When Menzies retired in 1951, and Major-General (Sir) John A. *Sinclair took over as 'C' or head of the service, Easton was appointed his deputy, with the clear understanding that he would eventually take over.

He made a substantial contribution towards rationalizing and uniting a service that had developed too fast in the war. Within the service he was liked and trusted. His one possible weakness was that, except for North America and Australia, foreign politics did not greatly interest him. When the treachery of H. A. R. ('Kim') *Philby, Guy *Burgess, and Donald *Maclean was discovered in 1951, Easton was one of those whose minds remained calm and objective at a time when Whitehall in general, and the Foreign Office in particular, were just wringing their hands. He decided in the summer of 1951, after a careful review of the evidence, that Philby was guilty. It was in this context that he first worked closely with (Sir) Dick White of MI5. He dealt with the Americans pragmatically over the case. He understood the clear distinction in Britain between a firm belief in guilt and the many difficult security problems involved in an open trial in a public court before a British jury. The fact that the Philby case did not destroy relations between MI6 and the CIA for very long was partly due to Easton's calm pragmatism.

For the next few years Easton worked closely with Sinclair. However, the world was changing and the influence of the armed services in Whitehall was gradually declining. The year 1956 was a climacteric, with the twentieth party congress in Moscow, the disaster and folly of the Suez affair, the Commander Lionel Crabbe incident, and the Soviet invasion of Hungary. The Crabbe case, in which Easton was in no way involved, was in itself of little importance and did not upset the Russians. But time and chance turned it into a political and govermental time bomb, and it was used as a reason for dismissing Sinclair. Dick White, the head of MI5, was appointed to replace him late in 1956. Easton served him loyally, and with grace, as his deputy, but he was told that the succession would not be his. He was not prepared to accept this. That he did not become chief of MI6, as planned, was not due to any failure on his part, but was the result of an inevitable switch of power in Whitehall from the armed forces to the Cabinet Office and the Foreign Office.

In 1958 Easton was offered a respectable job as consul-general in Detroit, Michigan. His wife had many friends in the area, and he accepted the post without outward bitterness. It worked out well, and he was for ten years a popular consul-general in a thriving, dynamic community. On his retirement in 1968 he decided to remain in the area which he had found so congenial. He became a much respected member of various Detroit-based industrial concerns, and a convivial golfing companion at the Grosse Pointe Country Club. In 1988 he caused a sensation when he publicly discussed the Kim Philby affair with the author Anthony Cave Brown before the latter's biography of Sir Stewart Menzies was published (*The Secret Servant*, 1988). Easton died 19 October 1990 at Grosse Point, Michigan.

Easton was neat, slim, dark, and conventionally dressed. He was appointed an officer of the US Legion of Merit in 1945, CBE in 1945, CB in 1952, and KCMG in 1956. His wife, Anna, died in 1977. They had a son and a daughter. In 1980 he married Jane, widow of William H. Walker, of Detroit, and daughter of Dr Joseph Stanley Leszynski, surgeon, also of Detroit.

[Private information; personal knowledge.]
JOHN BRUCE LOCKHART

EDE, Harold Stanley ('Jim') (1895–1990), curator, lecturer, and creator of Kettle's Yard, Cambridge, was born 7 April 1895 in Penarth, Glamorgan, the younger son and second of three children of Edward Hornby Ede, solicitor, of Penarth, and his wife Mildred Mary Furley, sometime schoolteacher, only daughter of Joseph Blanch, Methodist minister. At the Leys School, Cambridge (1909–12), where he began a lifelong friendship with Donald *Winnicott, he developed an interest in early Italian art which had burgeoned on a trip to Paris as a fourteen-year-old. He retained this passion throughout his life and in 1926 published *Florentine Drawings of the Quattrocento*.

Ede was a somewhat rebellious child who enjoyed reverie and nature rather than academic discipline. In his unpublished memoir Ede described himself as an effeminate young man. As he grew older he placed particular value on male friendships. However, he enjoyed the company of his maternal grandmother and of his aunt Maud, a painter whom he visited in Paris. He gained a passion for reading from his mother and his father was a bibliophile.

Leaving the Leys early he began to train as a painter at Newlyn and then Edinburgh College of Art before war service interrupted his studies.

In 1914 he joined the 6th battalion (Pioneers) of the South Wales Borderers. He served as a lieutenant in France, was invalided back, and was posted to Cambridge (officer cadet battalion) and then India, where he suffered serious illness for several months. He returned via Alexandria, which he described as the first place in which he felt at home. Earlier generations of his family had lived around the Mediterranean.

In 1919 Ede enrolled at the Slade School of Fine Art, leaving in March 1921 to become the photographer's assistant at the National Gallery and then, in 1922, an assistant at the Tate Gallery. During his fourteen years at the Tate (1922–36) Ede established close contacts with avant-garde artists in Paris but served under a director, J. B. *Manson, who was unable to recognize his talents. Had his friendships with Picasso, Braque, Chagall, Brancusi, Miró, and others been exploited, the Tate could have had an unrivalled collection of early twentieth-century art. Similarly his friendships with younger British artists such as Ben *Nicholson and (R.) Winifred *Nicholson, (Dame) (J.) Barbara *Hepworth, Henry *Moore, David *Jones, and Christopher Wood were also ignored.

Ede met the Nicholsons in 1923 and it was they who kindled his interest in contemporary art. Others whom he acknowledged as important influences on his life were Gertrude Harris (widow of Frederick Leverton *Harris), Lady Ottoline *Morrell, Helen Sutherland, and T. E. *Lawrence, with whom he regularly corresponded. Indeed, correspondence was a central activity in Ede's life.

In 1921 Ede married Helen, daughter of Otto Schlapp, professor of German at the University of Edinburgh. Scottish by birth, Helen began to call him Jim, a name which he was to adopt for the remainder of his life. Together they had two daughters. Within two years Ede acquired 1 Elm Row, Hampstead, with the help of his father, and there he and his wife entertained relentlessly, creating something of a salon for artists, collectors, and dignitaries. Ede was a collector of people as much as of art.

In 1926 Ede discovered the work of the sculptor Henri Gaudier-Brzeska (1819–1915), when his estate was offered to the Tate, but there was little enthusiasm for his work. After persuading a number of collectors to purchase sculptures and drawings, Ede was given permission to acquire the remainder. From that year onwards he championed the cause of Gaudier-Brzeska by publishing books—*A Life of Gaudier-Brzeska* (1930), which was republished as *Savage Messiah* (1931)—and making generous gifts to museums, notably the Tate Gallery, the Musée des Beaux-Arts in Orléans (1959), and the Musée National d'Art Moderne in Paris (1967). He was nominated chevalier (1959) and officer (1967) of the Legion of Honour.

In October 1936 Ede, a leading contender to be the next director, resigned from the Tate on grounds of ill health, unable to work further with Manson. Supporting himself by American lecture tours, and with financial aid from his father, he and his family moved to Tangier. He spent the war years in Tangier, North America, and England.

The Edes sold their house in 1952 and acquired a large, old farmhouse in the Loire valley. They returned to England in 1956 and in 1957 purchased a row of four derelict, seventeenth-century cottages in Cambridge. Ede converted them into a single dwelling and named it Kettle's Yard. Here he arranged his by then considerable collection of works of art, some given to him by his mother, who had purchased them on his advice, in a manner which would make modern art not merely approachable but alive, combining his twentieth-century enthusiasms with his love of artefacts and materials from the past. Works of art by Ben Nicholson and Brancusi would sit alongside antique country furniture, ancient stones, flints, and amphora. Old floorboards, tiles, and windows salvaged from demolished buildings found a natural home in a building which harmonized the modernist spirit of the 1930s with the experience of living in north Africa. A respect for light and space were the hub of Ede's vision. The house was infused with the spirituality which formed the core of his and his wife's life. They kept open house every afternoon and those fortunate to be there at closing time were invited to tea. In 1966 Ede gave Kettle's Yard to the University of Cambridge. He also endowed a student travel fund. Ede remained in residence until 1973, when he and his wife removed themselves to Edinburgh. She died in 1977. He maintained links with the curators of Kettle's Yard and published a book on it, *A Way of Life* (1984).

Although he was converted to the Church of England during his time in Cambridge, Ede's belief in God was unbound by the strictures of any one denomination or by his early Methodist formation. He believed in God's all-pervasiveness and Kettle's Yard was for him a manifestation of God. Determination, obstinacy, and a sense of rightness, mixed with a twinkling charm, were important traits of his character. His own description of David Jones best encapsulates him: 'Someone with a strange force which comes, not out of the strength of his body, but from the strength of his intention.' He died in Edinburgh, 15 March 1990.

[Unpublished memoir in the possession of the family; information from relatives; personal knowledge.]

JEREMY LEWISON

EDRICH, William John ('Bill') (1916–1986), cricketer, was born 26 March 1916 in Lingwood, Norfolk, the second son and second child in the family of four sons and a daughter of William Archer Edrich, tenant farmer, and his wife, Edith Mattocks, originally of Cumbrian farming stock, whose family had moved to Norfolk. Educated at Bracondale School, Norwich, where his cricketing prowess soon became evident, Bill Edrich was a member of a noted family of cricketers, which was able to field an entire eleven under the family name. His three brothers—Geoffrey, Eric, and Brian—all played first-class cricket, whilst his cousin, John McHugh Edrich, MBE, was to be a well-known Surrey and England batsman.

After several successful seasons with Norfolk in the Minor Counties championship, he was advised to seek an engagement with Middlesex. He qualified for Middlesex and lived in London, playing variously for the Marylebone Cricket Club and Norfolk. He made his first-class début for Minor Counties in 1934, and such was his progress that, in his first full season for Middlesex in 1937, he scored over 2,000 runs, and was chosen to accompany the third Baron Tennyson's tour of India the following winter. In spite of several failures, he retained his test place, and in South Africa in the winter of 1938–9 he scored a match-saving 219 at Durban. In 1938 he managed the unusual feat of 1,000 runs before the end of May. During World War II he served as a pilot with No. 21 Squadron, Coastal Command, rising from flight lieutenant to acting squadron-leader, and his bravery was rewarded with the DFC (1941).

Returning to the cricketing fray in 1946, he eventually regained his England place—his test career was always dogged by selectors' inconsistencies—and in 1947 he changed status from professional to amateur. The year 1947 proved to be his greatest. In partnership with the mercurial Denis Compton, he broke many records, and Middlesex and England flourished accordingly. In that summer he made 3,539 runs, including 12 centuries, and averaged 80.43. He captained Middlesex from 1951 to 1957, initially in harness with Denis Compton, and, after his retirement from first-class cricket in 1959, played for his native Norfolk until 1971.

In his 571 games in first-class cricket, Edrich scored 36,965 runs, including 86 centuries, with an average of 42.39. His highest score was 269, not out, versus Northamptonshire in 1947. He also took 479 wickets and 529 catches, and made a solitary stumping. In 39 test matches he scored 2,440 runs for an average of 40, and took 41 wickets.

Edrich approached his cricketing duties with much the same fervour with which he tackled his romantic ventures. Gusto and valour were his watchwords. As a batsman, he was a courageous player of quick bowling, relishing the hook and the pull-drive, and dealing plainly and authoritatively with much that he faced. As a bowler, he rushed intrepidly into the attack, hurling the ball awkwardly at often startled opponents. He was a most effective fielder, initially in the out-field, but mainly in the slips. Above all, he was, in cricket as in his domestic life, abundantly cheery and optimistic. A Robert *Bruce among cricketers, he was ever ready to try again. A very popular sportsman, he was only a little short of the highest rank of cricketers, and his fame was very much bound up with his sparkling relationship with Denis Compton. The sports journalist R. C. Robertson-Glasgow wrote that, while Compton was poetry, Edrich was 'prose, robust and clear'.

Edrich was short, dark, and keen-eyed, with brisk, lithe movements. A man of ardent amorous energies, he was married five times, each for relatively short periods. His first four marriages ended in divorce, and his fifth wife outlived him briefly. His first marriage, in 1936, was to Betty, typist, daughter of Sydney William Hobbs, railway official. The marriage ended in divorce in 1944 and in the same year he married Marion, an officer in the Women's Auxiliary Air Force, the divorced wife of Edward Reginald Fish and daughter of Albert Ernest Forster, works manager. They were divorced in 1948 and in 1949 he married Jessy Shaw, the divorced wife of Harold Tetley and daughter of Hubert Gomersall, building society manager. They had one son and the marriage ended with divorce in 1960. In the same year he married Brenda Valerie Terry, insurance consultant, whose previous marriage had been dissolved, the daughter of Constant Wells Ponder, medical practitioner. They had one son and the marriage ended with divorce in 1973. His fifth and final marriage, in 1983, was to Mary Elizabeth Somerville, hairdresser, whose previous marriage had been dissolved, daughter of Frederick Vincent Wesson, sales manager. Edrich died in Chesham as the result of a fall down the stairs around midnight at home, following a St George's day celebration, 23 or 24 April 1986.

[Ralph Barker, *The Cricketing Family Edrich*, 1975; Alan Hill, *Bill Edrich, a Biography*, 1994; *Wisden Cricketers' Almanack*, 1948 and 1987.]

ERIC MIDWINTER

EDWARDS, James Keith O'Neill ('Jimmy') (1920–1988), entertainer, was born 23 March 1920 in Barnes, London, the fifth of five sons and eighth of nine children of Reginald Walter Kenrick Edwards, professor of mathematics at King's College, London, and his wife, Phyllis Katherine Cowan, who was from New Zealand. He was educated at St Paul's Cathedral Choir School

and King's College School, Wimbledon, where he first developed what was to become a lifelong enthusiasm for brass instruments and learned to play the trombone. In 1938 he went to St John's College, Cambridge, where he read history and developed a mock 'professor' act for the Cambridge Footlights, in which he gave a musical lecture on the trombone.

His university career was interrupted by World War II and in 1939 he joined the Royal Air Force, eventually succeeding in his ambition to become a pilot. In 1944 he was flying a hazardous mission towing gliders and dropping supplies to the beleaguered troops at Arnhem when his Dakota was badly hit by a German Focke-Wulf. He made a successful landing, saving the lives of two men on board and sustaining burns to his face which he later disguised by growing the magnificent 'handlebar' moustache that was to become his trademark. He was awarded the DFC in 1945 for his skill and bravery.

Throughout his RAF career he had successfully entertained the troops with his 'professor' act, and so after demobilization in 1946 he contemplated life as an entertainer. He served his apprenticeship at London's Windmill theatre, where he met Frank Muir, who with Denis Norden was to write his most successful comedy material. In 1948 Muir and Norden created one of Edwards's best loved characters, the bibulous belligerent Pa Glum in the BBC radio programme *Take It From Here*. *Take It From Here* ran from 1948 until 1959, commanding audiences of over twenty million and making Edwards a wealthy man. He bought polo ponies, an aeroplane, and a farm in Fittleworth, Sussex, which was run by his elder brother Alan while Edwards played the local squire. Fox-hunting was one of his favourite pastimes and he was proud to be made master of foxhounds of the Old Surrey and Burstow Hunt. In 1951 he was elected lord rector of Aberdeen University, an appointment he held until 1954.

From 1957 until 1977 he appeared in *Does the Team Think?*, a radio panel game he had devised in which four comedians answered light-hearted questions from a studio audience. He attempted some 'straight' acting, turning in a creditable Sir Toby Belch in *Twelfth Night* and Falstaff in *The Merry Wives of Windsor* for BBC radio (both 1962). On television he found a tailor-made role in the series *Whack-O!* (1957–61 and 1971–2), in which he played the corpulent, conniving headmaster of Chiselbury School. His films included *Three Men in a Boat* (1957), *Bottoms Up* (1960), *The Plank* (1979), and *It's Your Move* (1982). Perhaps most surprising of all, in 1964 he stood as Conservative candidate for Paddington North, and although he did not win his seat, he polled

10,639 votes—more than his predecessor had gained.

His private life was less satisfactory. In 1958 he married Valerie, a British Overseas Airways Corporation ground stewardess, daughter of William Seymour, small landowner. They had no children and eventually divorced in 1969. She later told the press that on their honeymoon he had admitted that he was a homosexual 'trying to reform'. In 1976 Ramon Douglas, an Australian female impersonator, told the tabloid newspapers that for the past ten years he and Edwards had shared a 'loving relationship'. Even though he was personally devastated by the resulting publicity, Edwards found that his career did not suffer and in 1978 he was invited to reinvent his Pa Glum character when the Glums were revived for television. In 1984 he published his memoirs, *Six of the Best*, which followed an earlier autobiography, *Take It From Me* (1953).

By the early 1980s Edwards's blustering style of comedy was going out of fashion and he concentrated on touring in plays such as *Big Bad Mouse* with his friend Eric Sykes. He spent more time in the house he had bought in Perth, Western Australia, and it was there in 1988 that he became ill with bronchial pneumonia. He returned to England and died in the Cromwell Hospital, London, 7 July 1988.

[Jimmy Edwards, *Take It From Me*, 1953, and *Six of the Best*, 1984 (autobiographies); information from family and friends.]   VERONICA DAVIS

ELIAS, Norbert (1897–1990), sociologist, was born 22 June 1897 in Breslau, Germany (which later became Wrocław, Poland), the only child of Hermann Elias, businessman, and his wife, Sophie Galevski. He attended the Johannesgymnasium, Breslau, and, after service in the German army during World War I, read philosophy and medicine at Breslau University. He was awarded a doctorate in philosophy at Breslau in January 1924 for a thesis entitled *Idee und Individuum*. Financial difficulties caused by the great German inflation of 1922–3 interrupted his studies, but in 1925 he went to Heidelberg to work for his *Habilitation* in sociology, at first with Alfred Weber (1868–1958). In 1930, when Karl Mannheim (1893–1947) moved to Frankfurt as professor, Elias accompanied him as academic assistant. His *Habilitation* was rushed through early in 1933, after Adolf Hitler came to power, but shortly afterwards Elias, as a Jew, sought refuge first in Paris (1933–4) and then in London (from 1935), eventually becoming a British citizen in 1952.

In Paris and London Elias completed the two volumes of his *magnum opus*, *Über den Prozess der Zivilisation (The Civilizing Process*, 1994); they were published obscurely in Basle in 1939, and received very little notice at that unpropitious

moment. In 1939 Elias was awarded a senior research fellowship at the London School of Economics, interrupted by a period of internment as an enemy alien, and 'made himself useful' to the British security services. After the war he made a meagre living by extramural lecturing in London, and helped found the Group Analytic Society. Only in 1954, aged fifty-seven, did he obtain a post in a British university—at Leicester, from where he formally retired as reader in 1962. In 1962–4 he was professor of sociology at the University of Ghana.

His international reputation was gained in his long and productive old age. *Über den Prozess der Zivilisation* was republished in 1969, to acclaim in Germany, the Netherlands, and France. His later books, in their English versions, include *The Established and the Outsiders* (1965), *What Is Sociology?* (1978), *The Court Society* (on the court of Louis XIV, 1983), *The Loneliness of the Dying* (1985), *Involvement and Detachment* (essays on the sociology of knowledge and the sciences, 1987), *Quest for Excitement* (essays on the sociology of sport, 1986), *The Symbol Theory* (1991), *Time: an Essay* (1992), *Mozart: Portrait of a Genius* (1993), and *The Germans* (1995). A selection of his poems, *Los der Menschen*, appeared in 1987.

The Civilizing Process underlies all Elias's later work. The first volume begins by examining how the word 'civilization', derived from *civilité*, denoting the manners of courtiers, came to be used by nineteenth-century Europeans to express their sense of superiority over lower ranks or other cultures. The characteristics taken as evidence of this superiority had come to seem innate, and the Europeans were unaware that their own ancestors had acquired them through a long *process* of civilization. Through books about manners, from the Middle Ages to the nineteenth century, Elias traced the changing standards of good behaviour in matters such as spitting, nose-blowing, undressing, the toilet, and table manners. The threshold of repugnance had advanced, the expected standard of self-constraint had become more demanding, and many matters were hidden behind the scenes of social *and* mental life. Elias was, however, concerned not just with outward bodily propriety, but with violence and cruelty and changing feelings towards them. This provided a link to his second volume, dealing with state-formation processes, including the 'taming of warriors'. The monopolization of violence by the state, and longer chains of social interdependence, were associated with gradual changes in typical personality make-up.

Controversy about Elias's theory has concerned whether it is 'Eurocentric', whether twentieth-century 'permissive society' represents a reversal of the civilizing process, and whether his ideas are refuted by events such as the destruction of the Jews during World War II. Yet *The Civilizing Process* in part represents Elias's own attempt to grapple with unfolding events in Nazi Germany. The fact that his own mother died in Auschwitz was the cause of the major psychological trauma of Elias's life, and may possibly be one reason why he published little between 1939 and 1965. He could be quarrelsome, and in relation to his work was very sensitive. At the same time he was delightful company, immensely knowledgeable and stimulating, a fascinating conversationalist with a puckish interest in the trivial details of life. He was short in stature, stronger than he looked, and swam daily until his late eighties. Photographs can be found in *Human Figurations*, the 1977 Festschrift, edited by Peter Gleichmann *et al.*

In 1971 Elias was given the title and pension of professor emeritus of the University of Frankfurt. He was the first recipient of the Theodor W. Adorno prize, conferred by the city of Frankfurt in 1977, and had honorary doctorates from the universities of Bielefeld and Strasburg II. He was also awarded the German Grosskreuz des Bundesdienstordens (1986) and was a commander of the Order of Orange-Nassau (1987). In his adopted country of citizenship he enjoyed only a *succès d'estime*; from the mid-1970s he spent little time in Britain. Elias never married. He died peacefully in his study in Amsterdam, 1 August 1990.

[Norbert Elias, *Reflections on a Life*, 1994; Hermann Korte, *Über Norbert Elias*, Suhrkamp, 1988; personal knowledge.]   STEPHEN MENNELL

ELLIOT, SIR **John** (1898–1988), railway manager and chief of London Transport, was born John Elliot Blumenfeld 6 May 1898 at Albert Bridge Road, London, the younger son and third of four children of Ralph David *Blumenfeld, journalist and later editor of the *Daily Express*, and his wife, Teresa ('Daisie'), née Blumfeld [*sic*], a cousin. He was educated at Marlborough College and the Royal Military College, Sandhurst. In 1917 he was commissioned in the 3rd King's Own Hussars and went to France in October. He took part in the battles of Cambrai, Amiens, and Selle, returning to England in autumn 1919 as an acting adjutant. Reluctant to depend upon his family for the private income he would need as a cavalry officer, he resigned his commission and went to the United States to take up his father's profession of journalism.

After three years in New York on the *New York Times* he was recruited by the first Baron *Beaverbrook, the proprietor of the *Daily Express*, as assistant editor of the London *Evening Standard*. Knowing the disadvantage of having a German name, he had changed his name by deed

poll in 1922, taking his second forename as his surname. Within two years Beaverbrook sacked him and in 1925 he was taken on by Sir Herbert Walker, general manager of the Southern Railway, to improve that railway's image, as a public relations and advertising assistant. He soon moved from public relations to the traffic department, becoming deputy general manager of the Southern Railway in 1937. As such he played a major role in the electrification of the Southern Railway, the establishment of its World War II headquarters in Dorking, the evacuation of the children of London, and the transport of the survivors of Dunkirk. For his work in the war he became an officer of the Legion of Honour and received the American Medal of Freedom (1945).

After the end of the war, in 1947 he became general manager of Southern Railways, and, a year later, upon nationalization, chief regional officer of the Southern Region of British Railways. He moved to the same position in the London Midland Region in 1950 and in 1951 became chairman of the Railway Executive, which was abolished in 1953. In that year he became chairman of London Transport, a post he held until 1959, when he had to leave after the great seven-week London bus strike in mid-1958. He was responsible for the introduction of the Routemaster bus and the construction of the Victoria Line for the underground railway. He then assumed the chairmanship of Thomas Cook (1959–67) and the directorships of other organizations. Throughout this period he had travelled abroad extensively, to study other transport industries and to advise foreign governments on their transport problems. He was president of the Institute of Transport in 1953–4 and was knighted in 1954. He was also colonel (commanding) of the Engineer and Railway Staff Corps, Royal Engineers (1956–63). His last public appointment was as a director of the British Airports Authority in 1965–9, at the same time as he was campaigning against Stansted airport.

Elliot had a large circle of friends and many outside interests. He reviewed books on military history; wrote a newspaper column; shot, fished, and hunted; studied the campaigns of Napoleon, the American civil war, and the domestic life of Victorian London; and founded a dining club. In his late seventies he succumbed to the temptation to buy a small open sports car. He wrote three books—*Where Our Fathers Died* (1964), about the western front fifty years after World War I; *On and Off the Rails*, an autobiography (1982); and, perhaps his best, *The Way of the Tumbrils* (1958), a picture of the French revolution as seen from the streets of Paris in the 1950s, which *The Times* said should prove popular 'with every wanderer in Paris who wants, in kindred mood, to find history in stones'.

'Goo' Elliot was a short, stocky man, five feet six inches in height, and lost most of his hair by the time he was thirty. He lived in Great Easton, Essex, where he had a beautiful garden. In 1924 he married Elizabeth ('Betty'), daughter of Dr Arthur Stanbury Cobbledick, a general practitioner who later specialized in ophthalmology. He practised in a house in Bolton Street, London W1, in which Betty grew up. The Elliots had a son and a daughter. As Elliot approached the end of his life he remained always sprucely turned out, although he was physically frail. He died 18 September 1988 at St Stephen's Hospital, Fulham.

[Sir John Elliot, *On and Off the Rails* (autobiography), 1982; *The Times*, 20 September 1988; *Independent*, 21 September 1988.]   C. S. NICHOLLS

ELLMANN, Richard David (1918–1987), literary biographer and critic, was born 15 March 1918 in Highland Park, Detroit, Michigan, the second of the three sons (there were no daughters) of James Isaac Ellmann, lawyer, a Jewish Romanian immigrant, and his wife, Jeanette Barsook, an immigrant from Kiev. He attended local schools before going to Yale, where he graduated with exceptional distinction in English (1939), and completed an MA dissertation in 1941.

On America's entry into World War II in 1942 he joined the Office of Strategic Services, but that August he began his academic career as an instructor at Harvard. This was interrupted in 1943 when he enlisted in the US navy and was posted to a construction battalion. Although he disliked military service, he was to turn it to account in 1945 when he unexpectedly found himself seconded to the OSS in London. That September he visited the widow of W. B. *Yeats in Dublin. Impressed by his knowledge of her husband's work, she gave him access to her immense archive. He returned to Ireland immediately on his discharge from the navy in May 1946, and wrote a Litt.B. at Trinity College, Dublin, while simultaneously undertaking a Yale Ph.D. on Yeats's life and writings. This, the first Yale doctorate on a twentieth-century writer, was published in 1949 as *Yeats: the Man and the Masks* and remains one of the best introductions to the poet's work.

In 1947 he returned to teach at Harvard, where he met, and in August 1949 married, a talented Irish-American feminist critic, Mary Donahue, the daughter of William Henry Donahue, baker, of Newburyport, Massachusetts. Two years later he was appointed professor of English at Northwestern University, Evanston, Illinois. He had already begun research for his biography of James *Joyce, but his next book was a sophisticated critical study of Yeats's poetry, *The Identity of Yeats* (1954). His magisterial

James Joyce appeared in 1959 and immediately confirmed his reputation as the outstanding literary biographer of his generation, its research, narrative control, and wit setting new standards in the genre. His growing distinction was reflected in a series of academic honours, fellowships, and visiting professorships, and in 1963 by his promotion to the Franklin Bliss Snyder chair at Northwestern, which he held until 1968. Deeply involved in editing Joyce's writings and letters, he also found time to co-edit *The Modern Tradition* (1965), a collection of key Modernist texts, as well as anthologies of modern poetry. In 1967 he published *Eminent Domain*, a series of elegant essays on Yeats's various literary relationships. The following year he moved to Yale as professor of English, and it was supposed that he would see out his career at his old Alma Mater. But after only two years he was invited to apply for the Goldsmiths' chair of English literature at Oxford and was duly elected (1970), with a fellowship at New College. The move to Oxford was partly prompted by his proposed biography of Oscar *Wilde, but was also because, established at Yale, he could predict exactly which meetings he would be attending on any given day in the foreseeable future; Oxford offered no such predictability.

The move was marred when his wife suffered a cerebral haemorrhage that permanently confined her to a wheelchair. Of their three children, the eldest, Stephen, remained in America while the two daughters, Maud and Lucy, settled in England with their parents. The new professor delivered his inaugural lecture, *Literary Biography*, on 4 May 1971, and in 1972 he published *Ulysses on the Liffey*, which examined the principles of construction of Joyce's novel. A book of essays of the following year, *Golden Codgers*, ranged from George *Eliot to T. S. *Eliot, and *The Consciousness of Joyce* appeared in 1977. At once bemused and delighted by Oxford, Ellmann's forte was the seminar rather than the lecture, and he excelled in his supervision of graduate students.

In 1984 he retired as Goldsmiths' professor and took up the Woodruff chair at Emory University in Georgia. But he remained resident in Oxford, holding both an honorary fellowship at New College (1987) and an extraordinary fellowship at Wolfson College (1984), and he and his wife continued to keep open house at 39 St Giles to a wide circle of friends. All this time he had been working on his biography of Oscar Wilde, garnering new information and drafting and redrafting the book. He was elected a fellow of the British Academy in 1979. He had honorary degrees from several American universities and from Göteborg.

He was a tall man, balding, bespectacled, and tending to plumpness, with a warm smile and an infectious laugh. It was in the summer of 1986 that his friends began to notice a slight slurring of speech and an awkwardness of posture. These symptoms became more pronounced and motor neurone disease was diagnosed. With typical fortitude he refused to be intimidated by this terrible illness, and when speech finally failed he communicated through a tickertape machine, the messages showing that he had lost nothing of his intellectual edge and personal kindness. His final days were occupied with preparing *Oscar Wilde* (1987) for the press and he was able to read the proofs shortly before he died in Oxford 13 May 1987.

[Susan Dick *et al.* (eds.), *Omnium Gatherum: Essays for Richard Ellmann*, 1989; private information; personal knowledge.]   JOHN KELLY

ELWYN-JONES, BARON (1909–1989), lawyer and politician. [See JONES, (FREDERICK) ELWYN.]

EMETT, (Frederick) Rowland (1906–1990), cartoonist, depicter of fantastic trains, and inventor of whimsical machines, was born 22 October 1906 as Frederick Rowland Emett in New Southgate, Middlesex, the elder son (there were no daughters) of Arthur Emett, proprietor of a small advertising business, a perpetually optimistic, always disappointed, spare-time inventor, and his wife, Alice Veale. He was the grandson of William Henry Emett, lithographer and sometime court engraver to Queen *Victoria.

Emett did not achieve fame until his late thirties, although from his youngest days his future was well signposted. He was educated at Waverley Grammar School, Birmingham. Described as a lazy pupil, he invariably came top of the school in drawing and caricatured not only his masters, but also, prophetically, machinery and vehicles. At the age of eleven he wrote publishable poems; at fourteen he took out a world patent on a pneumatic volume-control for the acoustic gramophone. While studying briefly at Birmingham School of Arts and Crafts Emett aspired to become a landscape painter and in 1931 his 'Cornish Harbour' was hung on the line at the Royal Academy. During the depression he worked for an advertising agency, failed as a freelance commercial artist, then returned to agency work until his career was interrupted by World War II, throughout which he worked as a draughtsman for the Air Ministry. At the same time he discovered and perfected his gift for drawing cartoons.

On 12 April 1941 he married Mary, daughter of Albert Evans, silversmith, at Kings Norton church, Birmingham. They had one daughter, Claire. Mary Emett, a formidable personality who was methodical and firm in business matters, was shocked by her husband's insouciant attitude towards bookkeeping. Her offer to untangle his business affairs was gratefully accepted and from then until the end of his life she successfully propelled and managed his business interests.

Emett first contributed to *Punch* in 1939; there the originality of his humour was quickly recognized by the art editor, (C.) Kenneth *Bird ('Fougasse'). Soon his strange, bumbling, increasingly attenuated trains, called Nellie, or Bard of Avon, or Humphrey, unsteadily rode branch lines through the pages of *Punch* from Paddlecombe to Prawnmouth, from Friars Ambling to Little Figment. There was warmth in these endearing creations, which generally appeared as half-page drawings, some of them packed with gossamer-fine cross-hatching, others bathed in subtle washes. His occasional full-page colour work displayed a mastery of water-colour and gouache. Seeking a resident cartoonist, Arthur *Christiansen, the editor of the *Daily Express*, favoured Emett for the post, but the artist realized that his work, in which delicacy of line and thought played a major part, would suffer under the rigours of daily newspaper journalism and sensibly refused the offer. Among Emett's publications were *Engines, Aunties, and Others* (1943), *Sidings and Suchlike* (1946), *Saturday Slow* (1948), *The Early Morning Milk Train* (1976), and *Emett's Ministry of Transport* (1981).

In 1951 'Nellie', Emett's most famous steam engine—the first of three—was created in beaten copper and mahogany and rode the rails from Far Twittering to Oyster Creek to become one of the most popular attractions in the Festival of Britain. Emett's name began to spread beyond Britain and his work was much in demand in the United States and elsewhere. *Punch* had difficulty grasping the extent to which his reputation had increased and was unhappy at the encroachment upon his time and energy. In 1944 he had signed a contract to draw exclusively for the magazine, but in 1951, after several polite disagreements, financial and editorial, they parted company. Although Emett never entirely gave up drawing, he lost interest in drawing cartoons and devoted his energies to designing and naming the inventions which he called his 'things'.

The reality of Nellie had led to commissions for the Astro Terremare (for Shell Oil), the Hogmuddle Rotatory Niggler and Fidgeter, the Featherstone Openwork Basket-weave Gentleman's Flying Machine, and many others. In 1968 he designed machines for the film *Chitty Chitty Bang Bang*. Emett's work—Emettland—travelled around the world, leaving behind trails of laughter, and these large creations were destined to be housed in museums and galleries, not only in Britain but in the USA and Canada. The Smithsonian Institution, Washington, DC; the

Ontario Science Centre, Toronto; and the Museum of Science and Industry, Chicago, hold some of them. Nottingham's Victoria Centre has his Rhythmical Time Fountain (1974).

Devising, designing, and ultimately making the 'things' devoured Emett's time and energy. He rose at 5.15 each morning. In summer he might bicycle the three miles to the forge at Streat, where with several talented assistants he would shape his creations into their daft reality. Otherwise he would draw or paint in the studio-cum-guesthouse behind Wild Goose Cottage at Ditchling, the home he had bought on the proceeds of a multi-page spread in *Life* magazine. A conventional man, who dressed formally for formal occasions, he would wear an artist's smock when painting, or more usually, shirt, tie, sweater, old corduroys, and expensive, comfortable leather shoes. He kept in trim all year round by swimming in the heated pool in his garden. Emett rarely took holidays (claiming that his work *was* a holiday) and then only when a 'thing' had been completed. Then, drained of energy and sometimes speechless with exhaustion, he would, with Mary, rest and recuperate in France, or at a health farm, for a week or two.

A naturally shy, charming, mild-mannered person, Emett was occasionally mistaken for the actor-comedian Danny Kaye, to whom he bore a strong physical resemblance. Fair-haired and fresh-faced, even in old age he looked much younger than his years. He enjoyed classical music and would sometimes whistle with exceptional clarity excerpts from Beethoven and Mozart. In 1978 he was appointed OBE. Emett died in a nursing home in Hassocks 13 November 1990.

[*Punch* library archives, Ludgate House, Blackfriars Road, London; Reuter's archives, Reuters Ltd., Fleet Street, London; *Rowland Emett: from 'Punch' to 'Chitty Chitty Bang Bang and Beyond'* (exhibition catalogue), Beetles, 1988; private information; personal knowledge.]   JOHN JENSEN

EVANS, George Ewart (1909–1988), historian and writer, was born 1 April 1909 in Abercynon, Glamorgan, one of the eleven children, seven boys and four girls, of William Evans, shopkeeper, of Abercynon. He was one of the eight children of his father's second marriage, to Janet Hitchings, of Maesteg. He was educated at Mountain Ash Grammar School and then University College, Cardiff, where he went as a trainee teacher on a Glamorgan county council scholarship, winning a college bursary *en route*. He read classics and graduated in the summer of 1930 with a lower second-class degree. There followed a year of professional training, at the end of which he obtained his Dip.Ed. and became unemployed. As he himself bitterly remarked in his autobiography: 'You swore to teach but the Board of Education…could not provide you with the opportunity.'

When he finally found work in 1934 it was quite another aspect of his career which gave him the necessary qualifications. From his late boyhood Evans had been a fine rugby player and an excellent runner. He had played rugby for both the renowned Mountain Ash 'Old Firm' before university and for University College as an undergraduate. His running was in the rougher school of the old Welsh working-class semi-professional track, where, by side bets, he gained the money to finance part of his university career. It was this athleticism which got him his first job in 1934, as a games master at the newly opened Sawston Village College, Cambridgeshire, where he met Florence Knappett, who was later to become his wife.

His move to East Anglia, although it happened by chance, was to prove momentous in what was to be his final career—that of writer and historian of rural life. By 1934 he had already decided, as he later wrote, that 'I did not care ultimately what kind of job I took. I determined that my real work henceforth would be to write.' In the following years he published a number of short stories, poems, and articles and became closely associated with the group around Keidrych Rhys's magazine *Wales* and the London-based *Left Review*. These pieces are, in some ways, very much of their time, and yet they also show a close sense of the realities of life in south Wales which distinguish them from the run-of-the-mill socialist-realist fiction of the period.

In October 1941 Evans was called up into the Royal Air Force. Restricted because of his increasing deafness to home-based and ground-based duties, he served as a radio technician in No. 206 Squadron, Coastal Command. After his wartime service Evans published a full-length novel, *The Voices of the Children*, in 1947, but it was badly received outside Wales. In the 1940s he suffered recurrent moods of black depression, in which he constantly questioned his own abilities, and felt a despair which was exacerbated by his deafness, which made it virtually impossible to find work as a teacher.

In 1948 he moved to Blaxhall in Suffolk, where his wife had been appointed village schoolteacher, and it was out of Blaxhall that his first book about English rural life, *Ask the Fellows Who Cut the Hay*, came in 1956. The book was based on interviews with the older inhabitants of the village about their lives, their work, and their communities. This was a technique used in folk-life studies, and one which was beginning to find favour in the world of radio, but it was still well outside the bounds of conventional academic history. The book, however, was a success and in the next ten years three more followed. Part of their popularity certainly rested on the English nostalgia for a lost rural past, but, like Evans's earlier fiction, they contained a great deal more than that. Evans also lectured widely, particularly for the Workers' Educational Association. In the late 1960s, with the emergence of the technique of oral history in British academic life, there followed a period of stimulating, if not always easy, contact with academic life, especially the University of Essex, where Evans was Major Burrows lecturer in 1972 and a visiting fellow from 1973 to 1978.

His books from this period, particularly *Where Beards Wag All* (1970), *The Days That We Have Seen* (1975), and *From Mouths of Men* (1976), represent his best work. Careful and beautifully crafted, they remind the reader that Evans remained a writer as much as a historian. In the 1980s his relationship with academe, never easy, became more tense. His book on the myth of the hare, *The Leaping Hare*, written in 1972 with David Thomson, had been dismissed by academic anthropology, and he felt that oral history was moving away from its roots, into ever wilder areas of theory while neglecting the ordinary people. Some of these feelings are present in his fine volume of autobiography, *The Strength of the Hills* (1983), and in his last book, the much less satisfactory *Spoken History* (1987).

Through all this Evans retained much of his Welshness. Although not tall, he was an upright figure who kept his rugby-playing physique until late in life. He was a native Welsh speaker, and retained a clear Welsh accent all his life, which was often a shock to those who knew him only through his books and assumed he was East Anglian. His past also shaped him in other, more fundamental, ways. Politically he was born into a radical family; he was named Ewart after *Gladstone, and that radicalism never left him. He was

a member of the Communist party in the 1930s and remained very close to communism throughout his life. His politics and his Welshness drew him back in the 1970s to the subject-matter of Wales, and in his last books he became a chronicler of the end of the south Wales coal industry, as he had earlier been the recorder of the end of horse-based agriculture in England.

Evans remained very much an outsider to the academic world. His honesty, which was often blunt, and always based on a deep distrust of the English ruling élite, ill fitted him for English universities, and it is perhaps not surprising that it was at the politically radical University of Essex of the 1970s that he seemed happiest. He was awarded an honorary DU by Essex in 1982 and an honorary D.Litt. by the University of Keele in 1983. In 1971 he was president of the anthropology section of the British Association for the Advancement of Science meeting at Swansea.

In 1938 Evans married Florence Ellen, daughter of Albert George Knappett, clerk in the Stock Exchange. They had a son, who became a director of Faber & Faber, Evans's publishers, and three daughters, one of whom married David Gentleman, who illustrated many of Evans's books. Florence was a key figure in Evans's life, supporting him with her teaching in the 1940s and early 1950s, when otherwise he would not have been able to write, as well as being a gentle but firm commentator on his work, of which she said once, '[it was] a bit creepy...listening to all those dead voices'. Evans died 11 January 1988 at Brooke in Norfolk, where he had lived since the 1970s.

[George Ewart Evans, *The Strength of the Hills*, 1983; Gareth Williams, *George Ewart Evans*, 1991; personal knowledge.]   ALUN HOWKINS

F

FAIRBAIRN, SIR **Robert Duncan** (1910–1988), chairman of the Clydesdale Bank, was born 25 September 1910 in Longhirst, near Morpeth, Northumberland, the youngest of three sons and fourth of five children of Robert Fairbairn and his wife, Christina Robertson. His father was a Borderer who moved to Perth not long after Robert's birth to become head gamekeeper to the Dewar family. His mother, from the Highlands and a Gaelic speaker, had been a lady's maid. Fairbairn grew up in the strict but benign atmosphere of a happy, relatively simple, rural home, while mixing on terms of easy familiarity with the family his father served. His natural talent for ball games, and for cricket in particular, was developed in family games on the Dewar estate, where he benefited from tuition by the professional engaged in the summers for his son by the first Baron Forteviot. Fairbairn had many and varied talents, a robust character, and an attractive personality that, allied to his enthusiasm and industry, brought him distinction, and many friends, in widely different fields.

He was educated at Perth Academy, where he showed an aptitude for science. His teachers had intended him to develop this interest at St Andrews University, but when he left school in 1927 he secured an apprenticeship in the Perth branch of the Clydesdale Bank. By 1930 he had taken second place in the members' examination of the Institute of Bankers in Scotland and he was in due course transferred to the head office of the bank in Glasgow. Whilst there he studied for the examinations of the English Institute of Bankers and in the finals of 1934 won the Beckett memorial prize for first place overall, the Whitehead prize for practice and law of banking, and other distinctions.

In 1920 the Clydesdale had become affiliated with the Midland Bank, then in a period of acquisitive expansion, and in 1934 Fairbairn was invited by the Midland to work in London. He gained experience in London, Liverpool, and Bradford until 1939 when, having earlier joined the Royal Naval Volunteer Reserve in Liverpool, he was mobilized for war service in the Royal Navy. He served for six years, attaining the rank of lieutenant-commander (S) RNVR, and saw service first at Scapa Flow, then in the Admiralty, and finally, until the war ended, in India.

Fairbairn returned to the Midland Bank in 1946 and gained rapid promotion there, but in 1950 he was needed in Scotland to help with the amalgamation of the Clydesdale with another Midland 'affiliate', the North of Scotland Bank. After a period in Aberdeen on this assignment he was brought back to Glasgow as assistant general manager (1951) and in 1958 he was appointed general manager in succession to Sir John Campbell. In 1967 he was elected to the board and when he retired as general manager in 1971 he was invited to become vice-chairman. He was appointed chairman in 1975 and retired in 1985. It was a rare distinction at that time for a practising Scottish banker to become chairman of the bank in which he had served and clear evidence of the high esteem in which Fairbairn was held.

Throughout his career Fairbairn made his presence and his opinions powerfully and persuasively felt in many areas, not least in defending the distinctiveness of Scottish banking within the United Kingdom. Among his more notable initiatives at the Clydesdale was the radical review he instigated of the bank's public appearance and 'image', particularly as influenced by design, leading in the 1960s to the introduction of a fresh, modern, and much admired 'house style'. His academic and practical abilities as a banker, his interest in matters of design, and his concern for the economic development of Scotland brought him many awards and appointments, public and private. He was a director of several major companies including the Midland Bank, Scottish Amicable Life Assurance Society, British National Oil Corporation, and Newarthill Ltd. He held senior offices in many banking and business organizations and was a distinguished and effective chairman from 1972 until 1981 of the Scottish Industrial Development Advisory Board established under the Industry Act of 1970. In 1975 he was knighted in recognition of his services to economic development in Scotland.

Fairbairn's distinguished business career was matched by the development of his early promise as a sportsman. As a young man he played cricket—for Perthshire, West of Scotland, Cheshire, and eventually for the MCC and Scotland. His involvement in football led to his membership of Queens Park Football Club and of the celebrated Corinthian Casuals, for whom he played. When he turned to golf he was as competitive and as successful, winning the Silver Boomerang in his first year as a member of the Royal and Ancient and later captaining Royal Troon Golf Club.

Fairbairn was five feet ten inches in height, a strongly built, handsome man with a large head, blue-grey eyes, and a winning smile. He never lost his plentiful golden (later silver) hair, nor his robust, competitive, and cheerful athleticism and vitality. He had a quiet Scottish voice and an air of calm authority. In 1939 he married Sylvia Lucinda, daughter of Henry Coulter, a parish minister of the Church of Scotland in Glasgow. Their house in Bridge of Weir, Renfrewshire, bore witness to Fairbairn's interest in the visual arts. It was typical of his energy and zest even in retirement that when he was over seventy-five he and his wife enrolled as students at the Glasgow School of Art, where he was remembered as an assiduous and talented pupil. He died 26 March 1988 in Guildford, Surrey, at his daughter's home, following a hip replacement operation.

[Charles W. Munn, *Clydesdale Bank: the First One Hundred and Fifty Years*, 1988; private information; personal knowledge.]   THOMAS RISK

FAIRLIE, Henry Jones (1924–1990), political journalist and author, was born 13 January 1924 in Crouch End, London, the second son and fifth child in the family of two sons and four daughters of James Fairlie, journalist, and his wife, Marguerita Vernon. He was educated at Highgate School and Corpus Christi College, Oxford, where he read modern history, obtaining second-class honours in 1945 and becoming secretary of the Union in the Trinity term of 1945. A weak heart disqualified him from any form of military service, both during the war and after it, but an interest in Liberal politics led to his being appointed a lobby correspondent for the *Manchester Evening News* at the remarkably early age of twenty-one. He progressed from there to the *Observer* in 1948 and then in 1950 to *The Times*, where he wrote political leaders.

Anonymity, however, did not suit Fairlie and in 1954 he accepted an invitation to join the staff of the *Spectator*. Building there on the foundations laid by his former colleague, Hugh Massingham of the *Observer*, he perfected the journalistic art form of the modern political column. Irreverent, witty, and seldom anything but well informed, Fairlie's weekly columns (appearing first under the pseudonym of 'Trimmer' and later under his own byline) became required reading for politicians of all parties. This achievement was all the more notable as the time he spent at the *Spectator* was relatively short, barely two years in duration. But it was during this period that Fairlie made perhaps his most lasting contribution to the vocabulary of British politics, putting into circulation the term 'the Establishment' to describe those who, while often unelected, controlled the power points of British public life.

In some ways, it was an uncharacteristic notion for Fairlie to have propagated—the phrase had, in fact, first been coined by A. J. P. *Taylor—since by the mid-1950s his own political stance had become that of a romantic, if radical, Tory. It was this which gave him his curious affinity with Harold *Macmillan (later the first Earl of Stockton), to whom, especially after he started writing for the *Daily Mail*, he enjoyed regular access. Fairlie, however, was often wayward in his political judgements and it was typical of this flaw in his journalistic make-up that he should have predicted in the *Mail* that Labour under Hugh *Gaitskell would defeat Macmillan in the 1959 general election. The *Mail*, after the Tories had won a majority of 100, soon dispensed with his services. Thereafter he found an impecunious refuge in the columns of *Time and Tide*, where (as in *Encounter*) some of his more penetrating longer articles appeared in the early 1960s. He also enjoyed a brief Indian summer in another mass-circulation paper, the *Daily Express*, with some notable news scoops in the turbulent political year of 1963. Well before this, however, his personal difficulties had tended to overshadow his professional success, as marked in television and radio as it had originally been in the press. Always hospitable and, when in funds, generous to a fault, Fairlie exercised only the loosest control over the management of his own life. Pursued by debt, hounded by libel writs, and regularly the subject of bankruptcy proceedings (leading on one occasion to his imprisonment in Brixton), he eventually left Britain for the United States in 1965, never to return to his native land.

In America he built up a fresh, if equally controversial, journalistic reputation. Moving now steadily to the left, he early on attacked the power of money in US politics, as symbolized by the Kennedys. His assault on the funding of the Kennedy Library in Boston—originally published in the *Sunday Telegraph*—briefly became a *cause célèbre* in American newspapers, making him for a time something of a pariah in a Kennedy-nostalgic Washington. But even when denied his customary access to the power structure, Fairlie could feel that his own fame was secure. His first, and best, book, *The Life of Politics* (published in 1968 but largely written before he left Britain), drew on all his experience of Westminster and remains one of the most vivid defences of the parliamentary system. His subsequent two books—*The Kennedy Promise* (1973) and *The Spoiled Child of the Western World*

(1976)—concentrated on critical American themes but were respectfully received on both sides of the Atlantic.

Boyish in looks and capable, when sober, of being captivating in conversation, Fairlie exerted a powerful charm, particularly upon women. He was married in 1949 to Lisette Todd, daughter of Arthur Todd Phillips, architect. They had a son and two daughters. Fairlie's bohemian streak never allowed him to accept the normal constraints of matrimony. (Although never divorced, he and his wife separated in 1967.) The tales of his various *affaires* were legendary but were usually related, even by his romantic victims, with affection mingled with exasperated amusement.

Fairlie's last years were spent working for the *New Republic* in Washington, in whose offices he was eventually afforded the unusual facility of a bedroom in which to sleep. It was a striking testimony of the regard in which he was held by all those who shared his consuming interest in 'the life of politics'. He died in a Washington hospital 25 February 1990, of heart failure.

[*The Times* and *Independent*, 27 February 1990; private information; personal knowledge.]

ANTHONY HOWARD

FARR, Thomas George ('Tommy') (1913–1986), boxer, was born 12 March 1913 at 3 Railway Terrace, Blaenclydach, Rhondda, the sixth of eight children (four sons and four daughters) of George Farr, miner, and his wife, Sarah Ann Owen. Farr's mother died when he was ten, and his father was soon afterwards struck with paralysis, dying a few years later. Tommy, who grew up in extreme poverty and was always thereafter careful with money, was a schoolboy boxer, then briefly a miner, before he met a disabled miner turned saddler, Job Churchill, who unofficially guided his career throughout the interwar years.

At the age of fifteen Farr joined the boxing booth of Joe and Daisy Gess at Tylorstown as a handyman. As he grew, he boxed as 'Kid' Farr, occasionally facing five opponents in an evening. Beyond the booth, he was paid 3s. 6d. for a contest of six rounds, and when he had saved £109 in his Post Office account, he bought a house at 59 Court Street, Tonypandy, for himself and his younger brother and sister. By 1929 Farr was boxing contests of ten rounds all over the Rhondda Valley, and in the next five years he won and lost as a 'small hall' boxer whose style ('in-fighting was my speciality') did not appeal to major promoters. In Jack *Petersen, Wales had produced its first ever British heavyweight champion in 1932, and he had the attractive style that Farr lacked. In the economic depression Farr

could get few matches, and in 1933 he ignominiously lost his first London contest. At Tonypandy he won the Welsh light-heavyweight title, and in February 1935 at Mountain Ash challenged unsuccessfully for this British title, losing for the third time to the same man. Farr was not beaten again, however, until he met Joe Louis at the Yankee stadium in New York City in August 1937.

Seeking bigger purses in 1935, Farr signed with an experienced London manager, Ted Broadribb, and moved house to Slough. The boxer–manager relationship was stormy throughout the three years' contract, and Farr relied on the advice of Churchill, returning often to Tonypandy. Broadribb knew everybody, and he got a match with the former world light-heavyweight champion, Tommy Loughran of Philadelphia, whom Farr outpointed over ten rounds at the Royal Albert Hall. Farr's earnings in 1936 were modest by boxing standards, less than £150 a fight, though he outpointed another former world title holder, and won the Welsh heavyweight championship by a knockout. His jabbing and spoiling and clever inside work did not please spectators, and Farr remained in Petersen's shadow.

Farr's glory came in his five contests of 1937. Petersen had lost twice, including, surprisingly, to Ben Foord for his British and Empire heavyweight titles. Farr was Foord's first challenger, and gained the points decision in a pedestrian match at the recently opened Harringay arena. The Harringay promoters had brought over Max Baer, a charismatic Nebraskan who had been world heavyweight champion in 1935, and whom they had to match with a British boxer. Farr was his only feasible opponent, and a month after the Foord fiasco, with the arena packed, he outpointed Baer over twelve rounds. Two months later, with the British boxing market in his pocket, Farr decisively stopped Walter Neusel, the hefty German who had thrice beaten Petersen, and Harringay rang with Welsh song. Aged twenty-four, he signed to meet Max Schmeling at Harringay for a guaranteed £7,000, but broke this contract to sail to the USA with Broadribb for a $50,000 match (win, lose, or draw) with the new world heavyweight champion, Joe Louis.

The twenty-three-year-old Louis had been the first black man allowed to box for the world's heavyweight title since 1915, and he was a formidable champion. Possibly only Farr and Churchill fancied the challenger's chances. At fourteen and a half stones, Farr boxed brilliantly, never went down, and was outpointed over fifteen hard rounds. The fight commentary was broadcast by the BBC, the first sporting event to be relayed by transatlantic cable, and wirelesses were switched on in halls and homes in the early hours all over Britain. Farr's gritty loss was sporting memory's gain.

Farr lost as many contests as he won between this and retirement in 1940. He enlisted in the RAF but was soon discharged unfit. He tried to come back to boxing in 1950, but gave up after two years. As a fighter, he was awkward for opponents and difficult for promoters and managers; as a person, six feet tall and with a craggy face, he was a raconteur and could sing well enough to make six popular records. His Welshness stuck, and he retained his love of sport.

In 1939 he married Muriel Montgomery, daughter of Herbert Nicholas Germon, engineer. They had a daughter and two sons. Farr and his wife lived happily in Sussex until he died in Worthing, 1 March 1986.

[Gary Farr (ed.), *Thus Farr, by Tommy Farr*, 1989; Ted Broadribb, *Fighting Is My Life*, 1951; Fred Deakin, *Tommy Farr*, 1989; BBC television interview shown in May 1982.]   STAN SHIPLEY

FELL, DAME Honor Bridget (1900–1986), cell biologist, was born 22 May 1900 at Fowthorpe near Filey in Yorkshire, the youngest in the family of seven daughters and two sons of Colonel William Edwin Fell, soldier, landowner, and farmer, and his wife, Alice Pickersgill-Cunliffe, carpenter and architect, who designed the house at Fowthorpe. Her father was keenly interested in nature and animals and she may have inherited her deep commitment to biology from him. She was educated at Wychwood School in Oxford, Madras College in St Andrews, and Edinburgh University, where she was awarded a B.Sc. in zoology in 1923, a Ph.D. in 1924, and a D.Sc. in 1932.

She moved to Cambridge in 1923 to become scientific assistant to T. S. P. Strangeways, with a grant from the Medical Research Council. She was to remain in Cambridge for the rest of her working life, holding research fellowships until she was appointed to a Royal Society research professorship in 1963, having been elected FRS in 1952.

Honor Fell and Strangeways worked together on biomedical research at the Cambridge Research Hospital, until Strangeways died suddenly in December 1926. In 1929 Fell was appointed director of the hospital, which was renamed the Strangeways Research Laboratory in honour of its founder. She was to remain director until 1970 and during her tenure the laboratory developed into a unique institution for studies in cell biology, with an emphasis on *in vitro* techniques. Its staff rose from thirteen in 1933 to 121 in 1970, and various additions were made to the original building. It attracted many

visitors from all over the world, who came not only to learn the techniques of tissue and organ culture, but also to collaborate with Honor Fell and to gain from her imaginative and enthusiastic approach to biological research. In her own work she always stressed the importance of the application of a range of different disciplines in a research project. In consequence the staff of the laboratory came to include radiobiologists, immunologists, biochemists, and electron microscopists. She continually encouraged collaborations among the members of the laboratory, including the visitors, and with scientists in the University of Cambridge and other institutions. She was best known for her work on the histogenesis of bone and cartilage, the action of vitamin A on bone, skin, and membranes, the breakdown of tissues by lysosomal enzymes, and the role of synovial tissue in the breakdown of cartilage and bone.

She retired from the directorship of the Strangeways Research Laboratory in 1970 and then joined R. R. A. Coombs in the division of immunology of the department of pathology in Cambridge University. Her research continued unabated and she now initiated a whole new series of investigations on the effects of antiserum and complement on pig cartilage and bone in organ culture and on the role of synovial tissue in the breakdown of cartilage and bone. She returned to the Strangeways Laboratory in 1979, as a research worker, and continued to be active in research until a month before her death. Her work resulted in the publication of over 140 research papers and reviews. She was deeply interested in the education and training of young scientists and travelled as far afield as India and Japan to participate in courses on tissue and organ culture. She also made a major contribution to the development of societies for cell biology and tissue culture, and was elected into honorary membership or fellowship of many of them.

She received many honours, medals, and prizes and was appointed DBE in 1963. She was awarded eight honorary degrees. She was elected a fellow of Girton College in 1955 and a life fellow in 1970, honorary fellow of Somerville College, Oxford, in 1964, and a life fellow of King's College, London (1967), where she was senior biological adviser to the Medical Research Council biophysics unit for many years.

She was unmarried and throughout her working life lived alone, looked after at times by her old nanny and a succession of devoted daily ladies. As a young woman she was slim, with dark hair neatly brushed back. She changed very little with age and throughout her life her joy in science, her capacity for friendship, and her sense of fun were reflected in the brightness of her looks and the warmth of her smile. She died 22 April 1986 in Cambridge.

[Dame Janet Vaughan in *Biographical Memoirs of Fellows of the Royal Society*, vol. xxxiii, 1987; *Nature*, vol. cxcvi, 1962, pp. 316–18; private information; personal knowledge.]　　　　　　　　　　　AUDREY GLAUERT

FERRANTI, Basil Reginald Vincent Ziani de (1930–1988), industrialist and politician, was born 2 July 1930 in Alderley Edge, Cheshire, the younger son and youngest of five children of (Sir) Vincent Ziani de Ferranti, industrialist, of Henbury Hall, Macclesfield, and his wife Dorothy Hettie Campbell, daughter of Reginald Page Wilson, consultant engineer. 'Boz' was educated at Gilling Castle, the preparatory school for Ampleforth College, and Eton. He did his military service with the 4th/7th Royal Dragoon Guards in 1949–50 and then went to Trinity College, Cambridge, where he obtained a third class in part i of the mechanical sciences tripos (1953). He was sent by his father to D. T. Napier & Sons, a Glasgow engineering firm, to continue his training in preparation for entering the family business, Ferranti Ltd.

Ferranti Ltd. had been established by Boz's grandfather, Sebastian Ziani de *Ferranti, a leading electrical pioneer, and the firm had been built into a major electrical and electronics manufacturer by his father, Vincent. Boz joined Ferranti Ltd. in 1953 after having developed a domestic water-heating pump, and rose to the post of domestic appliances manager in the next year. It was always apparent, however, that he would play a subordinate role in the company, his elder brother Sebastian becoming chairman and managing director, and, although he was elevated to the board in 1957, he decided to pursue other interests.

A fascination with international affairs was later to dominate his life, but in the 1950s Ferranti was extremely keen to enter domestic politics, unsuccessfully fighting the Exchange division, Manchester, as a Conservative at the 1955 general election. He eventually gained a seat, at a 1958 by-election for the Morecambe and Lonsdale division, and in July 1962 rose to a junior ministerial post as parliamentary secretary at the Ministry of Aviation. The inevitable conflict of interest this created forced his resignation from the post in October.

With little prospect of a ministerial career, Ferranti gave up his seat at the 1964 general election, returning full-time to industry as deputy managing director (later sole managing director) of International Computers and Tabulators, the company which had recently purchased the Ferranti computer department. It was this experience in a high-technology company which convinced him of the need to create a single European trading area as a basis for competing against powerful American corporations like IBM. He incorporated this message into a report commissioned by the Confederation of British Industry in 1968, prompting that influential body into supporting (Sir) Edward Heath's successful application to join the European Economic Community.

When Britain became a member of the EEC in 1973, Heath invited Ferranti to sit on the economic and social committee, and such was his enthusiasm for European affairs that in 1976 he was elected chairman of that body. He thus gained an opportunity to publicize his ideas on the need to build an integrated market as the key to future prosperity. This message he also took into the first elections for the European Parliament in 1979, when he became Conservative MEP for Hampshire West (from 1984, Hampshire Central), and his influence increased after becoming vice-president of the Parliament (1979–82).

As an MEP Ferranti worked tirelessly for the cause of European integration, helping Karl von Wogau (the German Christian Democrat MEP) to form the Kangaroo Group, so-called because it wanted companies to be able to leap over trade barriers. Although Ferranti did not live to see the achievement of this dream in 1992, the Kangaroo Group of MEPs played an active role in persuading national governments to accept the need for European trading unity, and Ferranti was regarded as a major influence on the British Conservative government's policy. His natural charm and sunny disposition were always to the fore, and while he had a sturdily built figure his rounded face often carried a disarming smile, which he was able to use to good effect in conveying his message.

Ferranti became non-executive chairman of Ferranti Ltd. in 1982. The company had been semi-nationalized by the Labour government of 1974, after suffering serious losses in its transformer business, and his brother Sebastian, never at ease with the non-executive role he was given thereafter, decided to leave in 1982. When Ferranti Ltd. merged with the American company, International Signals and Control, in 1988, Ferranti was appointed president of the new business, Ferranti International, but a massive fraud perpetrated by the American partner eventually resulted in its demise.

Ferranti received an honorary D.Sc. from the City University, London, in 1970. He married three times, firstly Susan Sara in 1956, the daughter of Sir Christopher Gore, landowner; they had three sons, before divorcing in 1963. In 1964 he married Simone, daughter of Colonel Henry James Nangle; they had one daughter. He divorced her in 1971 to marry in the same year Jocelyn Hilary Mary, an Olympic skier, daughter of Wing Commander Arthur Thomas Laing.

Ferranti died of cancer at home in Ellisfield, Hampshire, 4 September 1988.

[Ferranti archives; private information; personal knowledge.]   JOHN F. WILSON

FIGGURES, SIR Frank Edward (1910–1990), civil servant, was born 5 March 1910 in Merton, London, the only son and elder child of Frank Thomas Figgures, an administrative assistant with the Crown Agents, and his wife, Alice Biggin. He passed from Rutlish School, Merton, to New College, Oxford, where he took a first class in modern history (1931), became a Harmsworth senior scholar at Merton College (1931), and received a much coveted Henry fellowship to Yale, where he attended the law school in 1933. After being called to the bar (Lincoln's Inn) in 1936, he practised up to the outbreak of World War II. There followed military service in the Royal Artillery from 1940 to 1946, where he attained the rank of lieutenant-colonel.

His public service began in 1946 with entry to the Treasury. He had a particularly happy start, not only because of the overriding importance of that department, but also because the Treasury was called upon to face quite new policy challenges at home and abroad. This, and the Treasury's traditional tolerance of individualism, was propitious for the exercise of Figgures's special talents and inclinations. He was concerned at once with overseas matters and was seconded to the recently created Organization of European Economic Co-operation (to which was later added 'and Development'), the heir of the Marshall plan, in the important post of director of trade and finance (1948–51). There he acquired an abiding skill in multilateral, international negotiation, and the ability to work harmoniously with a group of international public servants and politicians despite the clash of national interests.

In 1951 he returned to the Treasury and was promoted to under-secretary (1955–60). This was the period when the British government had to decide how to deal with the movement for European integration, which would culminate in the Treaty of Rome and the creation, by six countries, of the European Economic Community. Figgures was chosen as the chief developer and first director-general (1960–5) of the British government's European alternative, the European Free Trade Association, set up in May 1960. In 1964 he branded the British import surcharge policy as 'illegal'. To his relief (he had suffered two near-breakdowns), he returned in 1965 to the Treasury as third secretary. He was promoted in 1968 to second permanent secretary, a new post. He retired in 1971.

After his retirement from the Civil Service he became director-general of the National Eco-nomic Development Office (1971–3), at a time when it was hoped that this institution might make a decisive difference to the country's well-being, through developments such as an incomes policy. In 1973 Figgures was chosen to be chairman of the Pay Board, which, however, had no better success in these matters and was wound up after one year. This also marked his definite retirement from the public domain, with the exception of his membership of the BBC general advisory council (1978–82), but he continued to be active in the private sector as director and chairman of a number of companies.

Figgures had great abilities, particularly evident in the area of negotiation, especially in international matters. A large and affable man, he had an attractive personality, with a lively, amusing, kind, and understanding disposition. He knew much about music and his slight embonpoint, twinkling eyes, and widely cultured mind made him an agreeable companion. He was appointed CMG in 1959, CB in 1966, and KCB in 1970. He was an honorary D.Sc. of Aston University (1975).

In December 1941 he married Aline Martina, daughter of Professor Hugo Frey, an eminent Viennese laryngologist; they had a son and a daughter. His wife died in 1975 and in the same year he married a friend of the family and a matron at Uppingham School, Ismea, daughter of George Napier Magill, a rubber planter in Malaysia who had died in a Japanese prisoner-of-war camp, and widow of John Stanley Barker, a band leader and entertainment manager. Figgures died 27 November 1990 in Glaston, Rutland.

[Private information; personal knowledge.]
                                        ERIC ROLL

FINKELSTEIN, Moses (1912–1986), historian and sociologist. [See FINLEY, SIR MOSES I.]

FINLEY, SIR Moses I. (1912–1986), historian and sociologist, was born in New York 20 May 1912, the eldest in the family of three sons and one daughter of Nathan Finkelstein, mechanical engineer, of New York, and his wife, Anna Katzenellenbogen. Around 1936 he took the surname Finley. He had no second forename, but used the initial 'I'.

He was educated at Central High School, Syracuse, New York, and at Syracuse University, where in 1927, aged fifteen, he graduated BA *magna cum laude*, majoring in psychology, and was elected to Phi Beta Kappa. After taking an MA in public law at Columbia University, New York, in 1929, he worked as a legal clerk before holding several research posts (1930–9). Now, under W. L. Westermann, he began to study ancient history. Between 1930 and 1933 he was research assistant to A. A. Schiller at Columbia and also on the editorial staff of the *Encyclopaedia of the Social Sciences*. In 1934–5 he was a research fellow at Columbia, while also teaching (1934–42) at the City College of New York. From 1937 to 1939 he was an editor and translator at the Institute for Social Research, which Max Horkheimer had brought from Frankfurt in 1934.

After working for various war relief agencies (1942–7) Finley returned to Columbia in 1948 and was elected a fellow of the American Council of Learned Societies. From 1948 to 1952 he was lecturer, then assistant professor, at Rutgers University, Newark, New Jersey. Simultaneously he was working in the history faculty at Columbia for his Ph.D., which he took in 1950 with a thesis on 'Land and Credit in Ancient Athens' (published in 1953). From 1952 onwards he was active in a group around the Hungarian scholar, Karl Polanyi, who was then developing views on the pre-market economy, which had some influence on Finley.

In 1954, having come under attack for his left-wing opinions in the notorious committee run by Joseph McCarthy, he emigrated to England. Here he was appointed university lecturer in classics at Cambridge (1955–64) and, in 1957, elected to a fellowship at Jesus College. Finley spent the rest of his life domiciled in Cambridge (until 1976), becoming a British subject in 1962. He was reader in ancient social and economic history (1964–70) and professor of ancient history (1970–9), and from 1976 to 1982 master of Darwin College, Cambridge. He was knighted in 1979.

Finley's many writings on the society, economy, and political forms of ancient Greece were influential among fellow scholars and the general public alike. His vast published output included over a score of books and countless articles and reviews; and he was highly regarded abroad, especially in France and Italy, where he frequently lectured and organized conferences. His training in history and law had familiarized him with the ideas of such scholars as Marc Bloch, Henri Pirenne, Thorstein Veblen, and the Freudians; and his association with the Frankfurt school reinforced his interest in Karl Marx. Later, however, he became dissatisfied with Marxism, preferring Max Weber's emphasis on status rather than class as a tool of social analysis. By employing Weber's concept of 'ideal types' and the controlled use of comparative material from other societies, he tried to overcome the disadvantages of working on ancient Greece, where he found the evidence traditionally employed defective in range, variety, and quality. He insisted on regarding society as a whole;

institutions must be assessed within their own social context, and all anachronistic comparisons between primitive and more advanced societies avoided. Though strongly influenced by theoretical constructs, Finley never set out to discuss theory and method *per se*, preferring always to let his attitude emerge from examples of actual historical analysis.

A high point in his career and one that gave him great satisfaction was the invitation to return to the USA in 1972 to deliver the Sather lectures at Berkeley in California (published as *The Ancient Economy*, 1973, 2nd edn. 1985) and the Mason Welch Gross lectures at Rutgers University (published as *Democracy Ancient and Modern*, 1973). These two sets of lectures, which earned him the Wolfson literary award in history (1974), along with *The Use and Abuse of History* (1975), best exemplify his most mature work; though perhaps his most original book is *The World of Odysseus* (1956, 2nd edn. 1977).

Finley's distinction was widely recognized. He delivered endowed lectures in England, France, the USA, and Denmark. He was elected a fellow of the Royal Historical Society (1970), of the British Academy (1971), and of the Royal Society of Arts (1971). He was a foreign member of the Royal Danish Academy of Sciences and Letters (1975), the American Academy of Arts and Sciences (1979), and the Accademia Nazionale dei Lincei (1982), and received honorary degrees from the universities of Leicester (1972), Sheffield (1979), and Saskatchewan (1979), and from the City College of New York (1982). He was president of the Classical Association (1973–4), the Cambridge Philological Society (1974–6), and the Joint Association of Classical Teachers (1981–3); and he was a trustee of the British Museum from 1977 to 1984.

An insatiable controversialist in discussion and in print, Finley relished polemic. His interjections, usually introduced by a drawled 'I'm sorry, but...', were characterized by hard hitting. But to friends, colleagues, and students he was warm-hearted and generous and he built up a productive school to which he was both patron and Socratic gadfly. Finley was of medium height, with a dark complexion, slightly rugged features, and a lively countenance, expressive of his sharp mind. For most of his life he was a chain-smoker and, even after he stopped smoking for reasons of health, from ingrained habit he would hold the fingers of his right hand bent, as if still clutching a cigarette.

From 1932 Finley enjoyed a happy and mutually reinforcing marriage with his wife Mary (née Moscowitz, who later changed to her mother's surname, Thiers), schoolteacher. They had no children. On the day of her death he suffered a cerebral haemorrhage and he died the following day, 23 June 1986, at Addenbrooke's Hospital, Cambridge.

[B. D. Shaw and R. P. Saller, introduction to M. I. Finley, *Economy and Society in Ancient Greece*, 1981; P. D. A. Garnsey, *The Blackwell Dictionary of Historians*, 1988; information from Lawrence H. Finley (brother); personal knowledge.]   F. W. WALBANK

FISHER, Alan Wainwright (1922–1988), trade-union leader, was born in Birmingham 20 June 1922, the fourth of five sons (there were no daughters) of Thomas Wainwright Fisher, accountant, and his wife, Ethel Agnes Guest. He was educated at Sparkhill Commercial College, Birmingham. He went to work at the National Union of Public Employees (NUPE), becoming a junior clerk in 1939. On the outbreak of World War II that year, he began to serve in the Fleet Air Arm. After demobilization in 1945, he returned to NUPE.

By 1953 Fisher had become the midlands divisional officer and in 1962 he was appointed assistant general secretary. NUPE was the fastest-growing trade union at the time, its development assisted by Fisher in three main ways. First, as assistant general secretary in the early 1960s, he saw more clearly than most that NUPE needed to break with the organizational principles and oppositional ideology of the previous general secretary, the 'Welsh fire-eater', Bryn Jones. Jones was an old-time centralist-socialist, never so happy as when denouncing other Trades Union Congress leaders who refused to take seriously his version of militant industrial unionism. Fisher saw that NUPE must make its peace with the leaders of the 'general unions' within the general council of the TUC, seeking for allies in a common struggle against public sector employers and hostile governments.

Second, after involvement in his first major national dispute, the 'dirty jobs' strike of 1970, Fisher, who had become general secretary in 1968, sensed that NUPE itself was in need of radical reform. As he saw it, the key lay in the development and training of lay activists, integrated into union government as accredited shop stewards. He even came to argue that membership growth was a function of organizational effectiveness, and that this probably involved a process of constant change and adaptation. To this end he sponsored, and sought to implement, the findings of the 1974 'Warwick report', a radical plan for constitutional change written by three friendly sociologists. Most members of the general council would not have dared to commission and publish such an investigation into the working of their union. Nobody but Fisher would have handed the job to students of the subject.

Fisher's third major contribution was double-edged and ill-timed. He decided NUPE needed a rallying cry, to help to achieve real progress for its lowest paid members and attract further recruits. This took the form of a campaign for a national minimum wage, high enough to benefit the union's membership, and potential membership, in the National Health Service and local government. It was to be achieved partly by militant wage bargaining and partly by legislation. Unfortunately he converted the TUC to this policy just before Labour's prime minister, James Callaghan (later Baron Callaghan of Cardiff), committed his government to a pay limit of 5 per cent in 1978.

In the mythology of the Labour movement, the difference between Fisher's aspirations and Callaghan's inflexibility led inevitably to the series of disputes known as the 'winter of discontent'. This ended in the return of a Conservative government in April 1979. Of course the truth was more complex. The 5 per cent limit was unacceptable to many employers as well as to all other unions. Once into the dispute Fisher did his best to secure a settlement that would avoid a total government defeat. All the same, he could not quite escape some blame. He enjoyed his moment of history, until he realized the cost.

Fisher remained as NUPE's general secretary until 1982. He was a member of the TUC's general council from 1968 to 1982, and chairman of the TUC in 1980–1. He was also a member of the board of the British Overseas Airways Corporation (1970–2), British Airways (1972–82), and the London Electricity Board (1970–80). He was a director of Harland & Wolff, shipbuilders (1975–83), a governor of Henley Administrative Staff College (1977–83), and a member of the board of the Council for Educational Development Overseas (governor from 1970).

Fisher was a modest and extremely funny man, with the best line in trade-union repartee of any union leader of his generation. He had an effortless fluency, and his high-speed loquacity added to his charm. He was of average height, and until his long and fatal illness he looked younger than his years. Despite his illness, his high spirits and good nature did not desert him. He was married three times. In 1946 he married Peggy, daughter of Oscar Kinipple, technical representative. There were no children. Peggy died in 1956 and in 1958 he married Joyce Tinniswood, whose father was a farmer. They had two sons and one daughter. The marriage was dissolved in 1976 and in 1978 he married Ruth, formerly Woollerton, the daughter of Walter Henry Olliver, bank courier. There were no children of the third marriage. Fisher died of leukaemia 20 March 1988 in Maelor Hospital, Wrexham.

[Private information.]   WILLIAM McCARTHY
                                          C. S. NICHOLLS

FLEMING, (William) Launcelot (Scott) (1906–1990), geologist and bishop, was born 7 August 1906 in Edinburgh, the youngest of four sons (the second of whom died at the age of five months) and fifth of five children of Robert Alexander Fleming, MD, LL D, surgeon, of Edinburgh, and his wife Eleanor Mary, daughter of the Revd William Lyall Holland, rector of Cornhill-on-Tweed. Educated at Rugby and Trinity Hall, Cambridge, he obtained a second class in part i and a first in part ii of the natural sciences tripos (1927 and 1929), specializing in geology, and won a Commonwealth Fund fellowship to Yale University (1929–31). He then entered Westcott House, Cambridge, being ordained deacon in 1933 and priest 1934, as chaplain and fellow of Trinity Hall (1933–49).

Having accompanied summer university expeditions to Iceland (1932) and Spitsbergen (1933), with his dean's encouragement he joined the British Graham Land expedition to Antarctica (1934–7), as chaplain and geologist, and was one of the three-man dog-sledge party which explored the King George VI sound (including the Fleming glacier), thus proving that Graham Land was a peninsula. Returning to Trinity Hall as dean in 1937, he contributed to the *Geographical Journal*'s accounts (April, May, and June 1938, and September 1940) of the expedition's scientific findings. Commissioned as a chaplain in the Royal Naval Volunteer Reserve in 1940, his service included three years (of which 1941–2 were spent in the Mediterranean) in HMS *Queen Elizabeth*. In 1944 he became director of service ordination candidates. He returned to Cambridge in 1946 and became director of the Scott Polar Research Institute there in 1947. In 1949 he was appointed bishop of Portsmouth, and in 1959 bishop of Norwich. Struck by a rare spinal disorder, which seriously affected both legs, he resigned the see in 1971. The queen appointed him dean of Windsor and her domestic chaplain; he retired in 1976.

A great gift for friendship made him outstandingly effective pastorally; he genuinely cared about people. A remarkable rapport with young people led to his being made chairman of the Church of England Youth Council (1950–61). He helped plan the Duke of Edinburgh Award Scheme in 1954; was co-founder, with Dr Alec Dickson, of Voluntary Service Overseas in 1958; and played a part in inaugurating Atlantic College, the Prince's Trust, Project Trident, Outward Bound, and many similar projects to bring out young people's potential. The governor of numerous schools, he was much in demand for school confirmations.

Although he became a bishop without parochial experience or any great gift for preaching, his unassuming friendliness and humility won over clergy and laity. Portsmouth became an exceptionally well-run diocese, with more than its share of young clergy and ordinands. Norwich, with 650 churches and a shortage of clergy, presented greater problems; he tackled them resolutely and imaginatively, developing rural group ministries and again attracting good clergy. He also played a significant part in planning the University of East Anglia (which, unusually, has its own university chapel). He was an uncanny judge of character, excellent in 'one-to-one' situations. His desk might look chaotic, but he was a shrewd administrator with a clear grasp of priorities.

In 1968, most unusually for a bishop, he piloted a Bill (the Antarctic treaty) through the House of Lords. Well informed on environmental and ecological issues (he was a pre-war glaciologist of repute), he constantly urged responsible stewardship of the world (his maiden House of Lords speech was about cruelty to whales), and the need for international co-operation. He became vice-chairman of the parliamentary group for world government in 1969–71 and a member of the government standing advisory committee on environmental pollution (1970–3). At Windsor, he consolidated the reputation of St George's House. His influence on church policy would have been greater but for synodical government: off-the-cuff debate was not his forte.

Private means, which made his polar exploration possible, enabled him occasionally to inaugurate administrative improvements without waiting for official ecclesiastical sanction; and he was generous and hospitable. Proud of being a Scot, he loved the Highlands, where his holiday home at Innerhadden welcomed many undergraduates and clergy. His other enduring love was Trinity Hall, especially its Boat Club. His degrees included the MS (Yale, 1931), DD (Lambeth, 1950), and honorary DCL (East Anglia, 1976). He became an honorary fellow of Trinity Hall (1956), FRSE (1971), and honorary vice-president of the Royal Geographical Society (1961), and was awarded the Polar medal (1940). In 1976 he was appointed KCVO.

Fleming was slightly built, wiry, alert, and energetic. He still played a good game of squash in his fifties: it was physical fitness as well as mental discipline that made his prodigious workload possible. He was fifty-eight before he married in 1965, and then he contracted a happy union which lasted for twenty-five years. His wife was Jane, widow of Anthony Agutter and daughter of Henry Machen, landowner. There were no children. Fleming retired to Dorset and died in Sherborne, 30 July 1990.

[Donald Lindsay, *Friends for Life*, Lindel Publishing Company, 1981; *Geographical Journal*, vol. xcvi, no. 3, September 1940; personal knowledge.] GILES HUNT

FOOT, Hugh Mackintosh, BARON CARADON (1907–1990), colonial administrator and diplomat, was born 8 October 1907 in Plymouth, the second son and second child in the family of five sons and two daughters of Isaac *Foot, solicitor and Liberal MP for Bodmin, Cornwall, and his wife Eva, daughter of Dr Angus Mackintosh, DPH, of Fincastle, Perthshire. Isaac Foot's life centred on Liberal politics and Methodism. His children were brought up in a devout Christian home, over-brimming with books and the scholarship of radical philosophy. Hugh was the tallest and strongest of the children and the only one to win a scholarship to his school (the Quaker Leighton Park School in Reading). Unlike his father and three of his brothers, he did not enter the law, and whereas Dingle, John, Michael, and Christopher studied at Oxford, Hugh went to St John's College, Cambridge, where he rowed and played cricket. Politics and public speaking were a busy part of his life and, following his father's radical liberalism, he became president of the Liberal Club at Cambridge. Michael wrote of him later: 'He had acquired strange tastes and was ready to indulge in pastimes which the rest of us wouldn't be seen dead at—such as rowing, playing polo, dressing up in Goering-like uniforms and enjoying it, and occasionally even—at a pinch—placing some trust in the word of Tory Prime Ministers.' Four of the Foot brothers, including Hugh (1929), became presidents of their university unions. Hugh Foot obtained a second class (division I) in part i of the history tripos (1927) and a second class (division II) in part ii of the law tripos (1929).

In 1929 Foot joined the Colonial Service and was posted to Palestine. He became an Arab linguist and learned about the stresses and strains of the Middle East, developing an understanding which was invaluable when in later years he worked at the United Nations. He was back in London in the Colonial Office in 1938–9. On the outbreak of war he was appointed assistant British resident in Trans-Jordan, where he stayed until 1942. In 1943 he became lieutenant-colonel in charge of military administration in Cyrenaica and later in the same year was sent as colonial secretary to Cyprus, which was dangerously near to German-occupied Greece, Rhodes, and Crete.

In 1945 he went happily to Jamaica as colonial secretary and in 1947 he was posted to Nigeria as chief secretary. The preparatory work he did there contributed to Nigerian independence in 1962. He returned to Jamaica in 1951 as governor and captain-general. He was disappointed that plans for a federation of the West Indies were unsuccessful, Jamaica (which attained full independence in 1961) preferring to proceed alone.

Foot left the Caribbean in 1957 to become governor of the violent, riven island of Cyprus,

which had changed dramatically since 1943. Greece and the Greek Cypriots wanted Enosis (union), Turkey and the Turkish Cypriots desired partition, and the British government insisted on holding on to all of Cyprus. By 1960, after years of difficult diplomacy, independence was attained, with Britain retaining two sovereign bases on the island. The Conservative colonial secretary paid tribute in the House of Commons to Foot's 'unfailing imagination, courage and leadership'. Cyprus was Foot's last colony. For over thirty years he had moved with authority in lands of daunting complexity and engineered their metamorphoses from colonies into free countries, working as a mediator rather than a ruler. He believed that the only way to teach people responsibility was to give it to them. Everywhere he respected the individual dignity of his subjects, never patronizing them, and never remote from their human condition.

Foot's next move to the United Nations was consistent with his experience and his passionate belief that the UN was the only alternative to the division and destruction of the world. In 1961 he became the British representative on the trusteeship council, with special responsibility for Africa. However, Foot could not support the Conservative government's policy on Rhodesia. Deeply troubled, he resigned in 1962, writing: 'I do not feel able to speak in the UN or elsewhere in defence of our position in this matter. I simply cannot do it.' Foot was well aware that this might end his UN career. Yet his international reputation and popularity were such that he was invited by the UN to remain in charge of its own development programme.

After the Labour party's victory in 1964 Harold Wilson (later Baron Wilson of Rievaulx) appointed Foot minister of state at the Foreign Office and ambassador to the UN (1964–70). He was created a life peer as Baron Caradon (1964) and spoke on occasion forcefully in the House of Lords, particularly on the role of the UN charter in dealing with the world's dilemmas of violence and poverty. His efforts produced resolution 242 which formed the basis of the Egyptian-Israeli peace treaty. In New York his energy and robust optimism could be demanding and sometimes colleagues and staff could not keep up with the speed of his thinking and vision of his arguments. He certainly tried to implement the ideals of the charter. From 1971 he was consultant to the UN development programme, a post from which he retired in 1975, but he continued to advise in the troubled places of the world. He had a rare adaptability to peoples and places, which he happily shared with his talented, dedicated wife.

He was appointed OBE (1939), CMG (1946), KCMG (1951), and GCMG (1957). He became an honorary fellow of St John's College, Cambridge, in 1960 and was sworn of the Privy Council in 1968. Foot was often regarded as a colonial governor who ran out of colonies. He rejoiced that every colony he governed became independent. He was at the axis of an old empire swinging through conciliation to freedom and independence, enfranchising over six million people in twenty years.

In 1936 he married, in Haifa, (Florence) Sylvia (died 1985), daughter of Arthur White Millar Tod, OBE, director of the Steam Navigation Company of Baghdad. They had three sons, one of them the writer and journalist Paul Foot, and a daughter. Caradon died 5 September 1990 in Plymouth.

[Hugh Foot, *A Start in Freedom*, 1964; private information; personal knowledge.]   LENA M. JEGER

FORBES, SIR **Archibald Finlayson** (1903–1989), industrialist and banker, was born 6 March 1903 in Johnstone, Renfrewshire, the elder child and only son of Charles Forbes, chief constable of Johnstone, and his wife Elizabeth, daughter of James Robertson, slater and plasterer, also of Johnstone. He was educated at Paisley Grammar School and then joined the Glasgow firm of accountants, Thomson Mc-Lintock, and as part of his training attended Glasgow University. In 1927 he qualified as a member of the Scottish Institute of Chartered Accountants; his incisive brain, rapid grasp of detail, and capacity for hard work soon attracted the notice of Sir William *McLintock and marked the start of a close working relationship that continued for eight years. In 1930 he moved to the London office as McLintock's assistant.

In 1935 he was offered a partnership, but instead of taking this significant promotion he elected to accept an invitation to join Spillers, one of the milling clients, as finance director. This decision to leave the profession was an important milestone in his career, and was prompted partly by a realization that exceedingly able and more senior partners would succeed Sir William, and partly by his attraction to the challenge of and, at that time, more lucrative life in industry. Between 1939 and 1953 the food industry was under close operational control and the scope for the able and ambitious young finance director in Spillers was therefore very limited. In 1940 Forbes was seconded to the Air Ministry as director of capital finance, but soon afterwards he joined the first Baron *Beaverbrook, who, with a small hand-picked team, was charged by (Sir) Winston *Churchill with cutting through bureaucracy and red tape to speed up the production and repair of Spitfires and Hurricanes. He became first deputy secretary at the Ministry of Aircraft Production, where the stimulating and unorthodox life fully extended his talents. From 1943 until 1945 he was con-

troller of repair, equipment, and overseas supplies and from 1942 to 1945 a member of the Aircraft Supply Council.

In 1946 Forbes was appointed chairman of the Iron and Steel Board, which was disbanded on nationalization in 1949. After returning to office in 1951, the Conservatives denationalized steel, recreated the Board, and reappointed Forbes as chairman for a further six years (1953–9). He was president of the Federation of British Industries (subsequently the CBI) from 1951 to 1953, and on decontrol in 1953 returned to more active participation in Spillers's affairs, playing a major role in its growth and diversification; he became deputy chairman in 1960, chairman (1965–8), and president (1969–80). His financial acumen and experience were much in demand by other companies and between 1954 and 1964 he variously served as a non-executive director on the boards of Shell, English Electric, and Dunlop. From 1959 to 1964 he was chairman of the Central Mining and Investment Corporation. In 1959 he was appointed to the board of Midland Bank, whose deputy chairman he became in 1962. This signalled the final phase of his business career, which was to be devoted to the banking world. In 1964 he became chairman, but he suffered a minor heart attack in 1966 and was advised to cut back his activities. He gave up his other directorships, including in 1968 the chairmanship of Spillers.

As chairman of the Midland Bank he changed the traditional rôle of the office to one of a more executive character, while bringing the board much more closely in touch with the management. He was a strong advocate of diversification and between 1967 and 1974 played a direct personal part in negotiating some major deals. From his retirement in 1975 until 1983 he was president, an honorary office. While chairman of the Midland he served as chairman of the Committee of London Clearing Bankers and president of the British Bankers' Association (both 1970–2). He also sat on several government review bodies and committees, and was on the governing body of Imperial College, London (1959–75), and president of Epsom College (from 1964). He was knighted in 1943 and appointed GBE in 1957.

Forbes was urbane, courteous, and immaculately dressed, with a slim figure and iron-grey hair always in place; with a ready smile and at times acerbic wit he had great charm, particularly for women, who also found his soft Scottish accent an attraction. Occasionally he could infuriate his business colleagues by being indecisive or over-playing the role of 'devil's advocate', but his even temper ensured that this never led to bitterness. By no account mean, he had few extravagances and, despite his proclaimed enjoyment of golf, fishing on the Test, and playing bridge at Brooks's, his work was his paramount interest in life. Making money was never an ambition nor, considering his attainments, did he do so in any substantial way.

In 1937 he married Bina, daughter of Major Ronald Elliott, of Krickenbeek. They had no children. The marriage was dissolved in 1943 and in the same year he married Angela Gertrude, daughter of Horace Ely, of private means, of Arlington House, London SW1. They had two daughters and a son. His second wife brought him a happy social life that could otherwise so easily have been subordinated to his demanding career activities. Her sudden and untimely death in 1969 was a tremendous blow to him. He continued to lead an active life until about 1987, when he was confined increasingly to his flat in Portman Square, where he had lived for over fifty years. He died there 2 June 1989, from a heart condition.

[Private information; personal knowledge.]

W. MICHAEL VERNON

FORD, Edmund Brisco (1901–1988), geneticist, was born 23 April 1901 in Dalton, near Ulverston in Lancashire, the only child of the Revd Harold Dodsworth Ford, curate at Dalton in Furness, and his wife, Gertrude Emma Bennett. His interest in butterflies started as a boy, when he and his father observed each season a colony of the marsh fritillary butterfly in Cumberland. The numbers fluctuated greatly and in periods of rapid increase there was an extraordinary outburst of variability in pattern. When the population decreased again the common form was recognizably distinct from that which had prevailed before the period of abundance. An opportunity for evolution had occurred and the insect had made use of it. Ford was educated at St Bees School in Cumberland and then as an undergraduate at Wadham College, Oxford, where he gained a second class in zoology in 1924. He became a demonstrator in zoology and comparative anatomy at Oxford in 1930, then lecturer and later reader (1939) in genetics.

From 1952 to 1969 he was director of the genetics laboratory and from 1963 to 1969 professor of ecological genetics at Oxford. He was president of the Genetical Society of Great Britain from 1946 to 1949, and was elected to the Royal Society in 1946. From 1958 to 1971 he was a fellow of All Souls College, Oxford (serving two terms as senior dean); this was the first occasion for well over a century that a fellow of the Royal Society had been an All Souls man.

Ford devised elaborate techniques of mark-release-recapture, which enabled his team to estimate changes in frequency of particular forms of moths and butterflies, and of the genes controlling them, and to assess migration. This was classic work, done with Sir R. A. *Fisher, and

had a far-reaching effect on population genetics. The surveys were, however, characterized by a famous controversy with the American geneticist Sewell Wright over natural selection versus genetic drift—a chance process which can occur particularly in small populations. The moths provided an excellent example of Ford's conception of balanced polymorphism applied to the study of ecological genetics and of evolution in the wild. He was the first to predict that the human blood group polymorphic systems would influence susceptibility to disease. The association of cancer of the stomach and group A, and of duodenal ulcer and group O, bore this out. In the sickle cell haemoglobinopathy the dictum of the advantage of the heterozygote was excellently demonstrated, as this genotype protected children against malaria.

Ford was an inspiring teacher and his influence on genetics was worldwide. He had a particular gift for picking good research workers and then giving them their heads. Philip *Sheppard, with (Sir) C. A. Clarke, applied Ford's suggestion about the human blood groups to the Rh (rhesus) system, and with other researchers in the department of medicine at Liverpool University devised a successful method of preventing Rh haemolytic disease of the newborn. It was for this type of research that the Nuffield Foundation, of which Ford was a trustee, set up the Unit of Medical Genetics in Liverpool: Ford himself (he was always most generous) made a large personal contribution to this. It was a nice quirk that in the Rh polymorphism, when the mother is Rhesus negative, her heterozygous baby does not obey the rules, for it is always at a disadvantage.

In his later years Ford became interested in the genetics of the gypsy moth, *Lymantria dispar*, in relation to pest control. Using the heteropyknotic body technique, he and C. A. Clarke showed that R. B. Goldschmidt was wrong in thinking that unusual sex ratios in race crosses of the moth were the result of complete sex reversal. In fact the all-male broods were fully fertile and the result of the Haldane effect. Goldschmidt had thought his explanation would mean that these males were sterile and therefore would be useful in combating the pest, but this was not the case.

Known as 'Henry' to his friends, Ford's interests were very wide and included heraldry and archaeology. He contributed much to the Prehistoric Society, and with J. S. Haywood produced *Church Treasures in the Oxford District* in 1974. The titles of his genetics books also demonstrate his versatility—*Mendelism and Evolution* (1931), *The Study of Heredity* (1938), *Genetics for Medical Students* (1942), *Butterflies* (1945), *Moths* (1955), *Ecological Genetics* (1964), *Genetic Polymorphism* (1965), *Genetics and Adaptation* (1976),

Understanding Genetics (1979), and *Taking Genetics into the Countryside* (1981). Several went into many editions and every one is characterized by lucid prose. *Butterflies*, much to his surprise, proved a best seller.

He travelled widely, but in spite of this he knew virtually nothing about the wider political world, and cared for it even less. He would not allow radio and television in his house and he did not look at newspapers. In some respects time stood still for him and he regarded molecular geneticists as incomprehensible interlopers. He had a prickly manner and a feline skill in making his disapproval felt. Lecturing to an audience of mixed sex, he always began 'gentlemen'; once, when only women were present, he is said to have walked out.

In 1954 he was awarded the Darwin medal of the Royal Society. He won the Weldon memorial prize at Oxford University in 1959 and the medal of Helsinki University in 1967. He became an honorary fellow of the Royal College of Physicians of London in 1974 and was elected an honorary D.Sc. of Liverpool University in the same year. He was also an honorary fellow of Wadham College (1974) and, from 1977, senior dean and distinguished fellow of All Souls. He was a homosexual and misogynist, and he never married. He died in Oxford, 21 January 1988.

[*Munk's Roll*, vol. viii, 1989; R. Creed (ed.), *Ecological Genetics and Evolution: Essays in Honour of E. B. Ford*, 1971; personal knowledge.]   C. A. CLARKE

FOX, Felicity Lane-, BARONESS LANE-FOX (1918–1988), champion of the disabled. [See LANE-FOX, FELICITY.]

FOX, SIR Theodore Fortescue (1899–1989), medical editor, was born 26 November 1899 at Strathpeffer spa, Inverness-shire, the youngest in the family of two sons and three daughters of Dr Robert Fortescue Fox, a rheumatologist at the spa hospital, and his wife, Catharine Stuart McDougall. After Leighton Park School 'Robbie' served with the Friends' Ambulance Unit in 1918, and then in 1919 won a scholarship to Pembroke College, Cambridge, where he achieved a second class in part i of the natural sciences tripos (1921). He then obtained his LRCS and MRCP at the London Hospital in 1924. After one appointment as a houseman at the same hospital, he became a ship's surgeon before joining the *Lancet* in 1925. There he remained until 1964, save for his service in the Royal Army Medical Corps in 1939–44. He became B.Chir. in 1926, proceeded MD in 1936, and was elected FRCP in 1946, two years after becoming editor of the *Lancet*.

Fox was an excellent medical editor. He wrote well, could readily reduce a full-length book to a three-page article, and conducted negotiations

with wit and urbanity. The rate at which his assistant editors came and went reflected his exceptionally high standards. Fox's *Lancet* crucially influenced two major medical issues: the equitable delivery of health care, and publishing and interpreting breakthroughs in medical research. During negotiations about the setting up of a National Health Service in 1944–8 his low-key editorials balanced the advantages and disadvantages and eventually helped to persuade the profession to join the scheme. So esteemed then were Fox's contributions, both publicly and behind the scenes, that he was offered a knighthood, but declined lest he compromised the *Lancet*'s independence. He thought that any state system might threaten the doctor–patient relationship, something he had found in the USSR in 1936 and recorded in the *Lancet* and his MD thesis; this theme resurfaced in postwar accounts of visits to the USA, China, and the USSR again, as well as in major lectures (including the Harveian oration of the Royal College of Physicians in 1965). The *Lancet*'s scientific articles reported many postwar revolutionary discoveries, including the antibiotic explosion and unrecognized childhood conditions from adverse influences during pregnancy, such as thalidomide or X-irradiation. Fox judged papers without asking for expert opinions, a challengeable policy, but he took only a few days to decide whether to publish a piece, and, equally attractively, the *Lancet* printed articles within a few weeks of receipt.

Fox recruited experts to explain difficult concepts in editorials (whose anonymity also challenged current practices), which were then rewritten for non-experts. His *Lancet* also had space for debate, for developing new hypotheses, and for reminding readers that the traditional killers, such as famine, still coexisted with diseases of affluence. Unlike many editors, Fox insisted that campaigns should be short and crisp—to bore readers was to risk losing everything. He explained these policies in his Heath Clark lectures in 1963 (published in 1965 as *Crisis in Communication*), suggesting that the literature explosion could be contained by dividing journals into archival and newspaper forms.

All this made Fox's *Lancet* acknowledged as the best medical journal in the world, a most readable and prestigious exemplar, a fact that was reflected by the highest citation rate of any journal. Moreover, his public persona as a fighter of causes and as an engaging after-dinner speaker enabled him to promote new concepts (such as universal family planning, health centres, and postgraduate medical education) in other ways. Fox was prominent in the Royal College of Physicians and, uniquely for a non-clinician, a (narrowly defeated) candidate for the presidency in 1962. Knighted in 1962, and given honorary degrees by the universities of Birmingham (D.Litt., 1966) and Glasgow (LL D, 1958), after retirement in 1964 he was director of the Family Planning Association (1965–7).

Tall and thin, with a slight stoop, Fox had an attractive mild stammer, often (like his lifelong friend Russell *Brain) speaking after a disconcerting and lengthy silence, but then with good sense and wit. A puritan in most things, particularly clothes, food, and drink, his main interests after the *Lancet* were genealogy, the countryside, and his garden in Rotherfield, Sussex. As prizes for his pre-war intellectual parlour games he produced old copies of the rival *British Medical Journal* still in their wrappers.

In 1935 he married Margaret Eveline, daughter of William McDougall, Presbyterian minister. They had four sons, the youngest of whom, Robin, became editor of the *Lancet* in 1991. His wife died in 1970 and his eldest and second sons died in 1983 and 1970 respectively. Fox died at Rotherfield 19 June 1989.

[*Guardian*, 22 June 1989; *The Times*, 23 June 1989; *British Medical Journal*, 1 July 1989; *Lancet*, 1 July 1989; private information; personal knowledge.]

STEPHEN LOCK

FRANCIS, SIR **Frank Chalton** (1901–1988), director and principal librarian of the British Museum, was born 5 October 1901 in Liverpool, the only child of Frank William Francis, provision broker, who died in 1914, and his wife, Elizabeth Chalton, furrier; both parents were from Liverpool. He was educated at Liverpool Institute; at Liverpool University, where he took a first in classics; and at Emmanuel College, Cambridge, where he spent two years (1923–5) engaged in research upon early Greek philosophy and of which he became an honorary fellow in 1959.

In 1925–6 he taught at Holyhead County School, but in the latter year entered the British Museum as an assistant keeper in the department of printed books. He remained in the museum for the rest of his career. His work lay in the routines of the department, including, from 1930, the revision of the general catalogue, but like many of his colleagues he was also required to perform special language duties. For this purpose he acquired a knowledge of Swedish through classes at University College London. In 1936 he joined the Bibliographical Society and in the same year became editor of its transactions, *The Library*. Francis served as secretary of the British Museum from 1946 to 1947, and in the following year was appointed keeper of printed books. He had already served as chairman of the Library Association's committee on central cataloguing, and played a major part in the establishment of the *British National Bibliography*, which was first issued in 1950. He was also largely

responsible for terminating the revision of the museum's general catalogue, and replacing it with a photolithographically produced edition of the working copy of the catalogue. This was published between 1960 and 1966, when Francis had already become (in 1959) director and principal librarian of the museum (until 1968).

Within the Bibliographical Society, his editorship of *The Library* (until 1953) was combined with the honorary secretaryship, which he held jointly or solely from 1938 to 1964, guiding the society through World War II, and editing its *Studies in Retrospect* (1945). His position in the museum, his willingness to advise others, and his knowledge of historical bibliography involved him in the reconstruction and cataloguing of a number of older libraries, notably Lambeth Palace library and the cathedral libraries. He lectured in historical bibliography at University College London from 1945 to 1959.

The British Museum had been severely damaged in the war of 1939–45, and as director Francis continued the work of his predecessors in restoring galleries and in opening new ones (notably the Duveen gallery for the display of the Elgin marbles in 1962). He was particularly concerned to make the museum's collections more accessible to the public, and a feature of his directorship was the expansion of the museum's design, educational, and publication services. A notable example of the new attitude towards display was the Greek and Roman life room (1960). The museum's collections were greatly enriched, and one for which he had particular enthusiasm was the Ilbert collection of clocks (1958). Exhibitions were also brought in from outside the museum. The growth and improved display of both library and antiquities made the museum's need for more space imperative.

In line with his wish to make the collections of antiquities more accessible, Francis was also sympathetic to the growing demands that the museum's library should serve a wider public than its traditional clientele of scholars who sought manuscripts and older books in the humanities. In particular, a need had been voiced for a greatly improved reference service in the natural sciences. He believed that this must be met with the aid of the museum's existing privilege of legal deposit, and without jeopardizing the unity of the museum's library collections.

The British Museum Act of 1963, upon which he had a direct influence, embodied much of this thinking. Besides changing the composition of the body of trustees, it empowered them to house parts of the collections outside the museum buildings, thus enabling the transformation of the department of ethnography into the Museum of Mankind, creating a legal basis for a new library, and permitting the establishment of a National Library of Science and Invention. The integration of the Patent Office library into the department of printed books, as the basis of the new scientific service, was one of the landmarks of his directorship. Francis also initiated serious planning for a new library building. Architects were engaged, and plans for a new building on the south side of Great Russell Street had reached an advanced stage when in 1967 the government revoked the decision to build on the Bloomsbury site. Thus the establishment of the universal library for which he had worked was set back, though not permanently, by the government's ruling, and by the subsequent setting up of the national libraries committee.

Upon retirement in 1968 Francis moved to Nether Winchendon near Aylesbury, while maintaining his links with the bibliographical and library worlds, and in particular with facsimile publishing. He continued to visit the United States, where he was highly regarded and had many friends.

He was president of the Association of Special Libraries and Information Bureaux (1965–6), Bibliographical Society (1964–6), Library Association (1965), Museums Association (1965–6), and International Federation of Library Associations (1963–9). Honorary degrees were awarded by Oxford and Cambridge, and by other universities in Britain, Ireland, and North America. He was appointed CB in 1958 and KCB in 1960.

In appearance he was strong of profile, of medium height, and heavily built. He was handicapped by arthritis in later life. Genial and hospitable in private, he could be forceful and indeed dominating in public and official life. He married in 1927 Katrina Florence ('Kitty'), daughter of Thomas McLennon, warehouseman. They had two sons and one daughter. Francis died 15 September 1988 in Chilton House, Buckinghamshire.

[Private information; personal knowledge.]

R. J. ROBERTS

FRASER, SIR Hugh, second baronet (1936–1987), businessman, was born 18 December 1936 in Bearsden, Dunbartonshire, the only son and younger child of Hugh *Fraser, later first Baron Fraser of Allander, warehouseman and later chairman and managing director of the House of Fraser, and his wife Kate Hutcheon, daughter of Sir Andrew Jopp Williams Lewis, of Aberdeen, shipbuilder and former lord provost of Aberdeen. He was educated at St Mary's School, Melrose, and Kelvinside Academy. He left school at sixteen to go into the family business, which he joined on his seventeenth birthday,

starting work in McDonalds store in Buchanan Street, Glasgow.

Fraser worked closely with his father, and in 1957 he was given overall responsibility for the stores in Scotland, to prepare him for when he would take over the whole business. He was made assistant managing director in 1960. Following his father's heart attack in 1965, he was appointed deputy chairman.

Fraser was elected chairman of the House of Fraser and of the Scottish Universal Investment Trust (SUITS), his father's investment company, in 1966, just before his thirtieth birthday, following his father's death. He renounced the peerage, but was not able to disclaim the baronetcy. He was the fourth Hugh Fraser to head the family business, which his father had built up from a group of drapery stores in Scotland into a chain of seventy-five department stores headed by Harrods Ltd. Embarking on a policy of expansion and modernization, he introduced a new, more youthful style into existing stores. At Barkers of Kensington he staged a Youthquake, where models danced along the catwalk to pop music before a large audience of young people. He opened boutiques, shops within department stores, in an effort to revolutionize the sale of fashion wear in department stores and attract younger fashion-conscious people. One of the first, Way-In, opened in Harrods in 1967. At the same time, while selling some stores, such as Pontings in 1970, he was buying more stores, including James Howell & Co. in Cardiff and E. Dingle & Co., a group of stores in the southwest, with the intention of making the House of Fraser the best store in every large town in Britain.

Between 1966 and 1973 sales doubled to over £200 million, and profits doubled to over £10 million. But Fraser was fighting against competition from smaller specialist chains such as Laura Ashley, and when the recession began to bite in 1973 he was ready to give up the House of Fraser, partly because he had no son to whom to pass on the business, but also because he was tired of the relentless pressure of his hectic business life. When Boots Ltd. proposed a merger, Fraser supported the idea, intending to give up the chairmanship of the House of Fraser and concentrate on developing SUITS, but the proposed merger was blocked by the Monopolies and Mergers Commission in 1974, and Fraser decided to stay on.

The years after 1973 were difficult, and a Stock Exchange enquiry in 1976 revealed that Fraser had been selling his House of Fraser shares to finance his gambling. In 1976 he was fined £600 under the Companies Act for the misclassification of a loan, and for improper share dealings.

The company Lonrho first became involved in the fortunes of the House of Fraser in 1977, when it acquired nearly 30 per cent of the shares, and Roland ('Tiny') Rowland, the managing director, and Baron *Duncan-Sandys, the chairman, joined the board of directors. Lonrho gained control of SUITS in 1978 after buying Fraser's personal stake, and in 1980 turned its attention to acquiring the House of Fraser, and especially Harrods. In 1980 Lonrho started to harass the House of Fraser board, questioning decisions and circularizing shareholders. After Fraser and Rowland were reconciled in January 1981, Fraser lost the support of the directors, and he was removed as chairman at the end of January. He subsequently resigned from the chairmanship of Harrods, which he had just resumed, after giving it up in 1973. Lonrho then launched a take-over bid, which was turned down by the Monopolies and Mergers Commission in December 1981. Fraser resigned from the board in February 1982.

After 1981 Fraser spent most of his time in Scotland, settling into a quieter business life once he had severed his connections with the House of Fraser. He built up a chain of menswear shops, the Sir Hugh & Sir group, which he later sold, and he held a number of directorships, mainly in Scotland, as well as the chairmanship of Dumbarton Football Club.

Fraser was popular in Glasgow. He worked hard on behalf of the charitable trust set up by his father, the Hugh Fraser Trust, through which he bought the island of Iona for the National Trust of Scotland as a memorial to his father, and he gave his Mugdock estate near Glasgow to form the Mugdock country park. Although he was not interested in politics, he joined the Scottish National Party in 1974, partly out of anger at the Conservative government, which had referred the Boots merger to the Monopolies Commission. He served for a time on the Scottish Development Council.

A man of great personal charm and charisma, described by 'Tiny' Rowland as 'a charming man but a professional loser', Fraser worked long hours and was totally committed to the expansion and success of the House of Fraser. But, especially after 1973, he became addicted to gambling, playing for high stakes, and was rumoured to have lost over £1 million. He was chosen as Young Businessman of the Year by the *Guardian* in 1973, and was awarded an honorary doctorate by the University of Stirling in 1985.

He was very handsome as a young man, dark haired and popular with the sales assistants in the House of Fraser stores, which he visited regularly. In 1962 he married Patricia Mary, daughter of John Bowie, of Milngavie, Dunbartonshire, from an old Glasgow family. They were divorced in 1971 and in 1973 he married an international showjumper, Aileen Margaret (died 1984), daughter of George Paterson Ross. They were separated some years before the marriage was dissolved in 1982. There were three daughters from the first marriage. In 1979 Lynda Taylor, whom his friends thought would become his third wife, died of carbon monoxide poisoning in a garage of his lodge on Loch Lomond. In 1982 he was to marry Annabell Finlay, but he cancelled the marriage a few days before it was due to take place. Fraser died from lung cancer 5 May 1987 in Mugdock, near Milngavie, Dunbartonshire, Scotland.

[*The Times*, 5 January 1981 and 6 May 1987; *Guardian*, 22 February 1973; Michael Moss and Alison Turton, *A Legend of Retailing: House of Fraser*, 1989; House of Fraser archives in the Business Records Collection, Glasgow University.]   ANNE PIMLOTT BAKER

FRASER, (Walter) Ian (Reid), BARON FRASER OF TULLYBELTON (1911–1989), lord of appeal, was born in Glasgow 3 February 1911, the only child of Alexander Reid Fraser, stockbroker, and his wife, Margaret Russell MacFarlane. He was educated at Repton, where he distinguished himself academically. He then became a scholar of Balliol College, Oxford, and, after taking a first-class honours degree in philosophy, politics, and economics (1932), completed his education in the University of Glasgow, where he graduated LL B in 1935.

In 1936 he was admitted to the Faculty of Advocates and soon demonstrated the remarkable breadth of his legal quality both in practice and in lecturing in constitutional law, first at Glasgow University (1936) and, after World War II, at the University of Edinburgh (1948). His book, *Outline of Constitutional Law* (first edn. 1938 and second edn. 1948), became one of the standard textbooks of the law degree courses in Glasgow and elsewhere, and was a work which readily found its place in the libraries of practitioners. He was intellectually agile, clear and simple in his use of language, and, although not the outstanding advocate of his generation, excelled in debate and in appellate work, particularly in those cases which appealed to his academic cast of mind.

In 1939 his legal career was interrupted by the war. On its outbreak he was a subaltern in a Territorial Army anti-aircraft battery commanded by a fellow member of the faculty. He joined the Royal Artillery, reached the rank of major, and served in Burma, becoming deputy assistant adjutant-general in 1945. After the war, in spite of the fact that his practice was almost exclusively civil, he accepted service as an advocate depute, finally becoming home depute, the senior figure in the Crown Office under the law officers. In 1953 he took silk and in 1959 was elected dean of the Faculty of Advocates, an office which he held until 1964, when he became a senator of the College of Justice in Scotland (until 1974), with the judicial title of Lord Fraser.

As a judge he was not only respected but liked by the bar, and in both the Outer House and the Inner his acute intellect, coupled with the inherent diffidence of his quiet personality, was matched by his invariable courtesy, charm, and a healthy appetite for hard work. In 1974 he became a lord of appeal in ordinary, privy councillor, and life peer, and in the eleven succeeding years in which he sat in the appellate committee of the House of Lords (until 1985) and in the Privy Council, he made a notable contribution to the development and clarification of the law, delivering many lucid speeches on Scots appeals to the House of Lords. For example, in 1980 he clarified the duty of care owed by the occupier of premises to firemen fighting a fire there and in 1983 declared that the Court of Session's supervisory jurisdiction over decisions of administrative bodies was not enjoyed by the Sheriff Court.

While he was an advocate he was active in politics and unsuccessfully contested the East Edinburgh constituency as a Unionist in the general election of 1955. He became a member of the law reform committee (Scotland) in 1954, and of the royal commission on the police (1960–2). After he entered the House of Lords he was much concerned with legislation, especially with bills dealing with the administration of justice. When he retired from full-time judicial work he became chairman of the university commissioners, dealing with university and college constitutions which had been affected by the Education Reform Act of 1988.

Fraser was a member of the Queen's Body Guard for Scotland (Royal Company of Archers). In 1975 he became an honorary master of the bench at Gray's Inn, and in 1981 he was elected an honorary fellow of Balliol. He also became an honorary LL D of Glasgow (1970) and Edinburgh (1978).

He was a competent yachtsman but his main hobbies were shooting and walking, which he undertook on his small estate at Tullybelton in Perthshire. On foot, indeed, the normal pace of his tall spare frame over the ground was too rapid for most of his friends, who preferred to meet him when he had come to rest. Shy and reserved, he loved music and conversation. On 8 November 1943 he married (Mary Ursula) Cynthia (Gwendolen), the only daughter of Colonel Ian Harrison Macdonell, of the Highland Light Infantry. They had one son. On 17 February 1989 Fraser died in a road accident en route from Tullybelton House in Bankfoot to Edinburgh, on

the M90 between Perth and Edinburgh. He had been driving his car in blizzard conditions.

[Balliol College Record, 1989; records of the Faculty of Advocates, Advocates' library, Parliament House, Edinburgh; personal knowledge.]   EMSLIE

FRICKER, Peter Racine (1920–1990), composer and teacher, was born 5 September 1920 in Ealing, London, the elder child and only son of Edward Racine Fricker, civil servant, and his wife, Deborah Alice Parr, nurse. His middle name came from his great-grandmother, who was a direct descendant of the French dramatist. He was educated at St Paul's School, London. His father died when Peter was fifteen and about to enter the merchant navy, but this plan was prevented by his poor eyesight. He began studying organ as a schoolboy with Henry Wilson, then entered the Royal College of Music in 1937, where he continued his organ studies with (Sir) Ernest *Bullock and piano with Henry Wilson. He was assistant organist to Wilson while continuing his studies. Before the war, he also attended classes at Morley College. An early distinction was his election as a fellow of the Royal College of Organists at the age of nineteen. He studied theory and composition with R. O. Morris.

In 1940 his studies were interrupted by the war, during which he served as a radio operator in the Royal Air Force, in signals and intelligence. It was at the RCM that he had met (Audrey) Helen, a pianist, the daughter of Raymonde William Lee Clench, chartered accountant. They married in 1943, the same year he was posted to India to serve as an intelligence officer. There were no children of the marriage.

After the war years he resumed his composition studies with Mátyás Seiber, who became a strong influence and a close friend and colleague at Morley College, in London. During his years there he conducted, acted as rehearsal pianist for the choir, and, together with his wife, made a living copying and arranging music. From 1952 to 1964 he held a dual post as director of music at Morley College, where he succeeded (Sir) Michael Tippett, and was also professor of composition at the RCM. His career as a composer was launched when he won the A. J. Clements prize for his Wind Quintet in 1947, which was quickly followed by the Koussevitzky prize for his First Symphony in 1949, and by winning the Arts Council Festival of Britain competition for young composers prize for his Violin Concerto in 1951. These distinctions made him one of the most prominent British composers of his generation.

His music represented a departure from the nationalistic pastoralism coined by Ralph *Vaughan Williams, for he was one of the first in England to assimilate the contributions of Béla

Bartók, Arnold Schoenberg, and Igor Stravinsky, and to synthesize these influences with an expressively dissonant style of his own. During the 1950s he composed seven film scores and six works for radio. Other important works during this highly prolific period include two more symphonies (nos. 2 and 3), 'Dance Scene' (1954), 'Litany' (1955), and the large oratorio 'The Vision of Judgement' (1956–8).

In 1964 he was invited to the University of California at Santa Barbara, as visiting professor. He became enamoured of the school and its surroundings and excited about the possibility of establishing a centre for compositional study at the university. In 1965 he was appointed professor. His wife joined him in Santa Barbara, and they lived in nearby Goleta for the rest of his life. He held the Dorothy and Sherill C. Corwin chair in music and had a joint appointment in the university's innovative College of Creative Studies. He was a dedicated, patient teacher, and provided guidance to many composition students over the years. He was a tall, imposing figure of a man, but gentle and rather shy and reserved. His interests included bird-watching, word puzzles, mystery novels, travel, and cats.

His compositional output was extensive, and he was steadily prolific throughout his entire career. His *œuvre* included five symphonies, three string quartets, a ballet, an oratorio, concerti, various choral works, numerous chamber works, and others in all genres except staged opera, comprising a total of over 160 works in all. His reputation was international, and he composed works for important performers and ensembles such as Julian Bream, Dennis Brain, Henryk Szering, the Amadeus Quartet, and the Royal Philharmonic Orchestra. In 1976 his Symphony no. 5 was given its premier by the BBC Symphony Orchestra to commemorate the twenty-fifth anniversary of the Royal Festival Hall.

His honours and awards included an honorary RAM (1966), an honorary doctorate in music from the University of Leeds (1958), the freedom of the City of London, and the Order of Merit of West Germany (1965). He was an honorary professional fellow and research professor in the Institute of Creative Arts of University College, Cardiff, as well as an active member of the International Society for Contemporary Music, the Society of Composers International (formerly the American Society of University Professors), and the Composers' Guild of Great Britain (of which he was elected vice-president in 1986). During the summers of 1984–6 he served as president of the Cheltenham international festival.

In 1989 he was appointed composer-in-residence of the Santa Barbara Symphony Orchestra, for which he composed an orchestral work,

'Walk by Quiet Waters' (1988). It was while he was working on a second work for them and looking forward to retirement that he died 1 February 1990 in Santa Barbara, of cancer of the throat and larynx.

[*New Grove Dictionary of Music and Musicians*, ed. Stanley Sadie, vol. vi, 1980; *Dictionary of Contemporary Music*, ed. John Vinton, 1974; Fricker archives, Arts Library, University of California, Santa Barbara; private information; personal knowledge.]

JOHN J. CARBON

FROST, Dora (1901–1989), UK representative at the United Nations in the 1960s, and wife of Hugh Gaitskell, leader of the Labour party. [See GAITSKELL, ANNA DEBORAH ('DORA').]

FRY, (Edwin) Maxwell (1899–1987), architect, was born 2 August 1899 in Wallasey, Cheshire, the second of four children and elder son of Ambrose Fry, commercial traveller and later chemical manufacturer, and his wife, Lily Thomson. Fry was educated at the Liverpool Institute. He served in the King's Liverpool Regiment at the end of World War I and in the Allied occupation of Germany. An ex-serviceman's grant enabled him to enter Liverpool University school of architecture in 1920, under Professor (Sir) Charles *Reilly. A distinguished graduate of 1924, Fry worked in New York before joining the office of Thomas Adams and F. Longstreth Thompson, specialists in town planning, becoming a partner in 1930, after a period away as chief assistant in the architect's department of Southern Railways. His interest in planning, an important component of the Liverpool course, was to remain with him. As a partner in Adams, Thompson & Fry, he designed a garden village at Kemsley near Sittingbourne in 1929, and a house at Wentworth, Surrey, in 1932, in the refined neo-Georgian style typical of the Liverpool school in the 1920s.

The Canadian designer Wells Coates met Fry while working in the Adams and Thompson office in 1924, and encouraged him to set aside his classical training and follow the example of Le Corbusier, but Fry's conversion to Modernism was gradual, and came principally through his membership of the Design and Industries Association, which introduced him to modern German housing. He was also influenced by the Congrès International de l'Architecture Moderne, and was closely involved in its English branch, the Modern Architectural Research Group (MARS), following its establishment in 1933. The conversion is evident at Sassoon House in Peckham (1934), a block of working-class flats he designed with the engineer Kirkwood Dodds.

Fry became well known for two of the most elegant white Modernist houses of the mid-

1930s: Sun House, Frognal Lane, Hampstead (1936) and Miramonte in Kingston upon Thames (1937). With the housing consultant Elizabeth Denby he carried out an extensive social housing scheme at Kensal House, Ladbroke Grove (1936), with curving blocks of flats and a circular nursery school, a model of progressive architecture well publicized by the clients, the Gas Light and Coke Company.

Fry assisted Walter Gropius (1883–1969), the former director of the Bauhaus at Weimar and Dessau, on his arrival in England in 1934, by setting up a partnership which enabled Gropius to practise in England until his emigration to the USA in March 1937. This was a distinction from which Fry benefited, and his graphic skills and sympathetic attitude helped in the realization of Gropius's ideas in an alien culture. Their designs were not fully collaborative and can be separately attributed. To reduce its cost, Fry reworked Gropius's design for Impington Village College, Cambridgeshire, and supervised its construction after Gropius's departure. In 1939 he became a fellow of the Royal Institute of British Architects, of which he was vice-president in 1961–2.

Fry served in the Royal Engineers from 1939 to 1944, reaching the rank of major, and ended the war as town-planning adviser to the resident minister in west Africa. He worked during the early period of the war on a plan for London presented by MARS, some of which is described in his book *Fine Building* (1944), a testimony to his desire to efface the urban forms of the northern working-class suburbs known in his childhood.

In the immediate postwar period, Fry gathered a group of talented young assistants, and thereafter was to work in partnership with his second wife, the architect Jane Drew. The partnership designed Passfield Flats, Lewisham (1949), the Riverside restaurant for the South Bank exhibition (1951), and many educational buildings and offices in Ghana and Nigeria between 1946 and 1961, notably Ibadan University, Nigeria. These displayed the adaptability of Modernist methods to local climatic and cultural conditions, and Fry and Drew were instrumental in the establishment of a school of tropical architecture at the Architectural Association in London.

In 1951 Fry and Drew were invited to join the design team for the new capital of the Punjab at Chandigarh and were influential in causing Le Corbusier and Pierre Jeanneret to be invited as architects for the secretariat and law courts. Fry and his wife stayed in India for three years, working mainly on housing within Le Corbusier's masterplan. Fry, who was unique in his connection with two of modern architecture's masters, was content to take a less conspicuous role. He continued to work until the early 1970s, designing notable buildings such as the head offices for Pilkington Brothers at St Helen's (1959–65) and the mid-Glamorgan crematorium, a romantic late design revealing Fry's attachment to Scandinavian architecture. In retirement he devoted much time to painting. *Autobiographical Sketches* (1975), the last of his many publications, revealed an emotional, even sentimental aspect of his character which could hardly be deduced from his buildings. His friends and colleagues remember him as an ebullient, optimistic, unconventional but practical man. He was slim and elegant in appearance, with a high forehead and expressive mouth. In 1964 he was awarded the RIBA Royal gold medal. He was an honorary LL D of Ibadan University. He was appointed CBE (1955), ARA (1966), and RA (1972).

In 1926 Fry married Ethel, a secretary, the divorced wife of Charles Leese and daughter of Walter Speakman, schoolteacher. She was his elder by twelve years; they had one daughter. The marriage was dissolved in 1942, and in the same year Fry married Joyce Beverly ('Jane'), divorced wife of James Thomas Alliston and daughter of Harry Guy Radcliffe Drew, caterer. There were no children of this marriage. Fry died 3 September 1987 at Darlington Memorial Hospital.

[Maxwell Fry, *Autobiographical Sketches*, 1975, and *Art in a Machine Age*, 1969; private information.]

ALAN POWERS

FUCHS, (Emil Julius) Klaus (1911–1988), theoretical physicist, was born 29 December 1911 in Rüsselsheim, Germany, the third child in the family of two sons and two daughters of Emil Fuchs and his wife, Else Wagner. His father, renowned for his high Christian principles, was a pastor in the Lutheran church who joined the Quakers later in life and eventually became professor of theology at Leipzig University. The women in the family were all mentally unstable. His grandmother, mother, and one sister all took their own lives, while his other sister was diagnosed as schizophrenic.

He went to school in Eisenach and continued his education in the universities of Leipzig and Kiel. It was at the latter that he became involved in politics and, after some soul-searching, doubtless inspired by his father's idealistic attitude, the Communist party. After an altercation with the Nazis in 1933 he crossed the border into France and then, with the help of family connections, travelled to Bristol, where he studied under (Sir) Nevill Mott and obtained a Ph.D. He took a D.Sc. at Edinburgh University under the guidance of Max Born, one of the pioneers of the new quantum mechanics. After the outbreak of war in

1939 he was interned with other German refugees in camps on the Isle of Man and in Canada from June to December 1940.

In 1941 he was recruited by (Sir) Rudolf Peierls to work on Tube Alloys, the code name for the British project to develop the atomic bomb. The following year, in spite of wartime restrictions, he was granted British nationality as a special case, and signed the Official Secrets Act. In 1943 he went with Peierls to join the Manhattan District, which was the code name given to the American atomic bomb programme. He was posted to New York and then to Los Alamos in New Mexico, where he remained until after the resulting bombs had destroyed Hiroshima and Nagasaki. In 1946 he returned to England, where he was appointed by (Sir) John *Cockcroft as head of the theoretical physics division at the newly created Atomic Energy Research Establishment at Harwell, then under the Ministry of Supply. He was given the Civil Service rank of principal scientific officer. He soon became senior principal and in 1949 deputy chief scientific officer. He took personal charge of the mathematical work which underpinned the development of nuclear power.

In January 1950 he was arrested for transmitting significant information about Anglo-American work on nuclear weapons, including the hydrogen bomb, to secret agents of the Soviet Union. This he had been doing continuously since 1941, after Germany invaded Russia. He had felt so strongly that the details of atomic research should be shared with the Soviet Union that he made contact with a communist colleague he had known in Germany. He had been put in touch with someone working for the Soviet embassy. He was sentenced to fourteen years' imprisonment in February and his British citizenship was revoked in December 1950. Fuchs was released on 23 June 1959 after serving nine years and four months. Immediately after leaving Wakefield prison he joined his father and one of his nephews in what had become the German Democratic Republic, where he was appointed deputy director of the Institute for Nuclear Research in Rossendorf near Dresden; he retired in 1979. He never returned to the West.

In 1959 he married a friend from his student days, a fellow communist called Margarete ('Greta') Keilson, the widow of Max Keilson, president of the Association of Journalists in the GDR. They had no children. Fuchs achieved great prominence in East Germany and was elected to the Academy of Sciences and the Communist Party Central Committee. He was decorated with both the Order of Merit of the Fatherland and the Order of Karl Marx. He had probably saved the Soviet Union two years' work on nuclear weapons.

Of slight build, five feet nine inches in height, with fast receding hair, he was physically attractive with a warm smile, although he often seemed frail. Always tidily dressed and with impeccable manners, he could be kind and sensitive towards his friends. His legendary shyness and aloof manner, however, did not always quite succeed in concealing his innate arrogance and conceit and his belief that he was uniquely valuable. He was possessed of formidable self-control. Short-sighted and noticeably left-handed, he was also a heavy smoker, drank quite a lot, and suffered from respiratory problems, as did his older brother, who had tuberculosis for many years.

Whilst in the USA and Britain he enjoyed social occasions and prided himself on being a good dancer. He was also keen on family life and frequently dropped in on his married friends. Although he deliberately kept his distance from eligible women of his own age, he was not homosexual. It is believed that he formed a relationship at Harwell with an older woman who had psychiatric problems. She was married to a senior colleague of his at Harwell who was also his close friend. Fuchs died in Dresden, 28 January 1988.

[Emil Fuchs, *Mein Leben*, 2 vols., Leipzig, 1959; Norman Moss, *Klaus Fuchs*, 1987; personal knowledge.]   MARY FLOWERS

FULLER, Peter Michael (1947–1990), art critic and magazine editor, was born 31 August 1947 in Damascus, the second child and elder son in the family of two sons and a daughter of Harold William Charles Fuller, general medical practitioner, and his wife, Marjorie Dale Noyes, midwife. His childhood was largely spent in Eastleigh, a Hampshire railway town, where the family attended the Union Baptist church on Sundays. Fuller was baptized by complete immersion in 1961, just before he went away to board at Epsom College, a public school closely connected with the medical profession. Although he liked the fact that both John Piper and Graham *Sutherland went to Epsom College, Fuller was unhappy there. He doubted his religious convictions and felt bewildered by the loss of earlier certainties.

The sense of confusion intensified while he read English at Peterhouse, Cambridge, between 1965 and 1968. He obtained a second class (division II) in both parts of the English tripos (1967 and 1968). He later described his time at Cambridge as 'a period of personal crisis', and found his Baptist faith increasingly inadequate. Psychiatric problems aggravated his disquiet, and he consulted a psychoanalyst in his last year at Cambridge. By that time Fuller had fallen under the influence of Marxism and the far left. Revolution was in the air, and Marxist literature formed much of his reading. But he also staged an exhibition of his paintings at the Cambridge

Union, and in 1967 met his future wife, Colette Marie Méjean, a French student whose father was a village postmaster. They married in 1971, and five years later their only child, Sylvia Leda, was born.

After Cambridge Fuller worked at first as a journalist on *City Press*, a City of London newspaper, whose motto was 'The Voice of Honest Capitalism'. His interest in Marxism intensified, and he began writing for the underground press—most notably, *Black Dwarf* and *Seven Days*. A visit to Argentina allowed him to witness a struggle for national liberation, and he became an avid reader of the *New Left Review*. But his involvement with theoretical debate overlaid what he afterwards termed 'a deep sense of fragmentation'. Gambling and masochism grew into compulsive obsessions, and he began a five-year period of psychoanalysis in 1972.

Apart from editing a book on *The Psychology of Gambling* (1974), with Jon Halliday, Fuller became a regular contributor to *Arts Review*, *Connoisseur*, *Art and Artists*, *Art Monthly*, and *Studio International*. Some of his most substantial reviews appeared in *New Society*, to which he had been introduced by the writer who influenced him most powerfully during the 1970s, John Berger. They became friends, and Fuller also got to know the American painter Robert Natkin, about whom he wrote articles, catalogues, and finally a book (*Robert Natkin*, 1981). The most impressive outcome of his work during the 1970s was *Art and Psychoanalysis* (1980).

The advent of a new decade brought momentous changes. Colette left him in 1981, and they were divorced four years later. John Berger's influence was superseded by that of John *Ruskin, whose ideas dominated Fuller's book *Theoria: Art, and the Absence of Grace* (1988). He repudiated Marxism, along with most of the friends he had made in the 1970s. Berger came under particularly virulent attack, and Fuller revised an earlier publication called *Seeing Berger* (1980) under the new, caustic title *Seeing Through Berger* (1988). New friends, like the philosopher Roger Scruton, now aligned him more with the right than the left. He became a fierce opponent of the avant-garde, calling instead for a return to the romantic and figurative tradition in British art.

Marriage to the Australian sculptor Stephanie Jane Burns in 1985 brought him enormous happiness as well as a son, Laurence Ruskin Fuller, who was born in 1986. Stephanie was the daughter of Alan Robert Burns, company chairman and inventor. Two years later Fuller founded his own art magazine with the suitably Ruskinian title *Modern Painters*, as a pulpit for his views. It was an immediate success, not only because of Fuller's combative and controversial editorials, but also on account of his willingness to publish a lively range of views from novelists as well as critics. The attention attracted by the magazine helped to make Fuller more widely known, and his appointment as art critic of the *Sunday Telegraph* in 1989 gave him another public platform. A regular column there enabled him to champion artists like the painter John Bellany and the sculptor Glynn Williams, both of whom Fuller saw upholding the values he cherished.

Slight in build, and invariably pale, Fuller often looked as if he had just emerged from a long period incarcerated in his study. Behind spectacles, his eyes would often narrow as if to cope with the unaccustomed glare of daylight. Living in Bath, with a country cottage at Stowlangtoft in Suffolk, he enjoyed his greatest period of success and notoriety. But a motorway accident on 28 April 1990, when he was forty-two, cut everything short. His chauffeur-driven car crashed into a field off the M4 motorway, near Theale. Fuller died at the scene, of head and neck injuries. His wife, thirty-three weeks pregnant, broke a hip, damaged her spine, and lost her unborn child Gabriel as a result of the accident. Both Gabriel and Fuller were buried together at St George's church, Stowlangtoft. A large sculpture called 'Opening Chestnut', by Glynn Williams, stands at the head of the grave.

[Peter Fuller, *Marches Past*, 1986; John McDonald (ed.), *Modern Painters: Reflections on British Art by Peter Fuller*, 1993; private information; personal knowledge.]

RICHARD CORK

FULTON, John Scott, BARON FULTON (1902–1986), university administrator and public servant, was born in Dundee 27 May 1902, the younger son and youngest of three children of Angus Robertson Fulton, principal of University College, Dundee, and his wife, Annie Scott. He was educated at Dundee High School, St Andrews University, and Balliol College, Oxford, where he was awarded a second class in both classical honour moderations (1924) and *literae humaniores* (1926). After two years as a lecturer at the London School of Economics (1926–8), he returned to Balliol in 1928 as a fellow and tutor in philosophy. In 1935, when 'modern Greats' (philosophy, politics, and economics) had established itself, particularly in Balliol, the 'philosophy' in his title was changed to 'politics'. Fulton remained in that position until 1947, although during World War II he greatly widened his political and administrative experience, as principal assistant secretary in the mines department and later in the Ministry of Fuel and Power. Already a friend and admirer of Sir William (later Baron) *Beveridge, he now added to his range of friends and colleagues Harold Wilson (later Baron Wilson of Rievaulx), who worked with him as an economist and statistician.

Such personal relationships mattered greatly to Fulton and strongly influenced his career. Yet his success depended essentially on his own remarkable energy and, when inspired, his boundless enthusiasm. He demonstrated these qualities, not to universal acclaim, in his first, somewhat circumscribed, postwar field of action, as principal for twelve years (1947–59) of the University College of Swansea, with two spells, in 1952–4 and 1958–9, as vice-chancellor of the University of Wales. While in Swansea, he encouraged university expansion and furthered his interest in adult education, which had been stimulated in the past by Balliol's master, A. D. *Lindsay (Baron Lindsay of Birker). He was chairman of the Universities' Council for Adult Education and the council of the National Institute of Adult Education (both 1952–5).

An unprecedented opportunity to bring all his gifts into play came in 1959, when he was appointed principal of the University College of Sussex, the first of seven new English university institutions. When it took in its first students in 1961, its name had happily been changed from University College to University and his own title, his second significant change of title, from principal to vice-chancellor. By then, too, Fulton had assembled a small team of academics and administrators, most of them as energetic and enthusiastic as he was, all of them sharing his vision. Together they were committed to creating a university which from the start would reshape university curricula and organizational structures and develop a strong identity of its own. Critics were sceptical—or jealous—but the new university, which was sometimes called, though it never was, 'Balliol by the sea', proved highly attractive to applicants. Indeed, it came to symbolize the spirit of the 1960s. Fulton inspired the institution rather than managed it. He won friendship as well as loyalty.

Brighton was a more useful base than Swansea had been for the 'outside' activities which Fulton enjoyed. Some of them were directly concerned with university education in Britain and abroad. He was largely responsible in 1961, for instance, for speedily bringing into existence the University Central Council on Admissions (of which he was chairman in 1961–4), which transformed the system of university entrance, and a year later he became chairman of the BBC and ITA committees on adult education (both 1962–5). The BBC, of which he was to become vice-chairman in 1965, was uneasy about this dual role: Fulton, however, saw the two chairmanships as complementary. Later, he intervened personally with Harold Wilson, then prime minister, after proposals had been made in 1964 that the BBC should accept advertising.

Before he became chairman of the Inter-University Council for Higher Education Overseas (1964–8), Fulton had already been involved in university policy-making in Malta, Africa (Sierra Leone and Nigeria), and Asia. He was most successful in Hong Kong, where in 1962 he chaired the committee that established the new Chinese University. Its four-year pattern of courses was to survive him.

Fulton's major non-university public assignment concerned Britain's Civil Service. Invited by Wilson in 1966 to chair a departmental inquiry into it, he and his colleagues produced a report which criticized the dependence of the service on generalist all-rounders and pressed for a more professional and more specialized Civil Service. Other influences were brought to bear upon him in reaching this conclusion, notably that of Norman *Hunt (later Baron Crowther-Hunt), but the tone of the report, published in 1968, was his own. He always believed in opening access and in provoking change. Much criticized in Whitehall, his report had only limited results, although it was followed by the setting up of a new Civil Service department and to Fulton what was even more to the point—a Civil Service College.

Fulton was knighted in 1964 and became a life peer in 1966. He was an honorary fellow of Balliol (1972) and Swansea (1985), and had honorary degrees from ten universities.

A strong and confident believer in the claims of public service, official and voluntary, Fulton considered rightly that the various activities of his strenuous public life were all of one piece. Yet in private he owed much to the support of his wife Jacqueline, daughter of Kenneth Edward Towler Wilkinson, solicitor, of York. They married in 1939 and had three sons and one daughter. It was on his wife's initiative that, after Fulton's retirement from Sussex University in 1967, the two of them moved to Thornton le Dale in Yorkshire, an agreeable base, if less accessible than Brighton. He chose, however, to move frequently out of it. The motto of the University of Sussex of his own devising had been 'Be still and know', but to the end Fulton had little wish to be still. He was always full of vitality. The last of his big jobs was from 1968 to 1971 when he was a not entirely successful chairman of the British Council. In appearance he was short and wiry and in old age he looked far younger than his years. He died 14 March 1986 at his home, Brook House, Thornton le Dale, Pickering, north Yorkshire.

[Private information; personal knowledge.]

ASA BRIGGS

G

GAITSKELL, Anna Deborah ('Dora'), BARONESS GAITSKELL (1901–1989), UK representative at the United Nations in the 1960s, and wife of Hugh *Gaitskell, leader of the Labour party, was born 25 April 1901 near Riga in Latvia, then part of imperial Russia, the eldest in the family of four daughters and one son of Leon Creditor, Hebrew scholar and writer, and his wife, Tessa Jaffé. Her father emigrated to Britain in 1903 and, when his wife and daughter followed shortly afterwards, they settled in Stepney Green, in the East End of London. Dora Creditor won a scholarship to Coburn High School for Girls. She would have preferred to become a teacher, but was persuaded to study medicine, although she abandoned it when she married on 15 March 1921 Isaac ('David') Frost, lecturer in physiology, the son of Louis Frost, mechanical engineer. A son, Raymond, was born in 1925, but the marriage ended in divorce in 1937, having only continued because of what she was later to call 'the utterly shameful and disgraceful' state of the divorce laws.

Dora Creditor joined the Labour party at the age of sixteen and became politically active. She met Hugh Gaitskell at the Fitzroy tavern in Soho, then a popular haunt of artists, writers, journalists, dons, and aspiring politicians. Gaitskell had lately arrived in London to take up a teaching post at University College and was living a Bohemian social life in and around Fitzrovia, a milieu with which Dora Frost was already familiar. Gaitskell, who was five years younger, soon made her his confidante and, when he went to Vienna in 1933 on the eve of the climax of the counter-revolution against the Viennese socialists, led by Engelbert Dolfuss, she followed him. They lived together and then married at Hampstead town hall on 9 April 1937. Hugh Todd Naylor Gaitskell was the son of Arthur Gaitskell, of the Indian Civil Service.

Dora Gaitskell settled easily to domestic life. Her first child by this marriage, a daughter, Julia, was born in 1939, and a second, Cressida, in 1942. She proved an affectionate and caring mother, creating a family life of a fairly traditional kind. She was confident in her husband's love and ultimate loyalty and, in turn, became a devoted wife, a tigress in defending him from his political enemies, and committed and affectionate towards his friends.

Elected as MP for Leeds South East in 1945, Gaitskell was chosen as leader of the Labour party ten years later. This was a stormy period in Labour's history, and Gaitskell was frequently the object of bitter personal attacks. His wife was fierce in her defence of her husband and was thought, even by some of his friends, to exacerbate rather than soften his more extreme sentiments. During his lifetime, her political views were not easily distinguishable from his, but after his death she supported the 'yes' campaign in the European referendum of 1975, despite her husband's earlier opposition to Britain's membership of the Common Market. But she did not break with the Labour party when, in 1981, most of the remaining Gaitskellites left to form the SDP.

By that time Dora Gaitskell had enjoyed a substantial career of her own. Shortly after her husband's death, she was made a life peer in 1963 on the recommendation of the prime minister, Harold *Macmillan (later the first Earl of Stockton). Then when Harold Wilson (later Baron Wilson of Rievaulx) became prime minister in 1964, he arranged for her to become a member of the UK delegation to the general assembly of the United Nations. She became an outspoken champion of human rights, critical of the double standards of some Afro-Asian nations, but strong in her advocacy of the needs of the third world. She caused some anxiety in Foreign Office circles through her firm commitment to the state of Israel—but she was not an unthinking Zionist and was critical of the policies of right-wing Likud governments.

Dora Gaitskell was active in the House of Lords. Never afraid of controversy or of crossing swords, plump, a redhead in her earlier years, and only a little over five feet tall, she was spirited in her advocacy of libertarian causes and as direct as ever in personal relationships. At the time of her husband's death in 1963, Dora Gaitskell had every reason to believe that she would shortly accompany him to No. 10 Downing Street. It would be easy to see the remaining quarter century of her life as a pianissimo coda to the excitement and expectations of those earlier years. Yet, whilst always grieving for her lost husband, she established herself as a woman in her own right and contributed bravely to causes which were both his and her own. She died 1 July 1989 at her home, 18 Frognal Gardens, Hampstead, London.

[Philip Williams, *Hugh Gaitskell*, 1979; *Guardian*, 3 July 1989; private information; personal knowledge.]
WILLIAM RODGERS

GARDINER, Gerald Austin, BARON GARDINER (1900–1990), lord chancellor, was born 30 May 1900 at 67 Cadogan Square, London SW1, the second of three sons (there were no daughters) of (Sir) Robert Septimus Gardiner, a businessman with interests in the theatre and shipping, and his wife Alice Marie, daughter of Hermann von Ziegesar, a Prussian officer. He was educated at Harrow and served briefly in 1918 as a second lieutenant in the Coldstream Guards. At the end of World War I he joined the Peace Pledge Union. He then entered Magdalen College, Oxford, where he became president of the union and of the Oxford University Dramatic Society (both 1924). Acting remained a lasting attraction. He was rusticated for two terms in 1921 and was again threatened with rustication in November 1922, for publishing a pamphlet attacking restrictions on women undergraduates. He gained a fourth class in jurisprudence (1923) and was called to the bar at the Inner Temple in 1925.

Initially supported financially by his father, by the end of the 1930s he had a busy practice. His success lay in meticulous preparation of his cases and in the clarity and courteous, unrhetorical style with which he addressed judge, jury, or witnesses, although with the last he could, if necessary, be icy. In World War II he was not called up for active service, but, unhappy with a practice expanding at the expense of absent colleagues, joined the Friends' Ambulance Unit and served with, and finally commanded, its sections on the western front.

Returning to the bar, taking silk in 1948, and quickly developing a large practice, he served as chairman of the Bar Council in 1958 and 1959. His notable cases included the prosecution in 1960 under the Obscene Publications Act (1959) of Penguin Books for publishing *Lady Chatterley's Lover* by D. H. *Lawrence, in which the acquittal Gardiner won for the defendants led to a significant widening of the permissible boundaries in literature; and in 1961 the proceedings against the Electrical Trades Union, in which he exposed the ballot-rigging of its communist officials.

Gardiner had begun his law reform campaign in his own practice before the war by circularizing solicitors on how they could shorten litigation procedures. On leaving for the Friends'

Ambulance Unit he wrote to the lord chancellor, the first Viscount *Simon, about the legal-aid crisis arising from the departure for war service of the volunteers who provided the minimal aid then available. His initiative ultimately led to the Legal Aid and Advice Act of 1949. He had also joined the Haldane Society, which supported law reform. In 1945, when threatened with a take-over by communist sympathizers, Gardiner led a secession to form the Society of Labour Lawyers, of which he became chairman. In 1963, with a member of the Society, Andrew Martin, he co-edited and jointly contributed to *Law Reform Now*, which proposed a full-time permanent law reform commission making recommendations for law reform to Parliament. It was Gardiner's ten-year experience of the lord chancellor's law reform committee that had convinced him of the necessity for a full-time institution.

Gardiner had joined the Labour party in the 1930s. In the 1951 general election he stood unsuccessfully for Parliament at West Croydon. In 1963 Harold Wilson (later Baron Wilson of Rievaulx) nominated Gardiner for a life peerage and, after the Labour victory in 1964, chose him for lord chancellor. He was sworn of the Privy Council in the same year. Gardiner was then able by the Law Commissions Act (1965) to realize in its main features the proposal made in *Law Reform Now*. Gardiner also set up a royal commission (1966–9) to overhaul the machinery of the criminal courts. Its far-reaching recommendations were embodied in the 1971 Courts Act. He appointed the first woman High Court judge and instituted a compulsory training programme for JPs.

Under the auspices of the International Commission of Jurists Gardiner travelled to South Africa, Portugal, Tunisia, and Greece investigating alleged breaches of the 'rule of law', and in 1957 he helped to found 'Justice', the British branch of the Commission, which made the proposals culminating in the Parliamentary Commissioner ('Ombudsman') Act (1967) and the Rehabilitation of Offenders Act (1974), the latter's spirit being very close to Gardiner's own view of human nature as redeemable. In 1971 Gardiner was elected a member of the International Commission of Jurists. He served on its executive committee from 1971 to 1981, and on his retirement in 1986 remained an honorary member until his death.

The reform from which Gardiner drew the greatest satisfaction, however, was the suspension of the death penalty for murder in 1965 and its final abolition in 1969. He had argued against capital punishment in his book, *Capital Punishment as a Deterrent: and the Alternative* (1956) and had been joint chairman of the National Campaign for the Abolition of Capital Punishment. He retired as lord chancellor when the Labour government fell in 1970.

As lord chancellor Gardiner laid great emphasis on the quality of judges at all levels. He introduced systematic training for justices of the peace and sought to ensure that they were drawn from as wide as possible a cross section of the community. His reforming zeal stopped short when considering the legal profession, and especially the division between barristers and solicitors. He feared that in a single profession it would be more difficult to maintain the professional standards generally observed in a bar of limited size, and that, if the selection for the higher judiciary extended to the whole legal profession, there would be practical difficulties in ensuring candidates were all of the calibre required.

In 1972 Gardiner was one of three privy councillors (the others being the lord chief justice and a Conservative politician) appointed to investigate the alleged abuse of interrogation procedures in Northern Ireland. The majority were prepared to condone the practices complained of, but it was Gardiner's minority report which, in remarkable tribute to his legal and moral authority, was accepted by (Sir) Edward Heath's government. Nevertheless he could make practical compromises, as when as chairman of another committee on Northern Ireland in 1975 he approved the continuation for the time being of detention without trial.

He received honorary degrees from Southampton, York, London, Upper Canada, Manitoba, Birmingham, the Open University, Melbourne, and Surrey. In 1975 he was appointed CH.

Gardiner was a tall, thin man, of upright bearing, with finely chiselled features. His shy courtesy and painful inability to engage in small talk could be taken for coldness, but on closer acquaintance he soon revealed his warm spirit. He supported a very large number of liberal, humanitarian, and charitable causes. When he accepted the chancellorship of the Open University (1973–8) he himself enrolled for, and successfully completed, a three-year degree course in the social sciences (1977).

In 1925 Gardiner married Doris ('Lesly') (died 1966), daughter of Edwin Trounson, company director and later mayor of Southport; they had one daughter. In 1970 he married Mrs Muriel Violette Box, a distinguished film producer and writer, who survived him but died in 1991; they had no children. She was the daughter of Charles Baker, railway clerk, and divorced wife of Sydney Box, of J. Arthur Rank. Gardiner died 7 January 1990 at home, Mote End, Nan Clark's Lane, Mill Hill, London. There is a portrait by Norman Hepple in the Inner Temple.

[Muriel Box (Lady Gardiner), *Rebel Advocate*, 1983; *The Times* and *Daily Telegraph*, 9 January 1990; *Guardian* and *Independent*, 10 January 1990; Gardiner papers, Churchill Archives Centre, Cambridge; private information; personal knowledge.]   NORMAN S. MARSH

GARDNER, DAME Helen Louise (1908–1986), scholar, university teacher, and literary critic, was born in Finchley, north London, 13 February 1908, the middle child and only daughter of Charles Henry Gardner, journalist, of north London, and his wife, Helen Mary Roadnight Cockman. Helen was eleven when her father died and the family made their home with her grandparents. Mrs Gardner, a very musical woman, was ambitious for her gifted daughter and her encouragement was stimulating and sometimes a strain. Helen's education was at the North London Collegiate School, where she benefited from the excellent teaching of her English mistress, Florence Gibbons. In 1926 she went to St Hilda's College, Oxford, and in 1929 obtained first-class honours in English language and literature. Amateur dramatics revealed talents that could be discerned later in her style of lecturing and lively conversational habits.

She accepted a temporary post at the University of Birmingham. After three years (1931–4) as an assistant lecturer at the Royal Holloway College, London, she seized the chance of returning to Birmingham (1934–41), as a member of the English department. She extended the scope of her lecturing beyond the university audience; canvassed for Labour in a Conservative area; agonized over the Spanish civil war and refugees from Nazi Germany. It was on a dreary March day in 1940 that her spirits were roused by a first contact with 'East Coker' by T. S. *Eliot.

In 1941 she sought and took good advice and left Birmingham for Oxford to become a tutor (1941–54), and later fellow (1942–66) at her old college. The next thirteen years she regarded as her 'golden years'. She was memorably steady in her concern for the welfare of her own pupils. To the less able her tutorials were formidable, but to those who could take the wit and severity of her criticism of their essays the experience proved rewarding. In 1954 she was made reader in Renaissance studies and after one set-back she was elected in 1966 Merton professor of English language and literature, with a fellowship at Lady Margaret Hall. The distinction of being the first woman to hold this chair gave her special satisfaction. She exerted herself as a supervisor and she was as successful as she was strict. Forewords in many publications bear witness to her influence.

From 1961 to 1963 she served on the committee on higher education chaired by Baron *Robbins. She relished the discussion and travel involved and remained unabashed by some of the criticism of the extent of university expansion which was recommended. She served on the Council for National Academic Awards (1964–7) and enjoyed being a trustee for the National Portrait Gallery (1967–78). As a delegate to the Oxford University Press (1959–75) she made herself felt to the benefit of English studies. On subjects outside her range her judgements were sometimes less happy.

Meanwhile her work on the two poets with whom she will chiefly be associated—John *Donne and T. S. Eliot—went on concurrently. Her masterly edition of Donne's *Divine Poems* appeared in 1952 and was revised in 1978. The parallel edition of his *Elegies and Songs and Sonnets* followed in 1965. It was Helen Gardner's declared intent to supersede (Sir) Herbert *Grierson's text. She believed she had the advantage of more MSS to subject to the rigorous method of collation she favoured. The introductions and commentaries manifest the industry and intelligence she brought to this work. She continued to defend the readings and reorderings she proposed against subsequent criticism.

Her tribute to the genius of T. S. Eliot took a different form. In *The Art of T. S. Eliot* in 1949 she provided a way into an originality in thought and prosody in the poems that both fascinated and perplexed many readers. It was gratifying for her to learn that she had her author's approval. This book was written *con amore* and shows to advantage her critical enthusiasm. Later, in 1978, she was to take advantage of the publication of the drafts of *Four Quartets* to demonstrate a poem in the making (*The Composition of 'Four Quartets'*, 1978). She also wrote on *Shakespeare and *Milton's *Paradise Lost*. The British Academy lectures on Othello ('The Noble Moor', 1955) and on 'King Lear' (1967) draw out her best. The introductions to the World's Classics selections of Metaphysical Poets (1961) and of George *Herbert are admirable. She collaborated with Timothy Healy in selecting from Donne's sermons (*Selected Prose*, 1967), and with G. M. Story in an edition of William *Alabaster's poems (1959).

The popularity of Helen Gardner as a lecturer in Britain, America, European capitals, and the Far East, owed as much to her style as to her subject. Her enthusiasm could be infectious. She had a clear, strong voice and was aware of its attraction. The phrasing and rhythms of her prose echo in some measure their oral delivery. Her favourite unit of composition was about the length of a lecture, essay, long obituary, or university sermon.

Criticism she regarded as a serving art. She was not an innovator but chose rather to consolidate and conserve. Her endeavour was to increase the understanding and enjoyment of the best to be found in the literature of her own language. Later in life she was dismayed to realize how strong was the current of new methods of analysis, in the valuation of poetry and the style of theatrical production, and the effect it had on the teaching of English. She advertised her disapproval with fierce irony and then in more positive chapters reasserted her own beliefs in *In Defence of the Imagination* (1982). As a reviewer she was thorough, conscientious, severe, and open: everything was signed. She dealt with many of the most important publications of her peers and risked making enemies in the process. Twice she took on the thankless task of an anthologist with good will. The *Faber Book of Religious Verse* (1972) was followed in the same year by a more ambitious undertaking, *The New Oxford Book of English Verse* (1972).

To her Oxford D.Litt. (1963) and Cambridge honorary Litt.D. (1981) she added honorary degrees from eight other universities. She was appointed CBE (1962) and DBE (1967). She was made a fellow of the British Academy in 1958 and twice won the Crawshay prize (1952 and 1980). She was FRSL (1962).

In person she was small and sturdy. Vivacious, temperamental, occasionally overbearing, she appreciated good food and drink, liked to dress well, and revelled in parties where she talked well but, as she knew herself, too much. She was kinder in her actions than in her wit. She was no feminist: she liked to be a woman in a man's world, game to compete and reckoning that she could match anyone for scholarly hard work and tough argument. She made no secret of her satisfaction in her success. She was brave in a number of illnesses, and limped a little after a repeated hip replacement. She was a devout Anglican in the tradition of the seventeenth-century divines. Retirement in Eynsham, near Oxford, in 1975 did not greatly change her way of working except that she had more time to give to her pleasure in gardens and foreign travel. She died 4 June 1986 in a nursing home at Bicester after many months of a distressing illness. She never married.

[K. M. Lea in *Proceedings of the British Academy*, vol. lxxvi, 1990; private information; personal knowledge.]
K. M. LEA

GIBBONS, Stella Dorothea (1902–1989), novelist, was born 5 January 1902 in Malden Crescent, London, the only daughter and eldest of three children of (Charles James Preston) Telford Gibbons, medical doctor, and his wife, Maude Phoebe Standish Williams. She grew up in the dismal environment of Kentish Town where her father had his medical practice in Malden Crescent. Her childhood was unhappy and turbulent. She withdrew into stories and solitary games in her attic room to avoid the constant family rows which revolved around her preposterous father. He was unfaithful with a succession of governesses, against a noisy background of self-dramatizing uncles and aunts. Fortunately her mother was quiet and sensible, so she had some emotional refuge from the storms.

She was educated at home and then sent to the North London Collegiate School for Girls. At University College London she did a two-year course on journalism (set up for soldiers who had returned from the war of 1914–18). Her first job, in 1923, was as a cable decoder for British United Press. For the next decade she worked as a London journalist for various publications, including the *Evening Standard* and the *Lady*. Her first published book was a slim volume of poems (*The Mountain Beast*, 1930). No one could have guessed that the author of this neo-Georgian verse was about to spring a comic classic upon the world. *Cold Comfort Farm* (1932) was written as a parody of the novels of D. H. *Lawrence and Mary *Webb, with asterisks marking all the purple passages for the reader's delectation and mirth. Her characters soon became household names and her heroine Flora Poste a synonym for common sense. Flora goes to stay with her cousins, the Starkadders, on their decrepit farm in Sussex. From dawn to dusk the Starkadders live in a ferment of unruly passion but she manages them with cunning and dispatch, including the seething matriarch in the attic, Aunt Ada Doom.

Even minor characters like Mr Mybug, who is unable to look at a hill without thinking of women's breasts, are a comic delight, as are the cows, Feckless, Graceless, Pointless, and Aimless, who tend to lose their legs. All over the English-speaking world her fans quoted chunks of the novel to each other, rocking with laughter, and the expression 'something nasty in the woodshed' has a permanent place in the language.

After such a towering success so young the rest of Stella Gibbons's professional life was an anti-climax, despite her excessive industry and talent. Her second novel, *Bassett* (1934), was fuelled by an unhappy affair with a German businessman. In 1933 she met and married Allan Bourne Webb, an actor and singer, the son of the Revd Charles Johnston Bourne Webb. They had one daughter and lived happily ever after (not always grist to a writer's mill). Her subsequent writing (including poetry and short stories) was published at the rate of almost one book a year, until 1970. There were almost thirty of them. Some of the novels, like *Miss Linsey and Pa*

(1936), *My American* (1939), and *Here Be Dragons* (1956), were reasonably well received. The novel she preferred was *Ticky* (1943), a satire on army life, which flopped. In 1940 she tried to revive the magic formula with *Christmas at Cold Comfort Farm*, but it lacked the panache of the original, as did *Conference at Cold Comfort Farm* (short stories, 1949).

Stella Gibbons took her poetry more seriously than her prose and some of it, about nature and the pollution of the seas, was prophetic. Her *Collected Poems* were published in 1950. Longmans were her main publishers until 1955, when she moved to Hodder & Stoughton. She was a member of the Royal Society of Literature (fellow, 1950) and was awarded the Femina Vie Heureuse prize in 1933 for *Cold Comfort Farm*.

After her marriage Stella Gibbons had moved to 19 Oakeshott Avenue, London N6, a mock-Tudor house in a Hampstead backwater. She remained there after her husband's death in 1959. During their long marriage the only suffering he caused her was his absence in the army during World War II. In the last part of her life she held an 'At Home' once a month. She was known to expel guests from these tea parties if they were shrill, dramatic, or wrote tragic novels. The irony of her creative life is that the thing she hated most, overheated emotions, had given her the most inspiration. Ordinary life and personal goodness, which she enjoyed writing about, yielded a more pallid harvest. Many of her other novels have been dismissed unfairly, but some have dated. Her great joys were nature, music, and reading. She was an intensely private person, not easy to interview. Her appearance was of the blue-eyed, refined English variety and her beauty endured, as did her upright carriage, typical of Edwardian ladies who were forced as girls to walk around with a book balanced on their heads. She died 19 December 1989 at home in Oakeshott Avenue, London.

[*Publishers' Weekly*, 19 May 1934; Stanley J. Kunitz and Howard Haycraft (eds.), *Twentieth Century Authors*, 1942; private information; personal knowledge.]

JILL NEVILLE

GIBBS, SIR Humphrey Vicary (1902–1990), last governor of Southern Rhodesia, was born 22 November 1902 at 9 Portman Square, London, the third son and sixth and youngest child of Herbert Cokayne Gibbs, first Baron Hunsdon of Hunsdon, a partner in the guano-importing firm of Antony Gibbs & Sons, and his wife Anna Maria, fourth daughter of Richard Durant, of Sharpham. The family was wealthy and both his brothers, the fourth Baron Aldenham and Sir Geoffrey Gibbs, became distinguished City bankers. He was educated at Eton and Trinity College, Cambridge, which he left after a year. In 1928 he emigrated to Southern Rhodesia and bought a farm, some 6,000 acres, near Bulawayo. He acquired a high reputation as a farmer and became a recognized leader in the institutions concerned with agriculture and land. In 1947 he was persuaded to enter the legislative assembly as a member of the United Party for Wankie. He did not enjoy parliamentary life, perhaps because, as his leader and prime minister Sir Godfrey *Huggins (later first Viscount Malvern) said, 'he was far too honest a man to remain in politics very long'. He retired in 1953.

Five years later he was offered the post of governor of the colony. His integrity, reputation, tall stature, and distinguished appearance made him an obvious candidate, with the additional asset of being a 'Rhodesian', the first to hold the office. He accepted the honour, though with some reluctance. Southern Rhodesia since 1953 had been a 'territory' in the Federation of Rhodesia and Nyasaland—the area later covered by the independent states of Zimbabwe, Zambia, and Malawi. But it differed for historical reasons from the two northern territories in that the governor had only the limited powers of a constitutional monarch. In 1963 the Federation broke up. Zambia and Malawi became independent under black majority rule and it seemed all too likely that Southern Rhodesia would seek the same status, but under white minority rule. No British government could agree to this, and when Ian Smith made his foolish unilateral declaration of independence (UDI) on 11 November 1965 Gibbs found himself at the centre of a storm in Commonwealth relations as turbulent as anything since the Boston Tea Party. His position was virtually impossible. He was under immense pressure to go along with Smith. But he had been appointed by the queen and his loyalty to her was absolute and unquestionable. In all the convoluted, constitutional, and legal problems which followed he never put a foot wrong.

He would gladly have retired in 1965 and left Government House, but, at the request of Harold Wilson (later Baron Wilson of Rievaulx), he remained there for four unhappy and increasingly isolated years as a possible intermediary for a compromise settlement which never came. The Rhodesian government cut off his salary, his telephone, his official car, and his police escort. The British government offered to pay his salary, but he refused, saying that he could manage without it, and he communicated with Whitehall through a public telephone box. Constitutionally he was, under emergency legislation passed in Westminster, the sole ruler of Rhodesia since on British instructions in the name of the queen he had dismissed Smith and all his ministers from office after UDI. But this meant very little. Nevertheless dinners at Government House were still conducted in the old style—black tie, and the royal toast drunk at the end. This tended to be a perfunctory ceremony in Britain, but in Salisbury it really meant something. To drink to the queen was a hit at Smith.

Gibbs attended the abortive negotiations at Gibraltar in the warships *Tiger* and *Fearless*. In 1969 Smith declared Rhodesia a republic and Gibbs was at last released. He retired to his farm in Matabeleland, and served on the boards of various companies. He was chairman for many years of the local representatives of the Beit Trust which gave money to deserving causes in the three countries of the old federation. He was also very active in the cause of independent education. Disorder and crime in Matabeleland decided him in 1983 to give up his farm and move to Harare, where he lived for the rest of his life.

He was appointed OBE (1959), KCMG (1960), KCVO (1965), and GCVO (1969), when he was also sworn of the Privy Council. He was awarded £66,000 by Parliament as some recompense for his financial sacrifices as governor. He had honorary degrees from the universities of Birmingham (LL D) and East Anglia (DCL) in 1969. He married 17 January 1934 Molly Peel, second daughter of John Peel Nelson, businessman, of Bulawayo. She was appointed DBE in 1969. They had five sons. Gibbs died in Borrowdale, Harare, 5 November 1990.

[Private information; personal knowledge.]   BLAKE

GILMOUR, John Scott Lennox (1906–1986), botanist and horticulturist, was born 28 September 1906 at 1 St John's Wood Road, London, the youngest in the family of one daughter and three sons of Thomas Lennox Gilmour, Edinburgh lawyer, and his wife Elizabeth, daughter of Sir John Scott *Keltie, geographer. He was educated at Uppingham School, where he showed an early interest in botany, and then went to Clare College, Cambridge, to read natural sciences, in which he obtained a second class in both parts of the tripos (1928 and 1929). His first appointment (1930) was as curator of the university herbarium and botanical museum in the botany school, where he and other colleagues, notably Thomas *Tutin and William Stearn, were enthusiastic students of that remarkable teacher, Humphrey Gilbert-Carter, the first scientific director of the University Botanic Garden. These lifelong friendships were largely responsible for a considerable rebirth of interest in taxonomic botany in Britain during the expansion of universities after World War II.

Gilmour displayed early qualities of ability, tact, and charm, which undoubtedly helped his rapid promotion, in 1931, to the post of assistant director of the Royal Botanic Gardens at Kew. His career, interrupted by wartime service in the Ministry of Fuel and Power (1940–5), took him to the directorship of the Royal Horticultural

Society's garden at Wisley (1946–51) and then, on the retirement of Gilbert-Carter in 1951, back to Cambridge as director of the Botanic Garden and a fellow of Clare College. He held the directorship until his retirement in 1973.

The postwar years in Cambridge saw the expansion of the Botanic Garden: a 'golden age' made possible by a very generous private bequest and by the talents of the young director, whose sympathetic and humane administration educated many young people, some of whom became leading horticulturists. In this happy academic environment Gilmour made his mark on national and international botanical and horticultural science, in two particular directions. One of these concerned the philosophy of classification and its relevance to biology, a subject in which he had shown a surprisingly early interest, as evinced by his presentation in 1936 to the annual meeting of the British Association in Blackpool of a paper entitled 'Whither Taxonomy?'

An early friendship with (Sir) Julian *Huxley bore fruit, not least in the publication of his most important paper in this field in Huxley's The New Systematics (1940), a book that stimulated much-needed discussion involving botanists and zoologists in the newly formed Systematics Association. Radical ideas on the desirability of making a logical distinction between so-called 'natural classifications' and evolutionary (phylogenetic) ones underlay Gilmour's whole approach and, although most biologists remain unconverted, the impact of his ideas is still evident in modern academic controversies. His 1940 paper is suitable for modern students interested in this area of scientific activity. Among his other publications were British Botanists (1944), Wild Flowers of the Chalk (1947), Wild Flowers (jointly with S. M. Walters, 1954), and Some Verses (1977).

Unusually for philosophers of science, Gilmour remained throughout a pragmatist with an abiding interest in encouraging people to work out by rational argument how they should collectively proceed. These talents were much exercised in the field of horticultural nomenclature and taxonomy, where his second great contribution was made. In 1950 he and William Stearn represented the Royal Horticultural Society in the nomenclature sessions of the seventh international botanical congress held in Stockholm; from these meetings arose the International Code for the Nomenclature of Cultivated Plants (1953). His skill as a chairman was widely appreciated. A Dutch colleague, Frans Stafleu, who ran the International Association of Plant Taxonomy during those years, wrote in 1986 that 'for many of his contemporaries and colleagues Gilmour was the world's most charming botanist'.

Music and books were his main hobbies, both enjoyed best in the company of family and friends. He was a founder editor of the New Naturalist series of books published by Collins from 1945, and put his considerable knowledge of the second-hand book market to use in building the rich horticultural library in the Cambridge Botanic Garden. He became a fellow of the Linnean Society in 1932 and was awarded the Royal Horticultural Society's Victoria medal of honour in 1957.

Gilmour fervently believed that formal religion was on balance 'a bad thing', though characteristically his criticisms of religious colleagues and friends were full of charity. He was a founder member of the Cambridge Humanists in 1955, and enjoyed nothing so much as a tolerant, rational discussion of religion. He was dark haired and exceptionally handsome. Athletic in his youth, he became stocky later. In 1935 he married Molly, daughter of the Revd Maurice Berkley, an Anglican vicar. It was a singularly happy marriage and they had three daughters. Gilmour was troubled by incapacity and illness in his later years and died 3 June 1986 at his home, 25 Fitzwilliam Road, Cambridge.

[Memorial volume of Plant Systematics and Evolution, vol. clxvii (1, 2), 1989; tribute by W. T. Stearn in Garden (Journal of the Royal Horticultural Society), vol. cxii, 1987; private information; personal knowledge.]
MAX WALTERS

GINGOLD, Hermione Ferdinanda (1897–1987), actress, was born in London 9 December 1897, the elder daughter (there were no sons) of James Gingold, stockbroker, who had emigrated from Austria, and his wife, Kate Walter. She claimed Viennese, Turkish, and Romanian blood on her father's side. Her mother was Jewish.

La Gingold, or Herman or Toni, as she was often called in the theatre, first appeared on stage at the age of ten as the herald in Pinkie and the Fairies, produced by (Sir) Herbert Beerbohm *Tree. She later played the title role on tour and was cast by Tree as Falstaff's page, in The Merry Wives of Windsor. In 1912, aged fifteen, she played Cassandra at Stratford-upon-Avon in Troilus and Cressida, adventurously produced by William *Poel. (Dame) Edith *Evans was Cressida. For an actress who was subsequently to achieve fame for her flamboyant personality, her wit, her sophisticated but often grotesque comedy, and her basso profundo voice, described by J. C. Trewin as 'powdered glass in deep syrup', her surprising billing in the actor's directory Spotlight in the 1920s and early 1930s read 'Shakespearean and soprano'. She lost her high notes after suffering nodules on her vocal chords: 'One morning it was Mozart and the next "Old Man River".'

She played many parts in the theatre and on radio in the 1930s; but she found her true métier in revue. She was in *Spread It Abroad* at the Saville in 1936, *The Gate Revue* in 1939 which transferred to the Ambassadors theatre, and its sequel *Swinging the Gate* (1940). Her legendary partnership with Hermione *Baddeley ('the two Hermiones'), which was shorter lived than memory usually allows, began at the Comedy theatre in 1941 with *Rise Above It* (two editions) and continued in *Sky High* at the Phoenix theatre. It was during this show that their rivalry escalated in the press into a famous feud. She moved back to the Ambassadors for *Sweet and Low* (1943), *Sweeter and Lower* (1944), and *Sweetest and Lowest* (1946). Gingold became a special attraction for American soldiers and 'Thanks, Yanks' was one of her most appropriate numbers. During the astringent, name-dropping 'Sweet' series she played 1,676 performances, before 800,000 people, negotiating 17,010 costume changes.

She followed with *Slings and Arrows* at the Comedy in 1948 and appeared in cameo roles in English films, notably in *The Pickwick Papers* (1952), capturing a wider radio following with her weekly show *Home at Eight*, which featured Sid Colin's Addams-like family, the Dooms.

However, in spite of success with Baddeley in 1949 in *Fallen Angels*, by (Sir) Noël *Coward, achieved despite the author's disapproval of their overdoing the comic effects, she was determined to renew her American friendships. Her first significant appearance in New York was in *John Murray Anderson's Almanac* (Imperial, 1953). For the rest of her career she was based in America and became particularly well known on talk shows. She made other appearances in revue, toured in a number of plays and musicals—taking over from Jo Van Fleet the role of Madame Rose Pettle in Arthur Kopit's *Oh Dad, Poor Dad, Mama's Hung You in the Closet and I'm Feelin' So Sad*. She made many cameo appearances on television and in films, notably *Around The World in Eighty Days* (1956); *Bell, Book and Candle* (1958); and *The Music Man* (1962). She joined the San Francisco Opera to play the Duchess of Crackenthorp in Donizetti's *La Fille du Regiment* in 1975 and attacked the concert platform as a narrator.

There were two milestones in this period. She appeared with Maurice Chevalier in *Gigi* (1958), in which they sang Alan Jay Lerner and Frederick Loewe's song 'I Remember It Well' with exquisite wit and pathos. In 1973 she played Madame Armfeldt in Stephen Sondheim's *A Little Night Music*, triumphing with 'Liaisons', the memoirs of a *grande horizontale*. Once again she reminded audiences of her gift for pathos and the power of her acting.

In 1977 she took over the narrator's role in *Side by Side by Sondheim* on Broadway. Over eighty, she stayed with it gallantly on the gruelling 'bus and truck' tour of one-night stands,

travelling over 30,000 miles and visiting sixty cities until she tripped over an iron pole on Kansas City railway station in the small hours. A shattered knee and a dislocated arm effectively ended her performing career.

Hermione Gingold was an artist whose style and wit were unmistakable and who always held the promise of laughter and outrage. Adored as an icon and often underestimated as an actress, she is secure in her reputation as a queen of revue and one of the essential sights of London during World War II. She was a statuesque woman who exaggerated her gargoyle features for comic effect on the stage; but she could achieve a handsome aspect in repose.

In 1918 she married Michael Joseph (died 1958), publisher, the son of Moss Joseph, diamond merchant. They had two sons, the younger of whom, Stephen Joseph, pioneer of theatre in the round in Scarborough, later Alan Ayckbourn's base, died in 1967. They were brought up by her husband. The marriage was dissolved in 1926, and in the same year she married (Albert) Eric Maschwitz (died 1969), playwright, lyricist, and television executive, son of Albert Arthur Maschwitz, of Edgbaston. The marriage was dissolved in 1940. Hermione Gingold died of pneumonia and heart disease in the Lennox Hill Hospital, New York, 24 May 1987.

[Hermione Gingold, *How To Grow Old Disgracefully* (autobiography), 1989; G. Payn and S. Morley (eds.), *The Noël Coward Diaries*, 1982; Gerald Bordman, *American Musical Theatre*, 1978; personal knowledge.]

NED SHERRIN

GLASS, Ruth Adele (1912–1990), sociologist, was born 30 June 1912 in Berlin, Germany, the second of three daughters (there were no sons) of Eli Lazarus, described on her marriage certificate as a 'factory burner', a member of a distinguished Jewish family with a long rabbinical tradition, and his wife, Lilly Leszczynska. She embarked on a degree in social studies at the University of Berlin, and published a study of youth unemployment in Berlin in 1932 (reprinted in *Clichés of Urban Doom*, 1989), but following the rise of the Nazis she left Germany in 1932 before completing her degree. She studied at the University of Geneva and in Prague before arriving in London in the mid-1930s, where she resumed her sociological studies, at the London School of Economics. *Watling*, a study of a new London county council cottage estate in Hendon, on the outskirts of London, published in 1939, established her reputation as a social scientist.

From 1940 until 1942 she was senior research officer at the Bureau of Applied Social Research, Columbia University, New York, and was awarded an MA degree, but she returned to England in 1943 and became involved in town planning, as lecturer and research officer at the

Association for Planning and Regional Reconstruction. In 1947–8 she was a research officer for
PEP (Political and Economic Planning), and she
then spent 1948–50 at the Ministry of Town and
Country Planning, in charge of the new towns
research section. She returned to academic life
in 1950, to University College London, which
remained her academic base for the rest of her
life.

In 1951 she became director of the social
research unit at University College, working
under William (later Baron) Holford, professor
of town planning, and she founded the Centre
for Urban Studies in 1951, becoming director of
research in 1958, a post she retained until her
death. In addition, she was visiting professor at
University College in 1972–85, and at the University of Essex in 1980–6. She was chairman of
the urban sociology research committee of the
International Sociological Association (1958–75).
She was also on the editorial board of several
journals, including *Sage Urban Studies Abstracts*
and the *International Journal of Urban and
Regional Research*.

During the earlier part of her career her
interests centred on town planning, and *The
Social Background of a Plan: a Study of Middlesbrough*, based on a survey done in 1944,
appeared in 1948. She was always concerned
with the social aspects of town planning, constantly anxious that planners should not forget
human needs, especially those of people being
rehoused because their homes had been
destroyed during the war. She studied housing
problems in London, editing *London, Aspects of
Change* in 1964, and publishing *London's Housing
Needs* (1965) and *Housing in Camden* (1969). She
gave evidence to several government committees
and inquiries, most notably the royal commission
on local government in Greater London
(1957–60). She invented the term 'gentrification'
in 1962, giving warnings about the squeezing of
the poor out of London and the creation of
upper-class ghettos.

She became interested in the consequences of
immigration and the position of minorities in
British society. In *Newcomers: the West Indians in
London* (1960) she started from the premiss that
racial discrimination is an intolerable insult both
to the human dignity of an individual and to the
dignity of the society in which it is practised. She
did a study of the Notting Hill riots of 1958, and
in the 1960s she campaigned against the new
immigration laws. She was also concerned with
social change in the third world. In 1968 she set
up a one-year postgraduate course on urbaniza-
tion in developing countries. She was particularly drawn by India, which she visited for two
months every year from 1958 onwards.

Although she was a key figure in establishing
urban sociology as an academic discipline, pub-

lishing *Urban Sociology in Great Britain* in 1955,
Ruth Glass opposed the idea of research for its
own sake, believing that the purpose of sociological research was to influence government
policy and bring about social change, and to this
end she involved herself in political debate. A
Marxist all her life, she was never a member of
the Communist party, and after the compromises
made by the Labour party over immigration in
the 1960s she felt that radicals had no place in
any political party in Britain.

Abrasive and confident, with a powerful intellect, she could be devastating in argument, especially where she detected sloppy thinking. She
had no time for jargon and clichés. She had a
passion for justice and fought hard for those she
believed to be oppressed. She was a distinctive
figure, very short, always dressed in blue, with a
strong German accent.

She was made an honorary fellow of the Royal
Institute of British Architects in 1972 and was
awarded an honorary Litt.D. by Sheffield in
1982. In 1935 she married Henry William Durant, statistician and pioneer of public opinion
surveys, son of Henry William Durant, foreman
in a grain mill. They were divorced in 1941, and
in 1942 she married David Victor *Glass (the son
of Philip Glass, journeyman tailor), demogra-
pher, who became professor of sociology at the
London School of Economics in 1948. Together
they edited a series of 'Studies in Society', and at
the University of London they were known as
the Heloïse and Abelard of sociological research.
It was a very close marriage, and she never
recovered from his death in 1978. They had one
son and one daughter. In the last ten years of her
life, although she continued to lecture and to
work, she became increasingly lonely, and her
final few years were marred by illness. She died
7 March 1990 in Willow Lodge Nursing Home,
Sutton, Surrey.

[*Independent*, 13 March 1990; Ruth Glass, *Clichés of
Urban Doom and Other Essays*, 1988; Kenneth Leech,
The Birth of a Monster, 2nd edn., 1990.]

ANNE PIMLOTT BAKER

GLUBB, SIR **John Bagot** (1897–1986), soldier,
Arabist, and author, was born 16 April 1897 in
Preston, Lancashire, the only son and younger
child of (Sir) Frederic Manley Glubb, a major
(later major-general) in the Royal Engineers, and
his wife, Frances Letitia Bagot. 'Jack' Glubb was
educated at Cheltenham College and passed
second into the Royal Military Academy, Woolwich, in 1914. He was commissioned in the Royal
Engineers on 20 April 1915 and joined a field
company of the RE in France in November. He
served there throughout World War I, being
three times wounded, once nearly fatally in the
jaw, and was awarded the MC (1917).

In 1920 he was posted to Mesopotamia, where he later became a ground intelligence officer with the RAF. This was the beginning of his connection with the Arabs, for whom he formed an instant sympathy, so much so that in 1926 he left the army to join the British administration in Iraq. At that time the Iraqi bedouin and shepherd tribes in the southern desert were being terrorized by raids by Ibn Saud's Wahabis (*Al Ikhwan*). Glubb was posted there in 1928 as administrative inspector.

Partly by persuading the bedouin to join his armed police, and partly with RAF support, Glubb had ended the raiding by 1930, when he was invited to join the Arab Legion in Trans-Jordan, with a similar mission. This he accomplished within three years, raising a force of bedouin camel police, which became famous as the Desert Patrol. In 1939 Amir Abdullah appointed him to command the Arab Legion as *Feriq* (lieutenant-general), although he was better known perhaps as *Abu Hunaik* (Father of the Little Jaw), a reference to his 1917 war wound.

Glubb was probably the first man to succeed in turning the bedouin tribesmen into disciplined soldiers. Previously they had been considered untameable. Glubb was, however, careful to train his bedouins in accordance with their age-old customs. In 1941 he led them alongside the British army in Syria and Iraq, and was appointed to the DSO. His contribution to the capture of Baghdad in 1941 and the subsequent capture of the desert fortress of Palmyra in Syria was decisive, for it denied the eastern flank of the Middle East to Hitler. Later he formed a complete mechanized brigade, almost entirely bedouin. He was now known as Glubb Pasha, 'pasha' being an Ottoman honorific title.

On 15 May 1948 Glubb led the Arab Legion across the Jordan to occupy the West Bank, as laid down by the United Nations partition resolution of November 1947. He did not expect to have to fight for it, which is what actually happened. When the fighting ended with an armistice in March 1949, Glubb had the responsibility for defending the West Bank, but with far too few troops with which to do it. The Arab Legion had to be expanded with British financial support, but with the proviso that the British officers serving in the Arab Legion should be increased in number. They occupied all the important posts, which gave rise to resentment among many Jordanian officers. Glubb shared their disquiet, but the subsidy was vital. He was greatly reliant on King Abdullah's support, which vanished when the king was assassinated on 20 July 1951. His son Talal reigned only a few months before abdicating, and was succeeded by his son, Hussein, still only sixteen and a schoolboy at Harrow. Although Hussein respected Glubb, the gap between their ages proved impos-

sible to bridge and they soon fell out. Military and political developments were rapidly outgrowing Glubb, and the influential foreign adviser to an oriental monarch was becoming an anachronism.

Hussein, who came of age in 1953, particularly disagreed with Glubb's plan for the defence of the West Bank. Glubb sought to gain time by a planned withdrawal until Britain intervened in accordance with her treaty with Jordan. Hussein refused to countenance any withdrawal. The two views were irreconcilable and resulted in Hussein's dismissal of Glubb Pasha on 1 March 1956. The order giving him twenty-four hours to leave the country was intended to forestall any attempt to reinstate him. Glubb had in fact forbidden any bloodshed and had told his British officers to calm the situation. Soon they too were on their way. Glubb's abrupt dismissal caused a furore in Britain, and shocked many in Jordan.

Although Glubb was deeply hurt by the manner of his dismissal he behaved with exemplary dignity. Neither then nor later did he blame the king. He arrived in Britain with only £5, and was not awarded a general's pension by either Britain or Jordan. He was appointed KCB (1956) on his arrival and thereafter the British government washed its hands of him. He had been appointed OBE in 1925 and CMG in 1946. Glubb turned to his pen, and to lecturing, to provide for himself and his family of two sons and two daughters. He had married in 1938 Muriel Rosemary, daughter of James Graham Forbes, physician. They had a son in Jerusalem in 1939, whom they named Godfrey (later Faris), after the Crusader king. In 1944 they adopted a baby bedouin girl, and, after the death of another son who was born prematurely in 1947, adopted another daughter and son, both Palestinian refugees. Glubb was not impressive in appearance and was almost diffident in manner, speaking in rather a high-pitched voice. Yet there was about him an unmistakable air of authority, and when in uniform he wore no fewer than five rows of medal ribbons.

Glubb wrote twenty-two books, mostly on the Arabs, and lectured in Britain and the USA. His best book is perhaps *War in the Desert* (1960), which tells of his Iraq service. He had a soldier's aversion to politics—and to politicians. He had tried hard not to become involved, but as commander of Jordan's security forces some involvement was unavoidable. His dismissal was a political act, supported by Hussein's prime minister, Samir Rifai. Glubb remained nevertheless throughout his life a staunch supporter of Jordan and King Hussein. He was a devout Christian, an Edwardian in both manner and values. A servant of both Britain and Jordan, he was the last in the long line of powerful British proconsuls. He died from aplastic anaemia 17 March 1986 in May-field, Sussex.

[Sir John Glubb, *The Changing Scenes of Life* (autobiography), 1983; James Lunt, *Glubb Pasha*, 1984; Trevor Royle, *Glubb Pasha*, 1992; personal knowledge.]

JAMES LUNT

GOLDFINGER, Ernö (1902–1987), architect, was born 11 September 1902 in Budapest, second capital of the Austro-Hungarian empire, the eldest of three sons (there were no daughters) of Oscar Goldfinger, lawyer, landowner, and industrialist, and his wife, Regine Haiman. His early years were spent among the mountains of Transylvania, and later at school at the Budapest Gymnasium, but the well-to-do family left Hungary following the Communist *putsch* in 1919, and Goldfinger spent a year at Le Rosay School, Gstaad, before moving to Paris in 1920 to prepare for admission to the École des Beaux Arts. There he was a student, first of Léon Jaussely, pioneer in the field of town planning, then of Auguste Perret, pioneer in the architectural use of reinforced concrete.

These two interests—in the wider problems of planning and social architecture, and in the logical architectural expression of structure—were to remain with him and to define his mature work. But despite this apparently impersonal architectural commitment, his uncompromising character was inseparable from his work. The force of his personality, charming at times, explosive at others, was at the root of his achievement, and during his lifetime was almost better known than his architecture. His late work can now be seen, however, as the only major expression in Britain of the mature Modern architecture of the 1950s and 1960s, deriving directly from the radical architectural thought of continental Europe in the period of World War I.

As a student in Paris during the 1920s, Goldfinger moved in the avant-garde circles of the Left Bank, and was friendly with artists such as Man Ray, Max Ernst, Robert Delaunay (with whom he collaborated on film-set design), and Amédée Ozenfant (whose English pupil Ursula Blackwell he was later to marry), and with architects such as Adolf Loos, Pierre Charreau, and Le Corbusier himself, with whom, as French secretary of the Congrès International d'Architecture Moderne, he collaborated in the organization of the definitive Athens conference of 1933. At first in partnership with André Sizvessy (later Sive), he designed extremely austere, functional, but elegant shops, apartments, and furniture for an intellectually independent clientele. In 1927 he visited Britain for the first time, to build a salon for the cosmetics pioneer Helena Rubinstein, which has been described as the 'first Modern shop in London'.

Towards the end of 1934 he moved perma-nently to London, perhaps attracted by the nucleus of Modern architects forming there (many being refugees from Nazi Germany), perhaps looking to his wife's family connections for wider opportunities. In 1933 he had married Ursula Ruth (died 1991), daughter of Walter Reginald Blackwell, gentleman of leisure, a member of the founding family of the successful Crosse & Blackwell food company. But the work he obtained was self-generated. With a young family (finally two sons and one daughter), he made a speciality in design for children, designing toys and toyshops and the children's section of the British pavilion at the Paris exhibition of 1938. In 1937 he promoted the construction of a terrace of three houses in Hampstead, London (one being for his own occupation), his first significant building. These houses had highly modelled brick and concrete façades, rather than the smooth, white-painted surfaces favoured by most of his Modern architectural contemporaries. With these houses he effectively established his career, but he was obliged to spend the following war years largely producing exhibitions on economic and social themes for the armed services (he did not become a British citizen till 1945).

His political sympathies were with the left, and he designed offices both for the Communist party and the *Daily Worker* newspaper in the 1940s; but he was also unusual among architects of his background in receiving patronage from private developers, who gave him his first substantial opportunities. His small office building in Albemarle Street, London (1955–7), was highly praised for its Classical poise in a Modern idiom, and in 1959 he went on to win with the same client a development competition promoted by London county council for a much larger office block, conceived in the same manner, at the Elephant and Castle, London (which was to become the Ministry of Health). This won the Civic Trust award for architecture in 1964. Here he combined an emphatic expression of the concrete skeleton frame with an axial composition, reflecting his training at the École des Beaux Arts, and a powerful Constructivist sense of massing and spatial transparency. During the 1960s he won further commissions for two large public housing projects in London, each of which had as a dominant feature a thirty-storey slab of very dramatic outline, with a vertical circulation tower standing well clear at one end. The power of the composition was complemented by the elegance of the detail. He was elected FRIBA in 1963 and RA in 1975.

Goldfinger was a tall, handsome man, whose tightly compressed features bespoke the tense energy within. By the end of the 1960s his uncompromising commitment to concrete and high-rise housing solutions had become unfashionable, and he finally retired in 1977. He died 15 November 1987 at his home at 2 Willow Road, Hampstead, London, the house he had built nearly fifty years before.

[M. Major, *Ernö Goldfinger*, Budapest, 1973; James Dunnett and Gavin Stamp, *Catalogue 1920-1983*, Architectural Association exhibition catalogue, 1983; *Architectural Design*, special issue, January 1963; personal knowledge.]   JAMES DUNNETT

GOLDIE, Grace Murrell Wyndham (1900-1986), television producer, was born 26 March 1900 in Arisaig, Inverness, the only daughter and second of three children of Robert James Nisbet, civil engineer, and his wife, Alice Isabel Wright. Her father's work took him to Egypt and Grace's first school was the Convent of Notre Dame de Sion in Alexandria. In 1916 the family returned to England and she was educated at Cheltenham Ladies' College. Despite a warning that her early schooling abroad would prevent her from going on to tertiary education, she managed to enter Bristol University, where she took a first-class honours degree in history (1921). She then went to Somerville College, Oxford, and achieved a second class in philosophy, politics, and economics (1924).

For the next three years she taught history at Brighton and Hove School. Petite and bird-like, in 1928 she married the handsome actor Frank Wyndham Goldie, the son of Lewis Alexander Goldie, solicitor. They lived in Liverpool for six years, during which she lectured on drama, acted as an examiner in history, read plays for the repertory theatre where her husband was working, and wrote a book on its history (*The Liverpool Repertory Theatre, 1911-1934*, 1935).

In 1934 the Goldies moved to London and for the next seven years she wrote radio criticism for the *Listener*, turning her attention to television when it started in 1936. During World War II she spent two years (1942-4) at the Board of Trade before joining the BBC staff in 1944 as a talks producer, replacing Guy *Burgess.

She produced some major current affairs series such as *Atomic Energy* (1947) and *The Challenge of Our Time* (1948). In 1948 she moved to the television talks department at Alexandra Palace, to the disappointment of Bertrand (third Earl) *Russell, who said 'My dear girl, television will be of no importance in your lifetime or mine; I thought you were interested in ideas.' She was indeed; and she managed to translate political or international ideas into effective television programmes. She successfully enlisted academics, such as David Butler and Robert *McKenzie, to take part in the mammoth election results programmes which she mounted, beginning in 1951. She also encouraged political ministers to appear on the new medium in *Press Conference*.

In 1949 Goldie started *Foreign Correspondent*, shortly to be followed by *International Commentary*, *Race Relations in Africa*, and *India's Challenge*, all well researched programmes, with articulate presenters such as the war correspondents Chester Wilmot and Edward Ward (later seventh Viscount Bangor), as well as Christopher (later Baron) Mayhew and Aidan Crawley, then both former right-wing Labour MPs with considerable experience of the responsibilities of government and an interest in communication. Her regular use of these and other former Labour MPs led some Conservatives to complain that she was a well-known socialist. In fact her political instincts were conservative, and her husband worked part-time for the Conservative Central Office.

In 1954 a new head of television talks was appointed and Goldie became the assistant head of the department. Her high standards and her mastery of television techniques made her a valuable trainer of production staff who sought attachments to an expanding and highly regarded department. Without children herself, she particularly enjoyed recruiting and training youngsters. She excelled at starting new programmes, and making sure that they began well, but she tended to interfere with the minutiae of programme content, and it was not always easy for producers, especially the women, to work with her. She was described as having a whim of iron, and once a new series, such as the revamped current affairs vehicle *Panorama*, the daily magazine *Tonight*, or the arts programme *Monitor* had been successfully launched it was imperative to direct her restless energy elsewhere. She continued to produce major programmes herself, such as the tribute on Sir Winston *Churchill's eightieth birthday, and *Men Seeking God*.

After the death of her husband in 1957 she found relaxation difficult. Reluctant to return to an empty flat, she would remain late at the studios, arguing and dissecting programmes. Emboldened in the hospitality room, she would tell cabinet ministers, with the same asperity she showed to producers, what she thought of their performances. In 1962 she became head of talks and current affairs. After retirement in June 1965 she wrote *Facing the Nation* (1977), a definitive book about television and politics. She was appointed OBE in 1958. She died in London, at her Kensington flat, 3 June 1986.

[G. W. Goldie, *Facing the Nation*, 1977; personal knowledge.]   LEONARD MIALL

GOODALL, SIR Reginald (1901-1990), musician and conductor, was born in Lincoln 13 July 1901, the elder son of Albert Edward Goodall, solicitor's clerk, and his wife, Adelaide Jones. There was also a half-sister from Albert Goodall's previous marriage. Reginald went to Lincoln

Cathedral Choir School from 1910 to 1914, after which his education continued at Springfields, Massachusetts, USA, and in Burlington, Ontario, Canada, following the breakdown of his parents' marriage and their decision to emigrate, his mother to the United States and his father to Canada. He left school at fifteen and undertook a variety of work, as a messenger for the railways, a clerk in an engineering works, and in a bank in Burlington. His earnings enabled him to study at the Hamilton Conservatoire of Music, which led to his appointment as organist of St Alban the Martyr Cathedral, Toronto, and as a music master at Upper Canada College. As the result of meeting Sir Hugh *Allen in Canada, he became a student at the Royal College of Music, London, in 1925.

It was not until 1935 that Goodall conducted his first opera, *Carmen*, with a semi-professional company in London. In the mean time he had established himself as organist and choirmaster of St Alban's church, Holborn, and he gave the first performances in England of Bruckner's F Minor Mass and other works. Each year he travelled on the Continent as piano accompanist for the teacher and lieder singer Reinhold von Warlich. He was thus able to hear some of the world's great conductors, such as Wilhelm Furtwängler and Hans Knappertsbusch. In 1936 Goodall was engaged by Covent Garden to train the chorus for *Boris Godunov*, conducted by Albert Coates. He did this so well that he was asked to remain for the winter season. An invitation for the 1937 summer season followed, but he declined this in favour of other artistically less rewarding but financially more secure work. The 1930s were difficult for Goodall and the prospect of war filled him with gloom, as he envisaged the collapse of the German culture which he had come to know and love. Politically naïve, but at heart a serious pacifist, he supported Sir Oswald *Mosley and his demand for negotiations with Hitler.

Apart from a brief spell of military service, in the Royal Army Ordnance Corps from April to September 1943, Goodall spent the war conducting, first the Wessex Philharmonic Orchestra and then the Sadler's Wells Opera. The latter introduced him to a repertoire with which he was not familiar and much of which he did not admire. However, he conducted the première of *Peter Grimes* by Benjamin (later Baron) *Britten, at the reopening of the Sadler's Wells theatre on 7 June 1945. So impressed was the composer that he invited Goodall to conduct the première of *The Rape of Lucretia* at Glyndebourne's first postwar season the following year, although he shared the conducting with Ernest Ansermet. In 1947 Goodall became second conductor with the newly formed opera company at Covent Garden. This was a low period for him, with much of his time devoted to conducting Verdi, a composer he despised. In 1951 his contract as conductor was terminated and he continued as a coach. He was an invaluable teacher to the many singers who passed through his hands. There were occasional excursions into conducting for Covent Garden.

In 1968 Goodall conducted *The Mastersingers* at Sadler's Wells and again revealed his understanding of Richard Wagner. Following this huge success, Sadler's Wells invited him to conduct the four *Ring* operas at the Coliseum. These were nothing short of triumphant. He then went on to conduct *Tristan and Isolde* with the Welsh National Opera in 1979, and *Parsifal* with the English National Opera. Critical and public response was ecstatic, and both these performances were recorded.

A small, dishevelled, and sometimes cantankerous man, Goodall gave at first sight little indication of the strong inspirational force that he undoubtedly was as a conductor and coach. His conducting technique in a conventional sense was sketchy, but given time for preparation and rehearsal with singers and orchestra, which not every opera company could provide, the resulting performances were astonishing and profoundly moving in their revelations. He had a rare understanding of the architecture of Wagner's music. The long, slowly unfolding spans were wonderfully shaped and realized with unforced sonority. Goodall allowed the music to flow naturally and at the same time gave singers the greatest support without drowning them. He was appointed CBE in 1975 and knighted in 1985. He had honorary degrees from Leeds (1974), Newcastle (1974), and Oxford (1986).

In 1932 Goodall married Eleanor Katherine Edith (died 1979), schoolteacher, daughter of Montagu Gipps, of independent means. They had no children. Goodall died 5 May 1990 in a nursing home at Bridge, near Canterbury.

[John Lucas, *Reggie: the Life of Reginald Goodall*, 1993; personal knowledge.]   JOHN TOOLEY

GOOSSENS, Léon Jean (1897–1988), oboist, was born 12 June 1897 in Liverpool, the third of three sons and the fourth of five children of the conductor Eugene Goossens (1867–1958), himself the son of Eugene Goossens (1845–1906), conductor of the Carl Rosa Opera Company. His mother was Annie, daughter of the operatic bass singer Aynsley Cook. Of Belgian origin, the family had settled in England in the 1870s and 1880s; Léon's siblings were the conductor (Sir) Eugene *Goossens, the horn player Adolphe (who was killed in World War I), and the harpists Marie and Sidonie. He was educated at the Christian Brothers Catholic Institute in Liverpool and Liverpool College of Music. After some study of the piano, he began learning the oboe with Charles Reynolds at the age of eight, and by the time he was ten had played professionally. After further study with William Malsch at the Royal College of Music (1911–14), he was appointed principal oboe of the Queen's Hall Orchestra at the age of seventeen. Throughout his career (apart from a brief period when it was stolen) he played the same oboe, made for him by Lorée of Paris.

During World War I Goossens volunteered in the Middlesex Yeomanry and subsequently served in the 8th Royal Fusiliers before being commissioned into the Sherwood Foresters. On leaving for France in 1915 he was given a silver cigarette case as a keepsake by his brother Eugene, who had been given it by (Dame) Ethel *Smyth after a performance of one of her operas; it deflected a high-velocity bullet from the region of his heart, still wounding him sufficiently for him to be invalided home. He decided to accept an offer to join a friend on an Argentinian ranch; but, needing capital of £100, he began earning it by freelance oboe playing, which quickly brought so many engagements that the Argentinian plan was cancelled.

He rejoined the Queen's Hall Orchestra in 1918, moving to Covent Garden in 1924. In the same year he became professor of oboe at the Royal Academy of Music (until 1935) and at the Royal College of Music (until 1939). He also played in the Royal Philharmonic Society's orchestra and, on its foundation by Sir Thomas *Beecham in 1932, the London Philharmonic Orchestra. His playing with Beecham lent added distinction to a fine orchestra, as can be heard on records and was heard with admiration in an early broadcast of his music by the aged Frederick *Delius. Fritz Kreisler declared that among his greatest musical pleasures was listening to Goossens playing the solo in the Adagio of Brahms's Violin Concerto before his own entry. This, too, can be heard on records. Goossens was, in his own right, one of the most popular and prolific recording artists in the 1920s and 1930s. Recording companies were inexplicably slow to take him up again with the advent of the long-playing record, but he was making a comeback with a recording of J. S. Bach's Violin and Oboe Concerto, with Yehudi (later Baron) Menuhin, when an accident interrupted his career.

Goossens had by now acquired a world reputation (he frequently toured abroad) second to that of no other oboist. More, he had given the oboe standing as a solo instrument. He refined the sound from the conventional German breadth and reediness, while enriching the French slenderness but elegance of tone, to a warmth and sweetness hitherto unknown. By this, and by the highly personal elegance of his phrasing, he drew attention to lyrical possibilities that quickly excited the attention of composers,

while his brilliant finger technique opened up a new range of virtuosity. Almost every English composer of note was drawn to write music for him: works which he inspired and first performed included concertos by Ralph *Vaughan Williams and Rutland *Boughton, chamber pieces by Sir Arnold *Bax, Sir Arthur *Bliss, and Benjamin *Britten and an uncompleted suite by Sir Edward *Elgar. He was appointed CBE in 1950 and FRCM (1962). He also became honorary RAM (1932).

In 1962, still at the height of his powers, Goossens suffered a car accident that severely damaged his teeth and lips, rendering him incapable of playing. After many operations, borne with great physical courage, and the no less courageous confrontation of the apparent end of his career, he began practising again with a newly learned lip technique. He then played in film and recording orchestras away from the public view, always with the affectionate support of his colleagues. He was able to resume his professional life, though he privately insisted that the standard of his playing was not what it had been. He continued playing into his eighties, sometimes with small ensembles and modest orchestras to whom he felt an old loyalty.

In his prime, Goossens had earned himself a reputation as something of a prima donna among orchestral players. He would demand his own microphone in recording sessions, on the grounds that the oboe's tone needed special consideration. Colleagues in the wind section would feel obliged to fit in with phrasing that was always personal and at times became mannered and unstylish. But with this awareness of his own worth, seen in his gracious platform manner in concertos, went an essential musical humility and a high degree of personal kindness. Self-disciplined in his personal life, in the interests of a musical professionalism inherited from his strict father, he enjoyed physical activities, which included yachting and farming. He was always generous with his time to younger oboists, while sometimes resisting those who represented a newer stylistic wave. His charm and humour, among friends, were unaffected and engaging. He was a tall, well-built man, with a deep chest that would have helped his phenomenal breath control. Like his conductor brother Eugene, he went bald early and had the family's characteristic slightly hooded eyes and charming smile.

In 1926 he married Frances Alice, daughter of Harry Oswald Yeatman, a port shipper who worked in London for Taylor, Fladgate & Yeatman. They had one daughter. This marriage was dissolved in 1932 and in 1933 he married the dancer Leslie Burrowes (died 1985), daughter of Brigadier-General Arnold Robinson Burrowes, of the Royal Irish Fusiliers. There were two daughters of this marriage. Goossens died 13 February 1988 in Tunbridge Wells.

[Barry Wynne, *Music in the Wind: the Story of Léon Goossens*, 1967.] JOHN WARRACK

GOULD, SIR Ronald (1904–1986), teacher, educationist, and trade-union general secretary, was born 9 October 1904 in Midsomer Norton, the eldest in the family of two sons and a daughter of Frederick Gould, shoe worker, active trade unionist involved in local politics, and later MP for Frome, and his wife, Emma Gay, who was 'in service' until her marriage. It was a close-knit Methodist family, from Midsomer Norton, a Somerset mining village. Gould was educated, as a scholarship pupil, at Shepton Mallet Grammar School, which had fees of £5 a term. His parents struggled to pay for his books and daily travel. He then trained at the Methodist Westminster College in London, gaining his teaching certificate in 1924.

He started teaching at Radstock Council School in Somerset (1924–41). His career in local politics as a councillor began in 1924 and he became vice-chairman of Norton Radstock's urban district council four years later and was chairman from 1936 to 1946. In 1941 he was appointed headmaster of Welton Council School in Somerset, a post he held until 1946. Active in the National Union of Teachers from the start of his teaching career, within twelve years he was elected to the union's executive at the first attempt, becoming its president in 1943–4.

His talents had not gone unnoticed elsewhere. The postwar Labour government appointed him a member of the committee on conditions in the mining industry chaired by Sir John Forster. This was greeted with delight by his local mining community, who believed he would ensure the committee knew about the real conditions in the industry. He was also a founder member of the English advisory committee set up under the 1944 Education Act by the minister for education and architect of the Act, R. A. *Butler (later Baron Butler of Saffron Walden). The Act was the subject of lengthy consultation between the government and its partners in education, not least the NUT, in which Gould was so prominent.

From 1947 to 1970 Gould was general secretary of the NUT, the oldest, largest, and most influential teachers' organization. Under his leadership the union's influence grew further. Gould and the union argued in favour of comprehensive education, having recognized early on that every child had talent which was too often left dormant or underdeveloped. Gould did not define ability narrowly: in his opinion every child developed at different rates in different areas of knowledge. His underlying philosophy was that 'man can be improved'. This principle encour-

aged him to extend the 'professional' education work of the NUT, and to help establish the international teachers' organization, the World Confederation of Organizations of the Teaching Profession. He was unanimously elected president of WCOTP in 1952, and was regularly re-elected to this post until he retired in 1970. By then WCOTP represented six million teachers and was the teachers' voice in Unesco. In his last year as NUT general secretary he backed to the hilt a teachers' strike, which led to a raising of their salaries.

Gould and his counterpart Sir William Alexander (later Baron Alexander of Potterhill), chairman of the Association of Education Committees, dominated postwar education. Gould described their relationship as that of two boxers: 'He's only another brother earning a living,' he said. Together they averted the postponement of the raising of the school leaving age to fifteen in the late 1940s. But even they failed to convince a later Labour government, faced with another financial crisis combined with a teacher shortage, not to postpone its raising again, this time to sixteen. That reform had to wait until after Gould's retirement. However, they did prevent uncertificated staff from being brought in to ease the teacher shortage.

Gould was knighted in 1955 and held honorary degrees from Bristol (1943), British Columbia (1963), McGill (1964), St Francis Xavier (1969), Leeds (1971), and York (1972). A tall, warm-faced man, he was well aware of his own abilities but did not fail to recognize the talents of those around him. His upbringing and his years in education had taught him that wealth —or the lack of it—had nothing to do with intelligence or ability. In 1928 he married Nellie Denning, daughter of Joseph William Fish, a railway wagon repairer for the Great Western Railway. They had two sons. Nellie died in 1979 and in 1985 he married Evelyn Little, daughter of Frederick Box, Salvation Army officer. Gould died in his sleep at home in Worthing, 11 April 1986.

[Ronald Gould, *Chalk up the Memory, an Autobiography*, 1976; *Teacher* (newspaper of the National Union of Teachers), *passim*; private information.]

DOUG MCAVOY

GRAHAM, (William) Sydney (1918–1986), poet, was born in Greenock 19 November 1918, the elder child and elder son of Alexander Graham, marine engineer, of Greenock, and his wife Margaret McDermid, shopkeeper. After leaving Greenock High School at fourteen, he completed an apprenticeship in engineering. In 1938–9 he attended Newbattle Abbey Adult Education Residential College, near Edinburgh, where he responded enthusiastically to the literature and philosophy courses. Early

Scottish and Anglo-Saxon literature, modern writers including James *Joyce, Ezra Pound, and T. S. *Eliot, pre-Socratic philosophers and Martin Heidegger, were important influences, to which he later added Arthur Rimbaud, Marianne Moore, and Samuel Beckett.

After casual jobs in Ireland, he became a munitions engineer in Glasgow for a time during World War II, when he wrote *The Seven Journeys* (published later in 1944). David Archer, a publisher and philanthropist, provided him with practical support, publishing *Cage Without Grievance* (1942) and facilitating lively friendships in Glasgow and London with, amongst others, Jankel Adler, Robert *Colquhoun, Robert *MacBryde, Dylan *Thomas, and (F.) John *Minton. Bohemian life promoted both Graham's development and heavy drinking. *2nd Poems* (1945) continued the intense, romantic, semi-surreal language which both he and Dylan Thomas had derived in part from Joyce. Graham valued his early work (omissions from the *Collected Poems 1942–1977*, 1979, arose from misunderstandings about available space), which was intelligently evaluated by the critic Vivienne Koch in American journals. She became a close friend. His Atlantic award for literature in 1947 and his teaching at New York University in 1947–8 increased his circle of friends. He also visited Greece in 1964 and 1977 and Iceland in the 1960s; some of his poems drew on those experiences.

Faber & Faber accepted *The White Threshold* (1949) and became his principal publishers. T. S. Eliot, a director there, admired his excellent knowledge and craftsmanship and said at one of their meetings that Graham's poetry was difficult and would sell slowly because people did not like to think. His work certainly required the reader's full attention, which he gained at his impressive public readings in Britain and abroad, by the moving dramatic art and clarity of his definitive delivery. *The Nightfishing* (1955), *Malcolm Mooney's Land* (1970), and *Implements in their Places* (1977), the last two both Poetry Book Society choices, deployed a language increasingly transparent and exactly tuned to explore the essential separateness of each human experience in a world of flux. They displayed the desperate need to communicate, and the obdurate strangeness of language itself as medium and metaphor. Graham's themes were developed through sharply observed images, highly personal and presented with urgency through a musical poetry rich in structure and feeling. The work, like his own voice, had a Scottish timbre. The originality with which he enlivened and disturbed language was that of a thoroughly radical, modern, international tradition. This work, taken together with his simpler, lyrical pieces, made his achieve-ment outstanding and of permanent importance.

His poems, which did not fit any of the prevailing fashions, but nevertheless attracted a constant interest among serious readers, were published by several magazines in Britain, North America, and Europe, and were broadcast by the BBC. After 1944 Graham lived chiefly in Cornwall, often writing during the night after evenings spent with friends or literary visitors in his local pub. His work's excellence, together with his own professional integrity, inspired support from a number of friends, poets and painters who gave practical help or bought manuscripts. His remarkable letters, mostly in private hands, run parallel to his poetry, showing his loneliness, need to communicate, and deep feeling for his many friends. They throw light on his working methods, often containing verse and detailed criticism. Full of wordplay, they are startling, honest, sharp, and deeply humorous. He concentrated on poetry almost exclusively, having worked only very briefly on the land, as a copywriter, fisherman, or auxiliary coastguard when living at Gurnard's Head in Cornwall. Small grants from the Arts Council helped and a civil list pension of £500 a year was granted him in 1974.

Five feet eight inches in height, Graham had curly dark hair, very piercing blue eyes, and a slim physique. He loved music and had a good singing voice. Proud to be Scottish, he was witty, positive, and assertive, dominating conversations and demanding patience from his friends, which was usually freely given. His generosity of spirit inspired much affection and respect. In 1954 he married Agnes ('Nessie') Kilpatrick, daughter of David Dunsmuir, miner, of Blantyre. They had no children, but Graham acknowledged a daughter, Rosalind, born in 1944 to Mary Harris; he saw little of the child. Agnes had been a fellow student at Newbattle. During their close relationship they lived in distinctly spartan conditions; she provided material as well as moral support and always steadfast encouragement. From 1967 they lived at 4 Mountview Cottages, Madron, Cornwall, where Graham died from cancer, after a long illness, 9 January 1986.

[Jonathan Davidson, *The Constructed Space, a Celebration of the Poet W. S. Graham*, 1994; private information; personal knowledge.] MICHAEL SEWARD SNOW

GRANT, Cary (1904–1986), film actor, was born 18 January 1904 at 15 Hughenden Road, Ashley, Bristol, as Archibald Alec Leach, the son of Elias Leach, tailor's presser, and his wife, Elsie Maria Kingdon, daughter of a shipwright. An earlier baby brother had died before his birth. Years later, after he had left England, a half-brother was born. He attended Fairfield Secondary School, Bristol. When he was ten, his mother disappeared and he thought she had died. However, she had been committed to a mental hospital, where she remained for many years. Discovering the exciting life backstage at the Bristol Hippodrome, he was fascinated by Bob Pender's Knockabout Comedians, a visiting troupe of slapstick, acrobatic, and stilt artists, and joined them when he was fourteen. For two years they toured Britain, and then had a long run in New York in 1920, after which they spent a year touring the United States. When the troupe returned to England Leach, now eighteen, stayed on in America and took various jobs in vaudeville, at Coney Island and as a sandwich-board man on stilts. After a speaking part in revue, Arthur Hammerstein, the producer, cast him in an operetta by his nephew Oscar in 1927. He spent several years working in Broadway musicals, in theatrical touring companies, and in repertory. In the 1920s he went to and fro between England and America.

In 1931 he easily obtained a Hollywood contract with Paramount, adopted the name Cary Grant, and began five years as a handsome romantic lead in many unremarkable films. *Blonde Venus* (1932) with Marlene Dietrich and two Mae West films may not have been great pictures, but the exposure was good for his career. *Sylvia Scarlett* in 1935, although another indifferent film, was a turning-point for him as he began to evolve a style of his own.

In 1937 he became freelance, which he remained, choosing his films carefully and developing a light comedy touch. Over the next thirty years he was to make many huge box-office successes, taking a percentage rather than a fee. He changed his name legally in 1941 and became an American citizen in June 1942. Among his many sophisticated and 'screwball' comedies, romantic comedies, and comedy thrillers, perhaps the best remembered are *Bringing Up Baby* (1938) and *The Philadelphia Story* (1940). He worked with some of the best directors and with stars such as Katharine Hepburn, Irene Dunne, Ingrid Bergman, and Grace Kelly. Above all, it was (Sir) Alfred *Hitchcock who saw beyond the light comedian and jaunty man-about-town, giving him more subtle parts and being responsible for three of his best films, *Suspicion* (1941), *Notorious* (1946), and especially *North by Northwest* (1959). In 1966, at the age of sixty-two, he appeared in a part other than romantic lead for the first time. Not relishing the role of elderly character actor, and perhaps bored after seventy-two films, he made no more.

For many years one of the most glamorous and wealthy stars in Hollywood, playing opposite top actresses from Jean Harlow in the 1930s to Leslie Caron over a generation later, he was widely seen as an amiable performer who always played himself and, somewhat unjustly, was not taken seriously as an actor. He was nominated for the Best Actor award in 1941 and 1944 but did not win the Oscar. He finally got recognition from his peers in 1969 when, his film career over, the Academy belatedly gave him the survivor's consolation prize, an honorary award. The public loved him, however, and most of his films did well at the box office, some of them spectacularly so. He remained busy in old age, having a number of active directorships, including of the cosmetic firm Fabergé and Metro-Goldwyn-Mayer.

A tall, well-dressed man with thick dark hair and a marked cleft in his chin, he had a charming screen personality and self-deprecatory wit. He modified his west country working-class tones to an accent all his own, clipped and acceptable to American ears as upper-class British. So distinctive was his screen presence that it was easily mistaken for the man himself, but his private life suggests a deeply troubled individual. Rumoured to be bisexual, he had four unhappy marriages which collapsed quickly, with acrimony. His damaged childhood and vagabond youth had not equipped him for good personal relationships. Only a fifth marriage, when he was seventy-seven, to a much younger woman, seems to have brought him some tranquillity.

Cary Grant was married to actress Virginia Cherrill, formerly wife of Irving Adler and daughter of James Edward Cherrill, of independent means, 1934–5; Woolworth heiress Barbara Hutton, daughter of Franklyn Laws Hutton and his wife Edna, one of Frank Winfield Woolworth's two daughters, 1941–5; actress Betsy Drake 1949–59; actress Dyan Cannon (whose true name was Samile Dyan Friesen, daughter of an insurance executive), by whom he had his only child, a daughter, 1965–8; and former public relations director Barbara Harris in 1981. The first four marriages ended in divorce. He died of a stroke in Davenport, Iowa, 29 November 1986.

[*The Times* and *Independent*, 1 December 1986; Nicholas Thomas (ed.), *International Dictionary of Films and Filmmakers*, vol. iii, 1992; Chuck Ashman and Pamela Trescott, *Cary Grant*, 1987; William Currie McIntosh and William Weaver, *The Private Cary Grant*, 1983; Charles Higham and Roy Moseley, *Cary Grant, the Lonely Heart*, 1989.]   RACHAEL LOW

GRANVILLE, SIR KEITH (1910–1990), chairman and chief executive of the British Overseas Airways Corporation, was born Keith Granville Solomon 1 November 1910 in Faversham, Kent, the youngest of four children (all sons) of Albert James Solomon, sales representative, and his wife, Ada Miriam Chambers. He was educated at Tonbridge School. After he left he dropped the surname Solomon and used his second forename as his new surname. He joined Imperial Airways Ltd. at Croydon airport in 1929 as one of two original commercial trainees, and was paid ten shillings a week. His potential was immediately spotted, and he was one of the first trainees selected before World War II for service on overseas routes. During the 1930s he was successively station manager in Brindisi (Italy), Tanganyika, Southern and Northern Rhodesia, Egypt, and India, which were mainly Imperial Airways flying-boat bases.

By the end of the war he had made his mark in the airline, by then renamed the British Overseas Airways Corporation, and in 1947 was appointed manager, Africa and the Middle East. In 1948 he returned to London as general manager, mails, traffic, and catering, and he was promoted to sales director for all BOAC's overseas services in 1951. Further recognition followed in 1954 when he became commercial director. With the opening of Atlantic services, new routes to South America with Lockheed and Boeing aircraft, and the early jets of the 1950s and 1960s, he laid the foundation in BOAC of air travel marketing on a broad and popular scale. This was to be further developed through the arrival in service of the Boeing 747 (the 'jumbo jet') which, with its large passenger carrying capacity, brought a completely new concept to long-haul travel. In 1958 Granville became managing director under (Sir) Basil Smallpiece and was appointed CBE.

He joined the board of BOAC in 1959 and in 1960 was appointed chairman of the airline's associated companies, becoming deputy chairman under Sir Giles Guthrie in 1964. In 1969 he was named managing director to the new chairman, (Sir) Charles Hardie, retaining his post as deputy chairman. On 1 January 1971 he achieved the distinction of being the first member of the airline staff to be appointed chairman. His was a popular appointment because he was respected and admired by his colleagues as an able administrator with a keen sense of humour, who made a significant contribution to the fortunes of BOAC. He demonstrated sound judgement, was assertive, and liked to speak plainly. But his bluff, avuncular manner made him approachable and he was ever ready to help with problems and complaints. His wide experience and abundant common sense was equally well regarded by many other senior executives throughout the international airline community. He also helped guide the airline through difficult times, facing problems involving operating rights, industrial relations, government pressure in the choice and number of aircraft orders, and investment restrictions. He was pioneering, creative, and innovative.

Granville made a unique contribution to British civil aviation history when, in August 1972, he signed an order for five Concorde airliners, the world's first supersonic passenger aircraft. The order, later increased to seven aircraft, marked the culmination of more than ten years of close collaboration with the British and French manufacturers. When Concorde went into service to Bahrain for the first time in January 1976 it became the flagship of the British Airways fleet and the best known and most readily recognized aircraft in the world.

On the formation of the British Airways group in 1972 Granville became the first deputy chairman, and in September the same year he took up office as the president of the International Air Transport Association at its annual meeting in London. His international aviation career had thus come full circle, for he had represented his airline at IATA's first traffic conference in Rio de Janeiro just after the war. He also became president of the Institute of Transport in 1963–4 and chairman of International Aeradio Ltd. from 1965 to 1971. He was made an honorary fellow of the Royal Aeronautical Society in 1977 and was knighted in June 1973. He spanned a period of forty-five years, during which civil aviation developed from biplanes and flying boats to jet aircraft and supersonic air travel.

Granville was portly, about five feet ten inches tall, with smiling eyes and a firm, decisive nature. In 1933 he married Patricia Capstick; they had one daughter. The marriage was dissolved in 1945 and in 1946 he married Gertrude ('Truda'), daughter of Howard Belliss, gentleman farmer. They had one son and four daughters. On retirement in March 1974 Granville went to live in Château d'Oex, Switzerland, where he named his house Speedbird. He died in Lausanne, 7 April 1990.

[Private information; personal knowledge.]

COLIN MARSHALL

GRAY, Basil (1904–1989), keeper of oriental antiquities at the British Museum, was born 21 July 1904 at 13 Elvaston Place, London SW7, the younger son (there were no daughters) of Surgeon-Major Charles Gray of the Army Medical Corps, a passionate traveller, and his wife Florence Elworthy, daughter of the Revd Henry von der Heyde Cowell. He was educated at Bradfield and at New College, Oxford, where he gained a third class in *literae humaniores* (1926) and a second in modern history (1927).

On coming down from Oxford, in 1928 he worked for a season on the excavations at the great palace of the Byzantine emperors in Constantinople, where, however, his interests firmly turned to eastern rather than classical art, and then, for three months, in Vienna under Josef Strzygowski. He entered the British Museum late in 1928. There being no vacancy in the antiquities departments he spent an interim year in the department of printed books. In 1930 he transferred to the sub-department of oriental prints and drawings, then still a division of the department of prints and drawings, under R. Laurence *Binyon, the poet and distinguished orientalist whom he joined, with J. V. S. Wilkinson, to write the standard work, *Persian Miniature Painting* (1933). When the department of oriental antiquities was created in 1933 he was given the task of redisplaying the collection of Indian sculpture. The Chinese exhibition of 1935 then directed his attention to the Far East. By the outbreak of World War II his writings covered the whole field of eastern art, Islam, India, China, and Japan. His later work, however, dealt with the close relations between the arts of China and Persia, following the Mongol invasion and under the successors of Tamerlane—for example, in his important contributions, as editor and joint author, to *The Arts of the Book in Central Asia, 1307–1506* (1979), which definitively establish the prime role of princely patronage in the painting of eastern Islamic cultures.

Gray was placed in charge of the oriental collections in 1938, though, on account of his youth, he was appointed deputy keeper only in 1940 and keeper of oriental antiquities in 1946. Under his long keepership (until 1969) the immensely important collection of orientalia in the British Museum was complemented by a department of carefully chosen distinguished younger specialists. Gray was the friend and trusted adviser of many great collectors, stimulating their interest and moulding their taste. His confidence in their public-spiritedness was more than justified by their generosity to the British Museum.

Gray's outstanding career at the British Museum was recognized by the award of the CBE in 1957 and the CB in 1969, and by his appointment as acting director and principal librarian in 1968. In 1966 he was elected a fellow of the British Academy, and was closely associated with the British Institutes of Persian and of Afghan (later South Asian) Studies. His chairmanship of exhibitions of Islamic art in Cairo (1969) and Beirut (1974) culminated in the exhibition, The Arts of Islam, at the Hayward Gallery (1976), the most important of its kind since the Munich exhibition of 1910. His particular contribution to the study of Persian art was marked by his election as president of the Societas Iranologica Europaea (1983–7).

After his retirement in 1969 Gray continued to travel, lecture, write, and advise official committees, one of his few recreations being the Savile Club, of which he was a member for sixty years. He was a committed member of the Church of England and was church warden both at St George's, Bloomsbury, and at Long Wittenham, where he lived for the last twenty years of his life. He was elegantly neat in physique, with austere features offset by humorous eyes and bushy eyebrows. His suits and shirts were always tailor-made even when he was not well off. His colleagues remember him as forthright and rather autocratic in his earlier years. His works reveal, however, his patience and his eagle eye for decorative detail.

In 1933 he married Nicolete Mary, daughter of Laurence Binyon, herself a distinguished medievalist, designer of inscriptions, and historian of lettering. They had two sons and three daughters. Their eldest daughter, Camilla (died 1971), the historian of the Russian avant-garde, married the son of the composer Sergei Prokofiev. Gray died in the John Radcliffe Hospital, Oxford, 10 June 1989.

[J. M. Rogers, 'Basil Gray', *Iran*, vol. xvii, 1979, with a bibliography of his works to date; Denys Sutton, 'Basil Gray', *Apollo*, January 1989; Diana Scarisbrick, 'Basil Gray', *Apollo*, January 1989; Margaret Medley, 'Basil Gray CBE', *Transactions of the Oriental Ceramic Society 1988–89*, 1990; private information; personal knowledge.]　　　　　　　　　　　　　J. M. ROGERS

GREENE, SIR Hugh Carleton (1910–1987), journalist, broadcaster, and publisher, was born 15 November 1910 in Berkhamsted, the youngest of four sons and fifth of six children of Charles Henry Greene, headmaster of Berkhamsted School, and his wife Marion Raymond (his cousin), daughter of the Revd Carleton Greene, vicar of Great Barford. One of his brothers was the writer Graham Greene. He was educated at Berkhamsted School and at Merton College, Oxford, where he obtained a second class in both classical honour moderations (1931) and English (1933).

Having spent some time in Germany before he went to university, he joined the *Daily Telegraph*'s office in Berlin (1934) and became its chief correspondent in 1938. In May 1939, as a reprisal for the expulsion from London of a German correspondent, he was expelled from Germany. In his five years in Berlin he had become a forthright correspondent. He witnessed the rise of the Nazis and saw some of the evil at first hand, an experience which was a major influence in his life. As he put it: 'I learnt to hate intolerance and the degradation of character to which the deprivation of freedom leads.' The *Daily Telegraph* then stationed him in Warsaw. The Germans began to bomb Katowice on 1 September 1939 and within a week Greene had to leave Poland. He travelled to Romania, carrying only a bottle of beer and a gas mask. As the war spread, in the following months he reported from a number of European countries until in June 1940 he arrived at Falmouth, having left first Brussels and then Paris just ahead of the German armies.

After a brief period as a pilot officer in intelligence, while a member of the Royal Air

Force Volunteer Reserve, he arrived at the British Broadcasting Corporation in October 1940 to become assistant news editor of the German Service. It was the beginning of a new career and a relationship with the BBC that was to last for thirty-one years. In 1942 he flew in a Mosquito bomber over German-occupied Norway to neutral Stockholm, to hear for himself how the BBC output sounded through the German jamming. As a result, he changed the style in which the German news was written and broadcast. He concentrated on news, being less interested in features programmes, and made many hard decisions to dismiss staff. The broadcasts put out by his department eased the job of the postwar occupation and reconstruction of Germany, because, as he later learned, they had made a genuine impact on Germany, providing the core of Britain's anti-Nazi propaganda.

After the war Greene was seconded in 1946 to the British Control Commission in Hamburg to reorganize German broadcasting. Although he returned to the BBC briefly (from December 1948, to the Eastern European Service), he was seconded again in 1950, this time to the Colonial Office, to supervise psychological warfare against the communists in Malaya, in the Emergency Information Service. When he returned to London in September 1951, he had no clear view of what he wanted to do. He made enquiries about various jobs in journalism and intelligence but nothing came of them. At the invitation of Sir Ian Jacob, director-general of the BBC, he went back to Bush House and took on a number of senior appointments, eventually becoming controller, Overseas Services (1955–6). By 1956 it was clear that Jacob was grooming Greene as his successor. But first he had to learn about the non-journalistic side of the BBC. For two years he was director of administration and then, in 1958, director of news and current affairs. He was the first holder of that post and he succeeded where his predecessor, Tahu Hole (head of the news division), had failed. He restored the eminence of news and current affairs. The 1959 general election was the first reported by the BBC in its news bulletins and the first in which there was questioning of party leaders and some discussion of the issues.

The arrival of Hugh Greene as director-general on 2 January 1960 was the most important thing to happen to the BBC since World War II. For the first time a BBC man had been promoted to the top job. He changed the BBC for the better by doing three things. He made it clear that he was the editor-in-chief, exercising general editorial control over the BBC's output of programmes; he gave priority to television over radio; and he made the BBC realize that competition could be stimulating. This was an exciting and exhilarating time for those who worked in the BBC. For those who watched and listened to it the changes were challenging and occasionally disturbing, with programmes such as *That Was The Week That Was* and *Till Death Do Us Part*, as well as the series of 'Wednesday Plays'. In Greene's view, the BBC did a great service to the country by widening the limits of discussion and challenging the old taboos. He was dismissive of those who did not share those views—too dismissive, some felt. He played a major part in the establishment of the Open University, allocating thirty-two hours of broadcasting time each week.

He ensured the future well-being of the BBC by convincing the committee of inquiry into the future of broadcasting (1960–2), chaired by W. H. (later Baron) *Pilkington, that BBC television should have a second channel (BBC 2) and that colour television should call for an additional licence fee. Both these moves were delayed by the government. Financial pressures increased and so did criticisms of the BBC. Greene's relationship with the government became more testing and in 1967 Harold Wilson (later Baron Wilson of Rievaulx) switched Baron *Hill of Luton from the chairmanship of the Independent Broadcasting Authority to the BBC. Greene was enraged and thought of resigning at once, but he was persuaded to stay. The strain of working under a chairman he did not respect became too much and on 31 March 1969 Greene resigned. Three months later he was translated to the BBC board of governors. It was a mistaken move and after less than two years he resigned in 1971 and left the BBC, not bitter, but disappointed and depressed.

In retirement he made some programmes for both Independent Television and the BBC, advised the Greek and Israeli governments on broadcasting, wrote several books on the rivals of Sherlock Holmes, and became chairman of Bodley Head (1969–81), the publishing house of his brother, Graham Greene. Greene was appointed OBE in 1950 and KCMG in 1964. He was given an honorary DCL by East Anglia (1969) and a D.Univ. by York and the Open University (both 1973). Germany honoured him with the Grand Cross of the Order of Merit (1977).

In appearance, Greene was immensely tall (six feet six inches), with a striking skull, a chubby, cheerful face, and heavy spectacles. He was a kind man, though he could be ruthless. He was incisive, but he could also ponder. He was quick-witted, but enjoyed listening to and telling long stories. He had few close friends, having an aloof personality, which partly explained the failure of his first two marriages. His first wife (1934) was Helga, daughter of Samuel Guinness, banker, of London. They had two sons and were divorced in 1948. In 1951 he married Elaine Shaplen, daughter of Louis Gilbert, accountant, of New

York. They had two sons and were divorced in 1969. In 1970 he married Else Neumann (the German actress Tatjana Sais, with whom he had lived in 1948–50), daughter of Martin Hofler, of Frankfurt-am-Main, Germany. She died in 1981. In 1984 he married Sarah, daughter of David Grahame, concert manager, of Brisbane, Australia. Greene died of cancer in King Edward VII Hospital, London, 19 February 1987.

[Michael Tracey, *A Variety of Lives*, 1983; private information; personal knowledge.]   PAUL FOX

GREENWOOD, Joan Mary Waller (1921–1987), actress, was born 4 March 1921 at 122 Fulham Road, Chelsea, the only child of Sydney Earnshaw Greenwood, artist, and his wife, Ida Waller. The name 'Mary' does not appear on her birth certificate. She was educated at St Catherine's School in Bramley, Surrey, and at the Royal Academy of Dramatic Art. She first appeared on stage in 1939, when she was seventeen, in a small part in *The Robust Invalid*, a translation of Molière's *Le Malade imaginaire* at the Apollo and two years later in an unimportant film, *John Smith Wakes Up*.

Thereafter she was much in demand on both stage and screen, in every sort of production. Her first important film was *The Gentle Sex* in 1943, directed by Leslie *Howard, as one of a group of conscripts in the ATS (Auxiliary Training Service). Her first leading part was in a comedy of 1946 called *A Girl in a Million*, playing opposite Hugh Williams. It took her longer to make her mark in the theatre. During the war she took over from Deborah Kerr in *Heartbreak House*, toured with ENSA (the Entertainments National Service Association), did a season with Worthing Repertory Company, and toured with the company run by (Sir) Donald *Wolfit, playing Ophelia in *Hamlet* and Celia in *Volpone*. For several years after the war she concentrated on the cinema, becoming well known to the general public when she had roles in a number of Ealing films. *Saraband for Dead Lovers* (1948) was a historical romance with Stewart Granger, then at the height of his popularity. Her light touch as a comedian was particularly suitable for the gentle Ealing comedies of the day and she appeared in three of the best: *Whisky Galore!* (1948), *The Man in the White Suit* (1951), and, above all, *Kind Hearts and Coronets* (1949). In 1952 she was a piquant Gwendoline in the elegant film of *The Importance of Being Earnest*, directed by Anthony *Asquith.

She appeared in New York and made two disappointing films in Hollywood, where she disliked the lifestyle. After taking over from Lilli Palmer in *Bell, Book and Candle* at the Phoenix in 1955 she scored two critical successes with *Lysistrata* at the Royal Court in 1957, later transferred to the West End, and *Hedda Gabler* at the Oxford

Playhouse in 1960, which was repeated in the West End in 1964. She appeared at the Chichester festival of 1962 in *The Broken Heart*, and the following year in the film *Tom Jones*, Tony Richardson's rip-roaring adaptation from the novel by Henry *Fielding. This, however, was the last big film in which she had a role of any importance. She appeared in a few minor productions, the last being a partly animated Anglo-Polish version of *The Water Babies* which, despite a wonderful cast, was disappointingly flat. She later returned to the screen in 1987, the year of her death, for a small cameo part in the distinguished film *Little Dorrit*.

On the stage she gave a fine performance in *The Chalk Garden* in 1971 but, like her film career, her stage career virtually ended when she was in her mid-fifties, although she did appear in several television series later than this. She also returned to the stage later to take over the part in *The Understanding* played by Dame Celia *Johnson, when the latter died in 1982.

A versatile actress and a talented comedian, Joan Greenwood appeared in everything from sophisticated comedy, romance, and adventure to classical drama and even revue. Only five feet tall, slight, and with dazzling blonde hair, she was both sophisticated and elfin, quizzical and mocking, with her full pouting mouth and lingering glance. Her distinctive voice and almost exaggerated diction have been described as 'gargling with champagne', husky, purring, deliciously seductive. Her work as an intelligent and witty comedian endeared her to a discriminating minority, while her films, especially the Ealing comedies, brought her a wider public. However, both on stage and screen her career seems to have been strangely uneven. Perhaps the very distinctiveness of her style limited the opportunities offered to her. The strength and emotional power of her Lysistrata and even more her Hedda Gabler suggest possibilities not realized in the rest of her career.

When appearing in *Hedda Gabler* at Oxford in 1960, at the age of thirty-nine, she surprised everyone by eloping to Jamaica and secretly marrying an older fellow member of the cast, André Cecil Morrell (died 1978), son of André Mesritz Morrell. They had one son. Joan Greenwood died of acute bronchitis and asthma 27 February 1987, at her home in Chelsea.

[*The Times*, 3 March 1987; *Independent*, 4 March 1987; *Who's Who in the Theatre*, 17th edn., 1989; *Halliwell's Film Guide*, 8th edn., 1991.]   RACHAEL LOW

GRICE, (Herbert) Paul (1913–1988), philosopher, was born 15 March 1913 in Birmingham, the elder son (there were no daughters) of Herbert Grice, businessman and musician, and his wife, Mabel Felton, schoolmistress. He was educated at Clifton College, Bristol, where he was head boy and also distinguished himself in music and sports, and at Corpus Christi College, Oxford, where he was awarded first-class honours in classical honour moderations (1933) and *literae humaniores* (1935), and of which he later became an honorary fellow (1988). After a year as assistant master at Rossall School, Lancashire, and then two years as Harmsworth senior scholar at Merton College, Oxford, he was appointed lecturer and in 1939 fellow and tutor in philosophy at St John's College, Oxford, and university lecturer in the sub-faculty of philosophy.

During World War II he served in the Royal Navy in the Atlantic theatre and then in Admiralty intelligence from 1940 to 1945. By the middle 1950s he was widely recognized as one of the most original and independent philosophers in Oxford. At one time or another he taught an extraordinarily high number of those who were to become leading philosophers of the period, including (Sir) Peter Strawson. He held visiting appointments at Harvard, Brandeis, Stanford, and Cornell universities, and was invited again to Harvard to deliver the William James lectures in 1967. He was elected a fellow of the British Academy in 1966. He became an honorary fellow of St John's in 1980.

In 1967 he left Oxford for a new life in the United States, as professor of philosophy at the University of California, Berkeley. There he continued through teaching and informal discussion to influence and challenge a steadily growing group of devoted students and colleagues. He gave many distinguished lectures, seminars, and symposia at universities, conferences, and professional associations all across the country. He was elected president of the Pacific division of the American Philosophical Association in 1975, and was invited to give their Carus lectures in 1983. Near the end of his life he carefully prepared for publication *Studies in the Way of Words* (1989), which contains most of his major essays, the William James lectures, some previously unpublished papers, and a retrospective assessment. His Carus lectures and related material on the metaphysics of value appeared as *The Conception of Value* in 1991.

His most important and most influential work was in the philosophy of language, in particular the analysis of meaning. He proposed to define what a speaker means in saying something on a particular occasion in terms of the speaker's intentions to bring about certain effects in his audience through their recognition of those very intentions. He devised tests to reveal that many aspects of successful communication are due to the 'conversational implicatures' carried by a speaker's utterance rather than to logical implications carried by the meaning of the expression he uses or by what, strictly speaking, he says. He thereby showed how the meanings or semantics of many expressions in natural language are more adequately represented by the familiar structures of mathematical logic than had been widely supposed. This drew clearer limits to what can be concluded about meaning, necessity, and possibility from facts about linguistic usage. In these respects his work was a major factor in the fruitful *rapprochement* between Oxford philosophy of the 1960s and the more logically oriented philosophy then flourishing in the United States. His defence of the previously discredited causal theory of perception came to serve as prototype for an analytical strategy widely deployed elsewhere. In later years he concentrated on moral philosophy and, with characteristic imagination and metaphysical boldness, on the question of the objectivity of value, which, he held, required a realistic conception of finality or teleology in nature.

Though Grice thought continually about philosophy and wrote in manuscript a great deal, he published very little. This might have been thought attributable to practical inefficiency. His habits of life were in a way recklessly disorderly; the floor of his room in St John's was a dreadful litter of ashtrays, old clothes, scattered books and papers, cricket bats and balls, and (always unanswered, often unopened) correspondence. This apparent chaos was, however, deceptive. He was a man of formidable intellectual gifts, enormous energy, brooding temperament, and fiercely competitive spirit. His talents were well suited to his passions for chess, bridge, which he played for Oxfordshire for some years, and above all cricket, to which he largely devoted most of his summers while living in England. His musical talent was a more private, personal matter. His piano-playing was—like his considerable prowess as a batsman—fluent and forceful rather than elegant. It was understood by his friends that he was also a quite serious composer; but here, as in philosophy, he could not bring himself to think that any piece was ever really finished, and his works, it appeared, were permanently awaiting revision. That he published so little philosophy was due to this fixed idea that publication implied a claim to have got matters completely right, but a few months' further thought would always show this claim to be ill-founded.

In some ways the practices of teaching in Oxford did not suit him. In philosophy he throve on the stimulus of dialogue and debate, question and answer, thrust and counter-thrust; a silent, respectful, note-taking lecture audience bored and depressed him. Also, in private tutorials, he could be gloomily unforthcoming with pupils whose offerings were too feeble to be challenging. The seminar was his preferred habitat. He was a shrewd master of strategy, with the capacity to hold elaborate schemes or lines of argument in his mind and to unfold them slowly and deliberately, revealing the next step only when it was needed. His methodical, increasingly gleeful demolition of opposing philosophical theories, and occasionally his own, was a minor art form for the connoisseur. He was highly prolific in thought; he had more ideas, questions, and projects than he could ever have worked out in a dozen lifetimes. A man of strong appetites and impressive girth, he could be, when engaged, a deviously witty and highly convivial companion of fearsome endurance.

In 1942 he married Kathleen, daughter of George Watson, naval architect. They had a daughter and a son. Grice died in Berkeley 28 August 1988.

[University of California records; private information; personal knowledge.]　　　　　BARRY STROUD
　　　　　G. J. WARNOCK

GRIGSON, (Heather Mabel) Jane (1928–1990), writer on cookery, was born 13 March 1928 in Gloucester, the elder daughter (there were no sons) of George Shipley McIntire, deputy town clerk of Gloucester, and his wife, Doris Mabel Frampton Berkley, artist. When she was four her father became town clerk of Sunderland, and he bequeathed quietly left-wing politics to his daughters. It was the good fresh fish and the straightforwardness of north country food that first delighted Jane in her lifetime's study. In 1939 Wearside was a target for German bombing, and the sisters were sent to Casterton School (originally for clergy daughters) in Westmorland, where Jane encountered the outstanding English teaching of a Miss Bevis. In 1946 she followed her father to Cambridge, and attended Newnham College. She obtained a third class in part i of the English tripos (1948) and a second (division II) in part ii (1949).

Her first job was at Heffer's art gallery in Cambridge. In 1952 she went to work for the publisher Thames & Hudson, who recommended her as research assistant to Geoffrey *Grigson, man of letters, for his series of separate books People, Places, Things, and Ideas (1954). She had bought his anthology Visionary Poems and Passages, or the Poet's Eye, when she was fifteen. Geoffrey Harvey Grigson was the son of William Shuckforth Grigson, vicar of Pelynt. He was twenty-three years older than Jane, had been married twice before, and had three grown-up or adolescent children. They lived together and in the mid-1950s she changed her name by deed poll to Grigson; twenty years later they were able to marry. They had one daughter, Sophie, who also became a cookery expert. They lived partly at Broad Town Farm House near Wootton Bassett in Wiltshire, and partly at Troo, in the Loir [sic] valley. In both places they absorbed landscape and history, and gave news of them in different literary forms.

Jane Grigson's first published writing was for the Sunderland Echo, on the Venerable *Bede, and she made new translations of Carlo Lorenzini's Pinocchio (1959) and of Beccaria's Of Crimes and Punishments (1963, for which she jointly won the John Florio prize). She found her true vocation when a reader of Geoffrey Grigson's book Painted Caves (1957) wrote to him from Troo, asking if he knew that semi-troglodyte village. They went to see, and soon bought their own habitable cave.

Jane Grigson had started as Geoffrey's amanuensis, but in Troo she emerged as her own writer. The variety and excellence of the local raw materials, the skills of their neighbours, and her own developing conviction that because cooking is a central part of life it should be as carefully written about as any other art form, led to the first of her many books: Charcuterie and French Pork Cookery (1967). This was a breakthrough into a new literacy about cooking, and she was immediately recognized as a serious writer. Later landmark books were Fish Cookery (1973, enlarged as Jane Grigson's Fish Book, 1993), which restored fish cookery to its rightful place, and English Food (1974). The tiny Cooking of Normandy (1987), written for sale at Sainsburys, raised that often footling genre to a new level.

From 1968 till the week of her death she wrote for the Observer Magazine, to which Elizabeth David had recommended her. Several of her books were collections of articles. She campaigned against the bad as well as for the good, denouncing the degradation and sometimes danger inflicted on eaters by food adulterators in general.

Elizabeth David awoke postwar Britain from its devotion to oversized and overcooked food. Jane Grigson carried the awakening forward by opening the whole wide history and context of foods, dishes, utensils, and methods. Above all she sought to, and did, convey the reliable pleasures of knowledgeable cooking and eating. She herself put it: 'Cooking something delicious is really much more satisfactory than painting pictures or throwing pots. Food has the tact to disappear, leaving the room and opportunity for masterpieces to come. The mistakes don't hang on the walls or stand on the shelves to reproach you for ever.'

Jane Grigson was generous, scholarly, and deeply cheerful, combining outgoingness with equanimity; also smoothly and unobtrusively beautiful, with wavy fair hair and green eyes. When already mortally ill, she spoke and raised funds to fight off threats from developers to the great neolithic monument at nearby Avebury.

She died of cancer at Broad Town 12 March 1990 and was buried in the churchyard there beside her husband, who had died in 1985. Her collection of cookery books became the core of the Jane Grigson library at the Guildhall Library in the City of London.

[Private information; personal knowledge.]

WAYLAND KENNET

H

HALEY, Sir William John (1901–1987), editor of *The Times* and director-general of the BBC, was born 24 May 1901 in St Helier, Jersey, the only child of Frank Haley, clerk, originally from Bramley, Leeds, and his wife, Marie Berthe Sangan. He was educated at Oxenford School and Victoria College, Jersey. He left school at sixteen and for the next two years was a sea-going radio operator. Then journalism beckoned and, after a few months on the *Jersey Morning News*, he moved to *The Times* in London as a short-hand-telephonist.

There he soon convinced *The Times* management that the efficient way to channel European correspondents' messages was to set up a 'filter' system in Brussels, with himself as filterer-in-chief and the London end supervised by Edith Susie Gibbons, as editorial secretary. The plan worked so well that within months Miss Gibbons was recruited by the *Daily Mail* as their correspondent in Brussels, and it was there that she and Haley were married in November 1921. She was the daughter of John Thomas Gibbons, printer. There were two sons and two daughters of the marriage.

Thus, early in his career, the importance of journalism's double need of good writing and good administration had taken root in Haley's mind. It was a recurring theme for him in all the positions he held and was strikingly set out for his colleagues at *The Times* in a memorandum he wrote in November 1955: 'Editorial direction of a newspaper needs three things: judgement, imagination and drive. I am particularly concerned about the last. While the management properly has its own sphere in our affairs, there is plenty of editorial management which we can do for ourselves. The more efficient we make the editorial, the more successful the paper will be...Administration is important. But journalism is above all a writing profession. It is good for all of us to write.' His pen was busy in Brussels. He was contributing to the *Manchester Evening News* and in 1922 he joined the paper as a sub-editor. In 1925 he became chief sub-editor and by 1930 he had put before the manager, John Scott, a development plan which led to his appointment that year as managing editor, and a director of Manchester Guardian and Evening News Ltd.

He was the first to arrive in the office, and the last to go. His office contained no chair, only a reading desk for page proofs and his milk-and-bun lunch. He fought shy of personal contacts outside the office or family. It was a regime that earned him a reputation, among those not close to him, as a cold, austere man who could on occasion be ruthless. He played a large part in securing the future of the *Manchester Guardian* and *Evening News* and, when war came in 1939, Scott made him joint managing director of the two papers.

In 1939 Haley also became a director of the two great news agencies responsible for home and foreign news: the Press Association and Reuters. At Reuters financial problems had led the managing director, Sir (G.) Roderick *Jones, to discuss agreements with the government, an act some directors regarded as jeopardizing the agency's independence. At a dramatic meeting of the board, Haley accused Jones of withholding information and Jones resigned. Haley reorganized the Reuters service and its foreign contracts and drafted the trust deed which remains the foundation of its independence.

In 1943 the BBC offered Haley the new position of editor-in-chief; he accepted and within a year became director-general (1944–52). He thought of the BBC as the world's greatest educational institution and based his programme policy on the principle of a cultural pyramid by which listeners would progress from good to better: the Light Programme, the Home Service, and the Third Programme (the creation of which, with the inauguration of the Reith lectures, he regarded as one of his greatest achievements). He took firmer control of the BBC's finances, reorganized the top management, and fought to preserve the Corporation's monopoly of public-service broadcasting. He bitterly resisted the idea, already entering public debate, of commercial radio and television and in 1951, on being offered the editorship of *The Times*, felt that he could not leave the BBC until the future was clearer. That moment came in the following year and in June 1952 he was appointed editor of *The Times*, a task he considered to be the summit of his profession.

He at once defined the paper's threefold object to be a journal of record, a paper playing a useful part in the running of the country, and a balanced, interesting, and entertaining paper for intelligent readers of all ages and classes. Robust news coverage, supported by a devoted and vigorous staff, was a prime concern, but he broadened the paper's interest in drama, music, and art, enlarged features for women, introduced cartoons, and in May 1966 put news on the front page. He took an austere view of editorship: hobnobbing with politicians was discouraged. A minister with something worth to say would come to the newspaper. His written words could be full of warmth and humour, and none more so than in his weekly column on books written under the name of Oliver Edwards (an echo of his weekly columns, under the name of Joseph Sell, in his Manchester days). He conveyed his learning with infectious enthusiasm.

He waited seven months before writing his first leader—an appeal to the nation to listen to the voice of duty—and his most celebrated leader appeared on 11 July 1963, at the time of the Profumo scandal. It was headed 'It *is* a moral issue,' and proclaimed: 'Everyone has been so busy assuring the public that the affair is not one of morals, that it is time to assert that it is. Morals have been discounted for too long.' These were no idle reflections of a newspaper commentator. They sprang from a deep devotion to liberal principles and to unswerving uprightness in private and public life.

His editorship spanned a period of increasing financial difficulties for newspapers. In 1966 *The Times* was sold to Roy *Thomson, first Baron Thomson of Fleet. Haley was succeeded as editor by William (later Baron) Rees-Mogg. For a short time he remained as chairman of Times Newspapers Ltd. (1967) and later became editor-in-chief of the *Encyclopaedia Britannica* in Chicago (1968–9). This was not a happy choice and he retired to Jersey, where he kept up his omnivorous reading and reviewing until, well into his eighties, a prolonged and painful attack of shingles compelled him to give up his lifelong pleasure. Innately shy in conversation and personal contacts, Haley had a steely-eyed gaze that emanated from a handsome, lined, authoritative face.

Haley was appointed KCMG in 1946, became a chevalier of the Legion of Honour in 1948 and a grand officer of the Order of Orange Nassau in 1950, and had honorary degrees from the universities of Cambridge (1951), Dartmouth (USA) (1957), London (1963), and St Andrews (1965). In 1956 he became an honorary fellow of Jesus College, Cambridge.

Haley died in St Helier, Jersey, 6 September 1987. There is a bronze bust in the council chamber at the BBC, Broadcasting House, London.

[Iverach McDonald, *The History of The Times*, vol. v, 1984; family records; personal knowledge.]

EDWARD PICKERING

HALL, Henry Robert (1898–1989), dance orchestra conductor, impresario, and BBC chat show host, was born 2 May 1898 at 23 Bonar Road, Peckham, London, the eldest son in the family of three sons and three daughters of Henry Robert Hall, blacksmith, and his wife, Kate Ellen Smith. Part of his childhood in a poor but happy Salvation Army family in Peckham was spent learning the trumpet. Whilst still at the London county council school in Waller Road, Peckham, he won a scholarship to Trinity College of Music, London, for trumpet, piano, and musical theory lessons on Saturday mornings. He left school at fourteen, but his musical education fortunately continued when he was employed at the age of sixteen as a music copyist at the Salvation Army head office in Judd Street, King's Cross. His employer, Richard Slater, worked him hard but helped to develop his talents as player and composer. His 'Sunshine March' was later the basis for his BBC signature tune, 'Here's to the Next Time'.

In December 1916 he enlisted in the Royal Field Artillery. His musical prowess was quickly recognized and he spent much time playing at troop concerts. After the war he undertook desultory engagements in the seedier music halls and played a cinema piano to finance advanced piano lessons at the Guildhall School of Music. In 1922 he accepted a Christmas job as relief pianist at the Midland Hotel, Manchester. A Chopin study played at a minute's notice in the hotel cabaret stopped the show and Arthur Towle, general manager of Midland Hotels, signed up Hall as resident pianist. Within a year he was musical director of the hotel band, within ten he was in charge of the bands in all thirty-two hotels in the LMS railway group, and when the Gleneagles Hotel opened in 1924, Hall persuaded the BBC to broadcast his band on the opening night. This was the start of a broadcasting career which lasted forty years. In 1932 he succeeded Jack *Payne as musical director of the BBC Dance Orchestra, a move which involved a large cut in salary, but promised enhanced prospects.

Hall's purist style of music left some listeners lukewarm; but the impeccably played musical arrangements, often made by Hall himself, and his modest way of announcing the items were appealing. The repertoire of straight dance tunes interspersed with novelty items like 'The Teddy Bears' Picnic' soon made the band, broadcasting at teatime and in the evening, enormously popular. In 1934 he had the idea of inviting show-business stars to join him and his band in a programme called 'Henry Hall's Guest Night'. This was an instant success and ran for 972 performances over twenty-three years. The first chat show on British radio, it featured stars like (Sir) Noël *Coward, Stan *Laurel and Oliver Hardy, Danny Kaye, and (Dame) Gracie *Fields, with whom he always established an immediate rapport. The programme made him a major figure in the golden age of radio.

A royal command performance, a film *Music Hath Charms* (1935), and an engagement to conduct the ship's band on the maiden voyage of the *Queen Mary* showed a widening recognition of his star status. By 1937, when many other dance bands were broadcasting, he asked permission to leave the BBC and take his band with him. Sir John (later first Baron) *Reith granted it and agreed that they would not be replaced. It was said that forty million people listened to their final broadcast.

Hall now faced a freelance career touring the major variety theatres with his band topping the bill. Fears that the public would not support a wireless star in the theatre were groundless. 'Sold Out' boards were everywhere and Hall was frequently mobbed by the fans. The tours continued during the years of World War II, during which Hall also gave troop concerts and 'Guest Nights'. These strenuous and demanding years culminated in a second royal command performance (1948). After the war Hall began presenting stage shows, notably *Irma la Douce* (1958). Yet he continued to appear regularly on radio and television until 1964, finally announcing his retirement in 1970, when he was appointed CBE.

A tall dignified man, immaculately dressed, his dark hair brushed down, with a quizzical face and horn-rimmed glasses, Hall had flair and an engagingly hesitant style, which did not conceal a quiet authority inseparable from a lifetime of demanding high standards from himself and those around him. In return he received universal respect and affection. He was a showman completely in tune with the age in which he flourished. In 1924 he married Margery (died 1976), daughter of Robert Brook Harker, commercial traveller. It was a perfect partnership, and they had a son and a daughter. Hall died in Eastbourne after a long retirement, 28 October 1989.

[Henry Hall, *Here's to the Next Time*, 1955; BBC press books; private information; personal knowledge.]

IAN WALLACE

HALL, **Robert Lowe**, BARON ROBERTHALL (1901–1988), economist, was born 6 March 1901 in Tenterfield, New South Wales, the second of three sons (the eldest of whom was killed in action in 1917 in World War I) and third of five children of Edgar Hall, lecturer at the University of Sydney and later a mining engineer, who had emigrated to Australia, and his wife Rose Helen, daughter of Archibald Kennedy Cullen, of Undercliffe Station, New South Wales. His parents moved to Silverspur in Queensland when he was a baby and, after attending the local school there, he won a state scholarship to Ipswich Grammar School. He studied civil engineering at the University of Queensland, graduating B.Eng. in 1922, and going the following year to Magdalen College, Oxford, as a Rhodes scholar. He obtained first-class honours in philosophy, politics, and economics (1926) and was appointed to a college lectureship at Trinity College, Oxford. He was a fellow of Trinity from 1927 to 1950 (honorary fellow from 1958) and of Nuffield College, Oxford, from 1938 to 1947 (visiting fellow in 1961–4).

In the 1930s Hall became a prominent member of the Economists' Research Group, joining some younger Oxford dons who were sceptical of current economic doctrine, and undertook empirical research on how business actually behaved—for example, in fixing prices or reacting to price signals. Hall's contribution to this research included an article in 1939 on 'Price Theory and Business Behaviour', written in collaboration with the American Charles J. Hitch, which first introduced the idea of the kinked demand curve. (The article was reprinted in Thomas Wilson and Philip Andrews, eds., *Oxford Studies in the Price Mechanism*, 1951.)

On the outbreak of World War II in 1939 Hall joined the Ministry of Supply (raw materials department) and, after America's entry into the war, served for two years in 1942–4 with the British raw materials mission in Washington. In 1947 he succeeded James Meade as director of the economic section of the Cabinet Office, having meanwhile divided his time between Oxford and the Board of Trade, and continued as director for nearly fourteen years until April 1961.

Hall was in charge of the only substantial group of professional economists in Whitehall, and although he was not given the title of economic adviser to the government until 1953, when he moved to the Treasury, that accurately describes his role. Retaining this post until 1961, he served under eight chancellors of the Exchequer and exercised more influence on economic policy than any other official. Among the matters in which he took a prominent part were the devaluation of 1949, rearmament in 1950–1, the Robot proposal to float the pound in 1952, the introduction of the investment allowance in 1953, the credit squeeze that began in 1955, and the Treasury's evidence to the committee of 1957–9 chaired by Cyril (later Viscount) *Radcliffe. During his years in the economic section Hall kept a diary, contrary to the rules; it provides both a picture of the writer and a unique insight into the way in which economic policy took shape in the postwar years.

On leaving the Treasury, Hall returned to Oxford and in 1964 was elected principal of Hertford College, spending much of his three years there as a member of the commission of inquiry into Oxford University (1964-6), chaired by Baron Franks. He continued to maintain contact with Whitehall, for a short time as an adviser to the Ministry of Transport, and for six years as a member of the Commonwealth economic committee (1961-7). He also accepted two business appointments, one as an advisory director of Unilever (1961-71), and the second, at the invitation of Baron Plowden, as adviser to Tube Investments (1961-76). He took an active interest in the National Institute of Economic and Social Research, whose role as economic commentators and forecasters he had earlier done much to encourage, and served as chairman of the executive committee from 1962 to 1970.

In 1969 he was made a life baron and changed his name by deed poll to become Lord Roberthall. For the next two decades he was an active member of the House of Lords, latterly as a member of the Social Democratic party. He spoke in debates and served on many standing committees, taking the chair of a select committee on commodity prices in 1976-7.

He received many honours. Appointed CB in 1950 and KCMG in 1954, he was an honorary fellow of both Trinity College, Oxford (1958), and Hertford College (1969), and an honorary D.Sc. of the University of Queensland. He was president of the Royal Economic Society in 1958-60 and of the Society of Business Economists in 1968-73. Earlier, he had been chairman of an international group of experts at OEEC that was the forerunner of Working Party 3 of the OECD. He delivered the Sidney Ball lecture in Oxford in 1954 and the Rede lecture in Cambridge in 1962 (*Planning*, 1962).

Hall was not at his best as a theoretician and published relatively little: several articles and two books, of which the more substantial is *The Economic System in a Social State* (1937), based on lectures delivered in 1934. As is clear from his diaries, his gifts were those of a highly successful economic adviser. He had a remarkable feel for the state of the economy and could outdo his staff as a forecaster. He was outstanding as a draftsman, but a man of few words in committee. He was a realist, endowed with great common sense, appreciating the limits of what was feasible, and a good judge of men. He took great pains over recruitment of staff and initiated a scheme for borrowing economists from their universities for a two-year spell. His unaffected modesty, good humour, and thoughtfulness won

him the affection, as his abilities won the respect, of his colleagues.

Hall married twice. His first marriage in 1932 was to (Laura) Margaret (died 1995), daughter of George Edward Linfoot, musician, of Nottingham. She became a well-known economist in her own right and a fellow of Somerville College, Oxford. They had two daughters. When the marriage was dissolved in 1968 Hall married Perilla Thyme, daughter of Sir Richard Vynne *Southwell, aeronautical engineer, and former wife of Patrick Horace Nowell-Smith, philosopher and fellow of Trinity College, Oxford. The two spent much of the next twenty years in their house in north Cornwall. Hall was a passionate gardener, working on his Oxford allotment at weekends even when in the Treasury and winning prizes with his sweetcorn from the Treasury Horticultural Society. After a stroke in 1987 he never fully recovered; he died by his Cornwall garden next to the sea at Quarry, 17 September 1988.

[Alec Cairncross (ed.), *The Robert Hall Diaries 1947-1953*, 1989, and ibid., *1954-1961*, 1991; personal knowledge.]   ALEC CAIRNCROSS

HALLIWELL, (Robert James) Leslie (1929-1989), film buyer and encyclopaedist, was born 23 February 1929 in Bolton, Lancashire, the youngest child by thirteen years and only son in the family of three children of James Halliwell, cotton spinner, of Bolton, and his wife, Lily Haslam. He won a scholarship to Bolton School, and after national service in the Royal Army Education Corps he went to St Catharine's College, Cambridge, where he gained a second class (division I) in both parts of the English tripos (1951 and 1952).

Leslie Halliwell saw his first film at the age of four, and he spent his childhood going to the cinema, usually in the company of his mother. He claimed that at one time there were forty-seven cinemas within five miles of the centre of Bolton, and that he visited them all. At Cambridge, where he was editor of *Varsity*, he ran the university film society, and his first job after graduating was working as a journalist on *Picturegoer*.

At the end of 1952 Halliwell took on the job of running two cinemas in Cambridge. In 1956 he became a trainee publicity executive for the Rank Organization in London, moving in 1958 to Southern Television as a film buyer, and in 1959 he joined Granada Television as a film researcher, where he devised the *Cinema* series before moving to buy films for Granada from other companies.

In 1968 he became film buyer for the whole independent television network (ITV), and in 1982 Jeremy Isaacs, head of the new television channel, Channel 4, asked him to buy American films for Channel 4 as well. Isaacs described him as 'much more than a film buyer. Leslie Halliwell was a film buff, a walking encyclopaedia.' He visited Hollywood twice a year to search in the film libraries. At Channel 4 he was able to help schedule programmes, and he compiled very successful series such as *The British at War*, which he introduced himself. While he continued to buy for the other ITV companies, he earmarked interesting discoveries as 'obvious Channel 4 material', and his seasons of 'golden oldies', neglected films from the 1930s and 1940s, were very popular.

He was best known for his reference books. The first edition of *The Filmgoer's Companion*, the first comprehensive reference book of the cinema ever published, appeared in 1965, and revised editions appeared regularly thereafter. The first edition of *Halliwell's Film Guide*, with synopses and comments on 8,000 films, came out in 1977. Revised annually, it had grown to 16,000 entries by the time of the seventh edition in 1988. *Halliwell's Teleguide* (later with Philip Purser, *Halliwell's Television Companion*) was first published in 1979.

As well as compiling works of reference, Halliwell wrote about the cinema in such books as *The Clapperboard Book of the Cinema* (with G. Murray, 1975) and *Mountain of Dreams: the Golden Years of Paramount* (1965). In *Halliwell's Hundred* (1982) and its successor *Halliwell's Harvest* (1986) he considered some of his favourite films, claiming not that they were the greatest films ever made, or serious works of art, but that they all demonstrated an ability to entertain. In *The Dead That Walk* (1986) he wrote about horror films, with essays on films about Dracula, Frankenstein, and mummies, in which he argued that *Bride of Frankenstein* (1935) was the best horror film ever released. He also wrote a history of comedy, *Double Take and Fade Away* (1987). In the 1980s he published three books of short stories, wrote his autobiography, and also a novel, *Return to Shangri-La* (1987), a sequel to one of his favourite films, *Lost Horizon* (1937). After his retirement from ITV in 1986 he wrote a weekly television column in the *Daily Mail*.

Halliwell's work was directed at the general public, the middlebrow audience which went to the cinema for entertainment, and not at 'the egghead student of film culture who shuns commercial entertainments in favour of middle-European or Oriental masterpieces which never got further than the National Film Theatre' (introduction to the first edition of *The Filmgoer's Companion*). While he did not ignore foreign films, they did not appeal to him. Brought up in the 1930s and 1940s, he always regarded these years as the golden age of the cinema, the age when films were made in the studio in black and white. He liked very little that was produced

after 1950, and lamented the demise of the old studio crafts and film techniques. He found modern films crude and violent, and the language offensive, and he felt that the wit and style of the early movies were lacking. He dedicated *Halliwell's Harvest* to the proposition that art should not be despised because it is popular.

His most distinctive physical feature was his very long chin, which he later covered with a beard. In 1959 he married Ruth Porter, who had one son and one daughter from her previous marriage. She was the daughter of Samuel Edward Turner, clerk and Baptist minister, of Nottingham. The Halliwells had one son. Halliwell died of cancer 21 January 1989 in the Princess Alice Hospice, Esher, Surrey. At a memorial meeting at the National Film Theatre excerpts from some of his favourite films were shown, including *Citizen Kane* (1941), which he regarded as the greatest film ever made.

[*The Times*, 23 January 1989; Leslie Halliwell, *Seats in All Parts: Half a Lifetime at the Movies*, 1985.]

ANNE PIMLOTT BAKER

HAMILTON, SIR (Charles) Denis (1918–1988), editor-in-chief, Times Newspapers Ltd., was born 6 December 1918 in South Shields, the elder son (there were no daughters) of Charles Hamilton, engineer, and his wife, Helena Trafford. He left Middlesbrough High School at seventeen, became a reporter on the local *Evening Gazette*, and as a territorial in 1938 got a commission in the Durham Light Infantry. Two weeks after World War II began in 1939, part of the Territorial Army was embodied and Hamilton soon found himself in France. He was one of the few officers in his battalion who got back from Dunkirk. In 1940 he became a captain and in 1942 a major during a spell in Iceland. In 1944 he was promoted to lieutenant-colonel and commanded the 11th battalion, DLI, in the Normandy invasion. After the breakthrough in Normandy, Hamilton was posted to the 7th battalion of the Duke of Wellington's and led them in an inspired defensive action near Nijmegen, Holland, which won him a place in military history and a DSO (1944).

General B. L. *Montgomery (later first Viscount Montgomery of Alamein) wanted him to remain in the regular army after the end of the war. However, Hamilton went back to provincial journalism and within a few weeks J. G. *Berry, first Viscount Kemsley, summoned him to London to be his personal assistant (1946–50). Now he was at the centre of the Kemsley newspaper empire and was soon exercising influence. The brigadier, as the staff called him (he had ended the war as an acting brigadier), still looked a soldier with his discreet suits, polished shoes, slim, tall figure, and military moustache. If he never failed to find a military analogy to illustrate a newspaper problem, at least he never barked out his commands. He spoke quietly and could be disconcertingly silent when it was his turn to say something. Kemsley made him editorial director (1950–67) when he was thirty-one, whereupon he improved the organization and created a training scheme that became the model for a national scheme.

Turning his attention to the *Sunday Times*, edited by Henry Hodson, Hamilton believed that new readers would be attracted if they were given plenty to read every Sunday—the 'Big Read'. He persuaded his wartime friend, Viscount Montgomery, to let him serialize extracts from his memoirs, with the result that the circulation was increased by 100,000 copies over fourteen weeks; the new readers stayed. In 1959 Kemsley sold his newspaper group to Roy *Thomson (later first Baron Thomson of Fleet), a Canadian who had acquired the *Scotsman* and Scottish commercial television. Two years later Thomson made Hamilton editor of the *Sunday Times* (1961–7) and the paper became remarkably successful. Within six years it increased its sales by half a million copies. Hamilton, who did not himself write for the paper, recruited ardent young people and pioneered a bulky Sunday paper in separate sections, which included business news and a colour magazine. His 'insight' team of investigative journalists had outstanding successes. Thomson was a model proprietor, giving editors the widest freedom and in turn Hamilton delegated great responsibility to his assistants.

When Thomson acquired *The Times* in 1967, he made Hamilton editor-in-chief of both that and the *Sunday Times* and chief executive of Times Newspapers. Hamilton appointed as editors William (later Baron) Rees-Mogg for *The Times* and Harold Evans for the *Sunday Times*. He behaved very much as a constitutional monarch, guiding, encouraging, and occasionally warning both men. A successful promotion drive for *The Times* had to be dropped, for it was too costly to earn the expected profits.

Difficulties multiplied in the late 1970s. Both *The Times* and the *Sunday Times* were suffering severe losses because militant unionists, who resented wage restraint and feared the advent of new technology, were hampering production. Roy Thomson, who had died, was succeeded by his son, Kenneth, who wanted to know from his Canadian base what the strengthened hierarchy in London was going to do about the dispute. In the end it was decided, despite the reluctance of Hamilton and another director, to stop the presses, in the hope that this would bring the unions to their senses. It did not and the costly stoppage lasted almost a year (1979). Shortly after publication was resumed, the journalists decided to strike. This was the last straw for Hamilton, who advised Thomson to sell for what

he could get. The only bidder who looked likely to preserve the precious heritage and to stand up to the unions was the Australian Rupert Murdoch, who acquired Times Newspapers Ltd. in 1980.

Hamilton did not stay long after the take-over, resigning as chairman in 1981, and concentrated on his chairmanship of the expanding Reuters (1979–85). A trustee of the British Museum from 1969, he jointly sponsored the great Tutankhamun (1972) and Treasures of China (1973) exhibitions. He was an active trustee of the Henry Moore Foundation from 1980 and was president of the International Press Institute (1978–83), the worldwide protector of press freedom. He was president or chairman of many other institutions. Towards the end of his life, he struggled with the help of his son Nigel to produce a slim but valuable book of memoirs, *Editor-in-Chief* (1989). Appointed TD in 1975 and knighted in 1976, he had honorary degrees from Southampton (1975), City University (1977), and Newcastle upon Tyne (1979).

In 1939 he married Olive, younger daughter of Thomas Hedley Wanless, farmer. They had four sons, of whom one, Nigel, became a writer and produced a biography of the first Viscount Montgomery. Hamilton died, after a long illness, of cancer, 7 April 1988 at his home in Ashley Gardens, Victoria, London.

[Denis Hamilton, *Editor-in-Chief*, 1989; Eric Jacobs, *Stop Press*, 1980; Harold Evans, *Good Times, Bad Times*, 1983; personal knowledge.]   JOHN BEAVAN

HAMILTON, Hamish (1900–1988), publisher, was born James Hamilton 15 November 1900 in Indianapolis, USA, the only child of James Neilson Hamilton, businessman, and his wife, Alice van Valkenburg. He spent his childhood in Scotland. He was educated at Rugby School and Gonville and Caius College, Cambridge, reading medicine initially. He then changed to modern and medieval languages, in which he obtained a second class in part i (1921), and finally to law, in which he gained a third (1922). He travelled in the USA in 1922–3 and was called to the bar (Inner Temple) in 1925. The following year he became London manager for the American publishing company of Harper & Brothers, and in 1931 founded his own publishing company, Hamish Hamilton Ltd.

His American background and family connections enabled him to present to the British reading public a series of distinguished writers from the other side of the Atlantic, ranging from political and economic commentators such as Walter Lippmann, John Gunther, and John Kenneth Galbraith, to novelists like J. D. Salinger, Truman Capote, and William Styron. His tastes were eclectic, and commercial. A list which included writers of the variety of Sir D. W.

*Brogan, Nancy *Mitford, Alan *Moorehead, A. J. P. *Taylor, Angela *Thirkell, Eric *Partridge, Richard *Crossman, Georges Simenon, Raymond Chandler, James Thurber, Albert Camus, and Jean-Paul Sartre, as well as a number of *New Yorker* contributors (John Hersey, Charles Addams, Rachel Carson), was far from humdrum. He was not, perhaps, a great innovative publisher, in the mould of Sir Victor *Gollancz, and he was not wholly interested in the financial aspects of the business, but he was prepared, in an age when such things were still possible, to back his fancy. Over the years, he built up an extraordinary collection of acquaintances in the worlds of academe, politics, music, the theatre, and above all society. Though he had a surprisingly small coterie of close friends, he appeared to know everyone, however slightly.

This ability to draw so many disparate people into his circle stood him and his country in good stead during World War II. After a brief period in the army (he served in Holland and France during 1940), he was seconded in 1941 to the American division of the Ministry of Information, where he remained until the end of the war. During this period he was able to maintain his publishing company, when other publishers experienced great difficulty in obtaining essential paper for their books. After the war Hamish Hamilton Ltd. continued to flourish independently until it was bought by the Thomson Organization in 1965. Hamilton, however, remained as managing director until 1972, and chairman until 1981. Between that date and his death, he was president of the company.

Hamish Hamilton (he was actually christened James, and was almost universally known as Jamie, although later he changed his name by deed poll to Hamish) was a considerable sportsman in his youth. He was spare stroke of the Cambridge eight in 1921, stroke in the winning boat in the Grand Challenge Cup at Henley in 1927 and 1928, and rowed in the Olympics at Amsterdam in 1928, winning a silver medal. He played squash, skied, executed famously daring dives into the Mediterranean, and flew flimsy planes; in middle age, he took up golf. In appearance, he resembled a boxer, with a craggy face dominated by a broken nose. He was of medium height, and was noted for the cut of his suits and the high polish of his handmade shoes. But, though he had the friendship of a great many beautiful women, he was no extrovert. In the bar of the Garrick Club, or in the company of friends who could coax him out of his Scottish dourness, he flourished; with others he was reserved and curiously lacking in social graces. He entertained frequently, but his dinner parties were highly formal occasions, gatherings of public figures *en grande tenue*, many of whom he hoped would contribute books to his publishing

list. Inevitably, he was accused of snobbery, a criticism which contained more than a germ of truth, but which caused him disproportionate pain. Without his publishing partner, Roger Machell, and his second wife, Yvonne, both his public and his private lives would have been considerably less successful. Unlike Machell, he was not a real publisher, certainly not a man who appreciated new trends in writing; and, without his wife, who was born to be a hostess, invitations to parties at their house in Hamilton Terrace in London would have been less sought after.

Hamish Hamilton had an exceptionally low threshold of boredom. He hated meetings and committees, though he was honorary secretary of the Kinsmen Trust from 1942 to 1956, a governor of the Old Vic for thirty years from 1945, a member of the council of the English-speaking Union, and a governor of the British Institute in Florence. He also founded the Kathleen Ferrier memorial scholarships. None of these activities, however, was at the core of the publishing industry, and his refusal to serve on bodies such as the Publishers' Association was thought to have been the main reason why, unlike other publishers no more distinguished, he never received the knighthood he so much desired. Instead, he had to be content with being made a chevalier of the Legion of Honour, in 1953, and a grande ufficiale of Italy's Order of Merit, in 1976.

Hamish Hamilton married twice. In 1929 he married the actress Jean Forbes-Robertson, daughter of Sir Johnston *Forbes-Robertson, actor. This marriage was dissolved in 1933 and in 1940 he married Yvonne (died 1993), daughter of Giorgio Pallavicino, soldier. They had one son, Alastair, an academic and writer, who held various posts at the universities of Amsterdam, Leiden, and Urbino. Hamilton died of cancer, asthma, and emphysema 24 May 1988 in the St John and St Elizabeth Hospital in St John's Wood, London.

[Private information; personal knowledge.]

CHRISTOPHER SINCLAIR-STEVENSON

HAMILTON, James (1900–1988), publisher. [See HAMILTON, HAMISH.]

HAMILTON, Walter (1908–1988), headmaster of Westminster and Rugby and master of Magdalene College, Cambridge, was born 10 February 1908, the only child of Walter George Hamilton, tea-trader in the City, and his wife, Caroline Mary Stiff, schoolmistress. His paternal grandfather was treasurer of the National Union of Teachers, and his great-grandfather a Scottish rope-maker. His mother taught him devotedly at home until he was nine; his father was absent in France throughout World War I. In 1919 Hamilton went on a scholarship to Catford Grammar

School and in 1926 won a major scholarship to
Trinity College, Cambridge. He was placed in
the first class of parts i and ii of the classical
tripos (1927 and 1929), winning a Craven scholarship, the Porson prize, and the Chancellor's
classical medal. In 1931 he was elected to a prize
fellowship of Trinity. Two years later, encouraged by friends but in a temporary capacity, he
went to Eton, mainly to share the classics teaching of the headmaster's division. He fell on his
feet and stayed thirteen years. In 1937 he was
made master-in-college of the seventy King's
scholars.

This was the inspired appointment of his
career. He brought a keen intelligence and perception to his task and six years at Trinity had
done his wit no harm. Now his shy but amusing
and distinctive personality blossomed. The boys
were drawn to his strikingly low voice and
lugubrious manner, and, bright and competitive
(and often difficult!) though they were, he dis-
armed them with a trust and equality which
conveyed a sense that he and they depended on
one another. Shared experience of wartime conditions became a further strength; they enjoyed
his usually relaxed regime, accepted his strong
moral convictions, and knew that beneath the
surface he had much in reserve. He was also
cleverer than any of them. For himself, the years
at Eton were amongst his busiest; he felt at home
there, and thrived on the school's easy and
civilized style. He made many friends, and in
later life no honour gave him more pleasure than
his appointment as a fellow (1972–81).

In 1946, in need of change, Hamilton returned
to Trinity as fellow, university lecturer, and tutor
(the latter two from 1947). While there, a number of headmasterships were offered to him but
not until 1950 did he feel able to accept one, that
of Westminster. In the following year he married
a wife with whom he found lasting happiness and
companionship. At Westminster School, home
again after wartime evacuation, he at first seemed
withdrawn, even angular. But soon he was the
man for the hour. Buildings were restored and
reorganized, the number of boys doubled, and
his key appointments to the staff prospered. The
school developed a disciplined and new momentum and its learning and scholarship were transformed. Yet Dean's Yard was no place to bring
up a family of small children and after seven
years he accepted the headmastership of Rugby
in 1957. By now he was an illustrious figure and
it was the first time Westminster had lost its
headmaster to another school.

An Old Rugbeian wrote, 'This is the first time
they have appointed the *right man* since Thomas
Arnold.' Hamilton seemed to the staff larger than
life. With quick and warmly compelling rapport
he brought them on. As for the boys, he was
again a housemaster (with the assistance of

tutors) to seventy of them. He was shrewd and
wise, and always ready to listen. He would look,
often twinkling, over his half-moon spectacles,
puffing gently at his pipe, and the boys would
feel they were understood. Unless in difficulty,
no one at Rugby was allowed to take himself too
seriously, and Hamilton's own witticisms became
legendary. The absurd delighted him, pretension
he abhorred, and dishonesty aroused fierce
anger. He was physically a large man and on
formal occasions he presented a solemn appearance, which his tone of voice could dispel or
emphasize. He was master of the spoken as well
as written word. Some had hoped he would make
considerable changes in the school and he did
make some. But he was not given to change for
change's sake, preferring to make well-tried procedures work well. Given the increasingly questioning climate of the time, Hamilton knew
where he stood—in the liberal but nevertheless
firm tradition. Humanity was king and the
school's academic record of his time was
acclaimed.

Meanwhile his influence had spread wide,
especially in the schools belonging to the Headmasters' Conference and the Governing Bodies
Association. He was chairman of the first for four
years (1955, 1956, 1965, and 1966) and of the
second from 1969 to 1974. These were years of
ideological and political threat to selective education and to independent schools. Hamilton
strongly opposed the hostile proposals as being
untried, probably disastrous academically, and
anyway financially unrealistic.

In 1967 he was invited back to Cambridge as
master of Magdalene. He enjoyed presiding over
a college of traditional tendencies. But he disliked complacency and, when student unrest
impinged, his skill as chairman of the committee
of senior and junior members helped to restore
undergraduate goodwill. He warmed more to
undergraduates than dons, and regretted that
preoccupation with research had come to replace
scholarship as he knew it, and that publication
was deemed more significant than distinguished
teaching. His years as master were difficult ones
for universities and colleges, but when he retired
in 1978 he left Magdalene strengthened academically and financially on surer ground. He served
for five years on the council of the Senate
(1969–74) and frequently acted as the vice-
chancellor's deputy, notably as chairman of the
university examinations syndicate. He was an
honorary fellow of Magdalene from 1978.

He published for Penguin Books *A New
Translation of Plato's Symposium* (1951), *Plato's
Gorgias* (1960), *Plato's Phaedrus and Letters VII
and VIII* (1973), and (with A. F. Wallace-
Hadrill) *Ammianus Marcellinus* (1986). He was a
fellow of the Royal Society of Literature (1957)

and an honorary D.Litt. of Durham University (1958).

Hamilton deeply loved the Scottish Highlands, where he spent most of his holidays. There he was never happier, nor more relaxed and adventurous, with his family and friends. In 1951 he married Jane Elizabeth (she was nineteen and he was forty-two), daughter of (Sir) (Robert) John (Formby) Burrows, solicitor and president of the Law Society (1964–5); there were three sons and one daughter. Hamilton died 8 February 1988 in Cambridge.

[Donald Wright (ed.), *Walter Hamilton—a Portrait*, 1991; private information; personal knowledge.]

A. R. DONALD WRIGHT

HAMSON, Charles John Joseph ('Jack') (1905–1987), comparative lawyer and law teacher, was born in Constantinople 23 November 1905, the fourth child and elder son in the family of two sons and four daughters of Charles Edward Hamson, vice-consul in the Levant service, and his wife, Thérèse Boudon, whose father was a French architect-engineer engaged in building lighthouses in the Bosporus. He was at school at Downside, and in 1924 entered Trinity College, Cambridge, as a scholar, and read for the classical tripos, obtaining first classes in both parts i (1925) and ii (1927). He then turned to law, first in Cambridge, where he later won the Yorke prize (1932), and obtained the LL B (1934) and LL M (1935), and then at Harvard, as Davison scholar (1928–9). Despite a visibly bad eye, he fenced at Cambridge, and was captain of the university épée team in 1928.

Hamson began teaching at University College London, but in 1932 he returned to Cambridge as assistant lecturer, where, the war years apart, he spent the rest of his life as a fellow of Trinity, as university lecturer (1934) and then, by way of *ad hominem* appointment, first reader (1949) and later professor (1953–73) of comparative law. For twenty years (1955–74) he edited the *Cambridge Law Journal* with notable success and served on many university administrative bodies. He was chairman of the law faculty from 1954 to 1957 and was elected honorary fellow of St Edmund's House in 1976.

Hamson made no secret of his devotion to Cambridge and to Trinity. He also maintained a façade of English insularity, even to the extent of carrying an umbrella when visiting Persepolis, but the whole of his life belied it. He became an internationally recognized authority on comparative as well as common law and the admired friend of comparative lawyers throughout the world. He was president of the International Academy of Comparative Law from 1966 to 1979, chevalier of the Légion d'Honneur, correspondent of the Institut de France, and visiting professor in numerous universities overseas. He

held seven honorary degrees from foreign universities and received the extreme compliment of a translation into French of his book on the French *conseil d'état*.

Hamson was called to the bar by Gray's Inn in 1937. Though not a practitioner, he became a bencher in 1956 and, unusually for an academic, treasurer in 1975, when he was also appointed QC. He had a great affection for the Inn and earned the admiration and gratitude of all for his work there. It gave him particular pleasure, during his year of office, to call to the bar, and admit to the bench, the prince of Wales.

At the outset of World War II Hamson volunteered for service, sending his wife and young daughter to the United States. Seconded to the Special Operations Executive, he was sent clandestinely to Crete, where ultimately he was captured. In captivity (1941–5) he resumed his vocation by teaching law to his fellow prisoners, at first without the aid of any books. That, he used to say, meant that he did not have to waste time coping with the 'extravagant opinions of colleagues'. While a prisoner he wrote, perhaps as a means for coming to terms with his condition, a manuscript which is part personal history of the Cretan misadventure, part reminiscence, but in the main an analysis, in philosophical mood, of his understanding of himself and his own state of mind. This remarkable document, which remained virtually unknown until his death, was published by Trinity College in 1989 under the title *Liber in Vinculis*.

As a legal writer, Hamson's gift was to go directly to the heart of a question and to deal with it pithily and elegantly. He never indulged in lengthy exposition of a legal subject and his published work appears mainly in the form of articles or shorter notes. He wrote some memorable, even influential, pieces on both common law and comparative law topics, but the volume of his publications is relatively small. It was through his ability to convince others by the spoken word, at national and international gatherings as well as in the classroom, that he made his most important contributions to the law and its development.

Hamson was a great teacher. His knowledge of law was profound, but it was his style of presentation that set him apart. His gift of exposition and his evident delight in his subject made his lectures enthralling; his insistence on principle and his willingness to say things that more timid men might think inappropriate for undergraduate lectures made them memorable. Many of his pupils attained high office. To them he made it clear that the respect due to the dignity of office did not extend to the office holders. But they, along with all the others whom he taught—not least those whom he taught in prison camp—or who came to know him in other ways, held him in affection. His homes saw a stream of visitors to the day he died.

Hamson was not a tall man, but well built and physically strong. He could, at times, look severe, but he had a ready smile. With a high forehead and a slightly beaked nose, no one seeing him even briefly could doubt that behind his visible features there lay a formidable brain. In 1933 he married Isabella, daughter of Duncan Drummond, farmer, of Auchterarder, and his wife, Grace Gardiner. They had one daughter. His wife died in 1978, and Hamson returned to live in Trinity. A Roman Catholic, and a deeply religious man, whose religion was tempered by his irrepressible scepticism, he died in college 14 November 1987.

[J. Cann in *Liber in Vinculis*, 1989; J. A. Jolowicz in *Graya*, 1987–8; personal knowledge.] J. A. JOLOWICZ

HANCOCK, SIR (William) Keith (1898–1988), historian, was born in Melbourne 26 June 1898, the youngest in the family of three sons and two daughters of the Revd William Hancock, incumbent of St Mark's, Fitzroy, and later archdeacon of Gippsland, Australia, and his wife, Elizabeth Katharine McCrae. He was educated at Melbourne Grammar School, the University of Melbourne, and, after a short spell lecturing at the University of Western Australia, as a Rhodes scholar at Balliol College, Oxford, where in 1923 he gained first-class honours in modern history and became the first Australian to be elected to a fellowship of All Souls College (1924–30). From that base he wrote *Ricasoli and the Risorgimento in Tuscany* (1926). Like much of his later work, the book was about the complexities of nationalism. Already the prose was fluent, supple, and elegant.

From 1924 to 1933 he held the chair of modern history at the University of Adelaide. There he wrote *Australia* (1930), which remained the most professional and profound single volume about the country. The young professor had mixed feelings about his native land. Having been accepted at the heart of empire and now returned to a province, he would never be completely at home in either place. His speaking voice was neither quite English nor quite Australian. An account of his life to 1954 was entitled *Country and Calling*, signalling the tension.

Birmingham University called him to the chair of modern history in 1934 and Oxford to the Chichele chair of economic history in 1944. Dearly though he loved Oxford, he was not wholly comfortable in that chair, and left it for the University of London in 1949. Here he directed (until 1956) a new Institute of Commonwealth Studies, which was a monument to his own work. Hancock's *Survey of British Commonwealth Affairs* (3 vols., 1937–42), blending general perspectives with brilliant case histories and exhibiting what he often declared to be the historian's three cardinal virtues of attachment, justice, and span, had transformed the study of empire.

The British Commonwealth was in his vision the most benign of modern polities, able, if wisely led and liberally inspired, to deliver democracy and welfare not only to Australians and Canadians but also to Indians and Africans. Jan *Smuts, the subject of his two-volume biography (*Smuts: the Sanguine Years*, 1962, and *Smuts: the Fields of Force*, 1968), appealed to Hancock as avatar of the new commonwealth: a former enemy who freely chose imperial loyalty.

In World War I his brother Jim was named among the missing on the Somme. Keith was too young to join up without permission, which his bereaved parents refused. Like many young British men of his generation who missed the war, he lived after 1918 with a sense of shame and a high appreciation of bravery. In London during World War II he threw himself into the most active service he could find, by day directing (1941–6) the production of a thirty-volume civil series of official war histories, by night watching for fires from German bombs. Margaret Gowing, his co-author of the official volume *British War Economy* (1949), thought that by 1945, though not yet fifty, he looked venerable, with 'white hair and end-of-war exhaustion'.

His wife Theaden, daughter of John George Brocklebank, farmer, was even more exhausted. Like Jan Smuts, Keith Hancock had fallen in love with a fellow student of great ability who had had to settle for country school-teaching and then married a man needing (Hancock's words on Sybella Smuts) unfaltering support and heroic constancy. Theaden had been the wife of a busy, prolific, and preoccupied professor ever since their marriage in 1925. In *Country and Calling* he convicts himself of 'barbarous insensitiveness' to her. She found rewarding employment in wartime London as a producer of talks for the Overseas Service of the BBC, but collapsed into depression under the burdens of life and work. Her ill health was among reasons why Hancock did not accept until 1957 an invitation first extended some years earlier to go to Canberra as professor of history (until 1965) and director of the Research School of Social Sciences (until 1961) at the new Australian National University.

In Canberra, country and calling were now as nearly reconciled as they would ever be. Colleagues and postgraduate students in awe of a legend discovered that Hancock was short, slight, charming, and playful; he was also intellectually exacting, and tough and wily (some called him

'Sir Fox') in his determination to win resources for his school and distribute them according to his own judgement of quality. He had an undisguised sense of his own achievement, no envy, and a humble curiosity. He was good at coaxing under-producers to get on, as he would say, with their scribbling. He encouraged interdisciplinary and intercultural studies before they were fashionable in his world. He had blind spots, among them an Anglophile disdain for many things American and a patrician distaste for trade.

He became a kind of archbishop among Australian historians, at a time when most of the bishops, the professors of history in state universities, were Balliol men. The earliest and most enduring project of archiepiscopal inspiration was an *Australian Dictionary of Biography* modelled on the *DNB*, which he had served in Oxford as a member of the central committee; eleven gratifying volumes appeared during his lifetime.

Husband and wife lived happily in Canberra, enjoying both bush and society, until Theaden was stricken by cancer and died in 1960. In the following year, as she had counselled, Hancock married Marjorie Eyre (daughter of William Henry Eyre, of Enfield, Middlesex), who had worked for him on every project since the civil war histories, who gave him support and constancy for the next quarter of a century, and who survived him. There were no children from either marriage.

After retirement in 1965, country and calling led Hancock to the region south of Canberra, on which he wrote a pioneering study in environmental history, *Discovering Monaro* (1972). He became an activist in the cause of conservation, a member of an alliance which tried in vain to prevent a telecommunications tower from being installed on the forested peak he loved just behind the university, and he served as the group's war historian in *The Battle of Black Mountain* (1974). In a post-imperial epoch, and in his own eighties, he was attracted by the idea of armed neutrality for Australia, and campaigned against the presence of American communication bases on his country's soil. He went on writing, and talking in seminars and on the radio, almost to the end. 'Beyond all else,' wrote his close colleague and friend Anthony Low, 'he was the academic *animateur*.'

He was knighted in 1953 in recognition of a successful mission to Uganda as a negotiator, and appointed KBE in 1965. He was a fellow of the British Academy (1950) and universities and academies in four continents conferred honours on him. When asked to list his achievements, he might leave some out but included a medal of the Royal Humane Society won at the age of nine for rescuing another child from drowning. He died

13 August 1988 in Canberra, a few weeks after his ninetieth birthday.

[W. K. Hancock, *Country and Calling*, 1954, and *Professing History*, 1976; D. A. Low in *Proceedings of the British Academy*, vol. lxxxii, 1992; personal knowledge.]
K. S. INGLIS

HARDING, Allan Francis ('John'), first BARON HARDING OF PETHERTON (1896–1989), field-marshal, was born 10 February 1896 at Rock House, South Petherton, Somerset, the second child and only son in the family of four children of Francis Ebenezer Harding, solicitor's clerk and local rating officer, and his wife Elizabeth Ellen, daughter of Jethro Anstice, draper, of South Petherton. At the age of ten he was sent as a weekly boarder to Ilminster Grammar School. His headmaster, Robert Davidson, was a sound scholar; in later years, when already a lieutenant-general, Harding would attribute his capacity for hard work to Davidson's example and his gift of logical thinking to hours spent construing Ovid to him.

The family had not enough money to finance a career either in farming, his own preference, or the law, which Davidson recommended; he became at the age of fifteen a boy clerk in the Post Office Savings Bank. After attending night classes at King's College, London, he was promoted and in his new posting he was influenced by his superior in the office to apply for a commission in the Territorial Army. Two regular officers interviewed him and, although he was only eighteen and from a station in life different from that of most regular officers, they showed discernment and lack of prejudice in recognizing his quality. He was gazetted as second lieutenant in the 1/11th battalion of the London Regiment (the 'Finsbury Rifles') in May 1914.

He first saw action on 10 August 1915 in the Dardanelles campaign, where he was wounded after only five days. When Gallipoli was abandoned his battalion went to Egypt. Here he decided to apply for and in March 1917 was granted a regular commission as a lieutenant in his county regiment, the Somerset Light Infantry. By now he was specializing in machine-guns. In the third battle of Gaza he was divisional machine-gun officer, as acting major at the age of twenty-one, and was awarded the MC (1917). In 1918 he was made corps machine-gun officer at XXI Corps headquarters. From experience on the staff he learned, among other things, the value of strategic deception, which was practised with great success in both wars by British commanders in the Middle East.

Between the wars Harding served in India from 1919 to 1927, first with the Machine-Gun Corps and then with his regiment. From 1928 to 1930 he attended the Staff College. In May 1933 he was appointed brigade-major of the 13th Infantry brigade which was chosen as the British contingent in the international force which supervised the Saarland plebiscite. It was a good preparation for the tasks of collaborating with forces of different nationalities which were to fall to him later in the Mediterranean theatre; he also made a special study of the Italian contingent, whose light tanks were to prove so ineffective in the desert. In July 1939, at the age of forty-three, he was given command of the 1st battalion of his regiment, again in India. He earned a mention in dispatches for frontier operations, but his reputation ensured that he would soon be required for more serious service; in autumn 1940 he was posted to Egypt, where staff officers were required.

His first task was to plan Compass, the offensive against the Italian Tenth Army organized by Sir A. P. (later first Earl) *Wavell; he went on to become brigadier general staff to (Sir) Richard *O'Connor, commanding the Western Desert Force, later XIII Corps. Compass was brilliantly successful, expelling all Italian formations from Cyrenaica and capturing 125,000 prisoners, at little cost in British casualties. Harding's services were rewarded with a CBE (1940) and a second mention in dispatches. When the counter-attack led by Field-marshal Erwin Rommel overwhelmed the British in Cyrenaica, and both O'Connor and his successor, (Sir) Philip Neame, were taken prisoner it was Harding who took temporary charge, organized the defence of Tobruk, and persuaded Wavell that it could be held. After the first two misdirected German attacks on the fortress had been repulsed he was transferred to be brigadier general staff of a revived Western Desert Force at Matruh and appointed to the DSO (1941).

For Crusader, the operation which saw Rommel's army defeated in the field and the siege of Tobruk relieved, he was BGS to (Sir) A. R. Godwin-Austen, a robustly competent commander whose qualities were harmoniously supplemented by Harding's intellectual grasp of the often perplexing problems created by Rommel's ineffectual precipitancy. He received a bar to his DSO for this victory. In January 1942 he supported Godwin-Austen's correct appreciation of the capabilities of the German counter-offensive and found himself organizing for the second time a hurried withdrawal through western Cyrenaica. The differences between the army and the corps commanders being irreconcilable, Godwin-Austen was replaced. Harding considered he was also honour bound to ask for a transfer; he went to GHQ as director of military training. He was promoted to brigadier and then major-general in 1942.

In Cairo Harding found himself frequently at variance, in practical matters of organization, with the chief of staff and his deputy. It was a relief to be given command, in September, of 7th Armoured division, the original desert armoured formation. In the second battle of Alamein his division was originally employed on the southern flank, its purpose mainly to deceive General Stumme into maintaining the original faulty disposition of his armour; but, with the return of Rommel and the intensification of the struggle in the northern sector, 7th Armoured was transferred there. In the pursuit that followed the successful change of plan, Harding fretted at the constraints imposed on him, but drove hard, always up with the forward troops. In January 1943, when approaching Tripoli, he was severely wounded by a nearby shell burst. He received a second bar to his DSO but was not graded fit to return to duty until ten months had passed.

In November 1943 he took command of VIII Corps, having been promoted to lieutenant-general, but six weeks later, by the personal decision of Sir Alan *Brooke (later first Viscount Alanbrooke), chief of the imperial general staff, he was transferred to be chief of staff to Sir Harold *Alexander (later first Earl Alexander of Tunis), commander-in-chief, Allied Armies in Italy. This was an inspired appointment. Harding and Alexander not only got on well together but admirably complemented each other. Alexander was both an intellectual and a fighting soldier, combining a tactical grasp of the battlefield with the talent of an imaginative and fertile strategist. In Harding he had someone who could be relied on without reservation to implement his ideas.

After the capture of Rome Harding was appointed KCB (1944). He chose to be known as Sir John Harding, that being the name he had used in the regiment and the family since 1919. After fifteen months as chief of staff he was at last, in March 1945, given the chance to command a corps in action; he took over XIII Corps, with which he had served in the desert nearly five years earlier. The last battle in Italy was as hard fought as the first. Harding's corps, originally on the British left, changed direction in the closing stages and pursued the retreating enemy up to and across the Po with a speed and effectiveness greater than he had been allowed to achieve after Alamein. That headlong pursuit brought him to Trieste on 2 May, just after the Yugoslavs, and to the centre of a long-lasting dispute with Britain's former ally. The acute stage of the confrontation with the Yugoslavs was overcome when they backed down in June, the first victory, it has been called, in the cold war. For two years Harding ruled with popular acclaim over what became the free city of Trieste in reasonable tranquillity.

In the summer of 1947 he was appointed to Southern Command and two years later became commander-in-chief Far East. He arrived just as what was euphemistically called 'the emergency' was beginning in Malaya; it was destined to last for twelve years. The foundations of the system by which this formidable Chinese communist insurrection was eventually suppressed were laid by Harding. Malcolm *MacDonald, the special commissioner for the Far East, paid a firm tribute to the sagacity and tenacity of purpose with which Harding dominated the defence co-ordinating committee.

Promoted to general in 1949 and appointed GCB at the beginning of 1951 Harding was transferred in August 1951 to command the British Army of the Rhine. After the Russian take-over in Czechoslovakia and the Berlin blockade Britain had begun rearming and NATO set up the Supreme Headquarters, Allied Powers in Europe (SHAPE), commanded by Dwight Eisenhower. The British army was being transformed. New defence plans were studied. Harding had to display prodigies of inter-Allied tact, organizational flair, and determination. By contrast his period as chief of the imperial general staff, three years from 1952 to 1955, passed off with little more excitement than the Mau Mau rebellion in Kenya and the beginning of the dissolution of the British base in Egypt. In November 1953 he was promoted field-marshal and presented with his baton by the young queen.

As the end of the three-year term approached and Harding was making plans for his retirement, a proposal was made to him by the new prime minister, Sir Anthony *Eden (later the first Earl of Avon), that he should become governor of Cyprus. Eden considered that his experience in Malaya and Kenya would help him to control the demand for union with Greece, which was supported by the majority of Greek Cypriots. He accepted reluctantly, from a sense of duty. He realized at once that the only favourable prospect lay in negotiating with Archbishop *Makarios for some acceptable form of self-government. The two men were well matched in quickness of intelligence; Makarios later declared that Harding was both the cleverest and the most straightforward of the governors he had known. Though circumstances denied them the pleasure of a successful agreement, Harding's measures brought greatly improved security in the island, with the Greek Cypriot insurgent leader, George Grivas, reduced to impotent clandestinity. After the two years' term for which he had originally stipulated, Harding was able to hand over in October 1957 to his successor, Sir Hugh *Foot (later Baron Caradon), a sound basis for the eventual achievement of Cypriot independence.

In January 1958 he was raised to the peerage in acknowledgement of his service in Cyprus. In retirement he accepted several directorships, including one on the board of Plesseys, a major supplier of telecommunication equipment of which he became chairman in 1967. In 1961 he was invited to become the first chairman of the Horse Race Betting Levy Board. He was colonel of three regiments, the Somerset Light Infantry (from 1960 the Somerset and Cornwall Light Infantry), the 6th Gurkha Rifles, and the Lifeguards. He was awarded an honorary DCL of Durham University (1958).

He was slight in build with a frank and courteous expression, clear blue eyes, and a trim moustache. His manner was open and friendly; throughout a career that could have excited jealousy no one spoke badly of him. Apart from a notable skill in personal relationships, his leading characteristic was a lucidity of intellectual apprehension and strength of reasoning that enabled him to grasp the essence of every problem. Those who served with him were exhilarated by the speed and certainty with which he arrived at the right solution.

He married in 1927 Mary Gertrude Mabel, daughter of Joseph Wilson Rooke, solicitor and JP, of Knutsford, Cheshire, and sister of an officer in his regiment. She died in 1983. They had one son, John Charles (born 1928), who succeeded to the barony. Harding died 20 January 1989 at his home in Sherborne, Dorset.

[Michael Carver, *Harding of Petherton*, 1978; David Hunt, *A Don at War*, revised edn. 1990; I. S. O. Playfair *et al.*, *Official History of the Second World War. The Mediterranean and Middle East*, vols. i–vi, 1956–88; personal knowledge.]   DAVID HUNT

HARDING, SIR **Harold John Boyer** (1900–1986), civil engineer, was born in Wandsworth 6 January 1900, the younger son and younger child of Arthur Boyer Harding, who was employed by an insurance company, and his wife Helen Clinton, daughter of the Revd William Lowe. With the loss of his father in 1902, support through school, Christ's Hospital, and university depended on his mother's sister's husband, Jack Robinson. He entered the City and Guilds College (part of Imperial College) in 1917, serving through 1918 as a full-time Officers' Training Corps cadet. He resumed his studies in 1919, struggling in mathematics and excelling in geology. He received a B.Sc. (Eng.) in 1922.

In 1922 he joined the 'old, respected and feudal firm' of John Mowlem & Company, engineering contractors, where he was to become the outstanding engineer in soft ground tunnelling and shaft construction in Britain. His early work concerned underground railway development in and around London, including the reconstruction of Piccadilly Circus station (1926–9). The sheer complexity of this project spurred him to build, with his future wife, then a student at the Slade School of Art, a model of the underground works, subsequently displayed at the Science Museum and later at the London Transport Museum. His particular skills were soon exercised in overcoming major foundation problems encountered at Dagenham for the powerhouse for the Ford motor works, unwittingly placed exactly where Sir Cornelius *Vermuyden had closed a breach in the Thames 300 years before. This experience led to Harding's special interest in expedients for ground treatment, with pioneering work in Britain on the Joosten and Guttman processes of chemical consolidation. From 1936 to 1939 he directed construction of the Central line of London underground from Bow Road to Leytonstone.

During World War II he was responsible for defence works and emergency repairs to underground damage in London. In 1943–4 he organized the construction of precast concrete petrol barges and eight of the concrete floating monoliths of Mulberry harbour for the Normandy landings. During a night of air raids in 1941 he had a discussion with a distinguished colleague, which was to lead to a significant geotechnical advance in Britain, the foundation of Soil Mechanics Ltd. in 1942. From this date he was increasingly involved in the management of the firm, being a director from 1949 to 1955; from 1950 to 1956 he was also a director of the parent company, Mowlem. Subsequently, until 1978, he worked as a consultant and arbitrator. From 1958 to 1970 he was joint consultant, with René Malcor, to the Channel tunnel study group. In 1966–7 he was a member of the Aberfan disaster tribunal, chaired by Lord Justice Edmund Davies (later Baron Edmund-Davies), following a flow slide of mining waste, which engulfed a mining village in south Wales.

Harding was an active and loyal fellow of the Institution of Civil Engineers through a period of radical reform; he served as president in 1963–4. He was first chairman of the British Tunnelling Society (1971–3) and set the pattern for its instructive informal discussions, encouraging participation by young engineers, thus recreating an original objective of the parent institution. He gave great encouragement to others to undertake research to explain phenomena he had observed, for research often lagged behind their practical manifestation.

He was a governor of Westminster Technical College (1948–53), Northampton Engineering College (1950–3), and Imperial College (1955–75). In 1952 he was elected a fellow of the City and Guilds Institute. He was knighted in 1968 and received an honorary D.Sc. from City University in 1970. In 1976 he was elected a founder fellow of the Fellowship of Engineering

(later the Royal Academy of Engineering), and he became a fellow of Imperial College in 1968.

He was a man of great energy and application, an imposing figure with a high forehead, slightly aquiline nose and a severe expression which readily dissolved into a smile, and a penetrating eye which could be seen by the discerning to twinkle. His portrait, painted by Lady Harding, hangs in the Institution of Civil Engineers. To his school-days at Christ's Hospital, in the 'engineering side' taught by T. S. Usherwood, he attributed much of his command of English, interest in history, and facility for the apt quotation, learned under enthusiastic circumstances in association with science and technology. He was a witty and captivating speaker, dismissive of pomp and arrogance. He recognized that successful geotechnical projects depended on the early identification of unexpected change and the consequent need for modification of the scheme. This, he emphasized, required moral courage in those concerned to admit the errors in their original perceptions.

In 1927 he married Sophie Helen Blair, daughter of Edmund Blair Leighton, RI, artist. They had two sons and a daughter. Harding died in Topsham, Devon, 27 March 1986.

[Harold Harding, *Tunnelling History and My Own Involvement*, 1981; Institution of Civil Engineers archives; private information; personal knowledge.]

ALAN MUIR WOOD

HARLEY, John Laker ('Jack') (1911–1990), botanist, was born 17 November 1911 in Old Charlton, London, the elder son and second of four children of Charles Laker Harley, civil servant in the Post Office, and his wife Edith Sarah Smith, daughter of an armament artificer. His early childhood was spent in various parts of London. When he was twelve the family moved to Leeds, where his father took a post at the labour exchange. Harley entered Leeds Grammar School, originally intending to become a classicist, but switched to science in the sixth form. Three outstanding teachers made him interested and successful at biology, and he entered for the Oxford entrance examination. The hard work needed for this, combined with being prefect and house captain as well as playing first-XV rugby, taught him the efficient use of time and how to work early in the morning, a lesson he never forgot, to the later consternation of research collaborators, who found he often began preparing for experiments at dawn.

In 1930 he won an open exhibition to Wadham College, Oxford, but was unsure whether to read botany or zoology. He chose the former because the interviewers for the latter did not attract him. His undergraduate career was crowned with the awards both of a first-class honours degree (1933), and the Christopher Welch research scholarship, which financed the first four years (1933–7) of his postgraduate research on the mycorrhizas of the beech tree (mycorrhizas are very common and widespread symbiotic associations between fungi and the underground organs of plants, and the principal route for mineral nutrients such as phosphate to pass from soil to roots). This topic was chosen because he had carried out notable researches as an undergraduate into both fungi and plant ecology, but he was very dissatisfied with the outcome and, after his D.Phil. (1936), switched to studying the physiology of fungi, having been awarded an 1851 studentship. In 1939 he became a departmental demonstrator in the botany department.

War service intervened from 1940 to 1945, and he was commissioned in the Royal Signals. He joined the Army Operational Research Group no. 1 in 1943, serving first in the Burma theatre, and then in Ceylon as a staff officer at Supreme Allied Command headquarters, ending the war with the rank of lieutenant-colonel. His experiences left a marked impression, and the military way of life had some appeal for him. He returned to Oxford in 1945 as a university lecturer in the botany department, moving to the agriculture department in 1958. He was reader in plant nutrition from 1962 to 1965. He became a research fellow of Queen's College in 1946 (full fellow in 1952), a happy association which ended in 1965 when he moved to Sheffield University as a professor of botany. He returned to Oxford in 1969 as professor of forest science and fellow of St John's, a post he held until his retirement in 1979.

Harley's major contribution to science was that, over a period of nearly forty years after the war, he oversaw a pioneering series of researches into tree mycorrhizas which put the experimental study of these ecologically important symbioses firmly on the map; before his work, no one had a clear idea of their role. The initial stimulus to his studies was an invitation to write a review on mycorrhizas in 1947, which then inspired research with a succession of talented collaborators, many of whom were his own students. Two outstanding books were published, the second written with his daughter, herself an international expert on mycorrhizas: *The Biology of Mycorrhiza* (1959) and (with S. E. Smith) *Mycorrhizal Symbiosis* (1983).

Harley was elected a fellow of the Royal Society in 1964, and had honorary degrees from the universities of Sheffield (1989) and Uppsala (1981). He was president of the British Mycological Society (1967), the British Ecological Society (1970–2), and the Institute of Biology (1984–6), and had honorary fellowships of Wadham College, Oxford (1972), Wye College, London (1983), and the Indian National Academy of Sciences (1981). He was appointed CBE in 1979

and won the gold medal of the Linnean Society in 1989. His excellent analytical judgement benefited many national bodies, including the Agricultural Research Council, the Lawes Agricultural Trust, and the *New Phytologist*, the largest journal of general botany in Europe, which he served as both editor (1961–83) and a trustee.

Harley inspired intense loyalty and affection from his students and collaborators. Beneath his bluff, rather military style lay a remarkably perceptive and compassionate person, who combined courage and honesty with a zany sense of humour. He was six feet tall, erect, and slim, although he put on weight later in life. In 1938 he married (Elizabeth) Lindsay, daughter of Edward McCarthy Fitt, civil engineer. They had a son and a daughter. Harley died 13 December 1990 at his home in Old Marston, Oxford.

[D. C. Smith and D. H. Lewis in *Biographical Memoirs of Fellows of the Royal Society*, vol. xxxix, 1994; personal knowledge.]   DAVID SMITH

HARRISON, Francis Llewelyn ('Frank') (1905–1987), music scholar, was born 29 September 1905 in Dublin, the second son in the family of four sons and three daughters of Alfred Francis Harrison, an accountant with the Great Southern Railway and a talented amateur singer, and his wife Florence May Nash, who was of Welsh descent on her mother's side, and, on her father's (William Nash, of Kilrush, county Clare, craftsman in inlaid wood), of mixed English and Hiberno-Norman. Both sides of his family belonged to the Protestant, urban tradition of Irish society. The young Harrison showed a precocious talent for music, and was educated at the choir school of St Patrick's Cathedral, from which he won one of the two annual cathedral scholarships to Mountjoy School. He continued studies part-time at the Royal Irish Academy of Music, where he won prizes for organ, piano, and composition, and later at Trinity College, Dublin (Mus.B. 1926, Mus.D. 1930). After a short spell as organist at Kilkenny Cathedral (1929) he emigrated to Canada in 1930.

Harrison was to spend two decades on the other side of the Atlantic. His first posts were within the church music sphere in which he had established himself in Eire. Alongside this he built up a flourishing career as a private music teacher, organist, and composer. In 1933 he studied with Marcel Dupré in France, and in 1943 he won the Canadian Performing Rights Society's composers' award. But from 1935, when he was appointed resident musician to Queen's University, Kingston, Ontario, his career was to be chiefly within academic institutions. In 1940 he opened the university's new music department. After spending 1945–6 as Bradley-Keeler fellow at Yale, studying with

Paul Hindemith and Leo Schrade, and posts at Colgate University, New York (1946–7), and Washington University, St Louis (1947–50), he went to England in 1950 and settled in Oxford, as lecturer in music in 1952–6, senior lecturer in 1956–62, and reader in the history of music from 1962 to 1970. From 1965 to 1970 he was a senior research fellow of Jesus College.

The decade in Canadian and North American universities was responsible for changing the focus of Harrison's musical interests. Composition seems to have been virtually abandoned after he went to Oxford, and his appearances as a performer became sporadic. For a highly imaginative man, the challenge of devising humanities curricula from scratch, in a climate suffused with left-wing cultural politics, had left an indelible mark. The need to understand how processes of artistic production, and those of music in particular, related to social structures and assumptions, was to be the mainspring of his work for the rest of his life. In Oxford he immersed himself in a study of pre-Reformation insular liturgical music—then an uncharted field—and rapidly established himself as an expert of international repute. His *Music in Medieval Britain* (1958) is a remarkable combination of both encyclopaedic positivism, using mainly manuscript sources alongside liturgical evidence then rarely admitted into musicology, and a rigorous concern to establish the music's comprehensibility in terms of its context. He was also involved with two major editorial projects: *Polyphonic Music of the Fourteenth Century*, published by Oiseau-Lyre, from 1962 to 1986, and the *Early English Church Music* project initiated by the British Academy at his instigation (1961–72). Among his other publications was *The Eton Choirbook* in three volumes (1956–61).

By nature restlessly inquisitive, Harrison was not content with ploughing a single furrow. During the 1960s, while consolidating his reputation as a medievalist (he was elected a fellow of the British Academy in 1965), his interest in what he dubbed 'anthromusicology' led him to explore musical culture more widely, and he undertook important fieldwork in Latin America. This expansion of his activities led in 1970 to the offer of the chair in ethnomusicology at Amsterdam, which he held until 1976. In Amsterdam Harrison's formidable capacity for hard work was stretched in numerous directions. While establishing his department on a new footing and moulding it as a centre of international academic excellence, he also engaged in fieldwork on the music of Latin America and the Celtic peoples, as well as continuing research on medieval Europe. Throughout the 1970s he continued to accept visiting posts abroad, particularly in North America, where he was much in demand. On a return to Kingston in 1974 he was awarded

an honorary LL D, and was present at the inauguration of the Harrison–Le Caine concert hall, named in his honour.

Harrison was a stocky energetic figure, who spoke in tones that recalled both his homeland and his years in North America, and who always took great care with his appearance. A gregarious character, with personal as well as academic interest in people and their activities, he had a wide international circle of friends. As an émigré he carried with him a capacity to make a home almost anywhere, and he was an informed enthusiast for international cuisine. In 1927 he married Norah Lillian, daughter of William Thomas Drayton, antique dealer; they had two daughters. The marriage was not a happy one and there was a divorce in 1965. In 1966 he married Joan, daughter of Edmund Thomas Rimmer, schoolmaster. She had been since 1960 his companion in his exploration of the world's music. There were no children of the second marriage. Harrison died in Canterbury, where they retired, 29 December 1987.

[D. F. L. Chadd in *Proceedings of the British Academy*, vol. lxxv, 1989; private information; personal knowledge.]   DAVID CHADD

HARRISON, SIR Reginald Carey ('Rex') (1908–1990), actor, was born 5 March 1908 in Huyton, Lancashire, the youngest of three children and only son of William Reginald Harrison, stockbroker, and his wife, Edith Mary Carey. At the age of ten he adopted the name 'Rex', by which he was known for the rest of his life. He was a sickly child and a bout of measles left him with poor sight in his left eye. He was educated at Birkdale Preparatory School and Liverpool College. His appearances in school plays and regular visits to the Liverpool Playhouse confirmed an early desire to be an actor. At sixteen he was taken on at the Playhouse and after a year backstage made his acting début in 1924 in *Thirty Minutes in a Street*. After two and a half years playing small roles, he left Liverpool for London, where in 1927 he landed a part in a touring production of *Charley's Aunt*. Thus began six years of touring and repertory, in which he learned his craft. It was a five-month run as a caddish explorer in *Heroes Don't Care* in 1936 that provided his breakthrough. The critic of *Theatre World* proclaimed him 'one of the best light comedians on the English stage' and he maintained this position until his death.

On the basis of *Heroes Don't Care*, the producer (Sir) Alexander *Korda signed a contract with Harrison at London Films, and he was launched on a cinematic career, which he was to continue henceforth in tandem with his stage career. He achieved an early success in the delightful comedy *Storm in a Teacup* (1936), where as a crusading reporter he was taught by the director Victor Saville how to relax in front of the camera. He consolidated his theatrical reputation with long runs in *French Without Tears* (1936), *Design for Living* (1939), and *No Time for Comedy* (1941). From 1942 to 1944 he served in the Royal Air Force Volunteer Reserve as a flying control liaison officer. Emerging from the forces, he established himself as a major British film star in the screen version of *Blithe Spirit* (1945) and in *The Rake's Progress* (1945), in which he was excellent as a charming, feckless, parasitic playboy, who expiates a worthless life with a heroic death on the battlefield.

Hollywood inevitably beckoned and Twentieth Century-Fox signed a seven-year contract with him. They saw him not as a light comedian but as a character actor. The vehicles they provided for him, if not always to his taste, were invariably superbly mounted and stretched him as an actor. In *Anna and the King of Siam* (1946), Harrison was both comic and touching as the capricious but dedicated King Mongkut. In *The Ghost and Mrs Muir* (1947), playing the spirit of an old sea dog, he took to being blasphemous and bad tempered with evident glee. In *Unfaithfully Yours* (1948) he played an autocratic and egocentric orchestral conductor with a memorable line in vituperation. But his continuing unhappiness in Hollywood, his unflattering comments on the film capital, poor box-office returns on his later Fox films, and an unsavoury scandal surrounding the suicide of actress Carole Landis, with whom he was having an affair, led Harrison and Fox to terminate the contract by mutual consent. He returned to Broadway to play King Henry VIII in Maxwell Anderson's *Anne of the Thousand Days* (1948) at the Shubert theatre, New York, and promptly won a Tony award as best actor. Then in London and on Broadway he did John Van Druten's play *Bell, Book and Candle* (1950) and directed and starred in (Sir) Peter Ustinov's play *The Love of Four Colonels* (1953). He won the 1961 *Evening Standard* Best Actor award for his performance in Anton Chekhov's *Platonov* at the Royal Court theatre in 1960.

Harrison resolutely avoided Shakespeare, but became the supreme interpreter of the plays of Bernard *Shaw, bringing the necessary quality of civilized intelligence to his performances both on stage (*Heartbreak House* 1983, *The Devil's Disciple* 1977) and film (*Major Barbara* 1940–1). He will forever be associated with the role of Professor Henry Higgins in *My Fair Lady*, the Lerner and Loewe musical based on Shaw's *Pygmalion*. Harrison played the part for three years on stage in New York and London (1956–9), winning a second Tony award, and an Oscar for his performance in the film version (1964). So much did he make the part his own that he later said: 'For years I could never bear to

see anyone else do it—Higgins has become so much a part of me and I, of him.'

Harrison's success in *My Fair Lady* made him a major international star and led to appearances in several screen epics in the 1960s. There was more than a touch of Shaw's Julius Caesar in his drily witty and very human performance as the Roman conqueror in *Cleopatra* (1963). When Caesar expired half-way through, so did the film. The ponderous film about Michelangelo, *The Agony and the Ecstasy* (1965), was almost redeemed by Harrison's engaging interpretation of Pope Julius II as an urbane schemer.

In the late 1960s there was a string of expensive flops—*The Honey Pot* (1965), *Doctor Doolittle* (1966), *A Flea in her Ear* (1967)—and in the 1970s and 1980s Harrison's film appearances were mainly cameos, though he played Don Quixote in a notable 1973 BBC TV production. He concentrated his energies on the stage, displaying his gifts in London and New York in a series of Edwardian revivals: *Heartbreak House* 1983, *Aren't We All?* 1984–5, *The Admirable Crichton* 1988, and *The Circle* 1989. He was appearing in *The Circle* when his final illness was diagnosed.

Harrison was married six times, and allegedly mistreated all his wives. His first wife (1934) was the fashion model Collette Thomas (her real name was Marjorie). They had one son, the actor and singer Noel Harrison, born in 1935, and were divorced in 1943. His second wife was the émigré German Jewish actress Lilli Palmer (whose real name was Lilli Peiser), whom he married in 1943. They had one son, the playwright Carey Harrison, born in 1944, and were divorced in 1957. His third wife (1957) was the English actress Kay Kendall, who died of leukaemia in 1959 at the age of thirty-two. Their relationship was the basis of the play *After Lydia*, by Sir Terence *Rattigan, in which Harrison starred on Broadway in 1974, playing the role based on himself. He married his fourth wife in 1962, the Welsh actress Rachel Roberts, daughter of the Revd Richard Rhys Roberts. They divorced in 1971 and she committed suicide in 1980. His fifth wife (1971) was Mrs (Joan) Elizabeth Rees Harris, daughter of David Rees Rees-Williams, first Baron Ogmore, PC, and ex-wife of actor Richard Harris. They divorced in 1976. He married finally in 1978 an American, Mercia Tinker. Harrison wrote two volumes of autobiography and three of his wives left their impressions of him in their autobiographies.

Harrison was a man of enormous charm and this often compensated for the personal and professional self-centredness and perfectionism that sometimes tried the patience of colleagues and associates. He was perhaps the last Edwardian, compeer of Sir Gerald *du Maurier, Sir Charles *Hawtrey, and Sir (E.) Seymour *Hicks, actors who contrived to give the impression that they had just popped into the theatre for a spot of acting on the way to the club. Harrison had admired and closely studied the style and technique of the great Edwardians and had come to embody the same combination of elegance, authority, wit, and grace. He was appointed commendatore of Italy's Order of Merit in 1967, awarded an honorary degree by the University of Boston in 1973, and knighted in 1989. He died of cancer of the pancreas in New York, 2 June 1990.

[Rex Harrison, *Rex*, 1974, and *A Damned Serious Business*, 1990; Allen Eyles, *Rex Harrison*, 1985; Nicholas Wapshott, *Rex Harrison*, 1991; Alexander Walker, *Fatal Charm*, 1992; Lilli Palmer, *Change Lobsters and Dance*, 1976; Rachel Roberts and Alexander Walker, *No Bells on Sunday*, 1984; Elizabeth Rees Harrison, *Love, Honour and Dismay*, 1976.]   JEFFREY RICHARDS

HARTY, (Fredric) Russell (1934–1988), broadcaster, was born 5 September 1934 in Blackburn, the only son and elder child of Fred Harty, greengrocer (who, his son claimed, introduced Blackburn to the avocado pear), and his wife, Myrtle Rishton. He was educated at Queen Elizabeth's Grammar School, Blackburn, and Exeter College, Oxford, where he read English and was taught by Nevill *Coghill, who noted of an early essay on 'Sex in the Canterbury Tales', 'Energetic and zealous but very naïve'. He took a third-class degree (1957) and taught briefly at Blakey Moor Secondary Modern School in Blackburn before moving in 1958 to Giggleswick School in Yorkshire. Giggleswick was a school and a village with which he was to have close connections for the rest of his life. In 1964 there followed a spell at City College, New York, and at Bishop Lonsdale College of Education, Derby, but with many of his friends and contemporaries busy in the theatre and broadcasting he was increasingly dissatisfied with teaching.

In 1966 he made his first foray into television, an inglorious appearance as a contestant on Granada TV's *Criss Cross Quiz*; the only question he answered correctly was on Catherine of Braganza. It was such a public humiliation that his mother refused to speak to him. Still, it was a beginning and in 1967 he was taken on by BBC Radio as an arts programmes producer, his hankering to perform whetted by the occasional trip to the studio down the corridor whenever *Woman's Hour* wanted a letter read in a northern accent.

As an undergraduate Harty had invited Vivien *Leigh round for drinks and this precocious appetite for celebrity stood him in good stead when, in 1969, he became producer and occasional presenter of London Weekend TV's arts programme, *Aquarius*. He might not have seemed the best person to film Salvador Dali, but the elderly surrealist and the boy off Blackburn

market took to one another and the programme won an Emmy award; in another unlikely conjunction he set up an encounter on Capri between the eminent Lancashire exiles Sir William *Walton and Gracie *Fields. Harty was never abashed by the famous (his critics said that was the trouble), but it was his capacity for provocative half-truths and outrageous overstatement, which made him such a good schoolmaster, that now fitted him for a career as the host of a weekly talk show (*Eleven Plus* and later *Russell Harty*) and made him one of the most popular performers on television. Plump, cheerful, and unintimidating, he was particularly good at putting people at their ease, deflating the pompous and drawing out the shy.

In 1980 he returned to the BBC, but his output remained much as it had been for the last ten years, the same mixture of talk shows varied by occasional films like *The Black Madonna*, and his *Grand Tour*, shown in 1988. He wrote regularly for the *Observer* and the *Sunday Times*, publishing a book of his television interviews, *Russell Harty Plus* (1976) and also *Mr Harty's Grand Tour* (1988). He was a regular broadcaster on radio besides presenting the Radio 4 talk show, *Start the Week*.

'Private faces in public places are wiser and nicer than public faces in private places' (W. H. *Auden) did not anticipate television, where the distinction is not always plain. For his friends Harty was naturally a private face but for the public he seemed a private face too and one that had strayed on to the screen seemingly untouched by expertise. That was why, though it infuriated his critics, so many viewers liked him and took him to their hearts as they never did more polished performers. He giggled, he fumbled and seldom went for the right word rather than the next but two, and though his delivery could be as tortured as his mother's on the telephone, it did not matter. It was all part of his ordinariness, his deficiencies, his style.

Harty never made much of a secret of his homosexuality. He did not look on it as an affliction, but he was never one for a crusade either. His funniest stories were always of the absurdities of sex and the ludicrous situations it had led him into, and if he was never short of partners, it was because they knew there would always be laughs, sharing a joke being something rarer than sharing a bed.

In the second half of the 1980s the spread of AIDS enabled the tabloid press, and in particular those newspapers owned by Rupert Murdoch, to dress up their muckraking as a moral crusade, and they systematically trawled public life for sexual indiscretion. Harty, who had not scrupled to question his more celebrated interviewees about their sex lives, knew that he was in a vulnerable situation. Early in 1987 a young man, who had had a previous fling with Harty, was wired up with a tape recorder by two *News of the World* reporters and sent to call on Harty at his London flat. To the reporters' chagrin nothing newsworthy occurred, but the paper fell back on printing the young man's account of the previous association, thus initiating a campaign of sporadic vilification in the tabloid press, which only ended with Harty's death just over a year later.

The cause of his death was liver failure, the result of hepatitis B, but in the hope that he was suffering from AIDS the press laid siege firstly to his home in Giggleswick and then to St James's Hospital in Leeds, where he was in intensive care. A telescope was trained permanently on the window of his ward and a reporter tried to smuggle himself into the ward disguised as a junior doctor, in order to look at his case notes. When Harty was actually on his deathbed one of the journalists responsible for the original 'scoop' could not be restrained from retelling the tale of her exploits on television.

He died in Leeds 8 June 1988 and is buried in Giggleswick, the gravestone evidence of the vulgarity from which he never entirely managed to break free.

[Private information; personal knowledge.]

ALAN BENNETT

HASLER, Herbert George ('Blondie') (1914–1987), inventor, and founder of the Royal Marines Boom Patrol Detachment (the forerunner of the Special Boat Service) and shorthanded ocean racing, was born in Dublin 27 February 1914, the younger child and younger son of Lieutenant Arthur Thomas Hasler, quartermaster, of the Royal Army Medical Corps, and his wife, Annie Georgina Andrews. His father was drowned when the troop-ship *Transylvania* was torpedoed on 4 May 1917, leaving his mother to bring up the young boys on her own. She sent Herbert, with a bursary, to Wellington College, where he distinguished himself at cross-country running, rugby football, and as captain of swimming. He also boxed but, according to him, with rather less distinction.

'Blondie' Hasler (as he now became known, except to his family, because of his thinning blond hair and fair moustache) combined remarkable powers of physical endurance with above average strength and fitness (he was about six feet tall). Yet, throughout his subsequent career, he was loath to take advantage of these attributes, although they stood him in good stead in war and peace, preferring a well-reasoned, calm, and quietly conducted discussion to make his case. He also hated punishing men under his command, believing that their failure was the result of his lack of leadership. He had a totally original mind.

Hasler was commissioned into the Royal Marines on 1 September 1932, and by 1935 had already achieved yachting distinction by sailing a twelve-foot dinghy single-handed from Plymouth to Portsmouth and back again. It was then that he began expounding advanced nautical theories through illustrated articles in the international press—a hobby he pursued until his death. After World War II broke out, as fleet landing officer in Scapa Flow in 1940, he was sent to Narvik in support of the French Foreign Legion. In just a few weeks he was appointed OBE, mentioned in dispatches, and awarded the croix de guerre.

On his return he wrote a paper suggesting the use of canoes and underwater swimmers to attack enemy shipping, but this was rejected by Combined Operations as being too radical and impracticable. However, in January 1942 Hasler was appointed to the Combined Operations Development Centre where, after the Italians had severely damaged HMS *Queen Elizabeth* and HMS *Valiant* in Alexandria harbour by the use of 'human torpedoes', his paper was immediately resurrected. He was ordered to form the Royal Marines Boom Patrol Detachment (later to be dubbed the 'Cockleshell Heroes'—an expression of which he disapproved). When the problem of blockade-runners operating out of Bordeaux was identified in September, Hasler had his solution ready the next day. The submarine HMS *Tuna* launched a raid on the night of 7 December 1942. Four men out of the original twelve reached the target in tiny two-man canoes, and only two, including Hasler, returned, having made their way overland to Spain. Hasler was recommended for the VC, but was technically ineligible, having not been fired on. He was appointed to the DSO. The episode was turned into a film, which was only loosely based on fact, *Cockleshell Heroes*, starring José Ferrer and Trevor *Howard, in 1955.

Subsequently, Hasler experimented with different methods of attack, employing some of these ideas between 1944 and 1945 while serving as training and development officer with No. 385 Royal Marines detachment in the Small Operations Group (Ceylon), planning submarine-launched raids into Burma.

In 1946 he won the Royal Ocean Racing Club's class iii championships in his unconventional yacht, the thirty-square-metre *Tre Sang*. This was a remarkable achievement for a young officer. Hasler was invalided out of the Royal Marines in 1948 with the wartime rank of lieutenant-colonel. Retirement now allowed him time to concentrate on exploring, writing (in 1957 he wrote a play with Rosamund Pilcher, *The Tulip Major*, which was performed in Dundee), inventing, and developing a wide range of ideas, many of which are still in daily use. They included a floating breakwater and towed dracones (Hasler developed an earlier idea into a feasible design for transporting bulk oil).

In 1952 Hasler published *Harbours and Anchorages of the North Coast of Brittany* (revised 1965), which set the standard for the genre, but his greatest civilian triumphs of invention—and quiet, gentlemanly persuasion—were yet to come. In 1953 he conceived and built *Jester*, based on a modified twenty-six-foot Folkboat design, as a test bed for various sail plans (he eventually settled on the junk rig), and the internationally acclaimed, and first commercially successful, Hasler self-steering gear. *Jester* was a radical advance in British yacht design and she was not the last yacht to come from his drawing-board.

In 1957 he proposed the idea of a quadrennial single-handed transatlantic race for yachts and after many set-backs this was sailed in 1960 by five yachts; Hasler came second in *Jester*. He followed this in 1962 with a search for the Loch Ness monster and in 1966 by the first quadrennial two-handed round Britain and Ireland race, in which Hasler (again, the instigator) was crewed by his wife in the equally radical *Sumner*. These two races have spawned almost all modern, short-handed racing worldwide, with Hasler acknowledged as the founding father: he received a number of international awards. In his later years he moved to the west of Scotland, where he farmed organically and wrote *Practical Junk Rig* with J. K. McLeod (1988). His most important invention had been the self-steering gear, which became standard equipment and revolutionized sailing.

Hasler was married in 1965, when in his early fifties, to Bridget Mary Lindsay Fisher, then in her mid-twenties, the daughter of Rear-Admiral Ralph Lindsay Fisher, and an experienced yachtswoman in her own right. Despite the age difference the marriage brought them immense happiness and a son and a daughter. Hasler died of a heart attack in Glasgow, 5 May 1987.

[Mountbatten archives, Southampton University; C. E. Lucas Phillips, *Cockleshell Heroes*, 1956; Lloyd Foster, *OSTAR*, 1989; Ewen Southby-Tailyour, *Blondie Hasler, a Biography*, 1996; private archives; personal knowledge.]   EWEN SOUTHBY-TAILYOUR

HASSALL, Joan (1906–1988), artist and wood-engraver, was born 3 March 1906 at 88 Kensington Park Road, Notting Hill, London, the only daughter and elder child of John *Hassall, painter and illustrator, and his second wife Constance Maud, daughter of the Revd Albert Brooke-Webb, rector of Dallinghoe, Wickham Market, Suffolk. Her brother was the poet, biographer, and playwright Christopher *Hassall. She was educated at Parsons Mead School, Ashtead, and though wishing to study music, trained instead as a schoolteacher at the Froebel Educational Institute, Roehampton. For two years (1925–7) she worked at her father's London School of Art, but on its closure went herself to the Royal Academy Schools from 1928 to 1933, winning the Landseer scholarship in 1931. She learned to engrave on wood in 1931, being taught by R. J. Beedham at the London county council School of Photo-engraving and Lithography. At the time she felt she was *remembering* rather than learning how to handle the tools.

Her first substantial book illustration was for Francis Brett *Young's *Portrait of a Village* (1937), which established her as an illustrator of consequence. She studied nineteenth-century women's costume for the engravings for the 1940 edition of Elizabeth *Gaskell's *Cranford*, which were a pattern for much later work. During the war she taught printing and engraving at Edinburgh College of Art (1940–5), and between 1943 and 1951 designed and illustrated eleven chapbooks for the Saltire Society. The light-hearted designs for *A Child's Garden of Verses* by Robert Louis *Stevenson (1947 edition) had much of Thomas *Bewick about them, as did the thirty vignettes for the National Book League's *Reader's Guides* (1947–51). Mary Russell *Mitford's *Our Village* (1947) followed *Cranford* in its style, but with *The Strange World of Nature* (1950), by Bernard Gooch, she started a long series of engravings of wild life, conveying with consummate skill the textures of hair and feathers. For *Fifty-one Poems* by Mary *Webb (1946) and *Collected Poems* by Andrew *Young (1950) she cut a great many small vignettes that give visual life to the poems they decorate.

Troubled with arthritis in the early 1950s, she turned to scraperboard, drawing about 150 small designs for *The Oxford Nursery Rhyme Book*, edited by Peter *Opie and his wife, Iona (1955). She engraved some 120 blocks for the Folio Society, illustrating two collections of Anthony *Trollope's stories in 1949 and 1951, and, during periods of remission from the arthritis, a complete Jane *Austen in seven volumes (1957–63). The usual sobriety of her figures disappeared in the last of these, with a new excitement in their character, and this same vivacity was continued in the seventy-seven vignettes (two of them in colour) for *The Poems of Robert Burns* (1965). She added twenty-eight scraperboard drawings to a new edition of the Jane Austen, issued in 1975. In all she illustrated over eighty books.

She did a great deal of more ephemeral work, providing drawings and engravings for British Transport, the BBC, and various publishers and booksellers, as well as for a number of magazines including *Housewife*, *London Mystery Magazine*, and *The Masque*. She designed thirty-five bookplates, including twenty-four on wood, and was responsible for the £1 royal silver wedding stamp

(1948) and the queen's invitation card to her guests for the coronation (1953).

A fine artist, skilled as a water-colourist as well as at drawing, it was as an engraver that she excelled, cutting perhaps 1,000 blocks, which she proofed with great skill on an Albion hand-press. Inspired by Bewick, she preferred small vignettes to full-page illustrations, and enjoyed engraving for ordinary people, ordinary readers, rather than moneyed collectors. She preferred descriptive work to mere decoration. No more than the outlines of her designs would be drawn on the surface to be engraved, the detail coming from the burin, whose movement had sometimes the careless ease of a pencil. She was a slow worker, a perfectionist who would recut a design that had failed in some way, without regard for any urgencies of publication. Financial help from her brother and Sir Edward *Marsh enabled her to escape from home in 1937, but she always had to live very modestly. She lived in her father's house in Notting Hill after his death in 1948, moving in 1976 to a cottage in Malham, Yorkshire, that had been bequeathed to her by a friend. She was a friend of Sydney *Cockerell and her letters to him from Italy and France in April–May 1950 were published in 1991 as Dearest Sydney (edited by Brian North Lee).

She was a short plumpish woman, shy in her early years, but with a friendly disposition that made her many friends and admirers. She played the organ at Kirkby Malham church, and, at other times, the harpsichord, harp, viola da gamba, and flute.

In 1938 she was elected an associate, and in 1948 a fellow of the Royal Society of Painter-Etchers and Engravers, and in 1947 a member of the Society of Wood Engravers. She was made a fellow of the Society of Industrial Artists and Designers (1948), and was one of the first three women members of the Art Workers' Guild (1964) and its first woman master in 1972. She was awarded the bronze medal of the Paris Salon (1973) and was appointed OBE in 1987.

For many years suffering from arthritis, and latterly from failing sight, she died of broncho-pneumonia and diabetes 6 March 1988 in Airedale General Hospital, Keighley, Yorkshire. She never married.

[Ruari McLean, Wood Engravings of Joan Hassall, 1960; Brigid Peppin and Lucy Micklethwait, Dictionary of British Book Illustrators: the Twentieth Century, 1983; David Chambers, Joan Hassall, Engravings and Drawings, 1985; personal knowledge.]   DAVID CHAMBERS

HASTINGS, Francis John Clarence Westenra Plantagenet, fifteenth EARL OF HUNTINGDON (1901–1990), artist and politician, was born 30 January 1901 in Manchester Square, London, the only son and youngest of three children of Warner Francis John Plantagenet Hastings, four-

teenth Earl of Huntingdon (whom he succeeded in 1939), and his wife, (Maud) Margaret, daughter of Sir Samuel Wilson, MP for Portsmouth. He was educated at Eton and Christ Church, Oxford, where he played in the university polo team and obtained a third class in modern history in 1923. Descended from *George, Duke of Clarence, brother of Edward IV, he was the senior legitimate male Plantagenet. But the undoubted hereditary claim of his ancestor, Henry *Hastings, third Earl of Huntingdon, to succeed *Elizabeth I did not pass to him, being diverted through a female line. Huntingdon was more interested in an alleged but impossible descent from Robin *Hood, described in folklore as the Earl of Huntingdon.

In 1925 'Jack' Huntingdon, who painted under the name John Hastings, married (Maria) Cristina, daughter of the wealthy Marchese Casati, head of one of the families which had ruled Milan for centuries. They travelled extensively in Australia and the Pacific, living for a while on the island of Moorea, after which they named their only child, a daughter. In San Francisco the couple met Diego Rivera, the celebrated Mexican communist mural painter. Huntingdon, who had studied at the Slade School of Art after leaving Oxford, became a pupil of Rivera's and learned the technique of fresco. He became Rivera's assistant, branching out into mural painting on his own account. In 1933 he painted a mural depicting dentistry in the Hall of Science at the Chicago World Fair, to accompany a display of George Washington's teeth. Already inclined to be left wing at Oxford, he was further influenced by Rivera's ideology, and involved himself in the Spanish civil war, taking medical assistance to Republicans. His parents' anger at his marriage to a Roman Catholic foreigner, who shared their son's political outlook and eventually became a communist, was not assuaged by her high aristocratic lineage and there was a long breach during which the couple had little money other than a legacy from his grandmother.

On return to England, Huntingdon in 1935 painted a remarkable ten feet by twenty feet fresco on a wall in the Marx memorial library, Clerkenwell Green, London. It showed a 'Worker of the future upsetting the economic chaos of the present' and though slightly wooden in the Soviet realist manner, had distinctive original and pleasing touches. For his friend, the eccentric and rich socialist second Baron *Faringdon, he painted murals at Buscot Park depicting local Labour party activities. As his faith in socialism declined, his paintings abandoned ideology for almost surrealist shapes and writhings of serpents in bright colours, expressing cheerful distaste for conventional restraints, whatever their provenance. He was chairman of the Society of Mural Painters in 1951–8 and his works were widely exhibited.

Despite his far-left phase, he was a second lieutenant (Territorial Army) in the Royal Horseguards. He was deputy controller of civil defence for Andover from 1941 to July 1945, when he joined the government of Clement (later first Earl) *Attlee as parliamentary secretary at the Ministry of Agriculture and Fisheries. He stayed there until November 1950, when he left politics for the painting he preferred. Among his murals are those at Birmingham University (1965), the Women's Press Club in London (1950), and the Casa dello Strozzato, Tuscany (early 1970s). He taught fresco at the Camberwell and Central schools of art in London.

His marriage to the strong-willed Cristina, whose southern temperament did not easily fit with Huntingdon's gentler, more placid English ways, ended with divorce in 1943 and she married Wogan Phillips (previously married to Rosamund *Lehmann) who, as the second Baron Milford, was the first communist to take his seat in the House of Lords.

Tall, athletic, and an expert yachtsman, Huntingdon strongly resembled the portrait he owned of the Elizabethan third Earl in the reddish colour of his hair and finely delineated features. He played a number of musical instruments well and was a wine connoisseur with impeccable taste. He was the quintessence of a cultured, civilized man and in addition to his talents as a painter he was the author of two intelligently written books, *Commonsense about India* (1942) and *The Golden Octopus* (1928), a book of legends of the South Seas. A delightful, convivial companion with a lively, intelligent wit, full of kindness and amusing stories and quick to laugh at himself, he was vague, gentle, courteous, and charming, with exquisite manners sometimes taken for weakness, but he was politely resolute in avoiding inconvenience to himself. When his second wife, the author Margaret Lane, whom he married in 1944, proposed that her father should live with them he said nothing but quietly packed his bags ready to move out. She was formerly the wife of Bryan Wallace and daughter of Harry George Lane, newspaper editor, of Vernham Dean, Andover. This second marriage ran less excitingly and more smoothly than the first. From it there were two daughters, of whom one, Lady Selina Hastings, wrote a number of successful biographies.

Huntingdon died 24 August 1990 in a nursing home in Beaulieu, Hampshire. He was succeeded in the earldom by a first cousin once removed, William Edward Robin Hood Hastings Bass (born 1948).

[Personal knowledge; information from family, friends, and acquaintances.]   WOODROW WYATT

HAYTER, Stanley William (1901–1988), painter and printmaker, was born in Hackney 27 December 1901, the third of four children (two sons and two daughters) of William Harry Hayter, painter, and his wife, Ellen Mercy Palmer. Among his many artist ancestors was Sir George *Hayter, portrait and history painter to Queen *Victoria. He was educated at Whitgift Middle School, Croydon, and King's College, London (1918–21), where he obtained an honours degree in chemistry.

His scientific training, mathematical ability, and lifelong interest in science inform his art. Topological transformations, superimpositions of one space upon another, non-Euclidean spaces, wave motion, and moiré interferences of fields in continuous deformation characterize his imagery. The hallmarks of his work—energy, movement, and scintillating non-natural colour—reflect both his personality and his investigations into the psychology of vision. His technical innovations in colour printing were the work of a man equally at home in laboratory and atelier, in whom artistic sensibility and scientific curiosity were fused. He was as well read in poetry and literature as in science.

After university Hayter worked as a chemist for the Anglo-Iranian Oil Company in Abadan, Iran (1922–5). While there he drew and painted extensively. On his return he exhibited successfully in London. In 1926 he went to Paris, briefly attended the Académie Julian, and gravitated towards avant-garde artistic circles, making friends with Balthus, Alexander Calder, Anthony *Gross, André Masson, Joan Miró, and Alberto Giacometti. Joseph Hecht introduced him to engraving. Convinced that the potentialities of gravure had never been realized, he established in 1927 a printmaking workshop, which became the well-known Atelier 17 (so denominated in 1933)—a powerhouse of innovatory intaglio printmaking for the next sixty years. It was not based on master–pupil relations but on artists sharing ideas, exploring together the expressive possibilities of gravure. The list of those who worked in Atelier 17 between 1928 and 1939 reads like a roll of honour of artists of the interwar years.

Hayter divided his time equally between painting and printmaking and his output of paintings exceeds that of his prints. Until 1938 he associated with the Surrealists, exhibiting with them in Paris, London, and New York, and assisting in organizing the 1936 Surrealist exhibition in London. His imagery focused on mythological themes, war, and violence. His engraved line, the distinctive 'Hayter whiplash', bristled with aggressive energy.

In 1939 he returned to England and worked on camouflage techniques. Debarred by injury from military service, he went to New York (1940),

establishing Atelier 17 at the New School for
Social Research. The Atelier's exhibition at the
Museum of Modern Art (1944) brought renown.
Its impact on American printmaking was com-
pared with that of the Armory Show on Amer-
ican painting. In 1945 he moved the Atelier to
Greenwich Village. During his decade in New
York, it provided a fertile meeting place for
European expatriates, including Marc Chagall,
Le Corbusier, Max Ernst, André Masson, Joan
Miró, and Yves Tanguy, and American and
émigré artists such as Garo Antreasian, William
Baziotes, Willem de Kooning, Matta, Robert
Motherwell, Jackson Pollock, and Mark Rothko.
As a painter, Hayter was recognized as one of the
founders of abstract expressionism. In 1946 he
perfected a technique of simultaneous multi-
colour printing off a single plate in one passage
through the press (sometimes misnamed 'viscosity printing'), which, evolving under constant
experiment over the years, revolutionized colour
printmaking.

He returned to Paris in 1950 and reopened
Atelier 17, attracting artists from all over the
world and through them exercising worldwide
influence. Prominent themes in his paintings and
prints over the next four decades were gener-
alized depiction of light on water, wave motion,
water currents, the movement of objects in space
or in a fluid medium, and reflections. From 1957
his Surrealist imagery gave way to a quasi-
tachiste style, to be followed in the mid-1960s by
a decade of preoccupation with undulating line
and rhythm. With age his palette became increasingly brilliant, employing fluorescent paints and
inks in vibrant, energetic paintings and prints.
During his last decade figurative elements reap-
peared in his semi-abstract imagery.

Hayter was awarded the Legion of Honour
(1951), and made a chevalier de l'Ordre des Arts
et Lettres (1968) and commandeur des Arts et
Lettres (1986). British recognition came in the
form of an OBE (1959), CBE (1967), and honorary RA (1982). In 1988 the British Museum
purchased 400 prints from him, the largest purchase from a living artist it has ever made.

His books New Ways of Gravure (1949) and
About Prints (1962) reveal his gifts as a writer.
Though he hated to be thought of as a teacher, it
was his dynamic personality and enthusiasm
which made Atelier 17, and his Socratic methods
of awakening ideas which inspired so many of the
young artists who came to work with him. A true
bohemian to the last, Hayter cared little for
material comforts or rewards, but cared passionately for honesty in both art and life, and for
friendship. His generosity to younger artists was
well known. Hayter was a short, slim, and wiry
man of volcanic energy. A shock of blond hair fell
over his forehead. He had bushy eyebrows,
piercing blue eyes, and an aquiline nose. In old

age, his face was heavily lined—a striking face of
great forcefulness, mobile and expressive. His
voice was deep and gravelly.

In 1928 he married Edith Fletcher. They had
one son, who died of tuberculosis in New York in
1946. The marriage was dissolved in 1929 and in
1940 he married the sculptor Helen Phillips,
daughter of Lewis Henry Phillips, director of a
business college. There were two sons of the
marriage, which was dissolved in 1973. In 1974
he married Désirée, daughter of Aloysius Moor-
head, dentist. Hayter died suddenly at his Paris
home, 4 May 1988.

[Stanley William Hayter, New Ways of Gravure, revised
edn., 1981, and About Prints, 1962; P. M. S. Hacker
(ed.), The Renaissance of Gravure: the Art of S. W.
Hayter, 1988; Carla Esposito, Hayter e l'Atelier 17,
1990; personal knowledge.]　　　　P. M. S. HACKER

HELPMANN, SIR Robert Murray (1909–1986),
ballet dancer and choreographer, was born 9
April 1909 in Mount Gambier, South Australia,
the elder son and eldest of three children of
James Murray Helpman (the original spelling), a
rich sheep farmer, and his wife Mary, daughter
of Robert Gardiner, a sea captain in the whaling
business. Helpmann attended Prince Alfred's
College, Adelaide, but his education was marred
by his habitual truancy and his parents finally
withdrew him from the college, engaging a private tutor. This gave Helpmann the opportunity
to concentrate on his two passions, dancing and
acting; even at this early age he described himself
as 'the complete show-off'.

His appearance was certainly unusual. His
head was large, with a bulging forehead and
wide, protruding eyes: beneath a normally
shaped nose an exceptionally long upper lip
culminated in a small, thin mouth which revealed
many long, rather alarming teeth. Narrow shoulders, a large diaphragm, and thin, unmuscular
legs completed an image which he later used to
great effect in character roles, both balletic and
dramatic. Romantic performances were less successful and, in modern dress, he seemed too
fantastic to be believable. He added the final 'n'
to Helpman to avoid having a name of thirteen
letters for his theatrical career.

His first engagement was as a student-dancer
on the 1921 Australian tour by the company run
by Anna *Pavlova. He then appeared in J. C.
Williamson's productions of musicals and revues
until 1927. In pantomime in 1931 he was seen
and admired by the English actress, Margaret
Rawlings, then touring Australia. He joined her
company in New Zealand and sailed with her for
England in 1932.

Margaret Rawlings introduced Helpmann to
(Dame) Ninette de Valois, director of the
recently formed Vic-Wells (later Sadler's Wells)

Ballet. Intrigued by his appearance rather than his ability as a dancer, she employed him and, in 1933, he replaced (Sir) Anton *Dolin as Satan in de Valois' barefoot masque-ballet, *Job*. He created his first role in *The Haunted Ballroom* in 1934 and, in the following year, gave the first of many outstanding performances as the Rake in *The Rake's Progress*. In 1937, while forming his long partnership with the young ballerina, (Dame) Margot Fonteyn, he created another superb characterization as the old Red King in *Checkmate*.

These four de Valois ballets—and a fifth, *The Prospect Before Us* (1940), in which he played a wonderfully drunken stage manager—gave Helpmann the best roles of his career. His classical technique was barely adequate and none was required; all dancing and movement was in character, tragic or comic, and his superlative talent for mime was given full rein. No other actor-dancer matched him in this field.

His restlessness and determination for wider horizons took him to the Old Vic in 1937 to play Oberon in *A Midsummer Night's Dream*, his first essay into the English dramatic theatre. His light tenor voice had neither range nor power but his exotic appearance in this supernatural role was a success. He returned to the ballet and, while touring, met an Oxford undergraduate, Michael Pickersgill Benthall (died 1974). Helpmann, a flamboyant homosexual, made a lifelong companion of Benthall, who became a leading stage director and a major contributor to their partnership. He was the son of Sir Edward Charles Benthall, director of the Reserve Bank of India.

Leading the Sadler's Wells Company, Helpmann branched out into choreography. It was unsurprising that his few classically based ballets were pallid and derivative while his dramatic, character works were of genuine substance. Most notable were *Hamlet* in 1942 and *Miracle in the Gorbals* in 1944. In these, and in his future stage direction, he was guided by the taste and expert advice of Benthall. In 1950 Ninette de Valois, who had been fortunate to have Helpmann in her company in World War II because, as an Australian, he was unavailable for call-up into the armed services, gave Helpmann another perfect role for his talents in her ballet, *Don Quixote*. On an American tour later that year he resigned, abruptly and inexplicably, from the company.

Turning to the dramatic theatre, Helpmann played Hamlet, King John, Shylock, and Richard III at Stratford and the Old Vic; he appeared with Sir Laurence (later Baron) *Olivier and his wife Vivien *Leigh in the George Bernard *Shaw and *Shakespeare *Cleopatra*s in 1951 and with Katharine Hepburn in *The Millionairess* in 1952. He played supporting roles in films, including Olivier's *Henry V* (1944), *The Red Shoes* (in which he also choreographed the ballet

sequence, 1948), and *The Tales of Hoffmann* (1951). He directed *The Tempest* and *Murder in the Cathedral* (1953) at the Old Vic; *Madame Butterfly* (1950) and *Le Coq d'Or* (1956) at Covent Garden, and a number of plays, musicals, and pantomimes.

He returned to Australia to tour with the Oliviers and, later, with Katharine Hepburn. This experience was so successful and enjoyable that he decided, in 1962, to live many months of each year in his own country, visiting London less and less frequently. In 1965 he joined (Dame) Peggy van Praagh as an artistic director of the Australian Ballet and choreographed four productions for the company. His energy remaining undiminished, he acted in several Australian films and directed plays and musicals in New York and London. His last success was a production of Franz Lehár's *The Merry Widow* as a ballet at the Sydney Opera House in 1975.

Helpmann was the most theatrical of performers both on and off stage. He held court, always the centre of attention, and was considered a wit by close colleagues. Many found him amusing but not witty; his humour was always sharply malicious, at the expense of others, and, perhaps because of this, he evoked more wariness than affection. He was neither a great actor nor a great dancer, but he brought a singular and effective presence to the theatre, particularly the ballet stage. He was appointed CBE in 1964 and knighted in 1968. He died in the Royal North Shore Hospital, Sydney, 28 September 1986.

[D. C. Abrahams, *Robert Helpmann, Choreographer*, 1943; Anthony Gordon, *Robert Helpmann*, 1946; Kathrine S. Walker, *Robert Helpmann*, 1957; Elizabeth Salter, *Helpmann*, 1978; personal knowledge.]

MOIRA SHEARER

HEWITT, John Harold (1907–1987), poet, was born in Belfast 28 October 1907, the younger child and only son of Robert Telford Hewitt, principal of Agnes Street National School, and his wife, Elinor Robinson. He was educated at his father's school (c.1912–19), the Royal Belfast Academical Institution (1919–20), and the Methodist College, Belfast (1920–4). In 1924 he entered the Queen's University, Belfast, to read English and graduated in 1930 with a BA degree, having also (in 1927–9) taken a teacher training course at Stranmillis College, Belfast.

Hewitt's lifelong engagement with literature, art, and politics was fostered from the start by his parents, particularly by his father, a dedicated socialist. It was on his father's bookshelves that he discovered the English dissenting tradition which decisively influenced his political and literary development, as well as the magazines which stimulated his love of art. He wrote his first poems in 1924 and his earliest to appear in print were contributed (in 1928–9) to a wide variety of left-wing newspapers.

In November 1930 Hewitt was appointed art assistant at the Belfast Museum and Art Gallery. During an exhibition there (probably in autumn 1932) he met Roberta Black (born in Larne, county Antrim, 30 October 1904, the daughter of Robert Black, watchmaker); they were married in Belfast on 7 May 1934. Hewitt's energies found expression throughout the 1930s in a range of cultural activities. In 1934, for example, he helped to form the Ulster Unit, a progressive art group, and in 1937 he was involved in the founding of the *Irish Democrat* newspaper, acting as literary editor and occasional contributor. In 1936 he finished 'The Bloody Brae: a Dramatic Poem', his first extended treatment of the troubled relationship between English and Scottish planters and native Irish in the north of Ireland, thereafter a major theme in his writings.

During World War II Hewitt's work in the Belfast Museum and Art Gallery significantly broadened what he later described as his 'local imaginative mythology', in particular inspiring a lasting enthusiasm for the radical strain in Ulster Presbyterianism of the later eighteenth century. Hewitt's discovery of his own region, especially the glens of Antrim, made him acutely receptive to the 'regionalist' idea he encountered at this time in the works of Lewis Mumford and others.

Throughout the 1930s and 1940s Hewitt wrote numerous poems, publishing many in periodicals, and transcribing many more in his notebooks. He issued his first pamphlet of poems, *Conacre*, in 1943 and his second, *Compass: Two Poems*, in 1944, both privately published, and his first book-length collection, *No Rebel Word*, was published in 1948. Another key work of the period was the long autobiographical, 'regionalist' poem 'Freehold', which appeared in the literary magazine *Lagan* in 1946. In this and other poems he emerges as the liberal Ulsterman of planter stock searching for equilibrium and an abiding place in a province where his forebears were originally interlopers, and as the city-dweller whose spiritual home is the country, however marginalized he may sometimes feel there.

Having been promoted, in 1950, to deputy director and keeper of art at the Belfast Museum and Art Gallery, Hewitt had high hopes of being appointed director when the incumbent retired, but in 1953 he failed to gain this appointment, almost certainly because his radical and socialist ideals were unacceptable to the Belfast Unionist establishment. He remained as deputy director for four more years, then applied successfully for the directorship of the Herbert Art Gallery and Museum in Coventry, a post he held from 1957 to 1972. Coventry, recovering from the devastat-

ing air raids of 1940 and 1941, offered an exciting challenge to a man of his energies and ideals, though he maintained close contact with the north of Ireland. He travelled extensively during this period and shortly before his retirement his *Collected Poems 1932–1967* (1968) and *The Day of the Corncrake: Poems of the Nine Glens* (1969) were published.

He and Roberta returned to Belfast in 1972 at a time of violent unrest but also unprecedented creativity in Ulster, especially in the field of poetry. He produced new work as poet and art historian, salvaged and revised several decades of verse from his notebooks, published books more frequently than at any other time in his life, and enjoyed a degree of recognition and homage previously denied him. The bearded, silver-haired poet, who wore glasses, smoked a pipe, and carried a walking-stick, became a familiar figure at cultural gatherings in Belfast. Roberta Hewitt died 19 October 1975. The following year Hewitt became the first writer-in-residence at the Queen's University, Belfast, serving until 1979, and in 1983 he was made a freeman of Belfast.

He died 27 June 1987 in hospital in Belfast and in 1988 the John Hewitt international summer school was established in his memory.

[Tom Clyde (ed.), *Ancestral Voices: the Selected Prose of John Hewitt*, 1987; Frank Ormsby (ed.), *The Collected Poems of John Hewitt*, 1991; Gerald Dawe and John Wilson Foster (eds.), *The Poet's Place: Essays in Honour of John Hewitt*, 1991.]   FRANK ORMSBY

HEY, Donald Holroyde (1904–1987), organic chemist, was born in Swansea 2 September 1904, the second of three sons (there were no daughters) of Arthur Hey, FRCO, LRAM, professional musician, who had gone to Swansea from Yorkshire in 1888 to become organist at St James's church, and his wife, Frances Jane Baynham, from an established Swansea family. Donald Hey was brought up in a cultured home, where he gained his lifelong love of music. He played the piano and organ and was a chorister, winning a choral scholarship to Magdalen College School, Oxford. Since the school was a traditional classical establishment, with little opportunity to study science beyond school certificate, he thereafter taught himself. Such was his determination that he enrolled for the intermediate London science course while still at school. Because family finances did not allow him to go to Oxford University, he opted for the new college at Swansea. In 1924 he obtained a B.Sc. pass as an external student of London University. A first-class degree in chemistry followed in 1926 when, remarkably, he published his first scientific paper and sold his invention of a new type of chemical indicator to Imperial Chemical Industries. This was before he had even begun research for his Ph.D., which he gained in 1928.

Hey began his academic career in 1928 in the University of Manchester, as a temporary assistant lecturer. He was promoted to lecturer in 1930, with a three-year contract. In 1930 W. S. M. Grieve became his first research student. Out of their collaboration came one of two papers on the reactions of what Hey called phenyl radicals with benzene derivatives to give biphenyls. Up until then all chemical reactions in solution were assumed to involve positively charged (2-electron deficient) or negatively charged (2-electron rich) species. Grieve and Hey put forward the bold suggestion that in their reactions a third species, hitherto unsuspected, was involved—an electrically neutral phenyl radical carrying *one* unpaired electron. This was received with disbelief and ridicule, which persisted until 1948 in some quarters. The foremost British organic chemist, (Sir) Robert *Robinson, examined Grieve for his Ph.D. and remained unconvinced. Hey as sole author published his famous paper on the reactions of dibenzoyl peroxide in the *Journal of the Chemical Society*, part ii, 1934.

It was typical of Hey that he was prepared to take the offensive rather than retreat. In this he had an ally in W. A. *Waters at Durham and, later, Oxford. Waters was attracted by Hey's paper and looked at his own work in its light. In 1937 they co-authored one of the great reviews in chemistry—'Some Organic Reactions Involving the Occurrence of Free Radicals in Solution'—in which they postulated for the first time that a very large number of known chemical reactions proceeded via free radicals. They ended their review with an extraordinarily perceptive understatement: 'there may exist also several other reactions in organic chemistry in which transient free neutral radicals intervene' (*Chemical Review*, vol. xxi, 1937).

The study of free radicals henceforth dominated Hey's research career. He was a lecturer in chemistry at Manchester University from 1930 to 1938, and at Imperial College, London, from 1939 to 1941. In 1941 he became director of the British Research Institute, where he directed drug research. He was University professor of chemistry at King's College, London, from 1945 to 1950, when he became Daniell professor of chemistry, University of London, until his retirement in 1971.

By 1955 the importance of free radicals was universally accepted, critics disappeared or were silenced, and Hey was elected a fellow of the Royal Society. Then followed a period of remarkable administrative success, characterized by his inspired choice of supporting colleagues. His department at King's was small, with some fourteen staff, but in the 1960s six of his younger colleagues gained chairs in other departments and more were to follow in the period to his retirement. He did not shirk his responsibilities in the day-to-day operation of the college and the University of London. He served in every academic position, including that of assistant principal of the college and, as a devout Anglican, was particularly concerned with theological activities.

He became a fellow of Imperial College in 1968 and an honorary fellow of the Intra-Science Research Foundation (1971), Chelsea College (1973), and University College, Swansea (1986). The University of Wales gave him an honorary D.Sc. in 1970. As the first to publish experimental evidence for the existence of reactive free radicals (molecular species carrying an unpaired electron—the source of high unselective reactivity), Hey made a truly seminal contribution to science. His demonstration, and recognition, in 1934 that dibenzoyl peroxide decomposes in solution via phenyl radicals was the very genesis of the vast compass and knowledge of free radical chemistry, biochemistry, and biological processes.

Hey used to muse ruefully in his later years that if only he had realized the commercial implications of his discovery he could have become a rich man, but the success of his pupils and colleagues was the only reward he sought. His face had an unassuming expression; he was an accomplished pianist and organist. He kept his academic and home lives quite separate, and liked a simple way of life. He was a keen gardener, who loved Wales, family life, and family holidays. He was an unselfish, gentle, and modest scholar, with a great desire to help others. In 1931 he married a botanist, Jessie (died 1982), daughter of Thomas Jones, chemist. They had a son and a daughter. Hey died 21 January 1987 in Reigate, Surrey.

[J. I. G. Cadogan and D. I. Davies in *Biographical Memoirs of Fellows of the Royal Society*, vol. xxxiv, 1988; personal knowledge.]   JOHN CADOGAN

HICKS, SIR John Richard (1904–1989), economist and Nobel prize-winner, was born in Warwick 8 April 1904, the eldest of three children and only son of Edward Hicks, editor and part-proprietor of the *Warwick and Leamington Spa Courier*, of Leamington Spa, and his wife, Dorothy Catherine Stephens, who was one of five children of a Nonconformist minister. There was an intellectual tradition on both sides of his family, particularly that of his mother, where there was a connection with the political scientist Graham *Wallas. Hicks received much intellectual stimulus from the head of his preparatory school, Grey Friars, near Leamington—more stimulus, probably, than he received from his public school, Clifton College. None the less he acquitted himself perfectly adequately at Clifton, and in 1922 won a scholarship to Balliol College, Oxford, to study mathematics, in which he gained a first in moderations in 1923. His undergraduate contemporaries realized that his abilities were something out of the ordinary, as did his tutors. But he was not well taught, at least on the economics side of the new philosophy, politics, and economics school (to which he moved at the end of his first year). Something went seriously wrong with his performance in his final examinations, in which he obtained a second class (1925). His failure to get a first came as a serious set-back, and he was unsuccessful too in the All Souls fellowship examination.

He tried for some months to follow his father's profession as a journalist, on the *Manchester Guardian*; but that was not congenial. In 1927 he obtained a B.Litt. (under the supervision, surprisingly, of G. D. H. *Cole). He then made the decisive step in his life: in 1926 he moved to a teaching position at the London School of Economics, as a lecturer. His years there were the most important ones in his intellectual development. Hicks was the most eminent economic theorist of his generation in Britain. He was an economist's economist, much less well known to politicians and civil servants and to the general public than many other economists esteemed far less highly by their peers. Primarily, he was a conceptualizer. Concepts that he introduced were later used every day by economists who had almost forgotten their origin: income-effect/substitution-effect, 'Hicks-neutral' technical progress, the portfolio approach to the demand for money, 'fix-price/flex-price', and a host of others. He was not an ivory-tower economist: he believed the purpose of economic theory was to be useful. But he himself was more a toolmaker than a tool-user. His contribution did not lie in establishing specific empirical conclusions or policy recommendations. The book of his that came nearest to seeking to establish a definite conclusion was something of a *jeu d'esprit*, *A Theory of Economic History* (1969).

There is no school of Hicksian economics, although Hicks did have in his own mind a consistent system of thought, which evolved over the years, but which already by the time of the publication of *Value and Capital* (1939)—his most important book—was reasonably comprehensive in its scope. Hicks might, perhaps, have found congenial the genre of an earlier epoch: the comprehensive treatise, revised through several editions. As it was, he was unusual among modern economic theorists in putting forward many of his chief ideas in books, nearly twenty of them, ranging over almost the whole of economic theory, rather than in articles, though his collected articles also amounted to three substantial volumes. Among his articles were 'Mr Keynes and the Classic' (*Econometrica*, 1937), which

shaped economists' understanding of the Keynesian system for decades to come, and 'A Suggestion for Simplifying the Theory of Money' (*Economica*, 1935), which anticipated part of that system.

It may be conjectured that Hicks's approach was affected by the nearly complete *tabula rasa* that he brought to the LSE as a result of the weakness of his economic education in Oxford. He felt that he had to work things out for himself, almost from first principles, into his own consistent system of thought. That is not to say that his system of thought did not owe much to the great economists of the past—continental rather than British. The ideas of his contemporaries were also grist to his mill; but their status was no higher than that. 'I could not understand what others were doing,' he said, 'unless I could re-state it in my own terms.' His writings give an occasional impression of vanity. But the vanity was not for himself but on behalf of his work.

Hicks's later work continued to attract very serious attention. But with the vast proliferation in the literature of the subject, it inevitably seemed less innovative than what he had done in the golden years at the LSE. In addition, although the contemporary development of economic theory took its impetus in no small part from *Value and Capital*, he was out of sympathy with much of it. 'I have disappointed them,' he wrote, about his successors, largely American. 'I have felt little sympathy with the theory for theory's sake, which has been characteristic of one strand of American economics; nor with the idealisation of the free market, which has been characteristic of another; and I have little faith in the econometrics on which they have largely relied to make their contact with reality.'

At the LSE, but not later, Hicks worked in close association with others of his own age and standing—(Sir) R. G. D. Allen, Nicholas (later Baron) *Kaldor, A. P. Lerner, and several others, as well as the more senior Friedrich von Hayek. In later years he gave encouragement and discerning help to his graduate students, relatively few in number. They came mainly from overseas, particularly Italy.

Hicks left the LSE in 1935 to go to Cambridge as a university lecturer and fellow of Gonville and Caius College. In Cambridge (Sir) Dennis *Robertson became a good friend, and so remained till Robertson's death. But unfortunately the already powerful Keynesian school in the faculty made clear that it had room for only one god in the pantheon of economic theory: they were not interested in what Hicks was doing. So Hicks was glad to take the chair of political economy in Manchester in 1938, where he stayed till 1946. A fellowship (1946–58) in the newly established Nuffield College in Oxford then offered an attractive opportunity, with fewer administrative responsibilities. The LSE may have been the place that left its strongest intellectual imprint, but Oxford was where by far the largest part of his long life was spent. He moved to All Souls as Drummond professor of political economy in 1952, a post he held until 1965. In all he was a fellow of All Souls for thirty-five years. He was greatly devoted to the college. He was a very active delegate of the Oxford University Press.

Hicks received innumerable academic honours, in addition to his fellowship of the British Academy (1942) and his knighthood (1964). He was the first British scholar to win the Nobel prize in economics (1972); he gave the proceeds to the appeal then in progress for the new LSE library. He was an honorary fellow of the LSE (1969) and of Gonville and Caius (1971).

In 1935 he married an assistant lecturer at the LSE, Ursula Kathleen, the daughter of William Fisher Webb, solicitor, of Dublin. For the rest of his life, until her death in 1985, they were seldom separated, even for a few days. Their marriage was unusual by conventional standards and there were no children. Their characters were entirely unalike: he was shy, she was outgoing; she was direct, he was subtle. But she protected him and organized their lives; and their loyalty to each other was unswerving. They were both obsessive travellers. Hicks died suddenly, of a heart attack, 20 May 1989 in the house at Blockley, Worcestershire, which had been his principal home for many years.

[Dieter Helm (ed.), *The Economics of John Hicks*, 1984; private information; personal knowledge.]

R. C. O. MATTHEWS

HILL, CHARLES, BARON HILL OF LUTON (1904–1989), doctor, politician, and broadcaster, was born in Islington 15 January 1904, the youngest in the family of two sons and a daughter of Charles Hill, maker of pianoforte parts, who died in 1906, and his wife, Florence Madeleine Cook, bookkeeper, the seventh of eight children of a seller of mineral water. His mother remarried in 1916, her husband being W. E. Hulme, linotype operator in the *Morning Post*. Educated at St Olave's School, Tower Bridge, Hill was awarded a Drapers' Company scholarship and a sizarship at Trinity College, Cambridge, in 1921, and went on to read in parallel both medicine and part i of the natural sciences tripos, in which he received first-class honours in 1925. He completed his medical education at the London Hospital, obtaining his MRCS, LRCP in 1927 and MB, B.Chir. in 1929. He then took up a hospital post in Nottingham and became deputy medical officer of health in Oxford in 1930. He obtained his DPH in 1931. Determined and ambitious and more interested in administration than in medical practice, Hill was appointed

an assistant secretary of the British Medical Association in 1932. He stayed at the BMA headquarters in Tavistock Square for the next eighteen years (gaining his MD in 1936), climbing a ladder which took him to the top rung, when in 1944 he achieved the position of secretary, the senior full-time officer post, which he held until 1950.

Convinced of the importance of winning public support to buttress the BMA's cause, Hill had by 1944 become one of the best known figures in the country in his own right, though not under his own name, after being invited in 1941 to take part in the BBC's *Kitchen Front* programmes. In a remarkable series of wartime broadcasts, mainly given live, which came to cover a wide range of health problems, Hill, giving helpful advice as the 'radio doctor', soon won a huge audience. His rich, warm, and homely—if often booming—voice, so different from most BBC voices even in wartime, contributed to his success as a broadcaster, but did not guarantee it. His secret was careful preparation, meticulous selection of points to emphasize, and intuitive choice of exactly the right words. One of his broadcasts, which deserves the adjective classic, was delivered after the war on Boxing day in 1949. It began 'This is stomach speaking. Yes I mean it, *your* stomach'.

This broadcast was addressed to children. Hill, who in 1931 had married Marion Spencer Wallace, daughter of Moses Wallace, a Halifax mill owner, whom he had met at Cambridge, knew a lot about children. He had two sons and three daughters, and for all his ebullience always gave the reassuring air of being a real family doctor. As secretary of the BMA, he fought hard between 1945 and 1948 to ensure that the new National Health Service would incorporate family choice of doctor and that the profession would not become a state salaried service for general practitioners. Hill revelled in the rough and tumble of contest with Aneurin *Bevan, the minister of health, whose political skills he came greatly to admire, but he could also show patience and forbearance in dealing both with politicians and professional colleagues.

It was through struggles about health policy that Hill was drawn into party politics, which had never interested him at Cambridge, and eventually in 1957 into the cabinet, although his attitude to party was as unorthodox as that of the first Baron *Beaverbrook, the intermediary who arranged for him to be summoned to an interview at the Conservative party Central Office in 1944. Indeed, when Hill first stood (unsuccessfully) for Parliament, for Cambridge University, at the general election of 1945, it was not as a Conservative but as an Independent. When he won Luton at the next general election in 1950, it was as a Conservative *and* Liberal. Hill used his formidable oratorical talents at that election to deliver one of the outstanding controversial political broadcasts before the age of television.

He did not have to wait long for governmental office, and having served from 1951 to 1955 as parliamentary secretary to the Ministry of Food—an unenviable post, for most back-benchers in his party wished to see his ministry abolished—he was made postmaster-general by Sir Anthony *Eden (later the first Earl of Avon) in April 1955, being sworn of the Privy Council at the same time. This post greatly appealed to him, and, surviving Suez, he went on under Harold *Macmillan (later the first Earl of Stockton) to become chancellor of the Duchy of Lancaster in January 1957. His responsibilities for supervising government information services straddled these last two posts. Finally, Macmillan made him minister of housing and local government in October 1961, before removing him in his sudden, and to Hill premature, government reshuffle in July 1962. In any event Hill would have retired at the next election.

A new career now began, first in business and then in broadcasting. He was so successful a chairman of the Independent Television Authority, a post to which he was appointed in 1963, refurbishing its image and presiding over the recasting of the TV company structure, that a Labour prime minister, Harold Wilson (later Baron Wilson of Rievaulx), moved him from Brompton Road to become chairman of the BBC in 1967. This was a highly controversial move much resented in the BBC, particularly by Sir Hugh *Greene, the director-general, and Hill's first years there were difficult. But he outlasted Greene, and had his tenure extended in 1972 in order to preside over the BBC's golden jubilee. Hill was a strong and effective supporter of BBC autonomy.

Hill was made a life peer in 1963 and awarded an LL D by Saskatchewan University in 1950. He kept a diary during his years as chairman of the BBC and wrote two volumes of compact and readable memoirs, *Both Sides of the Hill* (1964) and *Behind the Screen* (1974). His only other published work, a joint one, was *What Is Osteopathy?* (1937). His appearance was as memorable as his voice. Short, plump, and brimful of energy, he was a favourite of cartoonists. He died in Harpenden 22 August 1989.

[Charles Hill, *Both Sides of the Hill*, 1964, and *Behind the Screen*, 1974; personal knowledge.] ASA BRIGGS

HIMMELWEIT, Hildegard Therese (1918–1989), professor of social psychology, was born 20 February 1918 in Berlin, Germany, the younger child and only daughter of Dr Siegfried Litthauer, chemist and industrialist, and his wife, Feodore Remak. Culturally and materially this Jewish family was of high standing. 'Hilde'

was proud of her great-grandfather, the first Jew to become a professor at a German university, though he had refused to be baptized. Her lifelong identification with Jewishness was based on the family's origin, not on Judaism as a religion; it was only strengthened by the advent of Adolf Hitler. A few days before her death she reminded a non-Jewish friend to bring a hat to her Jewish funeral.

It was the custom in well-to-do German families to send children abroad to finish their secondary education. Hers began in Berlin and continued from 1934 at the Hayes Court School, Kent; she returned to Germany during the holidays. Her father died in 1935; her mother emigrated to England in 1938. At Newnham College, Cambridge, she obtained a second class (division II) in part i of the economics tripos (1938) and a first in part ii of the medieval and modern languages tripos (1940). Two years later she earned another first-class degree in psychology at Cambridge. She qualified as an educational and clinical psychologist in 1943 and in 1945 she obtained a Ph.D. in psychology from the University of London.

Her first job was at the Maudsley Hospital (1945–8). During these years her professional identity as a social psychologist began to emerge. The transition from one culture to another, the experience of the war years and their aftermath, the fate of the Jews, and the fate of Germany predisposed her to emphasize in her professional work the impact of social conditions and political events on psychological phenomena. In 1949 she was appointed a lecturer at the London School of Economics, becoming a reader in 1954 and a professor in 1964.

Her first major contribution to the understanding of the contemporary world came when she was director of the Nuffield television enquiry (1954–8). Her resulting book (with A. N. Oppenheim and P. Vince), *Television and the Child* (1958), established her reputation in Europe and the United States; it also led to some heated discussions between her and some television personalities, who regarded empirical evidence as superfluous. That she exposed herself to such encounters was typical of her style of work: her studies were invariably meant for two audiences, the research community and policy-makers, even recalcitrant ones. Accordingly she spent much time and energy in giving research-based advice in formal and informal settings. From 1969 to 1974 she chaired the academic advisory committee of the Open University and from 1974 to 1977 she was a member of the committee on the future of broadcasting chaired by Baron Annan.

The second major aspect of her work was political psychology. With a team of gifted collaborators she followed a sample of young people for fifteen years, during which there were six general elections, to illuminate the process of decision-making by voters. Here again the resulting publications were intended for both researchers and politicians. Hitting two targets with one stone was, she realized, a difficult task. She agonized about how to combine her meticulous attention to the technical aspects of her work with readability. Her greatest satisfaction came not from writing the reports but from presenting the results personally and directly to potential users, and here she excelled.

As her international reputation grew she was invited to be a visiting professor and fellow at universities and institutes abroad. In 1981 she was given the Nevitt Sanford award for achievements in social psychology. She was also elected vice-president of the International Society for Political Psychology (1978–81). The distinction that pleased her most was an honorary doctorate from the Open University (1976). She was active in the British Psychological Society and on a committee of the Social Science Research Council.

Her friends enjoyed in equal measure her engaging personality, her mind, and her beauty, which she retained to the end of her life. Early in her career she may have had to prove to herself and others that there was more to her than met the eye. In her maturity she carried her beauty unselfconsciously, with grace and dignity, and had an unobtrusive elegance in dress. In 1940 she married Dr Freddy Himmelweit (died 1977), virologist. He came from a South African family, his father, Felix Himmelweit, being a businessman. They had one daughter. Hilde Himmelweit died of cancer 15 March 1989 at her home in Hampstead, London.

[Private information; personal knowledge.]

MARIE JAHODA

HOLTTUM, (Richard) Eric (1895–1990), botanist, was born 20 July 1895 in Linton, Cambridgeshire, the eldest in the family of two sons and one daughter of Richard Holttum, grocer and owner of a village general store, and his wife, Florence Bradley. His parents being Quakers, he was educated at the Friends' School, Saffron Walden, and then at Bootham School, York. He wrote in 1980 that his Quaker schooling 'conveyed a sense of responsibility and of respect for other people based on some appreciation of the spiritual basis of all living'. His long life of public service and research had that foundation. In 1914 he entered St John's College, Cambridge, with a scholarship to study botany, physics, and chemistry. He obtained a first class in part i of the natural sciences tripos in 1916. The horror of the 1914–18 world war led him to join in 1916 the

Friends Ambulance Unit, in which he served with the French army on the western front. In 1919 he received the croix de guerre. He returned to Cambridge, gaining first-class honours in part ii of the tripos (botany) (1920) and was awarded the university's Frank Smart prize.

In 1920 Professor Albert C. *Seward appointed Holttum as his assistant and as a junior demonstrator in botany at Cambridge, and together they went to Greenland in 1921 to investigate in fossil deposits its former tropical flora. Holttum was appointed assistant director of the botanic gardens, Singapore, in 1922. The Singapore herbarium was in a chaotic state and the general state of fern taxonomy was likewise unsatisfactory, with current classifications inconsistent, genera ill-defined, and specific descriptions inadequate. Holttum's research to remedy this led to his extensive fundamental pteridological publications. In 1925 he became director of the Singapore botanic gardens. An indefatigable field botanist, he was also a far-sighted, energetic administrator, intent both on botanical investigation and the encouragement of gardening in Malaya. Holttum used the method of raising orchid seedlings on nutrient media in glass test-tubes and flasks to raise new orchid hybrids. Out of his enterprise grew the important orchid-growing industry of Malaya.

After the Japanese conquest of Singapore in July 1942, Holttum's fate and that of the Singapore botanic garden was determined by Emperor Hirohito's instruction that such scientific institutions be maintained. Professor Hidezo Tanakadate ordered Holttum and the assistant director to continue their work. Later in 1942 Professor Kwan Koriba took over the administration. He treated Holttum 'with much kindness', as Holttum gratefully acknowledged, and for the next three years encouraged his scientific research on orchids, gingers, ferns, and bamboos, for which he previously had had too little time. Conscious, however, of the hardships of internees while he himself was exceptionally privileged, Holttum requested to be interned also, but Koriba ordered him to continue with research. Nevertheless his isolation caused him acute mental distress, near to utter despair.

After the Japanese surrender in September 1945 Holttum returned to England to recuperate. He then resumed direction of the neglected Singapore botanic garden, resigning in 1949 to become the first professor of botany in the newly founded University of Singapore, where he proved to be an enthusiastic and inspiring teacher. Never wasting time, he published *Plant Life in Malaya* (1954), *Gardening in the Lowlands of Malaya* (1953), and *Orchids of Malaya* (1953). With his department established and thriving,

Holttum retired in 1954, returned to England, settled at Kew, and worked in the herbarium of the Royal Botanic Gardens, Kew, principally on tropical ferns, until his death. His *Ferns of Malaya* (1955) was the prelude to major work on the ferns of Malaya, Indonesia, New Guinea, and the Philippines for the *Flora Malesiana* (section Pteridophyta). About 110 of his 500 or more publications on botany and horticulture relate to ferns, and all manifest his meticulous attention to detail, originality, and breadth of outlook.

Holttum was awarded a Cambridge Sc.D. (1951), and an honorary D.Sc. by Singapore (1954), the Victoria medal of honour of the Royal Horticultural Society (1972), the gold medal of the American Orchid Society (1963), and the gold medal of the Linnean Society of London (1964). The University of Malaya, which gave him an honorary D.Sc. in 1949, awards an Eric Holttum medal to an outstanding student of botany. At least twenty-three botanical specific names with the epithet *holttumi* or *holttumianus* commemorate him.

A lifelong member of the Society of Friends (Quakers), Holttum joined the Society's Brentford and Isleworth meeting in 1955. His spoken ministry there had its background in an extensive acquaintance with religious and philosophical literature, deep spiritual insight, and much thought. He published in 1975 *A Personal Christology* (reprinted 1995). His religious views also found expression in Quaker magazines and journals. From 1962 onwards he became increasingly deaf, and was ultimately completely deaf, although his eyesight, patience, and intellect remained unimpaired to the end. He had a modest, unassuming manner, and was helpful to all. Physically he was short and sparse in build, with sharp and alert features, a high forehead, and one-time ginger hair. In 1927 he married an artist, Ursula (died 1987), daughter of John William Massey, gentleman farmer at Finchingfield, Essex. They had two daughters. Holttum died from pneumonia 18 September 1990 in Queen Mary's Hospital, Roehampton.

[*Flora Malesiana Bulletin*, vol. xxx, 1975, pp. 2477–500 (autobiography and list of publications); *Kew Bulletin*, vol. xli, 1986, pp. 484–9; *The Friend*, 25 January 1991; W. T. Stearn in *Linnean*, vol. vii, no. 3, 1991; private information; personal knowledge.]

WILLIAM T. STEARN

HOPKINS, SIR Frank Henry Edward (1910–1990), admiral, was born 23 June 1910 at The Poplars, Maldon Road, Wallington, Surrey, the fourth child and only son of Edward Frank Lumley Hopkins, solicitor, and his wife, Sybil Mary Walrond. He was educated at the Nautical College at Pangbourne and joined the Royal Navy as a cadet on 16 September 1927. He served as a midshipman in the cruiser *London*, and then in destroyers before qualifying as an observer in 1934, flying from the aircraft-carriers *Furious* and *Courageous*. When war broke out in 1939, he was on the staff of HMS *Peregrine*, the naval observer school at Ford in Sussex. In 1940 he joined No. 826 naval air squadron, flying Fairey Albacores, covering the Dunkirk evacuation, bombing rail and road communications in Holland, and attacking enemy shipping off Zeebrugge, before operating for five months with RAF Coastal Command, making night attacks against targets in France, Belgium, and Holland. Hopkins was awarded the DSC in 1941.

In November 1940 his squadron embarked in the aircraft-carrier *Formidable* and sailed for the Mediterranean. On 28 March 1941 No. 826's aircraft made two torpedo attacks on ships of the Italian fleet off Cape Matapan. In a dusk attack, No. 826's aircraft torpedoed and crippled the heavy cruiser *Pola*. This led to a night action in which *Pola* and two more heavy cruisers, *Fiume* and *Zara*, were sunk with considerable loss of life. Hopkins was mentioned in dispatches (1941). On 6 December 1941 Hopkins took command of No. 830 naval air squadron, which flew Fairey Swordfish from Malta. Night after night he led his squadron on torpedo and bombing strikes which sank thousands of tons of Axis shipping, seriously affecting supplies to Rommel's army in North Africa.

Late in January 1942 Hopkins led a striking force through a gale to search for a large enemy convoy on its way to Tripoli. By the time the planes found the convoy they were too short of fuel to attack so they returned to Malta, refuelled, took off again, found the convoy a second time, and sank a 13,000-ton troop-ship. When Hopkins landed at Hal Far, the naval air station in Malta, just after dawn, he had been in the air for more than twelve hours in flying conditions normally considered impossible. He received an immediate DSO (1942), an award which his squadron thought by no means over-generous.

Hopkins then joined the staff of the British Air Commission in Washington DC, and he qualified as a pilot in 1944. As British naval air observer with the US Pacific Fleet, serving in the American carriers USS *Hancock* and *Intrepid*, he was present at the decisive defeat of the Japanese navy in the battle of Leyte Gulf in October 1944. In 1945 he went to the RN Staff College for two years on the directing staff. He went to Washington again in 1947, for two years as assistant naval air attaché. He was awarded the US Legion of Merit in 1948.

In 1949 he joined the light fleet aircraft-carrier *Theseus* as commander (air) and served in her in the Korean war from October 1950 until April 1951. Under Hopkins, *Theseus*'s air group was particularly energetic and successful in operations over Korea and in 1950 it won the Boyd trophy, awarded annually for the most outstanding feat of airmanship. Hopkins was again mentioned in dispatches (1950).

From 1951 to 1958 he was at the Admiralty as deputy director, naval air organization and training; was captain (D) of the No. 2 training squadron, commanding the destroyer *Myngs*; and was at the Admiralty again as director, naval air warfare. He also recommissioned the carrier *Ark Royal*, after a long and extensive refit, successfully commanding her through a difficult period with new aircraft, radar, and flight deck equipment. He then went to the Britannia Royal Naval College as the first naval aviator and the first public-school entry officer to command the college (1958–60). In 1960 (the year he was promoted rear-admiral) he became flag officer flying training and in 1962 flag officer, aircraft-carriers.

Having become vice-admiral in 1962, in 1963 he was appointed deputy chief of naval staff and fifth sea lord. He now had to fight for the navy's future air power. The RAF set out to destroy plans for the projected new carrier, known as CVA 01, claiming that shore-based aircraft could do all that carrier aircraft could do, and more. When CVA 01 was cancelled in February 1966, the first sea lord and the first lord both resigned. Hopkins wanted to follow suit but was prevailed upon to stay and became commander-in-chief, Portsmouth, which he said was the most miserable appointment of his life. He was promoted to admiral in 1966 and retired from the navy in 1967. He was made commander of the Swedish Order of the Sword in 1954, appointed CB in 1961, and promoted to KCB in 1964.

Hopkins worked his squadron hard, but with his reputation for gallantry and endurance, he could ask anything of his aircrew. He was always introspective, and his experience with No. 830, when he risked his life almost every night, left its mark on him, but he had great personal charm and was an excellent dinner-table companion. He was a keen and expert helmsman and a member of the Royal Yacht Squadron.

Hopkins was a handsome man, even into old age, with sharp features, high cheek-bones, and a keen gaze, quick to sum up a newcomer to ship or squadron. Although the marriage was not registered, in about 1933 he married Joan Mary, née Ashwin (died 1982), widow of Lieutenant-Commander John Standring, RN. They had one daughter. They were divorced in 1937 and in 1939 he married Lois Barbara, daughter of James Robert Cook, of Cheam, Surrey, director of Cook, Hammond & Kell, cartographers and printers. They had no children. Lois died in 1987 and he married in 1988 Georgianna Priest, the widow of an American naval officer he had

met during the war. Hopkins died in Hawaii, after a road accident there, 14 April 1990.

[*Daily Telegraph*, 18 April 1990; squadron records at the Fleet Air Arm Museum, Yeovilton, Somerset; memorial service address by Captain Desmond Vincent-Jones, 26 June 1990; private information; personal knowledge.]   JOHN WINTON

HOPKINSON, SIR (Henry) Thomas (1905–1990), journalist and editor, was born 19 April 1905 in Victoria Park, Manchester, the second child and second son in the family of four sons and one daughter of John Henry Hopkinson (son of Sir Alfred *Hopkinson), lecturer in classical archaeology at the University of Manchester, who soon took holy orders and eventually became archdeacon of Westmorland, and his wife Evelyn Mary, schoolteacher, daughter of the Revd Henry Thomas Fountaine, vicar of Sutton Bridge, Lincolnshire. Hopkinson went to St Edward's School, Oxford, with the financial assistance of a wealthy uncle, Austin Hopkinson, MP, and then won a classical scholarship to Pembroke College, Oxford, where he obtained a second class in classical honour moderations (1925) and a third in *literae humaniores* (1927).

For seven years Hopkinson lived in London by freelance journalism and copywriting in Crawford's advertising agency. After the publication of his first book, *A Strong Hand at the Helm* (1933), an acerbic commentary on the failings of J. Ramsay *MacDonald's government, Hopkinson transferred in 1934 to Odhams Press, where he became assistant editor of the *Clarion*, a weekly that combined cycling news with Labour youth propaganda. In the same year this was incorporated into *Weekly Illustrated*, which Stefan Lorant, a gifted Hungarian refugee, had persuaded Odhams to launch. When in the summer of 1938 Lorant achieved the backing of (Sir) Edward *Hulton in launching *Picture Post*, Hopkinson joined as assistant editor, taking over as editor when Lorant, fearing a German invasion, emigrated to the USA in July 1940. The magazine had been expected to sell 250,000 copies at most; soon it was selling more than 1,500,000 a week.

Lorant was an outstanding photo-journalist and trained Hopkinson to use pictures with equal flair. Hopkinson added a campaigning streak of his own, often contrasting the lives of the rich with the reality of poverty and deprivation, picturing, he hoped, the lives of ordinary people with the eye of a Rembrandt. Hopkinson was an excellent caption writer and always stressed the need for words to reinforce the message of his pictures. He gained the affection and devotion of his staff, displaying an almost donnish approach to their work and a total lack of pretension. His cool professional judgement contrasted with some turbulence in his emotional life, just as a remarkably tidy office contrasted with the turmoil and tension needed to bring out a weekly magazine. His slightly enigmatic personality and ability to adapt to people masked his true political convictions. He certainly attempted to encapsulate the socialist dream of a more just society. As World War II progressed, he paid particular attention to the problems that would arise when peace finally arrived. With a talented team of photographers and reporters, handpicked by Hopkinson, *Picture Post* became immensely influential in setting the mood of the country and may well have made a contribution to the Labour victory in the 1945 election.

Growing tension between Hulton, who was a Conservative, and Hopkinson finally came to a head in October 1950 over a powerful picture story, from photographer Bert Hardy and journalist (M.) James *Cameron, highlighting the appalling plight of so-called political prisoners in Korea, some of them children, under the western-backed regime of Syngman Rhee. Hulton refused to allow the magazine to print it and, with the support of a pliant board including his second wife Nika, sacked Hopkinson. Without his inspired editorship *Picture Post* soon lost its way and was closed in 1957.

After freelancing for a few years Hopkinson joined the *News Chronicle* in 1954. He resigned two years later because he believed the paper was destroying itself. In 1957 he was asked to edit *Drum*, the African picture magazine based in Johannesburg, and he took up the post early in 1958. However, the magazine did not offer quite the same opportunities and eventually he fell out with the proprietor, resigning in 1961, after three and a half years. In March 1963 he launched the International Press Institute's training centre for black journalists in Nairobi, Kenya, staying there as director until 1966. He then moved on to the academic training of journalists, becoming senior fellow in press studies at the University of Sussex (1967–9). Finally, in 1970 he became the first director of the centre for journalism studies at University College, Cardiff, a post he held until 1975. Eventually he became the virtual godfather of photo-journalism and did much to increase the standing of photographers in their profession. Hopkinson was also fairly successful as a writer of short stories and novels. As a writer he was a perfectionist, sometimes staying up all night to find the right word. He was appointed CBE in 1967 and knighted in 1978. He was an honorary fellow of the Royal Photographic Society (1976) and won its silver progress medal (1984), and had an honorary Litt.D. from Wales (1990).

Hopkinson was always beautifully dressed, a neat composed figure with a rather florid face, which gave him the air of a countryman. In 1930 he married Antonia White (died 1980), the novelist, daughter of Cecil George Botting, senior classics master at St Paul's School. She became increasingly unbalanced and they were divorced in 1938. In October 1938 he married Gerti Deutsch, an Austrian photographer, whose father Victor Deutsch was a rope manufacturer. The marriage was dissolved in 1953 and in the same year he married Dorothy, daughter of Thomas Vernon, musician, and widow of Hugh *Kingsmill. Hopkinson had one daughter by his first marriage and two by his second. Towards the end of his life he came to believe in reincarnation. He died of cancer in Oxford, 20 June 1990.

[Thomas Hopkinson, *In the Fiery Continent*, 1962, *Picture Post*, 1970, and *Of This Our Time*, 1982; private information; personal knowledge.]

CHARLES WINTOUR

HOWARD, Trevor Wallace (1913–1988), actor, was born Trevor Wallace Howard-Smith in Cliftonville, Kent, 29 September 1913, the only son and elder child of Arthur John Howard-Smith, who worked as Ceylon representative for Lloyd's of London, and his Canadian wife, Mabel Grey Wallace, nurse. Until he was five he lived in Colombo, but then travelled with his mother until the age of eight, when he was sent to school at Clifton College, Bristol. He was an isolated child and when neither of his parents returned to England holidays were spent either in seaside bed-and-breakfast accommodation or in the home of one of the housemasters. At school Howard was not strongly academic and it was sport that caught his interest, particularly boxing and cricket. The latter became one of the great loves of his life, together with jazz. Towards the end of his school career he started visiting the local theatre, and he left Clifton to become an actor, getting into the Royal Academy of Dramatic Art without any previous stage experience.

His first paid work was in the play *Revolt in a Reformatory* (1934), before he left RADA in 1935 to take small roles. That year he was spotted by a Paramount talent scout but turned down the offer of film work in favour of a career in theatre. This decision seemed justified when, in 1936, he was invited to join the Stratford Memorial Theatre and, in London, given the role of one of the students in *French Without Tears* by (Sir) Terence *Rattigan, which ran for two years. He returned to Stratford in 1939. At the outbreak of war he decided to enlist, but both the army and the Royal Air Force rejected him. However, in 1940, after working at the Colchester repertory theatre, he was called up into the Royal Corps of Signals, Airborne division, becoming a second lieutenant before he was invalided out in 1943.

The stories of Howard's war heroism were fabricated, without his consent, for publicity purposes.

Howard moved back to the theatre in *The Recruiting Officer* (1943). A short part in one of the best British war films, *The Way Ahead* (1944), provided a springboard into cinema. This was followed by *The Way to the Stars* (1945), which led to the role for which Howard became best known, the doctor in *Brief Encounter* (1945), in which his co-star was Celia *Johnson. Directed by (Sir) David Lean, the film won an award at the Cannes festival and considerable critical acclaim for Howard. Next came two successful Frank Launder and Sidney Gilliat thrillers, *I See a Dark Stranger* (1945) and *Green for Danger* (1946), followed by *They Made Me a Fugitive* (1947), in which the roots of British realism in cinema can be traced. In 1947 he was invited by Sir Laurence (later Baron) *Olivier to play Petruchio in an Old Vic production of *The Taming of the Shrew*. Despite *The Times* declaring 'We can remember no better Petruchio', the opportunity of working again with David Lean, in *The Passionate Friends* (1948), drew Howard back to film and, although he had a solid reputation as a theatre actor, his dislike of long runs, and the attractions of travel afforded by film, made him concentrate on cinema from this point.

Howard's film reputation was secured in *The Third Man* (1949). He played the character type with which he became most associated, the British military officer, but his capabilities were stretched by his role in this story of postwar Vienna by Graham Greene. Howard had a certain notoriety as a hell-raiser, based on his drinking capacity. Under the influence of alcohol he could embark on celebrated exploits, one of which led to his arrest in Vienna, for impersonating an officer. Despite his drinking, however, he always remained reliable and professional, never allowing alcohol to affect his work.

During the 1950s, while often eliciting good notices for his work, he frequently appeared in flawed films like *Odette* (1950) and *An Outcast of the Islands* (1951). An exception was *The Heart of the Matter* (1953), another Graham Greene story, in which he produced his best screen performance. Such opportunities were rare even though he shifted into the American market. In 1958 he received the Best Actor award from the British Film Academy for his performance in *The Key*, but this film, too, failed to meet his high standards.

Although *Sons and Lovers* (1960), for which he received an Oscar nomination for his performance as the father, and *Mutiny on the Bounty* (1962), in which he worked with Marlon Brando, enabled him to move away from playing military stereotypes, *Von Ryan's Express* (1965) and *The Long Duel* (1967), with Yul Brynner, saw a return to playing officer figures. Even the role of the pugnacious Cardigan in *The Charge of the Light Brigade* (1968) revisited military territory, and in this uneven yet innovative film Howard gave a fine performance. Working with Brando and Brynner proved frustrating experiences, leaving him with a mistrust of Hollywood. After the 1960s cinema gave him fewer opportunities to display his ability. His performance as the cynical priest in *Ryan's Daughter* (1971) is one of the most memorable in this over-long film, but for much of the 1970s he was increasingly relegated to cameo appearances in films such as *Ludwig* (1973) or disappointing movies such as *Persecution* (1974) and *Conduct Unbecoming* (1975). However, in 1978 he played a choric-narrator figure in *Stevie* with Glenda Jackson, an experience he found satisfying.

In television he began to find more substantial roles. In 1962 he played Lovborg in *Hedda Gabler* with Ingrid Bergman, and in 1963 won an Emmy award as Disraeli in *The Invincible Mr Disraeli*. In the 1970s he was acclaimed for his playing of an abbot in *Catholics* (1973) and in 1975 he received an Emmy nomination for his role as Abbé Faria in a television version of *The Count of Monte Cristo*. The decade ended with him reunited with Celia Johnson, giving a moving performance in the nostalgic *Staying On* (1980), written by Paul *Scott.

The 1980s saw a resurgence of Howard as a film actor. The exhilarating role of a Cheyenne Indian in *Windwalker* (1980) revitalized his acting. However, as was the case with *Sir Henry at Rawlinson End* (1980), a low budget, black and white film, this impressive movie never reached a wide audience. He continued with cameo roles, including Judge Broomfield in *Gandhi* (1982). His final films were *White Mischief* and *The Old Jest*, both released in 1988. Howard did not abandon the theatre altogether in 1947, returning to the stage on occasions, most notably as Lopakhin in *The Cherry Orchard* (1954) and the captain in *The Father* (1964). His last appearance on the British stage was in *Waltz of the Toreadors* in 1974.

Howard made seventy-four films. He embodied the traditional Englishman. His tight-lipped features and quiet, well-bred speaking voice caught the mood of postwar Britain while, in later years, his craggy face and gravelly voice animated the crusty character roles he played. He lacked the looks and physique to be an archetypal male hero, and his tall frame suited military roles. He failed to fulfil his potential, for he rarely played the lead roles he deserved. Supporting some of the most notable names in the world of cinema, he often received the highest critical acclaim.

In 1944 he married an actress, Helen, daughter

of William Cherry, who retired from the army at the end of World War I. They had no children. Howard died 7 January 1988, at Bushey Hospital in Hertfordshire, of bronchitis complicated by jaundice.

[Michael Munn, *Trevor Howard, the Man and his Films*, 1989; Vivienne Knight, *Trevor Howard: a Gentleman and a Player*, 1986; *The Times* and *Guardian*, 8 January 1988; *Observer*, 10 January 1988; private information.]

LIB TAYLOR

HOWARD-SMITH, Trevor Wallace (1913–1988), actor. [See HOWARD, TREVOR WALLACE.]

HOWARTH, Thomas Edward Brodie (1914–1988), schoolmaster and historian, was born 21 October 1914 in Rutherglen, the elder son (there were no daughters) of Frank Fielding Howarth, director of an insurance company, and his wife, Edith Brodie. From Rugby he won a scholarship to Clare College, Cambridge, where he achieved firsts in both parts of the history tripos (1935 and 1936).

His forte was teaching. He taught briefly at Canford, then at Winchester (1938–9), but then came World War II. He enlisted immediately, was commissioned in the King's (Liverpool) Regiment, reaching the rank of brigade-major, and in February 1945 joined the personal staff of Field-Marshal Bernard *Montgomery (later first Viscount Montgomery of Alamein). A significant friendship began. He wrote, 'After the first soul-stripping scrutiny which he [Montgomery] imposed on anybody crossing his path, he was to treat me with consistent kindness and consideration for the next twenty-five years.' He emerged from the war with an MC (1945) and returned to Winchester. In 1948 he was appointed headmaster of King Edward's School, Birmingham. He was instrumental in raising the school's academic standards, but he lacked the patience to deal with an oppressive governing body, and in 1952 was back at Winchester as second master. The accusation that he had run away from an important job stung him.

The second master of Winchester was housemaster of the scholars, who needed a sympathetic and inspiring pastor. Howarth, delighting in the company of intelligent young people, proved just that. One pupil described 'the taut wiry figure, keen eye, broad forehead, listening curled up in his chair, coiled for action with a mind never still, stabbing at words'. Often wit was at a premium, liberally spiced with gossip, and outrageous statements were uttered with a nasal intonation imitated by generations of his pupils, accompanied by great gusts of laughter. It was very exciting to be taught by him, and his courses on the French revolution and nineteenth-century France were particularly memorable.

In 1962 he was appointed high master of St Paul's School. His achievement there was the transplanting of the school from its gaunt Hammersmith setting to a superb site in Barnes. He never pandered to the confused but impassioned values of the 'revolting students' of the late 1960s. He left the detailed management of the school to people with less imagination than himself. He was uninterested in the minutiae of headmastering, preferring a more public life, as a member of the Public Schools Commission (1966) and then, in 1969, chairman of the Headmasters' Conference.

These roles enabled him to assert his views. He wrote that his experiences on the commission 'convinced me that the reformers are determined to sacrifice scholarship and a great many values which I regard as essential to a civilised community on the altar of a totally unattainable egalitarianism'. These values included a passionate commitment to meritocracy, together with active opposition to social élitism, and he expounded them, unfashionable as they were at the time, in a Public Schools Commission minority report.

Howarth left St Paul's in 1973 to become senior tutor of Magdalene College, Cambridge. Here he used his numerous contacts to good effect, lifting the quality while broadening the range of the college's entry. In 1980 he was invited to become headmaster of Campion International School in Athens, and briefed to sort out massive administrative problems. He left it in much better order in 1982, and spent his remaining years in London, enjoying a sociable life and writing copiously.

His published works included *Citizen-King* (1961), a biography of Louis Philippe, his most successful contribution to scholarship; a sharp polemic, *Culture, Anarchy and the Public Schools* (1969); *Cambridge Between Two Wars* (1978), in which he almost unmasked Anthony *Blunt; and *Prospect and Reality, Great Britain 1945–1955* (1985). He also edited a collection of reminiscences, *Monty at Close Quarters* (1985): his own account of his great friend and mentor is brilliantly observed. He was a governor of several schools, including his own old school Rugby, and was an active trustee of the Imperial War Museum (1964–79).

In 1943 he married Margaret, daughter of Norman Teakle, businessman. Sadly his wife became afflicted with mental illness, to a degree that made separation in the early 1960s unavoidable. There were three sons and a daughter of the marriage. The eldest son, Alan, became MP for Stratford-upon-Avon in 1983, serving as a junior minister in Margaret (later Baroness) Thatcher's government.

In an abundant and energetic life, Howarth made his mark as teacher, scholar, soldier, writer, housemaster, headmaster, and bon viveur. Yet he often seemed a solitary figure, rarely relaxed, grieved by the problems of his marriage, and in 1977 by the death from cancer in his twenties of his second son, Peter. He sometimes concealed his consequent unease behind a barrier of intellectual arrogance and less than charitable judgements. Much more often, however, he was a most warm-hearted man, delightful company, exulting in the success of his children, a patient and faithful friend, and a champion of excellence who achieved it himself, most especially as a teacher. He died in London 6 May 1988.

[Private information; personal knowledge.]

PATRICK HUTTON

HULL, SIR Richard Amyatt (1907–1989), field-marshal and chief of the defence staff, was born 7 May 1907 in Cosham, Hampshire, the only son and youngest of three children of Major-General Sir Charles Patrick Amyatt Hull, KCB, late of the Royal Scots Fusiliers, of Beacon Downe, Pinhoe, near Exeter, Devon, and his wife Muriel Helen, daughter of Richard Reid Dobell, businessman, of Beauvoir, Quebec, and Vancouver, Canada. He was educated at Charterhouse and Trinity College, Cambridge, where he took a pass degree. At Cambridge he was a close friend of (Sir) Peter *Scott, the naturalist, and it was there that he began to develop his great interest in wildlife and country sports.

He was commissioned as a university entrant into the 17th/21st Lancers in 1928 and went with the regiment to Egypt in 1930. It was then still horsed. Hull, who in any case lacked the money for expensive mounts, was a competent rather than enthusiastic horseman, but acquired a reputation as a polo umpire. His knowledge of the rules and firmness in applying them were paralleled by the attention to detail, energy, and integrity he showed in his professional life, qualities which underlay his successful career and brought him early promotion to captain and appointment as adjutant when the regiment moved to India in 1933.

He was a student at the Staff College, Quetta, in 1938–9, while the regiment was undergoing mechanization, a change which the forward-looking Hull strongly supported, and then supervised the return home of the regimental families in 1939. His efficiency in so doing brought him an appointment in the staff duties branch of the War Office, and promotion to lieutenant-colonel, but he soon chose to drop a rank and return to the 17th/21st as a squadron leader. He became commanding officer in 1941.

In 1942 he was promoted to colonel and given command of Blade Force, an all-arms group based on the 17th/21st, which had the mission during the North African landings of November 1942 of advancing from Algiers to capture Tunis. The force covered the 350 miles in two days but was thwarted fifteen miles from the city when German reinforcements secured it first. For the dash he had shown and his bravery under fire Hull was appointed to the DSO (1943) and promoted to brigadier to command 12th Infantry and then 26th Armoured brigade during the Tunisian campaign.

After another spell at the War Office, he was promoted to major-general and given command of 1st Armoured division in Italy in 1944. Its role was to outflank the Gothic Line on the Adriatic shore and lead a break-out into the plain of the Po. At Coriano on 5 September, however, its armoured brigade met heavy German resistance and was checked. Controversy surrounds this episode; terrain and weather were on the side of the enemy but Hull has also been criticized for his tactical dispositions.

This did not halt his progress. His formidable abilities as a staff officer had been recognized and, after commanding 5th Infantry division, he embarked on a long ascent of all the key staff appointments, interspersed with several important commands. He was commandant of the Staff College, Camberley (1946–8), director of staff duties, War Office (1948–50), chief army instructor, Imperial Defence College (1950–2), and chief of staff, Middle East Land Forces (1953–4). As lieutenant-general he then succeeded to the command of the British troops in Egypt and supervised the difficult evacuation from the canal zone in 1955–6.

On his return he became deputy chief of the imperial general staff (1956–8) and was at once embroiled in the series of defence reductions, imposed by Britain's shrinking world role and financial difficulties, that were to dominate the rest of his service career. He first chaired a committee whose task was to determine the future size of the army and, though he unsuccessfully opposed the army's reduction to a strength of 165,000, his doubts about its ability to meet its commitments with those numbers were proved right and the figure was later fixed at 185,000. He oversaw the abolition of national service in 1957, and the regimental amalgamations that resulted, but succeeded in sparing several threatened regiments. The shape of the army for the next thirty years was largely determined by his guidance.

Promoted to general in 1958, he was commander-in-chief, Far East Land Forces (1958–61), but then returned to the Ministry of Defence as chief of the imperial general staff (1961–5) ('imperial' was dropped in 1964 and so he was the last CIGS), and then chief of the defence staff (1965–7), in succession to the second holder of that office, the first Earl *Mountbatten of Burma. As CIGS and CGS he was responsible for the army's part in such operations as the deterrence of the Iraqi attack on Kuwait in 1961, 'confrontation' with Indonesia in Malaysia, the suppression of the East African mutinies, and the defeat of the Nasserist rebellion in the Radfan province of the Aden Protectorate.

His bitterest battles, however, were fought in Whitehall after he became CDS in July 1965. During his term of office Britain withdrew from Singapore and Aden and was challenged by rebellion in Rhodesia. At home, he found the navy and air force locked in conflict over the funding of air power, while Denis (later Baron) Healey, an imperious defence secretary, demanded budgetary sacrifices by all services. Hull, whose professional feelings for Mountbatten had amounted to loathing, was too upright to allow that to influence his arbitration of the dispute between the air marshals and the admirals. He perceived that the large carriers the navy wanted would cost too much and threw his weight behind the decision to spend available funds for the purchase of American aircraft for the Royal Air Force as a means of providing Britain with long-range strike capability. The small carriers that provided the Royal Navy with its later air support were the product of that chiefs of staff committee's decision.

Hull was promoted to field-marshal on appointment as CDS. On retirement in 1967 he became a director of Whitbreads (1967–76) and rationalized business in its western division. He held many state, army, and charitable appointments, including those of constable of the Tower of London (1970–5), deputy lieutenant of Devon (1973–8), high sheriff (1975), and lord-lieutenant (1978–82). He was president of the Army Benevolent Fund (1968–71), and was made an honorary LL D by Exeter University in 1965. Appointed CB in 1945, he was advanced to KCB in 1956 and GCB in 1961. He became a knight of the Garter in 1980.

Hull typified a certain sort of regular cavalry officer of his generation. A devout but undemonstrative Christian, a devoted husband and father, whose temperament often prevented him from disclosing his affections, a loyal friend to brother officers who won his favour, a devotee of regimental tradition, he was happiest shooting or fly fishing, two sports at which he excelled, and in his garden, where he knew the Latin, English, and Devon name of every plant. He was tall and of impressive bearing, with grave features.

In 1934 Hull married Antoinette Mary, only child of Francis Labouchère de Rougemont, of the Bank of Egypt. They had two daughters and a son and were a couple noted for their devotion. Hull died 17 September 1989, of cancer, at his home at Beacon Downe, Pinhoe, Exeter, which he had rebuilt after wartime bombing, was given a state funeral at Windsor, and was buried in the graveyard of the local church where he had regularly worshipped.

[Sir William Jackson and Edwin Bramall (as Bill Jackson and Dwin Bramall), *The Chiefs*, 1992; private information.]   JOHN KEEGAN

HULTON, SIR Edward George Warris (1906–1988), magazine publisher and writer, was born 29 November 1906 in London, the only son and elder child (the daughter died when she was twenty-two, in 1932) of (Sir) Edward *Hulton, baronet, of Downside, Surrey, a Manchester newspaper publisher, whose business expanded to include the London *Evening Standard* and the *Daily Sketch*. His mother, Millicent Warris, a beautiful actress, daughter of John Warris, was Edward Hulton's second wife, but the couple were unable to marry until ten years after their son's birth, and so the baronetcy conferred on Edward Hulton in 1921 became extinct on his death in 1925.

Hulton was a lonely, sensitive child. His parents descended at the weekend, when his mother would dote on him, while his father, ambitious for the boy's success, was awkward and irascible. From Harrow he won a history scholarship to Brasenose College, Oxford, which he entered in 1925 and where he edited the undergraduate magazine *Cherwell* and spoke frequently in Union debates. He left in December 1926 without a degree. Meanwhile his father sold the newspaper business, on medical advice, to the first Baron *Beaverbrook in 1923.

Hulton was called to the bar at the Inner Temple in 1936. He had stood unsuccessfully as a Conservative Unionist in the general elections of 1929 (the Leek division of Staffordshire) and 1931 (Harwich). Not until he was thirty did he realize control over his father's fortune and set about becoming a publisher in his own right. He founded the Hulton Press in 1937, with the prosaic purchase of *Farmers Weekly*. The business grew to include a variety of magazines, such as *World Review* and *Leader Magazine*. His children's magazines, notably *Eagle* and *Girl*, were highly successful in their day and set new standards of content and design. But the weekly publication which made Hulton widely known was *Picture Post*, launched on 1 October 1938. Its genius was the Hungarian refugee Stefan Lorant, who had founded (and now sold to Hulton) the popular monthly pocket magazine *Lilliput*. Under the steadying influence of Hulton's manager, Maxwell Raison, and Lorant's successor, (Sir H.) Thomas *Hopkinson, *Picture Post* developed a style of photo-journalism in which striking pictures and design were supported by good writing and a progressive editorial line. For more than a decade this formula was popular and profitable, with sales of nearly 1.5 million in the 1940s. Hulton used the magazine to boost the war effort, pioneering (and initially funding) the Home Guard training school at Osterley Park in 1940, and briefly even organizing the private supply of weapons from the USA. In August 1945 he gave 'a resounding welcome' to the government formed by C. R. (later first Earl) Attlee. 'I am not personally a socialist...Yet I rejoice that latter-day conservatism has been overthrown.' This attitude was foreshadowed by *Picture Post*'s publication of a postwar 'Plan for Britain' in 1941 and by Hulton's involvement in lobbying activities such as the progressive 1941 Committee, of which he was one of the founders and which met regularly in his house, and in support of the report by Sir William (later Baron) *Beveridge. His book *The New Age* (1943) summed up his support for a mixed economy and welfare state.

Hulton blamed shifts in reading habits more than the growth of television for *Picture Post*'s decline in the 1950s. His renewed support for the Conservative party provoked a break with Hopkinson, who resigned in 1950 when Hulton refused to publish a story about the ill-treatment of North Korean prisoners of war. A vacillating market strategy, frequent changes of editor, and mounting losses led Hulton to close the magazine in 1957. Two years later the Hulton Press was taken over by Odhams.

Increasingly Hulton spent time on European affairs. He was editor-in-chief of *European Review* and held office in the European Atlantic Group (president 1969–70), the European League for Economic Cooperation, and the British council of the European Movement. In 1957 he was knighted and in 1969 he received the NATO peace medal. The Hulton Picture Library, later to become the Hulton Deutsch Collection, which contained photographs taken for *Picture Post*, was founded in 1947.

Hulton had a lively, enquiring mind, as ready to experiment with a model farm at Salperton, his estate village in Gloucestershire, as with the possibilities of a new Sunday newspaper in the 1950s. He belonged to half a dozen London clubs and was fond of social life. He could be brusque and changeable in his opinions. Hopkinson found him donnish and kind-hearted but difficult to work with.

Hulton was stout, shortish, and florid. His manner was vague and authoritative, as if he were accustomed to both giving orders and having them disobeyed. His dress was always formal, as were his manners. He married first, in 1927, Kira Pavlovna, daughter of General Paul Goudime-Levkovitsch, of the Imperial Russian Army. There were no children. The marriage was dissolved in 1932 and in 1941 he again married a Russian, Princess Nika Yourievitch, whose father, Prince Serge Yourievitch, was a sculptor and had been a chamberlain at the court

of the tsar. Of this marriage there were two sons and a daughter. The marriage was dissolved in 1966, but the couple lived together for the last nine years of Hulton's life. Hulton died 8 October 1988 in his sleep at his home in Carlton Gardens, London, after a long illness.

[Edward Hulton, *The New Age*, 1943; *When I Was a Child*, 1952; Tom Hopkinson (ed.), *Picture Post*, 1970; *The Times*, 10 October 1988.] COLIN SEYMOUR-URE

HUMPHREY, John Herbert (1915–1987), immunologist and medical scientist, was born 16 December 1915 in West Byfleet, Surrey, the eldest in the family of three sons and two daughters of Herbert Alfred *Humphrey, inventor and co-founder of Imperial Chemical Industries (ICI) at Billingham, and his wife, Mary Elizabeth Horniblow. He was educated at the International School, Lausanne, Switzerland, before attending the preparatory school Bramcote (Yorkshire). Then followed a very formative period at Winchester College. From school he won a scholarship to Trinity College, Cambridge, where he read natural sciences in preparation for medicine. He obtained a first class in both parts of the natural sciences tripos (1936 and 1937). It was during this time that he became conscious of the evils and social injustices of his time. Such matters occupied him alongside his scientific career for the rest of his life.

In 1937 he enrolled at University College Hospital Medical School and qualified in medicine (MB, B.Chir.) in 1940 after the start of World War II. His first clinical appointment at the Royal Postgraduate Medical School (RPMS), Hammersmith, was soon interrupted when an attack of bronchitis was diagnosed as tuberculosis. After convalescence he spent a year (1941–2) as Jenner research fellow at the Lister Institute for Preventive Medicine, Stanmore, Middlesex, carrying out microbiological studies. As he was no longer eligible for service in the armed forces, he accepted in 1942 the post of assistant pathologist at the Central Middlesex Hospital (the chief pathologist being imprisoned by the Japanese). Under these difficult conditions he still managed to publish ten papers on his hospital work.

After the war he was able to carry out his passionate wish to do full-time research related to clinical problems. In 1946 he obtained an external Medical Research Council appointment in microbiology at UCHMS to work on bacterial enzymes. He became MD in 1947. In 1949 he joined the National Institute for Medical Research (NIMR) at Hampstead (later at Mill Hill), as a member of the scientific staff in the division of biological standards, which provided great opportunities for interdisciplinary research. By this time there was an urgent need to standardize biological substances, such as antibiotics, and he developed novel techniques for the quantitative analysis of their biological activities. He also found time to initiate collaborations with other institute members on basic immunological problems, which remained a major focus of his life's work.

In 1957 he was invited to become head of a newly founded immunology department at NIMR, where he served as deputy director from 1961 until 1976, when he accepted the chair of immunology at the RPMS, Hammersmith. His official retirement from the chair was in 1981; however, he continued his advisory and immunological activities as emeritus professor at RPMS until his death. Over many years he became increasingly deaf due to bilateral acoustic neuroma, diagnosed only late with advances in technology. Regardless of a serious cardiac condition, he continued undeterred with all his work, travelling widely, writing, lecturing, encouraging students and colleagues, and providing liberal advice.

Humphrey was a tireless worker; he was interested in all aspects of basic and clinical immunology; his encyclopaedic memory enabled his research to touch on diverse problems, with particular focus on cell-mediated immunity as well as immunopathology. At the time almost nothing was known about the complex cellular interactions responsible for the different immune reactivities. He is best known for his studies with radio-labelled antibodies, the cascade of events in allergic or anaphylactic reactions, the role of complement components in lysing cells, events underlying local antibody/antigen reactions *in vivo* (e.g., the release of histamine and other substances by different cell types), and the fate of administered foreign molecules or pathogens in relation to the generation of immunity. He published over 200 papers and several book chapters covering these studies. In 1963 he published a textbook (*Immunology for Students of Medicine*), with R. G. White; it made a great impact, presenting in a dynamic and exciting way the 'new' type of immunology in relation to clinical medicine. He was an important member of many national and international committees connected with the Royal Society, Medical Research Council, World Health Organization, and International Council of Scientific Unions.

Most importantly, Humphrey exerted a profound influence on his many young associates attracted from all over the world and on the direction of immunological thinking. His enthusiasm for immunology was infectious and he was generous with novel ideas. He always made time for any colleagues or students who sought him out.

In addition to his busy scientific career and influence, he found time to pursue his passionate concern for many socio-political issues. He was a founder member of the Medical Association for the Prevention of War (1951) and the Medical Campaign against Nuclear Weapons (chairman, 1981, and president from 1985), president of the Society for the Protection of Science and Learning (from 1978), and a supporter of Pugwash (a group of international scientists dedicated to preventing nuclear war). He wrote a number of articles concerning the physicians' peace movement and co-authored, with J. Ziman and P. *Sieghart, *The World of Science and the rule of Law* (1986).

Elected a fellow of the Royal Society in 1963, Humphrey became an honorary member of the American Association of Immunologists in the same year. He was appointed CBE in 1970. He was a fellow of Winchester College (1965–78), of the Institute of Biology (1968), of the Royal College of Physicians (1970), and a foreign honorary member of the American Academy of Arts and Sciences (1981). He had honorary memberships of scientific societies in The Netherlands, Hungary, South Africa, Germany, and Czechoslovakia. He was elected a foreign associate member of the US National Academy of Sciences (1986) and an honorary fellow of Trinity College, Cambridge (1986), and he was awarded an honorary doctorate by Brunel University (1979).

Humphrey was tall and thin, with uncombed and wispy light brown hair, lively eyes, and an alert and active stance. His friendly look conveyed genuine interest and concern for the other person. In 1939 he married Janet Rumney, daughter of Professor Archibald Vivian *Hill, CH, FRS, Nobel laureate in physiology. They had two sons and three daughters. Humphrey died 25 December 1987 at his country home in Ashwell, Hertfordshire.

[B. A. Askonas in *Biographical Memoirs of Fellows of the Royal Society*, vol. xxxvi, 1990; personal knowledge.]

B. A. ASKONAS

HUNT, John Henderson, BARON HUNT OF FAWLEY (1905–1987), general practitioner and medical politician, was born 3 July 1905 in Secunderabad, India, the eldest in the family of three sons and two daughters of Edmund Henderson Hunt, surgeon to the Hyderabad state railways, and his wife, Laura Mary Buckingham, the daughter of a tea planter. Mother and children returned to England before World War I and John was educated at Charterhouse, Balliol College, Oxford (where he obtained a second class in physiology in 1927) and St Bartholomew's Hospital, London. He qualified BM, B.Ch. and MRCS, LRCP in 1931.

After qualification Hunt seemed destined for a career in neurology and worked at the National Hospital for Nervous Diseases and then at St Bartholomew's, as chief assistant to the neurological clinic. During this period he obtained his

MRCP (London, 1934) and a DM (Oxford, 1935). He then decided to be a general practitioner. In 1937 he joined Dr George Cregan in practice at 83 Sloane Street as a partner, but he never went into financial partnership during his career.

During World War II he served in the Royal Air Force as a neurologist, with the rank of wing commander. He returned to general practice independently in 1945, at 54 Sloane Square. Always in private practice, he never really understood the National Health Service. His patients were in the main well off and had high expectations of health care, which he endeavoured to meet. He had his own laboratory and X-ray facilities and ran a practice where success was measured more by medical than financial standards. He had, as he confided to his brother, the ambition to be the best GP in England, even though his type of practice was vastly different from most. He had a high referral rate of patients for specialist opinions, but this was not because of personal lack of knowledge; his patients expected a second opinion. He consequently had close relationships with specialists. Although he preferred the organic aspects of medicine to the psycho-social, he always considered the personality and character of the patient when deciding the best course of management. Despite being a quick worker he seldom gave the impression he was hurrying or did not have time to listen. He would sit at breakfast with two telephones to hand, one for incoming calls and one for outgoing, and he rarely drove to visits, having a succession of lady drivers whilst he sat in the back of the car dictating his notes. The notes were typed in the car while he was in a house seeing his next patient.

In 1951 and 1952 Hunt played a crucial role in the establishment of a College of General Practitioners. The three royal colleges, which were implacably opposed to a separate college, set up their own committee, with Hunt as a member, to promote a joint faculty. However, Hunt knew that a full and independent college was required and gained support for it through meetings and letters to influential journals and people. Opposition was expressed by the press and in official circles, but, with Hunt as the honorary secretary of a steering committee, articles of association were signed on 19 November 1952. Within six months 2,000 practitioners joined, a foundation council was formed, and the college was launched. For the next thirteen years Hunt was honorary secretary of council, and never missed a meeting. He was a 'workaholic', with obsessional determination and attention to detail, who demanded as much from those who worked with him as he gave. He had an authoritarian demeanour, but his enthusiasm and energy were such that people responded with their best, although

several of them became exhausted by the attempt to keep pace.

Hunt received an avalanche of honours. He became FRCP (1964) and FRCS (1966) and was recognized by colleges in Canada, the USA, and Australia. He gave numerous important lectures and was the president of many of the prestigious medical societies in London. He was appointed CBE in 1970, was made a life peer in 1973, which enabled him to steer the Medical Act of 1978 through the House of Lords, and received the gold medal of the British Medical Association in 1980.

Hunt was a big man who, in spite of a hip problem, walked prodigiously, on one occasion from Land's End to John o' Groats. He played furious tennis and croquet at his country house in Henley. His eyes were always a problem to him. He was short-sighted in youth and lost the sight of one eye in 1967. Ten years later he began to lose the sight of the other and this greatly taxed his patience and that of his family. Later he developed Parkinson's disease.

In 1941 he married Elisabeth Ernestine, daughter of Norman Evill, FRIBA, architect. They had three sons and two daughters, two of whom became medical doctors. The eldest son died of leukaemia at the age of five; this deeply distressed Hunt, who could never bear to discuss it afterwards. His wife's help was essential in providing the stability on which his achievements were based. In spite of his rate of working, he always had time for his children and took great interest in their achievements, particularly those of a sporting nature. He died 28 December 1987 at his home, Seven Steep, in Fawley, near Henley-on-Thames.

[John Horder, *The Writings of John Hunt*, 1992; J. Fry, J. Hunt, and R. J. F. Pinsent (eds.), *A History of the Royal College of General Practitioners*, 1993; private information.]   MICHAEL DRURY

HUNT, Norman Crowther, BARON CROWTHER-HUNT (1920–1987), academic, constitutional expert, and broadcaster, was born 13 March 1920 at Bradford, Yorkshire, the elder son (there were no daughters) of Ernest Angus Hunt, master butcher, of Eccleshill, Bradford, and his wife, Florence Crowther. He was educated at Belle Vue High School, Bradford, and at Sidney Sussex College, Cambridge, where he was an exhibitioner (1939–40) and, after war service in the Royal Artillery and the War Office, a scholar (1945–7). He took a first in both parts of the history tripos (1946 and 1947), was a research fellow of Sidney Sussex (1949–51), and then spent a year as Commonwealth Fund fellow at Princeton, studying American politics. In 1952 he was elected to a tutorial fellowship in politics at Exeter College, Oxford, where he spent the rest of his academic career.

He was the very antithesis of the cloistered don, however. A square, stocky, round-faced man of enormous energy and indefatigable good humour, he took delight in challenging closed establishments, devising schemes and drafting papers for reform of matters great and small, and proving his stamina in new fields. He had won a Cambridge football blue as goalkeeper (1940), and continued to be an agile opponent in most ball games and in politics at every level. His years as domestic bursar of Exeter (1954–70) were christened the Norman Conquest by those who felt their impact. He was not a man for the long considered haul of quiet research. He published part of his historical Cambridge Ph.D. thesis (1951) as *Two Early Political Associations* (1961), edited *Whitehall and Beyond* (1964) and (with Graham Tayar) *Personality and Power* (1971), and wrote (with Peter Kellner) *The Civil Servants* (1980). But his academic gifts lay in teaching, not scholarship.

He was an invigorating, forceful tutor for generations of Oxford undergraduates, and, thanks to the BBC, a challenging political guide and familiar voice to a much wider audience. From 1961 he appeared regularly on both television and radio, and his 'People and Politics' was a weekly feature of the World Service for many years. His long service to the BBC culminated in his appointment as chairman of its general advisory council in 1986. It had also initiated a lasting friendship with Harold Wilson (later Baron Wilson of Rievaulx), a fellow Yorkshireman, whom Hunt interviewed (and greatly impressed) shortly after Wilson's election as leader of the Labour party in 1963. While Wilson was prime minister (1964–70, 1974–6), Hunt was able to promote the two constitutional issues about which he felt most deeply, and which he helped to place firmly on the political agenda: reform of the Civil Service, and devolution.

His was the chief radical voice in the committee on the Civil Service (1966–8), chaired by Baron *Fulton. He led its management consultancy group and drafted much of the final report which condemned the 'generalist' (and Oxbridge) bias of Civil Service recruitment and sought to open senior posts to specialists. In 1969 he was appointed to the royal commission on the constitution, chaired first by Baron *Crowther and then by C. J. D. *Shaw (later Baron Kilbrandon). Hunt was once again on the radical wing, though this time in a minority. He was principal author of a long memorandum of dissent to the final report (1973), in which he argued that devolution to the English regions must go hand in hand with the devolution to elected assemblies in Scotland and Wales which Kilbrandon recommended.

In 1973 he was made a life peer, and on Wilson's return to power in 1974 he was appointed constitutional adviser to the government (March–October), with a brief to develop its devolution proposals. He dealt with the same issue as minister in the Privy Council office in 1976. In the interim, from 1974 to 1976, he was minister of state at the Department of Education and Science; but he was less successful at handling the public controversies aroused by his proposals for manpower planning in higher education than he had been as a backroom advocate and elaborator of policy. He was disillusioned also by the extent to which narrowly party political considerations determined the government's attitude to devolution, and although Civil Service reform had proceeded further, he chafed at what he saw as continuing Whitehall obstruction. He returned to full-time teaching at Exeter College in 1976, not disappointed (he was the last man ever to have regrets), but with some relief.

His election as rector of the college in 1982 began the final, and personally most satisfying, part of his career. He enjoyed the distinction, as he enjoyed his honorary fellowship of Sidney Sussex (1982) and his honorary degrees from Bradford University (1974) and Williams College, Massachusetts (1985). But he was as determined as ever to use his position to reshape institutions and open their doors to fresh talent. He helped to reform the university's admissions procedures, and initiated an ambitious and successful college appeal. He made the rector's lodgings a welcoming centre of college activity, where undergraduates met public figures, where he could share his interests in music, and where his closeness to his family, and dependence upon them, were visible. He had married Joyce, daughter of the Revd Joseph Stackhouse, of Walsall Wood, Staffordshire, in 1944; they had three daughters. Still full of plans for the college, and with seven months to go before retiring from office, he died suddenly of a heart attack in the John Radcliffe Hospital, Oxford, 16 February 1987.

[Private information; personal knowledge.]

PAUL SLACK

HUNTINGDON, fifteenth EARL OF (1901–1990), artist and politician. [See HASTINGS, FRANCIS JOHN CLARENCE WESTENRA PLANTAGENET.]

HURST, Margery (1913–1989), recruitment agency founder, was born 23 May 1913, probably in Portsmouth, the second of four daughters (there were no sons) of Samuel Berney, cinema owner and builder, of Portsmouth, and his wife Deborah, née Rose. Her grandparents on both sides were Russian Jewish immigrants. She was educated at Brondesbury and Kilburn High School, London, and the Royal Academy of Dramatic Art. While at RADA she acted two nights a week with the repertory company at Collins music hall, which her father had just bought, but she decided she was too self-conscious to become an actress, and got a job as a typist. From there she moved on to work for her father, running the clerical side of his building business, and then became his office manager.

At the outbreak of World War II she became a secretary in an ambulance unit, and in 1943 she was commissioned into the Auxiliary Territorial Service (ATS). She later claimed that running a business was not very different from being in charge of a platoon. In 1944 she was invalided out of the army after having a nervous breakdown, worn out by the constant battle against army red tape.

In 1946, three weeks after the birth of her first child, her husband deserted her for another woman, and, driven by the need to support herself and her baby, she borrowed £50 and an old typewriter from her father, rented a small room at 62 Brook Street, opposite Claridge's in Mayfair, and started a typing agency. But overwork and the stress involved in leaving her baby with a nanny in Portsmouth while she spent the week in London led to another breakdown, and the typing agency collapsed. She started again, founding the Brook Street Bureau of Mayfair, this time supplying other businesses with temporary secretaries. From the beginning she would only take on secretaries with several years' experience, who had passed her skills test in shorthand and typing. In the early 1950s the Brook Street Bureau began to open branches in the London suburbs and then in other parts of the country. By 1961 there were thirty-three branches, providing about one third of Britain's agency-supplied staff, both temporary and permanent. In the early 1960s she opened branches in New York and Australia. In 1965 the company, now the largest office employment agency in the world, was floated on the London Stock Exchange. Because she was persuaded that it would be impossible to have a woman as chairman of a public company, Margery Hurst reluctantly agreed to remain as managing director, with her husband as chairman. The flotation was a success, and share prices doubled in fifteen months.

There were financial problems in the early 1970s, but profits rose again with the highly successful 'Brook Street Got Big by Bothering' advertising campaign on London underground trains, which lasted for a decade. The Brook Street Bureau suffered during the recession of the early 1980s and was forced to close 100 branches in Britain, as well as most of the branches in Australia and the United States. In 1985 it was sold for over £19 million to the Blue Arrow recruitment group. The Hursts, who owned 61 per cent of the shares, made £10 million out of the sale. Brook Street kept its identity, and Margery Hurst stayed on as non-executive chairman and consultant until 1988.

A member of the London county council children's committee for several years from 1956, she was involved in charities concerned with child welfare, and in 1973 she bought and founded a house in Gravesend to train autistic school-leavers for jobs. She was on the executive committee of the Mental Health Research Fund from 1967 to 1972. She also campaigned against discrimination in recruitment against ex-psychiatric patients, and in the 1970s Brook Street started a special project for the placement of those who had been mentally ill. She was appointed OBE in 1976 and was one of the first women to become a member of Lloyd's, in 1970. She was elected the first female member of the Worshipful Company of Marketors [sic] in 1981, became a freeman of the City of London the same year, and was also the first woman to be elected to the New York chamber of commerce.

She was very small, five feet tall, but had a dominating, if not domineering, personality. She was assertive and competitive, and even as a child she wanted to be in charge, not just part of a team. She was hot-tempered and liable to have violent arguments with members of her staff. Restless and energetic, she found it hard to relax and had a series of mental breakdowns. In 1940 she married Major William Baines, army officer. They had twin daughters, one of whom was stillborn. They were divorced and in 1948 she married Eric Kenneth Isaac Hurst, barrister and later her business partner, the son of Wilfred Hurst, cotton merchant. There was one daughter from this second marriage, which ended in divorce. Margery Hurst died 11 February 1989 at her London home in Eaton Square.

[*Independent*, 16 February 1989; Margery Hurst, *No Glass Slipper*, 1967; Margery Hurst with Sally Brompton, *Walking up Brook Street*, 1988.]

ANNE PIMLOTT BAKER

HUTCHINSON, SIR **Joseph Burtt** (1902–1988), geneticist, tropical plant breeder, and agriculturalist, was born 21 March 1902 in Burton Latimer, Northamptonshire, the eldest of three sons (there were no daughters) of Quaker parents Edmund Hutchinson, who farmed at Cransley Grange, and his wife, Lydia Mary Davy. 'Jack', as he was known within the family, was encouraged to participate in the activities of the farm, learning skills that were to serve him well in later years. He was educated at Ackworth and then Bootham School, where he showed an aptitude for science, winning an exhibition to St John's College, Cambridge. Though keen to farm, he was encouraged by his uncle, Joseph Burtt Davy, a distinguished African plant taxonomist, to read botany. After gaining second-class honours in both parts of the natural sciences tripos (1922 and 1923), he went to study at the Imperial College of Tropical Agriculture in Trinidad.

From his earliest years Hutchinson brought together the charity and discipline of his Quaker upbringing, a common-sense approach, learned through practical farming, and his excellence in science. With his direct and attentive gaze and upright bearing, his capacity to listen, speak clearly and with authority, and to blend the thoughts of those around him with his own radical and incisive thinking, were treasured by those he knew and with whom he worked.

From 1924, in Trinidad, he worked on the breeding of cotton, using the new genetical science. He was assigned research on the African and Asian species. Seizing a chance to work in India in 1933, Hutchinson went as geneticist and botanist to the Institute of Plant Industry at Indore, where he found the prevailing Indian Civil Service attitude to research utilitarian and myopically short-term. Here he excelled by harnessing the power of numerous young Indian scientists, whom he trained to work on the biodiversity of native cottons. He became a legend in India and left behind him an embryonic programme for improved crop breeding. He returned to Trinidad in 1937, to head the Empire Cotton Growing Corporation's cotton genetics programme. He was appointed CMG in 1944 before becoming chief geneticist at the Corporation's station near Khartoum, Sudan (1944–9).

Apart from his major taxonomic work on cotton, for which he became a fellow of the Royal Society in 1951, Hutchinson's principal plant-breeding achievement was in developing cotton varieties resistant to disease, the descendants of which formed the principal cottons grown in sub-Saharan Africa in the late twentieth century. He became director of the Cotton Corporation's Namulonge research station in Uganda in 1949. It was in Uganda that he ensured a continuing and high profile for agricultural research in English-speaking Africa. He never lost sight of the needs of the African smallholder. In Uganda, a country which depended on cotton and coffee, Hutchinson played a major role in developing agricultural education at school, technical, and university levels. He chaired the Makerere College council (1953–7) in the last days of a relatively enlightened Protectorate government. Knighted in 1956 for his services in East Africa, he 'retired' in 1957 when offered the Drapers' chair of agriculture at Cambridge and a fellowship at St John's College.

His Cambridge years were celebrated by the wide vision of his undergraduate teaching and writing, but they were uneasy, for in 1969 the school of agriculture was eventually forced to close, under government pressure, despite the reinvigoration that Hutchinson latterly brought to it. He was a figure of national standing in British agriculture and, with his global view, continually challenged the conventional wisdoms of his times. He was particularly proud of his governing body associations with the John Innes and Plant Breeding Institutes and the Norfolk Agricultural Station. He was president of the British Association in 1955–6, received the Royal Society medal in 1967, and had honorary D.Sc.s from Nottingham (1966) and East Anglia (1972). Among his books were *The Genetics of Gossypium* (1947) and *Application of Genetics to Cotton Improvement* (1959).

Hutchinson was a humble man who consistently and unobtrusively adhered to the precepts of the Society of Friends. He was chairman of the board of governors of a local Friends' school, a preacher in Cambridge churches and college chapels, and 'a weighty Friend' in his own Quaker meeting. He was an immensely positive person with a deep faith in the essential goodness of human beings.

In 1930 he married Martha Leonora ('Lena'), daughter of George Frederick Johnson, who trained as an engineer and worked in his own brass and ironmongery business in Malton, Yorkshire. It was a lifelong partnership marked by a real devotion; in their home simplicity and gravitas were combined with quiet humour and occasional frivolity. They had a son and a daughter. Hutchinson died 16 January 1988 at home in Girton, Cambridge.

[Sir Denis Rooke in *Biographical Memoirs of Fellows of the Royal Society*, vol. xxxvii, 1991; personal knowledge.]   STEPHEN P. TOMKINS

HUTTON, SIR Leonard (1916–1990), cricketer, was born 23 June 1916 in Fulneck, near Pudsey, Leeds, the youngest in the family of four sons and one daughter of Henry Hutton, builder, and his wife Lily Swithenbank, whose uncle, Seth Milner, had been a prominent cricketer in the 1880s. Fulneck, a Moravian religious community, had been founded in the 1730s by Count Zinzendorf, an exile from Bohemia. Generations of Huttons, some of whom became Moravian ministers, went to the community's school and chapel and were brought up in a terrace house dating from the eighteenth century. This moral, Nonconformist upbringing, which Len Hutton later described as 'strict but caring', gave him a reserved and thoughtful demeanour unusual among professional cricketers. He was educated at Littlemoor Council School, Pudsey.

His talent marked him out early for a career in the game, to which he took, he said, 'like a Sherpa to the mountains'. His three brothers all played Yorkshire league cricket for the Pudsey St Lawrence Club, where he joined them in the first

XI at the age of fourteen. An important event in his life was the return to Pudsey of Herbert *Sutcliffe, the opening batsman for Yorkshire and England, who had played in his youth with Hutton's father. Sutcliffe quickly saw the potential of the talented teenager who played on the concrete strip in Sutcliffe's garden and described him as 'a marvel—the discovery of a generation'. Hutton said he looked up to Sutcliffe at this time 'with the reverence that a pious Roman Catholic has for the Pope'.

It was Sutcliffe who introduced him to the Yorkshire County Cricket Club, where he was coached at the austere Headingley 'Winter Shed' in nearby Leeds by George *Hirst, the former England all-rounder, who soon pronounced that he could 'teach him nowt'. In 1930, when he was fourteen, Hutton sat enthralled in the Headingley crowd as the great Australian, (Sir) Donald Bradman, scored 309 runs in a day on his way to the record total of 334 which, eight years later, Hutton was to break at the Oval in the most famous innings of his life.

Yorkshire was the most powerful cricket county in England in the 1930s, winning the championship five times in the seven years before World War II, and to break into that team at all was an achievement. Hutton did this in 1934, at the age of seventeen, albeit with a duck (a feat he repeated three years later on his début for England). But he confirmed his class with an early innings of 196. Yorkshire, with talent to spare, nursed the young Hutton through his early seasons to avoid putting too much strain on his fragile physique. He later claimed to have learned all he knew about cricket from listening to the dressing-room talk of great players like Sutcliffe, Hedley *Verity, Maurice Leyland, and W. E. Bowes. It was an austere and rigorous apprenticeship designed to keep a young man, however talented, in his place. Even so, he was to say later of the Yorkshire dressing-room of his youth: 'Had I been ordered to walk on broken glass, I would have instantly obeyed.'

In 1937, just after his twenty-first birthday, he opened the batting for England against New Zealand and scored a century in his second test match. It was a year later, in the 'timeless' test at the Oval against Australia, that Hutton made history, scoring his record 364 in England's highest ever total of 903. It was a marathon feat of concentration over thirteen hours and seventeen minutes, the longest innings ever played, and the highest score by an England batsman. It made him an instant celebrity wherever cricket was played—a fame not entirely welcome to his reclusive personality.

In 1939, first in South Africa and then at home against the West Indies, he gave some of his finest batting performances and, in the view of many sound judges, was just reaching a peak

when his career was interrupted by six years of war, when he served in the Royal Artillery and the Army Physical Training Corps. In Hutton's case the war was a double tragedy, for he dislocated a wrist badly in a gymnasium accident in March 1941 and was left, after skin and bone graft operations, with one arm more than two inches shorter than the other. He was discharged from the army and for some time it seemed unlikely that he could ever play cricket again.

He returned to the international arena in 1946, and over the next decade established himself as England's greatest opening batsman since Sir Jack *Hobbs, scoring over 40,000 runs in his career, including 129 centuries, at an average of 55. But, as R. C. Robertson-Glasgow wrote, 'to admire Len Hutton merely for the quantity of his runs is like praising Milton for the length of Paradise Lost or Schubert for the number of his songs.' Despite the handicap to his left arm, which forced him to use a schoolboy's bat and restricted the range of his strokes, he was admired as a graceful, balanced, and classical batsman, perhaps the finest ever on a turning wicket. Only Bradman was unarguably his superior, and, for three or four years after Bradman's retirement in 1948, Hutton was undisputed as the greatest batsman in the world.

In 1951 he became England's first professional captain and never lost a series, recovering the Ashes against Australia in coronation year (1953) after a gap of fifteen years (and then retaining them in Australia). He was a cautious, uncommunicative captain, believing strongly in the use of fast bowlers, and was the first to slow down the over rate deliberately as a tactical ploy. In five series against the powerful Australian attack after the war he bore the brunt of the English batting, prompting the popular catch-phrase 'Hutton out, side out'. The physical and nervous strain took its toll, forcing his early retirement in 1956. He was the first professional cricketer to be elected an honorary member of the MCC and the second (after Hobbs) to be knighted (1956).

Curiously, though, Hutton was never appointed captain of Yorkshire, an omission which may in part explain his exile in Surrey for the rest of his life. After his retirement he became a director of Fenners, the mining equipment manufacturers, who made good use of his worldwide cricketing contacts. Always a shrewd judge of the game, he also became an England selector and wrote on cricket for the Observer for thirty years. He published three books on cricket. Len Hutton mellowed in later life and amused his friends greatly with a cryptic sense of humour, delivered with a crinkled smile from wide-apart blue eyes. His strong moral outlook shaped and directed one of the best natural talents in the history of the game.

He married, in September 1939, Dorothy Mary, daughter of George Dennis, foreman joiner on Lord Downe's estate at Wykeham, Yorkshire. Her brother played cricket for Yorkshire. Their happy marriage was a powerful source of strength. Their two sons, Richard and John, were both cricketers; Richard played one season for England in 1971 and became editorial director of the *Cricketer*. In January 1990, in a bid to heal the county's divisions, Hutton was invited to be president of Yorkshire CCC, an honour he deeply appreciated, but, before he could have much effect, he died 6 September 1990 in Kingston upon Thames Hospital, of a ruptured aorta.

[Donald Trelford, *Len Hutton Remembered*, 1992; Len Hutton, *Cricket is My life*, 1950, and *Just My Story*, 1956; Len Hutton with Alex Bannister, *Fifty Years in Cricket*, 1984; Gerald Howat, *Len Hutton*, 1988; personal knowledge.]   DONALD TRELFORD

I

ILLINGWORTH, Ronald Stanley (1909–1990), professor of child health, was born 7 October 1909 in Harrogate, the younger son and youngest of the three children of Herbert Edward Illingworth, architect, and his wife, Ellen Brayshaw. He was educated at Clifton House School in Harrogate and Bradford Grammar School, and went with a West Riding scholarship in classics to read medicine at Leeds University. He graduated MB, Ch.B. in 1934. In the following five years he held various posts and obtained the MD and MRCP in 1937, and the DPH with distinction and DCH in 1938. He worked at the Hospital for Sick Children at Great Ormond Street, London, before taking up a Nuffield research studentship at Oxford in 1939. Illingworth joined the Royal Army Medical Corps in 1941 and by the end of World War II was a lieutenant-colonel and in charge of a medical division in the Middle East.

After the war he worked at the Hammersmith and Great Ormond Street Hospitals in 1946, before going to the USA on a postponed Rockefeller research fellowship. In 1947, the year he became FRCP, he was appointed to the foundation chair of child health in the University of Sheffield. Over the next twenty-eight years he made the Sheffield Children's Hospital and his department of child health a port of call for aspirant academics and future consultants. When he arrived at Sheffield, the department was in a near-derelict house, and from there he led a team of clinical academics, which at any one time was composed of a stimulating mixture of doctors from home and abroad. Illingworth possessed a fine instinct for picking future leaders in paediatrics and child health. In the postwar years he was one of the medical magnets that drew bright young men from all over the Empire and Commonwealth to the Children's Hospital in Sheffield. When he retired in 1975 no fewer than fifteen of his former staff had become full professors and two had become ministers of health in their own countries.

Illingworth was an astute clinician and meticulous clinical researcher. By the time the endemic diseases of rheumatic fever, tuberculosis, and rickets had disappeared, he had become the foremost clinical expert on developmental paediatrics. It was in this area of clinical practice that he left his greatest legacy, through his prodigious output of papers and books. He had over 650 publications, including forty-six translations of new editions of his books. He was undoubtedly the most widely read paediatrician of his time. His best known books are *The Normal Child* (1953, ten editions), *The Development of the Infant and Young Child* (1960, nine editions), and *Common Symptoms of Disease in Children* (1967, nine editions). All three were translated into many languages. Illingworth had an eminently readable style of writing, being economical with words and precise in their use. His writings were a model of clarity and very popular with students and postgraduate scholars.

His hobby of photography, for which he received over seventy awards, was practised to a high professional standard. He was awarded the fellowship of the Royal Photographic Society in 1936, having exhibited at its annual international exhibition while still a medical student. His superb use of illustrated material, combined with his effortless and lucid style of delivery, made him a much sought-after lecturer. He gave over 500 invited lectures, including more than 180 abroad, in places as far apart as the Soviet Union and South Africa. On his eightieth birthday he gave masterly lectures on medical education and walking in the Alps without recourse to notes and, as always, illuminated by admirable photographic material.

He served on major committees of the Medical Research Council and Department of Health, and was the paediatric adviser to the parliamentary commissioner (ombudsman). For twenty-six years he was a member of the council of the Medical Defence Union. He was uncompromisingly honest in his expression of opinion whether in court, committee, or personal discussion. Illingworth was not a 'clubbable' person, for he was very modest and avoided self-publicity. He was elected an honorary fellow of five foreign academies of paediatrics and received the Aldrich award and medal of the American Academy of Pediatrics (1978). He also received the Spence medal of the British Paediatric Association (1979) and the Dawson Williams prize of the British Medical Association (1981). He was awarded the freedom of the city of Sheffield and honorary doctorates from Baghdad (1975), Sheffield (1976), and Leeds (1982). He was never awarded any civil honour although he had fought long and hard to develop and protect hospital services for children. He may well have antagonized those in authority, who were determined to see an end to children's hospitals in the 1950s and 1960s. After he retired in 1975 he started anew as a clinical medical officer running a well baby clinic in Derbyshire, and published a further seventy worthwhile papers and new revised editions of his books.

He was of medium height and relatively slender build, and could be of forbidding mien. With the exception of his taste in ties, his style of dress was subdued. In 1947 he married Cynthia, a paediatrician, daughter of Arthur Blenkinsop Redhead, engineer. They had one son and two daughters, and all the family were fellows or members of the Royal College of Physicians of London. Illingworth died in Bergen 4 June 1990 whilst on holiday, amongst the mountains and lakes, where he had been so fond of walking and taking photographs.

[*British Medical Journal*, vol. ccc, 23 June 1990; *Lancet*, 21 July 1990; personal knowledge.]   FRANK HARRIS

INCHYRA, first BARON (1900–1989), diplomat and Foreign Office official. [See MILLAR, FREDERICK ROBERT HOYER.]

IRVING, SIR Edmund George (1910–1990), hydrographer, was born 5 April 1910 in Sandakan, British North Borneo, the elder child and only son of George Clerk Irving, resident magistrate, British North Borneo, and his wife Ethel Mary Frances Poole, of Kimberley, South Africa. Arriving in England at the age of nine, Irving was sent to St Anthony's Preparatory School, Eastbourne, before being accepted for the Royal Naval College, Dartmouth, in 1923. Because of his notably prominent nose he was known to his classmates as 'Beaky'.

He went to sea as a cadet in HMS *Royal Oak* in 1927. On completion of sub-lieutenants' courses, in 1931 he joined the Royal Naval Surveying Service, in which he served for thirty-five years. In 1941 he was mentioned in dispatches for his skill as navigating officer in HMS *Scott*, when she was employed laying moored marker beacons in the Denmark strait to guide a squadron of British minelayers. On the staff of the commander-in-chief, Mediterranean, Irving was again mentioned in dispatches (1943) for putting in place on the western side of the straits of Messina three pairs of searchlights which, when illuminated vertically on the night of 2–3 September 1943, formed three sets of transit marks to guide the landing-craft of XIII Corps, Eighth Army, directly to their landing beaches in Reggio di Calabria.

In 1944, as a commander captaining HMS *Franklin*, he undertook rehabilitation surveys of a number of heavily damaged ports and harbours in north-west Europe as they fell into Allied hands. Finally, berthing his ship in Terneuzen, he was able to carry out surveys in the river Schelde, enabling Allied shipping to bring vital military supplies to Antwerp. For this he received not only appointment as OBE (1944) but also the thanks of Field Marshal *Montgomery (later first Viscount Montgomery of Alamein), who visited the ship and, at Irving's suggestion, 'spliced the mainbrace' (ordered the issue of an extra tot of rum), an action which was subsequently frowned upon by the Admiralty.

In 1948 'Egg' Irving, as he was now widely known, carried out in HMS *Sharpshooter* a number of sea trials of the newly developed Two Range Decca System for fixing surveying ships out of sight of land and in low visibility. This electronic invention brought about a radical change in sea surveying. As rear-admiral Irving was appointed hydrographer of the Royal Navy in 1960, a post he held with distinction. During this period he convinced the Admiralty that it was not satisfactory to convert warship hulls into surveying ships and that it would be more efficient to custom-build ships for this purpose. In December 1964 his wife launched *Hecla*, the first of four successful ocean-going survey ships.

Irving was a man of great energy and enthusiasm, with a love of people which made his retirement after 1966 a very full one. He continued for a number of years to work for the Decca Company, promoting the use of their electronic surveying equipment worldwide. He served on the council of the Royal Geographical Society, being chairman of the expeditions committee from 1965 to 1975, and president in 1969–71. In 1976 he was awarded the society's Patron's medal for 'services to the advancement of hydrographic science and encouragement for exploration'. As a member of the committee of management of the Royal National Lifeboat Institution from 1960, he was chairman of the boat committee from 1969 to 1978, during which period the institution developed the faster *Waveney* and *Arun* class lifeboats. He was a fellow of the Royal Institute of Navigation and its president from 1967 to 1969. He also served on the Natural Environment Research Council from 1967 to 1974, and was acting conservator of the river Mersey from 1975 to 1985. He was a trustee of the National Maritime Museum (1972–81) and an active member of the Society for Nautical Research. He was appointed CB in 1962 and KBE in 1966.

Irving was of middle height and fairly stout. He had a light complexion and sandy hair (although his beard was red when he grew it in wartime), with vivid blue eyes and bushy eye-brows. On 14 March 1936 he married Margaret Scudamore, daughter of Richard Edwards, of Ipswich and Birmingham. They had a son and a daughter. His first wife died in 1974 and in 1979 he married Esther Rebecca, daughter of Joseph Ellison, company director. Irving died of a heart attack at his home in Meopham, Kent, 1 October 1990.

[Private information; personal knowledge.]

G. S. RITCHIE

ISHERWOOD, Christopher William Brad-shaw (1904–1986), writer, was born 26 August 1904 at Wyberslegh Hall, Cheshire, the elder son (there were no daughters) of Francis Edward Bradshaw-Isherwood, professional soldier in the York and Lancaster Regiment, of Marple, and his wife Kathleen, the only child of Frederick Machell Smith, wine merchant, of Bury St Edmunds. He was educated at Repton, where he met his lifelong friend and the ultimate arbiter of his work, Edward Upward, with whom he wrote numerous surrealist-gothic stories about 'Mort-mere', a 'fantastic village' they had invented. He followed Upward to Cambridge, where, at Corpus Christi College, he studied history. He left after deliberately failing his tripos, and began earning his living as secretary to the International String Quartet.

He was deeply affected by World War I, in which his father had been killed and the certainties of the Edwardian world destroyed. Much of his life may be seen as a search for some creed to replace the traditional, public-school, Christian values of his childhood, against which he began rebelling as a young man. In 1925 he was reintroduced to W. H. *Auden, whom he had known at preparatory school, and through him met (Sir) Stephen Spender: the three men were to form a conspicuous literary, left-wing triumvirate of the 1930s. Isherwood's first novel, All the Conspirators (1928), is an oblique account of family discord, and is influenced by the work of Virginia *Woolf and E. M. *Forster. The conflict between mother and son was to be a frequent theme in his work (and, indeed, his life) and resurfaces in The Memorial (1932), a remarkably acute novel about the war between the generations, seen from both sides of the divide, and a key text of the period.

After a half-hearted attempt to train as a doctor at King's College, London (October 1928–March 1929), Isherwood followed Auden to Berlin, partly in order to pursue a homosexual life in the unfettered atmosphere of the Weimar Republic. He witnessed the rise of Nazism, and wrote two classic novels of the era, Mr. Norris Changes Trains (1935) and Goodbye to Berlin (1939). Both are sardonic tragi-comedies, and the latter contains the famous sentence 'I am a

camera with its shutter open, quite passive, recording, not thinking', which (to Isherwood's increasing irritation) was often quoted as a summation of his fictional method. To this period also belong collaborations with Auden: the three plays written for London's experimental Group Theatre—The Dog Beneath the Skin (1935), The Ascent of F6 (1936), and On the Frontier (1938)—and Journey to a War (1939), an account of their travels in China during the Sino-Japanese War. Lions and Shadows (1938) is an autobiography of the 1920s, in which many of Isherwood's preoccupations are outlined.

In January 1939 Isherwood and Auden emigrated to the United States, a controversial move seen in some quarters as little short of 'desertion'. Isherwood settled in Los Angeles, but, insecure, and wracked by feelings of guilt and literary impotence, he needed something to give form and order to his life. He found this in Vedantism and became a follower of Swami Prabhavananda, who had set up a temple in Hollywood. Isherwood had already worked in the British film industry (an experience he described in the novella Prater Violet, 1945), and now he found employment as a scriptwriter for Metro-Goldwyn–Mayer. His Hollywood career was largely undistinguished, and included scripts for Diane (1956), a lavish and miscast costume drama, and The Loved One (1965), a lamentably coarse adaptation of the novel by Evelyn *Waugh.

In 1941 he went to work in a Quaker-run camp for refugees fleeing Europe. When America entered the war, he registered as a conscientious objector and enrolled at a Vedanta monastery, where he worked with Prabhavananda on a new translation of the Bhagavad-Gita (1944) and became co-editor of the movement's magazine, Vedanta and the West. He left the monastery in 1945, the year he became an American citizen, and set up house with Bill Caskey, an ebullient, argumentative, and hard-drinking Irish-American. The Condor and the Cows (1949) is an account of their travels in South America.

In 1953 Isherwood met Don Bachardy, a student almost thirty years his junior, who later became a renowned portraitist: they were to live together until Isherwood's death. His first attempt at an 'American' novel, The World in the Evening (1954), took a great deal of time and effort to write and pleased its author as little as it pleased the critics. He returned to form with Down There on a Visit (1962), an autobiographical novel of four interlinking sections.

Isherwood had begun teaching English literature at the University of California in 1960, and an Isherwood-like professor is the protagonist of A Single Man (1964), a witty, sly, and touching book about the outsider in society. It is perhaps Isherwood's masterpiece. During the

1960s he published further books on Vedanta and a novel on related themes, *A Meeting by the River* (1967).

His three last books were *Kathleen and Frank* (1971), a portrait of his parents in which his interest in heredity is fully explored; *Christopher and His Kind* (1976), which retells in more explicit fashion the story of his Berlin years; and *My Guru and his Disciple* (1980), an account of his relationship with Prabhavananda.

Isherwood's principal characteristic, both in his life and his work, was an apparent candour. He was also a professional charmer, and these two qualities offset his considerable vanity. He was of short stature, with a disproportionately large head, a prominent nose, and deep-set, penetrating eyes. Although he maintained a strikingly boyish appearance well into old age, he was a lifelong hypochondriac. He eventually died of cancer at the age of eighty-one 4 January 1986, at his home at 145 Adelaide Drive, Santa Monica, California.

[Peter Parker, *Christopher Isherwood*, 1996; Isherwood's autobiographical books (see above) and unpublished diaries and papers, in the possession of Don Bachardy; Brian H. Finney, *Christopher Isherwood: a Critical Biography*, 1979; private information.] PETER PARKER

ISSIGONIS, SIR **Alexander Arnold Constantine** (1906–1988), motor engineer and designer, was born 18 November 1906 in Smyrna (later İzmir), Turkey, the only child of Constantine Issigonis, a marine engineer resident in Smyrna who was of Greek origin but had British citizenship, and his wife, Hulda Josephine Prokopp, whose family came from Bavaria and ran Smyrna's brewery. A comfortable childhood, during which 'Alec' was taught by private tutors, was abruptly ended by World War I, during which Greece and Turkey supported opposite sides and the Greeks in Smyrna were interned. Following the war, the city came under Greek control until 1922, when Turkey invaded and the Issigonis family was evacuated along with other British citizens. Constantine Issigonis died in Malta in 1922, and his wife and son travelled to London alone. Hulda Issigonis wanted her son to continue his broken education, but despite suggestions that his drawing talent pointed to art school, Alec enrolled at Battersea Polytechnic as an engineering student in 1923.

Though he failed his final exams because of his weakness in mathematics, Issigonis was determined to pursue an engineering career and joined Edward Gillett (London) in 1928, assisting in the design of a semi-automatic clutch. This earned him a job at Humber (Coventry) in 1934, as a technical draughtsman, and he began experimental designs for independent front suspension, which he continued after joining Morris Motors (Oxford) in 1936. During World War II Issigonis worked on various military projects, but simultaneously he began his first complete car design, which went into production in October 1948 as the Morris Minor. This small car was praised for its use of space, and its steering and road-holding capacities. It continued in production for twenty-four years, during which over 1.6 million were produced. Following this success, Issigonis was promoted to chief engineer in 1950. When Morris Motors merged with Austin Motors to form the British Motor Corporation (BMC) in 1952, he briefly moved to Alvis (Coventry), but in 1955 returned to BMC as deputy engineering co-ordinator, based in Birmingham.

Petrol-rationing, arising out of the 1956 Suez crisis, prompted motor manufacturers to think about small, fuel-efficient cars, and Issigonis was asked to head a team to design such a car for BMC. Just two years later, in 1959, the Mini was launched and was quickly recognized to be a revolutionary vehicle. A transverse-mounted engine with front-wheel drive gave maximum space utilization, with room for four adults, while the strikingly functional bodyshell, shaped like a box, and only ten feet long, resulted from Issigonis's insistence that a 'styled' car quickly dated. His instinct was vindicated by over three decades of continuous production, during which figures had reached 5 million by 1986. Though priced for the mass market, the Mini actually achieved its success as a 'cult' car, popular with the middle classes, particularly women, used by the rich and famous, and spectacularly successful in motor sport. It was probably the last great product of one man's vision the car industry is likely to see.

Issigonis's career was at its high point. In 1961 he became technical director of BMC, in 1963 he was given a seat on the board, and in 1964 he became engineering director. He continued to design successful cars, including the 1100/1300 range, launched in 1962 and the best-selling car of its day; but when BMC became part of the car giant British Leyland in 1968 innovation was sacrificed for 'market research', something Issigonis abhorred. In 1971 he officially retired, and though he was retained by the company as consultant, continuing to produce original designs for a steam-engined car and a gearless Mini, neither of these was ever manufactured.

Issigonis never married, but was a man of great personal charm, occasionally irascible, who formed enduring friendships. His working relationships seem to have been less relaxed, perhaps because of his need to be in complete control, his eye for detail, and his demanding work schedules. Colleagues were often irritated by his arrogant and impatient manner, but they also felt proud to be associated with one of his projects. His appearance was Mediterranean with his aquiline nose and large hands, yet his manner was very English and friends remembered his eloquent eyes and wry expression. He considered himself to be a creative artist rather than a number-cruncher, and his cars are very much the creation of an individual with a strong personality, not pieces of styled metal constructed by a committee.

His life was one of contrasts. His youth in Smyrna was relatively affluent but was followed by the privations caused by war. His middle years were spent in Oxford, where he built a career of personal achievement, while providing financial security for himself and his mother, who continued to live with him until her death. The years of his greatest success, which came when he was already over fifty, were spent in Birmingham, where he remained a man of simple tastes, which were reflected both in the practical-

ity of his designs and the austerity which characterized his private life. His recreations were also modest, and included a model railway and love of Meccano sets.

His contribution to society brought him a number of distinctions. In 1964 he was elected a Royal Designer for Industry and appointed CBE. In 1967 he became a fellow of the Royal Society. In 1969 he was knighted for 'services to automotive engineering'. He died at his home in Birmingham 2 October 1988, after suffering for several years from a progressive illness.

[Andrew Nahum, *Alec Issigonis*, 1988; Laurence Pomeroy, *The Mini Story*, 1964; *The Times*, 4 October 1988; Sir Diarmuid Downs in *Biographical Memoirs of Fellows of the Royal Society*, vol. xxxix, 1994; private information.]   GILLIAN BARDSLEY

J

JACOBSON, Sydney, BARON JACOBSON (1908–1988), editor and political commentator, was born 26 October 1908 in Zeerost, South Africa, the only son and elder child of Samuel and Anna Jacobson, a Jewish couple who had emigrated from Germany and were running an unsuccessful ostrich farm. In the summer of 1914 the family returned to Frankfurt to visit friends and were unfortunate enough to stay on until August, when they were all interned. Jacobson thus obtained his primary education in a German camp, a more humane version of the camps which were to fire his hatred of Germans in the 1930s and 1940s. His father was drowned when the ship in which he was attempting to return to South Africa sank off the south-west coast of England. The mother then took her children to live in Britain with relations, the family of Lewis (later first Baron) *Silkin, who was later a government minister.

Jacobson attended Strand School and King's College, London, where he obtained a diploma in journalism. He began his journalistic career on Sussex weekly papers. He soon left for India, however, where he became assistant editor of the *Statesman* (1934–6), a reservist with the Delhi Light Horse, and a daring steeplechase jockey. On his return to England he worked for the pocket-sized magazine, *Lilliput* (1936–9). He enlisted as a private immediately war was declared, was commissioned in the Middlesex Regiment, was awarded the MC (1944) for his resolute defence of a bridge during the 1944 fighting in the Low Countries, and was promoted lieutenant-colonel and given command of his battalion. On demobilization he wrote for *Picture Post* (1945–8) and obtained his first editorship at the *Leader Magazine* (1948–50), a paper which was a journalistic success but a financial failure. Soon after it ceased publication he began his association with the Mirror Group, writing first for the *Sunday Pictorial* (1951) under Hugh (later Baron) Cudlipp and then for the *Daily Mirror* as its political editor (1952–62).

The *Mirror* was a noisy, disputatious paper and Jacobson, a quiet man, who was erudite, sceptical, and mordant, nevertheless fitted in perfectly. With Cudlipp he produced coruscating attacks on the governments of *Churchill, *Eden, and Macmillan. Although he was on the far left when young he moved sufficiently to give notable support to Hugh *Gaitskell, whose speeches he occasionally helped to write. During the Suez crisis of 1956 Jacobson was instrumental in shifting the *Mirror* from early acquiescence to outright opposition, a policy which reduced its circulation by 70,000. In fact it was prepared to lose many more.

When the Mirror Group bought Odhams Press in 1961 Jacobson was made editor of the loss-making *Daily Herald* (1962–4), the organ of the Trades Union Congress and the Labour party. He remained editor (1964–5) after it was transmuted into the *Sun*, a middlebrow paper created to fill what was thought to be a gap in the market but which was proved not to exist. As its losses mounted the paper was almost given away to Rupert Murdoch in 1965 and Jacobson returned to the *Mirror*, where he became editorial director (1968–74) and later deputy chairman (1973–4) of the Group.

In the two general elections of 1974, in February and October, Jacobson was at his peak. Determined that the Labour party should win, he produced a series of famous poster-type front pages, inspired every leading article, and oversaw all the political stories. With election results as close as they were in both elections, Jacobson's contributions must have been significant. He had refused a knighthood when he was editing the *Daily Herald*, but after his retirement he accepted the offer of a life peerage in 1975.

He had hoped to play an active part in the House of Lords, but his later years were affected by ill health. They were also marred by the misfortunes of the Labour party and by what was happening at the *Daily Mirror*. After Robert Maxwell became its publisher in 1983 Jacobson stopped buying the paper he had served for so long.

Jacobson was a tall, distinguished-looking man with a large nose and sardonic smile. He married in 1938 Phyllis June, daughter of Frank Steele Buck, stockbroker; they had two sons and a daughter. He died 13 August 1988 in St Albans.

[Maurice Edelman, *The Mirror: a Political History*, 1966; Hugh Cudlipp, *Walking on the Water*, 1976; private information; personal knowledge.]

TERENCE LANCASTER

JAMES, (John) Morrice (Cairns), BARON SAINT
BRIDES (1916–1989), diplomat, was born 30 April
1916 in Finchley, the only son and younger child
of Lewis Cairns James, professor of drama and
elocution at the Royal College of Music, and his
second wife, Catherine Mary, daughter of John
Maitland Marshall, of Dulwich. He was educated
at Bradfield College and Balliol College, Oxford,
where he obtained second classes in classical
honour moderations (1936) and *literae humaniores*
(1938). He entered the Dominions Office as an
assistant principal in 1939. After war broke out
he joined the Royal Navy as an ordinary seaman
in 1940, before being commissioned into the
Royal Marines in 1941. He subsequently saw
action in the Middle East and Sicily, for which
he was appointed MBE (military) in 1944, and he
was demobilized in the rank of lieutenant-colonel
in the following year to return to the Dominions
(soon to become the Commonwealth Relations)
Office.

James was a born diplomat and an outstanding
negotiator, whose qualities were made full use of
by ministers of both parties, though his easy
manner and ready smile concealed a toughness
and ambition which did not always endear him to
his subordinates. Entries in successive editions of
Who's Who after his retirement described his
main recreation first as 'exploring the fallibility
of contemporary statesmen' and later as 'meeting
new and intelligent people'. He appears to have
made few lifelong friends among his immediate
colleagues, but his new friends invariably found
him congenial and sympathetic.

Having joined the Civil Service before the
war, his promotion when he rejoined it was
rapid. After a brief period as first secretary in the
high commission in South Africa (1946–7), he
became in quick succession head of the CRO
defence department (1949–51) and then of the
establishment department (1951–2). In 1952 he
was posted as deputy high commissioner to
Lahore, so beginning a unique series of postings
to the Indian subcontinent where, with a few
breaks, he served successively as deputy and high
commissioner in both Karachi and New Delhi.
During one of these breaks he accompanied
Harold *Macmillan (later the first Earl of Stockton) on his tour of Asia and the Far East in 1958,
and in another made a series of visits to Rhodesia
to set up what proved to be the abortive talks
between Harold Wilson (later Baron Wilson of
Rievaulx) and Ian Smith in HMS *Tiger* in 1966
and HMS *Fearless* in 1968. Smith's duplicity (or
weakness of character) was underlined by the fact
that he assured James before the *Tiger* talks that
he had 'full and unequivocal powers to settle',
but allowed his agreement to be overruled by his
cabinet colleagues on his return to Salisbury.

In the Indian subcontinent James initially
tended to be identified with Pakistan (deputy

high commissioner 1955–6, high commissioner
1961–6). With his opposite number in India,
John Freeman, he was closely involved in the
negotiations to settle the Rann of Kutch affair
which preceded the outbreak of war between
India and Pakistan in 1965, in which the Wilson
government gave some evidence of favouring
Pakistan. As a result, when James was posted to
Delhi as high commissioner in 1968, he faced
some initial hostility, though with characteristic
aplomb he quickly gained the confidence of
Indian ministers.

His appointment to Delhi came as the culmination of a curious sequence of events. Having
been deputy under-secretary of state for two
years, he had been appointed permanent under-
secretary of state at the Commonwealth Office
(formed two years earlier from the amalgamation
of the Colonial Office with the CRO) in early
1968, but within ten days of his appointment the
cup was dashed from his lips by Harold Wilson's
announcement that the CO itself was to be
amalgamated with the Foreign Office. He thus
served as PUS for only six months, but in
compensation was awarded the rare honour for a
civil servant of being appointed a privy councillor (1968). He ended his Diplomatic Service
career as high commissioner to Australia in
1971–6. He had to deal with Australian apprehension over Britain's entry to the Common
Market and with the affair of the runaway MP,
John *Stonehouse.

He was appointed CMG (1957), CVO (1961),
KCMG (1962), and GCMG (1975). In 1977 he
received a life peerage, taking the title of Baron
Saint Brides and accepting the ceremonial post of
king of arms of the Order of St Michael and St
George. After his retirement he took up a succession of academic appointments at American universities, including Harvard, the Foreign Policy
Research Institute at Philadelphia, and finally the
Center for International Security and Arms Control at Stanford, where he was remembered with
affection and admiration for his work on the
Asian–Pacific region and for his encouragement
of the younger students.

James was a big man in every way, who in his
earlier years waged a cheerful, but not wholly
successful, battle with corpulence by swimming
whenever he could during his lunch break. He
was married twice. His first marriage in 1948, to
the delightful Elizabeth Margaret Roper Piesse,
came as something of a surprise, many of his
colleagues having been under the impression that
he had been courting her mother. Elizabeth's
father was Francis Charles Roper Piesse, solicitor
and, later, hotelier. Of this marriage there were
two daughters and a son. Following Elizabeth's
untimely death in 1966, he married in 1968 Mrs
Geneviève ('Jenny') Christiane Sarasin, daughter
of Robert Henri Houdin, company director. On

their return from Australia he moved with her to live in France at St Tropez, where he died 26 November 1989.

[*The Times*, 30 November 1989; Foreign Office records; private information; personal knowledge.]

DAVID SCOTT

JAMESON, Margaret Ethel ('Storm') (1891–1986), novelist, was born 8 January 1891 in Whitby in the North Riding of Yorkshire, the eldest in the family of three daughters and a son of William Storm Jameson, sea captain, and his wife (who was also his stepsister), Hannah Margaret, daughter of George Gallilee, shipbuilder. As a child she accompanied her parents on several voyages, which marked the beginning of a lifelong passion for travel. Yet despite her self-imposed exile from Whitby, the harbour town remained central to her imagination and to many of her novels.

Her parents' marriage was unhappy and Storm Jameson's early life was dominated by her high-tempered, bitter mother whom she both feared and loved, and who encouraged her to receive an academic education. After being taught privately and at Scarborough Municipal School for a year, she won one of three county scholarships which enabled her to take a place at Leeds University, where she read English for three years, graduating in 1912 with a first-class degree. A research scholarship allowed her to go to London, first to University College, then to King's. She was awarded her MA in 1914 for a thesis on modern European drama, which was published in 1920 (*Modern Drama in Europe*).

On 15 January 1913 Jameson married Charles Dougan Clarke, schoolmaster, whom she had met in her second year at Leeds. He was the son of Charles Granville Clarke, doctor of medicine, an American Quaker. Their son, Charles William Storm, was born on 20 June 1915. The pair were temperamentally ill-matched and the marriage soon foundered, although there was no divorce until 1925. Meanwhile Storm Jameson had begun the extraordinarily prolific career of 'une machine à faire des livres', as she once described herself. The author of forty-five novels, numerous pamphlets, essays, and reviews, she freely admitted that she wrote too much, fuelled by her enormous energy and driven by the need to make money. Generous and spendthrift, constantly moving house and travelling in Europe whenever she could afford it, her career was shaped from the outset by her financial circumstances, which remained precarious throughout her life.

After refusing a job on the *Egoist*, which went to (Dame) Rebecca *West, she worked successively for an advertising agency, the *New Commonwealth*, and Alfred Knopf, the American publisher, but after 1928 most of her income was derived from writing. Her first novel, *The Pot Boils* (1919), was widely reviewed and her popularity increased with the publication of the Mary Hervey trilogy, *The Triumph of Time* (1927–31), which charted the fortunes of the Whitby shipbuilding community between 1841 and 1923. Jameson was by now happy in her personal life, having in 1926 married the historian and novelist, Guy Patterson Chapman (died 1972), son of George Walter Chapman, official receiver in bankruptcy. Chapman shared her love of France and tolerated her 'mania against domestic life' to the extent of living with her in a hotel for six years when he became professor of modern history at Leeds in 1945.

In 1930 Jameson began consciously to change her writing style in emulation of Stendhal. The result was three novellas about women, including the remarkably imagined meditations of an elderly prostitute in *A Day Off* (1933). Shortly afterwards she began a Balzacian quintet, *The Mirror in Darkness* (1934), that was based on the autobiographical figure of Mary Hervey Russell. Her own dissatisfaction as well as poor reviews caused her to abandon the series in 1936, although the related *The Journal of Mary Hervey Russell* (1945) and *The Black Laurel* (1947) are among her best novels, together with those inspired by her knowledge of Europe and love of France: *Cousin Honoré* (1940), *Europe to Let* (1940), and *Cloudless May* (1943).

During the 1930s Jameson became passionately involved in issues of social justice and anti-fascism. Between 1938 and 1944 she was president of the English section of PEN, for which she worked tirelessly on behalf of exiled European writers, earning herself a place on the 'Berlin death list'. After the war, although she continued to write indefatigably, her reputation as a novelist declined and the reprinting of some of her books by Virago Press in the 1980s did little to revive interest in her work. She noted her eclipse without resentment in her autobiography *Journey from the North* (2 vols., 1969, 1970), which contains a memorably honest self-portrait of the author as well as harrowing accounts of bereavement and war.

Jameson liked to remember that her Nordic ancestors had been peasants of the sea whom she resembled in her restlessness and endurance, as she did in her looks. Her large, long-sighted eyes were grey-blue, set in a round high-cheek-boned face. Sensual and physically strong, she experienced a series of romantic and sexual obsessions until the time of her second marriage. She received few public honours, although her honorary D.Litt. from Leeds (1943) gave her pleasure, as did her honorary membership of the American Academy and Institute of Arts and

Letters. She died in Cambridge 30 September 1986.

[*The Times*, 7 October 1986; Storm Jameson, *Journey from the North*, 2 vols., 1969, 1970.]

JUDITH PRIESTMAN

JASPER, Ronald Claud Dudley (1917–1990), liturgist and historian, was born 17 August 1917 in Plymouth, Devon, the only child of Claud Albert Jasper, dockyard craftsman, and his wife, Florence Lily Curtis. Educated at Plymouth College, he read history at Leeds University, obtaining a second-class degree in 1938. Responding to a call to ordination, he went to the College of the Resurrection at Mirfield to prepare for the priesthood, while completing an MA on constitutional history, gained with distinction. However, the academic world was not beckoning and on ordination he became curate of Ryhope, in the diocese of Durham (1940–2).

From the beginning of his time there, the bishop, A. T. P. *Williams, himself a distinguished historian, kept a benevolent eye on this young man with historical interests. At the first opportunity, he sent him to Durham as a curate of St Oswald's (1942–3). Later, two years as chaplain of University and Hatfield colleges in Durham (1946–8) gave him the opportunity for serious study, and the result was a BD (1950) and *Prayer Book Revision in England 1800–1900* (1954), the first of his many books. During this time he was also encouraged by (D.) Colin Dunlop, bishop of Jarrow, who used him as a lecturer at his clergy schools. In 1954 Bishop Dunlop, who had become dean of Lincoln, was asked by the archbishops of Canterbury and York to chair a commission 'to consider all matters of liturgical concern referred to it by the archbishops', and was given a free hand in choosing his team. He included Jasper, who was vicar of Stillington (1948–55) and who became succentor of Exeter Cathedral (1955–60).

The archbishop of York, Donald (later Baron) Coggan, who succeeded Dunlop on the liturgical commission in 1960, decided he must give up its chairmanship and persuaded Jasper to take it on (1964–81). By this time Jasper had left Exeter, had obtained his DD (1961) from Leeds, and was lecturing in liturgy at King's College, London (1960–7, reader 1967–8), and acquiring a reputation as an ecclesiastical biographer, with a life of A. C. *Headlam (1960) and the biography of George *Bell (1967) in progress. 'I was doing the very things in life I had always wanted to do and to take on the Commission would involve a serious disruption,' he said at the time. But he realized that his long study of the papers of Walter *Frere (*Walter Howard Frere: his Correspondence on Liturgical Revision and Construction*, 1954), who had been much involved in the abortive 1927–8 prayer book revision, had given

him a unique insight into the pitfalls awaiting those brave enough to attempt this kind of work in the Church of England. He also glimpsed the possibilities of ecumenical liturgical co-operation.

Jasper was responsible for convincing Archbishop Michael *Ramsey (later Baron Ramsey of Canterbury) to invite the mainstream British churches to form the Joint Liturgical Group, which was set up in 1963. Jasper served as its secretary until his retirement in 1984. During that time he edited a series of books which greatly influenced the revision of most denominational service books. His ecumenical vision was further widened when, in 1966, he was appointed an official observer to the Concilium Liturgicum, set up to work out the implications of the second Vatican Council's *Constitution on the Sacred Liturgy* (1963). From this work emerged the need for a forum at which the dilemmas of those engaged in liturgical revision in English-speaking countries could be shared. Roman Catholics were particularly anxious to be involved, being engaged in the problem of producing liturgical texts in the vernacular. In 1969 Jasper was elected president of Societas Liturgica, the international ecumenical society for liturgical study and research. At the same time he was engaged in all the major work of liturgical revision in his own Church of England, of which the *Alternative Service Book 1980* was to be the fruition.

Jasper was appointed a canon of Westminster (1968–75) and dean of York (1975–84). At York he saw through a liturgical reordering of the nave and significant work in the Lady chapel and the Zouche chapel. He also implemented the rescue, conservation, and restoration of the fifteenth-century St William's College. Jasper's time at York came to a dramatic conclusion. The fire which destroyed the roof and vault of the south transept occurred on 9 July 1984, four days before his retirement.

Under Jasper's leadership, major changes were made in the worship of the Church of England. Not all have been popular, but he courageously orchestrated change from a historian's knowledge of its inevitability and from a liturgist's appreciation of modern scholarship, never forgetting his ministry in the pit villages of Durham and never allowing the church's worship to become recherché or arcane. He retired to Ripon and produced an overview of 300 years of liturgical development in England in *The Development of the Anglican Liturgy 1662–1980* (1989). He was appointed CBE in 1981 and had an honorary D.Litt. from Susquehanna University, Pennsylvania (1976).

He was of average height, slim build, and always neatly and smartly dressed. He was one of those rare clergymen who took care in his choice of clothes when not in clerical dress. In 1943 he married Ethel ('Betty'), daughter of David Wiggins, solicitor's managing clerk. They had a daughter and a son, who became principal of St Chad's College, Durham. Jasper died 11 April 1990 in the District Hospital, Harrogate.

[Donald Gray, 'Dr Ronald Jasper and the Liturgical Commission', Friends of York Minster 62nd *Annual Report*, 1991; personal knowledge.]   DONALD GRAY

JEFFREYS, SIR Harold (1891–1989), geophysicist, was born 22 April 1891 in Fatfield, county Durham, the only child of Robert Hall Jeffreys, headmaster of the village school at Fatfield, and his wife Elizabeth Mary, schoolteacher, daughter of William Sharpe. His parents both came from families living near Morpeth, Northumberland. Jeffreys was educated at Rutherford College and Armstrong College (both in Newcastle upon Tyne) and at St John's College, Cambridge, of which he was a scholar. He obtained a first class in part i (1911) and was a wrangler in part ii (1913) of the mathematical tripos. He was awarded the Smith's prize in 1915. Inspired by the work of Sir George *Darwin on tides, he began research in celestial mechanics. He was elected a fellow of St John's in 1914, retaining his fellowship until his death. He obtained a Durham D.Sc. in 1917.

During World War I Jeffreys worked in the Cavendish Laboratory, Cambridge, on wartime problems, from 1915 to 1917. He then went to the Meteorological Office from 1917 to 1922, returning to Cambridge as lecturer in mathematics in 1922. He won the Adams prize in 1927. He became reader in geophysics in 1931 and was elected Plumian professor of astronomy and experimental philosophy in 1946, retiring in 1958.

Jeffreys worked in five branches of mathematics: hydrodynamics, celestial mechanics, seismology and the physics of the interior of the earth, probability, and pure mathematics. His wartime work led him to study fluid dynamics. He demonstrated the importance of eddy viscosity, identified by (Sir) G. I. *Taylor, in geophysical fluid motions, classified winds by their dynamical origins, and established the essential role of cyclones in the general circulation of the atmosphere. He was the first to identify the importance of viscosity in boundary conditions. He studied the mechanism for the generation of surface waves on water and developed the work of J. W. *Strutt (third Baron Rayleigh) on the initiation of convection.

Jeffreys had early realized the importance of seismology, which occupied him from 1921 to the end of his life, for investigating the interior of the earth, for which he established three major structural features. In 1921, with Dorothy Wrinch, he showed from records of an explosion in the Rhineland that the crust of the earth had at least two layers above the mantle; the study also demonstrated the value of explosions as seismic sources. In 1927 Jeffreys showed that the earth must have a dense core which must be effectively liquid, and this was amply confirmed subsequently. His third major discovery was the division between the upper and lower mantle of the earth, which he attributed to a change of crystal structure of olivine to a denser form at high pressure. He spent many years on calculations of travel times of seismic waves over the earth, and produced the Jeffreys–Bullen tables, first published in 1940, and still used in routine identification of earthquake epicentres and as reference times for both comparison with observations and calculations of models of the interior of the earth. Jeffreys also made many contributions to the theory of elastic waves.

Working mostly by himself and with few research students, Jeffreys wrote extensively on the dynamics of the earth and the solar system. In the years before artificial satellites were launched he analysed observations of gravity on the surface of the earth, another very laborious numerical project, and derived a consistent set of dynamical parameters of the earth and the moon. He studied the variations in the rotation of the earth and showed that the slowing down of the earth's rotation, found astronomically, was most probably due to eddy viscosity in shallow seas, another result that later seemed fully confirmed. Those studies, together with his theoretical work on the effect of the liquid core on the earth's rotation, dominated the subject.

Jeffreys's book, *The Earth* (1924), was the first systematic account of the physical state of the earth as a whole and had a profound influence on generations of geophysicists through its many successive editions. Jeffreys was not uncontroversial, and indeed he was involved in a number of major debates which seem to have called forth his tersest writing. In particular, he always opposed the ideas of continental drift and plate tectonics, although it was he who first pointed out that the earth's crust was just the upper layer of a rigid lithosphere about 100 km. thick, and he was a keen advocate (1936) of systematic studies of the floor of the oceans. Although his most significant work in geophysics was completed before the technical revolutions of artificial satellites, marine geophysics, and new methods of seismology changed the face of geophysics in the middle of the twentieth century, his major results were the foundation of subsequent developments. He showed, above all, how rigorous methods of classical mechanics should be applied to the study of the structure of the earth and the planets.

He had an early interest in scientific inference and, later, prompted by statistical problems arising from his work on seismic travel times, he constructed a comprehensive corpus of methods for estimation and tests of significance according to Bayesian principles. His *Theory of Probability* (1939), which presented a formal algebra of probability on an axiomatic basis, with many applications in various branches of physics, became very influential. Much of his original work in pure mathematics was incorporated in *Methods of Mathematical Physics* (1946, with his wife). His most important contributions were to the study of operational methods for the solution of differential equations and to asymptotic methods.

Jeffreys was elected a fellow of the Royal Society in 1925 and was president of the Royal Astronomical Society in 1955–7. He was a foreign member of a number of academies, among them the US Academy of Science, the Accademia Nazionale dei Lincei (Rome), and the royal academies of Sweden and Belgium. He was awarded, besides other prizes, the gold medal of the Royal Astronomical Society (1937), a Royal medal (1948) and the Copley medal (1960) of the Royal Society, the Vetlesen prize of Columbia University (1962), the Guy medal of the Royal Statistical Society (1963), and the Wollaston medal of the Geological Society (1964). He received five honorary degrees and was knighted in 1953.

Jeffreys had wide interests within and beyond science. Besides some prophetic papers on physics and stellar structure, he wrote on the ecology of county Durham and the Breckland and on psychology. He was a skilled photographer; a large collection of his negatives was given to St John's College. He was for many years active in national and international astronomical and geophysical societies. Undoubtedly one of the distinctive personalities of Cambridge in his time, he was difficult to talk to and was known for his intensive smoking and for his bicycling everywhere. Yet he was very sociable, dined regularly in his college, sang tenor for many years in the Cambridge Philharmonic Choir, and greatly enjoyed the dinners of the Royal Astronomical Society Club.

Jeffreys was somewhat over medium height and spare of frame. He wore glasses, had a small moustache, and was usually dressed informally, often wearing shorts in hot weather. In 1940 he married Bertha, daughter of William Alexander Swirles, commercial traveller in leather, and his wife, Harriet Blaxley, primary-school teacher. She was a cousin of Michael *Stewart (Baron Stewart of Fulham). There were no children of the marriage. Lady Jeffreys, a mathematician, was vice-mistress of Girton College, Cambridge, from 1966 to 1969. There is a portrait of Jeffreys

in St John's College. He died 18 March 1989 in Cambridge.

[Sir Alan Cook in *Biographical Memoirs of Fellows of the Royal Society*, vol. xxxvi, 1990; Harold and Bertha Jeffreys (eds.), *Collected Papers*, vols. i–vi, 1971–7; personal knowledge.]   ALAN COOK

JENNINGS, Paul Francis (1918–1989), humorous writer, was born in Leamington Spa 20 June 1918, the only son and second of three children of William Benedict Jennings, musician, and his wife, Mary Gertrude Hewitt, the daughter of a watchmaker. They soon moved to a Coventry Roman Catholic parish, where Paul's father was organist and choirmaster, and Paul became the city's boy soprano, performing solo at the Hippodrome. Music was an absorbing interest from Paul's youth, as was his religion. He won a scholarship to the King Henry VIII School at Coventry, but went on to Douai, his parents thinking he might have a vocation for the priesthood. He loved Douai and its admirable headmaster, Father Ignatius Rice, but decided he was not cut out for the priesthood. His grounding in the classics fed his literary imagination and his loving, lifelong, obsessive play with words.

His humour was innate, or at least formed very early. He joined the Royal Corps of Signals in World War II and, when he was a subaltern in India in 1943, *Lilliput* published a characteristic piece beginning: 'Have you ever watched a soldier marching, and wondered what he was thinking about? If he's a Young Soldier, I can tell you! He is thinking about a little booklet excitingly titled "Army Form B51".' *Punch* took an army piece in 1945. Jennings worked at the Central Office of Information (1946–7) and in advertising (1947–9). His celebrated parody of Jean-Paul Sartre appeared in the *Spectator* in 1948: 'Resistentialism is a philosophy of tragic grandeur ...deriving its name from the thesis that Things resist Men...*Les choses sont contre nous.*' Resistentialism's leading luminary was Pierre-Marie Ventre, who built on the work of his nineteenth-century predecessors, Friedegg and Heidansiecker. Jennings imagined the seminal play 'Puits Clos' about three old men endlessly stumbling over bricks in the bottom of a well. (It was used by *Time* magazine as a news story.) In 1949 he joined the staff of the *Observer*, with a regular column, 'Oddly Enough', which continued for seventeen years. His method was to start with something very familiar and then spin illogical and fantastic speculations around it, creating a brilliant and often subversive parody.

Those *Observer* years, which lasted until 1966, were years of fulfilment, establishing him, as *The Times* obituarist adjudged, as 'the most consistently original English comic writer of our century'. In the year Jennings joined the *Observer* so did Eric *Blom, as its music critic. Paul met his daughter, Celia. Their marriage, in 1952, was very happy and ended only with his death. There were three sons and three daughters. Jennings knew a great deal about music; he sang madrigals with the Oriana Society and enjoyed singing—as far afield as Istanbul—with the Philharmonia Chorus and the London Philharmonic Choir. 'For members of choirs, there's harmony beyond the heard harmony of music.'

The family moved from Hampstead to East Bergholt, in Suffolk, and Jennings's pieces in the *Observer* began to reflect his deep love of that county. His wife became involved in the work of the Suffolk Preservation Society. To celebrate its sixtieth anniversary in 1989, she edited a book to which her husband contributed inimitably—not only the title, *Suffolk For Ever*, but the last word. This was a clever discussion, disguised as a Platonic dialogue, of the complexities and the pitfalls confronting everyone moved to action by the erosions of our environs. In the wide-ranging book Jennings edited, and mostly wrote—*The English Difference* (1974)—he illustrated his speculative inclination: 'You can see on the face of a child, deep in a game, the kind of total absorption observable in the figure of Pythagoras, *Thinking*, carved on a portal at Chartres...Though children the world over play games, it is the English who, perhaps sensing the Death of God, once did unconsciously try to preserve religion in their untranslatable phrase *playing the game*.' After 1966 Jennings wrote freelance, and from this period emerged his compilation, *The Book of Nonsense* (1977). He mourned the loss of anything old-fashioned: steam trains, red telephone kiosks, the Fahrenheit classification of temperature. His prejudices were conservative and patriotic.

Jennings's *Observer* (and other) essays were collected and published with such titles as *Even Oddlier* (1952), and *Next to Oddliness* (1955), *Golden Oddlies* (1983), and *The Paul Jennings Reader* (1990). *The Living Village* (1968) was a picture of the Women's Institutes of Britain. He also wrote two children's books.

Jennings suffered serious illnesses—including tuberculosis and a heart attack—all belied by the laughter of that high, quick, musical voice and by lively, wide-open, grey eyes. He and his wife moved to Orford, on the Suffolk coast. He died there 26 December 1989, of liver cancer.

[*The Times*, 29 December 1989; private information; personal knowledge.] NORMAN SCARFE

JEWKES, John (1902–1988), economist, was born in Barrow-in-Furness 29 June 1902, the eldest of three children and only son of John Jewkes, sheet-metal worker and foreman in Vickers Armstrong's shipbuilding yard, and his wife, Fanny Cope. After attending Barrow Grammar School, he took a B.Comm. degree at the Uni-

versity of Manchester in 1923, with distinction in economics, and an M.Comm. by thesis in 1924. He then spent two years as assistant secretary of the Manchester Chamber of Commerce before being appointed to a lectureship at Manchester University in 1926. His early work was on the cotton industry and in 1935 he published with E. M. Gray a study of *Wages and Labour in the Lancashire Cotton Spinning Industry*. In 1930 he was appointed director of a new economic research section at Manchester University and concentrated on problems of industry and labour. With Alan Winterbottom he produced for the government in 1933 *An Industrial Survey of Cumberland and Furness* (one of a series for the 'development areas'), and in the same year with the same collaborator he published a study of juvenile employment—a subject to which he returned in 1938 with his wife in *The Juvenile Labour Market*. In 1936 his university appointed him to a chair in social economics, which he held until 1946.

In December 1939, after the outbreak of World War II, Jewkes was recruited, along with others, to provide economic advice to the war cabinet secretariat. In 1941 he became director of its newly formed economic section, which was a prime source of economic advice to the government. Jewkes had a boyish enthusiasm, a salty humour, and above all a grasp of the practical and the significant that fitted him for the job of feeding economic ideas into the administrative machine. Within a few months he was invited to review the need for some form of planning in the Ministry of Aircraft Production. He recommended in favour of this and was promptly invited to undertake the job. Lent initially for three months to that Ministry, he stayed for nearly three years, exercising as powerful an influence there as he had done in the Cabinet Office and recruiting a staff made up exclusively of economists. He proved himself a skilled planner in face of confusion and discouragement, his appointment as director-general of statistics and programmes coming only in 1943 after a struggle. Early in 1944 he moved on again, this time to the Ministry of Reconstruction. One of his main contributions there was to the drafting of the white paper on employment policy, a document which he defended in later years, emphasizing the limits of the commitments assumed. In wartime Whitehall he was an effective and capable head of a team, bold in his proposals and adroit in obtaining support for them.

After the war Jewkes never found the scope for his talents that the war had provided. For two years he returned to Manchester as Stanley Jevons professor of political economy, but in 1948 he moved to Oxford to a new chair in economic organization and a fellowship at Merton College. He was devoted to his college and as garden master did much to enhance the beauty of the garden. As an economist, however, he was swimming against the tide. He was not interested in pure theory, his views on policy were unfashionable with younger economists, and he missed the company of kindred spirits. But he remained in Oxford for the rest of his life, having, after his retirement in 1969, little contact with other members of the university.

In the early postwar years Jewkes played a leading part on the first of Sir (R.) Stafford *Cripps's working parties, on the cotton industry, and on the royal commission on betting, lotteries, and gaming (1949). He came to public attention with the publication in 1948 of his *Ordeal by Planning*. This established him as a leading critic of government intervention and control. He spent much of his time in the 1950s collecting material, with the help of two assistants, for his *magnum opus*, *The Sources of Invention*, which appeared in 1958. This studied the origin of over one hundred of the more important industrial inventions of the twentieth century. The results were in keeping with Jewkes's philosophy, derived from the American philosopher William James, of 'small is preferable'. He argued consistently against large organizations, pointing to the limits of economies of scale, the advantages of competition, the greater flexibility and inventiveness of small units, and the dangers of bureaucracy and monopoly. In 1957–60 Jewkes also served on the royal commission on doctors' and dentists' remuneration and developed a new interest in the economics of health care.

In 1978 Jewkes published his last work, *A Return to Free Market Economics?*, a symposium drawn from earlier writings. He was too extravagant in his attack on postwar controls, too sure that control of industry was not passing into fewer hands, and played down too much the advantages of large-scale research and development. He was more at home on issues of organization and micro-economics than on the major dilemmas of policy in postwar Britain, especially those associated with international balance. But he was a much underrated critic of government economic policy. The book contains a résumé of his work as director (1969–74) of the Industrial Policy Group, consisting of a score of top businessmen. This appointment arose out of his long association with Guinness as an economic adviser. He was appointed CBE in 1943 and awarded a D.Sc. by Hull University in 1973.

In appearance Jewkes was short and stocky with a broad, cheerful, bespectacled face and a soft, attractive voice. He was a man of many enthusiasms, a keen gardener and a house agent *manqué*. Although combative in his views, he was mild in manner, entertaining in conversation, full of humour, and a lover of paradox. In 1929 he

married (Frances) Sylvia, daughter of Harry Clementi Butterworth, a Manchester cotton merchant. She collaborated in much of his work and shared his views. They had one daughter. Jewkes died in Oxford 18 August 1988 and his wife died soon afterwards.

[Private information; personal knowledge.]

ALEC CAIRNCROSS

JOHNSON, SIR Henry Cecil (1906–1988), chairman of the British Railways Board, was born 11 September 1906 in Lavendon, Buckinghamshire, the third of three sons and the fifth of six children of William Longland Johnson, farmer and butcher, of Lavendon, and his wife, Alice Mary Osborne. He was educated at Bedford Modern School.

Johnson joined LNER (London and North Eastern Railway) as a traffic apprentice in 1923, the usual first step towards a career in railway management, and in 1926 became an assistant yard manager near Ely, entitled to wear a bowler hat, the symbol of a railway manager. After various posts in the operating department he was appointed assistant superintendent of Southern Area, LNER, in 1942. In 1955 he became chief operating superintendent of the Eastern Region, one of the six regions formed when the railways were nationalized in 1948. He was promoted to the position of assistant general manager of the Eastern Region at the end of 1955, becoming general manager in 1958. While at the Eastern Region he introduced the successful line management concept—an assistant general manager (traffic) co-ordinating the work of the line managers.

In 1962 Johnson became general manager of the London Midland Region, the most important of the British Railways regions, and he was also chairman in 1963–7. He took charge of the electrification of the Euston to Manchester and Liverpool line, the first main-line electrification, completed in 1966, which had been part of the modernization plan of 1955, and the new Euston station was opened in 1968. Johnson became vice-chairman of the British Railways board in 1967. Following the forced resignation of the chairman, Sir Stanley Raymond, at the end of 1967, after disagreements with the minister of transport, Barbara Castle (later Baroness Castle of Blackburn), Johnson was appointed chairman, a post he held from 1968 until 1971.

The finances of British Railways improved under Johnson, largely as a result of the 1968 Transport Act, in which the government promised specific grants to make unprofitable passenger services financially viable where they were providing a public service, in contrast to the recommendations of Richard (later Baron) *Beeching (chairman in 1963–5), who wanted to make the railways profitable by closing uneconomic lines. Although Richard (later Baron) Marsh, Johnson's successor, estimated in 1972 that the government invested five times as much each year in new motorways and trunk roads as in the railways, modernization continued: Inter-City, started in 1966 as a new operation of high-speed trains linking major cities, expanded, and in 1968 the last steam engines were taken out of service. In 1969 work began at the research centre in Derby on the Advanced Passenger Train, a high-speed train running on existing tracks, but it was withdrawn two weeks after it entered regular passenger service in 1981. Johnson took a particular interest in the commercial development of surplus railway land, and established and became chairman of the British Rail property board in 1970. In the 1970s British Railways earned £20 million a year from land sales.

Although there were large reductions in railway staff following modernization and the closure of uneconomic lines, there was some progress during the Johnson years towards improving industrial relations. The rail unions objected to pay being linked to productivity at a time when this was not the case in other industries, and Johnson had to steer British Railways through periods of 'work-to-rule', with the unions demanding large pay increases while British Railways proposals for price increases were being held back by the National Board for Prices and Incomes.

Johnson was not an innovator, and most of the changes which took place under his chairmanship had been put in motion by his predecessors. While he did not capture the public imagination in the way of Beeching, he was extremely popular with the railway employees, who admired him as the only railwayman to have started at the bottom and worked his way up through the ranks to become chairman of British Railways. He was fortunate to become chairman when the 1968 Transport Act had paved the way towards improving the financial situation, and he left British Railways with a surplus of £9.7 million. Johnson was appointed CBE in 1962, knighted in 1968, and became KBE in 1972. In 1981 a locomotive was named after him.

After his retirement he started a new career in the city, as chairman of Metropolitan Estate and Property Corporation (1971–6). He later held positions on the boards of Lloyds Bank, the Trident Life Assurance Company, and Imperial Life of Canada.

Always known as 'Bill' Johnson, he had a friendly and relaxed manner, but he was shrewd, a good listener, and expert at delegating. Sir Peter Parker, a later chairman, admired his honesty and courage, describing him as 'straight as a gun barrel'. He had an open, distinguished face, with silver-grey hair and large bushy eye-brows. In his younger days he was a keen rugby player and a cricketer, and he also enjoyed golf. He was a member of the Marylebone Cricket Club and the Royal and Ancient Golf Club. In 1932 he married Evelyn Mary ('Maisie'), daughter of Thomas Morton, corn merchant. They had two daughters. He died 13 March 1988 in Great Missenden, Buckinghamshire.

[*The Times*, 15 March 1988; T. R. Gourvish, *British Railways 1948–73, a Business History*, 1986; Michael Bonavia, *British Rail: the First 25 Years*, 1981; Sir Peter Parker, *For Starters: the Business of Life*, 1989; private information.]   ANNE PIMLOTT BAKER

JOHNSTON, SIR **Charles Hepburn** (1912–1986), diplomat, writer, poet, and translator, was born 11 March 1912 in Hampstead, the eldest in the family of four sons and two daughters of Ernest Johnston, an underwriter at Lloyd's, and his wife, Emma Florence Hepburn. (The family later moved to a larger house in Reigate, Surrey.) Studious and competitive, he won scholarships to Winchester and then to Balliol College, Oxford, where at first he was lonely and unhappy. He took first classes in both classical honour moderations (1932) and *literae humaniores* (1934) and taught for a term at his old school before choosing the Diplomatic Service, which he entered at the second attempt (1936).

For twenty years his career followed a conventional course, except that in Tokyo he and the rest of the embassy staff were interned for several months when Japan entered the war. Later, as first secretary in Cairo, he tried but was not allowed to transfer to the armed forces; he felt this keenly, especially after his brother Duncan was killed in action. He became first secretary in Madrid (1948), and counsellor at the Foreign Office (1951) and the embassy in Bonn (1955).

In 1956, aged only forty-four, he was picked to be ambassador to Jordan. His first task was to wind up the outdated Anglo-Jordan treaty, which he accomplished with skill and tact (1957). A year later, when King Hussein's position was threatened, it was his advocacy, backed by the prime minister Harold *Macmillan (later the first Earl of Stockton), which overcame the doubts felt elsewhere in London and led to the brief but successful deployment of British troops to Jordan. He was appointed KCMG in 1959. These events are described in his book *The Brink of Jordan* (1972), for which Macmillan wrote a preface awarding him 'a secure place in the list of great envoys who have represented Britain overseas'.

His next appointment, unusual for a non-member of the Colonial Service, was as (the last) governor of Aden. He worked to merge the colony of Aden with the Federation of South Arabia, promoting constitutional advance but keeping the British military base. So long as he was there (1960–3) this line was maintained, with some difficulty but on the whole with success, as he related in *The View From Steamer Point* (1964).

After Aden he might have risen higher if the Labour party had not won the general election of 1964. As it was, the top posts to which he aspired went to others, while those offered to him did not match his own estimate of his abilities. Finally, in 1965 he agreed to go as high commissioner to Australia, where he was more effective and more popular than many had expected. He continued to reject offers of other posts and retired with a GCMG in 1971, a year earlier than normal, with the idea of entering politics.

His last years brought some disappointments. He was judged too old for the House of Commons. A peerage was mentioned but not offered. A company chairmanship lapsed when the plan to build an airport in the Thames estuary was dropped. Despite his hopes he became neither chairman of the BBC nor poet laureate. A book of reminiscences built round the character of his long-serving Egyptian butler, *Mo And Other Originals* (1971), had a brief success, but his other prose and poetry found little market outside magazines.

Two things consoled him: his social work at Toynbee Hall, for which he showed an unexpected talent; and the world opened to him by his marriage. In Cairo he had met Princess Natasha Bagration, daughter of Prince Constantine Bagration-Mukhransky and of Princess Tatiana Konstantinovna, descended respectively from the royal house of Georgia and from Tsar Nicholas I of Russia. They were married in London in 1944. Though childless, it was a strange but successful union until her death in 1984 after several years of intermittent illness. Arrestingly tall, possessed of magnetic charm, and connected with royal families all over Europe, she vastly enlarged his mental and especially social horizons. From their flat in Knightsbridge they continued, almost to the last, to sustain their parts in the social round which he called 'the Belgraveyard'.

In collaboration with his wife he had produced in 1948 what is perhaps still the best English translation of Turgenev's *Sportsman's Notebook*. But his masterpiece is his rendering of *Eugene Onegin* into English verse preserving Pushkin's metre and rhyme scheme (1977). This received unqualified critical acclaim. His success as a translator did not help, and perhaps even hindered, the fortunes of his other work, though he continued to write, print, publish and circulate it to his friends, convinced that posterity would be kinder. *Poems and Journeys* (1979) contains much of his best work.

He developed a boisterous manner for social purposes, but remained shy and reserved at heart. The strong emotions reflected in his poetry, together with his deep vein of self-doubt, were well concealed. Physically tall, energetic but somewhat awkward, he was a good sailor and a keen shot. He managed his savings astutely and generously, and was a good judge of a painting. He died in his sleep 23 April 1986 at his home in London.

[Private papers; personal knowledge.]

JULIAN BULLARD

JONES, SIR **Eric Malcolm** (1907–1986), businessman, intelligence officer, and administrator, was born 27 April 1907 in Buxton, Derbyshire, the third in the family of four sons and one daughter of Samuel Jones, who ran the family business of Samuel Jones & Son, textile manufacturers, of Macclesfield, and his wife, Minnie Florence Grove, of Buxton. Jones went to King's School, Macclesfield, and left at the age of fifteen to join the business in Manchester. In 1925 he set up on his own, and built up a large textile agency, which he handed over in 1940 to a manager, in order to enlist in the Royal Air Force Volunteer Reserve.

He was posted to the Air Ministry intelligence branch. In 1942, as squadron-leader, he was sent to the Government Code and Cipher School at Bletchley Park to stand in temporarily for the senior RAF officer in Hut 3, which housed the group responsible for the analysis and dissemination of the deciphered German Enigma messages to the ministries and principal commands. So impressive was he to (Sir) Edward Travis, director GC&CS (later the Government Communications Headquarters or GCHQ) that in April 1943, when Travis decided that a formal head of Hut 3 was needed, he asked the RAF for Jones, who was then posted to Bletchley as head of Hut 3 and promoted to group captain. Jones provided the mainly academic staff in Hut 3 with wise leadership and demanded the highest standards of speed and accuracy in the production of their intelligence reports.

From 1945 to 1946 Jones was in Washington as representative of UK signal intelligence and it was his discussions with US agencies that were the basis for US–UK co-operation in this field in the future. This proved of great importance to both governments in the succeeding years, most notably in the cold-war period.

Jones was formally transferred from the RAF to GCHQ at assistant secretary level, was made deputy director in 1950, and succeeded Sir Edward Travis as director in April 1952. He stayed as director until 1960, when he took early retirement, believing that eight years was long enough in the post. During that time he established the organization and the ethos under which GCHQ was to operate in succeeding years. For a man who left school at fifteen, he had a remarkable interest in the English language. *A Dictionary of Modern English Usage* (1926) by H. W. *Fowler was a favourite work. Jones produced instructions, and a system for enforcing them, to ensure that GCHQ's reports and correspondence were of the highest possible accuracy and clarity.

His directorship spanned a period of great expansion in Soviet military capability, encompassing conventional and non-conventional weapons and rocketry to deliver them. With colleagues in the services, Jones made sure that UK signal intelligence had the staff and technical resources to provide information on these developments. He believed that his task was management of the intellectually brilliant and technically qualified staff by whom he was surrounded, to give them the best chance to exercise their skills. A man of the highest integrity, it was said of him that corruption was unthinkable in his presence.

He aimed, quite simply, to be the best, whether in his work, as a games player (he played golf at the highest amateur level), or in skiing, which he took up at the age of fifty. With the move of GCHQ to Cheltenham, he bought Bredons Hardwick Manor near Tewkesbury and with his wife and family became a keen gardener and grew high-quality carnations.

A handsome man, he was deliberate in both speech and gait, and some found him ponderous or pompous. Perhaps for this reason, or through a lack of empathy between Whitehall mandarins and a man from a quite different background, he was not given further government employment after his retirement in 1960, at the age of fifty-three. Thereafter he accepted non-executive directorships in a number of companies, including Simon Engineering Ltd. (1966–77).

He was appointed CBE in 1946, CB in 1953, and KCMG in 1957. His standing among US government and service officers was very high. He was awarded the US Legion of Merit in 1946. When the US Air Force decided to have its own signal intelligence organization in the early 1950s, the British government was asked to lend Jones to set it up. He felt bound to refuse the offer, but arranged to provide advice.

In 1929 he married Edith Mary ('Meg') (died 1984), daughter of Sir Thomas Taylor, silk merchant, of Macclesfield. They had a son and a daughter. Jones died 24 December 1986 in Gloucester.

[*The Times*, 1 January 1987; Ralph Bennett, *Ultra in the West*, 1979; private information; personal knowledge.]
D. R. NICOLL

JONES, (Frederick) Elwyn, BARON ELWYN-JONES (1909–1989), lawyer and politician, was born 24 October 1909 in Llanelli, the youngest in the family of three sons and a daughter of

Frederick Jones, tin-plate rollerman, and his wife Elizabeth Griffiths, daughter of a small farmer from Carmarthenshire. His father was a greatly respected member of the local community, an elder of the Tabernacle Congregational chapel, and a lifelong socialist, and his mother had an immensely strong and influential personality. The three other children all achieved success, in the worlds of science, business, and education respectively. Elwyn Jones was educated at Llanelli Grammar School, the University College of Wales at Aberystwyth, and Gonville and Caius College, Cambridge, where he became president of the Cambridge Union (1931). In the Cambridge history tripos he obtained a first-class (division II) in part i (1930) and a second class (division I) in part ii (1931). He went on to Gray's Inn and was called to the bar in 1935.

With his intense concern for human freedom and justice, he became politically involved with the Fabians and it was through this connection that he responded to a request to go out and give legal help to the beleaguered Austrian Social Democrats during the time of the chancellorship of Engelbert Dollfuss (1932–4). It was then that he became greatly involved with the European problem and attended political trials in Germany, Greece, Hungary, and Romania, organizing help for those accused. He wrote to various newspapers about the problems and went on to write three books for the Left Book Club on the Fascist threat—*Hitler's Drive to the East* (1937), *The Battle for Peace* (1938), and *The Attack from Within* (1939).

In the late 1930s Elwyn Jones rejected his earlier pacifism as the answer to the Nazi menace and became a Territorial Army volunteer. During World War II he served as a major in the Royal Artillery in North Africa and Italy but ended the war as deputy judge advocate (1943–5), attending many courts martial and inquiries into alleged Nazi brutalities. Following his election to Parliament in 1945, as Labour MP for Plaistow (West Ham), he soon became parliamentary private secretary (1946–51) to the attorney-general, Sir Hartley (later Baron) Shawcross, and joined the team of counsel for the prosecution at the Nuremberg war crimes trials.

In 1949 he was appointed recorder of Merthyr Tydfil; he took silk in 1953. He became recorder of Swansea in 1953, of Cardiff in 1960, the year he became a bencher of Gray's Inn, and of Kingston upon Thames in 1968 (until 1974). In the meantime he was reasonably active politically (as MP for West Ham South from 1950 to 1974) but still devoted a good deal of time to his practice on the Wales and Chester circuit. However, following the Labour victory in the 1964 general election, Elwyn Jones became attorney-general, holding that position until 1970, throughout the Labour government.

During his period as attorney-general, in co-operation with the lord chancellor, Gerald (Baron) *Gardiner, the most important achievement was the establishment in 1965 of the Law Commission, under the chairmanship of Sir Leslie (later Baron) Scarman. As attorney-general, Elwyn Jones was also counsel for the tribunal in the Aberfan inquiry, when over a hundred children had been killed in a Welsh village school by the movement of a coal slurry tip. He prosecuted in the Moors murder case and in cases arising from the Official Secrets Act.

Following the fall of the Labour government in 1970 he returned to his legal practice, by then mainly in London. When Labour returned in 1974, Elwyn Jones became lord chancellor, with a life peerage, and severed his long-standing tie with his beloved East End constituency. As lord chancellor he encouraged the growth of law centres, whose number had quadrupled by the time he left office.

Although a lord chancellor (until 1979, when he became a lord of appeal) and attorney-general of distinction, he was not a profound lawyer. Law as such was not his prime interest; politics were. He was very much a political lawyer of swift intelligence, good judgement, and rare sensibility; more concerned that the legal system should provide the means of achieving true justice than with handing down great judgments himself.

Elwyn Jones was a member of the Bar Council (1956–9) and chairman of the Society of Labour Lawyers. He was president of University College, Cardiff, from 1971 to 1988. He was an honorary fellow of his Cambridge college (1976) and received six honorary degrees. A privy councillor from 1964, he was knighted in the same year and appointed CH in 1976.

Elwyn Jones was tall and dark-haired, with aquiline features and a ready smile. He was a man of natural charm and dignity, with a warm personality, convivial disposition, and fine sense of humour. He was a superb raconteur and had a very fine light baritone singing voice, with which he entertained his friends and which he sometimes used on formal occasions. There was a disarming simplicity about his approach, and his shrewdness and capacity to grasp the essential points of a controversy, hidden behind an approach of urbanity and charming whimsicality, were often used to take the heat out of Commons debates, which might otherwise have become acrimonious. However, below the surface were to be found the true convictions from which he never wavered. When put to the test, his concern for social justice would manifest itself in passionate outbursts.

In 1937 he married Pearl ('Polly'), daughter of Morris Binder, a Jewish tailor in Salford. They had one son and two daughters. Pearl Binder was a lively and versatile writer, artist, radio and television personality, and expert on costume. The marriage was very happy. Elwyn Jones died in Brighton 4 December 1989 and his wife died seven weeks later.

[Frederick Elwyn-Jones, *In My Time* (autobiography), 1983; personal knowledge.]   EMLYN HOOSON

JONES, SIR Henry Frank Harding (1906–1987), gas engineer and company director, was born 13 July 1906 at Gloucester Terrace, Hyde Park, London, the only son and eldest of four children of Frank Harding Jones, gas engineer and company director, of Housham Tye, Harlow, Essex, and his wife Gertrude Octavia, daughter of Edmund Kimber, of Plumstead, Kent. He was educated at Harrow, where he won the Baker prize for mathematics, and at Pembroke College, Cambridge, where in 1927 he gained first-class honours in the mechanical sciences tripos. He was later elected to an honorary fellowship of Pembroke College (1973).

On leaving Cambridge Jones enrolled as a student member of the Institution of Civil Engineers and within two years had won the Miller prize for a paper on long-distance gas transmission. A fourth-generation gas engineer, he was articled to (Sir) George Evetts, a prominent consulting engineer, and until the war intervened was mainly occupied in merging over 100 individual gas companies into more economic units.

Called up in 1939, Jones served as an infantry lieutenant with the Essex Regiment in France and Belgium. Following Dunkirk, he served in staff appointments in Britain, India, and Burma. Promoted staff captain in 1941, major in 1942, lieutenant-colonel in 1943, and brigadier in 1945, he took part in the Arakan campaign and was awarded the MBE (military) in 1943. He returned from war service in 1945 and resumed his career in gas as a director of important gas companies, including the South Metropolitan Gas Company. When gas was nationalized in 1949, he was appointed as the first chairman of the East Midlands Gas Board. He was promoted as deputy chairman of the Gas Council in 1952, and became chairman in 1960.

On nationalization almost 1,000 separate companies were taken into public ownership. The immediate need was to rationalize them within the structure of twelve area boards and to integrate production, which was dominated by increasingly uncompetitive coal carbonization. Gas sales were stagnant and many saw the attempt of the Gas Council to establish new process routes as merely delaying the inevitable decline. But in the space of a decade the industry achieved two remarkable technological revolutions: first a move to the production of town gas by the total gasification of oil, and then a more fundamental change to the distribution and direct utilization of natural gas with the consequential need for the conversion of all gas-using appliances. Behind this transformation lay massive and radical changes in organization and technology.

Jones had a vision of the future, and his unrivalled grasp of technical detail, coupled with his propensity for detailed planning, a skill honed in war, bred confidence and provided the necessary drive. With the courage to allow his technical staff to make huge investments in innovative facilities, he faced, with evident imperturbability and remarkable success, the pressures of Westminster and Whitehall. It was a great team effort under a determined and inspiring leader and laid the foundations of the modern gas industry. He retired on 31 December 1971.

A quiet man, modest, at times even self-effacing, he was possessed of a notable inner strength. Punctilious and meticulous, his habit of making a cool clinical assessment of every situation did not prevent him from being sensitive to others and warm and generous in his friendships. He was tall, spare, upright in carriage, and from his early thirties had the characteristic pure white hair of his family. He had great pride in his family and was devoted to his wife, of whom he took especial care during the latter years of his life when she became blind.

Knighted in 1956, and appointed KBE in 1965, he was elevated to GBE in 1972. President of the Institution of Gas Engineers (1956–7), he was also a fellow of the Institutions of Civil and Chemical Engineers and a founder fellow of the Fellowship of Engineering. He was awarded an honorary LL D by Leeds University (1967) and honorary doctorates of science by Leicester (1970) and Salford (1971) universities. He was a member of the royal commission on standards of conduct in public life (1974–6). A liveryman of the Clothworkers' Company since 1928, he was master in 1972–3.

In December 1934 he married (Elizabeth) Angela, daughter of Spencer James Langton, of Little Hadham, Hertfordshire. They had three sons and one daughter. Jones died in Great Missenden 9 October 1987 of stomach cancer and is buried at Weston Turville, Buckinghamshire, his main postwar home.

[Trevor I. Williams, *A History of the British Gas Industry*, 1981; private information; personal knowledge.]   DENIS ROOKE

JONES, Reginald Teague- (1889–1988), intelligence officer. [See TEAGUE-JONES, REGINALD.]

JONES, (William) Clifford ('Cliff') (1914–1990), Welsh rugby player and administrator, was born 12 March 1914 in the Rhondda Valley at Porth near Pontypridd, Mid Glamorgan,

the second son in a family of two sons and two daughters of Daniel Jones, wholesale fruit and vegetable merchant, and his wife, Elizabeth Mary Lewis. He was educated at Porth Secondary School and, from the age of fourteen, at Llandovery College. From 1933 he attended Clare College, Cambridge, where he obtained a third class in part i of the law tripos (1935) and a second (division II) in part ii (1936). There he proved himself to be among the very first order of rugby players, winning a blue three times.

It was at Llandovery College that his extraordinary talent had been revealed. For five years, five afternoons a week, under the coaching of T. P. ('Pope') Williams, he had been initiated into the arts of rugby, for which, at five feet eight inches and only ten and a half stones, he was not well tailored. To survive, he relied on his quick wits and his electrifying speed off the mark. His swift, breathtaking sidestep (off either foot) he attributed, as he claimed in one of the embroidered anecdotes of which he was fond, to the daily necessity of avoiding the crowd, traffic, and lampposts of the narrow Welsh valleys and the clustered passages of his college. Having played for the Welsh secondary schools between 1931 and 1933, he left a legacy of virtuoso running. He played his first senior game for Wales (against England) at the age of nineteen. He continued to play for Wales while at university, but his national career lasted only four years. He was unable to escape the ravages of rugby's muscular confrontations: bones were cracked and joints displaced. He missed an international season because of injury in 1937. This prompted his early thoughts of quitting, so that he played only thirteen times for his country (as captain in 1938) and a mere twenty-two for his club, Cardiff. He was one of the greatest outside-halves to have graced the game.

While he was playing he insisted on assiduous preparation, bringing along his own masseur at a time when such assistance was unheard of. Although he was a supreme individualist he valued teamwork, as he emphasized in his book, *Rugby Football*, published in 1937. He benefited from the long pass from his partner at scrum-half, Haydn Tanner, while he in turn was able to utilize, as in the 1934 Oxford–Cambridge match, the powerful, long-striding skills of Wilfred Wooller outside him. This technique came to mature fruition in Wales's 13–12 victory against the New Zealand All Blacks in 1935, at Cardiff Arms Park.

Jones declared his temporary retirement in 1938 in order to concentrate on further legal studies, but he had played his last game for Wales. He returned to play for Cardiff against Bridgend on the first Saturday in September 1939, and war was declared the following day. In the same year he was appointed assistant solicitor to Glamorgan county council and assistant prosecuting solicitor to Glamorgan Police. However, he took up these posts only briefly, because when war broke out he joined the 77th Regiment of the Heavy Anti-Aircraft Royal Artillery (Territorial Army), where he rose to the rank of major. Stationed in Berlin at the end of the war he was assistant to the chief legal officer.

In 1946 he returned to Porth to join his father's business and later to start his own, Clun Fruits, in Pontyclun, where the family lived, before finally embarking on a property business. He had little contact with rugby for ten years and developed an enduring interest in water-colours, particularly marine and Victorian paintings.

In 1956 his interest in rugby revived and he became a member of the Welsh Rugby Union committee. In the following year he became a selector, a position he held until 1978. In the 1960s he was chairman of the committee which developed, in Wales, following the Welsh team's disastrous visit to South Africa in 1964, the world's first comprehensive rugby coaching scheme, from which was established a permanent coaching organizer, the first of its kind in the rugby world. He established a permanent national coaching organizer. He was the Union's president in the centenary year of 1980–1. He was also a member of the Sports Council of Great Britain (1967–71) and in 1971 was a founder member of the Sports Council for Wales. He presided over the 'golden age' of Welsh rugby football in the late 1960s and 1970s, being behind the squad training system which enabled Wales to dominate their European rivals. In 1979 he was appointed OBE.

Jones was dapper, with fair hair and, in later years, nicely rounded features. He was animated and gregarious, as vibrant in his conversation as he was on the field. He invariably wore his Hawks' club tie and Cambridge blues' scarf. In 1939 he married Gwendoline Mary, daughter of Frederick Bartle Thomas, wholesale butcher in Tonypandy. They had three sons. Jones died of a heart attack 27 November 1990 at his home in Bonvilston, near Cardiff, to which he and his wife had moved in later years.

[Interviews with Wilfred Wooller and J. B. G. Thomas; David Smith and Gareth Williams, *Fields of Praise, the Official History of the Welsh Rugby Union*, 1980; Wayne Thomas, *A Century of Welsh Rugby Players*, 1979; private information; personal knowledge.]

GERALD DAVIES

K

KAHN, Richard Ferdinand, BARON KAHN (1905–1989), economist, was born in London 10 August 1905, the second child and only son of four surviving children (two younger sons died) of Augustus Kahn, inspector of schools, and his wife, Regina Rosa Schoyer, of Germany. Kahn was educated at St Paul's School and King's College, Cambridge. He read mathematics for one year, obtaining a first in part i in 1925, physics for two years, obtaining a second in part ii of the natural sciences tripos in 1927, and economics, obtaining a first in part ii in 1928, a remarkable performance after only one year. J. M. (later Baron) *Keynes and Gerald Shove, his King's supervisors, and Piero *Sraffa encouraged Kahn to write a fellowship dissertation for King's, of which he became a fellow in 1930.

In only a year and a half, Kahn produced 'The Economics of the Short Period', a remarkable contribution to the then emerging theory of imperfect competition. It was associated with the beginning of Kahn's close intellectual friendship with Joan *Robinson. Kahn's dissertation contained many of the results in her *The Economics of Imperfect Competition* (1933) and the subsequent literature spawned by it and Edward Chamberlin's *The Theory of Monopolistic Competition* (1933): the use of a reverse L-shaped cost curve, the kinked demand curve, and the procedure of explaining empirical observations in terms of business people's perception of their situations rather than starting from a simple axiom. Showing that the unfit were not purged in a slump was the most grievous blow dealt to *laissez-faire* until Keynes established the possibility of under-employment equilibrium in 1936. Kahn's dissertation was not published in English until shortly after his death in 1989. (An Italian translation was published in 1983.) In retrospect Kahn regretted that he had not published it at the time. In his introduction to the 1989 book he described it as an impressive performance for its time and (economic) age of its author.

Kahn became a university lecturer in the faculty of economics and politics in 1933, second bursar to Keynes in 1935, and a teaching fellow at King's in 1936. He was the key figure in the famous 'circus' which 'argued out' the propositions of *A Treatise on Money* (2 vols., 1930) and discussed and criticized Keynes's drafts as Keynes moved from the *Treatise on Money* to *The General Theory of Employment, Interest and Money* (1936). Kahn also went regularly with Keynes to Tilton (the Sussex home of Keynes and his wife Lydia *Lopokova) to give him 'stiff supervisions' on the emerging drafts.

Cambridge was the scene for two theoretical revolutions in economic theory in the 1920s and 1930s. Kahn played crucial roles in both. His lifelong scepticism about the quantity theory of money as a causal explanation of the general price level increasingly sapped Keynes's acceptance of it (and Say's law) from his teacher, Alfred *Marshall. In a famous article in 1931 on the multiplier, 'The Relation of Home Investment to Unemployment' (*Economic Journal*, vol. xli), Kahn used the apparatus of Keynes's *Treatise on Money* to put a precise order of magnitude on the total increase in employment that would ultimately occur if a primary increase were created by public works. He showed, under carefully specified conditions, that the investment expenditure itself would create a matching volume of new saving. This concept allowed Keynes to create a key innovation, the propensity-to-consume schedule, which became an integral part of the theory of employment as a whole in *The General Theory*. That it was the investment dog which wagged the savings tail, rather than the other way around, owes much to Kahn's article. A mystery remains, though, as to why Kahn, who had provided a realistic and better alternative in his dissertation, allowed Keynes to return to Marshall to provide the theory of prices in *The General Theory*.

During the 1930s Kahn wrote a number of seminal papers on imperfect competition, welfare economics, and international trade. World War II saw Kahn, on Keynes's recommendation, in Whitehall. He started as a temporary principal in the Board of Trade. Oliver *Lyttelton (later first Viscount Chandos) liked his work and had Kahn seconded to him in a number of different sections: the Middle East Supply Centre (as economic adviser, 1941–3), then the Ministry of Production, the Ministry of Supply, and finally the Board of Trade again (1945). Kahn ended the war with the administrative grade of principal assistant secretary. He took to Whitehall like a duck to water, drafting memos, scheming to get his views through, while still having enough time and energy for the minutiae of administration. This intense interest in detail and a reluctance to delegate stayed with Kahn for the rest of his life. He had excellent ideas, was an acute and incisive critic, but was often difficult to work with, especially when his notorious anger was aroused.

After the war Kahn returned to Cambridge for the rest of his life (there were extended periods away working for the United Nations in the 1950s and 1960s). He became first bursar of King's in 1946 when Keynes died, a position which he held until he was elected to a personal chair in 1951. (He retired from this post in 1972.) He was appointed CBE in 1946, elected a fellow of the British Academy in 1960, and created a life peer in 1965. He remained, as he himself wished to be known, a disciple of Keynes, devoting himself, particularly through his selfless input into the work of others, to extending Keynes's ideas into the theory of the long period—especially with Joan Robinson and also with Nicholas (later Baron) *Kaldor, Sraffa, and Luigi Pasinetti—and to extending and defending Keynes's ideas on money and the stock market generally. Kahn had a substantial impact on the views of the committee of inquiry into the monetary and credit system (1957–9), chaired by Sir Cyril (later first Viscount) *Radcliffe. He also discussed the need for an incomes policy as he spelled out the implications for inflationary pressures and the balance of payments of successfully sustaining full employment, as opposed to reaching it (for obvious reasons, Keynes's main objective in the 1930s). In the 1970s and 1980s Kahn turned increasingly to the history of theory, providing authoritative evaluations of Keynes's achievements for the British Academy (1974), in the *Journal of Economic Literature* (1978), and in his Raffaele Mattioli Foundation lectures in Italy, *The Making of Keynes' General Theory* (1984).

Kahn lived in a splendid set of rooms in Webb's Court at King's until his final illness. To those who did not know him well, he seemed an intensely private person. Deafness and ill health in his last years made him a rather solitary public figure. In reality, he was kind, generous, and hospitable, a meticulously considerate host and, in his younger days, a vigorous walker and rock climber. He never lost his interest in what was happening in King's and the faculty, or ceased to disapprove if things did not turn out as he would have wished.

Kahn came from a deeply religious Jewish family who were devoted to education. Up until World War II Kahn's orthodoxy was a byword amongst Jewish students and others. After the war his strict observance fell away. In his last years, though, he returned to his earlier faith and asked that he be buried in the Jewish section of the Cambridge cemetery. There his body now lies. Kahn never married but he never lacked agreeable female company either. He died at the Evelyn Hospital, Cambridge, 6 June 1989.

[King's College *Annual Report*, 1990; L. L. Pasinetti, 'Kahn, Richard Ferdinand (born 1905)' in John Eatwell, Murray Milgate, and Peter Newman (eds.), *The New Palgrave: Dictionary of Economics*, vol. iii, 1987; L. L. Pasinetti in *Proceedings of the British Academy*, vol. lxxvi, 1990; Cristina Marcuzzo's (1988) interview with Kahn, mimeo, King's College library; personal knowledge; advice of relatives and friends.]

G. C. HARCOURT

KALDOR, Nicholas, BARON KALDOR (1908–1986), economist, was born in Budapest 12 May 1908, the youngest in the family of three sons (two of whom died in infancy) and one daughter of Gyula Kaldor, Jewish lawyer and legal adviser to the German legation in Budapest, and his wife, Jamba Adler. Miklós (he later Anglicized his name) was educated at the Minta Gymnasium in Budapest (1918–25), the University of Berlin (1925–7), and the London School of Economics (1927–30), where he obtained a first-class honours degree in economics and a research studentship to study the problems of the Danubian succession states. In 1932 he joined the staff of LSE as an assistant in economics (later assistant lecturer), then lecturer (1938), and reader (1945). He became an honorary fellow of LSE in 1970. In 1947 he resigned his post to become director of the research and planning division of the Economic Commission for Europe in Geneva. In 1949 he was appointed a fellow of King's College, Cambridge, and a lecturer in economics at Cambridge, where he taught and researched for the rest of his life. He became a reader in economics in 1952 and a professor in 1966, until his retirement in 1975.

During his academic life Kaldor held several advisory posts and visiting positions. In the war he worked on the two reports by Lord *Beveridge on *Social Insurance* (1942) and *Full Employment in a Free Society* (1944). After the war he took on several advisory roles as chief of the economic planning staff of the US Strategic Bombing Survey (1945), adviser to the Hungarian government (1946), adviser to the French commissariat general du plan (1947), member of the Berlin currency and trade committee (1948), and member of the UN group of experts on national and international measures for full employment (1949). In 1951 he was appointed to the royal commission on the taxation of profits and income and was the author of a famous memorandum of dissent attacking the majority report (1955) for its conservatism on matters relating to the taxation of capital gains, company taxation, and the treatment of expenses under schedule D. There followed several invitations from developing countries to give tax advice:

India (1956), Sri Lanka (1958), Mexico (1960), Ghana (1961), British Guiana (1961), Turkey (1962), Iran (1966), and Venezuela (1976). He was also special adviser (1964–8 and 1974–6) to the chancellor of the Exchequer in two British Labour governments. At this time he was associated in the popular mind with Thomas (later Baron) *Balogh. He accepted a life barony in 1974 and he contributed frequently to economic debates in the House of Lords, being a trenchant critic of Conservative economic policy during the early years of Margaret (later Baroness) Thatcher's government. Like J. M. (Baron) *Keynes, Kaldor was a public figure, but a socialist. He had a passionate concern for the underdog, and was the most prolific newspaper-letter-writing economist of his generation. His membership of the House of Lords gave him enormous pleasure. In many ways he was more English than the English. He admired their history and culture and revelled in their institutions.

His advisory work never seemed to interfere with his academic research and may even have enhanced it. In his early years at the LSE he made significant breakthroughs in several key areas including the theory of the firm, capital theory, trade cycle theory, and welfare economics. In 1936 Keynes produced his *General Theory* and Kaldor was an immediate convert. He later had close links with Keynes during World War II when the LSE was evacuated to Cambridge, and in the 1950s he was joint architect of the 'Cambridge school' which extended Keynesian modes of thinking to the analysis of growth and distribution in capitalist economies. At this time he also became a prominent tax expert, publishing a minor classic, *An Expenditure Tax* (1955). In the 1960s and 1970s he turned his attention to the applied economics of growth. He emphasized particularly the role of manufacturing industry in the growth process and argued that the ultimate constraint on growth in the world economy is the rate of land-saving innovations in agriculture. He was a strong critic of general equilibrium theory, regarding it as barren for an understanding of the dynamic and cumulative processes that propel economies in the real world. Kaldor also led the attack on the doctrine of monetarism, which he regarded as simply a euphemism for deflation, that afflicted both governments and the economics profession in the 1970s and 1980s. Between 1960 and 1980 he published eight volumes of collected essays which are testimony to his endeavour and creativity.

Kaldor was a unique figure in twentieth-century economics. It was not only his intellect and his non-orthodox approach to economics that made him dominant and controversial; it was also his style, charm, and sense of fun, which made it impossible not to listen to what he had to say. In lectures and seminars he would captivate his audience by the heavily accented flow of English prose which was so much a feature of his personality and an endearing quality in itself. The image of a rotund and jovial medieval monk holding forth in intellectual discourse fits him perfectly. While Kaldor worked in his ground-floor study, the ever-open door of his spacious Edwardian house would see a succession of family and friends coming and going. Kaldor might appear or not depending on the urgency of the task at hand. He was egocentric, but could also afford to be generous with his time. He liked to compartmentalize his intellectual effort, working for long periods and then relaxing. He had money enough to enjoy the summers at his home in the south of France.

Many honours came his way, including honorary doctorates from the universities of Dijon (1962) and Frankfurt (1982), fellowship of the British Academy (1963), the presidency of section F of the British Association for the Advancement of Science (1970) and of the Royal Economic Society (1974), and honorary membership of the American Economic Association (1975) and of the Hungarian Academy of Sciences (1979). He gave the Mattioli lectures (1984) and the Okun lectures (1985). Inexplicably, the Nobel prize eluded him.

Kaldor's love for economics and politics was superseded only by the love for his family, from which he derived so much of his self-confidence and inner happiness. In 1934, the year he was naturalized, he married Clarissa Elisabeth, daughter of Henry Frederick Goldschmidt, stockbroker. They had four daughters. Kaldor died from cardiac asthma at Papworth Hospital, Cambridge, 30 September 1986.

[A. P. Thirlwall in *Proceedings of the British Academy*, vol. lxxiii, 1987.]   A. P. THIRLWALL

KEIR, Thelma Cazalet- (1899–1989), politician. [See CAZALET-KEIR, THELMA.]

KENT, SIR Percy Edward ('Peter') (1913–1986), geologist, was born 18 March 1913 in West Bridgford, Nottingham, the youngest of three sons and third of four children of Edward Louis Kent, photo-engraver and commercial artist, of West Bridgford, and his wife Annie Kate, daughter of Luke Woodward, hosiery machine manufacturer and alderman, of Nottingham. He won scholarships to West Bridgford Grammar School (1924) and University College, Nottingham (1931), graduating with first-class honours in the London University B.Sc. degree (1934). He was awarded a Department of Scientific and Industrial Research studentship for postgraduate research and was invited to join the East African archaeological expedition led by L. S. B. *Leakey in 1934–5. He was the expedition geologist in western Kenya and northern Tanganyika; his

Ph.D. thesis (1941) was based on this work, and his lifelong fascination with East Africa dated from this period. His D.Sc. was awarded for published work in 1959.

Though he hankered after the British Geological Survey or an academic career, preferably in the east midlands, this was not to be, and in 1936 he took a temporary job with the Anglo Iranian Oil Company (later BP) and was posted to Eakring, seventeen miles from Nottingham. While there he worked on the petroleum prospects of the east midlands (oil was found at Eakring in 1939) and southern England, and then joined the Royal Air Force Volunteer Reserve in 1941, in spite of being in a reserved occupation. From 1941 to 1945 he served with the combined intelligence unit at Medmenham; he was mentioned in dispatches in 1944. After the Allied victory in Europe he worked at the US Pentagon on Japanese targets and was awarded the US silver medal of the Legion of Merit (1946). He went to Hiroshima and Nagasaki as a member of the US investigation team—an experience which he kept very much to himself.

On demobilization in 1946 he rejoined Anglo Iranian and for the next fifteen years worked in Iran, East Africa, Papua, and North and South America, returning to London in 1960. He became BP's chief geologist in 1966 and, though the title changed, the role did not; he retired from BP in 1973 as assistant general manager (exploration). On retirement from BP he went to the Natural Environment Research Council (NERC), where he was a very active full-time chairman in what was nominally a part-time job (1973–7). He joined NERC at a critical time and played a major part in the implementation of recommendations from the third Baron *Rothschild, which transformed relationships between the research council and spending ministries. On completing his term with NERC, in 1977 he returned to industry and was still active as a consultant and company director at the time of his death.

A meticulous field geologist and outstanding stratigrapher, he had a gift for the synthesis and interpretation of large masses of geological data. The author of 145 papers, he made major contributions to the understanding of the geology of eastern England, the North Sea basins, and the tectonic evolution of the north-west European continental shelf. His interests were global and his thinking powerfully influenced studies of sedimentary basins worldwide. Dedicated to his science, which was both profession and hobby, he acted throughout his career rather like an international professor of geology. He was demanding but fair, and always ready to discuss problems (when you could catch him in the office). Kent was neat, bespectacled, quietly spoken, and of medium height. Many thought him a retiring man, a listener rather than a talker, but he enjoyed social gatherings and was at his liveliest in the company of women. A landscape painter and gardener, he loved choral singing and he and his first wife were lifelong members of the Friary Congregational church in West Bridgford; their home at 38 Rodney Road, West Bridgford, was his base through all of his wanderings.

His honours included fellowship of the Royal Society (1966), the Geological Society's Murchison medal (1969), the MacRobert award (1970), a Royal Society Royal medal (1971), a knighthood (1973), and honorary degrees from Leicester (1972), Durham (1974), Bristol (1977), Glasgow (1977), Aberdeen (1978), Cambridge (1979), Hull (1981), and Birmingham (1983).

In 1940 he married Margaret Betty, daughter of George Frederick Hood, science master at Nottingham High School. She was a Nottingham JP for many years and died of cancer in 1974. They had two daughters, the younger of whom became a tutorial fellow in English at University College, Oxford. In 1976 he married Lorna Ogilvie, daughter of Henry James Scott, schoolteacher. As head of BP exploration's information branch, Lorna was a friend of long standing, and this too was a happy marriage. Kent, who had recovered well from an earlier heart attack, died suddenly 9 July 1986, while on a business trip to Sheffield.

[N. L. Falcon and Sir Kingsley Dunham in *Biographical Memoirs of Fellows of the Royal Society*, vol. xxiii, 1987, pp. 343–73; BP company records; private information; personal knowledge.]   GEOFFREY LARMINIE

KENTNER, Louis Philip (1905–1987), pianist, was born 19 July 1905 in Karwzn, Silesia, Hungary, the only son and elder child of Julius Kentner, stationmaster, and his wife, Gisela Buchsbaum. He was educated at the Gymnasium in Budapest and the Royal Franz Liszt Academy of Music, also in Budapest. This was a remarkable beginning: he was only six years old, and simultaneously a school pupil and an academician. He studied the piano with Arnold Szekely and composition with Hans Koessler, Leo Weiner, and Zoltan Kodály. Both Weiner and Kodály were lifetime influences. He gained a diploma in musical composition.

Composition was his first ambition. Three sonatinas were published (by Oxford University Press) in the 1930s, and there were later performances of a string quartet and a divertimento for chamber orchestra. But it was the piano that was to become the centre of his musical life. His concert career began with a recital in Budapest when he was thirteen. From the 1920s he undertook a ceaseless round of concerts around the world, his fame spreading rapidly. He went back to Hungary, but with the political situation worsening emigration beckoned, and he decided to move to England in 1935, becoming one of the mid-Europeans who transformed Britain's musical life. He became a British citizen in 1946, and London remained his home until his death.

In an early review (in the *Sunday Referee* of 11 October 1936), headed 'A new—and great—pianist comes to England', Constant *Lambert wrote: 'What gives Kentner's playing its exceptional quality, however, is not so much his technical ability, which he shares with several virtuosos, but the remarkable intelligence and musical instinct which direct this ability...I have never heard a pianist of such power who at the same time has such delicacy and subtlety of tone gradation...a pianist with a brilliant future.' Lambert immediately discerned Kentner's exceptional musicianship, as did (Sir) William *Walton and the *Sitwells, who were warm supporters and friends. He became an admired performer in solo recitals and concertos—an early Mozart concerto with Sir Thomas *Beecham was a landmark—as also in chamber music, a lifelong passion. For some years there was a trio with Yehudi (later Baron) Menuhin and the cellist Gaspar Cassado. Music-making with Menuhin, who married Kentner's second wife's sister, was an important activity over the years.

His repertory was enormous and ranged from Bach to Bartók. He was especially noted for his Chopin and Liszt, the latter being most remarkable. Liszt's music had been regarded as superficial and it was 'not done' to perform it. It was largely due to Kentner's championship and deeply felt performances that Liszt came to be treated as a composer of serious beauty. In 1951 he was one of the founders of the Liszt Society, and from 1965 to his death its president.

He gave the first performances of Bartok's Second Piano Concerto (conducted by Otto Klemperer, 1933) and—in Europe—his Third Concerto (conducted by Sir Adrian *Boult, 1946), the First Piano Concerto of Alan *Rawsthorne in 1942, the Piano Concerto of (Sir) Michael Tippett (1956), and, with Menuhin, of Walton's Sonata for Violin and Piano. He was gifted with a formidable technique and a faultless memory. But what governed his playing was a constant quest for musical truth and his faithfulness to the composer's intention, with which he wished to identify. So his performances moved one both through their effortlessness—though he never tried to dazzle—and his sensitivity, accuracy, and, above all, musical humility. He seemed to be communing with the composer, and this musicianship transmitted itself to the listener. He was one of the last great romantic pianists and his eightieth birthday concert in the Queen Elizabeth Hall, London, caused a spontaneous standing ovation. Fortunately, a number of splendid recordings were made.

The same qualities inspired his teaching,

whether in master classes at the Yehudi Menuhin School of Music or with individual pupils in his studio. His standards were high and criticisms tough, though spiced with good Hungarian sarcasm ('Why play the wrong note when the right one is next door?'). There was no didactic method, just a search for musical truth. Technique was taught *through* the music, and Kentner could translate brilliantly musical points into words. He wrote: 'no teacher can put anything into a pupil which is not already there. He can only awake what is already lying dormant, and guide it towards possible short cuts, tending and nurturing it as it grows.' And so his pupils were inspired. He also liked writing, and his little book, *Piano* (1976), is necessary reading for any aspiring pianist. He became an honorary member of the Royal Academy of Music in 1970 and was appointed CBE in 1978.

Physically, he was small in build, and he looked even smaller on his very low (collapsible) piano stool. He had a beautiful head, and an ever-hovering smile. A gentle warmth emanated from him, coupled with a special sense of humour, sometimes wicked, always witty. He was a brilliant raconteur, equalled only by his wife Griselda. His wide reading made him into a typically cultured mid-European.

In 1931 he married a pianist, Ilona, daughter of Ede Kabos, journalist and writer. They were divorced in 1945 and in 1946 he married Griselda Katharine, sister of Diana, who married Yehudi Menuhin the following year, and daughter of Gerard Louis Eugene Gould, of the special branch in the Foreign Office, who died in 1916, and his wife, the pianist Evelyn Suart. There were no children of either marriage. Kentner and Griselda shared the remainder of his life, and he spoke often of how central to his playing and life Griselda was: he wrote of her as 'beautiful, talented, angelic, highly musical withal'. Kentner died at their home at 1 Mallord Street, Chelsea, 22 September 1987.

[Harold Taylor (ed.), *Kentner: a Symposium*, 1987; personal knowledge.]   CLAUS MOSER

KESWICK, SIR **William Johnston** (1903–1990), chairman of Jardine, Matheson & Co. and banker, was born 6 December 1903 in Yokohama, Japan, the second of three sons (there were no daughters) of Major Henry Keswick, of Cowhill Tower, near Dumfries, and his wife, Winifred ('Ida') Johnston. Henry Keswick was a senior partner of Jardine, Matheson & Co. and was directly descended from Jean Jardine, the sister of Dr William *Jardine, one of the two founders of the company in 1832. William ('Tony') Keswick was thus Jardine's great-great-grandnephew. His younger brother, (Sir) John

Henry *Keswick, also became chairman of Jardine, Matheson. William Keswick went to Winchester College in 1917 and rowed for the school before going on to Trinity College, Cambridge, in 1922 to read economics and law for an ordinary degree (BA, 1925).

On leaving Cambridge he joined Jardine, Matheson in Harbin, Manchuria, in 1925, with a posting to the engineering department. He recalled Harbin as being a grim place in several respects and he welcomed later transfers to Beijing and Tianjin and subsequent promotion to the management team in Hong Kong, where he was taipan (head of the firm) in 1934–5, and in Shanghai, where he became taipan in 1935.

The decade of the 1930s was a difficult and dangerous time in China, and the international community in Shanghai was challenged both by the growth of communist ideology and by the aggressive policy of the Japanese government towards China, which led to attacks on Shanghai in 1932 and 1937. The authority of the Shanghai municipal council, of which Keswick had become chairman in 1938 (a post virtually equivalent to mayor), was also under attack, with the Japanese pressing for much greater representation, and he survived an assassination attempt by a Japanese member of the council at a ratepayers' meeting early in 1941.

By now the European war had already started and that in the Far East was about to begin. In 1941 Keswick was seconded as political adviser to the staff of (Alfred) Duff *Cooper (later first Viscount Norwich), then minister of state for the Far East, in Singapore. He joined the Special Operations Executive (SOE) and went as a staff officer to Washington, as a member of the British Shipping Mission under Sir J. Arthur (later Baron) *Salter. He then served on the staff of the 21st Army Group in North Africa, France, Belgium, and Holland, with the rank of brigadier. He also worked in the war cabinet offices, participating in the planning of the Normandy landings. Returning to London after the war, in 1947 he became a director of Matheson & Co. Ltd., the London correspondents of Jardine, Matheson, and subsequently served as chairman from 1949 to 1966: when he retired he remained on the board as a non-executive director until 1975. He was always a free-trader, feeling strongly that the market should be allowed to determine the business environment without bureaucratic intervention. His approach was down-to-earth and pragmatic and he was scrupulously fair in all his dealings.

A large and imposing figure and tall of stature, he had a presence and authority which marked his many years as a leading figure in the City of London. He was governor of the Hudson's Bay Company from 1952 to 1965 and a director of the Bank of England (1955–73) and of BP (1950–73).

He served as deputy chairman of Sun Alliance Insurance Ltd. and a trustee of the National Gallery (1964–71) and was knighted in 1972. He was a member of the King's (later Queen's) Body Guard for Scotland (the Royal Company of Archers) from 1949.

In 1937 Keswick married Mary Etheldreda, daughter of Sir Francis Oswald *Lindley, diplomat; they had three sons and one daughter. They shared a wide variety of interests and pastimes. Both loved gardening (a world in which the name of Lindley was honoured) and they created a much admired garden on the outskirts of Shanghai; later they were to create beautiful gardens at their homes at Theydon Bois in Essex and Glenkiln in south-west Scotland. An early friendship with Henry *Moore had resulted in a keen interest in sculpture and it was at Glenkiln that Keswick was to place his remarkable collection of statues by Moore, Sir Jacob *Epstein, and others on the Galloway moors, where art and nature complemented each other. The Keswicks also collected furniture and pictures, many of them closely associated with the early days of Jardine, Matheson, and they enjoyed tapestry, music, and even hot-air ballooning. Keswick died 16 February 1990 at the Lister Hospital, Westminster.

[Jardine, Matheson archives at Cambridge University Library; private information; personal knowledge.]

JEREMY BROWN

KEYS, William Herbert (1923–1990), trade unionist, was born 1 January 1923 at Elliots Row, Elephant and Castle, London SE1, the third child and second son in the family of four sons and one daughter of George William Keys, printer, and his wife, Jessie Powell. His elder brother and sister died before he was born. He spent his childhood in the Elephant and Castle and was educated at Archbishop Temple Grammar School there. He joined the army in 1939 and served in the Rifle Brigade throughout World War II, until 1946. He had a distinguished war record, becoming one of the youngest sergeant-majors. At one period in the war, cut off near the Nijmegen bridge, he was behind enemy lines for several days with a handful of his men. He was amongst the first Allied troops to enter Belsen concentration camp. This and his other wartime experiences confirmed his profound dedication to world peace, his total rejection of fascism, and his passionate support for nuclear disarmament.

'Bill' Keys started his career in the printing works of the Amalgamated Press, Summer Street, London SE1, but in 1953 he became a full-time official of the National Union of Printing, Bookbinding, and Paperworkers when he was appointed national organizer. From 1961 to 1970 he was the secretary of the union's London central branch, whilst from 1970 to 1974 he was the general president of the Society of Graphical and Allied Trades (SOGAT). On 1 January 1975 he became general secretary of SOGAT, a post he held until he retired in 1985. He served on the general council of the Trades Union Congress for eleven years from 1974.

He was a highly successful general secretary of SOGAT and its constituent unions and became one of the foremost leaders in the wider trade-union movement. On becoming general secretary, he changed SOGAT from being an inward-looking organization to one which became involved in mainstream issues. He believed strongly that it had a role and responsibility to be active within the Trades Union Congress, the Labour party, and society at large. He was always an internationalist and forged links with unions throughout the world, not only in the printing sphere but on a much broader basis. His stamina and tenacity made him a formidable negotiator, with the ability to take apart the most complex wage structure and put forward a solution to disputes. He was especially renowned for his habit of kicking off his shoes during the hard negotiating sessions with employers.

Of his many achievements, two stand out. He won a great victory for the continuation of his union's political fund, threatened by the Trade Union Act of 1984, which enforced periodic ballots on the issue. He spearheaded and co-ordinated the political fund ballots in trade unions—one of the few successes of the trade-union movement in the years of the government of Margaret (later Baroness) Thatcher. SOGAT was the first union to go to ballot and other unions followed. The other was his commitment to the creation of one union for the printing industry. He achieved a number of steps along this way with the merger in 1975 of the Scottish Graphical Association and SOGAT and then in 1982 of NATSOPA and SOGAT. Although his ultimate goal of one union evaded him before his retirement and death, he had put in place the basis of the SOGAT/NGA amalgamation, which took place in October 1991.

For all his successes, his biggest disappointment was his failure to persuade his old London central branch members in Fleet Street to accept modernization and new technology. If the 'Programme of Action' which he devised in 1977 had been accepted, the move of newspapers to Wapping and the demise of Fleet Street would not have happened in the brutal way it did. He foresaw what would ensue and wanted to avoid it.

On the wider trade-union scene Keys made a significant contribution to TUC policy-making at a national level, particularly in the role of chairman of the employment policy committee (1976–85) and of the printing industries committee (1974–85). He also presided over the TUC media committee (1977–85) and the equal rights committee (1974–85), and served on the race relations committee (1974–85) and the finance and general purposes committee (1982–5), which is regarded as the TUC's 'inner cabinet'. As one of the elder statesmen of the TUC, he was the trade-union nominee for the committee of inquiry which resolved the national steel strike (1980) and the national water strike (1983). He was one of the seven senior TUC leaders who tried to resolve the miners' strike of 1984–5. He was also the TUC nominee on the Commission for Racial Equality (1977–81), the Manpower Services Commission (1979–85), and the Central Arbitration Committee (from 1972). From 1981 to 1985 he was on the TUC–Labour party liaison committee, and he was a leading light in the Trades Unions for a Labour Victory organization.

Keys was warm, generous, and compassionate. He was well built, six feet in height, and some thirteen stones in weight. In 1941 he married Enid, daughter of William Gleadhill, who travelled all over the world doing many jobs, including work in the oilfields of the Persian Gulf. They had two sons, Ian and Keith. Keys died of heart trouble 19 May 1990 at his home, 242 Maplin Way, North Thorpe Bay, Essex.

[Private information.]   JOHN GENNARD

KILBRANDON, BARON (1906–1989), lord of appeal. [See SHAW, CHARLES JAMES DAL-RYMPLE.]

KING, Cecil Harmsworth (1901–1987), publisher, was born 20 February 1901 at Poynter's Hall, Totteridge, the fourth child in the family of three sons and three daughters of (Sir) Lucas White King, professor of oriental languages at Dublin University, and formerly of the Indian Civil Service, and his wife, Geraldine, daughter of Alfred Harmsworth, barrister, and sister of the first Viscounts *Rothermere and *Northcliffe. Cecil King's boyhood was unhappy. A brother was killed at Ypres, another when the ship taking him to school was torpedoed. 'Life has always been difficult for me because this is not my world,' he wrote in his candid autobiography. 'Until recently [1969] I have hated myself and always wanted to commit suicide.' He remembered his father as 'an irascible old gentleman' and his mother as violent and selfish. He hated his school, Winchester, and liked Oxford because at Christ Church (he gained a second class in modern history in 1922) he could always be alone. There he fell in love with Agnes Margaret (died 1985), whose father was George Albert *Cooke, canon of Christ Church and regius professor of Hebrew. He married her in 1923, and there were to be three sons and a daughter of the marriage (two sons were to die in his old age). King also adopted his deceased nephew's three children.

After Oxford King's uncle, Viscount Rothermere, arranged for him to begin work on two of his newspapers, the *Glasgow Record* and *Sunday Mail*. While in Glasgow he developed the skin disease, psoriasis, which troubled him for the rest of his life and precluded him from being called up in World War II. King then returned to the south and joined the staff of the *Daily Mail* in 1923, in the advertisement department. In 1926 he transferred to the *Daily Mirror*, of which he became a director in 1929. In its heyday the *Mirror* was not a comfortable habitat for a withdrawn Wykehamist, but when he joined the paper, it was Conservative, middle-class, and failing. With King's support, Guy Bartholomew, editorial director for many years, set about transforming it into an American-style tabloid, seeking a big working-class audience and willing to sympathize with Labour. King kept 'Bart's' extravagances at bay.

King was made editorial director of the *Sunday Pictorial* in 1937 and wisely appointed the twenty-four-year-old Hugh (later Baron) Cudlipp as editor. He was self-educated, had been brought up in socialist south Wales, was full of passion, and had the journalistic flair that King lacked. After the war, Bartholomew fired Cudlipp, but soon King ousted Bartholomew in 1951 and brought back Cudlipp as editorial director of Mirror Newspapers. King himself became chairman of the Mirror Group (1951–63).

King, Cudlipp, and the papers prospered. King built a vast world publishing empire on this small, rich base. In England, they acquired in 1958 the Amalgamated Press from the Berry family and then took over the Odham's Group in order to rationalize the women's magazines. In so doing, they acquired 'Labour's own (and only) paper', the *Daily Herald*. The Labour party's opposition to this was stifled when King promised to maintain the failing *Herald* for seven years. Halfway through this term the Trades Union Congress parted with their interest in the *Herald* and King changed its title to the *Sun*.

King and Cudlipp were now deeply involved in politics. The Mirror Group was almost a wing of the Labour movement. King had greater hopes of Harold Wilson (later Baron Wilson of Rievaulx) than he had had of his predecessor Hugh *Gaitskell, and believed that without the brilliant campaign conducted by Cudlipp, Wilson would not have won his marginal victory in 1964. Although King hoped to be Wilson's *éminence grise*, Wilson was unable to take his advice. Consequently when he offered to make King a peer and minister of state, King scornfully rejected the opportunity. As the government got into deeper economic difficulties, King became more hostile to Wilson and encouraged ministers to be disloyal to him.

In 1963 the Mirror Group was renamed the International Printing Corporation, with King as chairman. He was also a part-time member of the National Coal Board (1966–9) and a member of the National Parks Commission (1966–9). In 1965 he became a part-time director of the Bank of England. King felt that what he believed to be his special gifts as an administrator might be put at the service of the nation when the inevitable catastrophe came. He tried, at the dinner parties he gave in his ninth-floor suite in the *Mirror's* glass building, to persuade other business leaders that there would have to be an emergency government containing men like themselves. King feared there would be hyperinflation and even bloodshed in the streets. Cudlipp and his political executives had a hard time keeping this nonsense out of the paper. They tried in vain to convince King that, though the government deserved criticism, his fears were wildly excessive.

King got Cudlipp to take him to see Earl *Mountbatten of Burma in May 1968. He outlined his fears and asked Mountbatten if he would be titular head of an emergency government. Mountbatten had taken care to be accompanied by Sir Solly (later Baron) Zuckerman, the government's scientific adviser, who said at once that this was rank treachery and Mountbatten should have nothing to do with it. Mountbatten agreed with Zuckerman.

Two days later, King published an article in the *Mirror* under his own name entitled 'Enough Is Enough'. It read: 'Mr Wilson and his government have lost all credit and we are now threatened with the greatest financial crisis in history. It is not to be resolved by lies about our reserves but only by a fresh start under a fresh leader.' The City was appalled. King had resigned the previous night from his directorship of the Bank of England. The pound had a bad day. The Labour party's reaction was to give stronger support to Wilson. And three weeks later the directors of IPC unanimously dismissed King.

He had served Fleet Street well as chairman of the Newspaper Publishers Association (1961–8). He put a stop for a year or two to cheque-book journalism and made the Press Council more credible. In his retirement he wrote articles for *The Times*, and produced his autobiography and diaries. The diaries further injured his name because many people felt he had betrayed their confidences.

To lift his low spirits, King required stimulating company and people found him a likeable host at luncheons and dinners. He particularly appreciated the voluble Irish, the flamboyant Poles, and the ebullient Africans he met as a publisher. The whole of his professional life was spent in newspapers. He shared his uncle Rothermere's gift for finance but lacked his uncle Northcliffe's genius for popular journalism. King was six feet four inches tall, a commanding, burly figure with penetrating blue eyes, a quick smile, and, in later life, abundant grey hair.

He retired eventually to Ireland with (Dame) Ruth Railton, musician and founder and musical director of the National Youth Orchestra. They had married in 1962, after King and his first wife were divorced in the same year. She was the daughter of David Railton, army chaplain and rector of Liverpool. Her lively personality brought him prolonged happiness for the first time. King died 17 April 1987 at his home in Greenfield Park, Dublin, where he had lived for the last part of his life.

[*The Cecil King Diary 1965–70*, 1972; *The Cecil King Diary 1970–74*, 1975; Cecil King, *Strictly Personal* (autobiography), 1969; Hugh Cudlipp, *Walking on the Water*, 1976.]

JOHN BEAVAN

KING, Horace Maybray, BARON MAYBRAY-KING (1901–1986), Labour politician and Speaker of the House of Commons, was born 25 May 1901 at 91 Stapylton Street, Grangetown, near Middlesbrough, the second child in the family of two sons and two daughters of John William King, insurance agent (previously steel-worker), and his wife, Margaret Ann Maybray. He was educated at Norton Council School and Stockton Secondary School. He obtained first-class honours in English at King's College, London University, in 1922 and in the same year was appointed to a teaching post at Taunton's School in Southampton. He became head of English in 1930, and remained there until 1947, when he became headmaster of Regent's Park Secondary School in Southampton. He was an inspiring teacher, able to secure respect in a formal environment without heavy use of sanctions. A duodenal ulcer meant that he was not liable for military service in World War II. For several years he studied part-time for a Ph.D. on Shakespeare, and his thesis was accepted by King's College in 1940. King published widely on subjects as diverse as Homer, *Macaulay, Parliament, and Sherlock Holmes.

In December 1924 he married Victoria Florence, daughter of George Harris, bookseller. Born in Southwark, prior to her marriage she was a schoolteacher. Once in Southampton she became a significant political figure. A Labour councillor in 1928–31 and from 1933, she was coronation mayor in 1953 and played a leading role in hospital administration. In political circles Horace King initially tended to be viewed as Mrs King's husband. The couple had one daughter.

King joined the Socialist Society at university and was a Labour party member from his arrival

in Southampton. By the mid-1930s his concern over British foreign policy led to support for a United Front. He narrowly escaped expulsion from the Southampton Labour party after sharing a platform with communists.

In the Labour landslide of 1945 King unsuccessfully fought the safe Conservative constituency of New Forest and Christchurch. The following year he was elected to Hampshire county council, serving with one three-year break until 1965, and eventually becoming Labour party group leader. He was elected to the House of Commons in February 1950 as member for the extremely marginal Southampton Test constituency. Prior to the 1955 election King succeeded in transferring his candidacy to the adjacent and much safer Itchen constituency.

King quickly demonstrated a flair for publicity. He arrived at the House of Commons for the first time, wearing a cloth cap in memory of (James) Keir *Hardie, and made the first maiden speech of all the 1950 entrants. He was a very active back-bencher; within the Parliamentary Labour party he stood with the right. He was a keen supporter of the Anglo-American alliance, making frequent visits to the United States, and he backed Hugh *Gaitskell against unilateralism, but he was never a factionalist and attempted to remain on good terms with all sections of the party.

As early as 1953 King joined the Speaker's panel. In November 1964, following Labour's return to office, he became chairman of Ways and Means and deputy Speaker. Almost a year later, with the death of Sir Harry *Hylton-Foster in September 1965, he became the first Speaker from the Labour benches. At the same time he was sworn of the Privy Council.

He assumed the speakership in a context of increasing demands for parliamentary reform. Whilst no procedural die-hard, King was a traditionalist with a generally rosy view of established practices. One innovation, the speeding up of Question Time, probably reduced further the influence of the back-bencher. His speakership saw changes in parliamentary procedure that could seem significant by comparison with earlier inertia, but in real terms they were modest. Unlike many of his predecessors, he had no legal training but his headmasterly and avuncular style soon established his authority.

He retired as Speaker at the end of 1970. He became a life peer, as Baron Maybray-King, in 1971 and attended the House of Lords regularly for several years, serving as deputy Speaker there. His career contained much that was characteristic of Labour politics of the first half of the twentieth century. He was self-improving, cautiously reformist, and respectful of many venerable British practices. Yet there were paradoxes. The traditionalist was a showman; as Speaker he turned on the Blackpool illuminations. In Southampton he seemed a proper, somewhat puritanical, figure; at Westminster he was highly clubbable and well known in the bars. He was an accomplished player of the piano and piano accordion and loved entertaining children. The bonhomie masked a more complex and elusive character. Maybray-King had honorary degrees from Southampton (1967), London (1967), Durham (1968), Bath (1969), Ottawa (1969), and Loughborough (1971), and was honorary FRCP.

King's first wife died in 1966. He then married in July 1967 Una, daughter of William Herbert Porter, industrial manager. His second wife was a retired Southampton headmistress and had been King's honorary chauffeur in the last years of his political career. She died in 1978 and Maybray-King married in January 1981 Mrs Ivy Duncan Forster, a widow from county Durham. She was the daughter of John Edward Davison, miner. The marriage was dissolved in 1985, and finally, in March 1986, Maybray-King married Sheila Catherine, retired secretary and daughter of John Atkinson, dental mechanic. There were no children of the last three marriages. Maybray-King died in the Royal Hampshire Hospital, Southampton, 3 September 1986.

[Files at *Southampton Evening Echo*; *The Times* and *Daily Telegraph*, 4 September 1986; private information.]   DAVID HOWELL

KIRKLEY, SIR (Howard) Leslie (1911–1989), director of Oxfam, was born 13 March 1911 in Manchester, the youngest in the family of two sons and one daughter of Albert Kirkley, a Manchester schoolmaster, and his wife, Elizabeth Winifred Harris. He matriculated from Manchester Central High School, qualified in Manchester's local government examinations, and became an associate of the Chartered Institute of Secretaries. His early career in local government stirred a growing interest in politics which was reinforced by his staunchly Liberal father and by visits to the Rhondda, which was then suffering from the depression. His consequent involvement with social welfare issues at home was matched by concern for peace abroad. An active organizer for the Peace Pledge Union, he registered as a conscientious objector with unconditional exemption. In 1940 Manchester council decided to sack registered COs; Kirkley lost his job. It was a moment of truth which revealed his commitment, courage, and unyielding refusal to compromise on matters of principle.

A number of jobs followed before his appointment in 1942 as regional secretary for the Fellowship of Reconciliation based in Leeds. Here he became a founder member and honorary secretary to the Leeds European Relief Committee, sending food to war-torn Greece and, following the war, clothing to Germany and Austria. After the war came his first direct and successful experience of running a business, for the Quaker painting and decorating firm of Harry Seel. A secure future seemed assured when, in 1951, recruited by Cecil *Jackson-Cole, he moved to Oxford to become general secretary to the Oxford Committee for Famine Relief, one of whose founders was T. R. *Milford. Over the next twenty-four years he transformed this small local committee into a leading national and international organization.

The transformation began with the Committee's involvement in disaster relief after the Greek earthquake in 1953. There followed help to refugees: victims of the Korean war, the Chinese civil war, the Hungarian uprising, and the Algerian war, and displaced Palestinians. Kirkley's personal visits to disaster areas, and the Committee's high-profile role, together with the pioneering use of professional fund-raising methods, achieved rapid growth. As chairman of the World Refugee Year's public relations and publicity committee, Kirkley visited the Congo (1961), and the huge public response which the plight of the starving refugees invoked catapulted his organization—which in 1961 became Oxfam, with Kirkley as its first director—into the role of a major medium for prompt disaster relief.

The 1960s saw Oxfam move into long-term development work with a network of field staff. Kirkley played a key role within the Freedom from Hunger Campaign (1960–5) and consequently became interested in the causes of poverty. He began to campaign for a new interpretation of charity to include the examination of the causes of hunger and poverty as well as their relief. This soon brought complaints from the Charity Commission. Kirkley doggedly stood firm and successfully moved the frontier forward with his skilful and non-confrontational approach. His leadership also achieved a growing network of Oxfam shops, establishment of Oxfam Trading, encouragement of independent Oxfams overseas, provision of development education for schools, and establishment of the World Development Movement to campaign on issues which charity law prevented Oxfam from pursuing. Kirkley had succeeded handsomely in his aim 'to professionalize the whole business of charity without losing its soul in the process'. He left Oxfam in 1974 as a high-profile and flourishing organization of international renown while, in the United Kingdom, the antiquated concept of charity had been challenged.

Departure from Oxfam did not mean retirement. A further decade of involvement with voluntary and public organizations was to follow: as a member of the Board of Crown Agents (1974–80), chairman of the Standing Conference on Refugees and the British Refugee Council (1974–81), chairman of the Disasters' Emergency Committee (1977–81), and chief executive of the Voluntary and Christian Service Trust, the parent body of Help the Aged and Action Aid (1979–84). Here his organizational talents provided a cost-effective management structure which enabled Help the Aged to become a mainstream charity and to encourage an international network of similar indigenous organizations: Help the Aged International.

Colleagues from all stages of his working life remember Kirkley for his particular blend of warmth, optimism, energy, obstinacy, grit, and practical business sense. His efficient administrative skills were self-evident, but he was never a bureaucrat, disliking committees and preferring to work through personal contact. His were political skills. His management strengths lay in his ability to pick people of talent and commitment and motivate them to give of their best, allowing them freedom to operate creatively while, with his quiet style of leadership, he retained ultimate control.

He became a knight commander of the Order of St Sylvester (1963), and was given the Victor Gollancz humanity award (1974). He was appointed CBE in 1966 and knighted in 1977. Honorary MAs came from the universities of Oxford (1969), Leeds (1970), and Bradford (1974), and an honorary fellowship from Manchester Polytechnic (1971). He was also head shepherd of the Greek village of Livaderon.

Stocky in build, informal in dress and manner, with straightforward northern bluntness and a quizzical smile, he was outwardly easygoing, with a Quaker preference for compromise over confrontation. But the relaxed manner masked a steely determination, and his courage and tenacity could appear as obstinacy to frustrated colleagues. He had been raised an Anglican but his pacifism during the war led him to join the Quakers, and the deep sense of service which motivated him sprang from his Christian Socialist commitment.

A lover of music, theatre, and country walks, Kirkley drew rich pleasure from life. Devoted to his dogs and to his family—who had none the less to take their place—he was twice married, first in 1936 to Elsie May (died 1956), daughter of John Rothwell, accountant, and secondly to (Constance Nina) Mary, daughter of Thomas Bannister-Jones, clergyman. His family comprised three sons and two daughters, one daughter and one son being from the first marriage. Despite a serious heart attack in 1986 he continued to work for the things in which he believed. He died in the John Radcliffe Hospital, Oxford, 9 January 1989.

[Private and family information; Oxfam archives; personal knowledge.]   FRANK JUDD

L

LACEY, Janet (1903–1988), director of Christian Aid, was born in Sunderland 25 October 1903, the younger child and younger daughter of Joseph Lacey, property agent, who had been born within the sound of Bow Bells, and his wife, Elizabeth Smurthwaite, from the north of England. Her father died when Janet was ten and her sister, Sadie, died of cancer in mid-life. She went to various schools in Sunderland before going to drama school in Durham. Her family were fairly narrow Methodists, mostly teetotal, though her father 'drank whisky like water'. It may have been her father's death which caused Janet's mother to send her to live with an aunt in Durham.

Although she toured in the theatre world for three years, Janet Lacey found it hard to make a living. At the age of twenty-two she applied to the Young Women's Christian Association for work, and in 1926 was sent to the YWCA at Kendal to train as a youth leader. She stayed there for six years. Her skills in drama were fully used, and she received her first introduction to theology. Later she became an Anglican. During the general strike of 1926 she saw much poverty in Durham pit villages and became a Labour supporter. In 1932 she moved to Dagenham, to a job which used many of her gifts, in a mixed YMCA–YWCA community centre at the heart of a vast new housing estate which provided activities 'from the cradle to the grave'.

In 1945 she became YMCA education secretary to the British Army of the Rhine, which was slowly being demobilized. It was typical of her that she used the post to bring young British soldiers together with young Germans and with refugees. She learned much about running programmes of social aid and made her first contacts with ecumenical church leaders like Bishop Hans Lilje and Bishop George *Bell. She said she would go about whispering to herself: 'I must not get used to this devastation.' Her capacity for compassion shaped her career.

She was appointed youth secretary of the British Council of Churches in 1947, a job which introduced her to the World Council of Churches. She was a significant presence at its four assemblies: at Amsterdam, Evanston, New Delhi, and Uppsala. For the second assembly she wrote and produced a dramatic presentation, *By the Waters of Babylon* (1956). She got to know intimately many of the leaders of the world church, such as Visser t'Hooft. In Britain the peak of her work was the Bangor youth conference in 1951.

By 1952 Janet Lacey needed a task which would use her full talents. In December that year she was appointed secretary (the term director was only used later) of Inter-Church Aid (from 1960 Christian Aid), a post she held until 1968. She worked from both Geneva and London, helping to establish many other important bodies such as Voluntary Service Overseas and World Refugee Year, but her greatest contribution was to conceive Christian Aid Week. This was wholly her idea and she executed it with characteristic flair. The first week raised only £25,000 but by the time she retired it was raising £2 million a year. 'Need not creed' was Janet Lacey's slogan as she stumped not only Britain but the world.

She was tough and stocky; without being tall she confronted others as being a tower of strength. She was a formidable, autocratic leader, often infuriating, but her compassion in action caused even her critics to admire her. She was blunt to a fault. She was a skilled manager, but not as humane in her management as the really good manager needs to be, so that after she retired from Christian Aid, her years as director of the Family Welfare Association (1969–73) were not a total success. She more successfully reorganized the Churches' Council for Health and Healing (1973–7). Although she could run huge organizations, she could not boil an egg: nevertheless she loved entertaining her friends—at restaurants. She adored the theatre, music, and sculpture.

After her great contribution to World Refugee Year, she was appointed CBE in 1960. In 1967 she became the first woman to preach in St Paul's Cathedral. In 1970 her autobiographical volume, *A Cup of Water*, was published. Late in life she was prepared for confirmation by Father St John Groser, the socialist East End priest. She was awarded an honorary DD from Lambeth in 1975. Her retirement in her Westminster flat was happy—she would welcome her many friends from all corners of the globe—until she became a victim of Alzheimer's disease. She died in a Kensington nursing home, 11 July 1988, after having spent several years living there. She never married.

[Janet Lacey, *A Cup of Water* (autobiography), 1970; personal knowledge.]   ERIC JAMES

LAING, Ronald David (1927–1989), psychiatrist and psychoanalyst, was born 7 October 1927 at 21 Ardbeg Road, Glasgow, the only child of David Park McNair Laing, electrical engineer, and his wife, Amelia Elizabeth Kirkwood. He was educated at Cuthbertson Street Primary School, Hutcheson's Boys' Grammar School, and the University of Glasgow medical school, whence he graduated MB, Ch.B. in 1951. After a year at the Glasgow and western Scotland neurosurgical unit, Killearn (1951), he worked as a psychiatrist in the army (1952–3) and, after demobilization, in the department of psychological medicine, Glasgow (1953–6).

In 1956 he moved to London, having been accepted for training as a psychoanalyst under an experimental scheme, by which promising young psychiatrists from the provinces could be trained within the National Health Service by the Institute of Psychoanalysis, while working as registrars at the Tavistock Clinic. Despite opposition from some of his teachers, who found him arrogant and were offended by his failure to attend lectures regularly, he qualified as an analyst in 1960.

From 1956 until 1967 he worked at the Tavistock Clinic and Institute, first as a registrar, and then as a research fellow of the Foundations Fund for research in psychiatry, and principal investigator for the schizophrenia and family research unit. During his time at the Tavistock he was the leading co-author of two works, *Sanity, Madness and the Family* (1964) with A. Esterson, and *Interpersonal Perception: a Theory and a Method of Research* (1966) with H. Phillipson and A. R. Lee. In the former he produced clinical data in support of what became in the 1960s and 1970s the fashionable 'anti-psychiatric' idea that schizophrenia is not an illness but a mode of being into which the 'patient' has been forced by his family. As Laing put it in *The Politics of Experience* (1967), 'when one person comes to be regarded as schizophrenic, it seems to us that *without exception* the experience and behaviour that gets labelled schizophrenic is *a special strategy that a person invents in order to live in an unlivable situation*' (Laing's italics). This idea that schizophrenics, and, by extension, neurotics, are victims, the damaged but heroic survivors of impossible inhuman family and social pressures, was, coupled with Laing's charm and literary skill, largely responsible for the fact that he became the leading cult figure of the counter-culture of the 1960s.

In 1960 and 1961 Laing published the two books by which he became best known, *The Divided Self* and *The Self and Others*, the declared aims of which were to 'make madness, and the process of going mad, comprehensible' and to describe how one person can drive another one insane. They describe the subjective experiences of future or potential schizophrenics in language conspicuously free of the (pseudo-) objectifying jargon of psychoanalysis and psychiatry.

Around 1960 Laing came under the influence of Dr E. Graham Howe, a psychotherapist much interested in both Christianity and eastern religions, who in the 1930s had worked with Krishnamurti. This influence presumably explains the mystical, religious element that enters—some would say obtrudes—into Laing's writings from the mid-1960s onwards, and the fact that in 1971–2 he spent a year in Ceylon learning meditation with masters of the Hinayana Buddhist tradition. In 1962 Howe appointed Laing chairman of the Langham Clinic, a body that provided low-fee psychotherapy and trained psychotherapists. But in 1965 Howe asked him to resign on account of his interest in psychedelic drugs.

In the same year Laing was one of the founders of the Philadelphia Association, an organization devoted to establishing and running residential communities in which 'schizophrenics' could find sanctuary and make their own 'journey through madness' unimpeded by conventional psychiatric treatment. One of these communities, Kingsley Hall (1965–70), acquired fame and notoriety as a place where people could regress into infantile and uninhibited behaviour and then resurface with a new, true, and authentic sanity.

In 1972, after his return from Ceylon, Laing began a retreat from the extreme position he had taken in the 1960s. He had, he now maintained, never been an apostle of the drug culture, or an anti-psychiatrist, or an enemy of the family. In his *The Politics of the Family* (1971) he had merely tried to show how families can go wrong. His writings of the 1970s and 1980s, notably *The Facts of Life* (1976), *The Voice of Experience* (1982), and the autobiographical *Wisdom, Madness and Folly* (1985), are characterized by a sense of perplexity and uncertainty and marred by unbridled speculation. It is difficult to take seriously the idea that we are all traumatized by separation from 'our intra-uterine twin, lover, rival, double', the placenta.

Despite Laing's intelligence, charm, energy, and many talents—he wrote poetry and was a gifted pianist (LRAM, 1944, ARCM, 1945)—and his remarkable gift for rapport with the mentally disturbed, he was a flawed character. His ideas on schizophrenia were more derivative than his way of expressing them revealed; he maintained that his rise to fame had been more of a solitary struggle than in fact it was; and his account of his childhood in *Wisdom, Madness and Folly* is not strictly truthful. In his relationship to his 1960s followers, he must be convicted of playing to the gallery. His appearance was striking. He was dark and slender, with intense black eyes, and an air of abstraction about him.

Laing was married and divorced twice. He married his first wife Anne, daughter of Thomas George Charles Hearne, customs and excise officer, in October 1952, and had two sons and three daughters with her; they divorced in 1970. In March 1974 he married his second wife Jutta, daughter of Max Werner, clerk, and had two sons and one daughter with her. They divorced in 1986. He also had two illegitimate children. Laing died of a heart attack in St Tropez 23 August 1989.

[Adrian Laing (son), *R. D. Laing, a Biography*, 1994; private information; personal knowledge.]

CHARLES RYCROFT

LAITHWAITE, SIR (John) Gilbert (1894–1986), civil servant and diplomat, was born 5 July 1894 in Dublin, the eldest in the family of two sons and two daughters of John Gilbert Laithwaite, of the Post Office Survey, of Dublin, and his wife Mary, daughter of Bernard Kearney, of Clooncoose House, Castlerea, county Roscommon. He was educated at Clongowes, whence he won a scholarship to Trinity College, Oxford, of which he became an honorary fellow in 1955. He obtained a second class in both classical honour moderations (1914) and *literae humaniores* (1916).

During World War I he served in the front line in France in 1917–18, as a second lieutenant with the 10th Lancashire Fusiliers, and was wounded. In 1971 he published (privately printed in Lahore) a record of part of this service in *The 21st March 1918: Memories of an Infantry Officer*, which includes a lively, detailed account of the German attack at Havrincourt, near Cambrai, on 21 March 1918.

In 1919 Laithwaite was appointed to the India Office, and thus started a long career involved with the subcontinent. He became a principal in 1924 and in 1931 he was specially attached to the prime minister, J. Ramsay *Macdonald, for the second Indian Round Table conference in London. Two important secretaryships followed, of the Indian franchise (Lothian) committee under R. A. *Butler (later Baron Butler of Saffron Walden), which toured the subcontinent in 1932, and of the Indian delimitation committee from August 1935 to February 1936. From 1936 to 1943 he was principal private secretary to the viceroy of India, the second Marquess of *Linlithgow. It was a time of growing political tension following the India Act of 1935 and with provincial autonomy in 1937 imminent. The strains and stresses were greatly increased by the approach

of war. Laithwaite gave staunch support to the viceroy and his policies and deserves to share with Linlithgow the credit for ensuring that India's vital role as supply centre for the war effort, as well as a source of military manpower, was quickly and efficiently organized and maintained.

In 1943 he returned to England with Linlithgow and was appointed assistant under-secretary of state for India. He was then appointed an under-secretary (civil) of the war cabinet (1944–5) and secretary to the Commonwealth ministerial meeting in London in 1945. As deputy under-secretary of state for Burma (1945–7) he twice visited Rangoon and had a formative share in the negotiations leading to Burmese independence early in 1948. He was deputy under-secretary of state for India in 1947 and for Commonwealth relations in 1948–9, and he acted as one of the official secretaries of the conference of Commonwealth prime ministers in 1948.

In 1949 Laithwaite became the United Kingdom representative to the Republic of Ireland, a post upgraded to ambassador in 1950. In 1951 he was sent as high commissioner to Pakistan, where he already had friendly relations with members of the government, officials, and other leaders. He steadfastly promoted the British policy of friendship with both India and Pakistan in their disputes over the future of Kashmir and the distribution of the canal waters of the Punjab, and supported the efforts of the United Nations to reconcile the two countries. He left Pakistan in 1954 to be permanent under-secretary of state for Commonwealth relations from 1955 to 1959, first visiting Australia and New Zealand. From 1963–6 he was vice-chairman of the Commonwealth Institute.

He was also a governor of Queen Mary College, London, from 1959; president of the Hakluyt Society, 1964–9; vice-president of the Royal Central Asian Society in 1967; president of the Royal Geographical Society, 1966–9; and a member of the standing commission on museums and galleries from 1959 to 1971. After retirement in 1959 he played an active part in the life of the City as a director of Inchcape and of insurance companies. He was admitted a freeman of the City of London in 1960 and was master of the Tallow Chandlers' Company in 1972–3.

Laithwaite was an industrious and efficient worker, with an impressive grasp of problems and a reputation for fairness. He was rather tall and solidly built, dignified and precise in manner, but exceptionally friendly in a social context, even on first acquaintance, though still with a trace of formality. His outstanding qualities and affability, together with his sense of humour, made him many friends both at home and abroad. His diverse interests included a strong appreciation of fine artefacts and while in India and Pakistan he collected carpets and rugs with discrimination.

He came from a Lancastrian Roman Catholic family and adhered devoutly to that faith, which contributed to his success in the embassy in Dublin. In 1960 he was appointed a knight of Malta. He was appointed CIE (1935), CSI (1938), KCIE (1941), KCMG (1948), GCMG (1953), and KCB (1956). Laithwaite was a homosexual and unmarried. He died in London 21 December 1986.

[*The Times*, 24 December 1986; Gilbert Laithwaite, *The 21st March 1918: Memories of an Infantry Officer*, 1971, and *The Laithwaites: some Records of a Lancashire Family*, 1941 (revised edn., 1961); personal knowledge.]

MICHAEL MACLAGAN

LANCASTER, SIR Osbert (1908–1986), cartoonist, designer, writer, and wit, was born in London 4 August 1908, the only child of Robert Lancaster and his wife, Clare Bracebridge Manger. His grandfather, Sir William Lancaster, became secretary of the Prudential Assurance Company and his father had a job in the City but enlisted in the army in 1914. He was killed in the battle of the Somme (1916). Lancaster was sent to St Ronan's preparatory school in Worthing, and then to Charterhouse, an appropriate school for a caricaturist, as John *Leech, W. M. *Thackeray, and (Sir) Max *Beerbohm had all been there. (In the 1950s Lancaster received Beerbohm's warm compliments when he painted murals in the Randolph Hotel, Oxford, illustrating scenes from *Zuleika Dobson*.)

Lancaster did not shine at school (the headmaster's final report pronounced him 'irretrievably gauche') but was admitted to Lincoln College, Oxford, in 1926. Like his friend, (Sir) John *Betjeman, Lancaster became a 'figure' at Oxford. He wore loud checks, sported a monocle, and grew a large moustache. He contributed cartoons to *Cherwell*, the university magazine. He and Betjeman were fascinated by the Victorians and their architecture, an interest which began half in a spirit of mockery, but ended in expert championship. Lancaster obtained a fourth-class degree in English (1930), after an extra year of study. Intended for the bar, he failed his bar examinations.

He then went to the Slade School of Art, where he met his first wife, Karen, the second daughter of Sir Austin Harris, vice-chairman of Lloyds Bank. The couple were married in 1933 and had one son and one daughter. Lancaster found work alongside Betjeman, as an assistant editor at the *Architectural Review*. In 1936 his *Progress at Pelvis Bay* began the long sequence of his books satirizing architecture and mores. He was appointed cartoonist to the *Daily Express* in 1939 and on 1 January the first of his pocket

cartoons appeared in its William Hickey column. He was to draw roughly 10,000 cartoons, with only brief interruptions, over the next forty years. Lancaster's fusion of topicality and urbane wit was consistent. He depicted the world he knew—that of Canon Fontwater, Father O'Bubblegum, Mrs Frogmarch (the Tory lady), and, his most enduring creation, Maudie, countess of Littlehampton, and her dim, monocled husband Willy. Lancaster's satire was not splenetic, and, except in the cause of good architecture, he was never a crusader.

In World War II Lancaster joined the Press Censorship Bureau (1939) and then was sent to Greece, with which he fell in love, as a Foreign Office press attaché (1944–6). The British ambassador was being too high-handed with the press and Lancaster effectively smoothed things over. His first book to be published after the war was *Classical Landscape with Figures* (1947), a descriptive work based on his Greek experience. *The Saracen's Head* (1948) and *Draynflete Revealed* (1949) were in the manner of his prewar satires, though the former was pitched as a children's book.

In 1951 Lancaster worked with John Piper on designs for the Festival of Britain. In the same year, on Piper's recommendation, he designed his first stage set, for *Pineapple Poll* at Sadler's Wells. This and the many stage designs that were to follow (several of them for Glyndebourne) released him from the austerity of line and allowed him to indulge in the Mediterranean colour he loved. In 1953 the Lancasters moved to Leicester House, a stucco Regency mansion at Henley-on-Thames. Karen died of cancer in 1964 and in 1967 Lancaster married Anne Eleanor Scott-James, the magazine editor and garden expert. She was the daughter of Rolfe Arnold *Scott-James, journalist and author.

The 1960s, with their fashionable fads and fantasies, were perfect fodder for Lancaster's type of social satire. He would come into the *Express* office after having lunch at one of his four clubs and hold court for a while, telling jokes, before settling down with the day's newspapers. George Malcolm Thomson, right-hand man to Lord *Beaverbrook, said of Lancaster: 'The annoying thing at the *Express* was, not only was he the only one who could draw; he could also *write* better than anyone in the building.' The prose, admittedly, was an acquired taste, and it had to be taken on its own terms. When Betjeman wrote to congratulate Lancaster on 'that deliciously convoluted prose you write', the implied censure was not lost on Lancaster. The prose had to be taken as part of the rich plumcake fruitiness of the character Lancaster had created for himself. It was commonly said that he looked like one of his own cartoon characters and, as he aged, he resembled more and more an effigy of the English gentleman on a French carnival float: bulging eyes, bulbous nose, buffalo-horn moustache, bald head, striped shirt, pinstripe suit from Thresher & Glenny, old-fashioned shoes with rounded toes.

'Osbert, it quickly becomes clear,' wrote the architect Sir Hugh Casson, 'was a performance, meticulously practised and hilariously inflated and at times disturbing.' What, he wondered, was behind that 'elaborately woven yashmak of subsidiary clauses, this defensive portcullis of anecdotes, cranked into place at one's approach?' Lancaster was a work of art as memorable as any he created. It was as if he had chosen to be a 'living museum' exhibit, representing not the period of his own life but that of his lost father.

He was appointed CBE in 1953 and knighted in 1975, in which year he also received an honorary D.Litt. at Oxford. He also had honorary degrees from Birmingham (1964), Newcastle upon Tyne (1970), and St Andrews (1974). He was a fellow of University College London (1967), an honorary fellow of RIBA and of Lincoln College, Oxford (1979), and was made RDI (1979). He died in Chelsea 27 July 1986 and was buried at West Wing, Norfolk.

[Osbert Lancaster, *All Done From Memory*, 1953, and *With an Eye to the Future*, 1967; *Strand Magazine*, February 1947; *Sunday Times*, 25 July 1954; *The Times*, 26 July 1986; Myfanwy Piper, 'Osbert Lancaster', *Spectator*, 1 August 1986; Edward Lucie-Smith (ed.), *The Essential Osbert Lancaster*, 1988; Richard Boston, *Osbert: a Portrait of Osbert Lancaster*, 1989; personal knowledge.]   BEVIS HILLIER

LANE, DAME **Elizabeth Kathleen** (1905–1988), High Court judge, was born 9 August 1905 in Bowdon, Cheshire, the second of three children and only daughter of Edward Alexander Coulborn, mill owner at Bury in Lancashire, and his wife, Kate May Wilkinson. Her early years were spent in Bowdon and she was educated at home until the age of twelve. Her family moved to Switzerland in 1913, but returned in 1914 just before the outbreak of war. At Twizzletwig School in Hindhead and at Malvern Girls' College, she did not display any enthusiasm for academic studies, preferring to play games, especially hockey. Given the opportunity to study for Oxford or Cambridge, she decided not to embark on higher education and never regretted not going to university. She believed that, on leaving school, she would be 'done with academics and have a good time'.

In 1924 she spent a year in Montreal with her elder brother, and there she met (Henry Jerrold) Randall Lane, whom she married in 1926 when she was twenty, He was the son of a merchant of the same name. The couple went first to live in Manchester. Their only child, a son, was born in

1928. He was mentally disabled and died at the age of fourteen.

Her husband's decision to read for the bar changed her entire life, and led to her distinguished career at the bar and on the bench. They read law together, and in 1940 Elizabeth Lane was called to the bar by the Inner Temple. She was elected a bencher in 1965. She quickly made a name for herself in a profession where few women were, at that time, in practice, and prejudice was hard to overcome. She joined the Midland circuit and took silk in 1950, only the third woman to do this. In turn she became an assistant recorder of Birmingham (1953–61), the first woman recorder of Derby (1961–2), and a commissioner of the crown court at Manchester (1961–2). She also became a member of the Home Office committee on depositions in criminal cases (1948) and chairman of the Birmingham region mental health review tribunal (1960–2). In 1962 she was the first woman to be appointed a county court judge and she sat until 1965. She also sat as acting deputy chairman of London sessions.

In 1965 Elizabeth Lane was the first woman to be appointed to the High Court bench and was assigned to the Probate, Divorce, and Admiralty, later the Family, Division. On her appointment she was made DBE, an honour corresponding to the knighthood customarily conferred upon male High Court judges. In court she concealed, under a stern and even intimidating exterior, a warm, kindly, and understanding approach to the problems of families in the throes of separation and divorce. She was particularly understanding of the needs of children. When she went on circuit she enjoyed the opportunity to try both civil and criminal cases, in which she was always courteous. She was short in stature and wore glasses; correct in manner, she was conservative in outlook. Essentially a shy and modest person, she seldom relaxed except in private, when she was with close friends. She was very much aware that she was setting standards for the women judges of the future. Her portrait hangs in the Inner Temple; it shows a stern unbending mien, which was only part of her character. She was a kind and generous friend, with an excellent though rarely displayed sense of humour.

Between 1971 and 1973 she chaired the committee on the working of the Abortion Act, managing controversial and emotive problems with skill and understanding. Her report displayed a tolerant and unexpectedly liberal attitude.

Her husband, Randall, became legal adviser to the British Council. They were a devoted couple brought closer by the tragedy of their son. Randall was a great support to her in her career, and his death in 1975 was a very sad loss.

On her retirement in 1979 she left the Temple, where she had lived for many years, and moved to Winchester. There she had a garden, which she had missed in London. From time to time she sat in the Court of Appeal and much enjoyed it. She was very proud when the Western circuit made her an honorary member. She always encouraged young women contemplating a career at the bar. In 1986 she became an honorary fellow of Newnham College, Cambridge. She died in Winchester 17 June 1988.

[Elizabeth Lane, *Hear the Other Side* (autobiography), 1985; private information; personal knowledge.]

ELIZABETH BUTLER-SLOSS

LANE-FOX, Felicity, BARONESS LANE-FOX (1918–1988), champion of the disabled, was born 22 June 1918 in Newton Kyme, near Tadcaster, Yorkshire, the youngest child in the family of one son and three daughters of Captain Edward Lane-Fox, JP, and his wife, Enid Maud Bethell, herself later appointed MBE in 1967 for work for hospitals. Both her parents came from old Yorkshire families, her mother being the daughter of Alfred James Bethell, of Rise, and her father being the younger brother of George Richard Lane-Fox, the first and last Baron Bingley, of Bramham. At the age of two, Felicity developed periostitis, which left her with a permanently weak right arm. In 1930, at the age of twelve, on a summer holiday on the Yorkshire coast at Filey, she contracted poliomyelitis in a vicious form, which left her totally paralysed. Two years passed before she was able to sit up or to hold a cup or pencil. During this period she was living at home in the family house near Wetherby. Deprived of any formal education, she acquired knowledge by her own efforts supported by her mother's wide-ranging enthusiasms. Her mother, who lived until 1986, devoted the next fifty-five years of her life to the daily care of her crippled daughter. After her mother became incapable of looking after her, she was cared for by her sister.

When war came in 1939, Felicity Lane-Fox took on a job with the billeting officer in Wetherby. After the end of hostilities in 1945 she went into local politics as a councillor for the Wetherby division of the West Riding county council and became chairman of the local Conservative Association. Her interest in politics took her from there in 1960 to an appointment as assistant at the Conservative Research Department and in 1963 she became a member of the executive of the National Union of Conservative and Unionist Associations. Through these links with the party, she became known to Margaret (later Baroness) Thatcher, who, on becoming prime minister, offered her in 1981 a life peerage, which she was only persuaded to accept after her mother convinced her that the House of Lords would give her a forum for speaking on behalf of the disabled. This she assiduously did during the next seven years, making her maiden speech, a fortnight after taking her seat, on the integration of disabled children into ordinary schools. She was absent from the House on only three working days during her first year as a member.

Her work for the disabled had already won her an OBE in 1976, for in spite of her own disability, and with the indefatigable help of her mother, who combined the roles of nurse, chauffeuse, and counsellor, she travelled widely, spoke frequently, and carried on a large correspondence on behalf of a number of societies and projects connected with disabled people. Among these were the Nuffield Orthopaedic Centre at Oxford, where she was a member of the house committee, and the national fund-raising committee of the Disablement Income Group, of which she was chairman. In 1978 she became patron of the Handicapped Adventure Playground Association. To all these activities she paid full attention, regularly attending their meetings, to which she was driven in a specially adapted minicar into which she could be winched through the back window by her mother, who in spite of increasing age managed to propel her in the vehicle or on the ground with unflagging energy. For having learned to walk with the aid of a caliper and some human support, Felicity Lane-Fox in 1966 slipped on an icy patch of roadway, broke her pelvis, and was never able to walk again.

After becoming a baroness she accepted several further appointments to societies for the disabled, in particular becoming a member of the Prince of Wales's advisory group on disability and of the committee of inquiry into arts and disabled people. But the project which was closest to her heart was the Phipps Respiratory Unit Patients' Association (PRUPA). This unit, originally established in Clapham by Dr Geoffrey Spencer to provide relief and therapy for patients suffering from breathing maladies, was, thanks to her fund-raising efforts, later moved to become part of St Thomas's Hospital in Lambeth Palace Road, where it was renamed the Lane-Fox Respiratory Unit, and is a fitting memorial to her.

Felicity Lane-Fox leavened her arduous work for the disabled by a variety of other interests. She enjoyed watching cricket, tennis, racing, drama, and documentaries on television or listening to them on the radio, as well as a game of bridge and perhaps, most of all, social intercourse and conversation with her many friends. Her life was an example of how to overcome crippling physical infirmity and use the experience of it to alleviate the plight of fellow sufferers.

The fact that she was chair-bound, and also possessed a mane of thick brown hair, made it appear that her head was unusually large. With a high forehead, mischievous grey eyes, a classical nose, and a magnolia complexion, which never showed signs of ageing, her face gave an impression of being poised for laughter, into which it readily dissolved. She died unmarried in St Thomas's Hospital 17 April 1988.

[Private information; personal knowledge.]

EDWARD FORD

LANGLEY MOORE, Doris Elizabeth (1902–1989), founder of the Museum of Costume and Byron scholar. [See MOORE, DORIS ELIZABETH LANGLEY.]

LASKI, Esther Pearl ('Marghanita') (1915–1988), writer, broadcaster, journalist, and lexicographical irregular supreme, was born in Manchester 24 October 1915, the eldest child (she had one sister, two brothers, and an adopted brother and sister) of Neville Jonas Laski, barrister (later a crown court judge), and his wife, Seraphina Gaster. Her father called her 'Marghanita' (an affectionate adaptation of the Aramaic word for 'pearl') when she was small and she later adopted it herself. She was educated at Ladybarn House School in Manchester, St Paul's Girls' School, London, and Somerville College, Oxford, where she read English language and literature, giving as much time as the syllabus allowed to Anglo-Saxon and Middle English. She obtained a third-class degree in 1936. She also found time at Oxford for socializing and playing croquet and bridge. It was at Oxford that she met John Eldred Howard, whom she married in 1937; he was to become a publisher and founder of the Cresset Press. He was the son of John Howard, stockbroker and farmer. They lived in Oxford during the war and about 1948 moved to Capo di Monte, a picturesque house on the edge of Hampstead Heath, where they remained for the rest of their lives. In about 1965 they acquired a holiday house in the south of France, and it was there that a great deal of her book reviewing and her reading for the *Oxford English Dictionary (OED)* was done.

A primary influence on her early life in Manchester was her maternal grandfather, Moses *Gaster (1856–1939), scholar and chief rabbi of Sephardi Jews in England, 1887–1918, and she found his younger children, her near contemporaries, an intellectually stimulating group. She rarely spoke about her uncle, Harold *Laski, the political theorist, and it can be assumed that he played little part in shaping her beliefs. In view of the enduring influence of Moses Gaster it is a mark of Marghanita Laski's true independence of mind that, while remaining proud of her Jewishness, she renounced her faith even before she went up to Oxford and declared herself to be an atheist.

Her first novel, *Love on the Supertax*, was published in 1944, and this was followed by numerous other works (novels unless otherwise stated), including *The Patchwork Book* (an anthology, 1946); *To Bed with Grand Music* (written under the pseudonym Sarah Russell, 1946); *Stories of Adventure* (edited, 1946); *Victorian Tales* (edited, 1947); *Tory Heaven* (1948); *Little Boy Lost* (1949); *The Village* (1952); *The Victorian Chaise-Longue* (1953), and *The Offshore Island* (a play, 1959). The film rights of *Little Boy Lost* were sold to (Sir) John Mills, and she was furious and hurt when he turned it into a musical starring Bing Crosby (1953).

In the 1960s she turned away from the writing of fiction, and a string of thoughtful and literary works followed, including *Ecstasy* (1961), an ambitious book subtitled 'A Study of Some Secular and Religious Experiences'; a set of essays on the Victorian novelist Charlotte M. *Yonge (with E. G. Battiscombe, 1965); and a series of studies of the work of Jane *Austen (1969), George *Eliot (1973), and Rudyard *Kipling (1974). She also broadcast widely acclaimed radio programmes on the life and work of Kipling (1973, 1983).

To the general public she was best known as a broadcaster. 'Her clear, immediately recognisable voice with a slight touch of petulance or arrogance always there, was heard in programmes such as Any Questions, the Brains Trust, and the Critics' (*Daily Telegraph*, 8 February 1988). She also enjoyed speaking from pulpits, and her sermons were a demonstration of her profound and continuing interest in religion.

She gave much time and energy from 1974 onwards to the committee of inquiry into the future of broadcasting (1974–7, chaired by Lord Annan); and to the Arts Council (from 1979), serving as its vice-chairman (1982–6) and also as chairman of its literature advisory panel (1980–4).

Her extraordinary contribution as a voluntary reader for the *Supplement to the OED* was among her noblest deeds. From 1958 until the publication of the final volume in 1986 she supplied some 250,000 illustrative examples to the project, all copied out in her own hand. For this purpose she dredged numerous bulky Edwardian sales catalogues for the names of domestic articles, she read just about every work of crime fiction published in the twentieth century, and she scoured the whole rich literary world of twentieth-century (and some older) books and magazines for their unregistered vocabulary.

At Oxford and throughout her life she was renowned for her beauty, her forceful personality, and her obsession with religious and secular beliefs. She died in the Royal Brompton Hospital from a smoking-related lung problem 6 February 1988; her husband died in 1992. They had a son and a daughter.

[*Observer*, 7 February 1988; *The Times, Daily Telegraph*, and *Guardian*, 8 February 1988; *Independent*, 9 February 1988; family records; private information; personal knowledge.]   ROBERT BURCHFIELD

LAZARUS, Ruth Adele (1912–1990), sociologist. [See GLASS, RUTH ADELE.]

LEA, Sir George Harris (1912–1990), lieutenant-general, was born 28 December 1912 at Franche, Kidderminster, Worcestershire, the eldest in the family of two sons and three daughters of George Percy Lea, chairman of the family textile business, and his wife Jocelyn Clare, née Lea (his mother and father were distant cousins). Educated at Charterhouse and the Royal Military College, Sandhurst, he was commissioned into the Lancashire Fusiliers in 1933. Lea was handsome, broad, and tall—well over six feet—a robust and skilful games player, but a gentle and considerate man. He served in Britain, China, and India before World War II broke out in 1939.

In India in 1941, he was among the first to join airborne forces, becoming in 1943 brigade-major of 4th Parachute brigade during operations with the 1st Airborne division in Italy. Within this organization, he commanded the 11th battalion of the Parachute Regiment at Arnhem in September 1944. In the battle his force was overwhelmed by enemy armour. Wounded and captured with his soldiers, he mistakenly but characteristically blamed himself for this outcome. He spent the rest of the war in a German prison camp.

In the immediate postwar years he continued his service with airborne forces in India and at home, and in staff posts with the Royal Marine Commando brigade and NATO, as a lieutenant-colonel, prior to taking command of the Special Air Service Regiment in 1955. Revived for the emergency in Malaya, the unit lacked direction. Within ten days of his arrival, a sergeant remarked: 'the whole outfit came to life. He stretched us—and himself—to the limit, but we could see it was leading to an operational future.' During the next two years of his command, he developed the exacting standards and extraordinary skills for which the regiment became renowned.

As a consequence, he was promoted directly to a brigade command in England in 1957. He was then competing with peers in the favoured armoured warfare environment in Germany. Appointment to command the 42nd Lancashire territorial division and North-West District in 1962 appeared to limit his further employment. But he was selected in 1963 to the politically sensitive command of the armed forces of Northern Rhodesia and Nyasaland, colonies moving imminently to self-government. His political tact and decisive containment of dissident groups were judged exemplary. As this task concluded, he was chosen to succeed General (Sir) Walter Walker as director of Borneo operations early in 1965.

Responsibility for the civil government of the former British Borneo territories had passed to Malaysia, whose authority was disputed by neighbouring Indonesia and Chinese communists in Sarawak. Lea was required to secure a mountainous border 1,000 miles in length amidst dense jungle, and to pacify the communist faction. He served three authorities: the British commander-in-chief in Singapore, the Malaysian government in Kuala Lumpur, and, to an extent, the sultan of Brunei.

He possessed only a proportion of the powers necessary to ensure the co-operation of civil government, the Malaysian police and armed services, and the Australian and New Zealand sea, land, and air elements which reinforced his British forces from time to time. The rest depended upon good will, which he won by his open manner, humour, and modesty. Nothing ruffled him. Even when his wooden house caught fire and he lost in minutes the greater part of his personal possessions, he continued as if it were a matter of the least importance. Making adroit use of air and sea resources, Lea developed the policy of pre-emptive cross-border attacks by his troops, while containing the Chinese communists with police backed by military units. The success of these methods contributed to the change of political leadership in Jakarta and the emergence of an accord between Indonesia and Malaysia in 1966.

Promoted to lieutenant-general, he was posted in 1967 to Washington DC, as head of the British services joint mission, the link between the British and American joint chiefs of staff. Maintaining the close alliance in a period of British economic difficulty and defence retrenchment was not easy. But the Americans opened their offices and confidences to him more fully than protocol demanded, because they liked and respected him, as the chairman of the American joint chiefs observed on his retirement in 1970. He had evoked similar responses through the greater part of his professional life.

Colonel of the Lancashire Fusiliers from 1965 to 1968, Lea was deputy colonel and then colonel (1974–7) of the Royal Regiment of Fusiliers into which it was drawn. He was appointed MBE (1950), CB (1964), KCB (1967), and to the DSO (1957). For his services in Borneo, he was made

Dato Seri Setia, Order of Paduka Stia Negara, Brunei (1965). He retired to live in Jersey and was on the board of several commercial companies.

In 1948 he married Pamela Elizabeth, daughter of Brigadier Guy Lovett-Tayleur. His wife accompanied him wherever possible and contributed notably to his accomplishments. They had a son and two daughters. Lea died at home in St Brelade, Jersey, 27 December 1990.

[Regimental records; private reports; personal knowledge.]   ANTHONY FARRAR-HOCKLEY

LEACH, Archibald Alec (1904–1986), film actor. [See GRANT, CARY.]

LEACH, SIR Edmund Ronald (1910–1989), anthropologist, was born 7 November 1910 in Rochdale, the youngest of three children and second son of William Edmund Leach, owner and manager of sugar plantations in northern Argentina, and his wife Mildred Brierley, who like her husband came of a long line of successful Lancashire mill-owners. He was educated at Marlborough and Clare College, Cambridge, where, having changed his course from mathematics, in which he obtained a second in part i (1930), he gained first-class honours in the mechanical sciences tripos in 1932; he later obtained a Ph.D. in anthropology at the London School of Economics in 1947.

Restless and ambitious, it was some time before he found his true vocation. On leaving Cambridge, he first accepted a four-year contract with the Far Eastern trading firm of Butterfield & Swire, and left for China in 1933. Chinese art and thought deeply affected him. Fascinated by the alien culture, he collected jade and Sung pottery and studied Confucius. This probably helped him to throw off some of his early Christian upbringing and to suggest the lines of a possible future career. For, despite his acknowledged efficiency, he disliked the business atmosphere and determined 'never again to bind himself to an office stool'. Breaking his contract with the firm in 1937, he travelled slowly home, spending some months on the way among the Yami of Botel Tobago, taking ethnographic notes and making accurate drawings of their boats and houses. He began to consider an anthropological career. 'I feel that only then could the Hermit, the Wanderer and the pseudo-Philosopher within me, find mutual satisfaction,' he wrote.

Back in London, the anthropologist (Sir) Raymond Firth introduced him to seminars run by Bronisław *Malinowski at the London School of Economics. In 1938 he began a field study among the Kurds of Iraq. This was soon abandoned. A broken relationship, a touch of dysentery, and

the imminent threat of war all served to drive him home. He returned to London dispirited and uncertain about his future. He wrote: 'I've got an enormous amount of ability at almost anything, yet so far I've made absolutely no use of it...I seem to be a highly organised piece of mental apparatus for which nobody else has any use.' In July of 1939 he set out for a planned economic study in the Kachin hills of northern Burma. War intervened and interrupted his work. He volunteered to join the (2nd) Burma Rifles, and was involved in the disastrous British retreat from the Japanese. He faced much hardship, suffering serious illness. He later commanded Kachin irregular forces behind the enemy lines. But after demobilization in 1946, when he joined the staff of the London School of Economics as a lecturer and later reader in social anthropology, his future career seemed assured, and his rise to eminence was uninterrupted.

He moved to Cambridge in 1953 to work with Meyer *Fortes, was a university reader (1957–72), was made a fellow of King's College in 1960, and was given a personal chair in anthropology in 1972. He was elected provost of King's College in 1966, retiring in 1979. Knighted in 1975, he had honorary degrees from Chicago and Brandeis universities in 1976, honorary fellowships of the London School of Economics and of the School of Oriental and African studies in 1974, and of his old college Clare in 1986. He was elected a fellow of the British Academy in 1972, and a foreign honorary member of the American Academy of Arts and Sciences in 1968. He was a trustee of the British Museum from 1975 to 1980.

He delighted in this success and appreciated the uses of power, not for himself but for the things he cared for. As provost, he was proud to oversee the admission of women to King's, and an increasing intake of students from state schools. His real passion was for teaching, and disseminating anthropological insights to a wide public. He insisted that in studying 'other societies' we are really trying to understand our own.

He himself referred to his first major work, *Political Systems of Highland Burma* (1954), as 'idealist'; and so it was in the sense that his account of social organization emphasized the abstract patterns of Kachin social organization, and argued that what appeared to be distinct types of social organization were in fact different phases in a single process of oscillation between ideal forms. This was a brilliant exercise in abstraction and generalization, which sprang from the loss of his original field notes during the war and his consequent absorption in the work of previous observers of Kachin. His second major work, *Pul Eliya, a Village in Ceylon* (1961), by contrast presented an extremely detailed ethnography. He referred to it as 'materialist' for its attempt to show the economic basis for kinship and caste membership. But Leach was again concerned to explore the ideal world of Sinhalese villagers, and to discover the underlying principles of organization. These works are both classics; other shorter books and essays are often as brilliant. His reanalysis of some aspects of Malinowski's ethnography of the Trobriands again displayed his ability to master complex material and to discover unsuspected patterns. He applied this ability to kinship, particularly in disagreement with the French structuralist Claude Lévi-Strauss, and later to a wide range of subjects, including terms of abuse, children's stories, biblical studies, and the Sistine chapel. His book *Lévi-Strauss* (1970) was translated into six languages and ran to three editions. In it Leach presented his own version of structuralism, as he did more overtly in *Culture and Communication: the Logic by which Symbols are Connected* (1976).

Leach's originality was genuine and impressive, based in scholarly understanding of Asian society and in his ability to think abstractly about minutiae and to create grand patterns. His lectures were exciting, and he was a popular teacher. However, Leach said that he always reacted against his teachers (among whom he acknowledged Malinowski, Raymond Firth, Lévi-Strauss, and Roman Jakobson); and he did not himself look for followers, and founded no personal school. He was also a fearless controversialist: he was socially self-assured; he saw no particular virtue in consistency; he provoked on principle, and was surprised when his teachers, colleagues, and friends sometimes felt wounded. He was surprised too by the controversy aroused by his Reith lectures, published as *A Runaway World?* (1968), in which he asserted his belief in the relevance of anthropology to contemporary issues, and established himself as a witty, passionate, and uninhibited commenter on public affairs.

Disliking pomp and living simply, he used his personal inherited wealth to support research and publishing, particularly through the Royal Anthropological Institute, of which he was president (1971–5). A handsome man of indefatigable energy, humour, and insight, for several years he bore the painful and disfiguring illness of cancer of the head without complaint.

In 1940 he married Celia Joyce, daughter of Henry Stephen Guy Buckmaster, barrister. She was a talented painter who had also published two novels. Like him a lover of the countryside, good food, and wine, she provided the emotional stability his restlessness needed. They had a daughter in 1941 and a son in 1946. Leach died in a Cambridge hospice 6 January 1989, from an inoperable tumour of the brain.

[Stephen Hugh-Jones, *Edmund Leach, a Memoir*, privately printed by King's College, Cambridge, 1989; Chris Fuller and Jonathan Parry, 'Petulant Inconsistency? The Intellectual Achievement of Edmund Leach', *Anthropology Today*, 5 March 1989; Stephen Gudeman and Jean La Fontaine, *Edmund Leach, a Bibliography* (Occasional Papers of the Royal Anthropological Institute, 42), 1990; E. R. Leach, 'Glimpses of the Unmentionable in the History of British Social Anthropology', *Annual Review of Anthropology*, vol. xiii, 1984; personal knowledge; private letters.]

ROSEMARY FIRTH

LEE, JANET ('Jennie'), BARONESS LEE OF ASHERIDGE (1904–1988), politician, was born 3 November 1904 in Lochgelly, Fifeshire, the third of four children, two of whom died young, and only daughter of James Lee, miner and active member of the Independent Labour party, and his wife, Euphemia Greig. She was educated at Beath Secondary School from which she won her way to Edinburgh University and learned from the great English literature teacher, (Sir) Herbert *Grierson, how to read and how to write. She described her Scottish childhood in *To-morrow Is a New Day* (1939), a socialist classic suffused with her vibrant compassion.

Taking the finals of her Edinburgh MA in June 1926 (she also gained an LL B, a teacher's certificate, and a diploma in education), she longed to return home, where the miners' struggle was reaching a fresh climax as their communities were ruthlessly destroyed by the coalowners and the state. She began to earn her living as a schoolteacher, involved herself in politics, and, at a by-election in North Lanark in February 1929, she turned a Tory majority of 2,028 into a Labour majority of 6,578, and became the youngest woman ever elected to Westminster. Introduced into the House of Commons by Robert *Smillie, the miners' leader she most admired, and James *Maxton, she made many new friends, all on the left of the party: Ellen *Wilkinson, Sir Charles *Trevelyan, Aneurin *Bevan, and, most especially, Frank Wise, with whom she fell in love (he died suddenly in 1933). All were outraged by the failure of their own government to tackle the scourge of mass unemployment.

After her defeat in the general Labour rout of 1931, she became involved in a classic battle with the Labour leaders about party discipline; she believed the rules binding MPs not to vote against party decisions to be an infringement of their duties and rights and said so forcibly. This involved her in arguments with many of her closest associates, notably Aneurin Bevan. She recorded in her book one famous argument with him: 'as for you, I tell you what the epitaph of you Scottish dissenters is going to be—pure, but impotent...Why don't you get you into a nunnery and be done with it? Lock yourself up in a separate cell away from the world and its wickedness. My Salvation Army lassie.'

Bevan's brilliant remonstrance may have been part of his wooing. On 24 October 1934 they were married at Holborn Registry Office. Bevan, the Labour MP for Ebbw Vale, was the son of David Bevan, a Welsh miner. Jennie Lee's ego, like his, could take a collective form. She wanted her beloved working class to acquire a touch of arrogance. She created a series of homes for Bevan, with the aid of her own mother and father, and, to the surprise of her parliamentary colleagues, put herself second. The first of those blazing, comradely firesides was established at Lane End Cottage at Brimpton Common in Berkshire in 1939; in 1944 they moved to Cliveden Place in Chelsea; and finally to Asheridge Farm in Chesham, Buckinghamshire. For their closest friends, these homes were political havens, heavens on earth. The Bevans had no children.

Outside Parliament Jennie Lee played a big part in the politics of the 1930s, always insisting on the international allegiance of her socialism. She undertook annual lecture tours in America and some journalism. She went to Vienna in 1934, soon after the fascist attack on the socialists there. She was stirred from the start by the fascist attack on the democratic government in Spain, yet shamed by the feebleness of the British government's response and, worse, by the initial Labour party response. When full-scale war did come, she, like Bevan, had no doubts that the contest must be fought on two fronts: to defeat the fascist enemy and to prepare for democratic socialist victory afterwards. She accepted a job with the Ministry of Aircraft Production touring the aircraft factories and in 1941 went on a propaganda tour to the United States: 'Don't come back,' said Bevan, 'until you've brought them into the war.' When Hitler attacked the Soviet Union, she wrote a speedy good seller, Our Ally Russia (1941).

In 1943, at a by-election in Bristol Central, she stood as an independent in support of the two-front war, but lost. As peace came, she in turn sought her peace with the Labour party. In 1945 she won the mining constituency of Cannock for Labour with a 19,634 majority. Soon after the formation of the Labour government in 1945, Aneurin Bevan became one of its foremost and controversial figures. He was the chief architect of the National Health Service and Jennie Lee could see more closely than anyone what difficulties he had to encounter. She too wanted to see these principles established over wider fields. In the process she made friends with many of his friends: Jawaharlal *Nehru and Indira *Gandhi in India, Yigal Allon in Israel, and Milovan

Djilas in Yugoslavia. She could share his victories and his bitter defeats. She felt the attacks upon him more closely than anyone. When he died of cancer in 1960, she felt that he had been murdered.

However, even before the wounds were healed, she resumed her own political activity—notably in the Labour government formed by Harold Wilson (later Baron Wilson of Rievaulx) in 1964. The titles of her offices —parliamentary secretary at the Ministry of Public Buildings and Works (1964–5), parliamentary under-secretary of state, Department of Education and Science (1965–7), minister of state (1967–70)—give no proper indication of how she became one of the administration's most successful ministers. She was sworn of the Privy Council in 1966 and elected chairman of the Labour party the following year. She was, in effect, Britain's first 'minister for the arts', and thereafter no government could abandon the idea. She became an honorary fellow of the Royal Academy in 1981. Cambridge gave her an honorary LL D in 1974. Above all, she played the leading part in the establishment of the Open University. A commitment to experiment with a University of the Air had been included in Labour's manifesto and Wilson had always been an enthusiastic supporter. But, without Jennie Lee, the project would have been a pale imitation of a real university. She insisted that the highest academic standards must apply from the start. The new university received its first students in 1971, and by 1984 it was Britain's largest university, with 100,000 students.

Jennie lost her Cannock seat in the 1970 election and accepted a life peerage, as Baroness Lee of Asheridge. She lived happily at her Chester Row house in London for the next eighteen years, giving delight and good instruction to her family and friends. She never lost her zest for the causes of her youth, most of them celebrated in her last book of memoirs published in 1980, My Life with Nye. Dark, and strikingly beautiful in her youth, she had the physical, tough vivacity of many girls of mining families. She died 16 November 1988 at her London home, 67 Chester Row, Westminster.

[Jennie Lee, To-morrow Is a New Day, 1939, This Great Journey, 1963, and My Life with Nye, 1980; Michael Foot, Aneurin Bevan, 2 vols., 1962, 1973; personal knowledge.] MICHAEL FOOT

LEHMANN, Rosamond Nina (1901–1990), novelist, was born 3 February 1901 in Bourne End, Buckinghamshire, the second child and second daughter in the family of three daughters and one son of Rudolph Chambers *Lehmann, journalist, Liberal MP, and oarsman, and his wife, Alice Marie Davis. The Lehmanns were an affluent and gifted family. Rosamond Lehmann's great-grandfather was Robert *Chambers (1802–1871), who co-founded the publishing company Chambers; and her great-uncle was the artist Rudolf *Lehmann. Of the four Lehmann children, three grew up to distinguish themselves in the arts—Lehmann herself; her younger sister Beatrix, who became an actress; and John *Lehmann, the poet, editor, and publisher. 'I was bound to write,' Lehmann recalled in old age. 'I never considered anything else as a possibility.'

She was educated at the family home, Fieldhead, until she won a scholarship to read English at Girton College, Cambridge, in 1919. At Cambridge she contributed occasional pieces to *Granta*, the magazine founded by her father, and met (Walter) Leslie Runciman (from 1949 the second Viscount Runciman of Doxford), son of the Nonconformist shipping magnate and Liberal elder statesman, Walter *Runciman, first Viscount Runciman of Doxford. After graduating with second classes in English (1921) and modern and medieval languages (1922), she and Runciman married in December 1923 and moved to Newcastle. The marriage was brief and unsatisfactory, and it had already broken down when Lehmann's controversial first novel, *Dusty Answer*, was published in 1927. This was both a critical and a popular success, its sales enhanced by the author's reputation as a society beauty. Her second novel was, in contrast, poorly received by the critics, who were disconcerted by the glum northern setting and two unhappy marriages described in *A Note in Music* (1930). Lehmann's own marriage had been dissolved in 1928 and in the same year she had married the colourful Wogan Philipps, who in 1962 became the second Baron Milford (died 1994), artist and communist son of Laurence Richard Philipps, first Baron Milford, businessman. A son, Hugo, was born in 1929, and a daughter, Sarah ('Sally'), in 1934.

Between 1932 and 1953 Lehmann wrote the four novels by which she will be remembered: *Invitation to the Waltz* (1932), *The Weather in the Streets* (1936), *The Ballad and the Source* (1944), and *The Echoing Grove* (1953). The books are autobiographical in tone, with certain themes and preoccupations occurring throughout, notably the heroine's experience of compelling but destructive sexuality, and the conflict between intelligence and passion. Modern criticism now stresses Lehmann's role in asserting the centrality of female experience, whereas she was once stigmatized as a writer of 'women's novels'. She has been commended not only for her treatment of particular issues like homosexuality and abortion, but also for her technical skill, which became fully apparent in her handling of the non-linear chronological and narrative complexities of *The Echoing Grove*.

Between 1930 and 1939 Lehmann lived at

Ipsden House, Oxfordshire, where she entertained a wide circle of acquaintances, including the *Woolfs, Lytton *Strachey, Dora *Carrington, W. H. *Auden, Christopher *Isherwood, and (Sir) Stephen Spender. By 1939 her second marriage had also failed and in 1941 she began a relationship with the married poet Cecil *Day-Lewis, with whom she lived for several years. Her own marriage was dissolved in 1944, but when Day-Lewis was eventually divorced in 1951 he married Jill Balcon. The effect of his desertion was traumatic, although the tragic turning-point of Lehmann's life occurred in 1958 when her daughter, who had recently married the writer P. J. Kavanagh, contracted poliomyelitis in Jakarta and died, aged twenty-four. Lehmann wrote nothing of literary significance for many years afterwards and devoted herself instead to spiritualism. Her impressionistic autobiography, *The Swan in the Evening* (1967), reiterates her belief in Sally's continuing life, and in her last, confusing novel, *A Sea-Grape Tree* (1976), the spirit of Sibyl Jardine, monstrous protagonist of *The Ballad and the Source*, converses telepathically with the heroine. Other publications include translations of Jacques Lemarchand and Jean Cocteau; a play, *No More Music* (1939); *The Gipsy's Baby, and Other Stories* (1946), and several spiritualist works.

The reprinting of Lehmann's books by Virago Press in the 1980s brought her a new and appreciative audience. In 1982 she was created CBE and a fellow of the Royal Society of Literature. In 1986 she was made an honorary fellow of Girton College. She was also president of the English Centre of International PEN; a member of the council of the Society of Authors, and vice-president of the College of Psychic Studies.

Rosamond Lehmann was tall and beautiful, with almond-shaped eyes, a firm mouth, and a warm, impulsive manner. She died 12 March 1990 at her London home, 30 Clareville Grove.

[John Lehmann, *The Whispering Gallery*, 1955; Sean Day-Lewis, *C. Day-Lewis*, 1980; *Rosamond Lehmann's Album*, 1985; Judy Simons, *Rosamond Lehmann*, 1992.]

JUDITH PRIESTMAN

LEHMANN, (Rudolph) John (Frederick) (1907–1987), editor, publisher, and author, was born 2 June 1907 at Bourne End, Buckinghamshire, the fourth and youngest child and only son of Rudolph Chambers *Lehmann, oarsman, regular contributor to *Punch*, and from 1906 to 1911 Liberal MP for Market Harborough, and his wife Alice Marie, daughter of an American, Harrison Davis, and descended on her mother's side from Sir John *Wentworth, an eighteenth-century governor of New Hampshire. In the house and garden of Fieldhead, where he was brought up with his sisters, *Rosamond, Beatrix, and Helen, the profession of letters was powerful both as living presence and lively inheritance. His paternal grandmother belonged to the notable Scottish publishing family, W. & R. *Chambers (whence his father's second name), and a great-uncle of his father was W. H. *Wills, assistant editor with Charles *Dickens of *Household Words*.

He went as a King's scholar to Eton, where he edited *College Days*. Among his contemporaries were Eric *Blair (George Orwell), Henry *Yorke (Henry Green), and Cyril *Connolly; of the latter two he contributed notices to this Dictionary. He read history and modern languages at Trinity College, Cambridge, where he obtained a second class (division I) in both part i of the history tripos (1928) and part ii of the modern and medieval languages tripos (1930). There his close friendship with Julian Bell, nephew of Virginia *Woolf, plunged him so irresistibly into the Bloomsbury circle that by 1931 he was working as factotum at the Hogarth Press, which also published *A Garden Revisited* (1931), his first volume of poems. His verse, praised for metrical skill, elegiac tone, and clarity of diction, followed at rare intervals, ending with the *Collected Poems* of 1963, a self-critically thin volume.

As Nazism took grip in Germany, he left publishing to live as a poet in Vienna, a city he monitored as Christopher *Isherwood did Berlin. The first of his three volumes of autobiography, *The Whispering Gallery* (1955), reflects the hardening of his anti-fascist view of that 'pink' decade, while with heartache he faced the dilemma that was to dog him insolubly: whether to be impresario or artist. In 1935 he founded the twice-yearly (often irregular) hard-bound *New Writing*, which abruptly lost its left-wing élitism when in 1940 it burgeoned, as the paperback *Penguin New Writing*, into part of the war effort. This magazine was his masterpiece. Four or six issues a year during the war all sold out their 75,000 or more copies within days. A morale booster of high potency, a documentary record of war by the men fighting it, packed full of poets and story-writers who were his own discoveries, this was the voice of cultural survival.

In 1938 he had bought Virginia Woolf's share of the Hogarth Press, but when his partnership—vigorously described in *Thrown to the Woolfs* (1978)—ended in 1946, he launched his own firm, John Lehmann Ltd. His good-looking books—225 titles by 1954, when his supportive printers withdrew—reintroduced British readers to the wider world at a crucial postwar point. Saul Bellow, George Seferis, and Gore Vidal ornamented his list, as did the no less influential Elizabeth David. His services to European letters earned him the Legion of Honour (1958), the Greek Order of George I (1954), and an honorary D.Litt. at Birmingham (1980). He was appointed FRSL (1951) and CBE (1964).

His subsidy from the *Daily Mirror* in 1954 to found the *London Magazine* and maintain the aesthetics of humanism was soon dropped. The magazine tottered on too conservatively for the current *Zeitgeist* until Alan Ross took it over in 1961. For the remainder of his life Lehmann took visiting professorships in America and engaged in literary journalism and reminiscence of reflective quality, especially in his popular studies of *Lewis Carroll* (1972), *Virginia Woolf* (1975), and *Rupert Brooke* (1980). In his books, of which there were many, his writing was always courtly and finished, expressive only between the lines, except in the homosexually libidinous novel *In the Purely Pagan Sense* (1976), which he predicted would lose him his friends. It did not.

Lehmann was a tall, broad, and formidable figure, whose guttural voice and avuncular presence filled a room, with eyes, as William *Plomer put it, 'like forget-me-nots within a skull'. His gardens (and gardening) he loved. At his frequent parties at his Egerton Crescent home in London, where he had the generosity to confront young writers with their elder peers, his rooms were ablaze with massed flowers from the country. For much of his life he shared homes in London and near Crawley, West Sussex, with the dancer Alexis Rassine.

Lehmann died after a long illness, in which hip operations had interrupted his mobility, in a nursing home at 29 Devonshire Street, Westminster, 7 April 1987.

[*Daily Telegraph*, 9 April 1987; *Independent*, 10 April 1987; A. T. Tolley (ed.), *John Lehmann, a Tribute*, Ottawa, 1987; John Lehmann, *In My Own Time* (autobiography), 1969; personal knowledge.]

DAVID HUGHES

LEVY, Doris Elizabeth Langley (1902–1989), founder of the Museum of Costume and Byron scholar. [See MOORE, DORIS ELIZABETH LANGLEY.]

LILLIE, Beatrice Gladys, LADY PEEL (1894–1989), actress and singer, was born 29 May 1894 in Toronto, the younger daughter (there were no sons) of John Lillie, cigar seller, of Lisburn in Ireland, and his wife, Lucie Ann, eldest daughter of John Shaw, a Manchester draper. Following her parents' emigration to Toronto, the family grew up there and 'Bea' was educated at St Agnes' College in Belleville, Ontario; she began to appear in amateur concerts there with her mother and sister as the Lillie Trio. At the outbreak of World War I they all returned to London, and it was at the Chatham Music Hall in 1914 that Bea made her professional stage début.

Already it was clear that the Lillie Trio was not much of a success, and that if Beatrice Lillie was to succeed in the theatre it would have to be as a solo act. Almost immediately after her London début she formed an alliance with the leading World War I producer of intimate revues, André *Charlot, who saw in her not the serious singer she had set out to become, but a comedian of considerable if zany qualities. Charlot at this time was also fostering the very early careers of Gertrude *Lawrence (who for a time was Lillie's understudy), W. J. ('Jack') *Buchanan, and (Sir) Noël *Coward. In World War I Lillie became a favourite of troops on leave from the front, relying on spontaneity and an improvised response to her audiences, which Charlot had to restrain when it threatened to go too far. Lillie's great talents were the arched eyebrow, the curled lip, the fluttering eyelid, the tilted chin, the ability to suggest, even in apparently innocent material, the possible *double entendre*.

In 1920 she married Robert Peel, son of Robert Peel and great-grandson of Sir Robert *Peel, prime minister. He succeeded his father as fifth baronet in 1925. He died in 1934, leaving his wife with one beloved son, Robert, sixth and last baronet, who was killed in World War II, in 1942. The loss of first husband and then son comparatively early in her life (she never married again) left Lillie with a constant private sadness that she seemed able to overcome only on stage. Her career encompassed some fifty stage shows in the West End and Broadway as well as a dozen films, but she excelled in live performance, demolishing scripts and songs alike with her own particular brand of solo eccentricity. (Sir) Charles *Cochran, Coward, and Florenz Ziegfeld all employed her in their revues, but in 1932 American audiences saw her as the Nurse in the New York première of *Too Good to be True* by Bernard *Shaw, one of the comparatively few 'straight' roles she undertook: others were in Robert Morley's first play, *Staff Dance* (1944), and the non-musical version of *Auntie Mame*, which she brought to London after the war.

She made her cabaret début at the Café de Paris in 1933, worked in revue and troop concerts throughout the war, and made her own television series, based on her cabaret routines, as early as 1951. She then developed, and toured for many years around the world, a solo show called simply *An Evening with Beatrice Lillie*, which ranked alongside those of Joyce *Grenfell and Ruth Draper. Her career in films began with the silent film, *Exit Smiling*, in 1927 and continued intermittently right through to *Around the World in Eighty Days* (1956) and *Thoroughly Modern Millie* (her last, in 1967). But in films as on radio something was missing, the live audience to which she could respond and which she often made part of the act. She was excellent as the mad Auntie Mame, or as Madame Arcati in *High Spirits* (1964), a Broadway musical version of Coward's *Blithe Spirit*. Coward called her 'the

perfect comedienne' and wrote his 'Marvellous Party' for her to sing, while Cole Porter wrote her 'Mrs Lowsborough-Goodby'. Her entire career was a sustained monument to anarchic alternative comedy before those terms had ever been invented, and hers was a triumph of manic high spirits. With her long face, tall brow, lively eyes, natural poise, and radiant personality, she was one of the great female clowns.

Her last years were overshadowed by illness; she lived in Henley-on-Thames, a virtual recluse had it not been for her devoted manager John Philip, who shared the house with her for twenty years and who died of a stroke only a matter of hours after her death. She died 20 January 1989 in Henley.

[Beatrice Lillie, *Every Other Inch a Lady*, 1973; *The Times*, 21 January 1989; private information.]

SHERIDAN MORLEY

LITTHAUER, Hildegard Therese (1918–1989), professor of social psychology. [See HIMMELWEIT, HILDEGARD THERESE.]

LOCKSPEISER, SIR Ben (1891–1990), engineer and government administrator, was born 9 March 1891 at 7 President Street, St Luke's, London E1, the eldest son and second child in the family of three sons and two daughters of Leon Lockspeiser, diamond merchant, and his wife, Rosa Gleitzman, of a devout and industrious Jewish family, recently arrived from a farming background in Lubno, south-west Poland. Benny Lockspeiser—so named in his birth certficate, though he was Ben for most of his life—spent his early years at 21 Thornby Road, Clapham. He was educated at the Grocers' School, Hackney, and, at the age of seventeen, already a gifted pianist and cellist, he won an open scholarship to Sidney Sussex College, Cambridge. After gaining a first in part i of the natural sciences tripos (1912), he transferred to the mechanical sciences tripos and obtained a second class in part ii (1913). After a year at the Royal School of Mines, he immediately enlisted when World War I began. In 1915 he sailed for Gallipoli as a private with the Royal Army Medical Corps. There he was stricken with amoebic dysentery and invalided out to Egypt, where on his recovery he continued with the RAMC, identifying the type, causes, and treatment of that devastating malady.

After he came back home, having been demobilized in 1919, his MA degree in engineering gained him entry to the armaments and aerodynamics section of the Royal Aircraft Establishment at Farnborough, Hampshire, where in 1920, on a walking holiday at Newlands in Wales, he met his future wife. The young Lockspeisers set up home at 'Newlands', Victoria Road, Farnborough, where, with one move in the 1930s to

Waverley Road, they lived for the rest of their lives. Lockspeiser worked hard and also immersed himself in the social activities of the RAE, which included music, drama, and gardening, and he became a member of the local branch of the emerging Labour party. In 1922 he founded the RAE Orchestral Society, which later became the Farnborough Symphony Orchestra and which he himself conducted until 1939.

As one of a four-man elasticity research team, Lockspeiser began pioneering work on chemical means of de-icing aircraft wings and other surfaces. This led him to study how to prevent the freezing of aircrew oxygen systems and of moisture in gas-supply mains. At the same time he worked on metal fatigue and was closely involved in the design, construction, and operation of the RAE's wind tunnel, which had a diameter of twenty-four feet. In 1936 he succeeded Harold Roxbee Cox (later Baron Kings Norton) as head of the RAE's air defence department. Moved to the Air Ministry in 1939 as assistant director of scientific research, and then to the new Ministry of Aircraft Production in 1940, to become deputy director (armaments) in 1941, in 1943 he became the MAP's director of scientific research, and in 1945 director-general. He visited the German research centre at Volkenrode, near Brunswick, in 1945 and, as a result of seeing the advanced German technology, cancelled the contract for a Miles M52 straight-wing supersonic project in favour of an experimental series of swept-wing, radio-controlled, and rocket-powered models. Their failure caused criticism, but this was offset by his positive, and successful, backing of (Sir) Frederic Callan *Williams, of Ferranti and Manchester University, in producing the first electronic computers.

In 1946 Lockspeiser was appointed chief scientist of the Ministry of Supply, and thus masterminded British research into problems of nuclear physics, supersonic flight, and guided weapons. In 1949 he was appointed to succeed Sir Edward *Appleton as secretary to the committee of the Privy Council for scientific and industrial research. He was for seven years thereafter a formidable and beneficial influence upon British advances in science and industrial development. He was always a devastating debater and a competent administrator. Among major projects he espoused and advanced in this creative period were the Festival of Britain in 1951, the National Lending Library for Science and Technology in 1952, a major clean-up of the river Thames in 1953, (Sir) Bernard Lovell's Jodrell Bank radio telescope in 1954, and the creation of CERN (the European Council for Nuclear Research), of which he became the first president (1955–7). He retired in 1956 and became chairman of the technical advisory board of the Israeli government and a director of several companies,

notably Tube Investments, Staverley, H. R. Ricardo, and Warburg's.

Lockspeiser was knighted in 1946 and appointed KCB in 1950. Elected a fellow of the Royal Society in 1949, he was also F.Eng. (1976), F.I.Mech.E. (1946), and F.R.Ae.S. (1944). He was an honorary fellow of Sidney Sussex College (1953) and a life fellow of the RSA, and he was awarded the US medal of freedom (silver palms) in 1946. He had honorary degrees from Witwatersrand (1949), Haifa (1952), and Oxford (1954).

He was a chubby, gentle, kindly figure, of medium height, with a determined chin and full cheeks. He surveyed the world with a benevolent but quizzical air, through wire-rimmed spectacles, from beneath a broad forehead under a mane of white hair. In 1920 he married a botanist, Elsie, daughter of Alfred Shuttleworth, accountant, of Shuttleworth and Haworth, Manchester. They had one son and two daughters. Elsie died in 1964 and in 1966 he married the widow of an old friend from the RAE, Mary Alice Heywood, who died in 1983. Lockspeiser died 18 October 1990 at home in Farnborough, five months short of his one-hundredth birthday.

[A. J. P. Edwards in *Biographical Memoirs of Fellows of the Royal Society*, vol. xxix, 1994; private information; personal knowledge.]   PETER MASEFIELD

LOCKWOOD, Margaret Mary (1916–1990), actress, was born 15 September 1916 in Karachi, India (later Pakistan), the younger child and only daughter of Henry Francis Lockwood, district traffic superintendent (later chief superintendent) on the Indian railways, and his third wife, Margaret Eveline Waugh, a Scot, who had been a nurse. She also had an older stepbrother. Mother and children set up home in Upper Norwood, Middlesex, when Margaret was three and a half, after which they saw little of her father. She attended Sydenham Girls' High School, taking dancing lessons at the Italia Conti School. These led to her appearance as a fairy in *A Midsummer Night's Dream* at the Holborn Empire when she was twelve. She left Sydenham High for the Cone School of Dancing, and did the rounds of auditions, performing in clubs, concerts, cabarets, and tea dances. In 1929 she adopted a family name, Day, for her stage name Margie Day, finally leaving school altogether at fourteen.

In 1933 she was accepted by the Royal Academy of Dramatic Art at the age of sixteen, and showed both talent and dedication, completing the two-year course in fourteen months. Playing a leading part in the annual RADA show, she caught the attention of the London agent Herbert de Leon. He quickly secured her two brief London stage engagements and second lead in the film *Lorna Doone* (1934), directed by Basil *Dean. De Leon remained her manager, adviser, and friend until his death forty-five years later.

She was immediately put under contract by British Lion film company and during the next few years made over a dozen films, many of them quota quickies, often appearing on the London stage in the evenings as well. A beautiful girl with abundant dark hair, big eyes, delicate features, a beauty spot high on her left cheekbone (which was allowed to appear for the first time in *The Wicked Lady*, 1945), natural poise, and an unaffected speaking voice, she proved a hard-working and reliable actress and was much in demand. The important Gainsborough film company promoted her as a star, and in *Bank Holiday* (1938) and *The Lady Vanishes* (1938) she achieved critical success. Before long she was appearing in some of the best British films of the period, including *The Stars Look Down* and *Night Train to Munich*, both directed by (Sir) Carol *Reed.

Her career entered a new phase in 1943. Gainsborough had been acquired by J. Arthur *Rank, who launched a series of frankly escapist films to cheer up the war-weary British public. These were novelettish costume melodramas, dubbed 'Gainsborough Gothics', scorned by serious critics and not especially well made but an enormous success at the box office. Lockwood afterwards was always identified with her part in the best known of these, *The Wicked Lady*, in which she starred with James *Mason.

She was now at the peak of her career and earning a large salary, the biggest British film star of her time although no longer taken very seriously as an actress. But her films began to decline in quality and by 1948, still only thirty-two, her great days were over. Her contract with Rank was dissolved in 1951. A woman of spirit, she returned to the stage and turned also to television. Always professional, she continued to act on the London stage and on tour for another twenty-five years. She starred in two television series, *The Flying Swan* (1965) and *Justice* (1971–4). Her last film appearance was in the fairy tale, *The Slipper and the Rose*, in 1976, and her last stage part was Queen Alexandra in *Motherdear* in 1980.

Not a great emotional actress, she was a straightforward and intelligent woman who worked hard and lived quietly, earning the affection of the British public. Unpretentious, she disliked the attributes of stardom. She was nominated by the *Motion Picture Herald* as the top money-making star in Britain in 1945 and 1946, and won the *Daily Mail* film award as best actress in British films in 1946, 1947, and 1948. Later she received the *Daily Mirror* television award in 1961, and Best Actress award from the *Sun* in 1973 and from the *Television Times* in 1977. In 1981 she was appointed CBE.

In 1937 she married Rupert William Leon (who was not related to her agent), commercial clerk (later steel broker), the son of Emil Armand Leon, managing director of the British Iron and Steel Corporation. Her mother disapproved strongly of the marriage. Their daughter Julia, later the actress Julia Lockwood, was born in 1941 but the marriage failed soon afterwards. Margaret Lockwood wished to marry Keith Dobson, but her husband refused to give her a divorce. She then had a relationship with Theo Cowan, who was in charge of Rank's publicity. She later lived for seventeen years, apparently happily, with John Stone, a minor fellow actor considerably younger than herself, whom she met in 1959. She was afflicted by ear trouble and, after he left her in 1977, she gradually withdrew from the theatre. Two years later she was devastated by the death of her friend and mentor of Leon. For the last years of her life she lived as a recluse in Kingston upon Thames. She died of cirrhosis of the liver in the Cromwell Hospital, Kensington, 15 July 1990.

[*Daily Telegraph*, 16 and 17 July 1990; *Independent*, 17 July 1990; *The Times*, 16 and 17 July 1990; *Daily Mail*, 4 March 1946 and 22 June 1946; Margaret Lockwood, *My Life and Films*, 1948, and *Lucky Star*, 1955; Hilton Tims, *Once a Wicked Lady*, 1989; *Who's Who in the Theatre*, 17th edn., 1981; *Halliwell's Film Guide*, 7th edn., 1989.]　　　　　　　　　　RACHAEL LOW

LOGAN, SIR **Douglas William** (1910–1987), principal of London University, was born in Liverpool 27 March 1910, the younger son and youngest of three children of Robert Logan, cabinet-maker, of Newhaven, Edinburgh, and his wife, Euphemia Taylor Stevenson, of Kirkcaldy. He was educated at Liverpool Collegiate School and University College, Oxford, where he was a classical scholar and took firsts in classical honour moderations (1930), *literae humaniores* (1932), and jurisprudence (1933). In 1933 he was awarded an Oxford University senior studentship and the Harmsworth scholarship at the Middle Temple. During 1935–6 he held the Henry fellowship at Harvard, and in 1936–7 he was an assistant lecturer in law at the London School of Economics. In 1937 he was called to the bar (Middle Temple) and elected a fellow of Trinity College, Cambridge (until 1943).

During World War II he worked as a temporary civil servant at the Ministry of Supply from 1940 till 1944, when he was appointed clerk of the court of London University. In 1948 he became principal, a post which he held until 1975. When he took office Logan faced some formidable problems. In 1948 Britain was still suffering from the hardships imposed by the war. Rationing of food and petrol was still in force, many necessities were in short supply, and the devastation caused by German bombs on London meant that a huge building programme would have to be undertaken. At the same time such developments as the planning of new comprehensive schools marked the increased demand for university education. Added to these difficulties was the inescapable dilemma that London University itself was a large and complex organization, made up of a number of colleges, medical schools, and other institutions covering a variety of specialities, powered by machinery which could only work effectively if controlled by somebody equipped with the capacity to take clear decisions and the determination and energy required to put such decisions into effect. Logan's character, education, and experience gave him the toughness to make this machinery work even when hampered by financial stringency, student militancy, and occasional academic obduracy.

From the outset he concentrated on the problems of reconstruction necessitated by the shortage of accommodation for students and the cost of building sites in central London. The outcome was the acquisition or construction of seven university halls of residence and the purchase of an extensive site in Bloomsbury on which important new university buildings could be erected.

At this time London, the largest university in Britain, also had responsibility for a number of colleges outside London which took London degrees. Similarly, university colleges in Africa, the West Indies, and Malaya, together with the existing universities in Malta and Hong Kong, needed the assistance of London in maintaining their academic integrity through London degrees. Logan was actively involved in his membership of the Association of Commonwealth Universities, of which he was chairman in 1962–3.

Throughout his term of office as principal and after his retirement Logan worked industriously to better the conditions of university staff and students. He fought a long campaign for the improvement of the pensions of university teachers and was virtually the author of the Universities Superannuation Scheme, which came into force in 1974. He was its chairman in 1974–7, deputy chairman in 1977–80, and consultant from 1980 to 1986. In his youth he had been an enthusiastic player of rugby football, and, with the co-operation of his vice-chancellor, Sir David Hughes *Parry, he took a leading part in the provision of social and athletic facilities for students on a university as opposed to a college basis. He was also particularly concerned with the problems of medical education, and the establishment of the National Health Service seemed to him to call for constant vigilance to safeguard the efficiency of the London hospital medical schools.

Logan also sat for many years on committees dealing with scholarships and grants for students from both Britain and overseas, including Athlone fellowships and Marshall scholarships. He was a member of the board of the National Theatre (1962–8), a governor of the Old Vic (1957–80), and a trustee of the City Parochial Foundation (1953–67). He was knighted in 1959 and received honorary fellowships from LSE (1962), University College, Oxford (1973), and University College London (1975); honorary degrees were conferred upon him by universities from Melbourne to British Columbia. He was a chevalier of the Legion of Honour and an honorary bencher of the Middle Temple (1965).

In 1940 Logan married Vaire Olive, daughter of Sir Gerald Woods Wollaston, herald; they had two sons before they divorced in 1946. A year later he married Christine Peggy, daughter of William Arthur Walker, motor engineer inspector; they had one son and one daughter.

'Jock' Logan, as he was known to his colleagues, was well built, of medium height and somewhat shuffling gait. A prodigious worker, he had impressive organizing ability and was a consummate draughtsman. He was impatient with inadequacy and with opposition based on ignorance or vested interest, and his brusque and forceful manner alienated many. He died in University College Hospital, London, 19 October 1987, after suffering a stroke.

[*The Times*, 20 October 1987; Negley Harte, *The University of London 1836–1986*, 1986; Douglas Logan, *The University of London: an Introduction*, 1956; private information; personal knowledge.]   H. F. OXBURY

LORIMER, Maxwell George (1908–1990), comic entertainer and actor. [See WALL, MAX.]

LOSS, Joshua Alexander ('Joe') (1909–1990), bandleader, was born 22 June 1909 in Spitalfields, east London, the youngest of the family of two sons and two daughters of Israel Loss, of Russian origin, a cabinet-maker who had an office furnishing business, and his wife, Ada Loss. His mother and father were first cousins. Israel Loss recognized his son's musical talents and started him with violin lessons at the age of seven. It was hoped that he might become a concert violinist, and, after education at the Jewish Free School, Spitalfields, he studied at the Trinity College of Music and the London College of Music.

His interests lay in lighter fields and, after playing in cinemas during silent films and in various bands, at the end of 1930 he formed his own first band to play at the Astoria Ballroom (then known as the Astoria Danse Salon) in Charing Cross Road, becoming, at the age of twenty, the youngest bandleader in the West End of London. Under the name of Joe Loss and his Harlem Band, his musicians first played as the no. 2 unit, Joe Loss leading on violin, with three saxophones, trumpet, piano, and drums. Later they added a special tango section, which featured two accordions and two violins. Occasionally they deputized for the Percival Mackey Band at the Kit-Kat Club, and when Mackey left to go into vaudeville at the beginning of 1932, Joe Loss took over to initiate a new 'popular price' policy, playing for daily tea, dinner, and supper dances, supported by and often combining with Fred Spedbury's Coney Islanders. He returned to the Astoria in 1934 to become the no. 1 band and remained there until the outbreak of war in 1939.

During this period he began to record for the Regal-Zonophone label and his first really big hit came with a recording made in July 1939 of 'Begin the Beguine', with Chick Henderson (who was killed by shrapnel in 1944) as vocalist. During the war years Joe Loss toured the country and after D-Day played to the forces at various venues in Europe. His was to become the most prestigious society dance orchestra in the country, its qualities based on his love of a strong rhythm. From 1939 it played a regular engagement at Buckingham Palace and later at the weddings of Princess Margaret, Princess Anne, and Princess Alexandra. After the war there were residencies at the Hammersmith Palais, the Villa Marina in the Isle of Man, and Green's Playhouse, Glasgow, and there were frequent trips on the liner *Queen Elizabeth II*. The band was now always at least eighteen strong, usually with three vocalists—his singers, at various times, including Monte Rey, Howard Jones, Ross McManus, and Rose Brennan. (Dame) Vera Lynn was amongst those given encouragement in the early stages of an illustrious career. In 1970, when Loss left Hammersmith, the band, in the face of economic demands, became smaller.

His recording career was a busy one. In 1940 he had a second big hit with 'In the Mood', which became his signature tune, and many others followed. Despite the emergence of pop, he continued to record his swinging strict-tempo music and in the 1970s had two albums which sold a million copies—'Joe Loss Plays Glenn Miller' and 'Joe Loss Plays the Big Band Greats'. He continued to record with EMI until the end of his career, and became a well-known name on radio and television, notably with the long-running *Come Dancing* series.

Loss was a great supporter of such charities as the Variety Artists' Federation Sunshine Coach Fund. He was appointed OBE in 1978 and LVO in 1984. He was awarded the Queen's Silver Jubilee medal in 1978 and became a freeman of the City of London in 1979. Posthumously, he was made a fellow of the City University when his wife, who continued to run the Joe Loss Agency, started in the 1930s, presented the library with his collection of big-band scores.

Loss's generosity, kindness, and courtesy, and his dislike of star treatment, made him one of the best-liked figures in the world of popular music. He was five feet eight inches in height, with a trim figure and sleek black hair, which tumbled over his face when he was conducting in his typically energetic way. He was always well dressed, in later years in a white silk suit, and usually had a broad, friendly smile. Away from the relentless hard work of sixty years as a bandleader, celebrated by a Variety Club luncheon in 1989, he was a devoted family man. In 1938 he married Mildred Blanch Rose, daughter of a Latvian from Riga, Barnet Rosenberg (who later changed his name to Rose), master tailor. They had a son and a daughter and were delighted to have grandchildren who followed in Loss's musical footsteps. Loss died in a London hospital 6 June 1990.

[Private information; personal knowledge.]

PETER GAMMOND

LUBETKIN, **Berthold Romanovitch** (1901–1990), architect, was born 14 December 1901 in Tiflis, Georgia, the only child of Roman Aronovich Lubetkin, railway engineer, and his wife, Fenya. He was educated at Tenishevskaya Gymnasia, St Petersburg, and the Medvednikov Gymnasia, Moscow. He then attended the Charlottenburg School of Building in Berlin (1922–3) before moving to Warsaw Polytechnic, where he took his diploma in architecture in 1923.

In 1925 he assisted the architect K. Melnikov with his design for the Russian pavilion at the decorative arts exposition held in Paris in that year and himself settled in Paris for the following five years. He attended the École des Beaux Arts (where he studied under Auguste Perret, from whom he no doubt acquired the rigorous sense of structural form apparent in his own later work), the École Supérieure de Béton Armé, the Institut d'Urbanisme, and the Sorbonne. From 1927 he worked as an architect in partnership with Jean Ginsberg, designing with him a block of flats in the Avenue de Versailles.

In 1931 Lubetkin moved to London and in the following year formed, with a number of young architects who had recently qualified from the Architectural Association School, a partnership which called itself Tecton, under which name, in conjunction with his own, he practised until his retirement in 1939 when war broke out.

Tecton's most important early work was Highpoint, in Highgate, London (1935), a tall block of flats ingeniously and elegantly planned to give the maximum light and air to all its apartments. It was one of the first English buildings, other than industrial, to display the aesthetic potentialities of reinforced concrete. A second block was added in 1938 which aroused interest—and some alarm among purists—by its use of caryatids modelled on those of the Erectheion at Athens to support the entrance porch; an example of the intellectual perversity that relieved the doctrinaire nature of Lubetkin's thought. Other works, which brought his designs to the notice of a wider public, were the gorilla house (1934) and penguin pool (1935) at the London Zoo, which also revealed that concrete, a material hitherto used with much sophistication only on the Continent and considered in England strictly utilitarian, was capable of liveliness and gaiety. More zoo buildings followed at Whipsnade and at Dudley, Worcestershire, and in 1938 a health centre—Tecton's first municipal building—for the London borough of Finsbury.

The long-term significance of the Tecton office at this time is indicated by the number of young architects who gained their early experience there and afterwards became distinguished in the profession. They included Gordon Cullen, Peter Moro, and (Sir) Denys Lasdun. The group was dispersed in World War II, during which Lubetkin farmed in Gloucestershire, working his farm at Upper Kilcott himself while constantly challenging the validity of established farming practices. He had little help but that of his wife, whom he had married in 1939 soon after she joined the Tecton office as a young architect. An unusual aspect of their farm in wartime was the presence in it of a number of exotic animals and birds which they housed at the request of Sir Peter Chalmers Mitchell, secretary of the London Zoological Society, for whom Lubetkin had designed a house near Whipsnade in 1938. Lubetkin was naturalized on 24 February 1939.

In 1947 Lubetkin resumed architectural practice in London in partnership with Francis Skinner, one of the original Tecton group, and Douglas Bailey. They designed several housing schemes for Finsbury, which showed careful study of social needs but lacked some of the invention and vitality of Tecton's pre-war work. In 1948 Lubetkin was architect-planner of the new town of Peterlee in the coal-mining region of county Durham. His design was ambitious and unorthodox and a notable departure from the suburban style adopted by the other postwar new towns; so much so that it became the subject of long-running local argument, political and economic. It was finally rejected and Lubetkin resigned.

He thereupon retired altogether from architectural practice for reasons his friends and associates never fully understood. He became something of a recluse, living in a very private style at his Gloucestershire farm. In 1968 his wife's deteriorating health caused them to give up farming and move to a small flat at Clifton, Bristol, where she died ten years later. There, too, they lived in a modest style and there Lubetkin remained after her death, seeing few people and engaged in writing, the subject of which he did not disclose and nothing of which has been published.

In his later years Lubetkin found a gleeful enjoyment in the riskier aspects of motoring and had a number of road accidents, one of which, in 1972, resulted in a shattered femur and left him crippled for the rest of his life, giving him added reason to retreat from professional affairs. He did, however, make the journey to London to receive the RIBA Royal gold medal for architecture, which he was awarded in 1982 (he always refused to become a member of the RIBA). In 1987 he went to London again to attend in a wheelchair a ceremony marking the restoration of his penguin pool at the London Zoo.

Berthold Lubetkin (Tolek to all his friends) was a man of complex character whom some found difficult and devious and whose motivations often seemed mysterious. He had left-wing political allegiances and a distinguished analytical mind which ranged widely over many subjects. He was a stimulating conversationalist. His influence on the style and standards of architecture in Britain, especially in the 1930s, was considerable.

He married in 1939 Margaret Louise, the younger daughter of Harold Church, barrister. They had a son and two daughters. Lubetkin died at his home in Clifton 23 October 1990.

[Peter Coe and Malcolm Reading, *Lubetkin and Tecton: Architecture and Social Commitment*, 1981; John Allan, *Berthold Lubetkin: Architecture and the Tradition of Progress*, 1992; personal knowledge; information from his elder daughter.]   J. M. RICHARDS

M

McBEAN, Angus Rowland (1904–1990), photographer, was born 8 June 1904 in Newbridge, Monmouthshire, the elder child and only son of Clement Philip James McBean, surveyor, and his wife, Irene Sarah Thomas. He was educated at Monmouth Grammar School (1915–21) and, briefly, at Newport Technical College. His childhood was spent far away from the metropolitan sophistication which he later encountered in the 1930s and 1940s as Britain's most prominent and inventive theatre photographer. But photography had become significant to him long before he emerged as a professional. The teenage purchase of a simple Kodak camera gave him his first glimpse of the possibilities of the medium. Amateur dramatics, organized by an aunt, introduced McBean to the magical world of theatre—he designed posters and costumes, and began to experiment with the mask-making which intrigued him for the rest of his life.

McBean was a bank clerk from 1921 to 1924. After the death of his father in 1924, McBean's mother moved her family to London, and Angus joined the department store Liberty's (1926–33), as an antiques salesman. Like many of his generation, he was attracted by the Germanic cult of health and beauty and joined the Kibbu Kift movement, where he met Helena Wood, whom he married in 1923. They were separated in 1924 and there were no children.

By the end of the 1920s McBean was obsessed by theatre. He met the Motleys (Percy and Sophia Harris and Elizabeth Montgomery), three young stage designers who encouraged his interest in prop-making and helped him to secure his first design commission—work for the 1933 production of *Richard of Bordeaux*.

He continued to photograph, and in 1934 (after his first photographic exhibition, at the Pirates' Den teashop in London) he became assistant to the Bond Street portraitist Hugh Cecil. Though he disliked Cecil's soft-focus romanticism, he was an adept studio worker, and soon began to develop the aesthetic and technical skills which distinguished his later career. In 1935 McBean opened his own studio in London. He photographed Ivor *Novello in *The Happy Hypocrite* in 1936. His stage photographs were boldly lit and dramatic, and soon he was photographing at the Old Vic, documenting now

classic productions: Laurence (later Baron) *Olivier in *Hamlet*, (Dame) Edith *Evans in *The Country Wife*, and Diana Wynyard in *Pygmalion*. McBean's photographs were now appearing in all the London glossy magazines.

But it was the mounting in London of the 1936 exhibition of Surrealist art which inspired McBean to begin radical experiments with photographic portraiture. By 1937 he had begun to use the styles and devices of Surrealism to create fantastical portraits of theatrical stars —Vivien *Leigh, enveloped in a plaster-of-Paris gown and posed among cotton-wool clouds, (Dame) Flora *Robson erupting from a desolate landscape, the impresario H. G. ('Binkie') *Beaumont as a giant puppet-master, and Patricia Hilliard emerging from a sea shell. He photographed himself too, in striped pyjamas with an umbrella, in a neoclassical aquarium, as King Neptune, and as a Roman bust, and sent the photographs out as Christmas cards to an ever-widening circle of friends and associates. With his flowing beard and his deep theatrical voice, he became a well known and much admired character in the London of the 1930s. Immediately after the end of World War II (during the course of which he spent some time in prison as a conscientious objector), he opened a bigger studio in Covent Garden, and during the 1940s and 1950s he was inundated with commissions from London's major theatre companies.

In the early 1960s McBean photographed the Beatles for the cover of their first long-playing record. But as the decade wore on, and fashions in both theatre and photography began to alter, McBean's style, so rooted in the aesthetics of the 1950s, became unpopular. McBean had made those he portrayed into elegant stars. On the new realist stage, however, actors simply wanted to look like ordinary people.

Angus McBean's appearance was flamboyant. His thick beard marked him out immediately as one who wished to be considered an artist rather than a craftsman, and his colourful and often handmade clothes indicated an enduring interest in design and costume. When McBean retired in 1970 and moved to Flemings Hall near the village of Eye in Suffolk, he became almost immediately obscure. He sold his glass plate negatives to Harvard University and in Suffolk moved back into the design work which had so fascinated him in his early years. Flemings Hall, where he lived with his companion (and long-time assistant) David Ball, became a fitting arena for McBean's fantastical imagination. When his photographs were shown in 1976, as a retrospective exhibition at Impressions Gallery, York (and two years later at the National Theatre), the significance of his work within the history of British photography was finally recognized. Acknowledged too was his place as an elder statesman of the burgeoning and culturally progressive international gay community. During the 1980s there were major exhibitions of his work, TV documentaries, and numerous photographic commissions. No longer a half-forgotten name from the unfashionable past, Angus McBean, much to his delight, was once more in demand. He died 8 June 1990 at Ipswich Heath Road Hospital, Ipswich. The Harvard Theatre Museum has a collection of his photographs and plates.

[Colin Naylor (ed.), *Contemporary Photographers*, 2nd edn., 1988; Adrian Woodhouse, *Angus McBean*, 1982; typescript of an unpublished autobiography *c*.1972, Angus McBean papers in a private collection; information from David Ball; personal knowledge.]

VAL WILLIAMS

MacCOLL, Ewan (1915–1989), songwriter, singer, folk-song revivalist, and dramatist, was born James Miller 25 January 1915 in Salford, Lancashire, the youngest and only surviving child in the family of three sons and one daughter (one of each sex was stillborn and one son died at the age of four) of William Miller, iron-moulder, of Salford, and his wife Betsy Hendry, charwoman. He was educated at Grecian Street School, Salford. He left school at the age of fourteen after an elementary education and was immediately unemployed. He joined the Young Communists' League (he was not to leave the Communist party until the early 1960s) and then found work as a motor mechanic, factory worker, and street singer. He first began writing for factory newspapers, composing satirical songs and political poems, while also taking a keen interest in amateur dramatics, in 1931 forming a political street theatre group, the Red Megaphones, which performed sketches on the streets of Salford and Manchester. Both his parents were fine traditional singers, and he had begun to sing and write songs while a teenager. One of his first and finest protest songs, 'The Manchester Rambler', dealt with the 'mass trespass' campaigns of the 1930s, in which hikers fought pitched battles with gamekeepers when they invaded privately owned grouse moors.

It was two decades before he devoted his energies to music. He spent most of the 1930s involved in experimental theatre projects after joining forces with his future wife, Joan Littlewood, with whom he formed a 'workers' experimental theatre', the Theatre of Action, at Manchester in 1933. He wrote and co-produced a series of political satires and dance dramas, and was arrested and charged with disturbing the peace after the police stopped performances of his 'living newspaper', 'Last Edition'. In World War II he was called up, joined the army, and was arrested for desertion, although he claimed there had been a case of mistaken identity. He was discharged on medical grounds. He continued with his drama projects after the war, and he and Littlewood formed Theatre Workshop, for which he became art director and resident dramatist. He changed his name to Ewan Mac-Coll in 1945. Between 1945 and 1952 he wrote eleven plays, including *Uranium 235* (1952), a drama with music, and *Landscape with Chimneys* (1951), which included one of his best-known songs, 'Dirty Old Town', written in a matter of hours on the opening night to cover a scene change.

He severed his links with Littlewood in 1952 and gradually withdrew from the Theatre Workshop. From 1952 onwards he worked to establish a folk-song revival in Britain. He saw folk music not as some quaint historical curiosity but as a political force, an expression of working-class culture, and he wanted to develop a style in which 'songs of struggle would be immediately acceptable to a lot of young people'. With help from American folklorist Alan Lomax and A. L. ('Bert') Lloyd, he mixed politics, British and American folk music, and jazz in a radio series, *Ballads and Blues* (1953). He founded the Ballads and Blues Club, later renamed the Singers' Club, in London, and by the mid-1950s was considered one of the leading folk-singers in the country.

Initially, MacColl had encouraged the fashion for American folk and blues (he and Lomax had even started a skiffle group, which included another American singer and song-writer, Peggy Seeger, who was to become his third wife), but by the late 1950s he became concerned that British traditional music was being swamped by American styles. He therefore introduced his controversial 'policy rule'—singers had to perform songs from their own tradition, depending on whether they were British or American.

In 1957, when he claimed there were 1,500 folk clubs around Britain, he returned to experimental multi-media work, this time with a distinctively British flavour. The *Radio Ballads*, broadcast on the BBC Home Service (1958–64), dealt with the everyday lives of British workers, from railwaymen to boxers or fishermen, and used a montage of interviews and new songs written by MacColl. He wrote many of his best songs for this widely praised series, including 'Shoals of Herring' and 'Freeborn Man'.

A fiery, authoritative, opinionated figure, he never deviated from his staunch left-wing views. From 1965 to 1971 he trained young singers in folk-singing and theatre technique in his Critics Group, which performed an annual review of the year's news, the 'Festival of Fools'. He collected folk-songs, and co-wrote two books with Peggy Seeger (*Travellers' Songs from England and Scotland*, 1977, which was praised for its scholarship, and *Till Doomsday in the Afternoon, the Folklore of a Family of Scots Travellers*, 1986). With her he founded Blackthorne Records, which specialized in their own recordings. In the 1980s, by which time his jet-black hair and red beard had turned white, he wrote songs to support the miners' strike and the anti-apartheid movement. Considering his enormous and varied output, it was ironic that his only financial success came from his song 'The First Time Ever I Saw Your Face', a no. 1 hit in America for Roberta Flack in 1972. It won the Ivor Novello award in 1973. MacColl was awarded an honorary degree by Exeter University (1986).

In 1935 he married Joan Littlewood, who did not know the identity of her father, but was brought up by a stepfather, Jimmy Morritt, asphalter. They were divorced in 1948 and in 1949 he married Jean, daughter of William Newlove, a wartime director of regional supplies and part-time artist. They had a son, Hamish, and a daughter, Kirsty, a very successful singer-songwriter. They were divorced in 1974 and he married his third wife, the singer Peggy Seeger, with whom he had lived since the 1950s, in 1977. She was the daughter of Charles Seeger, musicologist, and sister of the singer Pete Seeger. MacColl died 22 October 1989 in the Brompton Hospital, London, after complications following heart surgery, and his autobiography *Journeyman* was published the following year.

[Interview with Ewan MacColl; Ewan MacColl, *Journeyman* (autobiography), 1990; Joan Littlewood, *Joan's Book*, 1994; *Independent*, 30 October 1989; private information.]   ROBIN DENSELOW

McELWAIN, Timothy John (1937–1990), cancer physician, was born 22 April 1937 in Wellington, New Zealand, the only child of Allan R. McElwain, freelance foreign correspondent, and his wife, Marjorie ('Miranda') Simpson, a commercial artist specializing in fashion. Because of the peripatetic nature of his father's employment, McElwain was educated in both Australia and England. He attended St Peter's College, Adelaide, from 1947 to 1949, and then transferred to Sloane School in London (1949–51). Back in Australia, he went to Haileybury College, Melbourne, from 1951 to 1957. He returned to London in 1957 to go to the London Polytechnic to study physics, chemistry, zoology, and botany for a first MB exemption. He duly

achieved this, with passes in all subjects. He also became president of the Students' Union, chairman of the Debating Society, and president of the Faculty Club. He was keen on water sports and rowing. He was admitted to St Bartholomew's Hospital Medical College in October 1960, being about five years older than the average student. His maturity is reflected in the fact that he had no difficulty with examinations, passing MB, BS finals with honours in 1965, when he obtained a distinction in applied pharmacology and therapeutics. He was awarded the Hayward prize in recognition of his contribution to student activities.

McElwain did his house physician appointments at Bart's, where he worked for Gordon Hamilton Fairley, a pioneer of the drug treatment of cancer. His interest and ability in therapeutics ensured Hamilton Fairley's support, and he obtained one of the first Leukaemia Research Fund fellowships (1968–70), to work on childhood leukaemia at the Hospital for Sick Children, Great Ormond Street. He passed his MRCP in 1968, and, after registrar appointments at Bart's (1967–8), and posts as lecturer (1970–1) and senior lecturer (1972–3) at the Royal Marsden Hospital, London, he was appointed in 1973 consultant physician at the Royal Marsden. He became head of the section of medicine in 1980, and was subsequently appointed Cancer Research Campaign professor of medical oncology in the University of London in 1983. He had been elected at an early age to the fellowship of the Royal College of Physicians of London, in 1977.

He brought to the Royal Marsden Hospital an appreciation of the importance of the discipline of internal medicine, not only in the proper use of drugs to combat cancer, but also in the expert general medical care necessary to the exploration of the drugs' potential. He pushed intensive therapy, using high doses of anti-cancer drugs, to the limit, and his resultant success in the care of myeloma, a highly malignant form of cancer, serves as a confirmation of the value of his work. This could not have been achieved without prolonged, intensive effort, and courage in facing the inevitable institutional resistance and resentments.

As professor of medical oncology he was in great demand from organizations abroad and at home. He was always generous with his time, holding such posts as consultant in medical oncology at the Tata Memorial Cancer Centre in Bombay, India, external assessor to the Chinese University of Hong Kong, and referee for research grant applications to the Medical Research Council of New Zealand. In Great Britain he was chairman or member of several important committees in such institutions as the Royal College of Physicians of London, the

Medical Research Council, and the Wolfson Foundation. However, the position that gave him most pleasure was his presidency of the Association of Cancer Physicians. He was a member of the editorial boards of many specialist journals. He was a popular member of societies, and of national and international committees, where his knowledge, combined with good common sense and a pithy expression of his views, could often rescue a meeting that was faltering.

McElwain was a large man, with a bald head, who loved food, wine, and music, and had a remarkable knowledge of contemporary literature. He had a library of over 2,000 records of classical music. With his wit and his expansive personality, he was a charming and thoughtful host, and an invitation to his home was not to be missed. In 1970 he married Sheila Glennis, daughter of Richard Howarth, accountant, after a whirlwind courtship while he was a junior doctor at the Hospital for Sick Children, Great Ormond Street. She brought love and security to his life and, while carving out a distinguished medical career for herself, was able to give him an elegant and happy home. There were no children. McElwain died at his home in Clapham, 26 November 1990.

[*British Medical Journal*, vol. cccii, 5 January 1991; *Lancet*, 8 December 1990; *British Journal of Cancer*, vol. lxiii, 1991; personal knowledge.]   J. S. MALPAS

MACFARLANE, (Robert) Gwyn (1907–1987), medical scientist, was born 26 June 1907 in Worthing, Sussex, the only child of Robert Gray Macfarlane, manager of the Siamese branch of the Bombay and Burma Trading Corporation in Bangkok, and his wife Eileen Montagu, daughter of the Revd Lancelot Sanderson, a schoolmaster at Harrow. Gwyn's father died of rabies in Bangkok soon after his marriage and before his son's birth, and as a baby and child Gwyn was brought up by his mother, who never remarried, grandmother, and nanny. Quite early in life he showed unusual interest in mechanical things, and at Cheltenham College he showed promise in mathematics and science and aimed to make a career in engineering. At the age of nineteen, however, he entered St Bartholomew's Hospital Medical College and qualified MRCS, LRCP and MB, BS (Lond.) in 1933.

While a student he showed a preference for laboratory work and began to investigate the clotting (coagulation) of blood. Macfarlane had become impressed with the tragedy of the bleeding disorder haemophilia, the cause of which was not understood. It was known, however, that the venom of certain snakes would promote coagulation and Macfarlane wondered whether snake venom could be used therapeutically. With the help of the London zoo, venom was collected from several species: that of the Russell's viper

was found to be most effective, not only in laboratory tests, but also when applied to the bleeding site in haemophiliacs. This was the start of Macfarlane's lifelong research into coagulation and the mechanisms of haemorrhage in haemophilia and other bleeding disorders, research that led to an international reputation and his recognition as *the* British expert in the field. Soon he realized that to understand the mechanisms of haemorrhage in disease it was essential to find out as much as possible about the mechanisms by which haemorrhage from small wounds ceased spontaneously in a healthy person. This enquiry resulted in his thesis for the degree of MD (London), for which he received a gold medal in 1938.

In 1936 Macfarlane moved to the newly founded British postgraduate medical school at Hammersmith Hospital to become assistant lecturer in clinical pathology, under the directorship of (Dame) Janet Vaughan. At the BPMS he developed his work on coagulation and assisted Janet Vaughan in her pioneering work in organizing blood banking in anticipation of war.

Early in 1939 Macfarlane left the BPMS to undertake work on bacterial toxins at the Wellcome research laboratories. In 1940 he was appointed clinical pathologist at the Radcliffe Infirmary, Oxford, where he remained until his retirement in 1967, except for a period in 1944-5, when he was seconded by the Medical Research Council to the Royal Army Medical Corps, with the rank of major, to undertake research into gas gangrene in battle casualties. After the war he continued his pioneering researches on coagulation and haemophilia, and the possibility of its treatment by extracts derived from normal blood. The success of these endeavours attracted to the Radcliffe Infirmary, and later to the Churchill Hospital (both in Oxford), a stream of assistants, who eventually disseminated his knowledge and expertise throughout the world.

His achievements were recognized by a succession of honours: he was elected a fellow of the Royal Society in 1956 and of the Royal College of Physicians in 1960. In 1959 he was appointed director of a newly established MRC Blood Coagulation Research Unit, and in 1964 he was appointed professor of haematology in the University of Oxford (having become a lecturer in 1948 and a reader in 1957). In 1963 he was elected a fellow of All Souls College and in 1964 appointed CBE. He became president of the Haemophilia Society in 1982, in recognition of his unique contribution to the welfare of haemophiliacs.

He was the author of about 140 scientific papers and chapters in books and wrote, with his long-standing collaborator Dr Rosemary Biggs, a major book entitled *Human Blood Coagulation and its Disorders* (1953); he also co-edited several other important books. After his retirement he wrote two notable biographies, *Howard Florey, the Making of a Great Scientist* (1979) and *Alexander Fleming, the Man and the Myth* (1984).

Macfarlane was of medium height and build, with pleasant features and a ready smile. He dressed somewhat informally. He had a brilliant intellect and was modest, kind and sensitive, witty and humorous, and a great raconteur. His early interest in mechanical things led him to devise a prototype machine for the mechanical counting of blood cells and, outside the laboratory, to the driving of fast cars. He was also a keen yachtsman.

Macfarlane married in 1936 Hilary Carson, also at the time a newly qualified doctor. She was the daughter of Harry Arthur Hamilton Carson, author of several standard surgical textbooks. They had four sons and one daughter and enjoyed a long and happy life together. When at Oxford they lived for most of the time at Downhill Farm, a farmhouse near Witney, surrounded by farm animals and usually with an added complement of friends. Hilary Macfarlane practised as a Witney general practitioner. After retirement they moved first to a cottage in Ramsden, a nearby Cotswold village, which they rebuilt, and ultimately in 1977 to a derelict crofter's cottage in Wester Ross, Scotland, which again they did much to restore with their own hands. There Macfarlane died 26 March 1987, of cardiac ischaemia.

[G. V. R. Born and D. J. Weatherall in *Biographical Memoirs of Fellows of the Royal Society*, vol. xxxv, 1990; Alastair Robb-Smith's address at a service of thanksgiving, 9 June 1987; personal knowledge.]   JOHN DACIE

McINTIRE, (Heather Mabel) Jane (1928–1990), writer on cookery. [See GRIGSON, (HEATHER MABEL) JANE.]

MACINTOSH, SIR Robert Reynolds (1897–1989), professor of anaesthetics at the University of Oxford, was born 17 October 1897 in Timaru, New Zealand. Christened Rewi Rawhiti (Maori names being popular at the time), he was the youngest in the family of two sons and one daughter of Charles Nicholson Macintosh, newspaper editor, businessman, farmer, and mayor of Timaru in 1901, and his wife, Lydia Beatrice Thompson. He spent part of his childhood in Argentina, but returned to New Zealand when he was thirteen years old. He was educated at Waitaki Boys' High School in the South Island, where he shone academically and athletically and was head of school. In December 1915 he travelled to Britain and was commissioned in the Royal Scots Fusiliers. After a short period in France he was transferred to the Royal Flying Corps, for which he had originally volunteered. He was mentioned in dispatches, but was shot down behind enemy lines on 26 May 1917 and

taken prisoner. There followed a remarkable series of attempted escapes from various prisoner-of-war camps, which have been documented in H. E. Hervey's *Cage-Birds* (1940).

After the war Macintosh entered Guy's Hospital medical school, qualifying MRCS, LRCP in 1924. Whilst working for the FRCS (Edin.), which he obtained in 1927, he undertook anaesthetic sessions in Guy's dental school. His skills were soon recognized and within a few years he had built up a large West End dental anaesthetic practice.

In February 1937 Macintosh was appointed to the first Nuffield chair of anaesthetics in Oxford and was awarded the DM (Oxon.). Since he had never received any formal academic training in anaesthesia, he spent some months visiting other departments, including that run by the only other professor of anaesthesia, Ralph Waters, in Madison, Wisconsin. Later in 1937 he anaesthetized for an American plastic surgeon who had volunteered to treat the wounded in the Spanish civil war. The experience of working under wartime conditions with very primitive equipment convinced Macintosh that there was a need for a simple, portable vaporizer, which would deliver known concentrations of ether when used under field conditions. When he returned to Oxford he invoked the aid of physicists in the Clarendon Laboratory, who produced the prototype Oxford vaporizer no. 1. Between 1941 and 1945 several thousand vaporizers were produced in the Morris car factory in Cowley, many being used in the armed services and, later, in underdeveloped countries. More sophisticated vaporizers and other items of equipment (such as the Macintosh laryngoscope) were subsequently developed and these, together with the superbly illustrated textbooks written by Macintosh and other members of department, had a major impact on the practice of anaesthesia.

During World War II Macintosh became an air commodore in the Royal Air Force in 1941, with responsibility for the anaesthetic services, but he retained his Oxford connections. The department provided training courses for many anaesthetists from the armed services and elsewhere, and was also deeply involved in hazardous physiological research into the provision of respirable atmospheres in submarines, survival during parachute descent from high altitudes, and the evaluation of life-jackets, using an anaesthetized volunteer submerged in a swimming-pool.

Macintosh's modesty and keen interest in his staff induced great personal loyalty. He delighted in his fellowship of Pembroke College (from 1937) and supported the college generously, later being made an honorary fellow (1965). He had great personal courage and did not hesitate to confront his colleagues over a matter of principle. He was one of the first to press for enquiries into the causes of death under anaesthesia and later travelled the world demonstrating simple, but safe, anaesthetic techniques. These tours resulted in his acquisition of a vast circle of friends, who regularly made the pilgrimage to Oxford.

He was knighted in 1955, and received many other distinctions, including honorary doctorates from the universities of Buenos Aires (1950), Aix-Marseilles (1952), Wales (1962), Poznan (1968), and the Medical College of Ohio (1977), and honorary fellowships of the Royal Society of Medicine (1966), the Royal College of Obstetricians and Gynaecologists (1973), the Royal College of Surgeons (1989), and three faculties of anaesthesia. He retired in 1965.

He was a skilled boxer in his youth, continued to take a keen interest in sport throughout his life, and remained very active in retirement. He was of average height and had a rubicund complexion and suntanned bald pate. He wore thick spectacles and had a soft voice. He rarely talked about himself, but interrogated dining companions kindly, if somewhat relentlessly. In 1925 he married Rosa Emily May, daughter of Ernest William Medway Henderson, builder; they had no children and Rosa died in 1956. In 1962 Macintosh married Ann Francis, daughter of Robert William Manning, an army officer. She had two sons by a previous marriage to Dennis Vincent Wilson Francis, who was employed in the motor industry. Macintosh suffered a fall whilst walking his dog and died in the Radcliffe Infirmary, Oxford, 28 August 1989.

[H. E. Hervey, *Cage-Birds*, 1940; Jennifer Beinart, *A History of the Nuffield Department of Anaesthetics, Oxford, 1937–1987*, 1987; private information; personal knowledge.]   KEITH SYKES

McKEOWN, Thomas (1912–1988), professor of social medicine at the University of Birmingham, was born 2 November 1912 in Portadown, Northern Ireland, the third in the family of three sons and one daughter of William McKeown, preacher, builder, and officer in the Salvation Army, and his wife, Matilda Duff, also a Salvation Army officer. The family later moved to Vancouver, Canada. McKeown was educated in Vancouver at Burnaby South High School. He went to the University of British Columbia, obtaining a first-class degree in chemistry (1932) at the age of nineteen. He then obtained a national research scholarship to McGill University and a first doctorate (1935) at the age of twenty-two. He proceeded to Trinity College, Oxford, as a Rhodes scholar, gaining his D.Phil. in 1938. He became Poulton research scholar and demonstrator in physiology at Guy's Hospital medical school, carrying out research in endocri-

nology. He achieved his MB, BS in 1942, and then was engaged for a while during World War II under Solly (later Baron) Zuckerman, on behalf of the Ministry of Home Security, investigating the effects of bombing.

In 1945 he was appointed to the new chair of social medicine at Birmingham University, where he remained until his retirement in 1977, acting as the university's pro-vice-chancellor in 1974–7. He was awarded a Birmingham MD in 1947 and became a member (1952) and then a fellow (1958) of the Royal College of Physicians of London. From 1950 to 1958 he was joint editor of the *British Journal of Preventive and Social Medicine*. He was the author of many scientific papers, which applied the broadening discipline of epidemiology to chronic as well as infective disease, the physiology and pathology of growth, nutrition and development, the growth of populations, and the evaluation and planning of health services. It was in this last field that he made his chief mark, forcing a realistic reappraisal of the origins of health improvements. He challenged the belief of many doctors that health changes, and the reductions in mortality during the previous century, had sprung from clinical practice, saying that rather they were due to social, economic, public-health-engineering, and dietary improvements. These ideas were developed with colleagues over a period of many years and gave rise to papers written jointly with R. G. Brown ('Medical Evidence Related to English Population Changes in the Eighteenth Century', *Population Studies*, vol. ix, 1955) and with R. G. Brown and R. G. Record ('An Interpretation of the Modern Rise of Population in Europe', *Population Studies*, vol. xxvii, 1972). These analyses eventually found a unified expression in McKeown's books. It was to the benefit and credit of medicine that this reappraisal should come from within the discipline rather than from outside. The social medicine movement (of which he was a founder), and the application of scientific analysis to health-care planning (of which he was the leading exponent), led the way to changes in public health practice in Britain and elsewhere. His books included *An Introduction to Social Medicine* (1966, jointly with C. R. Lowe), *The Modern Rise of Population* (1976), and *The Role of Medicine* (1979).

His reformulation of the role of medicine was often treated with suspicion, enmity, and misrepresentation. These ideas were too heretical, competing over-forcefully with fixed attitudes to planning, and with traditional pathways towards administrative power and professional status-building. It was therefore understandable if it took the medical and political worlds some time to catch up, and if they never quite made it. Yet, by the time he retired, McKeown was not so far in advance as to justify the disgraceful denial of civil honours. He became honorary FFCM (Ireland, 1980) and honorary FACP (1982), and was given an honorary D.Sc. by McGill University (1981).

McKeown was a gifted writer, and a polished and incisive speaker. He was an impressive lecturer, tall, slim, and good-looking, and he was always so much in command of his subject that he would never refer to notes. His interests covered walking, music, opera, and literature, and he had a special love of poetry, wine, and English puddings. In 1940 he married Esme Joan Bryan, daughter of Thomas William Widdowson, a London dentist. They had a son and a daughter. McKeown died from cancer 13 June 1988 in Birmingham.

[Private information; personal knowledge.]

E. G. KNOX

MACLEAN, Alistair Stuart (1922–1987), novelist, was born 21 April 1922 in Shettleston, Glasgow, the third of four sons (there were no daughters) of the Revd Alistair Maclean, Church of Scotland minister, of Glasgow and Daviot (Inverness), and his wife Mary, daughter of Archie Lamont, warehouseman, of Possil Park, Glasgow. He spent the first fourteen years of his life in the Highland districts of Daviot and Dunlichty, where his father was ministering. At home in the manse only Gaelic was spoken, a curious restriction when the father both wrote and delivered the English language with a fine eloquence and must have known that his children would require it later in life. Maclean was educated at Daviot School, Inverness Royal Academy, Hillhead High School in Glasgow, and Glasgow University, from which he graduated MA in 1950. In 1983 he was awarded an honorary D.Litt. by Glasgow University. He served in the Royal Navy from 1941 to 1946, much of the time as a leading torpedo operator on HMS *Royalist*, on the notorious Russian convoys to Murmansk.

From 1946 until 1956 he taught English, history, and geography at Gallowflat School, Rutherglen, Glasgow. After winning a short-story competition run by the *Glasgow Herald* he came to the attention of Ian Chapman, who worked at Collins publishers. Chapman persuaded him to write *HMS Ulysses*, which was published in October 1955. It was an instant best seller, with 250,000 copies sold in the first six months. *HMS Ulysses* was a Book Society choice, as was *Ice Station Zebra* (1963); they were followed by *The Guns of Navarone* (1957). Maclean then left his native Scotland and became a tax exile in Switzerland. In his subsequent nomadic life, he moved back to England and then to the South of France, California, and Yugoslavia. During these years he completed a total of thirty-two books, of which twenty-six were novels; they brought him gross earnings of around £20 million. Many of the books became films: *The Guns of Navarone* (1961), *Ice Station Zebra* (1968), *Where Eagles Dare* (1969), and *When Eight Bells Toll* (1971). The books were fast-moving thrillers, without great literary stature. Women rarely featured in them.

Maclean was of spare build and about five feet seven inches tall. He had sleek dark hair, with a middle parting: he was not unattractive, but was not an imposing figure. He had a thick Scottish Highland accent, which at times made him difficult to understand. He was highly intelligent, with a fascination for medical science in general and cancer research in particular. His life was greatly influenced by the early death of his brother, Lachlan, while a twenty-one-year-old medical student at Glasgow University. He was a very complex character, full of inhibitions and strange moods, with a wry sense of humour, which only appeared when he was relaxed in the company of friends. He was introverted and shy and, although his behaviour could be boorish, he was extremely generous, not only with his material possessions but in his willingness to encourage and help other writers in their careers. His charitable acts were never flamboyant or publicized.

On 2 July 1953 he married Gisela Heinrichsen, of Schleswig-Holstein, Germany. They had two sons of their own and adopted a third. Whether it was because, as a very shy and guilt-ridden man, Maclean found his success difficult to cope with or because of a growing drink problem, his marriage latterly was unhappy, and ended in divorce in 1972. In the same year he married, at Caxton Hall, London, Mary Marcelle Georgius, daughter of Georgius Guibourg, a well-known French music-hall entertainer. Marcelle wasted his money on attempted film productions and other extravagant enterprises and a lifestyle which was in total contrast to Maclean's very modest and unspectacular way of life. She died of cancer in Los Angeles in 1985, aged fifty and penniless, in spite of having had a substantial divorce settlement in 1977.

Maclean died 2 February 1987 at University Hospital, Munich, during a winter holiday with his first wife, Gisela, in the Black Forest. He had been controlling his hard drinking and his death followed a series of strokes. He lived the last eight years of his life alone in a rented villa just outside Dubrovnik, overlooking the Adriatic, with a view which reminded him of his Scottish west-coast origins. The landlord kept his apartment as a shrine after his death, but the typewriter, books, and other symbols of his writing den were plundered by federal troops during the break-up of Yugoslavia in 1991.

[Jack Webster, *Alistair Maclean*, 1991; personal knowledge.]   IAN CHAPMAN

MACMILLAN, (Maurice) Harold, first EARL OF STOCKTON (1894–1986), prime minister, was born 10 February 1894 at Cadogan Place, London, the youngest of three sons (there were no daughters) of Maurice Crawford Macmillan, publisher, and his wife, Helen ('Nellie') Artie, only surviving daughter of Joshua Tarleton Belles, surgeon, of Indianapolis, and his wife, Julia Reid. Nellie Belles's first husband, a young painter, died in November 1874, five months after their marriage. Ten years later she married Maurice Macmillan, a taciturn, austere workaholic, who left domestic matters exclusively to her. It has been often said, not least by Macmillan himself, that he was the grandson of a crofter. In fact he was the great-grandson; his grandfather Daniel left the croft at the age of eleven to become a bookseller's apprentice and to lay the foundations of the publishing firm which became one of the most prosperous and famous in Britain.

Nellie Macmillan was intensely and at times embarrassingly ambitious for her children. Neither Daniel ('Dan'), the brilliant donnish eldest son, nor Arthur, the gentle self-effacing second, were suitable instruments for her purpose. She concentrated on Harold, who later wrote: 'I can truthfully say that I owe everything all through my life to my mother's devotion and support.' But a price can be paid for matriarchal bossiness. Her constant vigilance and perpetual interference made her in the eyes of some members of the family 'a fiend'. Macmillan himself told a friend many years later when he was prime minister: 'I admired her but never really liked her... She dominated me and she still dominates me.' One asset she gave him was the ability to speak French. She had spent time in Paris before her marriage, and in London she employed French maids and insisted on her sons speaking French at meals 'downstairs'. Macmillan claimed that it was to be a help in dealing with General Charles de Gaulle. The combination of a reclusive father and an obsessive mother, together with two much older and not very sympathetic brothers, resulted in a solitary life for a small boy. He found solace to some extent, like Sir Winston *Churchill, in the affection of a devoted nanny, but he remained all his life a bit of a loner who found it hard, as did his brothers, to relate at all easily to his contemporaries, to his children, and to women. He was a shy and anxious child who hated to be conspicuous—curious characteristics in a future prime minister. To the end of his days he remained intensely nervous before making a speech. Of his famous 'unflappability'

he said that people little knew how much his stomach flapped on those occasions. He suffered all his life from sporadic moods of deep depression. He was also a hypochondriac, although, since he lived to ninety-two, his health cannot have been too bad.

He was educated at Summer Fields, Oxford, in those days a rather bleak factory programmed to produce scholars for the leading public schools. Although unhappy there, he gained a scholarship for Eton, where he was equally unhappy and from which in 1909 he was withdrawn early by his parents on grounds of health. Rumours of sexual impropriety have no foundation. Although he habitually wore an Old Etonian tie (that and the Guards' tie seemed in later life to be the only ones he possessed) he had little affection for the place. He never became a fellow and seldom revisited it.

To bridge the gap between leaving school early and the goal of Oxford set by his parents, a private tutor was needed. Their first choice was Dilwyn *Knox, son of the Anglican bishop of Manchester, who proved cold and unsympathetic; their second choice was his brother 'Ronnie' *Knox, an Eton and Balliol contemporary of Dan Macmillan and widely acclaimed at twenty-two as one of the intellectual stars of his time. He struck up a close friendship with his sixteen-year-old pupil. It was abruptly terminated in November 1910 by Nellie Macmillan, who may have suspected 'inordinate affection' and who certainly from her low-church angle disliked Knox's Anglo-Catholicism, which she saw, rightly in this case, as a stepping-stone to that arch-bugbear, 'Rome'. Their friendship was, however, renewed in 1912 at Oxford, where Macmillan was an exhibitioner at Balliol and Knox, also a Balliol man, had just become chaplain of Trinity College. Knox had loved Eton but was not keen on Balliol. Macmillan was exactly the opposite. He blossomed as never before at that supremely élitist college. He was secretary and then treasurer of the Oxford Union, and might well have become president but for World War I. He obtained a first class in classical honour moderations (1914). He made a host of friends, and many years later, when chancellor of the university, would dwell with nostalgia on the 'golden summer' of 1914—the last summer that so many of his Balliol companions were to see. Long after 1918, Oxford was to him a 'city of ghosts' and he could not bear to go back in the interwar years. Pictures show him at Oxford as a good-looking, dark-haired young man. He was tall and broad-shouldered. It was not till the war that he grew a bushy moustache which did not improve his appearance but which he kept for the rest of his life. Although he had the looks often associated with the Highlanders he had no trace of a Scottish accent but spoke the orthodox English of Eton and Oxford.

On the eve of war Macmillan, along with Knox and another Oxford friend, Guy Lawrence, seriously considered whether to 'Pope', in the jargon of their set. Lawrence did and Knox followed rather later, but Macmillan, to Knox's bitter disappointment, wrote in July 1915 to say that he intended to postpone a decision till after the war 'if I am alive'. In the end he resolved to remain an Anglican. He took his religion very seriously and continued to be a devout high churchman to the end of his life. In 1914 he was commissioned into the King's Royal Rifle Corps, but was soon transferred, thanks to wire-pulling by his mother, to the socially grander Grenadier Guards. He sailed to France in August 1915 and was wounded three times, a bullet permanently damaging his right hand on one occasion. The war left him with a limp handshake, a dragging gait, and sporadic pain. Mentally it gave him a deep sympathy with the largely working-class 'other ranks' and strong antipathy to the 'embusqués', who held office jobs far away from the front.

Yet, unlike so many 'demobbed' officers, he was financially secure, with a junior partnership in the publishing firm. Before taking it up he wanted to travel. His mother pulled wires again and in 1919 got him the job of aide-de-camp to Victor Christian William *Cavendish, ninth Duke of Devonshire, governor-general of Canada. There he fell in love with one of the duke's daughters, Lady Dorothy Evelyn Cavendish, to the consternation of the formidable duchess ('Evie'), who had intended her for the heir of the Duke of Buccleuch. On 21 April 1920 they were married, amid suitable pomp and circumstance, at St Margaret's, Westminster. The bride's side was lined with royals and peers, the bridegroom's with Macmillan authors, including six OMs. It seems to have been a genuine case of love at first sight although, as Alistair Horne says in the official biography, it is not clear 'what exactly it was that drew Dorothy to the earnest crofter's great-grandson, the ambitious middle-class publisher's son, with his shy, somewhat stilted manners, his Groucho moustache, and the shuffling walk that was a legacy of his war wounds'.

Macmillan's life was not entirely easy. The publishing firm was dominated by his father and his two uncles. He lived during working days at his parents' home in Chester Square and on weekends at Birch Grove, the family house in Sussex, which his father intended to leave to him, although he was the youngest son. A set of rooms on the top floor was kept for him and for his wife and children, who lived there most of the while, apparently not disconcerted by the presence of the formidable American matriarch, though it was hardly an ideal arrangement. Nor

was he at ease with the Cavendish clan and their closely related Cecil cousins. They called him 'the publisher' behind his back and regarded him as something of a snob. He certainly in those early days liked being a duke's son-in-law. But he was bored by the Cavendish passion for horse-racing, and they were bored by his prolixity. He cut a slightly uncomfortable figure at the vast Chatsworth house parties which, as Maurice Macmillan told Alistair Horne, must have been 'absolute hell' for his father. But he did genuinely enjoy shooting and made himself into a proficient, if slightly over-dressed, performer.

Macmillan, strongly encouraged by his mother, had for some time had parliamentary ambitions. Like more than one such aspirant he was not quite sure which side to join. He admired David *Lloyd George (later first Earl Lloyd-George of Dwyfor) but he sensed that the Liberal party was on its way out. He stood as a Conservative for Stockton-on-Tees in the election of 1923 and lost, but he won a few months later in the election of 1924, which was a Conservative triumph. His diffident electioneering was compensated for by his wife's outgoing energy. But he made little impression on the House of Commons, and was regarded as an earnest bore, destined at best for some minor office.

In 1926 Birch Grove was rebuilt by Nellie and converted into a vast neo-Georgian mansion. The result was a house that could not be divided and the young couple had no refuge. This may have been a contributory cause of marital disaster. No one can say how far his mother's dominating presence affected Harold's relations with Dorothy, but in 1929—a year of calamity for Harold in every respect—she fell in love with Robert (later Baron) *Boothby, a reckless, good-looking, 'bounderish' Conservative MP. The affair lasted in various ways till she died in 1966. She craved a divorce, but Macmillan, after some hesitation, decided against it and that, as the law then stood, settled the matter. They never separated. She continued to act as his hostess and canvass at his elections. But it was an empty shell of a marriage. They had three daughters and a son, Maurice, who died in 1984. Lady Dorothy claimed that their fourth child, Sarah, born in 1930, was Boothby's. But, although Boothby accepted responsibility, he did so with considerable doubt and it is by no means certain that she really was his daughter. Lady Dorothy's claim may have been a move to persuade Macmillan to divorce her. If so, it did not succeed. Sarah died in 1970.

The year 1929 brought another disaster. Macmillan lost his seat at Stockton and with it what slight chance he might have had of promotion when the Conservatives next regained office. After a brief flirtation with the 'New Party' run by Sir Oswald *Mosley, he was returned for Stockton in the landslide election of 1931. Shortly before that he had a serious nervous breakdown, which lasted for several months. He embarked upon the uneasy currents of the 1931 Parliament in a state of doubt and anxiety, which he sought to alleviate by writing some dull quasi-Keynesian pamphlets and a book, *The Middle Way* (1938). Their *dirigiste*, corporatist, and collectivist tone seemed very un-Conservative even then.

He was again returned for Stockton in 1935. He supported Winston Churchill's criticisms of defence policy and appeasement and signalled his dislike of the government's foreign policy by resigning the party whip when sanctions against Mussolini were lifted in 1936, the only back-bencher to do so. He was a rather solitary figure. His father and his two uncles died in 1936 and his mother in 1937. He now had far more responsibility as a publisher and found himself to be a good man of business. In politics and private life he ploughed a lonely furrow. In 1937 he applied successfully for the Conservative party whip, in the hope that the new prime minister, Neville *Chamberlain, would impart drive instead of drift to national policy. Chamberlain did, but, from Macmillan's point of view, the drive was in the wrong direction. He was dismayed at the resignation of Anthony *Eden (later the first Earl of Avon)—a heavy blow to the anti-appeasers. There were two groups, one centred on Churchill and called the 'Old Guard', the other on Eden and described by the whips as the 'Glamour Boys'. Macmillan joined the latter. On terms of outward friendship with Churchill, he was never a member of his 'court'. The presence of Boothby there was one reason. Moreover, Macmillan had disapproved of Churchill's attitude to India, and with his strong high-church views, disapproved even more strongly of Churchill's attitude to the abdication crisis. Churchill never personally liked him.

The Munich agreement had an ambivalent effect of Macmillan. He cheered in the House of Commons when Chamberlain announced his third visit to Hitler, but later took the view that Britain should have fought rather than accept Hitler's terms. He campaigned unsuccessfully in the Oxford City by-election against Quintin Hogg (later Baron Hailsham of St Marylebone), and in favour of the anti-Munich candidate A. D. *Lindsay (later first Baron Lindsay of Birker), the master of Balliol. For this rebellion he narrowly missed 'deselection' and expulsion from the Carlton Club.

When war came, Chamberlain had to give office to Churchill and Eden, but their followers were excluded. Macmillan was briefly involved in a fact-finding mission to Helsinki in January 1940, the idea being a possible Anglo-French expedition to help the Finns in their war with the USSR. Fortunately—though not thanks to Macmillan—this insane project came to nothing; the Finns had to sue for peace before any troops could be sent. The fall of Chamberlain in May 1940 at last brought Macmillan some recognition. He became parliamentary under-secretary to the Ministry of Supply (1940–2). His Civil Service private secretary was John *Wyndham (later first Baron Egremont), who was to be closely associated with him as aide and personal friend till he died in 1972. In June 1941 the first Baron *Beaverbrook became minister of supply, with quasi-dictatorial powers. As spokesman in the Commons Macmillan moved up a rung in the ladder. He coped with his strange and formidable chief both warily and successfully, laying on flattery, but keeping his distance, for he knew that Beaverbrook could morally seduce men as easily as he physically seduced women. To the end of Beaverbrook's life they remained on excellent terms. In February 1942 a reconstruction of the ministry suggested by Macmillan himself meant that Beaverbrook would cease to be represented by a parliamentary under-secretary in the Commons. Macmillan was shunted into the Colonial Office to represent the first Baron *Moyne and then Viscount Cranborne (later fifth Marquess of *Salisbury). It was, he said, 'like leaving a madhouse in order to enter a museum'. But he had the consolation of being made a privy councillor (1942), in those days a rare honour for a junior minister.

In the autumn of 1942 came the turning-point of his career. Churchill appointed him—his second choice—minister resident with cabinet rank at Allied Forces Headquarters in Algiers (1942–5). It was a make or break situation. It made Macmillan. He displayed remarkable diplomatic skill in dealing with such disparate characters as generals Eisenhower, Giraud, and de Gaulle, and with Robert Murphy, his American opposite number. He was helped by his American ancestry and his fluency in French. At the Casablanca conference shortly after his arrival he acquitted himself with notable success and was warmly congratulated by Eden. This warmth was not destined to last. Despite being badly burned and nearly killed in a plane accident soon afterwards, Macmillan was able to continue in his important office, much appreciated by Churchill, till the end of the war. He was head of the Allied Control Commission in Italy and thus in effect, as John Wyndham described him, 'viceroy of the Mediterranean'—a situation far from palatable to Eden.

His next major problem was Greece, where German withdrawal in October 1944 had left a situation of civil war between the Greek communists and the forces of the centre and the right. Macmillan spent some uncomfortable weeks during the bitter winter of 1944–5 in Athens, where the British army of occupation was very thin on the ground and the embassy was a beleaguered garrison under constant sniper fire. In the end Churchill and Eden made a personal foray; despite the hostility of the Americans and the *bien pensant* left–liberal media in England, the communists were ousted.

Then came the highly controversial question of the 'repatriation' of Soviet citizens who had been captured by the Germans. To be a prisoner at all was unforgivable by Stalin, and some of them had fought on the German side. Repatriation had been agreed at the Yalta conference (1945), but it did not apply to White Russians, who were also involved but had never been Soviet citizens. When the war ended large numbers of both categories were in British hands in northern Yugoslavia and Austria. Macmillan discussed the matter on 13 May with General Sir Charles *Keightley, who commanded V Corps at Klagenfurt. It is clear that repatriation (which also involved handing Chetniks and Ustasi over to Tito's partisan forces in Yugoslavia) was effected in deplorable circumstances of force and fraud, but there is no evidence of a conspiracy on the part of Macmillan, who had no executive authority nor any part in decisions taken at Yalta or the orders for their implementation made in Whitehall. The charge of being a war criminal, made many years later, haunted Macmillan in his old age, but it was baseless.

On 26 May 1945 Macmillan returned to Britain. By now he had made his mark. Churchill appointed him air minister in the caretaker government, pending the verdict of the general election to be announced on 26 July. The result was a disaster for the Conservatives and for Macmillan personally. The party was defeated by a huge majority and he lost Stockton. He might have been out of the house for two or three years and become a forgotten man but for a lucky chance. The sitting member for Bromley, a safe Conservative seat, died just before the election figures were announced. Macmillan was promptly adopted as candidate and was back in November with a majority of over 5,000.

For the next six years he devoted himself to the postwar problems of publishing and the opposition front bench. He had no difficulty in holding his seat in 1950 and 1951. On the personal side he had come to a bleak but balanced *modus vivendi* with his wife. She continued to support him socially and politically but her obsession with Boothby never waned. Politically Macmillan was active in trying to adapt the Conservative party to the challenge of its defeat. His theme was the occupation of the 'middle ground'—a Conservative heresy thirty years later but reasonable at the time, though it gave him a reputation among the right of being a 'neo-socialist', as Brendan (later Viscount) *Bracken described him. He hoped for an alliance with the Liberals and even toyed with proportional representation.

In foreign policy he was a 'European' up to a point. He regarded Clement (later first Earl) *Attlee's refusal in June 1950 to join the discussions of the six European nations about the Schuman plan as a disastrous error. But, like Churchill and other prominent Conservatives, he blew hot and cold. Although he served for three years on the Council of Europe at Strasburg, he wrote in 1949 'the Empire must always have first preference for us.'

When Churchill returned to office with a precarious majority in October 1951 he offered Macmillan the ministry of housing and local government. Macmillan nearly refused and only accepted with reluctance. The Conservative party conference, in a rush of blood to its collective head, had insisted on a mandate to build 300,000 houses a year compared with the 200,000 or so achieved by Labour. The target was widely regarded as unattainable—or only attainable at the unacceptable expense of industrial investment and infrastructure. Injecting into the ministry something of the hustle and bustle he had experienced under Beaverbrook, Macmillan reached the figure in 1953. He was helped inside the ministry by Dame Evelyn (later Baroness) *Sharp, the first woman to become a permanent under-secretary, outside it by Sir Percy *Mills, a Birmingham businessman. Equally valuable was his junior minister Ernest (later Baron) *Marples, who had also made his fortune from humble origins, as an engineer and road-builder. He introduced American principles into the torpid British building industry, with notable success. Macmillan told Alistair Horne: 'Marples made me PM: I was never heard of before housing.' The critics were probably right about the damage done to the balance of the economy, but politically the achievement was a notable feather in the caps of both the party and the minister.

In October 1954 there was a cabinet reshuffle and Macmillan became minister of defence for five unhappy months. At housing Churchill backed him and left him to get on with it. At defence he did neither and Macmillan became irritated at the ceaseless flow of memoranda on the most detailed topics from the aged prime minister. Perhaps this experience prompted him to take the lead in persuading Churchill to retire in favour of Eden. It was high time, but he was never forgiven by Clementine, Lady *Churchill, who had always mistrusted him. Eden succeeded on 5 April 1955, and the ensuing general election in May resulted in a Conservative majority of fifty-nine. Macmillan became secretary of state for foreign affairs, the post which he most wanted and believed would be the culmination of his political career. He was very much Eden's second choice. The prime minister would have preferred the fifth Marquess of Salisbury (the former Viscount—'Bobbety'—Cranborne), but feared a row about a peer in this position— unnecessarily, in view of the later appointments of lords Home and Carrington.

Like Churchill over defence, Eden could not keep his hands off foreign policy. At the end of the year he used the ill health of R. A. *Butler (later Baron Butler of Saffron Walden) to move him to the leadership of the Commons and replace him as chancellor of the Exchequer by Macmillan, who was replaced by Selwyn *Lloyd (later Baron Selwyn-Lloyd). Macmillan resented the change. He had never liked Eden, nor Eden him. He only introduced one budget. His more radical proposals were vetoed by the prime minister. The budget is mainly remembered for the introduction of premium bonds. The second half of 1956 was dominated by the Suez crisis. Macmillan does not come well out of it. He was a leading 'hawk', and he totally misjudged the American reaction. On 25 September he had a conversation with Eisenhower at the White House, from which he inferred that the American president would support British military action against Gamal Abdel Nasser, the Egyptian leader. Sir Roger Makins (later first Baron Sherfield), the British ambassador, was present and took notes. He was astonished to learn later that Macmillan had sent a dispatch to this effect to Eden, for the discussion in no way warranted such a version of the president's attitude. But the report inevitably reinforced Eden's already erroneous view of the American reaction.

Macmillan's second major error was one of omission. The Suez operation constituted an obvious risk to sterling. He took no precautions and failed to do what the French did, draw out a tranche of funds from the International Monetary Fund well in advance of the invasion. The ensuing run on the pound was exactly what a chancellor of the Exchequer might have anticipated and avoided. Instead he panicked and with all his power pressed the case for withdrawal. 'First in, first out,' was the justified jibe from Harold Wilson (later Baron Wilson of Rievaulx). Macmillan was unhappy about his role for ever afterwards. It was, he said, 'a very bad episode in my life'.

Credulous adherents of the conspiracy theory of history have seen in Macmillan's conduct a plot to oust and replace Eden. There is no evidence at all for this implausible theory. Eden resigned on 9 January 1957 on genuine grounds of health. He made no recommendation to the queen about his successor, merely advising her private secretary to consult Lord Salisbury as a senior peer who could not be a runner himself.

He and the lord chancellor interviewed each member of the cabinet separately and took slightly perfunctory soundings in the parliamentary party and the National Union. The result was a strong preference for Macmillan rather than Butler, whose attitude over Suez had been ambivalent, indecisive, and obscure. Macmillan was appointed by the queen at 2 p.m. next day.

The outlook for the Conservative party could hardly have been bleaker. Suez had been a fiasco and it looked as if Labour would have a walkover at the next general election. Macmillan transformed the situation. He soon dominated the House of Commons and his apparent confidence radiated out to the electorate. He also dominated his party, taking in his stride the resignation of Lord Salisbury over the release of Archbishop *Makarios in March 1957, and the resignations of Peter (later Baron) Thorneycroft, Enoch Powell, and Nigel *Birch (later Baron Rhyl)—the whole Treasury 'team'—nine months later in protest against his refusal to accept expenditure cuts of £50 million in the next budget. On the eve of his departure on a Commonwealth tour he dismissed the resignations as 'little local difficulties'. Meanwhile he had mended fences with Eisenhower and, in the 1958 crisis involving Iraq, Jordan, and Lebanon, the USA and Britain acted in harmony. Despite some awkward negotiations with the trade unions, he approached the election of 1959 at the head of a party in far better shape than in 1957. His ebullient behaviour caused the cartoonist *'Vicky' to depict him ironically as 'Supermac'. The joke backfired and made him in Horne's words 'something of a folk hero'. He was accused by many moralists of excessive 'materialism'. A famous phrase which he used—'most of our people have never had it so good'—was wrenched out of its context, which was a warning against rising prices and contained a forgotten qualification: 'Is it too good to be true?' On the foreign and colonial front there were difficulties—Cyprus, the Hola incident in Kenya, and other episodes. But Macmillan kept calm, plumped for autumn 1959 rather than spring for the election, and won easily, almost doubling the majority he had inherited from Eden.

His premiership lasted for another four years. But after the major triumph of the general election and the minor one of defeating Sir Oliver (later Baron) Franks in 1960 for the chancellorship of Oxford University, the tale is anything but a success story. It is clear now—and many people thought so then—that he spent too much time on foreign and post-colonial affairs, and too little on matters at home. These years were the period when France and Germany caught up and surpassed Britain in terms of economic success. The major British problems—

trade-union power and chronic inflation—were never recognized by Macmillan, who was not helped by two singularly mediocre chancellors of the Exchequer, nor by the expansionist advice of his economic guru, Sir Roy *Harrod. When unemployment rose from 500,000 to 800,000 Macmillan, obsessed by his memories of Stockton-on-Tees in the 1930s, was horrified. Attempts at an 'incomes policy' flopped as they always have. No serious effort was made to amend trade-union legislation. In July 1962 Macmillan got rid of his second chancellor of the Exchequer, Selwyn Lloyd, but made the major error of combining his dismissal with a reconstruction of the government, which involved sacking a third of the cabinet. It looked like panic and probably was. His prestige never recovered. He was not helped by the general anti-establishment sentiment that dominated the early 1960s. It was not exactly pro-Labour, but it was certainly anti-Conservative.

In external affairs Macmillan achieved a certain *réclame* in 'liberal' circles by his speech at Cape Town in 1960, on Monday 3 February, warning of the 'wind of change' which was blowing through Africa. To the Tory right it was anathema—'Black Monday'—and led to the formation of the Monday Club. Macmillan was of course correct about the strength of African nationalism, which was affecting the Central African Federation of the two Rhodesias and Nyasaland (later Zimbabwe, Zambia, and Malawi). The Federation had to be dissolved but the labyrinthine and disingenuous process won few friends even among the Africans and bitterly alienated its prime minister, Sir Roy Welensky, and his white supporters. They felt they had been double-crossed.

Macmillan was determined to keep in with America. He played the card of his American ancestry for all it was worth. The Cavendishes were related by marriage to the Kennedys, and the president genuinely admired the wit and wisdom of the older man. During the Cuban crisis of 1962 he kept in touch with Macmillan more closely than with any other European leader, but there is no evidence to suggest that the prime minister gave any advice which affected the course of events. He did, however, extract from Kennedy some concessions about the British independent nuclear deterrent, and the president paid full tribute to Macmillan for his part in negotiating the Atmospheric Test Ban treaty with the USSR on 5 August 1963. Macmillan came to regard this as one of the principal achievements of his premiership.

But long before that he had been in major trouble. Britain had applied in July 1961 to accede to the Treaty of Rome. From the start it was clear that President de Gaulle was hostile, but it was not clear that he could carry France with him till the referendum on the presidency in October 1962, followed by a sweeping electoral victory for his party a month later. Despite his earlier policy—he had tried to wreck the European Economic Community by setting up the European Free Trade Association in May 1960—Macmillan now put much political capital into accession to the EEC. But Britain was doomed. On 29 January 1963 de Gaulle delivered his formal veto. 'All our policies at home and abroad are ruined,' Macmillan wrote in his diary.

If that was not enough, a series of scandals, connected with espionage, security, and sex, erupted, culminating with the famous John Profumo affair when the secretary of state for war denied in Parliament in March 1963 a charge that he had slept with a woman who shared his favours with those of the Russian military attaché. A few weeks later Profumo had to retract and resign from public life. Macmillan was unfairly criticized as gullible and out of touch. Nigel Birch made a long-remembered attack, quoting Robert Browning's *The Lost Leader*, 'Never glad, confident morning again'. The government tottered but survived.

An election was due at the latest by autumn 1964. Macmillan, now nearly seventy and feeling none too well, had to decide whether to fight it himself or pass the lead to someone else. But whom? He resolved to go ahead. On the eve of the Conservative conference at Blackpool he was taken ill with an inflamed prostate gland, which necessitated an immediate operation. A prostate operation was a relatively minor matter but Macmillan, hypochondriac as ever, convinced himself that the malady was malignant and decided to resign at once. In fact it was not, and there was no need to retire at this singularly awkward political moment. He was to regret his decision for ever after.

When the operation was over, it was indicated that the queen would welcome his advice about the succession. He did not have to give it. Perhaps it would have been better if he had politely declined, like Bonar *Law in 1923 and Eden in 1957. But he was determined, despite later disclaimers, to block the obvious heir presumptive, R. A. Butler, whom he regarded as a ditherer. After complicated indirect consultations with the cabinet and other elements of the party—which have been the subject of controversy ever since—he plumped for the fourteenth Earl of Home (later Baron Home of the Hirsel) in preference to his first choice, Quintin Hogg, who was then second Viscount Hailsham. Both of them had taken advantage of a recent Act to disclaim their peerages. It was the last occasion when this informal and secretive system of consultation was employed.

Macmillan left the House of Commons at the election of October 1964. He declined for the time being the traditional earldom offered to ex-prime ministers. He recommended a barony for John Wyndham but took nothing for himself. He did not wish to damage the prospects of his only son Maurice, now at last a minister. He may also have dreamed of being recalled to office himself in a crisis as head of an all-party coalition. In 1966 his wife died. He missed her despite their latterly loveless marriage, but the Chatsworth connection remained and the reigning duke and duchess of Devonshire made ample hospitable amends for any snubs by an earlier Cavendish generation. Another consolation for his rather lonely life in the chilly emptiness of Birch Grove was Garsington Manor near Oxford, where he often stayed with Sir John *Wheeler-Bennett. Then there was clubland, which he regularly frequented.

In the long twilight—or perhaps Indian summer—of his career his chancellorship of Oxford University (from 1960) meant much to him. It also meant much to Oxford. He attended the various occasions—dinners, centenaries, laying of foundation stones, and the like—more assiduously than any previous chancellor. Dons and undergraduates alike were fascinated by his speeches and his conversation—an inimitable combination of wit, emotion, and nostalgia, which made it almost incredible that he had once been regarded as a parliamentary bore. He travelled a good deal, especially in America, where he raised money for Oxford. He even paid a visit to China, where he was fêted. He spent much time on his memoirs in six volumes (1966–73), published profitably by his firm, in which he took a renewed interest. They are in places somewhat heavy going but essential for historians. Much more 'fun', to use a favourite word of his, are his *The Past Masters* (1974), a series of political sketches and reminiscences from 1906 to 1939, and his diary of his time as minister resident in the Middle East, *War Diaries: Politics and War in the Mediterranean 1943–1945* (1984). He frequently appeared on television, almost always with great success. In the last ten years of his life he gave many long interviews at Birch Grove to Alistair Horne, his chosen official biographer. His relations with Margaret (later Baroness) Thatcher, who always treated him with respect, were ambivalent. She sought and followed his advice about the Falklands war in 1982. But he had led his party from left of centre whereas she did so from the right. Towards the end his coded criticism of her economic policy was abundantly clear.

He changed his mind about the peerage and, on his ninetieth birthday in 1984, his acceptance of an earldom was announced. Maurice was very ill (he died on 10 March) and the main reason for

refusal had gone. Macmillan took the title of Earl of Stockton, after his old constituency. By now he was almost blind—a great blow to such a voracious reader though relieved by his discovery of 'talking books'—and he made his thirty-two-minute maiden speech in November without a single note. It was a wonderful performance, which those who heard it will never forget.

Macmillan's political hero was Benjamin *Disraeli (first Earl of Beaconsfield), who had something of the same mixture of wit, irony, cynicism, romance, and sheer play-acting. To the end of his days Macmillan loved to put on a show. His last performance was a speech to the Tory Reform Group in November 1986. By now well distanced from Margaret Thatcher he compared privatization to 'selling the family silver'—a specious simile since the silver was, after all, being sold to the family. It is arguable whether Disraeli was a great prime minister, but he was certainly a great character. The same can be said of Harold Macmillan.

Macmillan was sworn of the Privy Council in 1942 and admitted to the Order of Merit in 1976. He became an honorary fellow of Balliol (1957), honorary DCL of Oxford (1958), and honorary LL D of Cambridge (1961). He died 29 December 1986 at Birch Grove, Hayward's Heath, East Sussex. He was succeeded in the earldom by his grandson, Alexander Daniel Alan Macmillan (born 1943).

[Macmillan's own writings mentioned in the text; Alistair Horne, *Macmillan, the Official Biography*, 2 vols., 1988, 1989; George Hutchinson, *The Last Edwardian at No 10*, 1980; Nigel Fisher, *Harold Macmillan, a Biography*, 1982; private information; personal knowledge.]   BLAKE

MADDEN, Cecil Charles (1902–1987), television pioneer and dramatic author, was born 29 November 1902 at the British consulate in Mogador, Morocco, the eldest of three sons (there were no daughters) of Archibald Maclean Madden, CMG, diplomat, and his wife Cecilia Catherine, daughter of Allen Page Moor, canon, of Truro. He was educated at French schools in Morocco, Spanish schools, Aldeburgh Lodge Preparatory School, and Dover College. He acquired fluent French and Spanish. While working in a secretarial post with the Rio Tinto Company in Spain, he wrote revues in Spanish and played Freddy Eynsford Hill in a translation of George Bernard *Shaw's *Pygmalion*. Four times a year his professional duties took him to New York, where he saw Broadway productions in his free time.

Between 1926 and 1932 every holiday was spent in Paris working in theatre management. Although he encountered famous stars like Fernandel, Maurice Chevalier, Mistinguett, and Miss Bluebell, he was very proud of the fact that he improved backstage conditions for the chorus girls. As well as writing revues in French and Spanish, he wrote several plays in English. In 1933 he joined the BBC talks department, where he produced a series entitled *Anywhere for a News Story* and subsequently produced the outside broadcasting spot on a popular Saturday evening programme, *In Town Tonight*.

Madden subsequently worked as a senior producer in the new Empire (later Overseas) Service of the BBC, and in 1936 joined Gerald Cock, the recently appointed first head of the BBC's Television Service. In August 1936 they were told to prepare programmes to open the first high definition service in the world on 2 November. Plans changed and Madden was told to produce a show to be transmitted to Radiolympia in ten days' time. *Here's Looking at You* was seen by visitors to the exhibition and the few television set owners then living around London. Madden then created *Picture Page*, a magazine programme transmitted from Alexandra Palace on the official opening of the Television Service. From 2 November 1936, until television shut down on 1 September 1939, Madden organized and produced live programmes of variety, ballets, and drama, as well as Disney cartoons. 'A play a day' was his motto. He created the series *100% Broadway, Cabaret Cartoons*, and *Starlight*.

On the outbreak of World War II Madden returned to radio, and in 1940 was made head of the overseas entertainment unit in the Criterion Theatre, broadcasting all radio programmes to British Commonwealth forces serving abroad. He presented the *American Eagle in Britain* programme from 17 November 1940 to 9 September 1945, earning the title of the 'GI's friend'. General Dwight D. Eisenhower visited the studio on 2 March 1944; on 7 June (D-Day plus one) his brainchild, the Allied Expeditionary Forces Programme of the BBC, began with Madden in charge of the integrated production. This programme informed and entertained its listeners until 25 July 1945. Artists included Gertrude *Lawrence, Marlene Dietrich, George Raft, Bing Crosby, and Bob Hope. Major Glenn Miller conducted the American band of AEF until he disappeared in December 1944, Madden being the last civilian to see him alive. He was also the man responsible for discovering Petula Clark in 1942 and the Beverley Sisters in 1944.

When television reopened on 7 June 1946, Madden returned to his former post of programmes organizer. In 1950 he was made acting head of children's programmes until April 1951. He then became assistant to the controller of television programmes and created *Picture Parade*, a magazine programme dealing with the film industry. He was also involved with a series of excerpts from West End plays, including *Look Back in Anger*.

Madden retired from the BBC in 1964, but he continued other activities, as a governor of Dulwich College Preparatory School, and president of both the Glenn Miller Society and the British Puppet and Model Theatre Guild. His interest in young entrants to the profession was reflected in his work for RADA, as vice-chairman of the RADA Associates. He was involved with the British Academy of Film and Television Arts (BAFTA) and took part in the National Film School. His personal scrapbooks, containing records of television since 1936, aided research for the 'fifty years of television' celebrations in November 1986, when he was videoed from the studio at Alexandra Palace on 2 November. In the Museum of Film, Photography, and Television at Bradford he is commemorated in a life-sized model, seated in the gallery at Alexandra Palace. He was a BAFTA award winner (1961) and a fellow of the Royal Society of Arts (1950). In 1952 he was appointed MBE. Madden laid the foundation of British television, always with taste and high standards. His popularity with those who worked with him was not always shared by the BBC administration. With his sound knowledge of theatre he was a discoverer of talent as well as an innovator.

Madden was tall, slim, and always immaculately dressed. He was charming, courteous, dignified, and had a great sense of fun, which prevented him from being pompous. In June 1932 he married Muriel Emily, daughter of Brigadier-General James Kilvington Cochrane; they had a son and daughter. Madden died in Westminster Hospital, London, 27 May 1987.

[BBC Written Archives Centre, Caversham Park, Reading; Peter Noble, *British Film and Television Yearbook 1957–8*, 1958; Cyrus Andrews, *Radio and Television Who's Who*, 2nd edn., 1950; personal knowledge.]

JUNE AVERILL

MAEGRAITH, Brian Gilmore (1907–1989), professor of tropical medicine, was born 26 August 1907 in Adelaide, Australia, the fourth son in a family of four sons and one daughter of Alfred Edward Robert Maegraith, accountant, and his wife, Louisa Blanche Gilmore. He was educated at St Peter's, Adelaide, and the University of Adelaide, from which he graduated MB, BS, first class (1930), and took up a South Australian Rhodes scholarship to Magdalen College, Oxford, in 1931. He graduated B.Sc. in 1933 and D.Phil. in 1934.

He was awarded a Beit fellowship in 1933 and the following year was appointed Staines medical fellow and tutor in physiology at Exeter College, Oxford, where he remained until 1940. In 1937 he became lecturer and demonstrator in pathology. One of his proudest boasts was that he came 'from the same town, the same school, the same University in Australia and the same College in

Oxford' as Baron *Florey, who developed penicillin.

World War II proved to be the crucial turning-point in his career. Having been in the territorial army since 1932, he was recruited in the Royal Army Medical Corps and dispatched to France in 1940. He was evacuated from Dunkirk and sent to Sierra Leone in west Africa. He returned to Oxford to lead, as a lieutenant-colonel, the Malaria Research Unit (1943-5), and he was honorary malariologist to the army from 1967 to 1973. While in Oxford he was also dean of the school of medicine from 1938 to 1944. He became FRCP (London, 1955, and Edinburgh, 1956).

Maegraith first came to prominence in the field of tropical medicine when he was pathologist for the British army in Sierra Leone, where his work on the kidney and malaria attracted a great deal of attention. It soon became clear to him that the pathophysiology of malaria and blackwater fever had been insufficiently studied and was poorly understood. With his background as an Oxford-trained physiologist and pathologist he was ideally suited to study this problem. On being appointed to the Alfred Jones and Warrington Yorke chair of tropical medicine at Liverpool University in 1944, his first task was to make a thorough review of the literature to date and he produced his most erudite publication, *Pathological Processes in Malaria and Blackwater Fever* (1948). The many ideas enunciated in that book were to form the basis of his and the department's research for the next twenty years. Another important achievement of his early days was his work on the anti-malarial drug Paludrine, in collaboration with A. R. D. Adams. In 1946, already at Liverpool, he was also appointed dean of the School of Tropical Medicine there, a post which he retained for nearly thirty years after he vacated his chair. As dean he was fully convinced that the School's impact had to be in the tropics and he pursued this objective relentlessly for the rest of his life.

The result was an intimate involvement with south-east Asia and the creation of the faculty of tropical medicine in Bangkok, which was later the best in the third world. He was also involved in west Africa, especially with the University of Ibadan and the Ghana medical school. He established Ghana's Institute of Health with the support of Kwame *Nkrumah, with whom he developed a personal friendship. He was the creator of the Association of European Schools of Tropical Medicine, whose meetings he regularly attended. As vice-president of the interim committee of the international congresses of tropical medicine and malaria he took a prominent part in the organization of a number of the congresses. He retired from his chair in 1972 and as dean in 1975.

A man of strong personality, he had vision and imagination, and ideas well ahead of his time. He envisaged the escalation of air travel and the increasing importance of imported diseases, with people arriving from tropical areas well within the incubation period of a potential infection, the most important of which was malaria. He wrote a classic paper in the *Lancet* (vol. i, 1963), 'Unde Venis?', emphasizing the importance of taking a patient's geographical history.

He was president of the Royal Society of Tropical Medicine and Hygiene (1969-71) and received many medals. He was appointed CMG in 1968. He received an honorary D.Sc. from Bangkok University in 1966, of which he was very proud, and was awarded the Order of the White Elephant of Thailand in 1982. The Liverpool School presented him with its highest award, the Mary Kingsley medal (1973) and also created the Maegraith wing, where he occupied a room.

For mental relaxation he taught himself to play the piano, one of his favourite pieces being Beethoven's 'Moonlight Sonata'. He was a talented amateur painter and won several prizes in competitions for physicians. He was also a good poet and short-story writer. Although Maegraith spent the whole of his career in Britain, he never lost his Australian approach to life, with its outspokenness, occasional brashness, and healthy disrespect for what he considered outmoded convention. A robust, fair-skinned, good-looking man, he had a striking appearance and strong personality. In 1934 he married Lorna, a schoolteacher, daughter of Edgar Langley, schoolmaster. They had one son, Michael, who went into publishing. Maegraith died in Liverpool 2 April 1989.

[*The Times*, 5 April 1989; *Independent*, 6 April 1989; *Lancet*, vol. i, 1989; personal knowledge.]

H. M. GILLES

MANIO, Jack de (1914-1988), broadcaster. [See DE MANIO, JACK.]

MANTON, Irene (1904-1988), plant cytologist, was born 17 April 1904 in Kensington, London, the youngest of three children and younger daughter of George Sidney Frederick Manton, dental surgeon, and his wife, Milana Angele Terese d'Humy. The eldest child, a son, had died in infancy and the elder daughter, Sidnie Milana *Manton, became a prominent zoologist. The family has been traced to Charles Manton (born 1620), chaplain to Charles II. Her father's hobbies were cabinet-making and gold- and silver-working and she undoubtedly owed her deftness to early exposure to these manual skills. She was educated at the Froebel Educational Institute and later at St Paul's Girls School. Oddly enough in view of her later abundant energy, her school found Manton an idle pupil with marked aptitude only in music. Nevertheless in 1923 she won a Clothworkers' scholarship, and an exhibition from the school, which took her to Girton College, Cambridge (of which she became an honorary fellow in 1985). She retained her musical interest and later became an accomplished violinist.

About this time she came across E. B. Wilson's book *The Cell in Developmental Inheritance* (1896) and decided to read botany and to spend her life counting chromosomes. She obtained first-class honours in both parts of the natural sciences tripos (1925 and 1926). She then elected to begin her postgraduate work in Sweden in Otto Rosenberg's laboratory. Though without a supervisor, after one year she managed to classify 250 species of the Cruciferae on the basis of chromosome counting, giving her the material for her first important publication, and on the way learned to speak Swedish. Back in Cambridge she completed the mandatory further year's residence with the aid of a Yarrow bursary. She gained her Ph.D. in 1930.

In 1929 she became assistant lecturer in botany at Manchester University, where she came under the influence of W. H. *Lang, who was working on *Osmunda* and turned her mind to the ferns, an interest which was to last all her life. By 1946 she had accumulated innumerable data on fern chromosomes, defining genera and species and their phylogenetic relationships, and later she gathered them into a book, *Problems of Cytology and Evolution in the Pteridophyta* (1950), which had enormous influence and established her as an authority.

In 1946 she was invited to become professor of botany at Leeds, a post she held until her retirement in 1969. Her medium figure in blouse or cardigan and tweed skirt, with its vigorous stride, strong face, and penetrating voice, became familiar. She had a heavy load of teaching and administration, and in consequence adopted a new lifestyle, working on her researches late into the evening every day, including weekends and holidays. She had no distracting domestic chores since she was, and remained, unmarried and had brought with her from Manchester her kindly, patient, and long-suffering housekeeper, Edith. She acquired an ultraviolet microscope and later took advantage of the extra microscopic resolution afforded by the first electron microscope, obtained in 1950. She dealt first with the flagella of the sperm of ferns and other plant groups, from which it was an easy step to the structure of the organelles inside plant cells. Because of this work, she became as distinguished for her electron microscopy as for her fern cytology. She took up the study of marine flagellates and published extensively on the remarkable structures they revealed. In the course of this work

she discovered a number of new species. Her ferns were not neglected either. By her own efforts and that of many students and colleagues she collected from various parts of the world and, with chromosomes as the guide, made the ferns the best-known group in the plant kingdom.

The early years of her retirement were traumatic since her housekeeper also retired, so that she had to fend for herself at home. She began work on the marine flagellates and was freely invited to use the facilities at Nottingham, Lancaster, and Imperial College, London, and occasionally laboratories at Ottawa and Marburg. She made frequent arduous journeys in places ranging from the Arctic to South Africa, discovering and recording innumerable new species. She also made a valuable collection of modern paintings, which she bequeathed to Leeds University.

She received many honours and medals. She had honorary doctorates from five universities (McGill, Durham, Lancaster, Leeds, and Oslo). Several societies elected her to honorary membership or fellowship. She was president of the Pteridological Society in 1971–2 and of the Linnean Society from 1973 to 1976. In 1961 she was elected FRS. As a final accolade, she and her sister Sidnie received posthumously the distinction of having a feature on the planet Venus named the Manton crater. She died 31 May 1988 in the Chapel Allerton Hospital, Leeds.

[R. D. Preston in *Biographical Memoirs of Fellows of the Royal Society*, vol. xxxv, 1990; personal knowledge.]

R. D. Preston

MANVELL, (Arnold) Roger (1909–1987), film critic and historian, was born 10 October 1909 at St Barnabas vicarage, Leicester, the only child of the Revd Arnold Edward William Manvell, later canon of Peterborough Cathedral, and his wife, Gertrude Theresa Baines. He was educated at King's School in Peterborough. He studied English literature at University College, Leicester, obtaining his Ph.D. on W. B. *Yeats at London University. He began work in 1931 as a schoolmaster and adult-education lecturer in Leicester, moving to the department of extramural studies at Bristol University in 1937.

In 1940 he joined the films division of the Ministry of Information, screening factual films and lecturing to non-theatrical audiences. Seizing the opportunities offered by current interest in 'film appreciation', he wrote *Film*, published in 1944, which broke new ground as a critical history of the great films of the past. It was an immediate best seller, introducing a whole generation to an understanding of film as an art form. In the following year he was appointed research officer and lecturer at the British Film Institute and was instrumental in setting up, and at first guiding, the institute's academic series of volumes on *The History of the British Film*.

In 1946 he began broadcasting and his name became a household word through the BBC series *The Critics*. He founded and edited the *Penguin Film Review* (1946–9), and in 1947 became the first director of the senior film-makers' own organization, the British Film Academy, the forerunner of the BAFTA, where he remained until 1959. All the while he busily produced books written or edited by himself alone or in collaboration with experts in various aspects of the cinema. After 1959 he acted as consultant to the British Film Academy, continuing to write, lecture, and sit on numerous committees. He was also prominent in the humanist movement, becoming associate editor of *New Humanist* (1967–75). Books of film criticism, analysis, and history continued thick and fast, interspersed with biographies of Sir Charles *Chaplin (1974) and of several great English actresses. In later years he was involved in film studies at Sussex University, Louisville University (1973), and the London Film School, of which he was a governor (1966–74), and did useful work for the Society of Authors and other bodies.

He also took up a new interest. Heinrich Fraenkel, a Jewish film journalist and scriptwriter, who had fled Germany in 1933, had founded a Free German movement in Britain and written several slight books to persuade his adopted country that not all Germans were Nazi. Manvell began a fruitful collaboration with him in 1959 with a thoughtful and well documented biography, *Doctor Goebbels* (1960). Together, during the next dozen years they produced eight solid books on the history of Nazism, including four biographies and an account of the 1944 July plot to kill Hitler. Fraenkel had gone to the Nuremberg trials and interviewed many key people. He had valuable contacts in Germany, as well as access to relevant archives. Manvell's expertise in scholarly presentation, as well as his wide contacts and fluent style, helped make this an important body of work.

By 1975 film studies in Britain and France had developed in directions uncongenial to a man of Manvell's generation and he felt more at home in American universities. He joined Boston University in 1975, was made a professor in 1982, and worked there for the rest of his life, continuing his large and varied output of books, of which two of the most notable were *Films and the Second World War* (1974) and *Elizabeth Inchbald, England's Leading Woman Dramatist* (1987).

In 1970 he was made commander of the Order of Merit of the Italian Republic, and in 1971 was awarded the Order of Merit (first class) of the German Federal Republic. A scholar-teacher of the year award for 1984–5 from Boston University followed, as well as an honorary DFA of New England College (1972), and honorary D.Litt.s from Sussex (1971), Leicester (1974) and Louisville (1979) universities.

These were meagre distinctions for an influential writer who had pioneered the serious study of film in his native land. Brisk and practical, he was a good organizer and a prolific writer, who combined accuracy with a readable middlebrow style. Even his puzzling insistence on the use of his academic title of 'Dr' played its part, perhaps, in the emergence of film as a respectable subject for academic study, belatedly accepted at last by British universities. His assiduous use of contacts, combined with great energy and drive, did much to spread a serious appreciation of the cinema in Britain.

Of medium height, fairly heavily built, and inclined to be pudgy, he always seemed in a hurry to get to the next opportunity that beckoned. As he grew older his hair receded fluffily and his eyes peered shrewdly from behind thick glasses. Ambition and determination almost hid a wry, slightly sardonic humour. In 1936 he married Edith Mary, daughter of John Cook Bulman; they had one son. The marriage was dissolved and in 1946 he married Margaret Hilda, daughter of Percy James Lee, dental surgeon, of Bristol. After a divorce, in 1956 he married Louise, daughter of Charles Luson Cribb, of London. They divorced in 1981 and in the same year he married Françoise Baylis, daughter of René Nautré, company director. There were no children of the final three marriages. Manvell died in Boston 30 November 1987.

[*The Times*, 2 December 1987; *Independent*, 3 December 1987; *Daily Telegraph*, 1 and 2 December 1987; private information; personal knowledge.]

RACHAEL LOW

MARC (pseudonym) (1931–1988), caricaturist, cartoonist, and magazine editor. [See BOXER, (CHARLES) MARK (EDWARD).]

MARKHAM, Beryl (1902–1986), aviator, horse trainer, and author, was born 26 October 1902 at Westfield House, Ashwell, Rutland, the younger child and only daughter of Charles Baldwin Clutterbuck, farmer and formerly a lieutenant in the King's Own Scottish Borderers, from which he was cashiered for absence without leave, and his wife Clara Agnes, daughter of Josiah William Alexander, of the Indian Civil Service. The Clutterbucks went to British East Africa in 1904 and in the following year bought Ndimu farm at Njoro, overlooking the Rift Valley, where they built a timber and flour mill. In July 1906 Clara left for England with her son and soon divorced her husband. Left with her father, Beryl did not see her mother again until she was twenty-one. She lived a wild childhood with the farm's

African children, particularly Kibii (whose name after initiation was arap Ruta), a Kipsigis boy.

In 1911 Beryl was sent to Nairobi European School, from which she was expelled in her third term. She returned to the farm and a possibly promiscuous early adolescence, not being sent to school again until 1916, when an army officer paid for her to attend Miss Seccombe's School in Nairobi, providing he could marry her. She was again expelled. On 15 October 1919, at the age of sixteen, she married the officer—Captain Alexander Laidlaw ('Jock') Purves, son of Dr William Laidlaw Purves, founder of the Royal St George's Golf Club in Scotland. Purves bought land adjoining Ndimu farm, but the marriage lasted only six months. Beryl began to train horses, as her father had done, and in 1921 left her husband to live on Soysambu, the farm on the floor of the Rift Valley owned by the third Baron *Delamere. She stayed there as a trainer until 1924, when she left for London, where she discovered she was pregnant. She claimed the child's father was Denys Finch Hatton, the lover of Karen Blixen, who later wrote *Out of Africa* (1937), but she had been so free with her sexual favours that any of a number of people could have been responsible. She had a late abortion and returned to Kenya, where she met Mansfield Markham, the son of Sir Arthur Basil Markham, first baronet, Liberal MP and owner of collieries in the north of England. He was wealthy and they married in 1927.

In 1928 *Edward, Prince of Wales, and his brother *Henry, Duke of Gloucester, visited Kenya. Beryl became mistress to Henry. She agreed to go to London to be with him, and he established her in a suite at the Grosvenor Hotel. On 25 February 1929 she had a son, about whom there was much speculation. However, he cannot have been fathered by Prince Henry, because Beryl must already have been pregnant when she met him. The boy was given to Markham's mother to bring up. When Markham threatened to cite Henry as co-respondent in a divorce, Queen *Mary, in an effort to avoid scandal, made Henry settle on Beryl a capital sum of £15,000, which provided her with an annuity of £500 until her death.

Beryl stayed in England until 1929, and learned to fly. Back in Kenya, she obtained her commercial pilot's licence in 1933. Following a dare, she decided to fly the Atlantic from east to west. On 4 September 1936 she took off from Abingdon, near Oxford, in a Vega Gull, without a radio. After 21 hours 35 minutes she landed in a bog at Baleine cove, near Louisburg, Nova Scotia, 100 yards from the ocean, having run out of fuel. She was the first woman to fly the Atlantic from east to west, and the first person to make a solo non-stop crossing in that direction.

Fêted in America, she returned there in 1939, and met Raoul Cottereau Schumacher, son of Henri Schumacher, farmer, of Minneapolis. A well-read and articulate man, Schumacher worked as a ghost writer. In 1942 Beryl married him, having divorced Markham in the same year. In June 1942 *West with the Night*, by Beryl Markham, was published in America. A remarkable account of her African childhood, it reached thirteen best-seller lists. The book was lyrically written, with many classical and Shakespearian allusions, and in a style similar in places to that of Antoine de Saint-Exupéry, who had befriended Beryl in Hollywood and who may well have been a help with the manuscript. Beryl later claimed that he encouraged her to write the book. Some short stories she wrote were later gathered together by her biographer, Mary Lovell, and published as *The Splendid Outcast* (1987). Schumacher divorced Beryl in 1960 and died in 1962.

In 1950 Beryl returned to Kenya without Schumacher. Her remaining days were spent training horses in Kenya, South Africa, and Rhodesia. She won the Kenya top trainer's award five times and the Kenya Derby six times. In 1971 her son, whom she had seldom seen, died after a car accident in France, leaving two daughters, and Markham died three months later.

In 1979 the Jockey Club of Kenya allocated Beryl a bungalow at its racecourse. *West with the Night* was republished in 1982 and hailed as a lost masterpiece. By 1987 140,000 copies had been sold and royalties began to pour in. At the last count the book had sold over a million copies.

Beryl Markham was five feet eight inches tall, of willowy build, with blue eyes, fair hair, slightly wide-spaced teeth, and slim, boyish hips. Her beautiful long oval face had a determined chin. She was exceptionally promiscuous, but retained the loyalty of her male friends. Women found her often ruthless and selfish, although they admitted her stamina, physical prowess, courage, and ability to withstand pain. She died in Nairobi Hospital, from pneumonia which followed a broken hip, 3 August 1986.

[Beryl Markham, *West with the Night*, 1942; Mary S. Lovell, *Straight on till Morning*, 1987; Errol Trzebinski, *The Lives of Beryl Markham*, 1993; private information; personal knowledge.]   C. S. NICHOLLS

MARRE, SIR Alan Samuel (1914–1990), civil servant and ombudsman, was born 25 February 1914 in Bow, London, the fourth child and second son in the family of three sons and three daughters of Joseph Moshinsky, who ran a tobacconist's shop near Aldgate East station, and his wife, Rebecca. His parents were Russian Jews who had settled in England in 1907. Marre (who, in 1941, like his elder brother, changed his name by deed poll) won a scholarship to St Olave's and St Saviour's Grammar School, Southwark, and an open scholarship to Trinity Hall, Cambridge. There he won the John Stewart of Rannoch scholarship and secured first-class honours in both parts of the classical tripos (1934 and 1935).

He entered the Ministry of Health in 1936, as an assistant principal. Though in a reserved occupation, he tried to volunteer for the Royal Air Force when war began in 1939, but he was rejected because of his very short sight. He worked in a variety of departmental posts, and helped to launch the National Health Service. He became a principal in 1941, assistant secretary in 1946, and under-secretary in 1952. Eleven years later he moved to the Ministry of Labour, where he handled policy on industrial relations. He returned to the Ministry of Health as deputy secretary in 1964, spent a further two years in the Department of Employment and Productivity, then went back to his home department in 1968 as second permanent under-secretary. This was a time of adjustment to the creation of the composite Department of Health and Social Security, of which Richard *Crossman was the first secretary of state. Crossman's personality was not well adapted to the role of departmental minister, and he was notoriously difficult to work with. It was not an easy or comfortable period for Marre; but he managed to establish and maintain a satisfactory relationship with Crossman, who in his diary referred to him as 'a charming sweet man'.

In 1971 Marre became parliamentary commissioner for administration (parliamentary ombudsman), the second holder of the post. In 1973 he additionally became the first Health Service commissioner, carrying both responsibilities until his retirement in 1976. He was subsequently requested by the government to carry out two difficult and sensitive inquiries, one into the position of children handicapped because of the drug thalidomide who had not benefited from an earlier overall settlement, the other into a £130 million discrepancy in the report on teachers' pay by the Standing Commission on Pay Comparability, chaired by Hugh Clegg (7th report, 1980). From 1979 to 1985 he was vice-chairman of the advisory committee on distinction awards for NHS consultants, and from 1983 to 1987 chairman of the newly established committee on rural dispensing, when he did much to defuse a bitter and long-standing dispute between the medical and pharmaceutical professions. He also devoted time and energy to a range of voluntary organizations, being chairman of Age Concern England in 1977–80. He was appointed CB in 1955 and KCB in 1970.

Marre, with his horn-rimmed spectacles and bald dome, was friendly and approachable, though cool and restrained. His gifts were not so much originality and imagination as excellent judgement and analytical ability, and he was also a good negotiator. His specific strengths included precision in thought and expression, thoroughness, respect for the facts, detachment, and a sense of justice. No one would have dreamed of questioning his intellectual or moral integrity. In his official work he maintained a scrupulous political neutrality, and the tradition of Civil Service anonymity was thoroughly congenial to him. There were some (including Crossman) who criticized his appointment as ombudsman, doubting whether, despite the strengths which had served him so well as a departmental civil servant, he had the public relations skills and the radically questioning, even aggressive, attitudes which the post required. In fact, he managed to come to terms with the public aspects of his task and, though unabrasive and disinclined to attack the general ethos of contemporary government, proved himself just, persistent, and firmly independent. He gained public credit for his handling of some of the difficult cases which came his way. His career is of particular interest because in its later years it reflects the transition from a Civil Service imbued with the traditions of neutrality and anonymity, begun in 1853 as a result of the report by Sir Charles *Trevelyan and Sir Stafford *Northcote, to one where senior officials appear in the public arena and are held personally accountable. For Marre, this change was against his personal grain, but he had the adaptability to adjust to it successfully.

Marre had a happy domestic life. In 1943 he married Romola Mary, daughter of Aubrey John Gilling, bank manager. She herself had a distinguished career of public service, particularly on the London Voluntary Service Council, being appointed CBE in 1979. They had one son and one daughter. Marre died of cancer 20 March 1990, at his home in Golders Green, London.

[Private information; personal knowledge.]

PATRICK BENNER

MARSHALL, (Charles) Arthur (Bertram) (1910–1989), humorist, writer, and broadcaster, was born 10 May 1910 in Barnes, London, the younger son of Charles Frederick Bertram Marshall, consulting engineer, and his wife, Dorothy Lee. His father was a loving husband, but although he quite liked the idea of children, to Arthur's disappointment he preferred to be where they were not. In 1920 the family moved to Newbury and Arthur was sent away to boarding-school. First he went to Edinburgh House, an uncomfortable but enjoyable preparatory school in Lee-on-Solent, and then to Oundle. He was happy at Oundle—he seems to have been happy almost everywhere—and during a debate in his last winter term a great burst of laughter at something he said gave him such a whiff of power and pleasure that he decided to make the raising of laughter the prime consideration of his life. He then went to Christ's College, Cambridge, where he obtained a second class (division II) in part i of the modern and medieval languages tripos (French, 1929, and German, 1930) and a third class in part ii (1931).

He acted at every opportunity at Oundle and at Christ's and was determined on a career in the theatre. He mostly played female parts at university, for which he collected some excellent press notices, notably for his playing of Lady Cicely, opposite (Sir) Michael *Redgrave, in *Captain Brassbound's Conversion*. He became president of Cambridge's Amateur Dramatic Society.

Down from Cambridge, armed with his glowing press cuttings, he had his heart set on going to the Royal Academy of Dramatic Art, but his mother pointed out that the acting profession would hardly give an ecstatic welcome to an amateur female impersonator. She persuaded him to go back to Oundle instead and make a career as a schoolmaster. In 1931 Oundle offered him a job as a house tutor and teacher of French and German, which he accepted, quaking in his shoes. To his own surprise he turned out to be a good teacher and, as the terms sped happily by, he spent a good deal of his free time writing and performing to friends what were then called 'turns', three-minute comic monologues in which, inspired by Angela *Brazil's girls' school stories which he found hilarious when read aloud, he impersonated hearty botany mistresses and stern school matrons. He wrote Angela Brazil's DNB entry.

In 1934 a BBC radio producer saw Arthur perform his botany-mistress turn at a party and booked him to broadcast it on *Charlot's Hour*. Thus his professional career began by his becoming the world's first radio drag act. In the same year (C.) Raymond *Mortimer, literary editor of the *New Statesman*, asked Arthur to review a clutch of schoolgirl stories. His review was much enjoyed and for many years was a popular Christmas feature of the magazine.

During World War II Marshall, like many a schoolmaster, was drafted into intelligence and he had a busy time, surviving the evacuation of Dunkirk in the British Expeditionary Force and working with Combined Operations headquarters and SHAEF (Supreme Headquarters, Allied Expeditionary Force). In 1945 he was a lieutenant-colonel on General Dwight D. Eisenhower's staff. He was appointed MBE in 1944. In 1943, still in uniform, he wrote and starred in a BBC comedy series on the radio, *A Date with Nurse Dugdale*, which was a wartime success.

After the war Marshall returned to Oundle in 1946 as a housemaster, but his fascination with the theatre was still strong and, afraid that he might end up as a rotund Mr Chips before his time, he left Oundle in 1954 at the age of forty-four and became a social secretary to his old friend, Victor, third Baron *Rothschild. In 1958 he changed jobs again and went to work as a script reader for one of the leading figures of Shaftesbury Avenue's commercial theatre, H. G. ('Binkie') *Beaumont of H. M. Tennent Ltd. Marshall was in his element at last. He was such pleasant company that everybody in the theatre seemed to know and like him and this charming, funny, and non-competitive person was invited everywhere. He spent many long weekends at W. Somerset *Maugham's Villa Mauresque at Cap Ferrat and months with Alfred Lunt and Lynn Fontanne in the USA. No doubt part of his attraction as a guest was that when conversation sagged his host would call upon him to entertain the company with a turn, and he was delighted to oblige.

In 1953 he began to publish his humorous prose pieces in book form, beginning with *Nineteen to the Dozen* (1953); there were many more. He also published some gratifyingly successful compilations from the *New Statesman* competitions and his own book reviews, *Salome Dear, Not in the Fridge!* (1968), *Girls Will Be Girls* (1974), *Whimpering in the Rhododendrons* (1982), and *Giggling in the Shrubbery* (1985). In 1975 he started writing a regular column for the *New Statesman* and another for the *Sunday Telegraph*. He also became a regular broadcaster and chat-show guest and in 1979 was enlisted as a team captain in the BBC TV game *Call My Bluff*, which he graced for ten years. A measure of his aggressive nature and will to win was evident in his first appearance on *Call My Bluff*. He led his team to an 8–0 defeat and laughed so much he was unable to say 'goodnight' to camera.

In the world of broadcast humour in the 1980s it was Arthur Marshall who was the 'alternative comedian'. This was the era dominated by young writers and comics, who appealed to young viewers and readers with a stunning display of aggressive, sexual, and politically simplistic routines nurtured on the students' union circuit. For those for whom this sort of comedy ceased to appeal much after the first excitement, Marshall's charming, intelligent, witty, *affectionate* humour came as a breath of fresh air. He was, perhaps, the last flowering of the humour which Joseph *Addison and Sir Richard *Steele pioneered in the early eighteenth century and called 'polite comedy'.

With his unconventional attitudes towards such things as religion and erudition, his distaste for foreigners (the 'Boche' and 'Frogs'), and his eyes sparkling and chins a-wobble at some absurdity he had noticed, a line of Rupert

*Brooke's should be bent to Arthur Marshall, this happiest of humorists, as 'an English unofficial sunbeam'.

He was unmarried. His last years were spent in Devon and during his final illness he was fortunate to have an old friend, Peter Kelland, a retired schoolmaster, to look after him and share his life. He died 27 January 1989.

[Arthur Marshall, *Life's Rich Pageant* (autobiography), 1984; private information.]   FRANK MUIR

MARTIN, SIR Harold Brownlow Morgan (1918–1988), air marshal, was born 27 February 1918 in Edgecliffe, Sydney, Australia, the only son and second of three children of Joseph Harold Osborne Morgan Martin, MD, medical practitioner, and his wife, Colina Elizabeth Dixon. He was educated at Randwick High School and Lyndfield College. An accomplished horseman, he became a cadet in the Australian Light Horse. In 1937, intent on world travel, he left Sydney as a crew member on a liner. In 1940, in England, he joined the Royal Air Force Volunteer Reserve.

During his first Bomber Command tour in No. 455 Squadron (Royal Australian Air Force) and No. 50 Squadron (Royal Air Force), flying Hampden, Manchester, and Lancaster bombers, Martin concluded that the most effective way of penetrating enemy defences at night was to disregard regulations and to fly at low level. By questioning higher policy and refusing to allow regulations to hinder chances of success he was already showing a boldness and independence of mind which was to characterize his entire career. His first DFC came in 1942, after twenty-five sorties.

Invited to join No. 617 (the 'Dambuster' squadron) in March 1943, he made a significant contribution to its night low-level training for the actual operation. The squadron flew at night at 150 feet all the way to its targets and released its bouncing bombs from 60 feet. Martin scored a direct hit. The Möhne and Eder dams were breached, and the Sorpe dam damaged. Martin was appointed to the DSO and this was soon followed with a bar to his DFC for his courage and resolution in a costly attack on the Dortmund Ems canal. Becoming No. 617's acting commander, Martin rebuilt the squadron before handing it over, well trained, to Leonard (later Baron) Cheshire in 1943. He also convinced Cheshire of the feasibility of low-level night target marking, a prerequisite for accurate bombing.

In February 1944 Martin's action during an attack with 'Blockbuster' bombs on a heavily defended viaduct in southern France, for which he received a bar to his DSO, was described by Cheshire as the supreme example of inspired fearless night marking. During his last operational tour in No. 515 Night Intruder Squadron, Martin again distinguished himself, gaining a second bar to his DFC (1944). He then attended the Haifa Staff College before returning to flying duties in No. 242 Transport Squadron (1946). With his war gratuity he bought a horse.

In 1947 Martin was awarded the Britannia trophy for a record-breaking Mosquito flight (21 hours, 31 minutes) from London to Cape Town, and the following year he received the AFC for his crucial contribution to the first jet crossing of the Atlantic, which was made by an RAF squadron. Serving in London as a squadron-leader (1948–51), he began to take an interest in painting, in which he displayed a natural talent, sculpture, and archaeology, subjects he pursued most of his life. From 1952 to 1955, as a wing commander, he was air attaché in Israel, a post in which he was a success because of his diplomatic flair and grasp of the political complexities of the Middle East. This posting, extended at the Israelis' request, marked a turning-point in his career, and steady progress followed.

A rewarding NATO staff post at Fontainebleau in France (1955–8) was followed by a course at the Joint Services Staff College and postings, first as group captain to Signals Command, and then to Cyprus, where he commanded the important Nicosia base. In 1963 he became an air commodore and was posted to No. 38 Support Group, where he enjoyed his contacts with the airborne forces but disagreed profoundly with the infantry over the control of the helicopter force. A course at the Imperial Defence College (1965), promotion to air vice-marshal (1967), and a return to Cyprus as the senior air staff officer prepared him for his last command appointments—air officer commanding No. 38 Group (1967–9), then, as air marshal (1970), AOC-in-C of the RAF in Germany, and commander of the NATO second tactical air force, with its force of Belgians, Dutch, Germans, and British.

Primarily because of frustration in his fight against Service cuts, he was unhappy in his last RAF post, as air member for personnel at the Ministry of Defence (1973–4). After his retirement in 1974 he spent three years in Beirut and Athens as Middle East marketing adviser to Hawker Siddeley International, before returning to London as a consultant. He was aide-de-camp to the queen (1963–6) and was appointed CB (1968) and KCB (1971).

Martin, a vital, alert man of medium height, and powerful, humorous eyes, was universally liked and respected. He was a man of great courage who always fought unselfishly for what he believed was right. In 1985 his lifestyle became restricted when he suffered brain damage after being knocked down by a coach, but he bore his lot with fortitude and patience.

In 1944 he married Wendy Lawrence, widow of Flight-lieutenant P. D. Walker, RAF, and daughter of Grenbry Outhwaite, lawyer, and Ida Rentoul, artist, of Melbourne. The marriage was very happy; there were two daughters. Martin died from cancer at home, 64 Warwick Gardens, London W14, 3 November 1988.

[*The Times* and *Daily Telegraph*, 4 November 1988; Paul Brickhill, *The Dambusters*, 1951; Russell Braddon, *Cheshire, VC*, 1954; Percy B. Lucas, *Wings of War*, 1983; private information; personal knowledge.]

FREDERICK ROSIER

MASON, SIR **Frank Trowbridge** (1900–1988), engineer officer in the Royal Navy, was born in Ipswich 25 April 1900, the elder son and elder child of Frank John Mason, MBE, draper and later JP and mayor of Ipswich, and his wife, Marian Elizabeth Trowbridge. He was educated at Ipswich School, passing into the Royal Navy (executive branch) as a special entry (public school) cadet in 1918. After two years as a cadet and midshipman in HMS *Collingwood* and *Queen Elizabeth*, he volunteered to specialize in engineering (E). He underwent specialist engineering training at the Royal Naval colleges at Greenwich and Keyham. In 1923 he qualified for his engineering watch-keeping certificate in HMS *Malaya* and was promoted to lieutenant (E), continuing his service in that ship as a fully qualified mechanical and marine engineer until appointed in 1925 to HM Dockyard, Malta.

In 1928 he was appointed to HMS *Rodney*, a new battleship then undergoing severe problems with her novel 16-inch guns. His engineering skill in securing improved reliability led him to specialize in ordnance engineering and to his reappointment after a short period with Messrs Vickers at Elswick. After promotion to lieutenant-commander (E) he served for three years in the Naval Ordnance Department and in 1933–4 he again served in HMS *Rodney*, but this time as 'senior (second) engineer', responsible to the commander (E) for all propulsion, electricity generating, and 'hotel services' machinery and equipment. Following his next promotion to commander (E) in December 1934, he served again for three years in the Naval Ordnance Department. From there he was appointed as 'engineer officer' (chief engineer) to a new cruiser, HMS *Galatea*, then flagship of the rear-admiral, destroyers. In 1939 he became the first commander (E) to serve in HMS *Excellent*, then the Naval Gunnery School. He was appointed in 1943 as fleet gunnery engineer officer to the Home Fleet in Scapa Flow, and at the same time received promotion to captain (E).

From 1944 he served again in the Naval Ordnance Department in the Admiralty (Bath) and in 1947 became chief gunnery engineer officer and deputy director of naval ordnance. In 1949 he was the first engineering specialist to become a student at the Imperial Defence College (later the Royal College of Defence Studies) and, on promotion to rear-admiral, from 1950 to 1952 he held the post of deputy engineer-in-chief of the Fleet. After a year on the staff of the commander-in-chief, The Nore, he was promoted to vice-admiral (E) in 1953 and assumed the post of engineer-in-chief of the Fleet. He was appointed CB in 1953 and KCB in 1955. He was placed on the inactive list of the Royal Navy in 1957.

By the 1950s Mason was among the last of those naval officers still serving who had entered under the Selborne–Fisher scheme of 1903, whose aim was to put engineers in the main stream of naval life. The scheme was cancelled in 1923 and the navy entered World War II technologically bereft. In the immediate postwar era Mason and others determined to resurrect it, in the face of great resistance. But Mason's influence and the battle experience of many senior officers of all specializations carried the day. In 1956 the new arrangements came into being. It was Mason's great service to the navy that he was at the centre of bringing about a general list of officers.

For thirty years after leaving the active list Mason devoted himself to the national, but greatly neglected, engineering aspects of manufacturing industry and to education in general. He was president of the Institution of Mechanical Engineers (1964) and of the Institute of Marine Engineers (1967), as well as being a member of the Institute of Plant Engineers and chairman or vice-chairman of many other professional bodies. He was a member of the National Council for Technological Awards (1960–4), a founder fellow of the Fellowship of Engineering (1976), a member of the Smeatonian Society of Civil Engineers, and assistant to the court of the Worshipful Company of Shipwrights. He served on the councils or governing bodies of the Further Education Staff College (1964–74), Brighton Polytechnic (1969–73), the Royal Naval School in Haslemere (1953–83), Hurstpierpoint College (1966–80), and Ipswich School (1961–72). He was an active member of the council of the Navy League (1967–73) and from 1967 held the life appointment of high steward of Ipswich. He was F.Eng., honorary F.I.Mech.E., honorary M.I.PlantE., and F.I.Mar.E.

Mason was good-looking and his expression was that of a man at peace with himself. Of medium build, he was always impeccably turned out, and, as he grew older, his white hair added to his aura of long and deep experience and benign but firm authority. He was a committed and practising Christian. In April 1924 he married Dora Margaret, daughter of Sydney Brand,

JP, who, like Mason's father, was a draper. They were a devoted couple who had one son, who became archdeacon of Tonbridge, and two daughters, one of whom was appointed OBE. While suffering from cancer of the lung, Mason died from heart failure at Townfield House, Hurstpierpoint, 29 August 1988.

[Private information; personal knowledge.]

LOUIS LE BAILLY

MATHER, SIR Kenneth (1911–1990), geneticist, was born 22 June 1911 in Nantwich, Cheshire, the elder child and only son of Richard Wilson Mather, furniture-maker, of Nantwich, and his wife Annie, daughter of John Mottram, agri-culturist, of Nantwich. His formal education started in 1915 at the Church of England Boys' Elementary School, Nantwich. He won a Chesh-ire county scholarship to Nantwich and Acton Grammar School (1922–8), where the head-master developed Mather's interest in mathe-matics but suggested a future in biological research. In 1928 he won a Cheshire county university scholarship to read botany at Man-chester University, where he obtained first-class honours in 1931. He was then awarded a research scholarship by the Ministry of Agriculture and Fisheries, to work at the John Innes Horti-cultural Institution, Merton, London, on chro-mosome behaviour (cytology) with C. D. *Darlington. Here Mather developed his skills and enthusiasm, within four months was writing his first paper (published in 1932), and within two years was awarded a London University Ph.D. (1933).

In 1933 Mather went to Svalöf, Sweden, where he decided that traditional genetics would not take the plant breeder very far with the problems that he encountered and that a differ-ent genetical methodology was needed. He returned in 1934 to work under (Sir) R. A. *Fisher in the Galton laboratory, University College London. 'My greatest gain was...working closely with Fisher and learning from him the principles and practice of statistical analysis, estimation and hypothesis testing; how to design experiments; how to wring information effi-ciently from data; and how to measure the amount of information available for the analytic purpose in mind. For this I owe him a debt which has lasted all my working life.'

A Rockefeller fellowship allowed Mather to visit the USA for the year 1937–8 and he spent time at the California Institute of Technology and Harvard. In 1938 he returned to the John Innes Institute as the head of the genetics depart-ment. While continuing his cytology work (for which he obtained a D.Sc. in 1940) and collabo-rating with Fisher, he paid increasing attention to the analysis of characters showing quantitative variation (biometrical genetics). In 1948 he

became the first professor of genetics at Birming-ham University. He built up his department, with support from the Agricultural Research Council (ARC), which established a unit of biometrical genetics. Mather expanded his work on biometrical genetics and published widely. In 1965 he was appointed vice-chancellor of the University of Southampton, where he experi-enced mixed fortunes. The student unrest of the 1960s and Mather's more traditional approach did not mix easily; he found this period trying and frustrating. Nevertheless, he was successful in persuading the University Grants Committee to authorize a new medical school, which he developed. In 1971 he returned to Birmingham as an honorary professor and senior research fellow, to concentrate his efforts on his passion—biometrical genetics. He worked there until the day before his death.

Mather wrote 283 scientific papers, gave twenty-four broadcasts, and published the fol-lowing books: The Measurement of Linkage in Heredity (1938), Statistical Analysis in Biology (1943), Elements of Genetics (1949), Biometrical Genetics (1st edn. 1949; 2nd and 3rd edns., with J. L. Jinks, 1971 and 1982), Human Diversity (1964), The Elements of Biometry (1967), Genet-ical Structure of Populations (1973), Introduction to Biometrical Genetics (1977), and (with C. D. *Darlington) The Elements of Genetics (1949) and Genes, Plants and People (1950).

Mather was appointed CBE in 1956 and knighted in 1979. He was presented with hon-orary degrees by Southampton (LLD, 1972), Bath (D.Sc., 1975), Manchester (D.Sc., 1980), and Wales (D.Sc., 1980). He was elected a fellow of the Royal Society in 1949 and was awarded the Weldon medal (Oxford, 1962) and the Darwin medal (Royal Society, 1964). He was president of the Genetical Society of Great Britain (1949–52) and an honorary member in 1981. He served on many research councils, advisory bodies, and committees.

Mather was short and stockily built, with swept-back hair and glasses, and invariably had a pipe in his mouth or hand. He did not suffer fools gladly and tended to make this clear, but he would spend whatever time was needed to explain an idea to a genuine enquirer. His determination and self-commitment were with-out question; he would sit with his pipe firmly gripped and would pursue an idea until he resolved it. Interruptions on trivial matters often resulted in large quantities of smoke and short sentences. The opportunity to try out an idea or the prospect of a new approach was welcomed warmly. Despite his commitment to genetics he showed a fascination and knowledge of British military (especially naval) history.

In 1937 he married a fellow botanist, Mona (died 1987), daughter of Harold Rhodes, managing director of a colour printer's firm in Saddleworth. They had one son. Mather died of a heart attack 20 March 1990, at his home in Edgbaston, Birmingham.

[Hand-written draft, 1988, of Kenneth Mather's personal record in the Royal Society archives, London; D. Lewis in *Biographical Memoirs of Fellows of the Royal Society*, vol. xxxviii, 1992; personal knowledge.]

PETER D. S. CALIGARI

MATTHEWS, SIR Bryan Harold Cabot (1906–1986), physiologist, was born 14 June 1906 in Clifton, Bristol, the younger son and youngest of three children of Harold Evan Matthews, manufacturing pharmacist, with a factory and shop in Clifton, and his wife, Sarah Susannah ('Ruby') Harrison, pharmacist. His elder brother was Leonard Harrison *Matthews, zoologist. Educated at Clifton College and King's College, Cambridge, he graduated with a second class in part i (1926) and a first in part ii (1927) of the natural sciences tripos.

Matthews worked in Cambridge all his life except during World War II. In 1928 he became Beit memorial fellow for medical research, and in 1932 assistant director of research, a post he held until 1948. Before the war Matthews made a major contribution to the development of neurophysiology. Previously single nerve impulses had been recorded, but only with difficulty and distortion; now Matthews developed an instrument, the moving iron oscillograph, with its associated amplifiers, which had the necessary sensitivity and frequency response to record single nerve impulses. Moreover, it was easily photographed, unlike the cathode ray oscilloscopes. With this system Matthews worked out the basic physiology of muscle spindles, including mammalian spindles, work which formed the basis of much subsequent receptor and control system physiology. With E. D. (later Baron) *Adrian, and using his newly developed differential amplifier, he investigated potentials from the surface of the brain and from the human brain through the skull, laying the foundation for later electroencephalography. He also worked with D. H. Barron on the potentials that could be recorded from spinal roots. This work advanced knowledge of the way nerve impulses converge on cells in the spinal cord and set up graded potential changes, which in turn initiate further impulses in other nerve cells.

During this time in Cambridge Matthews also developed his interest in high altitudes. He started with a theoretical study showing that heat lost through breathing becomes greater than that gained from the utilization of oxygen at altitudes above 30,000 feet. He participated as a subject in work on the effects of prolonged exposure to low oxygen tensions and in this and many experiments during the war he was prepared to act as a subject in situations which were potentially dangerous. In 1935 he was a member of an expedition to the Andes to study physiology at high altitudes. He spent longer at the highest camp than anyone else and made significant scientific as well as physical contributions to the expedition.

In August 1939 Matthews moved to Farnborough to head the Royal Air Force physiological laboratory, which in 1944 became the RAF Institute of Aviation Medicine, with Matthews as its first director. He had great success both in his own work and as director of the laboratory in finding quick and easy solutions to immediate and important problems facing aircrew: lack of oxygen, decompression sickness, and acceleration. At the same time he laid the foundations for the more sophisticated solutions needed for the jet age.

After the war he returned to Cambridge in 1946 and in 1948 became a reader in physiology. He was professor of physiology from 1952 to 1973. He continued his research on the nervous system, but his main task, as head of the department, was to build it up again once staff could be recruited. His overriding priority was to recruit only those of outstanding scientific ability. He made changes in the administration of the department, with a view to improving the distribution of resources, and left his staff to develop their own ideas. He was a fellow of King's College from 1929, director of studies there in 1948–52, and a life fellow from 1973. Matthews became a fellow of the Royal Society in 1940 and was a vice-president in 1957 and 1958. Appointed CBE in 1944, he was knighted in 1952.

An imposing bearded figure, he had a vigorous personality and was a friendly, likeable, and at times commanding person. He had a love of activities with an element of challenge to the natural elements, such as skiing, canoeing, and, above all, long-distance sailing. He cruised widely and spent much time at sea. He was an expert navigator and developed instruments and techniques for use in cruising short-handed, some of which became commonplace. In 1926 he married Rachel Katherine (died 1994), daughter of Gustav Eckhard, Manchester shipping agent, and sister of the wife of the economist F. W. *Paish. They had a son, Professor P. B. C. Matthews, FRS, neurophysiologist, and two daughters. The marriage broke up at the beginning of the war and he was then supported for nearly thirty years by the close friendship of his sailing companion, Constance Biron, who changed her name to Matthews by deed poll. In 1970, after his relationship with Constance had come to an end, he divorced Rachel and in the same year married Audrey Wentworth, widow of Air Vice-Marshal William Kilpatrick Stewart and daughter of Francis Tyndale, a lieutenant-colonel in the Royal Army Medical Corps. Matthews died in Cambridge 23 July 1986.

[D. A. Parry in *Annual Report* of King's College, Cambridge, 1987; John Gray in *Biographical Memoirs of Fellows of the Royal Society*, vol. xxxv, 1990; private information; personal knowledge.]   JOHN GRAY

MATTHEWS, Denis James (1919–1988), pianist, composer, and teacher, was born 27 February 1919 in Coventry, the only child of Arthur Matthews, director of the Norman Engineering Company at Leamington Spa, and his wife, Elsie Culver, schoolteacher. His father committed suicide when Denis was twelve. He was educated at Warwick Grammar School, where his musical gifts brought him to the attention of visiting adjudicators including Herbert *Howells, who encouraged him to consider a career in music. Another was the pianist Harold Craxton, who offered to teach him. Winning the Thalberg scholarship to the Royal Academy of Music in 1935, he studied composition with William Alwyn and the piano with Craxton, who welcomed him into a large and musical family circle, giving him a home as well as tuition and encouragement. His interests were initially in composition, and early works included songs and chamber music, which he later described as 'cosily derivative and romantic'. However, a piano trio, performed at a student concert, excited favourable press attention; and in 1937 he added a composition scholarship to that for piano. His performing and composing abilities were sometimes combined, as when Sir Henry *Wood conducted his Symphonic Movement for piano and orchestra. The list of his compositions eventually included a Violin Sonata, Five Sketches for violin and piano, a string quartet, and a Partita for wind quintet for a fellow student, the horn player Dennis *Brain.

Though some of his works were taken up by performers, and even published, Matthews found that his deepening interest in the classics—Bach, Mozart, and Beethoven, in particular—was directing him towards playing. His professional début came with a Promenade Concert in 1939, when he played Beethoven's Third Piano Concerto under Sir Henry Wood. Beethoven was to remain central to his interests, and was the subject of many lecture recitals, some records expounding the sketch-books, and two BBC Music Guide booklets, *Beethoven Piano Sonatas* (1967) and *Brahms Piano Music* (1978). Matthews's writings also included a chapter on Beethoven, Schubert, and Brahms in a symposium he edited, *Keyboard Music* (1972), *Arturo Toscanini* (1982), and an autobiography, *In Pursuit of Music* (1966).

Having graduated from the Royal Academy of Music in 1940 with the LRAM (to which he added the Royal College of Music's ARCM, as well as the Worshipful Company of Musicians' medal, 1938, for the most distinguished student), Matthews earned a living accompanying for opera and ballet classes, playing for social occasions such as City dinners, and occasionally giving concerts either alone or with student friends. He remained all his life an excellent sonata pianist, though latterly he seldom accompanied singers in lieder.

In 1940 he was called up, entered the Royal Air Force, and, together with a number of other musicians who were to go on to make distinguished careers, joined the central band at Uxbridge. He toured Germany at the end of the war with the central band, playing piano solos at the Potsdam conference to Josef Stalin, (Sir) Winston Churchill, and Harry S. Truman. He also shared the keyboard with Truman.

Demobilized in 1946, Matthews was taken up by musicians including Dame Myra *Hess, and solo engagements began to come in. He played concertos with (Sir) John *Barbirolli (Sir) Malcolm *Sargent, Sir Thomas *Beecham, Sir Adrian *Boult, and other leading conductors, and toured widely; he had also begun making records in 1941, in a repertory centring on Mozart and Beethoven (and including a classic version of Beethoven's Horn Sonata with Dennis Brain), but also embracing modern British composers. He was closely associated with the London Mozart Players, founded in 1949 by another friend from the central band, Harry Blech. Concerts and recordings brought him wide popularity, and he embarked upon a career that took him all round the world. In 1955 he settled in Henley, where he and his friends took part in festival music-making. However, divorce in 1960 brought him back to London.

With the emergence of a postwar generation of virtuosi, Matthews found his career prospering less well in the 1960s. To his friends, he was candid about his powers, believing that he had been fortunate to make a career at a time when competition was less fierce. He was never a great technician, but the musicality of his playing gave his performances at their best an illuminating quality, and a sense of the music's essential structure and meaning. His interest in conveying this found a new outlet when in 1971 he was invited to be the first professor of music at the University of Newcastle. He ran an enterprising and successful department, while continuing to maintain a performing career. He retired in 1984. He was appointed CBE in 1975, and had honorary degrees from St Andrews (1973), Hull (1978), and Warwick (1982).

Though prey to private melancholy, Matthews was an amusing and warm-hearted companion. He was slightly built, with sandy hair and an expressive face that remained impassive during performance but could take on a lively, animated expression in the discussions about music which were his greatest joy. He retained a somewhat boyish appearance and manner. He married three times. In 1941 he married Mira Howe, a cellist, and they had one son and three daughters. The marriage was dissolved in 1960 and in 1963 he married Brenda, who had been brought up by Dr Samuel McDermott, a general practitioner in Swindon, and taken his surname. They had one son and one daughter. The marriage was dissolved in 1985 and in 1986 he married Beryl, a piano teacher, daughter of Arthur Harold Jordan Perry, owner of a textile firm. Matthews died by his own hand in Birmingham, 24 December 1988, having suffered from bouts of severe depression, particularly after his marriage to Brenda McDermott broke up.

[Denis Matthews, *In Pursuit of Music* (autobiography), 1966; private information; personal knowledge.]

JOHN WARRACK

MATTHEWS, (Leonard) Harrison (1901–1986), zoologist and naturalist, was born 12 June 1901 in Clifton, Bristol, the elder son and eldest of three children of Harold Evan Matthews, manufacturing pharmacist, and his wife, Sarah Susannah ('Ruby') Harrison, pharmacist. His sister, Marjorie Violet (later Mrs Marshall Sisson), was an exhibitioner at Newnham College, Cambridge, and became an educational psychologist. His younger brother, (Sir) Bryan Harold Cabot *Matthews, became professor of physiology at Cambridge. Harrison or 'Leo' Matthews was brought up at Clifton, where his father had a pharmaceutical factory and chemist's shop, and went to Bristol Grammar School. In 1919 he went up to King's College, Cambridge, where he obtained a first class in part i of the natural sciences tripos (1922) and a second class in part ii (1923). He was also awarded the Frank Smart prize in zoology. He spent much time during his vacations studying the fauna of the Bristol channel and on trawlers, visiting the Faroes, Iceland, and the White Sea, confirming a liking for hands-on zoology that was to last his lifetime.

In 1924 he applied for, and obtained, a post with the *Discovery* committee to work on whale biology in South Georgia. This committee (known by the name of its research vessel) had been set up by the British government to conduct an intensive scientific research programme in the Southern Ocean to provide data for the rational management of the whaling industry, the expansion of which was causing concern. Matthews was attracted by the prospect of working in this remote spot on the largest and most impressive of all living things, and mixing with the hard men engaged in whaling. He travelled to South Georgia in the autumn of 1924 to establish a marine laboratory at King Edward cove, next to the whaling station where he was to do most of his work. This resulted in major monographs on humpback, sei, right, and sperm whales, published in *Discovery* reports. There were other papers on seals, birds, and invertebrates and his first book, *South Georgia: the British Empire's Subantarctic Outpost* (1931), which remained the definitive text for fifty years. Besides these, there were three books, *Wandering Albatross* (1951), *Sea Elephant* (1952), and *Penguin* (1977), aimed at the general public, which vividly captured the life of the sealers and whalers whose company Matthews had so relished.

Matthews relinquished his post with the *Discovery* committee in 1928, and returned to Bristol to work part-time in the family firm and help his brother develop scientific instruments. They established Clifton Instruments Ltd. He also took his Cambridge MA, which was followed by an Sc.D. in 1937. In 1935 he was appointed a special lecturer at Bristol University. Here he continued to work on his South Georgia material and widened his field to include African mammals. Reproductive physiology held a fascination for him and he was intrigued by the uncertainty surrounding the sex of the spotted hyena, regarded by Pliny as a facultative hermaphrodite. In 1935 he organized an expedition to the Balbal plains, west of the Ngorongoro crater in Tanganyika, and there collected and dissected 103 hyenas. He was the first to describe the extraordinary penile clitoris and apparent absence of a vulva in the female that had given rise to Pliny's misapprehension.

During World War II Matthews became a radio officer in Anti-Aircraft Command (1941), and senior scientific officer in the Telecommunications Research Establishment (1942). He worked at the Petersham radiolocation school, undertaking confidential work on radar gun-laying and, later, radar position-indicating systems for the Pathfinder bombers.

Matthews returned to Bristol in 1945 as research fellow. He continued to produce a wide variety of papers on the biology of animals, from bats to basking sharks. In 1952 he was appointed scientific director of the Zoological Society of London (the London zoo), a post he held till retirement in 1966. He was highly successful in developing the scientific activities of the society and his own research, particularly on reproduction in seals. In 1954 he was elected FRS. Unfortunately, his later years at the zoo were clouded by disagreement with the secretary, Sir Solly (later Baron) Zuckerman.

His retirement, at the Old Rectory, Stansfield, Suffolk, was an active period. He continued to produce important texts, including *The Life of Mammals* (2 vols., 1969 and 1971) and *The Natural History of the Whale* (1978). His last book was *Mammals in the British Isles* (1982). He was, perhaps, the last of the great 'naturalists', a man with a wide interest in animals, less concerned with laboratory experimentation than with animals' life in the field.

In appearance he was tall and well built and always well groomed, not to say dapper, which was surprising in one who had spent so much time in rigorous field conditions. In later life he sported a goatee beard and had a liking for bow-ties. He was excellent company, something of a bon viveur, and a most entertaining companion, always able to produce an appropriate yarn from his travels. He sketched and painted in a delightful free style and his illustrations appeared in several of his published works. He amassed a notable library and a remarkable collection of curios from his travels. In 1924 he married a dancer, Dorothy Hélène, daughter of Henry Charles Harris, of independent means. They had a son and a daughter. Matthews died at home at the Old Rectory, Stansfield, Suffolk, 27 November 1986.

[Sir Richard Harrison in *Biographical Memoirs of Fellows of the Royal Society*, vol. xxxiii, 1987; Nigel Bonner in *Journal of the Zoological Society of London*, vol. ccxiii, 1987, pp. 1–5; personal knowledge.]   NIGEL BONNER

MAURIER, DAME **Daphne du** (1907–1989), novelist. [See DU MAURIER, DAME DAPHNE.]

MAYBRAY-KING, BARON (1901–1986), Labour politician and Speaker of the House of Commons. [See KING, HORACE MAYBRAY.]

MEDAWAR, SIR **Peter Brian** (1915–1987), biologist and Nobel prize-winner, was born 28 February 1915 in Rio de Janeiro, the elder child and only son of Nicholas Agnatius Medawar, a Brazilian businessman of Lebanese extraction, and his British wife, Edith Muriel Dowling. He was educated at Marlborough College and Magdalen College, Oxford, where he took a first-class degree in zoology in 1935 and a D.Sc. in 1947. At Oxford he was successively a Christopher Welch scholar and senior demy of Magdalen (1935), a senior research fellow of St John's (1944), and a fellow by special election of Magdalen (1938–44 and 1946–7). From 1947 to 1951 he was Mason professor of zoology in the University of Birmingham, from 1951 to 1962 Jodrell professor of zoology and comparative anatomy in University College London, and from 1962 to 1971 director of the National Institute of Medical Research, Mill Hill. From 1971 to 1986 he was head of the transplantation section of the Medical Research Council's clinical research centre, Harrow.

He created a new branch of science, the immunology of transplantation. During the Battle of Britain in 1940 a plane crashed near Oxford, and Medawar, engaged there in research on tissue growth and repair, was asked whether he could help the badly burned pilot. Although he had nothing to offer at the time, this awoke in him an interest in transplantation of skin, which was to form the core of his scientific achievement. With the Glasgow surgeon Thomas Gibson he discovered the 'homograft reaction', the process whereby an immunological response causes the rejection of tissue that has been transplanted between unrelated individuals. It took another two decades and the work of many people to find ways of overcoming this reaction, by means of immunosuppressive drugs, but it was Medawar's first decisive step that made possible organ transplantation as it was later known.

Along the way he and his small research group, especially Leslie Brent and Rupert Billingham, made other important discoveries, most notably of immunological tolerance in 1954. The immune system discriminates efficiently between skin grafts of foreign and self origin, and under certain experimental conditions, which Medawar and his colleagues first defined, it can be misled into treating as self what is in fact foreign. Just as a new branch of surgery sprang from Medawar's seminal work on the homograft region, so also a new branch of developmental biology sprang from his work on tolerance. For this discovery he was awarded the Nobel prize for medicine in 1960, jointly with (Sir F.) Macfarlane Burnet.

It must not be thought that a scientist as clear-minded and creative as Medawar was never wrong. Indeed, it is precisely those qualities which make his few mistakes easy to identify. A conspicuous example was his idea, during the early 1950s, that pigment spreads in the skin by cell-to-cell passage of infective particles.

To a wider public he was known for his eloquent projection of ideas in and about biology. He was passionately convinced of the power of the scientific method not only to create what he called a magnificent 'articulated structure of hypotheses', but also to solve human problems. His deepest contribution was to expound the deductive view of scientific activity. For Medawar the place of honour is occupied by the 'act of creation', in which a new idea is formulated; experimentation has the humbler (but entirely necessary) role of verifying ideas. He happily accepted the consequence that an idea can never formally be proved true. Even the faintest whiff of induction was dismissed with contumely. He took pleasure in searching out the roots of this position in the English thinkers of the last three centuries. In all of this he was much influenced by his friends the philosophers T. D. ('Harry') Weldon, Sir Alfred *Ayer, and Sir Karl Popper. He conveyed these convictions with eloquence, elegance, and an unfailing sense of humour in ten books published between 1957 and 1986—including *The Uniqueness of the Individual* (1957),

The Future of Man (1960), *Advice to a Young Scientist* (1979), and *The Limits of Science* (1984)—and in some 200 articles and reviews. His 1959 Reith lectures on the future of man powerfully rejected the gloom-and-doom view of the impact of science on ordinary life. 'Is the Scientific Paper a Fraud?' (BBC Third Programme, 1963, reprinted in P. B. Medawar, *The Threat and the Glory*, 1990) was much enjoyed in scientific circles.

His autobiography, *Memoir of a Thinking Radish* (1986), relates that the Oxford senior common-rooms taught him to regard no subject as intellectually beyond his reach. Throughout his life he was quick to respond to the ideas of those around him: colleagues, students, friends, and family. How delighted were the undergraduates who attended his tutorials to find themselves acknowledged in his profound 1947 review of cellular inheritance and transformation. He never ran a large laboratory, and even as director of the National Institute of Medical Research he and two or three junior colleagues occupied just two rooms (where he continued to do his own research and his own washing up, on the Tuesdays and Thursdays that he kept free of administrative duties). He laughed at gigantic research programmes, and the possibility that government might perceive the practical benefits of research better than the individual scientist who carried it out. In his own experimental work, and above all in his writing, he set a standard which inspired the postwar flowering of immunology.

He needed and received the total love and support of his wife, from their first meeting as undergraduates at Oxford to his last paralysing illness. She was Jean, daughter of Charles Henry Shinglewood Taylor, surgeon; they had two sons and two daughters. Jean entered fully into his professional life, filling first their house in Edgbaston, and then successively Lawn House and Holly Hill, their large houses in Hampstead, with his students and colleagues, many of whom became her own friends. They had a wide circle of friends in the media, in music, and especially in opera, which he enjoyed intensely. A sudden visit to Covent Garden or Glyndebourne was one of the joys of his University College days. His wife collaborated in his later writings, and maintained a strong interest in birth control and in the environment.

Medawar was tall, physically strong (an excellent cricketer), with a voice which could hold a lecture theatre in suspense or reassure a doubting student. Always accessible and open to argument, he had no doubts about his own capacity: sitting at his typewriter in University College, cigarette in his mouth, he told James Gowans that 'It takes an effort to write undying prose'. His books are lucid and beautifully written.

He was elected a fellow of the Royal Society (1949), appointed CBE (1958) and CH (1972), knighted (1965), and admitted to the Order of Merit (1981). He became an honorary FBA in 1981. He was an honorary fellow of many colleges and was awarded numerous honorary degrees.

During his last fifteen years at the clinical research centre at Harrow he was partially paralysed from a stroke suffered in 1969, while reading the lesson in Exeter Cathedral at the British Association for the Advancement of Science (of which he was president in 1968–9), but his ideas continued to flow, and he both inspired and received support from devoted colleagues. He suffered several more strokes and eventually died from one, 2 October 1987, in the Royal Free Hospital, London.

[P. B. Medawar, *Memoir of a Thinking Radish*, 1986; N. A. Mitchison in *Biographical Memoirs of Fellows of the Royal Society*, vol. xxxv, 1990; personal knowledge.]

AVRION MITCHISON

MEIGGS, RUSSELL (1902–1989), ancient historian, was born 20 October 1902 in Balham, London, the only son and younger child of William Herrick Meiggs, of no fixed occupation but who described himself on his son's birth certificate as 'general merchant', and his wife, Mary Gertrude May, of Brantham, Suffolk. William Meiggs abandoned his family when his children were young, and they were brought up in great poverty. Russell Meiggs was educated at Christ's Hospital and Keble College, Oxford, taking first classes in both classical honour moderations (1923) and *literae humaniores* (1925). He then began to work on Ostia, the ancient port of Rome, as Pelham student at the British School at Rome. On his return he taught at his old school for two years; then in 1928 he was elected to a tutorship at his former college, becoming a fellow in 1930 and dean in 1935.

This smooth progress was interrupted when, in 1939, Meiggs left Keble and became a fellow of Balliol College, Oxford. Balliol's classical teaching had declined alarmingly, and Meiggs later described his move as 'like a First Division team needing to bring in a goalkeeper from a Third Division side'. He remained at Balliol until his retirement in 1970 and became profoundly identified with the college. During this period he was university lecturer in ancient history.

For many years he published little. He lavished his great energies on teaching, college activities, and that wide range of contacts which often enabled him to place a pupil. It was typical of his attitude to scholarship that he put so much energy into co-operative ventures and the revision of standard works. In 1951, with Antony Andrewes, he published a thoroughly revised version of Sir George *Hill's *Sources for Greek*

History (1897). He also revised the *History of Greece* by J. B. *Bury (third edition, 1951; fourth edition, 1975). *Roman Ostia* (1960, revised edition, 1973), his first major book, sprang from thirty-five years of work and reflection. It combines mastery of the evidence with a synthesis of archaeology, social history, economics, and religion, which goes far beyond most local histories. It anticipates interests which historians were to find increasingly central in the next thirty years. Meiggs was elected FBA in 1961. In 1969 he edited *A Selection of Greek Historical Inscriptions* with David M. Lewis. In 1972 appeared his second main work, *The Athenian Empire*. It handled the complex and controversial evidence without the violent disagreements which had infected that area of scholarship, and the book is almost surprisingly cool. The mastery of detail is impressive; the work is a judicious account of the views of its period.

The later years of Meiggs's retirement were darkened by increasing ill health, immobility, and, at the end, loss of sight. With great courage he battled to finish *Trees and Timber in the Ancient Mediterranean World* (1982). Meiggs had served in the war as chief labour officer in the Ministry of Supply, home timber production, and had published *Home Timber Production 1939–1945* (1949). His last major work was a pioneering one on a fundamental feature of ancient society: all the uses of timber and the history of forestation of the Mediterranean area. The work displayed so high a level of technical expertise that most classical scholars were daunted, and disappointingly few reviews appeared. It points forward to interests which are increasingly attracting historians. Meiggs continued to talk of finishing his long projected and much desired book on Herodotus, but ill health prevented him.

Meiggs was one of the great Oxford tutors. Amid growing specialization he taught both Greek and Roman history; he was an authority on Greek epigraphy who worked closely with archaeologists. His striking exterior, the mane of hair, the Aztec profile apparently hewn from some hard wood, the long shorts, and the uniquely shaped grey flannel trousers, made him a magnet for the cameras of tourists, especially as he tramped to and from his allotment with spade and wheelbarrow. His manner, much imitated, was no less individual. Challenging questions were accompanied with a piercing gaze under eyebrows of matchless bushiness, and his rather ferocious geniality loved to disconcert. In tutorials he liked pupils to put up a fight. Slipshod argument or carelessness over details did not pass unmauled, but he never had a 'line' for pupils to follow, nor a narrow or exclusive conception of history.

He suffered all his life from the alternation of periods of great elation with others of crippling depression. Physically he was robust and Spartan, famous for rolling in the snow in his bathing costume. He was a gardener, a Christian, a family man; quick to assess people and usually right about them. He did not aspire to promotion, and he published his first important book at the age of fifty-eight, giving his energies without reservation to pupils and college; British universities will see few such careers hereafter. He went his own way, choosing widely different subjects to work on, without regard to fashion.

In some ways a traditionalist, he welcomed the coming of co-education to Balliol, and he sympathized with the rebellious students of 1968. From 1945 to 1969 he was praefectus of Holywell Manor, the annexe of the college in which most students from overseas lived. He had many connections in North America and was frequently a visiting professor at Swarthmore.

Meiggs married in December 1941 the historian Pauline Gregg, daughter of Thomas James Nathaniel Gregg, Post Office sorter. They had two daughters. Meiggs died 24 June 1989 at his home in Garsington.

[Sir Kenneth Dover in *Proceedings* of the British Academy, vol. lxxx, 1991; private information; personal knowledge.]   JASPER GRIFFIN

MERCER, Joseph (1914–1990), footballer and football manager, was born 9 August 1914 at 32 Queen Street, Ellesmere Port, Wirral, Cheshire, the eldest in the family of three boys and one girl of Joseph Powell Mercer, professional footballer, of Ellesmere Port, and his wife, Ethel Breeze. He was educated at Cambridge Road School and John Street Senior Mixed School, Ellesmere Port, playing football for the Cheshire schools' team. His father, a former Nottingham Forest player, was wounded in World War I, and became a bricklayer. He died when Mercer was twelve. After leaving school, Mercer worked for Shell in a variety of unskilled jobs, and played football first for the village of Elton Green and the Shell Mex team, and later for Ellesmere Port. Spotted at Elton Green by an Everton scout, he played for Everton as an amateur for two years before signing on as a professional in 1931. He became a regular first-team player during the 1935–6 season as a wing-half, and got his first England cap in 1938. He appeared five times for England during the 1938–9 season, in which Everton won the League championship. In September 1939 Mercer joined the army after (Sir) Stanley *Rous, secretary of the Football Association, had circularized footballers urging them to join the Army Physical Training Corps, so that they would keep fit. He became a sergeant-instructor, and ended the war as a sergeant-major. He played in twenty-seven wartime internationals, captaining England on several occasions, and also played for Aldershot.

After the war he was unhappy at Everton, and suffered from knee trouble. He was contemplating retirement in order to devote himself to running a grocery business in Wallasey when Arsenal offered £7,000 for him in November 1946. He agreed to go on condition that he could live and train in Liverpool, and he continued to do so throughout his eight years with Arsenal. He became a half-back, and went on to captain Arsenal to two League championships, in 1948 and 1953, and to success in the FA Cup Final against Liverpool in 1950, a few days after being voted Footballer of the Year. In April 1954 he broke his leg, playing against Liverpool, and retired.

For the next twenty years Mercer pursued a successful career as a football manager. He became manager of Sheffield United, who were relegated to the second division at the end of his first season there, in 1955—an inauspicious start. In December 1958 he replaced Eric Houghton as manager of Aston Villa, who were also relegated at the end of the season. But, under his management, Aston Villa came top of the second division in the 1959–60 season, and won the League cup in 1961. Mercer had a nervous breakdown in 1964, after a disappointing season when the club came nineteenth in the League championship, and he resigned.

He was out of football for fourteen months before becoming manager of Manchester City in 1965. He brought in Malcolm Allison as assistant manager and coach, and for five seasons this was a highly successful partnership. Manchester City came top of the second division in Mercer's first season there, won the League championship in 1968 and the FA cup in 1969, and in 1970 won both the League cup and the European Cup-winners' cup, beating the Polish team, Gornik Zabrze, 2–1 in the final. It was the first English club to win a domestic and a European trophy in the same season. Mercer's relationship with Allison soured after Allison, ambitious for promotion, became involved in boardroom intrigues, and Mercer left in 1972 to become manager of Coventry City. In May 1974, after the resignation of Sir Alf Ramsey, the England manager, Mercer agreed to be caretaker manager for the rest of the season. He was in charge for seven matches, with a record of three wins, three draws, and one loss. He was appointed OBE in 1976.

Mercer was regarded as the greatest wing-half of his generation, and had the war not interrupted his career he would have won many more England caps. As a manager, his greatest successes were with Manchester City, previously overshadowed by their neighbours and rivals, Manchester United. He was a popular manager,

much loved for his amiable manner and his big smile. He was famous for his bandy legs and was often mistaken for the jockey Joe Mercer.

In 1942 he married Norah Fanny, daughter of Albert Edward Dyson, provision merchant. They had one son. Mercer died 9 August 1990 in Manchester.

[*Independent*, 11 August 1990; Joe Mercer, *The Great Ones*, 1964; Eric Thornton, *Manchester City*, 1969; Andrew Ward, *The Manchester City Story*, 1984.]

ANNE PIMLOTT BAKER

MERRISON, SIR **Alexander Walter** (1924–1989), nuclear physicist, was born 20 March 1924 in Wood Green, London, the only child of Henry Walter Merrison, fitter's mate, who rose to be service manager in the local gas board and a respected chairman of the Tottenham group of hospitals, and his wife, Violet Henrietta Mortimer, from Ipswich. 'Alec' attended Tottenham Grammar School and Enfield Grammar School. He went to King's College, London, where he graduated in physics in 1944, after which he was 'placed' on wartime radar at the Signals Research and Development Establishment at Christchurch. After two years he requested transfer to the Atomic Energy Research Establishment at Harwell (1946). There he helped to equip an electron accelerator to produce short pulses of neutrons, a new technique for probing the structure of matter, the subject on which he was to publish his first papers.

In 1951 Merrison accepted a lectureship at the University of Liverpool, where the physicists were constructing a proton cyclotron large enough to produce the newly discovered 'pi-mesons', the particles then thought to be responsible for binding together the atomic nucleus. Having assisted in the completion of the machine, he was awarded a Ph.D. in 1957 for his first experiments on the interaction of pi-mesons with nuclear matter. From that time on he was a dedicated particle physicist. He had a gift for designing clean experiments, creating new equipment and making it work properly, and inspiring physicists and engineers to work together hard but amicably. He also became an inspiring teacher, able to communicate his bubbling enthusiasm to his students. From 1957 to 1960 he was at CERN, the newly established European accelerator laboratory near Geneva. Together with G. Fidecaro he confirmed that the weak nuclear force responsible for radioactivity was a 'universal interaction'. In 1960 he returned to Liverpool as professor of experimental physics, but he remained closely connected with CERN for the rest of his life.

In 1962 Merrison was engaged by the Science Research Council (SRC) to build an electron synchotron at Daresbury in Cheshire, but was allowed to retain his chair. The machine was finished on time and on budget, and worked straight away. The Daresbury laboratory quickly became an important centre of research in particle and radiation physics and as its director he began to take an active part in policy matters at the SRC and elsewhere. He was a member of the government's Council for Scientific Policy (1967–72). Needing a change of home and work when his first wife died in 1968, he gladly accepted the vice-chancellorship of the University of Bristol (where the pi-mesons had originally been discovered). He was elected FRS in 1969.

Merrison arrived in Bristol in 1969 to find the university in confrontational turmoil and its academic quality depleted. He quickly gained the confidence of staff and students alike, made new academic appointments, and introduced far-reaching reforms of the senate, administration, and personnel management. He personally prepared a tough and detailed plan of action when faced with the financial cuts of 1981. It was unavoidably controversial, and difficult negotiations in the senate followed. Nevertheless, he eventually succeeded in his objective. Soon after becoming vice-chancellor, Merrison accepted a series of chairmanships of important government committees. The first was the committee of inquiry into the design and erection of box girder bridges (1970–3), which set new worldwide standards (the Merrison rules) for the design of such bridges. He was knighted in 1976 and became an honorary fellow of the Institution of Structural Engineers in 1981. Bristol gave him an honorary LL D in 1971 and he had six other honorary degrees. He also chaired the committee of inquiry into the regulation of the medical profession (1972–5). He was vice-chairman of the South West Regional Health Authority and was a popular choice to chair the royal commission on the National Health Service when it was appointed in 1976. This reviewed the entire service and in 1979 issued a report with suggestions about how it could be improved. Many of the proposals were gradually implemented by administrative action in the ensuing years.

Merrison played a full part in the committee of vice-chancellors and principals, being its chairman in 1979–81. During this time he had to deal with the government's new policy of high fees for overseas students. He became chairman of the advisory board for the research councils (1979–83), where he supervised the planning of the nation's basic research in the universities and research council laboratories and criticized the government's cuts. He was a devoted European, but never forgot the abiding value of the Commonwealth. He was president of the council of CERN in 1982–5, and simultaneously (1982–3) chairman of the council of the Association of Commonwealth Universities. At home he was elected president of the Institute of Physics (1984–6). He retired from the Bristol vice-chancellorship in 1984.

He was sought after by business for technological prowess as much as administrative flair. He became chairman of the Bristol Regional Board, and director of Lloyds Bank (1986–9) and of the Western Provident Association (1985–9), thereby extending his interests in medicine. He was a director of the Bristol Waterworks Company from 1984. Business was perhaps not his most natural habitat, but he threw himself into these new pursuits with characteristic zeal and open-minded curiosity. He became a governor in 1969, then chairman (1971–87), of the Bristol Old Vic, not only satisfying his love for the theatre but skilfully guiding it through its redevelopment programme. He was a director of the Bristol *Evening Post* (1979–89), was appointed deputy lieutenant of the county of Avon (1974), and served as high sheriff (1986–7).

Merrison was stockily built, five feet ten inches in height, with clear blue eyes and high cheek-bones. His voice became boisterous when he was excited. In 1948 he married Beryl Glencora (died 1968), daughter of Frank Bruce Le Marquand, a brewer in Jersey. They had two sons. In 1970 he married Maureen Michèle Barry, a lecturer in the history department at Bristol and daughter of John Michael Barry, entertainer. They had a daughter and a son. Their greatest pleasure was to entertain friends and colleagues at Maes-y-Ffyn, their farmhouse in the Llanthony valley, and, after Merrison's retirement, at Hinton Blewett, near Bristol. Merrison died in Bristol 19 February 1989.

[Private information; personal knowledge.]

BRIAN FLOWERS

MIDDLEDITCH, Edward Charles (1923–1987), painter, was born 23 March 1923 at 1 Park Avenue, Chelmsford, Essex, the younger son and second of three children of Charles Henry Middleditch, cabinet-maker and bat trimmer, and his wife, Esme Buckley. In the mid-1920s the family moved to the St Anne's district of Nottingham, where Edward went to Mundella School, but they returned to Chelmsford in 1939, where he attended King Edward VI Grammar School.

On leaving school he worked in an office until he joined the army in 1942, and two years later he was commissioned in the Middlesex Regiment, eventually reaching the rank of captain. He saw active service in Normandy during the winter campaign of 1944–5, and was wounded fighting in the Ardennes in 1945, when he was awarded the MC. His interest in art was first marked by the purchase, when on leave in Paris, of a book on Goya. After convalescence in

England he was posted to Burma, arriving in India in August 1945. He was then sent to West Africa and was invalided home from Nigeria in 1947 with malaria, and demobilized.

In 1948 he attended classes in painting and drawing at the Regent Street Polytechnic. With an ex-serviceman's grant he was accepted by the painting department of the Royal College of Art in September of that year, and he graduated in 1952. The strongest influences on him were (A. J.) Ruskin *Spear, who taught him to admire and to some degree emulate the sombre tones of Walter *Sickert, and (F.) John *Minton, who introduced him to modern French art. His friends and contemporaries at the RCA included Derrick Greaves, John Bratby, Jack Smith, and Malcolm Hughes.

In 1950 he exhibited and sold an oil painting, 'Trafalgar Square', at the Royal Academy, and the following year he showed views of the Thames in the exhibition 'Artists of Fame and Promise' at the Leicester Galleries. His pictures in the 'Young Contemporaries' exhibition of 1952 attracted the attention of John Berger, who wrote in the *New Statesman and Nation* (19 January 1952) that they were 'the most outstanding of all' in the exhibition. His stark picture 'Baby' (1952) was bought by the Arts Council, and his 'Crowd, Earls Court' (1954) reflected the austere mood of the time. Although, through friendship, he was associated with the group labelled 'Kitchen Sink Painters' by David Sylvester in *Encounter*, few of Middleditch's paintings, then or later, were of domestic subjects. Rather, his melancholy paintings (such as 'Sheffield Weir II', which was bought for the Tate Gallery from his first one-man exhibition in March 1954 at Helen Lessore's Beaux Arts Gallery), were mostly of landscape and cityscape. Characteristic of this period is the dark, bleak, elegiac 'Dead Chicken in a Stream' (1955, Tate Gallery).

In 1955 he was included in 'Giovani Pittori', an exhibition which travelled from Rome to Paris under the auspices of the Congrès pour la Liberté de la Culture, and won second prize in the *Daily Express* Young Artists exhibition. With Bratby, Greaves, and Smith he represented Britain at the twenty-eighth Venice Biennale in 1956. He visited Spain for the first time in 1957, and the Middleditch and Greaves families then began to share a large house in Buckinghamshire.

He taught at Chelsea School of Art from 1958 until 1963, and at Regent Street Polytechnic, the Cambridge School of Art, and St Martin's School of Art during the 1960s. In 1962 he was awarded a Gulbenkian Foundation scholarship. He moved to Boxford, Suffolk, and was appointed head of the department of fine art at Norwich School of Art in 1964. A gifted teacher and administrator, he had a profound influence on students. On his retirement in 1984 he became in 1985 keeper of the Royal Academy Schools, having been elected ARA in 1968 and RA in 1973.

From the 1960s Middleditch frequently painted flowers, and over the years the mood and colour of his painting lightened and became more decorative, without losing its serious commitment to the evocation of nature. At Norwich he made many silk-screen prints, and in 1981 he published *Books and Folios, Screenprints by Derrick Greaves, Robert Medley and Edward Middleditch*.

Middleditch dressed informally; his rounded forehead was furrowed under a widow's peak of hair, and deep creases from the side of his nose to his mouth were evidence, perhaps, of the injuries and illnesses he had suffered. In 1947 he married Jean Kathleen (died 1979), a student of engraving, daughter of Frank Joseph Thomas Whitehouse, assistant controller in the London and North-Eastern Railway. They had one daughter. Ill health forced Middleditch to retire as keeper of the Royal Academy in 1986, and he died in Chelmsford 29 July 1987, at the time of his major retrospective exhibition, mounted by the South Bank Centre, London.

[Lynda Morris, *Edward Middleditch: the South Bank Centre*, 1987–8; private information.] ALAN WINDSOR

MILES, SIR (**Arnold**) **Ashley** (1904–1988), microbiologist, was born 20 March 1904 in York, the second of three children and only son of Harry Miles, draper, and his wife, Kate Elizabeth Hindley. At Bootham School in York, a Quaker foundation that he remembered with great affection, he received a good grounding both in scientific subjects and literature. Thence he gained an exhibition to King's College, Cambridge, where his leanings towards pathology and bacteriology were encouraged by Henry Roy Dean, the professor of pathology, and Everitt G. D. Murray. He obtained second classes in both parts of the natural sciences tripos (1924 and 1925). After qualifying in medicine (MRCS, LRCP, 1928) at St Bartholomew's Hospital, Miles gave a remarkable foretaste of his academic abilities by obtaining in 1929 membership of the Royal College of Physicians while still a house physician (FRCP, 1937).

In 1929 he was appointed demonstrator at the London School of Hygiene and Tropical Medicine; this step was decisive in shaping his future career as a microbiologist with a strong interest in immunity to infection. His first researches, on the antigens of *Brucella*, were continued, in association with N. W. Pirie, when he returned two years later to Cambridge, as a demonstrator. In 1935 he became reader in bacteriology at the British Postgraduate Medical School, Hammersmith, and then, at the early age of thirty-three, was appointed in 1937 to the chair of bacteriology at University College Hospital medical school. Soon afterwards the outbreak of war brought many new responsibilities and difficulties. As well as continuing his professorial duties, Miles was a sector pathologist in the Emergency Medical Services, acting director of the Graham Medical Research Laboratories, and director of the Medical Research Council's wound infection unit in Birmingham. This last proved the most important post of all, for his researches on wound infections in collaboration with R. E. O. Williams resulted in effective recommendations for their control in surgical, industrial, and military contexts.

After the war Miles was appointed in 1946 deputy director of the National Institute for Medical Research and head of its department of biological standards, and took a prominent part in the work of the relevant national and international organizations. His own researches, some of which were published in collaboration with his wife, now centred on the mechanisms of inflammation and immunity.

In 1952 he was appointed director of the Lister Institute of Preventive Medicine, a private organization funded by endowments, grants, and the manufacture and sale of vaccines and antisera; it also housed several Medical Research Council units. In the same year he became MD and professor of experimental pathology in the University of London. In addition to directing these manifold activities and continuing his own investigative work, Miles characteristically shouldered other burdens, some of which alone would have occupied most of the time of lesser men. This capacity for work on a heroic scale, combined with his clear and incisive thinking, made him much in demand on boards and committees. He was elected a fellow of the Royal Society in 1961 and served for five years both as a vice-president and as biological secretary. His command of written English was superb; and as well as publishing more than 140 papers on his own work, he was joint editor, with Sir Graham S. *Wilson, of no fewer than five editions of *Topley and Wilson's Principles of Bacteriology and Immunity*.

After his official retirement from the Lister in 1971, he spent four years on laboratory studies at the Clinical Research Centre, after which he was invited in 1976 to become deputy director of the department of medical microbiology at the London Hospital Medical College. His last few years were marred by the results of a disabling stroke, despite which he continued to work until a few months before his death.

Miles's contributions to biomedical science were recognized by his appointment as CBE (1953) and a knighthood (1966); and by honorary fellowships of the Royal College of Pathologists

(1969); King's College, Cambridge (1972); the Institute of Biology (1975); the Infectious Diseases Society of America (1979); and the Royal Society of Medicine (1981). He also received a number of honorary memberships of learned societies and an honorary D.Sc. from the University of Newcastle upon Tyne (1969).

In addition to his other attainments, Miles had a wide knowledge of literature and music, and was an accomplished pianist. His ability to converse knowledgeably on these and other topics, including for example botany and the detailed anatomy of the Lake District, made him a delightful companion. His formidable intellectual capacity, set off by his large frame and imposing presence, could be daunting to students and junior staff; but he was a kindly person, who was intolerant only of those who contravened his own standards of personal and scientific integrity.

In 1930 he married a medical laboratory technician, Ellen Marguerite (died January 1988), daughter of Harald Dahl, a Norwegian shipbroker, of Cardiff, and his French wife, Sofie Magdalene Hesselberg. Ellen was the sister of the writer Roald *Dahl. They had no children. Miles died 11 February 1988 at his home in Hampstead.

[A. Neuberger in *Biographical Memoirs of Fellows of the Royal Society*, vol. xxxv, 1990; personal knowledge.]
LESLIE COLLIER

MILFORD, (Theodore) Richard (1895–1987), clergyman, liberal theologian, and first chairman of Oxfam, was born 10 June 1895 at Yockleton Hall in Shropshire, the eldest of three sons (there were no daughters) of Robert Theodore Milford, schoolmaster, and his wife, Elspeth Barter, granddaughter of George *Moberly, bishop of Salisbury. Both sides of his family contained notable academics and clerics. Milford went to Clifton College, where the traditional classical education was enhanced by a strong interest in music, unusual at that time. When World War I broke out in 1914 Milford volunteered for the army and was posted to the 19th Royal Fusiliers and then (1915–19) commissioned in the Oxford and Buckinghamshire Light Infantry, with whom he saw active service in Mesopotamia, with two spells of leave in India. He was sent to Cairo to train for the Royal Flying Corps in 1918, but was invalided home in 1919.

In 1919 he went to Magdalen College, Oxford, where he took a first in *literae humaniores* in 1921. His connection there with the Student Christian Movement led him to India, where he taught at Alwaye College in Travancore (1921–3) and St John's College, Agra (1923–4), with a two-year spell in Liverpool as local SCM secretary (1924–6) and a year at Westcott House (1930–1),

Cambridge, training for ordination. He was made priest in Lucknow, India, in 1934.

When he returned to England in 1935 he worked again for the SCM (until 1938), stimulating many young minds as the study secretary. At the same time (1935–7) he was a curate at All Hallows, Lombard Street, London. In 1938 he became vicar of St Mary's, the Oxford University church, where he stayed until 1947. Here a group, the Colloquy, gathered round him to discusss philosophical and theological topics. His rigorous logical mind and fearless questioning had a lasting influence on its members, many of whom attained later distinction.

Perhaps his most important contribution at this time was the part he played in the founding of Oxfam. Dick (he was never known by any other name) Milford and a few others met in the Old Library at St Mary's on 5 October 1942, in response to the idea brought to him by Henry Gillett, a Quaker, that in spite of the blockade something should be done to help the victims of starvation in Greece. The result was the foundation of the Oxford Committee for Famine Relief, later known as Oxfam. Many obstacles had to be overcome to get the government to agree to this idea. He remained chairman until 1947, returned for a second period from 1960 to 1965, and continued taking an active interest until his death.

In 1947 he was appointed canon and chancellor of Lincoln Cathedral, with special responsibility for religious education in the diocese, including the Scholae Cancellarii, the theological college at which successive ordinands profited from his pithy teaching. In 1958 Milford became master of the Temple. Here the social and intellectual climate was in total contrast to all that had gone before and he found himself at times in conflict with the benchers, notably in 1960 when he appeared for the defence in the Crown prosecution unsuccessfully brought under the obscenity laws against the publishers of the unexpurgated edition of *Lady Chatterley's Lover*, by D. H. *Lawrence, which had been banned since 1928. These London years also gave further scope for a varied ministry of preaching and counselling. In 1968 he retired to Shaftesbury, where his activities included running a group studying Teilhard de Chardin, with whose evolutionary philosophy and devotional intensity he found himself very much in sympathy.

Milford's influence was out of all proportion to his published work. *Foolishness to the Greeks* (1953), based on talks for a university mission, illustrates his style of Christian apologetic; *The Valley of Decision* (1961), the result of a working party of the British Council of Churches, explores the moral dilemma posed by atomic weapons; articles, broadcasts, and addresses

make up the rest except for a little book of verse (*Belated Harvest*, 1978) and some early memoirs published privately in his old age.

Milford was a handsome and gifted man with a first-class mind, dry wit, boundless intellectual curiosity which never left him, and wide interests including chess, music, and sailing. Though discriminating, he was a man of simple tastes. In 1932 he married Nancy Dickens Bourchier, daughter of Ernest Hawksley, solicitor, and great-grandaughter of Charles *Dickens; they had two daughters. After the death of his first wife in 1936, he married in 1937 Margaret Nowell Smith, daughter of Nowell Charles Smith, headmaster of Sherborne and former fellow of New College, Oxford. They had a son, who died in infancy, and two daughters. Milford died in Shaftesbury 19 January 1987.

[Information from the family; personal knowledge.]
OLIVER TOMKINS

MILLAR, Frederick Robert Hoyer, first BARON INCHYRA (1900–1989), diplomat and Foreign Office official, was born 6 June 1900 in Montrose, the third son and youngest of three children of Robert Hoyer Millar, timber merchant, of Blair castle, Culross, Fife, and his wife Alice Anne Combe, daughter of Dr James Simson. Frederick (known as Derick) was educated at Wellington College and New College, Oxford, where he took a second-class honours degree in modern history in 1922 and an MA in 1954 on his election as an honorary fellow of the college. He played rugby for the university without, however, getting a blue.

In 1922 he was an honorary attaché at the British embassy in Brussels. In the following year he entered the Diplomatic Service as a third secretary, first at Berlin and then in Paris. He returned to the Foreign Office in 1928 and moved to Cairo as second secretary in 1930. He returned to London in 1934 as assistant private secretary to the secretary of state and, since there was then no personnel department, was responsible for dealing with all appointments in the Foreign Office and Diplomatic Service. Millar managed this task with sympathy and skill. His judgement of men and events was eminently sound.

In 1939 he went to Washington as a first secretary and head of Chancery. It was a critical time. Both the ambassador and his minister were Christian Scientists and, during the final illness of the ambassador, the eleventh Marquess of *Lothian, Millar was in a difficult position. He also had to deal with the rapid build-up of the British departmental and military representation in Washington and the initial problems of the ambassadorship of the first Earl of *Halifax. He became counsellor in 1941 and was secretary of the British civil secretariat in Washington in 1943–4. His administrative skills and his Washington connections served him in good stead in this testing period.

In 1944 he became counsellor and in 1947 assistant under-secretary in the Foreign Office. He returned to Washington as minister in 1948. He played an important part in the establishment and early years of NATO, becoming in 1950 its UK deputy and in 1952 the permanent representative on the NATO council. In 1953 he was appointed UK high commissioner in Germany, where he had an influential role during the transition from Allied control to diplomatic recognition, and in 1955 he became the first postwar ambassador at Bonn.

An excellent administrator and effective operator in the Foreign Service, in 1957 he returned to the Foreign Office as permanent under-secretary of state and head of the Diplomatic Service, at a time when the Foreign Service had been badly shaken and divided by the Suez crisis. His robust but sympathetic manner and his administrative ability soon restored morale and made him an outstanding and popular head of the service. He retired in 1961, when he was created a hereditary peer as Baron Inchyra. He took his title from Inchyra House, his Perthshire home, and sat on the cross-benches. He was king-at-arms of the Order of St Michael and St George, and became a member of the Queen's Body Guard for Scotland. He was also a governor of Wellington College for many years.

On his retirement from the Foreign Service he accepted a number of appointments in banking, finance, industry, and insurance. He was also chairman of the British Red Cross and of the Anglo-Netherlands Society in London. In between these activities and in his final retirement he energetically pursued his favourite sport of shooting. He was appointed CVO (1938), CMG (1939), KCMG (1949), and GCMG (1956).

In appearance Inchyra was very tall and rather portly with a florid complexion and a bald head. He generally moved slowly in a dignified manner. He was a good companion, and had been a popular figure in Oxford and a member of the Bullingdon Club.

In 1931 he married (Anna Judith) Elizabeth ('Bunchie'), daughter of Reneke de Marees van Swinderen, the Netherlands minister in London, and his American wife. Bunchie was a strong and attractive character and a great help to her husband in his career. There were two sons and two daughters of the marriage. In April 1989 Inchyra was incapacitated by a massive stroke, but lingered on until he died at the Royal Infirmary, Perth, 16 October 1989. He was

succeeded in the barony by his elder son, Robert Charles Reneke Hoyer Millar (born 1935).

[Private information; personal knowledge.]

SHERFIELD

MILLER, James (1915–1989), songwriter, singer, folk-song revivalist, and dramatist. [See MACCOLL, EWAN.]

MITCHELL, Denis Holden (1911–1990), television and radio producer, was born 1 August 1911 in Cheadle, Cheshire, the younger child and only son of Ernest George Mitchell, Congregational minister, and his wife, Ethel Alderson. The family went to South Africa when he was six. When he was ten his mother returned with him to Britain to arrange his education and provide him with a home. He attended a Congregational public school in Caversham, Surrey, where he twice failed his matriculation examination.

He shared his mother's enthusiasm for drama, and as a teenager his temporary work included the carrying of spears at the Old Vic theatre. At the age of eighteen he was told by his father that he must return with his mother to South Africa, where he was to stay until 1949. His first work was as a bank clerk, and during his holidays he appeared as an actor in local stage productions, as well as acting and writing radio scripts for the South African Broadcasting Corporation.

On the outbreak of war Mitchell volunteered for service in the South African artillery, but because of his knowledge of drama and radio he was soon transferred to the entertainment unit of the Union Defence Force, being promoted to the rank of captain and placed in command of its operation in the Middle East and Italy. One of the members of his unit was Sidney *James.

At the end of the war he worked briefly for a local newspaper, and then joined the staff of the South African Broadcasting Corporation. His programme work covered a wide range, but his main concern, he insisted, was with 'real people and real voices', and his own personality, quiet and sympathetic, explains why no interviewer has extracted more by saying less. His passion for drama had already vanished, never to return.

On the advice of the BBC features producer, D. G. *Bridson, who had visited South Africa, he returned to Britain in 1949 and in 1950 became the BBC's features producer in Manchester, near to his birthplace. Most of his programmes were based on interviews with people whose voices were rarely heard: the homeless, nurses, the unemployed, and criminals. He always walked alone, often at night, usually finding people by chance. At a time when cameras and microphones were mainly studio-based, he worked out in the streets, recording people in their own surroundings.

In 1955 he was briefly attached to the BBC Television Service in London, where he made his first documentary film, about teenagers, which gained an award at the Brussels Experimental Film Festival. On his return to Manchester in 1956 he continued to make television documentaries, notably *Morning in the Streets* (1959), which won both the Prix Italia and an award of the Society of Film and Television Arts. He joined the Television Service at Shepherd's Bush in 1959, continuing his own style with *Soho Story*, about a London busker, but he also returned to Africa to make a series, *The Wind of Change*, and in 1961 he produced *Chicago*, the story of a city 'seen through the eyes of the people who live there, from the very poor to the extremely rich' (Denis Mitchell's notes proposing the film).

He left the BBC in 1962, and the following year formed Denis Mitchell Films Ltd., a small company which survived until his death. It made documentaries for many organizations, including ATV, the BBC, Rediffusion, Southern Television, and Channel 4. Much of his most personal work was made for Granada Television, based again in Manchester, and his subjects (especially in the series *This England*, 1964–7) were usually 'ordinary folk'; but his interviewing technique was equally effective in *Private Lives* (1972–3), in which the subjects came from many classes of society. A programme which he always regarded as one of his best was a portrait of Quentin Crisp. Towards the end of his life he became increasingly keen on making very short programmes, lasting between five and ten minutes, whose subjects were inevitably men and women in various walks of life. He made over 100 documentaries, and in 1975 received the SFTA's Desmond Davis award for his outstanding talent.

Mitchell was of medium height, with hazel eyes and brown hair; he was gentle and softly spoken, and frequently smiling. In 1938 he married in Durban Dorothea ('Sally'), daughter of William Arthur Bates, telegraphic engineer in the Post Office. They had two daughters, the younger of whom died in 1970. His first marriage was dissolved in South Africa in 1948, and in 1951 he married Betty Annie, a BBC secretary and the daughter of a transport inspector, Albert Elmer Horne. They had one son. His second marriage was dissolved in 1965, and in the same year he married (Norah) Linda, who had been his secretary in the BBC, the daughter of John Hastings Webster, chartered accountant. They were to live in the Norfolk countryside, the location of his film *Never and Always* (1977), which expressed its social history as seen by the local people. Mitchell died 30 September 1990 at his home in Great Massingham, Norfolk

(although his death certificate gives 1 October as the day of death).

[Broadcasting, Entertainment, Cinematograph, and Theatre Union history project, National Film and Television Archive, 21 Stephen Street, London; private information; personal knowledge.]

NORMAN SWALLOW

MITCHELL, Joseph Stanley (1909–1987), radiotherapist and physicist, was born in Birmingham 22 July 1909, the eldest of the three children and only son of Joseph Brown Mitchell, schoolteacher, and his wife, Ethel Maud Mary Arnold, also a schoolteacher. He won an open scholarship to King Edward VI High School, Birmingham, where he won a state scholarship, which he took up at Birmingham University in 1926, studying preclinical subjects. Two years later he won a scholarship to St John's College, Cambridge, where he read natural sciences and obtained first classes in both parts of the tripos (1930 and 1931).

He completed his clinical training in Birmingham, qualifying MB, B.Chir. (Cambridge) in 1934, and served as a house officer at Birmingham General Hospital. He returned to Cambridge to study for his Ph.D. (1937) on the physics of radiation. He held first an Elmore research studentship and then a Beit memorial fellowship. In 1936 he was elected to a fellowship of St John's College, which he held until his death. He took up the post of radiological officer at the Christie Hospital and Holt Radium Institute in Manchester (1937–8) and in 1938 was appointed assistant in research to the regius professor of physic at Cambridge, J. A. *Ryle.

In 1939 he became radiotherapist to the Emergency Medical Service in Cambridge and in 1944 was selected to go to Chalk River, Montreal, Canada, to take charge of medical investigations at the National Research Council laboratory, where the joint British and Canadian Atomic Energy Project was installed. He later described demanding a foot of concrete to be laid over the entire floor of the laboratory to protect the workers from the spilled radiation. He continued studies on the biological effects of radiation and was the first to realize the potential value of the gamma-emitting radiation of the isotope ^{60}Cobalt in the treatment of cancer.

After World War II Mitchell was elected to the new Cambridge chair of radiotherapeutics in 1946 and became the director of the radiotherapeutic centre at Addenbrooke's Hospital, Cambridge. He became internationally known for his work on the treatment of cancer by irradiation. He also tried to improve cancer treatment with a cancer-seeking drug (Synkavit) to carry radioactivity to cancer cells, but had limited success. The acme of his academic career came with his appointment as regius professor of physic at Cambridge in 1957. He set about establishing a postgraduate medical school. The first of the clinical chairs (medicine) was set up in 1963 and surgery in 1965. When the new professor of medicine initiated steps towards a clinical school (opened in 1976), Mitchell gave it his wholehearted support from the outset, and in 1974 he made a generous offer to vacate the regius chair in 1975, so that a new regius professor of physic could be in post before the clinical school was due to open. He reverted to his previous chair of radiotherapeutics, retiring in 1976 but continuing his research and training of Ph.D. students. He wrote numerous articles and a few books, including *Studies in Radiotherapeutics* (1960).

His skills were recognized in 1952 by the Royal Society electing him to their fellowship. He was appointed CBE (1951) and MD (1957), and a fellow of the Faculty (later Royal College) of Radiologists (1954) and the Royal College of Physicians (1958). He became Dunham lecturer at Harvard (1958), Withering lecturer at Birmingham University (1958), and honorary D.Sc. of Birmingham (1958). He was also Pirogoff medalist of the USSR Academy of Sciences (1967), an honorary member of the German Roentgen Society (1967), Silvanus Thompson lecturer of the British Institute of Radiologists (1968), and a foreign fellow of the Indian National Academy of Sciences. In 1970 he was Linacre lecturer of St John's College, Cambridge, and was appointed honorary consultant to the Atomic Energy Authority.

Mitchell was a well-built man, a little portly in later years, and with a well developed moustache. Although in public he appeared somewhat dour, in private he had a ready sense of humour. Even in the heat of summer he always wore the waistcoat of his three-piece suit. He was kind and gentle, and showed immense compassion when treating his cancer patients. He had a German grandfather and spoke fluent German. He showed a great interest in the Anglo-German Medical Society and was president of the British section from 1959 to 1968. In 1934 he married Lilian Mary Buxton, MB, Ch.B., and he later helped her direct the outfitting business she inherited from her father, George Buxton. She devoted her life to supporting him and his research until she died in 1983. They had a son and a daughter. Mitchell died in Cambridge 22 February 1987.

[D. H. Marrian in *Biographical Memoirs of Fellows of the Royal Society*, vol. xxxiv, 1988; personal knowledge.]   IVOR H. MILLS

MOMIGLIANO, Arnaldo Dante (1908–1987), ancient historian, was born 5 September 1908 in Caraglio, near Cuneo, Italy, the only son and eldest of three children of Riccardo Salomone Momigliano, grain merchant, and his wife, Ilda Levi. His was a prominent Jewish intellectual family; his father and mother died in a concentration camp in World War II. He was educated at home, and from 1925 at Turin University, where he came under the influence of Gaetano De Sanctis in ancient history and Augusto Rostagni in Greek literature.

Immediately after graduating in 1929, he followed De Sanctis to Rome, where he joined the group of scholars employed on the *Enciclopedia Italiana*, for which he wrote over 230 articles, including the long and important 'Roma in età imperiale' (1936). At the same time, from the age of twenty-four he was teaching Greek history at Rome University as assistant and from 1932 as substitute for De Sanctis.

Despite his connections with De Sanctis and Benedetto Croce (both openly opposed to Fascism) in 1936 he won the *concorso* for the post of professor of Roman history at Turin University; his inaugural lecture (published posthumously in 1989) was devoted to 'The Concept of Peace in the Graeco-Roman World'. In September 1938 he was dismissed on racial grounds.

His second book, on the emperor Claudius (1932), had been favourably noticed by Hugh *Last, professor of Roman history at Oxford, who arranged for its translation into English (1934); he therefore wrote to Last, who applied on his behalf to the Society for the Protection of Science and Learning (founded to assist academic refugees), which responded with an invitation and a small grant for a year to continue his researches in Oxford. He arrived on 30 March 1939, and his wife and daughter followed shortly. In 1940 he was interned briefly as an 'enemy alien' on the Isle of Man; throughout the war the family lived in rented rooms, supported first by the Society, then by research grants from the Rockefeller Foundation arranged through the Oxford University Press. During this period he was preparing a major book on 'Liberty and Peace in the Ancient World' (later abandoned, although substantial fragments survive). He was the youngest (and only Italian) member of that remarkable group of refugee classical scholars who congregated in the library of the Ashmolean Museum, and who subsequently repaid their debt to Britain by transforming classical studies in the Anglo-Saxon world.

After the war Momigliano was reinstated as supernumerary professor at Turin in 1945. In 1947 he was appointed lecturer at Bristol University and in 1949 he was promoted to reader. In 1951 he moved to the chair of ancient history at University College London, where he remained until 1975. From 1964 he was also professor at the Scuola Normale Superiore of Pisa.

For many years he played an important part

on the editorial boards of the *Journal of Roman Studies*, *Rivista Storica Italiana*, and *History and Theory*. After retirement he was appointed an associate member of All Souls College, Oxford (1975–82), and from 1983 a visiting (later honorary) fellow at Peterhouse, Cambridge. From 1975 to his death he was Alexander White visiting professor at Chicago, where he spent a semester each year, and he also lectured widely throughout Europe and in Israel. The deaths of most of his family and childhood friends in concentration camps meant that his connections with Germany remained distant.

Momigliano's early work was in the tradition of Italian idealist and critical historical studies, and showed a firm grounding in classical philology. His first book was on the Hellenistic Jewish book of Maccabees (1930); after his biography of Claudius, he wrote a study of Philip of Macedon (1934). These were all highly professional works, distinguished by critical use of sources, sympathy with the subject, and a mastery of the extensive bibliography. By the time of his exile his own bibliography already comprised 208 items (apart from encyclopaedia articles).

The move to England, with the need to master another culture and another language, coincided with a period of deep questioning of the meaning of European history. By the end of the war he had identified a new subject for research, the history of historiography from antiquity to the present day; his immense learning and sound judgement made him the acknowledged creator and master of a new area of study for a generation. The long delayed publication of the 1962 Sather lectures after his death (*The Classical Foundations of Modern Historiography*, 1990) showed that he had already then established the framework for researches which he pursued in detail over the next twenty-five years; these are included in his *Contributi alla Storia degli Studi Classici e del Mondo Antico* (1955 onwards), which when finally completed will run to fourteen large volumes. Many selections from these essays have been published, in English, Italian, French, and German. Some have criticized the fact that he preferred the essay to the book; but his choice relates to his conception of history as a way of life and an attitude of mind, rather than a set of permanent results.

His influence was felt in many areas. His work on Edward *Gibbon, George *Grote, and nineteenth-century continental scholarship is particularly important. He opened up the study of late antiquity in Britain (*The Conflict between Paganism and Christianity in the Fourth Century*, 1963). His work on early Rome inspired a new generation of Italian scholars. In 1972 he helped to establish a joint degree in anthropology and ancient history at University College London, and comparative themes are evident in his London seminar, culminating in *Alien Wisdom: the Limits of Hellenization* (1975). Since his early contacts with Croce, he had been interested in the idea of liberty and its relation to the concept of the person; this provoked a controversial study, *The Development of Greek Biography* (1971), and towards the end of his life papers on the idea of the person and biography in late antiquity. He retained a lifelong interest in Jewish history, and his latest work centred on the history of ancient religion.

It was in the lecture and the seminar that his distinctive combination of immense learning and facility with ideas had most impact. Although his accent remained impenetrably Piedmontese, he wrote English with an unacademic elegance and wit, and Italian 'like an Englishman'. His teaching presented no general theory of history, for he respected too much the autonomy of the past to wish to impose general patterns on it; as he said once: 'I have now lost faith in my own theories, but I have not yet acquired faith in the theories of my colleagues.' To him, theory was created by the historian, not by the facts; it was this emphasis on the role of the observer in the interpretation of history which was one of his most distinctive contributions to the study of history. Another was his insistence that methodology (as opposed to ideology) was the central theme of the history of historiography.

His teaching followed the continental tradition of seminars, and his efforts were directed towards the next generation of scholars. In England the main centre of his activity was the Warburg Institute: he contributed many lectures, and from 1967 to 1983 conducted a regular seminar there, which became the centre for young historians throughout Britain; in Italy his annual seminar at Pisa attracted audiences of hundreds; his Chicago seminar was equally famous. None who presented a paper on these occasions could forget the mixture of awe and fear which he inspired, as he summed up the problem with greater clarity and learning than the speaker could ever hope to achieve.

Widely held to be the most learned man of his age, he was 'a masters' master' (George Steiner), and one of the dominant figures in European historical studies for a generation, in which he seemed to many to be the embodiment of history itself. Stocky, untidy, and of immense vitality, a non-drinker always on the move, with his pockets full of medicines, carbon copy cash-books (for writing references in), and bunches of keys, his books in a string bag, his scarf attached by a safety pin, he took scant interest in administration, and lived for intellectual discussion. He was immediately approachable, and paid no attention to rank: he lacked all pomposity and most of the social graces, even forgetting his own retirement dinner—an act which he described as 'a triumph of the Id over the Ego'. He would move in a cloud of younger scholars; and an hour with him would often change their lives. He was fascinated by ideas, new and old; in his later years he became more insistent on the need to know, and returned to ancestral traditions of rabbinic learning and exact scholarship, but he never lost his delight in discussion. To those he respected intellectually, especially the young, he was generous to a fault; he would dismiss openly those who did not measure up to his standards. As a result he had many devoted friends and disciples, and not a few enemies. For he was a man of passion, capable of quarrelling magnificently and permanently; yet it must be said that he never did so without good cause, personal or intellectual.

Through his writing and his personality Momigliano made a major contribution to intellectual life in England, Italy, and America. But he remained true to his origins; during a lifetime of exile he retained his Italian citizenship, and as a free thinker was proud of his three inheritances, Celtic Piedmont, Italy of the Risorgimento, and the Jewish tradition of learning.

He held a number of visiting professorships in America; he became a fellow of the British Academy in 1954, and president of the Society for the Promotion of Roman Studies (1965–8); he received many honorary degrees, and an honorary KBE in 1974. He married in 1932 Gemma, daughter of Adolfo Segre, civil servant. They had one daughter, Anna Laura. Momigliano died 1 September 1987 in the Central Middlesex Hospital, London, and was buried in the Jewish cemetery at Cuneo.

[*Rivista Storica Italiana*, vol. c, 1988, fasc. II; Peter Brown in *Proceedings of the British Academy*, vol. lxxiv, 1988; Carlo Dionisotti, *Ricordo di Arnaldo Momigliano*, Bologna, 1989; L. Cracco Ruggini (ed.), *Omaggio ad Arnaldo Momigliano*, Como, 1989; *History and Theory* Beiheft, vol. xxx, 1991; Momigliano papers in Scuola Normale Pisa, Society for the Protection of Science and Learning (Bodleian Library, Oxford), and Oxford University Press; personal knowledge.]   OSWYN MURRAY

MOON, SIR (Edward) Penderel (1905–1987), Indian civil servant and writer, was born 13 November 1905 in Green Street, Mayfair, London, the only son and second of five children of Robert Oswald Moon, consultant cardiologist, and his wife, Ethel Rose Grant Waddington. Dr Moon wrote about philosophy and Greek medicine as well as diseases of the heart; he stood several times as a Liberal candidate for Parliament.

Penderel Moon followed his father to Winchester and New College, Oxford, was placed in the first class in *literae humaniores* (1927), and in the same year was elected to a fellowship at All Souls College, Oxford, which he held until 1935. In 1929 he was appointed to the Indian Civil Service, arriving in India on 29 November. He was posted to the Punjab and attached for instruction to Gurdaspur district under (Sir) Evan Jenkins, later private secretary to the viceroy and governor of the Punjab, who formed very early a high opinion of his administrative ability. By the time he had charge of the difficult district of Multan, it was known that Moon decided quickly and acted firmly but was not notably tolerant of the opinions of others, even his elders. None the less, he was appointed in 1938 private secretary to the governor of the Punjab, Sir Henry Craik; he was young for this key position and was also unusual in winning races on the governor's horses.

After his spell as private secretary, Moon was posted in 1941 as deputy commissioner to Amritsar, the focal point of the Sikh religion and of special importance in war in view of the Sikh contribution to the Indian army. Like many young British officers in the ICS, Moon considered that the government of the second Marquess of *Linlithgow was dragging its feet about Indian advance towards self-government. In November 1942 he addressed to the Punjab government a letter arguing that those imprisoned for preaching civil disobedience should receive better treatment; this was in order, but when he received an unsympathetic reply, explaining the critical war situation, Moon's reaction was not. He sent a copy of the government's letter, with his own acid comments, to a brother of Rajkumari Amrit Kaur, secretary to M. K. *Gandhi. She was at the time in gaol. This letter was intercepted and Moon was in serious trouble. Eventually the new governor, Sir Bertrand Glancy, persuaded him not to insist on dismissal, but to resign; he refused the suggestion of a proportionate pension.

Moon returned to England in April 1943, on six months' leave pending retirement, but in 1946 Viscount (later first Earl) *Wavell, now viceroy, on the advice of his private secretary, Sir Evan Jenkins, invited him to return, on contract, as secretary to the boards of development and planning. In April 1947 he became revenue minister of the state of Bahawalpur and stayed on after India's independence, serving as chief commissioner of Himachal Pradesh, as chief commissioner of Manipur state, and as adviser to the planning commission. The tone of an address to the Indian Administrative Staff College suggests that he was sometimes as critical of the new rulers of India as of the old.

During the war Moon had published *Strangers in India* (1944), in which he argued that the ills of India could not be solved by a foreign government; it was followed by *Warren Hastings* (1947), brilliantly written in a simple, lucid style and notable for its sympathy with *Hastings.

His last appointment in India ended in 1961.

He was knighted in 1962 for services to good relations between Britain and India, to which indeed he had notably contributed. After his return to England he held brief appointments with the World Bank and as adviser to the government of Thailand but soon put the main thrust of his life into scholarly work on India. In 1961 he published *Divide and Quit*, which he later believed the most likely to survive of any of his books. It contains a lucid account of the events leading up to the partition of India and Pakistan, and an unflinching assessment of responsibility together with a day-by-day account of his own actions and observations as revenue minister and district magistrate in the border state of Bahawalpur during the months immediately following the division of the Punjab and the slaughter that followed. There can be no doubt that his power of swift decision, and his application of common sense amounting to brilliance, saved many lives; his account constitutes first-hand historical evidence of a high order. His *Gandhi and Modern India* is an admirable counterpoise to his *Warren Hastings*.

From 1965 to 1972 he was a fellow of All Souls, being the college's estates bursar in 1966–9, and from 1972 to 1982 he was at the India Office Library and Records, preparing for publication, with Nicholas Mansergh, the India Office documents on *The Transfer of Power 1942–7* (twelve volumes). He found time also to edit *Wavell: the Viceroy's Journal* (1973), a labour of love carried out with his usual clarity and distinction. When he died his last and most substantial book, *The British Conquest and Dominion of India* (1989), was still in proof. It was written, as always, with clarity, detachment, and mastery of complex material.

Moon's life was not all spent toiling at a desk. Before retiring from All Souls he bought a mixed farm near Aylesbury, which he later enlarged. He employed a manager, but took pleasure not only in the business of the farm but in the physical work of haymaking and harvest; he was a generous employer. He was a good horseman and enjoyed both hunting and racing. He sang in Oxford in the Bach Choir and had a particular admiration for the music of *Handel.

Penderel Moon resembled in many ways an aristocrat of the Enlightenment. In appearance he was trim and slight; in personal habit, ascetic. In scholarship, as in farming, he combined the confident mastery of the professional with the detachment of the amateur of independent means. He was decisive in his opinions and often autocratic, a champion of the peasant but no egalitarian. In youth, he liked to surprise and even to shock, but he never took up a position merely for effect.

He married in 1966 Pauline Marion, daughter of the Revd William Everard Cecil Barns; the marriage was not a success and was soon dissolved; there were no children. Moon died 2 June 1987 at home at his farm in Wotton Underwood, Buckinghamshire.

[Private information; personal knowledge.]

PHILIP MASON

MOORE, (Charles) Garrett (Ponsonby), eleventh EARL OF DROGHEDA (1910–1989), chairman of the *Financial Times* and the Royal Opera House, Covent Garden, was born at 40 Wilton Crescent, London, 23 April 1910, the elder child and only son of Henry Charles Ponsonby Moore, tenth Earl of Drogheda, diplomat, and his wife Kathleen, daughter of Charles Maitland Pelham Burn, of Grange Park, Edinburgh. He was educated at Eton and Trinity College, Cambridge, which he left early, without a degree. After two years' bookkeeping at the Mining Trust, the first turning-point of his career came in 1932 when, at Brooks's Club in London, he met Brendan (later Viscount) *Bracken, and went to work for him at the *Financial News*, selling advertising space. He worked hard at mastering the detail of the newspaper business, made a considerable impression on Bracken, and developed a long, close relationship with him. In World War II he served briefly in France, as a captain with the 53rd battalion of the Heavy Anti-Aircraft Regiment, Royal Artillery, and was then appointed to the staff of the war cabinet secretariat (1941) and later the Ministry of Production (1942–5). By the end of the war he was back at the *Financial News*, as managing director.

In 1945, at Bracken's instruction, he went out and bought the *Financial Times*. The two newspapers merged under the one title. For twenty-five years, as managing director of the *Financial Times* (1945–70), Drogheda (who succeeded his father in 1957) devoted himself to its commercial expansion and editorial improvement, taking particular pleasure in stimulating its coverage of the arts, the other great passion and interest of his life. He allowed the editor, Sir L. Gordon Newton, to edit, but pursued him daily with a string of memoranda, demanding answers to pertinent questions. If none was received Drogheda persisted.

He used the same tactic at Covent Garden, where, after serving as secretary to the board from 1951, he was its chairman from 1958 to 1974. He bombarded the general administrators, Sir David *Webster and later Sir John Tooley, with the same missives, which were known as Droghedagrams. At Covent Garden Drogheda attempted to insist that the board was entitled to approve executive artistic decisions, such as the choice of designer for a particular opera. Webster resisted and (Sir) Georg Solti, engaged by Drogheda as musical director from 1961, never tolerated such interference. Solti's appointment, the decision to give opera in the original language rather than in English, and the high standards that resulted were the principal achievements of Drogheda's chairmanship, which also saw the birth and growth of the Friends of Covent Garden. The Droghedagrams were addressed also to those critics on the *Financial Times*'s pages and elsewhere whose views did not, in the author's opinion, do the opera house justice. These would arrive by messenger on a motor cycle early in the morning the review appeared. It was not unknown for them to be brought round, should the victim live close enough to his house in Lord North Street, by Drogheda himself, in slippers, pyjamas, and dressing-gown.

Drogheda's handsome looks and languid appearance concealed an iron determination to secure his ends. Charming, but obdurate; a dandy, but determined; debonair, but persistent, he would stop at nothing on the newspaper's or the opera house's commercial behalf, pursuing advertisers or possible benefactors without compunction. He struck up friendships with employees of every rank, and treated very many with great personal kindness. He had an acute mind, which expressed itself fluently and clearly on paper, but was guided, he himself thought, always by instinct.

Drogheda was chairman of Financial Times Ltd. (1971–5) and of the Newspaper Publishers' Association (1968–70). He chaired the London celebrations committee for the queen's silver jubilee in 1977. From 1941 he served as a director of the *Economist*, to which he was much attached. He was a commander of the Legion of Honour of France (1960) and of the Order of Merit of Italy (1968) and was grand officer of the Order of Leopold II of Belgium (1974). He was appointed OBE in 1946, KBE in 1964, and knight of the Garter in 1972.

He married in 1935 Joan Eleanor, daughter of William Henry Carr, who left her mother when she was born. She was an excellent pianist, whose immaculate musical taste served him often in good stead. They had one child, a son. Drogheda died 24 December 1989, at Englefield Green, Surrey, eight days after his wife. He was succeeded in the earldom by his son, Henry Dermot Ponsonby Moore (born 1937).

[David Kynaston, *The Financial Times: a Centenary History*, 1988; Frances Donaldson, *The Royal Opera House in the Twentieth Century*, 1988; Garrett Drogheda, *Double Harness, Memoirs*, 1978; private information; personal knowledge.]   JEREMY ISAACS

MOORE, Doris Elizabeth Langley (1902–1989), founder of the Museum of Costume and *Byron scholar, was born 23 July 1902 in Liverpool, the second daughter in the family of three daughters and one son of Joseph Langley Levy, writer and newspaper editor, and his wife, Mabel

Ada Rushden, theatrical designer. The family moved to South Africa when she was eight, and she was educated at convent schools there. In *Pleasure: a Discursive Guide Book* (1953) she described her comfortable and indulged childhood. Although she had no formal education, she read widely, under the guidance of her father.

She moved to London in the early 1920s, and her first book, *Anacreon: 29 Odes* (1926), was a verse translation from the Greek. This was followed by *The Technique of the Love Affair* (1928) by 'a Gentlewoman', a manual of advice to a woman on how to catch a husband. *Pandora's Letter Box, Being a Discourse on Fashionable Life* (1929) was written for her two-year-old daughter. She wrote six romantic novels between 1932 and 1959, and several books on household management, including *The Bride's Book* (1932, revised in 1936 as *Our Loving Duty*). Her biography of Edith *Nesbit (1933, revised 1967) drew on extensive conversations with members of the novelist's family and family letters, transcripts of which were invaluable for later biographers.

She was passionately interested in clothes, and dressed in the height of fashion each season. She loved hats, and early in life decided that when depressed one should go out and buy a hat. Her own clothes formed the basis of a collection of costumes, to which she added historical costumes, discovered in salerooms, country house auctions, and attics. She admitted to a certain amount of bargaining, plotting, and machination in obtaining such items. Her most exciting acquisition was the Albanian costume bought by Lord *Byron on his grand tour of 1809, which he wore for the portrait painted by Thomas *Phillips in 1814. She was one of the first to study the history of fashion seriously, and all her life she wrote and lectured on it, organized exhibitions, and produced television programmes. In 1949 she brought out *The Woman in Fashion*, a history of fashion in which some of the most famous beauties of the day, most of them personal friends, were photographed wearing costumes from her collection. In 1955 followed *The Child in Fashion*.

She campaigned for many years for a museum of costume to be founded in London, and she persuaded Christian Dior to bring his collection over from Paris in order to raise money for the project. The museum was opened in 1955, housed temporarily in Eridge castle, near Tunbridge Wells, Kent, and then in the Brighton Pavilion. It moved permanently to the rebuilt Assembly Rooms in Bath in 1963. The costumes were displayed by creating period tableaux with life-size dummies and furniture and objects from the correct historical period. There were also collections of babies' clothes and dolls' clothes, an underwear room with foundation garments from 200 years, a display of millinery, accessories such as fans, socks, ribbons, buttons, belts, gaiters, mittens, and bedroom slippers, and a collection of dresses worn by the royal family. She was anxious to keep the museum up to date, and created a modern room for clothes from 1907 to the current year. Each year new specimens were added, chosen as representative of current fashion, and a different fashion expert was asked to choose one outfit as 'dress of the year'. The dress for 1963 was designed by Mary Quant, and the 1967 'dress' was a trouser suit. Doris Langley Moore retired as adviser to the museum in 1974, and left her collection to the city of Bath.

Her interest in costume extended to the stage and to films, but the décor for her ballet *The Quest*, first performed at Sadler's Wells in 1943, was done by John Piper. The scenario was adapted by her from Edmund *Spenser's *The Faerie Queene*, showing the victory of St George over the forces of evil. (Sir) William *Walton wrote the score especially for the ballet, (Sir) Frederick *Ashton was the choreographer, and the soloists were (Dame) Margot Fonteyn, (Sir) Robert *Helpmann, (Dame) Beryl Grey, and Moira Shearer in her first role. She also worked as a costume designer for the theatre and films, and designed Katharine Hepburn's dresses for *The African Queen* (1951).

Doris Langley Moore first came across Byron when she was fifteen, when her father gave her a copy of *Don Juan*, She remained devoted to him all her life. 'I was perhaps the only woman to whom nothing but pleasure has come from loving that poet.' In 1924, the centenary of Byron's death, she was invited to join the commemoration committee, and in 1931 she accompanied the Greek prime minister on a visit to Byron's tomb. She was present when his tomb in Hucknall church was opened in 1938 to see if he really was buried there. She became a founding vice-president of the Byron Society in 1971. She was the first person, apart from Byron's family, to be allowed access to the large collection of uncatalogued Wentworth and Lovelace papers in the possession of Lady Wentworth, Byron's great-granddaughter. Her last novel, *My Caravaggio Style* (1959), about the forgery of the lost Byron memoirs, was written while she was immersed in these papers.

The first of her three scholarly works on Byron, *The Late Lord Byron*, appeared in 1961. In this, she started with the death of Byron and built up a picture of him from the attempts of others to write about him. *Lord Byron, Accounts Rendered* (1974) won the British Academy's Rose Mary Crawshay prize in 1975. Based on Byron's accounts, found among the papers of his Italian secretary, this book examines Byron's finances as a means of gaining insight into his domestic life. *Ada, Countess of Lovelace* (1977) is a biography of

Byron's daughter. The publication of these works had enormous influence on the subsequent course of Byron studies. Doris Langley Moore was appointed OBE in 1971.

She was an attractive woman, with a high forehead and a handsome profile. She moved in fashionable London circles, but she was a difficult person, and some of her friendships ended in bitterness. In 1926 she married Robert Sugden Moore, wool merchant, the son of Fred Denby Moore, also a wool merchant. They had one daughter, Pandora. They were divorced in 1942. She died in the Middlesex Hospital, London, 24 February 1989.

[*Independent*, 28 February 1989; *Guardian*, 2 March 1989; Doris Langley Moore, *The Museum of Costume: Guide to the Exhibition and Commentary on the Trends of Fashion*, 1967.] ANNE PIMLOTT BAKER

MOORE, Gerald (1899-1987), pianist and accompanist, was born 30 July 1899 in Watford, Hertfordshire, the eldest in the family of three sons and a daughter, who died in childhood, of David Frank Moore, who owned a men's outfitting establishment, and his Welsh-born wife, Chestina Jones. He was educated at Watford Grammar School. Musical, with perfect pitch, he learned the piano locally with Wallis Bandey. When, owing to a financial crisis, the family decided to emigrate to Toronto, Canada, the thirteen-year-old Gerald had to start again with his piano studies. His mother arranged an audition with Michael Hambourg, founder of a school of music in Toronto. This resulted in a scholarship and much expert coaching. Hambourg's cellist son, Boris, later took Moore as his accompanist on a tour of forty engagements in western Canada. When Moore finally was shipped back to London, in 1919, it was another Hambourg son—Mark *Hambourg, the well-known pianist—who offered to take over his training.

But Moore was not cut out for a career as a soloist and on the advice of (Sir) Landon *Ronald, then principal of the Guildhall School of Music, he concentrated on accompanying. He went on tour with baritone Peter Dawson and was engaged on an exclusive basis by the tenor John Coates. Coates taught him to work and awakened his realization of the importance of the piano part in the basic structure of the song: Moore said he owed everything to him.

In 1921 Moore made his first record (for HMV), with Renée Chemet, the French violinist. The studio had a large horn contraption into which the violinist played. In spite of the piece being a gentle lullaby Moore had to play fortissimo throughout in order to be heard at all on the record.

A vital step forward for Moore was the arrival on the recording scene of the microphone. At last his playing would be faithfully reproduced on records. At first he was greatly shocked by hearing himself. But by listening carefully he was able to improve, technically and musically, and raise his playing to a new standard, which took him to the top. Apart from many instrumentalists, his famous vocal partners included Elena Gerhardt, Elisabeth Schumann, (Dame) Maggie *Teyte, John McCormack, Hans Hotter, Kathleen *Ferrier, (Dame) Elisabeth Schwarzkopf, Victoria de los Angeles, Dietrich Fischer-Dieskau, and (Dame) Janet Baker.

When (Dame) Myra *Hess started her series of lunchtime concerts in the National Gallery, during World War II, she asked Moore to give a talk at the piano on his experiences as an accompanist. He revealed a sense of verbal timing of which any professional comic would be proud. His unique blend of wit and wisdom not only pleased the cognoscenti but also won over ordinary people who had no idea that classical music could be fun. This kind of treatment has its dangers, but not with Moore, who always put the music first and used the jokes to sugar the pill. The talk became immensely popular.

Moore played throughout the world as an accompanist and included many tours of America as a lecture-recitalist. His favourite festivals included Edinburgh, Salzburg, and King's Lynn (where he played piano duets with Ruth, Lady Fermoy).

Moore retired from the concert platform in 1967, at the comparatively early age of sixty-seven, when he was at the top of his form. A farewell concert, which was recorded, was given in his honour at the Royal Festival Hall on 20 February 1967. After Moore gave up public playing his great affection for Schubert became an obsession: he embarked on the huge task of recording over 500 Schubert songs. Three sets of these—'Schöne Müllerin', 'Winterreise', and 'Schwanengesang', all with Fischer-Dieskau—were issued on compact disc and form a lasting tribute to his work. His playing was remarkable for flawless technique and a rare ability to make the piano 'sing'.

Moore was a talented writer. His best-known book was the autobiography *Am I Too Loud?* (1962). He became CBE (1954), honorary RAM (1962), FRCM (1980), honorary D.Litt., Sussex (1968), and honorary Mus.D., Cambridge (1973).

Moore was a stocky, thickset figure not readily associable with the ravishingly delicate effects he could obtain from the piano. His zest for living, his enormous vitality, and his sense of humour were strong preservatives in a very hard-working life. Away from music Moore enjoyed in early life tennis and golf and, later, bridge, gardening, and watching cricket. He had an ideal partner in

his wife, Enid Kathleen (died 1994), daughter of Montague Richard, ironmonger, of Beckenham, whom he called 'the most perfect of all accompanists'. They had no children. Moore had had a previous marriage, in Canada in 1929, which lasted only three or four years and which ended in divorce. Moore died in his sleep at home in Penn, Buckinghamshire, 13 March 1987.

[Gerald Moore, *Am I Too Loud?*, 1962, *Furthermoore*, 1983, and *Collected Memoirs*, 1986; family information; personal knowledge.]   JOSEPH COOPER

MOORE, Henry Spencer (1898–1986), sculptor, was born 30 July 1898 at Castleford, Yorkshire, the youngest of four sons and seventh of eight children of Raymond Spencer Moore, coalminer, of Castleford, and his wife Mary, daughter of Neville Baker, coalminer, of Burntwood, Staffordshire. He was educated at Castleford Secondary (later High) School, where his natural talents were immediately recognized by the young art mistress, Alice Gostick.

Moore's father held responsible positions in the colliery, and the family lived on a newly built estate, with the children attending modern, well equipped schools. Raymond Moore was a self-improving man, with a taste for music and literature, and, as was the case with the family of D. H. *Lawrence, living not so far away in the Nottinghamshire coalfield, he saw schoolteaching as the way in which his clever children could better themselves and lead a more satisfying and less arduous life than his own. It was expected, therefore, that Henry would become a schoolteacher, like his older brother and his sisters. In 1915, on leaving school, he returned as a student teacher to his old elementary school at Castleford, in order to gain some practical experience before going to teacher training college. Meanwhile, his private ambition was to become a professional sculptor.

With a world war in progress, and compulsory conscription introduced in January 1916, Moore knew that his training was going to be interrupted. Rather than await his call up, he decided in 1917 to volunteer for a regiment of his own choice. Travelling to London for the first time, he tried for the Artists' Rifles—an indication of his secret wishes—but was rejected, and went into the Civil Service Rifles instead. After a brief training, Private Moore was sent in August 1917 to the front line in France; in December 1917 he was gassed in the assault on Cambrai and returned to England as a stretcher case, very fortunate to survive. After convalescence he returned to duty as a physical training and bayonet instructor, with the rank of lance-corporal. He went back to France just before the armistice was signed in November 1918, but as a teacher he was entitled to early demobilization, and he was back at his old school in Castleford in February 1919.

In later life, Moore rarely spoke about his wartime experiences, and then often in a somewhat light-hearted manner. He admitted to being a callow young man, pleased to have broken away from the parental home, and at the time unaware of the tragic implications of the war—in sharp contrast to slightly older contemporaries such as the Yorkshire-born (Sir) Herbert *Read, later to become Moore's close friend and champion.

It was expected that Moore would become a teacher specializing in art, and in September 1919, with an ex-serviceman's grant, he began his formal training at the Leeds School of Art, commuting by train from his home in Castleford. It was immediately clear that he was an outstanding student, and he completed the two-year drawing course in his first year. In his second year at Leeds Moore asked for sculpture lessons, and his progress was remarkable enough for him to win a scholarship to the Royal College of Art in London, which was, with the Slade School, the leading art school in Britain.

Moore studied in the sculpture school of the Royal College of Art from September 1921 until the summer of 1924, when he was awarded his diploma. He learned little from his teachers, but won the interest and support of the college's principal, (Sir) William *Rothenstein, and enjoyed the company of his fellow students, particularly those who had come with him from Leeds, the painters Raymond Coxon and Edna Ginesi, and the sculptor five years his junior, (Dame) Barbara *Hepworth. Together they visited exhibitions, made their first trips to look at art in Paris, and worked very hard with great confidence and dedication. Moore lived mainly in Hammersmith in west London, and for a time attended drawing classes in the local studio of the sculptor and painter, (G. C.) Leon *Underwood. Drawing always mattered for Moore, who saw it as the essential adjunct to sculpture.

The decisive experience for the young Moore was his hours spent studying the sculpture in the Victoria and Albert and, more importantly, the British Museum. The tradition of western sculpture had reached a culmination in the work of Auguste Rodin, and Moore knew instinctively that his generation would need to form a new language for this powerful but difficult three-dimensional art if it was to speak with a clear and distinctive twentieth-century voice. Following the examples of (Sir) Jacob *Epstein, Henri Gaudier-Brzeska, and Constantin Brancusi, Moore felt that the way forward must be to look at those other sculptures outside the classical/medieval/Renaissance/Rodin tradition: namely archaic Greek, Egyptian, Assyrian, and more significantly sculptures that until the twentieth century had not been recognized as art at all but as antiquities or curiosities, from pre-European Mexico, Africa, and Oceania.

It was this broad sculptural heritage, to which might be added such great archaeological remains as Stonehenge, that the young Moore studied. He visited Italy on a six-month travelling scholarship in 1925, and though he admired the paintings of Giotto and Masaccio he seems not to have wanted to look at sculpture: perhaps this is the reason why he surprisingly never competed for the prix de Rome. His appreciation of Donatello and Michelangelo came later in life. At the time Moore preferred to return to London, where he had a part-time teaching position in the sculpture school of the Royal College of Art. This gave him both financial security and enough time to make his own sculptures, and prepare for that crucial test that faces any artist—a first one-man exhibition.

This came for Moore in January 1928 at the Warren Gallery, where the artist showed forty-two sculptures and fifty-one drawings. Though giving rise to some controversy, it was an undoubted success. 'A very "advanced" show and one that will shock the orthodox, it contains much sculpture of overwhelming power,' said the Daily Herald. Moore was particularly pleased that among the purchasers of his work were artists of the calibre of Augustus *John and Jacob Epstein. There followed immediately, later in 1928, Moore's first public commission. On Epstein's recommendation he was asked to carve a relief for the façade of the new London underground headquarters near St James's Park, symbolizing the west wind, part of a decorative scheme to which (A.) Eric *Gill and Epstein himself also contributed. But providing sculpture for buildings was not the route forward that Moore wished to pursue, and in general he always avoided such commissions. At this stage in his career he also avoided making modelled sculpture for casting in bronze, believing that the future lay in the direct carving of wood and stone.

In July 1929 Moore married a student at the Royal College of Art, Irina Anatolia Radetzky. The daughter of Anatol Radetsky, who was lost in the Russian revolution, from an upper-class mercantile family, she had been born in Kiev in 1907 and had come to England in 1921–2 to stay with step-grandparents in Little Marlow, Buckinghamshire. A woman of striking and exotic beauty, she was Moore's support and best critic for the whole of his long career. They had one daughter. Irina died in 1989.

On their marriage, the Moores moved into a ground-floor studio with accommodation above at 11A Parkhill Road in Hampstead. The apartment was found by Barbara Hepworth, who lived nearby in The Mall Studios with, from 1931, the painter Ben *Nicholson. The poets Herbert Read and Geoffrey *Grigson, the writer Adrian *Stokes, and the painters Paul *Nash and Ivon *Hitchens were all close neighbours. This Hampstead circle became the most receptive to modern ideas in the visual arts in Britain, and its interests reflected the rival continental avant-garde movements of abstraction and Surrealism. At this time Moore's sculpture entered its most experimental phase, and, though still relatively small in size, his carvings in stone and wood, and the pages of drawings for sculpture, showed an astounding originality of invention, on which rests his international fame.

With the outbreak of war in September 1939 everything changed. During the 1930s Moore had led a regular and productive life, teaching part-time at the Chelsea School of Art, working in his Hampstead studio, and during the holidays making larger works in the garden of his cottage in Kent. The war stopped his teaching, and the bombing and the threat of invasion made it impossible to work in London or Kent. When his Hampstead studio was damaged by bombs in October 1940, he took the house at Perry Green, Much Hadham, Hertfordshire, in which he was to live and work until his death. With the gradual addition of land and studios this was the centre of all his later activity, rarely left for long.

Moore had more or less stopped making sculpture, and from 1940 to 1942 worked as an official war artist in the scheme supervised by Sir Kenneth (later Baron) *Clark, director of the National Gallery, and an admirer of Moore's art. He had begun to draw the women and children sheltering from the bombing on the platforms of London underground stations at night, and the coloured finished drawings he made from his sketches quickly won international attention. An artist hitherto associated exclusively with the avant-garde seemed uncannily able to capture the resignation and resistance felt by the ordinary people of London.

When Moore returned to sculpture in 1943–4 it was with two public commissions—a madonna and child for St Matthew's church, Northampton, and a family group, originally intended for the Village College at Impington, Cambridgeshire. In both cases Moore knew he had to make a sculpture that would speak directly to a wide community, and this led to fundamental changes in both his art and materials and techniques used to make it. Moore always held broad socialist principles, supporting the Labour party; he believed that the artist had a social responsibility, and he was pleased to find that his work could be appreciated in a public situation, and that his own obsession with the female human form could be shared by others.

This social commitment also led Moore to give his time generously to serve on public bodies. He was a trustee of the Tate Gallery (1941–8 and 1949–56), and of the National Gallery (1955–63 and 1964–74); a member of the Arts Council (1963–7), and of its art panel for many years from 1942 onwards. He was appointed a member of the National Theatre board in 1957 and the Royal Fine Art Commission (1947–71). He was elected a fellow of the British Academy in 1966. He accepted many prizes and twenty-one honorary degrees, and membership of a number of foreign academies.

In 1946 the first fully retrospective exhibition of Moore's work was held at the Museum of Modern Art in New York. Two years later he won the international sculpture prize at the Venice Biennale, and in 1956 he was commissioned to make a sculpture for the new Unesco headquarters in Paris. By the time he was sixty Moore was generally regarded as Britain's greatest artist and the world's greatest living sculptor. More than 200 museums worldwide own examples of his work, with particularly strong holdings in the Art Gallery of Ontario, Toronto, and the Tate Gallery, London. In over fifty cities his sculpture stands in prominent public places, notably outside the National Gallery of Art in Washington, the Lincoln Center in New York, the Houses of Parliament in London, and in Dallas, Chicago, Amsterdam, Zurich, Berlin, Singapore, and Hong Kong. By the time of his death he had had more exhibitions than any other artist, with the exception only of Pablo Picasso; particularly celebrated were those in Florence in 1972, Paris in 1977, and New York in 1983. The official bibliography devoted to his work published in 1992 lists over 10,000 publications.

Despite this public acclaim and celebrity, Moore's work in his last phase took on a more personal and private quality. Throughout the 1950s he had made a series of large seated and reclining female figures, but in the 1960s the sculptures became distinctly more abstract. The reclining figure was broken up into two, three, or even four parts, and sometimes made on a grand, monumental scale, much larger than life size. In such sculptures—the 'Sheep Piece' of 1971–2, the 'Three Piece Vertebrae' of 1968 and 1978–9, and the 'Large Four Piece Reclining Figure' of 1972–3, for example—Moore is at his most majestic, making work of a boldness no other sculptor has attempted. The figure references almost disappear, and in the big 'Arch' of 1963/9, 'Hill Arches' (1972), or the 'Mirror Knife Edge' in Washington (1977), the work takes on a powerful architectural quality that enhances the feeling of some mysterious timeless memorial.

Moore's working methods remained much the

same from 1944 onwards: ideas were developed by the artist as plaster maquettes, no more than hand size, which he could alter and shape like small carvings. Then, with the help of assistants, the forms could be enlarged to a human dimension or, if appropriate, to a monumental scale. The plaster sculpture was usually cast in bronze, the most durable material a sculptor can use, and works were sold in editions of three to ten copies. Nearly 1,000 works are listed in the complete catalogue of Moore's sculptures, and, as most were issued in editions, the probable complete tally must be over 6,000.

Such a production, spread over more than sixty years, made Moore a very wealthy man. In the mid-1970s he was paying over £1 million a year in tax, and it was partly this that led him in 1977, with the assistance of his only child Mary, who had been born in 1946, to set up the Henry Moore Foundation. This charitable foundation was established to advance public appreciation of the fine arts and in particular of the works of Henry Moore, and by the time of Moore's death it was already playing an active role arranging Moore exhibitions worldwide, and funding fellowships, publications, galleries, and exhibitions devoted to sculpture.

Moore's fame as a sculptor was matched by the renown that his drawings, water-colours, and graphic works brought him. As he grew older, so he spent more time drawing, not so much studies for sculpture, but drawings made for their own sake, of rocks, roots, and landscapes, as well as the human form. It was the natural world, and the human presence in it, that lay at the heart of all Moore's work, in whatever medium. He did not seek to express beauty, rather an image of power and vitality. Though without formal beliefs, Moore had a religious sense of life, and it is perhaps this quality that has given his best work a universal relevance which speaks to people of whatever race and religion in a way that no artist before Moore had been able to achieve. He was regarded as, and is likely to remain, a towering figure in twentieth-century art.

In personal appearance and manner Moore belied such an impression. It was often said that he looked more like a successful farmer than an artist. He had an attractive modesty that hid great self-confidence and ambition. He kept a light Yorkshire accent all his life, and expressed himself in simple straightforward terms, avoiding any philosophizing. Interpretations of his work he left to others; he was the maker, driven by some creative force that he could not and perhaps did not wish to understand. At times he seemed almost surprised at his own reputation, expressing a boyish delight at visits from prime ministers and presidents, accepting a CH in 1955 and the OM in 1963 but declining any title.

Moore died at Perry Green, Much Hadham, 31 August 1986, and was buried there.

[Herbert Read, *Henry Moore*, 1965; Donald Hall, *Henry Moore*, 1966; John Russell, *Henry Moore*, 1973; William Packer, *Henry Moore*, 1985; Roger Berthoud, *The Life of Henry Moore*, 1987; Susan Compton, *Henry Moore*, 1988; David Mitchison and Julian Stallabrass, *Henry Moore*, 1992; personal knowledge.]

ALAN BOWNESS

MOORES, Cecil (1902–1989), businessman, was born 10 August 1902 in Manchester, the fourth child and second son in the family of four sons and four daughters of John William Moores, builder, and his wife, Louisa Fethney. He completed state elementary and secondary education and in the early 1920s worked in a variety of jobs, which included training as an analytical chemist.

In 1924 he joined his elder brother, (Sir) John Moores, in helping to run the embryo Littlewoods Pools business. By 1932 it was so thriving and successful that John Moores concentrated his attention on diversification and left the core pools business in the safe control of his brother Cecil. Cecil Moores's name became synonymous with what was Britain's, indeed probably the world's, largest football pools business. He was also a director of the Littlewoods Organization, lending his considerable experience and talents to the progress of the other major businesses in the group, such as chain stores and mail order.

He was a loyal Briton, buying the famous Bapton herd of dairy shorthorn cattle in the early 1950s to prevent its being exported to America. Under his direction the herd won many prizes in national competitions and when he eventually came to sell it he imposed a rigid condition that it should stay in Aberdeenshire, to which he had moved it at the time of its acquisition.

His devotion to the work ethic was profound, his philosophy being 'it is fun to work hard and to build a business'. This went hand in hand with a concern for the working conditions and benefits available to his employees, all of whom referred to him affectionately as 'Mr Cecil'. He had a highly developed social conscience and provided the company's employees with numerous social benefits long before the welfare state became a reality. This concern was extended to his customers—for example, in 1957 he initiated a 'winners advisory service' to help winners of very large sums to adjust to their good fortune. He believed in practical involvement in management and his personal presence was manifest daily throughout the pools company. He arrived before most of the staff and usually did not depart until long after they had gone home.

His drive and organizing ability came to fruition with the outbreak of war in 1939. Virtually overnight the pools company was turned into an efficient war production machine, manufacturing and supplying everything from parachutes to Wellington bombers. The speed and efficiency with which a largely female clerical labour force was retrained and applied to these new activities was due in very large measure to the abilities of Cecil Moores. After the war he speedily guided Littlewoods Pools back to its pre-eminent position. He oversaw all the major developments in the pools industry, including, for example, the mechanization of the business, the provision of a nationwide coupon collector service (from 1957), and the use of Australian fixtures during the summer (from 1949).

He was also keenly interested in many sports. As a young man he was an amateur soccer player for Hyde United and later played for the amateur Liverpool side, the Azoics. Throughout his life he was a supporter of both Liverpool and Everton football clubs. He pursued numerous other sporting activities including golf, horse-racing, snooker, game shooting, and salmon and trout fishing—at all of which he characteristically became proficient. In 1975 he was the driving force behind the formation of the Football Ground Improvement Trust (later the Football Trust), which provided about £40 million per year to help football at all levels.

Cecil Moores was of medium height and stocky build, with straight brown hair and blue eyes. He was a devoted family man of simple tastes, who lived unostentatiously in the house he had bought in Formby before World War II. In 1930 he married Doris May (died 1988), daughter of Thomas Steel, electrician. They had a daughter and two sons, the elder of whom died as a result of a motor accident in 1977. Although he retired in 1979 as chairman of Littlewoods Pools, in old age Cecil Moores continued, as president of the business, to attend his office daily, maintaining regular contact with the business he loved. He died 29 July 1989 whilst on a fishing holiday at Loch Trool in Dumfries and Galloway, Scotland. He left £1,946,440 gross and £1,828,996 net.

[Private information; personal knowledge.]

MALCOLM A. DAVIDSON

MOORMAN, John Richard Humpidge (1905–1989), bishop of Ripon and ecumenist, was born in Leeds 4 June 1905, the younger son and second of three children of Frederic William Moorman, professor of English at Leeds University, and his wife, Frances Beatrice Humpidge. His father died when he was fourteen. He was educated at Gresham's School, Holt, and Emmanuel College, Cambridge, of which he was made an honorary fellow in 1959. In 1926 he obtained a second class (division II) in part i of the history tripos and in 1928 a second class in part i of the theology tripos. Whilst at Cambridge Professor F. C. *Burkitt encouraged him to make

the first of what became almost annual visits to Assisi, thus prompting a lifetime's interest in St Francis. He gained his BD with *The Sources for the Life of S. Francis of Assisi* (1940); and followed this with the more popular *Saint Francis of Assisi* (1950); his *magnum opus*, *A History of the Franciscan Order*, in 1968; and his final work, *Medieval Franciscan Houses*, in 1983. His library of Franciscan books (later given to St Deiniol's library, Hawarden) numbered well over 2,000 volumes, whilst Moorman himself achieved international recognition as the leading English Franciscan scholar.

Moorman's scholarly interests, however, were pursued not in an academic context but in the parishes and diocese he was to serve. He trained for ordination in the Church of England at Westcott House, Cambridge, under B. K. Cunningham, of whom he was later to write a memoir (1947). In 1929 he was ordained to a curacy at Holbeck in his native city of Leeds. He served his second curacy at Leighton Buzzard from 1933 until 1935, when he was appointed rector of Fallowfield, Manchester, where he remained until the early years of World War II. His innate pacifism, coupled with a concern to do work more obviously connected with the war effort, led him to resign his benefice and take employment as a farmhand in Wharfedale. At night, by the light of an oil lamp, he completed his *Church Life in England in the Thirteenth Century*, which gained him a doctorate of divinity at Cambridge in 1945.

Moorman's deep interest in the spiritual and scholarly training of Anglican clergy was first recognized in his appointment early in 1945 to Lanercost Priory, where men could be trained for the rural ministry. In the following year, however, Bishop George *Bell invited him south to reopen Chichester Theological College. Here Moorman restored both the financial fortunes and academic standing of the oldest of Anglican theological colleges, serving at the same time as chancellor of Chichester Cathedral. In 1953 his best-known work, *A History of the Church in England*, was published: it illustrated well the clarity of his mind, the independence of his judgements, and also his concern, like that of his father-in-law, that history should be both well written and enjoyable to read.

In 1956 Moorman resigned an appointment for the second occasion in his life, this time to concentrate on his Franciscan writings. The invitation in 1959 to become bishop of Ripon was both timely and inspired. Not only did the diocese include the great city of Leeds with its university, of which both he and his wife were to receive honorary doctorates, but also the dales which they enjoyed as keen walkers, bird-watchers, and lovers of rural life in general. The pastoral care of the clergy, their housing, pay, and continuing ministerial education, were paramount concerns of his sixteen-year episcopate and he saw administrative efficiency as subserving these ends.

The most significant development in Moorman's life, however, came in his appointment by Archbishop Michael *Ramsey (later Baron Ramsey of Canterbury) as chief Anglican observer at the second Vatican Council from 1962 to 1965. His fluency in the Italian tongue, coupled with his warm gift of friendship (not least his personal friendship with Cardinal Montini, who was to become pope in 1963), and his deep knowledge of Church history marked him out as one of the best-known visitors to Rome in those years. He thus became in 1967 the Anglican chairman of the preparatory commission which led to the setting up of the Anglican-Roman Catholic International Commission, of which he was a member from its inception in 1969 until 1983. During this time he was also the driving force in establishing the Anglican Centre in Rome and personally assembled books for its library.

Although Moorman was slight of stature and reserved by nature he had an authoritative presence. He was an accomplished pianist and a keen gardener. In 1930 he married Mary Caroline (died 1994), an authority on William *Wordsworth, daughter of George Macaulay *Trevelyan, regius professor of modern history at Cambridge. They had no children. From his mid-teens Moorman kept a diary, making daily entries until a week before his death 13 January 1989 in Durham, to which he had retired fourteen years earlier.

[Private information; personal knowledge.]

MICHAEL MANKTELOW

MORRIS, Charles Richard, BARON MORRIS OF GRASMERE (1898–1990), university teacher and administrator, was born 25 January 1898 in Sutton Valence, Kent, the elder child and elder son (the younger was (Sir) Philip Robert *Morris, educationist) of Meshach Charles Morris, inspector of schools, and his wife Jane, daughter of James Brasier, of St Cross, Winchester, Hampshire. He was educated at Tonbridge School and Trinity College, Oxford, where he obtained a first class in *literae humaniores* (1921). He then became a fellow and tutor in philosophy at Balliol College, Oxford (1921–43).

His natural inclination towards an educational career was fostered by his parents and augmented by the general ethos of Balliol under the inspiring mastership of A. D. *Lindsay (later first Baron Lindsay of Birker). The horror and carnage of World War I turned that inclination into an absolute commitment to education as the great liberating force beneficial to individuals and society alike. Morris gave this expression in many ways, including by financially supporting his younger sibling's education and by espousing movements to enlarge access to education at all levels at home and abroad.

The first dozen years at Balliol were 'paradise'. Morris had able and responsive pupils who admired him for his mastery of the subject and respected him for his remarkable insight into their nature and capability. He wrote three, largely expository, books. The first, *A History of Political Ideas* (1924), was written with his wife, Mary. She was the daughter of Ernest de *Selincourt, professor of English at Birmingham University. They had a long, mutually supportive marriage, based on shared values, of which there was a son and a daughter. Her brother introduced him to the Lake District, for which he developed a lasting affection. The other books were *Locke, Berkeley, Hume* (1931) and *Idealistic Logic* (1933).

The comfortable life of the archetypal Oxford don was challenged in the early 1930s by the vast social tragedy of the depression and the evident threat to democracy posed by the European dictators, especially Adolf Hitler. The Morrises responded privately by assisting refugees and publicly by Charles becoming an Oxford city councillor (1939–41) and campaigning against the election of a Conservative member in the Oxford parliamentary by-election of 1938, because he deemed inadequate and unacceptable the Conservative government's responses to the dictators' threat to democracy and to evident social injustice in Britain. In this period Morris joined with J. S. (later Baron) *Fulton to write *In Defence of Democracy* (1935).

In 1939 Morris became a wartime civil servant in the ministries of Supply (until 1942) and Production (1942–3), experiencing at first hand the workings of a 'command' economy and negotiating with counterparts in the USA for the supply of essential war materials. After this he did not return to Oxford but took up the post of headmaster of King Edward's School, Birmingham, to which he had been appointed in 1941. He stayed until 1948, when he became vice-chancellor of the University of Leeds. This brought him and his wife closer to the Lake District, where in 1943 she had inherited a house, gloriously situated above Grasmere, which was to become their real home for the next forty-seven years.

Morris was ideally suited to this vice-chancellorship, for which it seemed all his previous experience had been a preparation. Though he was short of stature, his bright eyes and lively intelligence commanded the affection and respect of colleagues and students. He led the university through postwar austerity and produced a development plan to ensure that Leeds was well placed to take early advantage of the resources which accompanied the government's acceptance of the report of the committee on higher education chaired by Baron *Robbins (1961-4). He also foresaw that internal structures of universities must change. He was an influential figure in the committee of vice-chancellors and principals, was its chairman from 1951 to 1955, and was much in demand for service on public bodies in the United Kingdom as diverse as the royal commission on local government in Greater London (1957), the Schools' Broadcasting Council (1954-64), and the advisory committee for the wool textile industry (1952). He made a major contribution to the development of universities overseas through his membership of the Inter-University Council for Higher Education Overseas (1957-64) and of the committee of inquiry into Australian universities (1957), whose definitive report was accepted. Some of these activities continued in retirement, when he also helped the newer universities of Bradford and Lancaster.

Morris was one of Britain's outstanding university administrators and was universally admired for his combination of practicality and total commitment to education. He was knighted in 1953, appointed KCMG in 1963, and made a life peer in 1967. He received eight honorary doctorates. He died, as he would have wished, at Grasmere, 30 May 1990, two years after his wife's death. There is a portrait of him in the University of Leeds by Robert *Buhler.

[Information from Balliol and Trinity Colleges, Oxford, and Leeds University; private information; personal knowledge.]   FREDERICK DAINTON

MORRIS, (John) Marcus (Harston) (1915-1989), magazine editor and publisher, and creator of *Eagle* and *Girl* strip cartoon magazines, was born 25 April 1915 in Preston, Lancashire, the second child and eldest of three sons, the youngest of whom died in childhood, of the Revd Walter Edmund Harston Morris and his wife, Edith Nield. In 1918 his parents moved to Southport. He was educated at Dean Close School in Cheltenham and Brasenose College, Oxford, where he obtained a second class in *literae humaniores* in 1937. He then moved to Wycliffe Hall and gained a second in theology in 1939. A curate in 1939-40 at St Bartholomew's, Roby, he was ordained priest in 1940 and moved to Great Yarmouth (1940-1). He was a chaplain in the Royal Air Force Volunteer Reserve from 1941 to 1943 and rector of Weeley thereafter. In 1945 he became vicar of St James's, Birkdale, Southport, where his talents as a Christian publicist were shown in a unique magazine, *Anvil*, which circulated far beyond the parish.

In 1948 he engaged a young artist, Frank *Hampson, to work first on *Anvil* and by 1949 on a new project, a strip cartoon magazine for boys. Morris saw clearly that boys were buying horror comics, produced for American servicemen of limited intelligence, because they wanted action stories in strip cartoon form, and not because they wanted pictures of savage sexual assaults on busty women. Hampson turned out to be a great strip cartoon artist, devising his own stories and characters and inventing spaceships and futuristic gadgets. He devised a cartoon about Dan Dare, space pilot, and he and Morris sent the dummy of a new paper, *Eagle*, to publishers. In October 1949 the dummy was bought by Hulton Press, which employed Morris and Hampson.

After unprecedented publicity, the first issue of *Eagle* went on sale on 14 April 1950 and was an immediate success. It was printed on good paper in four-colour rotogravure, on presses built by Eric Bemrose of Liverpool. The stories boys wanted—space adventure, cops and robbers, cowboys and Indians, fun and humour— and features they did not know they wanted until they had them, such as adventures of Christian heroes (these last proved fifth in popularity), were told in strip cartoon form. The depiction of historical scenes and clothing had to be accurate and the science in Dan Dare, space pilot of the future, must be beyond criticism: Hampson could invent what did not yet exist, provided there was no reason why it should not, but Dan must never do anything impossible, such as travelling at more than the speed of light.

The Morris family moved to Epsom in 1950 and Hampson's team was given a studio in the house. Although many girls read *Eagle*, the majority wanted their own paper, and *Girl* appeared in November 1951, to be followed in January 1953 by *Robin* (to teach smaller children to read) and in March 1954 *Swift* bridged the gap to the papers for older readers. The universal popularity of these magazines was not weakened by the fact that parents and teachers approved of them. They gave rise to annuals, the Eagle Club, and other expressions of belonging, including carol services, which filled St Paul's and other cathedrals. Morris dressed as a parson only for these events. His brilliance as an editor was recognized when (Sir) Edward *Hulton made him managing editor of *Housewife* (1954-9) and included him as a member of the Hulton Press management committee.

Morris left at the end of 1959 to join the National Magazine Company (a subsidiary of the Hearst Corporation of America) as editorial director in 1960. From 1964 until 1982 he was managing director and editor-in-chief. In the 1960s the company published eleven magazines, including *Good Housekeeping*, *She*, *Vanity Fair*, and *Connoisseur*. In the 1970s Morris bought *Queen* and amalgamated it with *Harper's*, and launched *Cosmopolitan* in Britain. In association with Condé Nast he formed COMAG, perhaps the biggest media distribution company in the country. He became deputy chairman of the

National Magazine Company in 1979 (the chairman had to be American). He increased the circulation of his company's magazines at a time when other magazines were struggling or going out of business. He retired in 1984. From 1952 to 1983 he was honorary chaplain of St Bride's, Fleet Street.

Morris's nine years at Hulton Press were exceeded in responsibility and success by his twenty-five years at the National Magazine Company, and yet it was for his creation of *Eagle* and *Girl* and for his powerful influence for good on a whole generation that he is remembered and revered. He was appointed OBE in 1983.

Morris was tall, thin, and fair, and looked like a sardonic Leslie *Howard. In 1941 he married Jessica, one of two actress daughters of John Hamlet Dunning, a representative for Clarks' shoes. They had a son, who died in a car accident in 1968, and three daughters. Morris died 16 March 1989 at King Edward VII Hospital for Officers, London. His memorial service filled St Bride's in Fleet Street to overflowing.

[Chad Varah, *Before I Die Again*, 1992; private information; personal knowledge.]   CHAD VARAH

MOSHINSKY, Alan Samuel (1914–1990), civil servant and ombudsman. [See MARRE, SIR ALAN SAMUEL.]

MOYNIHAN, (Herbert George) Rodrigo (1910–1990), painter, was born 17 October 1910 in Santa Cruz de Tenerife, Canary Islands, the elder son and elder child of Herbert James Moynihan, fruit broker, and his Spanish wife, Maria de la Puerta. His childhood and youth were peripatetic and between 1924 and 1927 he attended high school in Madison, New Jersey. In 1927–8 he was once more in Europe and declared his intention to study painting. In 1928 he was enrolled as a student at the Slade School of Fine Art, University of London, where he studied under Professor Henry *Tonks. A break in his progress occurred after his first year, when paternal pressure banished him to a broking office in the City; Tonks intervened on his behalf and from then onwards (he graduated in 1931) painting was his life.

An early cosmopolitanism in his outlook and tastes distinguished him from the run of his fellow students. At the same time there emerged characteristics of both innate conservatism and decided radicalism which were to shape the rest of his career and were marked features of his personality.

He first came to public notice through the exhibition 'Objective Abstractions' held at Zwemmer's Gallery, London, in March 1934, which he shared with Geoffrey Tibble, Graham Bell, and others. His works, evolved from elements of still life, were thickly encrusted, non-figurative paintings, indebted to the later paintings of J. M. W. *Turner and Claude Monet; in this, they ran counter to the prevailing geometric abstraction of, for example, Ben *Nicholson or Piet Mondrian. Although the works caused interest, he received little encouragement and, by the late 1930s, he returned to representational painting and gained considerable and increasing success over the following fifteen years. He was associated with, although not a member of, the Euston Road School (1937–9) through his friendship with (Sir) William *Coldstream, Victor Pasmore, Tibble, and Bell. Unlike them, he was not especially drawn to proletarian subject matter and his suave handling of paint and restricted colour range was distinct from, for example, Pasmore or Claude *Rogers at that time.

In the 1940s he became a celebrated 'conservative' artist known for his wartime paintings such as 'The Medical Inspection' (1943, Imperial War Museum) and 'Private Clarke, A.T.S.' (1943, Tate Gallery). He was called up in 1940, trained as a gunner, joined the camouflage section, and was invalided out after two years. He was an official war artist (1943–4) and became ARA (1944). After the war he became professor of painting at the Royal College of Art, London (1948–57), and in 1951 he produced his one book, *Goya*. In 1953 he was appointed CBE and in 1954 RA. It seemed he was cast in a mould all too familiar in the history of British art—of brilliant early achievement followed by establishment renown. By the mid-1950s he sensed he was trapped. The renewed possibilities of abstraction, the break-up of his first marriage, and his resignation from the Royal College and the Royal Academy (both 1957) all contributed to remarkable changes in his art and his personal circumstances.

The painterly daring of his early objective abstractions was harnessed to boldness of scale and dramatic colour to produce a handful of outstanding works. He was at first encouraged by the example of contemporary French *tachisme* and later by Sam Francis and American abstract expressionism, which he came to know well on several extended visits to New York in the 1960s with his second wife. It was during this period that they jointly edited (with Sonia Orwell and John Ashbery) the influential quarterly *Art and Literature* (1964–8).

Gradually the gestural freedom and liberality of options of this phase became burdensome; a hard-edge abstraction resulted in which areas of discrete colour are enlivened by bands, chevrons, and diamonds of contrasting hues. A 'sense of place' collides with severe geometric organization. At the same time Moynihan continued drawing from nature in the landscape near his homes in France (near Aix-en-Provence) and in Canada (New Brunswick).

In 1971 he resumed painting from life, chastened yet enriched by his second foray into abstraction. There then began what is perhaps his most notable contribution to painting—a series of still lifes of the quotidian objects on shelf or table top in his studio. They are painted in a light but intense scheme of colour, combining utmost dexterity of handling and subtle, unfussy composition. Such qualities also inform the portraits of the 1970s and 1980s which include penetrating studies of Francis Bacon, Sir William Coldstream, Friedrich von Hayek, and Benedict *Nicolson (the last two in the collection of the National Portrait Gallery, as is his 'The Rt. Hon. Margaret Thatcher, P.M.', 1984). In 1979 he was re-elected to the Royal Academy, the year after his full-scale retrospective was held there. He had been honoured by a fellowship of University College London in 1970.

Moynihan's personality mixed Spanish hauteur, English conservatism, and a mercurial intellectual curiosity. He was well read and well travelled and in conduct was both confidential and secretive, sybaritic yet disciplined. Attractive, attentive, and amorous, he had several love affairs. Early good looks, Mediterranean in cast, continued to give distinction to a face he recorded in a series of perceptive self-portraits. In later years poor health diminished his activities. In painting, his place is assured by the still lifes of his last decades in which visual values alone effect a brooding and magical transformation of the oppressive material of day-to-day life.

In 1931 Moynihan married the painter Elinor Bellingham Smith (died 1988), daughter of Guy Bellingham Smith, obstetrician and registrar at Guy's Hospital and collector of drawings and prints. They had one son. They were divorced in 1960 and in the same year he married the painter Anne Dunn, divorced wife of Michael Wishart and daughter of Sir James Hamet Dunn, first baronet, industrialist. They also had one son. Moynihan died in London in his South Kensington studio 6 November 1990.

[Richard Shone and John Ashbery, *Rodrigo Moynihan*, 1988; private information; personal knowledge.]

RICHARD SHONE

MUGGERIDGE, (Thomas) Malcolm (1903–1990), journalist and broadcaster, was born 24 March 1903 in Croydon, the third of five sons, one of whom died in 1922 (there were no daughters), of Henry Thomas Benjamin Muggeridge, Labour politician, and his wife Annie Booler, from Sheffield. His father, elected MP for Romford in 1929, was a self-educated Fabian with an unwavering dedication to socialism. He was the formative influence on his son's early years and as a small boy Malcolm accompanied him on his street-corner electioneering. After attending Selhurst Grammar School, Muggeridge went to Selwyn College, Cambridge, where he studied natural sciences but left with a pass degree (1923). It was here that, under the influence of Alec Vidler (a lifelong friend) and later of Wilfred *Knox, his religious instincts were first aroused and he even thought at one stage of following Vidler into the Anglican ministry. However he opted instead for a teaching post at Union Christian College, Alwaye, near Madras, India, where he remained for two years (1925–7).

But Muggeridge was perpetually restless and, after quarrelling with the college principal, he returned to England and took a job as a supply teacher in Birmingham. Shortly afterwards, in 1927, he married Katherine Rosalind ('Kitty'), daughter of George Cumberland Dobbs (an employee of the famous travel agent Sir Henry *Lunn) and his wife Rosie, the youngest sister of Beatrice *Webb. Kitty thereafter was to be the only permanent fixture in his life.

He taught English for a time at Cairo University (1927–30) and whilst there began to submit reports of the Egyptian political scene to the *Manchester Guardian*. In August 1930 he arrived in Manchester and was recruited on to the staff of the paper as a leader-writer, on the recommendation of Arthur *Ransome. He would perhaps have risen high on the staff but for the sudden death by drowning of E. T. Scott, who took over the editorship from his famous father C. P. *Scott. Muggeridge had developed a strong antipathy to Scott's successor, W. P. *Crozier, and was in a mood of disappointment following the formation of the national government in 1931. In September 1932 he and Kitty decided to go and live in Russia, which they regarded, like many young nonconformists of the time, as the new Jerusalem.

Muggeridge, however, was quickly disillusioned and after reporting first hand on the Ukraine famine—almost the only western journalist to do so—he went to Switzerland and worked for the League of Nations. In 1934 he took a job in India as assistant editor of the *Calcutta Statesman* and then worked for a short time on the staff of the London *Evening Standard*. Muggeridge always chafed at being a mere journalist and had already written a play and three novels (one of which, 'Picture Palace', a satirical account of his time on the *Manchester Guardian*, had been recalled and suppressed by the publisher). In 1936, encouraged by his great friend Hugh *Kingsmill, he abandoned full-time journalism and went to live at Whatlington in Sussex. In 1936 he published a critical biography of Samuel *Butler and in 1938 another novel, *In a Valley of This Restless Mind*. He also wrote *The Thirties* (1940), a social survey of the decade which first revealed his formidable powers as a political satirist and was remarkable for its anarchic wit and skilful use of quotation (a hallmark of Muggeridge's style).

At the outbreak of war Muggeridge joined the Intelligence Corps and after a few months was transferred to MI6. He was sent to Lourenço Marques in Mozambique, where he proved an effective agent in the fight to prevent the sinking of Allied shipping by German U-boats. He also served in North Africa, Italy, and, at the end of the war, in Paris, where he was instrumental in protecting (Sir) P. G. *Wodehouse, then under suspicion of collaborating with the Germans. He was decorated with the Legion of Honour and the croix de guerre with palm.

Muggeridge always liked to swim against the tide and in 1945 joined the Conservative *Daily Telegraph* as a leader-writer. He then became the *Telegraph*'s Washington correspondent (1946–7). He was the paper's deputy editor in 1950–2. In late 1952, to universal surprise, he accepted the editorship of *Punch*, the first non-member of staff ever to do so. He proved an effective editor, transforming the staid old periodical with his lively and satirical journalism. But, after an initial rise, the circulation fell again and Muggeridge resigned in 1957. By now he was already involved in television as a presenter of the BBC's *Panorama*, a magazine programme devoted to politics and the arts. Muggeridge had a natural flair for television and with his outspoken views, drawling voice, and long cigarette holder quickly became a household name. Briefly suspended by the BBC in late 1957, after he had published in the USA an article attacking the cult of monarchy, he appeared on a wide variety of programmes throughout the 1960s and 1970s, notably a series of autobiographical documentaries, including *Twilight of Empire* and *Ladies and Gentlemen It Is My Pleasure*—an account of a lecture tour in America.

All his life Muggeridge had been restless, dissatisfied, and tormented by strong appetites for women and drink. At about the age of sixty he made a series of renunciations—of drinking, meat-eating, smoking, and casual love affairs. He and Kitty had finally settled at Park Cottage in Robertsbridge, an idyllic setting at the end of a long farm track in the Sussex countryside. Here Muggeridge experienced for the first time a degree of contentment and peace. He developed a routine of early rising, writing, and long walks (in which visitors were expected to join). He rediscovered his faith and became in print and on television a formidable apologist for Christianity. He was the first to introduce Mother Teresa to a worldwide audience with his film *Something Beautiful for God*, later published in book form (1971). Muggeridge was received into the Roman Catholic Church in 1982.

Muggeridge was a man of middle height, with bright blue eyes and a bulbous nose. He had an enormous vitality and charm and was blessed with generous instincts which usually won over even his fiercest opponents (of whom there were many). He had no ambition for office of any kind and generally acted on impulse. His enormous success as a television personality came about by chance and may have encouraged a natural vanity. But he never lost the ability to laugh at himself. He was sustained throughout his life by the love of his wife, Kitty, who died in 1994. They had three sons and a daughter. Muggeridge died 14 November 1990 after a long decline and was buried near his father in Whatlington.

[Malcolm Muggeridge, *Chronicles of Wasted Time*: vol. i *The Green Stick*, 1972, vol. ii *The Infernal Grove*, 1973; Malcolm Muggeridge, *Like It Was* (diaries), 1981; Ian Hunter, *Malcolm Muggeridge: a Life*, 1980; Richard Ingrams, *God's Apology, a Chronicle of 3 Friends*, 1977, and *Muggeridge: the Biography*, 1995; Gregory Wolfe, *Malcolm Muggeridge: a Biography*, 1995; personal knowledge.]   RICHARD INGRAMS

MURDOCH, Richard Bernard (1907–1990), actor and comedian, was born 6 April 1907 at the family home in Keston, Kent, the only son of Bernard Murdoch, tea merchant, and his wife Amy Florence, daughter of Avison Terry Scott, archdeacon of Tonbridge. He was educated at Charterhouse School and Pembroke College, Cambridge, which he left without gaining a degree, his appetite for a career in show business being whetted by success with the Cambridge Footlights.

Murdoch's professional stage career began in 1927 at the King's theatre, Southsea, in the chorus of the musical play *The Blue Train*. He then worked in the chorus and played small parts in various musical comedies and revues including *That's a Good Girl* (1928), *Oh Letty!* (1929), *Cochran's 1930 Revue*, and *Stand Up and Sing* (1931). This was followed in the 1930s by André *Charlot's West End revues and the musical comedy *Over She Goes* (1936). By the mid-1930s his reputation as a first-class light comedian was growing.

In 1938 the BBC teamed Murdoch with Arthur *Askey in the radio series *Band Waggon*, in which they were alleged to live in a flat in Broadcasting House, and many sketches were based on this notion. Their humour was a forerunner of much radio comedy to come, for although their comic interludes only took up ten minutes of the weekly one-hour programme, the fantasy of their living in Broadcasting House, and the creation of such mythical characters as Mrs Bagwash the charlady and her daughter

Nausea and their pet animals, a goat called Lewis, and two pigeons Basil and Lucy, preceded *ITMA* and *Hancock's Half Hour* and was a strong influence on many nascent comedy scriptwriters.

In 1938, after two series, the stage rights to *Band Waggon* were acquired by the impresario Jack *Hylton, and Murdoch with Askey and a supporting cast toured the provincial music-halls and finished with a run at the London Palladium in 1939. The debonair, sophisticated West End style of Murdoch blended neatly with the more down-to-earth humour of Liverpudlian Arthur Askey, whose reputation was based on his successes in seaside concert party. It was Askey who gave Murdoch the nickname 'Stinker'. Together they were enormously successful.

In 1941 Murdoch joined the Royal Air Force as a pilot officer working in the intelligence sector of Bomber Command. Later he was posted to the Air Ministry in London, where he was promoted to squadron-leader in the directorate of administrative plans, under the command of Wing Commander Kenneth *Horne. The two quickly became friends and as both were regular broadcasters it was only a matter of time (1944) before they dreamed up the mythical RAF station *Much Binding in the Marsh*. This became the RAF segment of a Services series *Merry Go Round*, alternating with the Royal Navy show HMS *Waterlogged*, written by and starring Eric Barker, and the army contribution *Stand Easy*, with Charlie Chester.

Murdoch and Horne wrote the scripts of the *Much Binding* shows and when peace came in 1945 they duly transferred it to a civilian milieu, where it thrived until 1954. From then on Richard Murdoch's career was varied and interesting and included a tour of South Africa, a season in Canada playing William the waiter in G. B. *Shaw's *You Never Can Tell*, and a round-the-world trip for the Australian Broadcasting Corporation in a series of programmes called *Much Murdoch*.

His next major success was the BBC radio series *The Men from the Ministry* (1961–77), in which he co-starred first with Wilfrid Hyde-White and later with Deryck Guyler. Towards the end of his life Richard Murdoch appeared in several episodes of the television series *Rumpole of the Bailey*, playing the aged barrister 'Uncle Tom'.

Murdoch was six feet one inch tall and good looking. He was always polished and well mannered and was, to quote James Green, the show business columnist, 'a subtle and charming comic actor'. In 1932 he married Peggy, daughter of William Rawlings, solicitor. They had one son and two daughters. Richard Murdoch died 9 October 1990. As a keen golfer he could not have

wished for a better end, for he died while playing golf at Walton Heath, Surrey.

[Norman Hackforth, *Solo for Horne*, 1976; Barry Took, *Laughter in the Air*, 1976; personal knowledge.]

BARRY TOOK

MURLESS, SIR (**Charles Francis**) **Noel** (1910–1987), racehorse trainer, was born 24 March 1910 at Duckington Grange, Malpas, Cheshire, the elder son (there were no daughters) of Charles Herbert Murless, farmer, and his wife Mary Constance, daughter of Frank Lloyd, auctioneer, of Wrexham, north Wales. Having ridden and hunted from early boyhood, Noel Murless was inspired to make a career in racing by seeing Poethlyn, owned by his parents' neighbour, Mrs Hugh Peel, win the Grand National in 1919.

For a short time Noel Murless, while performing the duties of a stable lad, rode in steeplechases and hurdle races with limited success, as an amateur and then as a professional, for Frank Hartigan, a trainer in Weyhill, Hampshire. On leaving Weyhill in 1930, Murless commenced a period of five years as assistant to Hartigan's brother Hubert, first at the Curragh, and then at Penrith in Westmorland. In July 1935 he commenced training at Hambleton Lodge, near Thirsk in the North Riding of Yorkshire, with five horses belonging to Lady Maureen Stanley, Dick Taylor, J. T. Rogers, and Andrew Johnstone. On 2 September 1935 he obtained his first success with J. T. Rogers's Rubin Wood in the Lee plate at Lanark. He had only one winner again in 1936, but in 1939 he won ten races.

During World War II Murless conducted a small stable at Middleham in Yorkshire, having been rejected by the forces because of injuries to his feet, sustained in 1930. After the war Murless came further to the fore, and in 1946 he was leading northern trainer with thirty-four races worth £15,337 to his credit. He was leading northern trainer again in 1947, obtaining his first important success with Closeburn in the Stewards' cup at Goodwood. Following the retirement of Fred Darling at the end of 1947, Murless was invited to succeed him in the powerful Beckhampton stable, near Calne in Wiltshire, on the recommendation of the stable jockey (Sir) Gordon *Richards, who had been greatly impressed by his always carrying his own saddle and other evidence of personal attention to detail. Patrons of the stable included King *George VI, J. A. Dewar, the whisky millionaire, Sir Percy *Loraine, Major and Mrs Macdonald-Buchanan, and Colonel Giles Loder. In his first season at Beckhampton, Murless almost brought off the Newmarket classic double. The Cobbler was only beaten by a head in the Two Thousand Guineas, and Queenpot won the One Thousand Guineas. At the end of that season of 1948,

Murless was champion trainer, having won sixty-three races worth £66,542. In 1949 Major Macdonald-Buchanan's Abernant was beaten by a short head in the Two Thousand Guineas, but G. R. H. Smith's Ridgewood won the St Leger. The grey Abernant became an excellent sprinter, twice winning both the July cup at Newmarket and the Nunthorpe stakes at York (1949 and 1950).

Having moved to the palatial Warren Place stable at Newmarket towards the end of 1952, Murless performed a remarkable feat by winning the Two Thousand Guineas and Derby of 1957 with Sir Victor Sassoon's Crepello, a heavy-topped colt with far from the best legs. In 1957 he also won the Oaks with Carrozza, leased by the queen from the National Stud, and thus became that year's champion trainer, having won races worth £116,898. He was the first to amass a six-figure sum in a season. In 1959 he broke his own record by winning £145,727, when Ali Khan's grey filly, Petite Étoile, won the One Thousand Guineas, Oaks, Sussex stakes, Yorkshire Oaks, and Champion stakes.

During 1960 Murless won the Derby and St Leger with Sir Victor Sassoon's St Paddy. Although another St Leger was won with Vera Lilley's ill-tempered Aurelius in 1961, and Murless was champion trainer for the third consecutive time, the season was marred by Sir Victor's Pinturischio being so badly nobbled while favourite for the Derby that he could never run again. A third record was broken in 1967, when Murless won sixty races worth £256,899, including the Two Thousand Guineas and Derby with H. J. Joel's Royal Palace, and the One Thousand Guineas with R. C. Boucher's Fleet. The King George VI and Queen Elizabeth stakes and the Eclipse stakes were won by Stanhope Joel's Busted, who had improved greatly since joining Murless from Ireland. When champion trainer again in 1968, Murless won the One Thousand Guineas with Caergwrle, bred and owned by his wife. Murless was champion trainer for the ninth and final time in 1973, obtaining the last of his nineteen classic successes with G. Pope's Mysterious in the Oaks. He retired at the end of 1976, and sold Warren Place to his son-in-law, Henry Cecil.

A tall, handsome man, with rather aquiline features and large brown eyes in a weather-beaten face, Murless had brown hair, which was silver in late middle age, brushed straight back from his forehead. He was impatient with people who sought information about horses with a view to making money, something to which he himself was almost indifferent. On the other hand, he would go to a great deal of trouble, not least with younger people, to help those anxious to increase their knowledge of the thoroughbred. Although he had no liking for the limelight, he had many close friends, mainly amongst owners and breeders, who found him a generous and amusing host. He was knighted in the silver jubilee honours in June 1977, and elected to the Jockey Club the following month. To a great extent his success was due to his inexhaustible patience and natural empathy with his horses, whose hallmark was a muscular robustness. To conserve nervous energy, he always kept them absolutely relaxed. On taking over Beckhampton, he gave orders that the horses' heads should be held by one rack chain, instead of three, while being dressed over, so that they could cope with irritation by flies.

On 28 November 1940 Murless married Gwendolen Mary Lindsay, daughter of William Lindsay Carlow, coal exporter, of Craigend, Troon, Ayrshire. The only child of the marriage, Julia, married the future champion trainer Henry Cecil in 1966. Murless died 9 May 1987 of emphysema and chronic bronchitis at his home, The Bungalow, Woodditton, Newmarket.

[Tim Fitzgeorge-Parker, *The Guv'nor*, 1980; *Sporting Life*, 11 May 1987; private information; personal knowledge.]   RICHARD ONSLOW

MYNORS, SIR Roger Aubrey Baskerville (1903–1989), classical scholar, was born 28 July 1903 at Langley Burrell, Wiltshire, the eldest of four sons and second of five children of the Revd Aubrey Baskerville Mynors, rector of Langley Burrell, and his wife, Margery Musgrave, daughter of the Revd Charles Musgrave Harvey, prebendary of St Paul's Cathedral. His younger twin Humphrey (later first baronet), to whom he bore a confusing resemblance in earlier years, was to become deputy governor of the Bank of England, a position that had been held by his mother's brother, Sir Ernest Musgrave Harvey, first baronet. He was educated at Eton (scholar 1916) and Balliol College, Oxford (exhibitioner 1922), where he obtained firsts in classical honour moderations (1924) and *literae humaniores* (1926), as well as the Hertford (1924), Craven (1924), and Derby (1926) scholarships.

He was elected a fellow of Balliol in 1926; pupils remember how he introduced them to authors remote from the syllabus. In 1940 he went to the exchange control department of the Treasury as a temporary principal. In 1944 he was elected to the Kennedy chair of Latin at Cambridge, where he became a fellow of Pembroke College, but he never seemed to settle. In 1949 he was disappointed not to become master of Balliol, when Sir David *Keir was preferred. In 1953 he returned to Oxford as Corpus Christi professor of Latin in succession to Eduard *Fraenkel, and he remained at Corpus Christi College till his retirement in 1970.

His contribution to learning for most of his life centred on Latin manuscripts. He saw them as part of the cultural history of Europe; for him the scribes were not anonymous symbols at the foot of the page, but human beings and friends, who could be placed and dated and sometimes identified. He was a rapid and meticulous collator from an age without microfilms; his 'apparatus criticus' was always elegant and unfussy, like everything else including his handwriting, but he was not assertive enough to offer many conjectures of his own. He edited the *Institutiones* of Cassiodorus (1937), Catullus (1958), Pliny's letters (1963), the *Panegyrici Latini* (1964), and Virgil (1969). He was a medievalist at least as much as a classical scholar, and he did much to promote Nelson's Medieval Texts, where he was generous with unobtrusive help to others. He produced catalogues of the manuscripts of Durham Cathedral before 1200, a sumptuous book (1939), and of Balliol College, a conspicuously professional performance (1963). He was a precise and economical translator who contributed much to the Toronto translation of Erasmus (from 1974) and took part in the final revision of the New English Bible.

He was a fascinating lecturer whom undergraduates flocked to hear, not because he helped them for their examinations but because they found him so interesting. He supervised graduate students by describing his own researches and inspiring them to do likewise. He was a courteous chairman, yet with something in his manner that discouraged time-wasters. He was a delightful letter-writer to his friends, with great sympathy for the young, but did not hurry to reply on matters of business. He was not easy to find, but was there to help when it mattered most. His charm was memorable, but there was a touch of astringency towards the incompetent and self-important, and in spite of his urbanity he showed a diffidence that was not entirely assumed. Though the least didactic of teachers, he could throw off a remark that changed one's approach to the subject, and sensible people followed up his most tentative suggestions.

For many years he occupied himself with a commentary on Virgil's *Georgics* that appeared posthumously in 1990. It paid no particular regard to recent periodical articles, or to the fads and fancies of a younger generation of scholars. Instead it showed an expert knowledge of ancient and modern agriculture, a flair for integrating interesting things from a wide range of reading, and a sensitive ear for what the poet is actually saying. Above all it was directed by the author's feeling for the countryside, and particularly for Treago, the estate he inherited near St Weonards in Herefordshire. Anybody who wishes to know what Mynors was like should read this book.

He became a fellow of the British Academy in 1944 and was knighted in 1963. He was an honorary fellow of Balliol (1963) and Corpus Christi (1970) colleges, Oxford, of Pembroke College, Cambridge (1965), and of the Warburg Institute. He was an honorary member of the American Academy of Arts and Sciences, the American Philosophical Society, and the Istituto di Studi Romani. He held honorary degrees from the universities of Cambridge, Durham, Edinburgh, Sheffield, and Toronto.

In 1945 he married Lavinia Sybil, daughter of the Very Revd Cyril Argentine *Alington, dean of Durham and formerly his headmaster at Eton, and his wife, Hester Margaret, a daughter of the fourth Baron *Lyttelton; it was to prove an ideally happy union. There were no children. His sister-in-law Elizabeth was married to Lord Home of the Hirsel. Mynors died 17 October 1989 as the result of a road accident outside Hereford; he was driving back to Treago after working on his catalogue of the manuscripts in Hereford Cathedral library. As he left the cathedral he was heard to say that he had had a good day.

[R. G. M. Nisbet in *Gnomon*, vol. lxii, 1990; M. Winterbottom in *Proceedings of the British Academy*, vol. lxxx, 1991; personal knowledge.]   R. G. M. NISBET

MYRES, (John) Nowell (Linton) (1902–1989), historian, archaeologist, and Bodley's librarian at Oxford, was born at 1 Wellington Place, Oxford, 27 December 1902, the younger son and second of three children of (Sir) John Linton *Myres, archaeologist and historian, and his wife Sophia Florence Ballance, who was of Huguenot descent. Books brought over by her forebears in 1685, as well as sixteenth-century *incunabula* bought with his own pocket money, contributed to the boyhood inheritance of the future custodian of Bodley. From his preparatory school on the Surrey–Sussex border he won a scholarship to Winchester. Deeply influenced by the college architecture and the inspired history teaching of A. T. P. *Williams, later bishop of Durham and of Winchester, he went to New College, Oxford, in 1921 determined to make history his subject; substituting the history preliminary examination for classical honour moderations, he took a first in *literae humaniores* (1924) in three years and another in modern history (1926) in two.

After appointment as a college lecturer in modern history in 1926 he was elected a Student of Christ Church in 1928; thereafter, apart from wartime civil service (1940–5), in which he rose to be head of the fruit and vegetable products division of the Ministry of Food (he was a keen vegetable gardener), tutoring and lecturing were his formal occupation for the next twenty years.

They were also years of strenuous extra-collegial activity. Earlier excavations at St Catharine's Hill, Winchester, and at Caerleon amphitheatre were now followed by others at Colchester, Butley Priory in Suffolk, and Aldborough in Yorkshire. In 1931 he was invited to contribute a section on the English Settlements, based on archaeological as well as historical sources, to the first volume (*Roman Britain and the English Settlements*, 1936) of the new *Oxford History of England*. R. G. *Collingwood was his fellow author.

Librarian of Christ Church from 1938, Myres, with his versatile scholarship and proven ability as an administrator, was a natural choice in 1947 as successor to Sir H. H. Edmund Craster as Bodley's librarian, after a brief tenure by H. R. Creswick. His own tenure lasted for eighteen years and involved integrating the 1939 extension with the parent institution, the major repair and internal reordering of the buildings round the schools quadrangle, and supervision of a total structural overhaul of the fabric of Duke Humfrey, the fifteenth-century reading room above the vault of the Divinity School. He also presided over the establishment of the new law library in St Cross Road. He widened the Bodleian's status and repute by setting up and hosting the copyright libraries conference and establishing the standing conference of national and university libraries; also he founded the Society of Bodley's American Friends. Though a non-professional, in 1963 he was elected president of the Library Association. Bitter disagreement with the university authorities over their refusal to accept his defence of the Bodleian's claim to the premises of the Indian Institute led to his resignation after a dramatic debate in Congregation in 1965. (As Bodley's librarian he invariably wore a dark coat and striped trousers, even when riding a bicycle, and in later life grew a huge beard like his father's.)

From now on Myres gave his whole mind to archaeology and the pursuit of the course he had set himself in 1931. His Rhind lectures of 1964–5 appeared in 1969 as *Anglo-Saxon Pottery and the Settlement of England*; in 1973 came *The Anglo-Saxon Cemeteries of Caistor-by-Norwich and Markshall* (jointly with Barbara Green); 1977 saw the achievement of the long-envisaged *A Corpus of Anglo-Saxon Pottery of the Pagan Period*; finally, in 1986, he was able to bring out a revision and reassessment, as an independent volume of the *Oxford History*, of his *English Settlements* of fifty years earlier.

Many societies benefited from his unremitting involvement in their affairs, notably the Oxford University Archaeological Society, the Council for British Archaeology (of which he was a joint originator), the Sachsensymposium, and the Society for Medieval Archaeology. The Society of Antiquaries of London, whose president he was in 1970–5, awarded him their gold medal (1976) for services to archaeology. He was a valued member of many official bodies, amongst them the Royal Commission on Historical Monuments (1969–74) and the Ancient Monuments Board (1959–76). He was especially noted for his friendliness and sense of fun, as also for his helpfulness to younger scholars. Totally without pomposity, he brightened his later bedridden days with the use of one of his doctoral robes as a dressing-gown. Quick to apply modern terms to ancient situations, he chuckled a lot when giving the title 'Charlemagne on Miniskirts' to a learned but light-hearted note in *Antiquity* (vol. xlii, 1968, p. 125).

Myres was elected FBA in 1966 and appointed CBE in 1972. He was a fellow (1951–77) and sub-warden of Winchester, honorary fellow of New College (1973), and successively research, emeritus, and honorary Student (1971) of Christ Church. He received honorary doctorates from the universities of Toronto (1954), Reading (1964), Belfast (1965), and Durham (1983). In 1929 he married a teacher, Joan Mary Lovell (died 1991), sister of Charles Stevens, his school friend and fellow excavator of St Catharine's Hill, and daughter of George Lovell Stevens, farmer in southern Africa. They had two sons, the elder, Timothy, associate professor of zoology in the University of Calgary, the younger, Rear-Admiral John Myres, hydrographer of the Royal Navy. Myres died at his home, The Manor House, Kennington, 25 July 1989.

[*Oxford Times*, 24 January 1986; *The Times*, 26 July 1989; J. N. L. Myres, 'Recent Discoveries in the Bodleian Library', *Archaeologia*, vol. ci, 1967; A. J. Taylor in *Proceedings of the British Academy*, vol. lxxvi, 1990; bibliography (1926–78) in V. I. Evison (ed.), *Angles, Saxons and Jutes: Essays Presented to J. N. L. Myres*, 1981, continued to 1988 in British Academy *Proceedings*, as above; unpublished autobiography in the possession of the family; personal knowledge.]

ARNOLD J. TAYLOR

N

NEAGLE, DAME Anna (1904–1986), stage and film actress, and film producer, was born (Florence) Marjorie Robertson in Forest Gate, Essex, 20 October 1904, the only daughter and youngest of three children of Herbert William Robertson, a captain in the merchant navy, and his wife, Florence Neagle. She was educated at the High School, St Albans, and at Wordsworth's Physical Training College, South Kensington. After being a student dance teacher, from 1925 to 1930 she appeared in the chorus of revues produced by André *Charlot and (Sir) Charles *Cochran.

In 1930 she changed her name to Anna Neagle. Her first significant film part was in *Goodnight Vienna* (1932), directed by Herbert *Wilcox, who went on to direct thirty-two films with Neagle. Her first major film success was in *Nell Gwyn* (1934), and she gradually became synonymous with the historical picture, especially when Wilcox directed her in *Victoria the Great* (1937), an unexpectedly popular and critical success. It won the *Picturegoer* gold medal award and the gold cup at the Venice film festival. Neagle and Wilcox went to America to publicize its release and on their return repeated the formula successfully in Technicolor with *Sixty Glorious Years* (1938).

Anna Neagle went to America in 1939 and made four films with RKO studios: *Nurse Edith Cavell* (1939) and three musical comedies, *Irene* (1940), *No, No, Nanette* (1940), and *Sunny* (1941). She was the first actress to appear on the cover of *Life* magazine. On her return to Britain she started work on a film of the life of the aviator Amy *Johnson, *They Flew Alone* (1941). Her next film was *Yellow Canary* (1943), about a Women's Royal Naval Service intelligence worker mistaken for a Nazi spy.

In 1945 her films became less heroic, and more escapist light entertainment, as she continued to straddle her film career with stage appearances and tours. She appeared in the film *I Live in Grosvenor Square* (1945), co-starring (Sir) Rex *Harrison, and went on a European ENSA (Entertainments National Service Association) tour in the play *French Without Tears*. After the war Neagle starred in a distinctive series of musical comedies with Michael Wilding. The first of the 'London series' was *Piccadilly Incident* (1946), which won the *Daily Mail* national film

award, as did its successor, *The Courtneys of Curzon Street* (1947). For her performances in both films Neagle received the *Picturegoer* gold medal. The third film in the Neagle–Wilding partnership was *Spring in Park Lane* (1948).

Aware of her previous success in 'bio-pics', Herbert Wilcox directed Neagle as Odette Sansom, a Special Operations Executive undercover agent, who had been tortured by the Nazis, in the film *Odette* (1950). As a result Neagle was appointed an honorary ensign (1950) of the First Aid Nursing Yeomanry (FANY), an appropriate award for an actress who went on to play Florence Nightingale in *The Lady with a Lamp* (1951).

In 1957 Anna Neagle produced *These Dangerous Years*, starring Frankie Vaughan, and was directed for the first time by a person other than Herbert Wilcox (Cyril Frankel) in *No Time for Tears* (1957). After her first box-office flop, *The Lady Is a Square* (1958), financial problems beset Neagle and Wilcox and her attempt to start a dance school failed. Eventually, however, theatre appearances helped to resuscitate her flagging career.

Neagle was distinctive for her ability to maintain a 'regal presence' on screen. She was an 'English' beauty with a striking bone structure, who maintained her dancer's figure throughout her life. She could look equally at home in a glamorous ball gown or a practical flying-suit. Despite her variety of parts, her portrayals of heroines firmly placed her as a British icon in a patriotic style of film-making. She was appointed CBE in 1952 and DBE in 1969. She also received the freedom of the City of London (1981) and the Order of St John (1981).

In 1943 she married Herbert Sydney Wilcox (died 1977), film director and producer, the son of Joseph John Wilcox, sculptor and manager of a billiard hall. They had no children. Anna Neagle died 3 June 1986 at a nursing home in West Byfleet, Woking, Surrey.

[Anna Neagle, *It's Been Fun*, 1949, and *There's Always Tomorrow*, 1974; British Film Institute microfiche jackets.]   SARAH STREET

NICHOLSON, Norman Cornthwaite (1914–1987), poet and critic, was born 8 January 1914 at 14 St George's Terrace, Millom, Cumberland, the only child of Joseph Nicholson, tailor and draper, also of Millom, and his wife, Edith Cornthwaite, the daughter of a butcher. His mother died when he was five, and his father remarried three years later. He was educated at Millom Secondary School, but in his adolescence he developed tuberculosis, and from 1930 to 1932 was confined to hospital in Hampshire. One of his lungs was removed. This was the only period in Nicholson's life when he spent any considerable time away from his native and ancestral Millom, the source of much of his inspiration both in verse and prose.

He began writing at an early age. He was encouraged in this by a local clergyman, the Revd Samuel Taylor, who put him in touch with Brother George Every, poet, literary critic, and theologian, and a contributor to the *Criterion*; through Every, Nicholson was introduced in 1938 to the editor of that journal, T. S. *Eliot, who showed an interest in his poems. In the same year, Nicholson began to give lectures on literature to local Workers' Educational Association classes, material from which he used in his first critical book, *Man and Literature* (1943); but already, in 1942, he had edited a Penguin *Anthology of Religious Verse*, and before that had started to publish poems in periodicals, including some in the United States.

Nicholson's upbringing was in the Methodist church, to which his stepmother belonged, but in 1940 he was confirmed in the Church of England. His Christian faith was central to him throughout his life. Much of his poetry and his verse plays drew on this faith, nourished by his devotion to the landscapes, history, people, and stories of Cumberland. All are abundantly present in his first individual volume of poems, *Five Rivers*, which Eliot accepted for Faber & Faber and which was published in 1944. This had been preceded in 1943 by a selection of his work published in one volume alongside selections from Keith *Douglas and J. C. Hall. Nicholson went on to publish another ten books and pamphlets of poems, including a *Selected* volume in 1966, augmented in 1982. All were well received, as authentic and sometimes gently quirky products of a life which, though restricted by Nicholson's fragile health ('My ways are circumscribed,' he wrote in a poem, 'The Pot Geranium'), had broader visions of a universe of rock, rivers, hills, and the sea.

In appearance, he was craggy, increasingly bewhiskered with impressive sideburns. He had a fine head, brightly flashing and mischievous eyes, and an engaging and often roguish smile. His voice, as a result of lung operations, was hoarse but also strikingly vigorous: he was a splendid reader not only of his own poems but of other poets too, especially his beloved *Wordsworth,

parts of whose *Prelude* he read in a memorable series of BBC Third Programme broadcasts in the early 1960s. He was a much sought-after reader at literary gatherings up and down the country and, though these expeditions often exhausted him, he enjoyed them.

In 1956 he married a teacher, Yvonne Edith, daughter of John Oswald Gardner, engineering draughtsman. The partnership was a very happy one, until her death in 1982. Her loss left him desolate; and, much though he enjoyed the literary recognition and honours that increasingly came to him in his later years, they could not compensate for her absence. They had lived cheerfully in the small terraced house in Millom which had always been Nicholson's home (indeed, he had been born there, when it was also his father's shop), and he continued to live there after Yvonne's death. There were no children.

He was elected FRSL in 1945, and that year was given the Heinemann award. In 1967 he shared the Cholmondeley award for poetry with Seamus Heaney and Brian Jones. He received a Society of Authors' travelling bursary in 1973 (spent visiting Scandinavia) and an Arts Council bursary in 1977, which was also the year he was awarded the Queen's medal for poetry. He received an honorary MA from the University of Manchester in 1959 and another from the Open University in 1975. Manchester Polytechnic conferred on him an honorary fellowship in 1979, and he received a Litt.D. from the universities of Liverpool (1980) and Manchester (1984). One of his most treasured honours, which he delighted in showing to visitors, was the OBE, conferred in 1981. Perhaps even more, he was deeply moved by a volume of poems and prose pieces by many distinguished writers, *Between Comets* (edited by William Scammell), published and presented to him on his seventieth birthday in 1984.

Among Nicholson's many other publications were books and anthologies concerned with the history and topography of the Lake District, four verse plays, two early novels, and a life of William *Cowper (1951). The most individual and revealing of all is *Wednesday Early Closing* (1975), a memoir of his early years, full of the characters, anecdotes, sights, sounds, and smells of his Millom boyhood. He died 30 May 1987 at Whitehaven.

[Norman Nicholson, *Wednesday Early Closing*, 1975; Philip Gardner, *Norman Nicholson*, 1973; personal knowledge.]　　　　　　　ANTHONY THWAITE

NORWICH, first VISCOUNTESS (1892–1986), beauty, actress, memorable hostess and guest, and autobiographer. [See COOPER, LADY DIANA OLIVIA WINIFRED MAUD.]

O

OAKESHOTT, Michael Joseph (1901–1990), philosopher, was born 11 December 1901 at Chelsfield, Kent, the second of three sons (there were no daughters) of Joseph Francis Oakeshott, of Harpenden, a Fabian civil servant who had played a part in founding the London School of Economics, and his wife, Frances Maude Hellicar. Oakeshott was educated at St George's School, Harpenden, a progressive co-educational school, and has left moving accounts of the excitements a boy of scholarly disposition might enjoy as he came into contact with his classical inheritance. Oakeshott went to Gonville and Caius College, Cambridge, in 1920, and after a year in Germany in 1923–4 following graduation (he was placed in the second division of the first class in both parts—1922 and 1923—of the history tripos), and a short period as a school master at Lytham St Anne's Grammar School, became a history fellow of the college in 1925.

His early interests were in religion and historiography. Both led him on to philosophy and generated *Experience and Its Modes* (1933), in which he distinguished the different forms of human activity. R. G. *Collingwood admired particularly its treatment of history, but the reception of the book was cool. The 1,000 copies printed took over thirty years to sell out. In 1936 Oakeshott collaborated with Guy Griffith on *A Guide to the Classics: or How to Pick the Derby Winner*, an analysis of horse-racing whose second edition was called *How to Pick the Winner* (1947). In 1939 he published an anthology of political writings with commentary: *The Social and Political Doctrines of Contemporary Europe*.

During World War II he enlisted as a gunner and rose to be a captain in Phantom, a special unit whose dangerous work it was to report on the effect of artillery fire from close to the front. In 1945 he returned to Cambridge and wrote his famous introduction to *Hobbes's *Leviathan* (1946). Editing the *Cambridge Journal* from 1947 until its demise in 1954, he contributed actively to making it a centre of intellectual resistance to the ideas of social engineering, collectivism, and state planning dominant at that period. His love of freedom was so radical that his conservatism had anarchic tendencies. Most of the essays later reprinted in *Rationalism in Politics* (1962) first appeared in the journal. In 1949 he went to

Nuffield College, Oxford, as an official fellow, and in 1951 he was appointed to the chair of political science at the LSE.

The contrast between the public profile and enthusiastic socialism of Harold *Laski, his predecessor, and Oakeshott's sceptical conservatism made this a dramatic appointment, and Oakeshott's famous inaugural lecture, *Political Education* (1951), made an appropriate splash. Oakeshott lived during his years at the LSE in a small flat in Covent Garden. He administered the government department at the School with unostentatious efficiency, sending a stream of elegant handwritten notes to his colleagues, and was a familiar figure in the common-room. Avoiding committees when he could, he none the less played his part, and his unmistakable prose in, for example, describing the duties of a tutor, was to pass unscathed through several revisions of the B.Sc. (Econ.) degree.

In 1961 the University of London established the one-year master's degree, and although Oakeshott thought it an absurd idea, he set up an option within it on the history of political thought, which led to a distinguished seminar he ran with several colleagues. It drew scholars from all over the world, and he continued to attend until his late seventies. The work he did for this seminar, continually revised, appeared in *On History* (1983).

Oakeshott retired from the School in 1969 and eventually moved to Acton, near Langton Matravers in Dorset. Two cottages near a stone quarry had been knocked together, and Oakeshott lined the walls with book cases. Typically, he made something stylish out of the second-hand materials around him. There he lived until he died, though he often went to London to stay with his friends William and Shirley Letwin, or travelled to Hull or Durham, where favourite pupils were established in departments. He did venture to Harvard, and to Colorado College in Colorado Springs, a favourite place which elicited 'A Place of Learning', later republished among other essays on education in *The Voice of Liberal Learning* (1989), edited by Timothy Fuller. More commonly, he travelled to France.

Oakeshott was slight of build and elegant in his dress without being ostentatious. Many of his clothes, like the furniture of his cottage in Dorset, were picked up second-hand. In everything he did he was stylish without being precious. His voice was light, but carried remarkably well. No one could better him at making some sense out of the most opaque academic paper; he was a matchless discussant. The real passion of his life, however, was to understand the uniquely human. Philosophy he took to be the search for the postulates of human activities. As exclusively concerned to understand rather than control the world, it was a pure, almost morbid, preoccupation. In *Experience and Its Modes*, the most insidious of errors was found to be irrelevance, applying to one mode of activity the criteria appropriate to another. In his masterpiece *On Human Conduct* (1975), on which he had been working for years at the LSE but which came out after he had retired, the idea that experience is composed of a few discrete modes (practice, history, science, poetry) was loosened and replaced by 'conditional platforms of understanding', from which the enquirer casts his net to see what may be caught by any particular set of ideas.

Oakeshott argued that a modern state is best understood in terms of a distinction between two sorts of human association, which he called 'civil' and 'enterprise'. Characteristically, the first of the three essays in the book tells us what it is to inquire philosophically about human conduct, the second postulates the purely ideal forms of civil and enterprise association, and only in the third, long, historical essay does Oakeshott engage with the historical literature on the modern state, of which he had undoubtedly the most profound understanding of anyone in his generation. He has often been described as a 'Conservative philosopher', but he regarded this expression as a solipsism, for philosophers should not be partisans. Nevertheless he did eloquently characterize a Conservative disposition: it corresponded to his own character.

Oakeshott refused public honours and honorary doctorates from several universities, but he did accept honorary doctorates from Colorado, Durham, and Hull. In 1966 he became a fellow of the British Academy.

In 1927 he married Joyce Margaret, daughter of Guy Fricker, OBE, electrical engineer, of Harpenden. They had one son. The marriage was dissolved in 1938 and in the same year he married Katherine Alice (died 1964), daughter of Charles Frederick Burton, of Neuilly-sur-Seine. There were no children and the marriage was dissolved in 1951. In 1965 he married Christel, who had been brought up in Nuremberg, the daughter of Johann Schneider, bookkeeper and later dairy worker. They had no children. Oake-

shott died at his home in Acton, Dorset, 18 December 1990.

[Nevil Johnson in *Proceedings of the British Academy*, vol. lxxx, 1991; Jesse Norman (ed.), *The Achievement of Michael Oakeshott*, 1993; personal knowledge.]

KENNETH MINOGUE

OAKESHOTT, Sir Walter Fraser (1903–1987), schoolmaster and scholar, was born 11 November 1903, the second of two sons among the four children of Walter Oakeshott, medical practitioner, of Lydenberg, South Africa, and his wife, Kathleen Fraser. After Dr Oakeshott's early death, his wife brought the family home to England. Walter went to Tonbridge School, where he became head boy, leaving with an exhibition to Balliol College, Oxford, in 1922. He achieved first classes in classical honour moderations (1924) and *literae humaniores* (1926).

He became an assistant master at Tooting Bec School, whence in 1927 he proceeded to Merchant Taylors' School. In 1931, after a year spent working for the Kent county education committee, he was appointed an assistant master at Winchester College, where he remained till 1938. Two events of his time there were important for him. The first was his discovery, in 1934, among the manuscripts in the fellows' library, of the unique manuscript of *Morte d'Arthur* by Sir Thomas *Malory (his own full account of the find is given in *Essays on Malory*, ed. J. A. W. *Bennett, 1963). The second was the invitation to serve with the inquiry into unemployment sponsored by the Pilgrim Trust, for which he was given a year's leave of absence from the school (1936–7). He took a major part in writing up the findings of the inquiry, in William *Temple's *Men Without Work* (1938), a book which made a powerful impression and has since been twice reprinted.

In 1939 Oakeshott became high master of St Paul's School. On the outbreak of war he had to supervise the evacuation of the school from London to Crowthorne, Berkshire; the evacuation, and St Paul's adaptation to new surroundings and unfamiliar routines, were a triumph for his charismatic leadership. Soon after he had brought the school back to London in 1945 he was appointed headmaster of Winchester, a post which he held from 1946 to 1954. Apart from one dire confrontation at the very end of his time, when his request to a housemaster to resign was challenged and upheld by only a majority on the governing body, this was a period of successful stewardship in a highly individual style. Though capable in administration he had no great taste for it, and where he shone was as a teacher and inspirer of the young, especially of those whom he stirred to share his own keen appreciation of artistic beauty. His personal rapport with boys of all ages and tastes left a very strong impression, fondly recalled by Wykehamists who were in the school in his time.

In 1954 Oakeshott was elected rector of Lincoln College, Oxford, where he presided for the next eighteen years. His was a period of remarkable expansion for the college, which saw its tutorial fellowship more than double and a great increase in student accommodation. In 1962–4 he was vice-chancellor of Oxford, and during his term a commission of inquiry into Oxford University (1964–6) was initiated, under the chairmanship of Lord Franks.

Both at Winchester and at Oxford Oakeshott took a keen interest in buildings and restoration. At Winchester he was instrumental in the recovery of surviving panels of the college chapel's original medieval stained glass, dispersed in the nineteenth century, and their refitting in the windows of Thurbern's chantry. At Lincoln he was the moving spirit in the acquisition by the college of the redundant church of All Saints, for conversion into the college library. In Oxford he played a leading part in the restoration work made possible by the Oxford Historic Buildings Appeal, in particular in the restoration of the stonework, sculptures, and interior of the Sheldonian Theatre.

Oakeshott dedicated the interstices of his busy life to scholarship, where his interests were many-sided. He wrote on Renaissance cosmography and early exploration (*Founded upon the Seas*, 1942, and several learned articles). His purchase and subsequent identification of a notebook belonging to Sir Walter *Ralegh, written when he was collecting materials for *The History of the World* (1614), prompted research into the court culture of Elizabethan England and into Ralegh's poetry (*The Queen and the Poet*, 1962). His most abiding interest was in medieval art history, and his two studies of the Winchester Bible (*The Artists of the Winchester Bible*, 1945, and *The Two Winchester Bibles*, 1981) were authoritative and influential, especially the former, a pioneering work identifying the hands and styles of the painters who worked on the Bible and the influences that shaped their work. Among his other books were *Mosaics of Rome* (1967) and *Sigena Wall Paintings* (1972).

Oakeshott held honorary doctorates of the universities of St Andrews and East Anglia, and was an honorary fellow of both Balliol (1974) and Lincoln (1972). He was elected a fellow of the British Academy in 1971 and was knighted in 1980. He was master of the Skinners' Company (1960–1), a long-serving trustee of the Pilgrim Trust, and president of the Bibliographical Society (1966–8).

He was a tall man, of gracious bearing, with a high forehead, eyebrows that fluttered in animation, and a characteristically beaming smile.

His manner was gentle and courteous; he had an instinctive personal modesty, a delightfully whimsical wit, and a gift for friendship. In teaching, research, and life he strove continually for what he believed could inspire and elevate. He married in 1928 Noël Rose, daughter of Robert Oswald Moon, consultant physician. They had twin sons and two daughters, and the family was a close and affectionate one. His wife predeceased him in 1976, and he was buried beside her after he died, 13 October 1987, at his home in Eynsham, Oxfordshire.

[*Balliol College Register 1930–80*, 1983; F. R. Salter, *St Paul's School, 1909–1959*, 1959; *Lincoln College Record*, 1986–7; *The Trusty Servant* (Winchester old boys' periodical), December 1987; Jonathan Alexander and Maurice Keen in *Proceedings of the British Academy*, vol. lxxxiv, 1993; information from J. C. Dancy (preparing a biography); private information; personal knowledge.]   M. H. KEEN

ODELL, Noel Ewart (1890–1987), geologist and mountaineer, was born 25 December 1890 in St Lawrence, Isle of Wight, the third child in the family of two sons and three daughters of the Revd Robert William Odell, rector of St Lawrence, and his wife Mary Margaret, daughter of James Bell Ewart, timber merchant, of Dundas, Ontario, Canada. He was educated at Brighton College and at the Royal School of Mines at Imperial College, London, where he studied geology and gained the ARSM. During World War I he was commissioned as a lieutenant in 1915 in the Royal Engineers. Wounded three times, he returned to civilian life in 1919.

He embarked on a career in the petroleum and mining industries, first as a geologist with the Anglo-Persian Oil Company (1922–5) and then as a consultant in Canada (1927–30). In his late thirties he transferred to academic geology, first as a lecturer in geology and tutor at Harvard University (1928–30), then as a research student and lecturer at Cambridge, where he stayed on as a fellow commoner and supervisor of studies at Clare College (1931–40). His Ph.D., awarded in 1940, investigated the geology, glaciology, and geomorphology of north-east Greenland and northern Labrador. In 1940–2 he served as a major in the Bengal Sappers and Miners.

After World War II he took up various appointments at universities in Canada, New Zealand, and Pakistan. He lectured at McGill and was visiting professor at the University of British Columbia (1948–9). He was also professor of geology at the University of Otago (1950–6) and at Peshawar University (1960–2). On finally retiring, he returned to Clare and in 1983, at the age of ninety-two, was made an honorary fellow, an event which much pleased him.

Although Odell published several important papers on the geology of the Himalayas, and other mountain regions, and was a fellow or member of numerous geological, geographical, glaciological, and Arctic institutions, he probably never aspired to be in the front rank of academic research. It was in mountaineering that he made his name, and managed with singular success to combine the career of a geologist with the pleasures of mountaineering. Odell made his first discovery of the hills of the Lake District at the age of thirteen and soon acquired wide climbing experience in Britain and the Alps. Many an aspiring rock climber has cut his teeth on Odell's severe tennis shoe climb on the uncompromisingly smooth slabs of Cwm Idwal in north Wales (1919). He participated in the Oxford University Spitsbergen expedition (1921) and led the Merton College Arctic expedition (1923).

Odell was picked for the Everest expedition of 1924 and was the last man to see George *Mallory and Andrew Irvine before they disappeared in their attempt to scale the final slopes of the world's highest mountain. Odell was in close support. In a period of four days, he climbed mostly without oxygen, first alone to 25,000 feet to look for them, and then twice alone beyond Camp 6 to over 27,000 feet and back. On returning home he was invited to a private audience by King *George V.

There followed several visits for geological research, mountaineering, and exploration in the Canadian Rockies (1927–47) and with American friends to north Labrador (1931), north-east Greenland (1933), and the St Elias mountains in Yukon and Alaska (1949 and 1977). While at Harvard he inspired a generation of undergraduates to climb steep ice and to organize expeditions to the greater ranges of the world. An ice route he pioneered in the White Mountains bears his name, Odell Gully, and two mountains, a lake, and a glacier are also named after him.

Odell's greatest mountaineering achievement was the first ascent of Nanda Devi (25,695 feet) in 1936, with an Anglo-American party. H. W. *Tilman and Odell reached the summit, which for fourteen years remained the highest peak climbed. Two years later he again joined Tilman in the 1938 attempt on Everest, but deep powder snow made the last 1,500 feet impossible to climb. Odell continued to defy the normal limitations of old age. In 1984, at the age of ninety-three, he strode across the glacier to attend the seventy-fifth anniversary of the Britannia hut in the Alps, and recalled that as a young climber he had also been present at its opening. He was a founder member of the Himalayan Club and an honorary member of the Alpine Club and of kindred clubs in North America, Canada, South Africa, New Zealand, Switzerland, and Norway. He received the Livingstone gold medal (1944) of the Royal Scottish Geographical Society and,

unusually, a star in the constellation Lyra was named after him (*International Star Register*, 1925). He became a familiar figure at the Alpine Club and the Royal Geographical Society, retaining in old age his earnest enthusiasm and the tall, spare figure and purposeful gait which had carried him to record heights on the earth's surface. His genial nature and patriarchal figure earned him the nickname Noah, which he relished.

He married in 1917 Gwladys Mona (died 1977), daughter of Robert Jones, rector of Gyffin, north Wales. They had one son. Odell died suddenly 21 February 1987 at his home in Cambridge.

[*The Times*, 24 February 1987; *Alpine Journal*, vol. xciii, no. 337, 1988/9; personal knowledge.]

GEORGE BAND

OGDON, John Andrew Howard (1937–1989), pianist and composer, was born 27 January 1937 in Mansfield Woodhouse, Nottinghamshire, the youngest in the family of three sons and two daughters of Howard Ogdon, teacher, who wrote about music, and his wife, Dorothy Mutton, a former secretary, who also encouraged her children's musicianship by ensuring that they learned the piano from an early age. John began piano lessons when he was four years old. His gifts were such that at the age of eight he went to the Royal Manchester (later the Royal Northern) College of Music as a pupil of Iso Elinson. After attending Manchester Grammar School, he returned in his mid-teens to the college, where he found a gifted group of contemporaries— Alexander Goehr, (Sir) Harrison Birtwistle, (Sir) Peter Maxwell Davies, and Elgar Howarth—who were later known as the 'Manchester School'. Ogdon took piano with Elinson, Claude Biggs, and Gordon Green, and composition with Richard Hall.

Ogdon's superlative sight-reading gifts and his phenomenal musical memory enabled him to tackle the most difficult scores virtually at sight, but his technical mastery was allied to a deep intellectual grasp, which soon marked him out as a recreative musician of extraordinary range and depth. When he was still a child, his father had suffered a schizophrenic breakdown; it may well have been that this experience chastened Ogdon's own development: musically, he was prodigiously gifted, and physically he was (so described by Alexander Goehr) 'a big, clumsy, untidy, roly-poly boy'. His character was shy and reserved, his speech quietly withdrawn; only at the piano, it seemed, did his personality publicly flower, when he was overwhelming.

As a student he entered the Belgian Queen Elisabeth Competition in 1956 but was unsuccessful. On graduating soon afterwards (with distinction in every subject), he gave Brahms's D

Minor Concerto, conducted by Sir John *Barbi-rolli, which prompted Ogdon's Hallé Orchestra début at the age of twenty. Postgraduate work with Denis *Matthews in London and Egon Petri (a pupil of Ferruccio Busoni) in Basle led, in 1958, to Ogdon's playing Busoni's vast Piano Concerto from memory, conducted by (Sir) John *Pritchard in Liverpool. The Busoni perform-ance was much praised and on 8 August 1959, at less than forty-eight hours' notice, Ogdon made his Promenade Concert début in Franz Liszt's E Flat Concerto, after coming second in the Liver-pool International Piano Competition, and a month before his Wigmore Hall début in Lon-don.

Married in July 1960 to Brenda Lucas (Peter Maxwell Davies was best man), the newly-weds made a notable two-piano team. In December Ogdon began his record career with a Busoni–Liszt album for EMI. Although he later recorded for other labels, his main recorded legacy is with EMI. In January 1961 he took first prize in the Liszt Competition and achieved world fame as joint winner (with Vladimir Ashkenazy) of the first prize at the Tchaikovsky Competition in Moscow in 1962.

One of the most sought-after artists of his day, Ogdon travelled widely, notably to the USA and Russia, where he was adored. Unlike other vir-tuosos, he championed new and unusual music, including concertos written for him by Alun Hoddinott (with whom he founded the Cardiff music festival in 1967), Robert Simpson, and Gerard Schurmann, alongside standard reper-toire. He also found time to compose, among other music, a piano concerto, a symphony, solo piano works, and two string quartets. His immense energy ensured a full engagement book, yet his chain-smoking and excessive drinking, his unkempt appearance, and a tendency to over-work meant that the strains thus placed upon him took their toll.

In 1973 Ogdon began to exhibit symptoms of an alarming personality change. This previously gentle man became prone to degenerative mental and physical violence, eventually attacking his wife with such ferocity that she was hospitalized: he attempted suicide on numerous occasions. His condition at first eluded diagnosis, his treatment ranging from drugs and electric shock to psycho-therapy. Some of his earlier treatment was experimental; he seemed to suffer from paranoid schizophrenic psychosis. Ogdon spent eighteen months in London's Royal Maudsley Hospital; by 1977 he had improved enough to take his first teaching post, at Indiana University in Bloom-ington, where he stayed until 1980. Under care, he resumed concert-giving, which he had never really abandoned: an American doctor who had observed Ogdon for a year concluded that he was not schizophrenic but manic depressive and pre-scribed lithium, claiming Ogdon was an obses-sive genius living a vital inner life against which the 'real' world can appear remote.

The treatment was a success and, although never 'cured', he was able gradually to resume his career. His history meant that his condition was watched constantly; his earlier instability led to his affairs being taken over by the Court of Protection. Symptomatic of a new confidence was his recital of the legendary three-and-a-half-hour solo piano work Opus Clavicembalisticum by Kaikhosru *Sorabji in 1988, which he also recorded. Ogdon was a fellow of the Royal Manchester College of Music (1962) and the Royal Academy of Music (1974), and an hon-orary fellow of the Royal Northern College of Music (1986). He was also a recipient of the Harriet Cohen international award (1960). His publications included contributory chapters to Franz Liszt: the Man and his Music (ed. Alan Walker, 1976) and Keyboard Music (ed. Denis Mathews, 1972).

In 1960 Ogdon had married Brenda Mary, daughter of John Gregory Lucas, civil servant; they had a son and a daughter. In late July 1989 Ogdon complained of feeling unwell. He saw a new doctor, who asked if he had been diagnosed as diabetic, and who arranged for him to be examined by several specialists some days later. But his condition worsened, and his wife found him unconscious on the morning of 31 July, the day of his first specialist visit. Rushed to Charing Cross Hospital, he was found to be in a diabetic coma. He had, moreover, contracted bronchial pneumonia, from which he died in hospital early the following day, 1 August 1989.

[Brenda Lucas Ogdon and Michael Kerr, Virtuoso, 1981; Independent, 3 August 1989; private information; personal knowledge.]   ROBERT MATTHEW-WALKER

OLIVIER, Laurence Kerr, BARON OLIVIER (1907–1989), actor and director, was born in Dorking 22 May 1907, the second son and youngest of three children of the Revd Gerald Kerr Olivier, assistant priest at St Martin's church there, and his wife, Agnes Louise Crookenden. Educated at St Edward's School, Oxford, he showed precocious acting ability, which was recognized even by his clerically blinkered father, and made his stage début at the age of fifteen as Kate in a boys' performance of The Taming of the Shrew at the Shakespeare festival theatre, Stratford-upon-Avon. After leaving school, he won a scholarship to the Central School of Speech Training and Dramatic Art, founded by Elsie *Fogerty, and went on to join the touring company run by Lena *Ashwell and then (in 1927) the Birmingham repertory theatre, directed by (Sir) Barry *Jackson.

His first years on the stage were marked by fierce ambition and energy, but no clear sense of direction. An outstandingly good-looking young actor, he was in some danger of falling into the matinée idol trap—as when, having created the role of Stanhope in the try-out of *Journey's End*, by R. C. *Sherriff, he abandoned that fine play for the option of a short-lived lead in *Beau Geste* (1929). At the invitation of (Sir) Noël *Coward (to whom he remained lastingly in thrall) he took the tailor's dummy role of Victor Prynne in *Private Lives* (1930–1). He also began uncertainly in Hollywood as a Ronald *Colman look-alike; he was fired from the cast of *Queen Christina* in 1933 at the request of Greta Garbo.

After the failure of *Beau Geste* he went on to play five leading parts in under two years without ever achieving a decent run; an ominous experience for a young star in a hurry, though it forecast one of the greatest strengths of his maturity: the refusal ever to please the public by repeating himself. Late in his career, when he played James Tyrone in Eugene O'Neill's *Long Day's Journey into Night* (1971), there was a sense of personal horror in his portrait of a once hopeful young talent destroyed by years of profitable type-casting.

In Olivier's own view, the turning point in his career came with the 1934 production of *Queen of Scots*, by Gordon Daviot (the pseudonym of Elizabeth *Mackintosh): a long forgotten play which, again, met with small success, but which marked the beginning of a group of lifelong professional friendships with, among others, George *Devine, Glen *Byam-Shaw, Gwen Ffrangçon-Davies, and, supremely, the show's director, (Sir) John Gielgud. The fiery egoist had discovered his need for a family, and with it his future course as a company-based classical actor. The first fruits of this discovery were bitter when—playing Romeo to Gielgud's Mercutio (1935)—he ran into opposition from the London critics, who did not like his verse speaking. The fact that he then turned a flop into a triumph by switching roles with Gielgud, did not really heal the wound.

Olivier described his duel with Gielgud as one between 'earth and air'. The two stars were, and remained, opposites. But it was not long before the public learned to value both; to relish Olivier's animal magnetism, physical daring, and power to spring surprises, as much as his conversion of speech into another form of action. He struggled to extract every ounce of dramatic meaning from the text, often driven into harsh sardonic resonance and shock inflections, and detonating isolated words. Following Gielgud (whose theatrical families kept breaking up), Olivier's other main partnership was with his friend from the Birmingham rep, (Sir) Ralph *Richardson, with whom he played in two Old Vic seasons in the late 1930s—consolidating his Shakespearian position in a sequence of con-

trasted leading roles (Toby Belch, Henry V, Macbeth, Hamlet, Iago, and Coriolanus) before their reunion (with John P. Burrell) as directors of the postwar Old Vic company.

In the flush of his pre-war Shakespearian success, Olivier was wary of another summons from Hollywood. However, in 1939 he deigned to accept the role of Heathcliff in *Wuthering Heights*, and suffered a baptism of fire from his director, William Wyler, who criticized him unmercifully for his theatrically exaggerated style and patronizing attitude towards the art of film. Made ill by this treatment, Olivier endured it and emerged from the experience as a major star. 'Wyler,' he later acknowledged, 'taught me how to act in movies; taught me respect for them; taught me how to be real.' It was another victory for naturalism; and an apprenticeship in film-making which swiftly led to mastery in the first and best of his own films: *Henry V* (1943–4), probably the first successful Shakespeare film ever made, at once for its cunning blend of picturesque artifice and point-blank realism, and for Olivier's outstanding performance, which long outlived its patriotic morale-boosting intentions.

Olivier had entered the war in 1941 with the intention of putting acting away for the duration, and qualified as a pilot in the Fleet Air Arm. An incompetent aeronaut, he destroyed five aircraft in seven weeks. He was seconded into propaganda entertainment by the Ministry of Information and saw no active service. On completing *Henry V*, he led the Old Vic company in 1944 from their bombed-out Waterloo Road house into temporary West End premises at the New theatre. The company flowered as never before. These were the years of Olivier's Richard III, Hotspur, and Lear; and the inspired double bill of *Oedipus*, and *The Critic* by R. B. *Sheridan, in which Olivier, as Puff, was whisked off, still talking, up to the flies. Coupled with Richardson's Falstaff (to Olivier's Shallow) and Peer Gynt (to which Olivier, in a supreme stroke of luxury casting, played the tiny part of the Button Moulder) these seasons formed a glorious chapter in the Old Vic's history. But neither that, nor the knighthood Olivier received in 1947, inhibited the theatre's governors (headed by Viscount Esher) from picking a moment in 1948 when Olivier was leading the troupe on a tour of Australia, to inform him that the directors' joint contract would not be renewed.

Indignantly repulsing Esher's subsequent offer to re-engage him as sole director, Olivier set up his own management at the St James's theatre for a mixed classical and modern repertory, in which he directed and co-starred with his wife, Vivien *Leigh. These seasons included premières of plays by (Sir) Terence *Rattigan and Christopher Fry, new work from Thornton

Wilder and Tennessee Williams, and two Cleo-
patras from Vivien Leigh, with Olivier paying
successive court to her as *Shakespeare's Antony
and G. B. *Shaw's Caesar.

By this time, Olivier had reached the summit
of his worldly ambitions. All his desires had been
satisfied: as an actor, for whom audiences would
queue all night, he was the undisputed monarch
of the London stage; he had succeeded as a
director and as a manager; unlike Gielgud and
Richardson, he also had an international film
career, known to a vast public who had never set
foot in a theatre. He had made a fairy-tale
marriage; his residence was a twelfth-century
abbey including a home farm. But under the
glittering public image he felt he had come to a
stop; his work had again lost its sense of direction, and his private life was becoming a hostage
to Vivien Leigh's increasing manic depression.

To repair the 'aching void' he made some
random career changes: embarking on an uncon-
vincing singing début in the film of The Beggar's
Opera (1952), which at least forged an alliance
with Peter Brook, with whom he again broke new
Shakespearian ground in the 1955 Stratford production of Titus Andronicus; and directing and
playing the title role in the film of Rattigan's The
Prince and the Showgirl (1957), in which he was
outshone by Marilyn Monroe. By that time he
had already discovered the route to renewal in
the English Stage Company's new play-writing
revival at the Royal Court theatre, under his old
friend George Devine. Unlike the other leading
actors of his generation, Olivier took the plunge
into the new wave and, to the dismay of some
admirers, appeared as Archie Rice, the seedy
bottom-line comedian in John Osborne's The
Entertainer (1957), which became one of his
favourite parts. He discarded his West End
wardrobe with zest, swaggering on in a loud
check suit, exchanging all the obligations of
eminence for the free speech of the dregs of the
profession. 'Don't clap too loud, lady,' he leered
out to the house; 'it's a very old building.' This
was the time of the Suez crisis.

At the Royal Court (where he also played in
Eugène Ionesco's Rhinoceros, 1960) he met the
actress Joan Plowright, whom he married after
divorcing Vivien Leigh. His attachment to the
Court became crucial in 1963 when, after running the first seasons of the Chichester festival
theatre, he achieved his ultimate professional
goal as first director of the newly formed
National Theatre, where he confirmed his alliance with the young generation by engaging
Devine's protégés, John *Dexter and William
Gaskill, as his associate directors, and appointing the Observer's campaigning critic Kenneth
*Tynan (formerly an arch foe) as his literary
manager. Just as he transformed his stage physique from role to role, Olivier instinctively

altered his public identity according to the mood
of the times; and as head of the National Theatre
he put off West End glamour and re-emerged in
the likeness of a go-ahead bank manager, thoroughly at home in the new world of state subsidy
and permanent companies. He was uniquely
qualified for the job, as a natural leader who
commanded the loyalty of the whole profession,
and as an artist who had nothing more to
prove.

There remained one unscaled Shakespearian
peak, Othello, which he played (directed by
Dexter) in 1964 in a final burst of incandescent
sensuality. Otherwise, though he was a regular
NT player in roles ranging from punishing leads
like Edgar in August Strindberg's The Dance of
Death (1967) to walk-on parts like the Jewish
divorce lawyer in Home and Beauty (1969) by W.
Somerset *Maugham, his main energy went into
creating an ensemble that could tackle any play
in the world. The opening seasons were a surprise: plays by Harold Brighouse, Noël Coward,
Henrik Ibsen, Georges Feydeau—works with
nothing in common beyond the fact that almost
every one of them brought the theatre another
success and redefined the reputation of the
playwright.

One criticism of the National Theatre—
voiced, among others, by Olivier's former Old
Vic colleague, Sir W. Tyrone *Guthrie—was
that the ensemble was failing to present Britain's
leading actors. With the exception of Sir Michael
*Redgrave, no actor approaching Olivier's own
rank became a member of the team; and Olivier
unceremoniously sacked Redgrave and took over
his role in Ibsen's The Master Builder (1965),
mistaking the onset of Redgrave's Parkinson's
disease for drunkenness. Possibly the criticism he
received for importing Peter O'Toole over the
heads of the regular troupe for the opening
production of Hamlet (1963–4) made him shut
his door against visiting stars. What he did
achieve was a theatre that became a second home
to its actors and which developed its own stars—
including Colin Blakely, Derek Jacobi, Edward
Petherbridge, Geraldine McEwan, and Joan
Plowright.

Olivier's years at the National Theatre were
wracked with troubles of which the general
public knew little or nothing. His artistic associates' support for controversial work such as
Frank Wedekind's Spring Awakening and Rolf
Hochhuth's Soldiers brought him into collision
with the governors and completely estranged him
from their chairman, the first Viscount *Chandos. For the first time in his career, Olivier also
became plagued with stage fright and memory
loss. He suffered five major illnesses—including
thrombosis, cancer, and muscular dystrophy—
and came through them by sheer force of
will. But after appearing in Trevor Griffiths's

The Party (1974)—delivering a twenty-minute speech as an old Glaswegian Trotskyite—his stage career was at an end. In the previous year, with mixed feelings, he handed over the directorship of the National Theatre to (Sir) Peter Hall, who led the company from the Old Vic theatre into its new South Bank premises.

In his remaining years Olivier had a busy film and television life, though (with a few exceptions, such as the roles of Dr Christian Szell in *Marathon Man*, 1976, and Loren Hardemann in *The Betsy*, 1978) his film work consisted of cameo parts which he took to support his new young family. He was more scrupulous when it came to television, and the last flowering of his talent can be seen in his performances of Lord Marchmain in the Granada adaptation of Evelyn *Waugh's *Brideshead Revisited* (1981), the blind protagonist of John Mortimer's *A Voyage Round My Father* (1982), and a valedictory *King Lear* (1983). In his last decade he also published two books: *Confessions of an Actor* (1982) and *On Acting* (1986), both absorbingly informative but no guide to the man himself. As an author, as on stage, he disappeared into a role. He left behind a Dickensian gallery of characters, each one composed with the copious observation and imaginative investment of a novelist. Olivier did more to advance the art of acting than anyone since Sir Henry *Irving, and just as Irving had become the English theatre's first knight, so Olivier, in 1970, became its first life peer. In 1981 he was admitted to the Order of Merit. He had honorary degrees from Tufts, Massachusetts (1946), Oxford (1957), Edinburgh (1964), London (1968), Manchester (1968), and Sussex (1978). He had numerous foreign awards and in 1979 was given an honorary Oscar.

In 1930 he married an actress, Jill Esmond (died 1990), daughter of Henry Vernon Esmond, whose original surname was Jack, actor and playwright; they had one son. The marriage was dissolved in 1940 and in the same year he married the actress Vivien Leigh (died 1967), daughter of Ernest Richard Hartley, exchange broker in Calcutta, and former wife of Herbert Leigh Holman, barrister. There were no children and the marriage was dissolved in 1961. In the same year he married the actress Joan Ann Plowright, daughter of William Ernest Plowright, editor of the local newspaper in Brigg, Lincolnshire, and former wife of Roger Gage. They had one son and two daughters. Olivier also had several affairs, with both women and men. He died 11 July 1989 at his home in Steyning, West Sussex.

[Laurence Olivier, *Confessions of an Actor*, 1982, and *On Acting*, 1986; Felix Barker, *Laurence Olivier*, 1984; Melvyn Bragg, *Laurence Olivier*, 1984; Donald Spoto, *Laurence Olivier*, 1991.]   IRVING WARDLE

O'NEILL, Sir Con Douglas Walter (1912–1988), diplomat, was born in London 3 June 1912, the second of three surviving sons (there were no daughters) of (Sir) (Robert William) Hugh O'Neill, later first Baron Rathcavan, PC, politician, and his wife Sylvia Irene, daughter of Walter Albert Sandeman, of Morden House, Royston. He achieved early academic distinction with a scholarship from Eton to Balliol College, Oxford, a first class in English in 1934, and a law fellowship of All Souls College, Oxford, the following year (held until 1946). In 1936 he was called to the bar (Inner Temple), and in the same year he entered the Diplomatic Service.

He was posted to Berlin as third secretary in 1938; he resigned in 1939 because he disagreed with Neville *Chamberlain's policy of appeasement. He served in the Army Intelligence Corps from 1940 to 1943 and was then employed in the Foreign Office. In 1946 he left to become a leader-writer on *The Times* but returned to the Foreign Office the following year. From then on he rose steadily in the hierarchy; posts in Frankfurt and Bonn were followed by a period as head of the news department in 1954–5, chargé d'affaires in Peking (1955–7), return to the Foreign Office as assistant under-secretary in 1957, and posts as ambassador to Finland from 1961 to 1963 and ambassador to the European Communities in Brussels from 1963 to 1965. He returned to the Foreign Office as deputy under-secretary, and hoped in 1968 to go to Bonn as ambassador. Germany had been his first post; his German was impeccable and he would have carried considerable weight. But the foreign secretary, George *Brown (later Baron George-Brown), vetoed this proposal; it was a question of temperamental incompatibility. Con O'Neill did not dispute his right to do so but resigned to start a career in the City with Hill Samuel.

In 1969 he was recalled to the Foreign Office to head the team which would negotiate Britain's entry into the European Community. This task successfully accomplished, he left the Foreign Office for the last time in 1972, after writing the official history of the negotiations. From 1972 to 1974 he was chairman of the Intervention Board for Agricultural Produce. He was a director of Unigate from 1974 to 1983. In 1974 and 1975, the year of the referendum, he performed a last service to the European cause as director of the Britain in Europe campaign.

O'Neill was one of the outstanding diplomats of his generation. His intellect was impressive, his reasoning always a masterpiece of logic, his analysis of any situation penetrating and accurate. To this he brought a lucidity of expression which served him well as a leader-writer on *The Times*; some felt that he could have edited that newspaper with distinction. In appearance he resembled one of Anthony *Trollope's elders of the church, bald, bespectacled, with an air of measured dignity and a voice distinctly canonical. His manner had something of the formality of a previous generation, but those who dealt with him rapidly found that underneath there lurked a delightful sense of humour and a seemingly inexhaustible fund of Irish stories.

He was also a man of unbending principle. If he thought a policy was wrong he said so in clear and measured terms without any thought of the consequences for his career. It was most unusual for a diplomat to leave the Foreign Office three times before retirement and yet rise to posts of the highest distinction.

His greatest accomplishment was the British entry into the European Community. On this the country was bitterly divided and the complexities of the negotiation vast. In addition he had to carry with him the senior officials on the team who vigorously defended the interests of their departments. Through all these hazards O'Neill steered his team with imperturbable patience and skill, gaining the confidence and respect of all he dealt with, whether among Britain's European partners or in Whitehall. The success of the negotiations was one of the great achievements in the history of British diplomacy; it owed much to his efforts.

He was appointed CMG in 1953, KCMG in 1962, and GCMG in 1972. He married three times, first in 1940 Rosemary Margaret, daughter of the late Harold Pritchard, MD. They had a son and a daughter, Onora, who became principal of Newnham College, Cambridge. The marriage was dissolved in 1954 (his wife subsequently became Lady Garvey) and in that year he married Baroness Carola Hertha Adolphine Emma Harriet Luise ('Mädy') Marschall von Bieberstein, a widow and daughter of Baron Max Reinhard August von Holzing-Berstett. She died in 1960 and in 1961 he married Mrs Anne-Marie Lindberg, of Helsinki, daughter of Bertil Jungström, civil engineer, of Stockholm. Con O'Neill died 11 January 1988 at St Stephen's Hospital, London.

[Personal knowledge.]   ROY DENMAN

O'NEILL, Terence Marne, BARON O'NEILL OF THE MAINE (1914–1990), prime minister of Northern Ireland, was born 10 September 1914 at 29 Ennismore Gardens, Hyde Park, London, the third son and youngest of five children of Captain Arthur Edward Bruce O'Neill (2nd Life Guards), of Shane's Castle, Randalstown, county Antrim, MP for mid-Antrim and eldest son of the second Baron O'Neill, and his wife, Lady Annabel Hungerford Crewe-Milnes, eldest daughter of the Marquess of *Crewe, statesman. Terence O'Neill's father became the first MP to die at the front (5 November 1914) and his

mother married again in 1922. The young O'Neill was educated at West Downs School in Winchester, and at Eton. He spent much time in Abyssinia, where his stepfather was consul, and during the 1930s had several jobs, ending up at the Stock Exchange. After being commissioned at Sandhurst in May 1940, O'Neill joined the 2nd battalion of the Irish Guards, serving in Normandy and Holland. Both his brothers were killed in World War II.

In October 1946 O'Neill was returned unopposed as the Unionist member for Bannside in the Stormont parliament. He became parliamentary secretary to the minister of health in February 1948 and to the minister of home affairs in 1955. In 1956 he was sworn of the Privy Council (Northern Ireland) and became minister of home affairs and then of finance, forming a politically important relationship with a reform-minded private secretary, (Sir) Kenneth Bloomfield. Another important member of O'Neill's circle, *Belfast Telegraph* editor Jack Sayers, was 'never able to satisfy my mind about the Prime Minister's liberalism—it is far more intellectual than emotional and even then much of it emanates from Ken Bloomfield'. Nevertheless, the fact remains that when in 1963 O'Neill became prime minister of Northern Ireland—unlike his three Unionist predecessors—there was no trace of anti-Catholic bitterness on his record. Yet he was to disappoint some, at least, of his liberal friends.

The subsequent intensity of the sectarian conflict has obscured the fact that in his early years in office he was primarily concerned to win back Protestant support which the Unionist party had lost to the Northern Ireland Labour party in the period since 1958. 'Stealing Labour's thunder'—to use O'Neill's own term—rather than allaying Catholic resentments, was his main preoccupation.

O'Neill had a generous, even impulsive, streak and was capable of the occasional conciliatory grand gesture, such as his famous visit to a Catholic school. In the main, however, he espoused a rhetoric of planning and modernization by which nationalist grievances would be dissolved by shared participation in the benefits of economic growth. He saw little role for structural reform. His speeches in this early period resonate with a pious little-Ulsterism in which devolution emerges not just as an inevitable and reasonable historical compromise but as a responsive communal form of government superior to that of the class-based party system in the rest of the United Kingdom. That UK system was, however, economically sustaining the Stormont regime: a fact of which O'Neill was more aware than the Unionist electorate.

O'Neill's early lack of responsiveness to Catholic grievances was sharply criticized by liberal unionist groupings, such as the leadership of the Northern Ireland Labour party and the *Belfast Telegraph*, but in the short term O'Neillism was quite effective politically. The O'Neillite manifesto for the 1965 election crystallized the ideology of modernization—'Forward Ulster to Target 1970'. The result showed an average swing to the Unionist party of 7 per cent and was a major defeat for Labour.

Despite this electoral success, even then O'Neill was widely perceived to be a poor party manager. Normally secretive and aloof, at times he was capable of indiscreet and hurtful sarcasm at the expense of prickly senior colleagues. And, ironically, his 1965 triumph played a key role in marginalizing a party (Labour) which gave radicals from the Catholic community an outlet.

The emergence in 1968 of the civil rights movement, which included many such radicals, presented O'Neill with an excruciating dilemma: placating the reformers was likely to mean the consolidation of the internal unionist opposition. O'Neill chose the path of moderate, even modest, reform—'the five-point programme' of November 1968. For a brief moment, he seemed to have a real chance of gaining significant Catholic support whilst retaining that of a majority of Protestants. But the tactics of the radical wing of the civil rights movement, responding more to leftist politics than nationalist impulses, were to frustrate him.

The civil rights march led by the People's Democracy group in January 1969 was of decisive importance. This march was attacked at Burntollet bridge by Orange partisans and the subsequent deterioration in communal relations made O'Neill's position exceptionally difficult. Caught between the pressures generated by loyalist and nationalist militants, and having almost lost his seat in a snap election he called in February, he resigned in April 1969, though he retained substantial Protestant support even at the end. He accepted a life barony in 1970. In 1967 he had received an honorary LL D from Queen's University, Belfast.

O'Neill's legacy is ambiguous. Even the reputation of his path-breaking talks in 1965 with the taoiseach, Sean *Lemass, suffered, amongst unionists at any rate, from later claims by Lemass's widow (bitterly repudiated by O'Neill) that they had been about 'Irish unity'. His famous statement on resignation continues to haunt his reputation: 'It is frightfully hard to explain to Protestants that if you give Roman Catholics a good job and a good house, they will live like Protestants...they will refuse to have eighteen children on National Assistance...in spite of the authoritative nature of their church.' He was a patrician figure out of touch with large sections of the population. O'Neill's political failure is made all the more tragic by the fact that he was essentially a man of decent tolerant instincts.

In 1944 O'Neill married (Katharine) Jean, daughter of William Ingham Whitaker, of Pylewell Park, Lymington. They had a daughter and a son. O'Neill died 12 June 1990 at his home in Lymington, Hampshire.

[*Ballymena Observer*, 13 November 1914; Terence O'Neill, *The Autobiography of Terence O'Neill*, 1972; Andrew Gailey (ed.), *John Sayers, a Liberal Editor*, 1993; Paul Bew and Henry Patterson, *The British State and the Ulster Crisis*, 1985.]   PAUL BEW

OWEN, (Paul) **Robert** (1920–1990), engineer, was born 24 January 1920 in Dalston, London, the elder son (there were no daughters) of Joseph Owen, estate manager, and his wife, Deborah Grossmith. His secondary education was at the Central Foundation School (1933–8), a grammar school in the City of London. He then entered Queen Mary College, London University, to read engineering, specializing in aeronautics. On the outbreak of war in 1939 the college was evacuated to Cambridge. There Owen graduated in 1940 with first-class honours and won the Allen Low prize for the best student in engineering.

He started work at the aircraft firm Boulton-Paul, but his potential for research soon became evident and in 1941 he joined the aerodynamics department of the Royal Aircraft Establishment (RAE), Farnborough. The work there was varied and challenging, ranging from problems of immediate urgency for the RAF to matters of great importance for future aircraft designs. It was evident that high speeds, extending into supersonic flight, would in due course become a reality, calling for new experimental and theoretical research tools. Owen's progress with such problems was remarkable. He quickly matured from his initial junior status to become a creative leader, and his promotion was rapid. Topics he successfully addressed included the development of low-drag wings and bodies, the stability and control of high-speed aircraft, the aerodynamic problems of guided weapons, and supersonic flight. When the war ended in 1945 he expanded his interests to include other applications of fluid mechanics.

In 1953 he accepted an invitation to become reader and director of the Manchester University fluid motion laboratory, and three years later he was appointed professor and head of the newly formed mechanics of fluids department. In spite of his heavy administrative load, he became interested in meteorology and was also involved with local industrial problems—for example, cotton spinning, ventilation, and the dangers of coal dust in mines. He became a member of the Safety in Mines advisory board in 1956. This led him to investigate the transport of dust particles by air flows, including saltation (the lifting of particles from a surface and their subsequent trajectories). This became a major activity, with important applications to soil erosion and desertification.

In 1963 he moved to the Zaharoff chair of aviation at Imperial College, London. He there extended his interests even further, to the aerodynamics of buildings, heat exchangers, blood flow, and respiration. In 1966 a physiological flows unit was founded in his department. Meanwhile, however, Owen was an active member of the Aeronautical Research Council and in 1971 he was appointed its chairman, a position he retained for a record eight years. Since this was a time of major new developments in aeronautics, the work of the council was of first importance and Owen took great pride in it.

In 1984 he retired early, but he continued teaching and vigorously pursued his research, particularly in saltation. He developed fruitful contacts with workers elsewhere with similar interests, particularly in the Middle East, Africa, USA, Denmark, and France, and he contributed key papers to international symposia. In 1985 he developed heart trouble and had a bypass operation. Nevertheless, he soon resumed his research, travelling and lecturing extensively, and seemed to recover well.

He was passionately interested in music, drama, and the arts. His good looks and musical voice made him a natural choice in his youth for leading parts in the RAE dramatic society productions. He wrote and spoke with grace, wit, and a wry, kindly, self-deprecating humour. His sympathies were with the under-privileged and he constantly sought to apply himself to the problems of the third world. He was accorded various honours, including election as FRS in 1971, appointment as CBE in 1974, and election as F.Eng. in 1976.

In 1958 he married Margaret Ann, a law graduate of Oxford, daughter of Herbert Baron, solicitor. They had two sons and two daughters, in whom he took great pride and pleasure. In 1988 he fell ill again with what was thought to be a viral infection. He continued writing and collaborating with his international colleagues, but recovery eluded him. He died of cancer in St Mary's Hospital, London, 11 November 1990.

[A. D. Young and Sir James Lighthill in *Biographical Memoirs of Fellows of the Royal Society*, vol. xxxviii, 1992; personal knowledge.]   ALEC YOUNG

P

PÄCHT, Otto Ernst (1902–1988), art historian, was born in Vienna 7 September 1902, the elder son (there were no daughters) of David Pächt, a Jewish businessman, and his wife, Josephine Freundlich. He attended the Volkschule and Stadtgymnasium in Vienna and in 1920 proceeded to Vienna University where, with a brief interlude in Berlin, he studied art history and archaeology. He achieved his doctorate in 1925. His first book, devoted to Austrian Gothic panel painting, appeared in 1929. In 1933 he was appointed Privatdozent at the University of Heidelberg, but the Nazi embargo on Jews holding posts in Germany prevented him from taking up the position.

Frustrated and alarmed by the political situation, Pächt paid his first visit to London at the end of 1935 and settled there in 1938. He was invited to undertake a catalogue of illuminated manuscripts (a field new to him) at the British Museum, liaising with Francis Wormald, then assistant keeper in the manuscripts department, who rapidly became a close personal friend. The evacuation of the manuscripts in 1939 ended this scheme and in 1941 he moved to Oxford to begin a similar project at the Bodleian Library. The resulting three-volume catalogue, completed by his pupil Jonathan Alexander, appeared between 1966 and 1973. Specialists in the study of manuscript illumination were rare and the scope of this undertaking left Pächt with a virtually unrivalled expertise. During his two decades in Oxford he published on a wide variety of topics, paying particular attention to English work of the twelfth century, which he viewed within its wider European context. His contribution to the collaborative monograph on the St Albans Psalter (1960) is especially significant. During the same period he turned once more to his original fascination with northern painting of the fifteenth century, publishing *The Master of Mary of Burgundy* in 1948.

In March 1945 Pächt had been made fellow and lecturer in the history of medieval art at Oriel College, Oxford. In May 1947 he took British citizenship, which he retained for the remainder of his life. He became senior lecturer in the history faculty in 1952 and was advanced to reader in 1962. His subject was not, however, part of the formal syllabus and opportunities for direct teaching even at postgraduate level were disappointingly meagre. In 1963 he decided to accept an invitation to return to Vienna to fill the chair of art history in succession to K. M. Swoboda, thus becoming one of the few refugee scholars from Austria to return to his roots after the war. His work in England was acknowledged by election to the fellowship of the British Academy in 1956 and by the award of an honorary D.Litt. from Oxford in 1971.

In the 1960s Pächt's energies were directed almost entirely to his university commitments. His students welcomed him as an outstanding teacher and lecturer and he, in turn, was greatly stimulated by their enthusiasm. Fortunately for posterity, his carefully prepared lectures were all preserved in typescript and a series of publications, including *Buchmalerei des Mittelalters* in 1984, made their content and his methodology accessible to a wider audience. After his retirement in 1972 he returned to his own research and published extensively up to the time of his death, paying particular attention once more to the problems of northern painting in the fifteenth century. At the same time he was responsible, in collaboration with Dagmar Thoss and Ulrike Jenni, for the appearance of four volumes in the ambitious catalogue of illuminated manuscripts in the Vienna National Library, French in 1974 and 1977, Dutch in 1975, and Flemish in 1983 and 1990. A fellow of the Austrian Academy since 1967, he was awarded the Order of Merit by France in 1982 and became a commander of the Order of Arts and Letters in 1984.

Throughout his long career Pächt's circle of scholarly acquaintance was very wide. His attachment to the Bodleian Library brought him readily into contact with the international fraternity of manuscript specialists drawn there by their individual work. He maintained friendships with other members of the academic refugee community, notably colleagues from the Warburg Institute in London. Back in Vienna his many students found his approach inspiring. Pächt was stockily built and bespectacled, with thick dark eyebrows recalling the original colour of his sparse hair. Twenty-five years' residence in England did not entirely rob his speech of the evidence of his German origins.

Pächt married, on 11 January 1940, Jeanne Thalia (died 1971), an art historical researcher whom he met when she was working as assistant librarian at the Courtauld Institute, the daughter of Constantine A. Michalopulo, import–export merchant. They had one son. Pächt died in hospital in Vienna, 17 April 1988.

[J. J. G. Alexander in *Proceedings of the British Academy*, vol. lxxx, 1991; Otto Demus, 'Otto Pächt', *Almanach der Österreichischen Akademie der Wissenschaften*, vol. cxxxviii. 1988; private information; personal knowledge.]   JANET BACKHOUSE

PAGET, Reginald Thomas Guy Des Voeux, BARON PAGET OF NORTHAMPTON (1908–1990), politician, barrister, and master of foxhounds, was born 2 September 1908 at Sulby Hall, Northamptonshire, the younger son and second of three children of Major Thomas Guy Frederick Paget, sometime Independent Tory MP for the Bosworth division of Leicestershire, and his wife (Emma) Bettine, daughter of Sir (George) William *Des Voeux, colonial governor. He was educated at Eton and Trinity College, Cambridge, where he read law, receiving a third class in part i of the tripos in 1928. He then decided to read for an ordinary degree and passed parts i and ii of military studies, which would have enabled him to achieve an ordinary BA, for which, however, he never presented himself. It was while an undergraduate at Cambridge that he joined the Labour party, a decision not unusual in the political climate of the time but made perhaps more striking in his case by the fact that the previous five generations of his family had all been Tory MPs. During the 1930s he practised as a barrister, having been called to the bar in 1934.

Within the Labour party, for which he fought his first (unsuccessful) parliamentary election at Northampton in 1935, 'Reggie' Paget was always something of an anomaly. Once he reached Westminster in 1945, winning Northampton at his second attempt, he contrived to represent the voice of the squirearchy far more convincingly than anyone on the Conservative benches. His socialism was essentially paternalistic, and it was typical of him that he should have thought nothing of receiving a delegation of trade unionists while still dressed in his full hunting kit. He took silk in 1947.

Before becoming a life peer in 1974, Paget sat in the House of Commons for twenty-nine years. In all that time he was only briefly the recipient of preferment from his party. From 1960 to 1964 he was a junior opposition spokesman first for the Royal Navy (during World War II he had served in the Royal Naval Volunteer Reserve before being invalided out in 1943) and then for the army; but the death of Hugh *Gaitskell in 1963 put paid to any hopes he may have held of progressing to government office. An outspoken critic of Harold Wilson (later Baron Wilson of Rievaulx) during the leadership election which followed Gaitskell's death, he never relented in his belief that Wilson was quite the wrong man to lead the Labour party or, indeed, to be prime minister.

In appearance and diction more like a Whig grandee from an earlier age, Paget was nevertheless a man of parts. Said to be the slowest speaker in the House, Paget had a long chin and beetling brows. An intrepid yachtsman, a fearless rider to hounds (he must have been the only Labour MP ever to become master of the Pytchley, a position he held from 1968 to 1971), he was also a competent amateur painter (he held his first exhibition at the Fine Arts Gallery at Ebury Street, London, in 1988), as well as being the author of three books. The first, *Manstein, His Campaigns and His Trial* (1951), commemorated his spirited defence of Field-Marshal Fritz Erich von Manstein, for which he waived his normal barrister's fees, before one of the last war crimes tribunals in 1949; the second, co-authored with his fellow Labour MP, Sydney *Silverman, arose in part out of the Christopher Craig and Derek Bentley murder case of 1953 and conveyed its message in its title *Hanged—and Innocent?* (1953); while the third, and far the most ambitious, *The Human Journey*, published in 1979 well after his retirement from the Commons, represented an attempt to tell the whole story of the human race.

Courage, sometimes leading to recklessness, was in fact the hallmark of Paget's career. In 1963, after a row in the Commons over the extradition of Chief Enahoro of Nigeria who, he argued, should properly have been regarded as a political refugee, he insisted on reporting the attorney-general of the day, Sir John *Hobson, to the inn (the Inner Temple) to which they both belonged, almost certainly the first time a queen's counsel (and fellow bencher) had taken such action against a law officer of the Crown. But then no one was ever less a respecter of rank, station, or person, and it was this total lack of deference in his otherwise patrician character which clinched Paget's claim to be considered a genuine radical.

In 1931 Paget married Sybil Helen ('Nancy'), daughter of Sills Clifford Gibbons, of Scaynes Hill, Sussex, widow of Sir John Bridger Shiffner, sixth baronet, and former wife of Sir Victor Basil John Seely, fourth baronet. They had no children of their own. In London Paget tended to lead a faintly eighteenth-century bachelor life. But his roots were in the country and in particular at his family home, Lubenham Lodge, Market Harborough, where he and his wife brought up four adopted children, two boys and two girls. They were the offspring of an RAF pilot, whose wife died when the children were young. Paget adopted them because the father did not want them split up, and, when the father retired from the RAF, gave him a job and took him into the household too. He separated from his wife before his death, causing some embarrassment to his country friends. He died 2 January 1990, at his London home, 9 Grosvenor Cottages, SW1.

[*The Times*, 4 January 1990; *Independent*, 6 January 1990; private information; personal knowledge.]

ANTHONY HOWARD

PAISH, Frank Walter (1898–1988), economist, was born in Croydon 15 January 1898, the eldest of five sons (there were no daughters) of (Sir) George Paish, joint editor of the *Statist* (1900–16) and author of many publications on economic and social problems, and his wife Emily Mary, daughter of Thomas Whitehead, of Liverpool. He was educated at Winchester College before being commissioned into the Royal Field Artillery in 1916. He served in France in 1917–18 with the rank of lieutenant and was awarded the MC (1918) during the German offensive of March 1918, when he was wounded by shrapnel. In 1919–21 he was a student at Trinity College, Cambridge, where he obtained a second class (division I) in both part i of the history tripos (1920) and part ii of the economics tripos (1921).

On leaving university he joined the Standard Bank of South Africa, first in London in 1921 and then, from 1922 to 1932, in South Africa, at Aliwal North, where he was manager of a country branch, and finally in Cape Town, where his responsibility became that of economic intelligence and analysis. In 1932 he left the bank and was appointed a lecturer at the London School of Economics. His work for the Standard Bank led him to throw new light on the working of the gold standard and he was one of the first economists to emphasize the role of changes in national income and expenditure, in addition to the quantity of money, in bringing about balance of payments adjustments. He was made a reader at the University of London in 1938 and Sir Ernest Cassel professor of economics (with special reference to business finance) in 1949. During this period his publications included *Insurance Funds and Their Investment* (1934, with George *Schwartz) and a study of the cheap money policy of 1932. In 1941–5 he was deputy director of programmes in the Ministry of Aircraft Production. During the war he was also commissioned into the Home Guard, reaching the rank of captain.

He was elected president of section F of the British Association in 1953. He held his professorship until retirement in 1965, when he was appointed professor emeritus; and in 1970 he was made an honorary fellow of LSE. Between 1965 and 1970 he acted as consultant to Lloyds Bank on economic affairs. He had neither the training nor the taste for the mathematical theorizing and complex econometric testing which became prevalent in his profession. Instead, he had an unusually shrewd eye for applied economic problems and for the basic statistics needed to throw light on them. He always saw the formulation of economic theory as an art, and he was content to make contributions to the solution of difficult questions by means of a first approximation; econometric refinements he was content to leave to others. He had a rare understanding of the cyclical behaviour of the British economy and had a better forecasting record than most. He was one of the first economists to emphasize the need for a margin of spare capacity ('unused productive potential') to prevent inflation and the dangers of an ambitious policy of stimulating demand in the hope of stimulating long-term economic growth. In the conditions of the 1960s he argued that the spare capacity needed to prevent inflation would involve a level of unemployment of $2\frac{1}{2}$ per cent, a view which was the subject of hostility on the part of those who believed that economic policy should be less restrained, including trade unionists; although he held policy-makers rather than trade unions responsible for inflation and did not believe in the efficacy of 'incomes policy'.

Changes in the characteristics of the British economy in the 1970s and 1980s, like those in most other countries, rendered his original estimate of the level of unemployment implied by anti-inflationary policy much too low; and later all economists accepted the need for some margin of spare capacity, even though they might disagree on its precise level and on the role of different instruments of economic policy. In the 1960s Paish's views were unpopular in Whitehall, where his prescriptions were neither sought nor taken. The tension between the supporters of his approach, who included colleagues at LSE, and advocates of more ambitious demand policies, broadly identified with the Keynesian school in general and with economists in Cambridge in particular, made difficult his task as editor of the London and Cambridge Economic Service, which produced regular assessments of economic conditions by economists from LSE and Cambridge. He was its secretary in 1932–41 and again in 1945–9, and editor in 1947–9.

His publications included *The Post-war Financial Problem, and Other Essays* (1950), *Business Finance* (1953), *Studies in an Inflationary Economy* (1962), *Long-term and Short-term Interest Rates in the United Kingdom* (1966), (ed.), *Benham's Economics*, 5th–8th edns. (1962–7) and, with A. J. Culyer, 9th edn. (1973), *Rise and Fall of Incomes Policy* (1969), and *How the Economy Works, and Other Essays* (1970).

He was of medium height and fair-haired, with strikingly blue eyes. His war wound left him with a limited degree of movement in his right shoulder, which necessitated some unusual but spectacular shots at the table tennis which was an off-duty diversion of the senior common room at LSE. His writing and his teaching had a directness, clarity, and lack of pretentiousness which were characteristic of the man. He had a boyish sense of humour and would reach the heart of a subject by means of brief and pithy comment. He was always ready to help his students and was an amiable colleague; but behind his friendliness and humour there was a robustness and even a hint of steel, which owed something, perhaps, to his experience in World War I.

In 1927 he married Beatrice Mary (died 1992), sister of Rachel, who married Sir Bryan *Matthews, and daughter of Gustav Conrad Eckhard, shipping agent, of Manchester. They had two sons and a daughter. Paish died in Kentchurch, Hereford, 23 May 1988.

[Private information; personal knowledge.]

HAROLD ROSE

PARKES, SIR **Alan Sterling** (1900–1990), professor of the physiology of reproduction, was born 10 September 1900 in Bank House, Castleton, near Rochdale, the younger son and third of four children of Ebenezer Thomas Parkes, bank manager, and his wife Helena Louisa, daughter of Jonas Banks, brass founder, of Willenhall. He was educated at Hulme Grammar School in Oldham and Willaston School in Nantwich, Cheshire. After he failed his School Certificate, he went for a year to Harper Adams Agricultural College in Newport, Shropshire. He was called up in 1918 and did a brief period of military service in the Manchester Regiment. After demobilization, he went in 1919 to Christ's College, Cambridge, which waived entrance examinations for servicemen. He studied agriculture and obtained a second-class pass degree in 1921. After this inauspicious start, the opportunity to read for a Ph.D. degree (1923) in the University of Manchester on the mammalian sex ratio opened new doors into the world of biology and experimental research. Professor A. V. *Hill, his internal examiner, invited him to University College London in 1923, where he became Sharpey scholar in the department of physiology and subsequently Beit memorial research fellow (1924–30) and Foulerton student of the Royal Society (1930–4). He gained his Cambridge D.Sc. in 1931.

He had a clear and analytical mind and exceptional ingenuity as an experimentalist, and was an indefatigable and versatile worker. He was appointed in 1932 to the staff of the Medical Research Council, National Institute for Medical Research, Mill Hill. There his adventures in biology ranged from experimental endocrinology to setting up international standards for hormone preparations on the initiative of the director, Sir Henry *Dale. Distinguished in appearance, of average height, sturdy in build, and with a shock of white hair from an early age, he returned to Cambridge in 1961, as the first holder of the Mary Marshall and Arthur Walton chair of the physiology of reproduction (until 1967). He was a fellow of Christ's College from 1961 to 1969 and an honorary fellow from 1970.

His most influential research concerned the survival of cells, tissues, and whole animals at low temperature. He played a major part with Audrey Smith and Christopher Polge in developing the technique of storing and transporting at very low temperatures spermatozoa for artificial insemination, and in discovering that certain small rodents could survive cooling to low temperatures without showing apparent physiological or psychological impairment. Such work led to the formation of a new scientific society and the establishment of the journal *Cryobiology*, a name he and his colleagues coined 'to fill an etymological vacuum'.

His research into many aspects of reproductive physiology led to articles describing the patterns of reproduction in a number of wild and laboratory mammals, several of them written with his wife Ruth, whom he married in 1933. She was the daughter of Edward Deanesly, surgeon, of Cheltenham, and they had one son and two daughters. He published freely on the effects of X-rays on reproductive functions, the hormonal control of secondary sexual characteristics of birds, and, with Hilda Bruce, the remarkable capacity of certain pheromones to block the course of pregnancy. After his retirement from Cambridge he became consultant to the world's first sea turtle farm on Grand Cayman island (1973–80). Always retaining a very broad interest in biology, he was deeply involved in associated social and ethical questions, particularly those relating to human populations. His views about sensitive issues such as women's right to abortion, costly transplant surgery compared to simpler operations, and the quality of human populations are reflected in *Sex, Science and Society* (1966). Other important publications are his *The Internal Secretions of the Ovary* (1929) and *Patterns of Sexuality and Reproduction* (1976).

He gave numerous distinguished named lectures in different countries, and held presidencies, chairmanships, and medals of various learned societies. He was editor and prime mover of new journals and monumental primary volumes in the science he sought to foster. His devastating incisiveness and dynamism took him at an early age to fellowship of the Royal Society (1933), and to a CBE (1956) and a knighthood (1968). His lively sense of humour is displayed in two light-hearted and highly entertaining autobiographies, *Off-beat Biologist* (1985) and *Biologist at Large* (1988). One of the founders of modern reproductive biology, he died 17 July 1990 in Shepreth, Cambridgeshire.

[Alan S. Parkes, *Off-beat Biologist*, 1985, and *Biologist at Large*, 1988; R. W. J. Keay in *Biologist*, vol. xxxvii, 1990; personal knowledge.]   R. B. HEAP

PARKINSON, Norman (1913–1990), photographer, was born Ronald William Smith in Roehampton, London, 21 April 1913, the second of three children and younger son of William James Parkinson Smith, barrister and councillor of the borough of Wandsworth, and his wife, Louise Emily Cobley. Evacuated to the countryside during World War I, he returned to live in the family home at 32 Landford Road, Putney. Educated at Westminster School (1927–31), he described himself as 'scholastically abysmal', but received the encouragement of the art master, Henry S. Williamson, and was awarded the school's Henry Luce art prize. In 1931 he was apprenticed to the distinguished Bond Street court photographers, Speaight & Son. With a solid, if traditional, grounding in his craft he was able to set up in 1934 (initially in partnership with Norman Kibblewhite) the Norman Parkinson Portrait Studio at 1 Dover Street, London. It was after this that he adopted the name Norman Parkinson.

His earliest photographs, many of which were published in the *Bystander*, were principally of débutantes, but a chance meeting in 1935 with P. Joyce Reynolds, editor of *Harper's Bazaar*, changed the course of his career. Invited to try fashion photography, he was persuaded by the magazine's art director, A. Y. McPeake, to photograph outdoors. Parkinson became a pioneer in the genre, rejecting the static, posed artificiality of the studio and appropriating the naturalism and immediacy of contemporary news photography. He was also broadening his range, and notable early portraits include those of (Sir) Noël *Coward, the *Sitwells, and Edward James, a patron of the arts. His regular contributions of current affairs photographs to the *Bystander* included a report on unemployed Welsh miners and a weekly series, from 1937, on the armed forces preparing for war. Parkinson combined a modern style with traditional content in collaborating with the experimental photographer, Francis Bruguière, on photo-murals for the British pavilion at the 1937 Paris Exposition Universelle, images of quintessential 'Britishness' anticipating his neo-Elizabethan iconography of the postwar years. During World War II he combined farming, at Bushley, Worcestershire, with photography.

Parkinson's long association with *Vogue* began in 1940. Its art editor, John Parsons, was another catalyst in Parkinson's career, redirecting him to sources within the history of English painting and architecture. His photographs offered the solace of the English rural idyll during wartime deprivations, and served as a reaffirmation of enduring values in the years of postwar austerity. War damage destroyed most of his pre-war negatives.

From 1949 to 1955 Parkinson spent summer months in New York, working for American *Vogue*. He began to photograph increasingly in colour, in exotic locations throughout the world, a development which became a cornerstone of his later style. His contract with *Vogue* having expired in 1959, he became photographer and associate editor from 1960 to 1964 on *Queen* magazine, a base from which he launched his alternative view of the culture of the 1960s. In 1963 he bought a house in Tobago, subsequently dividing his time between there and Twickenham. It was in Tobago that he became a pig breeder and manufactured his well-known sausage, the Porkinson banger. In 1968 he was elected an honorary fellow of the Royal Photographic Society.

Parkinson combined hard work and perfectionism with a keen sense of humour. Six feet five inches tall, slim and mustachioed, he was an imposing figure, and his elegant if often unconventional mode of dress, which included a Kashmiri wedding cap, regularly gained him a place on British and international lists of best dressed men. He returned to *Vogue* from 1965 until he severed his connection with the Condé Nast organization following a dispute in 1978. His twenty-first birthday photographs of Princess Anne in 1971, and his coverage of her engagement and wedding in 1973, were widely considered a breakthrough in the glamorous and informal portrayal of royalty. Many similarly acclaimed commissions followed, including the queen mother's seventy-fifth birthday photographs, and the triple portrait with her daughters to mark her eightieth birthday.

Now recognized as a doyen of British photography, Parkinson was elected a fellow of the Institute of Incorporated Photographers in 1975, and in 1981 he was appointed CBE. His first major museum retrospective opened in London's National Portrait Gallery later in the same year. In 1978 he began regular assignments photographing the wealthy and famous for *Town and Country* magazine, which again brought his name to prominence in the USA. In 1983 he received the American Society of Magazine Photographers' 'lifetime of achievement' award.

In November 1935 he married Margaret, daughter of Sir Reginald Mitchell Banks, county court judge. The marriage was dissolved and in 1942 he married Thelma Woolley, daughter of George Blay, timber merchant. There were no children from either marriage. In 1947 Parkinson met Wenda (died 1987), second daughter of William Albert Rogerson, FRCP, FRCS, of the Royal Army Medical Corps, and she became for many years his favourite model and muse. Together they raised her son by a previous marriage, Simon (born 1945), as Simon Parkinson. Parkinson suffered a stroke while on assignment in Borneo, and died two weeks later in Singapore, 14 February 1990.

[Norman Parkinson, *Lifework*, 1983; private information.]   MARTIN HARRISON

PART, SIR Antony Alexander (1916–1990), civil servant, was born 28 June 1916 in Chelsea, London, the only son of Alexander Francis Part, barrister and company director, from a Lancashire family, and his second wife, Una Margaret Reynolds Snowdon, from Yorkshire. He had a younger sister, an older half-brother and half-sister, and a younger half-brother. His early childhood years were spent in happy and prosperous family surroundings in Chelsea, but his adolescence was overshadowed by his parents' divorce. After a good grounding in classics at a preparatory school he entered Harrow with a scholarship at the age of twelve and later specialized in French and German. He won a scholarship to Trinity College, Cambridge, where he achieved first-class honours in both parts of the modern and medieval languages tripos (1935 and 1937).

He entered the Board of Education in 1937 through the competitive examination for the administrative class of the Home Civil Service. Though he was soon lent to the newly created Ministry of Supply, a keen interest in education and training motivated the greater part of his Civil Service career.

He joined the Royal Ulster Rifles in 1940, but his knowledge of German quickly led to a commission in the Intelligence Corps, where by 1943 he had gained rapid promotion to lieutenant-colonel, serving in the Western Desert campaign and later in the 21st Army Group headquarters preparing for the invasion of France. His personality was changing. At school he had been shy and retiring. University had built his self-confidence. Finding in the army that he was thought somewhat over-assertive, he learned an important lesson about leadership which he never forgot.

He was recalled to the Ministry of Education at the end of 1944 and became principal private secretary to three successive ministers. His first major opportunity came in 1946 when he and the chief architect of the department as joint heads set up a new branch to assist education authorities to build the new schools needed to meet the demands of the rising birth rate and the raising of the school leaving age. The programme they developed was so effective in enabling good schools to be built quickly at acceptable cost that it earned international reputation. As a Commonwealth Fund fellow in the USA in 1950–1, Part found leading American experts in school building eager to learn from him about these British methods. He contracted tuberculosis in America and did not return to work until spring 1953.

Promoted to under-secretary in 1954 as head of the schools branch and later of the further education branch, he was active in the initiatives to improve and expand technical training at all levels through technical colleges and colleges of advanced technology. He became deputy secretary in 1960, covering teacher training and further education, served as a departmental assessor on the committee on higher education (1961–4) chaired by Baron *Robbins, and seemed well positioned by ability and experience to achieve his growing ambition to become permanent secretary of the Ministry of Education.

There were, however, other plans for him. In March 1963 he was moved to the Ministry of Works to organize a merger of departments into the Ministry of Public Building and Works, of which he became permanent secretary in 1965. It was as permanent secretary of the Board of Trade in 1968, of the newly created Department of Trade and Industry in 1970, and of the Department of Industry from 1974 to 1976 that he had the greatest scope for the exercise of his talents and experience. He worked hard to establish an industrial department as a major force in Whitehall and was greatly upset by the decision of the Labour government to split the DTI into three in 1974.

His strengths were his vision, his genuine interest in manufacturing industry, his ability to work constructively with most businessmen, trade unionists, and politicians, and his flair for public speaking. He exhibited great energy and determination in everything he undertook, whether in the fields of education or trade and industry. He put into practice his strong conviction that public administration should be efficient and financially prudent.

Retiring from the Civil Service in 1976, he took up a new career as a non-executive director of a number of firms, including chairmanship of Orion Insurance Company. He continued his active interest in education as deputy chairman of the court of governors of the London School of Economics.

Part was appointed MBE (1943), CB (1959), KCB (1966), and GCB (1974). He received honorary degrees from Brunel (1966), Aston (1974), and Cranfield (1976), and LSE honorary fellowship (1984). In his prime he was tall and dark with a confident bearing. However, he had poor health all his life and this greatly affected his appearance in his last years in the Civil Service and thereafter, major heart surgery causing him to have a pronounced stoop and to move very slowly. He enjoyed the performing arts, but his main interests were in his work in both public and private sectors, which despite his ready wit he took very seriously. In 1940 he married a ballet dancer, Isabella ('Ella'), daughter of Maurice Bennett, businessman. His marriage was happy and although they had no children, he and his wife maintained a close relationship with his siblings and their children. Part died of heart failure in Westminster Hospital, London, 11 January 1990.

[Sir Antony Part, *The Making of a Mandarin*, 1990; private information; personal knowledge.]

DOUGLAS ALLEN

PEARCE, Edward Holroyd, BARON PEARCE (1901–1990), lord of appeal, was born 9 February 1901 in Sidcup, Kent, the elder son (there were subsequently three daughters) of John William Ernest Pearce, headmaster of a preparatory school, and his wife Irene, daughter of Holroyd Chaplin. He was educated at Charterhouse and Corpus Christi College, Oxford, of which he became an honorary fellow in 1950. He obtained a first in classical honour moderations (1921) and a third class in *literae humaniores* (1923). While at Oxford he showed great prowess on the games field. He was called to the bar in 1925 by Lincoln's Inn and the Middle Temple.

In the decade before World War II his promising career as a junior barrister was interrupted by tuberculosis. After a period in Switzerland he was sufficiently cured to enable him to resume his practice, but ever afterwards he had to be particularly careful about his health. Exempt from war service, he continued his practice throughout World War II. Pearce became deputy chairman of East Sussex quarter-sessions in 1947 and was appointed a High Court judge in 1948, with the customary knighthood. He was first assigned to the Probate, Divorce, and Admiralty Division, moving to the Queen's Bench Division in 1954. In 1957 he was made a lord justice of appeal and a privy councillor. From 1962, when he was created a life peer, to 1969 he was a lord of appeal in ordinary. He was a popular and successful judge, with a clear and perceptive mind and friendly manner.

On his retirement in 1969 Pearce took over the chairmanship of the Press Council, which he held until 1974. He constantly emphasized the link between the freedom of the press and its responsibility. At the same time he became chairman of the appeals committee of the Take-over Panel (until 1976). He had also served on other important commissions and committees, notably (as chairman) the committee on ship-building costs (1947–9) and the royal commission on marriage and divorce (1951–5), of which he was an influential member. He was a leading figure in the committee of the four inns of court which set up a senate to iron out their differences (1971–3). He became a bencher of Lincoln's Inn in 1948 and treasurer in 1966. As past master and past member of the court of the Company of Skinners he was a governor of Charterhouse (1943–64), Tonbridge School (1945–78), and Sutton's Hospital in Charterhouse.

Pearce became a household name in 1971 when he became chairman of a commission set up to determine Rhodesia's reaction to a proposed constitutional settlement. The Pearce commission reported in May 1972 that the proposed terms were generally unacceptable and massively rejected by the Africans. The proposals were shelved and the status quo continued.

Pearce was exceptionally hard-working, cheerful, happy, and readily approachable. A distinctly attractive man, Pearce was ever-smiling and good-humoured. About five feet ten inches tall, he kept his light red hair to the end. He used plain language when unravelling problems at the bench and in the *Law Reports*. His simplicity of expression and manner made him an ideal chairman of committees. He was much in demand as a witty after-dinner speaker. Both he and his wife were talented artists, who held shows together or separately, and he exhibited regularly at the Royal Academy. He was also an ardent collector of pictures and sometimes sculpture. He became president of the Artists League of Great Britain (1950–74) and a trustee of the Chantrey Bequest. At their home in Crowborough he and his wife made a lovely garden. In later years Pearce suffered with trouble to both his hips.

In 1927 he married Erica (died 1985), daughter of Bertram Priestman, RA, artist. It was an extremely happy marriage and she did much to encourage his interest in art. They had two sons, both of whom became QCs, the elder of whom died in 1987 and the younger in 1985. Pearce was never a rich man—until the very end. His artistic eye had picked up a sculpture some thirty years beforehand, for about £15. Just before his death this 'dancing faun' turned out to be the work of a sixteenth-century Italian sculptor and was sold for £6.2 million in a London sale. Pearce died 26 November 1990 in Crowborough, Sussex.

[Personal knowledge.]

JAMES COMYN

PEARS, SIR Peter Neville Luard (1910–1986), tenor, was born 22 June 1910 at Newark House, Searle Road, Farnham, Surrey, the youngest in

345

the family of four daughters, one of whom died in infancy, and three sons of Arthur Grant Pears, civil engineer and later a director of Burma Railways, and his wife, Jessie Elizabeth de Visme Luard. Pears's parents were married in Bombay in 1893. Much of his father's working life was spent overseas, which meant that Peter had little contact with him until after 1923, when Arthur Pears retired, to live in England. Pears's mother too was often absent, though it is clear from his letters that his relationship with her was a fond one and sustained throughout his young manhood. His brothers followed naval careers, continuing a family tradition in which there was a strong service element: his mother's father had been a general. But there was also another and altogether different strand in Pears's ancestry, that of the Church and, more particularly, the influence of Pears's great-great-grandmother, Elizabeth *Fry, the Quaker reformer. A bonding with Quakerism was to continue throughout Pears's life and was reflected in his pacifism, his sense of values, and his virtues. There was indeed something of the patrician Quaker in his looks, manners, and deeds. His habitual charm and courtesy rarely deserted him.

Pears's childhood, even though it may have lacked the continuity of a settled home, seems to have been a happy one, as indeed were his school-days at Lancing College, Sussex, which he entered as a classical scholar in 1923. At Lancing he became aware of his homosexual nature, though it was to be some years before it found fulfilment. In this respect he was to live at ease with himself throughout his life. It was at school, too, that his musical and theatrical gifts and inclinations showed themselves. He was a capable pianist, took part in operatic and dramatic productions, and involved himself in the school's cultural life. He was an accomplished cricketer. As his school-days ended, his love of painting seems to have begun: his taste and judgement aided him in the acquisition across the years of a notable private collection which included many examples of the work of the best British artists of the period.

In 1928 he went to Keble College, Oxford, to study music, but again without a very clear musical goal in mind. For a while he had a post at Hertford College as temporary organist. But his Oxford career was short-lived. He failed his pass moderations, left Oxford, and never returned. He went back to his preparatory school, The Grange (Crowborough), in 1929, but this time as a teacher, and resumed his interest in cricket. At this point Pears's instinct for music finally located itself in his voice. This led to his undertaking, for the first time, professional vocal studies at the Royal College of Music in London, initially on a part-time basis and then, in 1934, as a full-time student (he was an operatic exhibi-

tioner). Again, however, he never completed the course. He left after only two terms, during which he participated in college operatic productions, to begin his professional career as a singer, with the BBC Singers (1934–7) and, in 1936, the New English Singers, with whom he made his first visit to the USA. In finally making his commitment specifically to a singer's life, he was helped by Nell Burra. She was the twin sister of Peter Burra, a close friend of Pears at Lancing and Oxford, whose life Pears was briefly to share in 1936 and 1937. It was a friendship which was to have a momentous consequence for Pears and indeed for the history of British music.

Burra, a gifted writer on the arts, had met the young composer, Benjamin (later Baron) *Britten, in Barcelona in 1936, and the two men became friends. This was before Pears and Britten themselves had met. It was Burra's untimely death in an air accident in 1937 that brought Pears and Britten together. Their remarkable partnership had its inception in April of that year when, as Burra's friends, they jointly sorted out his personal papers. Thus the end of one friendship was the beginning of another; and thereafter the careers of Pears and Britten were inextricably interlinked, as were their lives (they began to share a flat in 1938), though it was not in fact until 1939 in Canada that the love each had for the other finally declared itself. It was to be sustained over thirty-six years. Pears had left England for North America with Britten in the same year and they were not to return until 1942, when both men, convinced pacifists of long standing, sought and were granted exemption from military service, provided they continued their wartime work as performing musicians.

Pears, already in 1938, had had professional experience of opera as a member of the chorus at Glyndebourne, when he was described by a fellow artist as 'tall, fair-haired, reserved and poetic-looking', most of which characteristics were to remain unchanged. Britten's phenomenal development as a composer for the opera house, which had begun in the USA, inevitably brought with it a comparable development in Pears, for whom Britten wrote an extraordinary number and variety of leading roles in almost all of his principal operas, from *Peter Grimes* (1945) to *Death in Venice* (1973). It was in that last opera, dedicated to Pears, that Pears was to make his début at the Metropolitan Opera, New York, in 1974, at the age of sixty-four. But while it is true that Britten's operas shaped Pears's destiny as an opera singer, it must be remembered that Pears, on his return to England from America, had established himself independently as a notable member of the Sadler's Wells company, appearing in such roles as Alfredo in *La Traviata*, Ferrando in *Così fan tutte*, the Duke in *Rigoletto*,

Almaviva in *The Barber of Seville*, and Vašek in *The Bartered Bride*. His performances attracted critical attention for their exceptional musicality and intelligence and admiration from Britten, who was often in the theatre as a member of the audience. It was his growing confidence in Pears's theatrical and vocal skills that enabled Britten to write the title role of *Peter Grimes* with Pears's voice in mind (he had at one time thought of Grimes as a baritone). The famous world première of the opera on 7 June 1945 placed the composer in the front rank of musical dramatists of his time and Pears as his principal interpreter.

It was not only as a singer that Pears and his unique voice had an influential role to play in Britten's operas. In one of them, *A Midsummer Night's Dream* (1960), he collaborated with the composer in converting Shakespeare's text into a libretto. He was also the inspiration of the long series of song sets and song cycles that Britten composed between 1940 (the *Seven Sonnets of Michelangelo*) and 1975 (*A Birthday Hansel*), a legacy of song perhaps without equal in the twentieth century. This rich fund of songs reflected the prowess of Pears and Britten as performers. They were to establish themselves as one of the most celebrated and accomplished voice and piano duos of the postwar period, with an extensive repertory that included much of the work of Henry *Purcell (when his songs were by no means the staple diet of recital programmes) and the great nineteenth-century classic song cycles—for example, Schubert's *Winterreise* and Schumann's *Dichterliebe*—in interpretations which themselves achieved classic status, and have been preserved on gramophone records. His partnership with the lute virtuoso Julian Bream was to become almost as celebrated, perhaps especially for performances of the Elizabethan master, John *Dowland, of incomparable sensitivity and skill from both singer and accompanist. Of equal note was Pears's Evangelist in the Passions of Heinrich Schütz and J. S. Bach, roles to which he brought not only a predictable sensitivity but also an overwhelming sense of immediacy, as if he were a participant in the drama that was being unfolded. This was musical 'theatre' of an unusually exalted order.

The pattern of Pears's life, inextricably woven with the pattern of Britten's (until he suffered a slight stroke in 1973 as a result of his heart operation Britten was virtually the only pianist to accompany Pears), took the shape of strenuous recital tours, at home and abroad, recording and broadcasting; and planning the policy of the English Opera Group (of which he was a co-founder, in 1947) and the programmes of the annual Aldeburgh Festival (of which too he was a co-founder, in 1948). He played a leading role in both organizations as a performer and a stimulating, highly individual impresario.

It was Britten's name, as opera and song composer and pianist, that was inevitably most closely associated with Pears's. But his distinctive interpretations of roles other than Britten roles will not be forgotten: his Tamino in *The Magic Flute*, Idomeneo (in Mozart's opera), David in *The Mastersingers*, and Pandarus in *Troilus and Cressida* by (Sir) William *Walton, were all marked by the exceptional musicality and intelligence that characterized him as a singer and, above all, by his exceptional response to, and articulation of, words. He was as sensitive to the sounds of words as he was to pitches. It was a gift that enabled him to bring even a 'dead' classical language to life, as in his masterly performance as Oedipus in Igor Stravinsky's opera-oratorio, in which he collaborated with the composer. He was an enquiring and adventurous singer too, as the long list of first performances by living composers other than Britten amply demonstrates, among them commissions which he himself generously funded. His commitment to the singer's life and art, which had begun so tentatively in the 1930s, found further reflection in his later years when he was an active teacher in the Britten–Pears School for Advanced Musical Studies. This he had co-founded with Benjamin Britten in 1972, and, after the incapacitating stroke he suffered in 1980 which brought his career as a performer virtually to an end, he devoted more and more of his time to it. It was entirely appropriate that he should die at home at Aldeburgh, the focus of his personal and musical life for so many years, having completed, the day before, a full day's teaching at the School—a course, as it happened, on Bach's Passions—passing on to future generations his own unique experience of music, of creative partnership, of the spectrum of the arts, of life itself. It was the totality of all of these that coloured and informed Pears's voice and made it the unique instrument that it was. There were some who found it difficult to come to terms with its peculiar timbre. But his admirers, who were worldwide, rightly regarded it as a vehicle of civilization and sensibility without equal among English singers of his time.

He was appointed CBE in 1957 and knighted in 1978. He received honorary degrees from the universities of York (1969), Sussex (1971), Cambridge (1972), Edinburgh (1976), East Anglia (1980), Essex (1981), and Oxford (1981). Keble College made him an honorary fellow in 1978. From 1957 he and Britten lived together in the Red House in Aldeburgh, Suffolk. After Britten's death in 1976 Pears continued to live in the house until his own death there 3 April 1986. He was buried beside Britten in the churchyard of the parish church of St Peter and St Paul, Aldeburgh.

[Christopher Headington, *Peter Pears: a Biography*, 1992; Marion Thorpe (ed.), *Peter Pears: a Tribute on his 75th Birthday*, 1985; Donald Mitchell and Philip Reed, *Letters from a Life: the Selected Letters and Diaries of Benjamin Britten 1913–1976*, 2 vols., 1991; personal knowledge.]   DONALD MITCHELL

PEART, (Thomas) Frederick, BARON PEART (1914–1988), politician, the first parliamentarian since Benjamin *Disraeli to become leader of both houses of Parliament, was born in Durham 30 April 1914, the elder son (there were no daughters) of Emerson Featherstone Peart, a Weardale schoolmaster, and his wife, Florence Maud Hopper. The harsh realities of life for the families whose children his father taught gave Peart a lifelong commitment to the Labour movement. Starting his education at Crook Council School, he went on to Wolsingham Grammar and Henry Smith's School in Hartlepool. He read science at the College of the Venerable Bede (Durham University), becoming president of the Labour Club and of the university union. Excelling at boxing, he also represented his university at rugby and football.

Unusually for a science graduate, he began studying at the Inner Temple. He was not called to the bar, opting instead to return to his roots in Durham as a schoolteacher and a lecturer in economics, campaigning with characteristic vigour to improve educational opportunities in its mining communities. After serving from 1937 for three years on Easington rural district council, he enlisted in the Royal Artillery as a gunner in 1940. After distinguished war service in North Africa and Italy, he returned home as a captain in 1945 and was elected Labour MP for Workington, which he served for thirty-one years. From 1945 to 1951 he was parliamentary private secretary to Thomas *Williams (later Baron Williams of Barnburgh), minister of agriculture in the newly elected Labour government. They worked in total harmony; indeed, so identified was he with Tom Williams that he was the natural choice for the Ministry of Agriculture after Labour's return to office in 1964 under the leadership of Harold Wilson (later Baron Wilson of Rievaulx). At the same time he was sworn of the Privy Council.

Cabinet pressure led him to reduce farm subsidies in his first (1965) farm price review, which provoked farmers to civil disobedience, but he emerged from this baptism of fire a widely respected minister. His reputation was further enhanced by courageous and decisive handling of Britain's worst ever epidemic of foot and mouth disease. In the countryside he was ever more warmly received by farmers and farmworkers alike.

His reservations at that time about European Economic Community membership ran deep, echoing those in most farming communities. He opposed in cabinet the Labour government's 1967 application for EEC membership because he was convinced that the common agricultural policy (CAP) would deprive British farmers of secure incomes and make consumers worse off by excluding cheap food imports from the traditional suppliers and was concerned also about harmful effects of the CAP on the Commonwealth's poorer developing countries.

In 1968 he became leader of the Commons, first as lord privy seal (April–October) and then lord president of the Council. His courtesy, friendliness, generosity, and good humour made him as popular as leader of the House as he had been as minister of agriculture. With Labour's defeat in 1970, he became opposition spokesman on parliamentary affairs (1970–1), agriculture (1971–2), and defence (1972–4). He also served as leader of Labour's delegation to the Council of Europe, of which he was vice-president in 1973–4. In February 1974, with Labour back in office, he became minister of agriculture again. By then, exploitation by Commonwealth beef and sugar producers of rising world prices for their products led him reluctantly to come to terms with Britain's EEC membership, to which British farmers were now more favourably inclined.

In 1976, with James Callaghan (later Baron Callaghan of Cardiff) as prime minister, Peart received a life barony and, as lord privy seal, became leader of the House of Lords. Following Labour's defeat in 1979, he led the opposition peers until 1982. He was also chairman of the advisory council for applied research and development (1976–80) and the Retail Consortium (1979–81). He was an honorary D.Sc. of Cranfield Institute of Technology (1977), honorary FRCVS (1969), and a freeman of the City of London (1968).

Peart was one of the best-liked parliamentarians of his generation. Tall, gentlemanly, with patrician good looks and a naturally straightforward manner, he was always enjoyable company. In 1945 he married Sarah Elizabeth ('Bette'), daughter of Thomas Lewis, mining engineer in South America. They had one son. Welsh, articulate, highly principled, a history graduate and teacher, Bette shared her husband's passion for equality of educational opportunity. In 1984 Peart was savagely attacked by two armed robbers who had broken into his home. His health was shattered and he never fully recovered. He died 26 August 1988 in hospital in Tooting, London.

[Private information; personal knowledge.]
                    ALFRED MORRIS

PEDLEY, Robin (1914–1988), educationist, was born Robert Pedley in Grinton, north Yorkshire, 11 August 1914, the fourth in the family of four sons and one daughter of Edward Pedley, stonemason, of Grinton, and his wife Martha Jane, postmistress, daughter of William Hird, farmer of a smallholding, also of Grinton. All the family attended Fremington School (the local Church of England elementary school), most leaving at fourteen, though Pedley's three brothers all later achieved distinction in their careers in education, the Civil Service, and the police force. Pedley was articled as a pupil teacher, but north Yorkshire abolished the system at that time (1928) and he went to Richmond School (north Yorkshire) for his secondary education (1928–32). He won an Ellerton scholarship to Durham University and obtained an upper second-class degree in history and economics in 1935. He joined the education department at Durham and acquired his teacher's certificate in 1936. Elected a fellow of Durham University (1936–8), he was awarded the Gladstone memorial prize in modern history in 1937 and, in the same year, the Gibson prize in archaeology. In 1939 Pedley gained his doctorate for a study of the political and economic history of the northern Pennines. In addition to these scholarly achievements, Pedley proved himself an accomplished athlete at the university, excelling particularly in association football and cricket.

In 1938 Pedley was appointed to the Friends' School at Great Ayton. From 1943 to 1946 (Pedley was a conscientious objector) he was senior history master at the Crossley and Porter schools, Halifax, moving as a lecturer in education to the College of St Mark and St John, Chelsea, in 1946. In 1947 he was appointed as one of the founding members of the newly formed department of education at University College, Leicester.

It was at Leicester that Pedley fully developed his own outlook on educational policy and practice and soon made a national impact in his campaign for a comprehensive system of secondary education, based on what became known as the two-tier system. He believed in small schools as intimate communities and sought for a solution along these lines, rather than through the accepted policy of building large, 'all-through' schools catering for the entire eleven to nineteen age group.

The pattern Pedley favoured involved the division of secondary schooling at the age of fifteen. This had several advantages. First, comprehensive (or non-selective) education could be implemented in existing buildings, secondary modern schools taking in all local children at the age of eleven, and grammar schools those over fifteen. Secondly, both types of school, catering for local populations, could be developed as community schools, a project dear to Pedley's heart. Thirdly, both sets of schools could, in theory at least, be of reasonable size. Finally, senior pupils in upper schools could be treated as their increasing maturity required.

Pedley had already begun to develop his thinking along these lines in a set of articles published in the late 1940s. But the first breakthrough came in his *Comprehensive Schools Today* (1955), where articles on Pedley's proposed solution were commented on by leading educationists, especially those from local authorities. In 1956 his major book, *Comprehensive Education, a New Approach*, received wide publicity and was taken very seriously. At a meeting in that year with Sir David (later first Viscount) Eccles, minister of education, Pedley was left in no doubt about the Ministry's readiness to encourage experiment along the lines he suggested, and the county of Leicestershire announced its two-tier plan in 1957. In 1963 Pedley published what was to be his most influential book, the Pelican original entitled *The Comprehensive School*. This was immensely popular, going through five reprints or new editions by 1969, and is the book that brought the idea most closely to the attention of the general public during the 1960s and later.

It was at Leicester that Pedley made his main contribution to the movement for comprehensive education. Tall, handsome, and willowy in his prime, with an open, frank countenance, an accomplished sportsman and delightful colleague, he developed a persuasive style as a speaker and became adept in the presentation of his case to local authority representatives and others throughout the country.

Pedley remained at Leicester until 1963, when he accepted appointment as director of the Institute of Education at Exeter University. He was awarded a chair in 1970. In 1971 he was appointed professor of education and head of the school of education at Southampton University, where he acted as dean of the faculty for four years.

In 1951 Pedley married Jeanne Lesley, daughter of William Leslie Hitching, bank manager. They had one son and one daughter. Pedley died in Salisbury 20 November 1988, officially of pneumonia but in reality of Alzheimer's disease, from which he had suffered for some years.

[David Crook, 'The Disputed Origins of the Leicestershire Two-tier Comprehensive Schools Plan', *History of Education Society Bulletin*, no. 50, Autumn 1992; private information; personal knowledge.]   B. SIMON

PEEL, LADY (1894–1989), actress and singer. [See LILLIE, BEATRICE GLADYS.]

PETERSEN, John Charles ('Jack') (1911–1990), boxer, was born in Cardiff 2 September 1911, the only son (there was also a daughter) of

John Thomas Peterson, massage specialist, and his wife, Melinda Laura Rossiter. The family's name was Peterson, but Jack was known professionally as Petersen. It was a sporting family—his father (whom the press called 'Pa') had trained south Wales boxers who were near-British champions. The younger Petersen was never a 'mountain' fighter (a bare-knuckle boxer who fought illegally). He did well at school and was an enthusiastic boy scout. Not surprisingly, he took up amateur boxing, and by the age of eighteen had reached the Welsh Amateur Boxing Association finals at both middle and light-heavyweight. In the following season he won Welsh titles at light-heavy and heavyweight (1931), and the national ABA championships at the lighter weight.

Petersen immediately turned professional, managed by his father and backed by a syndicate of Welsh sportsmen. He won his first nine contests within the space of ten weeks at the stadium in Holborn, London. Cardiff was considered by professionals not to be a boxing city, though the Petersens lived in Whitchurch and Jack trained at St John Square, taking the train to go up for his Monday evening matches. Cardiff's Greyfriars Hall was soon used to display this stylish, hard-punching boxing prospect to his home supporters, and they became vociferously excited when he rescued a contest by a knockout in the fifteenth round.

The British light-heavyweight championship fell to Petersen at Holborn, and seven weeks later (July 1932), at Wimbledon stadium, he knocked out Reggie Meen, of Leicester, to become the British heavyweight champion, in his eighteenth professional contest, aged twenty. He was the first Welshman, and the youngest man, ever to win that title; and it was accomplished in ten months. The Cardiff press and the people of Wales glowed with pride. The light-heavyweight division did not draw crowds to boxing matches, and though Petersen could still weigh twelve stones and seven pounds he relinquished this title. As the champion at catchweights, he became extraordinarily popular, partly because his opponents often outweighed him by one or two stones. He was an attacking boxer, a dark-haired good-looking man, and the adjective 'gallant' appeared frequently in boxing reporters' commentary. On cinema newsreels, his modesty and pride in his own locality registered with the general public. Petersen was the most popular British boxer since Bombardier Billy Wells.

In 1933 an even younger man emerged as a contender. Jack Doyle, from county Cork via the Irish Guards, had won his ten fights by knockouts within two rounds, and he and Petersen were matched at the White City stadium in July. The largest crowd at a boxing match in Britain at that time (some 30,000) assembled, only to watch Doyle repeatedly punch Petersen below the belt and be disqualified in the second round. Petersen ignored the fouls, did not go down, and honourably matched the bigger man blow for blow. In his next contest Petersen unexpectedly lost the British title, to Len Harvey on points at the Royal Albert Hall (December 1933). It was his first defeat in twenty-five professional contests, and to a smaller, though exceptionally clever, man.

Six months later (June 1934) he beat Harvey to regain this title and also win the heavyweight championship of the British empire, for which black men were allowed to box. One such contender, Larry Gains from Canada, was the next boxer that Petersen defeated. The man from Cardiff defended both championships successfully until August 1936, when he lost heavily to Ben Foord, a Leicester-based white South African, who was qualified by residence for both titles. Whilst champion for the second time, however, Petersen had suffered international reverses. In 1935 he boxed only twice, and was beaten both times by a strong, young, fourteen-stone heavyweight from Germany, Walter Neusel. Petersen retired from boxing in February 1937, at the early age of twenty-five, after losing bruisingly to Neusel for a third time.

During World War II he was a physical training instructor in the Royal Air Force, and subsequently was heavily involved in Welsh affairs of the British Boxing Board of Control. In 1986 he became president of the BBBC and was appointed OBE for his services to sport. He was also vice-chairman of the Sports Council for Wales. Petersen lifted the low prestige of British heavyweights in the interwar years, and retired from boxing gracefully.

In October 1935 Petersen married Annie Elizabeth ('Betty'), daughter of Thomas Baker Williams, auctioneer, of Cardiff. His parents did not attend the long-planned ceremony. 'Pa' had been in his son's corner throughout his career, but the boxer–manager relationship stopped after the second contest with Neusel, and Petersen managed himself for the last four matches of his six years' career. He died 22 November 1990 at the Princess of Wales Hospital, Bridgend, of cancer of the lung.

[*Western Mail* and *South Wales Echo, passim*, 1930s; *Boxing, passim*; *The Times*, 23 November 1990.]

STAN SHIPLEY

PETERSON, Alexander Duncan Campbell (1908–1988), educational reformer, was born in Edinburgh 13 September 1908, the third of five sons, but the second to survive childhood (there were no daughters), of John Carlos Kennedy Peterson, of the Indian Civil Service, under-secretary in the finance department, government of Bengal, and his wife, Flora Campbell. He and his brothers were brought up largely by aunts and uncles. His parents had no home leave between 1915 and 1919, and when his mother eventually arrived at his preparatory school he failed to recognize her. He won scholarships to Radley College and Balliol College, Oxford, liking the second as much as he had disliked the first. At Oxford he showed the breadth of interest and taste for experiment which marked him throughout life. His activities as an undergraduate were multifarious, and in 1930 he missed a first in *literae humaniores*, apparently by a very narrow margin. He had received a second class in classical honour moderations in 1928.

Peterson's flair for communication did not stay hidden for long. His ascent up the teacher's ladder (as assistant master, Shrewsbury School, 1932–40; and as headmaster of Adams Grammar School, Newport, 1946–52, and of Dover College, 1954–7) was punctuated by two periods of 'psychological warfare' in the Far East. The first (1943–5), under Lord Louis *Mountbatten (later first Earl Mountbatten of Burma), earned him an OBE (1946); during the second (1952–4), under Sir Gerald *Templer in Malaya, his formidable chief judged him 'absolutely first class'.

The directorship of Oxford University's department of education, which he held from 1958 until his retirement in 1973, left him time for writing on educational problems and for outside activities. As the chairman of the Farmington Trust's council from 1964 to 1971 he helped to found the *Journal of Moral Education*. He acted for a time as the Liberal party's spokesman on education, and stood without any chance of success for Oxford in the 1966 election. He served from 1959 to 1966 as chairman of the Army Education Advisory Board. It was, however, as the advocate of broader sixth form studies that he became well known. He opened the campaign with a broadcast early in 1956 (*Listener*, 16 February), continued it in his Estlin Carpenter lectures at Oxford, 1957 (published as *Educating Our Rulers*, 1957), and brought it to a remarkable climax with the Oxford department's report, 'Arts and Science Sides in the Sixth Form', in 1960. This established beyond reasonable doubt that the early specialization characterizing English secondary schools not merely precluded sixth form courses appropriate to a scientific age, but reduced the flow of science graduates. About 40 per cent of the English sixteen-year-olds questioned for the report would have liked to combine arts with mathematics or science: under 6 per cent were actually doing so. When more than 700 pupils in French *lycées* and German *Gymnasien* were asked what subjects they would have chosen for the *baccalauréat* or *Abitur* had there been no restrictions on choice, only five chose entirely from mathematics or science. Peterson had won the argu-

ment; but, like many others in the decades which followed, he found that this did not open the road to the needed reforms.

Frustrated in England, Peterson turned abroad. The international sixth form which he had started at Dover brought him into contact with Kurt *Hahn; and in 1962, when Atlantic College was founded, he helped to plan its curriculum. No single syllabus could be made to conform to university entrance requirements, which varied from country to country; and in the same year plans for an 'international baccalaureate' were being discussed in Geneva. The Oxford department, which was then embarking on an investigation for the Council of Europe, was soon involved in the planning for this; and Peterson was the director of the International Baccalaureate Office during the crucial phase of growth, from 1966 to 1977. In the year of his death an IB, based on a balanced curriculum of six subjects, was in use in fifty-six countries and 2,643 IB diplomas were awarded. Five years later this figure had grown to 5,073, and the entry for the full diploma, or for certificates in the various subjects, exceeded 18,000. The United World Colleges, headed by Atlantic College, needed the IB and nourished it. Peterson, who was chairman of UWC (1978–80), helped with both organizations until he died. In *Schools Across Frontiers* (1987) he recorded the struggle to establish them. He was made an honorary doctor of the University of Trieste (1985).

Peterson was tall and good looking. A portrait by Henry Lamb hangs in Dover College. In December 1939 he married Ruth Pauline, daughter of William Anderson Armstrong, solicitor. This marriage ended in divorce in 1946, and in the same year he married Corinna May, daughter of Sir Arthur William Steuart Cochrane, Clarenceux king of arms. There were two sons and a daughter of the second marriage. Peterson died of a heart attack in St Mary's Hospital, Paddington, London, 17 October 1988.

[Bickham Sweet-Escott, *Baker Street Irregular*, 1965; Robert J. Leach, *International Schools and Their Role in the Field of International Education*, 1969; T. James Leasor, *Boarding Party*, 1978; John Cloake, *Templer, Tiger of Malaya*, 1985; Philip Ziegler, *Mountbatten*, 1985; Robert Blackburn, memorial tribute, Geneva (IBO Council of Foundation, 1988); private information; personal knowledge.]   MICHAEL BROCK

PHILBY, Harold Adrian Russell ('Kim') (1912–1988), Soviet agent, was born 1 January 1912 at Ambala in the Punjab, the only son and eldest of four children of Harry St John Bridger *Philby, Indian civil servant, explorer, and orientalist, and his wife Dora, daughter of Adrian Hope Johnston, of the Indian public works department. With unconscious prescience they nicknamed him Kim. He was educated at Westminster and Trinity College, Cambridge, where he joined the university Socialist Society and became a convinced communist. He obtained a third class in part i of the history tripos (1931) and a second class (division I) in part ii of the economics tripos (1933). Philby was of medium height with a seductive smile. In 1933 he went on a trip to Vienna, where he met Alice ('Litzi') Friedman, an Austrian communist, whose father was Israel Kohlman, a minor government official of Hungarian Jewish origin. They witnessed the street fighting, which ended with the defeat of the socialists in February 1934, when they had a hurried marriage and left for England. By this time she had persuaded him to become a Soviet agent. While he was in Vienna, the NKVD (the Soviet secret service) had talent-spotted Philby as a potential recruit.

In June 1934, at a secret meeting in Regents Park, Philby was approached by Arnold Deutsch, a Czech undercover Soviet intelligence officer operating in London. Philby welcomed the suggestion that he should penetrate 'the bourgeois institutions'. Another of his controllers was Teodor Maly, a Hungarian who had renounced the priesthood and become an idealistic convert to Bolshevism. Beginning his career as a journalist, Philby was instructed to sever all links with his communist past and swing over to the far right. Hence his involvement with the pro-Nazi Anglo-German Fellowship. First as a freelance and later for *The Times*, he went to Spain in February 1937 to cover the Spanish civil war from the point of view of General Franco (whose planned assassination was part of his original brief), who awarded him the red cross of military merit. He left Spain in August 1939 with his overt right-wing credentials established, while his covert faith in Joseph Stalin remained untarnished by the Terror of the mid-1930s, although he had an ambivalent attitude to the Nazi–Soviet pact in August 1939. His luck never deserted him, especially permitting him to survive the ups and downs of an alternating relationship with the Moscow centre.

After the outbreak of World War II Philby went to France as a war correspondent. Returning to England after Dunkirk, he was recruited, thanks to Guy *Burgess, his friend from Cambridge and a fellow NKVD agent, into the SIS (the Secret Intelligence Service or MI6) in July 1940 and soon joined Section Five (counter-intelligence) in 1941. A base in London eased his domestic problems with Aileen Furse (the daughter of Captain George Furse of the Royal Horse Artillery) with whom he had been living and producing children since 1940, but whom he did not marry until December 1946, a week after his divorce from Litzi. By then he was a rising star, having become in 1944 head of Section

Nine, whose remit was 'to collect and interpret information concerning communist espionage and subversion'. When Section Nine was merged with Section Five in 1945, he alerted Moscow to the intended defection in Istanbul of Konstantin Volkov, who could have unmasked Philby. He was appointed OBE in 1946.

In 1946 the SIS posted him to Turkey and in 1949 he became their representative in Washington, where he kept Moscow informed of Anglo-American intelligence collaboration. He also saw how the net was closing in on Donald *Maclean. In 1950 Guy Burgess was posted to Washington and lodged with Philby. When Maclean and Burgess fled to Moscow, Philby was summoned back to London and interrogated by MI5, who were persuaded of his guilt, but lacked the evidence of a confession to convict him. The SIS, however, in return for Philby's voluntary resignation, gave him a golden handshake. After his name had been cleared by Harold *Macmillan (later the first Earl of Stockton) in 1955, the SIS fixed his cover as a correspondent for the *Observer* and the *Economist*, based on Beirut, where he arrived in August 1956.

Aileen died in 1957. There were three sons and two daughters of the marriage; Philby had no other children. In 1959 he married Eleanor, from Seattle, who was formerly married to Sam Pope Brewer, Middle East correspondent of the *New York Times*. In Beirut, Philby was successfully reincarnated as a journalist until Anatoli Golitsyn's defection to the CIA in 1962 filled in the gaps in the case against him. The SIS and MI5 then confronted Philby with a prosecutor's brief in January 1963, plus an offer of immunity if he returned to London and made a full confession. Philby admitted he had been a Soviet agent but said no more. He quietly arranged his escape and arrived in Russia at the end of January 1963. Five months later he was granted Soviet citizenship.

Eleanor soon joined him, but she so disliked life in Moscow that she left for good in 1965; she died in America in 1968. Meanwhile, Philby had been awarded in 1965 the Order of Lenin and the Order of the Red Banner. He began an affair with Melinda, the wife of Donald Maclean, who had also defected to Moscow, but this did not last. Heavy drinking and smoking dominated his life until 1970, when George Blake, another defector, introduced him to Rufina Ivanova, half Polish and half Russian, whom he married in 1971. She was the daughter of an expert on the chemical treatment of furs. In 1980 his award of the Order of Friendship of Peoples preceded his East German, Hungarian, Bulgarian, and Cuban decorations. He died in Moscow 11 May 1988, receiving his final recognition in an elaborate funeral organized by the KGB. A private buyer purchased the lion's share of Philby's papers, which were auctioned at Sotheby's in July 1994.

[Christopher Andrew, *Secret Service*, 1985; Christopher Andrew and David Dilks (ed.), *The Missing Dimension*, 1984; Nicholas Bethell, *The Great Betrayal*, 1984; John Costello, *Mask of Treachery*, 1988; John Costello and Oleg Tsarev, *Deadly Illusions*, 1993; Phillip Knightley, *Philby, the Life and Views of the KGB Masterspy*, 1988; Patrick Seale and Maureen McConville, *Philby, the Long Road to Moscow*, 1973; Hugh Trevor-Roper, *The Philby Affair*, 1968; Kim Philby, *My Silent War*, 1968; Eleanor Philby, *The Spy I Loved*, 1968; Genrikh Borovik, *The Philby Files*, 1994; Yuri Modin, *My Five Cambridge Friends*, 1994; personal knowledge.]   NIGEL CLIVE

PHILLIPS, Owen Hood (1907–1986), constitutional lawyer, was born in Portsmouth 30 September 1907, the younger son and youngest of three children of Surgeon-Captain John Elphinstone Hood Phillips, of the Royal Navy and Southsea, and his wife, Kathleen Marian Esther Way. His mother died when he was two and his father when he was twenty. He was educated at Weymouth College and Merton College, Oxford, where he took a second class in both the honour school of jurisprudence (1929) and the BCL (1930). He always prided himself on being a Merton man. He was called to the bar (Gray's Inn, 1930) and served pupillages in both Common Law and Chancery chambers.

He did not practise but took his first academic appointment as an assistant lecturer in laws at King's College, London (1931–5). For two years after 1935 he held a lectureship in Trinity College, Dublin: to these years beside the river Liffey he attributed his liking for an occasional lunch-hour Guinness. In 1937 he returned to King's as reader in English law and vice-dean. During the 1939–45 war he served in the ministries of Labour and Aircraft Production. His years as a wartime civil servant assisted, he felt, his appreciation of the delicate constitutional relationship between a minister and his department. It also armed him with useful administrative experience when he was appointed in 1946 to the Lady Barber chair of jurisprudence at Birmingham University and in 1949 unexpectedly called upon to assume the deanship of the law faculty.

During the nineteen years which he served as dean (1949–68) the Birmingham law faculty expanded fourfold in staff and student numbers. It also won a deserved reputation for good teaching and sound scholarship. Phillips guided his team with a light rein, ever ready to let younger colleagues run their own course in teaching and research. He was for twelve years (1950–62) the university's public orator; his orations gave full scope to his gift for carefully crafted and elegant prose, delivered with clarity and grace. He was elected president of the Society of Public Teachers of Law (1963–4) and in this capacity played a prominent part in the setting up of the committee on legal education, chaired by Sir Roger Ormrod. Its report (1971) exercised a seminal influence on future developments in this field.

Phillips was the most eminent constitutional lawyer of his generation. His treatise on *Constitutional and Administrative Law* (1952), which was an original response to a request to produce a new edition of a far less valuable text, had reached its seventh edition by the time of his death and was widely regarded as the fullest modern exposition of the law on this subject. His worldwide reputation in the Commonwealth brought him invitations to serve as adviser to the Singapore constitutional commission (1953–4) and delegate to the Malta constitutional conferences in 1955 and 1958. His *A First Book on English Law* (1948) had much success as an introduction and went through several editions. He was a regular contributor to the *Law Quarterly Review* and *Public Law*: in his articles he anticipated the problem of trying to reconcile parliamentary sovereignty with British accession to the European Community. His later publications ranged more widely: *Reform of the Constitution* (1970) foreshadowed much of the subsequent debate, and in *Shakespeare and the Lawyers* (1972) his lifelong passion for the bard found a congenial theme.

He was understandably proud of the award of silk in 1970 and his Oxford DCL (1971). After his retirement in 1974 he kept his home in Edgbaston and continued to serve as a Birmingham lay magistrate. He also maintained his interest in the Schools of King Edward VI in Birmingham: he was a governor (1951–76) and, in his turn, bailiff (1958–9) of the foundation. Mindful of his years in Dublin, he encouraged the formation of the British and Irish Association of Law Librarians and was its first president (1972–6).

He liked to be known by all his three names: he was affectionately referred to by many as 'OHP'. He delighted in reading, classical music, gardening, and the countryside. Lean in stature and of above average height, he was of somewhat austere appearance; but he was an essentially kind man. He had a dry and exquisite wit which could enliven a lecture or debate of senate, grace an after-dinner speech, or delight a few friends. Reserved by nature, his personality expanded after his marriage. In 1949 he married Lucy Mary Carden, lecturer in physical education at Birmingham university and daughter of Arnold Philip, Admiralty chemist at the Portsmouth dockyard. They had no children. The quiet happiness which pervaded their home in Edgbaston or their cottage on the Clee Hills communicated itself to their extended family and the friends, colleagues, and students to whom they were ever generous in hospitality. For Commonwealth students, attracted to Birmingham by Phillips's reputation, he had a special solicitude. He died 25 May 1986, after a stroke, in the Queen Elizabeth Hospital, Birmingham.

[*Birmingham Post Yearbooks*; archives of Birmingham University; private information; personal knowledge.]

L. NEVILLE BROWN

PILCHER, SIR John Arthur (1912–1990), diplomat, was born 16 May 1912 in Quetta, India, the only child of Lieutenant-Colonel Arthur John Pilcher and his wife, Edith Blair. Both his parents shared a tradition of service in the Indian subcontinent in both the military and scholarly spheres, dating back to the eighteenth century. He was educated at Shrewsbury and Clare College, Cambridge. In 1932 he gained a second class (division I) in part i of the modern and medieval languages tripos and in 1935 a third class in part ii. His formal studies were supplemented by travel in Europe.

In 1936 he was accepted as a student interpreter in the Japan Consular Service and sent to Japan to learn the language. After one year in the embassy in Tokyo he went to study in the old capital of Kyoto, a city which he grew to love. He lived for two years in the temple of Sokokuji and developed an appreciation of Japanese Buddhism. He also learned to speak the Kyoto dialect and got to know Kanjiro Kawai and other potters and artists.

In 1939 he was transferred to Tsingtao, a consular post in Japanese-occupied China. While there he was received into the Roman Catholic Church. He returned to London in 1941 and worked mainly on Japanese affairs in the Ministry of Information and the Foreign Office.

In 1948 Pilcher was appointed first secretary (information) in the British embassy in Rome. He was sorry to return to London in 1951 on promotion to counsellor. He became head of the Japan and Pacific department of the Foreign Office, where he saw through the ratification of the peace treaty, the Korean war, and the rather difficult period in Anglo-Japanese relations which followed the peace treaty. In 1954 he was appointed counsellor in Madrid and in 1959 received his first ambassadorial appointment in Manila, in the Philippines.

He returned to London in 1963 to become assistant under-secretary in charge of information and cultural work. In 1965 he was appointed ambassador to Austria, which proved to be a very happy posting. In addition to his knowledge and understanding of European culture he was an enthusiastic student of the Austro-German musical tradition. An accomplished pianist, he

delighted in chamber music and accompanying singers and instrumentalists. In 1966 he was awarded the Austrian Grand Cross (gold) decoration of honour.

Pilcher was promoted to become ambassador in Tokyo in 1967. Having kept in touch with many of his pre-war Japanese friends, he was able to entertain widely on his return to Tokyo. He was assiduous in his contacts with the Japanese imperial family and accompanied the Showa emperor on the first Japanese state visit to London in 1971. On this occasion he was awarded the first class of the Japanese Order of the Rising Sun. His period in Japan coincided with the successful British week in Tokyo in 1969, attended by Princess Margaret, and the Expo in Osaka in 1970, visited by the prince of Wales. Pilcher retired in 1972.

He had been brought up in the old school of diplomacy where the first priority was to cultivate influential people in the country to which an ambassador was accredited. He did this very well. He was also a knowledgeable and wise observer, his dispatches being well written and to the point. He disliked having to be a tough negotiator and protector of narrow British interests and also found modern commercial diplomacy rather distasteful. However, he invariably supported fully his staff in their endeavours to promote British exports and threw himself enthusiastically into the task of educating hardheaded British businessmen about the realities of modern Japan, recognizing that for this purpose they needed a modicum of understanding of Japanese culture and history.

Pilcher was an accomplished raconteur and wit. He had a fund of stories, many with a Rabelaisian twist, and could keep an audience enthralled for a long time. He was a short, tubby man, with a round, partly bald, head and a twinkle in his eyes.

He was appointed CMG (1957), KCMG (1966), and GCMG (1973). In his retirement he became a director of the Foreign and Colonial Investment Trust (1973–82), chairman of the Brazil Fund (1975–82) and of the Fleming Japan Fund (1976–85), and adviser on Far Eastern affairs to Robert Fleming & Co. (1973–85). Of great interest to him personally were his membership of the Museums and Galleries Commission (1973–83) and of the committee of the Society for the Protection of Ancient Buildings (1974–82), which he represented on the council of the National Trust. He was also president of the Institute of Linguists (1982–4) and served twice (a total of six years) as chairman of the council of the Japan Society in Britain.

In 1942 he married Delia Margaret, daughter of Patrick Kirwan Taylor, a retired army officer who had been wounded in World War I. They had one daughter. Pilcher died 10 February 1990 in Barnes, London, after a protracted illness.

[*The Times*, 14 February 1990; *Independent*, 15 February 1990; information from widow; personal knowledge.]   HUGH CORTAZZI

PIPER, SIR David Towry (1918–1990), museum director and writer, was born 21 July 1918 in Wimbledon, London, the second of three sons (the oldest of whom was killed in action in 1941) of Stephen Harvey Piper, later professor of physics at Bristol University, and his wife, Mary Joyce Casswell. He was educated at Clifton College, and St Catharine's College, Cambridge, where he graduated with a first in the modern and medieval languages tripos in 1940, having obtained a first in French and a second in German in part i in 1938. He then joined the Indian Army (9th Jat Regiment). He was captured in the Malay peninsula in 1942, and endured three years as a prisoner of war in Formosa.

Piper then moved into the museum world. He was given his first job, as assistant keeper in the National Portrait Gallery, in 1946, when G. M. *Young, then a trustee, said, 'we must keep an eye on that young man; he will go far!' They were prescient words. He became its director (1964–7), director of the Fitzwilliam Museum and fellow of Christ's College, Cambridge (1967–73), and director of the Ashmolean Museum and fellow of Worcester College, Oxford (1973–85). He was Slade professor of fine art, Oxford (1966–7), Clark lecturer, Cambridge (1977–8), and Rede lecturer, Cambridge (1983). He was a member of the Royal Fine Art Commission (1970–86), trustee of the Watts Gallery (1966–88), and served on the Paul Mellon Foundation for British Art (1969–70), the Pilgrim Trust (1973–90), and the Leeds Castle Foundation (1981–8). This is a formidable list for any man, especially one whose physical health was blighted by three years as a prisoner of war. He never spoke much about this, but survivors have described how he encouraged the camp inmates with his civilized acceptance of a particularly horrendous experience.

Piper's twenty-one years at the NPG were marked by the publication of a pioneering volume in the Gallery's series of catalogues, *Seventeenth-Century Portraits* (1963), and by the initiation of the *Concise Catalogue*. The years were also remarkable for a number of exhibitions (Oliver Cromwell, William Shakespeare, and Elizabeth of Bohemia, the Winter Queen), and for some outstanding acquisitions, including portraits of John *Milton and Edmund *Halley, bought for £24 and £45. As a result, and because of his numerous broadcasts, lectures, and articles, the attendance figures rose to pass the quarter-million mark and the NPG became one

of the attractions of London. And Piper found time to write two outstanding books: *The English Face* (1957 and twice republished) repays frequent rereading; *The Companion Guide to London* (1964 and now in its sixth edition) has been judiciously compared to Richard *Ford's *Spain* and E. M. *Forster's *Alexandria*.

Piper left the NPG in 1967 to become director of the Fitzwilliam Museum, Cambridge, where he remained for six years, the highlights of which were the gift of Sir Hamilton Kerr's Mill House at Whittlesford, later to become the Hamilton Kerr Institute of Conservation of Works of Art, and Sir Robert Adeane's £100,000, given to launch the extension appeal fund. Acquisitions included pictures by George *Stubbs, John *Constable, Paulus Morelse, Nicolas Poussin, Jan van Goyen, and Meindert Hobbema, and a remarkable wooden sculpture of a Japanese warrior of the Kamakura period. Piper's eye for quality helped to draw the public towards whichever museum he served at the time, and his reward at the Fitzwilliam was to see the attendance figures increase by a third in the space of three years, and enough money raised for the new extension.

In 1973 Piper became the first director of the Ashmolean Museum, Oxford, having been appointed to bring in centralization and to keep the balance among the four departments. The new director's professional familiarity with the museum world greatly strengthened the Ashmolean, and his tactful handling of the many internal problems, arising in a difficult transitional period, endeared him to the museum staff. His departure in 1985 was marked by the acquisition of an Étienne Aubry 'Portrait of a Man'—an unknown Frenchman of the 1770s, whose genial smile and air of civilized self-doubt curiously enough suggest 'Pete' Piper himself. Striking in appearance, slim and elegant, Piper was tall and lolloping as a young man, with large brown eyes. Latterly a scholarly stoop disguised his height. At all times his rather lugubrious face could suddenly be lit by an enormous and friendly smile.

Piper was a prolific writer and broadcaster. His articles in the *Financial Times* and elsewhere drew attention to current exhibitions, books, and affairs in the art world. His own books include *Enjoying Paintings* (1964), *Shades: an Essay on Portrait Silhouettes* (1970), *London* (1971), *The Genius of British Painting* (1975), *The Treasures of Oxford* (1977), *Artists' London* (1982), and *The Image of the Poet* (1982). Among his novels (written as Peter Towry) were *It's Warm Inside* (1953), *Lord Minimus* (1955), a surprising account of Henrietta Maria's dwarf page, and *Trial by Battle* (1959).

He was appointed CBE in 1969, knighted in 1983, and made an honorary D.Litt. of Bristol

University in 1984 and an honorary fellow of the Royal Academy in 1985. In 1945 he married Anne Horatia, daughter of Oliffe Legh Richmond, professor of humanity in Edinburgh University. They had three daughters and a son. Piper died at home in Wytham, near Oxford, 29 December 1990, after suffering for many years from severe emphysema.

[Richard Walker in *Burlington Magazine*, vol. cxxxiii, March 1991; *Annual Reports* of National Portrait Gallery 1966–7, Fitzwilliam Museum 1973, Ashmolean Museum 1984–5; *Ashmolean*, no. 8, autumn 1985; personal knowledge.]   RICHARD WALKER

PLANT, Cyril Thomas Howe, BARON PLANT (1910–1986), trade-union official, was born 27 August 1910 in Leek, Staffordshire, the only son and elder child of Sidney Plant, manager of a Co-operative Society shop, and his wife, Rosina Edna Thomas, who previously ran a grocer's shop. He was educated at Leek High School, where he was head boy and captain of the cricket team. In 1927 he began work as a sorting clerk in the Post Office in Leek, where his interest in trade unions began. In these early years he was a keen local amateur association football player, and later became a referee, developing an interest in football that he retained throughout his life.

In 1934 he was successful in the limited competition for entry to the Civil Service clerical class. He joined the Inland Revenue in the collection service as an assistant collector. He quickly became a delegate to the newly formed Inland Revenue Staff Federation (IRSF) conference. He was elected to the executive committee of IRSF, and in 1937 became honorary secretary of the collection section. At this time the IRSF was still an unsettled alliance of former collection, inspectorate, and valuation divisions. Plant developed, and later finely tuned, his skills as a mediator and conciliator, helping to bind the union together. Later his skills as a 'fixer' were to be of great service to the international trade-union movement. He was appointed in 1944 to a full-time IRSF post as assistant secretary and then deputy general secretary. In 1960 he succeeded Douglas Houghton (later Baron Houghton of Sowerby) as general secretary of the IRSF. There were by then relatively few opportunities for the IRSF, through Plant, to obtain improvements significantly in advance of the rest of the Civil Service and he directed much of his energies and abilities into broader areas of trade-union and related activities.

He was a member of the TUC general council from 1964 to 1976 and served on the economic and international committees. His expertise on fiscal and economic subjects gave him far greater authority and respect than usual for someone from such a small union, and this was buttressed by his willingness to offer his colleagues good advice on income tax matters and frequent tips, some good and some less good, on horse-racing, which was a passionate interest of his. He was chairman of the TUC in 1975–6. He also fulfilled many TUC duties, including membership of public bodies such as the Community Relations Commission (1974–7), the Monopolies and Mergers Commission (1975–8), and the departmental committee of inquiry into police pay chaired by Baron Edmund-Davies (1977–8). After retirement in 1977 he became parliamentary adviser to the Police Federation and assiduously defended its interests in the House of Lords. A police band played at his funeral.

He was active at International Labour Office conferences from 1965 onwards, and the ILO gave him a major platform to press for the development of trade-union rights and improvements in working conditions, particularly of public service employees, throughout the world. He was a member of the governing body of the ILO from 1969 to 1977. He played a powerful role in the programme, financial, and administrative committee, a body which exerted great authority over finance and allocation of resources during the difficult period when the USA withdrew membership and subscriptions. In the international context Plant displayed the many virtues of British trade-union leaders in international settings. He grasped the importance of obtaining agreement and consensus from delegates, and his mastery of the complexities of procedural provisions allowed him to produce solutions that were acceptable to all. He spoke with eloquence, wit, and authority, earning respect from employers and government delegates alike.

He had a deep commitment to further education and was treasurer of the Workers' Educational Association from 1969 to 1981. He was a member of the governing body of Ruskin College, Oxford, and chairman of the governors from 1967 to 1979, helping to raise funds for one of the new buildings, which was named after him.

His interest in the Post Office and Civil Service Sanatorium Society began with his first job, and he was chairman of the committee of management from 1950 to 1975. It was his initiative which led to the queen mother becoming patron of the society, and under his guidance it developed into a large vocational health service, with a hospital which not only provides treatment for its members but encourages research. When he was made a life peer in 1978 he attached Benenden, the location of the hospital, to his title. This was the greatest of Plant's non-professional interests. He was appointed OBE in 1965 in recognition of his work for the Society and CBE in 1975.

Plant was a firm believer in the virtues of the

British Civil Service, with its concepts of duty and responsibilities, combined with a total commitment to the benefits of strong independent trade unions to protect the rights of public service employees. At the ILO he spoke in defence of the interests of the ILO employees and in particular sought to protect their pension rights.

Plant was a large, well-built man, six feet one inch tall, and broad-shouldered. In 1931 he married Gladys Sampson, daughter of Sampson Mayers, textile manufacturer. They had two sons and one daughter. Plant died from a burst aorta in hospital in Tours 9 August 1986, while on holiday with his wife in France.

[Minutes of the TUC, Congress House, London; minutes of the ILO, International Labour Office, Geneva; private information; personal knowledge.]

DEREK ROBINSON

PLATT, SIR HARRY, first baronet (1886–1986), surgeon, was born 7 October 1886 at 317 Rochdale Road, Thornham, Lancashire, the eldest of five sons, one of whom died in infancy, of Ernest Platt, master fustian cutter, and his wife Jessie Cameron, daughter of George Munro Lindsay, of Liverpool. At the age of five he developed tuberculosis of the knee. Having been taught mainly the classics and languages by home tutors, his decision to enter medicine in 1904 was a surprising one, especially as he had done very little science. He went to the Victoria University of Manchester, graduating MB, BS (Lond.) in 1909, with distinction in medicine and the gold medal in surgery. He obtained his FRCS in 1912 and was appointed resident surgical officer in the Royal National Orthopaedic Hospital, London.

In 1913 he spent a year in the USA, pursuing postgraduate studies at the Massachusetts General Hospital, Boston. This American experience finalized Platt's decision to devote his life to orthopaedics, which was then a much less fashionable or glamorous branch of surgery. He returned to Britain just before the outbreak of World War I, as honorary orthopaedic surgeon (1914–32) to Ancoats Hospital in Manchester, where he set up the first organized segregated fracture clinic in 1917. Because of his ankylosed knee and disability, he was made a captain in the Royal Army Medical Corps Territorial Forces, in charge of the Military Orthopaedic Centre in Manchester. In 1920 he joined the staff of the Shropshire Orthopaedic Hospital in Oswestry.

In 1921 Platt received the gold medal for his Manchester MD thesis, on peripheral nerve injuries. He became surgical director of the Ethel Hedley Hospital in Windermere, consultant to the Lancashire county council for education, public health, and tuberculosis, and in 1926 a lecturer in orthopaedic surgery to the University of Manchester. In 1932 the Manchester Royal Infirmary established an orthopaedic department away from the control of general surgery and Platt transferred there. Manchester University recognized his outstanding academic contribution to orthopaedics by creating a personal chair for him in 1939, which he held until 1951.

Having helped found the British Orthopaedic Association in 1917, he became its president (1934–5). He was also president of the Royal Society of Medicine orthopaedics section in 1931–2 and British delegate (1929–48) and later president (1948–53) of the international committee of the Société Internationale de Chirurgie Orthopédique et de Traumatologie. He served on the council of the Royal College of Surgeons of England (1940–58) and was its president in 1954–7. He was knighted in 1948 because of this work. He was consultant adviser in orthopaedic surgery to the Ministry of Health (1940–63), organizing general orthopaedics, and special fracture and peripheral nerve injury centres, as well as being honorary civilian consultant to the Army Medical Services (1942–54). Platt was actively involved in setting up the National Health Service before and after 1948.

In 1958 he was made a baronet, as was customary for presidents of the RCS. He received six honorary degrees and held sixteen honorary memberships of various societies and eight honorary fellowships of surgical colleges. Up to 1982 he wrote prolifically on orthopaedic subjects—their history, organization, staffing, nursing, and education. He was a competent musician and a member of council of the Royal Manchester College of Music (1949–73), as well as vice-president of the Wagner Society of Manchester. He had a fiery temper and was outspoken and intolerant of humbug. As a younger man he was intellectually arrogant and in the operating room he expressed his displeasure at delays by kicking over the nearest bucket.

Even when very old, this small, stockily built, vigorous person walked briskly despite a bad limp due to an ankylosed knee. His piercing deep blue eyes missed nothing around him and his obvious strength of character was reinforced by a strong jaw structure. In 1916 he married a nurse, Gertrude Sarah (died 1980), daughter of Richard Turney. They had four daughters and a son. Platt achieved his goal, to reach a hundred years of age with his mental faculties intact. He died 20 December 1986 in Manchester. He was succeeded in the baronetcy by his son, (Frank) Lindsey Platt (born 1919), barrister.

[Harold Riley (artist), *Conversations with Harry Platt*, 1986 (privately printed); official records of meetings of the Royal College of Surgeons; *Modern Medicine*, vol. i, 18 November 1968; *Lancet*, 10 January 1987; *British Medical Journal*, vol. ccxciii, 4 October 1986, and vol. ccxciv, 10 January 1987; private information; personal knowledge.]

R. B. DUTHIE

POCHIN, SIR Edward Eric (1909–1990), physician and specialist in the dangers of ionizing radiation, was born 22 September 1909 in Sale, Cheshire, the only child of Charles Davenport Pochin, mechanical engineer, and his wife, Agnes Collier. His father drowned soon after he was born and the family had little money, but he showed early determination by gaining a scholarship to Repton. He later went to St John's College, Cambridge, where he took first classes in both parts of the natural sciences tripos (1930 and 1931), stayed for some physiological research, and then went to University College Hospital (UCH) for his clinical training in 1932. He obtained his MRCS, LRCP in 1935, MB, B.Chir. in 1936, and MRCP in 1937. In 1941 he joined the Medical Research Council's department of clinical research at UCH, which was led by Sir Thomas *Lewis. After secondment to an army physiological laboratory, where he worked on the physiology and ergonomics of living in a tank, he returned to UCH as director of the department of clinical research in 1946 and remained there until his retirement in 1974. He became FRCP in 1946.

Known as 'Bill' to his friends from his student days, he determined early in his career that, to learn more about human physiology and disease, human studies needed to be carried out. He was a founder member of the pioneering UCH ethics committee, where he pursued the policy of informed consent. The clinical trials and clinical measurements that were later taken for granted were almost unknown then. His approach was successful and before long he was a world expert on endocrinology (the study of hormones and hormonal glands), especially the thyroid gland, which concentrates iodine to produce thyroid hormones.

With the development of nuclear power and the potential for releases of radioactive iodine, and the resulting risk to the thyroid gland, Pochin was well placed to advise the government on radiation protection. This led to his appointment to the MRC committee on protection against ionizing radiation. In those exciting but daunting years of the middle 1950s, when the first recognition was made of the dangers of fall-out from atmospheric testing of nuclear weapons, Pochin was appointed the first UK representative to the new United Nations Scientific Committee on the Effects of Atomic Radiation (UNSCEAR), a post he held for over twenty-five years (1956–82). At about the same time he also became involved with the work of the International Commission on Radiological Protection (IRCP), joining its main commission in 1959 and being chairman from 1962 to 1969. He was a member of the National Radiological Protection Board from 1971 to 1982.

He was deeply involved in the assessment of health consequences of the 1957 Windscale accident, when radioactive iodine was released into the atmosphere over Cumbria. He subsequently established with colleagues that a tablet of ordinary iodine could effectively prevent the body from taking up radioactive iodine. It was agreed throughout the world that this preventive measure would be adopted if there were a nuclear emergency. Some twenty years later in 1977 he returned to Windscale to become an assessor for the major planning inquiry into the expansion of the nuclear fuel reprocessing plant. In 1978 he conducted a government inquiry into radiological health and safety at the Atomic Weapons Establishment, Aldermaston. His report (1978) was highly critical of the poor protection afforded and led to the introduction of many improvements in health and safety.

The author of more than 120 articles or chapters in medical and scientific journals or textbooks, he was the first in the world to move radiation protection standards on to a quantitative basis and in 1977 he published *Problems Involved in Developing an Index of Harm* (IRCP publication 27). In 1984 there followed *Nuclear Radiation: Risks and Benefits*. He was appointed CBE in 1959 and knighted in 1975.

Pochin approached six feet in height and was of average build. He had a good head of hair, a healthy, clear complexion that went with his outdoor pursuits, and a rich, deep voice. He was kind and considerate, modest and unassuming, never pompous, often humorous. He had little time for the pretentious or devious, but managed to conceal this at important meetings. Those who were close to him knew when he was tested beyond endurance because of his habit of breaking a pencil in two as an alternative to an outburst. In addition to his scientific achievements, Pochin was an enthusiastic hill walker and an able painter. He was in the habit of using one of his sketches of a hill or rock face to produce his own personal Christmas card.

In 1940 he married Constance Margaret Julia (died 1971), daughter of Tobias Harry Tilly, solicitor. They had one son and one daughter. Pochin died 29 January 1990 at Hollington House, Woolton Hill, Newbury.

[Private information; personal knowledge.]

R. H. CLARKE

POND, SIR Desmond Arthur (1919–1986), psychiatrist, physician, and humanist, was born 2 September 1919 in Catford, London, the only child of Thomas Arthur Pond, electrical engineer and company director, and his wife, Ada Celia Clutten. He was educated at John Lyon School in Harrow, St Olave's in south-east London, and Clare College, Cambridge. At Cambridge he obtained a first class in both part i of the natural sciences tripos (1940) and part ii of the moral sciences tripos (1941). He gained a Rockefeller studentship to Duke University, North Carolina (1942–4). He followed this with clinical studies at University College Hospital Medical School, London, and thus qualified in medicine in both the United States and Britain (MB, B.Chir., 1945, DPM Eng. 1947). He proceeded to a Cambridge MD in 1951 and to fellowship of the Royal College of Physicians of London in 1960. By then he had trained in psychiatry at the Maudsley Hospital, specializing, though not exclusively, in child psychiatry.

British psychiatry, guided by (Sir) Aubrey *Lewis, flourished during the postwar years. Psychiatrists began to occupy important positions in medical affairs and councils. Others besides Pond contributed to this, but his personal effectiveness and standing placed him at the forefront. Psychiatrists respected him as a leading psychiatrist and physicians recognized him as a physician. He was helped by his particular speciality of epilepsy in children and its cerebral, psychiatric, and psychological causes and sequelae. In the eyes of the medical profession epilepsy was 'real medicine'. In 1961 he gave the Goulstonian lecture to the Royal College of Physicians of London, a rare honour for a psychiatrist, upon 'the psychiatric aspects of epileptic and brain damaged children'. His comprehensive approach to the epilepsies of childhood carefully balanced the respective importance of social, clinical, epidemiological, and electroencephalographic findings. Psychiatry was securing a larger place in medical education, and as a consultant at University College Hospital from 1952 to 1966, and later when occupying the Foundation chair of psychiatry at the London Hospital Medical College (1966–82), Pond raised both the clinical and academic status of the subject.

From 1978 to 1981 he was president of the Royal College of Psychiatrists, of which he had become a founder fellow in 1971. Previously he had served on its important committees and particularly furthered training in psychiatry for general practitioners. During his presidency he was chosen by fellow medical presidents to chair the Conference of Royal Medical Colleges, the first psychiatrist to do so. He thus became the spokesman on general matters for all the colleges. He was a member of the Medical Research Council (1968–72 and 1982–5) and from 1982 to 1985 chief scientist at the Department of Health, where he helped to develop the relationship between the Department of Health and the Medical Research Council to the benefit of medical science generally..

A deeply religious man, more humanitarian than pietistic, he was a founder member of the Institute of Religion and Medicine (1964). He served on the archbishop of Canterbury's group on divorce law reform from 1964 to 1966, which published *Putting Asunder*, and he helped set up the Richmond Fellowship, which provided residential homes with a marked but skilfully concealed spiritual background for psychiatric patients, wherein a long period of caring stability assisted in rehabilitating mentally disturbed young people.

He was a visiting professor to the Australian and New Zealand College of Psychiatrists in 1968 and at Western Reserve Institute, Pittsburg, in 1971. He served on a number of committees concerned with epilepsy, including the welfare and rehabilitation of epileptic subjects. These included committees of the World Health Organization, which adopted his classification of childhood epilepsies. He lectured widely and published upon his own subject and own research, and upon medical matters generally. *Counselling in Religion and Psychiatry* (1973) was based on his Riddell memorial lecture delivered in Newcastle upon Tyne in 1971. He was an honorary fellow of the British Psychological Society (1980) and the Royal College of General Practitioners (1981). He was knighted in 1981.

Personable, popular, and kind, with his ideas always well organized, Pond never seemed in a hurry. His build was slight, but there was an underlying firmness which ensured that others usually agreed with his proposals. He chiefly acted by encouragement, especially as a teacher. With colleagues, juniors, and students his emphasis was always on bringing out rather than stuffing in: 'I don't mind spoon-feeding students but I draw the line at moving their jaws up and down as well.' He had a great love of music and was a gifted pianist. In 1945 he married (Margaret) Helen, herself a physician, daughter of Louis Arnold Jordan, research scientist. It was a long and happy marriage and they had three daughters, two of whom became professional musicians. He and his wife retired to the Teign Valley in Devon. Pond died from cancer, after a long and painful illness, 29 June 1986 in Torquay Hospital.

[Private information; personal knowledge.]

NEIL KESSEL

PORTLAND, ninth DUKE OF (1897–1990), diplomat and international businessman. [See BENTINCK, VICTOR FREDERICK WILLIAM CAVENDISH-.]

POUNCEY, Philip Michael Rivers (1910–1990), connoisseur of Italian art, was born in Oxford 15 February 1910, the second of the three sons (there were no daughters) of (the Revd) George Ernest Pouncey, a bank manager who had decided to take holy orders, and his second wife Madeline Mary, daughter of Albin Roberts, cloth-maker. He was educated at Marlborough and Queens' College, Cambridge, where he obtained a third class in part i (1930) and a second (division II) in part ii (1931) of the English tripos. He then worked as a volunteer in the Fitzwilliam Museum, Cambridge, until 1934, when he was appointed assistant keeper in the National Gallery, London. He began by working on the catalogue of fourteenth-century Italian paintings, but as successive volumes of the catalogue (all published after he left the Gallery) show, his interests extended over the entire Italian school.

In the later part of the war of 1939–45 he was seconded to the Government Code and Cipher School at Bletchley Park, but for the first two years he was in charge of that part of the National Gallery collection moved for safety to the National Library of Wales at Aberystwyth. The drawings from the British Museum Printroom and the Royal Library at Windsor were also there under the care of A. E. *Popham, then deputy keeper of the Printroom, who took the opportunity of starting work on the catalogues of the Italian drawings in both collections. As problems arose Popham discussed them with two eminent art historians, Johannes *Wilde and Frederick *Antal, then also in Aberystwyth. Pouncey naturally took part in these discussions and realized that drawings, surviving as they have in far larger numbers than paintings and posing more difficult problems of attribution, offered greater scope for his particular gift for connoisseurship.

After the war he accordingly transferred to the British Museum and continued, now on an official basis, to collaborate with Popham on the catalogue of Italian drawings. The first volume, of fourteenth- and fifteenth-century drawings of all schools, appeared in 1950. Two later volumes, both in collaboration with J. A. Gere, were devoted to *Raphael and His Circle* (1962) and *Artists Working in Rome c.1550–c.1640* (1983). In 1954 he became deputy keeper, but succession to the keepership was blocked and he would have had to retire at sixty. The prospect of freedom from official routine and of again working with paintings led him in 1966 to join Sotheby's as a director, but he kept in close touch with his old department and continued to work there regularly on the third volume of the catalogue.

While still at Marlborough he had studied the classic history of Italian Renaissance painting (1864–71) by Sir Joseph *Crowe and G. B. Cavalcaselle. This pioneer work was the first to survey the field in a spirit of rigorous scientific enquiry, taking into account all available evidence, both documentary and stylistic. Pouncey's approach was similarly untheoretical and matter-of-fact. He saw the subject in terms of the complex interaction of a host of individual artistic personalities whose identification was the primary duty of the historian. His approach was

that of connoisseurship; he held that no critical generalization about an artist can be valid until his *œuvre* is correctly defined.

In the drawing-cabinets of Europe and the USA perplexed students see with relief inscriptions in his familiar neat handwriting. (It is estimated that in the Louvre alone he restored some 500 Italian drawings to their proper authors.) These annotations and his carefully indexed notes constitute the principal record of his life's work. Apart from the three British Museum catalogues, his publications were limited to short articles dealing with specific points, usually of attribution, and an occasional review (including a *tour de force*, of the 1964 Italian edition of Bernhard Berenson's *The Drawings of the Florentine Painters*). His one monograph, on the drawings of Lorenzo Lotto (1965), is an essay of only fifteen pages, but in them the essential facts are stated with concise clarity. His reluctance to publish was more than offset by the number and importance of his discoveries and by the encouraging generosity with which he always shared them with fellow students. A French friend described 'son allure juvénile et son air latin'. In spite of his solidly English descent, there was something *méridional* about his dark hair and pale lively features, his rapid speech, and flashing brown eyes—an effect in no way diminished by his invariable London uniform of dark suit, bowler hat, and high stiff collar.

In 1937 he married Myril, daughter of Colonel Albert Gros, a staff officer in the French army. She shared all his interests, and was felicitously described in an obituary notice as 'wife and colleague'. They had twin daughters, one of whom married Dr Marco Chiarini, director of the Galleria Palatina (Palazzo Pitti) in Florence. In 1975 Pouncey was elected a fellow of the British Academy and in 1987 was appointed CBE. His seventy-fifth birthday was celebrated at the Fitzwilliam Museum (where he was honorary keeper of Italian drawings from 1975) by a loan exhibition of his reattributions; and after his death, which took place at his house in Kensington 12 November 1990, he received the unique distinction of being similarly honoured by the Louvre (1992), the Uffizi (1992), and the British Museum (1994).

[J. A. Gere in *Proceedings of the British Academy*, vol. lxxvi, 1990; *Independent*, 16 November 1990; *The Times*, 20 November 1990; *Art Newspaper*, December 1990; private information; personal knowledge.]

J. A. GERE

POWELL, Michael Latham (1905–1990), film director, was born 30 September 1905 in Bekesbourne, near Canterbury, Kent, the second son and younger child of Thomas William Powell, farmer, and his wife Mabel, daughter of Frederick Corbett, of Worcester. He was educated at

King's School, Canterbury, where he was a King's scholar, and at Dulwich College. After joining the National Provincial Bank in 1922, Powell entered the film business in 1925 by joining Rex Ingram, a Hollywood director who was working at a studio in Nice, and Harry Lachman, a Chicago-born painter who secured employment for Powell with British International Pictures. In 1931 Powell formed Film Engineering with Jerry Jackson, an American lawyer, to produce 'quota quickies', British films given a market by the Cinematograph Act of 1927.

After a successful contract with Gaumont-British, Powell directed a personal project set on the island of Foula in the Shetlands, *Edge of the World* (1937), produced by the American Joe Rock. The film received good reviews and a cup for the best direction of a foreign film at the Venice film festival (1938). This led to a contract with (Sir) Alexander *Korda, who facilitated Powell's first collaboration with screenwriter Emeric *Pressburger on *The Spy in Black* (1939), the first of twenty-one films they made together, adopting a joint title in 1943, the 'Archers'. But before their partnership was more permanently forged Powell directed *The Lion Has Wings* (1939) and co-directed Korda's Technicolor *The Thief of Baghdad* (1940).

During World War II Powell and Pressburger produced some of their finest work, including *Forty Ninth Parallel* (1941), *One of Our Aircraft Is Missing* (1941), and *The Life and Death of Colonel Blimp* (1943), a film which was criticized by (Sir) Winston *Churchill and the Ministry of Information for its satirical portrayal of the military. The films were imaginative, creative, cinematic, and rather unconventional. Whereas most British films were made with an intense style of realism, Powell and Pressburger used fantastical situations, dream sequences, bold colour, and disjointed narratives. The Archers broke new ground with *A Canterbury Tale* (1944), a lyrical meditation for the postwar world which suffered from studio cuts to render it more conventional. At the time Powell's films were considered to stray beyond the critical boundaries of British films usually associated with 'quality' and realism. Nevertheless, the Rank Organization gave the Archers a firm production base and considerable freedom in the development of their projects. Powell excelled at location shooting and had a particularly poetic response to landscape. At the end of the war he directed *I Know Where I'm Going* (1945) and his favourite film, the spectacular *A Matter of Life and Death* (1946), starring David *Niven as a British pilot on the verge of death. It was an aesthetic experiment involving imaginative sets and innovative film techniques to represent the pilot's hallucinations. Powell's passion for experiment, risk tak-

ing, and creative use of colour influenced many film directors.

In a spirit of resourceful creativity *Black Narcissus* (1946) reproduced south India in a studio and *The Red Shoes* (1948) was an extravagant gamble. Rank allowed the Archers to produce a high budget film about ballet at a time when the British film industry was enjoying a brief period of protection against American film imports. Its excess stretched the limits of the relationship with Rank and ended the Archers' partnership with the studio until *The Battle of the River Plate* in 1956. From 1948 to 1955 Powell worked with Alexander Korda again on *The Small Back Room* (1949) and *The Tales of Hoffman* (1953), an experimental adaptation of Jacques Offenbach's opera. Powell's last film with Pressburger was *Ill Met by Moonlight* (1956). The Archers' partnership ended after a mutual distancing and several unsuccessful attempts to raise finance for film projects.

In 1959 Powell directed the controversial *Peeping Tom*, later widely regarded as a classic but at the time considered to be sadistic cheap horror. Its reception was so bad that Powell could get no further funding for his work and had to go to Australia in 1966 to make two films: *They're a Weird Mob* (1966) and *Age of Consent* (1969), the last feature film he was to direct. In the 1970s Powell's talent was fully recognized by critics and film-makers, especially Martin Scorsese and David Thomson, who encouraged him to move to America in 1980 to teach at Dartmouth College, New Hampshire. In 1981 he became director in residence at Francis Ford Coppola's Zoetrope Hollywood studio, where he also worked on his boastful and vengeful autobiographies, *A Life in Movies* (1986) and *Million-Dollar Movie* (1992). Powell was remarkable for his liveliness, enthusiasm, and passion for both cinema and Rudyard *Kipling. His physical appearance was distinctive: he had clear blue eyes, ruddy cheeks, and a moustache, and was bald from an early age. He loved the outdoors and always shot on location when possible.

In recognition of his work Powell received a number of awards, among them fellowship of the Royal Geographic Society; honorary doctorates from the universities of East Anglia (1978) and Kent (1984), and the Royal College of Art (1987); and the British Film Institute's special award in 1978 and a fellowship in 1983.

Powell was married three times. His first marriage was to an American dancer, 1927–36 (they were married in France and stayed together for three weeks only). In 1943 he married Frances, daughter of Dr Jeremiah Reidy JP, medical practitioner and mayor of Stepney in 1917–18. They had two sons. His wife died in 1983 and in 1984 Powell married film editor Thelma Schoonmaker, daughter of Bertram Schoonmaker, a clerical worker in the Standard Oil Company. Powell died of cancer 19 February 1990 in Avening, Gloucestershire.

[Ian Christie, *Arrows of Desire*, 1985; Michael Powell, *A Life in Movies*, 1986, and *Million-Dollar Movie*, 1992; private information.] SARAH STREET

PRÉ, Jacqueline Mary du (1945-1987), cellist. [See DU PRÉ, JACQUELINE MARY.]

PRESSBURGER, Emeric (1902-1988), author and screenwriter, was born Imre Josef Pressburger at 3 St Peter's Street, Miskolc, Hungary, 5 December 1902, the only son (he had one elder half-sister from his father's previous marriage) of Kálmán Pressburger, estate manager, and his second wife, Kätherina Wichs. He went to a boarding school in Temesvar. He then studied mathematics and engineering at the universities of Prague and Stuttgart before his father's death forced him to abandon his studies. He moved to Berlin in 1926 to work as a journalist and writer of short stories and film scripts. Ufa, the major European film studio, employed Pressburger as a contract writer and his first screen credit was for *Abschied* (1930), co-written with Erich Kästner, novelist, and directed by Robert Siodmak. Pressburger was not listed on the credits for a screen adaptation of Kästner's *Emil and the Detectives* (1931), which was signed by Billy Wilder. One Pressburger script, *Monsieur Sans-Gêne* (1935) was remade in Hollywood as *One Rainy Afternoon*. He also worked with Max Ophuls and Reinhold Schünzel.

After collaborating on many scripts in Germany (where he changed his name to Emmerich) and France, Pressburger went to Britain in 1935, on a stateless passport, to work for fellow Hungarian (Sir) Alexander *Korda, of London Film Productions. In England his name became Emeric. His first British assignment was *The Challenge* in 1938, the year he met Michael *Powell, his director and collaborator for the next eighteen years. Their first joint projects were *The Spy in Black* (1939), an espionage thriller filmed at Denham Studios, starring Conrad Veidt and Valerie Hobson, and *Contraband* (1940). Pressburger's most successful work was with Michael Powell as the 'Archers' production company, which they formed in 1943, with its distinctive trademark of nine arrows thrusting into a target.

During World War II Pressburger's screenplays provided excellent scope for Powell's distinctive visual style, which employed colour in an imaginary way, fantasy and unreal spectacle, complex and challenging narrative structures, and flamboyant visual and camera devices. The films involved were *Forty Ninth Parallel* (1941), *One of Our Aircraft Is Missing* (1941), *The Silver Fleet* (1943), *The Life and Death of Colonel Blimp*

(1943), based on the cartoon character created by David *Low, *A Canterbury Tale* (1944), and *I Know Where I'm Going* (1945). Pressburger's ability to see Britain from the point of view of a fascinated outsider suited the films' quizzical perspective on British society and history. Now regarded as a classic in a mystical tradition, *A Canterbury Tale* was misunderstood at the time of release, initiating the Archers' reputation as film-makers who were ahead of their time, and whose work was characterized by wit, fantasy, ambition, and originality. The film celebrated British heritage and freedom, two themes that were extremely important to Pressburger.

After the war Pressburger (who was naturalized in 1946) experimented with time in *A Matter of Life and Death* (1946) and with a clash of communities and values in *Black Narcissus* (1946), about a group of nuns in the Himalayas. *The Red Shoes* (1948, based on a Hans Christian Andersen story), showed how Powell's visual sense of colour could be assisted by Pressburger's ambitious screenplay. This was followed by adaptations of challenging material for *The Tales of Hoffman* (1953, adapted from a Jacques Offenbach opera at the suggestion of Sir Thomas *Beecham) and *Oh Rosalinda!* (1955, based on Johann Strauss's operetta *Die Fledermaus*). These films separated the Archers from the conventional canon of British film production, often to their cost, for puzzled critics dismissed their work as pretentious, extravagant, and confusing. In 1952 Pressburger directed for the only time, the film being *Twice Upon a Time*. The Battle of the River Plate* (1956) was chosen for the Royal film performance in 1956. After their last Archer collaboration, *Ill Met by Moonlight* (1956), Powell and Pressburger parted. Their work was beginning to lose its experimental edge and both agreed to separate as their interests began to diverge.

Pressburger wrote and produced *Miracle in Soho* (1957) and published two novels, *Killing a Mouse on Sunday* (1961), on which was based Fred Zinnemann's film *Behold a Pale Horse* (1964), and *The Glass Pearls* (1966). He worked again with Powell in 1972 when they collaborated on a film for the Children's Film Foundation, *The Boy Who Turned Yellow*, and on a novel of *The Red Shoes* (1978). Pressburger more or less retired after this, but enjoyed the critical appreciation of his work encouraged by Martin Scorsese and Francis Ford Coppola. A key event in the reappraisal of the Archers' work was the showing of a restored print of *The Life and Death of Colonel Blimp* at the National Film Theatre in 1978. Michael Powell was always keen to stress that his skill as a director was stretched to the best advantage when Pressburger had written the screenplay. There was a mutual sense of trust between them and a joint desire to explore the boundaries of word and image. A keen gastronome, Pressburger loved French food. He had a great sense of humour and his physical appearance contrasted with that of Michael Powell. Pressburger was short, wore glasses, and had a sagacious, bird-like facial expression. He was a keen supporter of Arsenal football team.

Pressburger received the British Film Institute special award (with Powell) in 1978 and fellowships from BAFTA in 1981 and the BFI in 1983. *Forty Ninth Parallel* earned an Oscar (1942) for Pressburger for best original story. In 1938 Pressburger married Agnes, daughter of Andrew Anderson, factory owner. This marriage was dissolved in 1941 and in 1947 he married Gwynneth May Zillah ('Wendy'), former wife of Abraham Jacob Greenbaum ('Jack Green'), gambler, and daughter of Edward Orme, professional soldier. They had two daughters, one of whom died as a baby in 1948. The marriage was dissolved at Reno, Nevada, in 1953 and in Britain in 1971. Pressburger died of bronchial pneumonia 5 February 1988 in Saxstead, Suffolk.

[Ian Christie, *Arrows of Desire*, 1985; Michael Powell, *A Life in Movies*, 1986, and *Million-Dollar Movie*, 1992; Kevin Macdonald, *Emeric Pressburger*, 1994; private information.]   SARAH STREET

PRITCHARD, SIR John Michael (1921–1989), operatic and orchestral conductor, was born 5 February 1921 at 17 Cromwell Road, Walthamstow, London, the younger son (there were no daughters) of Albert Edward Pritchard, violinist, and his wife, Amy Edith Shaylor. He was educated at Sir George Monoux School in London, and he studied privately with his father and other music teachers. In his teenage years he visited Italy to listen to opera. When World War II broke out Pritchard registered as a conscientious objector, to his father's dismay. He therefore underwent an army medical examination, but, because of an earlier attack of pleurisy, was registered unfit to serve. In 1943 he took over the Derby String Orchestra and was its principal conductor till 1951. Meanwhile he joined the music staff of Glyndebourne Opera (1947) and was appointed chorus master there (1949). He succeeded Reginald Jacques as conductor of the Jacques Orchestra (1950–2). By 1951 he was sharing with Fritz Busch major Mozart productions at Glyndebourne and at the Edinburgh Festival.

Important opportunities came his way in 1952. At Edinburgh he appeared with the Royal Philharmonic Orchestra, replacing Ernest Ansermet, who was ill; and he made his débuts at the Royal Opera House in Covent Garden, and at the Vienna State Opera. He appeared regularly with the Vienna Symphony Orchestra (1953–5). He continued to work at Glyndebourne, conducting their productions of Mozart's *Idomeneo* and Richard Strauss's *Ariadne auf Naxos* at the Edinburgh festivals of 1953 and 1954. After the latter he conducted the Glyndebourne production of Rossini's *La Cenerentola* at the Berlin Festival. The performance was a triumph.

At home, he was appointed principal conductor of the (Royal) Liverpool Philharmonic Orchestra (1957–63) and within a year had launched the Musica Viva series at which contemporary music was introduced, illustrated, performed, and then discussed. During five seasons, unfamiliar music by many living composers was heard for the first time in Britain. Pritchard's success in Liverpool led to his appointment as musical director of the London Philharmonic Orchestra (1962–6). At Glyndebourne he became music counsellor (1963), principal conductor (1968), and musical director (1969–77). In 1969 he took the London Philharmonic to the Far East and made his American début, at the Chicago Lyric Opera. Appearances at the San Francisco Opera (1970) and the Metropolitan Opera (1971) followed. In 1973 he conducted the London Philharmonic in China—the first visit by a western orchestra.

By 1980 Pritchard had conducted many of the world's greatest orchestras, including the Berlin Philharmonic, the Leipzig Gewandhaus, the Dresden Staatskapelle, and the Philadelphia Orchestra; he had appeared at the Salzburg festival, the Maggio Musicale in Florence, and the Munich State Opera. He was a regular guest at the Royal Opera House, Covent Garden, at the Proms, and with the BBC Symphony Orchestra, whose chief conductor he became in 1982. Overlapping posts included at that time the musical directorships of the Cologne Opera (1978), the Théâtre de la Monnaie, Brussels (1981), and the San Francisco Opera (1986).

Pritchard's innate musicality, his quick grasp, his range of sympathies, and his gift for getting the best out of the musicians (with whom he was very popular) combined to bring him a career of astonishing concentration and variety. No conductor can have had a fuller diary. Although this sometimes led to a perfunctoriness bordering upon indolence, he was, at his best, an interpreter of lasting distinction. His Mozart and Strauss were superbly idiomatic, but he also excelled in nineteenth-century Italian opera. And he could surprise his public with, for example, some tough Shostakovich. He was not, however, a great star; he did not make enough recordings to achieve that status. But he was appointed CBE in 1962 and was knighted in 1983. The coveted Shakespeare prize (Hamburg) was awarded him in 1975.

Pritchard's much imitated manner of speech—bland, almost epicene—was an outward sign of his unabashed homosexuality, but there was nothing effeminate about his music-making. He had friends in every walk and style of life and was loyal and generous to them. Witty and well-informed, he lived in some style (in a number of homes, including an elegant house near Glyndebourne and a villa in the Alpes-Maritimes above Nice). Indeed his enjoyment of good food and wine became a problem when he needed to lose weight for a hip replacement operation not long before his death. It was a problem he observed with rueful detachment. Though already ill, with a blood clot, he conducted the last night of the Proms on 16 September 1989 and made a touchingly prescient and self-deprecating speech. He died 5 December 1989 in San Francisco, where he was musical director of the San Francisco Opera. He left a large part of his estate to Terry MacInnes, his partner.

[Spike Hughes, *Glyndebourne*, 1965; Nicholas Kenyon, *The BBC Symphony Orchestra*, 1981; John Higgins (ed.), *Glyndebourne, a Celebration*, 1984; personal knowledge.]   ROBERT PONSONBY

Q

QUAYLE, SIR **(John) Anthony** (1913–1989), actor and stage director, was born 7 September 1913 at 2 Delamere Road, Ainsdale, Southport, Lancashire, the only child of Arthur Quayle, solicitor, and his wife, Esther Kate Overton. The Quayle family had Manx roots. During a rather lonely youth Anthony's interest in the theatre was encouraged by his lively and imaginative mother. He was educated at Rugby and the Royal Academy of Dramatic Art, where he stayed only a year. His first appearance on the professional stage, unpaid, was in *The Ghost Train* at the Q theatre while on holiday from RADA. He began his career in earnest playing both Richard Cœur de Lion and Will Scarlett in *Robin Hood* at the same theatre in 1931.

The following year, after touring as feed to a music-hall comic, he found his feet in classical theatre and met two men whose influence was to be an important factor in his career, (Sir) Tyrone *Guthrie and (Sir) John Gielgud. By 1939 he had appeared in many supporting roles, with Old Vic seasons in 1932 and 1937–8, had appeared in New York, and had played Laertes in the famous Guthrie production of *Hamlet* at Elsinore. Strongly drawn to the classics and especially to Shakespeare, he took over the lead from Laurence (later Baron) *Olivier in *Henry V* during an Old Vic tour of Europe and Egypt just before World War II. Though not yet at the top of his profession, he was known and liked by many who were.

He spent the war in the Royal Artillery, reaching the rank of major. Characteristically, he gave up an administrative job in Gibraltar, learned to parachute, and joined Albanian partisans behind German lines. He later wrote two slight novels suggested by his wartime experiences.

After the war he returned to the stage and as Enobarbus in *Antony and Cleopatra* (1946) was a great success in the first of the many supporting roles he was to make his own. He also turned to directing, and in 1946 his *Crime and Punishment*, starring John Gielgud, was considered outstanding.

In 1948, through Guthrie, he joined the Shakespeare memorial theatre in Stratford-upon-Avon as actor and stage director. He was soon promoted to run the whole memorial theatre. In eight years he transformed it from an unfashionable provincial theatre to a world-famous centre of classical drama. Because of his many contacts, he was able to attract illustrious players and directors to Stratford, as well as encourage such major new talents as Richard *Burton and (Sir) Peter Hall. He took companies on tours of Australasia in 1949 and 1953 and tried, although without success, to secure the kind of London shop window for the company which was later obtained by the Royal Shakespeare Company. With his 'Cycle of the Histories' for the Festival of Britain in 1951 he foreshadowed the later practice of staging Shakespeare's historical plays in chronological order. Among his own parts during these strenuous years were Henry VIII, Falstaff, and Othello. His work was not entirely confined to Stratford, but his enthusiastic leadership and hard work at the memorial theatre, proudly unsubsidized, put it on the map. He paved the way for the subsequent achievements of Peter Hall, Trevor Nunn, and the Royal Shakespeare Company.

In 1956 he resigned from Stratford and returned to mainstream theatre. For over twenty more years he continued to act and direct in the West End, having a steady if unspectacular career, occasionally taking the lead, as in *Tamburlaine* in 1956, but more often in highly praised supporting parts. He also appeared in over thirty films, most of them British, again in strong supporting roles. His portrayal of stiff-upper-lip Englishmen was much admired in films, especially in *The Battle of the River Plate* (1956), *The Guns of Navarone* (1961), and *Lawrence of Arabia* (1962). The first of his many television appearances was in 1961.

In 1978, at sixty-five, his career took a different course and he toured with the Prospect Theatre Company, playing leading roles in *The Rivals* and *King Lear*. The company closed, however, when its Arts Council subsidy was withdrawn. Several years later, in 1983, he formed his own Compass Theatre, which bravely stumped the country without subsidy, dedicated to bringing major plays to people who could otherwise never see them.

Quayle had a big physique, a vigorous personality, and a steadfast—even romantic—devotion to great plays and classical traditions. Despite his fine technique he had neither the personality nor the face for a great actor. As he grew older his face became more rugged but there was something about his amiable blue eyes which suggested a warm and pleasant person and deprived his acting of some of its emotional impact. However, as a man of great courage and integrity he was a natural leader and a major influence on the theatre in Britain.

He was appointed CBE in 1952 and knighted in 1985. He had honorary D.Litt. degrees from Hull (1987) and St Andrews (1989). He was guest professor of drama at the University of Tennessee in 1974, and was nominated for an Oscar as best supporting player for his perform-

ance as Cardinal Wolsey in the 1969 film about Anne Boleyn, *Anne of the Thousand Days*.

In 1935 he married Hermione (died 1983), actress daughter of actor Nicholas James Hannen, but the marriage was dissolved in 1943. In 1947 he married another actress, Dorothy Wardell, divorced wife of Robert Douglas Finlayson and daughter of another actress, Dorothy Dickson, and Carl Hyson, of independent means. They had a son and two daughters. He was still touring until two months before his death from cancer at his Chelsea home, 20 October 1989.

[*Daily Telegraph*, *The Times*, and *Independent*, 21 October 1989; Anthony Quayle, *A Time to Speak* (autobiography), 1990.]   RACHAEL LOW

R

RAMSEY, (Arthur) Michael, BARON RAMSEY OF CANTERBURY (1904–1988), archbishop of Canterbury, was born in Cambridge 14 November 1904, the younger son in the family of two sons and two daughters of Arthur Stanley Ramsey, a Cambridge mathematics don and Congregationalist elder, and his wife (Mary) Agnes, daughter of Plumpton Stravenson Wilson, vicar of Horbling, Lincolnshire. His elder brother Frank *Ramsey (died 1930) became the well-known Cambridge philosopher. Educated at Repton and then as a classical scholar at his father's college, Magdalene, he became a leading debater and president of the Cambridge Union (1926). He was committed to the Liberal party and was adopted as the Liberal candidate for Cambridgeshire. But during his third year at university he became convinced, to the surprise of his friends, that he should take holy orders. He gained a second class in part i of the classical tripos (1925) and a first class in part i of the theology tripos (1927). He then went to Cuddesdon College, near Oxford, to be trained for the priesthood. This training was almost wrecked, first by the death of his mother in a car accident in 1927, and then by the need for psychiatric treatment.

He was ordained to the curacy of St Nicholas, Liverpool, in September 1928 but stayed in the parish only eighteen months. He then became sub-warden of the theological college at Lincoln. Here he published in 1936 his best-known book, *The Gospel and the Catholic Church*. It was at once a persuasive to Protestants to take seriously the Catholic tradition of ministry and devotion, and a persuasive to Catholics to take seriously the Protestant conviction of the central biblical truths. The book was original in form and range of ideas and made him well known to the thinking and reading members of the church. After another curacy at Boston (Lincolnshire, 1936–8) and a year as vicar of St Bene'ts in Cambridge (1939–40), he was chosen in 1940 to be professor of divinity at Durham University. The post carried with it a canonry at the cathedral.

At Durham (1940–50) he was soon valued as the leader of sane Catholic thought and devotion in the Church of England, and after the war as an Anglican leader prominent in the ecumenical movement and the World Council of Churches.

After a brief spell as regius professor of divinity at Cambridge, with a fellowship at Magdalene College (1950–2), during which he was also canon and prebendary of Lincoln Cathedral (1951–2), he was chosen successively as bishop of Durham (1952–6), archbishop of York (1956–61), and archbishop of Canterbury (1961–74). As bishop of Durham he had the historic duty of standing at the queen's right hand during her coronation; his vast bald dome and mobile eyebrows attracted comment when the event was televised and introduced his colourful personality to the nation. His shining face, which looked old from the age of thirty-five, was attractive, though not at all handsome, with its abundant, beaming smiles.

His term at Canterbury coincided with the introduction of reforming legislation, in which he took a prominent part. He was weighty in the abolition of capital punishment, in changes in the laws on abortion, divorce, and homosexuality, and, especially, on the subject of race relations. As prime minister, Harold Wilson (later Baron Wilson of Rievaulx) made him the chairman of the national committee for Commonwealth immigrants, and as such he was in public dispute with Enoch Powell over immigration. His term also coincided with a prising apart of church and state. He was determined that Parliament should no longer have the final say in the doctrine and worship of the Church of England. To that end he helped with the creation of the general synod to secure a representative government for the church, with legislation to allow modern experiments in worship, with the abolition of the historic subscription by clergy to the Thirty-nine Articles of 1571, and with the transfer of the power over forms of prayer and doctrine to the authorities of the church instead of the state. This involved the repeal of the Act of Uniformity and was the biggest change in English church government since the restoration of Charles II.

What made Ramsey world-famous was his visit in March 1966 to Pope Paul VI, who received him with all honour and gave him his own bishop's ring. He had undertaken the mission with a certain reluctance, but once it was decided threw himself into its spirit of affection and charity. In public opinion the visit became an important symbol of the happier relations between churches in the modern age and the new attitudes of the Roman Catholic Church after the second Vatican Council. Afterwards, as Ramsey travelled the world on his visits to the Anglican provinces, he was much in demand as a speaker on the unity of the churches. He had long had an understanding of the eastern Orthodox tradition of spirituality and valued much that was best in the western Catholic inheritance. He stated his views in numerous books, of which the last was *Be Still and Know* (1982). His essays and addresses he gathered into three volumes.

His part in the movement for Christian reunion made him, despite his Anglo-Catholic convictions, an eloquent advocate of the proposed plan for union between Anglicans and Methodists. He just failed (1969 and 1971) to persuade a sufficient majority of his church to accept the plan. This was a blow to his confidence in the wisdom and charity of the representatives, to whom he was engaged in transferring authority from Parliament.

One strength of the Church of England had lain historically in its links, unconfessed, with the more tolerant sides of the Conservative party. Ramsey, however, swung away and became a Liberal advocate in the House of Lords, causing much criticism. He was accused of sanctioning modern services which lost the beauties of a beloved Prayer Book; of being kind to homosexuals; of being friendly to an open policy of immigration; of not denouncing the bishop of Hong Kong when he ordained two women as priests; and, above all, of sanctioning in 1965 military action by Britain to stop Ian Smith from making a racialist state in Rhodesia. This last matter incurred the strong displeasure of the far right, and Ramsey did not bear their abuse without suffering.

The attribute which commanded a vast discipleship and affection was Ramsey's obvious devotion. Despite an enchanting sense of humour, he was not good on television and was accused of sounding like a bumbling old parson. But his faith, and experience of God, and prayerfulness, came over unmistakably to nearly everyone who met him. He was an incompetent administrator if he was bored by the subject—such subjects included finance, the structure of a parish system, and constitution-mongering. Yet, where the subject interested him, where it concerned religion or religious thought, or something he otherwise cared about, he was a very good administrator. At conducting a retreat he was inspiring and lovable, at hearing confessions he was wise, and when he celebrated a quiet little sacrament it lifted the souls of the people heavenward. He distrusted his pastoral colleagues when they needed distrust, but occasionally he trusted too much someone who had won his

confidence. His conversation was fascinating when he was interested; his silences were profound when he was not or when he wanted to think about God. Some who sat next to him at dinner, especially women, despaired of making him say anything. His hobby was brass-rubbing.

Ramsey was an honorary master of the bench (Inner Temple, 1962), president of the World Council of Churches (1961–8), a trustee of the British Museum (1963–9), and an honorary FBA (1983). As well as a number from overseas universities, he held ten honorary degrees from universities in Britain, including Cambridge (1957) and Oxford (1960). He was an honorary fellow of several Oxford and Cambridge colleges, was sworn of the Privy Council (1956), and became a life peer in 1974.

In 1942 he married Joan Alice Chetwode Hamilton and the marriage, though childless, was happy. She was the daughter of Lieutenant-Colonel Francis Alexander Chetwode Hamilton. She shared her husband's vocation and helped him through the worst of the silences, especially when he was a host.

In 1974 he retired first to Cuddesdon, where he hoped to teach at his old college, and then in 1977 to Durham, where he loved to renew his association with the cathedral. He still paid many visits abroad to lecture. Nashotah House, Wisconsin, a college for training priests, became almost a second home, for he felt there a spirit in devotion and theology that he valued highly. In 1986 Ramsey and his wife began to age and moved to a ground-floor flat in the archbishop's house at Bishopthorpe outside York, and then to St John's Home in Oxford, where Ramsey died, 23 April 1988.

[Owen Chadwick, *Michael Ramsey*, 1990; J. B. Simpson, *The Hundredth Archbishop of Canterbury*, 1962; Michael De-la-Noy, *A Day in the Life of God*, 1971, and *Michael Ramsey, a Portrait*, 1990; D. L. Edwards, *Leaders of the Church of England*, 2nd edn., 1978; Adrian Hastings, *A History of English Christianity 1920–1985*, 1986; personal knowledge.]

OWEN CHADWICK

RAMSEY, (Mary) Dorothea (Whiting) (1904–1989), social worker, was born 10 January 1904 in Kensington, London, the only child of Robert William Ramsey, solicitor, and his wife, Anna Whiting Brown, of Clarendon Road, in the Notting Hill area of London. Of well-to-do parents, she was educated at St Paul's Girls' School, London, and at Newnham College, Cambridge, where she obtained third classes in both parts of the classical tripos (1926 and 1928). She then taught Greek and Latin in London until the outbreak of World War II in 1939. It was as a voluntary worker with the Bristol Council of Social Service in the War Emergency Bureau that she became alerted to the social problems of elderly people, and, henceforward, her career concentrated on that area.

In 1941 she helped to form the Bristol old people's welfare committee and became its secretary. Just as wartime threw into vivid perspective the needs of deprived children when they were evacuated, so was the distress of many old people made more apparent. Dorothea Ramsey was one of the first to stress the value of residential care for older people, especially compared with the isolation of living, often in a feeble condition, at home or floundering in the large dormitories of the workhouse or the chronic sick wards of the former poor law and other hospitals. She was to the fore in establishing, in 1942, the West Town House residential care home in Bristol, a small, model facility, only the second of its kind in the country.

Returning to London, in 1943 she became a member of the advisory case sub-committee of social service, a body dealing with old people in distress and the mobilization of people likely to care for them. This had been set up not least as a consequence of the bombing, involving both injury and homelessness. This small-scale agency received 2,000 requests for help each year, and was much pressed to find adequate residential and allied amenities for its needy elderly clients. As early as 1940 the National Council of Social Service, aware of the manifest difficulties of many older people, had convened a group of representatives of the major voluntary and statutory providers. Out of this initiative grew the National Old People's Welfare Committee, its remit the campaigning for and provision of decent social services for impoverished and sick old people. Soon it was to abandon its lengthy title, redolent of 1940s officialdom, in favour of the more user-friendly Age Concern.

Dorothea Ramsey became secretary of this new charity in 1945, and she fought hard and vigorously to improve conditions for its elderly clientele. During her seven-year secretaryship— she resigned in 1952—the number of groups grew rapidly from eight regional or county and eighty local committees to sixty-two regional or county and 831 local committees. Given her experience, it is not surprising that she concentrated on residential care, persuading both local old people's welfare groups and local authorities to build and sustain homes. She urged the value of professional training, successfully pressed for chiropody services, and sought for older people a reasonable degree of dignity and independence. Because of the work of men and women like Dorothea Ramsey during the postwar decades, a less negative attitude towards ageing began to develop. She was one of the first to take a more personal and less paternalist stand on social provision, insisting—at a time when welfare was granted grudgingly in rather chilling vein—that

the criterion should be 'what you would like in similar circumstances'. Her pioneering work led to recognition overseas, particularly in the USA, which she toured with a Smith–Mundt scholarship in 1952.

On retirement to the Lake District, she devoted herself to what had been a lifelong affection for music—she had studied the flute under Gustav *Holst as a girl—and she applied her considerable administrative skills to the furtherance of orchestral and choral activity in Cumbria. She also played in and became chairman of the Cumberland Symphony Orchestra. Severe eye problems, arthritis, and diabetes constrained her life over thirty years, but she bore these handicaps with admirable fortitude. She was dark, of medium height, with intelligent, bright looks, and penetrating eyes. A woman of committed conscience, if somewhat shy, she never married. In retirement she lived with a friend, Frances M. Birkett. She died in Keswick, Cumbria, 27 September 1989.

[Nesta Roberts, *Our Future Selves* (a history of Age Concern), 1970; *Independent*, 5 October 1989; interviews with colleagues.]   ERIC MIDWINTER

RATCLIFFE, John Ashworth (1902–1987), physicist, was born 12 December 1902 in Bacup, Lancashire, the elder son (there were no daughters) of Harry Heys Ratcliffe, partner in the stone-quarrying firm of Henry Heys & Co., and his wife Beatrice Alice, daughter of Richard Ashworth, founder of the firm of Mitchell, Ashworth, Stansfield & Co., felt manufacturers. He attended Giggleswick School, where he acquired a real interest in mathematics and science, and particularly physics. In 1921 he went to Sidney Sussex College, Cambridge, on a scholarship and obtained first classes in both parts of the natural sciences tripos (1923 and 1924).

In June 1924 he started research on radio wave propagation under (Sir) Edward *Appleton. His interest in this subject came through hearing Appleton's lecture course on 'Electrical Oscillations and Radio Telegraphy'. In 1927 he was elected a fellow of Sidney Sussex College (honorary fellow, 1962) and appointed a university demonstrator in the Cavendish Laboratory. He was promoted to lecturer (1933) and to reader in physics (1947). He played a major part in the organization of the teaching in the Cavendish. He enjoyed lecturing and had the highest reputation for clarity of presentation. His books—such as *Sun, Earth and Radio* (1970) and *An Introduction to the Ionosphere and Magnetosphere* (1972)— and papers are models of clear exposition and many of his students would say that in the use of English for scientific explanations he surpassed all others.

He became head of a group in the Cavendish Laboratory known as the radio ionosphere research group. Upgoing radio waves can be reflected back to earth by ionized regions of the upper atmosphere, once known as the 'Heaviside layer' but later called the 'ionosphere'. Ratcliffe had helped with experiments by Appleton and M. A. F. Barnett that established the existence of the reflecting layers and his research group was now concerned with studying how the radio waves were reflected, and how the ionized layers were formed. This work continued until 1939.

During World War II Ratcliffe was a member of the Air Ministry Research Establishment, which was later known as the TRE (Telecommunications Research Establishment). At first he was head of a group concerned with a new type of ground radar equipment, called CHL, for detecting low-flying aircraft that could be missed by the existing chain of radar stations. In September 1940 he moved to Petersham, Surrey, and there organized the AA Radio School, whose object was to train scientists to keep the anti-aircraft radars working on the gun sites, particularly those round London. In August 1941 he returned to TRE to become head of a new organization, later known as TRE Development Services, which tackled the problem of taking radar equipment that was new and untried and making it work in the field.

In 1945 he returned to the Cavendish Laboratory, where there were now better facilities. The work of the radio ionosphere group was resumed and expanded. (Sir) Martin *Ryle and some others from TRE joined the group and decided to follow up the discovery of radio emission from the sun, using techniques and skills derived from their work on radar. Thus the radio group divided into two sections, radio ionosphere under Ratcliffe and radio astronomy under Ryle, with Ratcliffe in overall charge. Both sections flourished and became internationally famous. Ratcliffe was elected a fellow of the Royal Society in 1951. It was through him, more than any other person, that the new subject ionospheric physics was launched as a major branch of science.

In 1960 he left Cambridge to take up the posts of director of radio research in the Department of Scientific and Industrial Research, and director of the Radio Research Station at Slough. The move gave him enlarged opportunities. Artificial satellites were then coming into use for studying the upper atmosphere and beyond it. This was part of the new subject of 'space physics'. In April 1965 the name of the station at Slough was changed to the Radio and Space Research Station.

Ratcliffe always carried a heavy load of administration. In Cambridge he served on numerous boards and committees. In 1954–5 he was a member of the council of the Royal Society and he served on several Royal Society committees. He was deeply interested in the advance of radio science as part of electrical engineering, and served on many committees of the Institution of Electrical Engineers, of which he became president in 1966–7. He accepted numerous other similar tasks. He retired in 1966 but remained active in many fields for another ten years. He was appointed OBE in 1947, CBE in 1959, and CB in 1965.

In 1930 he married Nora, daughter of Walter Disley, mill owner and manufacturer of blankets, of Waterfoot, Lancashire. They had two daughters, the younger of whom died in 1965. In 1937 they moved to a newly built house in Cambridge, which remained their home for most of the rest of his life. Nora's health declined and from about 1967 onwards Ratcliffe cared for her devotedly at home. She was moved to hospital in 1975 and died in 1977.

Ratcliffe was about six feet tall, with an upright stance and somewhat athletic appearance. He walked briskly and his speech, in conversation and in lecturing, was very clear, with a trace of a Lancashire accent. He had done some cross-country running and played fives and squash. From the age of seventy onwards he often joined groups of old school friends for walking in the hills. He suffered from asthma, which curtailed his activities in later years, and died at home in Cambridge 25 October 1987.

[K. G. Budden in *Biographical Memoirs of Fellows of the Royal Society*. vol. xxxiv, 1988; private information; personal knowledge.] K. G. BUDDEN

REED, Henry (1914–1986), poet and playwright, was born in Birmingham 22 February 1914, the elder child and only son of Henry Reed, master bricklayer and foreman in charge of forcing at Nocks Brickworks, and his wife, Mary Ann Ball. He was educated at King Edward VI Grammar School, Birmingham, where he specialized in classics. Since Greek was not taught, he taught himself, and went on to win the Temperley Latin prize and a scholarship to Birmingham University, gaining a first-class degree (1934) and an MA for a thesis on the novels of Thomas *Hardy (1936).

Like many other writers of the 1930s, he tried teaching and, again like most of them, hated it and left to make his way as a freelance writer and critic. In 1941 he was conscripted into the Royal Army Ordnance Corps, in which he served—'or rather *studied*', as he preferred to put it—until 1942 when, following a serious bout of pneumonia and a prolonged convalescence, he was transferred to the Government Code and Cipher School at Bletchley. At first employed as a cryptographer in the Italian section, he was subsequently moved to the Japanese section, where he learned the language and worked as a translator. In the evenings, he wrote much of his first radio play, *Moby Dick* (1947), and many of the poems later to be published in *A Map of Verona* (1946).

The most famous of these—indeed, the most famous English poem to emerge from World War II—derived from Reed's experience of basic training in the RAOC. A brilliant mimic, he would entertain his friends with a comic imitation of a sergeant instructing his recruits. After a few performances, he noticed that the words of the weapon-training instructor, couched in the style of the military manual, fell into certain rhythmic patterns which fascinated him and eventually provided the structure of 'Naming of Parts'. In this and two subsequent 'Lessons of the War', the military voice is wittily counterpointed by the inner voice—more civilized and still civilian—of a listening recruit with his mind on other matters. At approximately the same point in each of the first four stanzas, the recruit's attention wanders from the instructor's lesson in the unnatural art of handling a lethal weapon, back to the natural world: branches, blossom, Edenic life as opposed to death. The dialectical opposition of two voices, two views of a landscape associated with sexual desire, is a strategy refined in two remarkable poems of Reed's middle years: 'The Changeling', a brilliantly condensed (and disguised) autobiography, and 'The Auction Sale', a Forsterian or Hardyesque short story. Both deal with the loss of Eden, for which Reed, an unmarried, unhappy homosexual, would continue to search in vain. He came to associate the Great Good Place with Italy, the setting of some of his later poems, such as of his radio plays as 'Return to Naples' and *The Streets of Pompeii* (1971), and two fine verse plays about another poet whose work he was translating and with whom he identified strongly, Giacomo Leopardi.

In the mid-1950s Reed made a major liberating decision: he abandoned a projected biography of Hardy, which for years had burdened him with guilt like the Ancient Mariner's albatross. That failed quest, perhaps related to the failure of his earlier quest for lasting love, played out a dominant theme of his radio plays: from failure as a biographer, he turned to triumphant success in a radio play about a nervous young biographer, Herbert Reeve, engaged on just such a quest as he had himself abandoned. Reed's hero (whose name owes something to that of Herbert Read, the poet and critic, with whom he was tired of being confused) assembles a mass of conflicting testimony about his author, the novelist Richard Shewin. His witnesses include a waspish brother, his wife, two spinsters of uncertain virtue, and (the finest comic role he was to create for radio) the twelve-tone female composer Hilda Tablet.

The success of 'A Very Great Man Indeed' (1953) prompted six sequels, the best of them 'The Private Life of Hilda Tablet' (1954), in which Reeve is browbeaten into switching the subject of his biography from the dumb dead to the exuberantly vocal living female composer.

The modest income that Reed's work for radio brought him he supplemented with the still more modest rewards of book reviewing and translation. The reviewing was to result in a British Council booklet, *The Novel since 1939* (1946), and his published translations include Ugo Betti's *Three Plays* (1956) and *Crime on Goat Island* (1960), Honoré de Balzac's *Le Père Goriot* (1962) and *Eugénie Grandet* (1964), and Natalia Ginzburg's *The Advertisement* (1969). Several of his translations found their way into the theatre, and in the autumn of 1955 there were London premières of no fewer than three.

Reed's greatest imaginative investment, however, was in his poems, but as a perfectionist he could not bring himself to release what he must have recognized would be his last book until it was as good as he could make it, and it never was. Only with the posthumous publication of his *Collected Poems* (1991) would he take his rightful place 'among the English poets'. In his last years he became increasingly incapacitated and reclusive, but devoted friends never ceased to visit him in the London flat he continued to occupy in Upper Montagu Street, thanks to the generosity of a long-suffering landlady, until, removed to St Charles Hospital, Kensington, he died there 8 December 1986.

[Henry Reed, *Lessons of the War*, 1970, *The Streets of Pompeii and Other Plays for Radio*, 1971, *Hilda Tablet and Others, Four Pieces for Radio*, 1971, *Collected Poems*, ed. Jon Stallworthy, 1991.]   JON STALLWORTHY

REILLY, Paul, BARON REILLY (1912–1990), promoter of British modern design and director of the Design Council (formerly the Council of Industrial Design), was born 29 May 1912 in Dingle Bank, Toxteth, Liverpool, the third child and elder son of the family of four children, of which only one son and one daughter survived childhood, of (Sir) Charles Herbert *Reilly, professor of architecture at Liverpool University, and his wife, Dorothy Gladys, daughter of James Jerram Pratt, city merchant, of Highgate. His mother was a pupil of Henry *Tonks at the Slade School, but her career as a painter was cut short when she developed turberculosis soon after her marriage in 1904. Reilly was educated at Winchester College. He won an exhibition to Hertford College, Oxford, where he made lasting friendships, dabbled in left-wing politics, and left with a second class in philosophy, politics, and economics (1933). Although not really athletic, he was nimble and at Oxford gained a fencing half blue. He then spent the year 1933–4 at the

London School of Economics on a business administration course. He was always adept at making the best of unpropitious circumstances and his appointment, at a time of poor employment prospects, as a door-to-door salesman for the plywood firm Venesta (1934–6), brought him into contact with leading Modernist architects and clients.

With his innate verbal fluency and buoyant curiosity he was a born journalist. In 1936 he became assistant to the leader page editor of the *News Chronicle*. (Sir) Gerald *Barry, then editor, encouraged him to travel around Britain, with the photographer Barnett Saidman, reporting on buildings and design. He was promoted to features editor in 1940. After a *mouvementé* war, spent mainly in naval intelligence (he joined the Royal Armoured Corps in 1940 and was in the Royal Naval Volunteer Reserve from 1941 to 1946), he worked in New York on *Modern Plastics* magazine (1946). A chance meeting on the *Queen Elizabeth* returning home to England in 1948 with (Sir S.) Gordon *Russell, newly appointed director of the Council of Industrial Design, led to the offer of a job (1948) as public relations officer at the COID. The COID had been set up in wartime to 'promote by all practicable means the improvement of design in the products of British industry'. Reilly's aim was to raise consciousness of design standards in a public starved of visual stimulus in the years of austerity and rationing. He organized a series of design weeks in the provinces and drew on his journalistic experience to launch the COID's *Design* magazine. In the early 1950s his energies were focused on the Festival of Britain, an event to which his modernist proselytizing fervour and his liberal left attitudes were perfectly attuned.

The twelve years of double act between Russell, the craftsman–designer of integrity and vision, and the highly political, sophisticated Reilly were enormously successful for the COID. In 1956 the Design Centre in Haymarket, a selective exhibition through which the public could locate well designed products, was opened by the Duke of Edinburgh. Reilly was much involved in the setting up of annual Design Centre awards the next year, and was responsible for the introduction of what became the familiar triangular black-and-white label affixed to chosen products, the symbol of government approved design. His wily charm was useful in the COID's struggle to persuade corporate buyers, government and private, to make visually enterprising choices. He was the natural successor as director in 1960, Russell having retired in 1959.

Reilly faced serious underlying problems in the 1960s. In a sense the COID had done its job too thoroughly and commercial outlets began selecting products with more flair and catholicity

than the design committees at the COID. Moreover Reilly's own visual aesthetic, based on principles of functional fitness and truth to materials, was, in the more morally mobile 1960s, coming under threat. He identified the problem in an important article in the *Architectural Review* in 1967, 'The Challenge of Pop'. He subsequently shifted the COID sideways, concentrating on developing design in engineering at the expense of consumer education.

As an ambassador for British visual culture Reilly travelled widely on behalf of the Design Council (as the COID became in 1973) and the international crafts organizations: unlike many of his Modernist contemporaries he had great sympathy with the handmade product, and it was under his aegis that the craft advisory committee was set up in 1971. This committee burgeoned to become the Crafts Council. Although he played the power game with great skill and much enjoyment, he also delighted in the personal encounter and many young craftsmen and designers were spurred on by the warmth of his encouragement.

When he retired in 1977 he became a director of Conran Associates and chairman of the Conran Foundation Boilerhouse, precursor of the Design Museum. He received many awards, and honorary degrees from Loughborough (1977), Aston (1981), and Cranfield (1983). He became an honorary FRIBA in 1965, was knighted in 1967, and became an honorary doctor of the RCA in 1978. He was made a commander of the Royal Order of Vasa (Sweden) in 1961. He was delighted by his life peerage in 1978, regarding the House of Lords, where he sat on the crossbenches, until prevented by encroaching heart disease, as a glorified version of his old newspaper office: a place in which he would never feel unwanted or bored.

Reilly was small, twinkling, and benign enough to be mistaken for the archbishop of Canterbury, Michael *Ramsey, whom he much resembled. He was a great gossip and as eclectic a connoisseur of people as of things. His first marriage, in 1939, to the classical ballet dancer Pamela Wentworth Foster (daughter of Major Edward Bayntun Grove Foster, landowner, of Warmwell in Dorset and Clewer Manor in Berkshire), ended in divorce in 1952; their only child Victoria, a journalist, married the Czech artist-designer Daniel Spicka. In 1952 Reilly married his second wife, Annette Rose, daughter of Brigadier-General Clifton Inglis Stockwell; she had trained as a sculptor and became a fashion and design journalist and cookery correspondent on *The Times*. They had no children and lived and ate convivially in a South Kensington stuccoed terrace house, designed by George *Basevi, surrounded by the paintings, books, and objects of a lifetime's collecting. Reilly died 11 October 1990 in Kensington, London.

[Paul Reilly, *An Eye on Design* (autobiography), 1987; private information; personal knowledge.]

FIONA MACCARTHY

REVIE, Donald (1927–1989), footballer and football manager, was born 10 July 1927 in Middlesbrough, the youngest in the family of one son and twin daughters of Donald Revie, journeyman joiner, of Middlesbrough, and his wife, Margaret Emily Haston. His mother died when Revie was twelve. He was educated at Archibald Secondary Modern School, Middlesbrough, and left school at fourteen to become an apprentice bricklayer, before joining Leicester City Football Club in 1943. Hull City bought him for £20,000 in 1950.

Transferring to Manchester City in 1953, Revie reached his peak as a footballer in the mid-1950s, winning six England caps and being voted Footballer of the Year in 1955. Manchester City won the FA cup in 1956, using what became known as the 'Revie plan', with Revie, as centre forward, lying deep while feeding the ball to the other forwards and then moving through in the final stage, a tactic copied from the successful Hungarian team by the Manchester City manager.

Revie moved to Leeds United in 1958, after two years with Sunderland. At Leeds he was appointed manager in 1961, at a time when the club was struggling to avoid relegation to the third division. Revie not only avoided this, but brought Leeds to the top of the second division in 1964, and second to Manchester United in the first division in 1965, winning the League championship in 1969 with 67 points, the highest total in the history of the championship, and the FA cup in 1971. His ambitions for the club were not confined to the domestic scene, and in 1968 Leeds won the European Fairs cup, beating Ferencvaros 1–0, the first British club to win the cup. Despite these successes, Leeds had the reputation of being perpetual runners-up: they lost to Liverpool in the 1965 FA Cup Final, came second in the League championship in 1965, 1966, and 1967, lost to Chelsea in the FA Cup Final in 1967, were runners-up to Arsenal in the League championship in 1971, and lost to second-division Sunderland in the 1972 FA Cup Final. Revie never achieved his ambition for Leeds to win the European cup.

However, encouraged by the British media, which declared Leeds to have the best side in the world at the beginning of the 1969–70 season, Revie was confident of a treble victory: the European cup, the FA cup, and the League championship. In the end all three eluded Leeds, partly as a result of a pile-up of fixtures, compounded by injuries. In 1974, after Leeds United had won the League championship, remaining undefeated for the first 29 games of the season, Revie resigned to take up the position of England team manager, following the sacking of Sir Alf *Ramsey after England had failed to qualify for the 1974 World Cup Finals.

After a successful first season as the England manager, with the team undefeated after nine internationals, Revie encountered a set-back when England was eliminated from the European championship early in the 1975–6 season. He was faced with the task of building an international side with players from many different clubs, and it was hard to achieve the family atmosphere that had been so successful at Leeds. Moreover, his difficult relationship with Alan Hardaker, secretary of the Football League, made his task harder. While Revie was manager, England won 14 out of 29 matches, with 7 defeats and 8 draws. The poor results were attributed to the uncertainty and lack of continuity caused by frequent team changes rather than to the lack of outstanding players. He used 52 players in the 29 games, awarding 29 new caps, and he only once fielded an unchanged side. Morale sagged when England lost 2–0 to Italy in a World cup qualifying match in November 1976, and the press began to forecast England's elimination from the competition and Revie's dismissal.

In July 1977 the *Daily Mail*, to which Revie had sold his story, revealed that he had been in secret negotiations with the United Arab Emirates while the England team had been playing World cup qualifying matches in South America, had accepted the post of team manager to the UAE for four years at £60,000 a year, and had resigned from his England job. This led the Football Association to ban him from English football for ten years. Revie successfully appealed against the ban in the High Court in November 1979, on the grounds that the head of the tribunal, Sir Harold *Thompson, chairman of the Football Association, was biased. But the judge made it clear that it was still felt that Revie's conduct in leaving England so abruptly had brought English football into disrepute. He became manager of Al Nasr Football Club in 1980, and moved to the National Football Club, Cairo, in 1984.

At Leeds, Revie had aimed to make the club as famous as Real Madrid. By the time he left in 1974 some argued that Leeds was the greatest club side of all time, and that his achievements lay there, and not in his spell as England manager. He transformed Leeds from a club in danger of relegation into a club aiming at, and achieving, major honours at home and abroad.

Revie was appointed OBE in 1970, and was voted Manager of the Year in 1969, 1970, and

1972. Always well dressed, he had the pugnacious features of a boxer. He was very superstitious, and had a lucky blue suit, which he always wore on match days. In 1949 he married Elsie May Leonard, primary-school teacher, daughter of Thomas Grosett Duncan, professional footballer, and niece of the Leicester City manager, John Duncan. They had one son and one daughter. Revie died 26 May 1989 in Murrayfield Private Hospital, Edinburgh, of motor neurone disease.

[Donald Revie, *Soccer's Happy Wanderer*, 1955; Eric Thornton, *Leeds United and Don Revie*, 1970; Andrew Mourant, *Don Revie, Portrait of a Footballing Enigma*, 1990; Johnny Rogan, *The Football Managers*, 1989; *Independent*, 27 May 1989.]   ANNE PIMLOTT BAKER

RICHARDS, SIR Gordon (1904–1986), jockey and racehorse trainer, was born 5 May 1904 in Ivy Row at Donnington Wood, a district of Oakengates, Shropshire, the fourth child and third son of the eight surviving children (four died) of Nathan Richards, coalminer, and his wife Elizabeth, a former dressmaker, daughter of William Dean, miner and lay preacher. He was given a strict Methodist upbringing, and educated at the Infant School at Donnington Wood. In 1917 he became a junior clerk in the warehouse of the Lilleshall engineering works, Oakengates. Finding the work monotonous, he answered a newspaper advertisement for an apprentice to Martin Hartigan, who had the Foxhill stable near Swindon, Wiltshire, and on New Year's day 1920 left home for the first time to go to Foxhill.

Short, stocky, and very strong for his weight, he had the ideal physique for a jockey. He had dark brown eyes and a thick shock of black hair, which gave him the nickname of 'Moppy'. He weighed out at six stone nine pounds for his first mount in public on Clock-Work at Lingfield on 16 October 1920, and rode his first winner on Gay Lord at Leicester on 13 March 1921, but it was not until he had ridden forty-nine winners, and lost his apprentice allowance, in 1923, that his career got under way.

After coming out of his apprenticeship in 1924, he was first jockey to Captain Thomas Hogg's stable at Russley Park, Wiltshire, in 1925, and became champion jockey by winning 118 races. By the outset of 1926 his career was put in jeopardy by the diagnosis of a tubercular lung after he had ridden just five more winners, and he spent the rest of the year in a sanatorium. In the 1927 season he regained the championship with 164 winners. The first claim on his services in 1928 was held by the shipping magnate the first Baron Glanely, to whom Captain Hogg had become private trainer at Newmarket. Richards obtained his first classic successes in 1930 by winning the Oaks on Rose of England and the St

Leger on Singapore for Lord Glanely, but he narrowly lost the championship. After landing the Manchester November handicap on Lord Glanely's Glorious Devon, on the final day he had ridden one more winner than Freddie Fox, but Fox won the fourth and fifth races to be champion with 129 successes.

Richards was champion again with 141 winners in 1931, during which the Beckhampton trainer Fred Darling offered a substantial sum for first claim on him. With typical loyalty, he first asked Lord Glanely to match the offer, but on Glanely pleading poverty, he became first jockey to the Beckhampton stable. Always immensely popular with the public, Richards was a national hero in 1933, as he bid to break the seasonal record of 246 winners established by Frederick *Archer in 1885. After eleven consecutive successes at Chepstow in October, he rode his 247th winner on Golden King at Liverpool on 8 November, and finished the season with 259 winners. In 1934 he rode Easton to be second in the Derby, a race he was yet to win, and in 1936 may have been unlucky not to win it on the Aga Khan's Taj Akbar, who was badly hampered before being runner-up to the Aga Khan's second string Mahmoud. By 1938 his bad luck in the Derby was proverbial. That year Darling ran both Pasch, on whom Richards had won the Two Thousand Guineas, and the recent French importation Bois Roussel. Richards elected to ride Pasch, and was third to Bois Roussel.

As his tubercular record made him ineligible to serve in the armed forces, Richards continued to ride during World War II, but, after breaking a leg at Salisbury in May 1941, he missed the remainder of that season and lost the championship for the third time. In 1942 he wore the colours of King *George VI when winning substitute races for the One Thousand Guineas, Oaks, and St Leger on Sun Chariot. He also won a substitute Two Thousand Guineas for the king on Big Game, and was champion again. In 1943 he surpassed Archer's career total of 2,748 winners on Scotch Mist at Windsor, and was champion for the sixteenth time. After winning the Two Thousand Guineas by an extraordinarily easy eight lengths on that great miler Tudor Minstrel in 1947, Richards seemed certain to win the Derby at last. Heavily backed by the public, Tudor Minstrel started hot favourite, but failed to stay the course and finished only fourth. Champion for the twentieth time in 1947, Richard broke his own record of 1933 by riding 269 winners. After the retirement of Fred Darling at the end of that season, the Beckhampton stable continued to hold first claim on him when it was taken over by (Sir) Noel *Murless. The best horse he rode for Murless was the brilliant grey sprinter Abernant, on whom he won the Nunthorpe Stakes at York in 1949 and 1950.

The knighthood that Richards received in the coronation honours in 1953 was as much in recognition of his exemplary integrity as of his professional achievement. A few days after the queen had conferred it upon him, he won the Derby at his twenty-eighth and final attempt by riding Sir Victor Sassoon's Pinza to beat the queen's colt Aureole. A little over a year later, Richards had to retire from riding after breaking his pelvis and four ribs when he was thrown by Abergeldie in the paddock at Sandown Park on 10 July 1954.

With his body slewed round to the left, so that his weight was unevenly distributed as he rode his powerful finish, Richards had a most unorthodox style. All the same, horses ran as straight as a die for him. From 21,843 mounts, he rode 4,870 winners and was champion jockey twenty-six times.

Subsequently he trained at Beckhampton, Ogbourne Maisey, and finally Whitsbury, Hampshire. Although his success was not comparable to that which he had enjoyed as a jockey, he won a number of valuable races, notably the Middle Park Stakes with Pipe of Peace, who was to be third in the Derby in 1956, and the Champion stakes with Reform in 1967. Richards also managed the horses of Lady Beaverbrook and (Sir) Michael Sobell. He closed his stable in 1970. He was elected an honorary member of the Jockey Club the same year.

On 1 March 1928 Richards married Margery Gladys (died 1982), daughter of Thomas David Winckle, railway carriage fitter. They had two sons and a daughter. A third son, the daughter's twin, lived only a few hours. Richards died of a heart attack at his home at Kintbury, Berkshire, 10 November 1986.

[Sir Gordon Richards, *My Story*, 1955; Michael Seth-Smith, *Knight of the Turf*, 1980; *Sporting Life*, 11 November 1986; personal knowledge.]

RICHARD ONSLOW

RICHES, SIR Eric William (1897–1987), urological surgeon, was born 29 July 1897 in Alford, Lincolnshire, the second of three children and elder son of William Riches, schoolmaster, and his wife, Kate Rowbotham. He was educated at St Dunstan's School, Alford, and Queen Elizabeth Grammar School, Alford, before securing an entrance scholarship to Christ's Hospital, Horsham, where he won a number of prizes. After a further entrance scholarship to the Middlesex Hospital in 1915, he deferred his admission to join the army, serving first in the 10th Lincoln and then the 11th Suffolk regiments, in France and Flanders. Awarded the MC in 1917, he was demobilized in 1919 with the rank of captain and entered medical school, where he won a second-year exhibition, the Lyell gold medal in surgery, and the senior Broderip scholarship. He also played golf and rugby for the Middlesex Hospital. He obtained his MB, BS and MRCS, LRCP (both 1925), and his MS and FRCS (both 1927).

In 1925 he became surgical registrar to A. S. Blundell Bankart and Alfred (later Baron) *Webb-Johnson, before his appointment to the surgical staff of the Middlesex in 1930. He began primarily as a general surgeon, with a special interest in urology, and was also appointed to the Hospital of St John and St Elizabeth (before 1930) and to St Andrew's, Dollis Hill. He was consultant urologist to the army and to the Royal Masonic Hospital, and consulting surgeon to the Ministry of Pensions Spinal Injuries Centre.

Riches was a Hunterian professor at the Royal College of Surgeons in 1938, and both Hunterian professor and Jacksonian prizeman in 1942. He served six years on its court of examiners (1940–6) and sixteen years on the council, being vice-president in 1961–2. He was successively Bradshaw lecturer, Arnott demonstrator, and Gordon-Taylor lecturer. He developed a number of his own specialist surgical instruments and for many years acted as curator of historic surgical instruments at the RCS.

Riches was a superb surgical technician and innovator. He was a most energetic man who took an enthusiastic interest in teaching his students and training young surgeons. He published many urological papers and wrote or contributed to several books, including *Modern Trends in Urology* (1953, 1960, and 1969) and *Tumours of the Kidney and Ureter* (1964). He was also a lively and effective speaker at the many societies he supported, being a founder member of council of the British Association of Urological Surgeons, its president in 1951, and St Peter's medallist (1964), president and Lettsomian lecturer (1958) of the Medical Society of London, and president and orator (1967) of the Hunterian Society. At the Royal Society of Medicine, of which he became an honorary fellow in 1966, he was a vice-president and honorary librarian, and had been president of its urological, surgical, and clinical sections. He was chairman of the editorial committee and treasurer of the *British Journal of Urology*. His reputation was also international, for he was elected to the American Association of Genito-Urinary Surgeons in 1953, was vice-president of the International Society of Urology in 1961, and was president at that society's thirteenth congress in London in 1964. Riches retained a great love for his old school, Christ's Hospital, of which he became a governor in 1958 and a member of the council of almoners in 1960. He was knighted in 1958.

Riches, who went bald early, was a modest man of average height, with a friendly smile. He built up a large and highly successful private practice, which he continued for too many years after his retirement in 1962: indeed, he eventually had to be given very firm encouragement to stop operating. He included among his hobbies photography, golf, and music. In sad contrast to his lively character and exuberance in earlier times, he survived for the last few years of his life in poor and deteriorating health.

In 1928 he married Annie Margaret Sylvia, a doctor in general practice, daughter of Alexander Theodore Brand, medical practitioner, of Driffield, Yorkshire. They had two daughters, one of whom, Anne Riches, entered general medical practice. After the death of his first wife in 1952 he married in 1954 (Susan Elizabeth) Ann, a nurse at the Middlesex Hospital, daughter of Lieutenant-Colonel Leslie Holdsworth Kitton, regular army officer, of Wye, near Ashford, Kent. They had one daughter. Riches died 8 November 1987 at Thames Bank Nursing Home, Goring, Oxfordshire.

[Records of Royal College of Surgeons, London; *British Medical Journal*, vol. ccxcv, 1987, p. 1492; *Lancet*, vol. ii, 1987, p. 1347; *The Times*, 10 November 1987; personal knowledge.]   REGINALD MURLEY

ROBERTHALL, BARON (1901–1988), economist. [See HALL, ROBERT LOWE.]

ROBERTS, Colin Henderson (1909–1990), classical scholar and publisher, was born 8 June 1909 in Queen Elizabeth Walk, Stoke Newington, the second son and second of five children (four sons and one daughter) of Robert Lewis Roberts, the head of a family building firm founded in the previous generation, and his wife, Muriel Grace Henderson. The family had strong literary and clerical connections. Colin's elder brother, Brian (1906–1988), had a distinguished career in journalism, and was editor of the *Sunday Telegraph* (1961–76); like Colin, he ended his days as an honorary fellow of St John's College, Oxford. Colin followed Brian to Merchant Taylors' School and to St John's. At school he distinguished himself as a scholar (and sometimes on the stage, notably as Cassandra in Aeschylus' *Agamemnon*), and his university career followed its expected course, with first classes in both classical honour moderations and *literae humaniores* (1931), and a Craven fellowship (1932–4). His classics tutors, J. U. Powell and F. W. Hall, had both been interested in the discoveries of papyrology and in the history of the book in ancient times. This was the subject to which Roberts devoted himself. He took part in excavations in Egypt (Karanis) under the auspices of the University of Michigan in 1932–3 and 1933–4; he studied also with W. Schubart in Berlin; and in 1935–6 published important biblical papyri from the John Rylands Library. During all this period he was first a junior, then a senior research fellow of St John's.

World War II interrupted his studies, and, like many scholars of that time, he spent five years in intelligence work in London and at Bletchley. He returned to St John's in 1946 as fellow and tutor in classics. In 1947 he became a fellow of the British Academy, and he played an active part in the Academy's affairs, serving as foreign secretary (1960–9), until 1979, when its failure to expel Anthony *Blunt led him, with others, to resign his fellowship. In 1948 he became reader in documentary papyrology at Oxford, and in 1951–2 he spent a year at the Institute of Advanced Study at Princeton. His research in these years centred round the publication of the Antinoopolis papyri; but in 1955 he published a long essay, 'The Codex' (*Proceedings of the British Academy*, vol. xl), which gave a pioneering account of the most important development in book production before the invention of printing, namely the replacement of the papyrus roll by 'a collection of sheets, folded or fastened together at the back or spine, and usually protected by covers', in other words the book as we know it. With his close friend, T. C. Skeat, he revised and enlarged this essay in 1983.

Having rejected an opportunity to become professor of Greek at Edinburgh, in 1954 he gave up, as it seemed, his scholarly career to succeed (Sir) A. L. P. *Norrington as secretary to the delegates of the Oxford University Press (he had been a delegate since 1946). He thus had charge of a great publishing house for twenty years, in a time of much change and some difficulty. It was natural that he should have felt most deeply involved in the great enterprises in classical studies and theology which were a special excellence of the Press: the completion of *A Patristic Greek Lexicon* by Professor G. W. H. *Lampe, the continuation of E. A. Lowe's *Codices Latini Antiquiores*, the *Oxford Latin Dictionary* under Peter Glare, and above all the *New English Bible*. But his remarkable capacity for detail and rapid analysis enabled him to exercise his great administrative ability over a wide range of the Press's affairs, although they may have also led him to be less interested in systematic delegation than circumstances came to require. In the latter years of his tenure, the organization of the Press became seriously inappropriate to the increased scale of its operations. It comprised two separate businesses, one in Oxford, which undertook the learned publishing, and the other in London, which had responsibility for all distribution and marketing and for overseas operations other than those in New York. As the financial situation deteriorated, radical reform became necessary. Roberts was energetically engaged in his later years with the planning, which was to involve the transfer of the whole business to the Oxford site.

On his retirement in 1974, he once again became a senior research fellow of St John's, proposing to the college to work on 'Manuscript, Society, and Belief in Early Christian Egypt'. The book, given as the British Academy Schweich lectures, appeared in 1979. It demonstrates in its close argument Roberts's command of verbal scholarship, his historical insight (he viewed scholarship as a means to the understanding of the past, not as an end in itself), and his profound concern, grounded in his own spirituality, with the Christian tradition. After a time, he and his wife retired to Broadwindsor in west Dorset, where they enjoyed country life, animals, the village, and the church. As a lay reader (1982–5), he acquired a reputation for the excellence of his sermons.

Roberts was a notably handsome young man—to a famous refugee scholar in the 1930s he seemed the very type of Oxford youth—and he retained his slim and elegant physique until a car accident not long before he died left him bent and shrunken. He was a man whose gentle manners, immaculate courtesy, and great kindness (especially to the disadvantaged or insecure) sometimes concealed, but could never diminish, the sharpness of vision, strong sense of duty, and tireless energy with which he pursued his aims, whether in scholarship or in the wide world. He was appointed CBE in 1973.

In 1947 he married Alison Muriel, daughter of Reginald Haynes Barrow, classical scholar and inspector of schools. They had one daughter. Roberts died in Broadwindsor 11 February 1990.

[Merchant Taylors' School and St John's College records; D. A. F. M. Russell and P. J. Parsons in *Proceedings of the British Academy*, vol. lxxxiv, 1993; private information; personal knowledge.]

D. A. RUSSELL

ROBERTSON, ALAN (1920–1989), geneticist, was born 21 February 1920 in Preston, the only surviving child (he had one sister who died of tuberculosis before he was born) of John Mouat Robertson, Post Office signals engineer, of Liverpool, and his first wife Annie, daughter of William Grace, farmer, of Halewood, near Liverpool. His mother died soon after his birth, and he was brought up by his aunt, Bessie Grace, on the family farm. He obtained a scholarship to the Liverpool Institute, where he shone at all subjects, including languages and mathematics. From there he won a major entrance scholarship in natural sciences to Gonville and Caius College, Cambridge, and read chemistry. He was captain of the college soccer team and a keen tennis player, as he was to remain throughout his life. He obtained a second class (division I) in part ii of the natural sciences tripos in 1940 (he did not take part i).

He became a research student in physical chemistry under (Sir) E. K. *Rideal, working and publishing on combustion of hydrocarbons; but he did not complete his Ph.D., for in 1943 he moved into operational research on anti-shipping strikes with Coastal Command. His unit was led by C. H. *Waddington, who recognized Robertson's talents and, after the war, invited him in 1946 to join the new National Animal Breeding and Genetics Research Organization (NABGRO), initially in Hendon, and apply operational research methods to animal breeding. Thus Robertson became an animal geneticist without formal training, although with a farming background and mathematical talent. To gain experience he spent nine months with S. Wright and J. L. Lush in the USA.

Before this visit, he had married in 1947 Margaret Sidney ('Meg'), daughter of Maurice Bernheim, gem merchant. On their return they went to Edinburgh, where NABGRO had transferred. The Robertsons had two sons and a daughter and, at 47 Braid Road, were excellent hosts to colleagues, students, and visiting scientists. Robertson was a happy family man, with sport, gardening, and reading his main diversions.

He transferred to the Agricultural Research Council unit of animal genetics, based with the university department under Waddington in the Institute of Animal Genetics at King's Buildings, in which Robertson spent the rest of his career. The group there was the largest and strongest group of British geneticists and included eight in the 1950s who became fellows of the Royal Society. Robertson started work on dairy cattle improvement, initially with J. M. Rendel, and saw the potential role of artificial insemination in genetic improvement programmes. He made major contributions to predictions of rates of genetic progress and to statistical methods needed to evaluate the genetic merit of individual sires for milk production from records of daughters spread unequally over many herds, his contemporary comparison method being used worldwide. With students and colleagues he obtained estimates of the parameters and devised methods for optimizing breeding programmes. He obtained his D.Sc. (Edinburgh) in 1951.

Although his research on dairy cattle breeding established Robertson on the international stage, it was only part of his work. He was interested and effective over a broad range of quantitative genetics (the inheritance and evolution of continuous characters) and was unique in having the highest standing both in animal breeding and in evolutionary biology. Much of the research was mathematical, but he always had his own *Drosophila* experiments in progress and supervised the work of many students.

Among questions which concerned him was how variation was maintained in populations, and he studied particularly the roles of mutation and of stabilizing selection. He made original contributions to the theory of genetic change in small populations and introduced a theory of limits to artificial selection, which was a combination of mathematical insight, quantitative genetic principles, and practical context, of which only he was capable. In a paper on dairy cattle breeding he derived what has become known as the secondary theorem of natural selection. For many years, with the major results published near the time of his death, he worked on estimating the number and size of effects of genes influencing quantitative traits, which soon afterwards became a major research topic. He was far-sighted, appreciating the importance of molecular genetics to his field and writing with insight on the problems of exploiting transgenic methods in animal improvement.

Throughout he worked with a small group, took on no administrative position or trappings of power, and remained informal, approachable, and 'Alan' to all. His influence was through his papers, as a scientific referee, by personal contact (particularly in his famous morning coffee group), as a conference speaker and organizer, and as an example of efficient (if not organized) hard work. Although on the research staff, he lectured to generations of students for the diploma in animal genetics (breeding). He never wrote a book, but greatly influenced those of others who did. His achievements were recognized by an OBE (1965), election as a fellow of the Royal Society (1964) and the US National Academy of Sciences (1979), an honorary professorship at Edinburgh University (1967), and four honorary degrees (Stuttgart-Hohenheim 1968, Agricultural University of Norway 1984, Danish Agricultural University 1986, and Liège 1986).

Robertson was of above average height and of slim build, with a round face, dark brown hair, and a deep brow. He was very approachable, but had little small talk; he would enter an argument only with significant comments. He retired in 1985, but retained an office, although his faculties diminished from around that time. He died in the Royal Edinburgh Hospital 25 April 1989.

[W. G. Hill in *Biographical Memoirs of Fellows of the Royal Society*, vol. xxxvi, 1990; personal knowledge.]

WILLIAM G. HILL

ROBERTSON, SIR Alexander (1908–1990), veterinary academic and administrator, was born in Aberdeen 3 February 1908, the youngest of three children and second son of Alexander Robertson, private chauffeur, and his wife, Barbara Minty Strath. His two older siblings died in early infancy. His early childhood was spent in the neighbourhood of Stonehaven. He went to school in the village of Netherby and then attended Mackie Academy, Stonehaven. In 1926 he entered Aberdeen University, where he took an MA in 1929 and B.Sc. in 1930, majoring in chemistry. He won the Robbie scholarship for distinction in chemistry in 1928 and 1929. An indication of his fortitude and energy, so characteristic of his adult life, was the daily cycle ride of twenty miles to classes in Aberdeen.

In 1930 he entered the Royal (Dick) Veterinary College in Edinburgh, with a colonial office veterinary scholarship. He gained distinctions and prizes, and was admitted to membership of the Royal College of Veterinary Surgeons in 1934 with a Fitzwygram prize. As a veterinarian of great promise, he began an academic career as a demonstrator in anatomy at the Royal Dick, but within two months he joined the Ministry of Agriculture and Fisheries as a field inspector (1935–7). He moved to the veterinary research laboratories at Weybridge, where he worked on tuberculin testing and the development of a vaccine for bovine tuberculosis. In 1937 he returned to the Royal Dick as a lecturer in physiology, and was promoted to senior lecturer the following year. During the war years the teaching load was doubled by the inclusion of medical and dental students from the Royal College of Surgeons (Edinburgh). One account of this period describes Robertson providing blackboard illustrations to an overflow part of the class, while the rest were lectured in the adjoining theatre, the lecture being relayed to Robertson's group.

His interests proved wider than could be satisfied in physiology and in 1944 he secured the vacant chair of hygiene, dietetics, and animal husbandry, which became the William Dick chair in 1951, when the veterinary college was incorporated into the University of Edinburgh. In 1957 he was appointed director of the university's veterinary school, a post he held until the school became a faculty of the university and he was elected dean (1964–70). His conviction that veterinary preventive medicine, both at home and abroad, was a neglected but important field was evinced by the way he reorganized classes to reflect his views, and also by his revival of postgraduate diplomas in veterinary state medicine and some years later in tropical veterinary medicine. His overseas interests now began to proliferate, and he toured British African colonies and the dominions.

At the same time he was active in veterinary professional affairs, serving as president of the British Veterinary Association in 1954–5, and as councillor (1957–78), representing the University of Edinburgh, and later treasurer (1964–7) and then president (1968–9) of the Royal College of Veterinary Surgeons. These non-curricular activities made Robertson a well-known figure in veterinary and related public fields and he was called on to serve on numerous government bodies and to undertake state-supported activities. These included being on the governing bodies of the Animal Virus Research Institute at Pirbright (1954–62) and of the Rowett Research Institute (1962–77), and membership of the research advisory committee of the Meat and Livestock Commission (1969–73) and of the East African Natural Resources Research Council (1963–78). He also found time to edit the *International Encyclopaedia of Veterinary Medicine* (1966).

His intellect and capacity for hard work underlay the many and varied contributions he made to the veterinary profession, but it did not make him an easy colleague for those of his contemporaries who crossed him. At the same time he could be generous with help and advice to subordinates, while still expecting them to make good use of the opportunities he could provide. His lasting academic memorial is the University of Edinburgh Centre for Tropical Veterinary Medicine, which he persuaded the Ministry of Overseas Development to fund, and where he held the foundation chair from 1971 until his retirement in 1978. The CTVM provided both postgraduate teaching and research for hundreds of overseas veterinarians as well as on-site advice to fledgling overseas veterinary institutes in tropical countries. Robertson was appointed CBE in 1963 and knighted in 1970. He had honorary degrees from Aberdeen (LL D, 1971) and Melbourne (DVSc., 1973). Among his fellowships was that of the Royal Society of Edinburgh (1945). He was honorary FRCVS (1970) and an honorary member of the World Veterinary Association (1975).

In 1936 he married Janet (died 1988), daughter of John McKinlay, master butcher; they had two daughters. Robertson died 5 September 1990 at his home in Edinburgh.

[Private information; personal knowledge.]

AINSLEY IGGO

ROBERTSON, (Florence) Marjorie (1904–1986), stage and film actress, and film producer. [See NEAGLE, DAME ANNA.]

ROBERTSON, John Monteath (1900–1989), chemical crystallographer, was born 24 July 1900 at Nether Fordun, Auchterarder, Perthshire, the younger son and youngest of three children of William Robertson, farmer, and his second wife, Jane Monteath. He was educated in Auchterarder and at Perth Academy. Before he went to the Academy he was disturbed by the death of his mother, to whom he was much attached, and by his father's increasing blindness; in 1917 he was obliged to leave school in order to manage the farm. He liked the work, but he had always

been deeply interested in science, and when his brother returned from the war to take charge he turned to private study to qualify for entry to the University of Glasgow. In his first year (1919–20) he studied a miscellany of subjects which gained him a scholarship and also helped towards his later MA degree (1925). He then concentrated on pure science, obtaining his B.Sc., with special distinction in chemistry, in 1923. Under the supervision of G. G. *Henderson he went on to study structural relationships in sesquiterpenes, obtaining his Ph.D. in 1926.

In Henderson's laboratory Robertson acquired an enthusiasm for the study of molecular structure, but he foresaw that the methods then used by organic chemists would be largely supplanted by X-ray crystallography. With a £250 Carnegie post-doctoral fellowship, he therefore went to the Royal Institution to study with Sir W. H. *Bragg, the director, and for the rest of his life he devoted himself to X-ray crystallography. With a break (1928–30), during which he held a Commonwealth fellowship at the University of Michigan, Ann Arbor, sharing a flat with (Sir) Dick White, the future head of MI5, he remained at the Royal Institution until 1939, when he went to the University of Sheffield as a senior lecturer in physical chemistry. In 1941 he became scientific adviser (chemical) to Bomber Command and in 1942 honorary scientific adviser to the Royal Air Force. He returned to the University of Glasgow in 1942 as Gardiner professor of chemistry and (from 1955) director of the chemical laboratories. He retired with the title of emeritus professor in 1970.

At the Royal Institution in 1926 Robertson found himself in a group of able young people devoted to one broad objective, the elucidation of the structures of organic molecules by the new methods. The teachers from whom he learned his craft, W. T. *Astbury, J. D. *Bernal, and (Dame) Kathleen *Lonsdale, were about his own age; the whole atmosphere was one of youthful optimism, shared indeed by W. H. Bragg, who at that time was in his sixties. By the early 1930s Robertson's studies, together with those of Lonsdale and others, had shown that aromatic compounds were indeed, as the organic chemists had deduced earlier, based on the flat symmetrical C_6 hexagon, but the methodology was not yet adequate to enable crystallographers to deal successfully with molecules of unknown structure containing many atoms. The major obstacle (the 'phase problem') was that the experiments measure the *intensities* of the X-ray reflections, whereas the calculation of the atomic positions requires their *amplitudes*, the derivation of which from the intensities involves an ambiguity similar to, but more complex than, the extraction of a square root, which may be positive or negative.

Robertson's great achievement was to discover a method, very widely applicable, for circumventing the phase problem. In 1934 (Sir) R. P. *Linstead synthesized a new class of crystalline compounds, the phthalocyanines, of unknown structure. Robertson examined them and was at first discouraged by their complexity, but he then noticed that some of the compounds were isomorphous; he realized that, by comparing the reflections from two isomorphous substances differing only in having (say) a platinum atom instead of a copper atom, he could ascertain the phases of a sufficient number of reflections to determine the structure. Thus, for the first time, a previously unknown structure was elucidated completely and isomorphous substitution and heavy atom insertion entered the chemical crystallographer's armoury—immensely powerful methods, which in due course led to the unravelling of protein structures of the greatest complexity.

Robertson's heart was in his research laboratory, and he conscientiously organized the training of research students. The result was over 200 papers on the structures of a vast range of organic substances, one of the most impressive contributions to knowledge to come from any chemical laboratory in the middle of the twentieth century. Robertson was an efficient departmental head, but he left most of the management to competent and loyal colleagues. He did not seek prominence in public affairs, but did not shun assignments that came his way. He served on the councils of the Royal Societies of Edinburgh (1953–6) and London (1954–6); he was a member of the University Grants Committee (1960–4) and the Ramsay Trust (1970–8), and he was president of the Chemical Society (1962–4). His honours included FRSE (1943), FRS (1945), the Tilden lectureship (1945), the Davy medal of the Royal Society (1960), appointment as CBE (1962), honorary degrees from Aberdeen (1963) and Strathclyde (1970), and the Longstaff medal of the Chemical Society (1966).

Robertson was of middle height and solidly built. He was a gentle and courteous man, somewhat old-fashioned, with a quiet sense of humour and an attractive smile, all of which conveyed a true impression of his kindness and reliability, but did not so readily disclose his underlying strength of character. He hated to censure or criticize, but was nevertheless a good leader. In 1930 he married Stella Kennard, daughter of the Revd James Nairn, of Haslingden; it was, as he wrote later, 'the most important event in my life'. They had two sons and a daughter. He is commemorated by a tablet (unveiled by his wife a few weeks before he died) in the J. M. Robertson protein crystallography laboratory of the chemistry department of the University of Glasgow. Robertson died 27 December 1989 in Inverness.

[J. M. Robertson, personal reminiscences, in *Fifty Years of X-ray Diffraction*, ed. P. P. Ewald, Utrecht, 1962; S. Arnott in *Biographical Memoirs of Fellows of the Royal Society*, vol. xxxix, 1994; personal knowledge.]

E. G. Cox

ROBINSON, SIR David (1904–1987), entrepreneur, college founder, and philanthropist, was born 13 April 1904 in Cambridge, the third of six sons and third of nine children of Herbert Robinson, cycle shop and later garage owner, and his wife, Rosie Emily Tricker. He was educated at the Cambridgeshire High School for Boys, which he left at the age of fifteen in order to work in his father's bicycle shop in Cambridge. In 1930 he moved to Bedford, where he took over a garage and developed it into a large and prosperous firm.

His fortune, however, was made in the radio and television rental business. In the late 1930s he opened a radio and electrical shop in the High Street, Bedford, and in the late 1940s opened similar shops in Northampton, Kettering, Luton, Peterborough, Stamford, and Hitchin. Having observed the impact of the queen's coronation as a television spectacle in 1953, he set up his own television and rental business based at first on his chain of shops. By 1962 the Bedford firm of Robinson Rentals was making a profit of £1½ million a year and in 1968 he sold it to Granada for £8 million and turned his attention elsewhere.

The turf had interested him for a long time. Although his racing colours of green, red sleeves, and light blue cap were registered as early as 1946, and although in 1955 his Our Babu won the Two Thousand Guineas, it was not until 1968 that he seriously turned his mind to horseracing as a business. He set out to prove his theory that, given efficient and businesslike management, organization, and accounting, racehorse ownership could be made to pay. The results spoke for themselves. For eight seasons between 1968 and 1975 Robinson consistently headed the owners' list of individual winners and races. Although leading owner in terms of prize money only once (in 1969), he eventually won a total of 997 races. In the ten years from 1968 Robinson made a great contribution to British racing, at his peak having 120 horses in training.

He continued to apply and expect the same high standards of business efficiency even when it came to giving his money away. If potential recipients of his munificence did not come up to his own ideas of management efficiency, they went away disappointed and empty handed. He set up the Robinson Charitable Trust. Its beneficiaries included Bedford—a swimming pool; his old school—an arts centre; Addenbrooke's

Hospital—a large maternity unit ('Rosie') named after his mother; the Evelyn Nursing Home—a new wing; and Papworth Hospital—a large sum for heart transplants. When the Penlee lifeboat foundered with the loss of the entire crew in 1981, he provided £400,000 to purchase a new lifeboat named after his wife, *Mabel Alice*, and he went on to provide three more, including the *David Robinson* at the Lizard.

In the late 1960s it became known that he was considering a large academic benefaction, and eventually Cambridge University accepted his offer of £18 million to endow a large new college. Planning began in 1973. The design was prepared by the Glasgow firm of architects, Gillespie, Kidd & Coia; the building was started in 1977 and was virtually completed by October 1980, when the first sizeable number of undergraduates entered the college. By 1983 the college had grown to thirty-five fellows and 370 junior members and by 1993 had reached a steady state of fifty-six fellows and 485 junior members.

Robinson College was formally opened by the queen on 29 May 1981. Typically, Robinson avoided the opening ceremony, tendering his apologies to the queen on the grounds that he had become increasingly immobile and his wife had for some time been incapacitated. He was knighted in 1985.

Robinson's life was centred on his enterprises and his benefactions. He worked hard, with little relaxation and few social contacts; and he expected others to work hard. He kept up appearances, being tall, bald-headed and bespectacled, and always smartly dressed, but he was very reticent and shunned publicity to the end. He was not only a great entrepreneur, but also a self-effacing philanthropist who gave all his money away and, in spite of his disenchantment with academics, whom he regarded as vacillating and insufficiently businesslike, founded a college in his home town with a record benefaction in record time.

In 1922 he married Mabel Alice, daughter of Fred Baccus, stonemason, when they were both eighteen years old. A devoted couple, they had a daughter and a son, who died in 1981. Robinson died in Newmarket 10 January 1987 and was buried at sea off Great Yarmouth by the Royal National Lifeboat Institution.

[*Cambridge Review*, no. 2298, October 1987; private information; personal knowledge.]   GEORGE COUPE

ROSE, Francis Leslie (1909–1988), industrial research chemist, was born in Lincoln 27 June 1909, the second son in the family of two sons and one daughter of Frederick William Rose, solicitor's clerk, and his wife, Elizabeth Ann Watts. Frank, as he was invariably known to his colleagues, was educated at St Faith's Primary

School, Christ's Hospital Continuation School, and the City School in Lincoln. From the age of eight he was fascinated by science and developed a consuming passion for experimental chemistry, which he retained all his life. He entered Nottingham University College at the age of seventeen, won first-class honours in chemistry (London, 1930), and remained there with Professor F. S. *Kipping to carry out research on camphor and fluorene derivatives. This work had been partly supported by Imperial Chemical Industries Ltd. and, although very few people were being taken on at that period, he was recruited by ICI in 1932. He obtained his Ph.D. in 1934 and remained with ICI as a chemist, research manager, and finally consultant for fifty-six years. He was active scientifically until his death and was one of the best known and most innovative contributors to pharmaceutical research of his period.

His initial research concerned light-stable dyestuffs and the ways in which dyes bind to fibres. No doubt had he continued in this field he would have become eminent, but in 1936, just before World War II, ICI followed some of the other large chemical companies in setting up within its dyestuffs research group a small team to initiate pharmaceutical research. Rose was picked as one of the six chemists involved—a fortunate choice both for himself and for ICI.

The antibacterial sulphonamides had just been introduced to medicine and Rose soon devised a new route to one of the most widely used, Sulphamezathine. Unlike many of his chemical colleagues he became keenly interested in both the mode of action and the distribution of these agents. As a result he became and remained one of the leading exponents of antimetabolite theory and of pharmacodynamics.

The priorities of wartime soon required the ICI group to seek new anti-malarial drugs. The known synthetic agents came from Germany and the war in the Far East denied the Allies access to the quinine plantations. Rose led the chemical research team and over the next five years about 1,700 compounds were made and tested, resulting eventually in the discovery of Paludrine. Although Rose made many other therapeutic discoveries in areas as diverse as anti-bacterials, cancer, and bronchodilatation, it is for this wartime research that he is best remembered.

After the war the pharmaceutical work within ICI prospered and gave rise to a considerable business. Rose became research manager (1954–71) and at times was in charge of over 200 scientists, but until 1974 he still worked at the laboratory bench every day. He maintained a link between the ICI laboratories in Cheshire and Manchester University. From 1959 to 1972 he was honorary reader in organic chemistry at UMIST and he was a member of the courts of governors of the university and of UMIST and an honorary fellow of Manchester Polytechnic. He never retired. After relinquishing his research managership in 1971 he worked as a research fellow (1971–4) in his old department before joining a small team studying the potential carcinogenicity of compounds handled within ICI. He then remained an active consultant and was usually to be found every day in the laboratories which he helped to found at Alderley Park.

Rose retained a boyish enthusiasm for science. His knowledge of the interactions between chemicals and biological systems was immense and he was continually seeking new arguments to explain these interactions. His arguments were imaginative, sometimes wildly so, but they were given in such a hopeful and informed way as to be a great stimulus to the many who worked with him. He played an active part in the wider scientific community of learned societies and was also for many years a scientific adviser to the Home Office Forensic Science Committee (1965–78). He was elected FRS in 1957, appointed OBE in 1949 and CBE in 1978, and, to his especial delight, awarded a D.Sc. by his old university, Nottingham, in 1950. He had an honorary D.Sc. from Loughborough (1982) and several medals.

Rose was a lively, friendly man of medium height. He had blue eyes, fair and in later life grey hair, wore spectacles, and mostly moved with a quick purposeful step. The well-known scientist was also a very private person with deeply held Christian beliefs and a love of church music and sailing, totally devoted to his wife Ailsa (the daughter of Christopher Buckley, an ICI engineer), whom he married in 1935, and to their only child Peter, a schoolteacher who shared his father's love of church music. Frank Rose died of renal cancer in St Ann's Hospice, Heald Green, 3 March 1988.

[C. W. Suckling and B. W. Langley in *Biographical Memoirs of Fellows of the Royal Society*, vol. xxxvi, 1990; personal knowledge.]   BERNARD LANGLEY

ROSS, (John) Carl (1901–1986), magnate in the fisheries industry, was born in Cleethorpes 29 July 1901, the second of three sons and fourth of six children of Thomas Ross, Grimsby fish merchant, and his wife Marie, daughter of Herbert Bannister, trawler owner. He was educated at the East Anglian School at Culford and served for a short time in the Royal Navy, which he had joined shortly before armistice day in 1918. Upon demobilization, he entered the family fish merchanting firm of Thomas Ross Ltd., from which his father retired early, through illness, in 1928. From that year he initiated a steady decade of expansion, which included the import of frozen halibut and salmon from North America, a very innovative activity, which was to continue

well into the years following the end of World War II in 1945.

Whilst Carl Ross was developing his fish merchanting activities, he had the foresight to recognize that the future of the fishing industry might lie in integrating fish catching, processing, and merchanting, and he built the first diesel trawlers in the mid-1930s. However, his first major incursion into trawler-owning was when he purchased the nine vessels of the late Sir Alec Black, first baronet, in 1943. In 1944 he acquired a majority shareholding in Trawlers Grimsby Ltd., a publicly quoted company into which Thomas Ross Ltd. was injected. This was the foundation stone of what became the Ross Group.

It was at this stage that Ross demonstrated a remarkable ability to deal with financial and accountancy matters, although he had no formal training. He had a formidable talent for reading and understanding figures and gained great respect in City financial circles. This ability triggered off an extensive series of take-overs of companies engaged in all aspects of the fishing industry, including major catching and processing companies in Hull, which gave the Ross Group a dominant situation on the Humber. In 1956 the Ross Group acquired G. F. Sleight Ltd., owners of a substantial but ageing fleet, and thus, in one swoop, Carl Ross secured the services of twenty of the best North Sea skippers. It was a move that allowed him to announce a major North Sea and Middle Water trawler-building programme to accommodate these skippers. The programme was a resounding success and the subsequent profitable record of the Bird and Cat class of Ross vessels became a legend. The Ross Group built many more vessels, including deep-sea freezer trawlers, most of which were constructed at the Cochrane yards at Selby, which it acquired. At its peak, the Ross Group owned the largest fishing fleet in Europe.

In the very rapid growth of the Ross Group, the only set-back Carl Ross encountered was in 1966, when the Monopolies Commission refused to allow the Ross bid for Associated Fisheries Ltd., the other major publicly quoted company in the fishing industry, although the financial and business logic was irrefutable. Ironically, only two years later, the government itself was instrumental in bringing the fleets of the Ross group and Associated Fisheries together to form British United Trawlers. In the early 1950s, when Carl Ross recognized that the fish industry was but part of the food industry, he extended the Ross frozen fish business to become Ross Foods. An added dimension to the Ross Foods business was the acquisition of the Youngs shellfish company. Carl Ross established Ross Poultry (1961), which played a major role in the integration and rationalization of the British poultry industry; created Ross Vegetable (1960), the biggest single UK potato distributor; and developed a series of peripheral activities including the chain of Ross Motorway Services (1965).

Carl Ross parted company with the Ross Group after a somewhat acrimonious boardroom struggle in the late 1960s, which culminated in the take-over of the company by Imperial Group Ltd. in 1970. Although almost seventy, he then played a major role as chairman in developing Cosalt plc. He maintained an active interest in the affairs of that company until he died.

In his youth he was a distinguished county hockey player. Almost until his death he also enjoyed golf and shooting and for a period owned several racehorses. He obtained a pilot's licence in 1930 and played an active role in the Royal Air Force Volunteer Reserve cadet force during the 1939–45 war. He was a high steward of Grimsby (1970–86) and a member of the Companies of Poulterers and Fruiterers. He was a past president and leading member of the Fishing Industry Sports Association and a generous contributor to many charities. He was president of the Grimsby Conservative Association for some twenty-five years from 1954.

Ross was five feet nine inches tall, of medium build, with a strong face and distinguished appearance. In 1928 he married Elsie, daughter of Samuel Hartley, a cotton salesman based in Blackburn. They had two sons and two daughters. Ross died in Grimsby 9 January 1986.

[Archives of the *Grimsby Evening Telegraph*; private information; personal knowledge.] W. P. APPLEYARD

ROSS, William, BARON ROSS OF MARNOCK (1911–1988), educationist and politician, was born in Ayr 7 April 1911, the third of four children and only son of William Henry Ross, locomotive driver, of 7 Kirkholm Avenue, Ayr, who became senior bailie of Ayr town council. For the whole of his life his home was in Ayr, where his school-days were at Ayr Academy. From there he went on to Glasgow University on a Carnegie scholarship and graduated MA (1932). He then became a primary schoolteacher in Glasgow. The general strike of 1926, when his father was unemployed, and the depression of the 1930s intensified the political ideas he imbibed from his parents.

In 1936 he was selected as Labour candidate for Ayr constituency. He continued teaching until 1940, when he enlisted in the Highland Light Infantry, training in the Shetlands and Wales. He served in the North-West Frontier of India until seconded to Signals GHQ India in Delhi. In 1944 he became cipher officer to Lord Louis *Mountbatten (later first Earl Mountbatten of Burma), supreme commander, South-East Asia, in Ceylon and accompanied him on flights

to Burma and Singapore for the signing of the peace treaty with the Japanese. He was appointed MBE (military) in 1945 and demobilized in the rank of major.

At the 1945 election he unsuccessfully contested the Ayr Burgh constituency, but at a by-election in 1946 he was elected Labour member for Kilmarnock, Ayr, and Bute, which he continued to represent until he retired in 1979. His first government appointment was as parliamentary private secretary to Hector *McNeil, secretary of state for Scotland, a post he held until the defeat of the Labour government in 1951. From the back benches he worked as an aide to Douglas Houghton (later Baron Houghton of Sowerby) on pensions, insurance, and health. In 1962 he became shadow secretary of state for Scotland, and his energies were directed to changing public policy and narrowing the gap between the Scottish economy and that of the south of England.

In 1964 he became secretary of state for Scotland, the office he most desired. Carrying as it did responsibility for functions which in England are exercised by ministers for the home department, education, health, agriculture, electricity, and local government, it gave great scope to his boundless energy and gave him the opportunity to put into practice the policies for which he had fought with such zeal in opposition. Openly at Westminster and in Scotland, but also behind the scenes, he campaigned vigorously to achieve his aim of shifting industry from the south to Scotland and, under the auspices of the Scottish Development Department, he had much success in this. His creation of the Highlands and Islands Development Board changed for the better many aspects of life and work in the Highlands. He gave full support to the activities of the Scottish new towns, which were particularly successful in attracting new enterprises both from England and the USA. Relinquishing his position at the fall of the Labour government in 1970, Ross resumed as secretary of state for Scotland in the following Labour government elected in 1974. However, when Harold Wilson (later Baron Wilson of Rievaulx) resigned in 1976, Ross lost the Scottish Office because he was not in favour of devolution, which was then in vogue. He accepted a life barony in 1979.

In 1978–80 he was lord high commissioner to the general assembly of the Church of Scotland, an appointment for which his strong religious beliefs and lifelong membership of the Church made him highly suitable. He was fiercely loyal to everything he loved and believed in—family, friends, the Labour party, the Church, and Scotland. He was of medium height, with light red hair, strong features, cleft chin, and piercing grey eyes. He was unsympathetic to the ideals of the 'permissive society'. He was passionately fond of the works of Robert *Burns, of which he had an extensive knowledge. His rich Ayrshire voice made him a welcome speaker at numerous Burns suppers, where his proposal of the 'Immortal Memory' was unforgettable. In his speeches, both in Parliament and elsewhere, he made some of his most telling points by an apt quotation from Burns. His main leisure interest was watching Association Football, and he was very proud when the Scottish Football Association made him honorary president (1978).

He became an honorary LL D of the universities of St Andrews (1967), Strathclyde (1969), and Glasgow (1978), and a fellow of the Educational Institute of Scotland (1971). In 1948 he married Elizabeth Jane Elma, daughter of John Aitkenhead, marine engineer and hotel owner. They had two daughters. Ross had a happy marriage and family life, and was a kind and loving husband and father. He died at home in Ayr, of cancer, 10 June 1988.

[Information from relatives and friends; personal knowledge.]   WILLIAM HUGHES

ROTHSCHILD, SIR (**Nathaniel Mayer**) **Victor**, fourth baronet and third BARON ROTHSCHILD (1910–1990), zoologist and public servant, was born 31 October 1910 in Palace Green, Kensington, the only son and second of the four children of (Nathaniel) Charles Rothschild, banker and naturalist, and his wife Rozsika, daughter of Captain Alfred von Wertheimstein, of Cséhtelek, a part of Hungary since annexed by Romania. Charles, younger son of Nathan Meyer *Rothschild, first Baron Rothschild, took his life in 1923 while suffering from the effects of encephalitis (inflammation of the brain). During his schooldays at Harrow, Victor shone only as a cricketer. It was as an undergraduate at Trinity College, Cambridge, that he first revealed an ingenious mind. The university department of zoology was impressed enough to excuse him the long grind of the natural history tripos so that he could at once embark on research. A change of regulation required him nevertheless to sit for a pass degree. In 1935 he was elected to a fellowship at Trinity for work of high promise on the fertilization of frogs' eggs. He obtained a Ph.D. in 1937 and an Sc.D. in 1950.

Much was to be made in later years of his membership of the Apostles at Cambridge. Rothschild, like most of his Cambridge contemporaries, was mildly left-wing but never a Marxist. Nor did he share the belief of such Apostles and close friends as Anthony *Blunt and Guy *Burgess that the rise of Nazi Germany demanded uncritical adulation of the Soviet Union. And although he regarded homosexuals with amused tolerance at a time when their practices infringed the criminal law, he was not one himself. He excelled at tennis, golf, and cricket, as a driver of fast cars and a jazz pianist. Like most Rothschilds he was an obsessive collector. He began even as an undergraduate to assemble the finest library in private hands of English eighteenth-century first editions, manuscripts, and book bindings, some 3,000 items which he later presented to Trinity. He also pursued silver of the same period and Impressionist paintings.

He married in 1933 Barbara, only daughter of St John Hutchinson, barrister. Although Rothschild never subscribed to the beliefs and practices of Judaism, he thought it seemly that his wife should be converted to the Jewish faith. They had one son and two daughters.

Succession to the peerage of his bachelor uncle (Lionel) Walter in 1937 did not alter the rhythm of his laboratory life. Refusing to be burdened by possessions or a role in national affairs, he sold the family mansion, no. 148 Piccadilly, together with its plethoric contents, and most of the country estate at Tring. Rothschild spent much of the war of 1939–45 in charge of the tiny but effective counter-sabotage section of MI5. The precision with which he had learned to dissect frogs' eggs served him well in the defusing of explosive devices. For dismantling a new type of bomb placed by German agents in a cargo of Spanish onions bound for Britain, he was awarded the George medal (1944) after the personal intervention of (Sir) Winston *Churchill. Colonel Rothschild was also responsible for analysing anonymous gifts to the prime minister of food, wine, and cigars in case they concealed poison or explosives. The USA awarded him the Legion of Merit and the bronze star.

His marriage, exhilarating but precarious, ended in divorce in 1945. He married in 1946 his assistant in MI5, Teresa Georgina ('Tess') Mayor, MBE, daughter of Robert John Grote Mayor, civil servant. They had two sons, one of whom died at birth, and two daughters. Resuming his experiments at Cambridge on fertilization, Rothschild produced much original work on the speed and heat of spermatozoa, and with Michael (later Baron) *Swann discovered how a single sperm, on penetrating the egg of a sea urchin, was able to exclude all others. In 1953 he was elected a fellow of the Royal Society. He published, as well as many papers, *Fertilization* (1956) and *A Classification of Living Animals* (1961).

Only weeks after Labour's sweeping victory in the general election of 1945 he formally joined the Labour party: a mistimed gesture by a rich young patrician that invited cynical comment. He was appointed to several official bodies. As chairman of the Agricultural Research Council from 1948 to 1958 he increased both its budget and its standing. From 1961 to 1970 he was employed by Royal Dutch Shell, rising to be co-ordinator of research for the entire group worldwide. Shell accustomed him to a customer–contractor relationship, which he believed should also be imposed on government research establishments (even though he had opposed it at the ARC). *A Framework for Government Research and Development* (1971) was ill received by his colleagues in Cambridge laboratories and at the Royal Society, who felt betrayed at the application of payment by results to their work.

The report was the first fruit of the Central Policy Review Staff, popularly known as the Think Tank, set up by (Sir) Edward Heath in 1971 with Rothschild as its first director-general, to offer the cabinet independent advice on important issues, such as race relations, nuclear reactor policy, Concorde, and coal. Even under the influence of Rothschild's office hospitality—smoked salmon sandwiches and cider cup consisting almost entirely of brandy—permanent under-secretaries could see little merit in a band of intellectual *condottieri* sabotaging the established procedures of the Civil Service as they roamed the corridors of Whitehall. He was appointed GBE in 1975.

Retiring from the CPRS in 1974, Rothschild presided over the royal commission on gambling (1976–8) and was published in 1978 an exhaustive report. He was consulted by Margaret (later Baroness) Thatcher on the reform of local government finance, but bore no responsibility for the rigidity of the subsequent poll tax introduced by her government. In spite of an aversion to the practice of banking, he was persuaded in 1975 to become chairman of N. M. Rothschild & Sons, and from 1976 to 1988 chairman of Rothschilds Continuation Ltd.; he could not, however, heal its internal dissensions or prevent the departure of his son, Jacob Rothschild, to found his own more adventurous merchant bank—an episode that strained beyond repair an already uneasy relationship between father and son. Rothschild himself continued as a director and brought both scientific experience and flair to the chairmanship of its successful subsidiary, Biotechnology Investments Ltd. He had ten honorary degrees.

Byronically handsome in youth, he acquired a senatorial countenance in middle age. He was an accomplished host, but a guest only on his own terms: no formal clothes, a very small company, and an early night. He gave generously to charities and to individuals, often by stealth, and administered family trusts for the support of the Weizmann Institute in Rehovot and other Israeli causes. He preferred the pen to the telephone. The terseness of his epigrammatic style delighted his friends but was feared in controversy. He wrote, with professional help, two monographs on family history: one on N. M. Rothschild, founder of the English line, the other on Baron Lionel's role in acquiring the Suez canal shares in 1875.

The carefree friendships of his early Cambridge years that had continued throughout the war cast a shadow over the last decade of his life. The defection of Burgess to Russia and the uncovering of Blunt as a Soviet agent exposed Rothschild to innuendo and vilification in press and Parliament. Rather than let his name, his courage, and his record of public service speak for themselves, he sought unwisely to clear himself though the testimony of Peter Wright, who as an investigator employed by MI5 had every reason to know of his innocence. Clandestine association with so volatile a character aroused further suspicions that Rothschild had broken the Official Secrets Act. Only after voluntarily submitting himself to a long interrogation by Scotland Yard did he emerge with honour and patriotism intact. But the ordeal took a toll on both his pride and his health. He died of a heart attack at St James's Place, London, 20 March 1990 and at his express wish was buried near the tomb of N. M. Rothschild in a long-disused cemetery in Stepney. He was succeeded in the barony by his elder son, (Nathaniel Charles) Jacob Rothschild (born 1936).

[Lord Rothschild, *Meditations of a Broomstick*, 1977, and (with N. Logothetis) *Random Variables*, 1984; private information; personal knowledge.]

KENNETH ROSE

ROUS, SIR **Stanley Ford** (1895–1986), secretary of the Football Association, was born 25 April 1895 in Mutford, Suffolk, the eldest son and third child in the family of two sons and five daughters of Samuel George Rous, provision merchant, and his wife, Alice Coldham. He was educated at the Sir John Leman School, Beccles, and, after opting for a teaching career, at the town's teacher training centre. His passion for football was early apparent when, aged fifteen, he organized a village team. Tall and strongly built, he was an imposing figure in goal and showed considerable ability in local leagues. Watching Norwich play League football he also developed an interest in refereeing.

Then World War I intervened to take him to France, Palestine, Egypt, and Lebanon, as a non-commissioned officer in the 272nd brigade of the Royal Field Artillery (East Anglian). He acted as a referee in wartime Egypt, after a wrist broken by a shell impaired his playing ability. When demobilized he was attending an officer training centre.

After the war Rous returned to complete his education, going to St Luke's College, Exeter. His football and sporting interests were furthered by his appointment in 1921 as an assistant master at Watford Grammar School, where he was in charge of all sport. During his thirteen years at Watford he also became a leading football referee. In 1927 he was appointed a Football League referee. On 13 March that year he officiated at an international match in Antwerp, the first of thirty-four such games he refereed. In the week in which he submitted his application to succeed Sir Frederick Wall as Football Association secretary he refereed the Welsh Cup Final on Thursday, the Football Association Cup Final, in which he used the diagonal refereeing system he had invented, on Saturday, and an international in Antwerp on Sunday.

As secretary of the Football Association (1934–61) he made an immediate impact with his emphasis on training, coaching, and youth football. Firm but charismatic, he was a forceful character, who got his way more by humour and persuasion than reliance on authority. During World War II he was released as a lieutenant in the Royal Artillery from an anti-aircraft battery to organize sport and raise funds for the Red Cross. He proved an outstanding Football Association secretary, methodical, clear, and well reasoned in his judgements. Always open-minded and progressive, he was conservative only in preserving the essential simplicity of the game and its laws, which he believed to be its main attraction. Indeed, he wrote *A History of the Laws of Association Football* (1974). He was responsible for the codification of the laws of the game, redrafting the red and yellow card system for cautions and the linesman's signals. Otherwise he encouraged innovations and improvements, particularly in coaching and refereeing, in a variety of national courses, and in the introduction of floodlighting and of televised football. His close co-operation with the England team manager and director of coaching, (Sir) Walter Winterbottom, gave both men a worldwide reputation.

His international interest was much in contrast to previous officials' insular outlook. He played a constructive part in England's entry into World Cup football in 1950 and in the formation of the European football confederation (UEFA), of which he became a vice-president. He also helped Germany back into international football after the war. His international outlook led to his election in 1961 as president of the Fédération Internationale de Football Associations (FIFA). Travelling the world and working tirelessly for the game, he made a particular impact on the technical and educational side, which represented his special interest. He wrote a football coaching manual and a book of physical exercises (both 1942). His popularity also played a part in the World cup being awarded to England in 1966. He retired from FIFA in 1974.

His many other contributions to sport in general include being a founder member in 1935 of the Central Council of Physical Recreation,

of which he was chairman of the executive committee from 1945 to 1973. Work for the King George's Jubilee Trust, the 1948 Olympic Games, the 1951 Festival of Britain, and the Duke of Edinburgh's Award Scheme typified his dedication to his prime concept of 'work that others may play'. From 1943 to 1947 he was a member of Paddington borough council and he was a JP (1950). He held many foreign awards, was appointed CBE in 1943, and was knighted in 1949.

Rous was six feet three inches tall, with a straight back and distinguished presence that commanded respect, although his clear eyes and husky voice showed a warm-hearted and jovial personality. In 1924 he married Adrienne (died 1950), daughter of Victor Louis Gacon, silk merchant, originally of Lyons, France, who had a small silk-weaving factory in Hemel Hempstead. She was half German and half French. There were no children of the marriage. Rous died 18 July 1986 in St Mary's Hospital, Paddington, London, of chronic myelomonocyclic leukaemia.

[Stanley Rous, *Football World* (autobiography), 1978; private information.]   A. PAWSON

RUBBRA, (Charles) Edmund (Duncan) (1901–1986), composer, pianist, and symphonist, was born 23 May 1901 at 57 Cambridge Street, Northampton, the elder son (there were no daughters) of Edmund James Rubbra, journeyman, shoe-last maker, clock and watch repairer, and, later, jeweller, and his wife, Mary Jane Bailey. The name Duncan was not on his birth certificate; it was the surname of his first wife and he used it after his first marriage. According to family tradition, the Rubbras originated from Bologna in Italy. He left school at fourteen and worked briefly as an errand boy and then a railway clerk. In his home there was a deep love of music and as a youngster he was much drawn to the music of Cyril *Scott and Claude Debussy. Eventually he took lessons with Scott, and then went on to study composition at Reading University, where Gustav *Holst taught, and counterpoint at the Royal College of Music with one of the great theorists of the day, R. O. Morris.

After leaving the RCM in 1925, he pursued a freelance career as a pianist, taking whatever teaching, performing, and journalistic work came to hand. His repertoire included both Arnold Schoenberg and Alexander Scriabin, and he was a perceptive exponent of J. S. Bach. During the 1930s he attracted increasing attention with such works as the *Sinfonia Concertante* for piano and orchestra (1934) and his First Symphony (1937).

During World War II he served in the army, as an anti-aircraft gunner in the Royal Artillery and then in the army music unit, and made an appearance in battledress at London's Henry Wood Promenade Concerts to conduct the first performance of his Fourth Symphony (1942). Rubbra spent much of his army service entertaining the troops with the trio he had formed with Erich Gruenberg and William Pleeth (and was very fond of telling how the three were once introduced as being 'at the top of the tree in their various string combinations'). The Rubbra–Gruenberg–Pleeth trio continued for some years after the war until the combined pressures of Rubbra's creative work and teaching led to its demise. In 1947 he was appointed lecturer in music at Oxford University, becoming a fellow of Worcester College in 1963. He remained at Oxford until 1968. In 1961 he also joined the staff of the Guildhall School of Music, where he taught composition until 1974.

Rubbra belonged to the same generation as Sir William *Walton, Sir Lennox *Berkeley, and Sir Michael Tippett but had little in common with them and even less with such European contemporaries as Karl Amadeus Hartmann, Luigi Dallapiccola, and Dmitri Shostakovich. It has been said that his music was not of his time, yet could have been composed at no other. It is rooted in place—England—and, more specifically, England's musical heritage lies at its heart. There is little of the pastoral school in it, though Rubbra revered Ralph *Vaughan Williams and also possessed a keen sense of nature's power, which is clearly evident in the Fourth (1941–2) and Seventh symphonies (1957). Rubbra's outlook was far from insular: he set to music poetry ranging from the time of the Chinese T'ang dynasty and of Icelandic ballads to medieval Latin and French verse, and his interest in eastern culture, which arose in childhood, remained lifelong. In his book, *Counterpoint* (1960), Rubbra argued that western music had grown out of melody and in particular the interaction of independent melodic lines; this was certainly a dominant principle in his own music. Such was the eloquence and quality of his vocal music that some critics spoke of his symphonies as 'motets for orchestra'. His choral music was finely fashioned and elevated in feeling, and his symphonies likewise were touched by a preoccupation with linear growth. Matter, not manner, was his central concern.

His early symphonies are difficult, though not in the way that some contemporary music is, for the musical language itself is quite straightforward. There is nothing abstruse about the symphonies' tonality and harmony, which is basically diatonic, but they are difficult because the continuity of their melodic and polyphonic growth is logical and unremitting. The first two symphonies were composed in quick succession (both were finished in 1937) and it was obvious that, whatever their failings, Rubbra was a symphonist to be reckoned with. The Third, which he finished in 1939, was a positive reaction to the experience of the Second, and is outwardly the most genial and relaxed of the early symphonies. The orchestration is much cleaner and the first movement much closer to sonata form. The opening of the Fourth Symphony is beautiful and free from any kind of artifice, having serenity and quietude. This symphony, like the Third, is not so dense contrapuntally as the first two, and though practically every idea evolves in some way or another out of the opening figure, its first movement is a sonata design. Nothing could be further removed from the grim years of World War II than this symphony. In 1948 came the Fifth and most often played of the Rubbra symphonies; it enjoyed something of a vogue in the 1950s. Sir Adrian *Boult premièred it, Sir John *Barbirolli recorded it, and Leopold Stokowski briefly included it in his repertoire.

After the Seventh Symphony (1957), Rubbra's music fell on hard times and enjoyed relatively little exposure. His Eighth Symphony (1968) had to wait three years for a performance and the Ninth (*Sinfonia Sacra*, 1971–2), for soloists, chorus, and orchestra, possibly his masterpiece, also suffered relative neglect. It tells the story of the resurrection, and with its soloists and chorus would closely resemble a passion were it not for its symphonic cohesion. Like most of Rubbra's finest music, it unfolds with a seeming inevitability and naturalness, and a powerful sense of purpose that justify its inclusion in the symphonic canon. His scoring has been criticized, but conductors such as Arturo Toscanini, Eugene Ormandy, and Neeme Järvi recorded his orchestration of Brahms's *Variations and Fugue on a Theme of Handel*.

Rubbra was of medium height and was for most of his adult life bearded. He possessed a beatific smile and exercised great personal charm. Always courteous, a supportive and illuminating teacher, he radiated warmth and spirituality. His deeply religious nature shines through much of his music: the Canto movement of the Sixth Symphony (1954), for example, and the Eighth, subtitled *Hommage à Teilhard de Chardin*. (Although he was much influenced by Buddhist teachings, Rubbra was received into the Catholic faith in 1947.) He never lost this feeling for organic growth essential to the symphony: his Tenth (1974) and Eleventh (1979) are highly concentrated one-movement affairs of much substance.

His output was extensive and ran to over 160 works. Apart from the symphonies, his most important works included a Viola Concerto in A Major, op. 75 (1952); a Piano Concerto in G Major, op. 85 (1956); a Violin Concerto, op. 103

(1959); an Improvisation for Violin and Orchestra, op. 89; four string quartets: F Minor, op. 35 (1933, revised 1946), E flat, op. 55 (1952), op. 112 (1962–3), and op. 150 (1976–7); two piano trios: op. 68 (1950) and op. 138 (1973); two violin sonatas: op. 31 (1931) and op. 133 (1967); and a Cello Sonata in G Minor, op. 60 (1946). Eight of his symphonies have been commercially recorded, and there is an extensive discography which includes his two masses. His last work was the Sinfonietta for large string orchestra, op. 163, which he completed in 1980, in his late seventies, shortly before suffering a stroke, from which he eventually died.

Rubbra was appointed CBE in 1960. He became MRAM (1970) and FGSM (1968). He had honorary degrees from Leicester (LL D, 1959), Durham (D.Mus., 1949), and Reading (D.Litt., 1978). His music does not possess the dramatic power which characterizes that of Vaughan Williams and Walton but has a sense of organic continuity that is both highly developed and immediately evident to the listener. Perhaps the most distinctive and individual quality that shines through his most inspired music, such as the opening of the Seventh Symphony or the *Missa in Honorem Sancti Dominici* (op. 66, 1948), is breadth and serenity.

Rubbra's first marriage, which lasted only a few months, was to Lilian Annie Duncan. There were no children. In 1933 he married the violinist Antoinette Chaplin, from France, daughter of William Chaplin, engineer; they had two sons. He separated from his second wife during the 1950s and in 1975, following her death, he married Colette Muriel Marian Yardley, daughter of Harold Evans, a Sunbeam Motors salesman. They had one son. Rubbra died 14 February 1986 in Gerrards Cross.

[(Ronald) Lewis Foreman (ed.), *Edmund Rubbra: Composer*, 1977; Ralph Scott Grover, *The Music of Edmund Rubbra*, 1993; personal knowledge.] ROBERT LAYTON

RUNCIMAN, (Walter) Leslie, second VISCOUNT RUNCIMAN OF DOXFORD (1900–1989), shipowner, was born in Newcastle upon Tyne 26 August 1900, the eldest of five children and elder son of Walter *Runciman, first Viscount Runciman of Doxford, shipowner, Liberal MP, and president of the Board of Trade, and his wife Hilda, later an MP, daughter of James Cochran Stevenson, MP for South Shields, and a kinswoman of Robert Louis *Stevenson. The younger son, (Sir) Steven Runciman, became a well-known scholar of the Byzantine period. Leslie Runciman grew up at Doxford and was educated at Eton, where he was a King's scholar, and at Trinity College, Cambridge, also as a scholar. He once remarked, however, that he learned good manners from a gamekeeper. At Cambridge he took part i in classics (1920) and

achieved a second class (division II) in part ii of the economics tripos (1922).

After a year with the Blue Funnel Line in Liverpool he went into the family firm of Walter Runciman & Company, shipowners. Here he learned the basics of shipping affairs from his formidable grandfather, Sir Walter (later Baron) *Runciman, who had begun life as a boy in small merchant sailing vessels. In due course Leslie Runciman became chairman of the company and six other shipping and banking concerns. He was for fifty years a member of the Chamber of Shipping and a very successful president in 1952. He was also for many years a UK delegate to the International Chamber of Shipping. He was president of the Royal Institution of Naval Architects (1951–61) and chairman of the trustees of the National Maritime Museum from 1962 to 1972, a role for which his interests fitted him exactly, and of the government advisory committee on historic wreck sites from 1973 to 1986. He was an honorary elder brother of Trinity House. Like his grandfather, he was also a very practical seaman, cruising far and wide, first in the family's three-masted schooner *Sunbeam* and later in his motor ketch *Bondicar*. He succeeded Prince Philip, Duke of Edinburgh, as commodore of the Royal Yacht Squadron (1968–74). He was also a keen shot and an enthusiastic skier.

As a young man in the 1920s Runciman became interested in aviation. He qualified as a pilot, had some success in the King's Cup air races of the period, and founded his own aviation company. He raised and commanded the Durham Squadron of the Auxiliary Air Force and in 1937 was awarded the Air Force Cross. He joined the boards of both Imperial Airways and British Airways in 1938 and played a prominent part in their amalgamation into the British Overseas Airways Corporation. In 1939 he became its first director-general, but he resigned in 1943 in protest at the government's somewhat negative attitude to civil aviation. From 1943 to 1946 he was air attaché at the British embassy in Tehran, with the rank of air commodore, and he was a member (later vice-chairman) of the Air Transport Advisory Council from 1946 to 1954. His family shipping interests supplanted those of aviation when his father died in 1949 and he succeeded as second Viscount and third baronet. He became increasingly involved in the affairs of the Moor Line, Walter Runciman & Co., Runciman (London) Ltd., the Doxford Co. Ltd., and the Anchor Line.

Runciman's other interests included forty years of service on the board of Lloyds Bank, of which he was a deputy chairman from 1962 to 1971. He was among other things chairman of the committee on horticultural marketing (which determined the future location of Covent Garden market) in 1955–6, prime warden of the Goldsmiths' Company, and chairman of the British Hallmarking Council (1974–82).

Runciman was a tall and very handsome man with great personal charm. He carried natural authority which, however, he never used to overawe or dominate his colleagues and subordinates, and which, surprisingly, masked a certain diffidence. He was a natural chairman and finder of the middle way who gained the immediate respect of those with whom he worked. He was a doer, who became deeply involved in all his commitments. He was also an intellectual, an omnivorous reader, and chairman of the Horatian Society (1970–88), whose conversation was constantly illuminated with quotation. He greatly enjoyed Glyndebourne. Unfailingly courteous to all with whom he came into contact, he was very attractive to women. His attitude to them was that of his generation and background and he did not see them as members of the board. To work closely with him engendered not only respect, but also affection—and occasional mild exasperation with his insistence on the detached view. He was appointed OBE in 1946 and deputy lieutenant of Northumberland in 1961, and was awarded an honorary DCL by Durham University in 1937.

In 1923 Runciman married Rosamund Nina *Lehmann, novelist, daughter of Rudolph Chambers *Lehmann, journalist and MP. The marriage was dissolved in 1928 and in 1932 he married Katherine Schuyler, younger daughter of William R. Garrison, of New York, and Constance Clementine Schuyler, née Coudert. They had one son. Runciman died, following serious injury in an accident three years before, from which he never fully recovered, in King Edward VII Hospital in London, 1 September 1989. He was succeeded in the viscountcy by his son, Walter Garrison Runciman (born 1934).

[Private information; personal knowledge.]

BASIL GREENHILL

RUPP, (Ernest) Gordon (1910–1986), church historian, was born 7 January 1910 in Islington, the only son and elder child of John Henry Rupp, counting-house clerk, and his wife, Sarah Thomas, nurse. He learned to read at the Methodist Sunday school in Islington and, after an elementary education at Owen's School, became a messenger boy to a furniture dealer and then a bank clerk. At the bank he used his wage to buy one Everyman volume a week and so read many great novels and fell in love with the English language. He went out to Finsbury Park to preach on a box and became a Methodist local preacher. He decided to be a teacher, and the Methodist community gave him the money to spend a year at the London Institute of Education, and then a further year, studying history at King's College, London. The Methodist Church then wanted him as a minister and sent him to Wesley House at Cambridge (1933–6), where he gained a first class in both parts of the theology tripos (1935 and 1936). He was afterwards sent for a year to the universities of Strasburg and Basle. From 1938 to 1946 he was a Methodist minister at Chislehurst, and from 1947 to 1952 a tutor at the Methodist College in Richmond. He gained a Cambridge BD in 1946 and DD in 1955.

He was a born pamphleteer and was threatened with prosecution by Hilaire *Belloc for a wartime article in the *Record*. In 1944, replying to a pamphlet which accused Martin Luther of causing the rise of Hitler, because Luther was responsible for the German cult of the state, he published *Martin Luther, Hitler's Cause—or Cure?* This counter-pamphlet was persuasive and funny and its author was not afraid to pillory the revered Archbishop William *Temple; he also disclosed a rare knowledge of Luther's original texts, thereby showing Rupp to be a potential academic historian. As a result of his pamphlet, Rupp was invited to give the Birkbeck lectures in Cambridge (1947), which drew large audiences. In the same year he wrote *Studies in the Making of the English Protestant Tradition*. In 1952 Norman Sykes, who had taught him at London, found him a lectureship in Reformation history at Cambridge (1952–6). He subsequently became the first professor of ecclesiastical history at Manchester (1956–67). In 1968 he was appointed Dixie professor at Cambridge, with a fellowship at Emmanuel College (until 1977). But the professor at Manchester was also the deputy pianist at the Sunday school in Chorlton-cum-Hardy, as well as an observer at the second Vatican Council, and the professor at Cambridge was also the principal of Wesley House (1967–74) and for the year 1968–9 the president of the Methodist conference and a frustrated leader in the plan to unite the Methodists and the Anglicans. His university colleagues occasionally grumbled that, when they needed him for a meeting, he was speaking in a little chapel 300 miles away.

As a historian he reintroduced the British to Luther's thought with the publication of his Birkbeck lectures, *The Righteousness of God* (1953). He did not overstress the importance of Luther in the Reformation (he also studied other leading radicals in *Patterns of Reformation*, 1969) and he thought that social causes were given too much emphasis, to the detriment of the religious and theological ideas which lay at the heart of the Reformation. He was the first Briton to read the complete critical texts of Luther's works, and to understand the different interpretations in the two Germanies, whether Marxist or not. He also made himself familiar with Swedish Lutheran scholarship.

John *Wesley was almost as consuming an interest. Rupp was among the editors of the *History of the Methodist Churches in Great Britain* (4 vols., 1965–88) and his last book centred on the age of Wesley—*Religion in England 1688-1791* (1986). He was elected a fellow of the British Academy in 1970. An honorary fellow of King's College, London (1969), Fitzwilliam and Emmanuel colleges, Cambridge (1969 and 1983), Rupp had honorary degrees from Aberdeen, Manchester, and Paris.

Rupp never lost his simple tastes, retaining a liking for fish and chips and ginger beer. In an age when sermons had become much shorter, he was the supreme master of that art form. He had a husky voice and was small and impish, with a delightful command of satire and barbed wit. He was no man for tidy structures but looked to the heavens to probe the mystery of religion. He lit up with humour, historical example, and humane insight all that he encountered. In 1938 he married Marjorie, daughter of Frank Hibbard, toolmaker. They had one son. Rupp died in Cambridge 19 December 1986.

[*The Times*, 22 December 1986; P. N. Brooks in *Proceedings of the British Academy*, vol. lxxx, 1991; David Thompson in *Cambridge Review*, June 1987, pp. 91 ff.; P. N. Brooks (ed.), *Christian Spirituality, Essays in Honour of Gordon Rupp*, 1975, with a list of Rupp's writings to 1973; J. M. Turner, 'Gordon Rupp...as Historian', *Epworth Review*, January 1991, pp. 70–82; personal knowledge.]   OWEN CHADWICK

RUSSELL, Charles Ritchie, BARON RUSSELL OF KILLOWEN (1908–1986), lord of appeal, was born 12 January 1908 at 68 Elm Park Gardens, Chelsea, London, the youngest in the family of one son and two daughters (a third daughter died in infancy) of Francis Xavier Joseph *Russell, Baron Russell of Killowen, lord of appeal, and his wife, Mary Emily Ritchie. On his father's side Russell's family were Ulster Catholics who settled in Ireland in about 1300. His grandfather, Charles *Russell, Baron Russell of Killowen, became lord chief justice. Russell's father was a Chancery judge and a member of the Court of Appeal before being appointed to the House of Lords. On his mother's side Russell was descended from a Scottish family; his maternal grandfather was Charles Thomson *Ritchie, first Baron Ritchie of Dundee, chancellor of the Exchequer. Russell followed his father to Beaumont College and Oriel College, Oxford, where he was awarded a half blue in golf and a third class in jurisprudence (1929). He claimed to prefer the cinema to study and golf to both.

After being called to the bar in 1931 by Lincoln's Inn he worked hard in Old Buildings, where he quickly repaired any deficiencies in legal learning. During World War II he became a major in the Royal Artillery, was attached to the 6th Airborne division, and on D-Day flew into the Orne valley by glider. He subsequently took part in another glider drop over the Rhine and suffered abdominal wounds from shell fire. For his exploits on active service Russell was mentioned in dispatches and awarded the croix de guerre with star.

After the war Russell returned to the bar and took silk in 1948. He quickly became one of a triumvirate of distinguished Chancery counsel: (Sir) Andrew Clark pulverized witnesses and some judges, (Sir) E. Milner *Holland was successful with sweet reason, and Russell was the most formidable advocate. Russell was handsome, tall, slim, and elegant; he was dark with expressive eyes and a sensitive, sometimes sardonic expression. He was possessed of a warm melodious voice which made his well structured arguments almost irresistible. In 1960 he was appointed a judge of the Chancery Division and was knighted; two years later he went up to the Court of Appeal and was sworn of the Privy Council. As a judge Russell was urbane, courteous, and aloof; his flashing wit disconcerted some who were not suffered gladly. His judgments were models of analysis and lucidity, well suited to the complicated commercial and property disputes with which he was mainly concerned. Out of court he was kind and amusing to people of all ages and backgrounds. He was not very interested in the arts and his light reading was confined to Jane *Austen, and the novels and biographies of the nineteenth century, especially the works of Anthony *Trollope. He enjoyed claret, partridge, and a good cigar, but was not a gourmet. He was a sound bat and subtle bowler for Wisborough Green in village cricket as late as his forties. He played golf to a handicap of eight until he became lame in his seventies. He much enjoyed the Bar Golfing Society meetings at Sandwich, Rye, and Deal. He was tolerant towards his weaker partners and enjoyed the company of the young; he was a sparkling member of the Garrick Club.

Lincoln's Inn appealed to Russell's sense of history and he became treasurer in 1972. In his approach to the law, Russell was a firm believer in certainty and a follower of precedent; he did not approve of the purposive construction of statutes and did not admire the intellectual flexibility which enabled Lord Denning to his own satisfaction to temper the wind to the shorn lamb. Russell took refuge sometimes in a cold reserve and patrician arrogance, fortified on occasions by alcohol, which led to his suffering a great humiliation. In 1960 he pleaded guilty in a magistrate's court to driving with an unlawful level of alcohol. He was fined £25 and costs and his licence was suspended for a year. The incident was a severe blow to Russell. He was passed over in 1971 when a vacancy occurred in the House of Lords; he behaved with dignity and his work in the Court of Appeal did not suffer. When he had completed thirteen years' hard labour in that court the authorities relented and in 1975 he was appointed lord of appeal, to his surprise and to the relief of his friends. Russell took the same title as his father and grandfather. His work in the House of Lords followed the pattern of his earlier judicial career. The appellate committee was in 1975 dominated by lords Wilberforce and *Diplock. Russell was prepared to follow their lead, but he was not slow to dissent when he concluded that precedent was threatened.

In 1933 Russell married Joan Elizabeth, daughter of James Aubrey Torrens, consulting physician; she was a graduate of Somerville College, Oxford, keenly interested in literature and poetry, and was a help and companion to Russell when he was at the bar and on the bench. There were two sons and one daughter of the marriage. Another daughter died at the age of eight months. Joan died in 1976 and in 1979 Russell married Elizabeth Cecilia, the young widow of Edward Hey Laughton-Scott, circuit judge, and daughter of William Foster Mac-Neece Foster, air vice-marshal. She introduced her own children and her family and a wide circle of friends, and Russell perceptibly mellowed. He died in Southampton Hospital 23 June 1986, after a fall at home in which he struck his head on the fireplace.

[*The Times*, 24 June 1986; private information; personal knowledge.]   TEMPLEMAN

RUSSELL, Dora Winifred (1894–1986), feminist writer and campaigner, was born 3 April 1894 at 1 Mount Villas, Luna Road, Thornton Heath, Croydon, the second of three daughters and second of four children of (Sir) Frederick William Black, clerk in the Admiralty and later senior civil servant, and his wife, Sarah Isabella Davisson. She was educated at Sutton High School and Girton College, Cambridge, where she was awarded a first class in the medieval and modern languages tripos in 1915. She began research on eighteenth-century French philosophers at University College London, but in 1917 went to the United States as personal assistant to her father, who was head of a special government mission to persuade the American government to re-route some of its oil tankers to Britain. She was appointed MBE for this (1918). Shortly after her return she was elected to a fellowship by Girton, and returned to Cambridge in 1918.

In 1916 she had met Bertrand *Russell,

already famous as a mathematician and philosopher, and notorious as a pacifist. Bertrand Arthur William Russell was the grandson of Lord John *Russell, first Earl Russell, prime minister in 1846–52 and 1865–6, and the son of John Russell, Viscount Amberley, MP for Nottingham. He became third Earl Russell in 1931. They began an affair in 1919. She visited Russia in 1920, and on her return took to wearing peasant-style clothes. She remained an enthusiastic supporter of the Soviet Union all her life. In 1921 she wrote 'The Soul of Russia and the Body of America', which was finally incorporated in *The Religion of the Machine Age* (1983). She resigned her Girton fellowship in 1920 in order to accompany Russell to Russia and China.

Russell was married, although separated, and had no children. Although Dora disapproved of marriage she agreed to marry him when she became pregnant, as he was anxious to produce a legitimate heir. On their return from China he divorced his wife and married Dora in the same month, September 1921, two months before their son John, later fourth Earl Russell, was born.

They bought a house in Chelsea, and Dora soon became aware of the difficulties involved in being married to a much older, famous man. Although Russell supported women's suffrage, he believed that women were less intelligent than men, and that their main function was to be wives and mothers. His friends adopted a patronizing attitude towards Dora, assuming that any ideas she might express came from him. She was determined to have an identity separate from that of her husband, and to escape from the shadow of his reputation. She joined the Labour party, and stood unsuccessfully as Labour candidate for Chelsea in the autumn of 1924. She helped to form the Workers' Birth Control Group in 1924, and threw herself into the campaign for birth-control advice to be given to all women. In 1925 she published *Hypatia, or, Women and Knowledge*, followed by *The Right to Be Happy* in 1927.

In 1927 Dora and Bertrand Russell started Beacon Hill School at Telegraph House, on the South Downs, in order to educate their own children in the company of others, because no existing school seemed satisfactory. The plan was to do away with excessive discipline, religious instruction, and the tyranny of adults. It was a joint venture, although Dora was responsible for the day-to-day organization, while Bertrand financed it through writing popular books and lecture tours in the United States. The school was ridiculed in the press, and Bertrand Russell later claimed it was a failure, but it embodied many progressive ideas. Dora published *In Defence of Children* in 1932.

Betrand Russell left Dora, and the school, in 1932, after she had had two children by Griffin Barry, an American journalist. Although they had always insisted on their freedom to have affairs with other people, Russell could not accept her extending this to the freedom to have another man's child. They were divorced in 1935. She managed to carry on the school alone, moving several times after leaving Telegraph House in 1934. She had a brief affair with a communist, Paul Gillard, before he was murdered, and in 1940 married his friend, Gordon Grace ('Pat'), a working-class Irish communist who was helping her to run the school. He was the son of Patrick Grace, clothier, and he died in 1949.

She closed the school in 1943, and went to London to work at the Ministry of Information, moving to the Soviet relations division in 1944 to work on *British Ally*, a weekly paper published by the British government in Moscow. When the paper was closed down in 1950 she lost her job. Unable to find another, she devoted herself to feminist causes and the women's peace movement. She was a member of the Six Point Group (a discussion and political pressure organization) and the Married Women's Association. She attended peace conferences, and went to New York in 1954 to the United Nations Commission of Women, on behalf of the Women's International Democratic Federation. In 1958 she organized the Women's Caravan of Peace, a group of women who travelled across Europe to Moscow and back, protesting against nuclear weapons and calling for total disarmament, with the banner 'women of all lands want peace'.

In 1962 she returned to Cornwall, to Carn Voel, Porthcurno, the house she and Russell had bought in 1922. She devoted most of her time to writing, and to the care of her son John, who had had a mental breakdown in 1954. She continued to campaign for peace, leading a London CND rally in a wheelchair at the age of eighty-nine, and just before her death she took part in an anti-nuclear demonstration at the RAF base at St Mawgan, Cornwall. Dora Russell died 31 May 1986 at home in Porthcurno. She had four children, one son and one daughter from her first marriage, and one son and one daughter with Griffin Barry. The younger son was crippled in a mining accident in 1952 and was an invalid until his death in 1983.

She loved campaigning, enjoying public speaking—she had always wanted to be an actress—and writing letters to the press. A chain-smoker, she was small, red-haired, and untidy, and claimed to have been one of the first women in England to wear shorts, in the 1920s. Throughout her life she campaigned for sexual freedom for women. She believed passionately that hope for the future lay in women. Many of her ideas anticipated those of the feminist movement of the 1970s and 1980s.

[Dora Russell, *The Tamarisk Tree*, 3 vols., 1975, 1980, and 1985 (with portrait); Dora Russell, *The Dora Russell Reader: 57 Years of Writing and Journalism, 1925–1982*, 1983; Dale Spender, *There's Always Been a Women's Movement This Century*, 1983; Bertrand Russell, *The Autobiography of Bertrand Russell*, vol. ii, 1968; Caroline Moorehead, *Bertrand Russell*, 1992.]

ANNE PIMLOTT BAKER

RUSSELL, (Muriel) Audrey (1906–1989), radio broadcaster, was born 29 June 1906 in Dublin, Ireland, the only child of John Strangman Russell, director of the family woollen mill, of Dublin, and his wife Muriel Metcalfe, sister of E. Dudley ('Fruity') Metcalfe, the closest friend of the prince of Wales (later King *Edward VIII and duke of Windsor). From an Anglo-Irish Protestant background, her parents were part of Dublin society, and her father led the life of a country gentleman. She was educated at home by governesses, and later at Southlands, a private boarding-school in Harrow, before going to a finishing school at the Villa St Georges in Neuilly, Paris.

Back in London, she trained as an actress for six months at the Central School of Speech and Drama, and then worked for several years as a theatre dogsbody, preparing stage meals, understudying, and taking walk-on parts. She was assistant stage-manager for Rodney Ackland's play *After October*, which ran for a year in 1936, and then became stage-manager for the Group Theatre, an avant-garde theatre club at the Westminster Theatre.

With the outbreak of World War II imminent, Audrey Russell joined the London Fire Brigade (later the London Auxiliary Fire Service). She fought fires throughout the blitz. Stationed in Manchester Square, she was close to the BBC, and after she had been interviewed on the effects of the air raids she was asked to do a series of broadcasts on the work of the Auxiliary Fire Service, which included a description of the worst night of the blitz, 10 May 1941, when the House of Commons was bombed. This led to a secondment to the Air Ministry for six weeks, to do a series of talks on the work of the Women's Auxiliary Air Force.

In 1942 the BBC asked to have her released from national service in order to join the magazine programme *Radio Newsreel*. For two years she travelled all over the country, broadcasting from army camps, bomb sites, and rescue stations, interviewing those whose homes had been destroyed, and reporting on the damage done by flying bombs and rockets. On D-Day she was in Trafalgar Square interviewing people on their reactions to the Normandy landings. In 1944 she was accredited as a British war correspondent by the War Office, and went with the war reporting unit to Europe to send back dispatches from Belgium, Holland, Germany, and Norway. Suffering from influenza, she returned home in March 1945, and spent the rest of the war in London.

Determined to make a career in broadcasting rather than go back to the theatre, she accepted a post as a reporter in the new Home Service reporting unit, but she really wanted to be a commentator rather than a reporter. She was attracted by the tightrope quality of doing a live commentary, describing the action as it happens, which was very different from the work of a reporter, who could read from a script. She succeeded in 1947, when she was asked to join the outside broadcasts team commentating on the wedding of Princess Elizabeth, to cover the 'women's angle', describing the wedding dress and clothes worn by the guests.

She decided in 1948 to leave the news division and join the outside broadcasts department on a contract basis. She became one of the principal royal commentators on state occasions, covering eight royal weddings between 1947 and 1981. She covered the Festival of Britain in 1951, and went on the first of many royal tours in 1952. At the coronation in 1953 she was in Westminster Abbey to describe the processions, and then accompanied the six-month royal tour around the world by sea. Every year she broadcast from the Royal Maundy service. She covered the funerals of Sir Winston *Churchill and *Victoria (Mary), the princess royal, in 1965, and

described the silver jubilee in 1977 and the eightieth-birthday celebrations for the queen mother in 1980. In recognition of her work the queen gave her a hand-embroidered chair. Although she was never tempted to leave radio broacasting for television, she did a series of programmes on BBC television in the 1960s on the opening of the Queen's Gallery, Buckingham Palace, in 1962 and the first ten exhibitions held there.

Audrey Russell was the only woman to be an accredited war correspondent in World War II, and the first woman news reporter when she joined the Home Service in 1945. Her voice was instantly recognizable, and she was to radio coverage of state occasions what Richard *Dimbleby was to television. She became a freeman of the City of London in 1967, and was appointed MVO in 1976.

She was tall, blonde, and elegantly dressed, with a beautiful, calm speaking voice, with the slightest tinge of an Irish accent. She loved painting in oils, and collected art, as well as lecturing on art and antiques. She was unmarried, having broken off her engagement to Brent Grotrian, the heir to a baronetcy. He was later killed in Burma, in 1941. She died 8 August 1989 of Alzheimer's disease in Woking, Surrey.

[*The Times*, 10 August 1989; Audrey Russell, *A Certain Voice* (autobiography), 1984; Leonard Miall, *Inside the BBC, British Broadcasting Characters*, 1994; recordings in the National Sound Archive, 29 Exhibition Road, London.]   ANNE PIMLOTT BAKER

S

SAINT BRIDES, BARON (1916–1989), diplomat. [See JAMES, (JOHN) MORRICE (CAIRNS).]

SALOMON, SIR Walter Hans (1906–1987), banker, was born in Hamburg 16 April 1906, the elder son and second of three children of Henry Salomon, personal banker, and his wife, Rena Oppenheimer, from Vancouver. He was educated at the Oberrealschule, Eppendorf, Hamburg. He left at sixteen, partly because he upset its authorities by campaigning against a master active in extreme right-wing politics and partly to be independent of his father, who wanted him to sacrifice football to music.

He joined Bachach & Co., a small private bank, and became a partner at twenty-eight. He studied part-time at Hamburg University but, disillusioned by philosophy asking but not answering questions, did not take a degree. Asked to train as a middle-distance runner for the Olympics, he declined lest it delayed his career progression.

Quickly recognizing the full implications of Nazi policy for the Jews, he began in ingenious ways transferring funds for himself and his clients to London and New York. In 1937 he was investigated by the Gestapo and ordered to repatriate those funds. He immediately flew to London. His wife escaped across the Swiss border when security was slack at Christmas, and her parents joined them in London. Salomon's family escaped to Chile.

In London he formed Walter H. Salomon & Co., a private banking company, largely servicing other refugees. When war began he was interned near Liverpool and spent his time learning Spanish. If hard at work, he skipped roll-calls, asking a friend to answer for him since 'they're English, not German'. He was soon released and spent the rest of the war combining banking and helping to run a wartime factory. In 1946 he obtained British citizenship.

In 1948, by reverse take-over, he merged his business with the small merchant bank Rea Brothers, which became the hub of all his business activities for the rest of his life. He quickly became dominant in it, being its chairman from 1950 to 1984. He ran it on traditional German private banking lines, emphasizing confidentiality, personal commitment, and detailed control from the top. As well as accepting business from

England, he built strong links with clients in Germany and Brazil. In 1971 he became a commander of the Southern Cross of Brazil and in 1979 Germany gave him an officer's cross of the Order of Merit.

Over the years, Salomon became closely involved as adviser, director, or chairman with many other companies, particularly Furness Withy, Ocean Wilsons, Canal-Randolph, and Scottish & Mercantile.

In 1967 Rea Brothers was accepted into the prestigious Accepting Houses Committee, the only bank for generations to obtain this status without taking over an existing member. In the committee he showed little newcomer's diffidence, quickly becoming its most vociferous member. Frequently he hectored and irritated, but his views were never ignored. When talking, he often raised his left shoulder, turning his head to the right; many in the committee affectionately copied this gesture whilst passing on his latest *obiter dicta*.

In 1963 he demonstrated his belief in practical education by founding Young Enterprise, to teach young people business. Thirty years later 28,000 youngsters of school age throughout Britain were involved in 2,000 Young Enterprise companies. For this he was knighted in 1982.

As his status in the City grew, he became a prolific writer and commentator on public affairs, passionately proselytizing for individual freedom and against interference by government in business. His views were contained in his *One Man's View* (1973) and *Fair Warning* (1983), the latter a collection of essays. Although actively involved with the Liberal party in the 1950s, he later became an ardent supporter of Margaret (later Baroness) Thatcher, who valued his advice and individuality. Nevertheless, he fought bitterly against her government's imposition of new regulatory bodies on financial companies. He believed 'fonctionnaires' could not understand banking and threatened its cornerstone of secrecy.

Salomon was immensely proud of winning in 1964 a three-year battle in the courts with the customs, recovering £15 18s. excess duty on a camera. In private life, he was devoted to his family. He was an active club man, master of the Pattenmakers' Company (1977-8), keen on tennis and snooker, and excellent at bridge. He skied until late in life, enjoyed his large yacht, and built an outstanding collection of paintings, mainly of French Impressionists. He was slim, trim, and well proportioned, with an air of confident distinction. In town he always wore a bowler hat and a red carnation in his buttonhole.

In 1935 he married Kate, daughter of Walter Jacoby, sugar merchant. They had a son and a daughter. He died at his home in London, Castlemaine House in St James's, 16 June 1987, and was buried at Ohlsdorf in Hamburg.

[Private information; personal knowledge.]
GEORGE BLUNDEN

SAMUEL, Harold, BARON SAMUEL OF WYCH CROSS (1912–1987), businessman, was born 23 April 1912 at 8 Fairley Road, Finchley, northwest London, the second of three children and younger son of Vivian Samuel, master jeweller and later property developer, and his wife, Ada Cohen. He was educated at Mill Hill School and the College of Estate Management. He was then articled to surveyors and qualified as a fellow of the Royal Institution of Chartered Surveyors (1933). He set up as an estate agent in London, but subsequently decided to become a property developer and investor, and promptly ceased to practise, in order to avoid any conflict of interest.

In 1944 Samuel acquired the shares of an insignificant company, the Land Securities Investment Trust, which owned three properties with total assets of under £20,000. He foresaw that the key to the success of a property investment company was a strong base, a sound reputation, and the provision of fixed long-term finance at low interest rates. In 1947 profits from the Land Securities Investment Trust enabled him to provide the financial backing to secure bomb sites in provincial cities devastated during World War II. The associate company, which he formed for this purpose with colleagues and subsequently merged into Land Securities, succeeded in rebuilding the city centres of Plymouth, Exeter, Hull, Coventry, and Bristol.

Samuel adopted a revolving development policy, acquiring new sites to improve the portfolio and refurbishing or rebuilding existing holdings. His aims were to provide high-quality building in first-class locations, tenants of good standing, and architects' open competition to ensure innovative designs. He assembled throughout Britain a fine collection of income-producing commercial buildings of all types. He developed the financial muscle of his company, which enabled him to take over control of the United City Property Trust, Associated London Properties, the shares and assets of City Centre Properties, with its vast holdings and subsidiary companies, and the City of London Real Property Company,

with its exceptional portfolio of outstanding buildings. In 1953 he failed to gain control of the Savoy, an episode which ended in public acrimony. Eventually his company accounts showed assets of £3 billion. He donated generously to many charities, but liked to remain anonymous. Among others, he supported the Royal College of Surgeons and the universities of Cambridge and London. He was president of the Central London Housing Trust for the Aged, an honorary fellow of Magdalene College, Cambridge (1961), and University College London (1968), and vice-president of the British Heart Foundation. He was knighted in 1963 and became a life peer in 1972.

In 1936 Samuel married Edna, daughter of Harry Nedas, outfitter, of Manchester. They had three daughters, one of whom died in 1968. In 1947 the family moved from Hampstead to a house with extensive gardens in Regent's Park. There their love of horticulture and art was nurtured, and Samuel assembled an outstanding personal collection of paintings, which included works by Pieter Brueghel and Frans Hals. In 1952 he acquired an estate in Ashdown forest, Sussex, which provided more room for his growing art collection. He also completely renovated the mansion there and cultivated magnificent flower gardens. Samuel bequeathed his private art collection to the Corporation of London, where it hangs in the Mansion House.

Samuel was five feet ten inches tall, clean shaven, and with good regular features. He dressed immaculately, in formal and conservative style. He was a perfectionist, extremely precise, and a deep thinker with high standards of integrity. A shy man, he avoided public speaking. He died 28 August 1987 at Wych Cross Place, Forest Row, East Sussex.

[Edward Erdman, *People and Property*, 1982; personal knowledge.]
EDWARD ERDMAN

SANDYS, (Edwin) Duncan, BARON DUNCAN-SANDYS (1908–1987), politician, was born 24 January 1908 in Sandford Orcas, Dorset, the only child of Captain George John Sandys, of the 2nd Life Guards, later MP for Wells, and his wife, Mildred Cameron, of New Zealand. He had a Russian nanny and won the Newcastle prize for Russian at Eton, being the only entrant. At Magdalen College, Oxford, he read history, obtaining a second class in 1929. He then entered the Diplomatic Service in 1930, passing third in the competitive examination. Posted to the Berlin embassy, he improved his German and learned to fly.

He left the Diplomatic Service to stand successfully as Conservative candidate in the Norwood by-election in 1935. The same year he married Diana (died 1963), daughter of (Sir) Winston Leonard Spencer-*Churchill, and divorced wife of John Milner Bailey, the son of Churchill's friend, the multi-millionaire South African mine-owner, Sir Abe *Bailey, first baronet. Sandys struck up a close political relationship with his father-in-law, and was one of the few Conservative MPs who campaigned with Churchill to throw the Nazis out of the Rhineland by force in 1936 and for rearmament instead of appeasement. Like other young Conservative MPs, Sandys joined the Territorial Army and in 1938 he used inside knowledge for parliamentary questions designed to reveal anti-aircraft deficiencies. This angered the prime minister and the secretary of state for war, who knew that it was a Churchill ploy. Sandys was threatened with a court martial, but was exonerated by a select committee of privileges.

In 1940 Sandys went to Norway with the expeditionary force. On his return he commanded the Anti-Aircraft Rocket Regiment, driving through the night regularly to the launching base near Cardiff. On one of these trips he was involved in an accident and badly damaged both his feet. He suffered recurrent pain throughout his life, which may have affected his temperament but not his judgement. In the summer of 1944 the massive destruction of inner London by V1 and V2 flying bombs caused Churchill to put Sandys in charge of countermeasures. Sandys had been appointed chairman of a war cabinet committee on V weapons in 1943 when he was parliamentary secretary, Ministry of Supply, and become minister of works in 1944. With his scientific advisers he conceived the ingenious scheme of feeding the enemy false reports, through German spies who had been 'turned', about the landing zones of the bombs, in the hope the Germans would aim at less populated areas. Sandys transmitted a number of misleading signals, ignoring a cabinet directive, until at a second cabinet, despite Churchill's insistence, Herbert *Morrison (later Baron Morrison of Lambeth) vetoed the plan.

After his defeat in the Labour landslide of 1945 Sandys concentrated on helping his father-in-law in his campaign for a united Europe, accompanying him to Zurich for his famous speech. In 1950 he returned to the Commons as MP for Streatham. He became minister of supply in Churchill's postwar government in 1951, but by now Churchill's other son-in-law, Christopher (later Baron) *Soames, had superseded Sandys as the prime minister's chief confidant. Four years later Sandys was appointed minister of housing and local government by Sir Anthony *Eden (later the first Earl of Avon). He did not take a strong stand against the Suez war, although he expressed serious doubts in one letter to Eden, but, deeply disappointed over Eden's cold-shouldering of plans to form a Common Market at Messina in 1956, he buried himself in his own ministry. His enthusiasm for town planning lasted for the rest of his life and he was the pioneer of pedestrian town centres at home and abroad. He also inspired and inaugurated the Civic Trust. In 1957 Sandys became minister of defence and in 1959 of aviation. His 1957 defence white paper, the principles of which were accepted by successive governments, was largely drafted by him and called for drastic reductions in the armed forces and the end of conscription in favour of nuclear weapons; this made him unpopular with the services. In 1962 Sandys reached the peak of his career as secretary of state for the colonies, a post he held in tandem with that as secretary of state for Commonwealth relations, which he had become in 1960. The British empire was breaking up with demands for independence which could not be denied. Sandys, overcoming great difficulties, successfully negotiated independence for eleven former colonies including Cyprus, Malaya, Nigeria, Ghana, and Uganda. The continuous travel this demanded put a severe strain on his stamina and patience.

Sandys's front-bench career ended abruptly when (Sir) Edward Heath removed him from the shadow cabinet in 1964. According to Heath, this was because Sandys had been in the cabinet for thirteen years and, as it was likely to be five years until the next election, he wanted 'new faces'. Another factor may have been that Sandys, too outspoken for Heath and perhaps too right-wing, belonged to the landowning, aristocratic section of the parliamentary party with whom Heath did not always feel at home. He stayed active on the back benches, in 1969 unsuccessfully introducing a private Bill to limit Commonwealth immigration. He retired from the Commons in 1972 and in 1974 accepted a life barony. He continued to work for the European Movement and the Civic Trust, and took up abstract painting.

In his last years Sandys was privately bitter against Heath for dismissing him and for Heath's criticism of his role in Lonrho, of which he had become chairman in 1972, on the suggestion of the Bank of England. A Department of Trade report disclosed Sandys had been paid £130,000 by Lonrho in the Cayman Islands at a time when British residents were forbidden by exchange regulations to hold overseas accounts. Heath described this as 'the unacceptable face of capitalism'.

Sandys was one of the outstanding politicians of his generation, full of initiative and with a creative political mind. Tall and good looking, with red wavy hair, he might have reached higher office had he not been aloof and unwilling to go out of his way to cultivate his fellow MPs; he could also appear patronizing. He was always a master of his brief, never worsted at the dispatch box, but a slow worker who by over-stressing details could make his speeches dull. Nevertheless on occasions his colleagues were grateful to him for defusing a tense debate.

There were one son and two daughters from his first marriage. Diana became difficult to live with, and an embarrassment due to her heavy drinking, and there was a divorce on Sandys's petition in 1960. In 1962 he married Marie-Claire, daughter of Adrien Schmidt, of Paris, and former wife of Robert William Hudson, second Viscount Hudson. They had one daughter. His second marriage mellowed Sandys, helping him to appreciate the point of view of others. He became a privy councillor in 1944 and CH in 1973. After several years of ill health he died at his home in Warwick Square, London, 26 November 1987.

[Private information; personal knowledge.]

RICHARD LAMB

SARGANT, Thomas (1905–1988), law reformer, was born in Highgate, London, 17 August 1905, the fourth child in the family of five daughters and three sons of Norman Thomas Carr Sargant, commodity merchant, and his wife Alice Rose, daughter of William Davies Walters, a Methodist minister. Tom (as he was always known) was brought up in a household committed to devout Methodism, progressive politics (his father was four times a Liberal candidate), and high moral principles. He inherited all these commitments. He was educated at Highgate School, where he became head boy, won the public schools' mile, and gained a scholarship to Cambridge. However, his father got into financial difficulties and Sargant offered to join him in the family business instead of taking up his place at Cambridge. Eventually the business collapsed and Sargant went to work in the Royal Mint Refinery, where he later became commercial manager. He left the refinery in 1947 and held various jobs in the metal trade until at the end of 1955 he became ill with tuberculosis.

In 1941 he had published *These Things Shall Be*, a plea for a new and juster social order. The book came to the attention of Sir Richard *Acland, who invited Sargant to join the Christian Socialist movement, Common Wealth, which Acland was launching. Sargant stood for Common Wealth in a by-election in 1943 and in the general election of 1945. He then joined the Labour party, for which he stood in the 1950 and 1955 elections, again without success.

On his recovery from illness, Sargant found himself with no qualifications, no job, and no wish to return to the City. In November 1956 Peter Benenson, then a young barrister, asked Sargant to help in setting up an all-party group of lawyers to send observers to the trial of the leaders of the Hungarian revolution and to the treason trial in South Africa. Benenson persuaded leading lawyers from the three main political parties to convert their *ad hoc* group into a permanent organization for the protection of human rights and the rule of law, which was formally established under the name 'Justice' in June 1957, and became the British section of the International Commission of Jurists. Sargant's offer to act as the part-time secretary of Justice, at a salary of £500 a year, was accepted.

He remained the secretary of Justice for twenty-five years, until 1982. He had no legal training, but his concern with the legal process had been stimulated by his own experiences as a defendant in a libel action, in which he eventually succeeded, in the face of great difficulties, against a plaintiff supported by the General Medical Council. His sympathy for the underdog led him to begin taking up—contrary to instructions—the cases of individual prisoners who wrote to Justice complaining of wrongful convictions. His disregard of orders proved fortunate both for the prisoners whom he helped (he was able to secure the release of some twenty-five of them) and for Justice. Sargant's casework kept Justice firmly involved with the practical realities of the legal system and gave it an unrivalled expertise in the causes of miscarriages of justice and the problems of correcting them. He helped to make miscarriages of justice a matter of public concern through his co-operation with the BBC in producing a series of television programmes on the subject, under the title 'Rough Justice'.

Sargant was also actively involved in Justice's work on law reform. This was mainly achieved through reports prepared by expert committees, but he was influential in choosing the subjects, selecting the chairmen and members of the committees, and sometimes guiding their discussions. He was in no way overawed by the very distinguished lawyers, such as Lord *Gardiner, Sir John *Foster, and Lord Shawcross, who chaired the council of Justice. He was particularly proud of the part which Justice reports and his own efforts had played in the creation in 1967 of the post of 'ombudsman' (parliamentary commissioner for administration) and the extension of the ombudsman system into other fields; in the setting up of the Criminal Injuries Compensation Board; and in reforming the system of appeals in criminal cases. He also wrote, jointly, *More Rough Justice*, 1985, and *Criminal Trials: the Search for Truth*, 1986. He was appointed OBE in 1966, was awarded an honorary LL M by Queen's University, Belfast (1977), and sat for many years as a JP in Hampstead.

Sargant looked like a shabby eagle. Tall, angular, and untidy, he was usually covered in cigarette ash. In 1929 he married Marie, daughter of František Hloušek, shoemaker. They were divorced in 1942, and in that year he married

Dorothy, daughter of William Lattimer, headmaster. Sargant had two daughters by his first marriage and a son by his second. He died in Highgate 26 June 1988.

[Unpublished autobiography in the possession of the family; private information; personal knowledge.]

WILLIAM GOODHART

SAYERS, Richard Sidney (1908–1989), economist, was born 11 July 1908 in Bury St Edmunds, Suffolk, the fifth in the family of five sons (the eldest of whom died in infancy) and two daughters of Sidney James Sayers, county accountant for West Suffolk county council, and his wife, Caroline Mary Watson. He attended a succession of schools in Bury St Edmunds from 1912 to 1926, becoming head prefect in his last two years at West Suffolk County School. He entered St Catharine's College, Cambridge, in 1926, taking first classes (division II) in both parts of the economics tripos (1928 and 1929). Although he was made a member of J. M. (later Baron) *Keynes's Political Economy Club, it was to (Sir) Dennis *Robertson that he habitually sent drafts of his work before publication.

After postgraduate study in Cambridge he was appointed assistant lecturer at the London School of Economics in 1931 and remained there for four years before moving in 1935 to lecture in Oxford, where he became a fellow of Pembroke College in 1939. In 1936 he published *Bank of England Operations, 1890–1914*, which established Sayers's reputation as a monetary historian. Two years later, in need of additional income with the approaching birth of his second child, Sayers produced the first of seven editions of his internationally known textbook, *Modern Banking* (1938). Although a textbook, it gave expression to many original thoughts that are prominent in his later writings: his emphasis on liquidity; his judgement that the bank rate is a 'halting, clumsy, indeed a brutal instrument'; and his scepticism of unsupported monetary policy ('I know of no case in monetary history of a dear money policy alone producing a general deflation of money incomes').

During World War II Sayers worked in the Ministry of Supply, where his duties carried him into the secret area of the atomic bomb and negotiations for the development of uranium supplies. At the end of the war he was persuaded by James Meade to serve as deputy director of the economic section of the Cabinet Office, but after two years opted to resume his academic career, accepting the Sir Ernest Cassel chair of economics at the LSE in 1947 and remaining there until he took early retirement in 1968.

In the 1950s he produced or edited half a dozen books, including one of his major works—some would say his best—*Financial Policy 1939–45*, which was part of the official war history. This took over five years to complete, appearing finally in 1956. It recreated the atmosphere of the wartime Treasury and dealt with both economic and political issues with great skill. Another work—his favourite though not his best—was his history of Lloyds Bank (1957).

In the spring of 1957 he was appointed a member of the committee on the working of the monetary system, chaired by Baron (later Viscount) *Radcliffe, the most important assignment of his life. He played a dominant part in the committee's affairs, undertaking much of the examination of witnesses and drafting the key sections of its report (1959). The reception accorded to the report was a bitter disappointment to Sayers. 'Two years of my life—two years wasted!' he once exclaimed.

His disappointment did not prevent a considerable volume of new work, most of it essays and articles but also a centenary history of Gillett's discount house (1968). Sayers was much in demand as a historian of banking institutions. He was considered as a possible historian of the Federal Reserve System and invited to produce a sequel to Sir J. H. *Clapham's history of the Bank of England to 1914. This was completed in 1976, in three volumes covering the years from 1891 to 1944, in celebration of the 250th anniversary of the founding of the Bank. The history was highly praised but left Sayers dissatisfied.

Apart from his academic duties, Sayers was editorial adviser and 'chief architect' of the *Three Banks Review* for twenty years from its foundation in 1948, was closely associated for a time with the editorial side of *Economica*, and from 1969 to 1974 was publications secretary of the British Academy, of which he was made a fellow in 1957 and became vice-president in 1966–7.

He was a superb lecturer, taking immense pains over his lectures and expressing himself, both in lectures and in conversation, slowly and with deliberation. He took great trouble over his graduate students—most of them from abroad. His former pupils are said to have included nineteen ministers of finance.

He was temperamentally a loner who preferred to get on with his work without much social activity. This tendency was accentuated after the war by a bad back, which obliged him to rest for long spells. None the less he was basically a healthy and vigorous man and would walk for hours over rough country even with arthritic hips. Latterly, however, his health deteriorated and in his last few years he was more or less bedridden. Music, art, and walking were his main non-academic interests. In appearance he was tall and lean, clean-shaven, and good-looking.

In 1967 the universities of Warwick and Kent

conferred honorary degrees on him and the University of Cambridge sought to do so unsuccessfully. He was an honorary fellow of his old Cambridge college, St Catharine's, and of the LSE and the Institute of Bankers. After the publication of *The Bank of England* he was offered, but refused, a knighthood.

In 1930 Sayers married an old classmate, Millicent, daughter of William Henry John Hodson, bookkeeper in a brewery. They had a son and a daughter, but the marriage eventually broke down. In 1985 he finally left his wife and went to live with Audrey Taylor, an old associate, in Eastbourne, where he died after a long illness, separated from his family, 25 February 1989.

[Information from professors Theodore Barker, Leslie Pressnell, and J. S. G. Wilson and from Sayers's family; Alec Cairncross in *Proceedings of the British Academy*, vol. lxxvi, 1990; personal knowledge.]

ALEC CAIRNCROSS

SCHMITTHOFF, Clive Macmillan (1903–1990), legal scholar and barrister, was born Maximilian Schmitthoff in Berlin 24 March 1903, the eldest in the family of one son and two daughters of Hermann Schmitthoff, a prominent Berlin lawyer, and his wife Anna. After a classical education at the Friedrichsgymnasium in Berlin, he read law at the University of Freiburg im Breisgau and later at the University of Berlin, studying under the well-known jurist Professor Martin Wolff, with whom he quickly established a warm rapport and later collaborated in publications. Awarded his doctorate in law at Berlin in 1927, he joined his father's flourishing law practice and quickly became a successful advocate in the Berlin *Kammergericht* (court of appeal). But in 1933 he was forced to leave Germany for England, where he lived for the rest of his life, assuming the name Clive, and altering Maximilian to Macmillan. Having obtained an LL M degree at the London School of Economics in 1936 he was called to the bar in Gray's Inn, becoming a tenant in the chambers of (Sir) Valentine *Holmes, where he had served his pupillage. Lacking the contacts to make a full-time living at the bar, he became a part-time lecturer in German at the City of London College (later the City of London Polytechnic) and wrote books on commercial German and German poetry and prose. A cultured man, he maintained a keen interest in literature, art, and music throughout his life. He was naturalized in July 1946.

After wartime service in the Pioneer Corps and Canadian Engineers as a warrant officer, during which he took part in the Normandy landings and received several medals, he returned to England, to the War Office. He then went back to the City of London College, initially in the language department but later becoming a lecturer in law in the department of professional studies (lecturer 1948–58, senior lecturer 1958–63, principal lecturer 1963–71). Right up to the time of his retirement he had an abiding loyalty to his first academic home, resisting all blandishments to accept university chairs.

Schmitthoff was in love with the law in all its manifestations. A superb teacher and devoted to his students, he also maintained a successful consultancy practice at the bar. Of medium build and thoughtful demeanour, he had an infectious enthusiasm and humour which captivated students and clients alike. He combined prodigious energy with enterprise and vision. In 1948 he founded the Mansfield Law Club, also establishing a highly successful summer school in English law for foreign students. He developed the MA in business law, the first postgraduate law degree to be offered in the polytechnic sector. He co-founded the Association of Law Teachers in 1966 and was its honorary vice-president until the time of his death. He was a prolific and scholarly writer, with countless articles to his credit in legal periodicals around the world. His first major English law textbook, *A Textbook of the English Conflict of Laws*, was published in 1945. He also wrote a book on the sale of goods, and for many years from 1960 co-edited *Charlesworth's Mercantile Law*. He was general editor of *Palmer's Company Law* for nearly thirty years, from 1959. He was also the founder and editor of the *Journal of Business Law* (1957–89). In 1953 he received an LL D from the University of London in recognition of his scholarship.

Schmitthoff's most striking achievements lay in the field of international trade law, which he created as a subject of academic study and made peculiarly his own. His classic textbook, *The Export Trade*, first published in 1948 and translated into several languages, was the first work to give an overall picture of the law, practice, and institutional structure of international trade law and practice, and in 1979 he became vice-president of the Institute of Export. It was his report *The Progressive Development of the Law of International Trade* (1966), commissioned by the United Nations, that led to the establishment of the United Nations Commission on International Trade Law (UNCITRAL), devoted to the harmonization of international trade law; and it is he who is credited with first propounding the new *lex mercatoria*, the transnational law of international trade, a subject on which he wrote extensively.

Schmitthoff's retirement in 1971 was purely notional. His scholarly publications continued unabated. His seventieth birthday was celebrated with a Festschrift in his honour, *Law and International Trade* (ed. Fritz Fabricius). He continued to lecture extensively in England and abroad. He held the Gresham chair in law at City University, London (1976–86), and honorary and visiting professorships at a number of universities, including the University of Kent at Canterbury, City University, the Ruhr University Bochum, and Notre Dame University, and received honorary doctorates from several universities in Britain and abroad, and from the Council for National Academic Awards. In 1974 he received the grand cross of the German Order of Merit. In 1983 his colleagues at Kent published a collection of essays by way of tribute, *Essays for Clive Schmitthoff* (ed. John Adams).

The passing of the years seemed to have little impact on him. In 1985, his ninth decade, he became joint vice-chairman of the Centre for Commercial Law Studies at Queen Mary (later Queen Mary and Westfield) College, University of London, where he introduced and co-taught an LL M course on international trade law, at the same time establishing and organizing a series of annual conferences on international commercial law. A new edition of *Palmer* appeared in 1987 and of *The Export Trade* in 1990. A week before his death he was busy editing a set of conference papers and arranging a meeting with his publishers to discuss new projects. Despite his huge following he was essentially a private man, at his happiest working alone in his study.

In 1940 he married Ilse ('Twinkie'), daughter of a leading Frankfurt lawyer, Ernst Moritz Auerbach, and herself a lawyer. They had no children. He died 30 September 1990 at the Charing Cross Hospital, London.

[Fritz Fabricius (ed.), *Law and International Trade*, 1973; Chia-Jui Cheng (ed.), *Clive M. Schmitthoff's Select Essays on International Trade Law*, 1988; private information; personal knowledge.]   ROY GOODE

SCOTT, SIR Peter Markham (1909–1989), conservationist, painter, naturalist, sportsman, writer, and broadcaster, was born at 174 Buckingham Palace Road, London, 14 September 1909, the only child of Captain Robert Falcon *Scott, Antarctic explorer, and his wife Kathleen Bruce, sculptor, daughter of Canon Lloyd Stewart Bruce. His father died in 1912 and in 1922 his mother married Edward Hilton *Young, who became first Baron Kennet. There was one son of this marriage. In his last message home before he died Scott had urged his wife to make his son interested in natural history, which was better than sport. In the event, Peter Scott came to excel at both. He was an energetic child, with a passion for natural history, who spent much time drawing and painting. He also shone at sports, ice-skating, and sailing in small boats. From his preparatory school, West Downs, he went to

Oundle. He then studied at Trinity College, Cambridge (1927–30), where he hoped to take the natural sciences tripos, but failed his part i (1930). He stayed on for an extra term and obtained an ordinary degree in December 1930 (zoology, botany, and history of art). During his Cambridge days he took up wildfowling, and in 1929 *Country Life* magazine printed two articles on the sport written and illustrated by him.

From Cambridge he went to the Munich Academy for a term, and then spent two years at the Royal Academy Schools in London. In 1933 he held his first one-man exhibition, which was a huge success, at Ackermann's Galleries in London. He was able to make his living as a painter of wildfowl, producing his first book (entitled *Morning Flight* and published by *Country Life*) in 1935. This was followed by *Wild Chorus* in 1938. Lavishly illustrated with his paintings, both books became very popular and ran to twelve editions.

Scott excelled at sailing and won a bronze medal in the 1936 Olympic Games, for single-handed yachting. He also won the prestigious Prince of Wales cup for international fourteen-foot dinghies in 1937, 1938, and 1946. In the late 1950s he developed a passion for gliding, and won the British gliding championships in 1963.

At the outbreak of war in 1939 he volunteered for the Royal Naval Volunteer Reserve. After training he spent two years in destroyers, mainly in HMS *Broke* in the Western approaches, becoming a first lieutenant, and then he served in the coastal forces in steam gunboats. He became senior officer of the flotilla, was awarded a DSC (1943) and bar, and was thrice mentioned in dispatches. He also invented a night camouflage scheme for naval ships. His final appointment was the command of a new frigate, as a lieutenant-commander. With the war coming to a close, Scott was adopted as the Conservative candidate for Wembley North, but he failed to be elected by 435 votes, having had only two weeks to prepare for the election.

While visiting the river Severn at Slimbridge in Gloucestershire in 1945, in search of a rare goose amongst the wintering white-fronted geese, he decided to establish a research organization, which he had planned for many years, to study the swans, geese, and ducks of the world. The Severn Wildfowl Trust was set up at Slimbridge in 1946 and soon boasted the largest collection of wildfowl in the world. Later known as the Wildfowl and Wetlands Trust, it expanded into nine centres around Britain. Scott remained its honorary director until he died. Scientific research took Scott to Iceland in 1951 to study pink-footed geese on their breeding grounds, and to the Perry river region of northern Canada, where in 1949 he mapped this unknown area while in search of the breeding grounds of the ross goose. Scott did more than any British contemporary to save wildlife species from extinction.

When the BBC founded a television centre in Bristol Scott helped to establish the Natural History Unit there, planning a programme on natural history called *Look*, which he hosted for seventeen years. Many of the early programmes contained his own film which he shot on his travels. He took part in *Nature Parliament*, a radio programme which ran for twenty-one years, and was the narrator in many other programmes.

In the early 1950s Scott became involved with the International Union for the Conservation of Nature and Natural Resources (IUCN). He helped build up the Species Survival Commission of the union and became chairman (1962–81). With two friends, in 1961 he founded the World Wildlife Fund (later the World Wide Fund for Nature) to raise the money needed to finance nature conservation around the world. As its chairman from 1961, he designed its panda logo and invented the red data books listing endangered species. He travelled abroad extensively on behalf of the Fund, establishing national appeals, advising on conservation issues and areas for reserves, lecturing, and fundraising. He was also involved in numerous other conservation and naturalist societies. He became as much of an expert on coral fish as he was on birds and his records have proved scientifically useful.

His autobiography, *The Eye of the Wind*, was published in 1961 and was reprinted many times. He was a prolific author and illustrator, his final books being the three volumes of *Travel Diaries of a Naturalist*, published in 1983, 1985, and 1987 respectively.

He was elected rector of Aberdeen University (1960–3) and appointed chancellor of Birmingham University (1974–83). Appointed MBE (1942) and CBE (1953), he was knighted in 1973. In 1987 he became both CH and a fellow of the Royal Society. He had honorary degrees from the universities of Exeter, Aberdeen, Birmingham, Bristol, Liverpool, Bath, Guelph, and Ulster. He was also awarded numerous medals, prizes, and foreign honours.

Strongly built and of average height, Scott was warm and friendly, tackling everything with enthusiasm. He liked to paint every day. In 1942 he married the novelist Elizabeth Jane Howard, daughter of David Liddon Howard, timber merchant. They had a daughter. This marriage was dissolved in 1951 and in the same year he married (Felicity) Philippa, daughter of Commander Frederick William Talbot-Ponsonby, of the Royal Navy, and his wife Hannah (née Findlay). They had a daughter and a son. Peter

Scott died from a heart attack in hospital in Bristol 29 August 1989.

[Peter Scott, *The Eye of the Wind* (autobiography), 1961; Jonathan Benington, *Sir Peter Scott at 80: a Retrospective* (catalogue including a biography), 1989; Elspeth Huxley, *Peter Scott*, 1993; personal knowledge.]   PAUL WALKDEN

SCOTT, William George (1913–1989), painter and printmaker, was born 15 February 1913 in Greenock, Scotland, the third of eleven children and eldest son of William John Scott, a sign writer and house decorator from Enniskillen in county Fermanagh, Northern Ireland, and his Scottish wife, Agnes Murray. The family removed to Enniskillen in 1924, where he attended Enniskillen Technical School and, encouraged by his father, enrolled in evening classes in art. In 1928 he entered Belfast College of Art with a local scholarship. From 1931 to 1935 Scott studied at the Royal Academy Schools in London, where he won the silver medal for sculpture in 1933, the Landseer scholarship in painting (1934), and a Leverhulme travelling scholarship in 1935. Once freed from the restrictions of academic training, he sought alternatives to both English landscape painting and to the Surrealist and abstract modes of the day.

In 1937 he married (Hilda) Mary, daughter of William Lucas, a paint manufacturer of Bristol. She was a sculptor, and a fellow student at the Academy Schools. They were to have two sons. For the next two years they travelled in Italy and the south of France, and taught during the summers at a painting school at Pont Aven in Brittany. It was there that Scott did his first mature paintings. They prefigure his later work in their modesty of subject-matter (the single figure, still life, and landscape), a deliberate simplicity in composition, a painterly touch, and rich tonality. Cézanne was an important influence, and Scott was also affected by other French painters, notably Bonnard and Matisse. In November 1938 he exhibited at the Salon d'Automne, and was elected sociétaire.

At the outbreak of war in September 1939 the Scotts moved to Dublin, where their elder son, Robert, was born in January 1940. After a few months in London, in 1941 they took a cottage at Hallatrow in Somerset, where Scott created a market garden and taught part-time at Bath Academy of Art. James, his second son, was born in July 1941. In 1942, shortly before his first one-man exhibition at the Leger Gallery, London, Scott volunteered for the armed forces, and joined the Royal Engineers. As an ordnance mapmaker he learned lithography, and in north Wales made water-colour landscapes in the pervasive English Romantic mode of the time.

These were shown in London in 1944 and 1945.

In September 1946 Scott painted the seminal 'The Frying Pan', his first table-top still life featuring a frying-pan, bowl, and toasting-fork, props that with a number of other simple kitchen objects (saucepans, spoons, eggs, beans, fish, etc.) were to recur as motifs in his work. Scott invested these simple things with multivalent symbolic significance, first as attributes of the elemental life of the simple poor; later they seem to be the components of obscure sexual encounters in what Scott referred to as 'the secret in the picture'. This intensity of regard for domestic objects was derived from a French tradition of still-life painting (variously exemplified by J. B. S. Chardin, Paul Cézanne, and Georges Braque), with which Scott felt a particular affinity.

In 1946 Scott had returned to Hallatrow, and was appointed senior painting master at Bath Academy of Art, now at Corsham Court in Wiltshire. He taught there, highly regarded by staff and students, until 1956. During the late 1940s he made fruitful contacts with many of those St Ives artists associated with Ben *Nicholson, who were moving towards a simplifying abstraction of forms. These artists, among them Roger *Hilton, Terry Frost, (G.) Peter Lanyon, Bryan Winter, Patrick Heron, and Adrian Heath, formed the nucleus of a British school of abstract painting, within which Scott was to be a prime mover and major influence throughout the 1950s.

Scott maintained an individual creative course, the momentum and direction of which was determined by his own predilections towards a reductive simplification of forms and an evocative richness of surface texture. In 1953 in New York he was the first British painter to meet the abstract expressionists at first hand, and was impressed by the expansive scale and confidence of their work. The effect was to confirm his sense of identity as essentially a European painter, whose abstraction was derived from first-hand experience of the world of familiar objects and phenomena. He returned to the painterly evocation of figurative subjects, freed from direct description but never absolutely free of reference. In the mid-1960s Scott experimented with an even-surfaced decorative abstraction, but the flattened outlines of domestic utensils and ambiguous fruit and vegetable forms invariably found their way back into his work. These formal and symbolic elements of the pictorial drama are unmistakably personal in origin, and resolutely modern in their deployment on the flat surface of the canvas.

William Scott was widely recognized as an artist of international standing. He represented Britain at the twenty-ninth Venice Biennale in 1958, and at the sixth Bienal, São Paulo, in 1961.

He received honorary doctorates from the Royal College of Art (1975), Queen's University in Belfast (1976), and Trinity College, Dublin (1977). The Tate Gallery mounted a major retrospective in 1972. He was elected ARA in 1977 and RA in 1984. He was appointed CBE in 1966. Scott was unostentatious in appearance; but his emphatic dark brows and small beard were expressive of an intense temperament. Small and wiry, and compact of energy, he was quick and precise in his gestures, and deliberate in manner. He died in Coleford, Somerset, 28 December 1989, after suffering from Alzheimer's disease for several years. Scott's work is represented in many public collections, in Britain and abroad, including the Tate Gallery, the Ulster Museum, the Scottish National Gallery of Modern Art, and the Guggenheim Museum, New York.

[Ronald Alley, *William Scott*, 1963; Alan Bowness, *William Scott Paintings*, 1964, and *William Scott*, 1972; Norbert Lynton, *William Scott*, 1990; Tate Gallery catalogue, 1972; William Scott Foundation archives, 13 Edith Terrace, London SW10.]   MEL GOODING

SCUPHAM, John (1904–1990), educationist and broadcaster, was born 7 September 1904 in Market Rasen, Lincolnshire, the younger son and third of five children of Roger Scupham, master builder and monumental mason, and his wife Kate, daughter of Thomas Hulme Whittingham, proprietor of the *Rasen Mail* and bookseller. He was educated at Market Rasen Grammar School and then became a scholar of Emmanuel College, Cambridge, gaining first-class honours in part i of the history tripos (1925) and in English (1926).

He was a polymath, who would have been a scientist had his school been able to provide the grounding. His wide reading, together with an intense interest in people of all kinds, no doubt contributed to his success as a teacher. From 1927 to 1946 his experience was unusually varied, with teaching in grammar schools in Newcastle, Liverpool, and Derby, Workers' Educational Association tutoring in Forces Education, and running the department of liberal studies and adult education at Cambridge Technical College. He prided himself on the fact that he had done everything from teaching apprentices to write a few lines of literate English to examining open scholarships in history at a group of Cambridge colleges.

From 1946 to 1965 he worked in educational broadcasting at the BBC. Starting as an education officer with the School Broadcasting Council, a body representing the educational world within the Corporation, he progressed rapidly to become assistant head of school broadcasting and in 1954 was made head of educational broadcasting. His work with the Council, visiting schools and colleges and meeting other educationists, enabled him to guide the production departments in what was needed. His profound understanding of the issues involved in teaching and learning through broadcasts made him a formidable head of the complete production machine and in 1963 he was made the first controller, educational broadcasting. This enhanced role reflected the expansion that had occurred under his aegis as head.

The expansion, which he promoted with considerable energy and fortitude, was mainly exemplified by the creation of a School Television Department in 1959 and a Further Education Department in 1965, which, when added to the two equivalent radio departments, constituted a large output 'empire'. This was resented by a number of very senior managers in the television service. It took them some time to realize that Scupham's small yet precise physique, his quiet, reasonable negotiating style, and his absolute moral integrity concealed a steely will. He believed passionately in the importance of disseminating knowledge widely and saw broadcasting as a new, powerful medium through which to achieve this both at home and abroad. Like John (later first Baron) *Reith, the BBC's first director-general, he worked tirelessly in the arena of international broadcasting and, as he reveals in his books, *Broadcasting and the Community* (1967) and *The Revolution in Communications* (1970), believed that mass media have important social purposes. He was appointed OBE in 1961.

Towards the end of his BBC career he helped to devise plans for a College of the Air, but when the more ambitious Open University project emerged he worked assiduously and diplomatically to see that the BBC played a vital role. After retiring from the BBC in 1965 he sat on the ministerial committee to advise on the setting up of the university, and from 1969 to 1978 was a member of its council. He was awarded an Open University honorary doctorate in 1975. Among his many other activities were participation in the inquiry undertaken by (Sir) John *Newsom in 1961–3, which championed the educational needs of less able children, and in the Church of England board of education (1960–72), as well as the presidency of the educational section of the British Association (1965–6).

Scupham was a lifelong, but not uncritical, member of the Church of England, a proud provincial, who combined a sense of life's mysteries with an extensive knowledge of modern thinking. Like Matthew *Arnold he thought that 'the men of culture are the true apostles of equality', but was wise enough at the end of his life to see that times were changing.

In 1932 he married Dorothy Lacey (died 1987), daughter of Fred Clark, a Lincolnshire draper, and their happy marriage produced a son and a daughter. Scupham died 10 January 1990 in Norwich, near to his daughter, having lived much of his married life in Harpenden.

[Recorded interview with John Scupham, 1984, for BBC Oral History Project, Broadcasting House, London; BBC Written Archives Centre, Caversham Park, Reading; private information; personal knowledge.]

JOHN CAIN

SEEBOHM, Frederic, BARON SEEBOHM (1909–1990), banker and philanthropist, was born 18 January 1909 at Poynder's End, Hitchin, Hertfordshire, the second in the family of three sons and one daughter of Hugh Exton Seebohm, banker, of Poynder's End, and his wife Leslie, daughter of George James Gribble. He was the grandson of the historian Frederic *Seebohm. The Seebohm family had emigrated from Germany to York in the mid-nineteenth century, and subsequently had been for three generations Quakers and bankers at Hitchin; their bank had been one of the constituents of Barclays Bank Limited on its formation in 1896. Seebohm was educated at the Dragon School, Oxford, at Leighton Park School in Reading, and then at Trinity College, Cambridge, where he read economics but left after two years (having achieved a third class in part i in 1929) to enter Barclays Bank, Cambridge, in 1929. He spent most of the next twenty-five years in Sheffield, where he was posted in 1932, and after the war in York and Birmingham, as a local director. During this time he developed his interest in social services as treasurer of the Sheffield council of social service, chairman of the community council in York, and a member of the Joseph Rowntree Memorial Trust. The Seebohms were related to the Rowntree family.

In 1938 he joined the Territorial Army and in 1939 was commissioned in the Royal Artillery. After attending the Staff College in 1944, he was posted to Supreme Headquarters Allied Expeditionary Force, as a lieutenant-colonel (GSO 1). In 1945 he was mentioned in dispatches and awarded the bronze star of America.

He was appointed a director of Barclays Bank Limited in 1947 and in 1951 of Barclays Bank (Dominion, Colonial and Overseas). In 1957 he moved to London in a full-time executive position in Barclays Bank DCO, becoming a deputy chairman in 1959 and chairman in 1965. Seebohm developed DCO from a federation of retail banks in the ex-colonies and South Africa into an international bank operating on a worldwide basis.

In spite of constant travelling overseas he continued to extend his interests in the City as chairman of Friends' Provident Life Office (1962–8), the Export Guarantees Advisory Council (1967–72), and Barclays Bank Limited, where he became deputy chairman in 1968. In 1966–8 he was president of the Institute of Bankers. He was knighted in 1970. In 1972 he retired as chairman of DCO which, as part of his international strategy, had been taken over by Barclays Bank Limited in 1971 and renamed Barclays Bank International. He remained deputy chairman of Barclays until 1974 but, although he remained on the board until 1979, his interests were increasingly elsewhere. From 1974 to 1979 he was chairman of Finance for Industry, which had been set up by the banks in the aftermath of World War II to assist in the development of industry, a subject close to Seebohm's heart.

His wider reputation and his life peerage, in 1972, came from his other great interest, social service. His earlier experience made him a natural choice to head (1965–8) the government's inquiry into local authority and allied personal social services, which led to the Seebohm report (1968). The far-reaching conclusions, most of which were embodied in the Local Authority (Social Services) Act of 1970, owed much to his strong personal convictions, skilled chairmanship, and vigorous advocacy. He maintained from the House of Lords, where he sat as an independent, a close interest in subsequent developments in the social services, as well as in financial matters, and served as chairman of the Joseph Rowntree Memorial Trust, and president of Age Concern, the National Institute of Social Work, the Royal Africa Society, and the Overseas Development Institute. He was asked by the government to report on naval welfare (1974) and the British Council (1980). He was high sheriff of Hertfordshire in 1970–1. He received an honorary LL D from Nottingham in 1970 and an honorary D.Sc. from Aston in 1976.

Seebohm's rather military bearing, conciseness of speech, and formidable powers of chairmanship, combined with a very direct approach and strong, sometimes unconventional, views, won him respect and affection in the many fields to which he contributed. In later years he became a member of the Society of Friends, which his father had left on 'marrying out'. He was a keen shot, played real tennis, and was later a skilled gardener and competent water-colourist. He became an honorary member of the Royal Watercolour Society.

In 1932 he married Evangeline, daughter of Sir Gerald Hurst, QC; they had two daughters (one of them the writer Victoria Glendinning) and one son. Lady Seebohm died thirteen days after her husband as a result of a motor accident near Sutton Scotney in Hampshire. Seebohm died in the accident, 15 December 1990.

[Archives of Barclays Bank; private information.]

PETER LESLIE

SELLORS, Sir Thomas Holmes (1902–1987), cardiothoracic surgeon, was born 7 April 1902 in Wandsworth, the only son and younger child of Thomas Blanchard Sellors, a family doctor, and his wife, Anne Oliver McSparron. His father later practised at Westcliff-on-Sea, where Tom, as he was always known, was educated at Alleyn Court School. He then went to Loretto College, Musselburgh, and Oriel College, Oxford, where he received a second class in physiology (1923). He secured an entrance scholarship to the Middlesex Hospital, qualifying BM, Ch.B. and MRCS, LRCP in 1926 before holding resident and surgical registrar appointments there. After a thorough grounding in general surgery, including a year in Scandinavia as recipient of the first G. H. Hunt award by Oxford University in 1928, he decided to specialize in chest work, which was then a rather limited field. He became FRCS in 1930.

In 1934 he was appointed to the London Chest Hospital and then to various London county council hospitals and sanatoria, for some 90 per cent of thoracic surgery was then concerned with pulmonary tuberculosis. In 1933 he surprised many of his seniors with the publication of *Surgery of the Thorax*, and during the 1930s he started chest surgery units at the Radcliffe Infirmary, Oxford, and Leicester Royal Infirmary, which entailed even more travelling and a heavy workload. He became DM in 1933.

On the outbreak of World War II he became adviser in thoracic surgery to the north-west metropolitan region of the Emergency Medical Service, based on Harefield Hospital, Middlesex. In the next few years, in addition to his tuberculosis work, he did an increasing number of resections for lung and gullet cancer, whilst the nascent field of heart surgery slowly demanded more of his time and interest. On appointment as thoracic surgeon to the Middlesex Hospital in 1947 he enjoyed close and cordial relationships with the cardiologists D. Evan Bedford and Walter Somerville, which were to prove vital to the development of more complex heart surgery. He was responsible for the creation of three cardiac surgical units—at Harefield (which remained his first love), the Middlesex, and finally, in 1957, the National Heart Hospital.

Sellors showed a healthy conservatism in avoiding frankly experimental procedures, but was quick to utilize the significant advances of his contemporaries. Before there was a practicable heart–lung machine for open heart surgery he learned his hypothermic technique from Henry Swann in the United States and closed some 500 atrial septal defects with overall results which were unrivalled at that time. He and his team then acquired the early cardiopulmonary bypass technique from John Kirklin at the Mayo Clinic. Sellors became FRCP in 1963.

Ever courteous in the operation room, and never known to raise his voice (the fiercest reaction to an inept assistant was no more than his favourite admonition 'Juggins!'), Sellors was a superb craftsman, a master of sharp dissection. He did the first successful direct operation on the pulmonary heart valve for the relief of valvular stenosis, but, characteristically, was not the first to publish this success. He had retired from practice before coronary artery surgery was established and later frankly admitted that he had wrongly believed the successful and lasting anastomosis of such small vessels to be impracticable.

From the inception of the National Health Service Sellors was active in the medico-political field. Having been chairman of his regional consultants' and specialists' committee for some years, he was an inaugural member of the central committee and its chairman for five years. In 1958 he became chairman of the Joint Consultants' Committee, which linked the British Medical Association with the various royal colleges, an arduous task which he undertook for nine years. For this work, and his services to surgery, he was knighted in 1963. A Hunterian professor of the Royal College of Surgeons in 1944, he was elected to its council in 1957, and was vice-president in 1968–9 and president in 1969–72. He was president of the British Medical Association in 1972–3 and was awarded its gold medal in 1979. Throughout his busy surgical life he travelled widely abroad, lecturing and demonstrating. He was awarded honorary fellowships of the American (1971) and South African surgical colleges, as well as those of Edinburgh (1972) and the Royal College of Surgeons in Ireland (1975). He had honorary degrees from Groningen (1964), Liverpool (1970), and Southampton (1972), and was an honorary fellow of Oriel College, Oxford (1973).

Well after his retirement from surgical practice he laboured for many good causes. Apart from his early textbook he wrote a number of surgical papers and edited several cardiothoracic works. Outside his professional work he had a capacity for gracious living. He was a keen gardener, a fine draftsman, and a competent painter in water-colours. He had great sympathy and kindness, and a quiet wit.

Sellors was of medium height and portly build, with a fine Churchillian head; his reading spectacles were generally perched near the end of his nose. He was thrice married and thrice widowed. His first wife, Brenda Lyell, died of acute appendicitis a few weeks after their marriage in 1928. She was the daughter of William Darling Lyell, advocate and sheriff-substitute of Lanark. In 1932 he married (Dorothy) Elizabeth, daughter of John Chesshire, businessman. They had a son, Patrick, who became surgeon oculist

to the queen, and a daughter. Elizabeth died in 1953 and in 1955 Sellors married his secretary, Marie Hobson, who died in 1985. She was the daughter of Martin Greenwall or Grunwald, aeronautical engineer. Sellors died 12 September 1987 in Parkside Hospital, Wimbledon, of carcinoma of the colon and chronic prostatic obstruction.

[*Munk's Roll*, vol. viii, 1989; private information; personal knowledge.]   REGINALD MURLEY

SEMPRINI, (Fernando Riccardo) Alberto (1908–1990), pianist and conductor, was born 27 March 1908 in Bath, the second of three sons (there were no daughters) of Arturo Riccardo Fernando Semprini, musician, from Rimini, Italy, and his wife, Elizabeth Tilley, opera singer, from Dudley, Worcestershire. The family settled in Bath until Alberto was nine, when his father, a horn player, was appointed librarian to the Scala Opera House, Milan. The boy was intensely musical and won a state scholarship to the Conservatorio Verdi to study piano, composition, and conducting. When he was only sixteen Arturo Toscanini, chief conductor of the Scala, auditioned him for the fiendishly difficult orchestral piano part in Igor Stravinsky's ballet *Petroushka* and gave him the job.

On his vacations he played the piano on transatlantic liners, and while in New York was enthralled by jazz groups and the popular concert orchestra of André Kostelanetz. He discovered he could play this sort of repertoire far better than most classically trained pianists, and this seems to have proved a decisive influence in shaping his career. Another consideration was his marriage in Italy in 1931 to Brunilde Regarbagnati and the arrival of three sons to clothe, feed, and educate.

Semprini left the Conservatorio in 1929 with a doctorate of music and though he occasionally conducted at the Scala and elsewhere, the piano was his first love. In the 1930s he and another Italian pianist Bormioli toured Europe as a popular piano duo, and later he formed his own rhythm orchestra in Italy, with which he made records, broadcasted, and played in a number of musical films. The outbreak of war in 1939 halted his career. He had angered the Fascist authorities by playing western music against their orders, and though he had dual Italian and British citizenship, both passports were confiscated, obliging the family to keep a low profile. When eventually the Allies advanced into southern Italy he managed to get to Rome, where he volunteered for ENSA, the Services entertainments organization, and gave many front-line concerts, his piano on the back of an army truck.

Among his troop audiences was the actor Michael Brennan, who offered to be his manager if he ever came to England. But immediately after the war he went to work and study in Spain, where he fell in love with a young Spanish dancer, Maria de la Concepción Consuelo Garcia Cardoso, daughter of Generoso Jose Garcia Inglesias, house painter. Sadly his first marriage had not survived the stresses of a musician's peripatetic life. He took Consuelo to England in 1949 and after his divorce in 1952 married her the same year. There were two sons of this happy and enduring union.

When they arrived in England Brennan secured Semprini a BBC audition. He was immediately engaged to play in a series of fifteen-minute programmes in the style of the recently deceased Charlie Kunz, a popular pianist whose German name had caused public resentment. The style of Semprini quickly took over, pleased the listeners, and led to a short programme with orchestra, for which he chose, arranged, and orchestrated all the music. It was entitled *Semprini Serenade*, and was a subtle blend of classical pieces interspersed with selections from theatre and film music and the work of popular composers like George Gershwin, impeccably performed and introduced quietly and economically from the piano. Soon the programme stretched to an hour; it remained on the air for twenty-five years.

Semprini appeared rarely on television, but was a great favourite from 1952 in the surviving variety theatres, sharing the bill with rising stars like Peter *Sellers and (Sir) Harry Secombe, and touring the country in a caravan pulled by an ancient ambulance that contained a piano and a long table for doing orchestrations. Later, driving his beloved Jaguar, he gave many concerts with a more classical content both in Britain and abroad. Whenever possible he drove home through the night to *L'Espérance*, a sailing ship converted into a houseboat at West Mersea, where the family lived happily for many years.

Some critics regretted that Semprini did not pursue a more serious musical career. Certainly he could have performed at the very top of his profession, but he was master of his genre and millions of radio listeners and concert-goers loved his music. In 1972 he was made an officer of the Order of St John and he was appointed OBE in 1983—both recognitions of his considerable efforts for charity. He was a tall, dark, dignified man with fine features, always immaculately dressed, but his gravity was often dispelled by a strong sense of humour and a charming smile. He looked Italian, but he was an Englishman at heart. He died in Brixham from Alzheimer's disease, 19 January 1990.

[Information from relatives, friends, and Kathleen Davey, his personal assistant and music librarian for many years; personal knowledge.]   IAN WALLACE

SHACKLETON, Robert (1919–1986), professor of French literature and Bodley's librarian, was born in Todmorden 25 November 1919, the eldest in the family of two sons and one daughter of (Robert William) Albert Shackleton, a boot and shoe maker, and of his wife, Emily Sunderland. He attended Broomfield Boys' School and Todmorden Secondary School, and subsequently went to Oriel College, Oxford, as a scholar in modern languages, taking a first class in 1940. The next five years were spent in the Royal Corps of Signals, serving in North Africa and Italy. In 1946 he was elected the first modern languages fellow at Brasenose College, Oxford. The college became the physical and affective centre of his life; he resided there, served as senior dean in the difficult postwar years (1954–61), was college librarian (1948–66), and came close to the principalship. An enthusiastic gastronome and a connoisseur of wines, he was a generous host to both young and old.

Born and bred in north country nonconformity, he was a lifelong Liberal, taking an active part in politics early on and standing for Parliament, unsuccessfully, at Blackburn in 1945. A man of unusual elocution—his nasal intonation was a striking characteristic—he was nevertheless a good lecturer. Factually based academic research was, however, one of his real strengths and he soon gained a considerable reputation as both a scholar and an academic administrator. A leading member of his faculty, he was president of the conference of university teachers of French in 1958 and an editor of *French Studies* from 1960, and in 1965 succeeded Enid Starkie as university reader in French literature.

His early edition of Bernard de Fontenelle's *Entretiens sur la Pluralité des Mondes* (1955), linking his childhood love of astronomy with his deep devotion to the European Enlightenment, was followed by his magisterial, if dry, critical biography of Montesquieu (1961), which was translated into French in 1977. Shackleton's identification of Montesquieu's different scribes and the painstaking research behind this volume contributed largely to the resurgence of Montesquieu studies with which his name became synonymous. He took his Oxford D.Litt. in 1966. A regular traveller abroad and an easy speaker of French and Italian, Shackleton became a major figure in the international learned field, being president of the International Comparative Literature Association (1964–7) and of the International Society for Eighteenth-Century Studies (1975–9) (where in particular he did much to improve relationships), and chairman of committee of the Voltaire Foundation (from 1983), the transfer of which to Oxford University he did much to assist. From 1972 to 1981 he was a delegate of the Oxford University Press.

An expert committee man, he was, though often of firm views, notably articulate in their expression and deft at either compromise or the maintenance of an entrenched position. A frequenter of libraries at home and abroad and, from early days a bibliophile and book collector, he became a curator of the Bodleian Library in 1961 and in 1965–6 chaired the special Oxford committee on the university's libraries. Its report, written at the end of the period of postwar expansion, foresaw notable developments in storage, co-operation, and automation, but, in the manner of pre-oil crisis days, took funding for granted. The office of Bodley's librarian fell vacant in 1966 and Shackleton was elected to it. Retaining his rooms in Brasenose, he was active in promoting the cause of the Bodleian and that of sharing the labour and cost of cataloguing between major libraries by using automated techniques. He travelled much during these years and lectured throughout the world. Shackleton was an excellent ambassador but less effective as head librarian, in the changed financial and academic climate of the 1970s. The desire for a more active participation in the development of the Bodleian by staff, curators, university administrators, and library users did not chime easily with his autocratic management style. Already suffering from a blood complaint, he resigned the librarianship in 1979 in favour of a return to the more strictly academic post of Marshal Foch professor of French literature (1979–86).

This translation required removal from Brasenose to All Souls and to the, for him as an unmarried man, difficulties of practical domestic life. He had built up a renowned private library and an informal portrait of him by Margaret Foreman (later placed in the college), standing in his beloved rooms in Brasenose, depicts the man better than his formal portrait by Sir William *Coldstream in the Bodleian. His superlative Montesquieu collection, the basis of his 1983–4 Lyell lectures in bibliography, was ultimately bequeathed to the Bodleian while the rest of his books were sold to the John Rylands University Library of Manchester. He was appointed CBE (1986), was a fellow of the British Academy (1966), of which he was publications secretary (1974–7), and a chevalier of the Legion of Honour (1982), and held numerous other awards, including honorary degrees from Bordeaux (1966), Dublin (1967), Manchester (1980), and Leeds (1985).

Shackleton was tall with a domed brow and long arms, which at times made him appear ungainly in his movements. His last professorial years were clouded by illness and he died in Ravello 9 September 1986, a few weeks before he was due to retire.

[List of publications in G. Barber and C. P. Courtney (eds.), *Enlightenment Essays in Memory of Robert Shackleton*, 1988; Giles Barber in *Proceedings of the British Academy*, vol. lxxiii, 1987; personal knowledge.]

GILES BARBER

SHAW, Charles James Dalrymple, BARON KILBRANDON (1906–1989), lord of appeal, was born 15 August 1906 in Martnaham, near Maybole, Ayrshire, the only son and second of three children of James Edward Shaw, of High Greenan by Ayr, solicitor and county clerk of Ayrshire, and his wife, Gladys Elizabeth Lester. He was educated at Charterhouse, Balliol College, Oxford, and Edinburgh University. He obtained a second class in philosophy, politics, and economics at Oxford (1928) and an LL B at Edinburgh (1932).

Shaw was called to the Scottish bar in 1932. By 1939 he had a substantial junior practice, had been commissioned as a territorial officer in the Royal Artillery, and had sustained a knee injury while skiing, which made him lame for the rest of his life. In 1939 he was mobilized and served in the Royal Artillery, mostly on the staff in the rank of major (from 1941), until the end of World War II in 1945. On his return to the bar his practice rapidly increased. He took silk in 1949. It then became clear that, despite a tendency to be unbusinesslike and absent-minded, he was destined for the highest appointments. (He was liable to be found in Kilbrandon on the coast of Argyll, having forgotten a professional engagement in Edinburgh. The unaccountably missing brief would be found among his much-loved music.)

In 1957 he was elected dean of the Faculty of Advocates, the highest honour which can be conferred on a member of the Scots bar. As dean, Shaw was an anxious guardian of the Faculty's traditions. In May 1959 he was appointed to the bench of the Court of Session, taking the judicial title of Lord Kilbrandon. From the outset Kilbrandon displayed the highest judicial qualities—complete impartiality, patience and courtesy, legal scholarship, and a determination not to be prevented from doing justice by any rules of mere procedural law. His judicial career in Scotland ended with his appointment in 1965 as chairman of the Scottish Law Commission, for he retained that office until his elevation to the House of Lords in 1971, as a life peer, privy councillor, and lord of appeal in ordinary. As chairman Kilbrandon found in Sir Leslie (later Baron) Scarman, the first chairman of the English Law Commission, a kindred spirit. Kilbrandon was also a member of the royal commission on the constitution from 1969 to

1972 and its chairman in 1972–3. The commission's report was a major contribution to the contemporary debate on devolution. In 1969 Kilbrandon was elected an honorary fellow of Balliol, a distinction which he particularly cherished, and in 1974 he was appointed visitor, a position he held until 1986. He became an honorary LL D of Aberdeen (1965) and an honorary D.Sc. of Edinburgh (1970).

Kilbrandon's elevation to the Lords was predictable. For three years he sat as the junior Scottish colleague on the judicial committee of the octogenarian Baron *Reid. In an apt obituary of Reid, Kilbrandon wrote 'Counsel found him a formidable figure, and so did I'. Kilbrandon, on the other hand, did not have it in him to be what Ronald *Knox called an 'awful presence', unless dealing with someone whose conduct gave him no option. In a line of Scotsmen who have become lords of appeal in ordinary Kilbrandon was *sui generis*. Large of frame, heart, and mind, he had the traditional Scottish regard for legal principles but he had more. He had the breadth of outlook, culture, and philosophical learning of James *Dalrymple, first Viscount Stair, the father of Scots law. Endowed with a verbal dexterity, analogous to the cartoonist's art, he was able to compress profound and novel ideas into a synoptic phrase. In his Hamlyn lectures (1966) he derided the civil jury as a mere 'bingo session'. His observation in *Customs and Excise v. Thorn Electrical, Weekly Law Reports*, vol. i, 1975, that 'a modern Hampden would in many quarters be pilloried as a tax evader', was worthy of F. X. J. *Russell, Baron Russell of Killowen. Kilbrandon's most lasting memorial may be the Social Work (Scotland) Act (1968), which arose from his report for the departmental committee on the treatment of children and young persons in Scotland (1964). Kilbrandon retired as a lord of appeal in ordinary in 1976.

Kilbrandon was an outstandingly handsome man. Over six feet in height, he was a striking figure in his Inverness cape, limping at a smart pace from Westminster to Gray's Inn, where he lived during term. He was elected an honorary bencher in 1971. Until almost seventy he retained a boyish appearance enhanced by his thick, wavy hair. In old age he enjoyed a peaceful retirement in the beautiful setting of Kilbrandon House on the island of Seil in Argyll. The essential Kilbrandon was the man of religion whose faith pervaded his life and outlook. He liked to speak of himself as a Catholic although he was, denominationally, a Scottish Episcopalian of High Church outlook. One who knew him well described him as 'a practising Christian'. This was apt. His amiability, sweetness of character, freedom from prejudice, and kindness were all exceptional.

In 1937 he married (Ruth) Caroline, youngest daughter of Frank Morrison Seafield Grant, landowner, of Knockie, Whitebridge, Inverness. They had two sons and three daughters. Kilbrandon died from heart disease in Kilbrandon House, Balvicar, by Oban, Argyll, 10 September 1989.

[Private information; personal knowledge.]

D. W. R. BRAND

SHAW, Glencairn Alexander Byam ('Glen') (1904–1986), actor and director of theatre and opera. [See BYAM SHAW, GLENCAIRN ALEXANDER.]

SHEEHAN, Harold Leeming (1900–1988), expert on the pathology of pregnancy, was born 4 August 1900 in Carlisle, Cumberland, the second of six sons and second of thirteen children of Patrick Sheehan, general medical practitioner, and his wife Eliza, daughter of Francis Leeming, a businessman in the cotton trade. He was educated at Carlisle Grammar School and the University of Manchester, where he graduated MB, Ch.B., with second-class honours, in 1921. His father died in 1919 and as soon as Harold qualified he went back to Carlisle to assist his elder brother in the family medical practice for the next six years.

In 1927 he returned to Manchester University as a demonstrator, and later as a lecturer, in the department of pathology, where his researches into renal function earned him the degree of MD, with a gold medal, in 1931 and the M.Sc. in 1932. He gained a Rockefeller medical fellowship in 1934 and spent a year on further studies of the kidney in the department of pharmacology at the Johns Hopkins Medical School in Baltimore, Maryland, USA, after which he was appointed director of research at Glasgow Royal Maternity Hospital (1935–46). During the next five years he established himself as an international expert on the pathology of pregnancy by making important contributions on disease of the liver, brain, heart, and kidneys in pregnancy and, in particular, on the importance of shock and haemorrhage in causing necrosis of the anterior lobe of the pituitary gland.

Since he was a Territorial Army officer, on the declaration of war in 1939 he was mobilized and graded as a specialist in pathology, with the rank of major, in the Royal Army Medical Corps. He served in Britain until January 1944 and was then posted to Italy, with the rank of lieutenant-colonel. In January 1945 he became a full colonel and was director of pathology to the central Mediterranean forces until the end of the war. He was mentioned in dispatches.

In 1946 he was appointed to the chair of pathology in the University of Liverpool. Students found him informative, entertaining, and memorable; he challenged much accepted dogma. His well-deserved reputation as an exacting examiner, however, made him respected rather than popular. He continued his researches and accepted many invitations to lecture abroad. Gradually the effects of post-partum necrosis of the pituitary gland came to be known as Sheehan's syndrome. After his retirement Sheehan produced two books, *Pathology of Toxaemia of Pregnancy* (with J. B. Lynch, 1973) and *Postpartum Hypopituitarism* (with J. C. Davis, 1982).

In 1940 Sheehan became a D.Sc. of Manchester University. In 1941 he gained membership of the Royal College of Physicians of London and he was promoted to fellowship in 1947. He became a fellow of the Royal College of Obstetricians and Gynaecologists (1949) and a founder fellow of the Royal College of Pathologists (1964). His foreign honours included an honorary MD from the University of Szeged, Hungary, in 1982. He was an honorary member of endocrinological societies in Argentina, Chile, Romania, and Hungary. He was also an honorary fellow of the Obstetrical and Gynaecological Societies of America and of Belgium, while in France he was a foreign associate of the National Academy of Medicine.

Physically, though not obese, he looked portly and stooped slightly. He wore formal suits, even at informal times, but never looked smart. His hair became white at an early age, but his eyebrows remained black until he was old. When he was excited or emphatic his eyes would bulge slightly. He was enthusiastic, talkative, argumentative, and self-confident. He smoked his pipe while he worked—even in the autopsy room. He ate and drank with discrimination and was an excellent host. He was a strong swimmer and a successful gardener. His secrecy about his personal affairs was notorious, but he was certainly affluent when his position had become established.

In 1934 he married Eve Suzette Gertrude (died 1986), daughter of (Martin) Henry Potter, theatre manager. She was a good linguist, assisted in the preparation of Sheehan's publications, and travelled abroad with him. She was rather reserved, but her penetrating remarks gave balance to her husband's exuberance. They had no children. Sheehan died in Kendal, Cumbria, 25 October 1988, having become immobile due to a fracture of his hip in January of that year.

[Private information; personal knowledge.]

A. H. CRUICKSHANK

SHINWELL, Emanuel, BARON SHINWELL (1884–1986), politician, was born 18 October 1884 in Spitalfields, east London, the eldest in a family of thirteen children of Samuel Shinwell, a clothing manufacturer of Polish Jewish origin, and his Dutch wife, Rose Konigswinter. The family moved to Glasgow but Shinwell left school at the age of eleven to be apprenticed to the tailoring trade. He joined his first trade union, the Amalgamated Society of Clothing Operatives, at the age of seventeen and was elected to Glasgow Trades Council in 1906. He was to serve twice as its president. He became an early member of the Independent Labour party and was an active socialist crusader. In 1911 he was prominent on the Clyde during the national dock strike.

He continued his militant union activities during the war and was wrongly alleged to have been involved in the disturbances in George Square, Glasgow, between striking workers and the police on 'Red Friday' (31 January 1919). As a result, he spent over five months in Calton gaol, Edinburgh. He was now turning to thoughts of a political career. In the 1918 general election, he stood unsuccessfully as Labour candidate for Linlithgow (West Lothian); in 1922 he was elected to Parliament there.

He served as parliamentary secretary to the mines department in the first Labour government of Ramsay *MacDonald in 1924. Defeated in the 1924 general election, he was re-elected in a by-election in 1928 and served in junior offices in the second Labour government, as financial secretary to the War Office in 1929–30 and again in the mines department in 1930–1. He had an immense admiration for MacDonald and tried in vain to persuade him not to head the 'national' government in August 1931. In the subsequent general election, Shinwell was defeated again.

He now decided to challenge MacDonald directly and in the 1935 general election handsomely defeated his old leader at Seaham Harbour. After a redistribution of seats, the constituency was later renamed Easington. Shinwell was always a pugnacious member of Parliament. In 1938 he caused a sensation by striking a Conservative, Commander Robert Bower (as it happened, a former naval boxing champion), when the latter made a hostile interjection in debate. During the war years Shinwell was a vigorous, though always patriotic, critic of (Sir) Winston *Churchill's coalition government. He and the Tory sixth Earl *Winterton were popularly christened 'Arsenic and Old Lace'. Shinwell was also prominent in Labour's policy-making committees, notably those dealing with coal and energy.

When Labour won the 1945 general election, Attlee appointed Shinwell to the cabinet as minister of fuel and power. Here he achieved the nationalization of coal in 1946 and also negotiated the so-called miners' charter with the National Union of Mineworkers. He caused much controversy by declaring that the middle class was 'not worth a tinker's cuss'. He served as chairman of the Labour party in 1947–8. However, his reputation slumped during the acute fuel crisis of January–March 1947, at a time of an exceptionally severe winter. He was accused of complacency and failing to plan to deal with basic problems of coal production. That October, much to his chagrin, Shinwell was demoted by Attlee to the War Office, outside the cabinet. Hugh *Gaitskell took his place and thereby earned Shinwell's undying enmity, reinforced by Gaitskell's public school background. Shinwell was also attacked by younger men like James (later Baron) Callaghan for being less than ardent over nationalization. However, Shinwell proved to be a vigorous war minister, in tune with army sentiment, and Attlee reappointed him to the cabinet in March 1950 as minister of defence. Here Shinwell dealt energetically with the emergency in Malaya and war in Korea. In the summer of 1951 he urged the cabinet to send British troops to protect the oil refineries at Abadan, which the Persian government had nationalized, but he was successfully resisted by other ministers.

After Labour fell from office in 1951, Shinwell lost ground. He was defeated in elections for the party national executive in 1952 and left the shadow cabinet in 1955. Gaitskell was elected party leader that year; Shinwell had backed his fellow veteran, Herbert *Morrison (later Baron Morrison of Lambeth). However, despite being in his seventies, he continued to play a lively role in politics. He changed his stance on nuclear weapons and campaigned against the stationing of US Polaris submarines at Holy Loch. The election of Harold Wilson (later Baron Wilson of Rievaulx) as party leader after Gaitskell's death gave Shinwell new opportunities. Although now eighty, he was appointed by Wilson as chairman of the Parliamentary Labour party in October 1964, and worked hard to secure support for a government whose initial majority was only three. However, he came into conflict with ministers from 1966, especially with the equally aggressive foreign secretary, George *Brown (later Baron George-Brown), since Shinwell was a vehement enemy of British entry into the European Common Market. He resigned as party chairman in 1967; in 1970 he became a life peer.

His career was still far from over. He became chairman of the all-party Lords' defence study group. He voted against his own Labour government in 1976 and in March 1982 resigned the party whip in protest against left-wing militancy, though he remained a Labour party member. He was now a legendary figure, and his hundredth birthday was celebrated in the House of Lords in 1984 (during a national miners' strike) with considerable enthusiasm.

With his stocky figure and Glaswegian accent, 'Manny' Shinwell was pugnacious in Parliament and on the platform. Appropriately, his enthusiasms included professional boxing. Though not religious, he was also much involved with the Jewish community. His performance in office was marred by the 1947 fuel crisis, while as a service minister he showed a jingoism some thought inappropriate. However, he had the gift of striking up friendships across the spectrum, including with the first Viscount *Montgomery of Alamein and the editor of the *Sunday Express*, Sir John Junor. He was kindly towards the young. He was a major personality over sixty years, and a notable pioneer in Labour's long march to power in 1945. He wrote several autobiographical works, of which *Conflict Without Malice* (1955) is the most important. He was married (and widowed) three times. In 1903 he married Fay ('Fanny') Freeman (died 1954); they had two sons and a daughter. In 1956 he married Dinah (died 1971), daughter of Carol Ludwig Meyer, of Denmark. In 1972 he married Sarah, former wife of Alfred Hurst and daughter of Solomon Stungo. She died in 1977. Shinwell himself died 8 May 1986 at the age of 101, at his St John's Wood flat in London, and was cremated at Golders Green crematorium.

[Emanuel Shinwell, *Conflict Without Malice*, 1955, *I've Lived Through It All*, 1973, *Lead with the Left: my First Ninety-Six Years*, 1981, and *Shinwell Talking*, tape-recorded conversations edited by John Dexat, 1984; *The Times* and *Guardian*, 9 May 1986; Dalton papers, London School of Economics; Gaitskell papers, Nuffield College, Oxford; Labour party archives, Manchester; private information.] KENNETH O. MORGAN

SHOTTON, Frederick William (1906–1990), geologist, was born 8 October 1906 in Exhall, near Coventry, the younger child and only son of Frederick John Shotton, an industrialist specializing in drop forged products, who was manager of the Albion Drop Forging Company of Coventry, and his wife, Ada Brooks. He was educated at Bablake School in Coventry and Sidney Sussex College, Cambridge. He obtained first classes in both parts (1926 and 1927) of the natural sciences tripos (geology), and was awarded the Harkness scholarship in 1927. In 1929 he was appointed assistant lecturer at the University of Birmingham, where he remained until returning to Cambridge as a lecturer in 1936. After war service he became Sorby professor of geology at Sheffield University in 1945 and in 1949 he took up the post of Lapworth professor of geology at Birmingham University, from which he retired in 1974. He was vice-principal of Birmingham University in 1965–71.

Shotton made contributions in three main areas: as a military geologist, as a Quaternary stratigrapher and geomorphologist, and as a student of the Mesozoic and Palaeozoic. His career as a military geologist started in 1938 when he joined the Army Officers' Emergency Reserve. He was called up in May 1940 and commissioned into the Royal Engineers. He took responsibility for geological activities in North Africa and the Middle East and was particularly concerned with the provision of water supplies. Indeed, the success of the advance from El Alamein owed much to Shotton's hydrological studies in parched desert terrain. In 1943 Shotton, now a major, was recalled to Britain as geological adviser on the staff of the chief engineer at the headquarters of 21st Army Group under the command of Sir Bernard *Montgomery (later first Viscount Montgomery of Alamein). There he worked on the assessment of the character of the invasion beaches prior to Operation Overlord and, *inter alia*, cross-country mobility along the line of advance towards the Rhine. He was three times mentioned in dispatches. After demobilization he retained his links with the army and acted as the geological adviser to the chief scientist (army) until the post was disbanded in 1970.

Shotton's career as a Quaternary scientist was an important one and dominated the last three decades of his life. At Birmingham he created one of the outstanding British centres for Quaternary research, establishing a radiocarbon dating laboratory and a renowned centre for the study of Quaternary beetles. He helped to launch the Quaternary Field Study Group (eventually the Quaternary Research Association) in 1964 and presided at the International Quaternary Association (INQUA) in 1977. He made fundamental contributions to the study of Quaternary sediments and land-forms in the English midlands and was the editor of (and contributed to) *British Quaternary Studies* (1977). With characteristic vigour and forthrightness he argued and debated the issues until the end; he was one of the physical and intellectual giants of British Quaternary geology.

As a mainstream geologist Shotton wrote extensively on the stratigraphy, structures, and sedimentology of a range of rocks, particularly from the English midlands. Especially important was his work on the Bunter Sandstones, for which he reconstructed palaeo-wind patterns from aeolian cross stratification. As head of the geology department at Birmingham University he introduced both geophysics and hydrogeology into the curriculum and instituted M.Sc. courses in them.

Shotton was appointed MBE in 1945. He became a fellow of the Royal Society (1956), and president of the Geological Society of London (1964–6), Section C of the British Association for the Advancement of Science (1961–2), and INQUA. He was awarded honorary membership of the Royal Irish Academy (1970), the Prestwich medal of the Geological Society of London

(1954), and the Stopes medal of the Geologists' Association (1967).

Shotton was large, bespectacled, and a smoker. In 1930 he married Alice Louise, daughter of John Linnett, a draper from Coventry; they had two daughters. She died in 1979 and in September 1983 he married a widow, Lucille Frances Bailey, daughter of David Ray Matteson, chief accountant of the Spokane, Portland, and Seattle Railway in Portland, Oregon. Her career was in psychology and education. Shotton died 21 July 1990 in the East Birmingham Hospital.

[M. S. Rosenbaum in *Royal Engineers Journal*, vol. civ (3), 1990, pp. 289–90; P. Worsley in *Proceedings of the Geologists' Association of London*, vol. cii, 1991, pp. 322–3; E. P. F. Rose and M. S. Rosenbaum, 'British Military Geologists: through the Second World War to the End of the Cold War', ibid., vol. civ, 1993, pp. 95–108; Russell Coope in *Biographical Memoirs of Fellows of the Royal Society*, vol. xxx, 1994; private information; personal knowledge.]   A. S. GOUDIE

SIEGHART, (Henry Laurence) Paul (Alexander) (1927–1988), law reformer, was born 22 February 1927 in Vienna, the only child of Ernst Alexander and his wife Marguerite, daughter of Rudolph Sieghart. Following his parents' divorce in about 1930, his mother resumed her maiden name for herself and her son. Sieghart came from a remarkable background. His grandparents were Jewish by birth but had converted to Catholicism. He was brought up as a pious Roman Catholic, unaware of his Jewish ancestry until 1938. His maternal grandfather entered the Austro-Hungarian civil service and became *chef de cabinet* to the Emperor Franz Josef. Sieghart's mother was the first woman to obtain a doctorate of law at Vienna University.

In January 1939 Sieghart (knowing no English) and his mother fled to England from Austria. After one unhappy term at Harrow he moved to Berkhamsted School. He went on to read mathematics at University College London, but decided to leave without taking a degree, believing that he had not done enough work to obtain the outstanding result of which he was capable. After a succession of short-term and very varied jobs, Sieghart decided to read for the bar, to which he was called by Gray's Inn in 1953. He was talent-spotted by (Sir) John *Foster, who invited him to join his chambers. Sieghart quickly developed an enormous commercial and tax practice, but—probably because he had made enemies among the judiciary—his first application for silk was rejected in 1966. He promptly quit the bar.

Thereafter Sieghart earned money as a consultant and arbitrator, but devoted most of his time and energy to the advancement of human rights. Foster had introduced Sieghart to the law reform organization, Justice. This became his main forum and he chaired its executive committee from 1978 until shortly before his death. Sieghart was almost single-handedly responsible for the enactment of the Rehabilitation of Offenders Act (1974). He wrote and lectured frequently on human rights. His book, *The International Law of Human Rights* (1983), was a masterly analysis of the principal international human rights instruments. *The Lawful Rights of Mankind* (1985), aimed at a less expert readership, was also an outstanding book. Sieghart became a governor of the British Institute of Human Rights in 1974 and a trustee of the European Human Rights Foundation in 1980. The quickness of his mind, breadth of his intellectual interests, skill in argument, and enthusiasm for his causes made Sieghart a leading contributor to the development of human rights law both in Britain and beyond.

Sieghart was fascinated by many aspects of science, including computers and nuclear energy, and by medical ethics. He linked these interests with his concern for human rights by founding the Council for Science and Society in 1972 and by his publications *Privacy and Computers* (1986) and *Plutonium and Liberty* (a Justice report, 1978). He pushed the Home Office into setting up the committee (of which he was an influential member) which resulted in the Data Protection Act of 1984.

Although not devout, Sieghart retained close links with the Roman Catholic church and was a member of the hierarchy's Commission on International Justice and Peace (1976–80). One of his last acts was to address a Vatican conference, attended by the pope, on human rights. He was a regular contributor to the *Tablet* and a trustee of the Tablet Trust (from 1976). Sieghart proved to be a superb television performer as the moderator of discussion programmes. One of his programmes won a Royal Television Society award. He was a fellow of the Royal Society of Arts and a freeman of the City of London.

Gaunt, beak-nosed, a chain smoker (he died of lung cancer), Sieghart aroused strong personal reactions. He could be difficult and self-centred, but he could also exercise a compelling fascination. In 1954 he married Rosemary, daughter of Commander Charles E. Aglionby, DSO, of the Royal Navy. She died of cancer in 1956, leaving Sieghart with an infant son and daughter. In 1959 he married Felicity Anne Olga Howard, daughter of Alfred Max Baer, chairman of Rio Tinto Zinc, with whom he had a further son and daughter. Sieghart died in Islington 12 December 1988, shortly after returning home from a dinner given by Justice in his honour.

[Private information; personal knowledge.]

WILLIAM GOODHART

SILKIN, John Ernest (1923–1987), solicitor and Labour MP, was born 18 March 1923 in London, the third and youngest son (there were no daughters) of Lewis *Silkin (later first Baron Silkin), solicitor, who became minister of town and country planning in the Labour government of 1945–51, and his wife, Rosa Neft. It was a Jewish, intellectual, Labour family, and his brother Samuel *Silkin (later Baron Silkin of Dulwich), the second son, became a somewhat controversial attorney-general in the Labour governments of 1974–9. John Silkin was educated at Dulwich College and for a short period at the University College of Wales, Cardiff, before going to Trinity Hall, Cambridge, where he obtained a second class (division I) in part ii of the law tripos in 1942. He was then called up for the Royal Naval Volunteer Reserve. He became a lieutenant-commander in the intelligence branch and saw service in the Far East. On demobilization he entered the family firm of solicitors. He was admitted a solicitor in 1950.

His first attempt to enter Parliament in the Labour interest was in the general election of 1950 for the London constituency of St Marylebone. It was a hopeless seat for any Labour candidate. Having unsuccessfully contested West Woolwich in 1951 and South Nottingham in 1959, Silkin finally entered the House of Commons in July 1963 for the south London constituency of Deptford, and very soon began to move upwards within the Parliamentary Labour party. In 1966 he became chief whip in the government of Harold Wilson (later Baron Wilson of Rievaulx), a position which he filled with an agreeable competence until 1969, at a time when Labour had a majority of only three. He was deputy leader of the House of Commons in 1968–9 and minister of public building and works in 1969–70. It was in this period that he became close to Richard *Crossman, whose diaries for these years offer a favourable commentary on Silkin's personality and political skills.

In the last Wilson government of 1974–6 Silkin was given the office of minister for planning and local government. It was not a very happy appointment and in 1976 he was moved to the Ministry of Agriculture, where he was much more successful. During the years to 1979 he became well known through extensive press coverage of his disputes with the Brussels officials of the European community. Silkin's own personal politics were now directly involved. He belonged to the left of the Parliamentary Labour party, which clustered around the journal *Tribune*. In foreign affairs he was a unilateralist on the issue of the atom bomb, and a vigorous opponent of Britain's entry into the European community. His tenure at the Ministry of Agriculture was notable for the tough stance he took on European matters, using a strongly nationalist approach to the much debated issues of fishing rights, and agricultural policies in general. His public quarrels with Brussels greatly extended his political image among the British electorate. His general opposition to the European Economic Community was based upon his acceptance of what was known at the time as 'the alternative economic policy': import controls and the protection of Britain's industrial base, a withdrawal from Europe, and a renegotiation of the terms for a possible future entry.

The Labour party lost the general election of 1979 and a year later, after James Callaghan (later Baron Callaghan of Cardiff) had resigned from the leadership of the party, there was an election for his successor. For reasons which are difficult to justify, John Silkin confidently believed that he was a serious candidate as a compromise between Denis (later Baron) Healey on the right of the party and Michael Foot on the left. Barbara Castle (later Baroness Castle of Blackburn) wrote in her diary in 1976 that Silkin was 'the kindest chap, but has not yet proved himself a political heavyweight'; it must have been his success against the Brussels officials that warped his judgement. In the first round of the leadership election he received 38 votes against Healey's 112, Foot's 83, and Peter Shore's 32. Nor did Silkin succeed in the election for deputy leader. This serious miscalculation concerning his own position weakened his general standing in the Parliamentary Labour party.

In the years that followed, although he was on the Labour opposition's front bench, he became involved in various disputes that he was to find very wearing. His own constituency Labour party was much to the left of his own position and there were serious attempts to replace him as the candidate for the next election. They failed for the general election of 1983, but the continued friction helped to push Silkin into deciding in 1985 that he would not stand again. He was also much involved in a bitter internal quarrel over the control of *Tribune*, the organ of the moderate left.

Silkin had been brought up in an affluent family and he added to his inherited wealth during his own lifetime. His parliamentary salary was augmented by his continued practice as a solicitor. Among his clients was Robert Maxwell, which meant that Silkin had a place on the board of Pergamon Press. Silkin died before Maxwell was exposed as a fraudulent swindler on a very large scale. Silkin also benefited financially from property deals, one of which—a family affair involving his father in earlier years—prompted discussion in the national press in 1974. John Silkin publicly, and vigorously, defended his position.

Slightly taller than average, Silkin was well built. In 1950 he married an actress, (Nora)

Rosamund John, formerly the wife of Lieutenant-Commander (Hugh) Russell Lloyd, of the Royal Naval Volunteer Reserve, and daughter of Frederick Henry Jones. They had one son. Silkin died suddenly, of a heart attack, at his London home, 4 Dean's Yard, SW1, 26 April 1987.

[*Sunday Times*, 30 June 1974; R. H. S. Crossman, *The Diaries of a Cabinet Minister 1964–1970*, 3 vols., 1975, 1976, and 1977; *The Crossman Diaries: Selections* (ed. Anthony Howard), 1979; Barbara Castle, *The Castle Diaries, 1974–76*, 1980; N. Wapshott, 'Mr John Silkin', *The Times*, 3 November 1980; *The Times*, 27 April 1987.] JOHN SAVILLE

SILKIN, Samuel Charles, BARON SILKIN OF DULWICH (1918–1988), barrister and Labour MP, was born 6 March 1918 in Neath, Glamorgan, the second in the family of three sons of Lewis *Silkin, later first Baron Silkin, solicitor, who became minister of town and country planning in the Labour government of 1945–51, and his wife, Rosa Neft. Educated at Dulwich College and Trinity Hall, Cambridge, he obtained first classes in both parts of the law tripos (1938 and 1939), and in his bar finals was awarded a certificate of honour and the Harmsworth law scholarship. He was called to the bar by the Middle Temple in 1941. A formidable cricketer, he played for Glamorgan in 1938.

In World War II he achieved the rank of lieutenant-colonel in the Royal Artillery. He was on the staff of XII Corps during the invasion of France in 1944 and was mentioned in dispatches. He presided at two trials of major Japanese war criminals. After the war he practised from the chambers of Edmund Davies (later Baron Edmund-Davies). Careful and methodical in style, he acquired a substantial practice, particularly in the planning field.

He took silk in 1963 and in 1964 he entered Parliament as Labour member for Camberwell, Dulwich. He served on the royal commission on the penal system in 1965–6. An enthusiastic European, he led the British delegation to the Council of Europe in 1968–70; there he formed a friendship with Robert Maxwell. Unlike his brother John *Silkin, he was never associated with the left of the Labour party, and he was one of the sixty-nine Labour MPs who, in 1971, defied a three-line whip to support British entry to the European Economic Community. During this time he was also recorder of Bedford (1966–71). From 1970 to 1974 he served on the opposition front bench, on Law Office matters, and it was no surprise when in 1974 Harold Wilson (later Baron Wilson of Rievaulx), the incoming prime minister, appointed him attorney-general. He was then sworn of the Privy Council. He began on a controversial note, by declining to accept the knighthood which, for 400 years, had been bestowed upon law officers on their appointment. From 1974 to 1983 he was MP for Southwark, Dulwich.

Shortly afterwards the government introduced the Housing Finance (special provisions) Bill, granting retrospective immunity to the Clay Cross councillors, who faced surcharges and disqualification from office for refusing to increase council rents under the Housing Finance Act of 1972. It fell to Silkin to speak in the Commons on the legal aspects of the Bill and the opposition was able to produce a leaked letter written by him to a front-bench colleague advising against the principle of the Bill. He was the subject of press criticism, which seemed destined to continue throughout his period of office.

In 1974 the literary executors of Richard *Crossman proposed publication in the *Sunday Times* of his diaries, including his records of confidential discussions within the Labour government of 1964–70. In accordance with the established convention, they submitted them to the cabinet secretary, who declined to agree to their publication without excising the offending passages. The *Sunday Times* announced that it proposed nevertheless to publish. The affair was presented in sections of the press as a blatant attempt to suppress publication of embarrassing material. Ironically, the government would have preferred to see the material published, in order to establish that there were no secrets. But Silkin was his own man, and insisted that the public interest in the enforcement of constitutional conventions must take precedence over the political interests of the government. The lord chief justice (Lord *Widgery) held that the convention existed, and that the courts would enforce it, but that, given the long interval which had elapsed since the events which formed the subject-matter of the entries, no damage would be done by publication, and he declined to issue the injunction. The purpose of upholding the convention had been achieved, but the public perception was that Silkin had 'lost'.

In 1977, when he declined to authorize a relator action which would have enabled John Gouriet, of the National Association for Freedom, to proceed against the Union of Post Office Workers, Lord Denning, master of the Rolls, used language in the Court of Appeal which was construed by the press as imputing improper motives to Silkin. In the House of Lords he was completely vindicated, but the outcome received less publicity than the earlier judgment. Silkin ceased to be attorney-general in 1979, when the Labour government left office.

In court and in the House his contributions were quiet, well reasoned, and delivered in a slow, carefully formulated style, which did not appeal to the media. Arising as it did from a preoccupation with the logical form of the argument, it ensured that he was rarely guilty of

fallacious reasoning, but tended to conceal his passionate commitment to social justice and human rights. He retired from the Commons in 1983 and entered the House of Lords, as a life peer. There he found the style of debating more congenial. He became a director of two of Robert Maxwell's companies, Pergamon Press and BPCC.

Tall and well made, with the prominent nose and rather heavy jowls associated with his central European ancestry, his face was frequently softened in a smile. In 1941 he married Elaine Violet, daughter of Arthur Stamp, headmaster, of London; there were two sons and two daughters of the marriage. In 1984 she died, and in 1985 he married an old friend of the family, Sheila Marian, widow of Walter Swanston and daughter of Arthur Jeal, an executive of a small gas company who owned property and land. Silkin died in the Churchill Hospital, Oxford, 17 August 1988.

[Personal knowledge.]   ARCHER OF SANDWELL

SIMPSON, (Bessie) Wallis, DUCHESS OF WINDSOR (1896–1986), wife of the former King Edward VIII. [See WINDSOR, (BESSIE) WALLIS.]

SINCLAIR, Hugh Macdonald (1910–1990), nutritionist, was born 4 February 1910 at Duddingston House, Edinburgh, the second son and youngest of four children of Colonel Hugh Montgomerie Sinclair, of the Royal Engineers, and his wife Rosalie Sybil, daughter of Sir John Jackson, civil engineer and MP. He was educated at Winchester and Oriel College, Oxford, where he obtained a first class in physiology in 1932. He then went to University College Hospital, London, and qualified as LMSSA (he was master of the Society of Apothecaries in 1967–8) and BM, B.Ch. in 1936. Elected a university demonstrator and lecturer in biochemistry at Oxford, and a fellow of Magdalen College, in 1937, he chose to work on thiamine. He obtained his Oxford DM in 1939. In May 1941 he created the Oxford Nutrition Survey (ONS), of which he was director from 1942 to 1947. Scarcely out of his twenties, he had acquired a mastery of survey technique, and by 1944 was directing twenty-five trained and experienced staff. His work was a springboard for the postwar surveys in The Netherlands and Germany, which he was invited to undertake with the rank of brigadier after his success in assuring the British government that its food policy was working.

Sinclair's reports to the Ministry of Health were brief, but he kept his records well, and his 1940s data were still being written up in the 1990s. Some of the German data was lost as a result of administrative tangles, partly due to Sinclair's delight in twisting the tails of supposed superiors. He was a difficult man to work under, with, or over. He was appointed an officer of the Order of Oranje-Nassau in 1951 and was awarded the US medal of freedom with silver palm in 1946 for his postwar work. He became FRCP in 1964.

By 1947 the ONS had given place to the University Laboratory of Human Nutrition, of which Sinclair was director until 1955. He was reader in human nutrition from 1951 to 1958, but, in a titanic quest for better premises, he fell foul of authority, losing both the directorship (to Sir Hans *Krebs) and the readership in the struggle, a calamity that might have been prevented by a better record of publication. His fellowship at Magdalen lapsed with the readership, and he became a research fellow there, with some tutoring, at which he was excellent, in a much reduced stipend. Meanwhile, he was developing his fatty-acid hypothesis: having undertaken a compendious review, he concluded in the 'longest and rudest letter' in the *Lancet* (6 April 1956, p. 381) that a relative deficiency of essential polyunsaturated fatty acids was the main cause of various diseases of civilization. This was thought too speculative by his seniors, and weakened Sinclair's chances of re-election to the readership, for which he did not reapply. Encouraged by the first Earl of *Woolton, he decided to set up an independent nutrition institute, to which he dedicated his property. He sold his medical library in 1965 for £90,000, to escape insolvency. The rump of his library, including much erotica (the basis of his wide knowledge of sado-masochism), sold for £70,000 in 1992.

In 1972 Sinclair registered a nutrition 'association' as a charity, which was renamed the International Nutrition Foundation (INF) in 1982. He was its unpaid director and main sponsor, housing it rent-free at his estate in Sutton Courtenay, ten miles south of Oxford, where he planned to build a research centre. The INF failed to raise the £12 million needed, and after his death its trustees, as the sole heirs of his estate, decided to develop it to raise capital for a university chair of nutrition.

From 1970 to 1980 Sinclair was much appreciated as a visiting professor at Reading, and was still doing scientific work. In his seventieth year he followed an Eskimo diet, composed of water, seal, and fish, for three months. His bleeding time rose from three to fifty-seven minutes, thus supporting his view that the unsaturated fatty acids of fish decrease the aggregation of platelets and are effective in diminishing the incidence of coronary thrombosis in persons on a high-fat diet. Sinclair continued work on fatty acids to the end of his life, writing or editing ten books, giving lectures, composing critical chapters and reviews, and appearing on television. In all he published about 400 separate pieces, and much

enjoyed his final years as the doyen of an international branch of research. He was devoted to scientific truth, but slow to establish it by experiment. Claiming an allergy to publication, he produced some important speculation, which he thought more significant than reputation, and throughout his life scrupulously maintained his own education, relentlessly sacrificing home and wardrobe to the work of his beloved foundation, to the acquisition of new texts, and to the cultivation of friendships.

Sinclair's tall mesomorphic physique tempted him to work excessively far into the small and not necessarily productive hours, but, relishing deadlines and crises, he was never late for work in the morning. He had a broad and high forehead, fair colouring, and strongly slanting eyebrows, supercilious at the extremities and contracted downwards at the centre, above stone-blue eyes. He was engaged to be married twice, but one of his fiancées died in 1939 from cancer, and the other died from taking cyanide when captured behind German lines in 1940. He remained unmarried. He died 22 June 1990 in the John Radcliffe Hospital, Oxford, from a gastric carcinoma.

[Mary Gale and Brian Lloyd (eds.), *Sinclair* (Founders of Modern Nutrition no. 3, McCarrison Society), 1990; personal knowledge.] BRIAN LLOYD

SINCLAIR, Ronald (pseudonym) (1889–1988), intelligence officer. [See TEAGUE-JONES, REGINALD.]

SITWELL, SIR Sacheverell, sixth baronet (1897–1988), writer, was born in Scarborough 15 November 1897, the youngest of three children and younger son of Sir George Reresby *Sitwell, fourth baronet, of Renishaw Hall, Derbyshire, antiquarian, and his wife, Lady Ida Emily Augusta Denison, daughter of the first Earl of Londesborough. Sachie (as he was nicknamed) passed his childhood with his sister Edith *Sitwell and brother Osbert *Sitwell, mostly at Renishaw Hall or in his grandmothers' houses at Scarborough. At Eton he was fortunate in his tutor G. W. Headlam, who encouraged his mania for reading. He did not distinguish himself at games which he detested. In later life he looked back upon the school holidays as fraught with misery. This was largely caused by Lady Ida's imprisonment for heavy gambling debts, a traumatic experience for a doting son while still a schoolboy.

On leaving Eton in 1915 Sitwell was gazetted an ensign of the Grenadier Guards, although on account of a weak heart he was spared the trenches in France. His duties at Aldershot barracks were compensated for by an obsession with poetry. In June 1918 he published a first volume of poetry, *The People's Palace*, which had a moderate reception. John *Lehmann considered his poetic inspiration the fruit of great works of art rather than life's experiences. Yet it was deeply tinged by the blood bath in which 'my school friends were killed, with hardly an exception'. For the rest of his days he was haunted by a macabre pessimism made all the more tormenting by total lack of religious faith. Another obsession was with the Russian ballet. With Edith and Osbert he celebrated armistice night of 1918 entertaining Sergei Diaghilev and his *corps de ballet*. This led to Diaghilev commissioning from him in 1926 a libretto, *The Triumph of Nature*, set to music by Lord *Berners. By Christmas 1918 Sitwell was demobilized.

He immediately entered Balliol College, Oxford. But the university offered little to the ex-Guards officer, whose acquaintances were artists, writers, musicians, and actors. His intoxication with the stage sprang from memories of the Pierrot troupes who danced on the sands at Scarborough. After the summer term of 1919 he left Oxford and set up house with Osbert at 5 Swan Walk and then 2 Carlyle Square, Chelsea. Until his marriage the two brothers were inseparable, and indeed with Edith made a formidable phalanx of intellectuals against the philistines. Already a leader of the avant-garde, Sacheverell organized an exhibition of modern French painters in London and helped introduce Modigliani, Utrillo, and Dufy to the British public. He discovered the composer (Sir) William *Walton and promoted the author (A. A.) Ronald *Firbank.

In 1920 he made a quixotic expedition to Fiume to see its leader Gabriele d'Annunzio, whom he admired as the greatest poet of the age. In the autumn he accompanied Osbert to Naples and Caserta, and the next year to the southern extremities of Italy, then exceedingly remote and beyond the tourist horizon. These visits fired his enthusiasm for baroque and rococo architecture, the track of which he pursued to Spain, Portugal, Bavaria, and even Latin America. The outcome was *Southern Baroque Art* (1924). A masterpiece in the delineation of a style, the book caused a sensation among the *cognoscenti*. It was followed by *German Baroque Art* (1927).

Sacheverell, unlike Osbert and Edith, was modest and besettingly shy. He was an uneasy collaborator in his siblings' provocative *Façade* recitation to Walton's music in 1923. Tall, slender, with an oval face, small mouth, and attenuated nose, he conjured up the effigy of a Crusader knight on a tomb-table. His manner to old and young was exquisite, and towards children of the poor deeply compassionate. His memory, like his imagination, was prodigious. As a raconteur he was spellbinding: his humour impish and bubbling. Before exhausting one subject he was launched upon another.

In 1925 he married Georgia, younger daughter of Arthur Doble, banker, of Montreal. They had two sons. Marriage brought him great happiness. While inducting him into circles of the rich and raffish, Georgia also protected the privacy of his writing. The young couple lived comfortably at Weston Hall near Towcester, which his father on inheriting had passed to his younger son in 1923. Yet Sitwell always considered himself to be dogged by poverty. Devoted though he was to Weston, its family treasures and old-fashioned garden, he was never a countryman.

He wrote a great number of books. In spite of their diversity of subject, most are basically autobiographical. *The Gothic North* (3 vols., 1929-30) gave Sitwell as much rein for his fantasy as *Southern Baroque Art*. His sympathy for the age of chivalry was as pronounced as for that of rococo. *British Architects and Craftsmen* (1945) was a brilliant compendium of the master workers of Great Britain. Love of music led to the publication of *Mozart* (1932) and a life of *Liszt* (1934). The composers Constant *Lambert and F. B. Busoni, and the clavichord player Violet Woodhouse were among his intimate friends.

Mauretania (1940), *The Netherlands* (1948), *Spain* (1950), *Portugal and Madeira* (1954), *Denmark* (1956), and *Malta* (1958) poured from his pen. Half guidebook, half travelogue, they were idiosyncratic and subjective. Of even more serious consideration are his travel books of the mind and spirit, of which *Sacred and Profane Love* (1940), an aesthetic journey during the stress of World War II, was the first, and *For Want of the Golden City* (1973) the last.

He was a JP (1943) and high sheriff of Northamptonshire (1948-9). He was granted the freedom of the city of Lima (Peru) in 1960. In 1981 the Royal Society of Literature awarded him the Benson silver medal, and in 1984 he was appointed CH. On his wife's death in 1980 Sitwell gave up writing altogether. His remaining years were spent quietly at Weston where he died 1 October 1988. He was succeeded in the baronetcy by his elder son, (Sacheverell) Reresby (born 1927).

[Sarah Bradford, *Sacheverell Sitwell*, 1993; Max Wykes-Joyce, *Triad of Genius*, 1953; John Lehmann, *A Nest of Tigers*, 1968; Denys Sutton, 'The World of Sacheverell Sitwell', *Apollo*, part 1, September 1980, and part 2, October 1980; Neil Ritchie, *Sacheverell Sitwell: an Annotated and Descriptive Bibliography*, 1987; John Pearson, *Façades: Edith, Osbert and Sacheverell Sitwell*, 1978; personal knowledge.]

JAMES LEES-MILNE

SKYRME, Tony Hilton Royle (1922–1987), theoretical physicist, was born 5 December 1922 at 7 Blessington Road, Lewisham, Kent, the only child of John Hilton Royle Skyrme, bank clerk, and his wife, Muriel May Roberts. After attending a boarding school in Lewisham, he won a scholarship to Eton, where he distinguished himself by outstanding work in mathematics, gaining a number of prizes. In 1940 he became a scholar of Trinity College, Cambridge, reading mathematics, and there he maintained the high standard shown at Eton. He passed part ii of the mathematics tripos as a wrangler in 1942, and part iii in 1943.

On graduating, he was directed by the wartime central register of scientists to Birmingham, where a group under (Sir) Rudolf Peierls was working on the theoretical aspects of atomic energy, particularly atomic weapons. Here his great ability soon attracted attention. While capable of using abstract reasoning on difficult problems, he was prepared to look at experimental situations and at measurements which needed theoretical analysis. He wrote a number of useful reports, one of which, concerned with neutron scattering, remained in demand for many years. At the end of 1943 several scientists working on atomic energy, including Peierls, were transferred to the United States, to assist in the 'Manhattan Project'. Skyrme followed a little later, and worked first in New York, on problems concerning the diffusion plant for isotope separation, and then at Los Alamos.

After the end of World War II Skyrme spent two years (1946–7) as a research fellow at Birmingham University, where he acquired a command of modern theoretical physics. One of the results he obtained provided a rigorous mathematical proof of an important theorem in nuclear physics. He submitted this for publication, but the referee wanted one section expanded; Skyrme never complied with this request, and the paper remained unpublished. The academic years 1948–9 and 1949–50 were spent at the Massachusetts Institute of Technology and at the Institute for Advanced Study in Princeton, respectively.

From 1950 to 1962 Skyrme worked at the Atomic Energy Research Establishment at Harwell, and these were his most productive years. Apart from papers relating to the design or interpretation of experiments in nuclear physics, and much work on specific problems of nuclear structure, he made two pioneering contributions to nuclear physics. One was to show how to handle short-range forces in a three-body problem; the other, not unrelated, was a powerful approximation to nuclear forces, later widely used as the 'Skyrme model'. An even more original contribution was a treatment of fundamental particles, in which particles such as neutrons and protons, which obey the Pauli exclusion principle, appear as manifestations of fields such as that of mesons. These ideas were so

revolutionary that it was some years before they received adequate attention. Later the study of these 'Skyrmions' became a flourishing branch of theoretical physics. For this work Skyrme was awarded the Hughes medal of the Royal Society in 1985.

During a year's leave from Harwell, he and his wife spent a semester in the University of Pennsylvania and then returned via the United States, Australia, and the Far and Middle East, making all the land journeys by Land-Rover. They had enjoyed Malaysia, and when changes at Harwell made his condition there less congenial, he accepted a post in the University of Malaysia in Kuala Lumpur, where they arrived, again by Land-Rover, in the autumn of 1962. Since the staff of the department was much smaller than he had been led to believe, there were heavy teaching duties and few people interested in research. In 1964 Skyrme accepted an invitation to a professorship in Birmingham, initially as head of the department, but later he was relieved of the administrative duties. He remained in Birmingham until his death.

Skyrme was distinguished by a deep understanding of physics, by a great command of mathematics, and, above all, by an original and fertile imagination. He was of medium height, with light brown hair and brown eyes. As a young man he had a slim, athletic figure; in later life he put on much weight. He tended to be rather quiet, being a solitary person who did not like joint work, but preferred to think about problems on his own. In 1949 he married Dorothy Mildred, daughter of Francis Charles Millest, commercial traveller. They had no children. Skyrme died 25 June 1987 in Selly Oak Hospital, Birmingham, of an embolism after an operation.

[R. H. Dalitz, 'An Outline of the Life and Work of Tony Skyrme', *International Journal of Modern Physics* A, vol. iii, 1988, pp. 2719–44, 1988; personal knowledge.]   RUDOLF PEIERLS

SLACK, Kenneth (1917–1987), Nonconformist minister, was born 20 July 1917 in Wallasey, the second son in the family of two sons and one daughter of Reginald Slack, manager of a small grocery store, and his wife, Nellie Bennett. They lived on a grocer's wage and providing for Kenneth's education was a struggle. He was educated at Wallasey Grammar School and Liverpool University, from which he graduated with a BA honours degree in 1937. He then studied theology at Westminster College, Cambridge, on a Lewis Gibson scholarship. He was ordained into the Presbyterian Church of England in 1941.

Throughout the years of his ministry there was a continual and creative movement between service in local churches and leadership within the ecumenical agencies. In both he revealed talents for organization, and preaching and writing skills. His first pastorate was at St Nicholas church, Shrewsbury. In 1942 he entered the Royal Air Force Volunteer Reserve as a chaplain. From 1943 to 1946 he served in the Far East, from which he returned with an MBE (1946) and an international dimension to his thinking. He became minister of St James's, Edgware, where his abilities were soon recognized throughout the Presbyterian Church of England, as a vigorous pastor, forthright editor of the church journal, and supporter of ecumenical development.

In 1955 Slack was appointed general secretary of the British Council of Churches, the first Free Church minister to hold this position, and as such became the senior civil servant of the ecumenical movement in Britain. It was an ideal appointment, for he was quick to establish excellent personal relations with senior officers of the churches, becoming a trusted colleague at Lambeth Palace and at Archbishop's House, Westminster. The BCC had been a tender plant in its early years, but Slack was able to give it a higher public profile and a greater priority in the life of the churches. He was also concerned with the local expression of ecumenism, travelling constantly to encourage local councils of churches.

In 1965 he returned to local ministry, first at St Andrew's church in Cheam (1965–7), and then in central London at the City Temple (1967–75). During this time he became well known as a broadcaster, being frequently heard on the BBC's 'Thought for the Day'. So skilled was he at the brief pertinent message that a member of his congregation was moved to ask if he could not preach as briefly on Sundays. The cause of Christian unity remained a priority to him, and during the 1960s he took a leading part in the discussions between Presbyterians and Congregationalists, which led to the formation of the United Reformed Church in 1972. It was no surprise that he was elected moderator of the URC for 1973–4 and stimulated consultation about further unions. He had become a leading public exponent in Britain of the call to remove the ancient barriers between Christian churches.

The broader scene claimed him again from 1975 to 1982, when he was director of Christian Aid, the agency through which the churches provided help to the most needy people of the world. This task called for much travel and constant advocacy so that resources could be provided, not only for disaster relief, but to lift the chronic burdens of poverty. Another period of local church ministry followed for him, at Kensington, from 1982 until his death in 1987.

A steady and prolific writer, he produced a series of books on World Council of Churches assemblies, biographies of Martin Luther King

(1970) and Bishop George *Bell (1971), and biblical studies on the Lord's Prayer (1973) and the Psalms (*New Light on Old Songs*, 1975). But he was never a cloistered writer. Excelling in conversation and friendship, vigorous and challenging, he was good company, helping many to share his own confidence in the radical power of Christian faith. Tall, upright, and burly, he was a commanding figure, particularly when robed in the pulpit. His air of confidence, good humour, and frequent laughter gave him a welcoming appearance. Southampton University gave him an honorary degree in 1971.

In 1941 he married (Barbara) Millicent, daughter of William Spong Blake, a traveller for the family printing firm. They had two sons and one daughter. Slack died 4 October 1987 in East Finchley.

[Personal knowledge.]   BERNARD THOROGOOD

SMART, Elizabeth (1913–1986), writer, was born 27 December 1913 in Ottawa, Canada, the third child and third daughter in the family of four daughters (one of whom died in infancy) and one son of Russel Sutherland Smart, a prominent Ottawa lawyer, specializing in patents, and his wife, Emma Louise ('Louie'), daughter of James Alexander Parr, executive in the Montreal Telegraph Co. She grew up in affluent circumstances in Ottawa and Kingsmere, where the family had a second house on a lake. She was educated at Ottawa Normal School, Elmwood School, and Hatfield Hall in Cobourg, with the exception of one year during which she was obliged to lie in bed with a heart condition, and there began to write. She vacillated between becoming a musician or writer and did not go to university. She travelled around the world under the eye of a family friend. In London she studied to become a professional pianist with Katharine Goodson, but with the confidence born of what she called the 'huge luckiness' of her childhood she reacted against the hollowness of her social life and broke away to travel around the world, always gravitating towards artistic rebels. Although she had studied music for thirteen years and played the piano very well, she never played again. She lived on an allowance from her father.

She expressed her adventurous, romantic nature to the full when, after reading the poems of George Granville Barker in a Charing Cross bookshop, she promptly fell in love with the poet, who was then working unhappily in Japan. He was the son of George Barker, formerly of the Coldstream Guards, butler at Gray's Inn. In 1940 she invited Barker and his wife to Canada, raising the cash herself for both their fares, and they then moved to Monterey, California, where she was living. This was the pivotal act of her life and resulted in a passion-wracked affair, which began in July 1940, four children, and her extraordinary novel, *By Grand Central Station I Sat Down and Wept*, which she completed in 1941. First published in August 1945 by Tambimuttu just before the end of World War II, her novel (or narrative prose poem) remained largely unnoticed in the fray, although Cyril *Connolly gave it a certain grudging admiration in *Horizon*.

After the birth of her first love-child, a girl, in 1941, Smart went to England in 1943 on a convoy which was torpedoed. Shortly afterwards she produced a son by Barker, whose wife had twins five weeks later. The rigours of bringing up a family with very little money (she was still reliant on an allowance from her father) and without a permanent father-figure gagged her muse, but she became more settled when she moved to a mill-house in Essex. She wrote intermittently about the aftermath of her grand passion, but, understandably under the circumstances, her productivity was low. She had another of Barker's sons in 1945 and a daughter in 1947.

From 1949 to 1951 she was a sub-editor on *House and Garden*. Separated from Barker, who eventually had fifteen children by different women, she had occasional affairs. By the mid-1950s she supported her family by writing advertising copy. Her large flat at 9 Westbourne Terrace was a centre for London bohemians, many of them distinguished remnants from the old Soho 'Fitzrovia' days (the painters Robert *Colquhoun, Robert MacBryde, Patrick Swift, and Craigie Aitchison; the poets Patrick Kavanagh and W. S. *Graham, and the inspired drifter Jeffrey Bernard). In 1957, with Agnes Ryan, she published *Cooking the French Way*. Her life began to pick up considerably in 1964 as the children grew up and she began writing for the sparkling new magazine *Queen*, a job she held until 1966.

In 1966 her novel was republished by Panther Books in a silver paperback, with an introduction by Brigid Brophy, who described it as one of the half dozen masterpieces in the world: 'The entire book is a wound. Even when its rhythm expresses the throb of pleasure, the pleasure is so ardent it lays waste the personality which experiences it...it is one of the most shelled, skinned, nerve-exposed books ever written.' But some critics continued to be affronted by such a metaphor-laden, raw, female emotion, the eternal wail of a woman for her demon lover, and took their refuge in accusations of purple prose, discounting the passages of searing humour.

After her younger daughter became involved with drugs, she often had full responsibility for the daughter's two children, and she soon moved to a cottage near Bungay, Suffolk, where she became absorbed in creating a garden and writing poetry. She aimed for Blakean simplicity which did not appeal to the poetry Mafia of the period. However, her first collection, *A Bonus*, was published in 1977 (Polytantric Press) and she began to give poetry readings. The publication of *The Assumption of the Rogues and Rascals* in 1978 (Cape/Polytantric), her long-brewing aftermath novel, and the Canadian publication of her dazzling memoirs, *In the Meantime* (1984), reinforced her growing reputation. Meanwhile the now famous early book was translated into many languages and became something of a cult novel. In 1982 she spent a year as writer in residence at the University of Alberta.

Elizabeth Smart had occasional affairs with both men and women. She was a great beauty, not only in the classical blonde, blue-eyed, well-featured sense, but because of a radiance which, even later, ravaged by age and empathy, could draw so many people to her. She was a bohemian in the best sense of the word and died 4 March 1986, of a heart attack, in her son Christopher's flat in the Soho where she had spent so many hours in conviviality, good talk, and freedom from hypocritical moral restraints. Her younger daughter had died from drug-taking in 1982. Her journals, *Necessary Secrets*, were posthumously published by Harper Collins in 1986.

[Elizabeth Smart, *In the Meantime*, 1984; Rosemary Sullivan, *By Heart: Elizabeth Smart, a Life*, 1991; private information; personal knowledge.]

JILL NEVILLE

SMITH, SIR (**James**) **Eric** (1909–1990), marine biologist, was born in Hull 23 February 1909, the elder son and eldest of three children of Walter Smith, who had a wholesale grocery business, and his wife, Elsie Kate Pickett. He was educated at Hull Grammar School, where he was head boy and an all-round athlete. After a short period in his father's firm, he entered King's College, London, in 1927, where he gained a first class in zoology.

He began his scientific career in 1930, as a student probationer at the Plymouth laboratory of the Marine Biological Association, where he worked on the invertebrate fauna of the Eddystone shell gravels. He left Plymouth in 1932, and after three years as an assistant lecturer at Manchester University (1932–5) moved to Sheffield (1935–8), and thence to Cambridge as an assistant lecturer (1938–50). He then took the chair in zoology at Queen Mary College, London (1950–65), where he ran a most successful department with a strong marine biological side. Although much of his time was taken up by administrative duties (he was vice-principal of the college from 1963 during a period of expansion), he took an active part in lecturing and continued his research on echinoderms, recognized by his election as a fellow of the Royal Society in 1958.

From QMC he returned to Plymouth as director of the Marine Biological Association laboratory in 1965, a post he held until his retirement in 1974.

Soon after he became director at Plymouth, the wreck of the oil tanker *Torrey Canyon* in 1967 produced the first large-scale oil pollution incident. The work of the MBA during this episode resulted in a classic account of the incident, which Smith edited. He also acted as one of the three members of the commissions of Australia and of the state of Queensland dealing with possible oil drilling on the Great Barrier Reef. The scientific work for which Smith is chiefly known, the neurobiology of starfish, was begun at Manchester and continued at Cambridge and QMC. It resulted in a series of monumental papers. The study of the starfish nervous system presented challenging difficulties, and when Smith began, only rudimentary information about gross morphology was available. He was undaunted by the difficulties, and was able greatly to advance knowledge of the nervous system by careful histological work. He also made significant contributions to the study of the fine structure of the nervous system in another invertebrate group, the polychaete worms, using the methods he had developed for starfish.

Smith was a kindly and generous man, notable for his obvious and genuine interest in people, and an unusually able and diplomatic negotiator; these qualities made his advice and counsel much sought, and he undertook a good deal of committee work. Both at QMC and at Plymouth, Smith played an important role in British zoology by his membership of many committees. He was a member of the Science Research Council (1965–7); a council member (1953–6) and vice-president (1954–5) of the Linnean Society; twice a council member of the Zoological Society (1958–61 and 1964–7) and vice-president (1959–61); as well as serving twice (1962–3 and 1972–4) on the council of the Royal Society and as vice-president (1973–4). He was also a trustee of the British Museum (Natural History) in 1963–74 (chairman 1969–74), and chairman of the board of the Millport laboratory. After his retirement his skills on committees were still much in demand, and he acted as a member of the Advisory Board for the Research Councils (1974–7), president of the International Council of Scientific Unions, and chairman of its special committee on problems of the environment (1972). He also chaired the important ABRC review group on taxonomy in Britain, whose report was published in 1977.

Smith was appointed CBE in 1972 and knighted in 1977; amongst other honours, he received the gold medal of the Linnean Society in 1971, the Frink medal of the Zoological Society in 1981, and was elected a fellow of King's College, London (1964) and Queen Mary College (1967). He received an honorary D.Sc. from Exeter (1968), and was one of the first fellows of the Plymouth Polytechnic.

Smith was of medium height and build, blue-eyed and more or less bald in early life. He usually dressed simply, in a sports coat and flannel trousers, and his benevolent demeanour and charming smile made him very approachable. In retirement, as well as spending more time in his garden (he was a keen vegetable gardener), he continued a lifelong interest in the naturalists of the west country, and also worked on periwinkles, collected from the shore below his house at Saltash, and at many sites around the south-west. In 1934 he married Thelma Audrey (died 1989), daughter of John Lillicrap Cornish, auctioneer and house agent. They had a son and a daughter. Smith died in a nursing home in Plymouth, 3 September 1990.

[Q. Bone and D. Nichols in *Biographical Memoirs of Fellows of the Royal Society*, vol. xxxviii, 1992; private information; personal knowledge.]   QUENTIN BONE

SMITH, Ronald William (1913–1990), photographer. [See PARKINSON, NORMAN.]

SMITH, SIR Thomas Broun (1915–1988), academic lawyer, was born in Glasgow 3 December 1915, the second of four sons (there was also one daughter, the fourth child) of John Smith, DL, JP, restaurateur, of Pollokshields, Glasgow, and Symington, Lanarkshire, and his wife, Agnes Macfarlane. He was educated at the High School of Glasgow and Sedbergh School, went to Christ Church, Oxford, as Boulter exhibitioner, and graduated in 1937 with first-class honours in jurisprudence and the Eldon law scholarship. A year later, having achieved a first class and certificate of honour in the bar final, he was called to the bar by Gray's Inn, which in 1986 made him an honorary bencher.

Smith joined the Territorial Army in 1937 and served throughout World War II in the Gordon Highlanders and Royal Artillery, rising to the rank of lieutenant-colonel. He took part in the retreat from Dunkirk, served in the Mediterranean and the Middle East, and moved to intelligence work. He then returned to Scotland, passed advocate of the Scottish bar in 1947, and commenced practice. In 1949 he accepted the chair of Scots law in the University of Aberdeen, where he was very happy, made a great impression on students, and began the movement to change the study of law in the Scottish universities from a part-time complement to office training to a more thorough study. He became a QC (Scotland) in 1956 and in 1958 moved to the

chair of civil (Roman) law at Edinburgh, where
he transformed the course from classical civil law
to its later Romanist developments as the basis of
much modern European law. Ten years later, in
1968, he transferred to the chair of Scots law at
Edinburgh, which he held till 1972. In 1960 he
established the Scottish Universities Law Institute, a co-operative organization of the law faculties of the four Scottish universities, to secure the
writing and publication of new, modern textbooks in all the major fields of Scots law. He was
its director from 1960 to 1972.

Smith also made many contacts abroad,
becoming a visiting professor at, among other
universities, Cape Town (1958), Harvard
(1962–3), and, as Tagore professor, Calcutta
(1977). A member of the law reform committee
for Scotland from 1954, he became a commissioner when the Scottish Law Commission was
established in 1965 (full-time from 1972 to 1980);
on this body his breadth of scholarship made him
a stimulating and inspiring colleague. In retirement he took up in 1981 the onerous post of
general editor of the new *The Laws of Scotland:
Stair Memorial Encyclopaedia* (25 vols., 1986–
94).

He wrote extensively and entertainingly in
journals and some of his papers are collected in
Studies Critical and Comparative (1952). His
Hamlyn lectures, *British Justice: the Scottish
Contribution* (1961), strongly asserted the distinctive nature of Scots law. His biggest book,
requested as a chapter on Scotland for a volume
The United Kingdom in a series *The British
Commonwealth: the Development of its Laws and
Constitutions* (ed. G. W. Keeton and D. Lloyd),
emerged in 1955 as a full volume. It was also
issued as *A Short Commentary on the Law of
Scotland* (1962), to provide a better basic textbook for Scottish law students than was then
available. In this it was not a success, being too
general and discursive.

Physically Smith had a tendency to heaviness
and his cheerful round face and moustache
maintained to the end strong traces of his military years. He was a genial and jovial companion,
with a lively sense of humour; in discussion he
was courteous and stimulating, but tended sometimes to pontificate. He cared deeply about
Scotland and Scots law. He was much influenced
by T. M. *Cooper (Baron Cooper of Culross),
whom he revered. In particular he was interested
in the influence of civil law on Scots law and the
shared tradition of Scots and Roman-Dutch law.
He made a great contribution to raising to
importance Scots law and Scottish legal scholarship, modernizing it, and, more by his contacts
than by his writings, making it better known to
the world and better appreciated outside Scotland.

Smith's published work gained him a DCL

(Oxford, 1956) and LL D (Edinburgh, 1963). He
was elected FBA in 1958, FRSE in 1977, and a
foreign honorary member of the American Academy of Arts and Sciences (1969). He received
honorary LL D degrees from Cape Town (1959),
Aberdeen (1969), and Glasgow (1978), and was
knighted on his retirement in 1981. The *Juridical
Review* for 1982 was devoted to essays in his
honour.

In 1940 he married Ann Dorothea, crimino-
logist, daughter of Christian Tindall, CIE, of the
Indian civil service, of Exmouth, Devon. It was a
happy marriage, which produced a son, who died
in 1962, and two daughters, one of whom also
predeceased Smith in 1976. Smith died of cancer
in Edinburgh 15 October 1988. Till near the end
he continued to welcome friends and bombard
contributors to *The Laws of Scotland* with comments and encouragement. There is a portrait by
T. A. Cockburn in Edinburgh University.

[*Juridical Review*, 1982; *The Times* and *Daily Telegraph*,
18 October 1988; *Scotsman*, 19 October 1988; obituary
in *Scots Law Times* (News), 1988; *Yearbook of the Royal
Society of Edinburgh*, 1990; J. O. M. Hunter in *Proceedings of the British Academy*, vol. lxxxii, 1992; personal
knowledge.]   DAVID M. WALKER

SOAMES, (Arthur) Christopher (John),
BARON SOAMES (1920–1987), politician, was born
12 October 1920 in Penn, Buckinghamshire, the
only son and youngest of three children of
Captain Arthur Granville Soames, OBE, of the
Coldstream Guards and Ashwell Manor, Penn,
and his wife, Hope Mary Woodbyne, daughter of
Charles Woodbyne Parish. He was educated at
Eton and the Royal Military College at Sandhurst and commissioned in 1939 as a second
lieutenant in the Coldstream Guards. He served
in the Middle East, Italy, and France during the
war, winning the croix de guerre (1942) while on
attachment to the Free French brigade in the
Western Desert, where his right leg was shattered by a mine explosion. In 1946 he was
appointed assistant military attaché at the British
embassy in Paris. In the following year he married Mary, youngest daughter of (Sir) Winston
Leonard Spencer-*Churchill, former prime
minister.

In 1950 he entered Parliament as the Conservative member for Bedford. During Churchill's second premiership (1952–5), Soames acted
as his parliamentary private secretary. He did
much to keep the government going, masking the
seriousness of his father-in-law's illness, when
Churchill suffered a stroke in 1953. He went
through the ranks of junior ministerial office
before becoming secretary of state for war in
1958 (when he was sworn of the Privy Council),
and serving in the cabinet in 1960–4 as minister
of agriculture.

Having lost his seat in the 1966 election, he was an inspired choice by the government led by Harold Wilson (later Baron Wilson of Rievaulx) as British ambassador to France (1968–72). Soames took up his post at a difficult time, with President Charles de Gaulle continuing to obstruct British accession to the European Community. His term in Paris began inauspiciously with the leaking by the Foreign Office of the contents of a private conversation between him and de Gaulle (*l'affaire Soames*). A year later, de Gaulle was gone and Soames was able to establish a much warmer relationship with his successor, Georges Pompidou. This was the crucial period leading to the successful completion of negotiations for Britain's entry into the EC and Soames, himself a convinced European, played a major part in persuading the French government no longer to impede the negotiations. His excellent colloquial French, splendid hospitality, and ebullient personality endeared him to the Parisians.

Immediately following British entry into the EC, Soames became the first British vice-president of the European Commission and commissioner for external affairs, from 1973 to January 1977. He was a most effective commissioner. He played a major role in international trade negotiations and in establishing British influence in Brussels.

After a brief return to private life, Soames was invited to join Margaret (later Baroness) Thatcher's government in 1979 as lord president of the Council and leader of the House of Lords. Later that year he was given his most difficult task, being appointed governor of Southern Rhodesia to oversee the cease-fire and elections leading to the independence of Zimbabwe. When he set off from London the cease-fire had still not been agreed, much less brought into effect, and the prospects for the success of his mission were generally discounted by the press. Following the successful conclusion of the Lancaster House negotiations, a cease-fire was implemented under the supervision of the largely British Commonwealth monitoring force. Soames had the greatest difficulty with the Rhodesian military commanders on the one hand and sections of the Patriotic Front on the other throughout the period leading up to the elections, which were held in February 1980. He had to exercise responsibility with no more real power than he could win by bargaining with the contending parties. He set out to establish a personal relationship with the black political leaders, assuring Robert Mugabe that, if he won the elections, Soames would take the lead in helping the new government establish itself in a still uncertain, tense, and dangerous situation. When Mugabe did win he invited Soames to continue to serve as governor. In the ensuing period major steps were taken towards bringing together and forming into a single military command elements of the Rhodesian forces and those of the Patriotic Front, who themselves were split into two warring factions. Soames left Rhodesia having helped to bring an end to the war and to launch Zimbabwe as an independent nation, amidst near-universal plaudits.

On his return to Britain he had to deal with matters far less congenial to him, including a Civil Service strike. He found himself out of sympathy with the new economic strategy being pursued by Mrs Thatcher and her style of government. In 1981 he was dropped from the government. He remained thereafter very active in business, holding a number of important directorships until his death, including those of N. M. Rothschild's and the National Westminster Bank, and the chairmanship of ICL (UK).

Soames was a figure very much larger than life. His conversation could usually be heard in the next room. His convivial but forthright personality inspired strong loyalties among his friends and some resistance on the part of more sensitive souls. His hospitality and enjoyment of life were legendary. As ambassador in Paris, commissioner in Brussels, and governor of Rhodesia, he put up performances which could scarcely have been matched by anyone else. His success in all these capacities owed much to his wife, (Dame) Mary. They had three sons, one of whom, Nicholas, also became a Conservative MP and minister, and two daughters.

The academic distinctions Soames received included honorary doctorates from Oxford (1981) and St Andrews (1974). He was awarded the Robert Schuman prize in 1976. He was appointed CBE (1955) and GCMG and GCVO (1972), created a life baron in 1978, and appointed CH in 1980. He also was awarded, on his departure from Paris, the cross of grand officer of the Legion of Honour. He died from cancer 16 September 1987, at his home in Odiham, Hampshire.

[Private information; personal knowledge.]

ROBIN RENWICK

SOLOMON (1902–1988), pianist, was born 9 August 1902 at 39 Fournier Street, in the East End of London, the youngest in the family of four sons and three daughters of Harris Cutner (formerly Schneiderman), master tailor, the grandson of a Polish *émigré* from Cutnow, and his wife, Rose Piser. Showing exceptional musical talent from early childhood, at the age of seven he came to the attention of Mathilde Verne, a fashionable London piano teacher and former pupil of Clara Schumann. She persuaded Solomon's parents to sign a contract, relinquishing him into her care for five years, and within a year she had launched him successfully as a child prodigy, with a début at the Queen's Hall in June 1911, playing Mozart's Concerto in B♭ ('the little B♭'), the slow movement of Tchaikovsky's first Piano Concerto, and a Polacca by Alice Verne. The concert was conducted by Theodor Müller-Reuter, another of Clara Schumann's pupils. Billed from the outset as 'Solomon', sometimes wearing a sailor suit, sometimes in velvet knickerbockers and a lace collar, he captivated his audiences. He was invited to play at Buckingham Palace in 1912, and he made his Proms début in 1914 playing Beethoven's Second Piano Concerto.

After Solomon had spent five miserable years with Mathilde Verne, forced to practise for many hours a day in a locked room, his parents refused to sign another contract, and for a year he gave concerts throughout England chaperoned by one of his brothers. In 1916 he decided to give up all public performances, and, after a farewell recital at the Wigmore Hall shortly before his fourteenth birthday, he began studying with Dr Simon Rumschisky in London, while attending King Alfred School in the North End Road in the mornings. His studies were financed through a fund set up by an American, Mrs Colson. He spent three years with Rumschisky, a medical doctor who had studied the physiological aspects of playing the piano. Solomon later claimed that he was one of the greatest teachers in the world, and had taught him all his technique. In 1919, financed by Mrs Colson, Solomon went to Paris, where his teachers included Lazare Lévy, Marcel Dupré, and Alfred Cortot.

Still only nineteen, Solomon returned to the concert platform with a Wigmore Hall recital in 1921. The 1920s were difficult years for him, for English audiences then preferred foreign pianists such as Arthur Schnabel. Although he toured the USA in 1926, he remained relatively unknown outside England. Thanks to Sir Henry *Wood he performed regularly at the Queen's Hall Promenade Concerts. (Sir) Arthur *Bliss wrote his Viola Sonata (1933) for Solomon and Lionel *Tertis, and when Solomon was asked by the British Council to represent Great Britain at the New York World Fair in 1939, he commissioned Bliss to write a piano concerto. During World War II Solomon joined the Entertainments National Service Association (ENSA) and gave many concerts, both for troops abroad and in army camps and hospitals at home, making many converts to classical music. Through his concerts on the wards at St Mary's Hospital, Paddington, he came into contact with Sir Alexander *Fleming, and was successfully treated for a septic thumb through the inhalation of penicillin in the very early days of its development as an antibiotic.

After the war Solomon became an international celebrity, following an enthusiastic reception in the USA on his tour in 1949. He spent the next few years touring and recording, before a stroke ended his career in 1956. He was left with an active brain, but a speech impediment. Though he struggled to express himself his playing days were over. In the remaining years of his life he could take no interest in his career, achievements, or recordings.

Solomon was one of the three greatest English pianists of the twentieth century, with Dame Myra *Hess and Sir Clifford *Curzon, and possibly the greatest twentieth-century British interpreter of Schumann. During his early career he was best known for his performances of Chopin, but he later concentrated on Mozart, Beethoven, Schumann, and Brahms. Critics commented on the elegance and purity of his playing, its clarity and accuracy, and the controlled nature of his performances. Famous recordings from the early 1950s include those of the Brahms 'Variations and Fugue on a Theme by Handel', Beethoven's 'Moonlight' Sonata, the two Brahms piano concertos, and Schumann's 'Carnaval'. He also played chamber music, recording the Beethoven cello sonatas with Gregor Piatigorsky, and he formed a trio with Zino Francescatti and Pierre Fournier for the 1955 Edinburgh festival.

Solomon was short and stocky, almost completely bald from an early age, with short, thick fingers. He displayed none of the temperamental behaviour usually associated with great artists, and despite his years of adulation as a child prodigy he developed into a charming and modest person, nicknamed 'Solo' by Walter Legge, manager for artists and repertory at the Gramophone Company. He had a passion for betting and gambling, possibly originating in his trips to the races with the elderly mother of his landlady while he was studying in Paris, and he loved to visit the casinos in Cannes and Monte Carlo. He enjoyed bridge and golf, and for years played tennis daily with his old friend Gerald *Moore.

Solomon was appointed CBE in 1946 for his wartime work. He had honorary degrees from Cambridge (Mus.D., 1974) and St Andrews (LL D, 1960). In 1970 he married, after a long friendship begun in 1927, a former pupil, Gwendoline Harriet, daughter of Patrick Byrne, an Irish doctor and surgeon. They had not married earlier because Solomon was an orthodox Jew and Gwendoline a gentile. They had no children. Solomon died 22 February 1988 in London.

[Mathilde Verne, *Chords of Remembrance*, 1936; Gerald Moore, *Am I Too Loud?*, 1962; David Dubal, *The Art of the Piano*, 1990; Reginald Pound, *Sir Henry Wood*, 1969; Brian Crimp, *Solo*, 1995; BBC Sound Recordings archive; private information.] ANNE PIMLOTT BAKER

SOLOMON, Keith Granville (1910–1990), chairman and chief executive of the British

Overseas Airways Corporation. [See GRANVILLE, SIR KEITH.]

SOPWITH, SIR **Thomas Octave Murdoch** (1888–1989), engineer and pioneer airman, was born 18 January 1888 at 92 Cromwell Road, Kensington, west London, the eighth child and only son of Thomas Sopwith (1838–1898), managing director of the Spanish Lead Mines Company of Linares in southern Spain, and his wife Lydia Gertrude, daughter of William Messiter, of Wincanton, Somerset. Sopwith was educated at the Cottesmore School, Hove, Sussex, and, from 1902, the Seafield Park Engineering College at Lee-on-Solent, where he pursued his already deep interest in early motor cars, motor cycles, and all things mechanical. His childhood was deeply affected by an incident on a boating expedition during the family's annual summer holiday on the Isle of Lismore, off Oban in Scotland, when a gun, lying across the ten-year-old Sopwith's knee, went off and killed his father. This haunted Sopwith for the rest of his life. A substantial inheritance of £52,000 was divided, chiefly, between Sopwith and his mother, because five of the seven daughters had already married well.

Thus provided, on leaving Seafield Park in 1905, without academic attainments, but with a good, practical grasp of basic engineering, Sopwith plunged into the enjoyable pursuits of ballooning, motor-racing at Brooklands, and sailing in Channel waters. He bought a single-seat Avis monoplane and taught himself to fly (he gained the aviator's certificate no. 31). Before the end of 1910 he set up a British distance and duration record of 107 miles and 3 hours 10 minutes and, in December, with a flight of 169 miles in $3\frac{3}{4}$ hours, won the £4,000 Baron de Forest prize for the longest flight of the year from Britain into Europe. He won further prize money in America, which enabled him, in February 1912, to found the Sopwith School of Flying and, in June, the Sopwith Aviation Company Ltd.

By the outbreak of war in August 1914 the Sopwith Aviation Company had become one of the leading early British aircraft manufacturers, supplying aircraft to both the Admiralty and the War Office. Moreover, a Sopwith Tabloid on floats—a precursor of all subsequent single-seat fighters—had won for Britain the second Schneider Trophy air race at Monaco. Between August 1914 and November 1918 more than 18,000 Sopwith aircraft, of thirty-two different types, were designed and built for the Allied air forces. They included 5,747 Sopwith Camel single-seat fighters. The Camel was one of the most successful military aircraft of World War I, with 1,294 confirmed victories in air combat. Sopwith's contribution to the war was recognized by his appointment as CBE in 1918, but from the end of the war until September 1920 the Sopwith Company built only fifteen aircraft, while vainly endeavouring to maintain the employment of as many as possible of its workers by building motor-car bodies, motor cycles, and even aluminium saucepans. In September 1920 Sopwith put the company into liquidation while he was still able to pay creditors in full. Two months later he launched the H. G. Hawker Engineering Company Ltd., with himself as chairman, Fred Sigrist as chief engineer, and Harry Hawker as designer/test pilot. In June 1928 the Hawker Company's fortunes were truly founded, following the first flight at Brooklands of the outstanding Hawker Hart, a two-seat day bomber, designed by (Sir) Sydney *Camm, who had joined the Hawker Company in 1923. During the next ten years 3,036 Harts, and its seven variants, were built to form a substantial portion of the Royal Air Force.

Until 1963, under Sopwith's leadership and with Camm's design team, 26,800 aircraft of fifty-two different types flowed from the production lines of Hawkers and its associated companies. Chief among them was the Hawker Hurricane, a single-seat fighter, first flown on 6 November 1935, and put into production by Sopwith three months before an Air Ministry order had been received. Thanks to that hazardous but calculated risk, an additional 300 Hurricanes were able to be in service when the Battle of Britain began in 1940—a factor which contributed to Britain winning the world's first decisive air battle.

Meanwhile, in July 1935, with acumen and skill Sopwith had begun to weld a major portion of the British aircraft industry into the Hawker Siddeley Group—a combination of the Armstrong-Whitworth, Avro, Gloster, and Hawker aircraft companies, with the Armstrong Siddeley aero-engine and motor-car company and Air Service Training. During World War II the group delivered more than 40,000 aeroplanes of fifteen different types. They ranged from the Avro Lancaster bomber to the Gloster Meteor jet fighter. In 1959 the de Havilland Aircraft Company was added to the group and, in 1963, Blackburn and General Aircraft Ltd. Sopwith remained steadfastly in charge as chairman of the board, skilfully delegating his responsibilities until in 1963, at the age of seventy-five, he retired as chairman, but remained on the board until, on his ninetieth birthday, he was elected founder and life president. He was knighted in 1953.

Throughout his long life Sopwith maintained his cherished pursuits of fishing, shooting, and boating. In 1913 he set up a world speed record for powerboats of 48 knots, and between 1928 and 1930, with seventy-five first prizes, he became the leading British 12-metre yachtsman. In 1930 he was elected a member of the Royal Yacht Squadron. With his J-class sloop, *Endeavour*, he came close to winning the America's Cup for Britain in 1934. In 1937 he tried again, with *Endeavour II*, but lost to a better boat. In later years he confided, 'My one great regret is that I didn't bring home that Cup.' Between 1937 and 1939 Sopwith revelled in the ownership of the 1,600-ton, ocean-going diesel yacht, *Philante*, built to his own requirements.

Sopwith was six feet tall, somewhat chubby-faced, with full cheeks, and a high, broad, and clear forehead, topped by a mass of thick dark hair, always parted to the right. He had somewhat heavy eyebrows, hazel eyes, a broad, straight nose, a wide mouth, and a rather thin upper lip. In 1914 he married the forty-three-year-old Beatrix Mary Leslie, divorced wife of Charles Edward Malcolm and daughter of Walter James Ruthven, Baron Ruthven. To his great distress, she died of cancer in 1930. In 1932 he married Phyllis Brodie Leslie, daughter of Frederick Philip Augustus Gordon, inspector of gaols in the Indian Civil Service. She died in 1978. They had one son. In his ninetieth year Sopwith became completely blind, but he lost none of his memory, nor his interest in aviation, sport, and meeting old friends. In 1988 a great assembly of Sopwith's legion of friends attended a hundredth birthday party held for him at Brooklands, at which they contacted him in Hampshire by land line (a discreet telephone line). He died at his home, Compton Manor, at Kings Somborne in Hampshire, 27 January 1989.

[Bruce Robertson, *Sopwith the Man and His Aircraft*, 1970; Horace F. King, *Sopwith Aircraft 1912–1920*, 1981; Alan Bramson, *Pure Luck, the Authorized Biography of Sir Thomas Sopwith*, 1990; private information; personal knowledge.]   PETER MASEFIELD

SORABJI, Kaikhosru Shapurji (1892–1988), composer, pianist, and critic, was born 14 August 1892 in Buxton Road, Chingford, Essex, as Leon Dudley Sorabji, the only child of a Parsee father, Shapurji Sorabji, mining engineer and iron merchant, and his wife, Madeline Matilda Korthy, a Spanish-Sicilian opera singer. He adopted the baptismal Parsee name by which he was universally known early in life, though near the beginning of his career he signed himself with various forms combined with Leon and Dudley. Latterly, he rejected enquiries into his nomenclature, as into the date of his birth, with the jealousy of his privacy that characterized his life. This refusal to countenance journalistic curiosity, coupled with the challenging letters with which he would bombard those who displeased him, was in contrast to the good humour, humanity, and generosity which he would show

to those who came into personal contact with him.

Sorabji had a number of teachers, both as pianist and as composer, but no formal education. His keyboard technique was admired as 'fabulous' in the early part of his career, when he played in London, Paris, Vienna, Glasgow, and Bombay; but he came to dislike the circumstances of public music-making, and withdrew from the concert platform in December 1936. In part, this was a product of his distaste for playing to listeners of whom he knew nothing, and a preference for addressing himself to a circle of like-minded friends. Modest private means enabled him to pursue a life free from the commercial considerations he despised, though he continued to compose (up to 1982) and won himself a reputation as a trenchant and forceful critic. He wrote especially for the *New English Weekly* and for A. R. *Orage's New Age. Some of these articles were later reprinted in two collections, *Around Music* (1932) and *Mi Contra Fa* (1947).

The allusion in the latter title is to the medieval theorists' description of two harmonically opposed notes: 'mi contra fa, diabolus in musica'. However, Sorabji's criticism was generally on the side of the angels. Composers he championed included those who later won international recognition, such as Karol Szymanowski, Nicolai Medtner, Ferruccio Busoni, and Charles-Henri Alkan (all influences on him), and some who have remained neglected even in their homeland, such as Francis George Scott and Bernard van Dieren. Though he had strong opinions, his attacks were mostly reserved for individuals and organizations whose attitudes he saw as betraying the loftiest standards. He expressed himself forcefully, even vituperatively, but always with an expressive bravura in his widely ranging sentences that made his prose an entertainment to read. A characteristic sally is contained in the dedication of what is probably his masterpiece, the 'Opus Clavicembalisticum', to his friend Hugh *MacDiarmid, 'likewise to the everlasting glory of those few men blessed and sanctified in the curses and execration of those many whose praise is eternal damnation'.

The elaborate richness of Sorabji's own music reflects not so much the oriental luxuriance often attributed to it (nothing enraged him more than being described as Indian) as the profusion of his mind. His earliest music, such as 'In the Hothouse' (1918), is sensuously chromatic in a manner that might have appealed to Frederick *Delius (who admired his 'Le Jardin Parfumé' of 1923). His First Piano Sonata (1919) makes some use of thematic cells, but the Second (1920) lacks any clear controlling form; his Fourth (1929) was accompanied by a rare analytical account (probably written as a concert introduction) and gave the music more traditional forms, such as passacaglia. He claimed to have found his direction with the First Organ Symphony (1924), a work lasting two hours (the later organ symphonies are longer). In this, an opening passacaglia provides an admirable tether for his far-ranging fantasy, a fugue develops some ideas strictly, and in the complex finale all the ideas are woven into a complex tapestry. Other works drew, with great technical virtuosity, on established forms as providing the basis for elaborate fantasizing. The 'Opus Clavicembalisticum' (1930) for solo piano combines into its time-span of four and a half hours a wide range of disciplines, of which the principal is fugue.

Sorabji gave the first performance himself in Glasgow in December 1930. It caused a sensation, but then an inadequate London performance of the first part by an inferior pianist contributed to Sorabji withdrawing his music from being performed without his express permission. This 'ban' was relaxed when, in the 1970s, there began to emerge virtuosi with the technique to master the music's difficulties and the intellectual curiosity to explore its substance. Sorabji was happy with performances by John *Ogdon, Yonty Solomon, Michael Habermann, Geoffrey Douglas Madge, and the organist Kevin Bowyer.

He had by now long since withdrawn to what he called his 'granite tower', a small house on the outskirts of Corfe castle in Dorset, from which he repelled casual vistors with fierce notices, but welcomed friends with warmth and wit. Short of stature and bespectacled, with a shock of wild black hair that in later life became a heavy white mane, he was a delightful conversationalist whose independence of mind remained intact. Though he denied any formal doctrinal persuasion, he had a religious temperament that inclined towards Roman Catholicism while not excluding an interest in Parsee mysticism. He never married, and died in Winfrith Newburgh 15 October 1988.

[Sorabji archive, organized by Alistair Hinton, Easton Dene, Bailbrook Lane, Bath, BA1 7AA; personal knowledge.]   JOHN WARRACK

SOSNOW, Eric Charles (1910–1987), journalist, lawyer, and businessman, was born 18 August 1910 in Kolno, eastern Poland, the second son in the family of three boys and two girls of David Sosnow, a Jewish produce merchant, and his wife, Libby Markewitz. He spent his early years in Poland and was educated at Lomża Secondary School, Wilno University, law chambers in Warsaw, and the London School of Economics. In 1934 he left Poland for England and was employed as a foreign correspondent for Polish newspapers.

He worked briefly for Nahum Sokolov as his private secretary. In 1936 he became a graduate research student at the London School of Economics. As a foreign journalist he joined the Foreign Press Association and with his knowledge of politics and command of languages (he spoke eight) he specialized in articles on eastern Europe. In 1938 he started writing for the *Economist* under Donald *Tyerman, and in 1940 became an overseas correspondent for the *Sunday Times* and *Sunday Chronicle*. He was to continue writing for these papers for a further twenty years. His reputation grew and in 1944 he was asked to interview the Polish prime minister and, later, the president of Czechoslovakia before his ill-fated journey to Moscow. He mixed easily with foreign journalists of every nationality and political persuasion. He loved journalism for the contact it gave him with people and the outlet it provided for his writing. He was naturalized in October 1947.

While travelling and reporting he built a network of contacts around the world. Although his first love was journalism, the most obvious outlet for his talents and energy was international trade. On his arrival in England he worked with his uncle in the importation of fruit juices. In 1945 he took over a redundant orange–juice factory and started, together with his wife, the manufacture of inexpensive fashion clothing under the name 'Estrava'.

In 1955 he was asked by Joe Bradley, with whom he had developed a very close association, to take over the management of Carters Merchants, an import–export company. In 1961 Estrava and Carters Merchants were combined into Whiteley Stevens, a textile company quoted on the London Stock Exchange. In the same year the group bought Gordon Woodroffe, with its trading interests in India, China, Japan, and Africa. In 1962 Sosnow changed the name of the group to United City Merchants. He now had an international trading group, which was to continue to grow and keep him travelling.

Gaining a reputation for barter, he became a central figure in international trade, and particularly trade behind the iron curtain. When he retired as chairman in 1981, United City Merchants was an international trading company, with offices worldwide, involved in banking, shipping, leather, raw materials, industrial machinery, cars, and turnkey projects. He had hoped that his very talented son Norman would take over from him, but he was killed in an air crash in 1967, at the age of twenty-three, while working for the company.

From 1981 onwards Sosnow devoted more of his time to predominantly educational charities. He became a governor and honorary fellow of the London School of Economics and was elected a fellow-commoner of Christ's College, Cambridge. He endowed chairs and travelling scholarships in both universities in his son's name; he had a great affection for and understanding of young people. He was very much involved in the Hebrew University of Jerusalem and the Weizmann Institute in Israel, and was closely associated with the Oxford Centre for Postgraduate Hebrew Studies and with the Institute of Jewish Affairs in London. Among his decorations were the Polish Order of Merit (1985) and the rank of comendador of the Republic of Portugal (1973). He became a freeman of the City of London in 1960.

Sosnow was a short, affable, and energetic man, always immaculately dressed, and with a great sense of humour. He was never prepared to take 'no' for an answer. As a journalist he searched for the scoop. As a businessman he expanded his company, which grew, not only in spite of the controls in the 1960s and 1970s, but because of them. He was never prepared to contest take-over bids but was willing to fight the system. When dividend controls were instituted he used them as an opportunity to conserve cash with which he bought businesses. He developed a technique for issuing tax-free bonus shares to his shareholders which was widely copied. He enjoyed the pomp and ceremony of the City and was happy when he was made a freeman of the City of London. He believed the basic tools necessary for success in international trade were a knowledge of and aptitude for languages, training in economics and international law, a love of travel, and an interest in modern history and people.

He was a voracious reader and an excellent academic lawyer, from whom solicitors and counsel learned many lessons. As a lawyer he derived immense satisfaction from his successful appeal to the House of Lords in 1982, *United City Merchants Investments Ltd. v. Royal Bank of Canada*, which decided that where a letter of credit was in order on its face, refusal by a banker to pay on presentation did not extend to fraud to which the seller was not party.

In 1943 Sosnow married Sylvia, daughter of Mark Tafler, an authority on late nineteenth-century English engraved glass. They had a son, who died in 1967, and a daughter. They were a remarkable couple, Sylvia being an active partner in the business and contributing greatly to its success. Sosnow died at the Hospital of St John and St Elizabeth, London NW8, 20 February 1987, and his wife died in 1988.

[Private information; personal knowledge.] E. S. BIRK

SPEAR, (Augustus John) Ruskin (1911–1990), artist and teacher, was born 30 June 1911 in Hammersmith, London, the only son and youngest of five children of Augustus Spear, coachbuilder and coach-painter, and his wife, (Matilda) Jane Lemon, cook. He acquired his unusual and appropriate Christian names by being named Augustus after his father, John after his maternal grandfather, and Ruskin after a member of the artistically inclined family with whom his mother was in service at the time of his birth. Crippled by polio at an early age, Spear attended the Brook Green School, Hammersmith, for afflicted children, where his artistic talent was recognized. He went on to study at the Hammersmith School of Art on a scholarship, aged about fifteen, and then at the Royal College of Art in London (1930–4), on another scholarship, under Sir William *Rothenstein.

He subsidized his own work by teaching, stating that he 'tried to believe money unimportant', and he noted wryly: 'first teaching appointment Croydon School of Art. Fee for $2\frac{1}{2}$ hours, 16 shillings plus train fare. The Principal, interested in palmistry, read my hand, deciding it was promising, offered me four days per week.' He taught at Croydon, Sidcup, Bromley, St Martin's, Central, and Hammersmith schools of art, and—notably—as a visiting teacher in the painting school at the Royal College of Art (1952–77). He was also a gifted musician, and added to his income by playing jazz piano.

Throughout his life Spear regarded himself as 'a working-class cockney', while pursuing an extensive career as one of the liveliest members of the art world, loved by the public, fellow artists, and students, but only occasionally by the critics, by whom he was not taken seriously. He was a robust character, direct, colourful, pipe-smoking, and bearded. Known as a man with a prodigious thirst, he frequented his local pubs in Hammersmith and Chiswick, where his fellow drinkers formed a substantial proportion of his subject-matter. He summed up his life view thus: 'Painting, Breathing, Drinking, Ars Longa, Vita Brevis.' His polio caused a permanent limp and prevented active service in World War II. He did, however, contribute noteworthy paintings of working life on the home front, commissioned and purchased by the war artists' advisory committee.

He became an associate of the Royal Academy in 1944 and a fellow in 1954. This enabled him as of right to contribute to the Academy's summer exhibitions, where he had first exhibited in 1932. His facility with paint, and his fascination with low life and high life, and the foibles of both, often made his contributions newsworthy. Pub characters, members of the royal family, and politicians were his favourite subjects for Academy presentation, with the portraits of public figures often based on newspaper photographs. He was a gentle satirist, exaggerating what was there rather than turning to stereotypes. He also portrayed ordinary life with vivid sympathy; a painting of a mother potting a baby caused the president of the Royal Academy, Sir Alfred

*Munnings, such displeasure in 1944 that it was not shown. In 1942 Spear was elected to the London Group, becoming its president in 1949–50.

Spear had a thriving portrait practice among prominent figures. His subjects, which he proudly listed in his *Who's Who* entry, included lords *Butler, *Adrian, *Olivier as Macbeth (painted from life), and *Ramsey of Canterbury, Sir John *Betjeman in a rowing-boat, and Lords Goodman and Howe of Aberavon. He was a portrayer of the human comedy with a light touch, in spite of often using a dark palette. He never had regular showings or a contract with a commercial gallery. He did occasionally exhibit abroad, but the only substantial exhibition of his work ever held in Britain (or anywhere) was the retrospective in the Diploma Galleries in the Royal Academy in 1980. The National Portrait Gallery has several of his portraits.

In spite of the relatively conventional, if exuberant, nature of his own work, Spear promoted what he called the 'modern chaps', and was instrumental in turning the Academy away from its unhealthy nostalgia; he was assisted by his outstanding success as a teacher during a golden age at the Royal College (Ron Kitaj, Frank Auerbach, David Hockney, and Peter Blake were his students). 'We did a lot of teaching. The atmosphere tingled with the excitement of being *free.*' Spear himself produced portraits endowed with sympathy; he was also a fascinating reporter, but his portrayals often appeared skin-deep rather than profound, and his talent was 'made in England' and not for travel. He was appointed CBE in 1979.

In 1935 Spear married (Hilda) Mary, artist and only child of William Henry Freer Hill, civil engineer, and Hilda Anne Grose; they had a son. The existence of his long-lasting liaison with Claire Stafford, an artist's model, whom he met in 1956 when she was sixteen, was posthumously publicly revealed in 1993. They had a daughter Rachel Spear-Stafford (born 1957). Spear died in Hammersmith 17 January 1990.

[*Ruskin Spear RA: a Retrospective Exhibition*, Royal Academy, 1980; Mervyn Levy, *Ruskin Spear*, 1985; private information; personal knowledge.]

MARINA VAIZEY

STEERS, James Alfred (1899–1987), geographer and conservationist, was born 8 August 1899 in Bedford, the only child of James Alfred Steers, house agent and property owner, and his wife, Clara Blott. He was educated at Elstow School in Bedford. After joining the army in World War I and being stationed at Oswestry, he went to St Catharine's College, Cambridge, obtaining first-class honours in part ii of the geographical tripos (1921). After a year of teaching at Framlingham College, he returned to

Cambridge, where he became a fellow of St Catharine's in 1925 and stayed for the rest of his life. He subsequently became dean (1928), tutor (1939), and president (1946–66) of St Catharine's. He was a university demonstrator (1926–7), lecturer (1927–49), and professor of geography (1949–66).

At Framlingham he began studies of Orford Ness, which led him to more general coastal studies in East Anglia, Britain, and abroad. Numerous publications reported his meticulous and pioneering work, culminating in his major treatise *The Coastline of England and Wales*, first published in 1946. Altogether, he published fourteen books and well over 100 papers, mainly on physical geography and conservation.

In 1928–9 Steers participated in a major expedition to the Great Barrier Reef, during which he did important work on the evolution of coral reefs and atolls. His conclusions concerning sea-level changes and coral formation provided lively discussion; further work by himself and others generally substantiated the conclusions he drew in these two years.

In 1945 Steers, as adviser to the Ministry of Town and Country Planning, was asked to prepare a report on the coasts of England and Wales. Two years later he joined the wildlife conservation special committee; their report led to the formation of the Nature Conservancy in 1948. At the same time his influence was apparent in the establishment of the National Parks Commission, on which he served from 1960 to 1966. For the rest of his life Steers played an active part in promoting conservation, especially but not exclusively through his work for the Nature Conservancy and its successor, the Nature Conservancy Council. The call which he had made in a 1944 paper to the Royal Geographical Society, for a national policy of coastal planning and management, was heeded and acted upon.

Steers was elected professor of geography at Cambridge in 1949. He had already served on all of the major university committees during the 1940s. As head of department, Steers was able to enhance the standing of his subject within the university and more generally, especially through the staff appointments that were made and the calibre of the students attracted to the department, and in particular to St Catharine's College. In 1928 he persuaded the college to establish a scholarship in geography; on his retirement in 1966 he was presented with a silver salver bearing the signatures of forty-nine St Catharine's geographers who held university posts around the world.

A major storm surge in 1953 wrought havoc along the East Anglian coast. Steers sat on the departmental committee on coastal flooding, under John *Anderson, first Viscount Waverley, which recommended that new coastal protection measures were needed. For many years thereafter he was a member of the advisory committee to improve sea defences. The effectiveness of this work was demonstrated by the 1973 storm surge which, although as severe as that of 1953, caused minimal damage.

Steers left an enduring imprint within Cambridge, on the international standing of geography and, above all, on coastal studies. He was a national figure who played an influential role in shaping conservation and landscape management in the post-war period. He was a tall, imposing figure, commanding but generous to a fault. Never at ease in the lecture room, he excelled in more personal interaction, where his sense of humour showed at its best. He was a reserved man, with an aversion to controversy.

The Royal Geographical Society awarded him the Victoria medal in 1960 'for research in coastal geomorphology', and seventeen years later he and his wife were given honorary membership for their exceptional services to the society. The Royal Scottish Geographical Society awarded him the Scottish geographical medal in 1969. In 1973 he was appointed CBE, and he received honorary degrees from the universities of Aberdeen (LL D, 1971) and East Anglia (D.Sc., 1978).

In 1942 he married Harriet, daughter of John Alfred Wanklyn, mill owner; they had a son and a daughter. Steers died 10 March 1987 in Cambridge.

[*Geographical Journal*, vol. cliii, 1987, pp. 436–8; *Transactions of the Institute of British Geographers*, vol. xiii, 1988, pp. 109–15; D. R. Stoddart, 'Alfred Steers, 1899–1987', Department of Geography, Cambridge (mimeo); 1987; personal knowledge.]

MICHAEL CHISHOLM

STEPHENSON, SIR **William Samuel** (1896–1989), businessman and intelligence agent, was born 11 January 1896 of Scottish ancestry in Point Douglas, near Winnipeg, the son of Victor Stephenson, lumber mill owner, and his wife, Christiana. He was educated at Argyll High School, Winnipeg. In World War I he enlisted in the Royal Canadian Engineers, straight from school. He then served in the Royal Flying Corps, being shot down in July 1918. He was decorated with the MC and DFC and was officially credited with six air victories.

Between the wars he was in business in England, his principal interests being the radio transmission of photographs and film production. In 1940 he went to New York as head of an organization called British Security Co-ordination, intended to promote co-operation with the US Federal Bureau of Investigation. Originally sent by the Secret Intelligence Service (MI6), he was responsible also for security (MI5) until March 1942 and for the Special Operations Executive (SOE). Stephenson was energetic and effective. He formed close relationships with the powerful Herbert Hoover, head of the FBI, and with William Donovan, head of the Office of Strategic Services, who acknowledged Stephenson's aid in creating OSS. In 1945 he was knighted in recognition of his valuable services; from the United States he received the Medal for Merit, on Donovan's recommendation.

About fifteen years after the end of the war Stephenson began to commission books by various authors to give a more colourful and imaginative slant to his wartime career. The first choice was C. H. Ellis, a former SIS operative; but his draft was not flamboyant enough to satisfy its subject, who gave the task to H. Montgomery Hyde, an established biographer. The result, *The Quiet Canadian*, was published in 1962. Its numerous invented stories, based on briefing from Stephenson, created a certain sensation but it still came short of Stephenson's inflated ideas; and as fresh revelations of British successes in the intelligence sphere continued to appear—for instance the Ultra secret—he clearly wished to claim credit for them. He accordingly commissioned another biographer, William Stevenson (no relation of his) and provided him with careful guidance, a fund of fresh stories, and misleading and wrongly captioned photographs. The publication of Stevenson's book, *A Man Called Intrepid*, in 1976 brought enormous publicity and record sales, especially in North America. It is almost entirely a work of fiction.

Stephenson's World War I record was embellished with twenty extra air victories, the Legion of Honour, the croix de guerre with palms (in his *Who's Who* entry from 1984 onwards he added two bars to his DFC), and also the amateur lightweight boxing championship of the world. About World War II fantasy was unrestrained. The principal claim is that he was so close to (Sir) Winston *Churchill that he was appointed his 'personal representative in the western hemisphere'. In truth there is no evidence that he ever met Churchill and much evidence to the contrary. In 1976 he quoted in support a letter attributed to Churchill, which was immediately denounced as a fabrication; in a biographical note of 1982 he withdrew this claim and substituted another story that can also be proved fictitious. Stevenson used as his frontispiece a well-known press photograph of Churchill and Brendan (later Viscount) *Bracken; in the caption, supplied by his mentor, Bracken's name is changed to Stephenson.

The principal purpose of *A Man Called Intrepid* is to enumerate the best-known successes of British wartime skill and intelligence and ascribe them to Stephenson. The decipherment of German Enigma transmissions, the development of nuclear weapons, the organization of European resistance: he was supposedly involved in them all and found time also to invent petroleum warfare and the 'V' sign and help with the production of the Spitfire and the jet engine. He is described as an invisible man directing the work of all four intelligence agencies: SIS, SOE, Security Executive, and MI5; invisible is the *mot juste*. Film clips misrepresented as genuine archival material were used to suggest a wholly imaginary connection between Stephenson and the famous SOE agent Madeleine. The book, later made into a successful film, was strongly criticized by knowledgeable reviewers in Britain who called it 'worthless', 'ludicrous', and 'dishonest'; this did not affect Stephenson's reputation in North America.

Stephenson was short in stature and often called 'Little Bill'. He spent the last years of his life in Bermuda. In 1980 he was appointed a Companion of the Order of Canada. He married in 1924 Mary French (died 1978), daughter of William H. Simmons, of Springfield, Tennessee. Stephenson subsequently adopted as his daughter the person who had nursed Mary during her final illness. He died in Bermuda 31 January 1989 and was buried there.

[F. H. Hinsley and C. A. G. Simkins, *British Intelligence in the Second World War*, vol. iv, 1990; William Stevenson, *A Man Called Intrepid*, 1976; H. Montgomery Hyde, *The Quiet Canadian*, 1962, and *Secret Intelligence Agent*, 1982; David Stafford, 'A Myth Called Intrepid', in *Saturday Night Magazine* (Toronto), 1989; Sir David Hunt, 'Looking-Glass War' (review of *A Man Called Intrepid*), *Times Literary Supplement*, 1976; Timothy J. Naftali, 'Intrepid's Last Deception: Documenting the Career of Sir William Stephenson', *Intelligence and National Security*, vol. viii, no. 3, July 1993.]   DAVID HUNT

STEPTOE, Patrick Christopher (1913–1988), gynaecologist, was born 9 June 1913 in Witney, Oxfordshire, the sixth and youngest son and seventh of ten children of Harry Arthur Steptoe, who lived in Abingdon before moving to Witney as registrar of births, deaths, and marriages, and his wife, (Grace) Maud Minns. Steptoe attended Witney Grammar School. He developed an early interest in music and by the age of thirteen played incidental music for silent films at the local cinema, as well as the organ at St Mary's church. When eighteen he became director and organist of Christ Church Musical Society in Oxford.

At the age of twenty he entered King's College, London, as a medical student and qualified in 1939 with the degrees of MRCS, LRCP from St George's Hospital, London. Already a member of the Royal Naval Volunteer Reserve, he served in the navy from 1939 to 1946, reaching the rank of surgeon lieutenant-commander. His ship was torpedoed in the Mediterranean in 1941. After some hours in the water, he was rescued by the Italians and held as a prisoner of war for two years (1941–3). After demobilization Steptoe became chief assistant in obstetrics and gynaecology at St George's Hospital (1947–9) and then senior registrar at the Whittington Hospital, passing the MRCOG examination in 1948 and the FRCS (Edin.) in 1950. In 1951, after only five years of specialist training and with the need to support a young family, he obtained the post of consultant obstetrician and gynaecologist in Oldham.

Although his work covered all aspects of obstetrics and gynaecology, Steptoe developed at an early stage a special interest in female infertility. Diagnostic techniques, particularly in relation to pelvic pathology and endocrinology, were rudimentary, but laparoscopy and culdoscopy were being introduced at centres in Europe and North America. Steptoe visited these centres and established lasting friendships and collaboration with Raoul Palmer in Paris and Hans Frangenheim in Germany. He became the first gynaecologist to develop laparoscopy in Britain, lectured at the first international symposium in gynaecological laparoscopy in Palermo in 1964, and published the first English book on the subject, *Laparoscopy in Gynaecology*, in 1967. He described not only the potential for accurate diagnosis in relation to problems of infertility, pelvic infection and pain, ectopic pregnancy, and endometriosis, but also explored the therapeutic aspects of surgical laparoscopy. Within a decade this led to the incorporation of laparoscopy into everyday gynaecological practice.

It was at a meeting at the Royal Society of Medicine in 1968 that Robert Edwards first approached Steptoe. A young geneticist and embryologist, Edwards had already done outstanding work on *in vitro* fertilization in mice, other mammals, and human beings. The collaboration between the two men lasted for twenty years until Steptoe's death. It resulted in the delivery on 25 July 1978 of Louise Brown, the first 'test-tube' baby born after laparoscopic oocyte recovery, *in vitro* fertilization, and transfer of the eight-cell embryo into the mother's uterus. Steptoe and Edwards reported the bare facts in a dramatic letter to the *Lancet* (12 August 1978) and gave a full account of their work at a historic scientific meeting at the Royal College of Obstetricians and Gynaecologists on 26 January 1979.

Following Steptoe's retirement from the National Health Service in 1978, he and Edwards founded the Bourn Hall Clinic in 1980. Edwards was the first scientific director and Steptoe, as medical director, continued seeing patients until his death, whilst at the same time training juniors, lecturing worldwide, and collaborating in over fifty scientific papers.

Steptoe's impact on gynaecology was enormous. Following the introduction of carbon fibre optics to provide brilliant cold light illumination from an external source, laparoscopy became safe and efficient. Steptoe popularized the procedure, not only for direct visualization of the abdominal and pelvic organs, but also for laparoscopic photography, video recording, and surgery. Had he done no more, his fame would have been assured. His work with Edwards, overcoming what was previously insuperable infertility, resulted in the birth of over 1,000 babies from Bourn Hall Clinic alone in his lifetime. It ushered in the new speciality of assisted reproduction and led to a wealth of clinical work and scientific research, the setting up of the committee of inquiry into human fertilization and embryology chaired by Dame Mary (later Baroness) Warnock (1982–4), the establishment of the Voluntary Licensing Authority, and the passage in Parliament in 1990 of the Human Fertilization and Embryology Act. The fact that all the early work was done in a small provincial hospital, on shoestring budgets, in the face of scepticism, opposition, and even hostility, and with no financial support from the established bodies in medicine and research, is testimony to Steptoe's total dedication and exceptional perseverance.

He was elected FRCOG in 1961 and made an honorary D.Sc. of Hull University in 1983. The winner of many medals and awards both at home and in the USA, he was a founder member and first chairman of the British Fertility Society from 1973 to 1986 and president thereafter, and was president of the International Federation of Fertility Societies (1977–80). In 1987 he was elected FRS, the first gynaecologist thus honoured, and he was appointed CBE in 1988.

Steptoe was of medium height, thickset but not obese, with blue eyes and grey hair. He was genial, relaxed, tidy, and well dressed. Sailing and music remained lifelong hobbies, and many an international meeting finished with Steptoe at the piano. Something of a sybarite, good food and wines, travelling, opera, and theatre constituted his pleasures. He married in 1943 Sheena Macleod, daughter of Nina and Arthur Kennedy, a general practitioner in Kent. Trained at RADA, Sheena acted in repertory theatre during the war. A woman of beauty, charm, and warmth, she was a great support in Steptoe's professional life. She died from a second cerebral haemorrhage in 1990. They had two children: a daughter, Sally (1947), killed in a road traffic accident in 1992, and a son, Andrew (1951), who became professor of psychology at St George's Hospital medical school, London. Steptoe died of prostatic carcinoma at the Chaucer Hospital, Canterbury, 21 March 1988. His bust, sculpted

by Peter Wardle, stands in the Royal College of Obstetricians and Gynaecologists.

[Private information; personal knowledge.]

HERBERT REISS

STEVENS, Thomas Terry Hoar (1911–1990), actor and comedian. [See TERRY-THOMAS.]

STEVENSON, SIR (Aubrey) Melford (Steed) (1902–1987), judge, was born in Newquay 17 October 1902, the elder child and only son of the Revd John George Stevenson and his wife Olive, daughter of Joshua Steed, solicitor, of Long Melford, Suffolk, and sister of Henry Wickham *Steed, later editor of *The Times*. The father was a Congregational minister of distinction and eloquence who died in 1916 when his son was fourteen. The family was left impoverished, but, with the help of another uncle, also a solicitor in Long Melford, Stevenson was sent to Dulwich College. There he was a contemporary of Hartley (later Baron) Shawcross. His school career was unhappy. He was destined by his uncles for the family firm and to that end began articles in London. Funds did not permit a full university education, which he always regretted, but he took an external LL B at London University. He disliked articles and was determined to go to the bar. He joined the Inner Temple and was called by that Inn in 1925. He was to become its treasurer in 1972. After pupillage with (Sir) Hubert Wallington and a short tenancy in the chamber of Sir Patrick *Hastings, he moved to the chambers of (Sir) Wintringham ('Owlie') *Stable, where, save for the war years, he remained for the rest of his career at the bar.

His surviving fee books show a slow but steady increase in junior practice, almost always with small fees, until the outbreak of war in 1939. In view of his later reputation it is remarkable how little criminal work he did. His junior practice lay largely in the field of insolvency and running down cases. By the outbreak of war he would have been justified in applying for silk. But like most others in the Temple he left practice. He served in the army and from 1940 to 1945 acted as deputy judge advocate, with the rank of major. In October 1945 he served as judge advocate in the war crimes trial of former officers of the submarine *U852*, who were convicted and executed for the murder of the crew of the Greek ship *Peleus* after that ship had been torpedoed and sunk. The succinctness of Stevenson's summing up perhaps foretold his subsequent conduct of criminal trials.

Meanwhile, while on war service he had in a special wartime list in 1943 been given the silk the war had denied him. After a brief and unsuccessful foray into politics as a Conservative candidate—he was heavily defeated by Tom *Driberg (later Baron Bradwell) at Malden in the

1945 general election—he returned to practice in 1946. His gifts of speech with his fluent delivery, distinctive voice, remarkable sense of timing, and pungency of phrase soon marked him out as an advocate of note. He successively held the recorderships of Rye (1944–51) and Cambridge (1952–7), but his increasing practice still lay outside the criminal courts. He was employed in fashionable divorce and libel cases. He appeared for the Marten family in the Crichel Down enquiry, and he also prosecuted Jomo *Kenyatta in Kenya. His unsuccessful defence of Ruth Ellis (the last woman to be hanged for murder) and his appearances at the magistrates court and (with the attorney-general) at the Old Bailey in the notorious trial of Dr John Bodkin *Adams for the murder of his patients, brought him into the public eye.

Yet at the same time his uninhibited comments on people and affairs gained him another reputation, that of an eccentric and a maverick who might not always show the restraint traditionally required on the bench. It was perhaps for this reason that it was not until 1957 when he had been fourteen years in silk, eleven of them in full practice, that the lord chancellor, Viscount (later the Earl of) *Kilmuir, appointed him to the Probate, Divorce, and Admiralty Division of the High Court. In the same year he was knighted. He served in that division for four years without attracting attention, but far from content with the work that he was required to do under the existing divorce laws. It was only after his transfer to the Queen's Bench Division in 1961 that his strong personality, style, and penetrating and outspoken use of language made him one of the best known judges of the day. He had no time for those at the bar whom he saw as prolix, pompous fools or time-wasters and he made his views all too clear. But to the young and to beginners and many others (not least his former clerk) he could show great kindness and patience. He felt strongly that it was the duty of a judge in a criminal case to do everything he could to stop crime and above all to punish severely crime in all its forms. It was, however, by chance and not by choice that his country home in Sussex was named 'Truncheons'. His conduct of the Kray trial and of the Garden House 'riot' trial in Cambridge in 1970 brought notoriety and in the latter case much criticism, not only for the severity of the sentences which he passed but also for the force of some of his comments. But notwithstanding these criticisms, again and again he was entrusted with the conduct of sensitive and difficult cases and always fulfilled his task as he saw it, fearless and unmoved by criticism. He was ready to say things which others feared to say and had no time for judges who courted popularity.

It would be wrong to judge him simply by the notoriety of a few cases. There were others where with no publicity he showed great mercy to those whom he saw to be victims rather than aggressors. Those who sat in the Court of Appeal in the 1970s might sometimes find in the appeal papers a letter from Stevenson to the court suggesting that he might have been too severe and that the sentences which he passed should be reviewed. He never claimed to be a profound lawyer or interested in the theory of law as distinct from its practice. Though privately he could be critical of the Court of Appeal, especially when that court differed from him, he sometimes expressed disappointment that he had not become one of its members. He rejected a possible opportunity in mid-career and the chance did not recur. But his special appointment to the Privy Council in 1973 gave him great pleasure.

Stevenson was of medium height, but strongly built. Initially he gave an impression of severity, but on the shortest acquaintance his immense sense of humour became apparent. In private life he was very gregarious, often at the centre of a group at the bar of the Garrick Club, where occasionally his witticisms trespassed across the boundary into indiscretion. No moment spent in his company could ever be dull and he had a wide circle of friends both within and without his profession. In 1929 he married Anna Cecilia Francesca Imelda, daughter of Michael Rynston, musician. He divorced her in 1942. There was one daughter of that marriage. In 1947 he married Rosalind Monica, daughter of Orlando Henry Wagner, founder of Waynes, the well-known boys' day-school in Kensington, and sister of (Sir) Anthony Wagner, later Garter king of arms. There was one son (who later became a practising barrister) and one daughter of that marriage. Stevenson retired in 1979, after which he enjoyed appearing on television, where his gifts of expression made him a good performer in what was to him a novel medium. But failing health and eyesight led to gradual withdrawal from active life and he died in St Leonards on Sea 26 December 1987.

[*The Times*, 28 December 1987; *Independent*, 30 December 1987; family papers and information; personal knowledge.]   ROSKILL

STEWART, (Robert) Michael (Maitland), BARON STEWART OF FULHAM (1906–1990), politician, was born 6 November 1906 at 20 Minster Road, Bromley, the only son and youngest of three children of Robert Wallace Stewart, D.Sc., lecturer and author of scientific textbooks, and his wife Eva, daughter of Samuel Blaxley. In 1910 his father died and his mother, for whom Stewart had a deep affection, went to work in a mixed school. Stewart used to complain that she was paid four-fifths of the salary of her male colleagues, some of them bachelors. He gave this as one explanation for his passionate advocacy of equal pay and conditions for women teachers when he became secretary of state for education. After attending Brownhill Road Elementary School in Catford during World War I, in 1918 Stewart went by scholarship to Christ's Hospital, Horsham, which was unique among public schools for closing its doors to the sons of the rich, or even moderately well-off parents. In 1925 Stewart won an open scholarship to St John's College, Oxford, where he obtained first classes in classical honour moderations (1927) and philosophy, politics, and economics (1929). Stewart spent a formative summer vacation in Dresden in 1927, which accounted for the complaints from Intelligence Corps superiors during World War II that he had a Saxon accent. He was elected president of the Oxford Union in 1929, an unusual post for a Labour supporter.

After Oxford, Stewart became a teacher at Merchant Taylors' School (1930–1) and Coopers' Company School (1931–42), which gave him the opportunity to contest, unsuccessfully, the parliamentary seat of West Lewisham for the Labour party in 1931 and 1935. He joined the Army Intelligence Corps in 1942, transferred to the Army Educational Corps in 1943, and was commissioned and promoted to captain in 1944. In 1945 he was elected as Labour MP for Fulham East. He went into the government whips' office and took to parliamentary life with the greatest of ease. He was comptroller of the royal household in 1946–7 and then became under-secretary of state for war (1947–51), where his performance led R. H. S. *Crossman, for whom he had a mutual antipathy, to brand him 'an inveterate cold warrior'. Stewart's parliamentary seat from 1955 to 1974 was Fulham and from 1974 to 1979 Hammersmith and Fulham.

In thirteen years of Labour opposition (1951–64), Stewart was one of the workhorses of the opposition front bench, specializing in housing and local government. Appointed education secretary in 1964 by Harold Wilson (later Baron Wilson of Rievaulx), he became secretary of state for foreign affairs in January 1965 where he remained until August 1966, when George *Brown (later Baron George-Brown) had to be accommodated. Deeply resentful, Stewart became first secretary for economic affairs (1966–7), where it was thought that his clarity of mind would ease the government's difficulties over its prices and incomes policy. Such hopes were unfulfilled, partly because trade-union leaders, whose co-operation was essential, regarded Stewart as a 'cold fish'.

In March 1968 Stewart returned to the Foreign Office, which was now linked with Commonwealth affairs, after the resignation of George Brown. Vietnam apart, the main issues were Rhodesia, where Stewart was anathema to

the white population, and Nigeria. He returned to the back benches in 1970, when the Labour government fell, after suffering a crushing defeat in the elections in the Parliamentary Labour party for the shadow cabinet. Stewart was an excellent choice as leader of Labour's first delegation to the indirectly elected European Parliament (1976), where he enjoyed an Indian summer. The obvious quality of his mind and his dignity impressed European politicians. In the words of a conservative, Sir James Spicer, 'he was a steady hand on the tiller at a time when Labour was deeply divided over EEC membership.'

Stewart's two stints as foreign secretary involved him in bitter controversy. He infuriated the left by his unswerving support of the American position in the Vietnam war. Then he outraged a wider section of opinion by stridently supporting the federal government's crushing of the secessionist Biafrans in the ferocious Nigerian civil war. During his first stint, his relations with back-bench MPs were safeguarded by his parliamentary private secretary and friend, Laurence Pavitt, the popular MP for Willesden. When Pavitt, a committed member of the Campaign for Nuclear Disarmament, withdrew from Stewart's service on grounds of policy differences, the foreign secretary became curiously estranged from the Parliamentary Labour party. On the other hand, he was, according to Sir (J.) Nicholas Henderson, who was once his private secretary, 'an unsung foreign secretary'. Henderson argued that, by strength of reason and integrity, Stewart prevented many possible disasters, such as a serious deterioration in British relations with the US as a result of the Vietnam war, or the setting of a dangerous precedent for Africa, if he had equivocated over Biafra. Yet it was Russia that dominated Stewart's thinking.

When he retired from Parliament in 1979 he accepted a life peerage. He also became president of the Trade Union committee for transatlantic understanding and of the H. G. Wells Society (from 1982). St John's College, Oxford, elected him to an honorary fellowship in 1965, and he became a freeman of Hammersmith in 1967. He had honorary degrees from Leeds (1966) and Benin (1972). He was sworn of the Privy Council in 1964 and appointed CH in 1969.

Stewart was no orator but a good debater, in his nasal, flat, toneless voice. He made a memorable return to the Oxford Union in 1968, in a televised debate in which he put the American case for intervention in Vietnam better than the Americans. His capacity to speak from brief notes was remarkable, and yet he was not a good conversationalist. He tended to display his knowledge of the classics too readily, acting in a patient and expository manner which he probably acquired as a schoolmaster. He was inclined to be prim and austere. He was dapper, with soulful serious eyes; because of his dark hair, in his younger days some of his friends called him 'Black Michael'. Spare of frame, he became grey and distinguished in later years. He wrote five books on political subjects, as well as an auto-biography.

In 1941 Stewart married Mary Elizabeth Henderson, daughter of Herbert Birkenshaw, teacher. There were no children of the marriage. A pillar of the Fabian Society, his wife was created a life peer in her own right in 1974, as Baroness Stewart of Alvechurch. When she died, 28 December 1984, Stewart was stricken with grief, but contrived to speak fluently and logi-cally in the Lords until he died in a London hospital, 10 March 1990.

[Michael Stewart, *Life and Labour*, 1980; Sir Nicholas Henderson, *Private Office*, 1984; personal knowledge.]
TAM DALYELL

STIRLING, SIR (Archibald) David (1915–1990), founder of the Special Air Service Regi-ment, was born 15 November 1915 at Keir, Stirlingshire, the third son and fourth child in the family of four sons and two daughters of Brigadier-General Archibald Stirling of Keir, of the Scots Guards and later MP for West Perth-shire, and his wife Margaret Mary, daughter of Simon Fraser, fifteenth Baron Lovat. His child-hood, mostly spent at Keir, was a happy one. He was educated at Ampleforth and, for a brief period, at Trinity College, Cambridge. Soon after leaving Cambridge, without a degree, he decided that he wanted to climb Mount Everest and, with this in mind, spent some time climbing in Switzerland and later in the American and Canadian Rockies. On the outbreak of war in September 1939 he returned from North Amer-ica to join the Scots Guards Supplementary Reserve, of which he had become a member the previous year.

Early in 1941 the newly raised Guards Com-mando, for which he volunteered as soon as he had been commissioned and which he found more congenial than ordinary regimental soldier-ing, sailed for the Middle East as part of Lay-force, consisting of three commando units commanded by a friend of his, Brigadier (Sir) Robert *Laycock. Later in 1941 Layforce was disbanded, leaving Stirling at a loose end, but at least in a theatre of war. This offered him the opportunity he needed. The war in the desert had by this time settled down into a slogging match between the opposing armies and Stirling turned a fertile mind to the overall strategic situation. What he quickly grasped was the possibility of turning the enemy's flank by send-ing well-equipped raiding parties through the allegedly impassable Sand Sea to strike at worth-while targets far behind the enemy's front line.

Gaining access to the commander-in-chief Middle East, General Sir Claude *Auchinleck, by what can best be described as shock tactics, Stirling, still to all appearances an unremarkable subaltern of twenty-five, with little or no military experience, managed to win his confidence, con-vince him of the soundness of his ideas, and gain from him authority to recruit at the end of July 1941 six officers and sixty other ranks, a small-scale raiding force to be known, misleadingly, as L detachment Special Air Service brigade. He was promoted to captain.

Stirling's first operation, in November 1941 by parachute, was a total failure. But he did not let this deter him, and General Auchinleck, greatly to his credit, continued to back him. Fortunately L detachment's next, land-borne, raids, which followed immediately and were carried out with the invaluable help of the Long Range Desert Group, were spectacularly successful. In two weeks ninety enemy aircraft were destroyed on the ground. They were the first of a succession of no less brilliant operations planned and led by Stirling himself, who was quickly promoted to major (January 1942) and then to lieutenant-colonel (July 1942). In their planning he showed remarkable imagination and resourcefulness. In their execution his personal courage and utter determination were unsurpassed. He possessed above all the ultimate quality of a leader, the gift of carrying those he led with him on enterprises that by any rational standards seemed certain to fail and convincing them that under his leader-ship they were bound to succeed. Stirling was appointed to the DSO in 1942, and also became an officer of the Legion of Honour and of the Order of Orange Nassau.

By the time Stirling was taken prisoner in Tunisia in January 1943 the potential value of the SAS and of his contribution to military thinking had been generally recognized. As he had intended it should, the regiment went on to play an important part in the Mediterranean and later in the European theatres where, without their founder's outstanding leadership, but using his methods, they achieved a series of remarkable successes.

Stirling escaped from prison in Germany four times and was eventually shut up in Colditz. On his return to Great Britain in May 1945, his first thought was to take full advantage of the obvious opportunities for SAS operations offered by the war against Japan. But before he could put his plans into execution, the war in the Far East was over and by the end of 1945 the SAS had been disbanded. In due course the SAS was, however, reconstituted in the shape of one regular and two territorial regiments. With these Stirling, who as founder had been active in securing their recon-stitution, remained in continual contact.

After the war Stirling's imagination was captured by Africa and its problems, to which he was thereafter to devote much time and energy. He settled in Southern Rhodesia and in 1947 became president of the newly founded Capricorn Africa Society, set up, largely on his initiative, to help find a solution to Africa's innumerable racial, economic, social, and political problems, which he felt could not safely be ignored. His efforts were overtaken by political events and he returned to Britain in 1961. In 1974 he organized GB75, to run essential services, such as power stations, in the event of a general strike. He then turned to fighting left-wing extremism in trade unions, by backing the Movement for True Industrial Democracy (Truemid).

Six feet six inches tall, with a deceptively vague and casual manner, Stirling had a very strong personality. He was appointed OBE in 1946 and knighted in 1990 by when, half a century on, the full extent of his achievement had finally been recognized. He died in the London Clinic 4 November 1990. He never married.

[Alan Hoe, *David Stirling*, 1992; John Strawson, *A History of the SAS Regiment*, 1984; personal knowledge.]   FITZROY MACLEAN

STOCKTON, first EARL OF (1894–1986), prime minister. [See MACMILLAN, (MAURICE) HAROLD.]

STOCKWELL, SIR Hugh Charles (1903–1986), general, was born 16 June 1903 in Jersey, the only son and youngest of three children of Lieutenant-Colonel Hugh Charles Stockwell, OBE, of the Highland Light Infantry, later chief constable of Colchester, and his wife, Gertrude Forrest. He spent his early childhood in India with his parents before attending school at Cothill House in Abingdon, Marlborough College, and the Royal Military College, Sandhurst. Commissioned into the Royal Welch Fusiliers on 1 February 1923, he was one of a small number of postwar officers among the veterans of the war of 1914–18. High spirited, professionally keen, a proficient rugby football, hockey, and cricket player, he was quickly accepted by both groups.

Garrison life in England and Germany palled, however. 'Hughie' Stockwell was seconded to the Royal West African Frontier Force, serving from 1929 to 1935 as a Vickers machine-gun officer, a position which led to an instructor's post at the Small Arms School, Netheravon, in 1935–8. War approached. The Territorial Army was expanding and, without attending the Staff College, in 1938 he was made brigade-major of 158th—the Royal Welch—brigade at Wrexham, an exceptional appointment. However, his reputation as a leader suggested his employment in the 'special companies' formed hastily in April 1940, for independent tasks in the flagging Norwegian campaign. Promoted to lieutenant-colonel, he commanded a group of these units in the operations, and was appointed to the DSO (1940). He was then made commandant of the special forces training centre at Lochailort.

In June 1942 he led the 2nd Royal Welch Fusiliers in the Madagascar landings. He was promoted to brigadier, commanding the 30th East African and then, from January 1943, the 29th Independent Infantry brigade group during the battles for Arakan and northern Burma. For his leadership in lengthy operations, notably his personal influence in maintaining the morale of his soldiers, he was created CBE (1945).

In January 1945 he was appointed commander, 82nd West African division in Burma. This completed a rise from major to major-general in less than five years, and although he was only forty-two years of age he was confirmed as a general officer at the end of the war. Successively commander of the Home Counties District (1946–7) and 44th Territorial division, and the 6th Airborne division (1947–8), he was responsible for the evacuation of the latter and all other British troops from Palestine in 1948. His friendly but firm relationship with the Jewish authorities ensured a peaceful withdrawal despite late attempts to frustrate British demolition of selected facilities. Appointed CB in 1946, he was promoted to KBE in 1949.

An inspired selection placed him next as commandant of the Royal Military Academy, Sandhurst (1948–50). His early choice of a scooter bearing a major-general's two stars to carry him about the grounds characterized him: unpretentious, practical, and approachable, he moved easily between formal occasions, such as the sovereign's parade, to informal association in the training field with instructors and cadets. Unrecognized by two late returning cadets on one occasion, he helped to push them over the wall to avoid detection at the gate.

After two years with the 3rd division, he was promoted to lieutenant-general and command of the land forces in Malaya in 1952, augmenting the policies of General Sir Gerald *Templer to counter terrorism. He was active in the expansion of the Royal Malay Regiment at this time. Command of I British Corps followed (1954–6), from which he was withdrawn to lead the land forces in the Port Said and Suez canal operation in the latter part of 1956. In an environment of political and military fumbling, his resistance to impractical commitments spared his forces many difficulties. Following the seizure of the port and its southern approaches, the British forces were subjected to repeated acts of terrorism. Stockwell visited daily the areas most affected, explaining to the soldiers concerned in his friendly and direct way the need for restraint. His withdrawal plan was a model. It ensured the safety of his troops without jeopardizing the United Nations forces who relieved them. Stockwell's talents as an extrovert, practical commander were seen at their best in the politically fraught Port Said operation. He was also able to stimulate laughter in dismal circumstances. As a consequence, the army units involved disengaged in high morale.

Thereafter, as military secretary (1957–9) and adjutant-general (1959–60), in which appointment he was promoted to general in the army (1957), his name is associated with the well-being of officers and men, whose confidence he held absolutely. He was finally selected by the first Viscount *Montgomery of Alamein as his successor in the post of deputy supreme allied commander, Europe (1960–4). His first step, wisely, was to become the trusted friend of two American supreme commanders. On this firm basis he gathered considerable influence among the international commanders and staffs. He worked for the creation of strong mobile forces in Europe, advocating the use of tactical nuclear weapons only as a last resort.

Following his retirement in 1964, he was active in the development and maintenance of British waterways, not least as chairman of the Kennet and Avon Canal Trust from 1966 to 1975. Among many connections with the army, he was colonel of the Royal Welch Fusiliers (1952–65), Royal Malay Regiment (1954–9), and Army Air Corps (1957–63), and ADC-general to the queen (1959–62). He was further appointed KCB (1954), GCB (1959), and a grand officer of the Legion of Honour (1958). He was also awarded a bar to his DSO (1957).

Tall and fair, Stockwell had striking features, notably piercing blue eyes above a beaky nose, and an expression daunting when he was angry, but more frequently relieved by an engaging smile. In 1931 he married Joan Rickman, daughter of Charles and Marion Garrard, of independent means, of Kingston Lisle, Berkshire. They had two daughters. Stockwell died 27 November 1986 at the Royal Air Force Hospital, Wroughton.

[Royal Welch Fusilier archives, Regimental Headquarters, Caernarfon; private information; personal knowledge.]   ANTHONY FARRAR-HOCKLEY

STONEHOUSE, John Thomson (1925–1988), politician and confidence trickster, was born 28 July 1925 in Southampton, the youngest of four children and second son of William Mitchell Stonehouse, Post Office engineer and later dockyard engine-fitter, and his wife Rosina Marie, formerly a scullery maid in Cowes, Isle of Wight, daughter of Henry George Taylor, boilermaker. The family was active in the local Labour movement, the father becoming a trade union official

and the mother being an alderman (1936–70) and later mayor (1959) of Southampton. Stonehouse was educated at Tauntons School, Southampton, which he left at the age of sixteen to work in the Southampton probation department as a clerk and typist (1941–4). In 1944 he joined the Royal Air Force, training as a pilot in the USA. From 1947 to 1951 he studied at the London School of Economics, where he obtained a B.Sc. (Econ.) in 1951.

In the early 1950s he gained experience by working in the Co-operative movement both at home and abroad. In 1952 he established valuable African credentials by taking his wife and young family to Uganda, where they stayed until 1954, while he helped to organize the Co-operative movement among the African population. Some of his contemporaries said that his work in Uganda was not as pioneering as he subsequently claimed. Nevertheless, it gave him powerful authority in the political debate about decolonization, which was gathering strength in Britain and Africa. Stonehouse was certainly not out of step with his own party's developing policy on Africa.

In February 1957, at a by-election, he entered Parliament as Labour Co-operative member for Wednesbury, whose MP he remained until 1974. In March 1959 he was declared *persona non grata* by the government of the Federation of Rhodesia and Nyasaland. The cause of this heavy-handed treatment was a speech to an African audience in which he had urged the black people of Rhodesia to 'lift your heads high and behave as though the country belongs to you'. However, spats with minority regimes in Africa did no harm to Stonehouse's reputation as a coming man. He wrote a book about his experiences, *Prohibited Immigrant* (1960).

He also established a reputation on the domestic front when he became a director of the London Co-operative Society (1956–62, president 1962–4). The LCS was one of the jewels in the crown of the Co-operative movement and Stonehouse's role kept him in the public eye as a tough, if not always popular, political in-fighter and administrator. It was no surprise when Harold Wilson (later Baron Wilson of Rievaulx) sent him to the Ministry of Aviation as parliamentary under-secretary when Labour returned to power in October 1964. He held several subsequent posts in the 1964–70 Labour government: parliamentary under-secretary of state for the colonies (1966–7), minister of aviation (1967), minister of state for technology (1967–8), postmaster-general (1968–9), and minister of post and telecommunications (1969–70). However, he never made the cabinet and was dropped from the government shortly before Labour lost office in 1970.

In the early 1970s he turned his energies to a

variety of fund-raising and money-making activities, many associated with the new country of Bangladesh. He created a lattice-work of companies, in which he manipulated funds to conceal mismanagement and fraud. On 21 November 1974 he went missing, presumed dead, whilst supposedly swimming in the sea off Miami. Five weeks later he was discovered in Australia by Australian police, who thought he might be the missing Lord Lucan. The Stonehouse story then took on aspects of cheap fiction rather than real life. He had obtained two passports in the names of husbands of widows in his constituency. A beautiful mistress, his House of Commons secretary, Sheila Buckley, was identified as having conspired with him to fake the disappearance to enable them both to start a new life together in Australia with money salted away from the Stonehouse companies. At his trial the Stonehouse defences ranged from international conspiracy to mental breakdown. That he had not lived up to high expectations, his own and those of others, had caused him to retreat into a world of deceit and fraud. In 1976 he resigned his privy councillorship, to which he had been appointed in 1968, and applied for the Chiltern Hundreds, thus ceasing to be an MP (he had represented Walsall North from 1974).

His behaviour would have condemned most men to oblivion, but Stonehouse did not shun the public eye. He served three and a half years in prison, being released in 1979, and then, after a brief period of charity work, turned his hand to writing. Between 1982 and 1987 he had three novels published: *Ralph* (1982), *The Baring Fault* (1986), and *Oil on the Rift* (1987). A posthumous publication, in 1989, was *Who Sold Australia?* Earlier he had written an autobiography, *Death of an Idealist* (1975). Three years before his death he started a company which manufactured electronic safes.

Stonehouse was tall, handsome, and charming. In 1948 he married Barbara Joan, stenographer, daughter of Robert Charles Smith, insurance agent; they had one son and two daughters. The marriage was dissolved in 1978 and in 1981 he married Sheila Elizabeth Buckley, secretary, whose previous marriage had ended in divorce, daughter of Leslie William Black, master butcher. They had one son. Stonehouse, who had suffered a series of heart attacks and undergone heart surgery during his prison term, collapsed during the night of 15 April 1988 at his home in Totton, near Southampton, and was dead on his arrival at Southampton General Hospital.

[John Stonehouse, *Prohibited Immigrant*, 1960, and *Death of an Idealist*, 1975; *The Times*, 15 April 1988; information from House of Commons library.]

C. S. Nicholls
Tom McNally

STREATFEILD, (Mary) Noel (1895–1986), children's author, was born 24 December 1895 in Frant, Sussex, the second child and second daughter in a family of five daughters (the second youngest of whom died at the age of two) and one son of William Champion Streatfeild, Anglican vicar, and his wife Janet Mary, daughter of Henry Venn, vicar of Walmer. She grew up in Amberley, St Leonards-on-Sea, and Eastbourne, where her father was vicar (he later became suffragan bishop of Lewes). In the first part of her autobiography she describes overhearing her mother's friends identify her as 'the plain one'. That, and the genteel poverty in which they lived, made her fiercely resentful and in later years it was noticeable what an important part clothes played in her plots and her own life; she was always elegant. She was educated at the Hastings and St Leonard's Ladies College in St Leonards and Laleham School in Eastbourne. In 1916 she went to work in Woolwich Arsenal, but became ill.

In 1919 she joined the Academy of Dramatic Art in London (later to become RADA). She had moderate success as an *ingénue* playing in repertory, reviews, and pantomime. She also went on tour in South Africa, Rhodesia, New Zealand, and Australia. When her father died in 1929 she returned home and decided to adopt a more stable career, choosing to be a writer.

Her first efforts were three fairy stories published in a children's magazine and a novel, *The Whicharts* (1931), based on children's misunderstanding of the prayer 'Our Father which art...'. Its success encouraged her to write five other novels, including *I Ordered a Table for Six* (1942), which anticipated the bomb which destroyed the Café Royal a year later. It was about this time, after her agent suggested she try writing for children, that she rather unenthusiastically produced *Ballet Shoes* (1936), which became a runaway success, and which caused her to have no further worries about money.

Almost by accident she had found the perfect ingredients for a children's book. Into it she had put all her accumulated backstage knowledge of the theatre and of her sister's ballet training, as well as their childhood struggles with hardship and a genuine picture of family life. *Tennis Shoes* (1937) incorporated the advice given to her by John *Galsworthy, in the first fan letter she received, 'always remember to know at least three times as much as you are going to put on paper'. Her third book, *The Circus Is Coming* (1938), was the result of nearly a year spent travelling with a family circus and won her the Library Association's Carnegie medal.

On the outbreak of World War II she trained as an air-raid warden and joined the Women's Voluntary Service, running a canteen service for people in the Deptford shelters. In her spare time, she prettified London by scattering flower seeds on bomb sites. In 1941 her London flat was bombed and she lost almost everything. She wrote four more children's books, including *Party Frock* (1946). After the war she spent some time in Hollywood, from which came *The Painted Garden* (1949). In 1951 *White Boots*, a story about skating, appeared. She began to share a flat at 51A Elizabeth Street, London, with a friend, Margot Grey.

Noel Streatfeild believed that every detail in her books should be factually correct and she also developed her characters convincingly. Her writing for young readers had a reassuring warmth, or 'heart' as she described it, and almost all her stories were centred around families. The family background and rules of behaviour between parents and siblings had a warm quality which made them both fascinating and believable.

In all she wrote sixty-four books, all but seventeen for children, always drawing on her own experience to make them as authentic as possible. Many of them were broadcast on radio or television; it was the BBC who introduced her Bell family to radio; the serials were broadcast from 1949 to 1953. *The Growing Summer* (1966) was a television serial set in Ireland, and *Thursday's Child* (1970) was also serialized. She wrote her autobiography in three volumes, and a life of another renowned writer of children's books, Edith *Nesbit (*Magic and the Magician*, 1958). She was generous in encouraging young writers and replied kindly to every child who wrote to her. She was also indefatigable in her response to schools and libraries, never treating this as a duty, but taking the trouble to make her visits as exciting and glamorous as possible. On the days when she visited the yearly exhibition of the Puffin Club (the children's branch of Penguin Books, which published her work) huge queues formed to get her autograph. Mothers came with their daughters, bringing their own battered copies of *Ballet Shoes* to be signed. She was appointed OBE in 1983.

Noel Streatfeild was a tall woman, with a fine carriage. She often wore a mink coat, and her lovely hands were regularly manicured with rich red nail polish. She was physically somewhat clumsy, with a rather loud, commanding voice. She died 11 September 1986 in a nursing home in Vicarage Gate, London, after a stroke. She never married.

[Noel Streatfeild, *A Vicarage Family*, 1963, *Away from the Vicarage*, 1965, and *Beyond the Vicarage*, 1971 (three volumes of autobiography); Angela Bull, *Noel Streatfeild, a Biography*, 1984; Barbara Ker Wilson, *Noel Streatfeild*, 1961; personal knowledge.]

KAYE WEBB

STRONG, Patience (1907–1990), author and poet, was born Winifred Emma May 4 June 1907 in Catford, south-east London, the younger daughter and second of three children of Alfred William May, postal worker at Mount Pleasant, London, and his wife, Nell Mason. She played the piano by ear at the age of four and began composing verses when very young. She was educated at the local school in Catford and then at Cusack's College, where she learned shorthand and typing. She worked in a patent agency and subsequently in a music publisher's office, which stimulated her interest in writing lyrics for popular music. She was nurtured by Lawrence Wright, an influential music publisher of the time, and among the lyrics she subsequently wrote were those for the well-known tango, 'Jealousy', and the ballad, 'The Dream of Olwen'.

In August 1935, spurred by the success of the prose-poem writer, Wilhelmina Stitch, who wrote regularly for the *Daily Sketch*, she decided to try to perform a similar service for the rival newspaper the *Daily Mirror* and, 'with a poem in my pocket'—the subsequent title of her autobiography—she visited the paper's features editor with her proposal. He was impressed and invited her to return the following day with eighteen further poems, and a suitable pseudonym for a regular column. That evening, a friend visited her with the gift of a book by an American author, Adeline D. T. Whitney, with the title *Patience Strong* (1870). The next day she presented the editor with the further poems—and her new name.

Patience Strong continued to write a daily poem for the *Daily Mirror*, without interruption, from then onwards and throughout World War II, under the heading 'The Quiet Corner', which became synonymous with her work. Some critics derided her verse for its sentimentality, but readers responded warmly to her poems and to her philosophy, feeling that they knew her personally and could confide in her; she replied to each correspondent and her office at her home became something of an adjunct to the local post office, when service men and women, and those left at home, wrote to thank her for her poems and support, explaining that she had been able, through her verses, to speak for them. An example of her work is: 'Give me a window with a view that flows to meet the sky. Give me a garden where the trees can feel the winds blow by...Give me good days and sleep-blessed nights when I have closed the door—and anyone can have the world. I'll never ask for more.' (*Give Me A Quiet Corner*, 1972.)

In the late 1940s she transferred from the *Daily Mirror* to its sister Sunday newspaper, the *Pictorial* (subsequently the *Sunday Mirror*), and she also began contributing her poems to the weekly magazine, *Woman's Own*. Her sojourn with each was over forty years. Latterly, her poems appeared in the quarterly journal, *This England*.

In the late 1930s her books of prose poems began publication, with *Every Common Bush* (1937), and many titles followed, published by Frederick Muller, under which imprint her books appeared until her death, when posthumous compilations were issued. Her books, which numbered over seventy, include *Quiet Corner Reflections* (1938), *A Christmas Garland* (1948), *The Patience Strong Bedside Book* (1953), *The Blessings of the Years* (1963), *Come Happy Day* (1966), *A Joy Forever* (1973), *Poems from the Fighting Forties* (1982), and *Fifty Golden Years* (1985, to commemorate her fiftieth anniversary as Patience Strong). She also wrote many booklets with a specifically religious basis for the Henry E. Walter Company. Her posthumous publications included *Tapestries of Time* (1991) and many of her early titles were reissued by Grace Publishers. Patience Strong's poems appeared on calendars and greetings cards and similar publications for over fifty years and also continued to be published. Two gramophone records of the author reciting favourite poems were issued: 'The Quiet Hour' (Saga, 1963) and 'The Quiet Corner' (Meridian, 1978).

Patience Strong was attractive in personality and appearance, and her beauty could not better have complemented the nature of her work. She was a devout Christian, who explored many churches—Baptist, Methodist, Church of England, Christian Science, and, in later years, the British Israel movement. Her faith in God governed her life. She had a great gift for communication, and regarded this as her mission in life. She was a countrywoman, who found her inspiration in the changing seasons of the English countryside, in all its moods, as shown in her verse: 'This is what he dreamed about beneath the desert sky: brown earth breaking on the plough and white gulls wheeling by...This is what he fought for on a beach in Normandy: parish church and village green, his English legacy. These things did he know and love. He lived and died for them...Speak no word. The evening thrush will sing his requiem.' (*Magic Casements*, 1950.)

In 1931 she married the son of a master builder who was an alderman of the city of Liverpool, Frederick Arnold ('Paddy') Williams, architect. He died in 1965 and in 1967 she married Guy Cushing, buyer, who had retired from the John Lewis Partnership, the son of William Isaac Cushing, draper, and his wife Amanda, the great friend of the author, who had given her the book *Patience Strong* many years before. He predeceased her in 1979. There were no children of either marriage. Patience Strong was made a freeman of the City of London in

1970. She died 28 August 1990 at her home in Sedlescombe, East Sussex.

[Patience Strong, *With a Poem in my Pocket*, 1981; personal knowledge.]   DOREEN MONTGOMERY

SWANN, Michael Meredith, BARON SWANN (1920–1990), biologist and public servant, was born 1 March 1920 in Cambridge, the elder son and eldest of three children of Meredith Blake Robson Swann, university demonstrator in pathology, and his wife, Marjorie Dykes. He was educated at Winchester College and as a scholar at Gonville and Caius College, Cambridge, of which his father was a fellow, and of which he himself became an honorary fellow in 1977. He left Cambridge at Easter 1940, after six terms, and, as a result of a wartime dispensation, was given a BA (zoology) in 1943 and an MA in 1946.

During World War II he worked on radar at the War Office and on operational research in Normandy and Germany. He was mentioned in dispatches in 1944. In 1946, having registered as a research student at Cambridge, he was elected a fellow of his college. For the next six years he was a university demonstrator in zoology, and, during that period, was closely concerned with research on the structure during mitosis (the splitting of cell or nucleus) and with the process of fertilization of the eggs of sea urchins (sea urchins being one of those marine creatures that do not mate, but shed their eggs and sperm into the sea). His findings were recorded in a number of scientific papers which made Swann's reputation as a leading authority on cell biology. He obtained a Ph.D. in 1950.

In 1952 Swann moved to Edinburgh University as professor of natural history. He continued his research, but became increasingly involved in the administrative responsibilities of his post, and, by the time he was elected dean of the faculty of science in 1963, he had made his department one of the best centres for biological teaching and research in the United Kingdom. Having left his microscope for the instruments of academic business, he published his last scientific paper in 1962.

In 1965 he succeeded Sir Edward *Appleton as principal and vice-chancellor of Edinburgh University and was soon seen to be not only an able administrator within the university and the committee of vice-chancellors, but also a notable authority on educational problems in wider fields beyond Edinburgh. He was a member of the advisory council on education in Scotland (1957–61), the committee on manpower resources (1963–8), and the council for scientific policy (1965–9). However, his term of office as principal of the university coincided in the late 1960s with an upsurge of political activism among his students, and, although he dealt with the resultant problems with firmness and tact, he found the situation tedious and tiresome.

Meanwhile, relations between the chairman of the governors of the BBC, Baron *Hill of Luton, and the director-general and his staff had not been running smoothly, and (Sir) Edward Heath, the prime minister, was seeking as the new chairman somebody less assertive and blustering in carrying out the functions of that office. In 1973 Swann was offered and accepted the post. From the outset he made clear that he had no intention of trying to steer the ship, but would be prepared to help to hold her on course if rough weather were encountered. The next seven years were not without some rough weather. In 1977 the central policy review staff made recommendations regarding the external services of the BBC, which in the view of the corporation would have been disastrous if implemented. Swann took steps to ensure that the proposals were quietly shelved. In 1974 the committee on the future of broadcasting had been set up under Baron Annan. Its report, published in 1977, challenged the role of the governors. Having handled the committee with tact and good humour, Swann was able to ensure that the management of the corporation was not imperilled.

Throughout his term of office as chairman (1973–80), Swann earned not only the regard of the two directors-general with whom he worked, but also the respect and affection of all BBC staff. Sir Ian *Trethowan paid tribute to him as 'an outstanding chairman steering the BBC through a number of political crises'.

Swann was knighted in 1972. In 1981 he was created a life peer, and in the House of Lords continued to defend the independence of the BBC. During that year (1980–1) he was provost of Oriel College, Oxford, but he was not happy there, and resigned after twelve months. He found it difficult to cope with the minutiae of college life after facing the demands of public life for so long, and the college itself was unprepared for the amount of time that his outside activities were to take up. He was a member of many organizations, in which he took an active part, including the Medical Research Council (1962–5), Council for Science and Society (1974–8), and the Wellcome Trust, of which he was a trustee from 1973 to 1990. From 1979 to 1990 he was chancellor of York University. From 1981 to 1985 he chaired the committee of inquiry into the education of children from ethnic minority groups, and the Swann report of March 1985 was radical. He was also chairman of the Royal Academy of Music from 1983 to 1990, an appointment which gave him special pleasure, and a trustee of the British Museum (Natural History), 1982–6. He received many academic honours, including honorary degrees from Aber-

deen (1967), Leicester (1968), York (1968), and Heriot-Watt (1971). He was elected FRSE in 1952 and FRS in 1962.

Swann was a big, broad, heavy man, unathletic and with blond hair and a friendly manner. He never managed to look very smart, even when wearing his best clothes. In 1942 he married Tess Gleadowe, a keen musician, an associate of the Royal College of Music and of the Royal College of Organists. She was the daughter of Reginald Morier Yorke Gleadowe, Slade professor of fine art at Oxford. They had two sons and two daughters. Swann died 22 September 1990 of a ruptured aorta at his home, Tallat Steps, in Coln St Denys, Gloucestershire.

[*The Times* and *Independent*, 24 September 1990; J. M. Mitchison in *Biographical Memoirs of Fellows of the Royal Society*, vol. xxxvii, 1991.]   H. F. OXBURY

SYKES, Christopher Hugh (1907–1986), writer and traveller, was born 17 November 1907 in Sledmere, near Driffield, Yorkshire, the elder of twins and the second son and third child in the family of three sons and three daughters of (Sir) Mark *Sykes, later sixth baronet, and his wife Edith Violet, third daughter of Sir John Eldon *Gorst, solicitor-general. His father was first employed as honorary attaché to the British embassy in Constantinople, before helping to found the Arab Bureau with T. E. *Lawrence and signing the Sykes–Picot agreement of 1916. Christopher followed an undistinguished academic career at Downside and Christ Church, Oxford (which he left without a degree), by becoming honorary attaché at both the Berlin embassy (1928–9) and the British legation in Tehran (1930–1).

At Oxford he was thought of as a boisterous, if congenial, companion, given to acts of bravado, rather like his early hero, and close friend of his father, Aubrey *Herbert, the model for John *Buchan's Greenmantle. Unlike Herbert or his father, he was inhibited from embarking on a political career by a stutter, which grew more pronounced whenever the subject-matter was such as might inspire disbelief. Since Sykes was chiefly interested in those areas of discussion which lie on the borders between personal experience, artistic embellishment, and fantasy, it was thought that a political career was closed to him. He took a course in Persian studies at the School of Oriental Studies, London, and in 1933 left for two years' travel in Persia and Afghanistan with Robert *Byron. He wrote for *The Times*, *Spectator*, and *Observer*.

Of Sykes's writing before the war, little survived after it: *Wassmus* (1936), a biography of the German Arabist, was followed by two light novels, one of them written under the puzzling pseudonym of Waughburton in collaboration with Robert Byron. The war itself saw him commissioned in the 7th battalion of the Green Howards. Later, as part of Special Operations Executive, he adorned GHQ in Cairo when the presence of the Duff *Coopers and other cronies made it the most elegant place to be, before being posted to Tehran as a spy attached to the British legation. Transferring to the 2nd battalion of the Special Air Service, he worked with the French Resistance and was awarded the croix de guerre.

Many of these experiences came together in what will probably be seen as his masterpiece, *Four Studies in Loyalty* (1946), incorporating elements of biography and autobiography. It is memorable in particular for its study of a previous Christopher Sykes, his great-uncle. His *Two Studies in Virtue* (1953) was less successful in its treatment of Cardinal J. H. *Newman and E. B. *Pusey. Although Sykes was a cradle Catholic, intermittently devout and, like many Catholics of his class, enraged by the despoliation of the Roman liturgy after the second Vatican Council, his interest in the finer points of High Anglican conscience was limited.

After some foreign reporting, notably for the *Daily Mail* during the Azerbaijan campaign in Iran, he joined the BBC in 1948. Following a short spell as deputy controller of the Third Programme he joined the features department (1949–68), where he was suspected of having formed a Catholic mafia.

His biography of *Orde Wingate* (1959) may have described the sort of life he would have liked to live, but the life of Adam von Trott (*Troubled Loyalty*, 1968), the patriotic anti-Nazi, was closer to the world he eventually inhabited. After a life of Nancy *Astor (*Nancy*, 1971), generally seen as a bit of a pot-boiler, he came, after some delay, to write the authorized biography of his old friend and boon companion, the novelist Evelyn *Waugh (1975). This might have been his best book. He was chosen because he was the only one of Waugh's obituarists who caught something of the gaiety, as well as the recklessness of the man. Unfortunately, when he came to set pen to paper six years after his subject's death, the light had dimmed a little. Inhibited, as he said, by respect for Waugh's widow—she, in fact, had died two years before the book appeared—he had also suffered a decline in energy, a certain loss of optimism or hope. The book is marred not only by carelessness but also perhaps, by a certain resentment at the dying of the light. Sykes's life had been a reasonably successful one, but not so successful as that of his *arriviste* friend.

He was a most congenial man to meet, an excellent mimic, well-mannered, and witty even in his cups, much loved by the young to whom he was always pleasant and friendly. In appearance he was tall, with a dark, slightly saturnine

countenance. He carried himself well, with a debonair and jaunty manner, which remained with him when age brought a certain heaviness, not to say majesty, to his gait. In 1936 he married Camilla Georgiana (died 1983), daughter of Sir Thomas Wentworth *Russell, pasha, chief of police in Cairo from 1917 to 1946, but this did little to improve the parlous financial situation of a younger son. He spent his last years in a Kent nursing home. He died in the course of an agreeable house party at Sledmere, his childhood home, 8 December 1986. He was survived by an only son, Mark, publisher and second-hand bookseller.

[*The Times*, 10 December 1986; *Independent*, 11 December 1986; personal knowledge.]

AUBERON WAUGH

SYLVESTER, Albert James (1889–1989), political and private secretary, was born 24 November 1889 in Harlaston, Staffordshire, the eldest of three children and only son of Albert Sylvester, a tenant farmer reduced to the role of farm-worker by the agricultural depression, and his wife Edith, daughter of James Redfern, also from Staffordshire but of no traceable address. He was educated at Guild Street School, Burton-on-Trent, and while there studied Pitman's shorthand. After leaving school at fourteen to become a brewery clerk he devoted most of his leisure to perfecting his shorthand and typing, achieving the champion speeds of, respectively, 210 and 80 words a minute. As a young man he moved as a freelance typist to London, where his talents were soon in demand and he became a member, in 1911 and 1912, of the British international typewriting team, which competed (unsuccessfully) with the Americans.

In 1912, on the recommendation of a stranger whom he met on the underground after a concert at the Albert Hall, he was appointed to the secretarial staff of the royal commission on Indian public services. This took him to the subcontinent and introduced him to work in the official sphere. After the outbreak of war in 1914 he joined the staff of Colonel (later first Baron) M. P. A. *Hankey, secretary of the committee of imperial defence. The following year he became the first shorthand writer to record the proceedings of a cabinet committee.

When, in December 1916, David *Lloyd George (later first Earl Lloyd-George of Dwyfor) succeeded H. H. *Asquith (later the first Earl of Oxford and Asquith) as prime minister, he at once established a war cabinet secretariat under Hankey, who chose Sylvester as his private secretary. In this capacity he showed such diligence, discretion, and efficiency that at the end of the war he was given the status of a higher-grade civil servant, without having to sit the examination. Immediately after the war he accompanied

Hankey to the Paris peace conference, where he continued to work under intense pressure. In 1918 he was appointed OBE and in 1920 CBE.

His work for Hankey brought him into frequent contact with the prime minister, and in 1921 Lloyd George recruited him to the secretariat at 10 Downing Street. With Lloyd George he attended the Cannes and Genoa conferences, and he was also involved in the tortuous processes leading to the Anglo-Irish Treaty in 1921. When, eleven months later, the Lloyd George coalition was brought down, Sylvester stayed on for a time under two Conservative prime ministers, Andrew *Bonar Law and Stanley *Baldwin (later first Earl Baldwin of Bewdley). But in 1923 he left the Civil Service and rejoined Lloyd George.

Though Sylvester's chief motive for doing so was that he admired the Welshman and found working for him exciting, Lloyd George facilitated the move by paying him a higher salary, and also a substantial sum to compensate him for the loss of Civil Service pension rights. He was given the title of principal private secretary, though in reality that role belonged to Lloyd George's mistress (later his second wife), Frances Stevenson (later Countess *Lloyd George of Dwyfor).

Nevertheless, Sylvester accompanied Lloyd George on most of his travels abroad, including his controversial visit to Adolf Hitler in 1936, and at home ran the office at Thames House, Westminster, which at the height of Lloyd George's activity as an opposition politician had a staff of over twenty. Sylvester dealt with his master's enormous correspondence and, when he was working on his *War Memoirs* (6 vols., 1933–6), carried out much archival research and interviewing of former colleagues on his behalf. His services were indispensable, and he stayed at his post until Lloyd George's death in 1945.

Any hopes he may have had that Lloyd George's widow would invite him to be, as it were, joint guardian of the shrine, and to collaborate in work based on the papers that had been left to her, were soon dashed. In 1947 he published a book of his own, *The Real Lloyd George*, which has its good points but is on the whole rather disappointing. In 1975 a selection from his diary appeared, edited by Colin Cross and entitled *Life with Lloyd George*, and this is a far more valuable publication. The diary, kept in shorthand, gives a vivid impression of Lloyd George and a detailed account of his life, though unfortunately it covers only the last phase, from 1931 to the end. The full text of the diary is now in the National Library of Wales.

Always at heart a countryman, Sylvester bought during World War II 150 acres of farmland in Wiltshire. In 1949 he moved from his London home in Putney to another Wiltshire property, Rudloe Cottage near Corsham, where he cultivated a smallholding, his larger holding being let to a tenant. He spent the rest of his life at Rudloe, becoming a JP (1953) and, in 1962, chairman of the local bench. In old age he took to ballroom dancing for which, at eighty-five, he received the top amateur award, thereby earning himself a place in the *Guinness Book of Records*.

Sylvester was well above medium height, clean-shaven, with a high forehead, longish nose, and fresh complexion. His vigorous and humorous temperament came across most effectively in the many radio and television interviews that he gave in his later years. Even when very old and infirm his resilience was remarkable. A visitor to Rudloe would find him slumped in an armchair before a fire that was nearly out, and his first words would be a plaintive 'I am very, very ill.' But soon he would be standing erect, throwing logs on the fire and reliving past experiences with strong voice and eloquent gesture. No doubt it was his personality as much as his great professional competence that appealed to Lloyd George.

In 1917 he married Evelyn Annie (died 1962), daughter of William Welman, draper and Baptist lay preacher, of Norbiton. They had one daughter. Sylvester himself died at St Andrews Hospital, Chippenham, 27 October 1989, a month short of his hundredth birthday.

[A. J. Sylvester, *The Real Lloyd George*, 1947, and *Life with Lloyd George* (ed. Colin Cross), 1975; private information; personal knowledge.]   JOHN GRIGG

SYME, SIR Ronald (1903–1989), Roman historian, was born 11 March 1903 in Eltham, a small market town in the province of Taranaki in the north island of New Zealand. He was the elder son and eldest of three children of David Simpson Syme, solicitor, and his wife, Florence Mabel Selley. He was educated at Eltham Primary School and Stratford District High School, where his interest in Latin was strongly encouraged by a first-class teacher, Miss Tooman. In 1918–20 he attended New Plymouth Boys' High School, of which he was dux in 1919–20, winning a junior university scholarship. From 1921 to 1923 he was a student at Victoria University of Wellington, studying English, Latin, French, jurisprudence, and constitutional history. In the second year he added Greek; it is a very striking sign of his extraordinary linguistic aptitude, as demonstrated a few years later in Oxford, that it was only then that his formal study of Greek began. In 1922–4, while still technically a student at Victoria, he was studying extramurally at the University of Auckland, to which he transferred formally in 1924. In 1923–4 he acted as assistant to the professor of classics, H. S. Dettmann. The story that in this role, after the professor took a headmastership, he set, sat, and marked his own papers for the BA in 1923 is unfortunately only a legend.

In 1924–5 he studied for an MA in classics at Auckland, winning first-class honours in Latin, a senior scholarship in Greek, Latin, and French, and a postgraduate scholarship in arts, which brought him in the autumn of 1925 to Oriel College, Oxford, to study *literae humaniores*, which then consisted of ancient history and philosophy. He was not to return to New Zealand until 1950, but remained profoundly attached to it, its mountain scenery, and memories of seeing Halley's comet in the clear New Zealand sky of 1910. His first and best-known book, *The Roman Revolution* (1939), was dedicated to his parents and his homeland ('parentibus optimis patriaeque'), and he kept his New Zealand citizenship throughout his life, speaking with unusual passion of the state-sponsored terrorism practised there by the French government in the matter of the sinking of a Greenpeace ship.

In Oxford he was deeply influenced by his tutor in ancient history, Marcus Niebuhr Tod, a specialist in the illumination of Greek history through the careful study of inscriptions, and famed for the delicacy and precision of his language, both spoken and written. Syme's own linguistic gifts were shown in the remarkable feat of his winning the Chancellor's prize for Latin prose and the Gaisford prize for Greek prose in 1926 (some five years after beginning Greek); these were followed by the Gaisford prize for Greek verse in 1927.

This quite outstanding talent had two consequences, the one merely of incidental interest, the other fundamental to his whole career. The former was a brilliant series of vignettes of Oxford life of the 1930s, in both Latin and Greek and in prose and verse, published in the *Oxford Magazine* ('de coniuratione Bodleiana'; or a memorable evocation in Homeric verse of a scene involving Provost L. R. *Phelps at Oriel high table). More important was the fact that the areas of his attention, within Roman history, were always to be directed to those periods from which there survives contemporary literature in Latin. In his entire output Greek history is represented only by a single essay on Thucydides; and, with the exception of Strabo, the vast Greek historical literature of the Roman period did not engage his attention.

But first he had to take his degree, achieving a first (with rather modest marks in philosophy) in 1927; a typically elegant note from M. N. Tod informing him of the result is preserved in the archive of Syme's papers at Wolfson College, Oxford. Tod continued to lend him his support, which led very quickly, in the fashion of the Oxford of those days, to his election as fellow and tutor in ancient history of Trinity College, Oxford, in 1929.

The decade which he spent at Trinity until the outbreak of war was his happiest and most creative period. Indeed it had already begun in 1928, hence a year after he took his finals, with an article on the legions under Domitian. That was a sign of one enduring preoccupation: military history painstakingly reconstructed from literary sources and inscriptions, and set against the vast and varied landscapes of the Roman empire, from Spain to the Euphrates. With that went a deep engagement with European, especially German, scholarship. His command of both French and German was very considerable, but his knowledge of French was more typically deployed in an exhaustive acquaintance with modern novels. In German, however, there was not only a wide knowledge of literature, some of which—like parts of Goethe's *Faust*—he knew by heart, but also a profound relationship to the German scholarship of the previous few decades: not so much Theodor Mommsen, however, as W. Schulze's study of Roman names; the great article 'Legio' by E. Ritterling in Pauly-Wissowa's *Realencyclopaedie*; Friedrich Münzer on the history of Roman aristocratic families; perhaps (this is not so clear as might be supposed) Matthias Gelzer on 'the Roman nobility'; and above all the two editions of the *Prosopographia Imperii Romani* (1897 and 1933–). Reading in the library was supplemented by many visits to Germany and the Balkans, when he also walked long distances to gain a detailed understanding of the landscape.

Military history was perhaps the most obvious product of his studies until the end of the 1930s, culminating in his still unsurpassed article on 'Flavian Wars and Frontiers' in the *Cambridge Ancient History*, vol. x (1936). But already other dominating themes of his work were developing. Among his papers later given to Wolfson College, there is a manuscript draft dated 1934 of a book entitled 'The Provincial at Rome', to which he refers in the preface of his *Tacitus* (1958): 'It is suitable to confess in this place that the concluding section, "The New Romans" (Chapters XLIII–XLV), owes something to a book begun many years ago, soon interrupted, and not yet terminated—"The Provincial at Rome".' It never was to be terminated, though *Colonial Elites* (1958) also owes much to it. But it is now clear how rapidly the main lines of his thought had developed, and how consistently he maintained them to the end of his life.

An interest in the 'provincial' coming to the centre from the periphery must, obviously, have owed much to his background. But there are more general aspects to his use of prosopography, which he turned into a dominant mode in

Roman history: the study of families over generations, the interplay of literary and epigraphical evidence; the structure of public careers; the possibility of filling the stage of Roman history not just with the Pompeys, Caesars, and Augustuses, but with a host of lesser mortals. All these themes came together, along with his reactions to the rise of the interwar dictatorships and their gross misuse of language, to produce *The Roman Revolution*, finished in 1938 when he was thirty-five, and published in 1939. As a work of literature, and as an exercise in intellectual and stylistic control, it has no equal in the historiography of Rome, and few in that of any period or area.

The war then imposed a quite long hiatus, when he served in the Balkans, and was then professor of classical philosophy in Istanbul. He did indeed teach classics there; as to what other roles he played (as he certainly did), he never, to the end, gave the smallest hint.

The postwar period saw him back in Oxford, where in 1949 he succeeded H. M. *Last as Camden professor of ancient history, and fellow of Brasenose. It was very unfortunate that Last, a major figure but not to be compared with Syme in intellectual creativity, was there still as principal. Their profound disagreements, which the surviving correspondence shows to have been Last's fault, significantly soured his life at Brasenose and his attitude to it.

None the less it was in 1958 that he published the most original and creative of his works, the infinitely complex and fruitful two-volume work on *Tacitus*, accompanied by *Colonial Elites*, and followed by his Sather lectures on *Sallust* (1964). A wider recognition came: in 1959 a knighthood, in 1976 the Order of Merit, as well as twenty honorary doctorates, and memberships of foreign academies. In 1956 (though no earlier) he made the first of many, ever more frequent, journeys across the Atlantic. All his life an extremely private person, Syme rarely developed close relations with colleagues, and tended to gain more pleasure from passing, if repeated, contacts with academic acquaintances made during his travels.

Before his retirement in 1970 he had developed a fascination, possibly excessive, with the late fourth-century collection of imperial biographies in Latin known as the *Historia Augusta*. In the same period, however, the generous initiative of the newly founded Wolfson College, Oxford, led to his election as a fellow and to his occupation of a fine penthouse apartment overlooking the river Cherwell, where he worked with great contentment, very productively, publishing *History in Ovid* (1978), *Some Arval Brethren* (1980), and a work of remarkable complexity, interest, and novelty, *The Augustan Aristocracy* (1986), at the age of eighty-three—not to speak of over fifty papers published in the 1980s.

Always extremely sociable, provided that his essential reserve was respected, Syme never married, something which was not in the least a sign of aversion from the opposite sex, or even of an inability to form a long and deeply affectionate relationship. Never inclined to superfluous expenditure, on clothes or anything else, he none the less maintained to very near the end a brisk and military appearance, walking wherever possible, and at a pace which only very late began to slow to that of ordinary mortals. His reserve also softened somewhat in later years, when he found the support of younger scholars and their families, who regarded him with affection, without rivalry, and with no thought of obtrusion beyond what he wished. The cheerful, multinational society of Wolfson also offered him both stimulus and a more comfortable environment than he had ever enjoyed before, while respecting his privacy.

Late in August 1989, when already suffering from cancer, he collapsed in his room in Wolfson, and never fully regained consciousness, dying only four days before a party, to be held by the college, which would have celebrated the fiftieth anniversary of the publication of *The Roman Revolution*. This book, together with *Tacitus*, remains the main memorial to his unique contribution to Roman history; he is universally acknowledged as its greatest practitioner in the twentieth century. His particular qualities are not easy to summarize, and the true importance of his work can hardly yet be assessed. But his qualities included sheer intelligence, and a memory of legendary accuracy; great sensitivity to language, and vast reading; an intense engagement with the individual lives and family histories which can be brought out from behind the surface of Latin inscriptions and Roman literature; and a sense of style, which could lapse into idiosyncrasy. That style is shown at its best in the last paragraph of his *Tacitus*, which may also serve as his own epitaph: 'The irony is restrained and impressive. When Tacitus wrote, colonials and provincials from the Latin West occupied the place of the Caesars. There was only one higher pinnacle: literary renown. To that also the epoch of Trajan and Hadrian might confidently aspire. Men and dynasties pass, but style abides.' He died 4 September 1989 in the John Radcliffe Hospital, Oxford.

[G. W. Bowersock in *Proceedings of the British Academy*, vol. lxxxiv, 1993; F. Millar, 'Style Abides', *Journal of Roman Studies*, vol. lxxi, 1981; obituary by M. T. Griffin, ibid., vol. lxxx, 1990; personal information from Mrs Geraldine Gill (sister); Syme archive, Wolfson College, Oxford; personal knowledge.]

FERGUS MILLAR

T

TAYLOR, Alan John Percivale (1906–1990), historian, journalist, and broadcaster, was born 25 March 1906 in Birkdale, Lancashire, the only son (and sole surviving child) of Percy Lees Taylor, Preston cotton merchant, and his wife, Constance Sumner Thompson, schoolmistress. His well-to-do Edwardian Liberal parents subsequently became ardent Labour supporters, which shaped Taylor's lifelong commitment to left-wing causes, notably the first Campaign for Nuclear Disarmament. Precocious, learned, and spoilt, he was educated at Bootham School in York and Oriel College, Oxford, where, as something of a gilded youth who flirted with the Communist party, he took a first class in modern history as a medievalist in 1927.

Abandoning his intention of becoming a labour lawyer, Taylor went to Vienna in 1928 as a Rockefeller fellow to work on modern diplomatic history. Appointed a lecturer at Manchester University in 1930, he came under the influence, which he later denied, of his professor, (Sir) Lewis *Namier, and wrote the first of his more than thirty books, *The Italian Problem in European Diplomacy, 1847–1849* (1934) and *Germany's First Bid for Colonies, 1884–1885* (1938), both mischievous products of hard work, rarely repeated thereafter, in the archives. He schooled himself to lecture (and speak publicly) without notes, a craft he later brought to perfection; contributed regularly as reviewer and leader-writer on the *Manchester Guardian* under A. P. *Wadsworth; travelled widely; and cultivated his vegetable garden at Disley in the High Peak.

With Namier's crucial support, Taylor returned to Oxford in 1938 as a fellow of Magdalen College, to which he remained devoted until his retirement in 1976. Soon established as an outstanding tutor of responsive undergraduates and a charismatic, early-morning lecturer, he began to make a wider name for himself as an incisive speaker on current affairs, in person and on the radio. Throughout World War II his house at Holywell Ford was a centre for writers young and old, wayward musicians, and the grander Slav refugees clustered in north Oxford as well as his pupils coming on leave. In 1941 he published the most elegant of his books, the elegiac first version of *The Habsburg Monarchy*, and this was followed in 1945 by his initial best seller, *The Course of German History*, a graphic, opinionated *pièce d'occasion* and the clue to much of his later work in its anti-German assumptions.

Notorious as an early critic of the cold war, Taylor emerged as a national figure with the advent of television. On *In The News* and *Free Speech* he caught the viewers' fancy as a quick-witted debater, a Cobbett-like scourge of 'the establishment', and, quite simply, something of a card, much appreciated by the 'man on the Clapham omnibus', in the phrase of his exemplar, Lord *Macaulay. First of the television dons, he retained this primacy into old age as he delivered unscripted lectures direct to the camera on historical themes to a vast audience. Meanwhile he was taken up by Lord *Beaverbrook, a lover of maverick left-wingers, as the charms of Oxford faded. A highly paid, sometimes outrageous columnist on the *Sunday Express*, and the first (and last) director of the Beaverbrook library, Taylor paid uneasy tribute to an improbable but close friend in *Beaverbrook* (1972), the last of his substantial works and dedicated to the only man who ever persuaded him to cross the Atlantic.

Long before, Taylor had consolidated his academic reputation. In 1954 *The Struggle for Mastery in Europe, 1848–1918* was at once recognized as a model analysis, with its careful attention to the records. This massive work, with the brief but perceptive *Bismarck* (1955) and the self-indulgent Ford lectures, *The Trouble Makers* (1957), fully justified his election to the British Academy in 1956. (Perversely, he resigned on libertarian grounds in 1980 when Anthony *Blunt relinquished his fellowship.) Contrary to many expectations, however, Taylor was not appointed regius professor at Oxford in 1957. This failure, in which Namier played some part, remains a subject of uncertain legend, but it did not prevent an embittered man denigrating the university he loved. Thereafter he was consoled by honorary doctorates at Bristol, Manchester, New Brunswick, Warwick, and York, as well as honorary fellowships of both Magdalen (1976) and Oriel (1980).

Superficially, Taylor was an old-fashioned historian, holding that 'politics express the activities of man in society', with the addendum that economic and social circumstances must be taken into modest account. A master of narrative but essentially an analyst, he founded no school, despite his influence upon younger historians, and his methods could be a dangerous model. In his heyday Taylor came to rely upon assiduous reading in five languages and sheer intuition—'green fingers', in Namier's envious phrase. There was no elaborate filing system, but a prodigious memory could usually supply some evidence for the thousand words tapped out each well-organized morning. Despite his commitment to popular journalism, he was also a superb and creative essayist, and published several volumes based upon serious reviews in the learned journals and the *Observer*.

Ultimately, Taylor's scholarly standing depends upon three major achievements. *The Struggle for Mastery* remains unrivalled as a totally authoritative study of international relations in a complicated period. *English History, 1914–1945* (1965) is an enthralling, highly idiosyncratic account of his own times, regarded by some as his best book. *The Origins of the Second World War* (1961) was a dazzling exercise in revisionism, which earned him a mixture of international obloquy and acclaim. Whatever its flaws, this treatment of Hitler as a product of German tradition summed up Taylor's paradoxical, provocative, and inventive approach to historical explanation. A pragmatic loner, suspicious of philosophies of history and a brilliant stylist, he was admired even by his many critics for the range of his erudition, his clarity of presentation, and the fertility of his hypotheses.

Though he enjoyed portraying himself as a simple, true-born Englishman, Taylor was a cosmopolitan intellectual, with an expert knowledge of European architecture, music, and wine. An admirable but frugal host, his table talk was inimitable; a shrewd if nervous man of business, he was soothed by domestic chores; and in old age he became an indefatigable walker in town and country. Short, stocky, and bespectacled, he was vain about his appearance, but always happiest in a crumpled tweed or, more often, corduroy suit, invariably accompanied by a flamboyant bow-tie.

An emotional man, despite the brash exterior, Taylor was three times married and devoted to his six children. In 1931 he married a musician, Margaret, the daughter of Harold Adams, an English merchant trading in India; they had two sons and two daughters. Margaret was later an over-indulgent patron of Dylan *Thomas. This marriage was dissolved in 1951 and in the same year he married Eve, daughter of Joseph Beardsel Crosland, under-secretary at the War Office. There were two sons of this marriage, which was dissolved in 1974. In 1976 he married the Hungarian historian, Eva Haraszti, daughter of Mitse

Herczke, a textile merchant in Budapest. Taylor's last years were clouded by Parkinson's disease and he died at a nursing home in Barnet, 7 September 1990.

[Taylor's works *passim*, but especially *A Personal History*, 1983, and *Letters to Eva*, 1991; Adam Sisman, *A. J. P. Taylor*, 1994; C. J. Wrigley, *A. J. P. Taylor, a Complete Annotated Bibliography*, 1980; Chris Wrigley in *Proceedings of the British Academy*, vol. lxxxii, 1992; personal knowledge.]   A. F. THOMPSON

TEAGUE-JONES, Reginald (1889–1988), intelligence officer, known under the pseudonym of Ronald Sinclair, was born 30 July 1889 in Walton, Liverpool, the eldest of four children and only son of Frederick Jones, schoolmaster, and his wife, Elizabeth Deeley Smith. His father, who taught languages, died when he was about thirteen, leaving his mother in straitened circumstances, and friends living in St Petersburg offered to take him there and oversee his education. He attended St Anne's College in the tsarist capital and was soon fluent in German, French, and Russian. On return to England he studied at King's College, London, but left without a degree. He failed to pass the Foreign Office entry examination, instead joining the Indian Police in 1910. He quickly learned some Indian languages, plus Persian, and was used for frontier intelligence work—sometimes in disguise—before being transferred to the foreign and political department of the British Indian government, who had spotted his unusual talents, and for whom he was working at the outbreak of World War I. He was then commissioned into the Indian army reserve of officers.

The nature of his duties makes his career a shadowy one, but he appears to have spent most of the war as officer in charge of British intelligence in the Persian Gulf, and then as political officer in Basra. However, following the withdrawal of Russian forces from Persia and the Caucasus as a result of the Bolshevik coup in October 1917 and the peace treaty of Brest-Litovsk, he was engaged in the urgent task of assessing which groups, if any, of non-Bolshevik Russians or of the indigenous peoples would support the Allies in keeping the Germans and Turks from overrunning Persia, the Caucasus, and Transcaspia—and ultimately India.

Teague-Jones himself crossed into Transcaspia disguised as a Persian merchant and travelled along the Transcaspian railway—assessing the possibility of blowing it up if necessary—to Krasnovodsk on the eastern side of the Caspian. After successfully foiling German plans to acquire a large consignment of cotton from the Bolsheviks (for use in the manufacture of explosives), he crossed by ferry to Baku to liaise with the British representative there and to organize a network of intelligence agents in the area, before reporting back to Major-General (Sir) Wilfrid Malleson in Meshed. The Bolsheviks' brutality in Transcaspia led to their being overthrown there in July 1918 by Social Revolutionaries and the local Turcomans, and the new government, the 'Ashkhabad Committee', sought British help from Malleson, via Teague-Jones, who sent an urgent report to Meshed before returning to Baku, which was being hard pressed by the Turks. After a few weeks, however, Teague-Jones was summoned back to Transcaspia, where a Bolshevik force from Tashkent in Turkestan was fighting its way westwards along the railway and seemed likely to recapture the province.

A few days later he was hit in the thigh by a machine-gun bullet at a battle eighty miles east of Ashkhabad. He was removed to hospital in Ashkhabad and, as soon as he was able to hobble around, was appointed British political representative there. In the meantime Baku had fallen to the Turks, and in the frenzied exodus a large party of Bolshevik commissars who were making for Astrakhan, which was still in Bolshevik hands, had the misfortune to be delivered instead to Krasnovodsk, where they were seized by their enemies the Social Revolutionaries. The gaols of Transcaspia were already overflowing with the hated local Bolsheviks and there was little room for these new arrivals, so the Ashkhabad Committee asked Malleson whether the British could take them over. Malleson suggested to his authorities that the commissars might be useful in an exchange of prisoners with the Bolsheviks, but was unsure how he could transport them to India when he was very short of men. While the debate was proceeding the Social Revolutionaries pre-empted any decision by taking twenty-six of the prisoners out into the desert at dead of night, summarily executing them, and shovelling their bodies into a shallow grave (20 September 1918).

At the time this seemed just one more atrocity in the Russian civil war, but it was to have the gravest repercussions for Teague-Jones. Once World War I was over and the British had withdrawn from the region in 1919, the Bolsheviks soon recaptured Transcaspia and discovered the fate of their colleagues from Baku, some of whom had been personally known to Lenin. The Social Revolutionaries of the old Ashkhabad Committee, eager to exonerate themselves, blamed Teague-Jones for the decision to execute the commissars, and the affair escalated to the point where the twenty-six Baku commissars became revered martyrs in the Soviet Union, and Teague-Jones was regarded as a war criminal, denounced by Stalin and Trotsky personally. Such were the fears for his safety that he was forced to 'disappear' in 1922 and re-emerge as Ronald Sinclair. Thereafter he led a shadowy life, still apparently working for British intelli-

gence until his retirement, and keeping his true identity secret right up to his death at the age of ninety-nine. He received two honours: an MBE (military) (1919) as Reginald Teague-Jones, and an OBE (1923) as Ronald Sinclair.

A big ebullient man with a distinctive throaty voice, he was twice married: first—and very romantically—to a Russian girl, Valentina ('Valya') Alexeeva, whom he met in Transcaspia during the war. In July 1933 they were divorced in London, but remained friends. Her parents lived in Krasnovodsk. In October 1933 he married in Cairo his second wife Else ('Taddie'), daughter of Hermann Ferdinand Danecker, a German engineer. They subsequently lived in New York (where he seems to have worked for British intelligence during World War II), Florida, and Spain. After her death in 1986 he moved to a retirement home in Plymouth, where he was joined by Valya not long before her own death in 1988. He had no children.

Shortly before his death in Charlton House, Mannamead, Plymouth, 16 November 1988, his first book, *Adventures in Persia*, appeared, under the name of Sinclair, and it was as Ronald Sinclair that his obituary was published in *The Times* on 22 November. A corrected one, revealing his real identity and the reasons for his change of name, appeared three days later. His Transcaspian journals were published in 1990 under his true name, with the title *The Spy Who Disappeared*.

[Reginald Teague-Jones, *The Spy Who Disappeared*, with foreword and epilogue by Peter Hopkirk, 1990; Peter Hopkirk, *On Secret Service East of Constantinople*, 1994; Brian Pearce, articles on the fate of the twenty-six Baku commissars in the Soviet affairs journal, *Sbornik*, nos. 6–7 (1981), 9 (1983), and 11 (1985); personal investigations.]   PETER HOPKIRK

TERRY-THOMAS (1911–1990), actor and comedian, was born 14 July 1911 at his parents' home in Finchley, London, as Thomas Terry Hoar Stevens, the third child and third son in the family of four sons and one daughter of (Ernest) Frederick Stevens, managing director of a produce merchant's business, and his wife Ellen Elizabeth, daughter of Joseph Hoar, horsedealer, of London. He was educated at Ardingly College, Sussex. During World War II he served in the Royal Corps of Signals (1941–6) and with ENSA (the Entertainments National Service Association).

Thomas began his career as a clerk at Smithfield market, but his interest in amateur theatricals led him to work as a film extra. He took the stage name of Terry-Thomas, which he hyphenated to match the gap in his front teeth. His props were a diamond-encrusted cigarette holder, monocle, raffish waistcoat, and red carnation. Six feet in height, handsome in appearance, with a neat moustache and a natural upper-class accent, Terry-Thomas personified the English-man as an amiable bounder. With his drawling accent, he commonly used phrases such as 'rot-ter' and a leering 'jolly good show'. Once estab-lished, the character changed little from film to film. He toured with ENSA during World War II and, when demobilized, turned to cabaret work. In 1946 he found success with Sid Field in the West End hit, *Piccadilly Hayride*. He soon became popular on radio, with his own personal caddish humour, on *To Town with Terry* (1948–9) and *Top of the Town* (1951–2). He also presented his own television series—*Strictly T-T* (1949–56) and *How Do You View?* (1951–2).

The *Boulting brothers brought his natural comic talents to universal acclaim when they cast him, with Ian Carmichael, Dennis *Price, and Richard (later Baron) Attenborough, in their film *Private's Progress* (1956), in which he uttered the words 'You're an absolute shower' in his best upper-crust voice, words which were to become a catch-phrase. This led to a succession of memorable films, which included *Brothers in Law* (1957), *Carlton-Brown of the FO* (1958), *Lucky Jim* (1958), *I'm All Right, Jack* (1960), and *School for Scoundrels* (1960). In the early 1960s Terry-Thomas went to Hollywood, where he had to coarsen his already not very subtle persona, and he made several films, including *How to Murder Your Wife* (1964, his favourite film, in which he acted with Jack Lemmon), *Those Magnificent Men in Their Flying Machines* (1965), and *Monte Carlo or Bust* (1969). He was also a frequent performer on American television, appearing with Danny Kaye, Judy Garland, Andy Wil-liams, and others. A return to the BBC in 1968, with a series called *The Old Campaigner*, had only a modest impact. In the late 1970s he discovered that he was suffering from Parkinson's disease, which put an end to his career.

In 1938 Terry-Thomas married a dancer, Ida Florence (died 1983), the divorced wife of Ernest Stern and daughter of Philip Patlansky, hotel proprietor. There were no children of the mar-riage. After a divorce in 1962 he married in 1963 Belinda, daughter of Geoffrey Percy Cunning-ham, a lieutenant-colonel in the Royal Artillery. They had two sons.

A millionaire at the height of his fame, after his premature retirement he and his wife went to live in a villa on Ibiza, where he had built up land and property holdings. However, his illness caused him to spend £40,000 a year on medical bills and he had to return to Britain. Following a succession of house moves, he was discovered in the late 1980s living in reduced circumstances in a church charity flat in Barnes, south-west Lon-don, furnished by the Actors' Benevolent Fund. Friends in show business staged a benefit concert

for him at London's Drury Lane theatre in April 1989. The money that it raised enabled him to live in comfort at Busbridge Hall Nursing Home in Godalming, Surrey. He died there of pneu-monia 8 January 1990. At his funeral service, the organist played the theme tune to one of his favourite films, *Those Magnificent Men in Their Flying Machines*.

[Terry-Thomas, *Filling the Gap* (autobiography), 1959; Terry-Thomas and Terry Daum, *Terry-Thomas Tells Tales* (autobiography), 1990; *A Tribute to Terry-Thomas*, a documentary made by the Serendipity Film Company and screened by ITV in May 1990.]

RICHARD HOPE-HAWKINS
C. S. NICHOLLS

THALBEN-BALL, SIR George Thomas (1896–1987), organist, was born 18 June 1896 in Sydney, New South Wales, Australia, the elder son (there were no daughters) of George Charles Ball, who had gone to live temporarily in Aus-tralia on business, and his wife, Mary Hannah Spear, daughter of a miller, of Newquay, Corn-wall. The family returned to England in 1899, settling in Muswell Hill, where the father kept a shop. Both his parents were amateur musicians and George became a member of the choir of St James's church. The 'Thalben' of George's surname, which he added by deed poll in 1924, although he used it from 1917, has some Cornish connection. After attending Highfield, a private school in Muswell Hill, he entered the Royal College of Music on an exhibition in 1911, studying piano with Frits Hartvigson, Franklin Taylor, and Fanny Davies, organ with Sir Walter *Parratt and F. A. Sewell, and composition and history with Sir Charles *Stanford, Sir (C.) Hubert *Parry, and Charles *Wood. He quickly took part in ensemble and solo performances at the RCM, playing, among other works, Franz Liszt's Sonata in B Minor and, with the orches-tra conducted by Stanford, the solo part in Sergei Rachmaninov's Piano Concerto no. 3 in D Minor, the performance of which made a pro-found impression on his seniors and peers alike.

As an organist Thalben-Ball's energies were largely directed towards developing the music at the various churches where he held appoint-ments: as organist of Whitefield's tabernacle, Tottenham Court Road (1911); as organist and choir-master of Holy Trinity church, Castelnau, Barnes (1914–16), and St James's, Sussex Gar-dens (1916–19); and as acting organist (from 1919) and organist (1923–81) of the Temple church, near Fleet Street, London. His associa-tion with Sir (H.) Walford *Davies, which led eventually to Thalben-Ball's appointment at the Temple church, began with Saturday morning choir-training classes at the RCM, when he took part in conducting and accompanying the choir, and succeeded in getting Walford Davies to allow him to bring along his choristers from Barnes to take part. Thalben-Ball's work at the Temple was the cornerstone of his musical life. Throughout an association of more than sixty years he maintained a uniquely high standard of performance, and a musical style, traditional and in some ways limited, of extraordinary consistency. His achievement was all the more remarkable because the choir, for which the boys were drawn from the City of London School, had essentially to be re-established in the early 1950s following the ravages of World War II and the later rebuilding of the church. Thalben-Ball was helped, however, by a strong association of old choristers, which provided a continuing nucleus of singers.

The importance of church and choral music to Thalben-Ball makes his position as an organist somewhat paradoxical. Endowed with an exceptionally robust constitution, possessing impeccable technique and powers of co-ordination, showing concentration and alertness at all times, he became the best British organ recitalist for more than half a century. Together with his seniors, Sir Walter Alcock and George Dorrington Cunningham, he inaugurated the Royal Albert Hall organ in 1924, and was the preferred choice for many opening recitals. He became curator-organist of the Albert Hall in 1934, and was a regular soloist at the Henry Wood Promenade Concerts for many years, making a great effect with *Wood's transcription of Handel concertos for modern resources. After a recital at Birmingham Town Hall in 1948, following Cunningham's death, he was persuaded to take on the post of city organist in 1949, together with that of university organist. He always had reservations about this job, none the less enjoying the rail journeys from London, and performing a large repertory in more than 1,000 recitals before his retirement in 1982.

With his many-sided work and musical interests, Thalben-Ball was never a specialist organist, and this fact helps to explain why his reputation is more that of an executant than an interpreter; his natural sympathies lay firmly within the period bounded by the standard concert repertory of his time, which excluded 'early' music and, to a considerable extent, radical modern composition. His teaching was consistent with this outlook. He would work hard and long, even if somewhat spasmodically, with his pupils at the RCM, and yet a student often received the greatest enlightenment, not from explanation and discussion, but from persuading the master himself to get on the organ bench and demonstrate his way of doing things. He seemed most at home in music of the era from Mendelssohn to Sir Edward *Elgar, and produced memorable

accounts of the organ works of Liszt and Adolf Reubke. As an accompanist he performed extraordinary feats in turning the organ into an orchestra, such as when playing for Kathleen *Ferrier in *The Dream of Gerontius*.

Thalben-Ball was religious music adviser to the BBC from 1941, concerned with directing music for broadcast services and composing choral introits for them. This at first involved constant travel, as the department had been evacuated from London to Bedford. Even with the later commitments of Birmingham and the re-formed Temple church choir, Thalben-Ball was able to keep his BBC connection until 1970. He was appointed CBE in 1967 and knighted in 1982. He was FRCM (1951), FRCO (1915), FRSCM (1956, diploma 1963), FRSA (1971), and honorary RAM (1973). He was president of the Royal College of Organists in 1948–50 and an honorary bencher of the Inner Temple (1959). He won the grand prix de Chartres (1973) and the EMI gold disc (1963, for Mendelssohn's *Hear My Prayer*). He had an honorary D.Mus. and gold medal from Birmingham (1972).

Thalben-Ball was about five feet six inches in height, stockily built, with a small moustache and a ramrod-straight back. His dapper dress and turnout made him a man of the city. He married in 1926 a New Zealand artist, (Grace) Evelyn, daughter of Francis Chapman, a New Zealand wheat exporter. They had a son and a daughter. Evelyn died in 1961 and in 1968 Thalben-Ball married the organist Jennifer Lucy Bate, daughter of Horace Alfred Bate, organist of St James's, Muswell Hill. They had no children; the marriage was annulled in 1972. Thalben-Ball died at a nursing home in Wimbledon 18 January 1987.

[Jonathan Rennert, *George Thalben-Ball*, 1979; David Lewer, *A Spiritual Song, the Story of the Temple Choir*, 1961; private information; personal knowledge.]

JAMES DALTON

THOMAS, Howard (1909–1986), writer, broadcaster, and film and television impresario, was born 5 March 1909 in Cwm, Monmouthshire, the second son and third and youngest child of William George Thomas, stationer and postmaster, and his wife, Alice Maud Stephens. The family left south Wales when Thomas was eleven and moved to Beswick, Manchester. He went to local schools until he was old enough to start work.

He took evening classes in advertising and qualified as a copywriter, which led him to a small but aggressive Manchester advertising agency run by F. John Roe, where he developed the enterprise and showmanship on which he was to draw for the rest of his career. He moved to London in 1934. In 1937 he joined London Press

Exchange and obtained his first BBC commission. He set up LPE's commercial radio department in 1938, writing and producing most of its programmes himself, and also became one of BBC Radio's highest paid freelance script-writers.

Rejected for military service in 1940 because of his defective eyesight, Thomas was offered a BBC staff position and in the next three years produced over 500 programmes, among them two of the most notable of the war years. *Sincerely Yours* established (Dame) Vera Lynn as a musical link between servicemen and their partners back home and made her a star to be remembered ever afterwards as the 'Forces' Sweetheart'. In *The Brains Trust*, a panel of experts answered listeners' questions. This was a simple formula which became an outstanding popular success because of Thomas's selection of the panellists, whose three regulars—biologist (Sir) Julian *Huxley, philosopher C. E. M. *Joad, and retired naval commander A. B. Campbell—became national figures, answering questions, which ranged from 'What is the origin of life?' to 'How does a fly land upside down on the ceiling?'

In 1944 Thomas resigned from the BBC, where he saw no future for himself, and moved to the film industry as producer-in-chief of Pathé Pictures, the short-film subsidiary of the Associated British Picture Corporation, where he revitalized Pathé News and Pathé Pictorial and extended production into documentaries, such as his colour film of the coronation of Elizabeth II. Thomas was a passionate advocate of commercial television. When ABPC was invited by the Independent Television Authority in 1955 to apply for the weekend contract in the north and midlands, his lobbying was finally rewarded. ABC Television was formed as a subsidiary, with Thomas as managing director, and went on the air in February 1956.

ABC was the last and smallest of the original 'big four' contractors, alongside Associated-Rediffusion, ATV, and Granada. But Thomas's energy and enthusiasm, and his ability to pick the right like-minded lieutenants, propelled the little company into prominence. *Armchair Theatre*, under Sydney Newman, galvanized the single television play; arts programming was pioneered with *Tempo*, religious programming with *The Sunday Break*, adult education with *Sunday Session*; and London's dominance of popular entertainment at the weekend was successfully challenged with programmes like *Blackpool Night Out*, *Candid Camera*, and the stylish thriller series *The Avengers*.

When the structure of Independent Television was reshaped in 1967, the IBA offered the London weekday contract to a new company formed by the merger of Rediffusion and ABC Television, in which majority control was to be exercised by ABC, with Thomas as managing director. In the words of IBA chairman Baron *Hill of Luton, 'the combination of these two companies seemed to the Authority to offer the possibility of a programme company of real excellence.' Thames Television began transmission in August 1968 and realized the possibility of excellence in the ensuing years with a programme output high in both quantity and quality, ranging from *This Week* and *The World at War* to *Rumpole of the Bailey* and *Minder*, from *The Naked Civil Servant* and *Edward and Mrs Simpson* to *This Is Your Life* and *The Benny Hill Show*. In 1974 Thomas succeeded Baron Shawcross as chairman. He retired at the age of seventy in 1979.

Thomas was part of a particularly colourful period in the history of broadcasting in Britain, a bluff, burly showman in both radio and television. Among the founding fathers of Independent Television, he had the unique distinction of setting up and running two highly successful programme companies. He remained a programme-maker throughout his career, brimming with ideas himself and always respectful of the ideas of other programme-makers, whose talents he was quick to spot and ready to support. It was remarkable that, apart from his appointment as CBE in 1967, his achievement was never appropriately recognized. He was a governor of the British Film Institute (1974–82) and vice-president of the Royal Television Society (1976–84). He wrote five books, including *How to Write for Broadcasting* (1940). He also served three times as chairman of Independent Television News.

Thomas was above average height, thickset, balding from a quite early age, with a bluff manner and a forceful presence emphasized by his horn-rimmed spectacles. He was capable of great charm and persuasiveness, which served him well as a showman in both radio and television during a particularly colourful period in the history of British broadcasting. In 1934 he married Hilda, daughter of Harrison Fogg, a Manchester journalist. They had two daughters. Thomas died in hospital in Henley-on-Thames 6 November 1986.

[Howard Thomas, *With an Independent Air*, 1977; Asa Briggs, *History of Broadcasting in the United Kingdom*, vol. iii, 1970; Bernard Sendall, *Independent Television in Britain*, vol. i, 1982; Jeremy Potter, *Independent Television in Britain*, vol. iv, 1990; personal knowledge.]

BRIAN TESLER

THOMAS, (Lewis John) Wynford Vaughan- (1908–1987), author and broadcaster. [See VAUGHAN-THOMAS, (LEWIS JOHN) WYNFORD.]

THOMAS, Terry- (1911–1990), actor and comedian. [See TERRY-THOMAS.]

THROWER, Percy John (1913–1988), broadcaster and writer on gardening, was born 30 January 1913 in Little Horwood, Buckinghamshire, the second child and second son in the family of three sons and two daughters of Harry Thrower and his wife, Beatrice Dunnett. Just before Percy's birth his father had been appointed head gardener at Horwood House, near Winslow, where a new garden was to be made on an old site. An intelligent child but not a bookish one, Percy grew up with the new garden, becoming attuned to the daily rituals of garden nurture. With his ambition—'to be a head gardener, like my father'—already named, he was withdrawn from Little Horwood Church of England School shortly after his fourteenth birthday, in order to join his father's staff as pot-and-crock boy.

In 1931 Thrower was offered a job as an improver in the royal gardens at Windsor. In 1935 he moved to Leeds to sample municipal gardening as a journeyman, taking with him a sense of hierarchy and an adherence to the frugal and disciplined methods of Windsor. He was able to put some of these into practice from 1937, as deputy parks superintendent at Derby, where the job included maintaining the country's first public arboretum, opened in 1840. A century on, that now mature amenity was unregarded by the citizens, whose preferences, if any, inclined towards the formal bedding schemes that were the staple of municipal gardening. Thrower found a role in that style for fuchsias, whose seemingly exotic but generally very tolerant qualities he was to help popularize. In the summer of 1939 the focus of his work shifted to organizing the local 'dig for victory' effort. He spent the next five years instructing often motley groups of non-gardeners in the cultivation of roots and basic brassicas, supporting the wartime aim of self-sufficiency in food. Thus he discovered his distinguishing gift—as a natural teacher.

From 1946 until his retirement in 1974 Thrower was parks superintendent at Shrewsbury. His responsibilities included helping to revive the annual flower show after the war and maintaining its place near the top of the gardener's calendar. From its resumption in 1947 the show was covered by the BBC, which was keen to develop its treatment of all leisure interests. In the course of co-operating with BBC producers it became apparent that Thrower had the qualities of a natural broadcaster. The Corporation's principal gardening voice—C. H. Middleton, 'the best-known gardener since Adam'—had died prematurely in 1945 and an unofficial vacancy existed. Thrower's services were soon much in demand.

Most remarkably on the radio, and later on television, Thrower believed in letting his material speak for itself. Without a script, and with scarcely any comment or elaboration, he would describe a plant and its capabilities, its strengths and foibles, likes and dislikes, and how to draw out its best. The same technique was later brought to larger themes: how to discover the genius of a site, however small, by observation and experiment; how to create a microclimate by the judicious planting of trees and shrubs; how to reconcile the desire for immediate effect with long-term aims.

No attempt was made to change Thrower's not particularly appealing south midland accent, nor to soften a mode of utterance reminiscent of a mild-mannered sergeant-major. The tone of voice could be heard too in his journalism, principally for the *Daily Mail* and *Amateur Gardening*, and in the sixteen books, among them the often reprinted *In Your Garden Week by Week* (1959), commissioned as his reputation grew. When he proceeded from wireless to television it was not a surprise to behold a rather formal, somewhat top-heavy figure, who might put aside his pipe and often his jacket to demonstrate some arduous task, but seldom his tie. The image thus innocently created was that of the nation's head gardener.

Through simple education and encouragement Thrower helped to restore gardening as Britain's favourite leisure activity, bringing it back as a source of often productive pleasure after the unduly protracted season of the war and the allotment. As one who had known a little too much hands-and-knees drudgery during his early years in the garden, Thrower became a fervent advocate of all labour-saving machines and gadgets. His unrestrained use of chemicals and fungicides tended to isolate him from the new generation of gardeners who rose to prominence as his own career drew to a close. This was the indirect cause of the BBC's decision in 1976 to end his thirteen years as principal presenter of their leading garden programme, *Gardeners' World*. But Thrower had already started a new television career describing gardening on children's programmes, and with that audience he was soon an even bigger cult than he had been with their elders. His last broadcast was made a week before his death, from his hospital bed in Wolverhampton, where he was being treated for Hodgkin's disease.

Recognition from his peers came when the Royal Horticultural Society made him an associate of honour in 1963. Thrower took particular pleasure from the Society's Victoria medal of honour, awarded in 1974. He was appointed MBE in 1984.

On 9 September 1939 Thrower married Constance Margaret, whom he had courted since the days when he had worked under her father, Charles Cook, then head gardener at Windsor.

They had three daughters. Thrower died in hospital in Wolverhampton 18 March 1988.

[*The Times*, 19 March 1988; Percy Thrower, *My Lifetime of Gardening*, 1977; Timothy O'Sullivan, *Percy Thrower*, 1989; personal knowledge.]

TIMOTHY O'SULLIVAN

TINBERGEN, Nikolaas (1907–1988), authority on animal behaviour and Nobel prize-winner, was born 15 April 1907 in The Hague, the third of five children and second of four sons of Dirk Cornelis Tinbergen, schoolteacher, who taught Dutch language and history and was a scholar of medieval Dutch, and his wife, Jeannette van Eek, primary school teacher. 'Niko' Tinbergen went to school in The Hague. At Leiden University his career was at first undistinguished, and much of his time was spent on hockey or natural history. He was, however, very influenced by a number of amateur and professional ornithologists and, rebelling against the arid nature of the laboratory curriculum, he preferred to study wasps in the field. Perhaps affected by the rising influence of physiology, he resisted the subjectivism of A. F. J. Portielje and Bierens de Haan, and sought for more objective explanations of behaviour. As a result he was able to defend his behavioural work against the scepticism of the biological establishment and he received his Ph.D. in 1932 on a thesis only thirty-two pages long, the shortest on record in Leiden University.

In 1932 he married a chemistry student, Elisabeth ('Lies') Amélie, daughter of Louis Martien Rutter, geologist. They set off on a fourteen-month 'honeymoon' with a meteorological expedition to Greenland. They lived with an 'unwesternized' group of Inuit (Eskimos), learned their language, and acquired an interest in the hunter-gatherer's way of life. Tinbergen concentrated his research efforts on the snow bunting (*Plectrophenax nivalis*), a small bird that arrived as the snows melted, expended much energy in territorial battles with rivals, and bred in the brief summer. He also studied a variety of other Arctic animals.

When he returned he became an instructor at Leiden (1936), with the task of organizing laboratory practicals. For this he chose the three-spined stickleback (*Gasterosteus aculeatus*) and other animals that could easily be kept in the laboratory. The three-spined stickleback was a happy choice, for its natural environment could easily be imitated in an aquarium, and simple experiments were possible. Tinbergen mapped the reproductive cycle, analysed the stimuli eliciting attack and courtship, and showed that the complex zigzag courtship dance might be seen as a compromise between incompatible response systems. It is said that at this time Tinbergen wrote above the departmental library door

'Study Nature and not Books'. The stickleback became the classical animal of ethology, the work being subsequently continued by Jan van Iersel, Piet Sevenster, and many others. Around the same time Tinbergen started to study the herring gull (*Larus argentatus*), working on the reproductive cycle and setting up experiments on egg recognition and the stimuli releasing begging. This also became one of the classics of ethology, giving rise to a comparative study of gull behaviour in which many students participated and to a programme of experimental work, which continued under the leadership of Gerard Baerends.

In 1936 Tinbergen met Konrad Lorenz in Leiden, and he spent some of 1937 working with him near Vienna. Together they refined the methods of early ethology, Tinbergen inserting experimental probes into Lorenz's observations of hand-reared greylag geese. At this time Tinbergen and Lorenz had much in common. Both loved being in the open, observing wildlife and 'walking and wondering'. They were similarly unconventional and shared a common sense of humour. They associated easily with their students. But they also differed in critical ways. Whereas 'wondering' led Lorenz to an intuitive solution, with Tinbergen it led to patient experiments. Such differences were of great importance in the subsequent development of ethology.

Tinbergen became a senior lecturer in 1940. However, later in World War II he spent two years in a German hostage camp for refusing to co-operate with the occupation authorities in their attempts to 'nazify' Leiden University and for protesting against the removal of Jewish professors from the university.

After the war he returned to Leiden, becoming a full professor in 1947. At the suggestion of W. H. Thorpe, the Society for Experimental Biology organized a conference on physiological mechanisms of animal behaviour in 1949 in Cambridge. As a result, there was renewed contact between Tinbergen and Lorenz, and the conference provided a forum for open controversy between Lorenz, who defended the view that motor patterns were co-ordinated centrally, and (Sir) James *Gray and Hans Lissmann, of the Cambridge zoology department, who believed that peripheral reflexes were important. This led to the establishment of a biennial series of ethological conferences in which Tinbergen played a major role, and which became of enormous importance in the growth of ethology.

Tinbergen had paid a brief visit to the United States before the war, and saw that the generalizations made by comparative psychologists there were based on laboratory studies of a few species, mostly rodents. He thus conceived a desire to teach ethology in the English-speaking world, and in 1949 he resigned his professorship at

Leiden and accepted a less well paid and less prestigious lectureship at Oxford and a fellowship at Merton College (from 1950). Although the facilities that he had looked for at Oxford never fully materialized, he built up a research group that had a profound influence on the development of ethology. He was reader from 1960 to 1966 and professor in animal behaviour from 1966 to 1974, holding a fellowship at Wolfson College at the same time as his chair. He was never attracted, however, to college life.

One of Tinbergen's major contributions was to emphasize clearly the distinction between the four basic questions about behaviour—its immediate causation, development, function, and evolution, while at the same time showing how these factors are interrelated. *The Study of Instinct*, his first and perhaps most important book, appeared in 1951. It contained 127 pages on causation, but only 24 on development, 34 on function, and 26 on evolution. From then on, however, his emphasis changed to questions of function ('What is this behaviour for?') and evolution ('How did it evolve?'). In tackling these problems, Tinbergen worked primarily with gulls, and his work was especially noteworthy for his use of field experiments and detailed observation.

By the 1960s two ethologies had developed, one stemming from Lorenz, and more influential in Germany and the USA, and the other from Tinbergen, more prevalent in Britain and The Netherlands. Among the differences were Lorenz's adherence to an energy model of motivation which Tinbergen abandoned, Lorenz's more traditional approach to the nature/nurture controversy, and Tinbergen's clearer recognition of the importance of an individual selection approach to evolutionary questions. Tinbergen was an inspiring teacher. Unlike Lorenz, he was never paternalistic, but created an atmosphere, with his charm and simplicity of manner, in which his students felt that he was working with them. He was a man of boundless energy and enthusiasm and an inspiring leader, who also wrote various semi-popular books (such as *The Herring Gull's World*, 1953, and *Curious Naturalists*, 1958) and books for children, and was an expert photographer.

Tinbergen gave more and more of his time to establishing the science of ethology, writing freely in natural history journals. He took films of gull behaviour which won international prizes. He also played a part in establishing the Serengeti Research Institute in Tanzania in the mid-1960s. Later he put a lot of energy into the implications of ethology for human behaviour, and helped establish the human biology course at Oxford. He wrote on the effects of human activities on the environment, and drew lessons from animal behaviour about the incidence of human aggression. Throughout his career, his wife was a constant support and colleague. During the last years of his life they collaborated in a study of human autism, drawing lessons from animal behaviour for its treatment. They had two sons and three daughters. Small, energetic, and white-haired for the last thirty years of his life, Tinbergen always dressed in field clothes unless under strong pressure. He was an inveterate smoker until fifteen years before his death.

Tinbergen was awarded the Nobel prize in physiology or medicine (together with Lorenz and Karl von Frisch), the Swammerdam medal, and the Wilhelm Boelsche medal (all 1973). He received many other distinctions, including honorary D.Scs. from Edinburgh (1973) and Leicester (1974). He was elected a fellow of the Royal Society in 1962. He became a British subject in 1954 and died 21 December 1988 at his home, 88 Lonsdale Road, Oxford.

[R. A. Hinde in *Biographical Memoirs of Fellows of the Royal Society*, vol. xxxvi, 1990; personal knowledge.]

R. A. HINDE

TINLING, Cuthbert Collingwood ('Ted') (1910–1990), dress designer, was born 23 June 1910 in Eastbourne, Sussex, the youngest of the three sons (there were no daughters) of James Alexander Tinling, chartered accountant, and his wife, Florence Mary Elizabeth Buckland. He was christened Cuthbert after his great-grandfather, Admiral Cuthbert (first Baron) *Collingwood, but his parents changed his name to Teddy during World War I because Cuthbert was the name given to conscientious objectors in cartoons in the *Evening News*. Much later he shortened this to Ted, on the advice of his agent, when he became a popular guest on television chat shows in the United States. Because of his chronic asthma, the family moved to the French Riviera after the war, and he spent the rest of his childhood in Nice, on his own with his mother after his father had to return to England. He attended a Catholic day school.

As a schoolboy Tinling joined the Nice Tennis Club, umpiring a match for Suzanne Lenglen at the age of thirteen, and he became a devoted member of her entourage, mixing with high society on the French Riviera while still in his teens, umpiring and refereeing matches and organizing tournaments. Suzanne Lenglen, with her flowing pure silk dresses and silk bandeau around her head, became his idol and inspiration. His first tennis dress was designed for her, in 1937, for her last world tour.

In 1927 he was sent to London to study dress designing, and when he set up his own business there in 1931 many of his clients were friends he had made in the south of France. Within a year he had expanded into premises in Mayfair, and showed his first collection. He soon had a reputation in *haute couture* to rival that of (Sir) Hardy Amies and (Sir) Norman *Hartnell, and in 1938 he made fourteen wedding dresses for society weddings at St Margaret's, Westminster.

At the same time he remained involved in the world of tennis, especially at Wimbledon, where he worked from 1927 to 1949 during the two weeks of the championships as the 'call boy', responsible for escorting players from their dressing-rooms to the centre court and court no. 1 for their matches. In 1928 he was also asked to act as a liaison between the Wimbledon committee and the players, and he did this until 1949. A keen amateur player himself, he played on the amateur circuit from 1935 until 1950, captaining Sussex for many years, and he first played at Wimbledon in 1948.

During World War II Tinling served in the Intelligence Corps in Algiers and Germany, and he remained in the army until 1947. He reached the rank of lieutenant-colonel.

In 1947 he resumed his career as a couturier, and became known as a designer of tennis dresses. Tinling believed that women tennis players should wear clothes that stressed their femininity. He designed his first Wimbledon tennis dress for Joy Gannon in 1947, and became famous in 1949 when 'Gorgeous Gussy' Moran asked him to design her tennis dresses for Wimbledon, and the underwear to go with them. The lace-trimmed panties he made for her caused a sensation, and, told he had put vulgarity and sin into tennis, he was barred from working at Wimbledon for many years. But he continued to design tennis dresses for the leading women players. For ten successive years, from 1952 to 1961, he dressed the winner of the Wimbledon women's singles title, and in 1973 the five major championships in the world were won by players wearing his dresses. In 1970 he was appointed official designer to the Virginia Slims women's professional circuit, and in eight years he created more than 1,000 different dresses, embroidered with sequins, woven with silver threads, and covered with frills and bows. However, in the late 1970s the top players were attracted by large sponsorship contracts to wear sportswear separates designed by large manufacturers, and Tinling gave up designing tennis dresses. He settled in Philadelphia in 1976.

He made fourteen wedding dresses for tennis stars, including a dress for 'Little Mo' Connolly for her wedding in California in 1955, and ones for Christine Truman and Chris Evert. In June 1986, as part of the celebration of the centenary of the Wimbledon championships, the Victoria and Albert Museum put on an exhibition of Tinling's tennis creations. The exhibits included some of the coloured dresses he had designed during the war, when the all-white rule was suspended, such as Kay Stammers's pink dress of 1941. Also on display were Maria Bueno's dress with its 'Cleopatra' embroidery, Rosie Casals's black-sequined dress, and Billie Jean King's rhinestone-studded dress of 1973. In the 1980s he admired the ice dancer Jayne Torville, and always said that the movements of a good tennis player were as beautiful and graceful as those of an ice skater or ballerina.

In 1982 Tinling became assistant to the president of the International Tennis Federation in Paris, and shortly afterwards was invited to become head of the Wimbledon liaison committee once again, a job he continued to do until his death.

Very tall (6 feet 6 inches), with a shining bald head, shaved on the advice of Vidal Sassoon, Tinling wore a large diamond in one ear and several bracelets on his wrists. He was witty and outrageous, and was often compared with Oscar *Wilde and Sir Noël *Coward. Apart from tennis and fashion, his other enthusiasms included the music of Richard Wagner and tenpin bowling. Tinling died 23 May 1990 in Cambridge. He was unmarried.

[*Independent*, 24 May 1990; Teddy Tinling, *White Ladies*, 1963, and *Tinling, Sixty Years in Tennis*, 1983; Max Robertson (ed.), *The Encyclopedia of Tennis*, 1974 (article on fashion written by Tinling).]

ANNE PIMLOTT BAKER

TOPOLSKI, Feliks (1907–1989), draughtsman, painter, and stage designer, was born in Warsaw 14 August 1907, the only child of Edward Topolski, actor and manager, and his wife, Stanislawa Drutowska, who later divorced her husband and married an army officer. Topolski matriculated from Mikolaj Rey School in 1925, his artistic talent already evident and fostered by his mother. He was encouraged to develop his artistic abilities by Tadeus Pruszkowski, principal of the Warsaw Academy of Art, where Topolski studied from 1927 to 1932. A summer school at Kazimierz, over which Pruszkowski presided, was described by Topolski in his autobiography, *Fourteen Letters* (1988), as an important liberating influence, both artistically and socially. He made many friends, and began to enjoy the free love affairs with women which were a currency of his milieu, and which were woven into the pattern of his life.

In Warsaw Topolski joined the artillery reserve, in which he was commissioned as a second lieutenant. He became active in the city's artistic and literary life, besides during the early 1930s making extensive travels in Europe, beginning with a trip which included Vienna, Italy, France, and England in 1933.

In 1935 Topolski went to London with an assignment to record the jubilee of King George V. He found England enjoyably exotic, and was quickly accepted into a congenial set of talented people. An early commission was to draw the first cover of *Night and Day*, a short-lived periodical from which he gained literary friendships, including that of Graham Greene. Drawings for the *News Chronicle* formed the basis for his first English book, *The London Spectacle* (1935). His fluent graphic style was from the first equally effective in newspapers, magazines, or books; for example, George Bernard *Shaw became a firm admirer, and commissioned him to do illustrated editions of three of his plays. Shaw described him as 'an astonishing draughtsman; perhaps the greatest of all the impressionists in black and white'. He was also commissioned by Shaw to design stage sets.

The war years of 1939–45 consolidated Topolski's British reputation as an exceptionally gifted draughtsman, adept at recording history as it happened. He became an official war artist in 1940 and began by making drawings of the London blitz. In 1941 he was sent on an Arctic convoy to Russia to draw for both the Polish authorities and *Picture Post*. He subsequently worked for both the Polish and British authorities, as works in the Imperial War Museum and Warsaw testify.

Topolski published three wartime books of drawings (*Britain in Peace and War*, 1941, *Russia in War*, 1942, and *Three Continents, 1944–5*, 1946), and worked extensively for magazines in Britain and the United States. From 1944 he was officially posted variously to draw convoys, to Egypt, the Levant, East Africa, Burma, China, and Italy. After the invasion of France he followed the armies into Germany, where he was one of the witnesses of Belsen concentration camp; and, later, he attended the Nuremberg trials. He was naturalized in 1947.

Topolski had become internationally celebrated and remained so. He scored a popular success with portraits used for the British television programme *Face to Face*, published as a book in 1964. In all he produced twenty-two books. His gifts as a painter on a large scale were also recognized by commissions beginning with a mural for the Festival of Britain in 1951—'Cavalcade of the Commonwealth', later placed for ten years in the Victoria Memorial Hall, Singapore. In 1958 Philip, Duke of Edinburgh, commissioned a record of the coronation of Queen Elizabeth II for a corridor in Buckingham Palace. His culminating mural work was 'Memoir of the Century', begun in 1975, a vast panoramic interior under the railway arches of Hungerford bridge on London's South Bank, where he also had his postwar studio. A graphic published parallel was *Topolski's Chronicle* (1953–79 and 1982–9), which reproduced drawings from the artist's extensive travels throughout the world. His work was acquired by the British Museum,

Victoria and Albert Museum, Tate Gallery, and Imperial War Museum.

Topolski was small in stature with brown eyes, and a charm of manner which made him welcome at every level of society. In 1944 he married Marion (died 1985), daughter of Tom Mason Everall, businessman. They had a son and a daughter, Daniel and Teresa. Daniel became well known as the coach of the Oxford University boat crews which gained a succession of wins over Cambridge. Topolski's first marriage was dissolved in 1975, in which year he married Caryl Jane, architect, daughter of Theodore Stanley, company director. Topolski received many awards for his work, about which four television programmes were made. He was awarded a doctorate by the Jagiellonian University of Cracow in 1974, and was elected RA in 1989. He died in St Thomas's Hospital, London, from heart disease and diabetes, 24 August 1989.

[Feliks Topolski, *Fourteen Letters* (autobiography), 1988; private information.]   JOSEPH DARRACOTT

TREND, Burke Frederick St John, BARON TREND (1914–1987), civil servant, was born 2 January 1914 in Greenwich, the only child of Walter David St John Trend, journalist, and his wife, Marian Gertrude Tyers. He was educated at Whitgift School and Merton College, Oxford. He obtained first classes in both classical honour moderations (1934) and *literae humaniores* (1936).

In 1936 he passed into the Civil Service, and was appointed to the Ministry of Education. A year later he was transferred to the Treasury, where he remained, with a brief interruption, for twenty-five years. His first years at the Treasury were spent on work relating to defence. In 1939, shortly after the outbreak of war, he became assistant private secretary to the chancellor of the Exchequer, under Sir John (later first Viscount) *Simon and Sir H. Kingsley *Wood. In 1941, on promotion, he returned to dealing with the problems of defence equipment. After the war he was again appointed to the chancellor of the Exchequer's private office, serving as principal private secretary (1945–9) to Hugh (later Baron) *Dalton and later Sir Stafford *Cripps. During this time the Treasury had the tasks of returning to peacetime levels of expenditure, carrying the reorganization of the Civil Service, and handling the Labour government's economic policies of Keynesianism and nationalization.

In 1949 Trend became an under-secretary at the Treasury and assumed responsibility for the home finance division. In 1953 he moved to the central economic planning staff until his Treasury service was interrupted in 1955 for a year in the office of the lord privy seal, then R. A. *Butler (later Baron Butler of Saffron Walden), followed by three years (1956–9) as deputy secretary to the cabinet, the secretary to the cabinet then being Sir Norman *Brook (later Baron Normanbrook). Much of the day-to-day running of the affairs of the cabinet secretariat was Trend's responsibility. He returned to the Treasury in 1959 as third secretary and became second secretary a year later. On Brook's retirement at the end of 1962, he became secretary to the cabinet.

In this capacity Trend served under four prime ministers, Harold *Macmillan, Alec Douglas-Home, Harold Wilson, and Edward Heath, and proved himself a civil servant who ably gave an independent, balanced brief to his political masters regardless of their party colour. In particular he accepted responsibility for keeping them informed and advised on all nuclear matters, both civil and military, and maintained contacts on their behalf at the highest level with other governments involved. He also played a major part in organizing the Commonwealth conferences in conjunction with the cabinet secretaries of other member countries. His activities reflected Britain's position in the Commonwealth. He retired in 1973.

An interesting side to Trend's service in the Treasury is that from his early days he undertook the work of the accounting office for the secret vote. His responsibility was to secure value for money in expenditure on MI5 and MI6, but at the same time to ensure the safeguarding of these services. This experience was put to good use in 1974–5, when he carried out an official investigation into allegations that Sir Roger *Hollis had been an agent for the Soviet Union. He was unable to reach a definite decision.

In 1974 Trend became a life peer. Between 1973 and 1983 he was rector of Lincoln College, Oxford, and from 1975 to 1983 a pro-vice-chancellor of the university. He served as chairman of the trustees of the British Museum from 1979 to 1986 and was a member of the advisory council on public records (1974–82). He died holding three other prominent offices: chairman of the managing trustees of the Nuffield Foundation (from 1980), president of the Royal Commonwealth Society (from 1982), and high bailiff of Westminster Abbey and searcher of the sanctuary (from 1983), where during World War II he had been a fire-watcher.

Trend had a formidable intellect which he used to penetrate at once to the heart of any problem. At the same time he possessed a constructive and positive approach, which could set out with absolute clarity the possible alternative courses of action in any given situation. His minutes of meetings recorded the proceedings and conclusions with precision and accuracy. He never gave the least indication to those present, either by word or by facial expression, of his personal views or feelings. Tall and serious, he responded to the humour of others but seldom followed it up with his own. Everyone who dealt with him knew that in all circumstances his conduct would undeniably be correct. If to some outsiders he may have appeared somewhat strait-laced in Whitehall, at Oxford it was apparent to everyone that he was thoroughly enjoying himself. With an unchallengeable academic record from his undergraduate years he could hold his own in any assembly. At the same time he was completely relaxed in the company of young people, stimulating them with his conversation and sharing with them his views with theirs. If in Whitehall it was sometimes said that Trend tended to be academic in his approach, at Oxford he was regarded as very much a man of the world.

Trend was appointed CVO (1953), CB (1955), KCB (1962), and GCB (1968). He was sworn of the Privy Council in 1972 and became an honorary fellow of Merton College in 1964. He was given honorary degrees by Oxford (DCL, 1969), St Andrews (LL D, 1974), and Loughborough (D.Litt., 1984).

In 1949 Trend married Patricia Charlotte, daughter of the Revd Gilbert Shaw, by profession a barrister and later a priest. They had a daughter and two sons, one of whom, Michael, was elected MP for Windsor and Maidenhead at the general election of 1992. Trend died 21 July 1987 at his London home in Rochester Row, SW1.

[Private information; personal knowledge.]

EDWARD HEATH

TRETHOWAN, Sir (James) Ian (Raley) (1922–1990), journalist and broadcaster, was born 20 October 1922 in High Wycombe, the only child of Major James Jackson Raley Trethowan, MBE, a retired army officer, who combined a life in business and army welfare with writing about sport, and his wife, Winifred Timms. Trethowan followed in his father's footsteps to Christ's Hospital, where he displayed only modest academic achievement, leaving at the age of sixteen to pursue a career in journalism. A short spell as post-boy at the *Daily Sketch* led to a reporting job on the *Yorkshire Post*, before Trethowan joined the Fleet Air Arm during World War II, in 1941. After the war Trethowan rejoined the *Post* in 1946, working for its London staff, and rising rapidly to parliamentary lobby correspondent. There his meticulousness began to be widely noticed. His writing was mostly terse and to the point, and he had a good nose for what constituted a story. He also developed fine contacts within the Tory party, about which he made no secret, but which never became so blatant as to diminish Trethowan's effectiveness as a chronicler of politics across the board.

Trethowan moved to the *News Chronicle* in

1955 and from there was tempted by (Sir) Geoffrey Cox, at the fledgeling Independent Television News, to take an on-screen role (1958–63). Trethowan did not develop into a permanent newscaster, always preferring to involve himself in a little administration. He served as ITN's deputy editor, before moving on to the larger canvas of the BBC in 1963. Trethowan's main work at the BBC was again political, dealing both with Westminster direct, and with the broader world of politics through the weekly programme, *Gallery*. At the same time he was political commentator for the *Economist* (1953–8 and 1965–7) and *The Times* (1967–8).

In 1968 Baron *Hill of Luton, an old political comrade and now chairman of the BBC, needed a new managing director for BBC Radio to succeed F. G. Gillard, the veteran correspondent and administrator. Trethowan, somewhat to his surprise, was asked to apply. He was offered the job and took it—in part, he recorded, because he knew he would never be top-flight on television. 'Not a star,' (Sir) Huw *Wheldon had told him, firmly but with kindness.

Trethowan skilfully negotiated the pitfalls of radio management (1969–75). Radios 1, 2, 3, and 4 were introduced with less pain than had been anticipated. In 1976 he was switched back to television, this time as managing director, as part of a deliberate grooming for the top job. He succeeded Sir Charles *Curran as director-general in late 1977. In his own view he had had 'a lot of luck'.

In his first years at the top, he was fortunate that his chairman was Sir Michael (later Baron) *Swann, a clubbable man of clear view. In Swann's opinion, the BBC would work best if the director-general did the driving, while the chairman and his board assisted in reading the map. Although Trethowan was sometimes suspected by radical broadcasters of acting purely as the 'thirteenth governor', his own memoir, *Split Screen*, analyses in some detail a relationship of sturdy delicacy and shows why it worked well. The political world was sufficiently convinced both to renew the BBC charter, and to sustain the value of the licence fee even during difficult inflationary times. Trethowan suffered a heart attack in 1979, but recovered to continue in office until his official retirement in 1982.

Unlike most BBC directors-general, Trethowan had a full and active life beyond the BBC. He pursued his second love, the turf, as chairman of the Horserace Betting Levy Board (1982–90), took a directorship at Barclays Bank (1982–7), and eventually re-emerged in commercial television as director (1986–7), and then chairman (1987–90) of Thames TV. There controversy followed him over the 1988 programme, *Death on the Rock*, which asked hard questions about the killing of three IRA terrorists. Tretho-

wan stood by the programme and diverted much of the political animus. He again drew on that firm but unfailing courtesy, which had stood him in good stead in all his broadcasting and journalistic endeavours. He had a clear vision of the proper province of both commentators and those commentated upon, and throughout his career this enabled him to defuse potentially explosive editorial challenges. Although in appearance both unassertive and unassuming, he would stand his ground, his determination deepening with each twist and turn of external pressure.

Among his other activities, Trethowan was a trustee of Glyndebourne Arts Trust from 1982 and of the British Museum from 1984, a governor of the Ditchley Foundation from 1985, and on the board of the British Council (1980–7). The University of East Anglia gave him an honorary DCL (1979) and he was knighted in 1980.

Trethowan's life was cut short by the onset of motor neurone disease, which he bore with good grace, even in its latter wheelchair stages. In 1950 he married Patricia, daughter of Colonel John Elliott Nelson, retired army officer. They had no children. The marriage was dissolved in 1963 and in the same year he married Carolyn, daughter of Alfred Brian Challen Reynolds, retired army officer and company director. They had three daughters, and it was Trethowan's greatest consolation that he lived to see them into maturity. He died 12 December 1990 in the Cromwell Hospital, London.

[Ian Trethowan, *Split Screen: Memoirs*, 1984; personal knowledge.]   BRIAN WENHAM

TREVELYAN, Julian Otto (1910–1988), painter and printmaker, was born 20 February 1910 in Leith Hill, Surrey, the only surviving child (a first son had died at the age of two in 1909 and a daughter had died in infancy) of Robert Calverley Trevelyan, classical scholar and poet (the son of the historian Sir George Otto *Trevelyan and brother of the historian George Macaulay *Trevelyan), and his Dutch wife Elizabeth, daughter of Jan des Amorie van der Hoeven, of The Hague. He was educated at Bedales School and Trinity College, Cambridge, where he completed two years of the English tripos (obtaining a second class, division II, in part i, 1930) before leaving, without part ii of his degree, to study painting in Paris.

At Cambridge Trevelyan identified himself with the Modernist group associated with the magazine *Experiment*, which included (Sir) William *Empson, Jacob *Bronowski, Humphrey *Jennings, and Kathleen Raine. Through Jennings, he was introduced to French painting and Surrealist ideas. In Paris, after a false start at the Académie Moderne run by Fernand Léger and

Amédée Ozenfant, he enrolled at the printmaking workshop run by Stanley William *Hayter (later Atelier 17), and immersed himself in the cosmopolitan nocturnal life of Montparnasse, counting among his friends Massimo Campigli, Vieira da Silva, and Alexander Calder. His training under Hayter was technically and creatively rigorous, and he worked alongside such major contemporaries as Joan Miró, Max Ernst, Pablo Picasso, and John Buckland-Wright. His etchings of this period are wittily Surrealistic.

In 1935 Trevelyan established himself at Durham Wharf on the Thames at Hammersmith, where he was to live for the rest of his life. Here, in the mid-1930s, he made his first distinctively original works. Painted and scratched on wood and slate, these spiky linear images of whimsical buildings and transparent cities reflect an awareness of Paul Klee and Joan Miró, but their quirky invention is entirely personal, as is their dreamlike juxtaposition of image and sign. Paintings and etchings in this style were selected for the 1936 International Surrealist Exhibition at the New Burlington Galleries, London, and Trevelyan continued afterwards to take part in English Surrealist manifestations and exhibitions. His first one-man show was held at the Lefèvre Galleries in 1935. In 1937-8 he participated in Mass Observation, run by Tom *Harrisson, as a photographer, artist, and observer in Bolton and Blackpool, making *plein-air* collage landscapes of newspaper scraps, ephemera, and coloured paper, in which the fragments of the printed word relate ironically to the topographies depicted. In late 1938, inspired by the expressive authenticity of 'unprofessional painting', and excited by the infernal landscapes of the Potteries, he adopted a deliberately gauche painterly manner and a vehement colourism. This expressionist style matched his response to the vitality and violence of industrialism, and later to the fevered atmosphere of London during the blitz of 1940, the year in which he joined the Royal Engineers as a camouflage officer.

In 1943 Trevelyan was invalided out of the army on psychiatric grounds. His painting in the 1940s became more impressionistic and atmospheric, the handling lighter and less emphatically primitivist, his colours brighter and fresher. The best paintings of this period, the townscapes, riverscapes, and interiors of the late 1940s, have a newly sophisticated looseness of touch, a tonal subtlety and compositional sureness influenced by French painting, especially by Pierre Bonnard. During the 1950s he moved towards linear depiction and decorative colour, a simplification related to a renewed commitment to etching, which he taught at Chelsea School of Art from 1950 to 1960, and at the Royal College of Art from 1955 to 1963. This developed into the distinctive schematic stylization of his late manner, in which sharply delineated flat planes of colour are deployed across the canvas in jigsaw-like patterns to effect evocative distillations of mood and locale. Unpretentious and charming, this later work avoids false naïvety by disciplined design and a persistent visual wit. As a painter Trevelyan was modest in ambition and achievement, but his work was distinguished always by an authentic innocence of eye, and a spirit by turns passionate, ironic, and humorous. A brilliantly inventive etcher, his linear technique and imaginative texturing, often using found materials and objects, established him as one of the finest printmakers of his generation. He was a much loved and influential teacher.

Trevelyan was a tall, long-faced, and handsome man, whose sweetness of manner disguised a mercurial temperament. From a distinguished family he inherited a wide culture and a love of friendship; parties at Durham Wharf, especially on the day of the Oxford and Cambridge boat race, were famous. He travelled widely throughout his life, constantly recording his impressions in paint, but remained profoundly attached to his studio home by the Thames. In 1963 he suffered an unidentified viral infection of the brain, which badly affected his speech; with regret he had to give up teaching, driving, and playing the oboe. He soon returned to etching, and later to painting. He was made a senior fellow of the Royal College of Art and an honorary senior royal academician (both 1986). He had a mini-retrospective exhibition at the New Grafton Gallery in 1977 and his work is represented in the Tate Gallery and in many public collections.

In 1934 Trevelyan married Ursula Frances Elinor, potter, the daughter of Bernard Richard Meirion *Darwin, golfing journalist. Their son, Philip Erasmus, was born in 1943. This marriage ended in divorce in 1949, and in 1951 he married (Adye) Mary, painter, daughter of (Harry) Vincent Fedden, sugar broker. There were no children of the second marriage. Trevelyan died in Hammersmith 12 July 1988.

[Julian Trevelyan, *Indigo Days* (autobiography), 1957; private information; personal knowledge.]

MEL GOODING

TRINDER, Thomas Edward ('Tommy') (1909-1989), comedian, was born 24 March 1909 in Streatham, London, the eldest in the family of two sons and one daughter of Thomas Henry Trinder, tram driver and baker, and his wife, Jean Mills. Educated at Queensborough Road School and St Andrew's, Holborn, he left school early to work as an errand boy at Smithfield meat market. Giving up his job at the age of twelve he toured South Africa with a variety company, and then in the following year, 1922, he won a talent competition at Collins's Music Hall, Islington, which led to a week's engagement. He worked in a touring show, Will Murray's Casey's Court, using the name Red Nirt (his own name backwards) and played the halls for seventeen years before reaching the London Palladium in 1939 in *Band Waggon*. For the next eleven years he played there regularly, first as a supporting act in *Top of the World* (1940), with Bud *Flanagan and Chesney Allen, and *Gangway* (1941), with Ben Lyon and Bebe Daniels, and then topping the bill in *Best Bib and Tucker* (1942), *Happy and Glorious* (1944–6), which with 938 performances became the longest running of all Palladium shows, *Here, There and Everywhere* (1947), and *Starlight Rendezvous* (1950).

Trinder had a long, thin face, a jutting chin, and a wide smile; he always wore a trilby hat, even with evening dress. Soon after he arrived at the Palladium, he invested £265 a week for two weeks to advertise his chin on twenty-five strategically sited London hoardings. All but one read 'If it's laughter you're after, Trinder's the name. You lucky people!' The odd one out, opposite Aldgate station, was printed in Hebrew. With his shovel-like jaw, ready grin, quick-fire topical humour, and 'You lucky people' catch-phrase, Trinder became one of the most popular of variety entertainers.

His film career began in 1939, but it was not until his fifth film, *Sailors Three* (1940), with Claude Hulbert and Michael Wilding, that he made a mark. Of his fifteen films, *The Foreman Went to France* (1941), *The Bells Go Down* (1943), and *Champagne Charlie* (1944), in which he played Victorian music-hall star George Leybourne, are the most notable.

In 1943 he was singled out in the House of Commons for criticism for not having worked overseas for ENSA (Entertainments National Service Association), a criticism which ignored the fact that he had been entertaining troops at home since the outbreak of war. He later became the first major star to visit Italy and in 1946 took the last ENSA party to the Far East. It was Trinder who gave ENSA its soubriquet 'Every Night Something Awful'. Trinder holds a record unlikely to be beaten of playing the most West End theatres in a single night. During the London blitz, when audiences had to remain in their seats during air raids and Trinder was at the Palladium, he drove round the West End and managed to play a ten-minute spot in seventeen theatres before the all-clear sounded.

Known as the Mr Woolworth of show business, he could sometimes be earthy, though never crude, and he hated bad language. When he arrived at Scapa Flow to entertain the Royal Navy he found the padre sitting with his back to the stage watching the audience to see who laughed. He invariably worked alone without the aid of stooges, props, or even a microphone, and frequently without a script, relying on his ready wit. He was noted for his ability to deal with hecklers. When he opened his act at the Embassy Club with his usual 'Trinder's the name', a morose Orson Welles, having that day been divorced from Rita Hayworth, growled 'Well, change it', to which Trinder retorted 'Is that an offer of marriage?'

In 1955 he became the first host of *Sunday Night at the London Palladium*, one of the most successful television variety shows. He fell out with producer Val Parnell and left the show; his career, although he rarely stopped working, became a series of one-night stands, overseas tours, and pantomimes in the provinces. A firm favourite of the royal family, he appeared before the queen mother at the 1980 Royal Variety Show, in what must have been the oldest chorus line, when thirteen artists, including Arthur *Askey, Stanley *Holloway, Richard *Murdoch, Chesney Allen, and Trinder, with a combined age of 891 years, danced and sang their way through Flanagan and Allen's 'Strollin'.

A lifelong supporter of Fulham Football Club, Trinder was on the board for many years, becoming chairman in 1955, a post he held for twenty-one years despite being forced to apologize publicly for cracking jokes at his players' expense. He was appointed CBE in 1975 for his services to charity (he was thrice chief rat of the show business charity the Water Rats).

He married Gwyn ('Toni'), daughter of Major Gilbert Arthur Lancelyn Green, of the Royal Field Artillery. There was one daughter of the marriage. Trinder died 10 July 1989 in St Peter's Hospital, Chertsey.

[John Fisher, *Funny Way to Be a Hero*, 1973; *The Times*, 11 July 1989; private information; personal knowledge.]   RICHARD FAWKES

TURNBULL, Sir Alexander Cuthbert (1925–1990), obstetrician and gynaecologist, was born in Aberdeen 18 January 1925, the elder son (there were no daughters) of George Harley Turnbull, sales manager, and his wife, Anne Whyte Cuthbert. He was educated at Robert Gordon's College in Aberdeen, Merchant Taylors' School in Crosby, and Aberdeen Grammar School, where he was modern dux in 1942. He entered the University of Aberdeen in the same year to read medicine and graduated MB, Ch.B. in 1947. He then did his national service in the army, spending part of the time in India. His early general medical and specialist training took place in Aberdeen. He was awarded a Medical Research Council scholarship in 1951.

Turnbull had by then come under the influence of (Sir) Dugald *Baird, who made him his lecturer at Aberdeen in 1955. In 1957 he became senior lecturer in the University of Dundee and an honorary consultant obstetrician and gynaecologist to the Dundee Teaching Hospitals, only to return to a similar position in the University of Aberdeen in 1961. In 1966 he graduated MD with honours from the same university and gained the Thursfield award for the best thesis of the year.

Turnbull was appointed to the chair of obstetrics and gynaecology in the Welsh National School of Medicine in Cardiff in 1966. In 1973 he was invited to become Nuffield professor of obstetrics and gynaecology in the University of Oxford, to work within the new *John Radcliffe Maternity Hospital*. He was elected a fellow of Oriel College, Oxford, in the same year.

Early in his career he developed a scientific and clinical interest in the physiology and pathology of labour. During his time as senior lecturer in Aberdeen, he formed a highly productive professional association with Anne Anderson, which lasted until her death in 1983. In this synergistic scientific collaboration, it was frequently she who translated his exciting and novel ideas into successful projects. Basic observations on the mechanisms of labour were matched by important clinical studies on 'premature' (pre-term) labour, and safer pharmacological interventions to induce and stimulate labour. Turnbull developed an infusion pump designed to give sufficient oxytocin to cause the uterus to contract. The decade of the 1970s had been associated with an increasingly uncritical trend towards induction and acceleration of labour by uterine stimulants and Turnbull participated in an interview for the BBC television programme *Horizon* on the induction of labour. He was portrayed as an arch-interventionist—a gross misrepresentation of his caring and conservative nature. Deeply hurt by this, and using data collected at his instigation in Cardiff between 1964 and 1973, he undertook a critical review of his research and clinical approach, deciding that the scientific evidence indeed showed no real benefit to women or babies from induction. In the years that followed, an increasing amount of research from his team reinforced this conservative view. From 1973 to 1984 Turnbull played a major role in the influential triennial confidential enquiry into maternal mortality. He was a prolific author of original scientific papers and books.

Turnbull influenced a generation of young doctors and scientists, many of whom later held eminent positions at home and abroad; they felt great esteem and affection for him. He travelled widely and had friends in every part of the world. He became a member of the Royal College of Obstetricians and Gynaecologists in 1954, a fellow in 1966, and was vice-president from 1983 to 1986. In 1981 he was awarded the Semmelweiss medal of the Hungarian Society for Gynaecology. In 1990, not long before his untimely death, he received the Sir Eardley Holland medal of

the RCOG and the rarely conferred honorary fellowship, in recognition of his outstanding lifelong contribution to obstetrics and gynaecology. Turnbull was appointed CBE in 1982 and knighted in 1988. He was awarded an honorary D.Sc. of the University of Leicester in 1989.

Turnbull was strikingly handsome, with his aquiline nose, warm but penetrating blue eyes, and, in his later years, a profusion of white hair. His athletic build was rounded by middle age before being ravaged by his illness. Despite his talents and achievements, he had an underlying feeling of insecurity and always needed to drive himself a bit harder. As a result of not wanting to hurt anybody, he found it difficult to say 'no'. His innate drive helped greatly in his courageous ten-year fight with cancer. In 1953 he married Elizabeth Paterson Nicol ('Elsie'), daughter of Alexander Bell, farmer. Herself a doctor, she collaborated in his early research work. They had one daughter (a doctor) and one son. Turnbull died 18 August 1990 in Oxford from the late consequences of oesophageal cancer.

[Private information; personal knowledge.]

GORDON STIRRAT

TURNER, DAME Eva (1892–1990), soprano, was born 10 March 1892 in Oldham, Lancashire, the elder child and only daughter of Charles Turner, chief engineer of a cotton mill, and his wife, Elizabeth Park. She was educated at Werneth Council School until she was ten, when her father moved to Bristol to take up an appointment as manager of another mill in the southwest of England. There she heard her first opera, performed by the Royal Carl Rosa Opera Company, and so struck was she by this that she was determined to become a singer herself. Her parents were musical and gave her every encouragement, sending her for lessons to Daniel Rootham, who taught (Dame) Clara *Butt. Her studies were continued at the Royal Academy of Music in London from 1911 to 1915, during which time she was briefly betrothed. In 1915 she joined the chorus of the Royal Carl Rosa Opera Company and entered her new life with enthusiasm and with the serious determination and commitment that were to characterize her life. When not singing in the chorus, she never lost an opportunity to observe other performers from the wings, studying the action and learning the soprano repertory. Anxious for progress, she badgered the management to find her roles and she soon made her solo début as the page in *Tannhäuser*.

But she was still not satisfied and on the advice of the company's principal tenor she began to work with an Australian singer, Richard Broad, who had recently joined the management of the Carl Rosa. He had sung as a bass under Hans Richter at Covent Garden but it was as an authority on voice production that he was better known. This proved to be a most successful relationship and Broad continued as her coach, adviser, and friend until his death some twenty-five years later.

The small parts became larger and by 1920 she was assuming dramatic roles as her voice increased in power and weight. In that year the company gave a four-week season at Covent Garden, in which Eva Turner sang Santuzza (*Cavalleria Rusticana*), Musetta (*La Bohème*), Leonora (*Il Trovatore*), Butterfly (*Madame Butterfly*), Antonia (*The Tales of Hoffmann*), and Venus (*Tannhäuser*). *The Times* critic described her Leonora as promising. Another Covent Garden season followed a provincial tour in 1921. *Tosca* and *Lohengrin* were two operas added to her repertory that year. In 1922 she appeared as Eva in *The Mastersingers* with the Carl Rosa at Covent Garden and won a favourable review from *The Times*.

In 1924 the Carl Rosa was at the Scala Theatre, London, for a four weeks' season, which was to be a turning-point in her career. Amongst other roles she sang Butterfly on 3 June, a performance with which *The Times* did not find entire favour but which so impressed Ettore Panizza, Arturo Toscanini's assistant at La Scala, Milan, that he asked her to sing to the maestro. She auditioned successfully and was offered Freia and Sieglinde in the 1924–5 Scala season. Her characteristic loyalty persuaded her to tell the Scala that she was not free to accept because of her Carl Rosa contract. However, she was released from that and she spent the intervening period learning Italian and her roles in that language in preparation for her début, as Freia in *Das Rheingold*, conducted by Vittorio Gui.

Thus began the most important part of her career and a love affair with Italy, one of the outcomes of which was the Italianate colouring, with strongly enunciated consonants, that she applied to her speaking voice. She was then to sing in many Italian cities, including Brescia, where she first sang Turandot with conspicuous success. This became the role with which she was most identified, although from all accounts her portrayal of Aida was equally outstanding. She built and settled in a villa on Lake Lugano.

By now Eva Turner's international career was developing rapidly, with appearances in Europe and in North and South America. She returned to Covent Garden in 1928 in a season managed by the Covent Garden Syndicate and scored a major triumph with the press and public with Turandot. Nobody was prepared for such a magnificent performance. Nothing could then hold her back and with her glorious voice she took a leading place in the seasons at Covent Garden and abroad until the outbreak of war in 1939. Small of stature, Eva Turner had a vocal command which was astonishing, with a voice of extraordinary sumptuousness and steadiness that could project through the loudest orchestral sound without any loss of quality. She surmounted all the technical challenges of the German and Italian repertoire and left her audiences spellbound. Turner's colossal success did much to encourage British opera singers, who at that time were probably more noted for dependability than brilliance and rarely given chances to prove anything else. An English name was a handicap and Eva Turner was urged to change hers. Proud of her Lancastrian roots, she refused.

Undoubtedly the war deprived her of the final climax to her career, including the conquering of audiences at the Metropolitan in New York. After a performance of Turandot in Brescia in 1940 she returned to England, where she spent the war singing in concerts for the armed forces and the radio, and in the Proms. A staunch patriot, this was what she believed she needed to do and she declined invitations to work in America.

In the 1947 and the 1948–9 seasons at Covent Garden she joined the newly formed company for Turandot, in which once again she astonished and thrilled the public and press. Then, in 1949, she accepted an invitation to teach at the University of Oklahoma for one year and stayed for ten. After that she returned to London to teach at the Royal Academy of Music. Teaching occupied her for several more years and she passed on to many singers, established and young alike, her wealth of experience, with her inimitable generosity but also with a ferocious expectation of hard work and high standards in return. For her it was serious work which produced the results, however talented the individual. President of the Wagner Society from 1971 to 1985, she was appointed DBE in 1962. She was FRAM (1928), FRCM (1974), an honorary citizen of the state of Oklahoma (1982), and a first freeman of Oldham (1982). She was awarded an honorary D.Mus. from Manchester (1979) and Oxford (1984) and became an honorary fellow of St Hilda's College, Oxford (1984).

Well into her nineties and still immaculately groomed and handsome, she maintained her enthusiasm and capacity for work, serving on committees and lecturing endlessly to music clubs and societies. She was constantly to be seen at opera performances and concerts, travelling and coaching with an eagerness and display of energy that left many breathless. She never married, probably because she believed she could not find the time for the kind of relationship that marriage demanded. She led an intensely busy life, ably assisted by Ann Ridyard, her companion and secretary for thirty-five years, whose descent into senile dementia caused Eva Turner's last years to be burdensome. Eva Turner died 16 June 1990 in the Devonshire Hospital, Marylebone, London.

[*Record Collector*, vol. 11, no. 2, Feb./March 1957; John Steane, *The Grand Tradition*, 1974; Royal Opera House programme note by Harold Rosenthal for concert celebrating Eva Turner's ninetieth birthday, 14 March 1982; private information; personal knowledge.]

JOHN TOOLEY

TUTIN, Thomas Gaskell (1908–1987), botanist, was born 21 April 1908 in Kew, Surrey, the only son and elder child of Frank Tutin, biochemist, and his wife, Jane Ardern. He was educated at Cotham Grammar School, Bristol, and Downing College, Cambridge, where he gained a third class in part i (1929) and a second in part ii (1930) of the natural sciences tripos. As an undergraduate he was much involved with the Cambridge Natural History Society and, amongst many other activities, he participated in a botanical expedition to the Azores in 1929. After graduation, Tutin continued in Cambridge working on fossil plants from Greenland. He went on biological expeditions to southern Spain and Spanish Morocco (1931), British Guiana (1933), and Lake Titicaca (Peru/Bolivia, 1937), the last of these resulting in his important publication on the development and stability of lake plant communities ('The Hydrosere and Current Concepts of the Climax', *Journal of Ecology*, vol. xxix, 1941).

On his return from Peru, in 1938, Tutin held a part-time post as a demonstrator at King's College, London, before, in 1939, accepting an assistant lectureship in the University of Manchester. There, in addition to teaching and nocturnal fire-watching duties during World War II, he further developed his interests in lake algae begun during the Titicaca expedition. This led to frequent visits to the research station at Wray Castle on Lake Windermere, where he met his future wife. In 1942 Tutin joined the geographical section of the Admiralty's naval intelligence division in Cambridge, which was producing a new series of geographical handbooks for wartime use. In 1944 he was appointed lecturer in charge of the department of botany at Leicester University College, becoming the first professor of botany when university status was granted by royal charter in 1947. For the next twenty years he carried out the manifold duties of his post, conceived and developed the university botanic garden, and built up one of the more important university herbaria of flowering plants in the kingdom. In 1967 Tutin became the first occupant of the new chair of plant taxonomy in Leicester, from which he retired in 1973 to be awarded the titles of professor emeritus and university research fellow.

Shortly after World War II Tutin took afternoon tea with (Sir) Arthur G. *Tansley, the doyen of British ecology, who suggested that a modern account of the flowering plants and ferns of Britain was urgently needed. With characteristic verve, Tutin, together with A. R. *Clapham and E. F. *Warburg, wrote *Flora of the British Isles* (1952, 3rd edn. 1987). At the eighth International Botanical Congress in Paris (1954), participants drew attention to the need for an overall treatment of the plants of Europe. Tutin, again, gathered together a group of friends who galvanized the European botanical community into producing the first comprehensive account of the higher plants of Europe. *Flora Europaea* was published in five volumes between 1964 and 1980.

Tutin wrote over sixty scientific papers and took a leading part in writing thirteen books on the plants of Britain and the rest of Europe. In 1977 he was awarded the gold medal by the Linnean Society of London, whilst in 1982 he was elected a fellow of the Royal Society for his considerable contributions to the furtherance of plant taxonomy. The University of Dublin awarded him an honorary Sc.D. in 1979.

Tutin was of medium height, with a robust frame and a mop of grey-white hair. He enjoyed working in his garden, his glass of beer, Mozart, and, occasionally, playing his flute; always, however, there was his intellectual backbone of steel. In 1942 he married a palaeoecologist, Winifred Anne, daughter of Albert Roger Pennington, Post Office supervisor; they had a son and three daughters. She became a fellow of the Royal Society in 1979. Tutin died in Leicester 7 October 1987.

[A. R. Clapham in H. E. Street, *Essays in Plant Taxonomy*, 1978, pp. xi–xviii; A. D. Bradshaw in *Biographical Memoirs of Fellows of the Royal Society*, vol. xxxviii, 1992; private information; personal knowledge.]

D. M. MOORE

U

URQUHART, Robert Elliott (1901–1988), major-general, was born in Shepperton on Thames 28 November 1901, the eldest in the family of three sons and one daughter of Alexander Urquhart, MD, physician, and his wife, Isabel Gillespie. After attending St Paul's School and the Royal Military College, Sandhurst, he was commissioned as a second lieutenant in the Highland Light Infantry in 1920. Two years at the Staff College, Camberley (1936–7), were followed by staff appointments in India—staff captain (1938), deputy adjutant and quartermaster-general at army headquarters (1939–40), and deputy assistant adjutant-general and AA&QMG (3rd division, 1940–1), until he was given command of the 2nd battalion of the Duke of Cornwall's Light Infantry in 1941. In 1942 he became general staff officer grade 1 of the 51st Highland division and went through the campaign in North Africa which destroyed the Afrika Korps. He was given command of 231st brigade in Malta in 1943, and its distinguished performance in Sicily and Italy brought him appointment to the DSO.

He was then brigadier general staff of XII Corps and was chosen in 1944 for command of the 1st Airborne division. He led it in Operation Market Garden, which was designed to cross three main river obstacles in Holland in September 1944 and to join up with XXX Corps arriving from the south, to swing through into the German industrial heartland. Since Urquhart was over six feet tall, of robust build, and possibly at forty-two rather too old for parachuting, he moved into battle by glider. He faced immediate difficulties. British troops arrived in a piecemeal fashion over three days and had to move five miles to their allotted positions around Arnhem. Their route was blocked by German armour reorganizing after Normandy, and, to compound the difficulties, the Germans captured the plans of the entire operation on the body of an American soldier shot down in a glider. Communications were rarely satisfactory and the weather was atrocious, making air support and replenishment difficult. The worst stroke of ill luck was Urquhart's enforced absence (he was obliged to take refuge in the attic of a house surrounded by German troops) from his headquarters for thirty-six hours soon after his arrival, when decisive command was imperative and was lacking. Urquhart made mistakes: the high ground at Wester Bouwing, for example, dominating the divisional bridgehead, and the heavy ferry at Heveadorp were never secured, but he fought a great battle. The high morale of the troops under his command reflected his own, but the battle of Arnhem was a defeat for the British and the advance of XXX Corps was delayed. The remnants of Urquhart's division, withdrawn on 25 September 1944 across the Lower Rhine, numbered some 2,600 men of the 10,000 he had brought in.

Urquhart, appointed CB after Arnhem (1944), was next used to command an *ad hoc* airborne force, styled 1st Airborne division, which was sent to Norway to rescue King Haakon, but his division was never reconstituted and was disbanded in November 1945. He became a colonel in 1945 and major-general in 1946. He was awarded the Netherlands Bronze Lion (1944) and Norwegian Order of St Olaf (1945).

Urquhart's career thereafter puzzled and disappointed many who knew his qualities. For fourteen months while the Territorial Army was being reorganized he was its director-general (1945–6). He was general officer commanding 16th Airborne division, Territorial Army (1947–8), and commander, Lowland District (1948–50). In 1950 he was given command of 17th Gurkha division in Malaya and in the same year became general officer commanding Malaya. He moved to Austria in 1952 for three years as GOC-in-C British troops, in an agreeable if uninspiring assignment, which was his last in the service. From 1954 he was colonel of his regiment, the Highland Light Infantry, but when the Army Council decreed its amalgamation with the Royal Scots Fusiliers in 1957 he became embroiled in a disagreement, which concerned style, title, and above all dress. Would the new regiment be in kilt or trews? The two colonels negotiated an agreement, with the lord lyon's support, that the kilt should be worn with the tartan dress Erskine. The War Office insisted on trews and both colonels had to go (1958).

After Urquhart's retirement from the army in December 1955 he lived for some years at Drymen in Stirlingshire and thereafter at Bigram, Port of Menteith, nearby. In 1957 he joined the Davy & United Engineering Co., where his sound judgement and administrative experience found useful scope, first as personnel manager and then as director, in an industrial environment whose technical aspects were not perhaps among his deepest interests. He moved into complete retirement in 1970.

In 1939 Urquhart, always known as 'Roy', married Pamela, daughter of Brigadier William Edmund Hunt Condon, of the Indian Army. They had one son and three daughters. Urquhart died 13 December 1988 at his home in Port of Menteith.

[R. E. Urquhart, *Arnhem*, 1958; Sir John Hackett, *I Was a Stranger*, 1977; private information; personal knowledge.]   JOHN HACKETT

UTLEY, THOMAS EDWIN ('PETER') (1921–1988), political philosopher and journalist, was born 1 February 1921 in Hawarden, Flint, the second of five children (two sons, two daughters, and one deceased in infancy) of Thomas Cooper, chemist, of West Derby, Liverpool, and his wife, Emily Utley. In 1931 he was adopted by his maternal aunt, Anne Utley, by whose surname he was thenceforward known. He was born blind in one eye owing to infantile glaucoma and lost the sight of the other eye at the age of nine, but, with the help of a series of amanuenses, courageous determination, and a prodigious memory, offset this handicap almost completely in adult life. Educated privately, Utley took first-class honours in both parts i (1941) and ii (1942) of the history tripos at Corpus Christi College, Cambridge.

Utley joined the Royal Institute of International Affairs (Chatham House) in 1942, as secretary to the Anglo-French relations postwar reconstruction group, and worked there until 1944, when he became a temporary foreign leader writer for one year. From 1945 to 1947 he was foreign leader writer at the *Sunday Times*. He spent a year at the *Observer* in 1947–8, and then rejoined *The Times* as a leader writer. He stayed there for six years, becoming associate editor of the *Spectator* in 1954–5. In 1955 he began life as a freelance journalist and broadcaster, until in 1964 he joined the *Daily Telegraph* as a leader writer. He was that newspaper's chief assistant editor in 1986–7. From 1987 till his death a year later he was obituaries editor and a columnist at *The Times*.

His frequently signed articles on political subjects gained for him a widespread reputation as a political philosopher, and during his later years he was regarded as its most articulate and reflective exponent by that wing of the Conservative party which designated itself distinctively as high Tory. The party in general during the last twenty years of his life was influenced more than it might have cared to admit by the views expressed in Utley's leading and other articles in the *Daily Telegraph*.

Never inclined to inhabit an ivory tower, Utley served as chairman of the Paddington Conservative Association in 1977–9 (president, 1979–80) and as consultant director (1980–8) of the research department of Conservative Central Office; but his only venture into practical politics, when he contested Antrim North at the general election of February 1974 against the sitting Democratic Unionist member, Ian Paisley, proved abortive. Northern Ireland was one of the many subjects to which he brought his ability to provide policy with a well-developed structure of logically sustainable argument; but this quality was most practically effective during the premiership (1979–90) of Margaret (later Baroness) Thatcher, who held him in high regard. In some degree he paved the way intellectually for the changes in the direction of Conservative policy which she initiated and implemented. He also had an unswerving religious belief, and regretted changes to the Church of England which would damage its careful compromises.

A collection of Utley's signed publications appeared after his death under the title *A Tory Seer* (ed. Charles Moore and Simon Heffer, 1989). His own books included *Modern Political Thought* (1952), *Not Guilty: the Conservative Reply* (1957), *Occasion for Ombudsman* (1961), *Your Money and Your Life* (1964), *Enoch Powell: the Man and his Thinking* (1968), and *Lessons of Ulster* (1975). His influence was magnified by the spellbinding effect which his fluent and incisive discourse produced, especially upon young hearers. It was not without significance that the group of younger officials who sat at his feet at the Conservative research department became known as the 'Utley play school'.

Utley was of striking, if frail, appearance; and those introduced to him sensed no disposition on his part to conceal the severity of the disability under which he laboured. He wore a black patch over his right eye. An inveterate smoker, unable to see where he flicked his ash, he caused Mrs Thatcher to bob up and down from her chair to move the ashtray in order to preserve the carpets.

He married in 1951 Brigid Viola Mary, younger daughter of Dermot Michael Macgregor *Morrah, journalist, historian, and Arundel herald extraordinary. There were two sons and two daughters of the marriage. Utley was overtaken by a cancer-induced stroke while working at his home, and died the following evening at the Cromwell Hospital, London SW7, 21 June 1988.

[Private information; personal knowledge.]

J. ENOCH POWELL

V

VAN DAMM, Sheila (1922–1987), car rally driver and director of the Windmill theatre, London, was born 17 January 1922 in Gloucester Terrace, west London, the youngest of three daughters (there were no sons) of Vivian Van Damm and his wife, Natalie Lyons. Although her father had sponsored motor-cycle speedway events in the 1920s, before inheriting the Windmill theatre and initiating its format of non-stop revues, Sheila's upbringing in an all-girl Jewish family generated no interest in motoring beyond her training as a Women's Auxiliary Air Force driver. She subsequently trained privately as a pilot and joined the Royal Air Force Volunteer Reserve after World War II.

As a promotional stunt for the Windmill theatre, Sheila Van Damm was persuaded in November 1950 to enter her first motor sporting event, the MCC–*Daily Express* Car Rally, driving a factory-prepared Sunbeam Talbot, which her father had persuaded the Rootes Group to enter carrying the words 'Windmill Girl' on the side of the car. Navigated by her sister Nona, she claimed third place in the ladies' section—a performance which so impressed the Rootes team manager Norman Garrard that he invited her to join Nancy Mitchell and 'Bill' Wisdom to form an all-women crew of a Hillman Minx in the 1951 Monte Carlo Rally. She claimed further success in the 1951 RAC Rally, when she won the ladies' prize for closed cars under 1,500 cc at the wheel of her own Hillman Minx. This was the only occasion on which she competed as a private entrant. Subsequently, she would drive factory cars entered by the Rootes Group.

Her first major success was in the 1952 Motor Cycling Club Rally, when she won the ladies' prize in a Sunbeam Talbot. Despite disappointment in the 1953 Monte Carlo Rally, when a series of punctures forced her out of contention, she soon afterwards entered the record books, outpacing her more illustrious team-mate Stirling Moss to set a class record for 2–3-litre cars, driving the prototype Sunbeam Alpine sports car at an average of 120.135 m.p.h. at Jabbeke in Belgium.

Described in a contemporary report as 'a fresh faced woman, possessed of an infectious sense of fun', Sheila Van Damm had an ebullient and outgoing personality which masked a fearsomely competitive and determined approach to her sport. The 1953 Alpine Rally, one of Europe's toughest events, saw her, co-driven by Anne Hall, not only win the Coupe des Dames, but also one of the coveted Coupes des Alpes, for finishing the event without gaining penalty marks for lateness.

Van Damm competed in the Great American Mountain Rally before claiming, with Anne Hall, another Coupe des Dames in the 1954 Tulip Rally of Holland, a performance that also saw her winning outright the ten-lap race around the Zandvoort circuit. Winning a further ladies' award in the 1954 Viking Rally in Norway successfully clinched the Ladies' European championship for Van Damm and Hall, a feat that they were set to repeat again in 1955, after starting the season in fine style by gaining a Coupe des Dames after five years of trying, on the Monte Carlo Rally.

Despite covering over 14,000 miles a year on rallies, Sheila Van Damm still managed to combine motor sport with helping her father run the Windmill theatre. However, in October 1955 she asked Sir William (later first Baron) *Rootes to release her to devote her efforts more fully to the theatre. Her final rally for the Rootes team was the 1956 Monte Carlo, in which she overcame myriad problems to finish, but without award-winning success. She was also invited to partner Le Mans driver Peter Harper at the wheel of a Sunbeam Rapier in the 1956 Mille Miglia road race. Despite the severity of the event, she maintained intact her record of finishing every event which she started in her five-year career. Averaging 66.37 m.p.h., she and Harper won their class.

Van Damm published her autobiography, *No Excuses*, in 1957. In 1958 she was appointed the first honorary colonel of the Warwickshire and Worcestershire battalion of the Women's Royal Army Corps (Territorial Army). She maintained her contacts with the motoring world as president of the Doghouse Club for motor-racing wives and ladies and later as president of the Sunbeam Talbot Owners' Club. Her first love, however, remained the Windmill theatre. She continued its wartime reputation as 'the theatre that never closed' and its revue format, supporting young comedians including Peter *Sellers,

Tony *Hancock, (Sir) Harry Secombe, and Bruce Forsyth. She inherited the Windmill from her father on his death in 1960 and energetically presided over the theatre for a further four years, before relinquishing the battle against the advancing tide of strip shows and permissive cinemas in the Soho area, which forced it to close in 1964.

Sheila Van Damm was well built, with dark hair and a round face. She never married and in later life moved to West Chiltington in rural Sussex, where with her sister Nona she enjoyed running a small farm and stables, in addition to helping the handicapped as a fund-raiser for the International Spinal Research Trust. She died of cancer at the London Clinic 23 August 1987 and was subsequently commemorated by a memorial service at the west London synagogue.

[Sheila Van Damm, *No Excuses* (autobiography), 1957; *The Times*, 25 August 1987; *Classic & Sportscar Magazine*, November 1987; private information.]

STEPHEN SLATER

VAUGHAN-THOMAS, (Lewis John) Wynford (1908–1987), author and broadcaster, was born 15 August 1908 in Swansea, the second of three sons (there were no daughters) of Dr David Vaughan Thomas, professor of music, and his wife, Morfydd Lewis. He attended Swansea Grammar School, where he just overlapped with Dylan *Thomas, the poet, of whom he became a close friend. He won a history exhibition to Exeter College, Oxford, and obtained a second class in modern history in 1930.

Having graduated at the depths of the depression Vaughan-Thomas (he had added Vaughan to his name) made a precarious living by lecturing. In 1933 he became keeper of manuscripts and records at the National Library of Wales and in 1934 area officer of the south Wales council of social services. In 1937 he joined the outside broadcasts department of the BBC's office at Cardiff, in order to be close to the girl he was to marry ten years later. Outside broadcasts were then the only BBC programmes where words spoken were not read from a script. The challenging task of an outside broadcast commentator was to convert an event, as it unfolded, into vivid words and structured sentences which immediately conveyed the scene visually to audiences who could only use their ears.

Vaughan-Thomas was a dark-haired, somewhat chubby man of great vitality. His natural effervescence, his Celtic eloquence, his humour, and his well-stocked mind soon brought him to the fore as a commentator on major occasions in both English and Welsh. He gave the Welsh commentary on the coronation of King George VI. On the outbreak of war he transferred to the London outside broadcasts department as a home front reporter and in 1942, after covering the blitz, he became a war correspondent. He was the first BBC reporter to fly in a Lancaster bomber on a night raid on Berlin (1943). The bomb run which he brilliantly described, as the aircraft was caught by the German searchlights and dodged the flak, gave listeners a vivid picture of the gruelling perils the RAF crews endured.

Later he recorded memorable dispatches on the Anzio beachhead and covered the liberation of Rome. He also 'liberated' the vineyards of Burgundy, remarking typically, 'We had three marvellous days in a cellar and I emerged with the Croix de Guerre' (1945). The closing stages of the war found him in Hamburg, broadcasting from the studio which William *Joyce, Lord Haw-Haw, had been using only days before. He visited the Belsen concentration camp shortly after it was opened and was outraged by the assault on human dignity that he found there.

For the next three decades Vaughan-Thomas was a leading commentator on state occasions, most notably the wedding of Princess Elizabeth to the duke of Edinburgh. He covered the granting of independence to India and many similar celebrations as former colonial territories hauled down the Union Jack. He went on overseas tours with the royal family. He took the popularity of his broadcasts in his stride. In his television commentary at the memorial service in Westminster Abbey for Richard *Dimbleby he said: 'Ours is a transient art, our words and pictures make a powerful immediate impact, and then fade as if they never had been.'

He was happier as a performer on radio than on television, but in 1967 he became a leading member of the group headed by the fifth Baron *Harlech, which was unexpectedly awarded the franchise for the commercial television channel serving Wales and the west of England. Vaughan-Thomas became the first director of programmes for Harlech Television (HTV) in Cardiff and three years later was promoted to be executive director of HTV. His return to Wales brought him into active participation in the affairs of the principality. He was a director of the Welsh National Opera, chairman of the Council for the Preservation of Rural Wales, and an honorary druid (1974). He was also a governor of the British Film Institute (1977–80).

He wrote a number of books, especially about the countryside. He continued to broadcast radio talks about the changing seasons and made regular forays to London where he would regale his friends with scatological limericks involving complicated Welsh place-names, composed by himself. He had an infectious good humour.

Vaughan-Thomas became OBE in 1974, CBE in 1986, and an honorary MA of the Open University in 1982. In 1946 he married Charlotte, daughter of John Rowlands, civil servant.

There was one son of the marriage, who became a film director. Vaughan-Thomas died in Fishguard 4 February 1987.

[W. Vaughan-Thomas, *Trust to Talk* (autobiography), 1980; Leonard Miall (ed.), *Richard Dimbleby, Broadcaster*, 1966; *The Times*, 5 February 1987; *Independent*, 6 February 1987; Vaughan-Thomas papers in National Library of Wales; private information; personal knowledge.]   LEONARD MIALL

VERNON, Philip Ewart (1905–1987), professor of educational psychology, was born 6 June 1905 in Oxford, the second of three children and elder son of Horace Middleton Vernon, physiologist and fellow of Magdalen College, Oxford, and his wife, Katherine Dorothea, daughter of the Revd William Ewart, of Bishop Cannings, Wiltshire. He was educated at the Dragon School in Oxford, Oundle, and St John's College, Cambridge, where he graduated with first-class honours in physics, chemistry, and physiology in 1926 (natural sciences tripos, part i) and in 1927 with a first in psychology (moral sciences tripos, part ii). He then completed a Ph.D. on the psychology of musical appreciation. Vernon was a good amateur musician, possessing perfect pitch and able to play the piano, oboe, organ, and horn.

While a research student at St John's College in 1927, he won a Rockefeller fellowship for study in America. In 1929 he worked at Yale on personality assessment and spent a year at Harvard with Gordon Allport. From 1931 to 1933 he was a research and teaching fellow at St John's, which he left to work as a child psychologist at the Maudsley Hospital, London. There he gained important practical experience, which infused his work. In 1935 he was appointed head of the department of psychology in the Jordanhill Training Centre, Glasgow, which trained teachers. In 1938 he became head of Glasgow University's department of psychology. He remained there until 1947, working also at the War Office and Admiralty on personnel selection. In 1949 he was appointed to the professorship of educational psychology in the Institute of Education, University of London. He retired from that post in 1968 to take up a professorship of educational psychology in the University of Calgary, Alberta, Canada, from which he retired officially in 1975.

Vernon was an outstanding educational psychologist, who specialized in psychometrics, the measurement of human abilities and personality. His work was notable for his exceptional ability to synthesize in a balanced and fair-minded manner large quantities of apparently disparate findings. In addition, the clarity of his writing enabled generations of students, both in educa-

tion and psychology, to understand the statistical problems and complexities which render mental measurement such a difficult subject for many teachers.

In the field of human abilities Vernon synthesized two apparently opposing views, those of the British psychologists, who stressed the importance of a single general factor of ability, and the Americans, who thought that there were a number of separate human abilities. He showed that a hierarchical ordering of abilities with a broad general reasoning factor and important group factors such as verbal and spatial ability would fit the results. He also attempted to elucidate the environmental and genetic factors underlying general intelligence and his argument that there was a considerable genetic determination is generally accepted in the light of more recent data.

Unlike many psychometrists, Vernon believed that psychological findings should be applied to real-life situations. His writing was aimed at teachers and educationists in the hope that high standards of measurement would be employed in education—always, it should be noted, for the good of the children. During World War II his work for the War Office on officer selection hugely improved selection procedures. In 1949 he published, with J. B. Parry, *Personnel Selection in the British Forces*. Among his other books were *The Measurement of Abilities* (1940), *Personality Tests and Assessments* (1953), *Intelligence and Cultural Environment* (1969), and *Intelligence: Heredity and Environment* (1979).

Vernon was awarded the D.Sc. of the University of London and was a fellow of the American Psychological Association, life fellow of the Canadian Psychological Association, and honorary fellow of the British Psychological Society, of which he was the president in 1954–5. In 1980 he received an honorary LL D from the University of Calgary.

Vernon was a shy and highly introverted person who rarely seemed to relax. He was a tall man with an impressive demeanour and an almost military bearing. Like his books he appeared to be supremely rational, although he was human enough not to abandon smoking despite the respiratory problems which first led him to Calgary. His choice of psychology may well have been influenced by his father, who abandoned his fellowship at Oxford to alleviate the conditions of factory workers and who effectively became an industrial psychologist. His older sister, Magdalen Vernon, also became a professor of psychology, at Reading University.

In 1938 he married a schoolteacher, Annie Craig, daughter of Robert Gray, solicitor. In 1946 she met an early death through ill health and in 1947 he married Dorothy Anne Fairley, an educational psychologist and daughter of William Alexander Lawson, a civil and marine engineer. They had one child, Philip Anthony, a specialist in human intelligence. Vernon died of cancer in Calgary, Alberta, 28 July 1987.

[Obituary in *Bulletin of the British Psychological Society*, vol. xl, 1987; personal knowledge.] PAUL KLINE

W

WALL, Max (1908–1990), comic entertainer and actor, was born Maxwell George Lorimer 12 March 1908 at 37 Glenshaw Mansions, Brixton Road, Brixton, London, the second of the three children, all sons, of John Gillespie Lorimer, music-hall artiste, formerly of Forres, Scotland, and his wife Maud Clara, dancer and singer, the daughter of William and Maud Mitchison of Newcastle upon Tyne, both music-hall entertainers. He had sporadic schooling of a disjointed kind, being brought up in the music-hall theatre by his parents, who were known as Jack Lorimer and Stella Stahl. He was first taken on stage, in a kilt, at the age of two. Later he changed his name to Max Wall by deed poll.

After the break up of his parents' marriage and the death of his father, Max Wall began his long show-business career. At the age of fourteen he made his stage début in *Mother Goose* (1922), and, much encouraged by his stepfather, Harry Wallace—from whom he took his stage surname—he soon became a fully fledged professional entertainer, concentrating on eccentric dance routines and funny walks. He made his first London appearance in 1925 at the London Lyceum in *The London Revue*. Thereafter he appeared in several musical comedies and revues, including (Sir) C. B. *Cochran's *One Dam Thing After Another* (1927), and he appeared in the 1930 and 1950 Royal Variety performances. He now established himself as a prominent music-hall artiste, variously billed as 'the boy with the obedient feet' or 'Max Wall and his independent legs'. He served in the Royal Air Force from 1941 to 1943, when he was invalided out on account of 'anxiety neurosis', and returned to the musical stage.

With his inventive patter, he also enjoyed radio success, notably in *Hoopla!* (1944), *Our Shed* (in which he popularized the character of Humphrey, 1946), and *Petticoat Lane* (1949). He next had a major success as Hines in the musical *The Pajama Game* (1955), and soon starred in his first television series, *The Max Wall Show* (1956). He had also perfected his role as Professor Wallofski, a weird spidery figure of a musical clown, clad in black tights, straggling wig, a short dishevelled jacket, and monstrously huge boots. His idols were the clown Grock and Groucho Marx.

By now the old variety theatre was in decline, and, with domestic problems also taking some toll, Max Wall had a lean period, during which he mainly played dates in northern clubland. In 1966 his mordant style found fresh opportunites on the legitimate stage, first as Père Ubu in Ian Cuthbertson's adaptation of *Ubu Roi* (1966), and then, *inter alia*, in Arnold Wesker's *The Old Ones* (1972), as Archie Rice in John Osborne's *The Entertainer* (1974), and in Samuel Beckett's *Krapp's Last Tape* (1975) and *Waiting for Godot* (1980). He also appeared, in 1973, in *Cockie!*, a musical version of C. B. Cochran's life, and the *International Herald Tribune* said he was 'quite simply, the funniest comedian in the world'. He acted in several films, for instance as Flintwich in *Little Dorrit* (1987).

In 1974 he first produced what was to become a famous one-man show with songs, *Aspects of Max Wall*. In his later years he became something of a cult entertainer and in 1975 published his autobiography, *The Fool on the Hill*. He was a fluent mime, hilarious and eccentric dancer, competent musician, and acidic stand-up comedian. His stage persona had an air of melancholy, even of cynicism, and his countenance was clown-like, with glaring eyes, a prominent nose, and leering mouth.

Following an unstable upbringing, he married, in 1942, Marion Ethel ('Pola') Pollachek, dancer, the divorced wife of Thomas Patrick Charles and daughter of Alexander Pollachek, mechanical engineer, who ran a sponge rubber business in Islington. They had four sons and one daughter. The marriage was dissolved, with colourful attendant publicity, in 1956, and Wall became estranged from his family. In the same year he married a beauty queen, Jennifer Chimes, of north Staffordshire, daughter of John William Schumacher, master plumber. That marriage was dissolved in 1969, and he had a third, and extremely brief, third marriage, to Christine Clements, in 1970, which was dissolved in 1972.

Max Wall rarely sought the camaraderie of show business in his later years, and, despite considerable wealth, lived almost as a recluse in a bedsitting room in south London. He died in the Westminster Hospital, London, 22 May 1990, having fractured his skull in a fall outside a London restaurant.

[Max Wall, *The Fool on the Hill* (autobiography), 1975; *The Times*, *Guardian*, and *Independent*, 23 May 1990; Theatre Museum, London; private information.]

ERIC MIDWINTER

WARNER, Reginald Ernest ('Rex') (1905–1986), novelist, classicist, and translator, was born 9 March 1905 in Amberley, Gloucestershire, the only child of the Revd Frederic Ernest Warner, vicar ('of the modernist persuasion') of Amberley, and his schoolteacher wife Kathleen, daughter of Arthur Aston Luce, philosopher. He was educated first at St George's School, Harpenden, and then at Wadham College, Oxford, which he entered with an open scholarship in classics in 1923, in spite of having been, according to his tutor, (Sir) Maurice *Bowra, ill taught at school, so that he 'found in Greek and Latin all the charms of novelty'. No doubt better taught at Wadham, he took a first class in classical honour moderations in 1925, but suffered a nervous breakdown in the following year and, after leaving Oxford for a time, returned to take a third class in English in 1928.

Among his Oxford contemporaries and friends were the poets W. H. *Auden and (Sir) Stephen Spender, and particularly Cecil *Day-Lewis, who was at the same college and willing to share in some degree his athletic as well as his literary enthusiasms. Warner—tall, strongly built, and vigorous—captained a Wadham rugby team of which Day-Lewis was a member, and always retained his interest in and taste for energetic sporting pursuits. Day-Lewis, in his autobiography *The Buried Day* (1960), recalls his friend's 'Homeric boisterousness', which did not fade with the passing years.

Warner's entry upon the literary scene was not immediate. On leaving Oxford he took teaching appointments in various schools, including at one stage, in 1933, a post in Egypt. His début, when it came in 1937, was auspicious. His *Poems*, published in that year, made no great mark, and in later years verse was only a small part of his prolific output. But it was also in 1937 that there appeared his novel *The Wild Goose Chase*, written mainly in Egypt, and this strikingly original work made an immediate impression. His tale of three brothers and their quest in an unnamed country for the wild goose, symbol of hope and personal regeneration, was rightly seen as akin to the work of Franz Kafka; but it drew also on elements of classical mythology, and even of fairy tale, in a manner genuinely new in English fiction. *The Professor* (1938) was a very different work, a touching and almost purely naturalistic apology for traditional liberalism confronted, disastrously, with totalitarian amoralism. In *The*

Aerodrome (1941) he reverted in part to a non-realistic, expressionist technique. Generally regarded as his best novel, this deeply gloomy work also sees human values collapsing before a rising tide of nihilistic materialism. Warner had never shared the Marxist enthusiasms of his student contemporaries, and saw communist dictatorship as scarcely preferable to the fascist variety. His own position is vigorously stated in his book of essays, *The Cult of Power* (1946).

After a brief spell of service with the Allied Control Commission in Berlin Warner became director (1945–7) of the British Institute in Athens. Later he held academic appointments in America, chairs at Bowdoin College in 1962–3 and at the University of Connecticut from 1964 to 1974. He was awarded the Greek Royal Order of the Phoenix (1963), an honorary D.Litt. of Rider College (1968), and an honorary fellowship of his Oxford college, Wadham (1973).

From 1945 his output of fiction, criticism, translations, and particularly retellings of classical legend and history, was unceasing—some thirty publications in as many years. But, after his rather slight novel *Escapade* (1953), it mostly took the form of what he himself called 'uncreative writing'—writing based rather on classical and historical scholarship than on imaginative invention. The quality of the work, however, was unfailingly high. *Imperial Caesar* (1960) won the Tait memorial prize, and special mention should be made of his version of the *Confessions* of St Augustine (1963), and of his translations of Aeschylus, Euripides, Thucydides, and Plutarch.

He was married three times, in unusual circumstances. In 1929 he married Frances Chamier, daughter of Frank Grove, civil engineer, who was much employed, before World War I, in railway construction in China. They had two sons and a daughter. This marriage was dissolved in 1949 and in the same year he married Barbara Judith, divorced wife of the third Baron *Rothschild and daughter of St John Hutchinson, barrister and recorder of Hastings; they had a daughter. The marriage was dissolved in 1962 and in 1966 he remarried Frances Chamier Warner, his former wife. He died at Anchor House, St Leonard's Lane, Wallingford, 24 June 1986.

[Sir Maurice Bowra, *Memories*, 1966; Cecil Day-Lewis, *The Buried Day*, 1960; personal knowledge.]

G. J. WARNOCK

WATES, SIR Ronald Wallace (1907–1986), builder and benefactor, was born in Mitcham 4 June 1907, the second child in the family of three sons and one daughter of Edward Wates, builder, and his wife, Sarah Holmes. He was educated at Emanuel School, Wandsworth, to which he remained affectionately loyal, becoming a governor and generous benefactor. Leaving school at sixteen, he worked in an estate agency while qualifying as a surveyor in 1928 (later FRICS) before joining the family building firm, of which he became a director in 1931. Founded jointly by Wates's father, Edward, early in the twentieth century, by the 1920s the firm was well placed to take advantage of the suburban growth in south London between the wars. A good range of well-built houses was offered, and output rose to 2,000 a year.

Edward Wates's three sons were responsible for the business's expanding to become one of the largest family-owned firms in the country. The eldest, Norman, was undoubtedly the dominant force, but Ronald's sound financial sense, feel for property, and organizing ability played an important part. The youngest, Allan, was largely responsible for a skilled and contented workforce. Tight family control and a united external front were maintained.

During World War II Wates carried out much high priority work and a significant development in the firm was the successful fulfilment of a major wartime contract for sections of Mulberry harbour, made for the 1944 Normandy landings. In the postwar years the firm's reputation grew as its activities widened, extending to contract housing, tower blocks, City redevelopment, and other large-scale construction projects. Wates's contribution lay in his keen eye for a valuable site and, increasingly, his City contacts. In 1969 Wates unexpectedly took over as chairman when his brother Norman died suddenly. It was not an easy time. In a family firm, there was little career structure; the next generation, with new ideas, was waiting in the wings, but not yet deemed ready. Subordinating his other interests, Wates held the fort solidly until 1973, when Norman's eldest son Neil *Wates took over as chairman and he became president.

Wates's influence and interests had been growing steadily. A lifelong Conservative, he was a member of Wandsworth borough council (1937–46) and London county council (1949–52). He was made a freeman of the City of London in 1945 and a JP for inner London in 1947. He acquired the art of public speaking and was a good raconteur. He became master of the Worshipful Company of Innholders (1978–9), was a fellow of the Institute of Building, and a governor of the Brixton School of Building; he also gave his time to many other activities in support of the industry. He was for many years chairman of the Royal School for the Blind, Leatherhead (1971–82); a council member of King's College Hospital medical school; a trustee of the Historic Churches Preservation Trust; and a member of the Church Commissioners' committee on redundant churches. In 1966 he and his two brothers established from their personal resources the Wates Foundation, dedicated to improving the quality of life, especially for the disadvantaged young. By 1990 its annual income was £1.3 million.

Rubicund and dapper, with a twinkle in his eye, Wates was a congenial companion at ease with everyone. Careful of the pennies, he was shrewd and sound on large issues. He was, in every sense, a builder for both his firm and his family. He became a rich man but remained engagingly modest. Of strong Christian faith, he had a natural concern for others and a respect for traditional values, relishing all that was best in his country's heritage. In 1931 he married a childhood friend, Phyllis Mary, daughter of Harry Trace, innkeeper. The marriage was exceptionally happy—Wates's equable temperament played its part in this. They had four sons. In 1947 they acquired the Manor House, Headley, where Wates put down roots. He became absorbed in the upbringing of his children, passing on to them his love of horses and field sports. He farmed with enjoyment, hunted until he was seventy, and became a popular member of the old-established Surrey Club. He was an involved and generous benefactor to his parish church, of which he was church warden and treasurer, to Guildford Cathedral (council member) and to Surrey University (foundation fellow, and D.Univ. 1975). In 1972 he was made an honorary fellow of University College London. He was knighted in 1975 for his charitable and philanthropic services and was made deputy lieutenant for Surrey in 1981. He died of a cerebral thrombosis in Ashtead Hospital 25 January 1986. The value of his will, after allowing for liabilities, but before inheritance tax, was £1,124,010.

[*The Times*, 21 February 1986; private information; personal knowledge.] JOHN MORETON

WATT, (John) David (Henry) (1932–1987), journalist, was born 9 January 1932 in Edinburgh, the only son and second of three children of the Revd John Hunter Watt and his wife Helen Garioch, daughter of Reuben Bryce, accountant. His childhood years were spent principally in Kent, where his father was vicar of Boxley, near Maidstone. He was educated at Marlborough College, doing two years' national service with the Royal Artillery (partly in the canal zone and after that on secondment to the Mauritian Guard), before going up to Hertford College, Oxford, with a classics scholarship in 1951. He obtained second-class honours in both classical honour moderations and *literae humaniores* (1953 and 1956). He had only just taken moderations when his university career was interrupted by his falling victim to poliomyelitis. The effects were to stay with him all his life—bringing a slightly lopsided look to his previously tall, erect figure, with his left arm hanging limply by his side. He was seldom without pain, which he bore with remarkable stoicism. He continued to experience breathing difficulties, involving in later years the regular use of a portable respirator. Nevertheless, the illness forged and shaped his whole character, transforming a conventional, public school, games-playing product into the acerbic possessor of one of the shrewdest minds and sharpest pens in British political journalism.

Polio also gave him his start as a writer. His first published article was called simply 'Last Gasp' and appeared in the *Spectator* of 14 October 1955, when he had just ceased undergoing treatment in an iron lung. It was a detached description of what it felt like to live, as he put it, in 'a long box, monstrous and coffin-like, with bellows attached'. As a piece of spare, cool prose, it sufficiently impressed the *Spectator*'s editor, Ian Gilmour (later Baron Gilmour of Craigmillar), for Watt to be offered a job when, a year later, he left Oxford. He spent two years (1956–7) with the *Spectator*, ostensibly as the paper's dramatic critic, but in reality as the office dogsbody. In 1958 he moved to the *Scotsman* as its London-based diplomatic correspondent and from there was tempted in 1960 to rejoin a revamped *Daily Herald* as its Common Market correspondent. A year later the *Herald* passed into the ownership of the International Publishing Corporation and Watt did not, under the new proprietorship, linger long. Instead, he went back to the *Spectator*, this time in the rather grander capacity of political correspondent (1962–3).

It was his second coming at the *Spectator* that marked Watt's real arrival as an influential journalist. After a brief flowering with Henry *Fairlie—and a rather longer one with Bernard Levin—the *Spectator*'s political commentary had become spasmodic and patchy. In less than a year and a half Watt provided it with consistency, coherence, wit, and intelligence. It was no surprise when, towards the end of 1963, the *Financial Times* snapped him up to be its correspondent in Washington.

Although without any economic training, Watt soon vindicated his selection, becoming in the words of the *Financial Times*'s own official history, 'the pick of the [paper's] foreign correspondents'. Starting from scratch, he rapidly built up an impressive network of sources, prompting the International Monetary Fund once to complain that it had to read a London newspaper to discover what was going into its own minutes. But he was equally penetrating in covering American politics and by 1967 had returned to London—and to the important appointment as political editor of the paper. The next ten years, in which his Friday column came

to be recognized as the best-informed example of 'insider' journalism in Britain, probably represented the high point of Watt's influence over public affairs.

By 1977, having been disappointed in his bids for two editorships (the *Economist* in 1974 and the *Observer* in 1975), Watt had become bored. He had grown tired, as he characteristically phrased it, of 'turning the prayer wheel'. So, when the offer came in 1978 to take over from (Sir) Andrew *Shonfield as director of the Royal Institute of International Affairs (Chatham House), he accepted it. He was afterwards to regret doing so. Cut off from its Foreign Office subvention, Chatham House was going through a difficult phase and its new director had little appetite for fund-raising. It was with some relief that he laid down his burden at the end of his five-year term.

While at Chatham House, Watt had already put a toe back into journalism, writing a weekly column in *The Times* from 1981 until his death. He had been a visiting fellow of All Souls in 1972–3 and was a research fellow there in 1981–3—appointments which gave him great pleasure, as did his joint editorship of the *Political Quarterly* from 1979 to 1985. He was once described as having 'a clergy-boned face', and it was typical of this aspect of his personality that he should have served on the board of visitors of Wandsworth prison for five years (1977–81). In the last period of his life he also became a highly valued political consultant to the multinational company, Rio Tinto Zinc, which, a year after his death, established a prize for journalism in his memory.

In 1968 he married Susanne, daughter of Frank ('Fritz') Adolf Burchardt, statistician and fellow of Magdalen College, Oxford; they had four sons. Watt died 27 March 1987 at his country cottage in Lewknor near Oxford, after, on a stormy night, picking up an electric cable that turned out to be live. He was instantly electrocuted.

[David Kynaston, *The Financial Times: a Centenary History*, 1988; Ferdinand Mount (ed.), *The Inquiring Eye: the Writings of David Watt*, 1988; private information; personal knowledge.]   ANTHONY HOWARD

WAYNE, SIR Edward Johnson (1902–1990), physician, was born 3 June 1902 in Leeds, the elder child and only son of William Wayne, chief surveyor to a building society, of Roundhay, Leeds, and his wife, Ellen Rawding, of Leadenham, Lincolnshire. He attended Leeds Central High School and then entered Leeds University as Akroyd scholar, graduating with first-class honours in chemistry in 1923. At Manchester University he worked on the intermediary metabolism of the fatty acids with H. S. Raper, obtaining a Ph.D. in 1925. It was at this point that his instincts led him to medicine, and he returned to Leeds in 1926 to complete a medical course. He graduated MB, Ch.B. in 1929 with first-class honours and was awarded the Hey gold medal, as the most distinguished graduate of the year.

In 1931 he became an assistant in the department of clinical research in University College Hospital, London, under the directorship of Sir Thomas Lewis, and he carried out some of the earliest trials with digoxin and an investigation into angina. In 1934 he was appointed to the chair of pharmacology and therapeutics in the University of Sheffield. He became FRCP in 1937 and MD in 1938. In this pre-war period he coped with his university teaching commitment as well as his clinical duties. He had one lectureship, to which he appointed (Sir) Hans *Krebs, a refugee from Nazi Germany. Krebs completed his work on the citric acid cycle, for which he obtained the Nobel prize.

During World War II Wayne's clinical duties were expanded by his appointment as physician to the Children's Hospital, Sheffield, and to the Emergency Medical Services. He also had his private practice. After the war he became once again a full-time professor of therapeutics. He was appointed chairman of the joint formulary committee of the British Medical Association and the Pharmaceutical Society, and later chairman of the British Pharmacopoeia Commission (1958–63), which gave him unrivalled experience in the assessment of drugs. He recruited able young men returning from the armed forces to his department. At last his flair for directing clinical research was able to reach its full potential. His collaboration with his team led to advances in the use of radioiodine in the diagnosis and treatment of thyroid disease, as well as the use of angiography and cardiac catheterization for cardiac disease.

In 1954 he was appointed regius professor of the practice of medicine at Glasgow University, which had a purpose-built clinical research building (the Gardiner Institute) attached to the professorial wards of the Western Infirmary. Wayne was determined to continue his successful run in Sheffield and the Gardiner Institute was the ideal vehicle for his ambitions. From 1953 till his retirement in 1967 he sparked off and encouraged research in a number of areas—in his own field of thyroid disease, cardiovascular disease, osteoporosis, and blood disorders. He developed and encouraged the use of tapes and slide-tapes as ancillaries for clinical teaching. Coming from Sheffield he gradually, but successfully, integrated himself into the life and work of Scottish medicine.

From 1954 to 1967 he was honorary physician to the queen in Scotland and in 1958 he was recruited to the Medical Research Council,

becoming chairman of the clinical research board (1960–4). In 1959 he was elected Sims commonwealth travelling fellow and with his wife visited most of the medical schools in Canada. He was knighted in 1964 and became an honorary D.Sc. of Sheffield in 1967, the year he retired to Chipping Campden in the Cotswolds. After fourteen years he and his wife went to live with their son's family at Lingwood near Great Yarmouth.

Wayne was one of the new breed of full-time clinical scientific professors which evolved in the mid-twentieth century. His training as a young man in chemistry, biochemistry, and clinical science, and his appointment to various drug committees, gave him a unique opportunity to perceive and contribute to the therapeutic revolution. His drive and ability to attract younger men of merit allowed him to promote and superintend important advances. He was chairman of the BMA committee on alcohol and road accidents from 1948 and his work on this topic for two decades was responsible for the government's introduction of the blood alcohol limit of 80 mg per 100 ml of blood (Road Safety Act, 1967).

Of medium height, Wayne had a sturdy frame with slender limbs. He had iron grey hair brushed back to show a good forehead, and was strong-jawed and clean shaven until late in life, when he sported a grey beard which finally completed the mellow, venerable image. He was dynamic and his movements were mercurial, matching his quick enquiring mind. He kept those round him on their toes, but he was usually sensitive to their feelings, employing his Yorkshire wit in the most effective way. A man of wide reading, he enjoyed short poems and had a great love of music. In 1932 he married Honora Nancy (died 1992), a teacher of classics and daughter of David Halloran, schoolteacher. They had a son, who became a consultant physician, and a daughter. Wayne died 19 August 1990 in the James Paget Hospital, Gorleston, near Great Yarmouth, from heart failure.

[*Munk's Roll*, vol. ix, 1994; *British Medical Journal*, vol. ccci, 1990, p. 604; *Lancet*, vol. 2, 1990, p. 932; *Guardian*, 22 August 1990; private information; personal knowledge.]   ABRAHAM GOLDBERG

WECK, Richard (1913–1986), civil engineer, was born 5 March 1913 in Franzenbad, Bohemia, the elder son and eldest of three children of Francis Weck, manager of a small restaurant, and his wife, Katie Dauber. His early life was frugal, for his mother and younger sister died early, and he had to care for his younger brother and become accustomed to casual teaching work. Despite these set-backs he entered the Technical University of Prague to study civil and structural engineering in 1931, and graduated in 1936.

After he had gained some practical experience from 1937 to 1938, he was engaged with Professor J. Fritzsche in research on plastic theories of structural analysis and design. His life at this stage was dominated by the problems of his native country (which had become Czechoslovakia in 1918), and the adjacent Nazi rise to power, so that it is not surprising that he should have become a student activist, founding a Democratic Liberal society and engaging with the anti-fascist student movement. When Czechoslovakia was annexed by Germany in 1938, he and fifteen similar activists, with the help of leading members of the British Liberal party, were secretly evacuated to Britain, where Weck was joined by his wife.

At the age of twenty-six, already with worldly experience, and having a sparkling, seductively iconoclastic temperament, he was soon deeply involved in the war effort. He gave technical assistance to foundries, and then edited a handbook for welded structural steelwork on behalf of the Institute of Welding, thereby both improving his English and meeting the institute's originator J. F. (later Baron) *Baker. When Baker became professor of mechanical sciences at Cambridge in 1943, Weck joined him, as his research assistant, in teaching, research, and later in expanding the British Welding Research Association (BWRA). Their most pressing wartime research task was to understand and correct the mysterious blight of brittle fractures in welded steel ship hulls, which threatened the transatlantic supply lifeline to an extent only masked by submarine torpedo losses. His seminal research on welding residual stresses was rewarded with a Cambridge Ph.D. in 1948, and matched by metallurgical research conducted by Dr Constance Tipper at the same laboratory. Both co-operated in this work for more than a decade, but Weck increasingly turned his attention to fatigue testing of welded structures; both saw the culmination of their efforts even later, in the successful placement and service of welded steel oil platforms in the hostile environment of the North Sea.

Meanwhile, driven by the excessive bulk and noisy operation of his testing machines, Weck sought an outstation site, and discovered the derelict Abington Hall estate nearby, which then offered the desired space and remoteness. It soon became the home of BWRA, of whose fatigue laboratory he had been head since 1946, and a purpose-built fatigue testing laboratory was added in 1952, the first of several buildings there to employ the new plastic methods of Baker. Weck served BWRA at this juncture, but returned to Cambridge as a lecturer in 1951, and stayed there until 1957, creating a postgraduate course, which was both well supported and influential. He did, however, continue to live at Abington until his death.

He was appointed in 1957 as director of research at BWRA, and as director-general of the Institute of Welding and BWRA when they were merged as the Welding Institute in 1968. At the time of his retirement in 1977 the latter body had expanded greatly, and acquired a reputation for quality of service, confirmed by the substantial proportion of its revenue drawn from overseas, and in particular from the USA, Japan, and Europe. Weck was also for six years a visiting industrial professor at Imperial College, London (1968–74), and from 1976 he added a complementary post in the department of civil engineering.

The international outlook of Richard Weck gained respect and recognition in the International Institute of Welding, where for more than a decade he was chairman of the commission devoted to the study and control of welding residual stresses. He was a competent linguist, embracing German, Spanish, Russian, and later Japanese, and his many publications (he wrote over sixty articles) reflect this. His style as a leader was fearless and outspoken, but always both courteous and generous. He was appointed CBE in 1969, FRS in 1975, and F.Eng. in 1976. He also held honorary fellowships of the Welding Institute, the Institution of Mechanical Engineers, and the Institution of Civil Engineers. An array of medals for distinguished services included the Bessemer gold medal of the Metals Society (1975).

Weck was naturalized in 1946. In 1933 he married Katie, daughter of Karl Bartl, master tailor and cutter. They were a mutually devoted couple; although without children, they treasured those of others. Weck had a serious heart attack in March 1971. He was an expert grower of exotic plants. He had been typically in search of gifts on 9 January 1986 when he collapsed and died of a second heart attack on the train returning to Cambridge from London.

[A. A. Wells and E. G. West in *Biographical Memoirs of Fellows of the Royal Society*, vol. xxxii, 1986; personal knowledge.]   A. A. WELLS

WEX, Bernard Patrick (1922–1990), civil engineer, was born 24 April 1922 in Acton, London, the only child of Julius Wex, a lace merchant from Germany, who had gone to England in 1900, taken British nationality in 1911, and in the same year married Gertrude Brady, a fashion saleswoman. His father died of pneumonia two weeks before he was born, and his mother went to live with her mother in Acton. He attended Acton County Grammar School, where he showed all-round prowess, matriculating in 1938. On the outbreak of World War II his desire to become a Royal Air Force pilot was thwarted by minor astigmatism. After attending Sandhurst, in 1943 he became a tank commander (lieutenant) in the Royal Armoured Corps (23rd Hussars). Having suffered pleurisy and pneumonia in 1944, he was transferred to administrative work until demobilization as captain in March 1947. That October he was accepted by Imperial College, London, to read civil engineering and he graduated in 1950 with first-class honours, being top of his year and winning the Unwin medal.

He immediately started work with Freeman Fox & Partners under (Sir) Gilbert *Roberts and, later, Oleg *Kerensky. His early work included Auckland harbour bridge (built in 1955–9) and schemes for the 1000m Severn and Forth suspension spans. He gained site experience on the 600MW Castle Donington power station. Design work on another power station was followed by six 177m-span oil pipeline suspension bridges in India, and a further series of bridges to carry high-pressure gas in Pakistan, including the 1770m multi-span river Sutlej crossing, which was built entirely in one dry season.

Appointed a partner in Freeman Fox in 1969, he oversaw construction of the M5 Avonmouth bridge and took charge of the newly authorized Humber bridge project. This had originally been studied by the firm in 1927–8 and proposed as a single 1372m-span by Sir Ralph *Freeman in 1935. Wex directed its final design and construction, adopting 'slip-formed' concrete for the towers, rather than steel, thus making substantial cost savings. He also used novel methods for sinking the south tower and anchorage foundations through 40m of water and silt to reach the Kimmeridge clay. The construction period coincided with unprecedented inflation and worsening industrial relations, which caused severe delays and mounting costs. Undaunted, Wex piloted client and contractors through to a supremely successful conclusion. The bridge was opened by Queen Elizabeth II on 17 July 1981. At 1410m its main clear span was the world's longest by 110m. Wex was appointed OBE in the 1982 New Year honours list.

Although the Humber bridge was Wex's crowning achievement, he packed much else into the decade of the 1970s, including the cable-stayed box-girder Myton swing bridge in Hull and a slender 165m concrete arch bridge in South Africa. In 1979 he prepared a design for one of six contractors bidding in competition for the proposed river Foyle bridge near Londonderry, Northern Ireland. His graceful 234m-span twin-steel box-girder scheme was judged the winner for appearance by the Royal Fine Art Commission and was also the lowest priced. The bridge was completed in October 1984.

Wex led the seven-year inquiry into the 1969 collapse of the 381m Emley Moor television mast, and served energetically on many technical committees and on the council of the Welding Institute. He contributed much to the work of the International Association for Bridge and Structural Engineering, chairing its British group and technical committees; it made him an honorary member in 1990. He helped to found the Steel Construction Institute in 1986 and remained its chairman until shortly before his final illness. He wrote sixteen papers on six subjects, eleven of them between 1976 and 1984, which were published in ten countries, and he delivered many lectures at home and abroad.

With his lifelong enthusiasm, unquenchable good humour, and first-class brain, Wex became a most proficient and successful creator of bridges, the equal of any of his time. He was a perfectionist in all he attempted, becoming a skilful photographer and cabinet-maker. He was elected a member of the Institution of Civil Engineers (ICE) in 1956 (fellow, 1968), and a fellow of the Welding Institute, where he also took the practical welding course, in 1972. In 1982 he was elected to the Fellowship (later Royal Academy) of Engineering, and awarded the fellowship of the City and Guilds Institute. In 1985 he won the ICE's Telford gold medal and became a fellow of the Institution of Structural Engineers.

Wex was tall, of athletic build, fair-skinned with blond hair (which mostly disappeared in his early twenties), good-looking, and of extrovert personality. In 1945 he married Sheila Evelyn Lambert, the widow of Malcolm Kingsbury Lambert, RAF pilot, and daughter of Peter Thompson, a builder in north-west London. It was a very happy marriage, of which there were two sons. Wex died 31 July 1990 in St Bartholomew's Hospital, London, while undergoing chemotherapy treatment for myeloid leukaemia.

[Freeman Fox records in archives of Acer Group Ltd.; information from Wex's widow and colleagues; personal knowledge.]   RALPH FREEMAN

WHEATCROFT, George Shorrock Ashcombe (1905–1987), professor of English law at the London School of Economics, was born 29 October 1905 in Derby, the eldest of three children, a son and two daughters, of Hubert Ashcombe Wheatcroft, solicitor, and his wife Jane Eccles, daughter of a Liverpool cotton broker. He was educated at Rugby School and New College, Oxford, taking a third in mathematical moderations in 1924 and a second in jurisprudence in 1926. He qualified as a solicitor in 1929.

Always known as Ash, he had several successful careers. The first was from 1929 to 1951 as a practising solicitor in his father's firm, Corbin, Greener & Cook of 52 Bedford Row, London, with which he had been articled. This was interrupted by war service in 1940–5 with the Royal Army Service Corps, during the North

African and Italian campaigns, a period which included the task of running the port of Naples for a year. He was twice mentioned in dispatches and was released with the honorary rank of lieutenant-colonel. On returning to practice he specialized in company law and estate duty.

His second career, from 1951 to 1959, was as master of the Supreme Court (Chancery Division), where he was widely respected by those who appeared before him. Although this would have been a full-time job for most people, he regarded it as a part-time occupation which left him free to write and build up his reputation in taxation. His first book, *The Taxation of Gifts and Settlements* (1953), might claim to be the first book on tax planning. In 1956 he founded the first scholarly journal on taxation, the *British Tax Review*, which he edited until 1971, when he became consulting editor. A significant event, from the point of view of his later life, was his teaching of the first university course in England on taxation, at the London School of Economics in 1957. In 1959 he founded a tax discussion and dining society, the Addington Society, the membership of which was limited to sixty, with roughly equal representation from solicitors, barristers, accountants, and economists. His third career, which naturally followed, was as professor of English law at the London School of Economics from 1959 to 1968, during which he specialized in tax law and built up an international reputation. He played a full part in administering the law department, being its convenor, and during this period he also wrote *The Law of Income Tax, Surtax and Profits Tax* (1962) and, with A. E. W. Park, *Wheatcroft on Capital Gains Taxes* (1967). His fourth and final career was as a director and vice-chairman of Hambro Life Assurance, later known as Allied Dunbar Assurance. Outside his work, he was an excellent chess player, representing England at Stockholm in 1937 and serving as president of the British Chess Federation, and bridge player.

His contribution to taxation law was immense. Not only did he teach the first tax course at London University, but he did the same in Oxford and Cambridge, and such courses spread rapidly. In 1972 a survey showed that tax law was taught in thirty-two of the forty-one institutions offering law degrees, and, by the time of Wheatcroft's death, it would have been a matter of comment if any similar institution failed to offer such a course. Perhaps the previous neglect of tax law as a subject for academic study stemmed from its being a statute-based branch of law compared to the traditional judge-made common law, which is the basis of the study of law at universities. Wheatcroft demonstrated that this statutory basis did not imply any lack of principles, and that, on the contrary, the statutory basis was its virtue, particularly for postgraduates with

a thorough grounding in other branches of the law, for whom academic tax study formed an excellent start to subsequent tax practice. Certainly attitudes had changed completely by the time of his death. Among his other innovations was the founding of a course to help economists and lawyers understand each other's views on tax law, a subject they were approaching from different points of view. As a tall and solidly built person he made a commanding lecturer, who delighted in difficult problems. He was appointed honorary fellow of the LSE in 1976 and of University College, Buckingham, in 1978; he received an honorary LL D at Buckingham in 1979.

His writings, which included standard works on income tax, capital gains tax, and corporation tax, together formed the *British Tax Encyclopedia* published by Sweet & Maxwell (1962, looseleaf), and he also wrote books on VAT (value added tax), many of them later updated by succeeding authors. He wrote many articles on all aspects of taxation. He was honorary adviser to Customs and Excise on the introduction of VAT.

In 1930 he married Mildred Susan (died 1978), daughter of Canon Walter Lock, DD, formerly warden of Keble College, Oxford. They had two sons and a daughter. His wife had a first-class Oxford degree in philosophy, politics, and economics, and worked on management research, and also on economic intelligence at the British embassy in Washington, where she had taken the family during the war. Wheatcroft died in Berkhamsted 2 December 1987.

[Private information; personal knowledge.]

J. F. AVERY JONES

WHELDON, SIR **Huw Pyrs** (1916–1986), broadcaster, was born 7 May 1916 at his grandmother's home in Prestatyn, the eldest in a family of two sons and two daughters of (Sir) Wynn Powell Wheldon, solicitor and civil servant, and his wife, Margaret ('Megan') Edwards. His father worked in David Lloyd George's law practice before World War I, had a brave military career, and went on to become registrar of the University College of North Wales in Bangor and then permanent secretary to the Welsh department of the Ministry of Education. Huw Wheldon was educated at Friars School, Bangor (he did not speak English until he was seven) and later at the London School of Economics and Political Science where he gained a B.Sc.(Econ.) in 1938. He joined the staff of the Kent education committee, and then war interrupted his career. Enlisting in the East Kent Regiment as a private, he was commissioned into the Royal Welch Fusiliers (1940), and volunteered to join the airborne forces. He served in both the 1st and 6th Airborne divisions, ending the war as a major in the Royal Ulster Rifles, having won the MC shortly after D-Day in 1944.

In 1946 he became director of the Arts Council in Wales, and in 1949 joined the directorate of the Festival of Britain. He helped to ensure the festival reached all of Britain, and for his work he was appointed OBE in 1952, the year he joined the BBC as publicity officer, television. He wanted to be involved in programmes and first made his mark on the screen as the presenter of the children's programme, *All Your Own*. He became a national figure when he devised a conkers competition that drew 58,000 conkers from all over Britain. In 1954 he was appointed senior producer, television talks, although he had never directed or produced a programme. His first series was *Men in Battle* with Lieutenant-General Sir Brian *Horrocks, and his second *Orson Welles's Sketchbook*.

From 1958 to 1964 he devised, edited, and presented *Monitor*, the first arts programme on television. In this pioneering fortnightly programme he introduced a growing audience to major artists, in numbers and range remarkable for its time. He built around him a team of talented people, including John Schlesinger, Ken Russell, Humphrey Burton, David Jones, Patrick Garland, and Melvyn Bragg. He required of all his programmes fidelity and attention to the subject, to the audience, and to the integrity of the programme maker.

Inevitably, he progressed to the most senior posts in BBC television: he was the first television producer to become controller of programmes (1965–8) and he was the first holder of the new post of managing director (1969–75). This was the time when BBC television was at its best with some remarkable series (*Civilisation* with Sir Kenneth (later Baron) *Clark, *The Ascent of Man* with Jacob *Bronowski, and Alistair Cooke's *America*), challenging drama, refreshing comedy, and lively current affairs and sports programmes. Despite the restrictions of his office (concerned with the BBC's strategy, standards, and finances), programmes and programme makers were what Wheldon cared about most. In his own phrase, he wished programmes to 'give delight and insight'. Although he was a candidate for the post of director-general when Sir Hugh *Greene retired, the BBC governors, led by Baron *Hill of Luton, preferred to give the job to someone with a lower profile, (Sir) Charles *Curran. Wheldon served him loyally as his deputy until his own retirement in 1976, the year he was knighted.

Three factors helped to shape Wheldon's life: Wales and the advantages of a close-knit family life, the army and its discipline, and the BBC and its creative ethos. They gave him a reference for language and for institutions and for the need to protect them and keep them alive. Wheldon was

a tall man, slightly stooped. It was his face that was remarkable: piercing eyes, a pointed chin, a hawk's nose. He was the most generous and companionable of men, the best and sometimes longest teller of stories, and he had an enormous zest for life.

After he left the BBC, he returned to programme making and wrote and presented the *Royal Heritage* series (1977) and *Destination D-Day* (1984), on the fortieth anniversary of the Allied landings in Normandy. He became an honorary fellow (1973) and chairman of the court of governors of the London School of Economics (1975–85). He was the president of the Royal Television Society (1979–85) and received every honour possible in television. From 1976 he was a trustee of the National Portrait Gallery and from 1983 a trustee of the Royal Botanic Gardens, Kew. He had five honorary doctorates, from Ulster (1975), Wales (1978), London (1984), Loughborough (1985), and the Open University (1980), which he helped to establish.

In 1956 he married Jacqueline Mary (died 1993), the daughter of Hugh Clarke, who had a tool designing business in Chiswick. They had one son and two daughters. Their family house in Richmond was an exceptionally happy home and he died there, from cancer, 14 March 1986.

[Private information; personal knowledge.]   PAUL FOX

WILKINSON, James Hardy (1919–1986), mathematician, was born 27 September 1919 in Strood, Kent, the third child in the family of two sons and three daughters of James William Wilkinson, dairyman, and his wife, Kathleen Charlotte Hardy. The family, impoverished when their dairy business failed in the 1930s, was close and happy. As a boy, Wilkinson's exceptional qualities secured him a Foundation scholarship to Sir Joseph Williamson's Mathematical School in Rochester before he was eleven. He won a major scholarship to Trinity College, Cambridge, which he entered just after his seventeenth birthday in 1936. He won college prizes in 1937 and 1939 for being the most distinguished student of his year in any subject, became a wrangler in part ii of the mathematics tripos in 1938, and took his part iii in 1939.

After World War II broke out in 1939, Wilkinson, together with other leading young mathematicians, was drafted into the Ministry of Supply. After working mainly on pedestrian calculations, he sought a more demanding mathematical environment as soon as the war ended. In May 1946 he joined the mathematics division of the National Physical Laboratory, where E. T. Goodwin led a desk machine computing section, and where A. M. *Turing was busy designing the automatic computing engine (ACE). After a brief spell of desk machine work Wilkinson devoted himself to Turing's machine. The ACE project was hampered by erratic leadership from Turing and misdirection from above. But after Turing's departure in 1948 and the establishment of a new NPL regime, Wilkinson took a leading role in the development of a modified machine, known as Pilot ACE; this proved highly successful from its inception in May 1950. In that year Wilkinson was promoted to principal scientific officer and by 1974 he had become chief scientific officer.

The results that Wilkinson obtained from programmes run on the Pilot ACE and later machines spurred him to develop new analytical and numerical techniques. In succeeding years he described the fruits of his research in publications which came to form the very foundation of numerical linear algebra. He wrote over 100 papers and was the author of *Rounding Errors in Algebraic Processes* (1963) and the monumental *The Algebraic Eigenvalue Problem* (1965). In 1960 George Forsythe of Stanford, one of the most eminent numerical analysts of his generation, wrote 'In my opinion Wilkinson is single-handedly responsible for the creation of almost all of the current body of scientific knowledge about the computer solution of the problems of linear algebra.' This judgement was made when Wilkinson's most productive period still lay in the future. He spent his working life at NPL, but also made many visits to the USA. In particular he was an annual consultant to the Argonne National Laboratory for some twenty years, a visiting professor at Ann Arbor, Michigan (1957–73), and a professor at Stanford (1977–84). His lectures were legendary; his meticulous clarity owed much to painstaking preparation concealed by a highly individual, informal delivery.

He obtained an Sc.D. from Cambridge in 1962. He was elected FRS in 1969, and in the following year became the first person ever to receive both the A. M. Turing award of the Association for Computing Machinery and the J. von Neumann award of the Society for Industrial and Applied Mathematics in the same year. In the next fifteen years honours and distinctions (including honorary doctorates from Brunel, 1971, Heriot-Watt, 1973, Waterloo, 1978, and Essex, 1979) came regularly. Posthumous honours included the establishment of the J. H. Wilkinson fellowship at Argonne, and also the triennial Wilkinson prize sponsored jointly by NPL, the Numerical Algorithms Group, and Argonne.

Wilkinson was a jovial, round-faced, ruddy-complexioned man, once described as having 'all the aspects of a sailor on shore leave and ready to do the town'. He certainly had a great capacity for enjoying himself and his ready wit enlivened any gathering. He appeared to be interested in everything and everybody; boredom was impossible in his company. Of his specific interests, perhaps the greatest outside mathematics was music, of which his knowledge was wide and profound. He was also very knowledgeable about the wines with which he entertained his friends and which he consumed with such pleasure. Very many people felt that they knew Wilkinson, though in fact few knew him well; beneath the jocularity he was a very private individual.

In 1945 he married Heather Nora, daughter of William Henry Ware, buyer for a drapery warehouse. They had a daughter, who died in 1978, and a son. Wilkinson died at his home in Teddington 5 October 1986, from a heart attack.

[L. Fox in *Biographical Memoirs of Fellows of the Royal Society*, vol. xxxiii, 1987; personal knowledge.]

CHARLES CLENSHAW

WILKINSON, Sir (Robert Francis) Martin (1911–1990), stockbroker, was born 4 June 1911 in Blackheath, London, the elder son and eldest of four children of (Sir) Robert Pelham Wilkinson, a partner of de Zoete & Gorton from 1913 to 1960 and deputy chairman of the Stock Exchange from 1936 to 1946, and his wife, Phyllis Marion Bernard. He was educated at Repton School.

He joined de Zoete & Gorton straight from school in 1930 and became a partner in 1936, having become a member of the Stock Exchange in 1933. During World War II he served in the Royal Air Force in radar intelligence in Northern Ireland and Italy, and at Bushey Priory, attaining the rank of squadron leader. He returned to de Zoete & Gorton after the war and was elected to the council of the Stock Exchange in 1959. He became deputy chairman in 1963 and was elected chairman in 1965, having acted as chairman for the year before he took office, when he stood in for the third Baron Ritchie of Dundee during his illness. He became senior partner of de Zoete & Bevan following the merger of his firm with David A. Bevan & Simpson in 1970. He retired from the chairmanship of the Stock Exchange in March 1973 and from de Zoete & Bevan in 1976.

Wilkinson chaired the Stock Exchange during a difficult period. It was a time when international pressures were beginning to exert influence and reform was becoming necessary. He was himself not a natural reformer, being steeped in the traditions of the Exchange and the City. He was, however, open to ideas of reform and he encouraged his younger colleagues to come forward with them. He grasped ideas quickly and thoroughly and was a natural leader in the implementation of change.

During his period of office the settlement of Stock Exchange business was centralized, and stock exchanges throughout the United Kingdom and the Republic of Ireland came together in one organization. These two changes were interlinked. A single market authority was essential. Only one exchange could achieve the most efficient system of settlement and transfer of securities which was recommended by the City-wide Heasman committee in 1970. The exchanges were amalgamated in 1973 and this achievement led to the full computerization of the settlement procedures after Wilkinson's retirement. Furthermore, only one exchange could ensure the imposition of the best regulatory standards across the whole country and thus satisfy investors that their business was being fairly conducted and settled.

During Wilkinson's term of office the Stock Exchange's historic building, which had been extended many times on the same site since 1801, was pulled down and rebuilt, an extensive project which required the full backing of the voting members. He patiently achieved the necessary backing, explaining how essential the rebuilding was for the efficiency of the market place and particularly its worldwide communications.

Other reforms during his tenure of office included the abolition of the requirement of British nationality for membership of the Stock Exchange, the relaxation of some of the restrictions preventing member firms from competing in overseas markets, the easing of restraints on advertising, the tightening of the financial reporting requirements imposed on firms, the admission of women to the membership and to the trading floor, and the introduction of rules which allowed firms for the first time to seek external capital through the formation of limited partnerships or companies. These reforms arose from the need for Stock Exchange firms to be internationally competitive. It was no mean achievement to lead the Exchange through these changes in the face of much internal criticism from members who preferred to think of the Exchange more as a club than an international market place.

Wilkinson's years in office were also difficult because attitudes in Westminster towards the City of London and to the Exchange were hostile. Politicians were apt to describe the Exchange as a 'casino' and to draw unflattering comparisons between the paper shuffling of stock markets and the real world of manufacturing industry. Wilkinson continued the work of his predecessors in encouraging a greater public knowledge of the workings and *raison d'être* of the Exchange. He did not enjoy such public platforms, being himself a very private man, but he was not afraid to stand up and do his public duty as chairman. He left his listeners in no doubt about the role of the Exchange as the market through which industry could raise long-term risk capital and as the regulatory authority which demanded high standards of disclosure from listed companies and financial probity and ethical behaviour from its members, thus serving the interests of investors. He was a major influence on the introduction of legislation to make insider trading a criminal offence, having initiated this with a speech (of which he gave his colleagues no prior warning) in which he said it was 'no better than theft'.

Wilkinson served as chairman of two investment trusts—Altifund (1976–81) and the City of London Brewery Trust (1977–8). He was the seventh generation of his family to be a liveryman of the Worshipful Company of Needlemakers. He was knighted in 1969.

He was of medium height, well built, and well groomed. His movements and gestures were restrained, almost self-conscious. His somewhat aquiline features could be severe, but they frequently relaxed into a ready, impish smile. When he retired he lived part of the year near Cortona in Italy and indulged his passion for gardening at his home in England while continuing to act as consultant to de Zoete & Bevan. In 1946 he married Dore Esme, daughter of William John Arendt, timber trader. They had three daughters. Wilkinson died 22 January 1990 in Pembury Hospital, Kent.

[Stock Exchange archives in the Guildhall Library; private information; personal knowledge.]

NICHOLAS GOODISON

WILLIAMS, (George) Emlyn (1905–1987), actor and dramatist, was born 26 November 1905 at Pen-y-Ffordd, Mostyn, Clwyd (then Flintshire), the eldest of the three surviving sons (two older children, a boy and a girl, died in infancy) of Richard Williams, an ex-navy stoker become greengrocer, of Ffynnongroyw, Clwyd, and his wife Mary, a former maidservant, daughter of Job Williams, collier, of Treuddyn, Mold. He was educated at Holywell County School and St Julien, Switzerland, before winning an open scholarship to Christ Church, Oxford. At Holywell County School he had met Miss Sarah Cooke, the senior mistress, on whose character and personality he drew for much of Miss Moffett in *The Corn Is Green*. She encouraged him, fostered his gift for languages, paid for his stay in Switzerland, entered him for the Oxford scholarship, gave him much financial support, and remained a lifelong friend. At Oxford he did little work, spending his time acting with the Oxford University Dramatic Society and writing plays. In 1926 he suffered a nervous breakdown before his final examinations, mainly due to an emotional friendship with a fellow undergraduate (his autobiography is frank about his bisexuality). He sat his finals in 1927, when he was already a professional actor, and took a second class in modern languages. Williams was stagestruck, captivated by a glamorous popular theatre in which, through hard work and professional commitment, he became a dominant figure. Though he acquired great sophistication he remained, essentially, the daringly optimistic, emotional, and single-minded romantic who had worked his way up from humble beginnings.

When an undergraduate his one-act play, *Vigil* (1925) and a full-length drama, *Full Moon* (1927), were performed at the Playhouse theatre, Oxford. In London, after impressing with *Glamour* (1928) and *A Murder Has Been Arranged* (1930), he had his first commercial success with *The Late Christopher Bean* (1933), an adaptation of Sidney Howard's English version of Fauchois' *Prenez Garde à la Peinture*. *Night Must Fall* (1935) ran for over 400 performances; *The Corn Is Green* (1938) was very popular in both London and New York. His numerous plays include *The Druid's Rest* (1944), a Welsh comedy in which the young Richard *Burton made his début, *The Wind of Heaven* (1945), and *Someone Waiting* (1953). He wrote features for radio and one play, *Pepper and Sand* (1947), and two plays for television, *A Blue Movie* (1968) being the better known. His film-scripts include *The Citadel* (1938), in collaboration, and *The Last Days of Dolwyn* (1949).

His professional acting career began in 1927, at the Savoy, with a small part in *And So To Bed* by J. B. *Fagan. His first success was as Angelo in Edgar *Wallace's *On the Spot* (1930). In a long West End career he often starred in his own plays: he was a hit as Dan in *Night Must Fall* and an even greater one as Morgan Evans in *The Corn Is Green*. In 1937 he appeared in Shakespeare at the Old Vic. He was Sir Robert Morton in (Sir) Terence *Rattigan's *The Winslow Boy* (1946). At Stratford in 1956 he played Angelo, Shylock, and Iago. In 1955 he was Hjalmar Ekdal in *The Wild Duck*; he was Sir Thomas More in the New York production of *A Man for All Seasons* (1962). His films included *The Last Days of Dolwyn* (1949), *Ivanhoe* (1952), *The Deep Blue Sea* (1955), *The L-Shaped Room* (1962), and *David Copperfield* (1969).

In 1951 he began his acclaimed readings from Charles *Dickens, performing all over the world until he was well over eighty. From 1955 he performed a second one-man show, as Dylan Thomas in *A Boy Growing Up*. A third, based on

the writings of H. H. *Munro ('Saki'), began at the Apollo in 1977.

In 1961 he published the best-selling *George: an Early Autobiography*; its sequel, *Emlyn*, followed in 1973. His interest in the psychology of murderers led to *Beyond Belief* (1967), on the 'Moors murderers', and to *Dr. Crippen's Diary* (1987).

Given the high intellectual promise of Williams's beginnings his career is disappointing. He was a fine popular actor with lucid diction and a 'mesmeric' stage presence. But, though he had a success in *The Wild Duck* and as a 'superbly dangerous' Iago, his classical roles generally received mixed reviews. He was a determinedly commercial dramatist, with little interest in the avant-garde or in exploring social or political issues. His subjects were the psychology of murder and the supernatural, the conflict between innocence and experience, and the relationship between Wales and the outside world. But, too often, his desire for immediate effect led to melodrama, sentimentality, or theatrical cleverness. His portrayal of Welsh people tended to stereotype; claims that, in his Welsh plays, he perfected a rich poetic language reminiscent of J. M. *Synge are overstated. However, with such plays as *A Murder Has Been Arranged*, *Night Must Fall*, and *Someone Waiting* he contributed to the psychological thriller; his portrayal of ordinary people, particularly the rural Welsh, widened the narrow social range of West End 'drawing-room' plays. Above all, his fine command of the dramatist's craft made him a highly successful entertainer. His was the age of the well-made, middle-brow drama and the abrupt changes in British theatre during the 1950s, the advent of Samuel Beckett and John Osborne, effectively ended his writing for the stage. *Night Must Fall* and *The Corn Is Green* are occasionally revived and remain staple fare for amateurs, but he is now better remembered for his brilliantly accurate impersonation of Dickens the public reader.

His greatest literary achievement is *George*, a moving and detailed recreation of his childhood and adolescence in north Wales and an important study of a 'scholarship boy' in the 1920s. *George* is one of this century's finest autobiographies.

Williams's family was poor and Welsh-speaking. He remained proud of his roots and retained his Welsh. His upbringing made him careful with money; he died a wealthy man. He was an FRSL, received an honorary LL D at the University College of North Wales, Bangor, in 1949, and was appointed CBE in 1962. During his early career he lived with a fellow-actor, Bill Cronin-Wilson, who died in 1934. In 1935 he married Mary Marjorie ('Molly') (died 1970), formerly an actress, who was divorced from the barrister, Cecil Caradoc ('Jack') Carus-Wilson.

They had two sons. Mary's father was Theodore Walter O'Shann, chartered accountant.

Emlyn Williams died 25 September 1987, of cancer, at his London home, 123 Doverhouse Street, SW3.

[Emlyn Williams, *George* (autobiography), 1961, and *Emlyn*, 1973; Richard Findlater (K. B. F. Bain), *Emlyn Williams*, 1956; Don Dale-Jones, *Emlyn Williams*, 1979; James Harding, *Emlyn Williams, a Life*, 1993; *The Times*, 26 September 1987; information from John Atterbury.]   JAMES A. DAVIES

WILLIAMS, Kenneth Charles (1926–1988), actor and comedian, was born 22 February 1926 at Bingfield Street, off the Caledonian Road, London, the younger child and only son of Charles George Williams, manager of a hairdressing salon in Marchmont Street, King's Cross, London, and his wife, Louisa Alexandra Morgan, who assisted in the hairdresser's. He had theatrical aspirations from an early age, although his father, a Methodist, had a hatred of loose morals and effeminacy and thought the theatre epitomized both. The young Kenneth Williams, on the other hand, found acting 'instinctive, involuntary and authentic', attributes which marked his theatrical career in later years. He received his formal education at Lyulph Stanley School, Mornington Crescent, and from 1940 studied at the Bolt Court School of Lithography in Fleet Street, where he trained as a draughtsman.

Called up for national service in the army in 1944, he served as a sapper in the cartography section of the Royal Engineers and later as a poster designer and actor in CSE (Combined Services Entertainment), when stationed in Singapore. There, in company with such aspiring actors, playwrights, and directors as Stanley Baxter, Peter Nichols, and John Schlesinger, his theatrical aspirations hardened and developed, and he toured army bases in the Far East in the revue *At Your Service*.

He was demobilized in 1947 and by 1948 had become an established actor in various repertory companies, playing many different roles. By the early 1950s he had established his versatility. He made his début in films in a small part in the 1952 production of *Trent's Last Case*. In the same year he made his first television appearance in *The Wonderful Visit*, by H. G. *Wells, in which he played the Angel. This was followed by more repertory. In 1954 he played the Dauphin in G. B. *Shaw's *St Joan*, which led to his becoming the ubiquitous 'funny voice' man in the BBC radio success, *Hancock's Half Hour*.

In the theatre success followed success with Orson Welles's production of *Moby Dick* (1955), *Hotel Paradiso* (1956) with (Sir) Alec Guinness, *Share My Lettuce* (1957), *Pieces of Eight* (1959), and *One Over the Eight* (1957). Then, most importantly, with (Dame) Maggie Smith, to whom he was devoted, he acted in Peter Schaffer's *The Private Ear* and *The Public Eye* (double bill, 1962), followed by *Gentle Jack* (1963) with Dame Edith *Evans, and *Loot* (1965) by Joe *Orton, with whom Kenneth Williams developed a warm friendship. Later came *Captain Brassbound's Conversion* (1971), with Ingrid Bergman. His one flop was the 1956 production of Sandy Wilson's musical *The Buccaneer*, about a boys' magazine, in which Williams played the editor.

In 1958 he appeared in his first Carry On film, *Carry on Sergeant*, subsequently becoming a regular and playing in twenty-four Carry On films, all of them low farces. On radio he went from *Hancock's Half Hour* to *Beyond Our Ken* in 1958, and later to *Round the Horne* in 1965, where his brilliant characterizations contributed considerably to the show's success. In 1968 he became the star of the radio quiz *Just a Minute*, a game in which the panellists are asked to talk on a given topic 'without repetition, deviation, or hesitation'. Williams duly astonished chairman, cast, and listeners with his knowledge, erudition, humour, grasp of language, and simulated outrage when told he had deviated. One could hardly imagine him hesitating.

Williams, camp, slim, and dapper, was an amazingly versatile performer, able to switch from the vulgarities of the Carry On films and the louche characters of *Round the Horne* to more serious roles in plays by Jean Anouilh, Shakespeare, and Shaw. In addition he could be a sparkling raconteur, as he showed in the 1966–7 television series *International Cabaret*, where his long monologues happily punctuated the mundane procession of jugglers and acrobats. He was also a capable chat show guest, always ready with a new anecdote, and on more than one occasion successfully deputized for Terry Wogan as chat show host.

The public persona of a loud, brash, verbose vulgarian was very different from his private life, which was solitary, fastidious, and intellectual. He never married. His attitude to sex was ambivalent, for while he accepted his homosexual tendencies he found it difficult to consummate sexual relationships with either men or women. His writings included the books *Acid Drops* (theatrical anecdotes, 1980), *Back Drops* (personal anecdotes, 1983), and his autobiography *Just Williams* (1985). His diaries were published posthumously in 1993.

In the last entry in his diary, 14 April 1988, he complained of 'immense' exhaustion, pains in the back, and stomach trouble. He had never been physically robust, had a history of health problems, and it is likely he died as a result of accidentally taking an overdose of painkillers.

Williams died in his sleep at his home in Marlborough House, Osnaburgh Street, London, 15 April 1988.

[Kenneth Williams, *Just Williams, an Autobiography*, 1985; Russell Davies (ed.), *The Kenneth Williams Diaries*, 1993, and *The Kenneth Williams Letters*, 1994; personal knowledge.]   BARRY TOOK

WILLIAMS, Raymond Henry (1921–1988), writer and teacher, was born 31 August 1921 in Pandy, near Abergavenny, the only child of Henry Joseph Williams, railway signalman, of Pandy, and his wife (Esther) Gwendolene, daughter of James Bird, farm bailiff. He was educated at King Henry VIII Grammar School in Abergavenny and then went, in 1939 on a state scholarship, to read English at Trinity College, Cambridge. In part i of the tripos (1941) he gained a second class (division II). He was called up in 1941, commissioned in 1942, and fought with No. 21 Anti-Tank Regiment in the Normandy campaign and on to the Kiel canal. He attained the rank of captain.

In October 1945 he returned to Cambridge and took first-class honours in part ii of the tripos in 1946. Although he briefly considered a research degree, Williams entered the world of adult education as a staff tutor of the Oxford University Extra-Mural Delegacy (1946–61). He was based in East Sussex. He had married, in 1942, Joyce ('Joy') Mary (died 1991), daughter of Charles Dalling, coal factor, of Barnstaple. They had met at Cambridge when the London School of Economics was evacuated there during the war. They had two sons and one daughter. Joy Williams was a central influence on her husband's life and work. Later she was concerned with direct research for his books but throughout she was intimately involved with the evolution of his ideas and the publication of his numerous books. It was a deep and formidable partnership.

Although never a pupil of F. R. *Leavis, Williams was influenced by Leavis's emphasis on the life-enhancing properties of a close reading of literature. To this end he founded and edited, with Clifford Collins and Leavis's pupil Wolf Mankowitz, *The Critic* and *Politics and Letters* (which absorbed the former) in 1947–8. It was an uneasy marriage of socialist politics with cultural perspectives derived from Leavis. Despite severe disappointments with the wider social impact of any such approach, then and later, Williams consistently returned to the themes and principles of these early years. This firmness of purpose and integrity of behaviour, no less than an attractive diffidence and a generosity of spirit, were commented upon by all who met him throughout his lifetime. The public and private persona were all of a piece.

His first published books were on film and drama, notably *Drama from Ibsen to Eliot* (1952), and heralded a lifelong concern with the manner in which the form of literary works, no less than their content, was directly affected by the material changes wrought by social history. However, the key aspect of his work in the 1950s was his study of the connection between 'culture' and 'society', which was brought to its first conclusion in his path-breaking *Culture and Society* (1958). Its dissection of the meaning that British writers, and a wider society, had given to the word 'culture', since industrialization and under the pressures of democratic changes, had an immediate impact. It can be seen now as the main progenitor of the cultural studies which would flourish from the late 1960s. Williams followed it up with the important, though very different, volumes, *The Long Revolution* (1961), a provocative analysis of the interconnection between institutions, education, and ideas in Britain, and *The Country and the City* (1973), which used wide-ranging literary studies to dispute the notion of accepted boundaries between the rural and urban experience. All his critical writing challenged conventional boundaries of thought and their academic compartmentalization. The techniques of modern technology, advertising, and mass communications were, in a number of suggestive books, analysed as carefully as poems and novels had once been.

In 1961 he moved back to Cambridge as a lecturer in English and a fellow of Jesus College, and, from 1967 to 1974, reader in drama. He received a Cambridge Litt.D. in 1969 and was made the university's first professor of drama in 1974, retiring in 1983. Honours and appointments were many: membership of the Arts Council (1976–8), honorary doctorates from the universities of Wales (1980) and Kent (1984), and from the Open University (1975), and visiting professorships in Europe and the USA. He deeply affected a younger generation through weekly book reviews in the *Guardian* and revealed a keen interest in television, for which he wrote plays and presented documentary films, in a regular column in the *Listener*. His writing had made him a dominant figure, though slightly distanced in some respects, on the so-called 'new left'. In 1967 he largely edited the *May Day Manifesto* (a Pelican Special in 1968), a spirited but doomed attempt to redirect the merely pragmatic stance of the contemporary Labour party by reinvigorating the broader Labour movement with a sense of its socialist traditions and potential. Williams was active for a time in that party but more readily committed himself to wider left causes, such as the Campaign for Nuclear Disarmament. From the 1970s, as in his innovative interview/autobiography, *Politics and Letters* (1979), he called himself a 'Welsh European', a coupling as neat and as provocative as the phrases he used to signify his work, 'cultural materialism' and 'structure of feeling'. The whole corpus had established him, in his own lifetime, as a major socialist thinker. Steadfastly, *Towards 2000* (1983) rebutted nostalgia and defeatism.

He insisted that his fiction and better-known non-fiction writing should be seen as a unity. He had made his impressive début as a novelist with *Border Country* (1960); the first of a Welsh trilogy, *Second Generation* (1964); and *The Fight for Manod* (1979), in which his own individual background and general forces external to it, were given shape. *The Volunteers* (1978) was a political thriller of the near future, and *Loyalties* (1985) an indictment of political thrill-seekers of the near past. Two volumes of an incomplete historical novel, about the people of his native Black Mountains from the Ice Age to the present, appeared posthumously in 1989 and 1991. Their startling ability to be both realistic and experimental in tone again broke the mould at the very end of a life that had been heroically dedicated to the proposition that 'culture is ordinary'.

His tall, rather upright figure and long, etched face were instantly recognizable at conferences where, without ever striving for effect, he never failed to hold an audience. He was often said to look 'like a countryman' rather than a don and certainly the pipe, the rather deliberate drawl which was not quite a burr, and an unpretentious manner of dress and bearing all added to the image. Williams died 26 January 1988 at his home in Saffron Walden.

[*Independent*, 28 January 1988; *Guardian*, 27 January 1988; Raymond Williams, *Politics and Letters*, 1979; private information; personal knowledge.] DAI SMITH

WILLIAMS, Winifred (1907–1990), author and poet. [See STRONG, PATIENCE.]

WILLING, Victor James Arthur (1928–1988), artist, was born 15 January 1928 in Alexandria, Egypt, the only child of George Willing, professional soldier (captain), and his wife, Irene Cynthia Tomkins. He spent the first four years of his life in Egypt and, briefly, in Malta. Although he never consciously introduced the landscape of his childhood into his art, the paintings which made his reputation are notable for their sense of windless heat, bright light, vacant horizons, and undecorated enclosures. Through most of the 1930s Willing went to schools in various parts of southern England, including the Isle of Wight, but he enjoyed a more settled education during World War II at the Royal Grammar School, Guildford (1940–5), where he won the art prize. As a national serviceman (1946–8) he gained a commission in the Royal Artillery and, during this time, was confirmed in his ambition to be an artist by the Victoria and Albert Museum's pioneer showing in England of an exhibition of work by Pablo Picasso and Henri Matisse (1946). The force of Picasso's work, which he subsequently compared to being 'trapped in a stall with a stallion', particularly impressed him. On demobilization he was for a year at Guildford Art School before being accepted by the Slade School of Art, London University, where he spent four years (1949–53).

He had a rebellious streak and was admired by his contemporaries at the Slade—an outstanding intake, which included Michael Andrews and Euan Uglow—for his talent and intellectual zest, even being singled out by the influential critic David Sylvester as 'the spokesman for his generation'. He soon made friends in avant-garde circles, most influentially for his painting with (H. G.) Rodrigo *Moynihan and Francis Bacon. In 1955 he had a well-received first one-man show at Erica Brausen's Hanover Gallery, where Bacon exhibited.

This bright start as a painter was consolidated by his reputation as an intellectual. It is typical that his first, unpublished, article was preoccupied with the romantic and existential notion of the artist as hero, dandy, and gambler. It proved a false dawn. In 1951 he had married a girlfriend since school-days, Hazel, daughter of Harold Norman Whittington, FRICS, chartered surveyor. By the mid-1950s the marriage was failing and in December 1956 he left for Portugal to live with the painter Paula Rego, whom he had met at the Slade. She was the daughter of José Figueira Rego, electrical engineer. He continued to work but, by his own exacting standards, the results were not exhibitable and his loss to art seemed permanent when he took on the management of his father-in-law's business after the latter's death.

This coincided with the diagnosis that he was suffering from multiple sclerosis and when the Portuguese revolution of 1974 left the family affairs in chaos he settled in London with his wife (he had married Paula Rego in 1959, the year of his divorce from Hazel Whittington) and their children—Caroline (born 1956), Victoria (born 1959), and Nicholas (born 1961). He took a room in a condemned school in Stepney for a peppercorn rent and began to paint with renewed intensity, stimulated by the knowledge that time was short. Because he could only stand with the aid of a stick, for long periods he merely sat and stared. In states of reverie pictures would appear on the wall facing him. They were so vivid he called them 'visions'; and as soon as they were over he would draw them, later enlarging some into oil paintings. He exhibited the results in 1978 at the AIR (Artist Information Registry) Gallery.

The visions were the first pictures he felt 'exclusive to himself' and met with immediate critical success. Even after they disappeared, their effect remained. His last decade was a professional triumph. In 1980 he received a Thorne scholarship and in 1982 was made university artist in residence at Cambridge. There followed public exhibitions at the Serpentine and Whitechapel galleries—the latter a major retrospective in 1986; and his pictures entered several important collections, including those of the Arts Council and Tate Gallery. Even when greatly paralysed he managed to complete a series of powerful imaginative portraits, entitled 'Heads', exhibited at the Karsten Schubert Gallery (1987).

All Willing's paintings came from his large legacy of drawings, which he showed independently at the Hobson Gallery (1983), Bernard Jacobson Gallery (1983, 1984, and 1985), and the Hayward Gallery Annual (sponsored by the Arts Council) (1985). His most celebrated paintings are imaginative representations of empty rooms or deserted locations, pregnant with the presence of humans but never showing people. As in the work of Bacon, there is often a sense of existential anguish played out on a stage; but in Willing the drama is usually one of suspense and expectation. 'Place with a Red Thing' (1980, Tate Gallery) is an explicit exception, a masterpiece of ambiguity because of its clarity. A strange red form dripping and burgeoning dominates a space. 'Cythere' (1983, private collection) is also exceptional in showing a violently coloured plant simultaneously blooming and dying in front of a formal arrangement of cubic forms, apparently artificially lit against an indigo sky or backdrop. In pencil and brush Willing's handling is always expressive. His colours combine to enforce a sense of unease just as his geometry always avoids the right angle. His interest in stacked formal structures was realized in some sculptures towards the end of his life and he had unfulfilled plans to turn his fascination with the idea of the 'aedicula' or 'shelter', a place of refuge or retreat, into three dimensions.

Willing was slightly built, but with wide shoulders, sleek, handsome, and, unlike most artists, neatly dressed. He had an air of danger which made him a magnetic presence. He was given to quick, sudden movements and was a skilful and energetic dancer, with a sense of rhythm he brought to his painting. He died at home in Hampstead, London, of multiple sclerosis, 1 June 1988.

[*Victor Willing, a Retrospective Exhibition 1952–85*, Whitechapel Art Gallery, 1986; Karsten Schubert (ed.), *Victor Willing: Selected Writings and Two Conversations with John McEwen*, Karsten Schubert Ltd., 1993; personal knowledge.]							JOHN MCEWEN

WILSON, SIR Graham Selby (1895–1987), medical bacteriologist, was born 10 September 1895 in Newcastle upon Tyne, the youngest in the family of two daughters and a son of Ralph Graham Wilson, confectioner, and his wife, Caroline Elizabeth Dalgliesh. He was educated at various schools, including Mill Hill School and Epsom College, and entered King's College, London, in 1912. On the outbreak of war in 1914 he joined the clinical school at Charing Cross Hospital, where he qualified MRCS, LRCP in 1916; he joined the Royal Army Medical Corps and served, latterly as a captain and specialist in bacteriology, until 1920.

Returning from active service to Charing Cross Hospital, Wilson joined the department headed by W. W. C. *Topley, with whom he was to work for nearly twenty years and who was a great source of inspiration to him. Together they moved to the University of Manchester in 1923. In 1927 Wilson became reader in bacteriology at the University of London and in 1930 he was appointed professor of bacteriology as applied to hygiene at the newly established London School of Hygiene and Tropical Medicine.

In Manchester Wilson commenced studies of the hygiene of milk and demonstrated the frequency with which untreated milk was contaminated with disease-producing bacteria. He became an ardent advocate of pasteurization, demonstrating not only the efficacy of the process in ridding milk of dangerous bacteria, but also the enormous cost—in life and illness—of the mass consumption of untreated milk; sadly it was many years before the national authorities were convinced.

In the two or three years prior to the outbreak of war in 1939 Wilson assisted Topley in formulating plans for an emergency bacteriological service, to be mobilized in the event of war to help control the epidemics of infectious disease that were expected to result from the mass movement of people and the damage due to air raids. The Emergency Public Health Laboratory Service (EPHLS) started to function in September 1939. The epidemics did not, in fact, occur, but Wilson, inspired by Topley, saw the opportunity to develop a laboratory service that would be able to assist medical officers of health in the diagnosis and control of the infections that were endemic in the population. He proceeded to develop the EPHLS towards that end, and in 1941 he was formally appointed its director, a position that he held, through its metamorphosis into the permanent Public Health Laboratory Service, until he retired in 1963. During the postwar years he created a service comprising at one time nearly sixty area laboratories, many of which were housed in buildings that he himself had very largely designed, and a central reference laboratory, with a great international reputation.

At both Manchester and London, Topley and Wilson ran postgraduate courses for a diploma in bacteriology which provided unrivalled education in medical and public health bacteriology. Arising out of this teaching came the invitation to write a major postgraduate textbook and Topley and Wilson's *Principles of Bacteriology and Immunity*, first published in 1929 and continuing through seven editions with Wilson in charge, became and remained an excellent text. Wilson was elected a fellow of the Royal College of Physicians in 1930 and of the Royal Society in 1978, knighted in 1962, and received numerous medals, honorary fellowships, and other awards, among them an honorary LL D from Glasgow University (1962).

Physically, Wilson had a spare build and penetrating blue eyes; he rarely leavened scientific or administrative discussions with much humour, though he could lighten his conversation delightfully when right outside his working environment. If one adjective characterized him it would be 'meticulous'. It marked his work in the laboratory, his vision of planning and his work in designing both buildings and laboratory methods, and his mastery of the English language. It also affected his social manner: he was meticulous in never mixing professional and social activities. Indeed, even after many years of professional collaboration, he was reluctant to accept social invitations from his colleagues. He was also secretive, never revealing his plans until they were complete, even to his chief administrative staff, and refusing always to have a deputy, for fear that there might be premature leaks of proposals under discussion.

In 1924 Wilson married Mary Joyce (died 1976), daughter of Alfred Ayrton, banker, of Chester. They had two sons, one of whom was adopted. Wilson was an active gardener and a great lover of old churches, which he would prefer to reach on a bicycle. He used his bicycle whenever possible on the occasion of his annual visits to the laboratories, and he maintained well into his eighties a tradition of cycling 100 miles on or near his birthday each year. He was also a deeply religious man who served for twenty years as churchwarden at St Anne's Brookfield, in Highgate. He died 5 April 1987 in the Westminster Hospital, London.

[E. S. Anderson and Sir Robert Williams in *Biographical Memoirs of Fellows of the Royal Society*, vol. xxxiv, 1988; private information; personal knowledge.]

R. E. O. WILLIAMS

WINDSOR, (Bessie) Wallis, DUCHESS OF WINDSOR (1896–1986), wife of the former King *Edward VIII, was born 19 June 1896 in Blue Ridge Summit, Pennsylvania, the only child of Teackle Wallis Warfield, an unsuccessful businessman, and his wife, Alice Montague. The Warfields and Montagues were of distinguished Southern stock, but Wallis's parents were poor relations and her father died when she was only five months old. She spent her childhood in cheese-paring poverty, resentfully aware that her friends could afford nicer clothes and more lavish holidays. It seems reasonable to trace to this early deprivation the acquisitive streak which so strongly marked her character.

Though her jaw was too heavy for her to be counted beautiful, her fine violet-blue eyes and petite figure, quick wits, vitality, and capacity for total concentration on her interlocutor ensured that she had many admirers. When only nineteen she fell in love with a naval aviator, Lieutenant Earl Winfield Spencer (died 1950), son of Earl Winfield Spencer, a member of the Chicago Stock Exchange, and married him on 8 November 1916. It proved a disastrous match. Spencer's promising career disintegrated as he took to drink and Wallis, whose tolerance of weakness was never conspicuous, became increasingly alienated. While they were in Washington in 1922 they decided to separate and when Spencer was given command of a gunboat in the Far East, she remained behind, enjoying a flamboyant liaison with an Argentine diplomat.

In 1924 she joined her husband in China, but the reunion was not a success and they divorced in December 1927. By then she had already won the affections of Ernest Aldrich Simpson, whose own marriage was breaking up, the businessman son of an English father (Ernest Simpson, shipbroker and head of the firm of Simpson, Spence, & Young) and an American mother. She joined him in London, where he was managing the office of his family shipping company, and they married on 2 July 1928. Most of their friends were in the American colony in London; among them Benjamin Thaw of the US embassy, his wife Consuelo, and her younger sister Thelma, Viscountess Furness. Lady Furness was at that time mistress of the prince of Wales, and it was in her house at Melton Mowbray that Mrs Simpson, on 10 January 1931, met the man who was to become her third husband—Edward Albert Christian George Andrew Patrick David, the eldest child of King *George V. He was called David by his friends and family.

The precise nature of Mrs Simpson's appeal to the prince of Wales could only be understood by him; probably he hardly understood it himself. It is sufficient to say that by early 1934 the prince had become slavishly dependent on her and was to remain so until he died. The courtiers at first thought that this was just another of his recurrent infatuations, but throughout 1935 they became increasingly alarmed as her role became

more prominent and impinged on the performance of his duties. It seems unlikely that Mrs
Simpson seriously entertained the possibility
that she might become queen; indeed, all the
indications are that she enjoyed her role of
maîtresse en titre and would have been satisfied to
retain it. The prince, however, convinced himself
that his happiness depended on securing Mrs
Simpson as his wife. From his accession to the
throne on 20 January 1936 his main preoccupation was to bring this about.

Edward VIII's reign was marked by swelling
scandal as his relationship with Mrs Simpson
became more widely known. The cruise which
the couple undertook in the yacht *Nahlin* around
the eastern Mediterranean in September 1936
attracted keen interest everywhere except in the
British Isles, where the press maintained a discreet silence. It was, however, the Simpsons'
imminent divorce which convinced the prime
minister, Stanley *Baldwin (later first Earl
Baldwin of Bewdley), that he was faced by a
serious constitutional crisis. On 20 October he
confronted Edward at the king's country house,
Fort Belvedere, but it was only a month later
that Edward VIII stated categorically that he
intended to marry Mrs Simpson. Baldwin was
convinced that this must lead to abdication; the
king played with the idea of a morganatic marriage, a solution that would certainly have
appealed to Mrs Simpson, but was determined to
renounce the throne if that was the price he had
to pay.

Once she realized that marriage to her would
cost the king his throne, Mrs Simpson tried to
change his resolve. Anticipating much hostile
publicity when the story broke in the United
Kingdom, she retreated first to Fort Belvedere,
and then to the South of France. From there, in
a series of distraught telephone calls, she tried to
persuade Edward not to abdicate, even if this
meant giving her up. She accomplished nothing;
this was the only subject on which she was
unable to dominate her future husband.

On 10 December 1936 Edward VIII abdicated,
became duke of Windsor, and went into exile.
There followed six months of separation while
Mrs Simpson was waiting for her decree absolute
(3 May 1937), before, on 3 June 1937, the couple
were married at the Château de Candé in Tour-
aine. No member of the royal family was present
and the new duchess, on doubtful legal grounds,
was denied the title of Her Royal Highness. The
refusal of her husband's relations to accept her as
part of the family caused embittered and undying
resentment in the duchess.

Until the outbreak of war the Windsors lived
mainly in Austria and France. The duchess
accompanied her husband on his visit to Germany in 1937; it was popularly believed that she
had fascist sympathies and it has even been

claimed that she worked for German intelligence,
but there is no evidence that she held any
considered political views, still less indulged in
such activities. When war broke out in 1939 she
returned with the duke to Britain and then to
France. When the Germans overran France in
June 1940 the Windsors escaped into Spain and
thence to Portugal. From there they left for the
Bahamas, where the duke took up the post of
governor in August 1940.

The duchess hated their five years in Nassau
and made no secret of her views to those close to
her, but on the whole she performed the duties of
governor's lady conscientiously and well. She
entertained stylishly and went through the rituals
of opening bazaars and inspecting hospitals with
unexpected grace. Her happiest weeks, however,
were spent on shopping expeditions in the
United States and she was much criticized for
irresponsible extravagance at a time when Britain
was under assault.

After the war the Windsors settled in France
and their life became a dreary—though to her,
presumably, satisfying—merry-go-round featuring principally Antibes, Paris, New York, and
Palm Beach. The duchess entertained lavishly
and was counted among the best dressed and
fashionable figures in international society. Some
of her friends were raffish, a few even vicious,
but it was the sterility of her life that was most
remarkable. Though her husband resumed a
somewhat cool relationship with his mother and
siblings, the duchess was never received by the
royal family and remained fiercely hostile to
them. In 1956 she published her memoirs, *The
Heart Has Its Reasons*, an on the whole good-
tempered and balanced book, which was largely
ghosted but still reflected fairly her wit and
considerable common sense. When the duke died
on 28 May 1972 she was invited to Buckingham
Palace, but it was too late for the reconciliation to
mean much to her. The last fourteen years of her
life were spent in increasing decrepitude; during
the final five she lived in total seclusion. She died
at her home near Paris 24 April 1986 and was
buried beside her husband in the royal burial
ground at Frogmore.

[Duchess of Windsor, *The Heart Has Its Reasons*, 1956;
Michael Bloch, *Wallis and Edward: Letters 1931–1937*,
1986; Ralph G. Martin, *The Woman He Loved*, 1974;
private information.]   PHILIP ZIEGLER

WINNER, DAME **Albertine Louisa** (1907–
1988), physician and administrator, was born 4
March 1907 in Coulsdon, Surrey, the only child
of Isidore Winner (who had changed his name
from Isidor Wiener on leaving The Netherlands
some years previously), hide merchant, and his
wife, Annie Stonex. She was brought up in
London, which she always thought of as essentially composed of villages, and lived there all

her life. She was educated at the Francis Holland School, Clarence Gate, and from there she went to University College London, where she took a B.Sc. with honours in physiology. She went on to study medicine at University College Medical School, qualifying MB, BS in 1933 and winning the gold medal. An outstanding physician, she also became MD (1934), MRCP (1935), and FRCP (1959).

In her early career she worked with, and was much influenced by, Sir Thomas *Lewis and (Sir) Francis *Walshe. From the latter she gained her interest and skill in neurology, which she maintained throughout her life, culminating in the work of St Christopher's Hospice with patients in the terminal stages of motor neurone disease. She was appointed physician to the Elizabeth Garrett Anderson Hospital and the Mothers' Hospital (1937) but in 1940 she joined the Royal Army Medical Corps, becoming a lieutenant-colonel and later consultant to the Women's Services (1946–70).

Having acquired a taste for administration, she decided to become a medical administrator and joined the Ministry of Health, where she worked from 1947 to 1967. She saw the introduction of the National Health Service in 1948 and, with her intense interest in each individual patient, was especially concerned with the development of services for the long-term sick and disabled. She was the first woman to become deputy chief medical officer of health (1962). She brought a very human touch to the detailed implementation of administrative developments. At this time she was also a visiting lecturer at the London School of Economics (1951–63). Her interest was aroused both by the aims for the disabled of Group Captain (later Baron) Leonard Cheshire and (Dame) Cicely Saunders's plans for a research and teaching hospice for the terminally ill. Her background support and her encouragement to potential supporters of the projected plans for St Christopher's Hospice in south-east London, the first in the modern movement, was invaluable. When she retired in 1967 she went on a clinical refresher course and became the first deputy medical director at St Christopher's. She was later chairman (1973) and finally president (1985). Her clinical and administrative skills did much to establish the ensuing hospice movement on a sound footing.

She became Linacre fellow at the Royal College of Physicians from 1967 to 1978, being responsible for postgraduate education in medicine. Her experience of administration was greatly valued as a vice-president of the Medical Defence Union and within the Disabled Living Foundation. She was president of the Medical Women's Federation in 1971–2 and editor of the MWF newsletter from 1973 to 1981. She was appointed OBE in 1945 and DBE in 1967.

She reckoned that she had enjoyed at least five careers, to all of which she brought her vital interest and concern for people, whether they were patients or fellow workers. She never married but had time for many friends, to whom she gave unstinting support in any need. In her early years she was a keen sportswoman and she drove a Jaguar. She had a knowledgeable love of opera and a capacity for adventurous travelling holidays. Among her varied acquisitions was a valuable collection of Japanese prints. With all this she had her lonely and vulnerable side, although she could appear formidable. Of average height and robust figure, she gave the impression of being larger than she really was but this was offset by her warm smile. From her integrity stemmed her capacity for the attentive and skilful kindness that constitutes the very best moral support, which she gave so generously. For many years she affirmed her agnosticism while holding a great regard for the faith of others, but in her later years she became committed to Judaism, the faith of her father. After a long illness she died 13 May 1988 at Lancaster Lodge, a Wimbledon nursing home, where she was kindly and skilfully cared for and given a grand party for her eightieth birthday.

[*British Medical Journal*, vol. ccxcvi, 1988; *Medical Women's Federation Newsletter*, summer 1988; *Independent* and *Times*, 24 May 1988; personal knowledge.]

CICELY SAUNDERS

WINTERBOTHAM, Frederick William (1897–1990), airman and intelligence officer, was born 16 April 1897 in Stroud, Gloucestershire, the younger child and only son of Frederick Winterbotham, solicitor, of Painswick, Gloucestershire, and his wife, Florence Vernon Graham. He was educated at Charterhouse. On the outbreak of World War I in 1914 he joined the Royal Gloucestershire Hussars, transferring to the Royal Flying Corps when it was formed in 1916. The following year he was taken prisoner after being shot down during a dogfight over Passchendaele. His family thought he was dead, for he was reported as killed in action, and he was later to read his own obituary in a local paper. Upon his release in 1918 he went to Christ Church, Oxford, to study law, taking the shortened course for returning servicemen. He obtained his BA in 1920 (such degrees were unclassified).

He spent nine years as a pedigree stockbreeder, but in 1929 had a complete change of career when the deputy chief of air staff drew him into MI6, to run a new air intelligence section. From 1934 to 1938 he spent much time in Germany, with a cover story that he was 'persuading people in Britain to see things the Nazi way', but in actuality spying on German developments in air warfare. He used Baron

William de Ropp and Alfred Rosenberg as his main contacts, through them arranging meetings with Nazi leaders, from Hitler downwards. He learned much by listening, but was disappointed by the reception of his reports in Britain. He later wrote about this period in *Secret and Personal* (1969), which was revised as *The Nazi Connection* (1978). With Sydney Cotton he developed a pioneer system of high-altitude photo-reconnaissance, which was to be extremely useful in World War II. He was also a firm supporter of (Sir) Barnes *Wallis's bouncing bomb, being instrumental in getting it taken seriously by the air staff, who sanctioned the 'dambuster' raid.

In 1940 Winterbotham moved to the Government Code and Cipher School (GC&CS) at Bletchley Park, to work on the penetration of German ciphers encoded by the Enigma machine. This began to succeed when the Luftwaffe signals were broken; the next step was to convey the information to commanders in the field. Winterbotham devised and supervised the special liaison units of young officers and technical sergeants stationed at battle-command headquarters, who received enciphered radio messages from Bletchley (Ultra) and communicated them to the commanders. He was also the route by which Ultra intelligence reached the prime minister. His other role was, upon (Sir) Winston *Churchill's instructions, to indoctrinate American commanders before they could receive Ultra messages, for Churchill was concerned about the security of the Ultra system when America joined the war. Winterbotham thus became known to and respected by the American military leaders—Generals Dwight Eisenhower, Omar Bradley, and Karl Spaatz.

The Americans soon began to develop their own system of special liaison units. In March 1944 the Allies signed an agreement to unify the handling of Ultra intelligence throughout the world. That this happened was mainly due to Winterbotham. The 'Ultra secret' was never known by the Germans. It is ironic, therefore, that a confidential system known to thousands who honoured their wartime oath of silence was ultimately revealed by Winterbotham himself. This corporate act of silence was broken in 1974, when he produced *The Ultra Secret*, which aroused universal interest. Ultra was shown to be a factor of the highest importance in the Allied prosecution of the war; the book described how World War II was really won. Winterbotham was criticized by many for revealing the truth, but he had had the text of his book vetted by the authorities, who finally allowed him to publish it, though they did not endorse it.

In 1943 Winterbotham was appointed CBE. From 1945 to 1948 he worked for the British Overseas Airways Corporation. Thereafter he ran a small farm in Devon. In 1989 he produced his autobiography, *The Ultra Spy*. He was a charming and companionable man, tall, clean-shaven, with a fresh complexion, fair hair, and blue eyes. Distinctly handsome, he had a disciplined air. In 1921 he married Erica, daughter of Frederick John *Horniman, tea merchant, MP, and founder of the Horniman Museum. They had one son and two daughters. They were divorced in 1939 and he had a brief second marriage, which lasted until 1946. In 1947 he married Petrea, formerly wife of John Jowitt, army officer, and daughter of Alfred Samuel Trant, ironmonger, of Brixham, Devon. They had one daughter. After his third wife's death in 1986 he married in 1987 Kathleen Price, an old friend from his youth. Winterbotham died 28 January 1990 at his cottage in Tarrant Gunville, Dorset.

[F. W. Winterbotham, *The Ultra Secret*, 1974, *The Nazi Connection*, 1978, and *The Ultra Spy* (autobiography), 1989; F. H. Hinsley et al., *British Intelligence in the Second World War*, 4 vols., 1979–90; Ronald Lewin, *Ultra Goes to War*, 1978; R. V. Jones, *Most Secret War*, 1978; private information.]   C. S. NICHOLLS

WITTRICK, William Henry (1922–1986), professor of civil engineering, was born in Huddersfield 29 October 1922, the elder son and eldest of four children of Frank Wittrick (1894–1960), who had been wounded during World War I, had a variety of jobs, and finally worked for an engineering firm in Huddersfield, and his wife Jessie, the eldest child of Walter Jury, a local builder. Jessie was a proficient pianist and, prior to her marriage, had sung in the Huddersfield Choral Society. Wittrick's secondary education was at Huddersfield College where, because of his excellent higher school certificate results in July 1939, his parents were persuaded to allow him to stay for another year to try for a Cambridge scholarship. He was awarded an open exhibition in mathematics at St Catharine's College, while he later resat the HSC, obtaining such outstanding results that he was awarded both a state scholarship and the Jubilee exhibition of the Huddersfield education committee, thus relieving his parents of further financial burdens. Because of the war he decided to read mechanical sciences, in which he achieved first-class honours in the tripos in 1942, after only two years, and the award of the Archibald Denny prize for the theory of structures.

After a brief spell in 1942 with the Hawker Aircraft Company, he was interviewed by C. P. (later Baron) *Snow, the archetypal talent spotter of the day, and sent back to Cambridge as a junior demonstrator (1942–4). After another interview in October 1944 he was directed to the Royal Aircraft Establishment, Farnborough, where he undertook a theoretical investigation into the possible efficiency of 'sandwich construction', which resulted in the first of his seventy-seven research publications.

In 1945, following a recommendation by Professor J. F. (later Baron) *Baker, Wittrick accepted an invitation to become a senior lecturer in the University of Sydney, Australia. There he was able to spend considerable time on research into such topics as the coupling between torsion and flexure in swept-back wings, and the elastic stability of panels in such wings. In 1953 he spent six months at the California Institute of Technology with Professor Y. C. Fung investigating a structural 'boundary layer' at the free edges of thin plates in the large-deflexion regime. On his return to Sydney he became a reader in 1954 and in 1956 the Lawrence Hargrave professor of aeronautical engineering. His most important researches at that time were to determine stress concentrations around uniformly reinforced holes of various shapes, for which he was awarded the Orville Wright prize of the Royal Aeronautical Society (1961).

In 1964 he returned to England to accept the chair of structural engineering at Birmingham University, where his main research, much of it in co-operation with F. W. Williams, was to provide aerospace designers with the means to calculate the buckling loads or the natural modes and frequencies of vibration of thin-walled prismatic structures subjected to uniform biaxial compression and shear. This massive undertaking lasted about fifteen years and resulted in over twenty publications. It involved the development of novel mathematical techniques and spawned various computer programmes that were made available to British Aerospace, NASA, and all major aerospace firms in the USA.

In 1969 Wittrick became Beale professor of civil engineering at Birmingham University, a post he held until his retirement in 1982. He was appointed the general editor of the Oxford Engineering Science series of books and monographs in 1972. He was also on the editorial board of the *Aeronautical Quarterly* and the *International Journal of Mechanical Sciences*. From 1980 to 1984 he served on the British National Committee for Theoretical and Applied Mechanics and from 1980 to 1986 on the general assembly of the International Union of Theoretical and Applied Mechanics.

Wittrick was elected a fellow of the Australian Academy of Science in 1958 and a fellow of the Royal Aeronautical Society in 1961. He was awarded the Sc.D. degree at Cambridge in 1967. In 1980 he became a fellow of the Royal Society and in 1981 a fellow of the Royal Academy of Engineering. He was also awarded honorary degrees by Chalmers University of Technology

at Göteborg in Sweden (1984) and by the University of Wales (1985).

Wittrick, or 'Bill' as he was known to his many friends, had a cheerful personality and was the epitome of an English gentleman in family and public life. One cannot envisage him having other than friendly relations with all who knew him. He was of average height but muscular build, in keeping with his playing fly half in rugby while at college, and, in later years, squash and tennis. He had a ruddy complexion and brown hair, which thinned and greyed at a relatively early age. In June 1945 he married Joyce, daughter of Arthur Farrington, wholesale food merchant. They had two daughters. Since about 1976 Wittrick had suffered increasingly from emphysema, which caused his death 2 July 1986 at Warwick Hospital.

[Private information; personal knowledge.]

E. H. MANSFIELD

WOLPE, Berthold Ludwig (1905–1989), graphic artist and typographer, was born 29 October 1905 in Offenbach am Main, the younger son and third child of Simon Wolpe, dentist, and his wife, Agathe Goldschmidt. He was educated at a technical school (Realschule) as he was good even then at metalwork (through experience in his father's dental laboratory). He was expected to become an engineer, but in 1924 he went to Offenbach Art School and began his career. He worked under the great calligrapher Rudolf Koch, whose assistant he was from 1929 to 1934. Their association is celebrated in their book *Das ABC-Büchlein* (1934, English edition 1976), an elegant little collection of roman and Gothic alphabets drawn by both men. He learned goldsmith work under Theodor Wende at Pforzheim Art School and taught in both Frankfurt and Offenbach from 1930 to 1933.

In 1932 he visited London and met Stanley *Morison, who was interested in some bronze lettering of Wolpe's of which he had seen photographs. Morison asked Wolpe to design a printing type of capital letters in the same style for the Monotype Corporation. This was the birth of 'Albertus', first cut in 1934 and used in 1935, which quickly became the most widely used display face (i.e. for advertising, not books) in Britain. Its apparent simplicity made it look easy to copy, or reproduce photographically, and since there was no copyright in lettering, it was 'stolen' by every sign-writer in the country who had any taste. It appeared everywhere on buildings, shop fronts (e.g. Austin Reed), vans, paper bags, and posters, and if Wolpe had been paid a royalty for every time it was used (which he should have been) he would have soon become a rich man.

Wolpe, who was Jewish, settled in England in 1935, and from then until 1940 worked under

Ernest Ingham at the Fanfare Press in St Martin's Lane. While there he was designing a lowercase for Albertus, issued in 1938, a new display face 'Tempest', designed for Fanfare in 1935, a range of type ornaments for Fanfare published in his *A Book of Fanfare Ornaments* (with an introduction by James *Laver) in 1939, a new text face 'Pegasus', for the Monotype Corporation (cut only in 16 pt.) in 1937–40, and between 1935 and 1939 a series of innovative typographic yellow book jackets, printed by Fanfare, for Gollancz. He applied for naturalization in 1936, but it was not granted until 1947, and in 1940–1 he was interned in Hays Camp, central Australia.

When he returned to Britain in 1941 he moved to the publishers Faber & Faber in charge of jacket design, and remained there until his retirement in 1975. For Fabers Wolpe designed many books and more than 1,500 jackets and covers. While working there, he also taught lettering one day a week at Camberwell School of Art (1949–53) and at the Royal College of Art (1956–75), and, for about the last ten years of his life, he ran a unique lettering course at the City & Guilds of London School of Art. In 1966 he was invited to draw a new masthead for *The Times*, which was in use from 3 May 1966 to 20 September 1970.

Apart from his work as a designer (which included several other typefaces, distinguished emblems and devices, and lettering for permanent and ephemeral use) Wolpe was also an author and scholar of printing history and collector of any equipment or tools connected with writing, lettering, or measuring. He was vice-president of the Printing Historical Society in 1977. Among his books was *Renaissance Handwriting* (1960), written jointly with Alfred *Fairbank. When living in Chelsea, he found on a stall next door to his house a metal instrument thought by the stallholder to be something surgical, but which Wolpe had recognized as a pair of dividers, later established to be earlier than any in the British Museum. The bulging briefcase he used for carrying work to and from home was apt to be full of newly acquired treasures.

Whenever Wolpe rose to speak, for example at the Double Crown Club, of which he was an honorary member, or the Printing Historical Society, he always produced, with his diffident but entrancing smile, something wildly unexpected but totally apposite. He had a most striking head, with a big nose, which should have been drawn by Daumier or Dürer. It was in fact drawn by Charles Mozley in his little book, *Wolperiana: an Illustrated Guide to Berthold Wolpe*, published by the Merrion Press for his friends in 1960. This book also contains one of the best photographs of him, taken outside Fabers, by Frank Herrmann, who worked there.

Wolpe was made a Royal Designer for Industry in 1959 and appointed OBE in 1983. In 1981 he was Lyell reader in bibliography at Oxford University. The Society of Designer-Craftsmen made him an honorary fellow in 1984 and the Royal College of Art awarded him an honorary doctorate in 1968. He had retrospective exhibitions at the Victoria and Albert Museum (1980), the National Library of Scotland in Edinburgh (1982), and the Klingspor Museum in Offenbach (1983).

In November 1941 he made a most happy marriage with a sculptress, Margaret Leslie, daughter of Leslie Howard Smith, butcher, of Lewes. They had two sons and two daughters. Wolpe's essential Jewishness was expressed in the closeness of his relationship with his family. He died in St Thomas's Hospital, London, after a heart attack, 5 July 1989.

[*Berthold Wolpe: a Retrospective Survey*, Victoria and Albert Museum and Faber & Faber, 1980; private information; personal knowledge.]   RUARI MCLEAN

WOOLLEY, SIR **Richard van der Riet** (1906–1986), astronomer, was born 24 April 1906 in Weymouth, Dorset, the fourth of five children of Charles Edward Allen Woolley, paymaster rear-admiral in the Royal Navy, and his wife, Julia van der Riet, of Simonstown, South Africa. He went to Allhallows School, Honiton, Devon, from 1919 to 1921, when the family moved to Cape Town. He entered its university to study mathematics and physics, and by the age of nineteen he had the degrees of B.Sc. (1924) and M.Sc. (1925). Reverting to undergraduate status, in 1926 he entered Gonville and Caius College, Cambridge. He spent his first summer there with the scientific expedition led by H. G. ('Gino') *Watkins, exploring Edge Island, east of Spitsbergen. After graduating as a wrangler in the mathematical tripos (1928), he worked from 1928 to 1932 for his Ph.D. under Sir Arthur *Eddington, spending 1929–31 at Mt Wilson observatory, California, as a Commonwealth Fund fellow.

In 1933 he became chief assistant to the astronomer royal, (Sir) Harold Spencer *Jones, at the Royal Observatory, Greenwich. Seeking more scope for initiatives of his own, he returned to Cambridge in 1937 as John Couch Adams astronomer. From 1939 to 1955 he was Commonwealth astronomer and director of Mt Stromlo observatory, Australia. In 1940 the Australian government converted the observatory into an optical munitions factory, with Woolley as director. So impressed were they by his unfolding personality and resourcefulness that they also made him head of the army inventions directorate. His resulting acquaintance with leaders in scientific and public life led him to play an influential part in the phenomenal postwar development of Australian science.

From 1956 to 1971, as eleventh astronomer royal and director of the Royal Greenwich Observatory (RGO) at Herstmonceux, Sussex, he initiated far-reaching developments in British astronomy. He had also general oversight of the Royal Observatory, Cape of Good Hope, from 1960, and in 1971 the British and South African governments concluded an agreement whereby it became the headquarters of a new South African astronomical observatory (SAAO). In December 1971 Woolley retired from the Royal Observatory, forthwith becoming director of SAAO. He retired in December 1976.

Woolley's career had a remarkable coherence. His aim was the discovery of the physical constitution of the universe and the way in which the known laws of physics determine its operation. Pursuing this aim on three different continents, he erected large telescopes and promoted the education and training of astronomers, thereby creating the environment in which modern observational astrophysics could flourish. He was honorary professor in the formative years of the Australian National University and became an active visiting professor at the University of Sussex and later the University of Cape Town. He created vacation courses at the RGO, where he won young scientists' interest by having them join in *doing* astronomy. He made Stromlo the leading observatory in the southern hemisphere and generated the concept of the Anglo-Australian telescope. His friendship with leaders of Australian science and government eventually led to its becoming a reality on Siding Spring mountain. He strongly supported the construction there of the UK Schmidt telescope. At Herstmonceux he activated construction of the Isaac Newton telescope. When it was inaugurated in 1967 it was the largest in Europe (it was later moved to La Palma).

Telescope building and other duties were never allowed to halt Woolley's own observational researches. He made important and pioneering studies of the passage of radiation through both stellar and terrestrial atmospheres, the temperature of the sun's corona, the statistical mechanics of star clusters, the Magellanic clouds, and the stars within seventy-five light years of the sun. He was particularly concerned with determination of the kinematics and dynamics of the Galaxy and the presence of 'dark matter' within it. The resurgence of British optical astronomy and the related developments in Australia and South Africa owe their inception to Woolley and the telescopes he started. He was himself neither a popularizer nor a proponent of revolutionary ideas, although he respected some who were.

In 1952–8 he was vice-president of the International Astronomical Union, and in 1963–5 president and in 1971 gold medallist of the Royal Astronomical Society. He was elected a fellow of the Royal Society in 1953 and in 1956 an honorary fellow of Gonville and Caius College. He was master of the Worshipful Company of Clockmakers (1969) and had honorary degrees from Melbourne (1955), Uppsala (1956), Cape Town (1969), and Sussex (1970). He was appointed OBE (1953) and knighted in 1963.

Woolley was about six feet tall, with a fine presence; he had exceptional friendliness and charm and was an obvious leader. He was a man of open spaces, with an instinctive feeling for the countryside around him. On Stromlo he kept horses and rode a lot, and he enjoyed walking on Table Mountain. He was a talented pianist and liked country dancing and bell ringing. He played a whole range of ball games and encouraged others to participate.

In 1932 he married Gwyneth Jane Margaret, daughter of Hugh Harries Meyler, of independent means. She enhanced his love of the arts and greatly supported him in entertaining guests. He was devastated by her unexpected death in 1979 in Sussex. His health suffered, but (Emily May) Patricia, widow of Ronald Marples, a Royal Air Force gunner missing over Malta, and daughter of John Mowley, mining engineer, helped him back to normality. She became his second wife in 1979 and they went to live in South Africa, where many visiting astronomers enjoyed their hospitality. Patricia died in 1985. At the end of that year he married Sheila, former wife of David George Gillham, professor of English at Cape Town University, and daughter of William Penry Hammett, shipping agent. Woolley had no children. He had a bad fall and died 24 December 1986 at Somerset West, Cape Province, South Africa.

[Sir William McCrea in *Biographical Memoirs of Fellows of the Royal Society*, vol. xxxiv, 1988; personal knowledge.]

WILLIAM McCREA
DONALD LYNDEN-BELL

WOOTTON, Barbara Frances, BARONESS WOOTTON OF ABINGER (1897–1988), professor of social studies, was born 14 April 1897 in Cambridge, the only daughter and youngest of three children of James Adam, tutor at Emmanuel College, Cambridge, and his wife, Adela Marion Kensington, classicist and a fellow of Girton. Her father had been born into the family of a farm worker in Aberdeenshire, whence he made his way by scholarship from village school to Cambridge University and a degree in classics.

Barbara herself was healthy, good-looking, and precocious. Her father died when she was ten and he only forty-seven. Her best schoolfriend died at school and her brother Arthur in war. She was then widowed by war. Her husband, John

Wesley ('Jack') Wootton, a research student at Trinity College, Cambridge, and the son of Arthur Wootton, from a Nonconformist manufacturing family in Nottingham, was a friend of her elder brother Neil. They were married on 5 September 1917 and had thirty-six hours together before she saw him off to France at Victoria station. He died of wounds on 11 October 1917 and in due course the War Office returned to her his blood-stained uniform. We can reasonably speculate that the phobias and obsessions which plagued her had their origins in these adversities. Yet she herself remained resolutely pre-Freudian in her attitudes towards responsibility in the face of disaster. Utter self-reliance was her creed. 'We would do better,' she thought, 'to encourage children from the earliest possible age, however wretched their backgrounds, to believe that they are, or at least soon will be, masters of their fates.'

Though she prayed earnestly to be sent away to school like her brothers, she did not escape the home nursery until at thirteen she was allowed to enter the Perse High School in Cambridge as a day pupil. Her mother wanted her to study classics at Girton College and she was dutifully successful in the entrance examinations, becoming a candidate for the first part of the tripos, even though her strong personal inclination was to abandon dead languages for Alfred *Marshall and modern economics. As her final examinations approached she succumbed, apparently psychosomatically, to virulent tonsillitis. Her illness caused her to get an *aegrotat* degree (1918). Liberation from the well-intentioned matriarchal dominion of her childhood began with part ii of the tripos. She put aside the Greek and Latin texts and turned to read economics with determined enthusiasm. She gained a first class in 1919. Yet, ironically, as a woman she was prevented from appending BA to her name.

After leaving Cambridge she took up a research studentship at the London School of Economics. In 1920 Girton recalled her to a fellowship and the directorship of social studies in the college, and the board of economics invited her to lecture on economics and the State. The University of Cambridge at this time did not officially allow the admission of women and therefore could not license lectures by a non-member. (Sir) Hubert *Henderson intervened gallantly, offering himself as the advertised lecturer but on the understanding that the university would add in brackets that the lectures would be delivered by Mrs Wootton.

She married again in 1935, her husband being George Percival Wright, the son of Thomas Wright, of 29 Prothero Road, London SW6. He was her colleague in adult education and London government, who was temporarily a cab driver. There was no permanent peace, for Wright turned out to be a 'natural polygamist', who kept a succession of 'secondary wives' round the corner, though making it clear to each that his loyalty to Barbara was paramount. She nursed him through a long illness till he died of cancer in 1964. There were no children of the marriage.

She forsook not only the classics but also conventional scholarship and institutional religion. Her circumstances and her temperament gradually formed her into a rationalist, an agnostic, and a socialist—a method, a philosophy, and a commitment which lent steady consistency to a long professional and public life. Her rationalism evolved, no doubt, in part from sheer intellectual power but also from the experience of bereavement and the illogicality of a gifted woman's place in her society. Her agnosticism was nurtured by deep scepticism about the benevolence of any conceivable deity or principle of cosmic order in World War I. Her socialism was rooted in the same experiences which convinced her that, given sympathy for others, critical reason was the only road to salvation on this earth.

She worked for the research department of the Labour party and the Trades Union Congress from 1922, as principal of Morley College from 1926, and as director of studies for tutorial classes at London University from 1927 until she took up a readership at Bedford College in 1944. In 1944 she was disappointed in a competition for the chair and headship of the department of social science at the LSE, which went to T. H. *Marshall. Within academe her preoccupation was always with practical problems. She was promoted to the rank of professor in 1948. She became an acknowledged expert in criminology, penology, and social work, writing many books on those subjects. Her *Social Science and Social Pathology* (with V. G. Seal and R. Chambers, 1959) remains a classic in the application of utilitarian philosophy and empirical sociology to the enlightened management of society. From 1952 to 1957 she was Nuffield research fellow at Bedford College.

She became an outstandingly vigorous public figure. She was a governor of the BBC from 1950 to 1956 and served on four royal commissions (workmen's compensation 1938–44, the press 1947–9, the Civil Service 1953–5, and the penal system 1964–6). She was also chairman of the Countryside Commission (1968–70). Created a life peer in 1958, she was the first woman to sit on the woolsack in the House of Lords, as deputy speaker from 1967. Her ambivalence to the upper chamber surprised some democratic socialists. She recognized that it was 'totally indefensible in a democracy'. 'No one in his senses would invent the present house if it did not already exist... but...ancient monuments are not light-heartedly to be destroyed.' More generally she made the best of the institutions she found and was unwilling to see her country pay the price in misery to ordinary people that revolution along Stalinist lines would entail. She preferred to work piecemeal and her service as a justice of the peace for London, to which she was appointed in 1926 at the age of twenty-nine, that is, before she was entitled as a woman to vote, is a long record of humane public effort. She held thirteen honorary doctorates and was made a CH in 1977. She died 11 July 1988 at Holmesdale Park, Nutfield, Surrey, admired by those who knew her, honoured by a Festschrift, and widely revered as a woman whose steadfast faith was in argument and persuasion towards a socialist commonwealth.

[Philip Bean and Vera G. Seal (eds.), *Barbara Wootton: Selected Writings*, 4 vols., 1993; Philip Bean and D. Whynes (eds.), *Barbara Wootton: Essays in her Honour*, 1986; Barbara Wootton, *In a World I Never Made*, 1967; Terence Morris, 'In Memoriam: Barbara Wootton 1897–1988', *British Journal of Sociology*, vol. xl, no. 2, June 1989; personal knowledge.]   A. H. HALSEY

WRIGHT, Basil Charles (1907–1987), documentary film-maker and author, was born 12 June 1907 in Sutton, Surrey, the only son (there were also younger twin sisters) of Major Lawrence Wright, TD, and his wife, Gladys Marsden, and was brought up in a comfortably well-off middle-class family. He was educated at Sherborne School and entered Corpus Christi College, Cambridge, as a Mawson scholar in 1926 to read classics. He took a first in part i of the classical tripos (1928) and a third in part ii of economics (1929), having already decided while an undergraduate that he would become either a poet, dramatist, or film-maker.

A double chance—he had happened to attend the première of *Drifters*, directed by John *Grierson, the first 'documentary' film in the particular British definition of the genre (which struck him as 'the sort of film I wanted to make'), and Grierson happened to have seen an amateur film of his while looking for an editor to work in his film unit at the Empire Marketing Board—determined that he would become a film-maker and a documentarist. He was one of the first to join the small band of documentarists being gathered together at the EMB and he remained throughout his professional life one of the most devoted, unquestioning, and faithful members of the British documentary movement and a follower of its mercurial and magnetic leader, John Grierson. He followed Grierson to the GPO Film Unit in 1933; he resigned when Grierson was pushed out in 1937, and co-founded the Realist Film Unit, an independent commissioning and production unit for sponsored productions. In 1936 he co-directed, with Harry Watt, *Night Mail*.

He joined the Film Centre in 1939 as executive producer, a post he retained until 1944.

During this time of war (the golden age of the documentary with, for once, ample resources available), although by nature a personal film-maker, he worked tirelessly and selflessly as producer, administrator, and adviser to no fewer than thirty-six films, which were directed by others. His creative contribution to many of these was substantial, including to some of the classics, such as *Diary for Timothy* (1946).

He finished the war as producer in charge of the Crown Film Unit (1945) and adviser to the director-general of the Ministry of Information. This should have provided him with the means for resuming his creative career, but he responded unhesitatingly to Grierson's call to join him at International Realist in New York. This was an abortive attempt by Grierson to restart his own production career after leaving Canada in the wake of revelations by Igor *Gouzenko about Soviet infiltration. Wright then followed Grierson to Unesco and devoted his energies again primarily to paperwork.

His creative career restarted in 1953, although he sensed that he was now too old. Only six more films followed before his swansong, *A Place for Gold*, in 1960. He devoted the remaining twenty-seven years of his life to studying, writing, and teaching about film, trying to keep alive the ideals of the Griersonian documentary. He taught at the University of Southern California (1962–8), was senior lecturer in film history at the National Film School (1971–3), and visiting professor at other institutions such as Temple University, Philadelphia (1977), and Houston University (1978). He also taught film-making in developing countries, and held many honorific positions, including those of governor of the British Film Institute (1953) and fellow of the British Film Academy (1955).

His most influential and important film, in some ways never quite matched later, came early in his career. *Song of Ceylon* (1936), which won the gold medal and prix du gouvernement at Brussels, put the British documentary movement on the map, showing that film could be an art form, the first time the British film was recognized in that way. Of his other films, *Children at School* (1938) and *The Immortal Land* (1959, for which he was awarded the Council of Europe award) are perhaps the most representative of his special poetic and aesthetic gifts, as well as his technical mastery of the craft of documentary film-making. In 1936 he was awarded the gold cross of the Royal Order of King George I of Greece.

As a film-maker, his contribution to the development of the documentary lies essentially in bringing to it an aesthetic sensitivity. He was widely recognized as the 'poet of the documentary movement'. However, the insistence of Grierson on public service and his strident, if not always consistent, opposition to his documentarists being 'aestheticky' and personal, prevented those poetic shoots from their full flowering. As the critic David Thomson fairly said, Wright's work at its best was sensitive, graceful, and pictorial, but it was also without dynamic personality or heart.

As a writer he contributed greatly to the critical and theoretical debates essential to the development of the documentary movement, especially during World War II, when through the pages of the *Documentary Newsletter* he took over part of the role of the intellectual leader of the documentary movement while Grierson was in Canada. He was film critic of the *Spectator* and *Sight and Sound* in the late 1940s. He published two books, *The Use of the Film* (1948) and *The Long View* (1974), the latter one of the classic histories of the cinema from an aesthetic perspective.

Basil Wright had an attractive personality, at once cultured, scholarly, and sensitive, and yet efficiently practical and with a quiet sense of humour. His lifelong recreational interests were opera, ballet, and gardening. In appearance he was of medium height, with a lightly built, trim body and regular features, his scholarly appearance emphasized by dark-rimmed spectacles. He never married and lived for the latter half of his life with a long-time companion, Kassim Bin Said, at Little Adam Farm, Frieth, Henley on Thames. He died 14 October 1987 at Little Adam Farm, of bronchopneumonia and cerebral atrophy.

[David Thomson, *A Biographical Dictionary of the Cinema*, 1975; G. Roy Levin, *Documentary Explorations*, 1971; information from members of the documentary movement and others; personal knowledge.]

NICHOLAS PRONAY

WYNDHAM GOLDIE, Grace Murrell (1900–1986), television producer. [See GOLDIE, GRACE MURRELL WYNDHAM.]

WYNNE, Greville Maynard (1919–1990), businessman and intelligence agent, was born 19 March 1919 in Wrockwardine Wood, east of Shrewsbury, Shropshire, the only son to grow up of Ethelbert Wynne, plater, and his wife, Ada Pritchard. He had three elder sisters; an elder brother had died aged one in 1915. He was brought up at Ystradymynach, a mining village a dozen miles north of Cardiff, where his father was a foreman in an engineering works. His mother died when he was fourteen. He worked in his middle teens as an electrician, and took evening courses in engineering at Nottingham University.

Called up into the army in 1939, he spent the war as a sergeant in the Field Security Police, looking after elementary security in various parts of Great Britain. He acquired the vocabulary of the Intelligence Corps, in which he served. On being demobilized in 1946 he married, on 21 September, at St Anne's, Wandsworth, Sheila Margaret, daughter of Gordon Beaton, chemist. They had a son.

He already described himself, on his marriage certificate, as a consulting engineer—a trade in which he made himself useful to exporters, with whom lay the country's best hope of staying solvent. In a decade and a half he built up a profitable small business, and came to specialize in assisting exports to eastern Europe, then under rigid communist control from Moscow. He occasionally visited the USSR to forward his clients' interests. He was a short, stocky man, with a brisk, cheerful manner, a toothbrush moustache, and smooth dark hair.

As a matter of routine, MI6 (the Secret Intelligence Service) briefed many British businessmen who travelled behind the iron curtain about points for which they might like to look out while there; Wynne was among them. Chance turned him into an important pawn in the 'great game'. Oleg Penkovsky, a colonel in Russian secret military intelligence, had been demoted from work he enjoyed in Turkey to run a Moscow committee that enquired into scientific matters—a cover for industrial espionage against the capitalist powers. Entirely disillusioned with the Soviet regime, Penkovsky sought to change sides, and through several intermediaries approached the American Central Intelligence Agency, without securing a response. He then approached Wynne, who informed MI6, which decided to take the case up, and to handle it jointly with the CIA. MI6 accepted Wynne as one of the conduits through which material could from time to time be passed to and from Penkovsky.

Some of this material was of world strategic importance, for it enabled the Americans to outface the Russians in the Cuban missile crisis of 1962. Shortly thereafter, Wynne, who may have shown unprofessional enthusiasm at finding himself in Penkovsky's presence, unaware of the strictness with which Soviet citizens kept watch on each other, was abruptly arrested in Budapest, on 2 November 1962. He discovered after he had been flown to Moscow that Penkovsky was already in jail. After nine months' intermittent, fierce interrogation, the two were given a public show trial there on 7–11 May 1963.

Wynne stuck to his cover story that he was a simple businessman, admitting to having carried packets, but denying any knowledge of their contents. Penkovsky was sentenced to death, Wynne to eight years. After less than a year of hideous discomfort at Vladimir, some 120 miles east of Moscow, Wynne was, again abruptly, flown to Berlin and exchanged for a leading

Soviet agent, Conon Molody ('Gordon Lonsdale'), early on 22 April 1964. The exchange received a torrent of publicity in the free world's news media. MI6 and the CIA paid Wynne over $200,000 compensation.

His wife had stood by him loyally; but his marriage swiftly broke up. He went off to Majorca with his secretary, Johanna Hermania, the daughter of Dirk van Buren, civil servant. They married on 31 July 1970 at Kensington register office; his first wife had divorced him in 1968. There were no children of the second marriage. Wynne wrote two books, to try to make money out of what had happened to him: *The Man from Moscow*, a life of Penkovsky and himself (1967), and the much more fanciful *The Man from Odessa* (1981), in which, for example, he claimed to have held an army commission, which he never did. He never went back to business and died of cancer in the Cromwell Hospital, Kensington, 27 February 1990.

[Greville Wynne, *The Man from Moscow*, 1967; J. L. Schechetr and P. S. Deriabin, *The Spy Who Saved the World*, 1992; private information.]   M. R. D. Foot

Y

YONGE, SIR (Charles) Maurice (1899–1986), marine biologist, was born 9 December 1899 at Silcoates School, near Wakefield, Yorkshire, the younger child and only son of John Arthur Yonge, headmaster of the school, and his wife, Sarah Edith Carr. Silcoates School was a private establishment which Maurice joined as a pupil in 1908. As the son of the headmaster he did not enjoy his schooling. Shy, sensitive, with a stammer, he became ever more self-conscious and isolated. Influenced by his mother, he found solace in reading and developed a lifelong love of history. He left school at seventeen and for a year read history at Leeds University. In 1918 he was commissioned into the Green Howards, only to be demobilized shortly afterwards. For one glorious summer he read modern history at Lincoln College, Oxford, but then, believing it important to take up a more practical subject, persuaded his father to let him study forestry at Edinburgh, a city he had loved visiting with his mother.

The forestry degree included courses in natural history and these turned his interests to zoology. In his second year, after spending Easter at the Marine Station, Millport, 'in unspeakable weather and living conditions of the crudest', he returned 'a committed marine biologist'. In 1922 he completed a degree in zoology with distinction and was awarded the Baxter natural science scholarship.

Yonge spent a further two years in Edinburgh working for his Ph.D. on the physiology of digestion in marine invertebrates. He met Lancelot *Hogben, who suggested that the clam *Mya* might be of interest. That remark led Yonge to world renown for his studies on the bivalve molluscs. During the year 1924–5 a Carnegie research scholarship took him to Naples, and on his return he joined the staff of the Marine Biological Association at Plymouth, where for two years (1925–7) he worked mainly on feeding in oysters. These remained a special interest, which was expressed in his book *Oysters* (1960). At Plymouth also he joined with (Sir) Frederick *Russell in writing *The Seas* (1928), a classic that inspired budding marine biologists of the 1930s and 1940s.

In 1927 Yonge was invited to Cambridge as Balfour student, with the initially hidden object of his leading the Great Barrier Reef expedition, then being planned in some confusion. The same year he married a medical student he had met in postgraduate days, Martha Jane ('Mattie'), daughter of Robert Torrance Lennox, of Newmilns, Ayrshire. They married on 30 June 1927, the day after Yonge was awarded his D.Sc. degree. Mattie joined the expedition as medical officer; both the marriage and the expedition of 1928–9 were resounding successes.

From Australia Yonge returned to Plymouth as physiologist. After three years he was disenchanted with his progress and accepted the chair of zoology at Bristol in 1933. In 1944 he became regius professor of zoology at Glasgow. By then with immense determination he had controlled his stammer and become a most effective lecturer and administrator.

Initially at Glasgow there was great sadness, for his wife, who had spent the war years away from Bristol with the children (a son and daughter), became seriously ill, required brain surgery, and died shortly afterwards in 1945. Thereafter Yonge wrote *The Sea Shore* (1949), which he dedicated to her. In 1954 he married Dr Phyllis Greenlaw ('Phyll') Fraser, helminthologist and daughter of Douglas Morrison Milne Fraser, physician, of Eastry, Kent. They had one son.

Now in demand nationally and internationally, Yonge chaired the colonial fisheries advisory committee, served on the Natural Environment Research Council, was vice-president of the Scottish Marine Biological Association, and was twice on the council of the Royal Society. He was one of a few who controlled British biological science between 1950 and 1970. In 1964 he resigned his chair at Glasgow, remaining as research fellow until 1970. In 1965 he and his wife set up house in Edinburgh and on his retirement in 1970 he became an honorary research fellow in zoology at the University of Edinburgh. The circle was complete, but his scientific output and travel continued until his Parkinson's disease became too disabling when he was eighty-three.

Although his overwhelming concern lay with molluscs, Yonge published sufficient work on corals and decapod Crustacea to have been lauded for this alone. His output of popular marine science was also immense, for he had a journalistic bent and at Oxford had considered journalism as a career. He kept up historical interests, amassed a fine library, and indulged in carpentry.

Yonge was a fellow of the Royal Society of Edinburgh (1945, president 1970–3) and of London (1946) (Darwin medal, 1968). He was appointed CBE in 1954 and knighted in 1967. He was a member of the Royal Danish Academy of Sciences (1956) and had honorary degrees from the universities of Bristol (1959), Heriot-Watt (1971), Manchester (1975), and Edinburgh (1983). His last scientific paper was published three days before he died in Edinburgh, 17 March 1986.

[B. Morton in *Biographical Memoirs of Fellows of the Royal Society*, vol. xxxviii, 1992; personal knowledge.]
JOHN A. ALLEN

YOUNG, SIR Frank George (1908–1988), biochemist and educationist, was born 25 March 1908 at 2 Bond Street, Holford Square, Clerkenwell, the eldest in the family of two sons and one daughter of Frank Edgar Young, solicitor's clerk, and his wife, Jane Eleanor Pinkney. His childhood years were spent in Clerkenwell and Dulwich. He was educated at Alleyn's School, Dulwich, and University College London, graduating with first-class honours in chemistry in 1929. He rowed for both college and university.

On graduation he decided to take up biochemistry and joined the department of physiology, pharmacology, and biochemistry at University College. He obtained his Ph.D. in 1933. He was a Beit memorial research fellow at University College (1932–3 and 1935–6) and in between at Aberdeen and Toronto. In 1936 he moved to the National Institute for Medical Research in London as a member of the scientific staff. Within a year he had discovered that a permanent form of diabetes could be induced in suitable species of animal by a short period of injection of extracts of the anterior lobe of the pituitary gland. This discovery was of major importance, because it was the first time that permanent diabetes had been induced by a natural substance (later to be identified by him as the pituitary growth hormone). His work from 1936 to 1952, on this theme and on other aspects of the regulation of growth and metabolism by hormones, gave him a substantial national and international reputation.

In 1942 he left the National Institute to become professor of biochemistry at St Thomas's Hospital Medical School (1942–5) and then at University College London (1945–9). In 1949 he was appointed to the Sir William Dunn professorship of biochemistry at Cambridge, where he stayed until his retirement in 1975. From about 1952 onwards he abandoned personal research and teaching and concentrated increasingly on educational, scientific, and medical affairs in Cambridge and at national and international level. Two major themes were the needs of postgraduate students and relations between medicine and the sciences. In Cambridge Young was among the first to recognize the need for postgraduate colleges, and with the senior tutor of Corpus Christi (Michael McCrum) he set out in 1956 to advocate their establishment. Their campaign bore fruit in 1963, when the founding of Darwin College, with Young as its first master, was announced; and in 1964, with the report of the council of the senate which led to the establishment of Wolfson College. Young was a highly successful first master of Darwin (1964–76). He also played a decisive part in the founding of the Cambridge University clinical school in 1975. He was a member of the royal commission on medical education (1965–8), which provided the opportunity, and as chairman (1969–75) of the school planning committee, brought the opportunity to fruition. He served on the Medical Research Council, the council and other committees of the Royal Society, committees of the Department of Health, the Ciba Foundation, and the medical and scientific section of the British Diabetic Association (founding chairman), and as president of the European Association for the Study of Diabetes and of the International Diabetes Federation. He was knighted in 1973. He had intended to resume laboratory research on retirement, but a serious episode of food poisoning in 1977 impaired his mobility and made this impractical.

He was elected FRS in 1949 and his scientific achievements were further recognized by the Croonian lectureship of the Royal Society (1962), the Banting lectureships of the British and American Diabetic Associations (1948 and 1950), the Upjohn award of the American Endocrine Society (1963), and honorary degrees from the universities of Chile (Catolica) (1950), Montpelier (1959), Aberdeen (1965), and Zimbabwe (1975).

Young was a tall, broad-shouldered man, whose vitality showed in his face. In 1933 he married Ruth Eleanor, daughter of Thomas Turner, a Home Office civil servant, of Beckenham, Kent. He and Ruth were fellow students at University College (she qualified in medicine after a general sciences degree). They had three sons, and one daughter, who died in 1988. Ruth was a staunch supporter of his activities in Cambridge and elsewhere and her services to Darwin were recognized with an honorary fellowship in 1989. Young died 20 September 1988 in the Evelyn Nursing Home, Cambridge.

[Sir Philip Randle in *Biographical Memoirs of Fellows of the Royal Society*, vol. xxxvi, 1990; personal knowledge.]
PHILIP RANDLE

YOUNG, George Kennedy (1911–1990), intelligence officer, was born in Dumfries 8 April 1911, the youngest of three children and younger son of George Stuart Young, grocer, and his wife, Margaret Kennedy. He was brought up in the Old Covenanting traditions of the United Free Church to which his parents belonged. He was educated at Dumfries Academy and St Andrews University, where he was an outstanding figure, with his great height, red hair, outstanding intellectual ability, quick wit, and strong Independent Labour party views. He took six years to obtain his degree, during which he spent a year each at Giessen and Dijon universities, and he achieved first-class honours in both French and German in 1934. He was then awarded a Commonwealth scholarship (1934–6) to Yale University, where he obtained an MA in political science.

In 1936 he joined the staff of the *Glasgow Herald*, which he left in 1938 to join the British United Press. When war was declared in 1939 he joined the King's Own Scottish Borderers, and was commissioned in 1940, finally achieving the rank of lieutenant-colonel. He was transferred to field security, on the basis of a rather sketchy knowledge of Italian, and served with distinction in the Abyssinian campaign, being mentioned in dispatches (1941). He joined MI6 in Cairo in 1943. After the war he did a stint as British United Press correspondent in Berlin in 1946. He was then invited to rejoin MI6 (1946) and accepted. His first job was to investigate the ramifications of German penetration of British intelligence activities in the Low Countries.

Young had the qualities to make a success in this field—a deep knowledge of and interest in politics, a first-class brain, a gift for languages, and an ability to attract the loyalty of his staff. After stints in London and Vienna, he was posted to Cyprus in 1951 as the controller of all MI6 personnel and operations in the Middle East. This task he discharged with a firm hand, and in the process became a believer in 'covert action', encouraged in this by the success in 1952 of MI6, working with the CIA, in restoring the shah of Iran to his throne. As the Middle East drifted nearer to a major crisis and confrontation, some people in London became anxious about Young's independent plans. Sir Dick White had been appointed head of MI6, and Young was recalled to London late in 1956. He was put in charge of that part of the office concerned with the collation and distribution of intelligence. In this capacity he modernized an out-of-date system, particularly in the scientific and technological field. He was disappointed that he was unable to acquire an unmanned high-flying photo-reconnaissance plane.

After the resignation of Sir James *Easton in 1958 he was appointed vice-chief of MI6, with the rank of under-secretary in the Ministry of Defence from 1960. He became much involved in the Far East, studying the dangers of further involvement by the Americans in Vietnam. By the end of the 1950s his political views, particularly on racial matters, had moved so far to the right that he found it increasingly difficult to conform to official policies, whichever of the major parties was in power. His position as vice-chief of MI6 became difficult to sustain, and it was with some relief on both sides that he resigned in 1961.

Shortly afterwards he joined the merchant bankers Kleinwort, Benson. He worked with them more or less full-time from 1961 to 1976. The two banks had only recently amalgamated, and had decided to expand their overseas business. Young's international contacts enabled him to play a quasi-ambassadorial role in this expansion, particularly in Iran, France, and Belgium. He quickly learned the broad principles of banking, but was not involved in day-to-day banking operations. This happy arrangement with Kleinworts suited both of them. It gave Young space to develop his increasing interest in home politics, and time to write several books on contemporary problems. These included *Masters of Indecision* (1962), a diatribe against Whitehall in general and the Foreign Office in particular, *Merchant Banking* (1966), *Who Is My Liege?* (1972), and *Subversion* (1984). He stood as Conservative parliamentary candidate at Brent East in 1974—a gesture of principle rather than political ambition.

Young's influence on many people lay in what he was, rather than what he achieved. His ability might have taken him to the top in several fields. If he never quite succeeded it was perhaps because, while his views on policies and people were strongly held and pungently expressed, they were often unfashionable, and just occasionally his judgement was suspect. Whether politically involved with the left, or the right, his attraction and influence lay in his total independence of outlook. He remained at heart a militant Scottish Covenanter, believing deeply in the rights of the individual against the central forces of bureaucracy. He was appointed MBE (1945), CMG (1955), and CB (1960).

In 1939 he married Géryke, daughter of Dr Martin August Gustav Harthoorn, a distinguished Dutch lawyer, who had spent most of his life in Batavia, Dutch East Indies; there were no children. They remained devoted to each other. She was a strong-minded person who forcibly expressed her views about the roles of different ethnic groups. It is hard to estimate the degree of influence she had over Young's change from the left-wing student of the 1930s to a powerful figure in the right-wing Monday Club, but it was substantial. Young died in the Charing Cross Hospital, London, 9 May 1990.

[Private information; personal knowledge.]

JOHN BRUCE LOCKHART

YOUNG, Stuart (1934–1986), chartered accountant and chairman of the BBC board of governors, was born 23 April 1934 at home in Stamford Hill, London, the younger child and younger son of Joseph Young, who was in the flour business, and his wife, Rebecca ('Betty') Sterling. The family were religious Jews and his mother made him very conscious of his religious and charitable duties. Indeed, he met his wife on a charity committee when he was only sixteen, and he continued to be active in Jewish and other charities until his death. His brother, David, later became Baron Young of Graffham. He was educated at Woodhouse Grammar School, north Finchley, London, left school at sixteen, and qualified as a chartered accountant in 1956.

Young was a highly successful accountant. He set up his own practice in 1958, when he was only twenty-four. From 1960 he was the senior partner of his own firm, Hacker Young. He was hard working and decisive, with a very logical financial mind. In the early 1960s, when his practice was already well established, he began to get business from the interests of Sir Isaac Wolfson, including Great Universal Stores. He became a director of many companies, including Tesco, the food store group (from 1982), and Caledonian Airways (from 1973).

In the summer of 1981 Young was appointed a governor of the British Broadcasting Corporation. From the beginning of his term he was uneasy about what he regarded as the financial laxity and overmanning of the Corporation, though he felt great admiration for its broadcasting quality. This contrast between financial concern and admiration for the broadcast product marked his work both as a governor and as chairman of the BBC. Within a few weeks the financial concern led to a confrontation, which he won. The governors had to approve a new contract to promote BBC sales in American television. Young and another governor asked to see the contract; they were told it would not be customary, and that Alasdair Milne, the managing director of television, was reluctant to agree. Young told the chairman, George Howard (later Baron Howard of Henderskelfe), that he would not approve a contract he had not read, whereupon he was shown the contract. When Howard's term came to an end in 1983, Young was appointed chairman of the BBC governors. Margaret (later Baroness) Thatcher, as prime minister, wanted the BBC to be put under strong financial control. By that time Alasdair Milne had succeeded Sir (J.) Ian *Trethowan as director-general. Young promoted and encouraged

Michael Checkland, who was eventually to succeed Milne as director-general, as the member of the board of management who was to carry out the financial reforms he considered urgently necessary.

Within a few weeks of his appointment as chairman, Young suffered the first symptoms of the lung cancer which proved fatal to him, and his whole period as chairman was conducted under this disability, which he bore with great courage. His illness allowed him to form a personal link with Alasdair Milne, whose wife suffered from recurrent cancer; Milne had a sympathetic understanding of Young's condition. Yet Young did not feel that Milne had an adequate grasp of the business aspects of running so large a corporation, and did not find in him the partner who might have welcomed necessary reforms. If he had been in better health he might have been more ruthless in dealing with problems which he recognized. None the less, the reforms and demanning, which were later associated with the chairmanship of Marmaduke Hussey, his successor, were started in Young's time.

During his chairmanship, which he regarded as a high honour, there were a number of BBC crises of a characteristic kind. One was the libel action which arose out of 'Maggie's Militant Tendency', a television attack, which proved to be defamatory, on some right-wing Conservative MPs; another was the dispute in late July 1985 between the board of governors and the board of management over the 'Real Lives' interviews with Irish terrorists (done contrary to BBC producer guidelines), and a third was the dismissal of Richard Francis as managing director, radio, by Alasdair Milne. In all of these matters Young took a moderate position, trying to reconcile the warring parties in the interest of the BBC as a whole. His period as chairman was circumscribed by his illness; instead of being the radical reforming chairman he, and Margaret Thatcher, had hoped, he could only start to turn the tide from the extravagant BBC triumphalism of Howard and Milne toward the neo-puritanism of Hussey and John Birt, a later director-general. Young was courteous and friendly to his colleagues and staff. His balanced judgement and diplomatic approach were matched by firmness of purpose.

Young did much charitable work, which included aid for Israel; he was the treasurer of the Joint Israel appeal, but he was also involved in local charities in north London, and in heritage appeals. He was a trustee of the National Gallery from 1980. From 1977 he was a member of the finance and investment committee of Wolfson College, Cambridge, of which he became an honorary fellow in 1983. He was six feet tall, good-looking, and always well dressed, and he had a calm and friendly expression. His two passions were chess and golf. In 1956 he married Shirley, daughter of Harry Aarons, fashion company director. There were two daughters of the marriage. Young died of lung cancer at his home in Hampstead Garden Suburb, 29 August 1986.

[Private information; personal knowledge.]

REES-MOGG

Z

ZANGWILL, Oliver Louis (1913–1987), a founder of neuropsychology, was born 29 October 1913 in East Preston, Sussex, the youngest of three children and second son in the family of Israel *Zangwill, the Anglo-Jewish literary and political figure, and his wife, Edith Ayrton, who was active in the establishment of the League of Nations. A cousin was the painter and writer Michael Ayrton, the common grandfather being the physicist William *Ayrton, FRS. Oliver was educated at University College School, London (1928–31), and King's College, Cambridge, where he obtained a second class in part i of the natural sciences tripos (1934) and a first in part ii of the moral sciences tripos (1935).

At Cambridge Zangwill was influenced by (Sir) Frederic *Bartlett, while carrying out experiments on recognition and memory. With his lifelong friend R. C. Oldfield, he wrote a critique of the celebrated concept of mental schema put forward by Sir Henry *Head and Bartlett. Another influence was J. T. McCurdy, who intrigued Zangwill with hypnosis, which he later demonstrated to great effect on his students. Zangwill studied patients with Korsakoff psychosis, his paper 'Amnesia and the Generic Image' (*Quarterly Journal of Experimental Psychology*, vol. ii, 1950) remaining significant for the subject of whether semantic memory remains intact in amnesia. There is a story of a Korsakoff patient he saw each week when, taking a pen from his pocket, he asked: 'Have you seen this before?' Every week the patient would say 'No'. At the final session Zangwill asked: 'Have you seen *me* before?' The patient replied: 'Are you the man with all those pens?'

Zangwill became a research psychologist at the Brain Injuries Unit in Edinburgh (1940–5), which was directed by Norman Dott. There he did original, influential work on the psychological effects of penetrating wounds to the brain. His studies of cases of parietal lobe injury, with Andrew Patterson, led to his interest in hemispheric specialization and the complexities of right/left-handedness. His central aim was to use clinical abnormalities, especially symptoms of localized brain damage, to suggest how the normal brain functions.

While assistant director of the Institute of Experimental Psychology, University of Oxford (1945–52), Zangwill promoted the teaching of psychology when it was not considered a major subject, in spite of its importance at Cambridge. By establishing connections with the National Institute of Neurology in Queen Square, London, and the Radcliffe Infirmary in Oxford, he introduced a generation of psychologists to the study of neurological patients. His students included George Ettlinger, John McFie, Malcolm Piercy, Maria Wyke, Elizabeth Warrington, and Brenda Milner, all of whom became distinguished neuropsychologists. Appointed to the Cambridge chair (1952–81), with a fellowship of King's College, in his inaugural lecture he defined psychology as 'the study of behaviour', though he was never a behaviourist. Zangwill brought Lawrence Weiskrantz from America to set up a primate laboratory, with far-reaching consequences, especially as a result of Weiskrantz's continuing work as professor of psychology at Oxford.

Zangwill took a major part in setting up the Experimental Psychology Group, which was very influential, though it was sometimes critically described as an élitist Cambridge and Oxford club. It became the larger Experimental Psychology Society, with its quarterly *Journal*, which Zangwill edited from 1958 to 1966, serving also on the editorial board of *Neuropsychologia* (1963–81). His *An Introduction to Modern Psychology* (1950) set out pathways to be followed. He also wrote *Amnesia* (1966) and edited, with W. H. Thorpe, *Current Problems in Animal Behaviour* (1961).

Zangwill was elected FRS in 1977. He had honorary degrees from Stirling (1979) and St Andrews (1980). He held the honorary post of visiting psychologist at the National Hospital for Nervous Diseases (1947–79), and had close connections with European clinical neurology and in the United States, with Hans-Lukas Teuber at the Massachusetts Institute of Technology.

A tall stooping figure, with dark hair and green-grey eyes that looked everywhere, Zangwill had an elusive, almost haunted personality with moments of witty appreciation. He had several close friendships but was generally a very private person, whose thoughts were hard to interpret and whose decisions were often unpredictable, though not lacking in shrewdness.

In 1947 he married Joy Sylvia, daughter of Thomas Moult, poet. They had one son, who died in infancy. The marriage was dissolved in 1976 and in the same year he married Shirley Florence Tribe, daughter of Leonard Frank Punter, businessman. They had one adopted son. Zangwill died in Cambridge 12 October 1987, following a long illness in which he succumbed to the losses of memory that had so much concerned him throughout his professional life.

[Personal knowledge.]   RICHARD GREGORY

ZULUETA, SIR Philip Francis de (1925–1989), civil servant and businessman, was born in Oxford 2 January 1925, the only child of Francis (Francisco Maria José) de *Zulueta, regius professor of civil law and fellow of All Souls College, Oxford, and his wife Marie Louise, daughter of Henry Alexander Lyne Stephens. His childhood was spent in Oxford, where his parents had a house in Norham Road. His father was of distinguished Spanish descent and a cousin of Cardinal Merry de Val, the secretary of state at the Vatican, but took British nationality in order to fight in World War I. De Zulueta was educated at the Dragon School, Oxford, and the Roman Catholic Beaumont College, from where he won a scholarship to New College, Oxford. After taking a wartime second class in modern history in 1943 he joined the Welsh Guards the same year and served with the regiment in north-west Europe until 1947, participating in the liberation of Brussels with the Guards Armoured division and attaining the rank of captain. Thus did he gain early experience of two institutions to which he was to remain loyal throughout his life: the Brigade of Guards and the Roman Catholic church.

Returning to New College in 1947, de Zulueta studied jurisprudence but found it hard to settle down to study after the war and in 1948 left with a third-class degree. After Oxford he read for the bar, with the encouragement of his father, who was a strong influence on him. However, he decided not to proceed with his legal studies and joined the Foreign Service in 1949, serving in Moscow from 1950 to 1952 as private secretary to the ambassador, Sir David *Kelly. Returning to London, he became resident clerk at the Foreign Office; then in 1955 he began his long association with three prime ministers when Sir Anthony *Eden (later the Earl of Avon) took him to 10 Downing Street as one of his two private secretaries for foreign affairs.

He soon showed great aptitude for this work and after Harold *Macmillan (later the first Earl of Stockton) became prime minister in 1957 de Zulueta was the only representative of the Foreign Office among the private secretaries. He stayed on with Sir Alec Douglas-Home (later Baron Home of the Hirsel) from October 1963 to October 1964, but of all his masters it was Macmillan with whom he built up the greatest rapport, admiring his style of government, intellect, and wit and accompanying him often on foreign tours. Macmillan came to depend upon de Zulueta's loyalty, calm in a crisis, knowledge of the main foreign-policy issues of the time, and linguistic ability, using him as an interpreter at several of his meetings with Charles de Gaulle. 'Philip knows my mind,' he observed, and he remarked teasingly on de Zulueta's gravitas, determination, and strength of personality, for with the intelligence and fundamental kindness came a tendency to be impatient with the foolish or the slow. In Macmillan's resignation honours list of 1963 de Zulueta was given a knighthood.

In 1964, having always been interested in financial affairs and feeling that a diplomatic posting might be an anticlimax after his years in 10 Downing Street, de Zulueta left the Foreign Office for the City. Here he spent a six-month training period before joining Philip Hill-Higginson, Erlangers. He was a director of the newly merged Hill Samuel from 1965 to 1972. In 1973 he joined Antony Gibbs Holdings, serving as chief executive from 1973 to 1976 and chairman from 1976 to 1981. He was made chairman of Tanks Consolidated Investments in 1983 and a director of the Belgian Société Générale when that company took over Tanks in 1982. In 1984 he became a director of Abbott Laboratories of Chicago. Among his outside interests were the Franco-British Council, the Institute of Directors, and the Trilateral Commission. Increasingly he suffered from serious heart trouble.

De Zulueta was extremely hard working and energetic, deriving much self-confidence from an exceptionally happy family life. Tall, dark-haired, thickset, always immaculately dressed, quiet of voice, and often leaning forward slightly in a rather courtly way to catch every nuance of the conversation, he had an urbane, formidable presence and high standards; the morality and certainty of his strong religious faith never left him. Beneath this, however, lay humour and sympathy, qualities particularly evident at his homes in London and later at Eastergate in West Sussex, where he was a relaxed and generous host. In 1984 he became an officer of the Legion of Honour.

In 1955 he married Marie-Louise, daughter of James Bryan George Hennessy, second Baron Windlesham; they had a daughter and a son. De Zulueta died 15 April 1989 on board a British Airways flight, when returning from a business trip to the United States. He had a fatal coronary thrombosis as the aeroplane was coming in to land at London.

[Private information; personal knowledge.]

MAX EGREMONT

OCCUPATIONAL INDEX

Writing
Braine, John
Chatwin, Bruce
Dahl, Roald
Dennis, Nigel
Du Maurier, Dame Daphne
Durrell, Lawrence
Gibbons, Stella
Graham, W. S.
Grigson, Jane
Hewitt, John
Isherwood, Christopher
Jameson, Storm
Jennings, Paul
Lancaster, Sir Osbert
Laski, Marghanita
Lehmann, John
Lehmann, Rosamond
Maclean, Alistair
Nicholson, Norman
Reed, Henry
Scott, Sir Peter
Sitwell, Sir Sacheverell
Smart, Elizabeth
Streatfeild, Noel
Strong, Patience
Sykes, Christopher
Warner, Rex
Williams, Raymond

Scholarship
Ashmole, Bernard
Ayer, Sir Alfred
Blunt, C. E.
Braithwaite, Richard
Brenan, Gerald
Burrow, Thomas
Cecil, Lord David
Cheney, C. R.
Daniel, Glyn
De Beer, Esmond
Ellmann, Richard
Evans, George Ewart
Finley, Sir Moses
Francis, Sir Frank
Gardner, Dame Helen
Gray, Basil
Grice, Paul
Hancock, Sir Keith
Hunt, Norman Crowther
   (Lord Crowther-Hunt)
Meiggs, Russell
Momigliano, Arnaldo
Morris, Charles (Lord
   Morris of Grasmere)
Mynors, Sir Roger

Myres, Nowell
Oakeshott, Michael
Oakeshott, Sir Walter
Pächt, Otto
Piper, Sir David
Roberts, Colin
Shackleton, Robert
Syme, Sir Ronald
Taylor, A. J. P.

Government

a) POLITICS
Acland, Sir Richard
Boothby, Robert (Lord
   Boothby)
Brockway, Fenner (Lord
   Brockway)
Cazalet-Keir, Thelma
Gaitskell, Dora (Baroness
   Gaitskell)
King, Horace (Lord
   Maybray-King)
Lee, Jennie (Baroness Lee of
   Asheridge)
Macmillan, Harold (Earl of
   Stockton)
O'Neill, Terence (Lord
   O'Neill of the Maine)
Paget, Reginald (Lord Paget
   of Northampton)
Peart, Frederick (Lord Peart)
Ross, William (Lord Ross of
   Marnock)
Sandys, Duncan (Lord
   Duncan-Sandys)
Shinwell, Emanuel (Lord
   Shinwell)
Silkin, John
Soames, Christopher (Lord
   Soames)
Stewart, Michael (Lord
   Stewart of Fulham)
Stonehouse, John

b) CIVIL SERVICE AND LOCAL GOVERNMENT
Colville, Sir John
Cook, Sir William
Hall, Robert (Lord
   Roberthall)
Laithwaite, Sir Gilbert
Marre, Sir Alan
Part, Sir Antony
Sylvester, A. J.
Trend, Burke (Lord Trend)
Zulueta, Sir Philip de

c) CENTRAL GOVERNMENT AND DIPLOMACY
Berthoud, Sir Eric
Caccia, Harold (Lord Caccia)
Figgures, Sir Frank
James, Morrice (Lord Saint
   Brides)
Millar, F. R. H. (Lord
   Inchyra)
O'Neill, Sir Con
Pilcher, Sir John

d) COLONIAL GOVERNMENT AND ADMINISTRATION
Abell, Sir George
Foot, Hugh (Lord Caradon)
Gibbs, Sir Humphrey
Johnston, Sir Charles
Moon, Sir Penderel

The Management of Society

a) SOCIAL SCIENCES, ECONOMICS, PSYCHOLOGY, AND ANTHROPOLOGY
Blacking, John
Burn, Duncan
Clark, Colin
Elias, Norbert
Glass, Ruth
Hicks, Sir John
Himmelweit, Hilde
Jewkes, John
Kahn, Richard (Lord Kahn)
Kaldor, Nicholas (Lord
   Kaldor)
Leach, Sir Edmund
Paish, Frank
Sayers, Richard
Vernon, Philip
Zangwill, Oliver

b) TRADE UNIONS
Basnett, David (Lord
   Basnett)
Boyd, Sir John
Cousins, Frank
Fisher, Alan
Keys, William
Plant, Cyril (Lord Plant)

c) SOCIAL SERVICES AND CHARITIES
Aves, Dame Geraldine
Baxter, Kathleen
Bramwell-Booth, Catherine
Kirkley, Sir Leslie

CUMULATIVE INDEX

TO THE BIOGRAPHIES CONTAINED IN THE SUPPLEMENTS

OF THE DICTIONARY OF NATIONAL BIOGRAPHY

1901–1990

# indicates twentieth-century entrants to the *Missing Persons* volume of the *DNB*.

Abbey, Edwin Austin	1852–1911
Abbey, John Roland	1894–1969
Abbott, Edwin Abbott	1838–1926
Abbott, Eric Symes	1906–1983
Abbott, Evelyn	1843–1901
À Beckett, Arthur William	1844–1909
Abel, Sir Frederick Augustus	1827–1902
Abell, Sir George Edmond Brackenbury	1904–1989
Abell, Sir Westcott Stile	1877–1961
Aberconway, Baron. See McLaren, Charles Benjamin Bright	1850–1934
Aberconway, Baron. See McLaren, Henry Duncan	1879–1953
Abercorn, Duke of. See Hamilton, James	1838–1913
Abercrombie, Lascelles	1881–1938
Abercrombie, Sir (Leslie) Patrick	1879–1957
Abercrombie, Michael	1912–1979
Aberdare, Baron. See Bruce, Clarence Napier	1885–1957
Aberdeen and Temair, Marquess of. See Gordon, John Campbell	1847–1934
Aberdeen and Temair, Marchioness of (1857–1939). See under Gordon, John Campbell	
Aberhart, William	1878–1943
Abney, Sir William de Wiveleslie	1843–1920
Abraham, Charles John	1814–1903
Abraham, Gerald Ernest Heal	1904–1988
Abraham, William	1842–1922
Abrahams, Doris Caroline. See Brahms, Caryl	1901–1982
Abrahams, Harold Maurice	1899–1978
Abramsky, Yehezkel	1886–1976
Abu Bakar Tafawa Balewa, Alhaji Sir. See Tafawa Balewa	1912–1966
Abul Kalam Azad, Maulana. See Azad	1888–1958
Ackerley, Joe Randolph	#1896–1967
Acland, Sir Arthur Herbert Dyke	1847–1926

Acland, Sir Richard Thomas Dyke	1906–1990
Acton, Sir Edward	1865–1945
Acton, John Adams-. See Adams-Acton	1830–1910
Acton, Sir John Emerich Edward Dalberg, Baron	1834–1902
Acworth, Sir William Mitchell	1850–1925
Adair, Gilbert Smithson	1896–1979
Adam, James	1860–1907
Adam Smith, Sir George. See Smith	1856–1942
Adami, John George	1862–1926
Adams, Sir Grantley Herbert	1898–1971
Adams, James Williams	1839–1903
Adams, Sir John	1857–1934
Adams, Sir John Bertram	1920–1984
Adams, John Bodkin	1899–1983
Adams, (John) Frank	1930–1989
Adams, John Michael Geoffrey Manningham ('Tom')	1931–1985
Adams, Mary Grace Agnes	1898–1984
Adams, Sir Walter	1906–1975
Adams, William	#1825–1904
Adams, William Bridges-. See Bridges-Adams	1889–1965
Adams, William Davenport	1851–1904
Adams, William George Stewart	1874–1966
Adams-Acton, John	1830–1910
Adamson, Sir John Ernest	1867–1950
Adamson, Robert	1852–1902
Adcock, Sir Frank Ezra	1886–1968
Adderley, Charles Bowyer, Baron Norton	1814–1905
Addison, Christopher, Viscount	1869–1951
Adeane, Michael Edward, Baron	1910–1984
Adler, Hermann	1839–1911
Adrian, Edgar Douglas, Baron	1889–1977
Adshead, Stanley Davenport	1868–1946
AE, *pseudonym*. See Russell, George William	1867–1935
Aga Khan, Aga Sultan Sir Mohammed Shah	1877–1957

Agate, James Evershed	1877–1947
Aglen, Sir Francis Arthur	#1869–1932
Agnew, Sir James Wilson	1815–1901
Agnew, Sir William	1825–1910
Agnew, Sir William Gladstone	1898–1960
Aidé, Charles Hamilton	1826–1906
Aikman, George	1830–1905
Ainger, Alfred	1837–1904
Ainley, Henry Hinchliffe	1879–1945
Aird, Sir John	1833–1911
Airedale, Baron. See Kitson, James	1835–1911
Aitchison, Craigie Mason, Lord	1882–1941
Aitchison, George	1825–1910
Aitken, Alexander Craig	1895–1967
Aitken, John	#1839–1919
Aitken, William Maxwell, Baron Beaverbrook	1879–1964
Akers, Sir Wallace Alan	1888–1954
Akers-Douglas, Aretas, Viscount Chilston	1851–1926
Akers-Douglas, Aretas, Viscount Chilston	1876–1947
Alanbrooke, Viscount. See Brooke, Alan Francis	1883–1963
Albani, Dame Marie Louise Cécilie Emma	1852–1930
Albery, Sir Bronson James	1881–1971
Albery, Sir Donald Rolleston	1914–1988
Alcock, Sir John William	1892–1919
Aldenham, Baron. See Gibbs, Henry Hucks	1819–1907
Alderson, Sir Edwin Alfred Hervey	1859–1927
Alderson, Henry James	1834–1909
Aldington, Edward Godfree ('Richard')	1892–1962
Aldrich-Blake, Dame Louisa Brandreth	1865–1925
Aldridge, John Arthur Malcolm	1905–1983
Alexander, Mrs, *pseudonym*. See Hector, Annie French	1825–1902
Alexander, Albert Victor, Earl Alexander of Hillsborough	1885–1965
Alexander, Boyd	1873–1910
Alexander, (Conel) Hugh (O'Donel)	1909–1974
Alexander, Sir George	1858–1918
Alexander, Harold Rupert Leofric George, Earl Alexander of Tunis	1891–1969
Alexander, Samuel	1859–1938
Alexander, William	1824–1911
Alexander-Sinclair, Sir Edwyn Sinclair	1865–1945
Alexandra, Queen	1844–1925
Alexandra Victoria Alberta Edwina Louise Duff, Princess Arthur of Connaught, Duchess of Fife	1891–1959
Alger, John Goldworth	1836–1907
Algeranoff, Harcourt	1903–1967
Algy, Father. See Robertson, (William) Strowan (Amherst)	#1894–1955
Alice Mary Victoria Augusta Pauline, Princess of Great Britain and Ireland and Countess of Athlone	1883–1981
Alington, Baron. See Sturt, Henry Gerard	1825–1904
Alington, Cyril Argentine	1872–1955
Alison, Sir Archibald	1826–1907
Allan, Sir William	1837–1903
Allbutt, Sir Thomas Clifford	1836–1925
Allen, Sir Carleton Kemp	1887–1966
Allen, George	1832–1907
Allen, Sir George Oswald Browning ('Gubby')	1902–1989
Allen, (Herbert) Warner	1881–1968
Allen, Sir Hugh Percy	1869–1946
Allen, Sir James	1855–1942
Allen, John Romilly	1847–1907
Allen, Norman Percy	1903–1972
Allen, Percy Stafford	1869–1933
Allen, Reginald Clifford, Baron Allen of Hurtwood	1889–1939
Allen, Robert Calder	1812–1903
Allenby, Edmund Henry Hynman, Viscount Allenby of Megiddo	1861–1936
Allerton, Baron. See Jackson, William Lawies	1840–1917
Allies, Thomas William	1813–1903
Allingham, Margery Louise	1904–1966
Allman, George Johnston	1824–1904
Alma-Tadema, Sir Lawrence	1836–1912
Almond, Hely Hutchinson	1832–1903
Altham, Harry Surtees	1888–1965
Altrincham, Baron. See Grigg, Edward William Macleay	1879–1955
Alverstone, Viscount. See Webster, Richard Everard	1842–1915
Ambedkar, Bhimrao Ramji	1891–1956
Ameer Ali, Syed	1849–1928
Amery, John	#1912–1945
Amery, Leopold Charles Maurice Stennett	1873–1955
Amherst, William Amhurst Tyssen-, Baron Amherst of Hackney	1835–1909
Amoroso, Emmanuel Ciprian	1901–1982
Amory, Derick Heathcoat, Viscount	1899–1981

Arnold, Sir Thomas Walker	1864–1930	Asquith, Cyril, Baron Asquith	
Arnold, William Thomas	1852–1904	of Bishopstone	1890–1954
Arnold-Forster, Hugh		Asquith, Emma Alice	
Oakeley	1855–1909	Margaret ('Margot'),	
Arrol, Sir William	1839–1913	Countess of Oxford and	
Arthur of Connaught,		Asquith	1864–1945
Princess. See Alexandra		Asquith, Herbert Henry,	
Victoria Alberta Edwina		Earl of Oxford and	
Louise Duff	1891–1959	Asquith	1852–1928
Arthur Frederick Patrick		Asquith of Yarnbury,	
Albert, prince of Great		Baroness. See Bonham	
Britain	1883–1938	Carter, (Helen) Violet	1887–1969
Arthur William Patrick		Assheton, Ralph, Baron	
Albert, Duke of Connaught		Clitheroe	1901–1984
and Strathearn	1850–1942	Astbury, Sir John Meir	1860–1939
Arthur, William	1819–1901	Astbury, William Thomas	1898–1961
Arup, Sir Ove Nyquist	1895–1988	Aston, Francis William	1877–1945
Asche, (Thomas Stange		Aston, Sir George Grey	1861–1938
Heiss) Oscar	1871–1936	Aston, William George	1841–1911
Ashbee, Charles Robert	1863–1942	Astor, John Jacob, Baron	
Ashbourne, Baron. See		Astor of Hever	1886–1971
Gibson, Edward	1837–1913	Astor, Nancy Witcher,	
Ashbridge, Sir Noel	1889–1975	Viscountess	1879–1964
Ashby, Arthur Wilfred	1886–1953	Astor, Waldorf, Viscount	1879–1952
Ashby, Henry	1846–1908	Astor, William Waldorf,	
Ashby, Dame Margery		Viscount	#1848–1919
Irene Corbett. See Corbett		Atcherley, Sir Richard	
Ashby	1882–1981	Llewellyn Roger	1904–1970
Ashby, Thomas	1874–1931	Athlone, Countess of. See	
Asher, Alexander	1835–1905	Alice Mary Victoria	
Ashfield, Baron. See Stanley,		Augusta Pauline	1883–1981
Albert Henry	1874–1948	Athlone, Earl of. See	
Ashford, Margaret Mary Julia		Cambridge, Alexander	
('Daisy')	1881–1972	Augustus Frederick	
Ashley, Evelyn	1836–1907	William Alfred George	1874–1957
Ashley, Laura	1925–1985	Atholl, Duchess of. See	
Ashley, Wilfrid William,		Stewart-Murray, Katharine	
Baron Mount Temple	1867–1938	Marjory	1874–1960
Ashley, Sir William James	1860–1927	Atholstan, Baron. See	
Ashmead Bartlett, Sir Ellis.		Graham, Hugh	1848–1938
See Bartlett	1849–1902	Atkin, James Richard,	
Ashmole, Bernard	1894–1988	Baron	1867–1944
Ashton, Baron. See		Atkins, Sir Ivor Algernon	1869–1953
Williamson, James	#1842–1930	Atkins, Sir William Sydney	
Ashton, Sir Frederick William		Albert	1902–1989
Mallandaine	1904–1988	Atkinson, Sir Edward Hale	
Ashton, Thomas Gair, Baron		Tindal	1878–1957
Ashton of Hyde	1855–1933	Atkinson, Edward Leicester	#1881–1929
Ashton, Thomas Southcliffe	1889–1968	Atkinson, John, Baron	1844–1932
Ashton, Winifred, 'Clemence		Atkinson, Robert	1839–1908
Dane'	1888–1965	Atthill, Lombe	1827–1910
Ashwell, Lena Margaret	1872–1957	Attlee, Clement Richard, Earl	1883–1967
Askey, Arthur Bowden	1900–1982	Attwell, Mabel Lucie	1879–1964
Askwith, George Ranken,		Aubrey, Melbourn Evans	1885–1957
Baron	1861–1942	Auchinleck, Sir Claude John	
Aslin, Charles Herbert	1893–1959	Eyre	1884–1981
Aspinall, Sir John Audley		Auden, Wystan Hugh	1907–1973
Frederick	#1851–1937	Aumonier, James	1832–1911
Asquith, Anthony	1902–1968	Austen, Henry Haversham	
Asquith, Lady Cynthia Mary		Godwin-. See	
Evelyn	1887–1960	Godwin-Austen	1834–1923

Balfour, Sir Isaac Bayley	1853–1922
Balfour, John Blair, Baron	
Kinross	1837–1905
Balfour, Sir Thomas Graham	1858–1929
Balfour of Burleigh, Baron.	
See Bruce, Alexander Hugh	1849–1921
Balfour-Browne, William	
Alexander Francis	1874–1967
Ball, Albert	1896–1917
Ball, Francis Elrington	1863–1928
Ball, Sir (George) Joseph	1885–1961
Ball, Sir George Thomas	
Thalben-. See Thalben-Ball	1896–1987
Ball, John	1861–1940
Ball, Sir Robert Stawell	1840–1913
Ballance, Sir Charles Alfred	1856–1936
Ballantrae, Baron. See	
Fergusson, Bernard	
Edward	1911–1980
Ballinger, Sir John	#1860–1933
Balniel, Lord. See Lindsay,	
David Alexander Robert	1900–1975
Balogh, Thomas, Baron	1905–1985
Banbury, Frederick George,	
Baron Banbury of Southam	1850–1936
Bancroft, Marie Effie	
(formerly Wilton), Lady	
(1839–1921). See under	
Bancroft, Sir Squire	
Bancroft	
Bancroft, Sir Squire Bancroft	1841–1926
Bandaranaike, Solomon West	
Ridgeway Dias	1899–1959
Bandon, Earl of. See Bernard,	
Percy Ronald Gardner	1904–1979
Banham, (Peter) Reyner	1922–1988
Bankes, Sir John Eldon	1854–1946
Banks, Sir John Thomas	1815?–1908
Banks, Leslie James	1890–1952
Banks, Sir William Mitchell	1842–1904
Bannerman, Sir Henry	
Campbell-. See	
Campbell-Bannerman	1836–1908
Banting, Sir Frederick Grant	1891–1941
Bantock, Sir Granville	
Ransome	1868–1946
Barbellion, W. N. P.,	
pseudonym. See Cummings,	
Bruce Frederick	1889–1919
Barbirolli, Sir John (Giovanni	
Battista)	1899–1970
Barbour, Sir David Miller	1841–1928
Barcroft, Sir Joseph	1872–1947
Bardsley, John Wareing	1835–1904
Barger, George	1878–1939
Baring, (Charles) Evelyn,	
Baron Howick of Glendale	1903–1973
Baring, Evelyn, Earl of	
Cromer	1841–1917
Baring, John, Baron	
Revelstoke	#1863–1929

Baring, Maurice	1874–1945
Baring, Rowland Thomas,	
Earl of Cromer	1877–1953
Baring, Thomas George, Earl	
of Northbrook	1826–1904
Baring-Gould, Sabine	1834–1924
Barker, Sir Ernest	1874–1960
Barker, Harley Granville	
Granville-. See	
Granville-Barker	1877–1946
Barker, Sir Herbert Atkinson	1869–1950
Barker, Dame Lilian	
Charlotte	1874–1955
Barker, Thomas	1838–1907
Barkla, Charles Glover	1877–1944
Barling, Sir (Harry) Gilbert	1855–1940
Barlow, Harold Everard	
Monteagle	1899–1989
Barlow, Sir (James) Alan	
(Noel)	1881–1968
Barlow, Sir Thomas	1845–1945
Barlow, Sir Thomas	
Dalmahoy	1883–1964
Barlow, William Hagger	1833–1908
Barlow, William Henry	1812–1902
Barnaby, Sir Nathaniel	1829–1915
Barnard, Howard Clive	1884–1985
Barnard, Joseph Edwin	#1868–1949
Barnardo, Thomas John	1845–1905
Barnes, Alfred John	1887–1974
Barnes, Ernest William	1874–1953
Barnes, George Nicoll	1859–1940
Barnes, Sir George Reginald	1904–1960
Barnes, John Gorell, Baron	
Gorell	1848–1913
Barnes, John Morrison	1913–1975
Barnes, Sir Kenneth Ralph	1878–1957
Barnes, Robert	1817–1907
Barnes, Sydney Francis	1873–1967
Barnes, Sir Thomas James	1888–1964
Barnes, William Emery	1859–1939
Barnetson, William Denholm,	
Baron	1917–1981
Barnett, Dame Henrietta	
Octavia Weston	1851–1936
Barnett, Lionel David	1871–1960
Barnett, Samuel Augustus	1844–1913
Baroda, Sir Sayaji Rao,	
Maharaja Gaekwar of	1863–1939
Baron, Bernhard	1850–1929
Barr, Archibald	1855–1931
Barraclough, Geoffrey	1908–1984
Barrett, Wilson	1846–1904
Barrie, Sir James Matthew	1860–1937
Barrington, Rutland	1853–1922
Barrington-Ward, Sir	
Lancelot Edward	1884–1953
Barrington-Ward, Robert	
McGowan	1891–1948
Barron, (Arthur) Oswald	#1868–1939
Barry, Alfred	1826–1910

Belisha, (Isaac) Leslie Hore-,
Baron Hore-Belisha. See
Hore-Belisha   1893–1957
Bell, Alexander Graham   1847–1922
Bell, (Arthur) Clive (Heward)   1881–1964
Bell, Sir Charles Alfred   1870–1945
Bell, Charles Frederic
Moberly   1847–1911
Bell, Sir Francis Henry
Dillon   1851–1936
Bell, George Kennedy Allen   1883–1958
Bell, Gertrude Margaret
Lowthian   1868–1926
Bell, Sir (Harold) Idris   1879–1967
Bell, Sir Henry Hesketh
Joudou   1864–1952
Bell, Horace   1839–1903
Bell, Sir Isaac Lowthian   1816–1904
Bell, James   1824–1908
Bell, John Stewart   1928–1990
Bell, Joseph   #1837–1911
Bell, Sir Thomas   1865–1952
Bell, Valentine Graeme   1839–1908
Bell, Vanessa   1879–1961
Bellamy, James   1819–1909
Bellew, Harold Kyrle   1855–1911
Bellman, Sir (Charles) Harold   1886–1963
Bello, Sir Ahmadu, Sardauna
of Sokoto   1910–1966
Belloc, Joseph Hilaire Pierre
René   1870–1953
Bellows, John   1831–1902
Beloe, Robert   1905–1984
Bemrose, William   1831–1908
Bendall, Cecil   1856–1906
Benham, William   1831–1910
Benn, Sir Ernest John
Pickstone   1875–1954
Benn, William Wedgwood,
Viscount Stansgate   1877–1960
Bennet-Clark, Thomas
Archibald   1903–1975
Bennett, Alfred Rosling   #1850–1928
Bennett, Alfred William   1833–1902
Bennett, Donald Clifford
Tyndall   1910–1986
Bennett, Edward Hallaran   1837–1907
Bennett, (Enoch) Arnold   1867–1931
Bennett, George Macdonald   1892–1959
Bennett, Jack Arthur Walter   1911–1981
Bennett, Sir John Wheeler
Wheeler-. See
Wheeler-Bennett   1902–1975
Bennett, (Nora Noel) Jill   1929?–1990
Bennett, Peter Frederick
Blaker, Baron Bennett of
Edgbaston   1880–1957
Bennett, Richard Bedford,
Viscount   1870–1947
Bennett, Sir Thomas
Penberthy   1887–1980

Benson, Arthur Christopher   1862–1925
Benson, Edward Frederic   1867–1940
Benson, Sir Francis Robert
(Frank)   1858–1939
Benson, Godfrey Rathbone,
Baron Charnwood   1864–1945
Benson, Sir Reginald Lindsay
('Rex')   1889–1968
Benson, Richard Meux   1824–1915
Benson, Robert Hugh   1871–1914
Benson, Stella. See Anderson   1892–1933
Benson, William Arthur
Smith   #1854–1924
Bent, Sir Thomas   1838–1909
Bentinck, Victor Frederick
William Cavendish-, Duke
of Portland   1897–1990
Bentley, Edmund Clerihew   1875–1956
Bentley, John Francis   1839–1902
Bentley, Nicholas Clerihew   1907–1978
Bentley, Phyllis Eleanor   1894–1977
Bentley, Walter Owen   #1888–1971
Benton, Sir John   1850–1927
Bentwich, Norman de Mattos   1883–1971
Beresford, Lord Charles
William De La Poer, Baron   1846–1919
Beresford, Jack   1899–1977
Bergel, Franz   1900–1987
Bergne, Sir John Henry
Gibbs   1842–1908
Berkeley, Sir George   1819–1905
Berkeley, Sir Lennox Randal
Francis   1903–1989
Berkeley, Randal Mowbray
Thomas Rawdon, Earl of
Berkeley   1865–1942
Bernal, (John) Desmond   1901–1971
Bernard, Sir Charles Edward   1837–1901
Bernard, John Henry   1860–1927
Bernard, Oliver Percy   #1881–1939
Bernard, Percy Ronald
Gardner, Earl of Bandon   1904–1979
Bernard, Thomas Dehany   1815–1904
Berners, Baron. See
Tyrwhitt-Wilson, Sir
Gerald Hugh   1883–1950
Berney, Margery. See Hurst   1913–1989
Berry, Sir Graham   1822–1904
Berry, (James) Gomer,
Viscount Kemsley   1883–1968
Berry, Sidney Malcolm   1881–1961
Berry, William Ewert,
Viscount Camrose   1879–1954
Berthoud, Sir Eric Alfred   1900–1989
Bertie, Francis Leveson,
Viscount Bertie of
Thame   1844–1919
Besant, Annie   1847–1933
Besant, Sir Walter   1836–1901
Besicovitch, Abram
Samoilovitch   1891–1970

Blake, Dame Louisa
Brandreth Aldrich-. See
Aldrich-Blake   1865–1925
Blakenham, Viscount. See
Hare, John Hugh   1911–1982
Blakiston, Herbert Edward
Douglas   1862–1942
Blamey, Sir Thomas Albert   1884–1951
Bland, Edith, 'E. Nesbit'   1858–1924
Bland, John Otway Percy   1863–1945
Bland-Sutton, Sir John. See
Sutton   1855–1936
Blandford, George Fielding   1829–1911
Blanesburgh, Baron. See
Younger, Robert   1861–1946
Blaney, Thomas   1823–1903
Blanford, William Thomas   1832–1905
Blatchford, Robert Peel
Glanville   1851–1943
Blaydes, Frederick Henry
Marvell   1818–1908
Bledisloe, Viscount. See
Bathurst, Charles   1867–1958
Blennerhassett, Sir Rowland   1839–1909
Blind, Karl   1826–1907
Bliss, Sir Arthur Edward
Drummond   1891–1975
Bliss, Kathleen Mary Amelia   1908–1989
Blogg, Henry George   1876–1954
Blom, Eric Walter   #1888–1959
Blomfield, Sir Reginald
Theodore   1856–1942
Blood, Sir Bindon   1842–1940
Blood, Sir Hilary Rudolph
Robert   1893–1967
Bloomfield, Georgiana, Lady   1822–1905
Blouet, Léon Paul, 'Max
O'Rell'   1848–1903
Blount, Sir Edward Charles   1809–1905
Blumenfeld, John Elliot. See
Elliot, Sir John   1898–1988
Blumenfeld, Ralph David   1864–1948
Blumenthal, Jacques ('Jacob')   1829–1908
Blumlein, Alan Dower   #1903–1942
Blunden, Edmund Charles   1896–1974
Blunt, Lady Anne Isabella
Noel (1837–1917). See
under Blunt, Wilfrid
Scawen
Blunt, Anthony Frederick   1907–1983
Blunt, Christopher Evelyn   1904–1987
Blunt, Wilfrid Scawen   1840–1922
Blythswood, Baron. See
Campbell, Archibald
Campbell   1835–1908
Blyton, Enid Mary   1897–1968
Boase, Frederic   #1843–1916
Boase, Thomas Sherrer Ross   1898–1974
Bodda Pyne, Louisa Fanny   1832–1904
Bodington, Sir Nathan   1848–1911
Bodkin, Sir Archibald Henry   1862–1957

Bodkin, Thomas Patrick   1887–1961
Bodley, George Frederick   1827–1907
Bodley, John Edward
Courtenay   #1853–1925
Bodley Scott, Sir Ronald   1906–1982
Body, George   1840–1911
Boldero, Sir Harold Esmond
Arnison   1889–1960
Bols, Sir Louis Jean   1867–1930
Bolton, Arthur Thomas   #1864–1945
Bomberg, David Garshen   1890–1957
Bompas, Henry Mason
(1836–1909). See under
Bompas, William Carpenter
Bompas, William Carpenter   1834–1906
Bonar, James   1852–1941
Bonar Law, Andrew. See
Law   1858–1923
Bonavia-Hunt, Henry George.
See Hunt   #1847–1917
Bond, Sir (Charles) Hubert   1870–1945
Bond, Sir Robert   1857–1927
Bond, William Bennett   1815–1906
Bondfield, Margaret Grace   1873–1953
Bone, James   1872–1962
Bone, Sir Muirhead   1876–1953
Bone, Stephen   1904–1958
Bone, William Arthur   1871–1938
Bonham-Carter, Sir Edgar   1870–1956
Bonham Carter, (Helen)
Violet, Baroness Asquith of
Yarnbury   1887–1969
Bonney, Thomas George   1833–1923
Bonney, (William Francis)
Victor   1872–1953
Bonwick, James   1817–1906
Boosey, Leslie Arthur   1887–1979
Boot, Henry Albert Howard   1917–1983
Boot, Jesse, Baron Trent   1850–1931
Booth, Catherine Bramwell-.
See Bramwell-Booth   1883–1987
Booth, Charles   1840–1916
Booth, Hubert Cecil   1871–1955
Booth, Paul Henry Gore-,
Baron Gore-Booth. See
Gore-Booth   1909–1984
Booth, William ('General'
Booth)   1829–1912
Booth, William Bramwell   1856–1929
Boothby, Guy Newell   1867–1905
Boothby, Robert John
Graham, Baron   1900–1986
Boothman, Sir John Nelson   1901–1957
Borden, Sir Robert Laird   1854–1937
Borg Olivier, Giorgio
(George). See Olivier   1911–1980
Borthwick, Algernon, Baron
Glenesk   1830–1908
Bosanquet, Bernard   1848–1923
Bosanquet, Sir Frederick
Albert   1837–1923

Braine, John Gerard	1922–1986	Bridges, Sir William Throsby	1861–1915
Braithwaite, Dame (Florence)		Bridges-Adams, William	1889–1965
Lilian	1873–1948	Bridie, James, *pseudonym*. See	
Braithwaite, Richard Bevan	1900–1990	Mavor, Osborne Henry	1888–1951
Braithwaite, Sir Walter Pipon	1865–1945	Bridson, (Douglas) Geoffrey	1910–1980
Bramah, Ernest	#1868–1942	Brierly, James Leslie	1881–1955
Brambell, Francis William		Briggs, John	1862–1902
Rogers	1901–1970	Bright, Gerald Walcan-,	
Brampton, Baron. See		'Geraldo'. See	
Hawkins, Henry	1817–1907	Walcan-Bright	1904–1974
Bramwell, Sir Byrom	1847–1931	Bright, James Franck	1832–1920
Bramwell, Sir Frederick		Bright, William	1824–1901
Joseph	1818–1903	Brightman, Frank Edward	1856–1932
Bramwell-Booth, Catherine	1883–1987	Brightwen, Eliza	1830–1906
Brancker, Sir William Sefton	1877–1930	Brind, Sir (Eric James)	
Brand, Henry Robert,		Patrick	1892–1963
Viscount Hampden	1841–1906	Brise, Sir Evelyn John	
Brand, Herbert Charles		Ruggles-. See	
Alexander	1839–1901	Ruggles-Brise	1857–1935
Brand, Robert Henry, Baron	1878–1963	Brittain, Sir Henry Ernest	
Brandis, Sir Dietrich	1824–1907	(Harry)	1873–1974
Brandt, Hermann Wilhelm		Brittain, Vera Mary	1893–1970
('Bill')	1904–1983	Britten, (Edward) Benjamin,	
Brangwyn, Sir Frank		Baron	1913–1976
(François Guillaume)	1867–1956	Broad, Sir Charles Noel	
Brassey, Thomas, Earl	1836–1918	Frank	1882–1976
Bray, Caroline	1814–1905	Broad, Charlie Dunbar	1887–1971
Bray, Sir Reginald More	1842–1923	Broadbent, Sir William Henry	1835–1907
Brayley, (John) Desmond,		Broadhurst, Henry	1840–1911
Baron	1917–1977	Brock, Sir Osmond de	
Brazil, Angela	1868–1947	Beauvoir	1869–1947
Brearley, Harry	#1871–1948	Brock, Russell Claude, Baron	1903–1980
Brenan, (Edward Fitz) Gerald	1894–1987	Brock, Sir Thomas	1847–1922
Brennan, Louis	1852–1932	Brockway, (Archibald)	
Brentford, Viscount. See		Fenner, Baron	1888–1988
Hicks, William Joynson-	1865–1932	Brodetsky, Selig	1888–1954
Brereton, Joseph Lloyd	1822–1901	Brodie, Sir Israel	1895–1979
Bressey, Sir Charles Herbert	1874–1951	Brodribb, Charles William	1878–1945
Brett, John	1831–1902	Brodribb, William Jackson	1829–1905
Brett, Reginald Baliol,		Brodrick, George Charles	1831–1903
Viscount Esher	1852–1930	Brodrick, (William) St John	
Brewer, Sir Alfred Herbert	1865–1928	(Fremantle), Earl of	
Brewtnall, Edward Frederick	1846–1902	Midleton	1856–1942
Brian, (William) Havergal	1876–1972	Brogan, Sir Denis William	1900–1974
Bridge, Sir Cyprian Arthur		Bromby, Charles Hamilton	
George	1839–1924	(1843–1904). See under	
Bridge, Frank	1879–1941	Bromby, Charles Henry	
Bridge, Sir John Frederick	1844–1924	Bromby, Charles Henry	1814–1907
Bridge, (Stephen Henry)		Bronowski, Jacob	1908–1974
Peter	1925–1982	Broodbank, Sir Joseph	
Bridge, Thomas William	1848–1909	Guinness	1857–1944
Bridgeman, Sir Francis		Brook, Norman Craven,	
Charles Bridgeman	1848–1929	Baron Normanbrook	1902–1967
Bridgeman, William Clive,		Brooke, Alan England	1863–1939
Viscount	#1864–1935	Brooke, Alan Francis,	
Bridges, Edward Ettingdene,		Viscount Alanbrooke	1883–1963
Baron	1892–1969	Brooke, Basil Stanlake,	
Bridges, Sir (George) Tom		Viscount Brookeborough	1888–1973
(Molesworth)	1871–1939	Brooke, Sir Charles Anthony	
Bridges, John Henry	1832–1906	Johnson	1829–1917
Bridges, Robert Seymour	1844–1930	Brooke, Sir Charles Vyner	#1874–1963

Buckland, William Warwick	1859–1946	Burn, Robert	1829–1904
Buckle, George Earle	1854–1935	Burn-Murdoch, John	1852–1909
Buckley, Henry Burton,		Burnand, Sir Francis Cowley	1836–1917
Baron Wrenbury	1845–1935	Burne, Sir Owen Tudor	1837–1909
Buckmaster, Stanley Owen,		Burnell, Charles Desborough	1876–1969
Viscount	1861–1934	Burnet, John	1863–1928
Buckton, George Bowdler	1818–1905	Burnet, Sir John James	1857–1938
Budge, Sir Ernest Alfred		Burnett, Sir Charles Stuart	1882–1945
Thompson Wallis	1857–1934	Burnett, Frances Eliza	
Buhler, Robert	1916–1989	Hodgson	#1849–1924
Bülbring, Edith	1903–1990	Burnett, Dame Ivy	
Bulfin, Sir Edward Stanislaus	1862–1939	Compton-. See	
Bull, Sir Graham MacGregor	1918–1987	Compton-Burnett	1884–1969
Bullard, Sir Edward Crisp	1907–1980	Burnett, Sir Robert Lindsay	1887–1959
Bullard, Sir Reader William	1885–1976	Burnett-Stuart, Sir John	
Bulleid, Oliver Vaughan		Theodosius	1875–1958
Snell	#1882–1970	Burney, Sir Cecil	1858–1929
Bullen, Arthur Henry	1857–1920	Burney, Sir (Charles)	
Bullen, Frank Thomas	#1857–1915	Dennistoun	1888–1968
Buller, Arthur Henry		Burnham, Baron. See	
Reginald	1874–1944	Levy-Lawson, Edward	1833–1916
Buller, Sir Redvers Henry	1839–1908	Burnham, Baron. See	
Buller, Reginald Edward		Lawson, Edward Frederick	1890–1963
Manningham-. See		Burnham, Viscount. See	
Manningham-Buller	1905–1980	Lawson, Harry Lawson	
Buller, Sir Walter Lawry	1838–1906	Webster Levy-	1862–1933
Bulloch, William	1868–1941	Burns, Sir Alan Cuthbert	
Bullock, Sir Christopher		Maxwell	1887–1980
Llewellyn	1891–1972	Burns, Dawson	1828–1909
Bullock, Sir Ernest	1890–1979	Burns, John Elliot	1858–1943
Bulman, Oliver Meredith		Burnside, William	1852–1927
Boone	1902–1974	Burra, Edward John	1905–1976
Bulwer, Sir Edward Earle		Burrell, Sir William	1861–1958
Gascoyne	1829–1910	Burroughs (afterwards	
Bulwer-Lytton, Victor		Traill-Burroughs), Sir	
Alexander George Robert,		Frederick William	1831–1905
Earl of Lytton	1876–1947	Burrow, Thomas	1909–1986
Bunsen, Ernest de	1819–1903	Burrows, Christine Mary	
Bunsen, Sir Maurice William		Elizabeth	1872–1959
Ernest de. See de Bunsen	1852–1932	Burrows, Sir Frederick John	1887–1973
Bunting, Basil	1900–1985	Burrows, Montagu	1819–1905
Bunting, Sir Percy William	1836–1911	Burrows, Ronald Montagu	#1867–1920
Burbidge, Edward	1839–1903	Burt, Sir Cyril Lodowic	1883–1971
Burbidge, Frederick William	1847–1905	Burt, Thomas	1837–1922
Burbury, Samuel Hawksley	1831–1911	Burton, Baron. See Bass,	
Burch, Cecil Reginald	1901–1983	Michael Arthur	1837–1909
Burdett-Coutts, Angela		Burton, Sir Montague	
Georgina, Baroness	1814–1906	Maurice	1885–1952
Burdon, John Shaw	1826–1907	Burton, Richard	1925–1984
Burdon-Sanderson, Sir John		Bury, John Bagnell	1861–1927
Scott	1828–1905	Bush, Eric Wheler	1899–1985
Burge, Hubert Murray	1862–1925	Bushell, Stephen Wootton	1844–1908
Burgess, Guy Francis de		Busk, Rachel Harriette	1831–1907
Moncy	#1911–1963	Bustamante, Sir William	
Burgh Canning, Hubert		Alexander	1884–1977
George De, Marquess of		Butcher, Samuel Henry	1850–1910
Clanricarde	1832–1916	Butler, Arthur Gray	1831–1909
Burghley, Baron. See Cecil,		Butler, Arthur John	1844–1910
David George Brownlow	1905–1981	Butler, Basil Edward	
Burkitt, Francis Crawford	1864–1935	('Christopher')	1902–1986
Burn, Duncan Lyall	1902–1988	Butler, (Christina) Violet	#1884–1982

Campbell, James Henry
Mussen, Baron Glenavy — 1851–1931
Campbell, Sir James Macnabb — 1846–1903
Campbell, Dame Janet Mary — 1877–1954
Campbell, John Charles — 1894–1942
Campbell, John Douglas
Sutherland, Duke of Argyll — 1845–1914
Campbell, Lewis — 1830–1908
Campbell, Sir Malcolm — 1885–1948
Campbell, Patrick Gordon,
Baron Glenavy — 1913–1980
Campbell, (Renton) Stuart — 1908–1966
Campbell, Sir Ronald Hugh — 1883–1953
Campbell, William Howard — 1859–1910
Campbell-Bannerman, Sir
Henry — 1836–1908
Campion, Gilbert Francis
Montriou, Baron — 1882–1958
Camps, Francis Edward — 1905–1972
Camrose, Viscount. See
Berry, William Ewert — 1879–1954
Cannan, Charles — 1858–1919
Cannan, Edwin — 1861–1935
Canning, Sir Samuel — 1823–1908
Cannon, Herbert Graham — 1897–1963
Cannon, Thomas — #1846–1917
Canton, William — 1845–1926
Cape, Herbert Jonathan — 1879–1960
Capel, Thomas John — 1836–1911
Capes, William Wolfe — 1834–1914
Capper, Sir Thompson — 1863–1915
Caradon, Baron. See Foot,
Hugh Mackintosh — 1907–1990
Carden, Sir Sackville
Hamilton — 1857–1930
Cardew, Michael Ambrose — 1901–1983
Cardew, Philip — 1851–1910
Cardus, Sir (John Frederick)
Neville — 1889–1975
Carey, Rosa Nouchette — 1840–1909
Carlile, Wilson — 1847–1942
Carline, Richard Cotton — 1896–1980
Carling, Sir Ernest Rock — 1877–1960
Carlisle, Earl of. See Howard,
George James — 1843–1911
Carlisle, Countess of. See
Howard, Rosalind Frances — 1845–1921
Carlyle, Alexander James — 1861–1943
Carlyle, Benjamin Fearnley
(Dom Aelred) — 1874–1955
Carlyle, Sir Robert Warrand — 1859–1934
Carman, William Bliss — 1861–1929
Carmichael, Sir Thomas
David Gibson-, Baron — 1859–1926
Carnarvon, Earl of. See
Herbert, George Edward
Stanhope Molyneux — 1866–1923
Carnegie, Andrew — 1835–1919
Carnegie, James, Earl of
Southesk — 1827–1905
Carnell, Edward John — 1912–1972

Carnock, Baron. See
Nicolson, Sir Arthur — 1849–1928
Caroe, Sir Olaf Kirkpatrick
Kruuse — 1892–1981
Caröe, William Douglas — 1857–1938
Carpenter, Alfred Francis
Blakeney — 1881–1955
Carpenter, Edward — 1844–1929
Carpenter, George Alfred — 1859–1910
Carpenter, Sir (Henry Cort)
Harold — 1875–1940
Carpenter, Joseph Estlin — 1844–1927
Carpenter, Robert — 1830–1901
Carpenter, William Boyd — 1841–1918
Carr, Sir Cecil Thomas — 1878–1966
Carr, Edward Hallett — 1892–1982
Carreras, Sir James Enrique — 1909–1990
Carrington, Dora de
Houghton — #1893–1932
Carrington, Sir Frederick — 1844–1913
Carritt, (Hugh) David
(Graham) — 1927–1982
Carr-Saunders, Sir Alexander
Morris — 1886–1966
Carruthers, (Alexander)
Douglas (Mitchell) — 1882–1962
Carson, Edward Henry, Baron — 1854–1935
Carte, Dame Bridget D'Oyly.
See D'Oyly Carte — 1908–1985
Carte, Richard D'Oyly — 1844–1901
Carter, Sir Edgar Bonham-.
See Bonham-Carter — 1870–1956
Carter, (Helen) Violet
Bonham, Baroness Asquith
of Yarnbury. See Bonham
Carter — 1887–1969
Carter, Howard — 1874–1939
Carter, Hugh — 1837–1903
Carter, John Waynflete — 1905–1975
Carter, Thomas Thellusson — 1808–1901
Carton, Richard Claude — 1856–1928
Carton de Wiart, Sir Adrian — 1880–1963
Carus-Wilson, Eleanora Mary — 1897–1977
Carver, Alfred James — 1826–1909
Cary, Arthur Joyce Lunel — 1888–1957
Cary, Sir (Arthur Lucius)
Michael — 1917–1976
Case, Thomas — 1844–1925
Casement, Roger David — 1864–1916
Casey, Richard Gardiner,
Baron — 1890–1976
Casey, William Francis — 1884–1957
Cash, John Theodore — 1854–1936
Cassel, Sir Ernest Joseph — 1852–1921
Cassels, Sir Robert Archibald — 1876–1959
Cassels, Walter Richard — 1826–1907
Catchpool, (Egerton) St John
(Pettifor) — #1890–1971
Cates, Arthur — 1829–1901
Cathcart, Edward Provan — 1877–1954
Caton-Thompson, Gertrude — 1888–1985

Charrington, Frederick Nicholas	1850–1936
Charteris, Archibald Hamilton	1835–1908
Chase, Drummond Percy	1820–1902
Chase, Frederic Henry	1853–1925
Chase, Marian Emma	1844–1905
Chase, William St Lucian	1856–1908
Chatfield, Alfred Ernle Montacute, Baron	1873–1967
Chatterjee, Sir Atul Chandra	1874–1955
Chatwin, (Charles) Bruce	1940–1989
Chauvel, Sir Henry George	1865–1945
Chavasse, Christopher Maude	1884–1962
Chavasse, Francis James	1846–1928
Cheadle, Walter Butler	1835–1910
Cheatle, Arthur Henry	1866–1929
Cheesman, Robert Ernest	1878–1962
Cheetham, Samuel	1827–1908
Chelmsford, Baron. See Thesiger, Frederic Augustus	1827–1905
Chelmsford, Viscount. See Thesiger, Frederic John Napier	1868–1933
Chenevix-Trench, Anthony	1919–1979
Cheney, Christopher Robert	1906–1987
Chermside, Sir Herbert Charles	1850–1929
Cherry-Garrard, Apsley George Benet	1886–1959
Cherwell, Viscount. See Lindemann, Frederick Alexander	1886–1957
Cheshire, Geoffrey Chevalier	1886–1978
Chester, Sir (Daniel) Norman	1907–1986
Chesterton, Cecil Edward	#1879–1918
Chesterton, Gilbert Keith	1874–1936
Chetwode, Sir Philip Walhouse, Baron	1869–1950
Chevalier, Albert	1861–1923
Cheylesmore, Baron. See Eaton, Herbert Francis	1848–1925
Cheylesmore, Baron. See Eaton, William Meriton	1843–1902
Cheyne, Thomas Kelly	1841–1915
Cheyne, Sir (William) Watson	1852–1932
Chibnall, Albert Charles	1894–1988
Chichester, Sir Francis Charles	1901–1972
Chick, Dame Harriette	1875–1977
Chifley, Joseph Benedict	1885–1951
Child, Harold Hannyngton	1869–1945
Child, Thomas	1839–1906
Child-Villiers, Margaret Elizabeth, Countess of Jersey. See Villiers	1849–1945
Child-Villiers, Victor Albert George, Earl of Jersey. See Villiers	1845–1915
Childe, Vere Gordon	1892–1957
Childers, Robert Erskine	1870–1922
Childs, William Macbride	1869–1939
Chilston, Viscount. See Akers-Douglas, Aretas	1851–1926
Chilston, Viscount. See Akers-Douglas, Aretas	1876–1947
Chipperfield, James Seaton Methuen	1912–1990
Chirol, Sir (Ignatius) Valentine	1852–1929
Chisholm, Hugh	1866–1924
Cholmondeley, Hugh, Baron Delamere	1870–1931
Chorley, Robert Samuel Theodore, Baron	1895–1978
Christiansen, Arthur	1904–1963
Christie, Dame Agatha Mary Clarissa	1890–1976
Christie, John	1882–1962
Christie, John Reginald Halliday	#1899–1953
Christie, John Traill	1899–1980
Christie, Sir William Henry Mahoney	1845–1922
Christophers, Sir (Samuel) Rickard	1873–1978
Chrystal, George	1851–1911
Chubb, Sir Lawrence Wensley	1873–1948
Church, Charles James Gregory	1942–1989
Church, Sir William Selby	1837–1928
Churchill, Clementine Ogilvy Spencer-, Baroness Spencer-Churchill	1885–1977
Churchill, Jeanette ('Jennie'), Lady Randolph Churchill	#1854–1921
Churchill, Peter Morland	1909–1972
Churchill, Randolph Frederick Edward Spencer-	#1911–1968
Churchill, Sir Winston Leonard Spencer-	1874–1965
Churchward, George Jackson	#1857–1933
Chuter-Ede, James Chuter, Baron Chuter-Ede	1882–1965
Cilcennin, Viscount. See Thomas, James Purdon Lewes	1903–1960
Citrine, Walter McLennan, Baron	1887–1983
Clanricarde, Marquess of. See Burgh Canning, Hubert George De	1832–1916
Clanwilliam, Earl of. See Meade, Richard James	1832–1907
Clapham, Sir Alfred William	1883–1950
Clapham, (Arthur) Roy	1904–1990
Clapham, Sir John Harold	1873–1946

Cochrane-Baillie, Charles Wallace Alexander Napier Ross, Baron Lamington. See Baillie	1860–1940
Cockayne, Dame Elizabeth	1894–1988
Cockburn, (Francis) Claud	1904–1981
Cockcroft, Sir John Douglas	1897–1967
Cockerell, Douglas Bennett	1870–1945
Cockerell, Sir Sydney Carlyle	1867–1962
Cockerell, Sydney Morris	1906–1987
Cocks, Arthur Herbert Tennyson Somers-, Baron Somers. See Somers-Cocks	1887–1944
Codner, Maurice Frederick	1888–1958
Cody, Samuel Franklin	#1861–1913
Coghill, Nevill Henry Kendal Aylmer	1899–1980
Coghlan, Sir Charles Patrick John	1863–1927
Cohen, Sir Andrew Benjamin	1909–1968
Cohen, Arthur	1829–1914
Cohen, Harriet	1896–1967
Cohen, Henry, Baron Cohen of Birkenhead	1900–1977
Cohen, Sir John Edward ('Jack')	1898–1979
Cohen, Lionel Leonard, Baron	1888–1973
Cohen, Sir Robert Waley	1877–1952
Coia, Jack Antonio	1898–1981
Coillard, François	1834–1904
Cokayne, George Edward	1825–1911
Coke, Gerald Edward	1907–1990
Coke, Thomas William, Earl of Leicester	1822–1909
Coker, Ernest George	1869–1946
Colbeck, William	#1871–1930
Coldstream, Sir William Menzies	1908–1987
Cole, Cecil Jackson-. See Jackson-Cole	1901–1979
Cole, George Douglas Howard	1889–1959
Cole, George James, Baron	1906–1979
Cole, Dame Margaret Isabel	1893–1980
Colebrook, Leonard	1883–1967
Coleman, William Stephen	1829–1904
Coleraine, Baron. See Law, Richard Kidston	1901–1980
Coleridge, Bernard John Seymour, Baron	1851–1927
Coleridge, Mary Elizabeth	1861–1907
Coleridge, Stephen William Buchanan	1854–1936
Coleridge-Taylor, Samuel	1875–1912
Coles, Charles Edward, Coles Pasha	1853–1926
Coles, Vincent Stuckey Stratton	1845–1929
Collar, (Arthur) Roderick	1908–1986
Collen, Sir Edwin Henry Hayter	1843–1911
Colles, Henry Cope	1879–1943
Collett, Sir Henry	1836–1901
Collie, John Norman	1859–1942
Collier, John	1850–1934
Collings, Jesse	1831–1920
Collingwood, Cuthbert	1826–1908
Collingwood, Sir Edward Foyle	1900–1970
Collingwood, Robin George	1889–1943
Collins, Cecil James Henry	1908–1989
Collins, John Churton	1848–1908
Collins, Josephine ('José')	1887–1958
Collins, (Lewis) John	1905–1982
Collins, Michael	1890–1922
Collins, Norman Richard	1907–1982
Collins, Richard Henn, Baron	1842–1911
Collins, Sir William Alexander Roy	1900–1976
Collins, William Edward	1867–1911
Colman, Ronald Charles	#1891–1958
Colnaghi, Martin Henry	1821–1908
Colomb, Sir John Charles Ready	1838–1909
Colquhoun, Robert	1914–1962
Colton, Sir John	1823–1902
Colvile, Sir Henry Edward	1852–1907
Colville, David John, Baron Clydesmuir	1894–1954
Colville, Sir John Rupert	1915–1987
Colville, Sir Stanley Cecil James	1861–1939
Colvin, Sir Auckland	1838–1908
Colvin, Ian Duncan	1877–1938
Colvin, Sir Sidney	1845–1927
Colvin, Sir Walter Mytton. See under Colvin, Sir Auckland	
Commerell, Sir John Edmund	1829–1901
Common, Andrew Ainslie	1841–1903
Comper, Sir (John) Ninian	1864–1960
Compton, Lord Alwyne Frederick	1825–1906
Compton, Fay	1894–1978
Compton-Burnett, Dame Ivy	1884–1969
Comrie, Leslie John	1893–1950
Conder, Charles	1868–1909
Conder, Claude Reignier	1848–1910
Condy, Henry Bollmann	#1826–1907
Conesford, Baron. See Strauss, Henry George	1892–1974
Congreve, Sir Walter Norris	1862–1927
Coningham, Sir Arthur	1895–1948
Connard, Philip	1875–1958
Connaught and Strathearn, Duke of. See Arthur William Patrick Albert	1850–1942
Connell, Amyas Douglas	1901–1980
Connemara, Baron. See Bourke, Robert	1827–1902

Courtauld, Augustine	1904–1959	Crankshaw, Edward	1909–1984
Courtauld, Samuel	1876–1947	Crathorne, Baron. See	
Courthope, William John	1842–1917	Dugdale, Thomas Lionel	1897–1977
Courtneidge, Dame		Craven, Hawes	1837–1910
(Esmeralda) Cicely	1893–1980	Craven, Henry Thornton	1818–1905
Courtney, Sir Christopher		Crawford, Earl of. See	
Lloyd	1890–1976	Lindsay, David Alexander	
Courtney, Dame Kathleen		Edward	1871–1940
D'Olier	#1878–1974	Crawford, Earl of. See	
Courtney, Leonard Henry,		Lindsay, David Alexander	
Baron Courtney of Penwith	1832–1918	Robert	1900–1975
Courtney, William Leonard	1850–1928	Crawford, Earl of. See	
Cousin, Anne Ross	1824–1906	Lindsay, James Ludovic	1847–1913
Cousins, Frank	1904–1986	Crawford, Osbert Guy	
Cowan, Sir Walter Henry	1871–1956	Stanhope	1886–1957
Cowans, Sir John Steven	1862–1921	Crawfurd, Oswald John	
Coward, Sir Henry	1849–1944	Frederick	1834–1909
Coward, Sir Noël Peirce	1899–1973	Crawfurd, Sir Raymond	
Cowdray, Viscount. See		Henry Payne	1865–1938
Pearson, Weetman		Crawley, Leonard George	1903–1981
Dickinson	1856–1927	Creagh, Sir Garrett	
Cowell, Edward Byles	1826–1903	O'Moore	1848–1923
Cowen, Sir Frederic Hymen	1852–1935	Creagh, William	1828–1901
Cowie, William Garden	1831–1902	Creasy, Sir George Elvey	1895–1972
Cowley, Sir Arthur Ernest	1861–1931	Creditor, Dora. See Gaitskell,	
Cowper, Francis Thomas de		Anna Deborah	1901–1989
Grey, Earl	1834–1905	Creech Jones, Arthur. See	
Cox, Alfred	1866–1954	Jones	1891–1964
Cox, Sir Christopher William		Creed, John Martin	1889–1940
Machell	1899–1982	Creed, Sir Thomas Percival	1897–1969
Cox, George (called Sir		Creedy, Sir Herbert James	1878–1973
George) William	1827–1902	Cremer, Robert Wyndham	
Cox, Harold	1859–1936	Ketton-. See	
Cox, Leslie Reginald	1897–1965	Ketton-Cremer	1906–1969
Cox, Sir Percy Zachariah	1864–1937	Cremer, Sir William Randal	1838–1908
Cozens-Hardy, Herbert		Crewe-Milnes, Robert Offley	
Hardy, Baron	1838–1920	Ashburton, Marquess of	
Craddock, Sir Reginald Henry	1864–1937	Crewe	1858–1945
Cradock, Sir Christopher		Crichton-Browne, Sir James.	
George Francis Maurice	1862–1914	See Browne	1840–1938
Craig, (Edward Henry)		Cripps, Charles Alfred, Baron	
Gordon	1872–1966	Parmoor	1852–1941
Craig, Isa. See Knox	1831–1903	Cripps, Dame Isobel	1891–1979
Craig, James, Viscount		Cripps, Sir (Richard) Stafford	1889–1952
Craigavon	1871–1940	Cripps, Wilfred Joseph	1841–1903
Craig, Sir John	1874–1957	Crispin, Edmund, *pseudonym.*	
Craig, William James	1843–1906	See Montgomery, Robert	
Craigavon, Viscount. See		Bruce	1921–1978
Craig, James	1871–1940	Crocker, Henry Radcliffe-.	
Craigie, Pearl Mary Teresa,		See Radcliffe-Crocker	1845–1909
'John Oliver Hobbes'	1867–1906	Crockett, Samuel Rutherford	1860–1914
Craigie, Sir Robert Leslie	1883–1959	Croft, Henry Page, Baron	1881–1947
Craigie, Sir William		Croft, John	1833–1905
Alexander	1867–1957	Croft, (John) Michael	1922–1986
Craigmyle, Baron. See Shaw,		Crofts, Ernest	1847–1911
Thomas	1850–1937	Croke, Thomas William	1824–1902
Craik, Sir Henry	1846–1927	Cromer, Earl of. See Baring,	
Cranbrook, Earl of. See		Evelyn	1841–1917
Gathorne-Hardy, Gathorne	1814–1906	Cromer, Earl of. See Baring,	
Crane, Walter	1845–1915	Rowland Thomas	1877–1953
Cranko, John Cyril	1927–1973	Crompton, Henry	1836–1904

Dadabhoy, Sir Maneckji Byramji	1865–1953
Dafoe, John Wesley	1866–1944
Dahl, Roald	1916–1990
Dain, Sir (Harry) Guy	1870–1966
Dakin, Henry Drysdale	1880–1952
Dale, Sir David	1829–1906
Dale, Sir Henry Hallett	1875–1968
Daley, Sir (William) Allen	1887–1969
Dallinger, William Henry	1842–1909
Dalrymple-Hamilton, Sir Frederick Hew George	1890–1974
Dalrymple-Hay, Sir Harley Hugh. See Hay	1861–1940
Dalton, (Edward) Hugh (John Neale), Baron	1887–1962
Dalton, Ormonde Maddock	1866–1945
Dalziel, Davison Alexander, Baron	1854–1928
Dalziel, Edward	1817–1905
Dalziel, George	1815–1902
Dalziel, James Henry, Baron Dalziel of Kirkcaldy	1868–1935
Dalziel, Thomas Bolton Gilchrist Septimus	1823–1906
Damm, Sheila Van. See Van Damm	1922–1987
Dampier, Sir William Cecil Dampier (formerly Whetham)	1867–1952
Danckwerts, Peter Victor	1916–1984
Dane, Clemence, pseudonym. See Ashton, Winifred	1888–1965
Dane, Sir Louis William	1856–1946
Daniel, Charles Henry Olive	1836–1919
Daniel, Evan	1837–1904
Daniel, Glyn Edmund	1914–1986
Danielli, James Frederic	1911–1984
Danquah, Joseph Boakye	1895–1965
Dansey, Sir Claude Edward Marjoribanks	#1876–1947
Danvers, Frederic Charles	1833–1906
D'Aranyi, Jelly (1893–1966). See under Fachiri, Adila	1886–1962
Darbishire, Helen	1881–1961
Darbyshire, Alfred	1839–1908
D'Arcy, Charles Frederick	1859–1938
D'Arcy, Martin Cyril	1888–1976
D'Arcy, William Knox	#1849–1917
Darling, Charles John, Baron	1849–1936
Darling, Sir Frank Fraser	1903–1979
Darlington, Cyril Dean	1903–1981
Darlington, William Aubrey Cecil	1890–1979
Dart, (Robert) Thurston	1921–1971
Darwin, Bernard Richard Meirion	1876–1961
Darwin, Sir Charles Galton	1887–1962
Darwin, Sir Francis	1848–1925
Darwin, Sir George Howard	1845–1912
Darwin, Sir Horace	1851–1928
Darwin, Sir Robert Vere ('Robin')	1910–1974
Dashwood, Edmée Elizabeth Monica, 'E. M. Delafield'	1890–1943
Daubeney, Sir Henry Charles Barnston	1810–1903
Daubeny, Sir Peter Lauderdale	1921–1975
Davenport, Ernest Harold ('Nicholas')	1893–1979
Davenport, Harold	1907–1969
Davenport-Hill, Rosamond. See Hill	1825–1902
Davey, Horace, Baron	1833–1907
David, Albert Augustus	1867–1950
David, Sir Percival Victor David Ezekiel	#1892–1964
David, Sir (Tannatt William) Edgeworth	1858–1934
Davids, Thomas William Rhys	1843–1922
Davidson, Andrew Bruce	1831–1902
Davidson, Charles	1824–1902
Davidson, (Frances) Joan, Baroness Northchurch and Viscountess	1894–1985
Davidson, James Leigh Strachan-. See Strachan-Davidson	1843–1916
Davidson, (James) Norman	1911–1972
Davidson, John	1857–1909
Davidson, John Colin Campbell, Viscount	1889–1970
Davidson, Sir John Humphrey	1876–1954
Davidson, John Thain	1833–1904
Davidson, Sir (Leybourne) Stanley (Patrick)	1894–1981
Davidson, Randall Thomas, Baron Davidson of Lambeth	1848–1930
Davie, Thomas Benjamin	1895–1955
Davies, Charles Maurice	1828–1910
Davies, Clement Edward	1884–1962
Davies, David, Baron	1880–1944
Davies, Duncan Sheppey	1921–1987
Davies, Sir (Henry) Walford	1869–1941
Davies, John Emerson Harding	1916–1979
Davies, John Llewelyn	1826–1916
Davies, Margaret Caroline Llewelyn. See Llewelyn Davies	#1861–1944
Davies, Sir Martin	1908–1975
Davies, Rhys	1901–1978
Davies, Richard Llewelyn, Baron Llewelyn-Davies. See Llewelyn Davies	1912–1981
Davies, Robert	1816–1905
Davies, (Sarah) Emily	1830–1921
Davies, William Henry	1871–1940

De Robeck, Sir John Michael	1862–1928	Dickinson, Lowes (Cato)	1819–1908
De Saulles, George William	1862–1903	Dicksee, Sir Francis Bernard	
Desborough, Baron. See		('Frank')	1853–1928
Grenfell, William Henry	1855–1945	Dickson, Sir Collingwood	1817–1904
Desch, Cecil Henry	#1874–1958	Dickson, Sir William	
De Selincourt, Ernest. See		Forster	1898–1987
Selincourt	1870–1943	Dickson, William Purdie	1823–1901
De Soissons, Louis		Dickson-Poynder, Sir John	
Emmanuel Jean Guy de		Poynder, Baron Islington.	
Savoie-Carignan	1890–1962	See Poynder	1866–1936
Despard, Charlotte	#1844–1939	Diefenbaker, John George	1895–1979
De Stein, Sir Edward Sinauer	1887–1965	Digby, William	1849–1904
De Syllas, Stelios Messinesos		Dilhorne, Viscount. See	
(Leo)	1917–1964	Manningham-Buller,	
Des Voeux, Sir (George)		Reginald Edward	1905–1980
William	1834–1909	Dilke, Sir Charles Wentworth	1843–1911
Detmold, Charles Maurice	1883–1908	Dilke, Emilia Frances, Lady	1840–1904
De Valera, Eamon	1882–1975	Dill, Sir John Greer	1881–1944
De Vere, Aubrey Thomas	1814–1902	Dill, Sir Samuel	1844–1924
De Vere, Sir Stephen Edward	1812–1904	Dillon, Emile Joseph	1854–1933
Deverell, Sir Cyril John	1874–1947	Dillon, Frank	1823–1909
De Villiers, John Henry,		Dillon, Harold Arthur Lee-,	
Baron	1842–1914	Viscount Dillon	1844–1932
Devine, George Alexander		Dillon, John	1851–1927
Cassady	1910–1966	Dillwyn, (Elizabeth) Amy	#1845–1935
Devlin, Joseph	1871–1934	Dimbleby, Richard Frederick	1913–1965
Devonport, Viscount. See		Dimock, Nathaniel	1825–1909
Kearley, Hudson Ewbanke	1856–1934	Dines, William Henry	1855–1927
Devons, Ely	1913–1967	Diplock, (William John)	
Devonshire, Duke of. See		Kenneth, Baron	1907–1985
Cavendish, Spencer		Dirac, Paul Adrien Maurice	1902–1984
Compton	1833–1908	Dix, George Eglington Alston	
Devonshire, Duke of. See		(Dom Gregory)	1901–1952
Cavendish, Victor Christian		Dixey, Sir Frank	1892–1982
William	1868–1938	Dixie, Lady Florence	
Dewar, Sir James	1842–1923	Caroline	1857–1905
De Wet, Christiaan Rudolph	1854–1922	Dixon, Sir Arthur Lewis	1881–1969
De Wiart, Sir Adrian Carton.		Dixon, Henry Horatio	1869–1953
See Carton de Wiart	1880–1963	Dixon, Sir Pierson John	1904–1965
De Winton, Sir Francis		Dixon, Sir Robert Bland	1867–1939
Walter	1835–1901	Dixon, Walter Ernest	1870–1931
De Worms, Henry, Baron		Dobb, Maurice Herbert	1900–1976
Pirbright	1840–1903	Dobbie, Sir William George	
Dewrance, Sir John	1858–1937	Shedden	#1879–1964
Dexter, John	1925–1990	Dobbs, Sir Henry Robert	
D'Eyncourt, Sir Eustace		Conway	1871–1934
Henry William Tennyson-.		Dobell, Bertram	1842–1914
See Tennyson-d'Eyncourt	1868–1951	Dobrée, Bonamy	1891–1974
De Zulueta, Sir Philip		Dobson, Frank Owen	1886–1963
Francis. See Zulueta	1929–1989	Dobson, Gordon Miller	
Dibbs, Sir George Richard	1834–1904	Bourne	1889–1976
Dibdin, Sir Lewis Tonna	1852–1938	Dobson, (Henry) Austin	1840–1921
Dicey, Albert Venn	1835–1922	Dobson, Sir Roy Hardy	1891–1968
Dicey, Edward James Stephen	1832–1911	Dod, Charlotte ('Lottie')	#1871–1960
Dick, Sir William Reid	1878–1961	Dodd, Charles Harold	1884–1973
Dick-Read, Grantly	1890–1959	Dodd, Francis	1874–1949
Dickens, Frank	1899–1986	Dodds, Sir (Edward) Charles	1899–1973
Dickinson, Goldsworthy		Dodds, Eric Robertson	1893–1979
Lowes	1862–1932	Dodgson, Campbell	1867–1948
Dickinson, Henry Winram	1870–1952	Dodgson, Frances Catharine	1883–1954
Dickinson, Hercules Henry	1827–1905	Dods, Marcus	1834–1909

Duckworth, Wynfrid	
Laurence Henry	1870–1956
Du Cros, Sir Arthur Philip	1871–1955
Dudgeon, (John) Alastair	1916–1989
Dudgeon, Leonard Stanley	1876–1938
Dudgeon, Robert Ellis	1820–1904
Dudley, Earl of. See Ward,	
William Humble	1867–1932
Duff, Sir Alexander Ludovic	1862–1933
Duff, Sir Beauchamp	1855–1918
Duff, Edward Gordon	#1863–1924
Duff, Sir James Fitzjames	1898–1970
Duff, Sir Lyman Poore	1865–1955
Duff, Sir Mountstuart	
Elphinstone Grant. See	
Grant Duff	1829–1906
Dufferin and Ava, Marquess	
of. See Blackwood,	
Frederick Temple	
Hamilton-Temple	1826–1902
Duffy, Sir Charles Gavan	1816–1903
Duffy, Sir Frank Gavan	1852–1936
Duffy, Patrick Vincent	1836–1909
Duffy, Terence	1922–1985
Dugdale, Thomas Lionel,	
Baron Crathorne	1897–1977
Duke, Sir Frederick William	1863–1924
Duke, Henry Edward, Baron	
Merrivale	1855–1939
Duke-Elder, Sir (William)	
Stewart	1898–1978
Dukes, Ashley	1885–1959
Dulac, Edmund	1882–1953
Du Maurier, Dame Daphne	1907–1989
Du Maurier, Sir Gerald	
Hubert Edward Busson	1873–1934
Duncan, Sir Andrew Rae	1884–1952
Duncan, George Simpson	1884–1965
Duncan, Sir John Norman	
Valette ('Val')	1913–1975
Duncan, Sir Patrick	1870–1943
Duncan-Sandys, Baron. See	
Sandys, (Edwin) Duncan	1908–1987
Dundas, Lawrence John	
Lumley, Marquess of	
Zetland	1876–1961
Dunderdale, Wilfred Albert	1899–1990
Dundonald, Earl of. See	
Cochrane, Douglas	
Mackinnon Baillie	
Hamilton	1852–1935
Dunedin, Viscount. See	
Murray, Andrew Graham	1849–1942
Dunhill, Thomas Frederick	1877–1946
Dunhill, Sir Thomas Peel	1876–1957
Dunlop, Sir Derrick Melville	1902–1980
Dunlop, John Boyd	1840–1921
Dunmore, Earl of. See	
Murray, Charles Adolphus	1841–1907
Dunne, John William	#1875–1949
Dunne, Sir Laurence Rivers	1893–1970

Dunphie, Charles James	1820–1908
Dunraven and Mount-Earl,	
Earl of. See Quin,	
Windham Thomas	
Wyndham-	1841–1926
Dunrossil, Viscount. See	
Morrison, William	
Shepherd	1893–1961
Dunsany, Baron of. See	
Plunkett, Edward John	
Moreton Drax	1878–1957
Dunstan, Sir Wyndham	
Rowland	1861–1949
Du Parcq, Herbert, Baron	1880–1949
Dupré, August	1835–1907
Du Pré, Jacqueline Mary	1945–1987
Durand, Sir Henry Mortimer	1850–1924
Durham, (Mary) Edith	#1863–1944
Durnford, Sir Walter	1847–1926
Durrell, Lawrence George	1912–1990
Dutt, (Rajani) Palme	1896–1974
Dutt, Romesh Chunder	1848–1909
Dutton, Joseph Everett	1874–1905
Duveen, Joseph, Baron	1869–1939
Duveen, Sir Joseph Joel	1843–1908
Dwyer, George Patrick	1908–1987
Dyer, Reginald Edward Harry	1864–1927
Dyer, Sir William Turner	
Thiselton-. See	
Thiselton-Dyer	1843–1928
Dyke, Sir William Hart	1837–1931
Dykes Bower, Sir John	1905–1981
Dyson, Sir Frank Watson	1868–1939
Dyson, Sir George	1883–1964
Dyson, William Henry ('Will')	1880–1938
Eady, Charles Swinfen, Baron	
Swinfen	1851–1919
Eady, Sir (Crawfurd) Wilfrid	
(Griffin)	1890–1962
Eady, Eric Thomas	#1915–1966
Eardley-Wilmot, Sir Sainthill.	
See Wilmot	1852–1929
Earle, John	1824–1903
Earle, Sir Lionel	1866–1948
East, Sir Alfred	1849–1913
East, Sir Cecil James	1837–1908
East, Sir (William) Norwood	1872–1953
Eastlake, Charles Locke	1836–1906
Easton, Hugh Ray	1906–1965
Easton, Sir James Alfred	1908–1990
Eastwood, Sir Eric	1910–1981
Eaton, Herbert Francis, Baron	
Cheylesmore	1848–1925
Eaton, William Meriton,	
Baron Cheylesmore	1843–1902
Ebbutt, Norman	1894–1968
Ebert, (Anton) Charles	1887–1980
Ebsworth, Joseph Woodfall	1824–1908
Eccles, William Henry	1875–1966

Emden, Alfred Brotherston	#1888–1979	Evatt, Herbert Vere	1894–1965
Emery, Richard Gilbert		Eve, Sir Harry Trelawney	1856–1940
('Dick')	1915–1983	Everard, Harry Stirling	
Emery, (Walter) Bryan	1903–1971	Crawfurd	1848–1909
Emery, William	1825–1910	Everett, Joseph David	1831–1904
Emett, (Frederick) Rowland	1906–1990	Everett, Sir William	1844–1908
Emmott, Alfred, Baron	1858–1926	Evershed, (Francis) Raymond,	
Empson, Sir William	1906–1984	Baron	1899–1966
Engledow, Sir Frank Leonard	1890–1985	Evershed, John	1864–1956
Ensor, Sir Robert Charles		Eversley, Baron. See	
Kirkwood	1877–1958	Shaw-Lefevre, George	
Entwistle, William James	1895–1952	John	1831–1928
Epstein, Sir Jacob	1880–1959	Eves, Reginald Grenville	1876–1941
Erdélyi, Arthur	1908–1977	Evill, Sir Douglas Claude	
Erith, Raymond Charles	1904–1973	Strathern	1892–1971
Ernle, Baron. See Prothero,		Ewart, Alfred James	1872–1937
Rowland Edmund	1851–1937	Ewart, Charles Brisbane	1827–1903
Ervine, (John) St John		Ewart, Sir John Alexander	1821–1904
(Greer)	1883–1971	Ewart, Sir John Spencer	1861–1930
Escott, Bickham Aldred		Ewer, William Norman	1885–1977
Cowan Sweet-. See		Ewing, Sir (James) Alfred	1855–1935
Sweet-Escott	1907–1981	Ewins, Arthur James	1882–1957
Esdaile, Katharine Ada	1881–1950	Exeter, Marquess of. See	
Esher, Viscount. See Brett,		Cecil, David George	
Reginald Baliol	1852–1930	Brownlow	1905–1981
Esmond, Henry Vernon	1869–1922	Eyre, Charles Petrie	#1817–1902
Etheridge, Robert	1819–1903	Eyre, Edward John	1815–1901
Euan-Smith, Sir Charles Bean	1842–1910	Eyston, George Edward	
Eumorfopoulos, George	1863–1939	Thomas	1897–1979
Eva, *pseudonym*. See under			
O'Doherty, Kevin Izod	1823–1905		
Evan-Thomas, Sir Hugh	1862–1928	Faber, Sir Geoffrey Cust	1889–1961
Evans, Sir Arthur John	1851–1941	Faber, Oscar	1886–1956
Evans, (Benjamin) Ifor, Baron		Fachiri, Adila Adrienne	
Evans of Hungershall	1899–1982	Adalbertina Maria	1886–1962
Evans, Sir Charles Arthur		Faed, John	1819–1902
Lovatt	1884–1968	Fagan, James Bernard	1873–1933
Evans, Daniel Silvan	1818–1903	Fagan, Louis Alexander	1845–1903
Evans, Sir David Gwynne	1909–1984	Fairbairn, Andrew Martin	1838–1912
Evans, Dame Edith Mary	1888–1976	Fairbairn, Sir Robert Duncan	1910–1988
Evans, Edmund	1826–1905	Fairbairn, Stephen	1862–1938
Evans, Edward Ratcliffe		Fairbank, Alfred John	#1895–1982
Garth Russell, Baron		Fairbridge, Kingsley Ogilvie	1885–1924
Mountevans	1880–1957	Fairburn, Charles Edward	#1887–1945
Evans, Sir (Evan) Vincent	1851–1934	Fairey, Sir (Charles) Richard	1887–1956
Evans, George Essex	1863–1909	Fairfield, Baron. See Greer,	
Evans, George Ewart	1909–1988	(Frederick) Arthur	1863–1945
Evans, Sir Guildhaume		Fairfield, Cicily Isabel. See	
Myrddin-. See		West, Dame Rebecca	1892–1983
Myrddin-Evans	1894–1964	Fairley, Sir Neil Hamilton	1891–1966
Evans, Horace, Baron	1903–1963	Fairlie, Henry Jones	1924–1990
Evans, Sir John	1823–1908	Falcke, Isaac	1819–1909
Evans, John Gwenogvryn	1852–1930	Falconer, Lanoe, *pseudonym*.	
Evans, Meredith Gwynne	1904–1952	See Hawker, Mary	
Evans, Sir Samuel Thomas	1859–1918	Elizabeth	1848–1908
Evans, Sebastian	1830–1909	Falconer, Sir Robert	
Evans, Sir Trevor Maldwyn	1902–1981	Alexander	1867–1943
Evans, Sir (Worthington)		Falkiner, Caesar Litton	1863–1908
Laming Worthington-	1868–1931	Falkiner, Sir Frederick	
Evans-Pritchard, Sir Edward		Richard	1831–1908
Evan	1902–1973	Falkner, John Meade	1858–1932

Finley, Sir Moses I.	1912–1986	Flecker, Herman Elroy	
Finnie, John	1829–1907	('James Elroy')	1884–1915
Finzi, Gerald Raphael	1901–1956	Fleming, Sir Alexander	1881–1955
Firbank, (Arthur Annesley)		Fleming, Sir Arthur Percy	
Ronald	#1886–1926	Morris	1881–1960
Firth, Sir Charles Harding	1857–1936	Fleming, David Hay	1849–1931
Firth, John Rupert	1890–1960	Fleming, David Pinkerton,	
Firth, Sir William John	1881–1957	Lord	1877–1944
Fischer Williams, Sir John.		Fleming, George	1833–1901
See Williams	1870–1947	Fleming, Ian Lancaster	1908–1964
Fisher, Alan Wainwright	1922–1988	Fleming, James	1830–1908
Fisher, Andrew	1862–1928	Fleming, Sir (John) Ambrose	1849–1945
Fisher, Geoffrey Francis,		Fleming, (Robert) Peter	1907–1971
Baron Fisher of Lambeth	1887–1972	Fleming, Sir Sandford	1827–1915
Fisher, Herbert Albert		Fleming, (William) Launcelot	
Laurens	1865–1940	(Scott)	1906–1990
Fisher, James Maxwell		Fletcher, Sir Banister Flight	1866–1953
McConnell	1912–1970	Fletcher, Charles Robert	
Fisher, John Arbuthnot,		Leslie	1857–1934
Baron	1841–1920	Fletcher, Sir Frank	1870–1954
Fisher, Sir (Norman Fenwick)		Fletcher, James	1852–1908
Warren	1879–1948	Fletcher, Reginald Thomas	
Fisher, Robert Howie	1861–1934	Herbert, Baron Winster	1885–1961
Fisher, Sir Ronald Aylmer	1890–1962	Fletcher, Sir Walter Morley	1873–1933
Fisher, Sir William		Flett, Sir John Smith	1869–1947
Wordsworth	1875–1937	Fleure, Herbert John	1877–1969
Fison, Lorimer	1832–1907	Flint, Robert	1838–1910
Fitch, Sir Joshua Girling	1824–1903	Flint, Sir William Russell	1880–1969
Fitton, James	1899–1982	Florey, Howard Walter,	
FitzAlan of Derwent,		Baron	1898–1968
Viscount. See Howard,		Flower, Sir Cyril Thomas	1879–1961
Edmund Bernard FitzAlan-	1855–1947	Flower, Robin Ernest William	1881–1946
FitzAlan-Howard, Bernard		Floyer, Ernest Ayscoghe	1852–1903
Marmaduke, Duke of		Fluck, Diana Mary. See Dors,	
Norfolk. See Howard	1908–1975	Diana	1931–1984
FitzAlan-Howard, Henry,		Flux, Sir Alfred William	1867–1942
Duke of Norfolk. See		Foakes Jackson, Frederick	
Howard	1847–1917	John. See Jackson	1855–1941
Fitzclarence, Charles	1865–1914	Fogerty, Elsie	1865–1945
FitzGerald, George Francis	1851–1901	Folley, (Sydney) John	1906–1970
FitzGerald, Sir Thomas		Foot, Sir Dingle Mackintosh	1905–1978
Naghten	1838–1908	Foot, Hugh Mackintosh,	
FitzGibbon, Gerald	1837–1909	Baron Caradon	1907–1990
FitzGibbon, (Robert Louis)		Foot, Isaac	1880–1960
Constantine (Lee-Dillon)	1919–1983	Forbes, Sir Archibald	
Fitzmaurice, Baron. See		Finlayson	1903–1989
Petty-Fitzmaurice, Edmond		Forbes, Sir Charles Morton	1880–1960
George	1846–1935	Forbes, George	#1849–1936
Fitzmaurice, Sir Gerald		Forbes, George William	1869–1947
Gray	1901–1982	Forbes, James Staats	1823–1904
Fitzmaurice, Sir Maurice	1861–1924	Forbes, (Joan) Rosita	1890–1967
Fitzmaurice-Kelly, James	1857–1923	Forbes, Stanhope Alexander	1857–1947
Fitzpatrick, Sir Dennis	1837–1920	Forbes-Robertson, Sir	
FitzPatrick, Sir (James) Percy	1862–1931	Johnston. See Robertson	1853–1937
FitzRoy, Edward Algernon	1869–1943	Forbes-Sempill, William	
Fitzsimmons, Robert	#1863–1917	Francis, Baron Sempill	1893–1965
Flanagan, Bud	1896–1968	Ford, Edmund Brisco	1901–1988
Flanders, Allan David	1910–1973	Ford, Edward Onslow	1852–1901
Flanders, Michael Henry	1922–1975	Ford, Ford Madox (formerly	
Fleay, Frederick Gard	1831–1909	Ford Hermann Hueffer)	1873–1939
Fleck, Alexander, Baron	1889–1968	Ford, Patrick	1837–1913

Frazer, Sir James George	1854–1941	Fuller, John Frederick	
Fream, William	1854–1906	Charles	1878–1966
Fréchette, Louis Honoré	1839–1908	Fuller, Sir (Joseph)	
Freedman, Barnett	1901–1958	Bampfylde	1854–1935
Freeman, Gage Earle	1820–1903	Fuller, Peter Michael	1947–1990
Freeman, John	1880–1929	Fuller, Sir Thomas Ekins	1831–1910
Freeman, John Peere		Fuller-Maitland, John	
Williams-. See		Alexander. See Maitland	1856–1936
Williams-Freeman	1858–1943	Fulleylove, John	1845–1908
Freeman, Sir Ralph	1880–1950	Fulton, John Scott, Baron	1902–1986
Freeman, Richard Austin	#1862–1943	Furneaux, William Mordaunt	1848–1928
Freeman, Sir Wilfrid		Furness, Christopher, Baron	1852–1912
Rhodes	1888–1953	Furniss, Harry	1854–1925
Freeman-Mitford, Algernon		Furniss, Henry Sanderson,	
Bertram, Baron Redesdale.		Baron Sanderson	1868–1939
See Mitford	1837–1916	Furnivall, Frederick James	1825–1910
Freeman-Thomas, Freeman,		Furse, Charles Wellington	1868–1904
Marquess of Willingdon	1866–1941	Furse, Dame Katharine	1875–1952
Freeth, Francis Arthur	1884–1970	Furse, Sir Ralph Dolignon	1887–1973
Fremantle, Sir Edmund		Fury, Billy	1941–1983
Robert	1836–1929	Fust, Herbert Jenner-. See	
French, Evangeline Francis	1869–1960	Jenner-Fust	1806–1904
French, Francesca Law	1871–1960	Fyfe, David Patrick Maxwell,	
French, Sir Henry Leon	1883–1966	Earl of Kilmuir	1900–1967
French, John Denton		Fyfe, Henry Hamilton	1869–1951
Pinkstone, Earl of Ypres	1852–1925	Fyfe, Sir William Hamilton	1878–1965
Frere, Alexander Stuart	1892–1984	Fyleman, Rose Amy	1877–1957
Frere, Mary Eliza Isabella	1845–1911		
Frere, Walter Howard	1863–1938		
Freshfield, Douglas William	1845–1934	Gabor, Dennis	1900–1979
Freud, Anna	1895–1982	Gaddum, Sir John Henry	1900–1965
Freund, Sir Otto Kahn-. See		Gadsby, Henry Robert	1842–1907
Kahn-Freund	1900–1979	Gainford, Baron. See Pease,	
Freyberg, Bernard Cyril,		Joseph Albert	1860–1943
Baron	1889–1963	Gairdner, James	1828–1912
Freyer, Sir Peter Johnston	1851–1921	Gairdner, Sir William	
Fricker, Peter Racine	1920–1990	Tennant	1824–1907
Friese-Greene, William. See		Gaitskell, Anna Deborah	
Greene	1855–1921	('Dora'), Baroness	1901–1989
Frisch, Otto Robert	1904–1979	Gaitskell, Hugh Todd Naylor	1906–1963
Frith, William Powell	1819–1909	Galbraith, Vivian Hunter	1889–1976
Fritsch, Felix Eugen	1879–1954	Gale, Frederick	1823–1904
Frost, Dora. See Gaitskell,		Gale, Sir Humfrey	
Anna Deborah	1901–1989	Myddelton	1890–1971
Frowde, Henry	1841–1927	Gale, Sir Richard Nelson	1896–1982
Fry, Charles Burgess	1872–1956	Gallacher, William	1881–1965
Fry, Danby Palmer	1818–1903	Galloway, Sir Alexander	1895–1977
Fry, Sir Edward	1827–1918	Galloway, Sir William	1840–1927
Fry, (Edwin) Maxwell	1899–1987	Gallwey, Peter	1820–1906
Fry, Joseph Storrs	1826–1913	Galsworthy, John	1867–1933
Fry, Roger Eliot	1866–1934	Galton, Sir Francis	1822–1911
Fry, Sara Margery	1874–1958	Game, Sir Philip Woolcott	1876–1961
Fry, Thomas Charles	1846–1930	Gamgee, Arthur	1841–1909
Fryatt, Charles Algernon	1872–1916	Gandhi, Indira Priyadarshani	1917–1984
Frye, Leslie Legge Sarony.		Gandhi, Mohandas	
See Sarony, Leslie	1897–1985	Karamchand	1869–1948
Fuchs, (Emil Julius) Klaus	1911–1988	Gann, Thomas William	
Fulford, Sir Roger Thomas		Francis	1867–1938
Baldwin	1902–1983	Garbett, Cyril Forster	1875–1955
Fuller, Sir Cyril Thomas		García, Manuel Patricio	
Moulden	1874–1942	Rodríguez	1805–1906

Gibbs, Vicary	1853–1932	Glenavy, Baron. See	
Gibson, Edward, Baron		Campbell, James Henry	
Ashbourne	1837–1913	Mussen	1851–1931
Gibson, Guy Penrose	1918–1944	Glenavy, Baron. See	
Gibson, Sir John Watson	1885–1947	Campbell, Patrick Gordon	1913–1980
Gibson, Reginald Oswald	#1902–1983	Glenesk, Baron. See	
Gibson, Wilfrid Wilson	1878–1962	Borthwick, Algernon	1830–1908
Gibson, William Pettigrew	1902–1960	Glenny, Alexander Thomas	1882–1965
Gielgud, Val Henry	1900–1981	Glenvil Hall, William George.	
Giffard, Sir George James	1886–1964	See Hall	1887–1962
Giffard, Hardinge Stanley,		Gloag, Paton James	1823–1906
Earl of Halsbury	1823–1921	Gloag, William Ellis, Lord	
Giffen, Sir Robert	1837–1910	Kincairney	1828–1909
Gifford, Edwin Hamilton	1820–1905	Gloag, William Murray	#1865–1934
Gigliucci, Countess. See		Gloucester, Duke of. See	
Novello, Clara Anastasia	1818–1908	Henry William Frederick	
Gilbert, Sir Alfred	1854–1934	Albert	1900–1974
Gilbert, Sir Joseph Henry	1817–1901	Glover, John	#1817–1902
Gilbert, Sir William		Glover, Terrot Reaveley	1869–1943
Schwenck	1836–1911	Glubb, Sir John Bagot	1897–1986
Gilchrist, Percy Carlyle	#1851–1935	Gluckman, (Herman) Max	1911–1975
Giles, Herbert Allen	1845–1935	Glyn, Elinor	1864–1943
Giles, Peter	1860–1935	Godber, Frederick, Baron	1888–1976
Gill, (Arthur) Eric (Rowton)	1882–1940	Goddard, Rayner, Baron	1877–1971
Gill, Sir David	1843–1914	Godfrey, Daniel	1831–1903
Gilliatt, Sir William	1884–1956	Godfrey, John Henry	1888–1971
Gillie, Dame Annis Calder	1900–1985	Godfrey, Walter Hindes	1881–1961
Gillies, Duncan	1834–1903	Godfrey, William	1889–1963
Gillies, Sir Harold Delf	1882–1960	Godkin, Edwin Lawrence	1831–1902
Gillies, Sir William George	1898–1973	Godlee, Sir Rickman John	1849–1925
Gilman, Harold John Wilde	#1876–1919	Godley, Sir Alexander John	1867–1957
Gilmour, Sir John	1876–1940	Godley, Alfred Denis	1856–1925
Gilmour, John Scott Lennox	1906–1986	Godley, (John) Arthur, Baron	
Gilson, Julius Parnell	1868–1929	Kilbracken	1847–1932
Gimson, Ernest William	#1864–1919	Godwin, George Nelson	1846–1907
Gingold, Hermione		Godwin, Sir Harry	1901–1985
Ferdinanda	1897–1987	Godwin-Austen, Henry	
Ginner, Isaac Charles	1878–1952	Haversham	1834–1923
Ginsberg, Morris	1889–1970	Gogarty, Oliver Joseph St	
Ginsburg, Christian David	1831–1914	John	1878–1957
Girdlestone, Gathorne		Gold, Ernest	1881–1976
Robert	1881–1950	Gold, Sir Harcourt Gilbey	1876–1952
Girouard, Désiré	1836–1911	Goldfinger, Ernö	1902–1987
Girouard, Sir (Edouard)		Goldie, Sir George Dashwood	
Percy (Cranwill)	1867–1932	Taubman	1846–1925
Gissing, George Robert	1857–1903	Goldie, Grace Murrell	
Gladstone, Herbert John,		Wyndham	1900–1986
Viscount	1854–1930	Goldschmidt, Otto	1829–1907
Gladstone, John Hall	1827–1902	Goldsmid, Sir Frederic John	1818–1908
Glaisher, James	1809–1903	Goldsmid, Sir Henry Joseph	
Glaisher, James Whitbread		D'Avigdor-. See	
Lee	1848–1928	D'Avigdor-Goldsmid	1909–1976
Glanville, Sir William Henry	1900–1976	Goldsmid-Montefiore, Claude	
Glass, David Victor	1911–1978	Joseph. See Montefiore	1858–1938
Glass, Ruth Adele	1912–1990	Gollan, John	1911–1977
Glazebrook, Michael George	1853–1926	Gollancz, Sir Hermann	1852–1930
Glazebrook, Sir Richard		Gollancz, Sir Israel	1863–1930
Tetley	1854–1935	Gollancz, Sir Victor	1893–1967
Gleichen, Lady Feodora		Gonne, Maud Edith	#1866–1953
Georgina Maud	1861–1922	Gooch, George Peabody	1873–1968
Gleitze, Mercedes	#1900–1979	Goodall, Frederick	1822–1904

Graham, Hugh, Baron	
Atholstan	1848–1938
Graham, John Anderson	1861–1942
Graham, Robert Bontine	
Cunninghame	1852–1936
Graham, Sir Ronald William	1870–1949
Graham, Thomas Alexander	
Ferguson	1840–1906
Graham, William	1839–1911
Graham, William	1887–1932
Graham, (William) Sydney	1918–1986
Graham Brown, Thomas. See	
Brown	1882–1965
Graham-Harrison, Sir	
William Montagu	1871–1949
Graham-Little, Sir Ernest	
Gordon Graham	1867–1950
Grahame, Kenneth	1859–1932
Grahame-White, Claude	1879–1959
Granet, Sir (William) Guy	1867–1943
Grant, Sir (Alfred) Hamilton	1872–1937
Grant, Cary	1904–1986
Grant, Sir Charles (1836–	
1903). See under Grant, Sir	
Robert	
Grant, Duncan James	
Corrowr	1885–1978
Grant, George Monro	1835–1902
Grant, Sir Robert	1837–1904
Grant Duff, Sir Mountstuart	
Elphinstone	1829–1906
Grantham, Sir William	1835–1911
Granville, Sir Keith	1910–1990
Granville-Barker, Harley	
Granville	1877–1946
Graves, Alfred Perceval	1846–1931
Graves, George Windsor	1873?–1949
Graves, Robert Ranke	1895–1985
Gray, Sir Alexander	1882–1968
Gray, Sir Archibald	
Montague Henry	1880–1967
Gray, Basil	1904–1989
Gray, Benjamin Kirkman	1862–1907
Gray, George Buchanan	1865–1922
Gray, George Edward Kruger	1880–1943
Gray, Herbert Branston	1851–1929
Gray, Sir James	1891–1975
Gray, (Kathleen) Eileen	
(Moray)	1879–1976
Gray, Louis Harold	1905–1965
Greame, Philip Lloyd-, Earl	
of Swinton. See	
Cunliffe-Lister	1884–1972
Greaves, Walter	1846–1930
Green, Alice Sophia Amelia	
(Mrs Stopford Green)	1847–1929
Green, Charles Alfred Howell	1864–1944
Green, Frederick William	
Edridge-. See	
Edridge-Green	1863–1953
Green, Gustavus	1865–1964

Green, Henry, *pseudonym*. See	
Yorke, Henry Vincent	1905–1973
Green, Samuel Gosnell	1822–1905
Green, William Curtis	1875–1960
Greenaway, Catherine ('Kate')	1846–1901
Greene, Harry Plunket	1865–1936
Greene, Sir Hugh Carleton	1910–1987
Greene, Wilfrid Arthur,	
Baron	1883–1952
Greene, William Friese-	1855–1921
Greene, Sir (William)	
Graham	1857–1950
Greenidge, Abel Hendy Jones	1865–1906
Greenly, Edward	#1861–1951
Greenly, Henry	#1876–1947
Greenwell, William	1820–1918
Greenwood, Arthur	1880–1954
Greenwood, Arthur William	
James ('Anthony'),	
Baron Greenwood of	
Rossendale	1911–1982
Greenwood, Frederick	1830–1909
Greenwood, Hamar, Viscount	1870–1948
Greenwood, Joan Mary	
Waller	1921–1987
Greenwood, Thomas	1851–1908
Greenwood, Walter	1903–1974
Greer, (Frederick) Arthur,	
Baron Fairfield	1863–1945
Greer, William Derrick	
Lindsay	1902–1972
Greet, Sir Philip Barling Ben	1857–1936
Greg, Sir Walter Wilson	1875–1959
Grego, Joseph	1843–1908
Gregory, Sir Augustus	
Charles	1819–1905
Gregory, Edward John	1850–1909
Gregory, Frederick	
Gugenheim	1893–1961
Gregory, Isabella Augusta,	
Lady	1852–1932
Gregory, John Walter	1864–1932
Gregory, Sir Richard Arman	1864–1952
Gregory, Robert	1819–1911
Greiffenhagen, Maurice	
William	1862–1931
Grenfell, Bernard Pyne	1869–1926
Grenfell, Edward Charles,	
Baron St Just	1870–1941
Grenfell, Francis Wallace,	
Baron	1841–1925
Grenfell, George	1849–1906
Grenfell, Hubert Henry	1845–1906
Grenfell, Joyce Irene	1910–1979
Grenfell, Julian Henry	
Francis	1888–1915
Grenfell, Sir Wilfred	
Thomason	1865–1940
Grenfell, William Henry,	
Baron Desborough	1855–1945
Gresley, Sir (Herbert) Nigel	#1876–1941

Haddon, Alfred Cort	1855–1940
Haddow, Sir Alexander	1907–1976
Haden, Sir Francis Seymour	1818–1910
Hadfield, Sir Robert Abbott	1858–1940
Hadley, Patrick Arthur Sheldon	1899–1973
Hadley, William Waite	1866–1960
Hadow, Grace Eleanor	1875–1940
Hadow, Sir (William) Henry	1859–1937
Hadrill, (John) Michael Wallace-. See Wallace-Hadrill	1916–1985
Haggard, Sir Henry Rider	1856–1925
Hahn, Kurt Matthias Robert Martin	1886–1974
Haig, Douglas, Earl	1861–1928
Haig Brown, William	1823–1907
Haigh, Arthur Elam	1855–1905
Hailes, Baron. See Buchan-Hepburn, Patrick George Thomas	1901–1974
Hailey, (William) Malcolm, Baron	1872–1969
Hailsham, Viscount. See Hogg, Douglas McGarel	1872–1950
Hailwood, (Stanley) Michael (Bailey)	1940–1981
Haines, Sir Frederick Paul	1819–1909
Haking, Sir Richard Cyril Byrne	1862–1945
Halcrow, Sir William Thomson	1883–1958
Haldane, Elizabeth Sanderson	1862–1937
Haldane, John Burdon Sanderson	1892–1964
Haldane, John Scott	1860–1936
Haldane, Richard Burdon, Viscount	1856–1928
Hale-White, Sir William	1857–1949
Haley, Sir William John	1901–1987
Halford, Frank Bernard	1894–1955
Haliburton, Arthur Lawrence, Baron	1832–1907
Halifax, Viscount. See Wood, Charles Lindley	1839–1934
Halifax, Earl of. See Wood, Edward Frederick Lindley	1881–1959
Hall, Sir (Alfred) Daniel	1864–1942
Hall, Arthur Henry	1876–1949
Hall, Sir Arthur John	1866–1951
Hall, Christopher Newman	1816–1902
Hall, Sir Edward Marshall	1858–1927
Hall, FitzEdward	1825–1901
Hall, Harry Reginald Holland	1873–1930
Hall, Henry Robert	1898–1989
Hall, Hubert	1857–1944
Hall, Sir John	1824–1907
Hall, Philip	1904–1982
Hall, Radclyffe. See Radclyffe-Hall, Marguerite Antonia	#1880–1943
Hall, Robert Lowe, Baron Roberthall	1901–1988
Hall, William George Glenvil	1887–1962
Hall, Sir (William) Reginald	1870–1943
Hall, (William) Stephen (Richard) King-, Baron King-Hall. See King-Hall	1893–1966
Hall-Patch, Sir Edmund Leo	1896–1975
Hallé (formerly Norman-Neruda), Wilma Maria Francisca, Lady	1839–1911
Hallett, John Hughes-. See Hughes-Hallett	1901–1972
Halliburton, William Dobinson	1860–1931
Halliday, Edward Irvine	1902–1984
Halliday, Sir Frederick James	1806–1901
Halliley, John Elton. See Le Mesurier, John	1912–1983
Halliwell, (Robert James) Leslie	1929–1989
Halsbury, Earl of. See Giffard, Hardinge Stanley	1823–1921
Halsey, Sir Lionel	1872–1949
Hambleden, Viscount. See Smith, William Frederick Danvers	1868–1928
Hamblin Smith, James. See Smith	1829–1901
Hambourg, Mark	1879–1960
Hambro, Sir Charles Jocelyn	1897–1963
Hamidullah, Nawab of Bhopal. See Bhopal	1894–1960
Hamilton, Sir (Charles) Denis	1918–1988
Hamilton, Charles Harold St John, 'Frank Richards'	1876–1961
Hamilton, David James	1849–1909
Hamilton, Sir Edward Walter	1847–1908
Hamilton, Eugene Jacob Lee-. See Lee-Hamilton	1845–1907
Hamilton, Sir Frederick Hew George Dalrymple-. See Dalrymple-Hamilton	1890–1974
Hamilton, Lord George Francis	1845–1927
Hamilton, Hamish	1900–1988
Hamilton, Sir Ian Standish Monteith	1853–1947
Hamilton, James, Duke of Abercorn	1838–1913
Hamilton, James. See Hamilton, Hamish	1900–1988
Hamilton, John Andrew, Viscount Sumner	1859–1934
Hamilton, Sir Richard Vesey	1829–1912
Hamilton, Walter	1908–1988
Hamilton Fairley, Sir Neil. See Fairley	1891–1966
Hamilton Fyfe, Sir William. See Fyfe	1878–1965

Harmsworth, Alfred Charles William, Viscount Northcliffe	1865–1922
Harmsworth, Esmond Cecil, Viscount Rothermere	1898–1978
Harmsworth, Harold Sidney, Viscount Rothermere	1868–1940
Harper, Sir George Montague	1865–1922
Harraden, Beatrice	1864–1936
Harrel, Sir David	1841–1939
Harrington, Timothy Charles	1851–1910
Harris, Sir Arthur Travers	1892–1984
Harris, Frederick Leverton	1864–1926
Harris, Geoffrey Wingfield	#1913–1971
Harris, George Robert Canning, Baron	1851–1932
Harris, (Henry) Wilson	1883–1955
Harris, James Rendel	1852–1941
Harris, James Thomas ('Frank')	1856–1931
Harris, John Wyndham Parkes Lucas Beynon, 'John Wyndham'	1903–1969
Harris, Sir Percy Alfred	1876–1952
Harris, Sir Percy Wyn-. See Wyn-Harris	1903–1979
Harris, Thomas Lake	1823–1906
Harris, Tomás	1908–1964
Harris, Sir William Henry	1883–1973
Harrison, Francis Llewelyn ('Frank')	1905–1987
Harrison, Frederic	1831–1923
Harrison, Henry	1867–1954
Harrison, Jane Ellen	1850–1928
Harrison, Mary St Leger, 'Lucas Malet'	1852–1931
Harrison, Reginald	1837–1908
Harrison, Sir Reginald Carey ('Rex')	1908–1990
Harrison, Sir William Montagu Graham-. See Graham-Harrison	1871–1949
Harrisson, Thomas Harnett ('Tom')	1911–1976
Harrod, Sir (Henry) Roy (Forbes)	1900–1978
Hart, Sir Basil Henry Liddell	1895–1970
Hart, Horace Henry	#1840–1916
Hart, Sir Raymund George	1899–1960
Hart, Sir Robert	1835–1911
Hartington, Marquess of. See Cavendish, Spencer Compton	1833–1908
Hartley, Arthur Clifford	1889–1960
Hartley, Sir Charles Augustus	1825–1915
Hartley, Sir Harold Brewer	1878–1972
Hartley, Leslie Poles	1895–1972
Hartnell, Sir Norman Bishop	1901–1979
Hartog, Sir Philip(pe) Joseph	1864–1947
Hartree, Douglas Rayner	1897–1958
Hartshorn, Vernon	1872–1931

Hartshorne, Albert	1839–1910
Harty, (Fredric) Russell	1934–1988
Harty, Sir (Herbert) Hamilton	1879–1941
Harvey, Hildebrand Wolfe	1887–1970
Harvey, Sir John Martin Martin-. See Martin-Harvey	1863–1944
Harvey, Sir Oliver Charles, Baron Harvey of Tasburgh	1893–1968
Harwood, Basil	1859–1949
Harwood, Sir Henry Harwood	1888–1950
Haskell, Arnold Lionel David	1903–1980
Haslam, Sir Alfred Seale	#1844–1927
Hasler, Herbert George ('Blondie')	1914–1987
Haslett, Dame Caroline Harriet	1895–1957
Hassall, Christopher Vernon	1912–1963
Hassall, Joan	1906–1988
Hassall, John	1868–1948
Hastie, William	1842–1903
Hastings, Anthea Esther	1924–1981
Hastings, Francis John Clarence Westenra Plantagenet, Earl of Huntingdon	1901–1990
Hastings, James	1852–1922
Hastings, Sir Patrick Gardiner	1880–1952
Hatch, Frederick Henry	#1864–1932
Hathaway, Dame Sibyl Mary	#1884–1974
Hatry, Clarence Charles	1888–1965
Hatton, Harold Heneage Finch-. See Finch-Hatton	1856–1904
Hatton, Joseph	1841–1907
Hatton, Sir Ronald George	1886–1965
Havell, Ernest Binfield	#1861–1934
Havelock, Sir Arthur Elibank	1844–1908
Havelock, Sir Thomas Henry	1877–1968
Haverfield, Francis John	1860–1919
Havilland, Sir Geoffrey de. See de Havilland	1882–1965
Haweis, Hugh Reginald	1838–1901
Haweis, Mary (d. 1898). See under Haweis, Hugh Reginald	
Hawke, Sir (Edward) Anthony	1895–1964
Hawke, Sir (John) Anthony	1869–1941
Hawke, Martin Bladen, Baron Hawke of Towton	1860–1938
Hawker, Mary Elizabeth, 'Lanoe Falconer'	1848–1908
Hawkins, Sir Anthony Hope, 'Anthony Hope'	1863–1933
Hawkins, Henry, Baron Brampton	1817–1907
Hawkins, Herbert Leader	1887–1968
Haworth, Sir (Walter) Norman	1883–1950

Herbert, Sir Robert George Wyndham	1831–1905
Herdman, Sir William Abbott	1858–1924
Herford, Brooke	1830–1903
Herford, Charles Harold	1853–1931
Herford, William Henry	1820–1908
Herkomer, Sir Hubert von	1849–1914
Hermes, Gertrude Anna Bertha	1901–1983
Herring, George	1832–1906
Herringham, Sir Wilmot Parker	1855–1936
Herschel, Alexander Stewart	1836–1907
Herschel, Sir William James	#1833–1917
Hertslet, Sir Edward	1824–1902
Hertz, Joseph Herman	1872–1946
Hertzog, James Barry Munnik	1866–1942
Heseltine, Philip Arnold, 'Peter Warlock'	1894–1930
Heslop, Richard Henry	1907–1973
Hess, Dame (Julia) Myra	1890–1965
Hetherington, Sir Hector James Wright	1888–1965
Hewart, Gordon, Viscount	1870–1943
Hewett, Sir John Prescott	1854–1941
Hewins, William Albert Samuel	1865–1931
Hewitt, Sir Edgar Rainey Ludlow-. See Ludlow-Hewitt	1886–1973
Hewitt, John Harold	1907–1987
Hewlett, Maurice Henry	1861–1923
Hey, Donald Holroyde	1904–1987
Heyer, Georgette	1902–1974
Heyworth, Geoffrey, Baron	1894–1974
Hibberd, (Andrew) Stuart	1893–1983
Hibbert, Sir John Tomlinson	1824–1908
Hichens, Robert Smythe	1864–1950
Hichens, (William) Lionel	1874–1940
Hicks, Edward Lee	1843–1919
Hicks, Sir (Edward) Seymour (George)	1871–1949
Hicks, George Dawes	1862–1941
Hicks, George Ernest	1879–1954
Hicks, Sir John Richard	1904–1989
Hicks, Robert Drew	1850–1929
Hicks, William Joynson-, Viscount Brentford	1865–1932
Hicks Beach, Sir Michael Edward, Earl St Aldwyn	1837–1916
Higgins, Edward John	1864–1947
Higgins, Sir John Frederick Andrews	1875–1948
Hilbery, Sir (George) Malcolm	1883–1965
Hilditch, Thomas Percy	1886–1965
Hiles, Henry	1828–1904
Hill, Alexander Staveley	1825–1905
Hill, Alsager Hay	1839–1906
Hill, Archibald Vivian	1886–1977
Hill, Sir Arthur William	1875–1941

Hill, Charles, Baron Hill of Luton	1904–1989
Hill, Sir (Edward) Maurice	1862–1934
Hill, Frank Harrison	1830–1910
Hill, George Birkbeck Norman	1835–1903
Hill, Sir George Francis	1867–1948
Hill, Sir (John) Denis (Nelson)	1913–1982
Hill, Sir Leonard Erskine	1866–1952
Hill, Leonard Raven-. See Raven-Hill	1867–1942
Hill, (Norman) Graham	1929–1975
Hill, Octavia	1838–1912
Hill, Oliver Falvey	#1887–1968
Hill, Philip Ernest	#1873–1944
Hill, Sir Roderic Maxwell	1894–1954
Hill, Rosamund Davenport-	1825–1902
Hill, William	#1903–1971
Hillary, Richard Hope	#1919–1943
Hillgarth, Alan Hugh	1899–1978
Hillier, Sir Harold George Knight	1905–1985
Hillier, Tristram Paul	1905–1983
Hills, Arnold Frank	1857–1927
Hills, Sir John	1834–1902
Hilton, James	1900–1954
Hilton, Roger	1911–1975
Himmelweit, Hildegard Therese	1918–1989
Hinchley, John William	#1871–1931
Hind, Arthur Mayger	1880–1957
Hind, Henry Youle	1823–1908
Hind, Richard Dacre Archer-. See Archer-Hind	1849–1910
Hindley, Sir Clement Daniel Maggs	1874–1944
Hindley, John Scott, Viscount Hyndley	1883–1963
Hingeston-Randolph (formerly Hingston), Francis Charles	1833–1910
Hingley, Sir Benjamin	1830–1905
Hingston, Sir William Hales	1829–1907
Hinks, Arthur Robert	1873–1945
Hinkson (formerly Tynan), Katharine	1861–1931
Hinshelwood, Sir Cyril Norman	1897–1967
Hinsley, Arthur	1865–1943
Hinton, Christopher, Baron Hinton of Bankside	1901–1983
Hipkins, Alfred James	1826–1903
Hirst, Sir Edmund Langley	1898–1975
Hirst, Francis Wrigley	1873–1953
Hirst, George Herbert	1871–1954
Hirst, Hugo, Baron	1863–1943
Hislop, Joseph Dewar	#1884–1977
Hitchcock, Sir Alfred Joseph	1899–1980
Hitchcock, Sir Eldred Frederick	1887–1959

Hone, Evie	1894–1955	Horne, Henry Sinclair, Baron	1861–1929
Hood, Arthur William		Horne, Herbert Percy	#1864–1916
Acland, Baron	1824–1901	Horne, John	#1848–1928
Hood, Sir Horace Lambert		Horne, Robert Stevenson,	
Alexander	1870–1916	Viscount Horne of	
Hook, James Clarke	1819–1907	Slamannan	1871–1940
Hooke, Samuel Henry	1874–1968	Horner, Arthur Lewis	1894–1968
Hooker, Sir Joseph Dalton	1817–1911	Horniman, Annie Elizabeth	
Hooker, Sir Stanley George	1907–1984	Fredericka	1860–1937
Hooley, Ernest Terah	#1859–1947	Horniman, Frederick John	1835–1906
Hooper, Sir Frederic Collins	1892–1963	Hornung, Ernest William	#1866–1921
Hope, Anthony, *pseudonym*.		Horrabin, James Francis	1884–1962
See Hawkins, Sir Anthony		Horridge, Sir Thomas	
Hope	1863–1933	Gardner	1857–1938
Hope, James Fitzalan, Baron		Horrocks, Sir Brian Gwynne	1895–1985
Rankeillour	1870–1949	Horsbrugh, Florence	
Hope, John Adrian Louis,		Gertrude, Baroness	1889–1969
Earl of Hopetoun and		Horsley, John Callcott	1817–1903
Marquess of Linlithgow	1860–1908	Horsley, John William	1845–1921
Hope, Laurence, *pseudonym*.		Horsley, Sir Victor Alexander	
See Nicolson, Adela		Haden	1857–1916
Florence	1865–1904	Horton, Sir Max Kennedy	1883–1951
Hope, Victor Alexander John,		Horton, Percy Frederick	1897–1970
Marquess of Linlithgow	1887–1952	Horton, Robert Forman	1855–1934
Hope, Sir William Henry St		Hose, Charles	1863–1929
John	1854–1919	Hosie, Sir Alexander	1853–1925
Hope-Wallace, Philip Adrian	1911–1979	Hosier, Arthur Julius	1877–1963
Hopetoun, Earl of. See Hope,		Hoskins, Sir Anthony Hiley	1828–1901
John Adrian Louis	1860–1908	Hoskyns, Sir Edwyn Clement	1884–1937
Hopkins, Edward John	1818–1901	Hotine, Martin	1898–1968
Hopkins, Sir Frank Henry		Houghton, William Stanley	1881–1913
Edward	1910–1990	Houldsworth, Sir Hubert	
Hopkins, Sir Frederick		Stanley	1889–1956
Gowland	1861–1947	House, (Arthur) Humphry	1908–1955
Hopkins, Jane Ellice	1836–1904	Housman, Alfred Edward	1859–1936
Hopkins, Sir Richard		Housman, Laurence	1865–1959
Valentine Nind	1880–1955	Houston, Dame Fanny	
Hopkinson, Sir Alfred	1851–1939	Lucy	1857–1936
Hopkinson, Bertram	1874–1918	Howard, Bernard Marmaduke	
Hopkinson, Sir (Henry)		FitzAlan-, sixteenth Duke	
Thomas	1905–1990	of Norfolk	1908–1975
Hoppé, Emil Otto	#1878–1972	Howard, David	#1839–1916
Hopwood, Charles Henry	1829–1904	Howard, Sir Ebenezer	1850–1928
Hopwood, Francis John		Howard, Edmund Bernard	
Stephens, Baron		FitzAlan-, Viscount	
Southborough	1860–1947	FitzAlan of Derwent	1855–1947
Horder, Percy (Richard)		Howard, Esme William,	
Morley	1870–1944	Baron Howard of Penrith	1863–1939
Horder, Thomas Jeeves,		Howard, George James, Earl	
Baron	1871–1955	of Carlisle	1843–1911
Hore-Belisha, (Isaac) Leslie,		Howard, Henry FitzAlan-,	
Baron	1893–1957	Duke of Norfolk	1847–1917
Hore-Ruthven, Alexander		Howard, Leslie	1893–1943
Gore Arkwright, Earl of		Howard, Louise Ernestine,	
Gowrie	1872–1955	Lady	#1880–1969
Hornby, Charles Harry St		Howard, Rosalind Frances,	
John	1867–1946	Countess of Carlisle	1845–1921
Hornby, Frank	#1863–1936	Howard, Trevor Wallace	1913–1988
Hornby, James John	1826–1909	Howard de Walden, Baron.	
Horne, (Charles) Kenneth	#1907–1969	See Scott-Ellis, Thomas	
Horne, (Charles) Silvester	#1865–1914	Evelyn	1880–1946

Hutchinson, Horatio Gordon
('Horace')   1859–1932
Hutchinson, John   1884–1972
Hutchinson, Sir Jonathan   1828–1913
Hutchinson, Sir Joseph Burtt   1902–1988
Hutchinson, Richard Walter
  John Hely-, Earl of
  Donoughmore. See
  Hely-Hutchinson   1875–1948
Hutchison, Sir Robert   1871–1960
Hutchison, Sir William
  Oliphant   1889–1970
Huth, Alfred Henry   1850–1910
Hutton, Alfred   1839–1910
Hutton, Frederick Wollaston   1836–1905
Hutton, George Clark   1825–1908
Hutton, Sir Leonard   1916–1990
Hutton, William Holden   1860–1930
Huxley, Aldous Leonard   1894–1963
Huxley, Sir Julian Sorell   1887–1975
Huxley, Leonard   1860–1933
Hwfa Môn. See Williams,
  Rowland   1823–1905
Hyde, Douglas   1860–1949
Hyde, Sir Robert Robertson   1878–1967
Hylton, Jack   1892–1965
Hylton-Foster, Sir Harry
  Braustyn Hylton   1905–1965
Hyndley, Viscount. See
  Hindley, John Scott   1883–1963
Hyndman, Henry Mayers   1842–1921

Ibbetson, Sir Denzil Charles
  Jelf   1847–1908
Ibbetson, Henry John
  Selwin-, Baron Rookwood.
  See Selwin-Ibbetson   1826–1902
Ignatius, Father. See Lyne,
  Joseph Leycester   1837–1908
Ilbert, Sir Courtenay
  Peregrine   1841–1924
Ilchester, Earl of. See
  Fox-Strangways, Giles
  Stephen Holland   1874–1959
Iliffe, Edward Mauger, Baron   1877–1960
Illing, Vincent Charles   1890–1969
Illingworth, Ronald Stanley   1909–1990
Image, Selwyn   1849–1930
Imms, Augustus Daniel   1880–1949
Ince, Sir Godfrey Herbert   1891–1960
Ince, William   1825–1910
Inchcape, Earl of. See
  Mackay, James Lyle   1852–1932
Inchyra, Baron. See Millar,
  Frederick Robert Hoyer   1900–1989
Inderwick, Frederick Andrew   1836–1904
Ing, (Harry) Raymond   1899–1974
Inge, William Ralph   1860–1954
Ingham, Albert Edward   1900–1967
Inglis, Sir Charles Edward   1875–1952

Inglis, Sir Claude Cavendish   1883–1974
Inglis, Elsie Maud   1864–1917
Ingold, Sir Christopher Kelk   1893–1970
Ingram, Arthur Foley
  Winnington-. See
  Winnington-Ingram   1858–1946
Ingram, Sir Bruce Stirling   1877–1963
Ingram, John Kells   1823–1907
Ingram, Thomas Dunbar   1826–1901
Innes, James John McLeod   1830–1907
Innes, Sir James Rose-. See
  Rose-Innes   1855–1942
Innes of Learney, Sir Thomas   1893–1971
Inskip, Thomas Walker
  Hobart, Viscount Caldecote   1876–1947
Inverchapel, Baron. See Clark
  Kerr, Archibald John Kerr   1882–1951
Inverforth, Baron. See Weir,
  Andrew   1865–1955
Invernairn, Baron. See
  Beardmore, William   1856–1936
Iqbal, Sir Muhammad   1876–1938
Irby, Leonard Howard Loyd   1836–1905
Ireland, John Nicholson   1879–1962
Ireland, William Wotherspoon   1832–1909
Ironside, Robin Cunliffe   1912–1965
Ironside, William Edmund,
  Baron   1880–1959
Irvine, Sir James Colquhoun   1877–1952
Irvine, William   1840–1911
Irving, Sir Edmund George   1910–1990
Irving, Sir Henry   1838–1905
Isaacs, Alick   1921–1967
Isaacs, George Alfred   1883–1979
Isaacs, Sir Isaac Alfred   1855–1948
Isaacs, Rufus Daniel,
  Marquess of Reading   1860–1935
Isaacs, Stella, Marchioness of
  Reading and Baroness
  Swanborough   1894–1971
Isherwood, Christopher
  William Bradshaw   1904–1986
Isherwood, Sir Joseph
  William   1870–1937
Isitt, Dame Adeline Genée-.
  See Genée   1878–1970
Islington, Baron. See
  Poynder, Sir John Poynder
  Dickson-   1866–1936
Ismail, Sir Mirza Mohammad   1883–1959
Ismay, Hastings Lionel, Baron   1887–1965
Ismay, Joseph Bruce   1862–1937
Issigonis, Sir Alexander
  Arnold Constantine   1906–1988
Iveagh, Countess of (1881–
  1966). See under Guinness,
  Rupert Edward Cecil Lee
Iveagh, Earl of. See Guinness,
  Edward Cecil   1847–1927
Iveagh, Earl of. See Guinness,
  Rupert Edward Cecil Lee   1874–1967

Jessop, Gilbert Laird	1874–1955	Jones, Lady. See Bagnold,	
Jessopp, Augustus	1823–1914	Enid Algerine	1889–1981
Jeune, Francis Henry, Baron		Jones, Adrian	1845–1938
St Helier	1843–1905	Jones, (Alfred) Ernest	1879–1958
Jewkes, John	1902–1988	Jones, Sir Alfred Lewis	1845–1909
Jex-Blake, Sophia Louisa	1840–1912	Jones, Allan Gwynne-. See	
Jex-Blake, Thomas William	1832–1915	Gwynne-Jones	1892–1982
Jinnah, Mahomed Ali	1876–1948	Jones, Arnold Hugh	
Joachim, Harold Henry	1868–1938	Martin	1904–1970
Joad, Cyril Edwin Mitchinson	1891–1953	Jones, Arthur Creech	1891–1964
Joel, Jack Barnato (1862–		Jones, Sir (Bennett) Melvill	1887–1975
1940). See under Joel,		Jones, Bernard Mouat	1882–1953
Solomon Barnato		Jones, David	1895–1974
Joel, Solomon Barnato	1865–1931	Jones, Sir Eric Malcolm	1907–1986
John, Augustus Edwin	1878–1961	Jones, (Frederic) Wood	1879–1954
John, Sir Caspar	1903–1984	Jones, (Frederick) Elwyn,	
John, Gwendolen Mary	#1876–1939	Baron Elwyn-Jones	1909–1989
John, Sir William Goscombe	1860–1952	Jones, Sir (George) Roderick	1877–1962
Johns, Claude Hermann		Jones, Sir Harold Spencer	1890–1960
Walter	1857–1920	Jones, Sir Henry	1852–1922
Johns, William Earl	1893–1968	Jones, Henry Arthur	1851–1929
Johnson, Alan Woodworth	1917–1982	Jones, Henry Cadman	1818–1902
Johnson, Alfred Edward		Jones, Sir Henry Frank	
Webb-, Baron		Harding	1906–1987
Webb-Johnson. See		Jones, Sir Henry Stuart-	1867–1939
Webb-Johnson	1880–1958	Jones, (James) Sidney	1861–1946
Johnson, Amy	1903–1941	Jones, John Daniel	1865–1942
Johnson, Bertha Jane	#1846–1927	Jones, Sir John Edward	
Johnson, Dame Celia	1908–1982	Lennard-. See	
Johnson, Charles	1870–1961	Lennard-Jones	1894–1954
Johnson, Harry Gordon	1923–1977	Jones, Sir John Morris-. See	
Johnson, Sir Henry Cecil	1906–1988	Morris-Jones	1864–1929
Johnson, Hewlett	1874–1966	Jones, John Viriamu	1856–1901
Johnson, John de Monins	1882–1956	Jones, Owen Thomas	1878–1967
Johnson, Lionel Pigot	1867–1902	Jones, Reginald Teague-. See	
Johnson, Sir Nelson King	1892–1954	Teague-Jones	1889–1988
Johnson, Pamela Hansford,		Jones, Sir Robert	1857–1933
Lady Snow	1912–1981	Jones, Sir Robert Armstrong-.	
Johnson, William Ernest	1858–1931	See Armstrong-Jones	1857–1943
Johnson, William Percival	1854–1928	Jones, Thomas	1870–1955
Johnson-Marshall, Sir Stirrat		Jones, Thomas Gwynn	#1871–1949
Andrew William	1912–1981	Jones, Thomas Rupert	1819–1911
Johnston, Sir Charles		Jones, (William) Clifford	1914–1990
Hepburn	1912–1986	Jones, William West	1838–1908
Johnston, Christopher		Jordan, (Heinrich Ernst) Karl	1861–1959
Nicholson, Lord Sands	1857–1934	Jordan, Sir John Newell	1852–1925
Johnston, Edward	1872–1944	Jordan Lloyd, Dorothy. See	
Johnston, George Lawson,		Lloyd	1889–1946
Baron Luke	1873–1943	Joseph, Horace William	
Johnston, Sir Harry		Brindley	1867–1943
Hamilton	1858–1927	Joseph, Sir Maxwell	1910–1982
Johnston, Sir Reginald		Joubert de la Ferté, Sir Philip	
Fleming	1874–1938	Bennet	1887–1965
Johnston, Thomas	1881–1965	Jourdain, (Emily) Margaret	#1876–1951
Johnston, William	1829–1902	Jourdain, Francis Charles	
Joicey, James, Baron	1846–1954	Robert	1865–1940
Jolowicz, Herbert Felix	1890–1954	Jowitt, William Allen, Earl	1885–1957
Joly, Charles Jasper	1864–1906	Joy, David	#1825–1903
Joly, John	1857–1933	Joyce, James Augustine	1882–1941
Joly de Lotbinière, Sir Henry		Joyce, Sir Matthew Ingle	1839–1930
Gustave	1829–1908	Joyce, William Brooke	#1906–1946

Ker, Neil Ripley	1908–1982	King, Earl Judson	1901–1962
Ker, William Paton	1855–1923	King, Edward	1829–1910
Kerensky, Oleg Alexander	1905–1984	King, Sir (Frederic) Truby	1858–1938
Kermack, William Ogilvy	1898–1970	King, Sir George	1840–1909
Kerr, Archibald John Kerr		King, Harold	1887–1956
Clark, Baron Inverchapel.		King, Haynes	1831–1904
See Clark Kerr	1882–1951	King, Horace Maybray, Baron	
Kerr, John	1824–1907	Maybray-King	1901–1986
Kerr, Sir John Graham	1869–1957	King, William Bernard	
Kerr, (John Martin) Munro	1868–1960	Robinson	1889–1963
Kerr, Philip Henry, Marquess		King, William Lyon	
of Lothian	1882–1940	Mackenzie	1874–1950
Kerr, Robert	1823–1904	King-Hall, (William) Stephen	
Kerr, Lord Walter Talbot	1839–1927	(Richard), Baron	1893–1966
Keswick, Sir John Henry	1906–1982	Kingdon-Ward, Francis	
Keswick, Sir William		('Frank')	1885–1958
Johnston	1903–1990	Kingsburgh, Lord. See	
Ketèlbey, Albert William	1875–1959	Macdonald, John Hay	
Kettle, Edgar Hartley	1882–1936	Athole	1836–1919
Ketton-Cremer, Robert		Kingscote, Sir Robert Nigel	
Wyndham	1906–1969	Fitzhardinge	1830–1908
Keyes, Roger John Brownlow,		Kingsford, Charles	
Baron	1872–1945	Lethbridge	1862–1926
Keyes, Sidney Arthur		Kingsmill, Hugh. See Lunn,	
Kilworth	#1922–1943	Hugh Kingsmill	#1889–1949
Keynes, Lady. See Lopokova,		Kingston, Charles Cameron	1850–1908
Lydia Vasilievna	1892–1981	Kinnear, Alexander Smith,	
Keynes, Sir Geoffrey		Baron	1833–1917
Langdon	1887–1982	Kinnear, Sir Norman Boyd	1882–1957
Keynes, John Maynard, Baron	1883–1946	Kinns, Samuel	1826–1903
Keys, William Herbert	1923–1990	Kinross, Baron. See Balfour,	
Khama, Sir Seretse	1921–1980	John Blair	1837–1905
Khan Sahib	1883–1958	Kipling, (Joseph) Rudyard	1865–1936
Kidd, Benjamin	1858–1916	Kipping, Frederic Stanley	1863–1949
Kiggell, Sir Launcelot		Kipping, Sir Norman Victor	1901–1979
Edward	1862–1954	Kirk, Sir John	1832–1922
Kilbracken, Baron. See		Kirk, Sir John	1847–1922
Godley, (John) Arthur	1847–1932	Kirk, Kenneth Escott	1886–1954
Kilbrandon, Baron. See Shaw,		Kirk, Norman Eric	1923–1974
Charles James Dalrymple	1906–1989	Kirkbride, Sir Alec Seath	1897–1978
Killearn, Baron. See		Kirkley, Sir (Howard) Leslie	1911–1989
Lampson, Miles		Kirkman, Sir Sidney	
Wedderburn	1880–1964	Chevalier	1895–1982
Killen, William Dool	1806–1902	Kirkpatrick, Sir Ivone	
Kilmaine, Baron. See Browne,		Augustine	1897–1964
John Francis Archibald	1902–1978	Kirkwood, David, Baron	1872–1955
Kilmuir, Earl of. See Fyfe,		Kitchener, Horatio Herbert,	
David Patrick Maxwell	1900–1967	Earl	1850–1916
Kimber, William	#1872–1961	Kitchin, George William	1827–1912
Kimberley, Earl of. See		Kitson, James, Baron Airedale	1835–1911
Wodehouse, John	1826–1902	Kitson Clark, George Sidney	
Kimmins, Dame Grace		Roberts	1900–1975
Thyrza	1870–1954	Kitton, Frederick George	1856–1904
Kinahan, George Henry	1829–1908	Klein, Melanie	1882–1960
Kincairney, Lord. See Gloag,		Klugmann, Norman John	
William Ellis	1828–1909	('James')	1912–1977
Kindersley, Hugh Kenyon		Knatchbull-Hugessen, Sir	
Molesworth, Baron	1899–1976	Hughe Montgomery	1886–1971
Kindersley, Robert		Knight, (George) Wilson	1897–1985
Molesworth, Baron	1871–1954	Knight, Harold	1874–1961
King, Cecil Harmsworth	1901–1987	Knight, Joseph	1829–1907

Langford, John Alfred	1823–1903	Lawrence, (Arabella) Susan	1871–1947
Langley, John Newport	1852–1925	Lawrence, David Herbert	1885–1930
Langley Moore, Doris		Lawrence, Sir (Frederick)	
Elizabeth. See Moore	1902–1989	Geoffrey	1902–1967
Langton, Sir George Philip	1881–1942	Lawrence, Frederick William	
Langtry, Emilie Charlotte		Pethick-, Baron. See	
('Lillie')	#1853–1929	Pethick-Lawrence	1871–1961
Lankester, Sir Edwin Ray	1847–1929	Lawrence, Geoffrey, Baron	
Lansbury, George	1859–1940	Trevethin and Baron	
Lansdowne, Marquess of. See		Oaksey	#1880–1971
Petty-Fitzmaurice, Henry		Lawrence, Gertrude	1898–1952
Charles Keith	1845–1927	Lawrence, Sir Herbert	
Lapworth, Arthur	#1872–1941	Alexander	1861–1943
Lapworth, Charles	#1842–1920	Lawrence, Sir Paul Ogden	1861–1952
Larke, Sir William James	1875–1959	Lawrence, Thomas Edward	
Larkin, James	#1876–1947	(Lawrence of Arabia)	1888–1935
Larkin, Philip Arthur	1922–1985	Lawrence, Sir Walter Roper	1857–1940
Larmor, Sir Joseph	1857–1942	Laws, Robert	1851–1934
Lascelles, Sir Alan Frederick	1887–1981	Lawson, Edward Frederick,	
Lascelles, Sir Frank		Baron Burnham	1890–1963
Cavendish	1841–1920	Lawson, Edward Levy-,	
Lascelles, Henry George		Baron Burnham. See	
Charles, Earl of Harewood	1882–1947	Levy-Lawson	1833–1916
Laski, Esther Pearl		Lawson, Frederick Henry	1897–1983
('Marghanita')	1915–1988	Lawson, George	1831–1903
Laski, Harold Joseph	1893–1950	Lawson, George Anderson	1832–1904
Last, Hugo Macilwain	1894–1957	Lawson, Harry Lawson	
László de Lombos, Philip		Webster Levy-, Viscount	
Alexius	1869–1937	Burnham	1862–1933
Laszowska, (Jane) Emily de.		Lawson, Sir Wilfrid	1829–1906
See Gerard	1849–1905	Lawther, Sir William	1889–1976
Latey, John	1842–1902	Laycock, Sir Robert Edward	1907–1968
Latham, Charles, Baron	1888–1970	Layton, Walter Thomas,	
Latham, Henry	1821–1902	Baron	1884–1966
Latham, Peter Walter	1865–1953	Lazarus, Ruth Adele. See	
Lathbury, Sir Gerald William	1906–1978	Glass	1912–1990
Lauder, Sir Harry	1870–1950	Lea, Sir George Harris	1912–1990
Laughton, Charles	#1899–1962	Leach, Archibald Alec. See	
Laughton, Sir John Knox	1830–1915	Grant, Cary	1904–1986
Laurel, Stan	#1890–1965	Leach, Arthur Francis	1851–1915
Laurie, James Stuart	1832–1904	Leach, Bernard Howell	1887–1979
Laurie, Simon Somerville	1829–1909	Leach, Sir Edmund Rònald	1910–1989
Laurier, Sir Wilfrid	1841–1919	Leacock, Stephen Butler	1869–1944
Lauterpacht, Sir Hersch	1897–1960	Leader, Benjamin Williams	1831–1923
Lauwerys, Joseph Albert	1902–1981	Leader, John Temple	1810–1903
Laver, James	1899–1975	Leaf, Walter	1852–1927
Lavery, Sir John	1856–1941	Leake, George	1856–1902
Law, Andrew Bonar	1858–1923	Leakey, Louis Seymour	
Law, David	1831–1901	Bazett	1903–1972
Law, Sir Edward FitzGerald	1846–1908	Learmonth, Sir James	
Law, Richard Kidston, Baron		Rögnvald	1895–1967
Coleraine	1901–1980	Leathers, Frederick James,	
Law, Thomas Graves	1836–1904	Viscount	1883–1965
Lawes (afterwards		Leathes, Sir Stanley	
Lawes-Wittewronge), Sir		Mordaunt	1861–1938
Charles Bennet	1843–1911	Leavis, Frank Raymond	1895–1978
Lawes, William George	1839–1907	Le Bas, Edward	1904–1966
Lawley, Francis Charles	1825–1901	Lecky, Squire Thornton	
Lawrence, Alfred Kingsley	1893–1975	Stratford	1838–1902
Lawrence, Alfred Tristram,		Lecky, William Edward	
Baron Trevethin	1843–1936	Hartpole	1838–1903

Lewis, Cecil Day-. See	
Day-Lewis	1904–1972
Lewis, Clive Staples	1898–1963
Lewis, David (1814–1895).	
See under Lewis, Evan	
Lewis, (Dominic) Bevan	
(Wyndham)	#1891–1969
Lewis, Evan	1818–1901
Lewis, Sir George Henry	1833–1911
Lewis, John Spedan	1885–1963
Lewis, John Travers	1825–1901
Lewis, Percy Wyndham	1882–1957
Lewis, Richard	1821–1905
Lewis, Rosa	1867–1952
Lewis, Ted, 'Kid'	#1894–1970
Lewis, Sir Thomas	1881–1945
Lewis, Sir Wilfrid Hubert	
Poyer	1881–1950
Lewis, William Cudmore	
McCullagh	1885–1956
Lewis, William Thomas,	
Baron Merthyr	1837–1914
Lewis, Sir Willmott Harsant	1877–1950
Ley, Henry George	1887–1962
Leyel, Hilda Winifred Ivy	
(Mrs C. F. Leyel)	1880–1957
Liaqat Ali Khan	1895–1951
Liberty, Sir Arthur Lasenby	1843–1917
Liddell, Edward George	
Tandy	1895–1981
Liddell, Eric Henry	#1902–1945
Liddell Hart, Sir Basil Henry.	
See Hart	1895–1970
Lidderdale, William	1832–1902
Lidell, (Tord) Alvar (Quan)	1908–1981
Lidgett, John Scott	1854–1953
Lightwood, John Mason	1852–1947
Lillicrap, Sir Charles Swift	1887–1966
Lillie, Beatrice Gladys, Lady	
Peel	1894–1989
Limerick, Countess of. See	
Pery, Angela Olivia	1897–1981
Lincolnshire, Marquess of.	
See Wynn-Carrington,	
Charles Robert	1843–1928
Lindemann, Frederick	
Alexander, Viscount	
Cherwell	1886–1957
Lindley, Sir Francis Oswald	1872–1950
Lindley, Nathaniel, Baron	1828–1921
Lindrum, Walter Albert	1898–1960
Lindsay, Alexander Dunlop,	
Baron Lindsay of Birker	1879–1952
Lindsay, David	1856–1922
Lindsay, David Alexander	
Edward, Earl of Crawford	1871–1940
Lindsay, David Alexander	
Robert, Lord Balniel,	
Baron Wigan, Earl of	
Crawford, Earl of Balcarres	1900–1975
Lindsay, George Mackintosh	1880–1956
Lindsay, James Gavin	1835–1903
Lindsay, James Ludovic, Earl	
of Crawford	1847–1913
Lindsay, John Seymour	1882–1966
Lindsay, Sir Martin	
Alexander	1905–1981
Lindsay (afterwards	
Loyd-Lindsay), Robert	
James, Baron Wantage	1832–1901
Lindsay, Sir Ronald Charles	1877–1945
Lindsay, Thomas Martin	1843–1914
Lindsay, Wallace Martin	1858–1937
Lindsell, Sir Wilfrid Gordon	1884–1973
Lingen, Ralph Robert	
Wheeler, Baron	1819–1905
Linklater, Eric Robert Russell	1899–1974
Linlithgow, Marquess of.	
See Hope, John Adrian	
Louis	1860–1908
Linlithgow, Marquess of. See	
Hope, Victor Alexander	
John	1887–1952
Linnett, John Wilfrid	1913–1975
Linstead, Sir (Reginald)	
Patrick	1902–1966
Lipson, Ephraim	1888–1960
Lipton, Sir Thomas	
Johnstone	1850–1931
Lister, Arthur	1830–1908
Lister, Joseph, Baron	1827–1912
Lister, Philip Cunliffe-, Earl	
of Swinton. See	
Cunliffe-Lister	1884–1972
Lister, Sir (Robert) Ashton	#1845–1929
Lister, Samuel Cunliffe,	
Baron Masham	1815–1906
Lithgow, Sir James	1883–1952
Litthauer, Hildegard Therese.	
See Himmelweit	1918–1989
Little, Andrew George	1863–1945
Little, Sir Charles James	
Colebrooke	1882–1973
Little, Sir Ernest Gordon	
Graham Graham-. See	
Graham-Little	1867–1950
Little, William John Knox-.	
See Knox-Little	1839–1918
Littler, Sir Ralph Daniel	
Makinson	1835–1908
Littlewood, John Edensor	1885–1977
Littlewood, Sir Sydney	
Charles Thomas	1895–1967
Liveing, George Downing	1827–1924
Livens, William Howard	1889–1964
Livesey, Sir George Thomas	1834–1908
Livingstone, Sir Richard	
Winn	1880–1960
Llandaff, Viscount. See	
Matthews, Henry	1826–1913
Llewellin, John Jestyn,	
Baron	1893–1957

Lowe, Sir Drury Curzon Drury-. See Drury-Lowe	1830–1908
Lowe, Eveline Mary	1869–1956
Lowke, Wenman Joseph Bassett-. See Bassett-Lowke	1877–1953
Lowry, Clarence Malcolm	1909–1957
Lowry, Henry Dawson	1869–1906
Lowry, Laurence Stephen	1887–1976
Lowry, Thomas Martin	1874–1936
Lowson, Sir Denys Colquhoun Flowerdew	1906–1975
Lowther, Hugh Cecil, Earl of Lonsdale	1857–1944
Lowther, James	1840–1904
Lowther, James William, Viscount Ullswater	1855–1949
Löwy, Albert or Abraham	1816–1908
Loyd-Lindsay, Robert James, Baron Wantage. See Lindsay	1832–1901
Luard, Sir William Garnham	1820–1910
Lubbock, Sir John, Baron Avebury	1834–1913
Lubbock, Percy	1879–1965
Lubetkin, Berthold Romanovitch	1901–1990
Luby, Thomas Clarke	1821–1901
Lucas, Baron. See Herbert, Auberon Thomas	1876–1916
Lucas, Sir Charles Prestwood	1853–1931
Lucas, Edward Verrall	1868–1938
Lucas, Frank Laurence	1894–1967
Lucas, Keith	1879–1916
Luckock, Herbert Mortimer	1833–1909
Lucy, Sir Henry William	1843–1924
Ludlow, John Malcolm Forbes	1821–1911
Ludlow-Hewitt, Sir Edgar Rainey	1886–1973
Lugard, Frederick John Dealtry, Baron	1858–1945
Luke, Baron. See Johnston, George Lawson	1873–1943
Luke, Sir Harry Charles	1884–1969
Luke, Jemima	1813–1906
Lukin, Sir Henry Timson	1860–1925
Lumley, Lawrence Roger, Earl of Scarbrough	1896–1969
Lunn, Sir Arnold Henry Moore	1888–1974
Lunn, Sir Henry Simpson	1859–1939
Lunn, Hugh Kingsmill, 'Hugh Kingsmill'	#1889–1949
Lupton, Joseph Hirst	1836–1905
Lush, Sir Charles Montague	1853–1930
Lusk, Sir Andrew	1810–1909
Luthuli, Albert John	1898?–1967
Lutyens, (Agnes) Elisabeth	1906–1983
Lutyens, Sir Edwin Landseer	1869–1944
Lutz, (Wilhelm) Meyer	1829–1903

Luxmoore, Sir (Arthur) Fairfax (Charles Coryndon)	1876–1944
Lyall, Sir Alfred Comyn	1835–1911
Lyall, Sir Charles James	1845–1920
Lyall, Edna, pseudonym. See Bayly, Ada Ellen	1857–1903
Lygon, William, Earl Beauchamp	1872–1938
Lyle, Charles Ernest Leonard, Baron Lyle of Westbourne	1882–1954
Lynam, Charles Cotterill	#1858–1938
Lynch, Arthur Alfred	1861–1934
Lynch, Benjamin	#1913–1946
Lynd, Robert Wilson	1879–1949
Lyne, Joseph Leycester (Father Ignatius)	1837–1908
Lyne, Sir William John	1844–1913
Lynn, Ralph Clifford	#1882–1962
Lynskey, Sir George Justin	1888–1957
Lyon, Claude George Bowes-, Earl of Strathmore and Kinghorne. See Bowes-Lyon	1855–1944
Lyons, Sir Algernon McLennan	1833–1908
Lyons, (Francis Stewart) Leland	1923–1983
Lyons, Sir Henry George	1864–1944
Lyons, Joseph Aloysius	1879–1939
Lyons, Sir Joseph Nathaniel	#1847–1917
Lyons, Sir William	1901–1985
Lyte, Sir Henry Churchill Maxwell	1848–1940
Lyttelton, Alfred	1857–1913
Lyttelton, Arthur Temple	1852–1903
Lyttelton, Edward	1855–1942
Lyttelton, Sir Neville Gerald	1845–1931
Lyttelton, Oliver, Viscount Chandos	1893–1972
Lytton, Earl of. See Bulwer-Lytton, Victor Alexander George Robert	1876–1947
Lytton, Lady Constance Georgina	#1869–1923
Lytton, Sir Henry Alfred	1865–1936
MacAlister, Sir Donald	1854–1934
MacAlister, Sir (George) Ian	1878–1957
McAlpine, (Archibald) Douglas	1890–1981
Macan, Sir Arthur Vernon	1843–1908
Macara, Sir Charles Wright	1845–1929
McArthur, Charles	1844–1910
MacArthur, John Stewart	#1856–1920
Macarthur, Mary Reid. See Anderson	1880–1921
MacArthur, Sir William Porter	1884–1964
Macartney, Sir George	1867–1945

Macintosh, Sir Robert Reynolds	1897–1989
M'Intosh, William Carmichael	1838–1931
Macintyre, Donald	1831–1903
Macintyre, Donald George Frederick Wyville	1904–1981
MacIver, David Randall-. See Randall-MacIver	1873–1945
Mackail, John William	1859–1945
Mackay, Æneas James George	1839–1911
Mackay, Alexander	1833–1902
Mackay, Donald James, Baron Reay	1839–1921
Mackay, James Lyle, Earl of Inchcape	1852–1932
Mackay, Mary, 'Marie Corelli'	1855–1924
McKechnie, William Sharp	1863–1930
McKenna, Reginald	1863–1943
Mackennal, Alexander	1835–1904
Mackennal, Sir (Edgar) Bertram	1863–1931
Mackenzie, Sir Alexander	1842–1902
McKenzie, Alexander	1869–1951
Mackenzie, Sir Alexander Campbell	1847–1935
Mackenzie, Sir (Edward Montague) Compton	1883–1972
Mackenzie, Sir George Sutherland	1844–1910
Mackenzie, Sir James	1853–1925
M'Kenzie, Sir John	1836–1901
MacKenzie, John Stuart	1860–1935
McKenzie, (Robert) Tait	1867–1938
McKenzie, Robert Trelford	1917–1981
Mackenzie, Sir Stephen	1844–1909
Mackenzie, Sir William	1849–1923
Mackenzie, William Warrender, Baron Amulree	1860–1942
Mackenzie King, William Lyon. See King	1874–1950
McKeown, Thomas	1912–1988
McKerrow, Ronald Brunlees	1872–1940
McKie, Douglas	1896–1967
McKie, Sir William Neil	1901–1984
Mackinder, Sir Halford John	1861–1947
MacKinlay, Antoinette. See Sterling	1843–1904
Mackinnon, Sir Frank Douglas	1871–1946
Mackinnon, Sir William Henry	1852–1929
Mackintosh, Sir Alexander	1858–1948
Mackintosh, Charles Rennie	1868–1928
Mackintosh, Elizabeth, 'Josephine Tey' and 'Gordon Daviot'	#1896–1952
Mackintosh, Harold Vincent, Viscount Mackintosh of Halifax	1891–1964

Mackintosh, Hugh Ross	1870–1936
Mackintosh, James Macalister	1891–1966
Mackintosh, John	1833–1907
Mackintosh, John Pitcairn	1929–1978
Mackmurdo, Arthur Heygate	#1851–1942
Mackworth-Young, Gerard	1884–1965
McLachlan, Robert	1837–1904
Maclagan, Christian	1811–1901
Maclagan, Sir Eric Robert Dalrymple	1879–1951
Maclagan, William Dalrymple	1826–1910
Maclaren, Alexander	1826–1910
MacLaren, Archibald Campbell	1871–1944
McLaren, Charles Benjamin Bright, Baron Aberconway	1850–1934
McLaren, Henry Duncan, Baron Aberconway	1879–1953
Maclaren, Ian, pseudonym. See Watson, John	1850–1907
McLaren, John, Lord	1831–1910
Maclaren-Ross, James ('Julian')	#1912–1964
Maclay, Joseph Paton, Baron	1857–1951
Maclean, Alistair Stuart	1922–1987
Maclean, Sir Donald	1864–1932
Maclean, Donald Duart	1913–1983
Maclean, Sir Harry Aubrey de Vere	1848–1920
Maclean, Ida Smedley	#1877–1944
Maclean, James Mackenzie	1835–1906
Maclean, John	#1879–1923
McLean, Norman	1865–1947
Maclear, George Frederick	1833–1902
Maclear, John Fiot Lee Pearse	1838–1907
McLennan, Sir John Cunningham	1867–1935
Macleod, Fiona, pseudonym. See Sharp, William	1855–1905
Macleod, Henry Dunning	1821–1902
Macleod, Iain Norman	1913–1970
McLeod, (James) Walter	1887–1978
Macleod, John James Rickard	1876–1935
McLintock, Sir William	1873–1947
McLintock, William Francis Porter	1887–1960
Maclure, Edward Craig	1833–1906
Maclure, Sir John William (1835–1901). See under Maclure, Edward Craig	
McMahon, Sir (Arthur) Henry	1862–1949
McMahon, Charles Alexander	1830–1904
MacMahon, Percy Alexander	1854–1929
MacMichael, Sir Harold Alfred	1882–1969
Macmillan, Sir Frederick Orridge	1851–1936
Macmillan, Hugh	1833–1903

Manns, Sir August	1825–1907
Mansbridge, Albert	1876–1952
Mansel-Pleydell, John Clavell	1817–1902
Mansergh, James	1834–1905
Mansfield, Sir John Maurice	1893–1949
Mansfield, Katherine, *pseudonym*. See Murry, Kathleen	1888–1923
Mansfield, Robert Blachford	1824–1908
Manson, James Bolivar	1879–1945
Manson, Sir Patrick	1844–1922
Manson, Thomas Walter	1893–1958
Manton, Irene	1904–1988
Manton, Sidnie Milana	1902–1979
Manvell, (Arnold) Roger	1909–1987
Maple, Sir John Blundell	1845–1903
Mapleson, James Henry	1830–1901
Mapother, Edward Dillon	1835–1908
Mappin, Sir Frederick Thorpe	1821–1910
Mapson, Leslie William	1907–1970
Marc, *pseudonym*. See Boxer, (Charles) Mark (Edward)	1931–1988
Marconi, Guglielmo	#1874–1937
Marett, Robert Ranulph	1866–1943
Margesson, (Henry) David (Reginald), Viscount	1890–1965
Margoliouth, David Samuel	1858–1940
Marie Louise, Princess	1872–1956
Marillier, Henry Currie	1865–1951
Marina, Duchess of Kent	1906–1968
Marjoribanks, Edward, Baron Tweedmouth	1849–1909
Markham, Sir Albert Hastings	1841–1918
Markham, Beryl	1902–1986
Markham, Sir Clements Robert	1830–1916
Markham, Violet Rosa	1872–1959
Markievicz, Countess. See Gore-Booth, Constance	#1868–1927
Marks, David Woolf	1811–1909
Marks, George Croydon, Baron	#1858–1938
Marks, Simon, Baron Marks of Broughton	1888–1964
Marples, Alfred Ernest, Baron Marples	1907–1978
Marquand, Hilary Adair	1901–1972
Marquis, Frederick James, Earl of Woolton	1883–1964
Marr, John Edward	1857–1933
Marre, Sir Alan Samuel	1914–1990
Marrian, Guy Frederic	1904–1981
Marriott, Sir John Arthur Ransome	1859–1945
Marriott, Sir William Thackeray	1834–1903
Marris, Sir William Sinclair	1873–1945
Marsden, Alexander Edwin	1832–1902
Marsden, Sir Ernest	1889–1970
Marsh, Dame (Edith) Ngaio	1899–1982

Marsh, Sir Edward Howard	1872–1953
Marshall, Alfred	1842–1924
Marshall, (Charles) Arthur (Bertram)	1910–1989
Marshall, George William	1839–1905
Marshall, Sir Guy Anstruther Knox	1871–1959
Marshall, Sir John Hubert	1876–1958
Marshall, Julian	1836–1903
Marshall, Sir Stirrat Andrew William Johnson-. See Johnson-Marshall	1912–1981
Marshall, Thomas Humphrey	1893–1981
Marshall, Sir William Raine	1865–1939
Marshall-Cornwall, Sir James Handyside	1887–1985
Marshall Hall, Sir Edward. See Hall	1858–1929
Martel, Sir Giffard Le Quesne	1889–1958
Marten, Sir (Clarence) Henry (Kennett)	1872–1948
Martin, Alexander	1857–1946
Martin, (Basil) Kingsley	1897–1969
Martin, Sir Charles James	1866–1955
Martin, Sir David Christie	1914–1976
Martin, Sir Douglas Eric ('Deric') Holland-. See Holland-Martin	1906–1977
Martin, Sir Harold Brownlow Morgan	1918–1988
Martin, Herbert Henry	1881–1954
Martin, Hugh	1890–1964
Martin, Sir Theodore	1816–1909
Martin, Sir Thomas Acquin	1850–1906
Martin, Violet Florence, 'Martin Ross'	1862–1915
Martin, William Keble	1877–1969
Martin-Harvey, Sir John Martin	1863–1944
Martindale, Cyril Charlie	1879–1963
Martindale, Hilda	1875–1952
Marwick, Sir James David	1826–1908
Mary, Queen	1867–1953
Masefield, John Edward	1878–1967
Masham, Baron. See Lister, Samuel Cunliffe	1815–1906
Maskelyne, John Nevil	#1839–1917
Maskelyne, Mervyn Herbert Nevil Story-. See Story-Maskelyne	1823–1911
Mason, Alfred Edward Woodley	1865–1948
Mason, Arthur James	1851–1928
Mason, Charlotte Maria Shaw	#1842–1923
Mason, Sir Frank Trowbridge	1900–1988
Mason, James Neville	1909–1984
Mason-MacFarlane, Sir (Frank) Noel	1889–1953
Massey, (Charles) Vincent	1887–1967
Massey, Gerald	1828–1907

Meldola, Raphael	#1849–1915
Meldrum, Charles	1821–1901
Mellanby, Sir Edward	1884–1955
Mellanby, John	1878–1939
Mellon (formerly Woolgar), Sarah Jane	1824–1909
Melville, Arthur	1855–1904
Mendelsohn, Eric	1887–1953
Mendl, Sir Charles Ferdinand	1871–1958
Menon, Vapal Pangunni	1894–1966
Menon, Vengalil Krishnan Kunji-Krishna	1896–1974
Menzies, Sir Frederick Norton Kay	1875–1949
Menzies, Sir Robert Gordon	1894–1978
Menzies, Sir Stewart Graham	1890–1968
Mercer, Cecil William, 'Dornford Yates'	1885–1960
Mercer, James	1883–1932
Mercer, Joseph	1914–1990
Meredith, George	1828–1909
Meredith, Sir William Ralph	1840–1923
Merivale, Herman Charles	1839–1906
Merriman, Frank Boyd, Baron	1880–1962
Merriman, Henry Seton, *pseudonym*. See Scott, Hugh Stowell	1862–1903
Merriman, John Xavier	1841–1926
Merrison, Sir Alexander Walter	1924–1989
Merrivale, Baron. See Duke, Henry Edward	1885–1939
Merry, William Walter	1835–1918
Merry del Val, Rafael	1865–1930
Mersey, Viscount. See Bigham, John Charles	1840–1929
Merthyr, Baron. See Lewis, William Thomas	1837–1914
Merton, Sir Thomas Ralph	1888–1969
Merz, Charles Hesterman	1874–1940
Messel, Oliver Hilary Sambourne	1904–1978
Messel, Rudolph	#1848–1920
Messervy, Sir Frank Walter	1893–1973
Meston, James Scorgie, Baron	1865–1943
Metcalfe, Sir Charles Herbert Theophilus	1853–1928
Methuen, Sir Algernon Methuen Marshall	1856–1924
Methuen, Paul Ayshford, Baron	#1886–1974
Methuen, Paul Sanford, Baron	1845–1932
Methven, Sir (Malcolm) John	1926–1980
Meux (formerly Lambton), Sir Hedworth	1856–1929
Mew, Charlotte Mary	1869–1928
Meyer, Frederick Brotherton	1847–1929
Meyer, Sir William Stevenson	1860–1922

Meynell, Alice Christiana Gertrude	1847–1922
Meynell, Sir Francis Meredith Wilfrid	1891–1975
Meyrick, Edward	1854–1938
Meyrick, Frederick	1827–1906
Michell, Anthony George Maldon	1870–1959
Michell, Sir Lewis Loyd	1842–1928
Michie, Alexander	1833–1902
Micklem, Nathaniel	1888–1976
Micklethwaite, John Thomas	1843–1906
Middleditch, Edward Charles	1923–1987
Middleton, James Smith	1878–1962
Midlane, Albert	1825–1909
Midleton, Earl of. See Brodrick, (William) St John (Fremantle)	1856–1942
Miers, Sir Anthony Cecil Capel	1906–1985
Miers, Sir Henry Alexander	1858–1942
Milbanke, Ralph Gordon Noel King, Earl of Lovelace	1839–1906
Mildmay, Anthony Bingham, Baron Mildmay of Flete	1909–1950
Miles, Sir (Arnold) Ashley	1904–1988
Milford, David Sumner	1905–1984
Milford, Sir Humphrey Sumner	1877–1952
Milford, (Theodore) Richard	1895–1987
Milford Haven, Marquess of. See Mountbatten, Louis Alexander	1854–1921
Mill, Hugh Robert	1861–1950
Millar, Frederick Robert Hoyer, Baron Inchyra	1900–1989
Millar, Gertie	1879–1952
Miller, Florence Fenwick	#1854–1935
Miller, Henry George	#1913–1976
Miller, James. See MacColl, Ewan	1915–1989
Miller, Sir James Percy	1864–1906
Miller, William	1864–1945
Milligan, George	1860–1934
Milligan, Sir William	1864–1929
Mills, Bertram Wagstaff	1873–1938
Mills, Percy Herbert, Viscount	1890–1968
Mills, Sir William	1856–1932
Mills, William Hobson	1873–1959
Milne, Alan Alexander	1882–1956
Milne, Sir (Archibald) Berkeley	1855–1938
Milne, Edward Arthur	1896–1950
Milne, George Francis, Baron	1866–1948
Milne, John	1850–1913
Milne-Watson, Sir David Milne	1869–1945
Milner, Alfred, Viscount	1854–1925
Milner, Henry Ernest	#1845–1906

Montmorency, Raymond Harvey de, Viscount Frankfort de Montmorency. See de Montmorency	1835–1902
Monypenny, William Flavelle	1866–1912
Moody, Harold Arundel	1882–1947
Moon, Sir (Edward) Penderel	1905–1987
Moor, Sir Frederick Robert	1853–1927
Moor, Sir Ralph Denham Rayment	1860–1909
Moore, Arthur William	1853–1909
Moore, (Charles) Garrett (Ponsonby), Earl of Drogheda	1910–1989
Moore, Doris Elizabeth Langley	1902–1989
Moore, Edward	1835–1916
Moore, George Augustus	1852–1933
Moore, George Edward	1873–1958
Moore, Gerald	1899–1987
Moore, Henry Spencer	1898–1986
Moore, Mary. See Wyndham, Mary, Lady	1861–1931
Moore, Stuart Archibald	1842–1907
Moore, Temple Lushington	1856–1920
Moore-Brabazon, John Theodore Cuthbert, Baron Brabazon of Tara. See Brabazon	1884–1964
Moorehead, Alan McCrae	1910–1983
Moores, Cecil	1902–1989
Moorhouse, James	1826–1915
Moorman, John Richard Humpidge	1905–1989
Moran, Baron. See Wilson, Charles McMoran	1882–1977
Moran, Patrick Francis	1830–1911
Morant, Geoffrey Miles	1899–1964
Morant, Sir Robert Laurie	1863–1920
Mordell, Louis Joel	1888–1972
More-Molyneux, Sir Robert Henry	1838–1904
Morecambe, Eric	1926–1984
Morel, Edmund Dene	#1873–1924
Moresby, John	1830–1922
Morfill, William Richard	1834–1909
Morgan, Charles Langbridge	1894–1958
Morgan, Conwy Lloyd	1852–1936
Morgan, Edward Delmar	1840–1909
Morgan, Sir Frederick Edgworth	1894–1967
Morgan, Sir Gilbert Thomas	1872–1940
Morgan, John Hartman	1876–1955
Morgan, Sir Morien Bedford	1912–1978
Moriarty, Henry Augustus	1815–1906
Morison, Stanley Arthur	1889–1967
Morison, Sir Theodore	1863–1936
Morland, Sir Thomas Lethbridge Napier	1865–1925

Morley, Earl of. See Parker, Albert Edmund	1843–1905
Morley, Iris	#1910–1953
Morley, John, Viscount Morley of Blackburn	1838–1923
Morley Horder, Percy (Richard). See Horder	1870–1944
Morrah, Dermot Michael Macgregor	1896–1974
Morrell, Lady Ottoline Violet Anne	1873–1938
Morris, (Alfred) Edwin	1894–1971
Morris, Sir Cedric Lockwood	#1889–1982
Morris, Charles Richard, Baron Morris of Grasmere	1898–1990
Morris, Edward Patrick, Baron	1859–1935
Morris, Sir Harold Spencer	1876–1967
Morris, John Humphrey Carlile	1910–1984
Morris, (John) Marcus (Harston)	1915–1989
Morris, John William, Baron Morris of Borth-y-Gest	1896–1979
Morris, Sir Lewis	1833–1907
Morris, Mary ('May')	#1862–1938
Morris, Michael, Baron Morris and Killanin	1826–1901
Morris, Philip Richard	1836–1902
Morris, Sir Philip Robert	1901–1979
Morris, Tom	1821–1908
Morris, William O'Connor	1824–1904
Morris, William Richard, Viscount Nuffield	1877–1963
Morris-Jones, Sir John	1864–1929
Morrison, George Ernest	#1862–1920
Morrison, Herbert Stanley, Baron Morrison of Lambeth	1888–1965
Morrison, Walter	1836–1921
Morrison, William Shepherd, Viscount Dunrossil	1893–1961
Morshead, Sir Leslie James	1889–1959
Mortimer, (Charles) Raymond (Bell)	1895–1980
Mortimer, John Robert	#1825–1911
Mortimer, Robert Cecil	1902–1976
Morton, Sir Desmond John Falkiner	1891–1971
Morton, Fergus Dunlop, Baron Morton of Henryton	1887–1973
Morton, John Cameron Andrieu Bingham Michael, 'Beachcomber'	1893–1979
Morton, Richard Alan	1899–1977
Moseley, Henry Gwyn Jeffreys	1887–1915
Moshinsky, Alan Samuel. See Marre	1914–1990
Mosley, Sir Oswald Ernald	1896–1980

Naipaul, Shivadhar Srinivasa
(Shiva) 1945–1985
Nair, Sir Chettur Sankaran.
See Sankaran Nair 1857–1934
Nairne, Alexander 1863–1936
Namier, Sir Lewis Bernstein 1888–1960
Naoroji, Dadabhai #1825–1917
Narbeth, John Harper 1863–1944
Nares, Sir George Strong 1831–1915
Nash, John Northcote 1893–1977
Nash, Paul 1889–1946
Nash, Sir Walter 1882–1968
Nathan, Harry Louis, Baron 1889–1963
Nathan, Sir Matthew 1862–1939
Nawanagar, Maharaja Shri
Ranjitsinhji Vibhaji,
Maharaja Jam Saheb of 1872–1933
Neagle, Dame Anna 1904–1986
Neale, Sir John Ernest 1890–1975
Neave, Airey Middleton
Sheffield 1916–1979
Neel, (Louis) Boyd 1905–1981
Nehru, Jawaharlal 1889–1964
Nehru, Pandit Motilal 1861–1931
Neil, Robert Alexander 1852–1901
Neil, Samuel 1825–1901
Neill, Alexander Sutherland 1883–1973
Neill, Stephen Charles 1900–1984
Neilson, George 1858–1923
Neilson, Julia Emilie 1868–1957
Nelson, Eliza (1827–1908).
See under Craven, Henry
Thornton 1818–1905
Nelson, Sir Frank 1883–1966
Nelson, George Horatio,
Baron Nelson of Stafford 1887–1962
Nelson, Sir Hugh Muir 1835–1906
Nemon, Oscar 1906–1985
Neruda, Wilma Maria
Francisca. See Hallé, Lady 1839–1911
Nesbit, Edith. See Bland 1858–1924
Nettleship, Edward 1845–1913
Nettleship, John Trivett 1841–1902
Neubauer, Adolf 1832–1907
Nevill, Lady Dorothy Fanny #1826–1913
Neville, Henry 1837–1910
Nevinson, Christopher
Richard Wynne 1889–1946
Nevinson, Henry Woodd 1856–1941
Newall (formerly Phillpotts),
Dame Bertha Surtees 1877–1932
Newall, Cyril Louis Norton,
Baron 1886–1963
Newall, Hugh Frank 1857–1944
Newberry, Percy Edward 1869–1949
Newbigin, Marion Isabel #1869–1934
Newbold, Sir Douglas 1894–1945
Newbolt, Sir Henry John 1862–1938
Newbolt, William Charles
Edmund 1844–1930
Newitt, Dudley Maurice 1894–1980

Newman, Ernest 1868–1959
Newman, Sir George 1870–1948
Newman, Maxwell Herman,
Alexander 1897–1984
Newman, William Lambert 1834–1923
Newmarch, Charles Henry 1824–1903
Newnes, Sir George 1851–1910
Newsam, Sir Frank Aubrey 1893–1964
Newsholme, Sir Arthur 1857–1943
Newsom, Sir John Hubert 1910–1971
Newton, Baron. See Legh,
Thomas Wodehouse 1857–1942
Newton, Alfred 1829–1907
Newton, Ernest 1856–1922
Nichol Smith, David. See
Smith 1875–1962
Nicholls, Frederick William 1889–1974
Nichols, (John) Beverley 1898–1983
Nichols, Robert Malise
Bowyer 1893–1944
Nicholson, Benjamin Lauder
('Ben') 1894–1982
Nicholson, Sir Charles 1808–1903
Nicholson, Sir Charles
Archibald 1867–1949
Nicholson, Charles Ernest 1868–1954
Nicholson, Edward William
Byron 1849–1912
Nicholson, George 1847–1908
Nicholson, Joseph Shield 1850–1927
Nicholson, Norman
Cornthwaite 1914–1987
Nicholson, Reynold Alleyne 1868–1945
Nicholson, (Rosa) Winifred #1893–1981
Nicholson, Sir Sydney
Hugo 1875–1947
Nicholson, William Gustavus,
Baron 1845–1918
Nicholson, Sir William
Newzam Prior 1872–1949
Nickalls, Guy 1866–1935
Nicol, Erskine 1825–1904
Nicoll, (John Ramsay)
Allardyce 1894–1976
Nicoll, Sir William Robertson 1851–1923
Nicolson, Adela Florence,
'Laurence Hope' 1865–1904
Nicolson, Sir Arthur, Baron
Carnock 1849–1928
Nicolson, Sir Harold George 1886–1968
Nicolson, (Lionel) Benedict 1914–1978
Nicolson, Malcolm Hassels
(1843–1904). See under
Nicolson, Adela Florence
Nicolson, Victoria Mary,
Lady. See Sackville-West 1892–1962
Niemeyer, Sir Otto Ernst 1883–1971
Nightingale, Florence 1820–1910
Nimptsch, Uli 1897–1977
Niven, (James) David
(Graham) 1910–1983

O'Doherty (formerly Kelly),
  Mary Anne (1826–1910).
  See under O'Doherty,
  Kevin Izod
O'Donnell, Patrick   1856–1927
O'Dwyer, Sir Michael Francis   1864–1940
Ogden, Charles Kay   1889–1957
Ogdon, John Andrew Howard   1937–1989
Ogg, Sir William Gammie   1891–1979
Ogilvie, Sir Frederick Wolff   1893–1949
Ogle, John William   1824–1905
O'Hanlon, John   1821–1905
O'Higgins, Kevin Christopher   1892–1927
O'Kelly, Sean Thomas   1882–1966
Oldfield, Sir Maurice   1915–1981
Oldham, Charles James
  (1843–1907). See under
  Oldham, Henry
Oldham, Henry   1815–1902
Oldham, Joseph Houldsworth   1874–1969
Oldham, Richard Dixon   #1858–1936
Oldman, Cecil Bernard   #1894–1969
O'Leary, John   1830–1907
Oliver, David Thomas   1863–1947
Oliver, Francis Wall   1864–1951
Oliver, Frederick Scott   1864–1934
Oliver, Sir Geoffrey Nigel   1898–1980
Oliver, Sir Henry Francis   1865–1965
Oliver, Samuel Pasfield   1838–1907
Oliver, Sir Thomas   1853–1942
Olivier, Giorgio Borg
  ('George')   1911–1980
Olivier, Laurence Kerr, Baron   1907–1989
Olivier, Sydney Haldane,
  Baron   1859–1943
Olpherts, Sir William   1822–1902
Olsson, Julius   1864–1942
Oman, Sir Charles William
  Chadwick   1860–1946
Oman, John Wood   1860–1939
Ommanney, Sir Erasmus   1814–1904
Ommanney, George Druce
  Wynne   1819–1902
O'Neill, Sir Con Douglas
  Walter   1912–1988
O'Neill, Terence Marne,
  Baron O'Neill of the Maine   1914–1990
Onions, Charles Talbut   1873–1965
Onslow, Sir Richard George   1904–1975
Onslow, William Hillier, Earl
  of Onslow   1853–1911
Opie, Peter Mason   1918–1982
Oppé, Adolph Paul   1878–1957
Oppenheim, Edward Phillips   1866–1946
Oppenheim, Lassa Francis
  Lawrence   1858–1919
Oppenheimer, Sir Ernest   1880–1957
Orage, Alfred Richard   1873–1934
Oram, Sir Henry John   1858–1939
Orchardson, Sir William
  Quiller   1832–1910

Orczy, Emma Magdalena
  Rosalia Marie Josepha
  Barbara, Baroness   1865–1947
Ord, Bernhard ('Boris')   1897–1961
Ord, William Miller   1834–1902
Orde, Cuthbert Julian   1888–1968
O'Rell, Max, pseudonym. See
  Blouet, Léon Paul   1848–1903
Orme, Eliza   #1848–1937
Ormerod, Eleanor Anne   1828–1901
Ormsby Gore, (William)
  David, Baron Harlech   1918–1985
Ormsby-Gore, William
  George Arthur, Baron
  Harlech   1885–1964
Orpen, Sir William
  Newenham Montague   1878–1931
Orr, Alexandra Sutherland   1828–1903
Orr, John Boyd, Baron Boyd
  Orr   1880–1971
Orr, William McFadden   1866–1934
Orton, Charles William
  Previté-. See Previté-Orton   1877–1947
Orton, John Kingsley ('Joe')   1933–1967
Orwell, George, pseudonym.
  See Blair, Eric Arthur   1903–1950
Orwin, Charles Stewart   1876–1955
Osborn, Sir Frederic James   1885–1978
Osborne, Walter Frederick   1859–1903
O'Shea, John Augustus   1839–1905
O'Shea, William Henry   1840–1905
Osler, Abraham Follett   1808–1903
Osler, Sir William   1849–1919
O'Sullivan, Cornelius   1841–1907
Otté, Elise   1818–1903
Ottley, Sir Charles Langdale   1858–1932
Ouida, pseudonym. See De la
  Ramée, Marie Louise   1839–1908
Ouless, Walter William   1848–1933
Overton, John Henry   1835–1903
Overtoun, Baron. See White,
  John Campbell   1843–1908
Owen, Sir (Arthur) David
  (Kemp)   1904–1970
Owen, (Humphrey) Frank   1905–1979
Owen, John   1854–1926
Owen, (Paul) Robert   1920–1990
Owen, Robert   1820–1902
Owen, Wilfred Edward Salter   #1893–1918
Owen, Sir (William) Leonard   1897–1971
Oxford and Asquith,
  Countess of. See Asquith,
  Emma Alice Margaret
  ('Margot')   1864–1945
Oxford and Asquith, Earl of.
  See Asquith, Herbert
  Henry   1852–1928

Pächt, Otto Ernst   1902–1988
Page, Sir Archibald   1875–1949

Pattison, Andrew Seth Pringle- (formerly Andrew Seth)	1856–1931	Peel, Lady. See Lillie, Beatrice Gladys	1894–1989
Paul, Charles Kegan	1828–1902	Peel, Arthur Wellesley, Viscount	1829–1912
Paul, Herbert Woodfield	1853–1935	Peel, Sir Frederick	1823–1906
Paul, Leslie Allen	1905–1985	Peel, James	1811–1906
Paul, William	1822–1905	Peel, William Robert	
Pauncefote, Julian, Baron	1828–1902	Wellesley, Earl	1867–1937
Pavlova, Anna	#1881–1931	Peers, Sir Charles Reed	1868–1952
Pavy, Frederick William	1829–1911	Peers, Edgar Allison	1891–1952
Payne, Ben Iden	1881–1976	Peet, Thomas Eric	1882–1934
Payne, Edward John	1844–1904	Peile, Sir James Braithwaite	1833–1906
Payne, Humfry Gilbert Garth	1902–1936	Peile, John	1837–1910
Payne, John Wesley Vivian ('Jack')	1899–1969	Pelham, Henry Francis	1846–1907
Payne, Joseph Frank	1840–1910	Pélissier, Harry Gabriel	1874–1913
Peach, Benjamin Neeve	#1842–1926	Pell, Albert	1820–1907
Peacock, Sir Edward Robert	1871–1962	Pember, Edward Henry	1833–1911
Peacocke, Joseph Ferguson	1835–1916	Pemberton, Thomas Edgar	1849–1905
Peake, Arthur Samuel	1865–1929	Pemberton Billing, Noel. See Billing	#1881–1948
Peake, Sir Charles Brinsley Pemberton	1897–1958	Pembrey, Marcus Seymour	1868–1934
Peake, Frederick Gerard	1886–1970	Penley, William Sydney	1852–1912
Peake, Harold John Edward	1867–1946	Pennant, George Sholto Gordon Douglas-, Baron Penrhyn. See Douglas-Pennant	1836–1907
Peake, Mervyn Laurence	1911–1968		
Pearce, Edward Holroyd, Baron	1901–1990	Penrhyn, Baron. See Douglas-Pennant, George Sholto Gordon	1836–1907
Pearce, Ernest Harold	1865–1930		
Pearce, Sir George Foster	1870–1952	Penrose, Dame Emily	1858–1942
Pearce, Sir (Standen) Leonard	1873–1947	Penrose, Francis Cranmer	1817–1903
Pearce, Stephen	1819–1904	Penrose, Lionel Sharples	1898–1972
Pearce, Sir William George	1861–1907	Penrose, Sir Roland Algernon	1900–1984
Pears, Sir Edwin	1835–1919	Penson, Dame Lillian Margery	1896–1963
Pears, Sir Peter Neville Luard	1910–1986	Pentland, Baron. See Sinclair, John	1860–1925
Pearsall, William Harold	1891–1964		
Pearsall Smith, (Lloyd) Logan. See Smith	1865–1946	Pepler, Sir George Lionel	1882–1959
		Peppiatt, Sir Leslie Ernest	1891–1968
Pearse, Patrick Henry	#1879–1916	Percival, John	1834–1918
Pearson, Alfred Chilton	1861–1935	Percy, Alan Ian, Duke of Northumberland	1880–1930
Pearson, Charles John, Lord	1843–1910		
Pearson, Colin Hargreaves, Baron	1899–1980	Percy, Eustace Sutherland Campbell, Baron Percy of Newcastle	1887–1958
Pearson, Sir Cyril Arthur	1866–1921		
Pearson, (Edward) Hesketh (Gibbons)	#1887–1964	Percy, Henry Algernon George, Earl	1871–1909
Pearson, Egon Sharpe	1895–1980	Pereira, George Edward	1865–1923
Pearson, Karl	1857–1936	Perham, Dame Margery Freda	1895–1982
Pearson, Lester Bowles	1897–1972		
Pearson, Weetman Dickinson, Viscount Cowdray	1856–1927	Perkin, Arthur George	1861–1937
		Perkin, Sir William Henry	1838–1907
Peart, (Thomas) Frederick, Baron	1914–1988	Perkin, William Henry	1860–1929
		Perkins, Sir Æneas	1834–1901
Pease, Sir Arthur Francis	1866–1927	Perkins, John Bryan Ward-. See Ward-Perkins	1912–1981
Pease, Edward Reynolds	1857–1955		
Pease, Joseph Albert, Baron Gainford	1860–1943	Perkins, Robert Cyril Layton	1866–1955
		Perks, Sir Robert William	1849–1934
Pease, Sir Joseph Whitwell	1828–1903	Perowne, Edward Henry	1826–1906
Peat, Stanley	1902–1969	Perowne, John James Stewart	1823–1904
Pedley, Robin	1914–1988		
Peek, Sir Cuthbert Edgar	1855–1901		

Pleydell, John Clavell Mansel-. See	
Mansel-Pleydell	1817–1902
Plimmer, Robert Henry Aders	1877–1955
Plomer, William Charles Franklyn	1903–1973
Plomley, (Francis) Roy	1914–1985
Plucknett, Theodore Frank Thomas	1897–1965
Plumer, Herbert Charles Onslow, Viscount	1857–1932
Plummer, Henry Crozier Keating	1875–1946
Plunkett, Edward John Moreton Drax, Baron of Dunsany	1878–1957
Plunkett, Sir Francis Richard	1835–1907
Plunkett, Sir Horace Curzon	1854–1932
Plunkett-Ernle-Erle-Drax, Sir Reginald Aylmer Ranfurly	1880–1967
Plurenden, Baron. See Sternberg, Rudy	1917–1978
Pochin, Sir Edward Eric	1909–1990
Pode, Sir (Edward) Julian	1902–1968
Podmore, Frank	1855–1910
Poel, William	1852–1934
Poland, Sir Harry Bodkin	1829–1928
Polanyi, Michael	1891–1976
Pole, Sir Felix John Clewett	1877–1956
Pollard, Albert Frederick	1869–1948
Pollard, Alfred William	1859–1944
Pollen, Arthur Joseph Hungerford	#1866–1937
Pollen, John Hungerford	1820–1902
Pollitt, George Paton	1878–1964
Pollitt, Harry	1890–1960
Pollock, Bertram	1863–1943
Pollock, Ernest Murray, Viscount Hanworth	1861–1936
Pollock, Sir Frederick	1845–1937
Pollock, Hugh McDowell	1852–1937
Pollock, Sir (John) Donald	1868–1962
Polunin, Oleg	1914–1985
Pond, Sir Desmond Arthur	1919–1986
Ponsonby, Arthur Augustus William Harry, Baron Ponsonby of Shulbrede	1871–1946
Ponsonby, Vere Brabazon, Earl of Bessborough	1880–1956
Pont. See Laidler, (Gavin) Graham	#1908–1940
Poole, Reginald Lane	1857–1939
Poole, Stanley Edward Lane-	1854–1931
Pooley, Sir Ernest Henry	1876–1966
Poore, George Vivian	1843–1904
Pope, George Uglow	1820–1908
Pope, Samuel	1826–1901
Pope, Walter James Macqueen-. See Macqueen-Pope	1888–1960
Pope, William Burt	1822–1903

Pope, Sir William Jackson	1870–1939
Pope-Hennessy, (Richard) James (Arthur)	1916–1974
Popham, Arthur Ewart	1889–1970
Popham, Sir (Henry) Robert (Moore) Brooke-. See Brooke-Popham	1878–1953
Portal, Charles Frederick Algernon, Viscount Portal of Hungerford	1893–1971
Portal, Melville	1819–1904
Portal, Sir Wyndham Raymond, Viscount	1885–1949
Porter, Sir Andrew Marshall	1837–1919
Porter, Rodney Robert	1917–1985
Porter, Samuel Lowry, Baron	1877–1956
Portland, Duke of. See Bentinck, Victor Frederick William Cavendish-	1897–1990
Postan (formerly Power), Eileen Edna le Poer	1889–1940
Postan, Sir Michael Moïssey	1899–1981
Postgate, John Percival	1853–1926
Postgate, Raymond William	1896–1971
Pott, Alfred	1822–1908
Potter, (Helen), Beatrix (Mrs Heelis)	1866–1943
Potter, Stephen Meredith	1900–1969
Poulton, Sir Edward Bagnall	1856–1943
Pouncey, Philip Michael Rivers	1910–1990
Pound, Sir (Alfred) Dudley (Pickman Rogers)	1877–1943
Powell, Cecil Frank	1903–1969
Powell, Frederick York	1850–1904
Powell, Sir (George) Allan	1876–1948
Powell, Lawrenceson Fitzroy	#1881–1975
Powell, Michael Latham	1905–1990
Powell, Olave St Clair Baden-, Lady Baden-Powell. See Baden-Powell	1889–1977
Powell, Sir Richard Douglas	1842–1925
Powell, Robert Stephenson Smyth Baden-, Baron Baden-Powell. See Baden-Powell	1857–1941
Power, Sir Arthur John	1889–1960
Power, Sir D'Arcy	1855–1941
Power, Eileen Edna le Poer. See Postan	1889–1940
Power, Sir John Cecil	1870–1950
Power, Sir William Henry	1842–1916
Powicke, Sir (Frederick) Maurice	1879–1963
Pownall, Sir Henry Royds	1887–1961
Powys, John Cowper	1872–1963
Poynder, Sir John Poynder Dickson-, Baron Islington	1866–1936
Poynter, Sir Edward John	1836–1919

Rajagopalachari, Chakravarti	1878–1972	Rau, Sir Benegal Narsing	1887–1953
Raleigh, Sir Walter Alexander	1861–1922	Raven, Charles Earle	1885–1964
Ralston, James Layton	1881–1948	Raven, John James	1833–1906
Ram, Sir (Lucius Abel John)		Raven-Hill, Leonard	1867–1942
Granville	1885–1952	Raverat, Gwendolen Mary	1885–1957
Raman, Sir (Chandrasekhara)		Raverty, Henry George	1825–1906
Venkata	1888–1970	Ravilious, Eric William	1903–1942
Ramberg, Cyvia Myriam. See		Rawcliffe, Gordon Hindle	1910–1979
Rambert, Dame Marie	1888–1982	Rawling, Cecil Godfrey	1870–1917
Rambert, Dame Marie	1888–1982	Rawlinson, George	1812–1902
Rambush, Niels Edvard	#1889–1957	Rawlinson, Sir Henry	
Ramé, Marie Louise, 'Ouida'.		Seymour, Baron	1864–1925
See De la Ramée	1839–1908	Rawlinson, William George	1840–1928
Ramsay, Alexander	1822–1909	Rawnsley, Hardwicke	
Ramsay, Sir Bertram Home	1883–1945	Drummond	#1851–1920
Ramsay, Sir James Henry	1832–1925	Rawson, Sir Harry	
Ramsay, Lady (Victoria)		Holdsworth	1843–1910
Patricia (Helena Elizabeth)	1886–1974	Rawsthorne, Alan	1905–1971
Ramsay, Sir William	1852–1916	Rayleigh, Baron. See Strutt,	
Ramsay, Sir William Mitchell	1851–1939	John William	1842–1919
Ramsay-Steel-Maitland, Sir		Rayleigh, Baron. See Strutt,	
Arthur Herbert		Robert John	1875–1947
Drummond. See		Raynor, Geoffrey Vincent	1913–1983
Steel-Maitland	1876–1935	Read, Sir Charles Hercules	1857–1929
Ramsbottom, John	1885–1974	Read, Clare Sewell	1826–1905
Ramsden, Omar	1873–1939	Read, Grantly Dick-. See	
Ramsey, (Arthur) Michael,		Dick-Read	1890–1959
Baron Ramsey of		Read, Sir Herbert Edward	1893–1968
Canterbury	1904–1988	Read, Herbert Harold	1889–1970
Ramsey, Frank Plumpton	#1903–1930	Read, Sir Herbert James	1863–1949
Ramsey, Ian Thomas	1915–1972	Read, John	1884–1963
Ramsey, (Mary) Dorothea		Read, Walter William	1855–1907
(Whiting)	1904–1989	Reade, Thomas Mellard	1832–1909
Randall, Sir John Turton	1905–1984	Reading, Marchioness of. See	
Randall, Richard William	1824–1906	Isaacs, Stella	1894–1971
Randall-MacIver, David	1873–1945	Reading, Marquess of. See	
Randegger, Alberto	1832–1911	Isaacs, Rufus Daniel	1860–1935
Randles, Marshall	1826–1904	Reay, Baron. See Mackay,	
Randolph, Francis Charles		Donald James	1839–1921
Hingeston-. See		Reckitt, Maurice Benington	1888–1980
Hingeston-Randolph	1833–1910	Redcliffe-Maud. See Maud,	
Randolph, Sir George		John Primatt Redcliffe	1906–1982
Granville	1818–1907	Redesdale, Baron. See	
Ranjitsinhji, Maharaja Jam		Mitford, Algernon Bertram	
Saheb of Nawanagar. See		Freeman-	1837–1916
Nawanagar	1872–1933	Redgrave, Sir Michael	
Rank, (Joseph) Arthur, Baron	1888–1972	Scudamore	1908–1985
Rankeillour, Baron. See Hope,		Redmayne, Martin, Baron	1910–1983
James Fitzalan	1870–1949	Redmayne, Sir Richard	
Rankin, Sir George Claus	1877–1946	Augustine Studdert	1865–1955
Ransom, William Henry	1824–1907	Redmond, John Edward	1856–1918
Ransome, Arthur Michell	1884–1967	Redmond, William Hoey	
Raper, Robert William	1842–1915	Kearney	1861–1917
Rapson, Edward James	1861–1937	Redpath, Anne	1895–1965
Rashdall, Hastings	1858–1924	Redpath, Henry Adeney	1848–1908
Rassam, Hormuzd	1826–1910	Reed, Sir Andrew	#1837–1914
Ratcliffe, John Ashworth	1902–1987	Reed, Austin Leonard	1873–1954
Rathbone, Eleanor Florence	1872–1946	Reed, Sir Carol	1906–1976
Rathbone, William	1819–1902	Reed, Sir Edward James	1830–1906
Rattigan, Sir Terence Mervyn	1911–1977	Reed, Edward Tennyson	1860–1933
Rattigan, Sir William Henry	1842–1904	Reed, Henry	1914–1986

Ringer, Sydney	1835–1910
Ripon, Marquess of. See Robinson, George Frederick Samuel	1827–1909
Risley, Sir Herbert Hope	1851–1911
Ritchie, Anne Isabella, Lady (1837–1919). See under Ritchie, Sir Richmond Thackeray Willoughby	
Ritchie, Charles Thomson, Baron Ritchie of Dundee	1838–1906
Ritchie, David George	1853–1903
Ritchie, Sir John Neish	1904–1977
Ritchie, Sir Neil Methuen	1897–1983
Ritchie, Sir Richmond Thackeray Willoughby	1854–1912
Ritchie-Calder, Baron. See Calder	1906–1982
Rivaz, Sir Charles Montgomery	1845–1926
Riverdale, Baron. See Balfour, Arthur	1873–1957
Rivers, William Halse Rivers	#1864–1922
Riviere, Briton	1840–1920
Robbins, Lionel Charles, Baron	1898–1984
Robeck, Sir John Michael De. See De Robeck	1862–1928
Roberthall, Baron. See Hall, Robert Lowe	1901–1988
Roberton, Sir Hugh Stevenson	#1874–1952
Roberts, Alexander	1826–1901
Roberts, Colin Henderson	1909–1990
Roberts, Frederick Sleigh, Earl	1832–1914
Roberts, George Henry	1869–1928
Roberts, Sir Gilbert	#1899–1978
Roberts, Isaac	1829–1904
Roberts, Robert Davies	1851–1911
Roberts, Thomas d'Esterre	1893–1976
Roberts, William Patrick	1895–1980
Roberts-Austen, Sir William Chandler	1843–1902
Robertson, Alan	1920–1989
Robertson, Alexander	1896–1970
Robertson, Sir Alexander	1908–1990
Robertson, Andrew	1883–1977
Robertson, Archibald	1853–1931
Robertson, Brian Hubert, Baron Robertson of Oakbridge	1896–1974
Robertson, Sir Charles Grant	1869–1948
Robertson, Sir Dennis Holme	1890–1963
Robertson, Donald Struan	1885–1961
Robertson, Douglas Moray Cooper Lamb Argyll	1837–1909
Robertson, (Florence) Marjorie. See Neagle, Dame Anna	1904–1986
Robertson, George Matthew	1864–1932

Robertson, Sir George Scott	1852–1916
Robertson, Sir Howard Morley	1888–1963
Robertson, James Patrick Bannerman, Baron	1845–1909
Robertson, Sir James Wilson	1899–1983
Robertson, John Mackinnon	1856–1933
Robertson, John Monteath	1900–1989
Robertson, Sir Johnston Forbes-	1853–1937
Robertson, Sir Robert	1869–1949
Robertson, Sir William Robert	1860–1933
Robertson, (William) Strowan (Amherst) ('Father Algy')	#1894–1955
Robertson Scott, John William	1866–1962
Robey, Sir George Edward	1869–1954
Robins, Elizabeth	#1862–1952
Robins, Thomas Ellis, Baron	1884–1962
Robinson, Sir David	1904–1987
Robinson, (Esmé Stuart) Lennox	1886–1958
Robinson, Frederick William	1830–1901
Robinson, George Frederick Samuel, Marquess of Ripon	1827–1909
Robinson, (George) Geoffrey. See Dawson	1874–1944
Robinson, Henry Wheeler	1872–1945
Robinson, Joan Violet	1903–1983
Robinson, Sir John	1839–1903
Robinson, John Arthur Thomas	1919–1983
Robinson, Sir John Charles	1824–1913
Robinson, John George	#1856–1943
Robinson, Sir John Richard	1828–1903
Robinson, Joseph Armitage	1858–1933
Robinson, Sir Joseph Benjamin	1840–1929
Robinson, Philip Stewart ('Phil')	1847–1902
Robinson, Sir Robert	1886–1975
Robinson, Roy Lister, Baron	1883–1952
Robinson, Vincent Joseph	1829–1910
Robinson, William	#1838–1935
Robinson, Sir (William) Arthur	1874–1950
Robinson, William Heath	1872–1944
Robinson, William Leefe	1895–1918
Robison, Robert	1883–1941
Robson, Dame Flora	1902–1984
Robson, William Alexander	1895–1980
Robson, William Snowdon, Baron	1852–1918
Roby, Henry John	1830–1915
Roche, Alexander Adair, Baron	1871–1956
Rochfort, Sir Cecil Charles Boyd-. See Boyd-Rochfort	1887–1983
Rodd, Francis James Rennell, Baron Rennell of Rodd	1895–1978

Royden, Sir Thomas, Baron	1871–1950
Rubbra, (Charles) Edmund (Duncan)	1901–1986
Ruck, Amy Roberta ('Berta')	1878–1978
Rücker, Sir Arthur William	#1848–1915
Rudolf, Edward de Montjoie	1852–1933
Ruffside, Viscount. See Brown, Douglas Clifton	1879–1958
Rugby, Baron. See Maffey, John Loader	1877–1969
Ruggles-Brise, Sir Evelyn John	1857–1935
Ruggles Gates, Reginald. See Gates	1882–1962
Rumbold, Sir Horace	1829–1913
Rumbold, Sir Horace George Montagu	1869–1941
Runciman, Walter, Baron	1847–1937
Runciman, Walter, Viscount Runciman of Doxford	1870–1949
Runciman, (Walter) Leslie, Viscount Runciman of Doxford	1900–1989
Rundall, Francis Hornblow	1823–1908
Rundle, Sir (Henry Macleod) Leslie	1856–1934
Rupp, (Ernest) Gordon	1910–1986
Rusden, George William	1819–1903
Rushbrooke, James Henry	1870–1947
Rushbury, Sir Henry George	1889–1968
Rushcliffe, Baron. See Betterton, Henry Bucknall	1872–1949
Rushton, William Albert Hugh	1901–1980
Russell, Arthur Oliver Villiers, Baron Ampthill	1869–1935
Russell, Bertrand Arthur William, Earl	1872–1970
Russell, Sir Charles	1863–1928
Russell, Charles Ritchie, Baron Russell of Killowen	1908–1986
Russell, Dora Winifred	1894–1986
Russell, Dorothy Stuart	1895–1983
Russell, Edward Frederick Langley, Baron Russell of Liverpool	1895–1981
Russell, Sir (Edward) John	1872–1965
Russell, Edward Stuart	1887–1954
Russell, Francis Xavier Joseph ('Frank'), Baron Russell of Killowen	1867–1946
Russell, Sir Frederick Stratten	1897–1984
Russell, George William, 'AE'	1867–1935
Russell, George William Erskine	#1853–1919
Russell, Sir Guy Herbrand Edward	1898–1977
Russell, Henry Chamberlaine	1836–1907
Russell, Herbrand Arthur, Duke of Bedford	1858–1940

Russell, John Hugo, Baron Ampthill	1896–1973
Russell, Mary Annette, Countess	1866–1941
Russell, Mary du Caurroy, Duchess of Bedford (1865–1937). See under Russell, Herbrand Arthur	
Russell, (Muriel) Audrey	1906–1989
Russell, Sir (Sydney) Gordon	1892–1980
Russell, Thomas O'Neill	1828–1908
Russell, Sir Thomas Wentworth, Russell Pasha	1879–1954
Russell, Sir Walter Westley	1867–1949
Russell, William Clark	1844–1911
Russell, Sir William Howard	1820–1907
Russell, William James	1830–1909
Russell, (William) Ritchie	1903–1980
Russell Flint, Sir William. See Flint	1880–1969
Rutherford, Ernest, Baron Rutherford of Nelson	1871–1937
Rutherford, Dame Margaret	1892–1972
Rutherford, Mark, pseudonym. See White, William Hale	1831–1913
Rutherford, William Gunion	1853–1907
Rutland, Duke of. See Manners, (Lord) John James Robert	1818–1906
Ruttledge, Hugh	1884–1961
Ryan, Elizabeth Montague	1892–1979
Ryde, John Walter	1898–1961
Ryder, Charles Henry Dudley	1868–1945
Rye, Maria Susan	1829–1903
Rye, William Brenchley	1818–1901
Ryle, Gilbert	1900–1976
Ryle, Herbert Edward	1856–1925
Ryle, John Alfred	1889–1950
Ryle, Sir Martin	1918–1984
Ryrie, Sir Granville de Laune	1865–1937
Sabatini, Rafael	#1875–1950
Sachs, Sir Eric Leopold Otho	1898–1979
Sackville, Herbrand Edward Dundonald Brassey, Earl De La Warr	1900–1976
Sackville-West, Edward Charles, Baron Sackville	1901–1965
Sackville-West, Lionel Sackville, Baron Sackville	1827–1908
Sackville-West, Victoria Mary	1892–1962
Sadleir, Michael Thomas Harvey	1888–1957
Sadler, Sir Michael Ernest	1861–1943
Saha, Meghnad. See Meghnad Saha	1893–1956
St Aldwyn, Earl. See Hicks Beach, Sir Michael Edward	1837–1916

Satow, Sir Ernest Mason	1843–1929	Scott, Geoffrey	#1884–1929
Saumarez, Thomas	1827–1903	Scott, George Herbert	1888–1930
Saunders, Sir Alexander		Scott, Sir Giles Gilbert	1880–1960
Morris Carr-. See		Scott, (Guthrie) Michael	1907–1983
Carr–Saunders	1886–1966	Scott, Sir Harold Richard	#1887–1969
Saunders, Edith Rebecca	#1865–1945	Scott, Hugh Stowell, 'Henry	
Saunders, Edward	1848–1910	Seton Merriman'	1862–1903
Saunders, Sir Edwin	1814–1901	Scott, Sir (James) George	1851–1935
Saunders, Howard	1835–1907	Scott, John	1830–1903
Saunderson, Edward James	1837–1906	Scott, Sir John	1841–1904
Savage, Sir (Edward) Graham	1886–1981	Scott, Sir John Arthur	
Savage (formerly Dell), Ethel		Guillum	1910–1983
Mary	1881–1939	Scott, John William	
Savage-Armstrong, George		Robertson. See Robertson	
Francis	1845–1906	Scott	1866–1962
Savill, Sir Eric Humphrey	1895–1980	Scott, Kathleen. See Kennet,	
Savill, Thomas Dixon	1855–1910	(Edith Agnes) Kathleen,	
Saxe-Weimar, Prince Edward		Lady	1878–1947
of. See Edward of		Scott, Leader, pseudonym. See	
Saxe-Weimar	1823–1902	Baxter, Lucy	1837–1902
Saxl, Friedrich ('Fritz')	1890–1948	Scott, Sir Leslie Frederic	1869–1950
Sayce, Archibald	1845–1933	Scott, (Mackay Hugh) Baillie	#1865–1945
Sayers, Dorothy Leigh	1893–1957	Scott, Paul Mark	1920–1978
Sayers, Richard Sidney	1908–1989	Scott, Sir Percy Moreton	1853–1924
Scamp, Sir (Athelstan) Jack	1913–1977	Scott, Sir Peter Markham	1901–1989
Scarbrough, Earl of. See		Scott, Robert Falcon	1868–1912
Lumley, Lawrence Roger	1896–1969	Scott, Sir Robert Heatlie	1905–1982
Schafer, Sir Edward Albert		Scott, Robert Henry	#1833–1916
Sharpey-	1850–1935	Scott, Sir Ronald Bodley. See	
Schapiro, Leonard Bertram	1908–1983	Bodley Scott	1906–1982
Scharlieb, Dame Mary Ann		Scott, William George	1913–1989
Dacomb	1845–1930	Scott-Ellis, Thomas Evelyn,	
Schiller, Ferdinand Canning		Baron Howard de Walden	1880–1946
Scott	1864–1937	Scott-James, Rolfe Arnold	1878–1959
Schlich, Sir William	1840–1925	Scott-Paine, Charles Hubert	1891–1954
Schmitthoff, Clive Macmillan	1903–1990	Scrutton, Sir Thomas Edward	1856–1934
Scholes, Percy Alfred	1877–1958	Scupham, John	1904–1990
Schonland, Sir Basil		Seago, Edward Brian	1910–1974
Ferdinand Jamieson	1896–1972	Seale-Hayne, Charles Hayne	1833–1903
Schreiner, Olive Emilie		Seaman, Sir Owen	1861–1936
Albertina (1855–1920). See		Searle, Humphrey	1915–1982
under Schreiner, William		Seccombe, Thomas	1866–1923
Philip		Seddon, Richard John	1845–1906
Schreiner, William Philip	1857–1919	Sedgwick, Adam	1854–1913
Schumacher, Ernst Friedrich	1911–1977	See, Sir John	1844–1907
Schunck, Henry Edward	1820–1903	Seebohm, Frederic	1833–1912
Schuster, Sir Arthur	1851–1934	Seebohm, Frederic, Baron	1909–1990
Schuster, Claud, Baron	1869–1956	Seeley, Harry Govier	1839–1909
Schuster, Sir Felix Otto	1854–1936	Seely, John Edward Bernard,	
Schuster, Sir George Ernest	1881–1982	Baron Mottistone	1868–1947
Schwabe, Randolph	1885–1948	Segrave, Sir Henry O'Neal de	
Schwartz, George Leopold	1891–1983	Hane	#1896–1930
Scott, Archibald	1837–1909	Selbie, William Boothby	1862–1944
Scott, Charles Prestwich	1846–1932	Selborne, Earl of. See Palmer,	
Scott, Lord Charles Thomas		Roundell Cecil	1887–1971
Montagu-Douglas-	1839–1911	Selborne, Earl of. See Palmer,	
Scott, Clement William	1841–1904	William Waldegrave	1859–1942
Scott, Cyril Meir	1879–1970	Selby, Viscount. See Gully,	
Scott, Dukinfield Henry	1854–1934	William Court	1835–1909
Scott, Lord Francis George		Selby, Thomas Gunn	1846–1910
Montagu-Douglas-	1879–1952	Selfridge, Harry Gordon	1858–1947

Shippard, Sir Sidney Godolphin Alexander	1837–1902
Shipton, Eric Earle	1907–1977
Shirley, Frederick Joseph John	1890–1967
Shirreff, Maria Georgina. See Grey	1816–1906
Shoenberg, Sir Isaac	1880–1963
Shonfield, Sir Andrew Akiba	1917–1981
Shore, Thomas William	1840–1905
Short, Sir Francis Job ('Frank')	1857–1945
Short, (Hugh) Oswald	1883–1969
Shorter, Clement King	1857–1926
Shorthouse, Joseph Henry	1834–1903
Shortt, Edward	1862–1935
Shotton, Frederick William	1906–1990
Showering, Sir Keith Stanley	1930–1982
Shrewsbury, Arthur	1856–1903
Shuckburgh, Evelyn Shirley	1843–1906
Shuckburgh, Sir John Evelyn	1877–1953
Shute, Nevil, *pseudonym*. See Norway, Nevil Shute	1899–1960
Sibly, Sir (Thomas) Franklin	1883–1948
Sickert, Walter Richard	1860–1942
Sidebotham, Herbert	1872–1940
Sidgreaves, Sir Arthur Frederick	1882–1948
Sidgwick, Eleanor Mildred	1845–1936
Sidgwick, Nevil Vincent	1873–1952
Sieff, Israel Moses, Baron Sieff	1889–1972
Sieghart, (Henry Laurence) Paul (Alexander)	1927–1988
Siepmann, Otto	1861–1947
Sieveking, Sir Edward Henry	1816–1904
Sieveking, Lancelot de Giberne	1896–1972
Sifton, Sir Clifford	1861–1929
Silberrad, Oswald John	1878–1960
Silkin, John Ernest	1923–1987
Silkin, Lewis, Baron	1889–1972
Silkin, Samuel Charles, Baron Silkin of Dulwich	1918–1988
Sillitoe, Sir Percy Joseph	1888–1962
Silverman, (Samuel) Sydney	1895–1968
Silvester, Victor Marlborough	1900–1978
Sim, Alastair George Bell	1900–1976
Simmons, Sir John Lintorn Arabin	1821–1903
Simon, Ernest Emil Darwin, Baron Simon of Wythenshawe	1879–1960
Simon, Sir Francis Eugen ('Franz')	1893–1956
Simon, Sir John	1816–1904
Simon, John Allsebrook, Viscount	1873–1954
Simon, Oliver Joseph	1895–1956
Simonds, Gavin Turnbull, Viscount	1881–1971
Simonds, James Beart	1810–1904
Simonsen, Sir John Lionel	1884–1957
Simpson, (Bessie) Wallis. See Windsor	1896–1986
Simpson, (Cedric) Keith	1907–1985
Simpson, Frederick Arthur	1883–1974
Simpson, Sir George Clarke	1878–1965
Simpson, Sir John William	1858–1933
Simpson, Maxwell	1815–1902
Simpson, Percy	1865–1962
Simpson, Wilfred Hudleston. See Hudleston	1828–1909
Simpson, Sir William John Ritchie	1855–1931
Sims, Sir Alfred John	1907–1977
Sims, Charles	1873–1928
Sims, George Robert	#1847–1922
Sinclair, Sir Archibald Henry Macdonald, Viscount Thurso	1890–1970
Sinclair, Sir Edwyn Sinclair Alexander-. See Alexander-Sinclair	1865–1945
Sinclair, Sir Hugh Francis Paget	#1873–1939
Sinclair, Hugh Macdonald	1910–1990
Sinclair, John, Baron Pentland	1860–1925
Sinclair, Sir John Alexander	1897–1977
Sinclair, Mary Amelia St Clair ('May')	#1863–1946
Sinclair, Ronald, *pseudonym*. See Teague-Jones, Reginald	1889–1988
Singer, Charles Joseph	1876–1960
Singer, Simeon	#1848–1906
Singleton, Sir John Edward	1885–1957
Singleton, Mary Montgomerie. See Currie, Lady	1843–1905
Sinha, Satyendra Prasanno, Baron	1864–1928
Sitwell, Dame Edith Louisa	1887–1964
Sitwell, Sir (Francis) Osbert (Sacheverell)	1892–1969
Sitwell, Sir George Reresby	1860–1943
Sitwell, Sir Sacheverell	1897–1988
Skeat, Walter William	1835–1912
Skelton, Raleigh Ashlin	1906–1970
Skipsey, Joseph	1832–1903
Skyrme, Tony Hilton Royle	1922–1987
Slack, Kenneth	1917–1987
Slaney, William Slaney Kenyon-. See Kenyon-Slaney	1847–1908
Slater, Sir William Kershaw	1893–1970
Slessor, Sir John Cotesworth	1897–1979
Slessor, Mary Mitchell	#1848–1915
Slim, William Joseph, Viscount	1891–1970
Slingsby, William Cecil	#1849–1929
Smallwood, Norah Evelyn	1909–1984

Solomon, Solomon Joseph	1860–1927
Somers-Cocks, Arthur Herbert Tennyson, Baron Somers	1887–1944
Somerset, Henry Hugh Arthur FitzRoy, Duke of Beaufort	1900–1984
Somerset, Lady Isabella Caroline (Lady Henry Somerset)	1851–1921
Somervell, Donald Bradley, Baron Somervell of Harrow	1889–1960
Somervell, (Theodore) Howard	1890–1975
Somerville, Edith Anna Œnone	1858–1949
Somerville, Sir James Fownes	1882–1949
Somerville, Mary	1897–1963
Somerville, Sir William	1860–1932
Sonnenschein, Edward Adolf	1851–1929
Sopwith, Sir Thomas Octave Murdoch	1888–1989
Sorabji, Cornelia	1866–1954
Sorabji, Kaikhosru Shapurji	1892–1988
Sorby, Henry Clifton	1826–1908
Sorley, Charles Hamilton	#1895–1915
Sorley, Sir Ralph Squire	1898–1974
Sorley, William Ritchie	1855–1935
Soskice, Frank, Baron Stow Hill	1902–1979
Sosnow, Eric Charles	1910–1987
Sotheby, Sir Edward Southwell	1831–1902
Soutar, Ellen. See Farren	1848–1904
Southborough, Baron. See Hopwood, Francis John Stephens	1860–1947
Southesk, Earl of. See Carnegie, James	1827–1905
Southey, Sir Richard	1808–1901
Southward, John	1840–1902
Southwell, Sir Richard Vynne	1888–1970
Southwell, Thomas	1831–1909
Southwood, Viscount. See Elias, Julius Salter	1873–1946
Souttar, Sir Henry Sessions	1875–1964
Spare, Austin Osman	1886–1956
Spartali, Marie. See Stillman, Marie	#1843–1927
Speaight, Robert William	1904–1976
Spear, (Augustus John) Ruskin	1911–1990
Spear, (Thomas George) Percival	1901–1982
Spearman, Charles Edward	1863–1945
Spears, Sir Edward Louis	1886–1974
Spence, Sir Basil Urwin	1907–1976
Spence, Sir James Calvert	1892–1954
Spencer, Gilbert	1892–1979
Spencer, Sir Henry Francis	1892–1964
Spencer, Herbert	1820–1903

Spencer, John Poyntz, Earl Spencer	1835–1910
Spencer, Leonard James	1870–1959
Spencer, Sir Stanley	1891–1959
Spencer, Sir Walter Baldwin	1860–1929
Spencer-Churchill, Baroness. See Churchill, Clementine Ogilvy Spencer-	1885–1977
Spencer-Churchill, Randolph Frederick Edward. See Churchill	#1911–1968
Spender, John Alfred	1862–1942
Spens, Sir William ('Will')	1882–1962
Spens, (William) Patrick, Baron	1885–1973
Speyer, Sir Edgar	1862–1932
Spiers, Richard Phené	1838–1916
Spiers, Walter Lewis	#1848–1917
Spilsbury, Sir Bernard Henry	1877–1947
Spinks, Alfred	1917–1982
Spofforth, Frederick Robert	1853–1926
Spooner, William Archibald	1844–1930
Sporborg, Henry Nathan	1905–1985
Sprengel, Hermann Johann Philipp	1834–1906
Sprigg, Sir John Gordon	1830–1913
Sprigge, Sir (Samuel) Squire	1860–1937
Spring, (Robert) Howard	1889–1965
Spring-Rice, Sir Cecil Arthur	1859–1918
Sprott, George Washington	1829–1909
Spry, Constance	1886–1960
Spy, pseudonym. See Ward, Sir Leslie	1851–1922
Squire, Sir John Collings	1884–1958
Squire, William Barclay	1855–1927
Sraffa, Piero	1898–1983
Stable, Sir Wintringham Norton	1888–1977
Stables, William Gordon	1840–1910
Stack, Sir Lee Oliver Fitzmaurice	1868–1924
Stacpoole, Frederick	1813–1907
Stacpoole, Henry de Vere	1863–1951
Stafford, Sir Edward William	1819–1901
Stainer, Sir John	1840–1901
Stalbridge, Baron. See Grosvenor, Richard de Aquila	1837–1912
Stallard, Hyla Bristow	1901–1973
Stallybrass, William Teulon Swan	1883–1948
Stamer, Sir Lovelace Tomlinson	1829–1908
Stamfordham, Baron. See Bigge, Arthur John	1849–1931
Stamp, Josiah Charles, Baron	1880–1941
Stamp, Sir (Laurence) Dudley	1898–1966
Stanford, Sir Charles Villiers	1852–1924
Stanford, Edward	#1827–1904
Stanier, Sir William Arthur	1876–1965

Stirling, Sir James	1836–1916	Strachey, (Giles) Lytton	1880–1932
Stirling, James Hutchison	1820–1909	Strachey, Sir John	1823–1907
Stirling, Walter Francis	1880–1958	Strachey, John St Loe	1860–1927
Stockdale, Sir Frank Arthur	1883–1949	Strachey, Rachel Conn ('Ray')	#1887–1940
Stocks, John Leofric	1882–1937	Strachey, Sir Richard	1817–1908
Stocks, Mary Danvers,		Strachie, Baron. See Strachey,	
Baroness	1891–1975	Sir Edward	1858–1936
Stockton, Earl of. See		Stradling, Sir Reginald	
Macmillan, (Maurice)		Edward	1891–1952
Harold	1894–1986	Strahan, Sir Aubrey	#1852–1928
Stockwell, Sir Hugh Charles	1903–1986	Straight, Whitney Willard	1912–1979
Stoddart, Andrew Ernest	1863–1915	Strakosch, Sir Henry	1871–1943
Stoker, Abraham ('Bram')	#1847–1912	Strang, William	1859–1921
Stokes, Adrian	1887–1927	Strang, William, Baron	1893–1978
Stokes, Adrian Durham	1902–1972	Strangways, Arthur Henry	
Stokes, Sir Frederick Wilfrid		Fox	1859–1948
Scott	1860–1927	Strangways, Giles Stephen	
Stokes, Sir George Gabriel	1819–1903	Holland Fox-, Earl of	
Stokes, Sir John	1825–1902	Ilchester. See	
Stokes, Whitley	1830–1909	Fox-Strangways	1874–1959
Stokowski, Leopold Anthony	1882–1977	Strathalmond, Baron. See	
Stoll, Sir Oswald	1866–1942	Fraser, William	1888–1970
Stone, (Alan) Reynolds	1909–1979	Strathcarron, Baron. See	
Stone, Darwell	1859–1941	Macpherson, (James) Ian	1880–1937
Stonehouse, John Thomson	1925–1988	Strathclyde, Baron. See Ure,	
Stoner, Edmund Clifton	1899–1968	Alexander	1853–1928
Stoney, Bindon Blood	1828–1909	Strathcona, Baron. See Smith,	
Stoney, George Gerald	1863–1942	Donald Alexander	1820–1914
Stoney, George Johnstone	1826–1911	Strathmore and Kinghorne,	
Stoop, Adrian Dura	1883–1957	Earl of. See Bowes-Lyon,	
Stopes, Marie Charlotte		Claude George	1855–1944
Carmichael	1880–1958	Stratton, Frederick John	
Stopford, Sir Frederick		Marrian	1881–1960
William	1854–1929	Strauss, Henry George, Baron	
Stopford, John Sebastian		Conesford	1892–1974
Bach, Baron Stopford of		Streatfeild, (Mary) Noel	1895–1986
Fallowfield	1888–1961	Street, Arthur George	1892–1966
Stopford, Robert Wright	1901–1976	Street, Sir Arthur William	1892–1951
Storrs, Sir Ronald Henry		Streeter, Burnett Hillman	1874–1937
Amherst	1881–1955	Stretton, Hesba, *pseudonym*.	
Storry, (George) Richard	1913–1982	See Smith, Sarah	1832–1911
Story, Robert Herbert	1835–1907	Strickland, Gerald, Baron	1861–1940
Story-Maskelyne, Mervyn		Strijdom, Johannes Gerhardus	1893–1958
Herbert Nevil	1823–1911	Strong, Eugénie	1860–1943
Stout, George Frederick	1860–1944	Strong, Sir Kenneth William	
Stout, Sir Robert	1844–1930	Dobson	1900–1982
Stow Hill, Baron. See		Strong, Leonard Alfred	
Soskice, Frank	1902–1979	George	1896–1958
Strachan, Douglas	1875–1950	Strong, Patience	1907–1990
Strachan, John	1862–1907	Strong, Sir Samuel Henry	1825–1909
Strachan-Davidson, James		Strong, Sandford Arthur	1863–1904
Leigh	1843–1916	Strong, Thomas Banks	1861–1944
Strachey, Sir Arthur (1858–		Struthers, Sir John	1857–1925
1901). See under Strachey,		Strutt, Edward Gerald	1854–1930
Sir John		Strutt, John William, Baron	
Strachey, Christopher	1916–1975	Rayleigh	1842–1919
Strachey, Sir Edward	1812–1901	Strutt, Robert John, Baron	
Strachey, Sir Edward, Baron		Rayleigh	1875–1947
Strachie	1858–1936	Stuart, Sir Campbell Arthur	1885–1972
Strachey, (Evelyn) John (St		Stuart, Herbert Akroyd	#1864–1927
Loe)	1901–1963	Stuart, James	#1843–1913

Tait, Sir (William Eric)	
Campbell	1886–1946
Talbot, Edward Stuart	1844–1934
Talbot, Sir George John	1861–1938
Tallack, William	1831–1908
Tallents, Sir Stephen George	1884–1958
Tangley, Baron. See Herbert,	
Edwin Savory	1899–1973
Tangye, Sir Richard	1833–1906
Tanner, Joseph Robson	1860–1931
Tansley, Sir Arthur George	1871–1955
Tarn, Sir William	
Woodthorpe	1869–1957
Tarte, Joseph Israel	1848–1907
Taschereau, Sir Henri Elzéar	1836–1911
Taschereau, Sir Henri	
Thomas	1841–1909
Tata, Sir Dorabji Jamsetji	1859–1932
Tata, Jamsetji Nasarwanji	1839–1904
Tate, Maurice William	#1895–1956
Tatlow, Tissington	1876–1957
Tattersfield, Frederick	1881–1959
Tauber, Richard	#1891–1948
Taunton, Ethelred Luke	1857–1907
Tawney, Richard Henry	1880–1962
Taylor, Alan John Percivale	1906–1990
Taylor, Alec Clifton-. See	
Clifton-Taylor	1907–1985
Taylor, Alfred Edward	1869–1945
Taylor, Charles	1840–1908
Taylor, Charles Bell	1829–1909
Taylor, Eva Germaine	
Rimington	1879–1966
Taylor, Frank Sherwood	1897–1956
Taylor, Sir Geoffrey Ingram	1886–1975
Taylor, Sir Gordon Gordon-.	
See Gordon-Taylor	1878–1960
Taylor, Helen	1831–1907
Taylor, Henry Martyn	1842–1927
Taylor, Isaac	1829–1901
Taylor, James Haward	1909–1968
Taylor, (James) Hudson	#1832–1905
Taylor, Sir John	1833–1912
Taylor, John Edward	1830–1905
Taylor, John Henry	1871–1963
Taylor, Louisa. See Parr	d.1903
Taylor, Sir Thomas Murray	1897–1962
Taylor, Sir Thomas Weston	
Johns	1895–1953
Taylor, Walter Ross	1838–1907
Taylor, William	1865–1937
Taylor, William Ernest	#1856–1927
Teague-Jones, Reginald	1889–1988
Teale, Thomas Pridgin	1831–1923
Teall, Sir Jethro Justinian	
Harris	1849–1924
Tearle, (George) Osmond	1852–1901
Tearle, Sir Godfrey Seymour	1884–1953
Tedder, Arthur William,	
Baron	1890–1967
Tegart, Sir Charles Augustus	1881–1946

Teichman, Sir Eric	1884–1944
Temperley, Harold William	
Vazeille	1879–1939
Tempest, Dame Marie	1864–1942
Temple, Frederick	1821–1902
Temple, Sir Richard	1826–1902
Temple, Sir Richard Carnac	1850–1931
Temple, William	1881–1944
Templer, Sir Gerald Walter	
Robert	1898–1979
Templewood, Viscount. See	
Hoare, Sir Samuel John	
Gurney	1880–1959
Tenby, Viscount. See	
Lloyd-George, Gwilym	1894–1967
Tennant, Sir Charles	1823–1906
Tennant, Sir David	1829–1905
Tennant, Margaret Mary	
Edith ('May')	1869–1946
Tenniel, Sir John	1820–1914
Tennyson-d'Eyncourt, Sir	
Eustace Henry William	1868–1951
Terry, Dame (Alice) Ellen	1847–1928
Terry, Charles Sanford	1864–1936
Terry, Fred	1863–1933
Terry, Sir Richard Runciman	1865–1938
Terry-Thomas	1911–1990
Tertis, Lionel	1876–1975
Tetlow, Norman	1899–1982
Tewson, Sir (Harold) Vincent	1898–1981
Tey, Josephine. See	
Mackintosh, Elizabeth	#1896–1952
Teyte, Dame Margaret	
('Maggie')	1888–1976
Thalben-Ball, Sir George	
Thomas	1896–1987
Thankerton, Baron. See	
Watson, William	1873–1948
Thesiger, Frederic Augustus,	
Baron Chelmsford	1827–1905
Thesiger, Frederic John	
Napier, Viscount	
Chelmsford	1868–1933
Thirkell, Angela Margaret	1890–1961
Thiselton-Dyer, Sir William	
Turner	1843–1928
Thoday, David	1883–1964
Thom, Alexander	#1894–1985
Thomas, Bertram Sidney	1892–1950
Thomas, David Alfred,	
Viscount Rhondda	1856–1918
Thomas, Dylan Marlais	1914–1953
Thomas, Forest Frederic	
Edward Yeo-. See	
Yeo-Thomas	1902–1964
Thomas, Frederick William	1867–1956
Thomas, Freeman Freeman-,	
Marquess of Willingdon.	
See Freeman-Thomas	1866–1941
Thomas, Sir George Alan	1881–1972
Thomas, George Holt	1869–1929

Tonks, Henry	1862–1937	Tristram, Ernest William	1882–1952
Toole, John Lawrence	1830–1906	Tristram, Henry Baker	1822–1906
Topley, William Whiteman		Tritton, Sir William Ashbee	1875–1946
Carlton	1886–1944	Trotter, Wilfred Batten	
Topolski, Feliks	1907–1989	Lewis	1872–1939
Torrance, George William	1835–1907	Troubridge, Sir Ernest	
Tosti, Sir (Francesco) Paolo	#1846–1916	Charles Thomas	1862–1926
Tout, Thomas Frederick	1855–1929	Troubridge, Sir Thomas	
Tovey, Sir Donald Francis	1875–1940	Hope	1895–1949
Tovey, John Cronyn, Baron	1885–1971	Troup, Robert Scott	1874–1939
Townsend, Charles Harrison	#1851–1928	Trueman, Sir Arthur Elijah	1894–1956
Townsend, Sir John Sealy		Trueta, Josep Anthony	1897–1977
Edward	1868–1957	Truman, Edwin Thomas	1818–1905
Townsend, Meredith White	1831–1911	Truscot, Bruce, *pseudonym*.	
Townshend, Sir Charles Vere		See Peers, Edgar Allison	1891–1952
Ferrers	1861–1924	Tshekedi Khama	1905–1959
Towse, Sir (Ernest)		Tucker, Alfred Robert	1849–1914
Beachcroft (Beckwith)	1864–1948	Tucker, Sir Charles	1838–1935
Toynbee, Arnold Joseph	1889–1975	Tucker, (Frederick) James,	
Toynbee, Paget Jackson	1855–1932	Baron	1888–1975
Toynbee, (Theodore) Philip	1916–1981	Tucker, Henry William	1830–1902
Tozer, Henry Fanshawe	#1829–1916	Tuckwell, Gertrude Mary	1861–1951
Tracey, Sir Richard Edward	1837–1907	Tuke, Henry Scott	1858–1929
Trafford, F. G., *pseudonym*.		Tuker, Sir Francis Ivan	
See Riddell, Charlotte Eliza		Simms	1894–1967
Lawson	1832–1906	Tulloch, William John	1887–1966
Traill, Anthony	1838–1914	Tunnicliffe, Charles Frederick	1901–1979
Traill-Burroughs, Sir		Tupper, Sir Charles	1821–1915
Frederick William. See		Tupper, Sir Charles Lewis	1848–1910
Burroughs	1831–1905	Turing, Alan Mathison	1912–1954
Travers, Benjamin	1886–1980	Turnbull, Sir Alexander	
Travers, Morris William	1872–1961	Cuthbert	1925–1990
Tredgold, Sir Robert		Turnbull, Hubert Maitland	1875–1955
Clarkson	1899–1977	Turner, Sir Ben	1863–1942
Tree, Sir Herbert Beerbohm	1852–1917	Turner, Charles Edward	1831–1903
Treloar, Sir William Purdie	1843–1923	Turner, Cuthbert Hamilton	1860–1930
Trench, Anthony Chenevix-.		Turner, Eustace Ebenezer	1893–1966
See Chenevix-Trench	1919–1979	Turner, Dame Eva	1892–1990
Trench, Frederic Herbert	1865–1923	Turner, George Charlewood	1891–1967
Trenchard, Hugh Montague,		Turner, George Grey	1877–1951
Viscount	1873–1956	Turner, Harold	1909–1962
Trend, Burke Frederick St		Turner, Herbert Hall	1861–1930
John, Baron	1914–1987	Turner, James Smith	1832–1904
Trent, Baron. See Boot, Jesse	1850–1931	Turner, Sir Ralph Lilley	#1888–1983
Trethowan, Sir (James) Ian		Turner, Walter James	
(Raley)	1922–1990	Redfern	1889–1946
Trevelyan, Sir Charles Philips	1870–1958	Turner, Sir William	1832–1916
Trevelyan, George Macaulay	1876–1962	Turner, William Ernest	
Trevelyan, Sir George Otto	1838–1928	Stephen	1881–1963
Trevelyan, Hilda	1877–1959	Turnor, Christopher Hatton	1873–1940
Trevelyan, Humphrey, Baron	1905–1985	Turnour, Edward, Earl	
Trevelyan, Julian Otto	1910–1988	Winterton and Baron	
Treves, Sir Frederick	1853–1923	Turnour	1883–1962
Trevethin, Baron. See		Turpin, Edmund Hart	1835–1907
Lawrence, Alfred Tristram	1843–1936	Turrill, William Bertram	1890–1961
Trevethin, Baron. See		Tutin, Thomas Gaskell	1908–1987
Lawrence, Geoffrey	#1880–1971	Tutton, Alfred Edwin	
Trevor, John	#1855–1930	Howard	1864–1938
Trevor, William Spottiswoode	1831–1907	Tweed, John	1869–1933
Trinder, Thomas Edward		Tweedmouth, Baron. See	
('Tommy')	1909–1989	Marjoribanks, Edward	1849–1909

Victoria Alexandra Alice Mary, Princess Royal of Great Britain	1897–1965
Victoria Alexandra Olga Mary, princess of Great Britain	1868–1935
Victoria Eugénie Julia Ena, Queen of Spain	1887–1969
Villiers, George Herbert Hyde, Earl of Clarendon	1877–1955
Villiers, John Henry De, Baron. See De Villiers	1842–1914
Villiers, Margaret Elizabeth Child-, Countess of Jersey	1849–1945
Villiers, Victor Albert George Child-, Earl of Jersey	1845–1915
Vincent, Sir (Charles Edward) Howard	1849–1908
Vincent, Sir Edgar, Viscount D'Abernon	1857–1941
Vincent, James Edmund	1857–1909
Vines, Sydney Howard	1849–1934
Vinogradoff, Sir Paul Gavrilovitch	1854–1925
Voce, William	1909–1984
Voigt, Frederick Augustus	1892–1957
Von Hügel, Friedrich, Baron of the Holy Roman Empire	1852–1925
Voyce, (Anthony) Thomas	1897–1980
Voysey, Charles	1828–1912
Voysey, Charles Francis Annesley	1857–1941
Wace, Henry	1836–1924
Waddell, Helen Jane	1889–1965
Waddell, Lawrence Augustine (later Austine)	1854–1938
Waddington, Conrad Hal	1905–1975
Wade, George Edward	#1853–1933
Wade, Sir Willoughby Francis	1827–1906
Wadsworth, Alfred Powell	1891–1956
Wadsworth, Edward Alexander	1889–1949
Wager, Lawrence Rickard	1904–1965
Waggett, Philip Napier	1862–1939
Wain, Louis William	1860–1939
Waismann, Friedrich	#1896–1959
Wake-Walker, Sir William Frederic	1888–1945
Wakefield, Charles Cheers, Viscount	1859–1941
Wakefield, (William) Wavell, Baron Wakefield of Kendal	1898–1983
Wakley, Thomas (1851–1909). See under Wakley, Thomas Henry	
Wakley, Thomas Henry	1821–1907
Walcan-Bright, Gerald, 'Geraldo'	1904–1974
Walcot, William	1874–1943

Waldock, Sir (Claud) Humphrey (Meredith)	1904–1981
Waley, Arthur David	1889–1966
Waley, Sir (Sigismund) David	1887–1962
Walkden, Alexander George, Baron	1873–1951
Walker, Sir Byron Edmund	1848–1924
Walker, Sir Emery	1851–1933
Walker, Ernest	1870–1949
Walker, Dame Ethel	1861–1951
Walker, Frederic John	1896–1944
Walker, Frederick William	1830–1910
Walker, Sir Frederick William Edward Forestier Forestier-. See Forestier-Walker	1844–1910
Walker, Sir Gilbert Thomas	1868–1958
Walker, Sir Herbert Ashcombe	#1868–1949
Walker, Sir James	1863–1935
Walker, John	1900–1964
Walker, Sir Mark	1827–1902
Walker, Sir Norman Purvis	1862–1942
Walker, Patrick Chrestien Gordon, Baron Gordon-Walker. See Gordon Walker	1907–1980
Walker, Sir Samuel	1832–1911
Walker, Vyell Edward	1837–1906
Walker, Sir William Frederic Wake-. See Wake-Walker	1888–1945
Walkley, Arthur Bingham	1855–1926
Wall, Max	1908–1990
Wallace, Alfred Russel	1823–1913
Wallace, Sir Cuthbert Sidney	1867–1944
Wallace, Sir Donald Mackenzie	1841–1919
Wallace, Philip Adrian Hope-. See Hope-Wallace	1911–1979
Wallace, (Richard Horatio) Edgar	1875–1932
Wallace, Thomas	1891–1965
Wallace, William Arthur James	1842–1902
Wallace-Hadrill, (John) Michael	1916–1985
Wallas, Graham	1858–1932
Waller, Augustus Désiré	#1856–1922
Waller, Charles Henry	1840–1910
Waller, Lewis	1860–1915
Waller, Samuel Edmund	1850–1903
Wallis, Sir Barnes Neville	1887–1979
Wallis, Henry	#1830–1916
Walls, Tom Kirby	1883–1949
Walpole, Sir Hugh Seymour	1884–1941
Walpole, Sir Spencer	1839–1907
Walsh, Stephen	1859–1929
Walsh, William Joseph	#1841–1921
Walsh, William Pakenham	1820–1902
Walsham, Sir John	1830–1905
Walsham, William Johnson	1847–1903

Watson, Sir Patrick Heron	1832–1907	Webster, Richard Everard,	
Watson, Robert Spence	1837–1911	Viscount Alverstone	1842–1915
Watson, Robert William		Webster, Wentworth	1829–1907
Seton-. See Seton-Watson	1879–1951	Weck, Richard	1913–1986
Watson, William, Baron		Wedgwood, Josiah Clement,	
Thankerton	1873–1948	Baron	1872–1943
Watson-Watt, Sir Robert		Wedgwood, Sir Ralph Lewis	1874–1956
Alexander	1892–1973	Weeks, Ronald Morce, Baron	1890–1960
Watt, Alexander Stuart	1892–1985	Weir, Andrew, Baron	
Watt, George Fiddes	1873–1960	Inverforth	1865–1955
Watt, (John) David (Henry)	1932–1987	Weir, Sir Cecil McAlpine	1890–1960
Watt, Margaret Rose	1868–1948	Weir, Harrison William	1824–1906
Watt, Sir Robert Alexander		Weir, Sir John	1879–1971
Watson-. See Watson-Watt	1892–1973	Weir, William Douglas,	
Watts, George Frederic	1817–1904	Viscount	1877–1959
Watts, Henry Edward	1826–1904	Weisz, Victor, 'Vicky'	1913–1966
Watts, John	1861–1902	Weizmann, Chaim	1874–1952
Watts, Sir Philip	1846–1926	Welby, Reginald Earle,	
Watts–Dunton, Walter		Baron	1832–1915
Theodore	1832–1914	Welch, Adam Cleghorn	1864–1943
Wauchope, Sir Arthur		Welch, (Maurice) Denton	#1915–1948
Grenfell	1874–1947	Welchman, (William) Gordon	1906–1985
Waugh, Alexander Raban		Weldon, Walter Frank	
('Alec')	1898–1981	Raphael	1860–1906
Waugh, Benjamin	1839–1908	Wellcome, Sir Henry	
Waugh, Evelyn Arthur St		Solomon	1853–1936
John	1903–1966	Welldon, James Edward	
Waugh, James	1831–1905	Cowell	1854–1937
Wavell, Archibald Percival,		Wellesley, Dorothy Violet,	
Earl	1883–1950	Duchess of Wellington	1889–1956
Wavell, Arthur John Byng	1882–1916	Wellesley, Sir George	
Waverley, Viscount. See		Greville	1814–1901
Anderson, John	1882–1958	Wellesley, Sir Victor	
Wayne, Sir Edward Johnson	1902–1990	Alexander Augustus Henry	1876–1954
Weatherhead, Leslie Dixon	1893–1976	Wellesz, Egon Joseph	1885–1974
Weaver, Sir Lawrence	1876–1930	Wellington, Duchess of. See	
Webb, Alfred John	1834–1908	Wellesley, Dorothy Violet	1889–1956
Webb, Allan Becher	1839–1907	Wellington, Hubert Lindsay	1879–1967
Webb, Sir Aston	1849–1930	Wells, Henry Tanworth	1828–1903
Webb, Clement Charles		Wells, Herbert George	1866–1946
Julian	1865–1954	Wemyss, Rosslyn Erskine,	
Webb, Francis William	1836–1906	Baron Wester Wemyss	1864–1933
Webb, Geoffrey Fairbank	1898–1970	Wemyss-Charteris-Douglas,	
Webb, (Martha) Beatrice		Francis, Earl of Wemyss	1818–1914
(1858–1943). See under		Werner, Alice	#1859–1935
Webb, Sidney James		Wernher, Sir Julius Charles	1850–1912
Webb, Mary Gladys	1881–1927	West, Sir Algernon Edward	1832–1921
Webb, Philip Speakman	1831–1915	West, Edward Charles	
Webb, Sidney James, Baron		Sackville-, Baron Sackville.	
Passfield	1859–1947	See Sackville-West	1901–1965
Webb, Thomas Ebenezer	1821–1903	West, Edward William	1824–1905
Webb-Johnson, Alfred		West, Lionel Sackville-,	
Edward, Baron	1880–1958	Baron Sackville. See	
Webber, Charles Edmund	1838–1904	Sackville-West	1827–1908
Webster, Benjamin	1864–1947	West, Sir Raymond	1832–1912
Webster, Sir Charles Kingsley	1886–1961	West, Dame Rebecca	1892–1983
Webster, Sir David Lumsden	1903–1971	West, Victoria Mary	
Webster, (Gilbert) Tom	1886–1962	Sackville-. See	
Webster, Dame Mary Louise		Sackville-West	1892–1962
('May') (1865–1948). See		Westall, William (Bury)	1834–1903
under Webster, Benjamin		Westcott, Brooke Foss	1825–1901

Wilkie, Sir David Percival	
Dalbreck	1882–1938
Wilkins, Augustus Samuel	1843–1905
Wilkins, Sir (George) Hubert	1888–1958
Wilkins, William Henry	1860–1905
Wilkinson, Ellen Cicely	1891–1947
Wilkinson, George Howard	1833–1907
Wilkinson, (Henry) Spenser	1853–1937
Wilkinson, James Hardy	1919–1986
Wilkinson, Sir Nevile	
Rodwell	1869–1940
Wilkinson, Norman	1882–1934
Wilkinson, Sir (Robert	
Francis) Martin	1911–1990
Wilks, Sir Samuel	1824–1911
Will, John Shiress	1840–1910
Willcocks, Sir James	1857–1926
Willcox, Sir William Henry	1870–1941
Willes, Sir George	
Ommanney	1823–1901
Willett, William	1856–1915
William Henry Andrew	
Frederick, prince of Great	
Britain (1941–1972). See	
under Henry William	
Frederick Albert, Duke of	
Gloucester	
Williams, Alfred	1832–1905
Williams, Alwyn Terrell	
Petre	1888–1968
Williams, (Arthur Frederic)	
Basil	1867–1950
Williams, Charles	1838–1904
Williams, Charles Hanson	
Greville	1829–1910
Williams, Charles Walter	
Stansby	1886–1945
Williams, Edward Francis,	
Baron Francis-Williams	1903–1970
Williams, Sir Edward Leader	1828–1910
Williams, Ella Gwendolen	
Rees, 'Jean Rhys'	1890?–1979
Williams, Eric Ernest	1911–1983
Williams, Evan James	#1903–1945
Williams, Sir Frederic	
Calland	1911–1977
Williams, Sir George	1821–1905
Williams, (George) Emlyn	1905–1987
Williams, Sir Harold Herbert	1880–1964
Williams, Hugh	1843–1911
Williams, Ivy	1877–1966
Williams, John Carvell	1821–1907
Williams, Sir John Coldbrook	
Hanbury-. See	
Hanbury-Williams	1892–1965
Williams, Sir John Fischer	1870–1947
Williams, Kenneth Charles	1926–1988
Williams, (Laurence	
Frederick) Rushbrook	1890–1978
Williams, Norman Powell	1883–1943
Williams, (Owen) Alfred	#1877–1930

Williams, Ralph Vaughan. See	
Vaughan Williams	1872–1958
Williams, Raymond Henry	1921–1988
Williams, (Richard) Tecwyn	1909–1979
Williams, Sir Roland Bowdler	
Vaughan	1838–1916
Williams, Rowland, 'Hwfa	
Môn'	1823–1905
Williams, Thomas, Baron	
Williams of Barnburgh	1888–1967
Williams, Watkin Hezekiah,	
'Watcyn Wyn'	1844–1905
Williams, Sir William Emrys	1896–1977
Williams, Winifred. See	
Strong, Patience	1907–1990
Williams-Ellis, Sir (Bertram)	
Clough	1883–1978
Williams-Freeman, John	
Peere	1858–1943
Williamson, Alexander	
William	1824–1904
Williamson, Henry	1895–1977
Williamson, James, Baron	
Ashton	#1842–1930
Williamson, John Thoburn	1907–1958
Willing, Victor James Arthur	1928–1988
Willingdon, Marquess of. See	
Freeman-Thomas, Freeman	1866–1941
Willink, Sir Henry Urmston	1894–1973
Willis, Sir Algernon Usborne	1889–1976
Willis, Henry	1821–1901
Willis, William	1835–1911
Willock, Henry Davis	1830–1903
Willoughby, Digby	1845–1901
Wills, Sir George Alfred	1854–1928
Wills, Leonard Johnston	1884–1979
Wills, William Henry, Baron	
Winterstoke	1830–1911
Wilmot, John, Baron Wilmot	
of Selmeston	1895–1964
Wilmot, Sir Sainthill Eardley-	1852–1929
Wilshaw, Sir Edward	1879–1968
Wilson, Sir Arnold Talbot	1884–1940
Wilson, Arthur (1836–1909).	
See under Wilson, Charles	
Henry, Baron	
Nunburnholme	
Wilson, Sir Arthur Knyvet	1842–1921
Wilson, Charles Henry, Baron	
Nunburnholme	1833–1907
Wilson, Charles McMoran,	
Baron Moran	1882–1977
Wilson, Sir Charles Rivers	1831–1916
Wilson, Charles Robert	1863–1904
Wilson, Charles Thomson	
Rees	1869–1959
Wilson, Sir Charles William	1836–1905
Wilson, Edward Adrian	1872–1912
Wilson, Eleanora Mary	
Carus-. See Carus-Wilson	1897–1977
Wilson, Ernest Henry	#1876–1930

Woodgate, Walter Bradford	1840–1920	Wright, Helena Rosa	1887–1982
Woodham-Smith, Cecil		Wright, Joseph	1855–1930
Blanche	1896–1977	Wright, Sir Norman Charles	1900–1970
Woodruff, (John) Douglas	1897–1978	Wright, Robert Alderson,	
Woods, Sir Albert William	1816–1904	Baron	1869–1964
Woods, Donald Devereux	1912–1964	Wright, Sir Robert Samuel	1839–1904
Woods, Edward	1814–1903	Wright, Whitaker	1845–1904
Woods, Henry	1868–1952	Wright, William Aldis	1831–1914
Woods, Sir John Harold		Wright, Sir (William) Charles	1876–1950
Edmund	1895–1962	Wrong, Sir George	
Woods, Samuel Moses James	#1867–1931	Mackinnon	1860–1948
Woodward, Sir Arthur Smith	1864–1944	Wroth, Warwick William	1858–1911
Woodward, Sir (Ernest)		Wrottesley, Sir Frederic John	1880–1948
Llewellyn	1890–1971	Wrottesley, George	1827–1909
Woodward, Herbert Hall	1847–1909	Wycherley, Ronald. See Fury,	
Woolavington, Baron. See		Billy	1941–1983
Buchanan, James	1849–1935	Wyld, Henry Cecil Kennedy	1870–1945
Wooldridge, Harry Ellis	1845–1917	Wylie, Charles Hotham	
Wooldridge, Sidney William	1900–1963	Montagu Doughty-. See	
Woolf, (Adeline) Virginia	1882–1941	Doughty-Wylie	1868–1915
Woolf, Leonard Sidney	1880–1969	Wylie, Sir Francis James	1865–1952
Woolgar, Sarah Jane. See		Wyllie, Sir William Hutt	
Mellon	1824–1909	Curzon	1848–1909
Woollard, Frank George	1883–1957	Wyllie, William Lionel	1851–1931
Woolley, Sir (Charles)		Wyndham, Sir Charles	1837–1919
Leonard	1880–1960	Wyndham, George	1863–1913
Woolley, Frank Edward	1887–1978	Wyndham, John. See Harris,	
Woolley, Sir Richard van der		John Wyndham Parkes	
Riet	1906–1986	Lucas Beynon	1903–1969
Woolton, Earl of. See		Wyndham, John Edward	
Marquis, Frederick James	1883–1964	Reginald, Baron Egremont	
Wootton, Barbara Frances,		and Baron Leconfield	1920–1972
Baroness Wootton of		Wyndham (formerly Moore),	
Abinger	1897–1988	Mary, Lady	1861–1931
Worboys, Sir Walter John	1900–1969	Wyndham Goldie, Grace	
Wordie, Sir James Mann	1889–1962	Murrell. See Goldie	1900–1986
Wordsworth, Dame Elizabeth	1840–1932	Wyndham-Quin, Windham	
Wordsworth, John	1843–1911	Thomas, Earl of Dunraven	
Workman, Herbert Brook	1862–1951	and Mount-Earl. See Quin	1841–1926
Wormall, Arthur	1900–1964	Wyn-Harris, Sir Percy	1903–1979
Worms, Henry De, Baron		Wynn-Carrington, Charles	
Pirbright. See De Worms	1840–1903	Robert, Baron Carrington	
Worrell, Sir Frank Mortimer		and Marquess of	
Maglinne	1924–1967	Lincolnshire	1843–1928
Worthington, Sir Hubert	1886–1963	Wynne, Greville Maynard	1919–1990
Worthington, Sir Percy Scott	1864–1939	Wynne-Edwards, Sir Robert	
Worthington-Evans, Sir		Meredydd	1897–1974
(Worthington) Laming. See		Wynyard, Diana	1906–1964
Evans	1868–1931	Wyon, Allan	1843–1907
Wren, Percival Christopher	#1875–1941		
Wrenbury, Baron. See			
Buckley, Henry Burton	1845–1935		
Wrench, Sir (John) Evelyn		Yapp, Sir Arthur Keysall	1869–1936
(Leslie)	1882–1966	Yarrow, Sir Alfred Fernandez	1842–1932
Wright, Sir Almroth Edward	1861–1947	Yate, Sir Charles Edward	1849–1940
Wright, Basil Charles	1907–1987	Yates, Dornford, *pseudonym*.	
Wright, Charles Henry		See Mercer, Cecil William	1885–1960
Hamilton	1836–1909	Yates, Dame Frances Amelia	1899–1981
Wright, Sir Charles Theodore		Yeats, Jack Butler	1871–1957
Hagberg	1862–1940	Yeats, William Butler	1865–1939
Wright, Edward Perceval	1834–1910	Yeo, Gerald Francis	1845–1909